THE
HOTEL
GUIDE
2015

AA Lifestyle Guides

Published by AA Publishing, a trading name of AA Media Limited, whose registered office is Fanum House, Basing View, Basingstoke, Hampshire RG21 4EA. Registered number 06112600

First published by the Automobile Association as the Hotel and Restaurant Guide, 1967
© AA Media Limited 2014.
48th edition September 2014.

Assessments of AA inspected establishments are based on the experience of the Hotel and Restaurant Inspectors on the occasion(s) of their visit(s) and therefore descriptions given in this guide necessarily contain an element of subjective opinion which may not reflect or dictate a reader's own opinion on another occasion. See 'AA Star Classification' in the preliminary section for a clear explanation of how, based on our Inspectors' inspection experiences, establishments are graded. If the meal or meals experienced by an Inspector or Inspectors during an inspection fall between award levels the restaurant concerned may be awarded the lower of any award levels considered applicable.

AA Media Limited strives to ensure accuracy of the information in this guide at the time of printing. Due to the constantly evolving nature of the subject matter the information is subject to change. AA Media Limited will gratefully receive any advice from our readers of any necessary updated information.

Please contact:
Advertising Sales Department: advertisingsales@theAA.com
Editorial Department: lifestyleguides@theAA.com
AA Hotel Scheme Enquiries: 01256 844455

Typesetting and Repro by Servis Filmsetting Ltd, Stockport
Printed in Italy by Printer Trento SRL, Trento

This directory is compiled by AA Lifestyle Guides; managed in the Librios Information Management System and generated by the AA establishment database system.

Maps prepared by the Mapping Services Department of AA Publishing.

Maps © AA Media Limited 2014.

Contains Ordnance Survey data © Crown copyright and database right 2014.

Information on National Parks in England provided by the Countryside Agency (Natural England).

Information on National Parks in Scotland provided by Scottish Natural Heritage.

Information on National Parks in Wales provided by The Countryside Council for Wales.

A CIP catalogue record for this book is available from the British Library.

ISBN: 978-0-7495-7616-5

A05152

Contents

Welcome to the AA Hotel Guide 2015

We know that people use the AA Hotel Guide for finding many different types of accommodation, and for a variety of reasons. As the AA inspects such a wide range of establishments, we hope that this guide will prove an invaluable asset in helping you to find just the right place to stay.

Who's in the guide?

From the most opulent and sophisticated of London's elite hotels to personally run small hotels in the British countryside; from the practical and convenient budget hotel aimed at business or air travellers, to the luxurious country house hotel catering for leisure and sporting guests, *The AA Hotel Guide 2015* has it all. All year round our specially trained team of expert inspectors are visiting, grading and advising the hotels that appear in this guide. Each one is judged on presentation, quality of accommodation, leisure and sporting facilities, food operation, service, hospitality, conference facilities and cleanliness. It is then rated according to our Classification System (see pages 18–19).

Any hotel applying for AA recognition receives an annual unannounced visit to check standards. If the hotel changes hands, the new owners must reapply for classification, as AA recognition is not transferable.

Our inspectors have also chosen their Hotels of the Year, for England, Scotland, Wales, Northern Ireland and the Republic of Ireland, as well as Hotel Group and Small Hotel Group of the Year (see pages 11–13).

Red Stars and Inspectors' Choice

All of the hotels in this guide should be of a high standard, but some are a cut above, and these are specially selected by our inspectors. At these establishments you can expect a little more of everything: more comfort, more facilities, more extras and more attention. From 2 red stars to 5 red stars, these are the best of British hotels. Every Red Star hotel is highlighted as an INSPECTORS' CHOICE, but these are not the only places that are singled out in this way.

Rosettes

Most of the hotels in this guide have their own restaurants, and a large proportion of them serve food that has attained the award of AA Rosettes; including some that have reached the four and five Rosette level, making them among the finest restaurants in the world. These are regularly visited by the AA inspectorate and awarded Rosettes strictly on the basis of the inspector's experience alone.

Some of the establishments in the guide are known as Restaurants with Rooms. Most will have been awarded AA Rosettes for their food, and the accommodation they offer meets the required AA standard, making them worthy of inclusion in this guide.

Anonymous inspection

All hotel and restaurant inspections are made anonymously, and the inspector always pays his or her own bill (rather than it being paid by the establishment). After taking a meal or staying overnight at the hotel, the inspector will announce to a member of staff and ask to speak to the manager, or the chef, in the case of a Rosette visit.

Tell us what you think

We welcome your feedback about the hotels included in this guide, and about the guide itself. A Readers' Report form appears at the back of the guide, so please write in, or email us at: **lifestyleguides@theaa.com**.

The hotels, along with guest accommodation, pubs, golf courses, days out and restaurants feature on the AA website: **theAA.com** and on a number of AA mobile apps.

How to use the guide

LOWER BEEDING
West Sussex

Map 6 TQ22

South Lodge, an Exclusive Hotel

★★★★★ 84% ◉◉◉ COUNTRY HOUSE HOTEL

SOUTH LODGE
AN EXCLUSIVE HOTEL

tel: 01403 891711 **Brighton Rd RH13 6PS**
email: enquiries@southlodgehotel.co.uk **web:** www.southlodgehotel.co.uk
dir: A23, onto B2110. Right, through Handcross to A281 junct. Left, hotel on right

This impeccably presented 19th-century lodge with stunning views of the rolling South Downs is an ideal retreat. There is the traditional and elegant Camellia Restaurant, offering memorable, seasonal dishes, and The Pass Restaurant, which is an innovative take on the chef's table concept - a mini-restaurant within the kitchen itself. Guests can take a tour of the restored Victorian wine cellar, either with a sommelier or on their own. The elegant lounge is popular for afternoon teas. Bedrooms are individually designed with character and quality throughout. The conference facilities are impressive.

Rooms 89 (11 fmly) (19 GF) 🐾 **S** £275-£695; **D** £275-£695 (incl. bkfst)*
Facilities STV WiFi ♨ ♨ 36 ♨ Putt green Fishing ♨ Gym Mountain bikes Archery Clay pigeon shooting Xmas New Year **Conf** Class 100 Board 50 Thtr 170
Del from £0* **Services** Lift **Parking** 200 **Notes** LB Civ Wed 130

1. Location
Town listed alphabetically within country (the county name appears under the town name)

2. Map reference
Map page number followed by a 2-figure National Grid reference (see also page 9)

3. Hotel name
Where the name appears in italic type the information that follows has not been confirmed by the establishment for 2015

4. Grading
Hotels are listed in star rating and merit score order within each location (for full explanation of ratings and awards see page 18)
★ Star rating
% Merit score
◉ Rosette award

5. Type of hotel
See opposite

6. Hotel logo
If a symbol appears here it represents a hotel group or consortium (see pages 29–35)

7. Picture
Optional photograph supplied by the establishment

8. Address and contact details

9. Directions
Brief details of how to find the hotel

10. Description
Written by the AA inspector at the time of the last visit

11. Rooms
Number of rooms and prices
(see page 8)

12. Facilities
Additional facilities including those for
children and for leisure activities

13. Conference
Conference facilities as available (see
page 8)

14. Notes
Additional information (see pages 8–9)

Types of hotel
The majority of establishments in this
guide come under the category of Hotel;
other categories are listed below.

Town House Hotel A small, individual city
or town centre property, which provides
a high degree of personal service and
privacy.

Country House Hotel These are quietly
located in a rural area.

Small Hotel Has fewer than 20
bedrooms and is owner-managed.

Metro Hotel A hotel in an urban location
that does not offer an evening meal.

Budget Hotel These are usually
purpose-built modern properties offering
inexpensive accommodation. Often
located near motorways and in town or
city centres.

Restaurant with Rooms This category
of accommodation is now assessed
under the AA's Guest Accommodation
scheme, therefore, although they
continue to have an entry in this guide,
we do not include their star rating. Most
Restaurants with Rooms have been
awarded AA Rosettes for their food and
the rooms will meet the required AA
standard. For more detailed information
about any Restaurant with Rooms please

Key to symbols and abbreviations

★	Black stars	HL	Hearing loop installed
★	Red stars – indicate AA	Air con	Air conditioning
	Inspectors' Choice	⌧	Heated indoor swimming pool
◉	AA Rosettes – indicate an	⌁	Outdoor swimming pool
	AA award for food	⌁	Heated outdoor swimming pool
%	Inspectors' Merit score (see page 6)	♫	Entertainment
Ⓐ	Associate Hotels (see below)	Child facilities	
○	Hotel due to open during the		Children's facilities (see page 8)
	currency of the guide	Xmas/New Year	
Ⓤ	Star rating not confirmed		Special programme for
	(see below)		Christmas/New Year
Fmly	Number of family rooms available	♨	Tennis court
GF	Ground floors rooms available	⚘	Croquet lawn
U	Bedrooms with walk-in	⛳	Golf course
	showers available	CONF	Conference facilities
Smoking	Number of bedrooms allocated	Thtr	Number of theatre style seats
	for smokers	Class	Number of classroom style seats
pri facs	Bedroom with separate private	Board	Number of boardroom style seats
	facilities (Restaurant with	⊗	No dogs allowed (guide dogs for the
	Rooms only)		blind and assist dogs should
S	Single room		be allowed)
D	Double room	No children	
✳	2013 prices		Children cannot be accommodated
fr	From	RS	Restricted opening time
incl. bkfst	Breakfast included in the price	Civ Wed	Establishment licensed for civil
FTV	Freeview television		weddings (+ maximum number
STV	Satellite television		of guests at ceremony)
Wi-fi	Wireless network connection	LB	Special leisure breaks available
⬉	High speed internet connection	Spa	Hotel has its own spa
	(bedrooms)		

consult *The AA Bed and Breakfast
Guide* or see www.theAA.com/bed-and-
breakfast-and-hotel.

Ⓐ These are establishments that have
not been inspected by the AA, but
which have been inspected by the
national tourist boards in Britain and
Northern Ireland. An establishment
marked as "Associate" has paid to
belong to the AA Associate Hotel
Scheme and therefore receives a
limited entry in the guide.
Descriptions of these hotels can be
found on theAA.com.

Ⓤ A small number of hotels in the guide
have this symbol because their star
classification was not confirmed at
the time of going to press. This may
be due to a change of ownership or
because the hotel has only recently
joined the AA rating scheme.

AA Advertised
These establishments are not rated or
inspected by theAA, but are displayed
for advertising purposes only.

○ These hotels were not open at the time
of going to press, but will open in late
2014, or in 2015.

How to use the guide *continued*

Merit score (%)

AA inspectors supplement their reports with an additional quality assessment of everything the hotel provides, including hospitality, based on their findings as a 'mystery guest'. This wider ranging quality assessment results in an overall Merit Score which is shown as a percentage beside the hotel name. When making your selection of hotel accommodation this enables you to see at a glance that a three star hotel with a Merit Score of 79% offers a higher standard overall than one in the same star classification but with a Merit Score of 69%. To gain AA recognition, a hotel must achieve a minimum score of 50%.

AA Awards

Every year the AA presents a range of awards to the finest AA-inspected and rated hotels from England, Scotland, Wales, Northern Ireland and the Republic of Ireland. The Hotel of the Year is our ultimate accolade and is awarded to those hotels that are recognised as outstanding examples in their field. Often innovative, the winning hotels always set high standards in hotel keeping. The winners for all the 2014–2015 awards are listed on pages 11–16.

Rooms

Each entry shows the total number of en suite rooms available (this total will include any annexe rooms). The total number may be followed by a breakdown of the type of rooms available, i.e. the number of annexe rooms; number of family rooms (fmly); number of ground-floor rooms (GF); number of rooms available for smokers.

Bedrooms in an annexe or extension are only noted if they are at least equivalent in quality to those in the main building, but facilities and prices may differ. In some hotels all bedrooms are in an annexe or extension.

If the hotel has highspeed or broadband internet access in the bedrooms, this may be chargeable.

Prices

Prices are per room per night and are provided by the hoteliers in good faith. These prices are indications and not firm quotations. An asterisk (*) indicates 2014 prices. Many hotels have special rates so it is worth looking at their websites for the latest information.

Payment

Credit cards may be subject to a surcharge – check when booking if this is how you intend to pay.

Children

Child facilities may include baby intercom, baby sitting service, playroom, playground, laundry, drying/ironing facilities, cots, high chairs or special meals. In some hotels children can sleep in parents' rooms at no extra cost – check when booking.

If 'No children' is indicated, a minimum age may be also given e.g. No children 4yrs indicates that no children under 4 years of age would be accepted.

Some hotels, although accepting children, may not have any special facilities for them.

Leisure breaks (LB)

Some hotels offer special leisure breaks. The cost of these may differ from those quoted in this guide and availability may vary through the year.

Parking

We indicate the number of parking spaces available for guests. This may include covered parking. Please note that some hotels make a charge for the use of their car park.

Civil weddings (Civ Wed)

Indicates that the establishment holds a civil wedding licence, and we indicate the number of guests that can be accommodated at the ceremony.

Conference facilities

We include three types of meeting layouts – Theatre, Classroom and Boardroom style and include the maximum number of delegates for each. The price shown is the maximum 24-hour rate per delegate. Please note that as arrangements vary between a hotel and a business client, VAT may or may not be included in the price quoted in the guide. We also show if WiFi connectivity is available, but please check with the hotel that this is suitable for your requirements.

Dogs

Although many hotels allow dogs, they may be excluded from some areas of the hotel and some breeds, particularly those requiring an exceptional licence, may not be acceptable at all. Under the Equality Act 2010 access should be allowed for guide dogs and assistance dogs. Please check the hotel's policy when making your booking.

Entertainment (♪)
This indicates that live entertainment will be available at least once a week all year. Some hotels provide live entertainment only in summer or on special occasions.

Hotel logos
If an establishment belongs to a hotel group or consortium their logo is included in their entry (see pages 29–37).

Map references
Each town is given a map reference – the map page number and a two-figure map reference based on the National Grid. For example: **Map 05 SU 48**:
05 refers to the page number of the map section at back of the guide
SU is the National Grid lettered square (representing 100,000sq metres) in which the location will be found
4 is the figure reading across the top or bottom of the map page
8 is the figure reading down at each side of the map page

Restricted service
Some hotels have restricted service (RS) during quieter months, usually during the winter, and at this time some of the listed facilities will not be available. If your booking is out-of-season, check with the hotel and enquire specifically.

Smoking regulations
If a bedroom has been allocated for smokers, the hotel is obliged to clearly indicate that this is the case. If either the freedom to smoke, or to be in a non-smoking environment is important to you, please check with the hotel when you book.

Spa
For the purposes of this guide the word Spa in an entry indicates that the hotel has its own spa which is either managed by themselves or outsourced to an external management company. Facilities will vary but will include a minimum of two treatment rooms. Any specific details are also given, and these are as provided to us by the establishment (i.e. steam room, beauty therapy etc).

INSPIRED BY THE FUTURE, EXPERIENCE TODAY

With an innovative social hub to relax, dine and work in, the new Novotel London Brentford is the first of our next generation hotels. It's perfectly located for Kew Gardens, Twickenham and Central London, so book your future stay today.

Novotel.com | Accorhotels.com

Image is for illustrative purposes only.

NOVOTEL
HOTELS

AA Hotels of the Year

ENGLAND

DORMY HOUSE HOTEL & SPA ★★★★ 87% ◉◉
BROADWAY page 101

Re-opened in Summer 2013 after a major refurbishment, Dormy House was originally a farmhouse, built in the 17th century. Its history can be plainly seen in the flagstone floors, log fires and heavily beamed ceilings. There are also extensive grounds and some stunning views of the surrounding Cotswolds. In the 1940s, the original farmhouse was bought by the golf club next door and given its current name. 'Dormy' is a golfing term for an unbeatable round of golf, and is also a common name for rooming houses next to golf courses. This house has been in the same family since 1977, and has truly gone from strength to strength, building a loyal following on the way. It is part of the Farncombe Estate, which covers some 400 acres, and goes from Broadway to the top of Fish Hill. Recent refurbishment has seen a redesign of bedrooms and the opening of a new spa facility. There are two restaurants: the Potting Shed, which proves very popular, and the more formal Garden Room. Rooms are rated 'Intimate', 'Comfy', 'Splendid' and 'Top Notch', and there are some delightful suites, including a Rose Cottage in the grounds. A worthy winner with a professional management team.

LONDON

ROSEWOOD LONDON ★★★★★ 88% ◉◉
LONDON page 291

Formerly the Renaissance Chancery Court, under the same existing ownership, this splendid hotel has been completely refurbished and re-launched as the Rosewood London. The results are stunning, as befits a building built in 1912, designed by H. Percy Monkton in a flamboyant Edwardian style. The building has been expanded on for over 50 years, during which time it was the HQ of the Pearl Assurance Company. The new overall design of the public areas and bedrooms was done by Tony Chi, and is stylish, striking and unconventional, conveying a London residential feel which is sympathetic to the building's history and features. Accommodation ranges across four key categories, including an impressive range of suites and unique split-level house rooms. These include some amazing features like Nespresso machines, salon-grade hairdryers, Czech & Speake toiletries, and some very large flat-screen TVs. Public areas include a spacious bar, Holborn Dining Room and the striking Mirror Room salon. There are also a ballroom and a spa. The Rosewood is an exciting addition to the 5-star market, and is a worthy winner of our London Hotel award.

AA Hotels of the Year *continued*

SCOTLAND

MELDRUM HOUSE ★★★★ 83% 🌹🌹
ABERDEEN page 538

Meldrum House is an impressive baronial mansion, now serving as a country house hotel located a few miles from Aberdeen, providing a popular base for corporate and leisure guests. The name comes from the Gaelic *Meall Druim*, which means 'ridge on a hill'; this refers to the location of the 13th-century tower house which still forms part of the hotel today. Some claim it once belonged to the Knights Templar, but it is more certain that it was redesigned in the 19th century, and has been a hotel since the 1950s. The last decade has seen major refurbishment, including the addition of a championship golf course, and remodelling of bedrooms and public areas. Approaching the hotel up the long driveway makes for an impressive and relaxing introduction, passing small ponds and golf greens, arriving at the car park with its central fountain. The bedrooms are traditionally decorated yet come with all the modern amenities you'd expect in such a prestigious hotel. Obviously Meldrum House is a great place for a golf break, but is also popular for weddings and conferences, all handled with efficiency and attention to detail.

WALES

PLAS YNYSHIR HALL HOTEL ★★★★ 🌹🌹🌹
EGLWYS FACH page 570

Dating back to the 15th century, and once owned by Queen Victoria, Plas Ynyshir is a delightful bijou country house hotel in a peaceful location between the Cambrian Mountains and the golden sands of Borth Beach. Joan and Rob Reen, who were previous owners of the Hall, have re-purchased it back from Von Essen, and gone in for some serious re-investment, invigorating this delightful house in the process. Public areas have had a superb make-over, including artwork by Rob Reen himself, who is an esteemed artist, well known for his portraits of local sheep. The bedrooms continue the artistic theme, each named after and reflecting the works of famous artists including Hogarth, Matisse, Monet, Goya, Chagall and Miro. There are also a number of suites, and most of the rooms enjoy beautiful garden and mountain views. The cooking, overseen by Head Chef Gareth Ward, is impressive, which is hardly surprising considering Gareth has worked at Restaurant Sat Bains, Hambleton Hall and Seaham Hall. The therapy rooms offer a natural holistic approach to health and well-being.

NORTHERN IRELAND

BUSHMILLS INN HOTEL ★★★★ 80% ◉
BUSHMILLS page 592

This delightful hotel is located in the quiet town of Bushmills, just a short drive away from the Giants Causeway, and within easy reach of the distillery which shares its name. This is a quirky operation which dates back in part to 1608. It has grown, modernised and kept abreast with the trends in a subtle manner which has made sure its kept its charm. To give you an idea, the bar is lit by gaslight and has a peat-burning fire, while in another part of the hotel is a 30-seat state-of-the-art cinema with surround sound. Overall though, the feel remains small and intimate and the hospitality matches that homely feel, from a friendly professional team. Bedrooms are spacious and well appointed, and the food is Irish through and through. The AA Rosette worthy cuisine focuses heavily on local produce, and serves to a cosy restaurant with wooden booths and mood lighting. The bar serves plenty of whiskies and the ubiquitous 'black stuff', a.k.a. Guinness, and is a great place to get involved in the craic, which often involves local singers and musicians. Bushmills Inn Hotel is certainly something special in a very special area.

REPUBLIC OF IRELAND

MARYBOROUGH HOUSE HOTEL ★★★★ 80% ◉
CORK page 599

Dating from 1715, Maryborough House is set in the leafy suburbs of Cork, and was renovated and extended to become a fine hotel with beautifully landscaped grounds featuring rare plant species. The stylish suites in the main house are reached by a lavish marble staircase and boast beautiful views of the surrounding gardens. Each suite is furnished to complement the 18th-century interior architecture, while still providing all mod cons. Exposed beams and marble fireplaces add to the romantic setting. The bedrooms in the wing are comfortably furnished with modern features and beautiful garden views. The bar and lounge are very popular throughout the day; Bellini's Restaurant offers a mix of classic and contemporary dishes. There are impressive spa, leisure and conference facilities, plus activities for children. Maryborough House is the perfect setting for a wedding. A large green area provides a splendid location for outdoor entertaining, while the mood-lit ballroom is perfect for a sumptuous banquet. Service is a definite strength here, and a natural and friendly approach can be expected. Recent refurbishment of the dining areas and bar has added greatly to the facilities.

THE RED CARNATION
HOTEL COLLECTION

AA Hotel Group of the Year

QHotels

![QHotels logo]

QHotels prides itself in its collection of 21 carefully nurtured, unique four-star hotels throughout the UK. Some can be found in the most beautiful countryside, some preside over bustling city centres, but each has its own defining characteristics, ensuring guests enjoy a truly special experience - whether staying for business or pleasure. A team of dedicated staff are on hand to cater to guests' every need. There are over 2,900 bedrooms across the collection, and an abundance of first-rate flexible meeting rooms for up to 700 delegates.

The Collection was founded in 2003, has rapidly grown from 2 to 21 hotels, and has also seen a large investment for development.

QHotels has 5 golf resorts, 17 spa hotels and 2 city centre hotels. Recognition includes AA Eco Hotel Group of the Year 2011, and a shelf's worth of awards from the Green Tourism Business Scheme. Their newest eco-initiative is the introduction of a carbon offsetting scheme to aid reforestation in Uganda.

QHotels believe that training and development is the responsibility of everyone, not just the training team. This is why their group specialists, and many of their hotel managers, as well as their training teams, are dedicated to providing expert, inspired and creative training programmes which will give staff new or improved skills to help them progress their careers.

QHotels is one of a rare breed of hotel groups that has won the accolade of AA Hotel Group of the Year for a second time. The first was in 2009, but their recent impact and consistent performance across all key areas points clearly to QHotels being a deserving winner once again.

QHOTELS COLLECTION

ENGLAND

ALDWARK, North Yorkshire	Aldwark Manor Golf & Spa Hotel
ASHFORD, Kent	Ashford International Hotel
BASINGSTOKE, Hampshire	The Hampshire Court Hotel
CAMBOURNE, Cambridgeshire	The Cambridge Belfry
CHATHAM, Kent	Bridgewood Manor
CHELTENHAM, Gloucestershire	The Cheltenham Chase Hotel
CREWE, Cheshire	Crewe Hall
HELLIDON, Northamptonshire	Hellidon Lakes Golf & Spa Hotel
KENILWORTH, Warwickshire	Chesford Grange
LEEDS, West Yorkshire	The Queens
MANCHESTER, Greater Manchester	The Midland
MILTON COMMON, Oxfordshire	The Oxford Belfry
NOTTINGHAM, Nottinghamshire	The Nottingham Belfry
SCUNTHORPE, Lincolnshire	Forest Pines Hotel & Golf Resort
STRATFORD-UPON-AVON, Warwickshire	Stratford Manor
STRATFORD-UPON-AVON, Warwickshire	The Stratford
SUTTON SCOTNEY, Hampshire	Norton Park
TANKERSLEY, South Yorkshire	Tankersley Manor
TELFORD, Shropshire	Telford Hotel & Golf Resort
WARRINGTON, Cheshire	The Park Royal

SCOTLAND

CUMBERNAULD, North Lanarkshire	The Westerwood Hotel & Golf Resort

AA Small Hotel Group of the Year

Eden Hotel Collection

The Eden Hotel Collection is privately owned by IT entrepreneur Sir Peter Rigby. It consists of seven hotels that focus on quality, and are set in outstanding locations. Sir Peter has said of his collection that it "does not operate as a big company, indeed it isn't. The strength of our hotels is in their individual nature and the care and attention which comes from a personal ownership and a group of highly capable, dedicated professionals who care about their product, service and the guest experience."

Team spirit is of key importance, and development is on a case-by-case basis. The amount of long-term employees speaks volumes in terms of staff retention.

Mark Chambers, Managing Director of the Collection, is adamant that as more properties are added, the focus has to be on improving standards across the group, to ensure that all guests experience the same high quality of care and service.

Investment isn't just confined to the fabric of the buildings, but there is also a special focus on improvement of the kitchen gardens across the collection. Head gardener Chris Holdsworth and his team work closely with chefs to produce even more fresh, seasonal and organic produce for guests to enjoy.

EDEN HOTEL COLLECTION

CHADDESLEY CORBETT, Worcestershire	Brockencote Hall
CHELTENHAM, Gloucestershire	The Greenway Hotel
CHIPPING CAMPDEN, Gloucestershire	The Kings
LEAMINGTON SPA (ROYAL), Warwickshire	Mallory Court
KINGSBRIDGE, Devon	Buckland-Tout-Saints
STRATFORD-UPON-AVON, Warwickshire	The Arden
TAUNTON, Somerset	The Mount Somerset

Big city adventure or countryside retreat

There's a PH Hotel for everyone

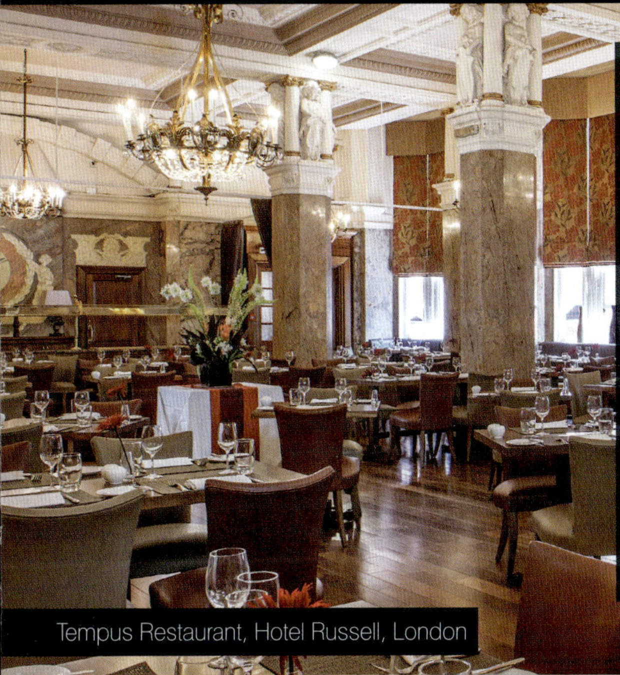

Tempus Restaurant, Hotel Russell, London

With stylish city centre destinations and stunning country house hotels to choose from, PH Hotels has a leisure break just for you.

Many of our hotels and venues include state-of-the-art leisure facilities. We take our golf pretty seriously too, enjoying some of the finest courses in England.

And of course an essential part of any hotel stay is the fine dining. With modern cuisine on the menu at our Tempus Restaurants, you won't be disappointed.

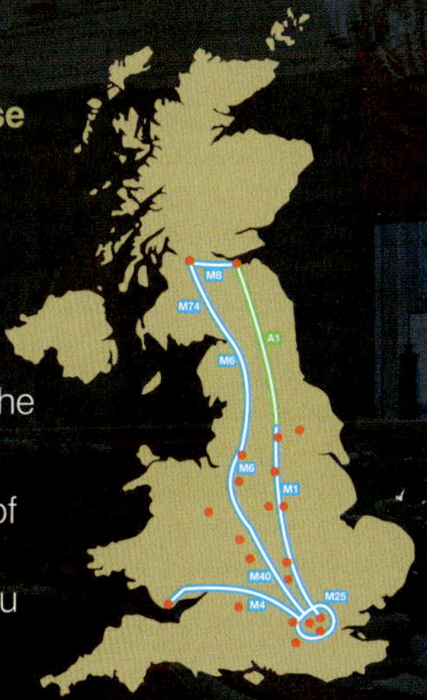

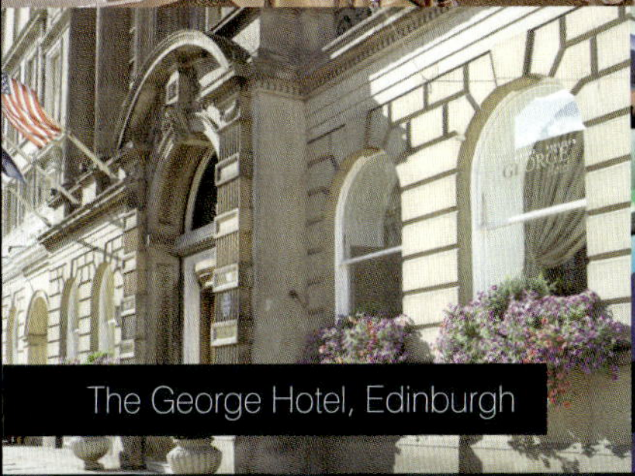

The George Hotel, Edinburgh

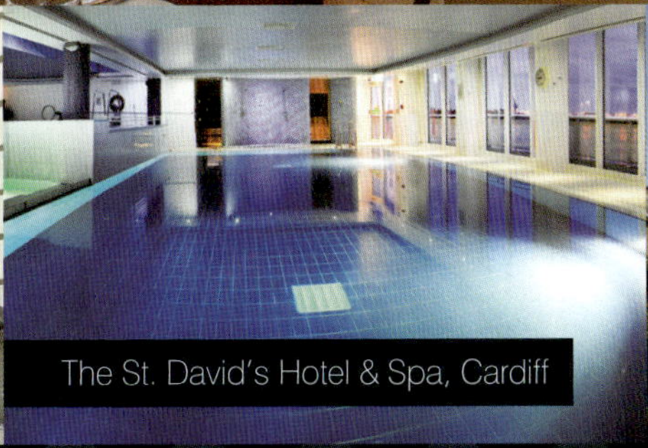

The St. David's Hotel & Spa, Cardiff

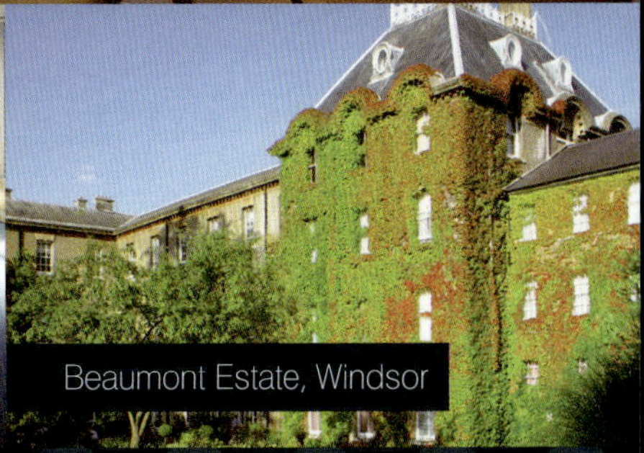

Beaumont Estate, Windsor

Discover your favourite PH Hotels break at **www.ph-hotels.com** or call **0844 824 6171**

PH hotels

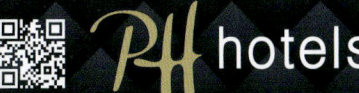

AA classifications and awards

AA assessment

In collaboration with VisitBritain, VisitScotland and VisitWales, the AA has developed Common Quality Standards for inspecting and rating accommodation. These standards and rating categories are now applied throughout the British Isles.

Any hotel applying for AA recognition receives an unannounced visit from an AA inspector to check standards. AA inspectors pay as a guest for their inspection visit, they do not accept free hospitality of any kind. Although AA inspectors do not stay overnight at Budget Hotels, they do carry out regular visits to verify standards and procedures.

A guide to some of the general expectations for each star classification is as follows:

★ One Star

Polite, courteous staff providing a relatively informal yet competent style of service, available during the day and evening to receive guests

- At least one designated eating area open to residents for breakfast
- If dinner is offered it should be on at least five days a week, with last orders no earlier than 6.30pm
- Television in bedroom
- Majority of rooms en suite, bath or shower room available at all times

★★ Two Star

As for one star, plus

- At least one restaurant or dining room open to residents for breakfast (and for dinner at least five days a week)
- Last orders for dinner no earlier than 7pm
- En suite or private bath or shower and WC

★★★ Three Star

- Management and staff smartly and professionally presented and usually uniformed
- A dedicated receptionist on duty at peak times
- At least one restaurant or dining room open to residents and non-residents for breakfast and dinner whenever the hotel is open
- Last orders for dinner no earlier than 8pm
- Remote-control television, direct-dial telephone
- En suite bath or shower and WC

★★★★ Four Star

- A formal, professional staffing structure with smartly presented, uniformed staff anticipating and responding to your needs or requests. Usually spacious, well-appointed public areas
- Reception staffed 24 hours by well-trained staff
- Express checkout facilities where appropriate
- Porterage available on request
- Night porter available
- At least one restaurant open to residents and non-residents for breakfast and dinner seven days per week, and lunch to be available in a designated eating area
- Last orders for dinner no earlier than 9pm
- En suite bath with fixed overhead shower and WC

★★★★★ Five Star

- Luxurious accommodation and public areas with a range of extra facilities. First time guests shown to their bedroom
- Multilingual service
- Guest accounts well explained and presented
- Porterage offered
- Guests greeted at hotel entrance, full concierge service provided
- At least one restaurant open to residents and non-residents for all meals seven days per week
- Last orders for dinner no earlier than 10pm
- High-quality menu and wine list
- Evening service to turn down the beds. Remote-control television, direct-dial telephone at bedside and desk, a range of luxury toiletries, bath sheets and robes. En suite bathroom incorporating fixed overhead shower and WC

★ Inspectors' Choice

Each year we select the best hotels in each rating. These hotels stand out as the very best in the British Isles, regardless of style. Red Star hotels appear in highlighted panels throughout the guide. Inspectors' Choice Restaurants with Rooms are establishments that have been awarded the highest accommodation rating under the AA Guest Accommodation scheme.

AA Rosette awards

Out of the many thousands of restaurants in the UK, the AA identifies over 2,000 as the best. The following is an outline of what to expect from restaurants with AA Rosette awards.

◉ Excellent local restaurants serving food prepared with care, understanding and skill, using good quality ingredients.

◉◉ The best local restaurants, which aim for and achieve higher standards, and better consistency; where a greater precision is apparent in the cooking. There will be obvious attention to the selection of quality ingredients.

◉◉◉ Outstanding restaurants that demand recognition well beyond their local area.

◉◉◉◉ Among the very best restaurants in the British Isles, where the cooking demands national recognition.

◉◉◉◉◉ The finest restaurants in the British Isles, where the cooking stands comparison with the best in the world.

Additional Information

Hints on booking your stay

It's always worth booking as early as possible, particularly for the peak holiday period from the beginning of June to the end of September. Bear in mind that Easter and other public holidays may be busy too and in some parts of Scotland, the ski season is a peak holiday period.

Some hotels will ask for a deposit or full payment in advance, especially for one-night bookings. Some hotels charge half-board (bed, breakfast and dinner) whether you require the meals or not, while others may only accept full-board bookings. Not all hotels will accept advance bookings for bed and breakfast, overnight or short stays. Some will not take reservations from mid week.

Once a booking is confirmed, let the hotel know at once if you are unable to keep your reservation. If the hotel cannot re-let your room you may be liable to pay about two-thirds of the room price (a deposit will count towards this payment). In Britain a legally binding contract is made when you accept an offer of accommodation, either in writing or by telephone, and illness is not accepted as a release from this contract. You are advised to take out insurance against possible cancellation, for example AA Single Trip Insurance (telephone 0800 975 5819).

Booking online

Locating and booking somewhere to stay can be a time-consuming process, but you can search quickly and easily online for a place that best suits your needs. Simply visit theAA.com to search for full details of over 5,700 quality rated hotels and B&Bs in Great Britain and Ireland. Check availability and click on the 'Book it' button.

Prices

The AA encourages the use of the Hotel Industry Voluntary Code of Booking Practice, which aims to ensure that guests know how much they will have to pay and what services and facilities are included, before entering a financially binding agreement. If the price has not previously been confirmed in writing, guests should be given a card stipulating the total obligatory charge when they register at reception.

Facilities for disabled guests

The Equality Act 2010 provides legal rights for disabled people including access to goods, services and facilities, and means that service providers may have to consider making adjustments to their premises. For more information about the Act see: www.gov.uk/government/policies/creating-a-fairer-and-more-equal-society or www.gov.uk/definition-of-disability-under-equality-act-2010

The establishments in this guide should be aware of their obligations under the Act. We recommend that you always telephone in advance to ensure that the establishment you have chosen has appropriate facilities.

Please note: AA inspectors are not accredited to make inspections under the National Accessibility Scheme. We indicate in entries if an establishment has ground floor rooms, walk-in showers and whether the hotel has a hearing loop system; and if a hotel tells us that they have disabled facilities this is included in the description.

Licensing laws

Licensing laws differ in England, Wales, Scotland, the Republic of Ireland, the Isle of Man, the Isles of Scilly and the Channel Islands. Public houses are generally open from mid morning to early afternoon, and from about 6 or 7pm until 11pm, although closing times may be earlier or later and some pubs are open all afternoon. Unless otherwise stated, establishments listed are licensed to serve alcohol. Hotel residents can obtain alcoholic drinks at all times, if the licensee is prepared to serve them. Non-residents eating at the hotel restaurant can have drinks with meals. Children under 14 may be excluded from bars where no food is served. Those under 18 may not purchase or consume alcoholic drinks.

Club licence means that drinks are served to club members only, 48 hours must lapse between joining and ordering.

The Fire Precautions Act does not apply to the Channel Islands, Republic of Ireland, or the Isle of Man, which have their own rules. As far as we are aware, all hotels listed in Great Britain have applied for and not been refused a fire certificate.

For information on Ireland see page 590.

Bank and Public Holidays 2015

New Year's Day	1st January
2nd January (Scotland)	2nd January
St Patrick's Day (NI & ROI)	17th March
Good Friday	3rd April
Easter Monday	6th April
Early May Bank Holiday	4th May
Spring Bank Holiday	25th May
Orangeman's Day (NI)	13th July
Summer Bank Holiday (Scotland)	3rd August
Summer Bank Holiday	31st August
St Andrew's Day (Scotland)	30th November
Christmas Day	25th December
Boxing Day (Substitute Day)	28th December

Visiting the northeast

by Sean Callery

The northeast doesn't always get the kind of attention other British regions may be used to, but this area has a giant wilderness and other landscapes much loved by walkers, a beautiful coastline, intriguing wildlife and some fascinating history. If you haven't been yet, you're missing out.

Northumberland has the lowest population of any English region. That means quiet roads, and a fantastic sense of space. It's easy to let the imagination run riot, and this is a great area in which to picture yourself in another period of history altogether

Be a Roman soldier

The area's best known landmark, Hadrian's Wall, is an extraordinary feat of military engineering. Amazingly it took only eight years to complete and kept the Caledonian tribes out for hundreds of years – although when you consider it had a gate every mile, it's clear it controlled movement more than preventing invasion. Stand on the ramparts and it's easy to imagine yourself as a Roman soldier cursing the cold wind and looking forward to a soak in the hot baths.

One of the best places to see and understand this world of 2,000 years ago is Housesteads, the site of a fort on the wall. There's a museum full of treasures illustrating Roman life, and you can see the deep ruts worn in the stone by Roman cartwheels – it really brings history to life. There's an impressive full-size reconstruction of a fort entrance at Arbeia Roman Fort in South Shields, and numerous artefacts from this era at the Great North Museum in Newcastle upon Tyne.

Be a monk

You could picture yourself as an 11th-century monk on Holy Island. Also known as Lindisfarne, the bare and windswept site was one of the earliest Christian centres in England. It housed a monastery from the 11th century,. and the Castle on the island dates from the 1540s. It was carefully restored from 1903, but rather confusingly it was decorated in the style of a 17th-century Dutch mansion. Mind your head as you negotiate narrow stairways and crane your neck round the many four-poster beds that dwarf the tiny windows through which you can glimpse the lovely small flower garden designed by Gertrude Jekyll in 1911.

Elaine Tang of Tillmouth Park Country House Hotel finds guests love the combination of beautiful scenery and history: "Many people visit us for historical reasons: we are surrounded by castles and battlefields the bloodiest being Flodden, where virtually all the Scottish nobility were slaughtered in 1513; there is a somber atmosphere which is offset with outstanding views. And Berwick's Elizabethan walls, the most complete bastioned town defences in Britain are a must – simply stunning!"

Be a pilgrim

Keeping with the religious theme, you could be a medieval pilgrim visiting

"The Northumberland National Park covers almost 400 square miles, and is a walker's paradise"

Durham Cathedral that shares a rocky base with the castle overlooking the River Wear. Work on this iconic structure began in 1093, and it remains one of Europe's finest Norman churches. Sophie Cook of Whitworth Hall Hotel says: "Durham became more popular with children when it was used in the Harry Potter movies, because they filmed around Durham School. The countryside is fantastic round here and we get a lot of walkers and bike riders who really enjoy getting muddy on the fells of the North Pennines."

Nick Homes of Rockliffe Hall in Hurworth, County Durham, echoes this: "We're right between the North York Moors and the Yorkshire Dales, so we get a lot of walkers. Many go to High Force, which is a very scenic walk to a 21-metre high waterfall. The number of cyclists has gone crazy since the Olympics and the Tour de France that came nearby in July 2014."

Become a wizard

The Harry Potter theme continues at Alnwick Castle, which took the part of Hogwarts School in the films about the boy wizard. This Norman stronghold has been altered over the centuries, including by the powerful Percy family (Dukes of Northumberland) adding a wall with seven towers to enclose the castle. The interior is magnificent, as is the 40-acre landscaped garden with many characterful features (poison garden, anyone?) and a massive treehouse.

By the way, Alnwick also has one of the largest secondhand bookstores in Europe and attracts bibliophiles from afar. It is also where a 1939 poster with the slogan 'Keep Calm and Carry On' was rediscovered in a box of books in 2000. The slogan has since been used and abused on countless mugs, tea towels and the like.

Get to work

Beamish's Living Museum of the North gives you the chance to work with heavy horses, fashion Victorian sweets or drive a steam engine, among many other activities. Costumed staff and volunteers bring Georgian, Victorian and Edwardian times to life among buildings that have been dismantled and rebuilt on the site.

"It's a real example of a living museum with amazing attention to detail and constantly evolving, like the new 1940s farm I drive through on the way to work, complete with land girls who just appear out of the mist and make you think you've driven back in time!" says Kerry McCabe of Beamish Hall Hotel.

Become a railway pioneer at the National Railway Museum in Shildon near Darlington. Here you can see one of the rivals that Stephenson's *Rocket* defeated at the famous Rainhill Trials in 1829. The site is close to the home of the Stockton and Darlington Railway, the world's first passenger railway, which dates from 1825.

The museum at Woodhorn brings to life the world of the Northumberland collieries. There was a coal mine on the site for 80 years and among the displays are massive metal blades inspired by the monster cutting machines that gouge out the coal below.

Turn yourself into a technology pioneer at Cragside, where inventor and head of the Vickers arms company Lord William Armstrong installed an array of new technology in the 19th century. The house was the first in the world to be entirely lit by electricity. It also boasts hydraulically-operated lifts and kitchen spit, telephones, electric gongs and other 'hi-tech' of the past.

Get digging

One of the garden highlights of the area is Howick Hall, once home to the second Earl Grey, who gave his name to the popular tea blend. It's famous for its rhododendrons, and has many rare plants and shrubs growing in its network of paths and glades. Howick's gardens were founded in the 1920s, but other popular gardens are even younger in garden years. Head to Netherwitton near Morpeth for the Bide-a-Wee gardens where hundreds of ferns, shrubs and grasses flourish in what was a sandstone quarry 25 years ago. At Herterton House, an almost derelict Tudor house and grounds have been transformed into a delightful set of very different gardens which boasts topiary, physic and flower gardens among many others. All this has only taken place since 1976.

Go wild

Too formal? Well, Northumberland offers unspoilt wilderness too. The Northumberland National Park covers almost 400 square miles and is a walker's paradise. It is barely inhabited by people,

△ Lindisfarne

and boasts curlew-haunted moorlands, wooded valleys and an expanse of green hills. The lack of habitation cuts light pollution and this makes for the darkest skies in England, a fact acknowledged by the International Dark Sky Association. In December 2013, the Park was awarded the title Northumberland Dark Sky Park. These black nights can be enjoyed from the Kielder Observatory, offering virtual tours of the universe and child-friendly explanations of how to use the powerful telescopes.

If you prefer to keep your eyes down, try Kielder Water, Europe's largest artificial lake with 27 miles of shoreline and home to Britain's largest forest - 153,140 acres of woodland. It hosts a wide range of wildlife, from roe deer and red squirrels to ospreys and kestrels.

Get on the ramparts

If castles are your thing, you're in the right place – with over 70, Northumberland is home to more castles than any other English county. If you want proof, climb to the top of Ros Castle and spot the seven castles surrounding you – Alnwick, Bamburgh, Chillingham (allegedly a favourite with ghosts), the romantic ruins of Dunstanburgh, Ford (now an activity centre), the spectacularly tall Warkworth and the holy retreat of Lindisfarne.

The region's castles reflect the history of what were very violent lands. Fortresses were needed to defend against the notorious Border Reiver gangs who raided across the Anglo-Scottish border, while others perch on the coast, looking out for Viking sea attacks.

Bamburgh Castle is one of the best preserved, sitting on a rocky outcrop that has formed a stronghold for thousands of years. Stand on the formidable ramparts to enjoy a fantastic panoramic view of Lindisfarne and the Farne Islands. The castle has a museum devoted to Grace Darling, a lighthouse keeper's daughter who famously rowed rough seas in 1838, to rescue nine people stranded on a wreck.

"I just love Bamburgh. It's the first place I recommend", says Peter Rae of Doxford Hall. "It's a quaint little village, very quiet, and I never get sick of looking at the castle – it's surprising how many films it's been a background to. And it's just above a clean and beautiful beach!"

From castles to sandcastles

Many of these castles sit on the Northumberland coast, which also boasts 30 miles of sweeping beaches and pretty villages. Among the most popular of these are Newbiggin by the Sea, which has a stylish beach promenade, a quirky free outdoor art trail and the UK's first permanent offshore sculpture.

Another gem is Seahouses, from where fishing boats still sail in search of a shoal, while other boats set off on trips to the Farne Islands to spot seals and seabirds. The curious can still hear stories of the many ships wrecked on the nearby rocks.

However, the major metropolis in this part of the world is Newcastle upon Tyne, a vibrant city which has a busy nightlife and is also a major cultural centre with several theatres and galleries. You can't miss the elegant curves of the Tyne Bridge, and a few miles away off the A1 in Gateshead is *The Angel of the North*; a newer but equally iconic Tyneside image. This 54-metre wide, 20-metre tall sculpture was created by Antony Gormley, and unveiled in 1998.

This mighty symbol of the Northeast is an ideal end-point for our exploration of the history of the area, as it brings together the image of the timeless, otherworldly angel, created by a modern sculptor, using the materials of the industrial age. A fine combination of heroic past, thoughtful present and hopeful future.

A clean getaway

by Jim Barker

From elegant clawfoot baths to hot tubs and Jacuzzis, and from bog standard showers to a rainforest shower experience, bathrooms are an essential part of a hotel stay.

One aspect of hotel accommodation that can make our time away from home special is the bathroom experience; the fact that alongside our clean, tidy and well-equipped bedroom is a bathroom that is (hopefully) cleaner, more nicely decorated, and better equipped than what most of us have at home. It is also cleaned and replenished by someone else.

Opulent bathing

Hotel bathrooms can come equipped with some pretty impressive modern equipment, but there are still plenty of places that do their best to provide us with a more timeless experience, using bathroom fittings and furniture that hark back to thoughts of a more opulent age, where a servant would fill your bath with buckets of piping hot water, rather than a simple turn of the tap. Even though they all have their own taps now, the object that really takes you back to a time before efficient indoor plumbing is the roll-top bath. Either in the middle of the room, or against a wall, these free-standing tubs sometimes sit on four legs, which are often designed to look like animal legs or feet, (clawfoot baths) or sometimes on a pedestal (pedestal baths), and look like they are just waiting for a Victorian to plant themselves among the suds. They can be quite tricky to get in and out of, especially if they are not against a wall, and therefore are not ideal for all guests, but they always add a touch of elegance to a hotel bathroom.

Some establishments mix up the bedroom and the bathroom by having the bath in the bedroom (or the bed in the bathroom, depending on your point of view). This is quite rare, which is probably good news for most, who don't relish the merging of the two, but even when the tub is visible from the bed, there's some kind of screening available.

Immerse yourself

As well as the classic bath tub, many hotels offer variations on the immersion principle. Hot tubs and Jacuzzis are very popular, offering a feel of Hollywood glamour; exchanging Edwardian opulence for a hint of hot California nights. Essentially, the Jacuzzi injects air into the water, creating a whirlpool which relaxes and soothes. Created in the 1920s by a firm of Italian brothers who had started as aircraft engineers in the US, the Jacuzzi, along with other similar products, such as the Infinity Bath, is pretty much standard in many high-end British hotels. For many, they offer a unique blend of hydrotherapy and high living.

Enough about baths; what about showers? In the last generation showers have become more common in the UK, to such a point that some hotels don't offer baths at all. Not only can showers be more accessible for disabled guests, there are also many who feel that taking a bath is tantamount to sitting in your own dirty water. The most common kind of shower is one that's over a bath, allowing the guest to choose either option, but many hotels now offer walk-in showers; basically wetrooms without a bath.

The walk-in shower or wetroom has a distinct advantage for hotel cleaning staff, as it's much easier to keep clean; no ring around the tub or awkward bits to reach. Also for the guest it allows a simple experience that amounts to disrobing, walking in, turning on the water, washing, turning off the water and walking out. No waiting for the bath to fill, or awkward lowering and raising. Although this is a comparatively new thing in the UK, it has been a staple in homes in much of Europe for decades.

Showers come in many shapes and sizes, from the old-fashioned shower head attached to the hot and cold taps to the rainforest shower, rain bar or power shower. The rainforest shower has shower heads that are much wider than the usual type and sit directly above the bather, rather than at the usual 45° angle. The premise is that it's more like being rained on than taking a shower, which apparently means a more natural start to the day.

A good soak

If you get bored soaking – we all know how easy it is to nod off and wake up in a bath full of lukewarm water – some hotels have TVs in their bathrooms, set into the wall at the end of the tub. All very well, unless you get involved in a good film and end up with fingers like raisins. Still, not an unwelcome innovation.

Most high-end hotels now provide luxury toiletries. Gone are the days of tiny soaps that turn to mush in your hands, and shampoo bottles that contain enough shampoo for half your head. These days you're as likely to see Molton Brown, Baylis & Harding, or Arran Aromatics. Leaving the bathroom smelling as good as possible can't help but make your stay even better, and when you've finished in the bath or shower, you're ready to face the day, whatever it may bring.

AA GUIDES

WE KNOW BRITAIN

- THE BEST PLACES TO VISIT
- CLEAR TOWN PLANS AND MAPPING
- WRITTEN BY LOCAL EXPERTS
- RECOMMENDED PLACES TO EAT
- TRUSTED LISTINGS

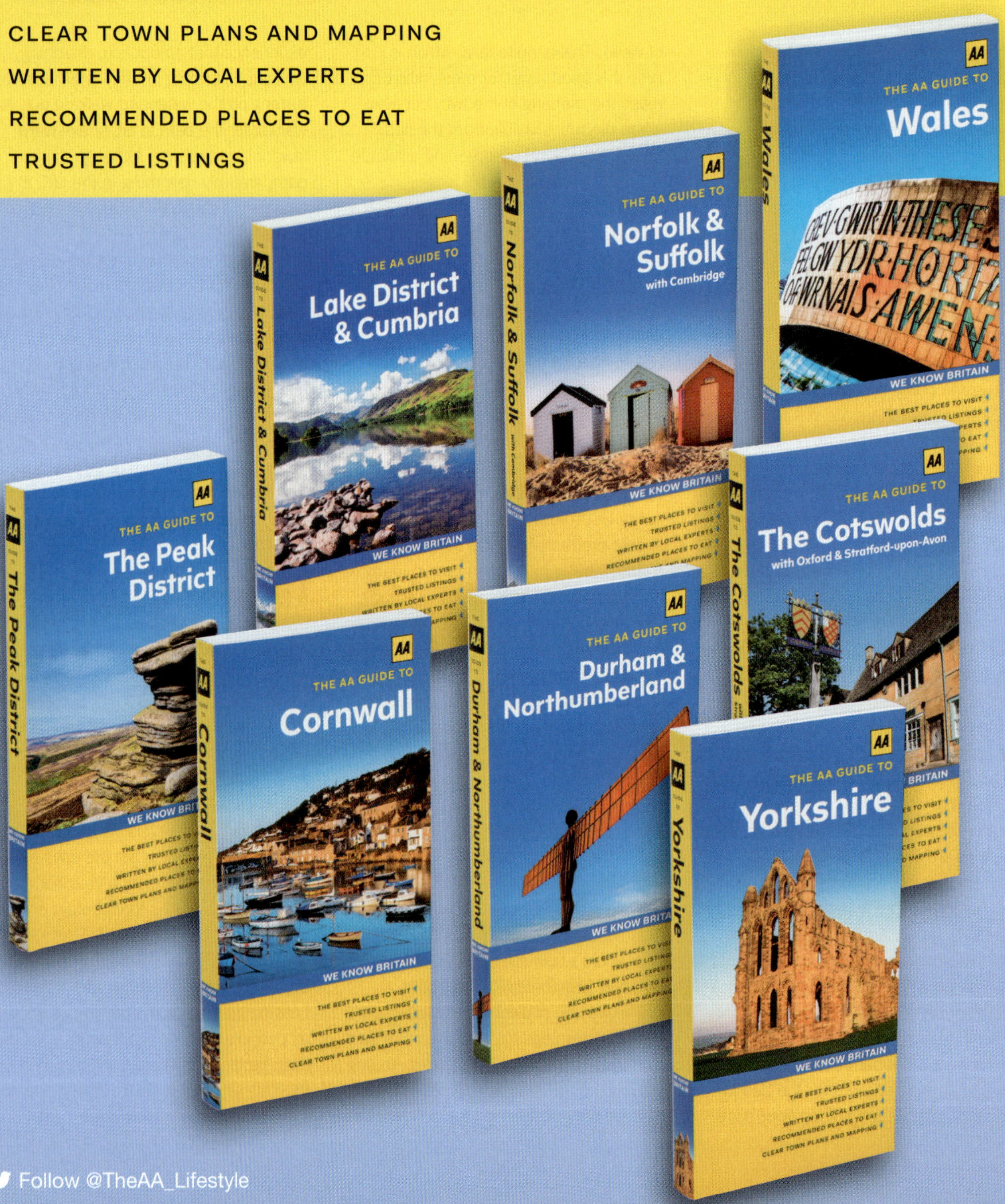

THE AA GUIDE TO
Wales

WE KNOW BRITAIN

THE AA GUIDE TO
Lake District & Cumbria

WE KNOW BRITAIN

THE AA GUIDE TO
Norfolk & Suffolk
with Cambridge

WE KNOW BRITAIN

THE AA GUIDE TO
The Peak District

WE KNOW BRIT...

THE AA GUIDE TO
The Cotswolds
with Oxford & Stratford-upon-Avon

THE AA GUIDE TO
Cornwall

WE KNOW BRITAIN

THE AA GUIDE TO
Durham & Northumberland

WE KNOW BRIT...

THE AA GUIDE TO
Yorkshire

WE KNOW BRITAIN

Follow @TheAA_Lifestyle

Hotel groups information

Adobe Hotels A contemporary collection of four city centre hotels in Canterbury, Chester, Exeter and Manchester that have a wide variety of dining outlets and are well geared to both corporate and leisure markets.		www.abodehotels.co.uk
Apex Hotels A group of contemporary mainly four star hotels. One in Dundee, four in Edinburgh and three in London. Spa and gym facilities are available at a number of the hotels.		0845 365 0000 www.apexhotels.co.uk
Best Western Britain's largest consortia group has over 280 independently owned and managed hotels, modern and traditional, in the two, three and four star range. Many have leisure facilities and rosette awards.		08457 76 76 76 www.bestwestern.co.uk
Best Western Premier These hotels are selected for their beautiful settings, range of facilities and enhanced levels of service. There are currently 6 Best Western Great Britain hotels that have achieved Premier status. These join over 45 Best Western Premier accredited hotels across Europe and Asia.		08457 76 76 76 www.bestwestern.co.uk
Best Western Plus 30 independently owned and managed hotels that offer that little something extra in the three and four star range. Some of these hotels have AA Rosette awards.		08457 76 76 76 www.bestwestern.co.uk
Bewley's Hotels Part of the Moran Hotel Group. A privately owned group of high quality, contemporary three star hotels in key locations in the UK and Ireland.		0845 234 5959 www.bewleyshotels.com
Brend A privately owned group of 11 three and four star hotels in Devon and Cornwall.		01271 344 496 www.brend-hotels.co.uk
Campanile An American owned and French managed company, Campanile has 15 properties in the UK offering modern accommodation in budget hotels.		www.campanile.com
Choice Choice has four different brands in the UK: Clarion and Quality Hotels are three and four star hotels, Comfort Inns are two and three star hotels, and Sleep Inns are budget hotels.		0800 44 44 44 www.choicehotelseurope.com
Classic British Hotels An exclusive upmarket collection of four star and quality three star independent hotels throughout the UK, noted for its comforts, fine dining, spas, golf and event facilities.		0845 070 7090 www.classicbritishhotels.com
Classic Lodges A small group of four star hotels.		0845 603 8892 www.classiclodges.co.uk
Copthorne Part of the Millennium and Copthorne group, with 12 three and four star hotels in primary provincial locations as well as London.		0800 41 47 41 www.millenniumhotels.com
Cotswold Inns & Hotels Charming three and four star small hotels located in the Cotswolds.		www.cotswold-inns-hotels.co.uk
Crowne Plaza Four star hotels predominantly found in key city centre locations.		0871 423 4876 www.crowneplaza.co.uk

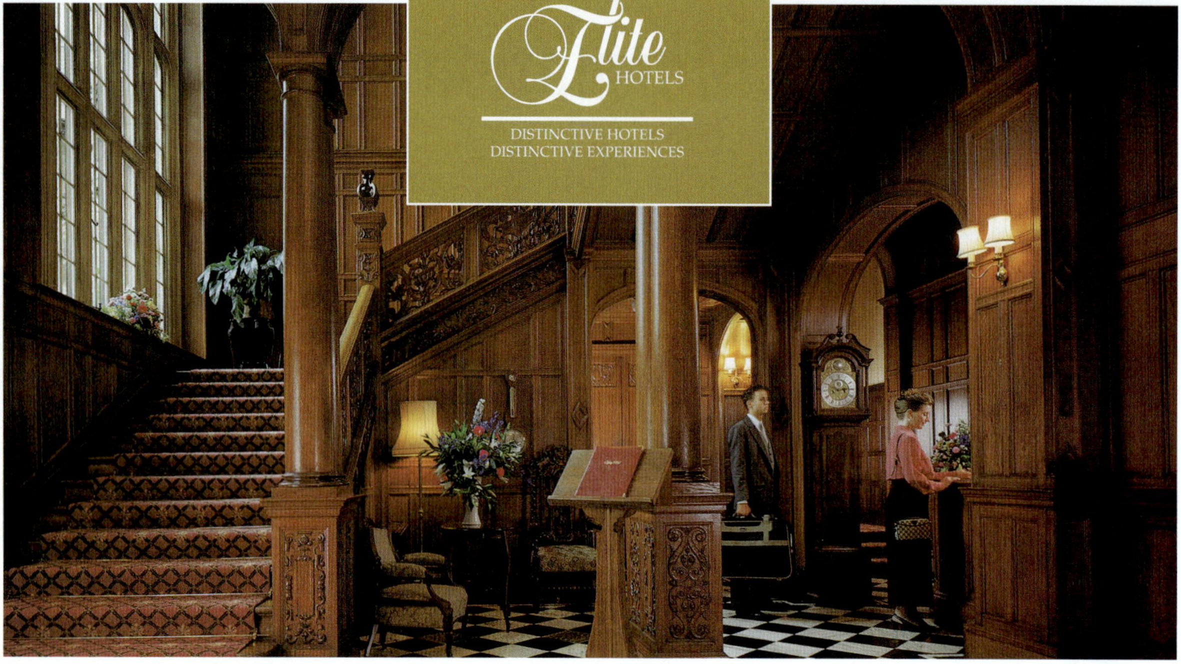

Hotel groups information *continued*

Days Inn Good quality modern budget hotels with good coverage across the UK.	*0800 028 0400* *www.daysinn.com*
De Vere Hotels & Resorts A group of four star hotels with good coverage across the UK.	*0845 375 2808* *www.devere.co.uk*
Eden Hotel Collection A privately owned collection of individual hotels, featuring award winning dining in quality surroundings.	*0845 351 0980* *www.edenhotelcollection.com*
English Lakes Hotels A collection of individually styled four star hotels located in and around the Lake District.	*015394 33773* *www.englishlakes.co.uk*
Exclusive Hotels A small privately owned group of luxury five star hotels, all located in the south of England.	*01276 471 774* *www.exclusivehotels.co.uk*
FBD Hotels & Resorts An Irish owned and operated group offering quality hotels in convenient locations.	*353 (0)1 428 2400* *www.fdbhotels.com*
Focus Hotels A group of three and four star hotels in both city and country locations across England. All offer Wi-fi and a number have spa facilities.	*0844 225 1625* *www.focushotels.co.uk*
Four Pillars Hotels A group of mainly four star hotels located in Oxfordshire and Gloucestershire. Most hotels have leisure facilities and all offer free Wi-Fi.	*0800 374 692* *www.four-pillars.co.uk*
Gidleigh Collection A small group of country hotels each with unique qualities, personalised service, memorable locations and a strong focus on food and wine.	*www.gidleighcollection.co.uk*
Hallmark Hotels A collection of seven hotels that provide comfortable accommodation; some have leisure facilities.	*0113 307 6760* *www.hallmarkhotels.co.uk*
Hand Picked Hotels A group of 19 predominantly four star, high quality country house hotels, with a real emphasis on quality food. Some provide stylish spa facilities.	*0845 458 0901* *www.handpickedhotels.co.uk*
Hillbrooke Hotels A growing portfolio of hotels and inns under the banner 'Quirky Luxury'. Excellent locations, comfortable surroundings, relaxed informal service.	*hillbrookehotels.co.uk*
Holiday Inn A major international group with many hotels across the UK.	*0871 423 4896* *www.holidayinn.co.uk*
Holiday Inn Express A major international hotel brand with over 100 hotels across the UK.	*www.hiexpress.co.uk*
Hotel du Vin A small expanding group of high quality four star hotels, that places a strong emphasis on its destination restaurant concept and appealing menus.	*0845 365 4438* *www.hotelduvin.com*

Hotel groups information *continued*

THE HOTEL COLLECTION	**The Hotel Collection** Formerly Puma Hotels, The Hotel Collection operates 20 four star hotels in locations across the UK.	*0800 808 9596* *www.thehotelcollection.co.uk*
ibis	**Ibis** A growing chain of modern budget hotels with properties across the UK.	*www.ibishotel.com*
THE INDEPENDENTS HOTEL ASSOCIATION	**The Independents** A consortium of independently owned, mainly two, three and four star hotels across Britain.	*0844 800 9965* *www.theindependents.co.uk*
IRELAND'S BLUE BOOK	**Ireland's Blue Book** A collection of country houses, historic hotels, castles and restaurants throughout Ireland.	*00 353 1 676 9914* *www.irelands-blue-book.ie*
IRISH COUNTRY HOTELS	**Irish Country Hotels** A collection of family-run hotels, located all across Ireland.	*00 353 1 295 8900 (local)* *0818 281 281* *www.irishcountryhotels.com*
LAKE DISTRICT HOTELS	**Lake District Hotels** A small collection of hotels situated in some of the most beautiful parts of the Lake District countryside and in Lakeland towns.	*0800 840 1240* *www.lakedistricthotels.net*
LEGACY HOTELS	**Legacy Hotels** A small group of three and four star hotels growing its coverage across the UK.	*0844 411 9011* *www.legacy-hotels.co.uk*
Leisureplex	**Leisureplex** A group of 20 two star hotels located in many popular seaside resorts.	*08451 305 888* *www.leisureplex.co.uk*
MACDONALD HOTELS & RESORTS	**Macdonald** A large group of predominantly four star hotels, both traditional and modern in style and located across the UK. Many hotels enjoy rural settings and state-of-the-art spa facilities. 10 Macdonald Hotels fall under the 'Signature Collection' banner	*0844 879 9000* *www.macdonaldhotels.co.uk*
Malmaison	**Malmaison** A growing brand of modern, luxurious city centre hotels that provide deeply comfortable bedrooms, exciting restaurants and carefully selected wine lists.	*0845 365 4247* *www.malmaison.com*
MANOR HOUSE HOTELS	**Manor House** Located throughout Ireland, this group offers a selection of independent, high quality country and manor house hotels.	*00 353 1 295 8900 (local)* *0818 281 281* *www.manorhousehotels.com*
Marriott	**Marriott** This international brand has four and five star hotels in primary locations. Most are modern and have leisure facilities with a focus on activities such as golf.	*00800 1927 1927* *www.marriott.co.uk*
MAYBOURNE HOTEL GROUP	**Maybourne Hotels** A hotel group representing the prestigious London five star hotels – The Berkeley, Claridge's and The Connaught.	*020 7107 8800 (Head Office)* *www.maybourne.com*
MenziesHotels	**Menzies Hotels** A group of predominantly four star hotels in key locations across the UK.	*0845 850 3013* *www.menzieshotels.co.uk*
Mercure	**Mercure Hotels** A large group of three and four star hotels throughout England, Scotland and Wales.	*0871 663 0627* *www.mercure.com*

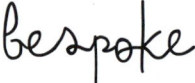

Hotel groups information *continued*

Logo	Description	Contact
MILLENNIUM MILLENNIUM · COPTHORNE	**Millennium** Part of the Millennium and Copthorne group with 7 high-quality four star hotels, mainly in central London.	*0800 41 47 41* *www.millenniumhotels.com*
MORAN HOTELS	**Moran Hotels** A privately owned group with 4 four star Moran Hotels, and 6 three star Bewley's Hotels. All have strategic locations in the UK and Ireland.	*00 353 1 459 3650* *www.moranhotels.com*
NEW FOREST HOTELS	**New Forest Hotels** A collection of properties situated in the New Forest National Park, each with its own distinct character. All have an AA Rosette award for culinary excellence.	*0800 44 44 41* *www.newforesthotels.co.uk*
NOVOTEL	**Novotel** Part of French group Accor, Novotel provides mainly modern three star hotels and a new generation of four star hotels in key locations throughout the UK.	*0871 663 0626* *www.novotel.com*
OldEnglish	**Old English Inns** A large collection of former coaching inns that are mainly graded at two and three stars.	*0845 608 6040* *www.oldenglishinns.co.uk*
Park Plaza Hotels & Resorts	**Park Plaza Hotels** A European based group increasing its presence in the UK with quality four star hotels in primary locations.	*0800 169 6128* *www.parkplaza.com*
PEEL HOTELS PLC	**Peel Hotels** A group of mainly three and four star hotels located across the UK.	*0845 601 7335* *www.peelhotels.co.uk*
Premier Inn	**Premier Inns** The largest and fastest growing budget hotel group with over 600 hotels offering quality, modern accommodation in key locations throughout the UK and Ireland. Each hotel is located adjacent to a family restaurant and bar.	*0871 527 8000* *www.premierinn.com*
PRIDE OF BRITAIN HOTELS	**Pride of Britain** A consortium of privately owned high quality British hotels, often in the country house style, many of which have been awarded Red Stars and AA Rosettes.	*0800 089 3929* *www.prideofbritainhotels.com*
PRIMA HOTELS GROUP	**Prima Hotels** A small hotel group which currently has 5 four star hotels. Four hotels are in England and one is in Scotland.	*www.primahotels.co.uk*
PH principal hayley	**Principal Hayley** A collection of luxury properties from Victorian grandeur to iconic city centre hotels.	*0844 824 6171* *www.ph-hotels.com*
QHOTELS	**QHotels** A hotel group with 21 individually styled four star hotels across the UK.	*0845 241 9783* *www.qhotels.co.uk*
RAMADA	**Ramada** A large hotel group with many properties throughout the UK in three brands – Ramada Plaza, Ramada and Ramada Hotel & Resort.	*0845 2070 100* *www.ramada.co.uk*

Britain's most complete guide to where to eat

AA Rosette Award for Culinary Excellence

- Over 2,000 professionally inspected restaurants, from village inns to smart city eateries

- Every establishment rated using the AA's renowned Rosette award scheme

- AA Restaurants of the Year and Wine Awards – recognising excellence in hospitality

- Authoritative and reliable – over 40 years of experience

- AA mapping makes restaurants easy to find

- Full details including email, websites, prices and facilities

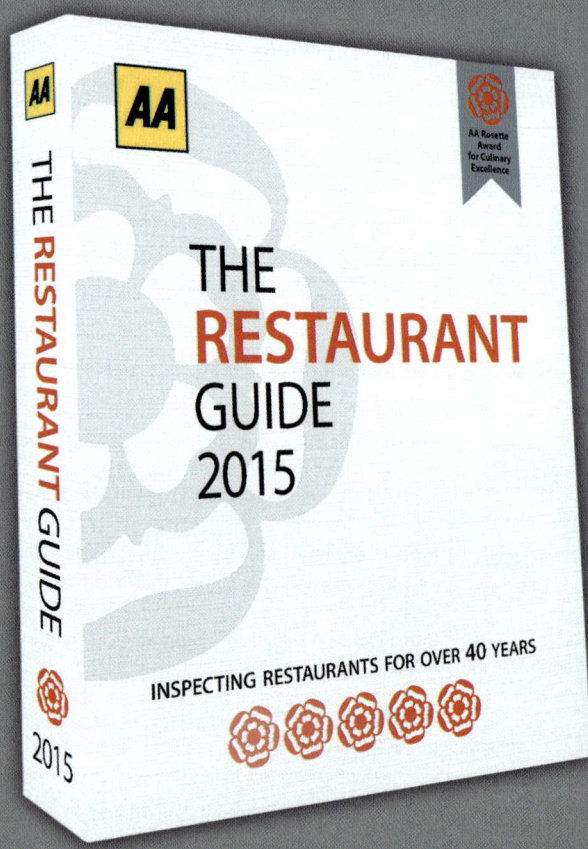

AA

THE RESTAURANT GUIDE

AA Rosette Award for Culinary Excellence

THE **RESTAURANT** GUIDE 2015

INSPECTING RESTAURANTS FOR OVER 40 YEARS

2015

Follow @TheAA_Lifestyle

Hotel groups information *continued*

Red Carnation A unique collection of prestigious four and five star hotels in Dorset, the Channel Islands and Ireland providing luxurious surroundings and attentive service.		*www.redcarnationhotels.com*
Relais et Chateaux An international consortium of rural, privately owned hotels, mainly in the country house style.		*00800 2000 0002* *www.relaischateaux.com*
Renaissance One of the Marriott brands, Renaissance is a collection of individual hotels offering comfortable guest rooms, quality cuisine and good levels of service.		*00800 1927 1927* *www.marriott.co.uk*
Richardson Hotels A group of 5 three and four star hotels located in Cornwall and Devon, plus one hotel in Lancashire.		*www.richardsonhotels.co.uk*
Rocco Forte Hotels A small group of luxury hotels spread across Europe. Owned by Sir Rocco Forte, with three hotels in the UK, all situated in major city locations.		*0870 458 4040* *www.roccofortehotels.com*
Scotland's Hotels of Distinction A consortium of independent Scottish hotels in the three and four star range.		*www.hotels-of-distinction.com*
Sheraton Represented in the UK by a small number of four and five star hotels in London and Scotland.		*www.starwoodhotels.com*
Shire A small group of four star hotels which feature spa facilities and well-equipped bedrooms ideal for both business and leisure guests.		*www.shirehotels.com*
Small Luxury Hotels of the World Part of an international consortium of mainly privately owned hotels, often in the country house style.		*0800 037 1888* *www.slh.com*
TA Hotel Collection A privately owned collection of three and four star hotels across Suffolk		*01728 452176* *www.tahotelcollection.co.uk*
The Circle A consortium of independently owned, mainly two and three star hotels, across Britain.		*0845 345 1965* *www.circlehotels.co.uk*
Warner Leisure Hotels A collection of 3 and 4 star country hotels and villages, exclusively for adults. Renowned for their restaurants, daytime activities and live entertainment.		*0844 871 4523* *www.warnerleisurehotels.co.uk*
Welcome Break Good quality, modern, budget accommodation at motorway services.		*01908 299 700* *www.welcomebreak.co.uk*

England

A

ABINGDON-ON-THAMES
Oxfordshire

Map 5 SU49

Oxford Abingdon Four Pillars Hotel

★★★ 77% HOTEL

tel: 0800 374692 & 01235 553456 **Marcham Rd OX14 1TZ**
email: abingdon@four-pillars.co.uk **web:** www.four-pillars.co.uk/abingdon
dir: A34 at junct with A415, in Abingdon, turn right at rdbt, hotel on right

On the outskirts of Abingdon, this busy commercial hotel is well located for access to major roads. The bedrooms are comfortable and well equipped with extras such as safes and trouser presses. All day refreshments are offered in the stylish lounge and conservatory.

Rooms 66 (5 fmly) (32 GF) ✆ **S** £60-£150; **D** £60-£150 **Facilities** FTV WiFi ⌕ Xmas New Year **Conf** Class 70 Board 40 Thtr 140 Del from £110 to £147 **Parking** 85 **Notes** LB ⊗ Civ Wed 120

Upper Reaches Hotel

★★★ 73% HOTEL

tel: 01235 522536 & 462143 **Thames St OX14 3JA**
email: info@upperreaches-abingdon.co.uk **web:** www.upperreaches-abingdon.co.uk
dir: From A415 in Abingdon follow Dorchester signs, turn left just before bridge over Thames

Built from Abingdon Abbey's old corn mill, the hotel enjoys an attractive location. It offers well-appointed rooms, individually styled and with a wide range of amenities. The aptly named Millrace Restaurant is situated in the ancient mill house which still features a working wheel, and the river can be seen flowing beneath.

Rooms 31 (5 GF) **Facilities** FTV WiFi ⌕ Fishing Xmas New Year **Parking** 60 **Notes** ⊗

Premier Inn Abingdon

BUDGET HOTEL

tel: 0871 527 8014 **Marcham Rd OX14 1AD**
web: www.premierinn.com
dir: On A415. Approx 0.5m from A34 at Abingdon South junct (Marcham Interchange)

High quality, budget accommodation ideal for both families and business travellers. Spacious, en suite bedrooms feature tea and coffee making facilities, and Freeview TV in most hotels. Internet access and WiFi are available for a small fee. The adjacent family restaurant features a wide and varied menu. See also the Hotel Groups pages.

Rooms 27

ACCRINGTON
Lancashire

Map 18 SD72

Mercure Blackburn Dunkenhalgh Hotel & Spa

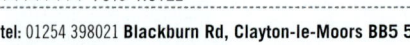

★★★★ 73% HOTEL

tel: 01254 398021 **Blackburn Rd, Clayton-le-Moors BB5 5JP**
email: H6617@accor.com **web:** www.mercure.com
dir: M65 junct 7, left at rdbt, left at lights, hotel 100yds on left

Set in delightfully tended grounds yet only a stone's throw from the M65, this fine mansion has conference and banqueting facilities that attract the wedding and corporate markets. The state-of-the-art thermal suite allows guests to relax and take life easy. Bedrooms come in a variety of styles, sizes and standards; some are located away from the main hotel building.

Rooms 175 (119 annexe) (36 fmly) (43 GF) ✆ **Facilities** Spa STV WiFi HL ⊗ Gym Thermal suite Aerobics studio Xmas New Year **Conf** Class 200 Board 100 Thtr 400 **Services** Lift **Parking** 400 **Notes** ⊗ Civ Wed 300

Sparth House Hotel

★★★ 74% SMALL HOTEL

tel: 01254 872263 **Whalley Rd, Clayton Le Moors BB5 5RP**
email: info@sparthhousehotel.co.uk **web:** www.sparthhousehotel.co.uk
dir: A6185 to Clitheroe along Dunkenhalgh Way, right at lights onto A678, left at next lights, A680 to Whalley. Hotel on left after 2 sets of lights

This 18th-century listed building sits in three acres of well-tended gardens. Bedrooms come in a choice of styles, from the cosy modern rooms ideal for business guests, to the spacious classical rooms - including one with furnishings from one of the great cruise liners. Public rooms feature a panelled restaurant and plush lounge bar.

Rooms 16 (3 fmly) **S** £60-£80; **D** £75-£95 (incl. bkfst)* **Facilities** FTV WiFi **Conf** Class 50 Board 40 Thtr 160 Del from £95 to £105* **Parking** 50 **Notes** ⊗ Civ Wed 100

ADDINGHAM
West Yorkshire

Map 19 SE05

Craven Heifer

 RESTAURANT WITH ROOMS

tel: 01943 830106 **Main St LS29 0PL**
email: info@wellfedpubs.co.uk **web:** www.thecravenheifer.com

The Craven Heifer is located close to the town of Skipton and boasts themed rooms based on Yorkshire celebrities. The bar is a traditional 'Dalesway' inn with stone and oak floors, open fires, leather seating, real ale and outstanding food. The two AA Rosette cuisine is beautifully complemented by a carefully chosen wine list. A warm and very friendly welcome from the well-informed staff is guaranteed.

Rooms 7

ALBURGH	Map 13 TM28
Norfolk	

The Dove Restaurant with Rooms

 RESTAURANT WITH ROOMS

tel: 01986 788315 📄 01986 788315 **Holbrook Hill IP20 OEP**
email: info@thedoverestaurant.co.uk **web:** www.thedoverestaurant.co.uk
dir: Between Harleston & Bungay at junct A143 & B1062

A warm welcome awaits at The Dove Restaurant with Rooms. Bedrooms are pleasantly decorated, furnished with pine pieces and have modern facilities. Public rooms include a lounge area with a small bar, and a smart restaurant with well-spaced tables and excellent food.

Rooms 2 (1 fmly)

ALCESTER	Map 10 SP05
Warwickshire	

Kings Court Hotel

★★★ 77% HOTEL

tel: 01789 763111 **Kings Coughton B49 5QQ**
email: info@kingscourthotel.co.uk **web:** www.kingscourthotel.co.uk
dir: 1m N on A435

This privately owned hotel dates back to Tudor times and the bedrooms in the original house have oak beams. Most guests are accommodated in the well-appointed modern wings. The bar and restaurant offer very good dishes from interesting menus. The hotel is licensed to hold civil ceremonies and the pretty garden is ideal for summer weddings.

Rooms 61 (57 annexe) (2 fmly) (30 GF) **Facilities** FTV WiFi Gym Xmas New Year **Conf** Class 60 Board 40 Thtr 100 Del £125* **Parking** 100 **Notes** Civ Wed 100

ALDEBURGH	Map 13 TM45
Suffolk	

Brudenell Hotel

T|A|HOTEL
COLLECTION

★★★★ 85% HOTEL

tel: 01728 452071 **The Parade IP15 5BU**
email: info@brudenellhotel.co.uk **web:** www.brudenellhotel.co.uk
dir: A12, A1094. In town, right into High St. Hotel on seafront adjoining Fort Green car park

Situated at the far end of the town centre just a step away from the beach, this hotel has a contemporary appearance, enhanced by subtle lighting and quality soft furnishings. Many of the bedrooms have superb sea views; they include deluxe rooms with king-sized beds and superior rooms suitable for families. The informal restaurant showcases skilfully prepared dishes that use fresh, seasonal produce, especially local fish, seafood and game.

Rooms 44 (17 fmly) **Facilities** STV WiFi Xmas New Year **Conf** Class 20 Board 20 Thtr 20 **Services** Lift **Parking** 18

Wentworth Hotel

★★★ 88% HOTEL

tel: 01728 452312 **Wentworth Rd IP15 5BD**
email: stay@wentworth-aldeburgh.co.uk **web:** www.wentworth-aldeburgh.com
dir: A12 onto A1094, 6m to Aldeburgh, with church on left, left at bottom of hill

Wentworth Hotel is a delightful, privately-owned building overlooking the beach. The attractive, well-maintained public rooms include three stylish lounges as well as a cocktail bar and elegant restaurant. Bedrooms are smartly decorated with co-ordinated fabrics and have many thoughtful touches; some rooms have superb sea views. Several very spacious Mediterranean-style rooms are located across the road.

Rooms 35 (7 annexe) (2 fmly) (5 GF) **S** £94-£142; **D** £156-£320 (incl. bkfst & dinner) **Facilities** FTV WiFi Xmas New Year **Parking** 30 **Notes** LB

The White Lion Hotel

T|A|HOTEL
COLLECTION

★★★ 88% HOTEL

tel: 01728 452720 **Market Cross Place IP15 5BJ**
email: info@whitelion.co.uk **web:** www.whitelion.co.uk
dir: A12 onto A1094, follow signs to Aldeburgh at junct on left. Hotel on right

A popular 15th-century hotel situated at the quiet end of town overlooking the sea. Bedrooms are pleasantly decorated and thoughtfully equipped, many rooms have lovely sea views. Public areas include two lounges and an elegant restaurant, where locally-caught fish and seafood are served. There is also a modern brasserie.

Rooms 38 **Facilities** STV WiFi Xmas New Year **Conf** Class 50 Board 30 Thtr 80 **Parking** 10 **Notes** Civ Wed 90

Read all about
Visiting the Northeast in our feature on page 22

A

ALDERLEY EDGE
Cheshire

Map 16 SJ87

Alderley Edge Hotel

★★★★ 79% 🌸🌸🌸 HOTEL

tel: 01625 583033 **Macclesfield Rd SK9 7BJ**
email: reservations@alderleyedgehotel.com **web:** www.alderleyedgehotel.com
dir: From A34 in Alderley Edge onto B5087 towards Macclesfield. Hotel 200yds on right

This well-furnished hotel, with its charming grounds, was originally a country house built for one of the region's 'cotton kings'. The bedrooms and suites are attractively furnished, offering excellent quality and comfort. The welcoming bar and adjacent lounge lead into the conservatory restaurant where imaginative, memorable food and friendly, attentive service are highlights of any visit.

Rooms 50 (4 fmly) (6 GF) 🐾 **Facilities** STV WiFi ➷ **Conf** Class 40 Board 30 Thtr 120 **Services** Lift **Parking** 90 **Notes** ⊗ Closed 1 Jan RS 25-26 Dec Civ Wed 114

Premier Inn Alderley Edge

BUDGET HOTEL

tel: 0871 527 8016 **Congleton Rd SK9 7AA**
web: www.premierinn.com
dir: From N: M56 junct 6, A538 towards Wilmslow, onto A34 towards Birmingham. From S: M6 junct 17, A534 towards Congleton, onto A34 towards Manchester. Hotel adjacent to De Trafford Arms

High quality, budget accommodation ideal for both families and business travellers. Spacious, en suite bedrooms feature tea and coffee making facilities, and Freeview TV in most hotels. Internet access and WiFi are available for a small fee. The adjacent family restaurant features a wide and varied menu. See also the Hotel Groups pages.

Rooms 37

ALDERMINSTER
Warwickshire

Map 10 SP24

Ettington Park Hotel

★★★★ 🌸🌸 COUNTRY HOUSE HOTEL

Hand PICKED HOTELS
BUILT FOR PLEASURE

tel: 01789 450123 & 0845 072 7454 **CV37 8BU**
email: ettingtonpark@handpicked.co.uk
web: www.handpickedhotels.co.uk/ettingtonpark
dir: Off A3400, 5m S of Stratford, just outside Alderminster

Set in 40-acre grounds in the picturesque Stour Valley, Ettington Park offers the best of both worlds - the peace of the countryside and easy access to main roads and motorway networks. Bedrooms are spacious and individually decorated; views include the delightful grounds and gardens, or the historic chapel. Luxurious day rooms extend to the period drawing room, the oak-panelled dining room with inlays of family crests, a range of contemporary meeting rooms and an indoor leisure centre.

Rooms 48 (20 annexe) (5 fmly) (10 GF) 🐾 **S** £95-£347; **D** £104-£357 (incl. bkfst)*
Facilities STV WiFi ⓢ ♨ ♨ Clay pigeon shooting Archery Sauna Steam room Xmas New Year **Conf** Class 48 Board 48 Thtr 90 Del from £150 to £215* **Services** Lift **Parking** 100 **Notes** LB ⊗ Civ Wed 96

ALDERSHOT
Hampshire

Map 5 SU85

Potters International Hotel

★★★ 70% HOTEL

tel: 01252 344000 **1 Fleet Rd GU11 2ET**
email: reservations@pottersinthotel.com **web:** www.pottersinthotel.com
dir: Access via A325 & A321 towards Fleet

This modern hotel is located within easy reach of Aldershot. Extensive air-conditioned public areas include ample lounge areas, a pub and a more formal restaurant; there are also conference rooms and a very good leisure club. Bedrooms, mostly spacious, are well equipped and have been attractively decorated and furnished.

Rooms 103 (9 fmly) (9 GF) **Facilities** STV WiFi ⓢ Gym Beauty treatment room **Conf** Class 250 Board 100 Thtr 400 **Services** Lift **Parking** 120 **Notes** ⊗

A

Premier Inn Aldershot

BUDGET HOTEL

tel: 0871 527 8018 **7 Wellington Av GU11 1SQ**
web: www.premierinn.com
dir: M3 junct 4, A331. A325 through Farnborough. Pass Barons BMW then Queens Rdbt. Adjacent to Willems Park Brewers Fayre

High quality, budget accommodation ideal for both families and business travellers. Spacious, en suite bedrooms feature tea and coffee making facilities, and Freeview TV in most hotels. Internet access and WiFi are available for a small fee. The adjacent family restaurant features a wide and varied menu. See also the Hotel Groups pages.

Rooms 60

| **ALDWARK** | **Map 19 SE46** |
| North Yorkshire | |

Aldwark Manor Golf & Spa Hotel

★★★★ 77% HOTEL

QHOTELS
INSPIRED BY YOU

tel: 01347 838146 **YO61 1UF**
email: aldwarkmanor@qhotels.co.uk **web:** www.qhotels.co.uk
dir: A1/A59 towards Green Hammerton, then B6265 Little Ouseburn. Follow signs for Aldwark Bridge/Manor. A19 through Linton-on-Ouse

Mature parkland forms the impressive backdrop for this rambling 19th-century mansion, with the River Ure flowing gently through the hotel's own 18-hole golf course. Bedrooms vary - the main-house rooms are traditional and those in the extension are modern in design. Impressive conference and banqueting facilities and a stylish, very well equipped leisure club are available. QHotels is the AA Hotel Group of the Year 2014-15.

Rooms 54 (6 fmly) ♠ **Facilities** Spa FTV WiFi ⚒ ♨ 18 Putt green Gym Health & beauty Xmas New Year **Conf** Class 100 Board 80 Thtr 240 Del from £135 to £165 **Services** Lift **Parking** 150 **Notes** Civ Wed 140

| **ALFRISTON** | **Map 6 TQ50** |
| East Sussex | |

Deans Place

★★★ 86% ⚅⚅ HOTEL

CLASSIC
BRITISH HOTELS

tel: 01323 870248 **Seaford Rd BN26 5TW**
email: mail@deansplacehotel.co.uk **web:** www.deansplacehotel.co.uk
dir: Exit A27 between Eastbourne & Brighton, signed Alfriston & Drusillas Zoo Park. S through village towards Seaford

Situated on the southern fringe of the village, this friendly hotel is set in attractive gardens. Bedrooms vary in size and are well appointed with good facilities. A wide range of food is offered including an extensive bar menu and a fine dining option in Harcourt's Restaurant.

Rooms 36 (4 fmly) (8 GF) **S** £25-£95; **D** £65-£135* **Facilities** FTV WiFi ⚒ Putt green ♨ Boules Xmas New Year **Conf** Class 100 Board 60 Thtr 200 Del £140* **Parking** 100 **Notes** LB Civ Wed 150

The Star Alfriston

★★★ 77% HOTEL

tel: 01323 870495 **BN26 5TA**
email: bookings@thestaralfriston.co.uk **web:** www.thestaralfriston.co.uk
dir: 2m from A27, at Drusillas rdbt follow Alfriston signs. Hotel on right in centre of High St

Built in the 13th century and reputedly one of the country's oldest inns, this charming establishment is ideally situated for walking the South Downs or exploring the Sussex coast. Bedrooms, including two feature rooms and a mini suite, are traditionally decorated but with comfortable, modern facilities. Public areas include cosy lounges with open log fires, a bar and a popular restaurant serving a wide choice of dishes using mainly local produce. Guests can also enjoy luxury spa treatments by appointment.

Rooms 37 (1 fmly) (11 GF) **S** £70-£90; **D** £99-£135 (incl. bkfst) **Facilities** FTV WiFi Xmas New Year **Conf** Class 60 Board 46 Thtr 85 Del from £125 to £145 **Parking** 35 **Notes** LB Civ Wed 120

| **ALMONDSBURY** | **Map 4 ST68** |
| Gloucestershire | |

Aztec Hotel & Spa

★★★★ 80% ⚅ HOTEL

shire

tel: 01454 201090 **Aztec West Business Park, Almondsbury BS32 4TS**
email: aztec@shirehotels.com **web:** www.aztechotelbristol.com

(For full entry see Bristol)

| **ALNWICK** | |
| *See* **Embleton** | |

A

ALSTON
Cumbria   Map 18 NY74

Lovelady Shield Country House Hotel

★★★ 82% ◉◉ COUNTRY HOUSE HOTEL

tel: 01434 381203 & 381305 **CA9 3LF**
email: enquiries@lovelady.co.uk **web:** www.lovelady.co.uk
dir: 2m E, signed off A689 at junct with B6294

Located in the heart of the Pennines close to England's highest market town, this delightful country house is set in three acres of landscaped gardens. Accommodation is provided in stylish, thoughtfully equipped bedrooms. Carefully prepared meals are served in the elegant dining room and there is a choice of appealing lounges with log fires in the cooler months.

Rooms 10 (1 fmly) ☏ S £110-£120; **D** £120-£170 (incl. bkfst)* **Facilities** FTV WiFi New Year **Conf** Class 12 Board 12 Del from £120 to £150* **Parking** 20 **Notes** LB Civ Wed 100

Alston House

RESTAURANT WITH ROOMS

tel: 01434 382200 ◷ 01434 382493 **Townfoot CA9 3RN**
email: alstonhouse@fsmail.net **web:** www.alstonhouse.co.uk
dir: On A686 opposite Spar garage

Located at the foot of the town, this family-owned restaurant with rooms provides well-equipped, stylish and comfortable accommodation. The kitchen serves both modern and traditional dishes with flair and creativity. Alston House runs a café during the day serving light meals and afternoon teas.

Rooms 7 (3 fmly)

ALTON
Hampshire   Map 5 SU73

The Anchor Inn

◉◉ RESTAURANT WITH ROOMS

tel: 01420 23261 **Lower Froyle GU34 4NA**
email: info@anchorinnatlowerfroyle.co.uk **web:** www.anchorinnatlowerfroyle.co.uk
dir: From A3 follow Bentley signs & inn signs

The Anchor Inn is located in the tranquil village of Lower Froyle. Luxury rooms are designed to reflect the traditional English inn style with charming decor, pictures and a selection of books. The restaurant welcomes both residents and non-residents with classic pub cooking, in impressive surroundings, that feature wooden floors and period furnishings.

Rooms 5

ALTRINCHAM
Greater Manchester   Map 15 SJ78

Mercure Altrincham Bowden Hotel

★★★ 78% HOTEL

tel: 0161 928 7121 & 941 1866 **Langham Rd, Bowdon WA14 2HT**
email: enquiries@hotels-altrincham.com **web:** www.hotels-altrincham.com
dir: A556 towards Manchester, into Park Rd at lights, hotel 1m on right

Situated within easy access of Manchester and the Airport, this hotel offers comfortable and well equipped bedrooms. Public areas include the Café Bar and The Restaurant, both serving a good choice of dishes. A well-equipped leisure centre has an indoor heated pool, spa, sauna and comprehensive air-conditioned gym. There is free WiFi throughout.

Rooms 87 (8 fmly) (13 GF) **Facilities** FTV WiFi ⊗ Gym Sauna Steam room Xmas New Year **Conf** Class 48 Board 50 Thtr 120 **Parking** 125 **Notes** Civ Wed 120

Premier Inn Manchester Altrincham

BUDGET HOTEL

tel: 0871 527 8738 **Manchester Rd WA14 4PH**
web: www.premierinn.com
dir: From N: M60 junct 7, A56 towards Altrincham. From S: M6 junct 19, A556 then A56 towards Sale

High quality, budget accommodation ideal for both families and business travellers. Spacious, en suite bedrooms feature tea and coffee making facilities, and Freeview TV in most hotels. Internet access and WiFi are available for a small fee. The adjacent family restaurant features a wide and varied menu. See also the Hotel Groups pages.

Rooms 46

ALVESTON
Gloucestershire   Map 4 ST68

Alveston House Hotel

★★★ 83% ◉ HOTEL

tel: 01454 415050 **Davids Ln BS35 2LA**
email: info@alvestonhousehotel.co.uk **web:** www.alvestonhousehotel.co.uk
dir: M5 junct 14 from N or junct 16 from S, on A38

In a quiet area with easy access to the city and a short drive from both the M4 and M5, this smartly presented hotel provides an impressive combination of good service, friendly hospitality and a relaxed atmosphere. The comfortable bedrooms are well equipped for both business and leisure guests. The restaurant offers carefully prepared fresh food, and the pleasant bar and conservatory area is perfect for enjoying a pre-dinner drink.

Rooms 29 (1 fmly) (6 GF) ☏ S £80-£105; **D** £125-£150 (incl. bkfst)* **Facilities** FTV WiFi ↻ Beauty treatments Xmas New Year **Conf** Class 48 Board 50 Thtr 85 Del from £135 to £150* **Parking** 75 **Notes** LB Civ Wed 75

A

AMBERLEY
West Sussex

Map 6 TQ01

Amberley Castle

★★★★ @@@ COUNTRY HOUSE HOTEL

GIDLEIGH COLLECTION

tel: 01798 831992 **BN18 9LT**
email: info@amberleycastle.co.uk **web:** www.amberleycastle.co.uk
dir: On B2139, off A29 between Bury & Storrington

The delightful castle hotel is idyllically set in the Sussex countryside, and boasts 900 years of history. The battlements (complete with mighty portcullis ;one of the few in Europe that still works) enclose the hotel. Beyond these walls are acres of stunning parkland that feature formal gardens, Koi ponds and a thatched treehouse accessed by a rope bridge. Guests can enjoy award-winning cuisine in the magnificent restaurant - pre-booking is essential. Named after Sussex castles, each of the sumptuously furnished bedrooms and suites is unique in design. Luxury amenities are provided in all rooms.

Rooms 19 (5 annexe) (5 fmly) (5 GF) ☏ **D** £265-£615 (incl. bkfst)* **Facilities** FTV WiFi ▷ ⛳ Putt green ⛵ Xmas New Year **Conf** Class 30 Board 30 Thtr 56 Del from £350 to £450* **Parking** 40 **Notes** ⊗ No children 5yrs Civ Wed 56

AMBLESIDE
Cumbria

Map 18 NY30

See also **Elterwater**

Waterhead Hotel

English Lakes
Hotels Resorts & Venues

★★★★ 78% @ TOWN HOUSE HOTEL

tel: 015394 32566 **Lake Rd LA22 OER**
email: waterhead@englishlakes.co.uk **web:** www.englishlakes.co.uk
dir: A591 to Ambleside. Hotel opposite Waterhead Pier

With an enviable location opposite the bay, this well-established hotel offers contemporary and comfortable accommodation with CD/DVD players, plasma screens and internet access. There is a bar with a garden terrace overlooking the lake and a stylish restaurant serving classical cuisine with a modern twist. Staff are very attentive and friendly. Guests can enjoy full use of the leisure facilities at a nearby hotel.

Rooms 41 (3 fmly) (7 GF) **S** £105-£198; **D** £135-£226 (incl. bkfst)* **Facilities** FTV WiFi ▷ Free use of leisure facilities at sister hotel (1m) Xmas New Year **Conf** Class 30 Board 26 Thtr 40 Del from £122* **Parking** 43 **Notes** LB Civ Wed 80

BEST WESTERN Ambleside Salutation Hotel

★★★ 86% HOTEL

Best Western

tel: 015394 32244 **Lake Rd LA22 9BX**
email: ambleside@hotelslakedistrict.com **web:** www.hotelslakedistrict.com
dir: A591 to Ambleside, onto one-way system, Wansfell Rd into Compston Rd. Right at lights into village

A former coaching inn, this hotel lies in the centre of the town. Bedrooms are tastefully appointed and thoughtfully equipped; many boast balconies and fine views. Inviting public areas include an attractive restaurant and a choice of comfortable lounges for relaxing. For the more energetic there is a swimming pool and small gym, and for relaxation a spa and treatment rooms.

Rooms 54 (12 annexe) (4 fmly) (1 GF) ☏ **S** £60-£80; **D** £120-£160 (incl. bkfst)* **Facilities** Spa WiFi ⊗ Gym Sauna Steam room Xmas New Year **Conf** Class 36 Board 26 Thtr 80 Del from £128 to £158* **Services** Lift **Parking** 54 **Notes** LB Closed 14-15 Dec

See advert on page 46

A

AMBLESIDE *continued*

Regent Hotel

★★★ 82% HOTEL

tel: 015394 32254 **Waterhead Bay LA22 0ES**
email: info@regentlakes.co.uk **web:** www.regentlakes.co.uk
dir: M6 junct 36, 1m S on A591

This attractive holiday hotel, situated close to Waterhead Bay, offers a warm welcome. Bedrooms come in a variety of styles, including three suites and five bedrooms in the garden wing. Public areas are contemporary and comfortable; the light, airy restaurant is the setting for hearty, enjoyable meals.

Rooms 30 (7 fmly) (7 GF) ↖ **S** £75-£139; **D** £85-£149 (incl. bkfst)* **Facilities** FTV WiFi New Year **Parking** 39 **Notes** LB Closed 21-27 Dec

Rothay Manor

★★★ 81% HOTEL

tel: 015394 33605 **Rothay Bridge LA22 0EH**
email: hotel@rothaymanor.co.uk **web:** www.rothaymanor.co.uk/aa
dir: In Ambleside follow signs for Coniston (A593). Hotel 0.25m SW of Ambleside opposite rugby pitch

A long-established hotel, this attractive listed building built in Regency style, is a short walk from both the town centre and Lake Windermere. Spacious bedrooms, including suites, family rooms and rooms with balconies, are comfortably equipped and furnished to a very high standard. Public areas include a choice of lounges, a spacious restaurant and conference facilities.

Rooms 19 (2 annexe) (7 fmly) (3 GF) ↖ **S** £85-£175; **D** £99-£220 (incl. bkfst)* **Facilities** STV WiFi ⌖ Free use of nearby leisure centre Free fishing permit Xmas New Year **Conf** Board 18 Thtr 22 **Parking** 45 **Notes** ⊗ Closed 2-22 Jan

AMESBURY
Wiltshire
Map 5 SU14

Holiday Inn Salisbury - Stonehenge

★★★★ 75% ◉ HOTEL

Holiday Inn

tel: 0845 241 3535 **Midsummer Place, Solstice Park SP4 7SQ**
email: reservations@hisalisbury-stonehenge.co.uk
web: www.hisalisbury-stonehenge.co.uk
dir: Exit A303, follow signs into Solstice Park. Hotel adjacent to service area

This hotel of striking modern design is located on the A303 very close to Stonehenge. All bedrooms have been appointed to the highest standards with unique headboards, air conditioning and broadband connection included in the generous amenities. Fluffy towels and powerful showers are provided in the modern bathrooms. The Solstice Bar and Grill is open from 7am-11pm and offers a range of snacks and meals.

Rooms 103 (24 fmly) (8 GF) ↖ **D** fr £9 **Facilities** FTV WiFi ⌖ Xmas New Year **Conf** Class 20 Board 20 Thtr 25 **Services** Lift Air con **Parking** 168 **Notes** ⊗

A

ANDOVER
Hampshire   Map 5 SU34

Esseborne Manor

★★★ 80% HOTEL

tel: 01264 736444 **Hurstbourne Tarrant SP11 OER**
email: info@esseborne-manor.co.uk **web:** www.esseborne-manor.co.uk
dir: Halfway between Andover & Newbury on A343, 1m N of Hurstbourne Tarrant

Set in two acres of well-tended gardens, this attractive manor house is surrounded by the open countryside of the North Wessex Downs. Bedrooms are delightfully individual and are split between the main house, an adjoining courtyard and separate garden cottage. There's a wonderfully relaxed atmosphere throughout, and public rooms combine elegance with comfort.

Rooms 18 (7 annexe) (5 fmly) (6 GF) ⌁ **S** £92-£133; **D** £100-£180 (incl. bkfst)*
Facilities STV FTV WiFi ⌁ ⌁ New Year **Conf** Class 40 Board 30 Thtr 60 Del £145*
Parking 50 **Notes** LB Civ Wed 100

Premier Inn Andover

BUDGET HOTEL

tel: 0871 527 8020 **West Portway Industrial Estate, Joule Rd SP10 3UX**
web: www.premierinn.com
dir: From A303 follow A342/A343 signs. Hotel at rdbt junct of A342 & A343 adjacent to Portway Inn Brewers Fayre

High quality, budget accommodation ideal for both families and business travellers. Spacious, en suite bedrooms feature tea and coffee making facilities, and Freeview TV in most hotels. Internet access and WiFi are available for a small fee. The adjacent family restaurant features a wide and varied menu. See also the Hotel Groups pages.

Rooms 50

ANSTY
Warwickshire   Map 11 SP48

Macdonald Ansty Hall

★★★★ 75% HOTEL   MACDONALD HOTELS & RESORTS

tel: 0844 879 9031 **Main Rd CV7 9HZ**
email: ansty@macdonald-hotels.co.uk **web:** www.macdonald-hotels.co.uk/anstyhall
dir: M6 junct 2 onto B4065 signed Ansty. Hotel 1.5m on left

Dating back to 1678, this Grade II listed Georgian house is set in eight acres of attractive grounds and woodland. The hotel enjoys a central yet tranquil location. Spacious bedrooms feature a traditional decorative style and a range of extras. Rooms are divided between the main house and the newer annexe.

Rooms 62 (39 annexe) (4 fmly) (22 GF) **Facilities** FTV WiFi ⌁ Xmas New Year
Conf Class 60 Board 60 Thtr 150 Del from £120 to £180* **Services** Lift **Parking** 100
Notes Civ Wed 100

APPLEBY-IN-WESTMORLAND
Cumbria   Map 18 NY62

Appleby Manor Country House Hotel

★★★★ 79% COUNTRY HOUSE HOTEL

tel: 017683 51571 **Roman Rd CA16 6JB**
email: reception@applebymanor.co.uk **web:** www.applebymanor.co.uk
dir: M6 junct 40, A66 towards Brough. Take Appleby turn, immediately right. 0.5m to hotel

This imposing country mansion is set in extensive grounds amid stunning Cumbrian scenery. The Dunbobbin family and their experienced staff ensure a warm welcome and attentive service. The thoughtfully equipped bedrooms vary in style and include the impressive Heelis Suite; some rooms also have patio areas. The bar offers a wide range of malt whiskies and the restaurant serves carefully prepared meals. AA Eco Hotel of the Year 2014-2015.

Rooms 30 (7 annexe) (9 fmly) (10 GF) ⌁ **D** £99-£240 (incl. bkfst)* **Facilities** FTV
WiFi ⌁ ⌁ Putt green Steam room Spa bath Sauna Table tennis Pool table New Year
Conf Class 25 Board 28 Thtr 38 Del £140* **Parking** 51 **Notes** LB ⌀ Closed 24-26
Dec RS 6-13 Jun Civ Wed 60

ARLINGHAM
Gloucestershire   Map 4 SO71

The Old Passage Inn

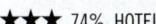 RESTAURANT WITH ROOMS

tel: 01452 740547 **Passage Rd GL2 7JR**
email: oldpassage@btconnect.com **web:** www.theoldpassage.com
dir: A38 onto B4071 through Frampton on Severn. 4m to Arlingham, through village to river

Delightfully located on the very edge of the River Severn, this relaxing restaurant with rooms combines high quality food with an air of tranquillity. Bedrooms and bathrooms are decorated in a modern style and include a collection of welcome extras such as air conditioning and a well-stocked mini-bar. The menu offers a wide range of seafood and shellfish dishes including crab, oysters and lobsters from Cornwall (kept alive in seawater tanks) and has been recognised for its excellence with two AA Rosettes. An outdoor terrace is available in warmer months.

Rooms 3

ARUNDEL
West Sussex   Map 6 TQ00

Comfort Inn Arundel

★★★ 74% HOTEL

tel: 01903 840840 **Lyminster Rd, Crossbush Services BN17 7QQ**
web: www.comfortinnarundel.com
dir: A27/A284, 1st right into services

A modern, purpose-built hotel ideally situated for exploring the nearby historic town and castle. The present owners have totally refurbished the property which now has a smart brasserie restaurant and bar. There is a range of meeting rooms, all air-conditioned, which makes this an ideal venue for business guests. Bedrooms are spacious, smartly decorated and well equipped.

Rooms 53 **Facilities** WiFi ⌁ **Conf** Class 35 Board 35 Thtr 35

ARUNDEL *continued*

A

Premier Inn Arundel

BUDGET HOTEL

tel: 0871 527 8022 **Crossbush Ln BN18 9PQ**
web: www.premierinn.com
dir: At junct of A27 &A284, 1m E of Arundel

High quality, budget accommodation ideal for both families and business travellers. Spacious, en suite bedrooms feature tea and coffee making facilities, and Freeview TV in most hotels. Internet access and WiFi are available for a small fee. The adjacent family restaurant features a wide and varied menu. See also the Hotel Groups pages.

Rooms 30

The Town House

 RESTAURANT WITH ROOMS

tel: 01903 883847 **65 High St BN18 9AJ**
email: enquiries@thetownhouse.co.uk **web:** www.thetownhouse.co.uk
dir: A27 to Arundel, into High Street, establishment on left at top of hill

This is an elegant, Grade II listed Regency building overlooking Arundel Castle, just a short walk from the shops and centre of the town. Bedrooms and public areas retain the building's unspoilt character. The ceiling in the dining room is particularly spectacular and originated in Florence in the 16th century.

Rooms 4

ASCOT	Map 6 SU96
Berkshire	

Coworth Park

★★★★★ 86% ⊛ COUNTRY HOUSE HOTEL

tel: 01344 876600 **London Rd SL5 7SE**
email: info.coworthpark@dorchestercollection.com **web:** www.coworthpark.com
dir: M25 junct 13 S onto A30 Egham/Bagshot. Past Wentworth Golf Club turn right at lights onto Blacknest Rd (A329) hotel on left

Set in 240 acres of stunning parkland, Coworth Park is part of the luxury Dorchester Collection, sister to The Dorchester in London. The hotel offers luxurious guest rooms and suites, polo grounds, stables and a spa. Children are well cared for too, with a 'Kids Concierge' who can arrange a wide variety of activities for them. The hotel maintains a strong 'green' policy, as does the kitchen team where local quality suppliers are a priority. Casual dining is available in the popular Barn restaurant (1 AA Rosette), in a converted stable block. The AA Rosette award for the fine-dining Restaurant Coworth Park is suspended due to a change of chef. The award will be in place once the inspectors have assessed the food created by the new kitchen regime.

Rooms 70 (40 fmly) (27 GF) ⌦ **D** £255-£550 (incl. bkfst)* **Facilities** Spa STV FTV WiFi ⌕ 🐾 ♨ 🏌 Gym Polo Equestrian centre Archery Laser clays Falconry Duck herding ♫ Xmas New Year Child facilities **Conf** Class 54 Board 40 Thtr 100 Del from £305 to £425* **Services** Lift Air con **Parking** 100 **Notes** LB ⊗ Civ Wed 250

Macdonald Berystede Hotel & Spa

★★★★ 78% ⊛ HOTEL

tel: 0844 879 9104 **Bagshot Rd, Sunninghill SL5 9JH**
email: general.berystede@macdonald-hotels.co.uk
web: www.macdonald-hotels.co.uk/berystede
dir: A30, B3020 (Windmill Pub). 1.25m to hotel on left just before junct with A330

This impressive Victorian mansion, close to Ascot Racecourse, offers executive bedrooms that are spacious, comfortable and particularly well equipped. Public rooms include a cosy bar and an elegant restaurant which serves creative dishes. The impressive self-contained conference centre and spa facility appeal to both conference and leisure guests.

Rooms 126 (61 fmly) (33 GF) **Facilities** Spa STV WiFi ⌕ 🐾 🏌 Gym Leisure complex (thermal & beauty treatments) Outdoor garden spa Xmas New Year **Conf** Class 220 Board 150 Thtr 330 **Services** Lift **Parking** 200 **Notes** Civ Wed 300

ASENBY	Map 19 SE37
North Yorkshire	

Crab Manor

⊛⊛ RESTAURANT WITH ROOMS

tel: 01845 577286 📄 01845 577496 **YO7 3QL**
web: www.crabandlobster.co.uk
dir: A1(M) junct 49, on outskirts of village

This stunning, 18th-century Grade II listed Georgian manor is located in the heart of the North Yorkshire Dales. Each bedroom is themed around the world's most famous hotels and has high-quality furnishings, beautiful wallpaper, and thoughtful extras. Scandinavian log cabins are also available within the grounds, which have their own terrace with hot tubs. There is a comfortable lounge bar where guests can relax in the Manor before enjoying dinner next door in the Crab & Lobster Restaurant, which specialises in fresh local seafood. The attractive gardens offer a lovely backdrop.

Rooms 14 (6 annexe) (3 fmly)

ASHBOURNE	Map 10 SK14
Derbyshire	

Callow Hall Hotel

★★★ 82% ⊛⊛ HOTEL

tel: 01335 300900 **Mappleton Rd DE6 2AA**
email: info@callowhall.co.uk **web:** www.callowhall.co.uk
dir: Telephone for directions

This delightful, creeper-clad, early Victorian house, set on a 44-acre estate, enjoys views over Bentley Brook and the Dove Valley. The atmosphere is relaxed and welcoming, and some of the bedrooms in the main house have comfortable sitting areas. Public rooms feature high ceilings, ornate plaster work and antique furniture. The elegant restaurant offers accomplished cuisine.

Rooms 16 (1 fmly) (2 GF) ⌦ **Facilities** FTV WiFi ⌕ ♨ Xmas New Year **Conf** Class 40 Board 20 Thtr 40 **Parking** 20 **Notes** Civ Wed 100

Station Hotel

★★ 76% SMALL HOTEL

tel: 01335 3000035 **Station Rd DE6 1AA**
email: stationhotel@ashbourne.myzen.co.uk **web:** www.stationhotel.eu

The Station Hotel is conveniently located close to the station and the centre of Ashbourne. The public areas are welcoming and spacious. Bedrooms are equally strong in their size and quality. The hotel is family owned and run ensuring a personal and very friendly welcome. Dinner is served five nights a week and available by reservation the rest. Ample car parking is also available.

Rooms 12 **S** £65-£85; **D** £80-£135 (incl. bkfst) **Facilities** FTV WiFi ⊬ **Conf** Class 12 Board 14 Thtr 20 Del from £105 to £195 **Parking** 15 **Notes** ⊗ No children 14yrs

ASHBY-DE-LA-ZOUCH	Map 11 SK31
Leicestershire	

Premier Inn Ashby De La Zouch

BUDGET HOTEL

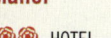

tel: 0871 527 8026 **Flagstaff Island LE65 1DS**
web: www.premierinn.com
dir: M1 junct 23a, follow A42 (M42), Tamworth & Birmingham signs. Hotel at rdbt at A42 junct 13. (NB for Sat Nav use LE65 1JP)

High quality, budget accommodation ideal for both families and business travellers. Spacious, en suite bedrooms feature tea and coffee making facilities, and Freeview TV in most hotels. Internet access and WiFi are available for a small fee. The adjacent family restaurant features a wide and varied menu. See also the Hotel Groups pages.

Rooms 40

ASHFORD	Map 7 TR04
Kent	

INSPECTORS' CHOICE

Eastwell Manor

★★★★ HOTEL

tel: 01233 213000 & 213020 **Eastwell Park, Boughton Lees TN25 4HR**
email: enquiries@eastwellmanor.co.uk **web:** www.eastwellmanor.co.uk
dir: M20 junct 9, follow Faversham A251 signs. On A251 hotel on left on entering Boughton Lees

Set in 62 acres of landscaped grounds, this lovely hotel dates back to the Norman Conquest and boasts a number of interesting features, including carved wood-panelled rooms and huge baronial stone fireplaces. Accommodation is divided between the manor house and the courtyard mews cottages. The luxury Pavilion Spa in the grounds has an all-day brasserie, and award-winning fine dining is offered in the main restaurant.

Rooms 62 (39 annexe) (2 fmly) (15 GF) ⊠ **S** £85-£450; **D** £85-£450 (incl. bkfst)* **Facilities** Spa FTV WiFi ⊠ ⊬ ♪ 9 ⊊ Putt green ⇲ Gym Boules ♫ Xmas New Year **Conf** Class 70 Board 60 Thtr 180 Del from £159* **Services** Lift **Parking** 200 **Notes** LB ⊗ Civ Wed 450

Ashford International Hotel

★★★★ 81% HOTEL

tel: 01233 219988 **Simone Weil Av TN24 8UX**
email: ashford@qhotels.co.uk **web:** www.qhotels.co.uk
dir: M20 junct 9, exit for Ashford/Canterbury. Left at 1st rdbt, hotel 200mtrs on left

Situated just off the M20 and with easy links to the Eurotunnel, Eurostar and ferry terminals, this hotel has been stunningly appointed. The slick, stylishly presented bedrooms are equipped with the latest amenities. Public areas include the spacious Horizons Wine Bar and Restaurant serving a competitively priced menu, and Quench Sports Bar for relaxing drinks. The Reflections leisure club boasts a pool, fully-equipped gym, spa facilities and treatment rooms. QHotels is the AA Hotel Group of the Year 2014-15.

Rooms 179 (29 fmly) (57 GF) ⊠ **S** £75-£189; **D** £87-£201 **Facilities** Spa WiFi ⊠ Gym Aroma steam room Rock sauna Feature shower Ice fountain Xmas New Year **Conf** Class 180 Board 26 Thtr 400 Del from £119 to £189 **Services** Lift Air con **Parking** 400 **Notes** LB Civ Wed 400

Premier Inn Ashford Central

BUDGET HOTEL

tel: 0871 527 8030 **Hall Av, Orbital Park, Sevington TN24 0GN**
web: www.premierinn.com
dir: M20 junct 10 S'bound; 4th exit at rdbt. (N'bound: 1st exit onto A2070 signed Brenzett). Hotel on right at next rdbt

High quality, budget accommodation ideal for both families and business travellers. Spacious, en suite bedrooms feature tea and coffee making facilities, and Freeview TV in most hotels. Internet access and WiFi are available for a small fee. The adjacent family restaurant features a wide and varied menu. See also the Hotel Groups pages.

Rooms 60

Premier Inn Ashford (Eureka Leisure Park)

BUDGET HOTEL

tel: 0871 527 8028 **Eureka Leisure Park TN25 4BN**
web: www.premierinn.com
dir: M20 junct 9, take 1st exit on left

Rooms 74

Premier Inn Ashford North

BUDGET HOTEL

tel: 0871 527 8032 **Maidstone Road (A20), Hothfield Common TN26 1AP**
web: www.premierinn.com
dir: M20 junct 9, A20 follow Lenham signs. Hotel between Ashford & Charing

Rooms 60

A

ASHINGTON
Northumberland   Map 21 NZ28

Premier Inn Ashington

BUDGET HOTEL

tel: 0871 527 8034 **Queen Elizabeth Country Park, Woodhorn NE63 9AT**
web: www.premierinn.com
dir: From A1 follow signs to Morpeth then Woodhorn Colliery Museum/Ashington. Through Ashington. Hotel in Queen Elizabeth II Country Park

High quality, budget accommodation ideal for both families and business travellers. Spacious, en suite bedrooms feature tea and coffee making facilities, and Freeview TV in most hotels. Internet access and WiFi are available for a small fee. The adjacent family restaurant features a wide and varied menu. See also the Hotel Groups pages.

Rooms 20

ASPLEY GUISE
Bedfordshire   Map 11 SP93

BEST WESTERN Moore Place Hotel

★★★ 79% HOTEL

tel: 01908 282000 **The Square MK17 8DW**
email: business@mooreplace.com **web:** www.mooreplace.com
dir: M1 junct 13, A507 signed Aspley Guise & Woburn Sands. Hotel on left in village square

This impressive Georgian house, set in delightful gardens in the village centre, is very conveniently located for the M1. Bedrooms do vary in size, but consideration has been given to guest comfort, with many thoughtful extras provided. There is a wide range of meeting rooms and private dining options.

Rooms 62 (27 annexe) (2 fmly) (16 GF) ₣ **Facilities** FTV WiFi ⊳ **Conf** Class 24 Board 20 Thtr 50 **Parking** 70 **Notes** Civ Wed 65

ATTLEBOROUGH
Norfolk   Map 13 TM09

Sherbourne House Hotel

★★★ 77% SMALL HOTEL

tel: 01953 454363 **8 Attleborough Rd NR17 2JX**
email: stay@sherbourne-house.co.uk **web:** www.sherbourne-house.co.uk
dir: A11 from London/Thetford towards Attleborough, through town centre, pass church on right, next left, hotel on right after 500mtrs

Built in 1740 this fine manor house is set among beautifully landscaped gardens and is a short walk from the historic market town of Attleborough. Much of the house has been refurbished and many of the original features sympathetically restored. Bedrooms are spacious, comfortable and there is a light-filled conservatory lounge for guests. An extensive dinner menu is available in the evenings and freshly prepared breakfasts are served in the charming breakfast room overlooking the gardens. WiFi is available throughout the property and the hotel is ideally placed for visitors to Snetterton motor racing circuit.

Rooms 8 (1 fmly) (1 GF) ₣ **S** £55-£60; **D** £85-£109 (incl. bkfst)* **Facilities** FTV WiFi **Conf** Class 18 Board 22 Thtr 30 Del £100* **Parking** 20

AUSTWICK
North Yorkshire   Map 18 SD76

The Traddock

◉◉ RESTAURANT WITH ROOMS

tel: 015242 51224 ▤ 015242 51796 **LA2 8BY**
email: info@thetraddock.co.uk **web:** www.thetraddock.co.uk
dir: From Skipton take A65 towards Kendal, 3m after Settle turn right signed Austwick, cross hump back bridge, 100yds on left

Situated within the Yorkshire Dales National Park and a peaceful village environment, this fine Georgian country house with well-tended gardens offers a haven of calm and good hospitality. There are two comfortable lounges with real fires and fine furnishings, as well as a cosy bar and an elegant dining room serving fine cuisine. Bedrooms are individually styled with many homely touches.

Rooms 12 (2 fmly)

AXBRIDGE
Somerset   Map 4 ST45

The Oak House

◉◉ RESTAURANT WITH ROOMS

tel: 01934 732444 ▤ 01934 733112 **The Square BS26 2AP**
email: info@theoakhousesomerset.com **web:** www.theoakhousesomerset.com
dir: M5 junct 22, A38 N, turn right towards Axbridge & Cheddar

This impressive restaurant with rooms is located in the middle of the village and has undergone a considerable transformation in recent years. It now provides a relaxed, high quality experience, whether guests are coming to enjoy the restaurant or to stay in one of the nine bedrooms above. Hospitality and service are delivered in an efficient and helpful manner by a young and enthusiastic team. The kitchen has a serious approach and delivers delightful dishes full of flavour, utilising the best quality produce.

Rooms 9 (2 fmly)

AXMINSTER
Devon   Map 4 SY29

See also **Colyford**

Fairwater Head Hotel

★★★ 77% ◉ HOTEL

tel: 01297 678349 **Hawkchurch EX13 5TX**
email: stay@fairwaterheadhotel.co.uk **web:** www.fairwaterheadhotel.co.uk
dir: From B3165 Crewkerne to Lyme Regis road, follow Hawkchurch signs

This elegant Edwardian country house provides a perfect location for anyone looking for a peaceful break. Surrounded by extensive gardens and rolling countryside, the setting guarantees relaxation. Bedrooms are located both within the main house and the garden wing, and all provide good levels of comfort. Public areas are very appealing and include lounge areas, a bar and an elegant restaurant. Food is a highlight with excellent local produce prepared with care and skill.

Rooms 16 (4 annexe) (8 GF) ₣ **Facilities** FTV WiFi Library Xmas New Year **Conf** Class 25 Board 20 Thtr 35 **Parking** 30 **Notes** Closed 1-30 Jan Civ Wed 50

B

AYCLIFFE
County Durham   Map 19 NZ22

The County

RESTAURANT WITH ROOMS

tel: 01325 312273 📠 01325 317131 **12 The Green DL5 6LX**
email: info@thecountyaycliffevillage.com web: www.thecountyaycliffevillage.com
dir: A1(M) junct 59, A167 towards Newton Aycliffe. In Aycliffe turn onto village green

Located overlooking the pretty village green yet convenient for the A1, the focus here is on fresh, home-cooked meals, real ales and friendly service. There is a relaxed atmosphere in the bar area, and the restaurant where attractive artwork is displayed. The bedrooms in the smart town house next door are all furnished to a high standard.

Rooms 7

AYLESBURY
Buckinghamshire   Map 11 SP81

INSPECTORS' CHOICE

Hartwell House Hotel, Restaurant & Spa

★★★★ ◎◎ HOTEL

tel: 01296 747444 **Oxford Rd HP17 8NR**
email: info@hartwell-house.com web: www.hartwell-house.com
dir: From S: M40 junct 7, A329 to Thame, then A418 towards Aylesbury. After 6m, through Stone, hotel on left. From N: M40 junct 9 for Bicester. A41 to Aylesbury, A418 to Oxford for 2m. Hotel on right

This beautiful, historic house is set in 90 acres of unspoilt parkland. The grand public rooms are truly magnificent, and feature many fine works of art. The service standards are very high; guests will find that the staff offer attentive and traditional hospitality without stuffiness. There is an elegant, award-winning restaurant where carefully prepared dishes use the best local produce. Bedrooms are spacious, elegant and very comfortable. Most are in the main house, but some, including suites, are in the nearby, renovated coach house, which also houses an excellent spa.

Rooms 46 (16 annexe) (3 fmly) (10 GF) ✦ S £175; D £290-£700 (incl. bkfst)*
Facilities Spa STV WiFi Ꮧ supervised ⌔ ⌔ Gym Sauna Steam rooms Spa bath ♫ Xmas New Year Conf Class 40 Board 40 Thtr 100 Del from £235* Services Lift Parking 91 Notes LB No children 4yrs RS Xmas/New Year Civ Wed 120

Premier Inn Aylesbury

BUDGET HOTEL

tel: 0871 527 8036 **Buckingham Rd HP19 9QL**
web: www.premierinn.com
dir: From Aylesbury on A413 towards Buckingham. Hotel in 1m on left adjacent to lights

High quality, budget accommodation ideal for both families and business travellers. Spacious, en suite bedrooms feature tea and coffee making facilities, and Freeview TV in most hotels. Internet access and WiFi are available for a small fee. The adjacent family restaurant features a wide and varied menu. See also the Hotel Groups pages.

Rooms 64

AYNHO
Northamptonshire   Map 11 SP53

Cartwright Hotel

★★★ 79% HOTEL

tel: 01869 811885 **1-5 Croughton Rd OX17 3BE**
email: cartwright@oxfordshire-hotels.co.uk web: www.oxfordshire-hotels.co.uk
dir: M40 junct 10, A43, B4100 to Aynho

This former coaching inn is located between Banbury and Oxford, making it ideally located for visiting the many tourist attractions the area has to offer including Blenheim Palace and the circuit at Silverstone. The hotel features individually designed bedrooms which range from double to executive, and premiere standards with flat-screen digital TVs and complimentary WiFi. Secure parking is available.

Rooms 21 (12 annexe) (2 fmly) (12 GF) ✦ S £65-£135; D £75-£145 (incl. bkfst)*
Facilities FTV WiFi Ꮧ Xmas New Year Conf Class 40 Board 20 Thtr 45 Del from £135 to £165* Parking 15 Notes LB ⊗

BABBACOMBE
See Torquay

BACTON
Norfolk   Map 13 TG33

The Keswick Hotel

★★★ 70% ◎ HOTEL

tel: 01692 650468 **Walcott Rd NR12 OLS**
email: margaret@keswickhotelbacton.co.uk web: www.keswickhotelbacton.co.uk
dir: On B1159 (coast road)

A small personally run hotel situated by the sea within easy driving distance of the Broads and north Norfolk coastline. The individually decorated bedrooms are pleasantly appointed, have modern facilities and either sea or countryside views. Public areas include a cosy lounge bar with plush sofas, a further lounge area, a restaurant and a conservatory.

Rooms 9 (1 fmly) (3 GF) Facilities FTV WiFi Parking 75 Notes No children

B

BAGSHOT
Surrey   Map 6 SU96

Pennyhill Park, an Exclusive Hotel & Spa

★★★★★ @@@@@ COUNTRY HOUSE HOTEL

tel: 01276 471774 & 486150 **London Rd GU19 5EU**
email: enquiries@pennyhillpark.co.uk **web:** www.pennyhillpark.co.uk
dir: M3 junct 3, follow signs to Camberley. On A30 between Bagshot & Camberley

This delightful country-house hotel, set in 120 acres of grounds, provides every modern comfort. The stylish bedrooms are individually designed and have impressive bathrooms. Leisure facilities include a jogging trail, a golf course and a state-of-the-art spa with a thermal sequencing experience, ozone treated swimming and hydrotherapy pools, along with a comprehensive range of therapies and treatments. The Latymer restaurant, overseen by chef Michael Wignall, has become a true dining destination. There is an eight-seater chef's table for enjoying the tasting menu while watching the action in the kitchen. In addition there are other eating options, and lounges and bars to relax in.

Rooms 123 (97 annexe) (6 fmly) (26 GF) 🛏 **S** £235-£1250; **D** £235-£1250*
Facilities Spa STV WiFi 🏊 🦢 ♿ 9 🎱 Fishing 🦢 Gym Archery Clay shooting Plunge pool Turkish steam room Rugby pitch Bike hire 🎵 Xmas New Year **Conf** Class 108 Board 55 Thtr 140 Del from £325* **Services** Lift **Parking** 500 **Notes** LB Civ Wed 140

Premier Inn Bagshot

BUDGET HOTEL

tel: 0871 527 8040 **1 London Rd GU19 5HR**
web: www.premierinn.com
dir: On A30 (London Rd) just before junct with A322 (Bracknell Rd). Adjacent to Cricketers Beefeater

High quality, budget accommodation ideal for both families and business travellers. Spacious, en suite bedrooms feature tea and coffee making facilities, and Freeview TV in most hotels. Internet access and WiFi are available for a small fee. The adjacent family restaurant features a wide and varied menu. See also the Hotel Groups pages.

Rooms 39

BAINBRIDGE
North Yorkshire   Map 18 SD99

Yorebridge House

@@@ RESTAURANT WITH ROOMS

tel: 01969 652060 📠 01969 650258 **DL8 3EE**
email: enquiries@yorebridgehouse.co.uk **web:** www.yorebridgehouse.co.uk
dir: A648 to Bainbridge. Yorebridge House N of centre on right before river

Yorebridge House is situated by the river on the edge of Bainbridge, in the heart of the North Yorkshire Dales. In the Victorian era this was a schoolmaster's house and school, the building now offers luxury boutique-style accommodation. Each bedroom is individually designed with high-quality furnishings and thoughtful extras. All rooms have stunning views of the Dales and some have their own terrace with hot tub. There is a comfortable lounge bar where guests can relax before enjoying dinner in the attractive and elegant dining room.

Rooms 11 (4 annexe) (11 fmly)

BALDOCK
Hertfordshire   Map 12 TL23

Days Inn Stevenage North - A1

BUDGET HOTEL

tel: 01462 730598 **Baldock Extra Motorways, A1(M) Junction 10, Radwell SG7 5TR**
email: stevenage.hotel@welcomebreak.co.uk **web:** www.welcomebreak.co.uk
dir: A1(M) junct 10 Baldock Extra Services

This modern, purpose built accommodation offers smartly appointed, well-equipped bedrooms, with good power showers. There is a choice of adjacent food outlets where guests may enjoy breakfast, snacks and meals. See also the Hotel Groups pages.

Rooms 62 (14 fmly) (30 GF) (8 smoking)

BALSALL COMMON
West Midlands   Map 10 SP27

Nailcote Hall

★★★★ 76% @ HOTEL

tel: 024 7646 6174 **Nailcote Ln, Berkswell CV7 7DE**
email: info@nailcotehall.co.uk **web:** www.nailcotehall.co.uk
dir: On B4101

This 17th-century house, set in 15 acres of grounds, boasts a 9-hole championship golf course and Roman bath-style swimming pool amongst its many facilities. The bedrooms are spacious and elegantly furnished. The eating options are the fine dining restaurant where smart casual dress is required, or The Piano Bar where more informal meals are served.

Rooms 40 (19 annexe) (2 fmly) (15 GF) **Facilities** STV FTV WiFi 🏊 supervised ♿ 9 🎱 Putt green 🦢 Gym 🎵 Xmas New Year **Conf** Class 80 Board 44 Thtr 140 **Services** Lift **Parking** 200 **Notes** ⊗ Civ Wed 120

Premier Inn Balsall Common (Near NEC)

BUDGET HOTEL

tel: 0871 527 8042 **Kenilworth Rd CV7 7EX**
web: www.premierinn.com
dir: M42 junct 6, A45 towards Coventry for 0.5m. A452 signed Leamington/Kenilworth. In 3m hotel on right

High quality, budget accommodation ideal for both families and business travellers. Spacious, en suite bedrooms feature tea and coffee making facilities, and Freeview TV in most hotels. Internet access and WiFi are available for a small fee. The adjacent family restaurant features a wide and varied menu. See also the Hotel Groups pages.

Rooms 42

| BAMBURGH | Map 21 NU13 |
| Northumberland | |

Waren House Hotel

★★★ 85% COUNTRY HOUSE HOTEL

tel: 01668 214581 **Waren Mill NE70 7EE**
email: enquiries@warenhousehotel.co.uk **web:** www.warenhousehotel.co.uk
dir: 2m E of A1 turn onto B1342 to Waren Mill, at T-junct turn right, hotel 100yds on right

This delightful Georgian mansion is set in six acres of woodland and offers a welcoming atmosphere and views of the coast. The individually themed bedrooms and suites include many with large bathrooms. Good, home-cooked food is served in the elegant dining room. A comfortable lounge and library are also available.

Rooms 15 (4 annexe) (3 GF) ↝ **S** £100-£150; **D** £150-£250 (incl. bkfst & dinner)* **Facilities** FTV WiFi Xmas New Year **Parking** 20 **Notes** No children 14yrs

The Lord Crewe

★★★ 82% HOTEL

tel: 01668 214243 & 214613 **Front St NE69 7BL**
email: enquiries@lordcrewe.co.uk **web:** www.lordcrewe.co.uk
dir: Just below castle

Located in the heart of the village in the shadow of impressive Bamburgh Castle, this hotel has been developed from an old inn. Public areas combine modern and traditional very well and include a choice of lounges, a cosy bar and a smart contemporary Italian restaurant. Bedrooms vary in size, but all are well equipped and offer expected amenities.

Rooms 17 **Facilities** FTV WiFi **Parking** 20 **Notes** ⊗ No children 5yrs Closed 25-26 Dec & 6 Jan-1 Feb

Victoria Hotel

★★★ 78% HOTEL

tel: 01668 214431 **Front St NE69 7BP**
email: enquiries@thevictoriahotelbamburgh.co.uk
web: www.thevictoriahotelbamburgh.co.uk
dir: Turn off A1, N of Alnwick onto B1342, follow signs to Bamburgh. Hotel opposite village green

Set on the delightful village green and overlooked by Bamburgh Castle, this hotel offers bedrooms with high quality furnishings and modern conveniences including LCD TV, a hairdryer, trouser press and complimentary refreshment tray. Bailey's Bar

and Restaurant offers locally sourced food on menus served throughout the day. The staff pay great attention to detail and the hotel makes an ideal base from which to tour this beautiful area of Northumberland.

Rooms 36 (3 fmly) (2 GF) ↝ **S** £35-£65; **D** £75-£185 (incl. bkfst)* **Facilities** FTV WiFi Xmas New Year **Conf** Class 20 Board 12 Thtr 25 Del from £60 to £100* **Parking** 20 **Notes** Civ Wed 40

| BAMPTON | Map 5 SP30 |
| Oxfordshire | |

Biztro at Wheelgate House

RESTAURANT WITH ROOMS

tel: 01993 851151 & 07747 466151 **Wheelgate House, Market Square OX18 2JH**
email: enquiries@wheelgatehouse.co.uk **web:** www.wheelgatehouse.co.uk
dir: In village centre opposite war memorial

This restaurant with rooms is set in the pretty village of Bampton at the edge of the Cotswolds, and extends a warm and friendly welcome to all its guests. Bedrooms are individual in design offering a cosy experience. The ground floor is 'Biztro', where breakfast is served daily along with lunches and dinners available from Tuesday to Saturday.

Rooms 3

| BANBURY | Map 11 SP44 |
| Oxfordshire | |

BEST WESTERN PLUS Wroxton House Hotel

★★★ 86% HOTEL

tel: 01295 730777 **Wroxton St Mary OX15 6QB**
email: reservations@wroxtonhousehotel.com **web:** www.wroxtonhousehotel.com
dir: M40 junct 11, A422 signed Banbury & Wroxton. Approx 3m, hotel on right on entering Wroxton

Dating in part from 1649, this partially thatched hotel is set just off the main road. Bedrooms, either created from cottages or situated in a contemporary wing, are comfortable and well equipped with WiFi and LCD TVs. The public areas are open plan and the low-beamed Restaurant 1649 has a peaceful atmosphere for dining.

Rooms 32 (3 annexe) (5 fmly) (8 GF) ↝ **Facilities** FTV WiFi ↜ Xmas New Year **Conf** Class 40 Board 40 Thtr 90 Del from £125 to £142* **Parking** 60 **Notes** ⊗ Civ Wed 90

Mercure Banbury Whately Hall Hotel

★★★ 78% HOTEL

tel: 01295 253261 **Banbury Cross OX16 0AN**
email: h6633@accor.com **web:** www.mercure.com
dir: M40 junct 11, straight over 2 rdbts, left at 3rd, 0.25m to Banbury Cross, hotel on right

Dating back to 1677, this historic inn boasts many original features such as stone passages, priests' holes and a fine wooden staircase. Spacious public areas include the oak-panelled restaurant, which overlooks the attractive well-tended gardens, a choice of lounges and a traditional bar. Smartly appointed bedrooms vary in size and style but all are thoughtfully equipped.

Rooms 69 (6 fmly) (2 GF) **Facilities** FTV WiFi Xmas New Year **Conf** Class 40 Board 40 Thtr 120 **Services** Lift **Parking** 52 **Notes** ⊗ Civ Wed 120

B

BANBURY *continued*

Premier Inn Banbury

BUDGET HOTEL

tel: 0871 527 8044 **Warwick Rd, Warmington OX17 1JJ**
web: www.premierinn.com
dir: From N: M40 junct 12, B4451, B4100 towards Warmington. From S: M40 junct 11, A423, A422, B4100. Hotel adjacent to Wobbly Wheel Brewers Fayre

High quality, budget accommodation ideal for both families and business travellers. Spacious, en suite bedrooms feature tea and coffee making facilities, and Freeview TV in most hotels. Internet access and WiFi are available for a small fee. The adjacent family restaurant features a wide and varied menu. See also the Hotel Groups pages.

Rooms 39

BARKING
Greater London · Map 6 TQ48

Ibis London East Barking

BUDGET HOTEL

tel: 020 8477 4100 **Highbridge Rd IG11 7BA**
email: H2042@accor.com **web:** www.ibishotel.com
dir: Exit Barking from A406 or A13

Modern, budget hotel offering comfortable accommodation in bright and practical bedrooms. Breakfast is self-service and dinner is available in the restaurant. See also the Hotel Groups pages.

Rooms 86 (26 GF)

Premier Inn Barking

BUDGET HOTEL

tel: 0871 527 8048 **Highbridge Rd IG11 7BA**
web: www.premierinn.com
dir: A13 onto A406 signed Barking/Ilford. At Barking, exit at Tesco/A406 slip road. Hotel on left

High quality, budget accommodation ideal for both families and business travellers. Spacious, en suite bedrooms feature tea and coffee making facilities, and Freeview TV in most hotels. Internet access and WiFi are available for a small fee. The adjacent family restaurant features a wide and varied menu. See also the Hotel Groups pages.

Rooms 88

BARLBOROUGH
Derbyshire · Map 16 SK47

Ibis Sheffield North

BUDGET HOTEL

tel: 01246 813222 **Tallys End, Chesterfield Rd S43 4TX**
email: H3157@accor.com **web:** www.ibishotel.com
dir: M1 junct 30. Towards A619, right at rdbt towards Chesterfield. Hotel immediately left

Modern, budget hotel offering comfortable accommodation in bright and practical bedrooms. Breakfast is self-service and dinner is available in the restaurant. See also the Hotel Groups pages.

Rooms 86 (11 fmly) 🐾 **Conf** Board 18 Thtr 35

BARNBY MOOR
Nottinghamshire · Map 16 SK68

Ye Olde Bell Hotel & Restaurant

★★★★ 79% HOTEL

tel: 01777 705121 **DN22 8QS**
email: enquiries@yeoldebell-hotel.co.uk **web:** www.yeoldebell-hotel.co.uk
dir: A1(M) south near junct 34, exit Barnby Moor or A1(M) north exit A620 Retford. Hotel on A638 between Retford & Bawtry

This beautifully refurbished 17th-century coaching inn is located in the rural village of Barnby Moor near Retford. Public rooms have a wealth of original character such as traditional log fires and ornate plaster work, and there is an outside terrace also available at the front of the main bar. Restaurant 1650 features elegant wood panelling as well as a striking contemporary bar. The tastefully appointed bedrooms are furnished to a high standard and are attractively co-ordinated. All benefit from modern bathrooms. The hotel also features a stylish hair and beauty treatment salon and a fitness suite. The gardens are another highlight and are perfect for weddings or outside entertaining in warmer weather.

Rooms 57 (8 annexe) (5 fmly) (8 GF) 🐾 **Facilities** FTV WiFi 🏋 Gym Hair salon Beauty treatment room Xmas New Year Child facilities **Conf** Class 100 Board 50 Thtr 250 Del from £99 to £145 **Parking** 200 **Notes** ⊗ Civ Wed 250

BARNET
Greater London

Map 6 TQ29

Savoro Restaurant with Rooms

 RESTAURANT WITH ROOMS

tel: 020 8449 9888 020 8449 7444 **206 High St EN5 5SZ**
email: savoro@savoro.co.uk **web:** www.savoro.co.uk
dir: M25 junct 23, A1000. Establishment in crescent behind Hadley Green Jaguar Garage

Set back from the main high street, the traditional frontage of this establishment belies the stylishly modern bedrooms and well designed bathrooms within. The award-winning restaurant is an additional bonus.

Rooms 11 (2 fmly)

BARNHAM BROOM
Norfolk

Map 13 TG00

Barnham Broom

★★★★ 78% ◉◉ HOTEL

tel: 01603 759393 **NR9 4DD**
web: www.barnham-broom.co.uk
dir: A11/A47 towards Swaffham, follow brown tourist signs

Situated in a peaceful rural location just a short drive from Norwich, this hotel offers contemporary style bedrooms that are tastefully furnished and thoughtfully equipped. The Sports Bar serves a range of snacks and meals throughout the day, or guests can choose from the carte menu in Flints Restaurant. There are also extensive leisure, conference and banqueting facilities.

Rooms 46 (5 fmly) (22 GF) **S** £58-£139; **D** £88-£172 (incl. bkfst)* **Facilities** Spa STV WiFi supervised 36 Putt green Gym Squash Sauna Steam room Personal trainers Xmas New Year **Conf** Class 100 Board 50 Thtr 150 Del from £130 to £160 **Services** Air con **Parking** 150 **Notes** LB Civ Wed 150

BARNSLEY
South Yorkshire

Map 16 SE30

Tankersley Manor

★★★★ 77% HOTEL

QHOTELS
INSPIRED BY YOU

tel: 01226 744700 **Church Ln S75 3DQ**
email: tankersleymanor@qhotels.co.uk **web:** www.qhotels.co.uk

(For full entry see Tankersley)

Premier Inn Barnsley Central M1 Jct 37

BUDGET HOTEL

Premier Inn

tel: 0871 527 9204 **Gateway Plaza, Sackville St S70 2RD**
web: www.premierinn.com
dir: M1 junct 37, A628 (Dodworth Rd) signed Barnsley. In approx 1m 2nd exit at rdbt into Shambles St, car park entrance on left

High quality, budget accommodation ideal for both families and business travellers. Spacious, en suite bedrooms feature tea and coffee making facilities, and Freeview TV in most hotels. Internet access and WiFi are available for a small fee. The adjacent family restaurant features a wide and varied menu. See also the Hotel Groups pages.

Rooms 110

BARNSTAPLE
Devon

Map 3 SS53

The Imperial Hotel

Brend Hotels

B

★★★★ 75% HOTEL

tel: 01271 345861 **Taw Vale Pde EX32 8NB**
email: reservations@brend-imperial.co.uk **web:** www.brend-imperial.co.uk
dir: M5 junct 27/A361 to Barnstaple. Follow town centre signs, passing Tesco. Straight on at next 2 rdbts. Hotel on right

This smart and attractive hotel is pleasantly located at the centre of Barnstaple and overlooks the River Taw. Staff are friendly and offer attentive service. The comfortable bedrooms are of various sizes; some have balconies and many enjoy river views. Afternoon tea is available in the lounge, and the appetising cuisine is freshly prepared.

Rooms 63 (8 annexe) (9 fmly) (4 GF) **S** £80-£245; **D** £95-£245* **Facilities** FTV WiFi Leisure facilities at sister hotel Xmas New Year **Conf** Class 40 Board 30 Thtr 60 **Services** Lift **Parking** 80 **Notes** LB Civ Wed 50

See advert on page 56

BARNSTAPLE *continued*

The Barnstaple Hotel

★★★ 80% HOTEL

tel: 01271 376221 **Braunton Rd EX31 1LE**
email: reservations@barnstaplehotel.co.uk **web:** www.barnstaplehotel.co.uk
dir: Outskirts of Barnstaple on A361

This well-established hotel enjoys a convenient location on the edge of town. Bedrooms are spacious and well equipped, many with access to a balcony overlooking the outdoor pool and garden. A wide choice is offered from various menus based on local produce, served in the Brasserie Restaurant. There is an extensive range of leisure and conference facilities.

Rooms 60 (4 fmly) (17 GF) 🐾 **S** £66-£114; **D** £74-£129* **Facilities** FTV WiFi 🏊 🏋 Gym Beauty treatment room Saunas Chill out sanctuary Xmas New Year Child facilities **Conf** Class 100 Board 50 Thtr 250 **Parking** 250 **Notes** LB ⊗ Civ Wed 150

The Royal & Fortescue Hotel

★★★ 79% HOTEL

tel: 01271 342289 **Boutport St EX31 1HG**
email: reservations@royalfortescue.co.uk **web:** www.royalfortescue.co.uk
dir: From A361 onto Barbican Rd signed town centre, right into Queen St, left into Boutport St, hotel on left

Formerly a coaching inn, this friendly and convivial hotel is conveniently located in the centre of town. Bedrooms vary in size and all are decorated and furnished to a consistently high standard. In addition to the formal restaurant, guests can take snacks in the popular coffee shop or dine more informally in The Bank, a bistro and café bar.

Rooms 49 (4 fmly) (4 GF) 🐾 **S** £59-£125; **D** £75-£155* **Facilities** FTV WiFi 🏊 Leisure facilities available at sister hotel Xmas New Year **Conf** Class 25 Board 25 Thtr 25 **Services** Lift **Parking** 40 **Notes** LB ⊗

The Park Hotel

★★★ 78% HOTEL

tel: 01271 372166 **Taw Vale EX32 9AE**
email: reservations@parkhotel.co.uk **web:** www.parkhotel.co.uk
dir: A361 to Barnstaple, 0.5m from town centre. Opposite Rock Park

Enjoying views across the park and within easy walking distance of the town centre, this modern hotel offers a choice of bedrooms in both the main building and the Garden Court, just across the car park. Public rooms are open-plan in style and the friendly staff offer attentive service in a relaxed atmosphere.

Rooms 40 (17 annexe) (3 fmly) (2 GF) ♠ **S** £52-£79; **D** £67-£89* **Facilities** FTV WiFi ↘ Leisure facilities available at sister hotel Xmas New Year **Conf** Class 50 Board 30 Thtr 80 **Parking** 100 **Notes** LB ⊗ Civ Wed 100

Premier Inn Barnstaple

BUDGET HOTEL

tel: 0871 527 8052 **Whiddon Dr, off Eastern Av EX32 8RY**
web: www.premierinn.com
dir: Exit A361 (North Devon Link Rd) towards Barnstaple. Right at Portmore rdbt

High quality, budget accommodation ideal for both families and business travellers. Spacious, en suite bedrooms feature tea and coffee making facilities, and Freeview TV in most hotels. Internet access and WiFi are available for a small fee. The adjacent family restaurant features a wide and varied menu. See also the Hotel Groups pages.

Rooms 40

BARROW-IN-FURNESS	Map 18 SD26
Cumbria	

Clarence House Country Hotel & Restaurant

★★★★ 72% ⊛⊛ HOTEL

tel: 01229 462508 **Skelgate, Dalton-in-Furness LA15 8BQ**
email: clarencehsehotel@aol.com **web:** www.clarencehouse-hotel.co.uk
dir: A590 through Ulverston & Lindal, 2nd exit at rdbt & 1st exit at next. Follow signs to Dalton, hotel at top of hill on right

This hotel is located in ornamental grounds with unrestricted countryside views. Bedrooms are individually themed with those in the main hotel being particularly stylish and comfortable. The public rooms are spacious and also furnished to a high standard. The popular conservatory restaurant and contemporary brasserie

offer well-prepared dishes from extensive menus. There is a delightful barn conversion that is ideal for weddings.

Rooms 18 (11 annexe) (1 fmly) (5 GF) ♠ **S** fr £99; **D** fr £130 (incl. bkfst)* **Facilities** FTV WiFi ♫ New Year **Conf** Class 40 Board 15 Thtr 100 **Parking** 40 **Notes** LB Closed 24-26 Dec Civ Wed 100

Abbey House Hotel

★★★ 79% HOTEL

tel: 01229 838282 & 0844 826 2091 **Abbey Rd LA13 0PA**
email: enquiries@abbeyhousehotel.com **web:** www.abbeyhousehotel.com
dir: From A590 follow signs for Furness General Hospital & Furness Abbey. Hotel approx 100yds on left

Set in its own gardens, this smart hotel provides stylish public areas, as well as extensive function and conference facilities. The well-equipped bedrooms vary in style - the more traditional rooms are in the main house while more contemporary accommodation can be found in the extension. Service is friendly and helpful.

Rooms 61 (4 annexe) (6 fmly) (2 GF) ♠ **Facilities** STV FTV WiFi ↘ Xmas New Year **Conf** Class 120 Board 80 Thtr 300 **Services** Lift **Parking** 100 **Notes** Civ Wed 120

Clarke's Hotel

★★★ 74% HOTEL

tel: 01229 820303 **Rampside LA13 0PX**
email: bookings@clarkeshotel.co.uk **web:** www.clarkeshotel.co.uk
dir: A590 to Ulverston then A5087, take coast road for 8m, turn left at rdbt into Rampside

This smart, well-maintained hotel enjoys a peaceful location on the south Cumbrian coast, overlooking Morecambe Bay. The tastefully appointed bedrooms come in a variety of sizes and are thoughtfully equipped, particularly for the business guest. Inviting public areas include an open-plan bar and a brasserie offering freshly prepared food throughout the day.

Rooms 14 (1 fmly) **Facilities** FTV WiFi ↘ **Parking** 50

Premier Inn Barrow-in-Furness

BUDGET HOTEL

tel: 0871 527 9470 **North Rd LA14 2PW**
web: www.premierinn.com
dir: M6 junct 36, A590. In 3m take slip road signed Barrow-in-Furness. Follow signs for Barrow-In-Furness & A590. At rdbt 2nd exit signed Walney Island & A590. Approx 0.5m, hotel on right

High quality, budget accommodation ideal for both families and business travellers. Spacious, en suite bedrooms feature tea and coffee making facilities, and Freeview TV in most hotels. Internet access and WiFi are available for a small fee. The adjacent family restaurant features a wide and varied menu. See also the Hotel Groups pages.

Rooms 62

BARTON	Map 18 SD53
Lancashire	

Barton Grange Hotel

★★★★ 79% HOTEL

tel: 01772 862551 **Garstang Rd PR3 5AA**
email: stay@bartongrangehotel.com **web:** www.bartongrangehotel.co.uk
dir: M6 junct 32, follow Garstang (A6) signs for 2.5m. Hotel on right

Situated close to the M6, this modern, stylish hotel benefits from extensive public areas that include leisure facilities with a swimming pool, sauna and gym. Comfortable, well-appointed bedrooms include executive rooms and family rooms, as well as attractive accommodation in an adjacent cottage. The unique Walled Garden Bistro offers all-day eating.

Rooms 51 (8 annexe) (4 fmly) (4 GF) **Facilities** STV WiFi ♨ ✪ Gym Sauna Xmas New Year **Conf** Class 100 Board 80 Thtr 300 **Services** Lift **Parking** 250 **Notes** ⊗ Civ Wed 300

BARTON-ON-SEA	Map 5 SZ29
Hampshire	

Pebble Beach

⊛ RESTAURANT WITH ROOMS

tel: 01425 627777 📄 01425 610689 **Marine Dr BH25 7DZ**
email: mail@pebblebeach-uk.com **web:** www.pebblebeach-uk.com
dir: A35 from Southampton onto A337 to New Milton, left into Barton Court Av to clifftop

Situated on the clifftop, the restaurant at Pebble Beach boasts stunning views towards The Needles. Bedrooms and bathrooms, (situated above the restaurant), are well equipped and provide a range of accessories to enhance guest comfort. A freshly cooked breakfast is served in the main restaurant.

Rooms 4

BASILDON	Map 6 TQ78
Essex	

Holiday Inn Basildon

★★★ 81% HOTEL

tel: 0871 942 9003 & 01268 824000 **Waterfront Walk, Festival Leisure Park SS14 3DG**
email: reservations-basildon@ihg.com **web:** www.hibasildonhotel.co.uk
dir: From A127 take A176/Basildon Billericay exit. Follow brown signs to Festival Leisure Park

This modern hotel sits alongside the river in a convenient location in the heart of town. It enjoys delightful views and is ideally placed for leisurely walks beside the river or for easy access to the town. The contemporary bedrooms are comfortable and particularly well equipped, with safes, WiFi and flat-screen TVs. There are a host of other facilities including a range of meeting rooms and leisure facilities, as well as a car park.

Rooms 148 (10 fmly) (8 GF) (16 smoking) **Facilities** STV WiFi ♨ Free use of nearby leisure club to over 18's New Year **Conf** Class 80 Board 80 Thtr 300 **Services** Lift Air con **Parking** 152 **Notes** ⊗ Civ Wed 300

Chichester Hotel

★★★ 75% HOTEL

tel: 01268 560555 **Old London Rd, Wickford SS11 8UE**
email: reception@chichester-hotel.com **web:** www.chichester-hotel.com
dir: Signed from A129 between Wickford & Rayleigh

Set in landscaped gardens and surrounded by farmland, this friendly hotel has been owned and run by the same family for over 25 years. Spacious bedrooms are located around an attractive courtyard, and each is pleasantly decorated and thoughtfully equipped. Public rooms include a cosy lounge bar and a smart restaurant.

Rooms 35 (32 annexe) (12 fmly) (17 GF) **Facilities** FTV WiFi **Parking** 150 **Notes** ⊗

Premier Inn Basildon (East Mayne)

BUDGET HOTEL

tel: 0871 527 8054 **Felmores, East Mayne SS13 1BW**
web: www.premierinn.com
dir: M25 junct 29 , A127 towards Southend, take A132 S signed Basildon & Wickford at Neverdon exit. Hotel on left

High quality, budget accommodation ideal for both families and business travellers. Spacious, en suite bedrooms feature tea and coffee making facilities, and Freeview TV in most hotels. Internet access and WiFi are available for a small fee. The adjacent family restaurant features a wide and varied menu. See also the Hotel Groups pages.

Rooms 32

Premier Inn Basildon (Festival Park)

BUDGET HOTEL

tel: 0871 527 8056 **Festival Leisure Park, Pipps Hill Road South, Off Cranes Farm Rd SS14 3WB**
web: www.premierinn.com
dir: M25 junct 9, A217 towards Basildon. Take A17. Hotel just off A1235 adjacent to David Lloyd Leisure Club

Rooms 64

Premier Inn Basildon South

BUDGET HOTEL

tel: 0871 527 8060 **High Rd, Fobbing, Stanford-Le-Hope SS17 9NR**
web: www.premierinn.com
dir: M2 junct 30/31, A13 towards Southend. 10m to Five Bells Rdbt junct with A176. Right into Fobbing High Rd. Hotel on left

Rooms 61

B

BASINGSTOKE
Hampshire — Map 5 SU65

INSPECTORS' CHOICE

Tylney Hall Hotel

★★★★ HOTEL

tel: 01256 764881 **RG27 9AZ**
email: sales@tylneyhall.com web: www.tylneyhall.com

(For full entry see Rotherwick)

Oakley Hall Hotel
★★★★ 84% COUNTRY HOUSE HOTEL

tel: 01256 783350 **Rectory Rd RG23 7EL**
email: enquiries@oakleyhall-park.com web: www.oakleyhall-park.com
dir: M3 junct 7, follow Basingstoke signs. In 500yds before lights turn left onto A30 towards Oakley, immediately right onto unclass road towards Oakley. In 3m left at T-junct into Rectory Rd. Left onto B3400. Hotel signed 1st on left

An impressive drive leads to this country house which benefits from delightful country views across north Hampshire. Built in 1795, it was once owned by the Bramston family who were friends of Jane Austen. An ideal wedding venue, Oakley Hall also has an excellent range of conference facilities, and is a great place to spend a relaxing leisure break. The bedrooms are spacious; many are located in the impressively restored courtyard and are particularly well equipped; there is also the delightful Garden Cottage. Service is delivered by a friendly team, and cuisine is contemporary and satisfying.

Rooms 18 (18 annexe) (8 fmly) (18 GF) Facilities FTV WiFi Clay pigeon shooting Xmas New Year Conf Class 82 Board 50 Thtr 300 Del from £145 to £169* Services Air con Parking 100 Notes Civ Wed 100

Audleys Wood Hotel

★★★★ 81% HOTEL

tel: 01256 817555 **Alton Rd RG25 2JT**
email: audleyswood@handpicked.co.uk web: www.handpickedhotels.co.uk/audleyswood
dir: M3 junct 6. From Basingstoke take A339 towards Alton, hotel on right

A long sweeping drive leads to what was once a Victorian hunting lodge. This traditional country-house hotel offers bedrooms with flat-screen TVs and MP3 player connections. Smart and traditional public areas have log fires, and the dining options include the award-winning Simonds Room and a contemporary conservatory with a small minstrels' gallery.

Rooms 72 (23 fmly) (34 GF) Facilities STV FTV WiFi HL Xmas New Year Conf Class 80 Board 60 Thtr 200 Parking 100 Notes Civ Wed 100

The Hampshire Court Hotel
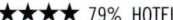
★★★★ 79% HOTEL

tel: 01256 319700 **Centre Dr, Chineham RG24 8FY**
email: hampshirecourt@qhotels.co.uk web: www.qhotels.co.uk
dir: Off A33 (Reading road) behind Chineham Shopping Centre via Great Binfields Rd

This hotel boasts a range of smart, comfortable and stylish bedrooms, and leisure facilities that are unrivalled locally. Facilities include indoor and outdoor tennis courts, two swimming pools, a gym and a number of treatment rooms. QHotels is the AA Hotel Group of the Year 2014-15.

Rooms 90 (6 fmly) Facilities Spa STV WiFi HL Gym Steam room Sauna Exercise studios Xmas New Year Conf Class 800 Board 60 Thtr 1500 Services Lift Parking 220 Notes Civ Wed 1500

Basingstoke Country Hotel

★★★★ 76% HOTEL

tel: 01256 764161 **Scures Hill, Nately Scures, Hook RG27 9JS**
email: basingstokecountry.reservations@pumahotels.co.uk web: www.pumahotels.co.uk
dir: M3 junct 5, A287 towards Newnham. Left at lights. Hotel 200mtrs on right

This popular hotel is close to Basingstoke, and its country location ensures a peaceful stay. Bedrooms are available in a number of styles - all have air conditioning, WiFi, in-room safes and hairdryers. Guests have a choice of dining in the formal restaurant, or for lighter meals and snacks there is a relaxed café and a smart bar. Extensive wedding, conference and leisure facilities complete the picture.

Rooms 100 (26 GF) S £55-£259; D £55-£299* Facilities Spa STV WiFi supervised Gym Sauna Solarium Steam room Dance studio Beauty treatments New Year Conf Class 85 Board 80 Thtr 240 Services Lift Air con Parking 200 Notes LB RS 24 Dec-2 Jan Civ Wed 90

Apollo Hotel
★★★★ 72% HOTEL

tel: 01256 796700 **Aldermaston Roundabout RG24 9NU**
email: admin@apollohotels.com web: www.apollohotels.com
dir: M3 junct 6. Follow ring road N towards Newbury. Follow A340 Aldermaston signs. Hotel on rdbt, 5th exit into Popley Way for access

This modern hotel provides well-equipped accommodation and spacious public areas, appealing to both the leisure and business guest. Facilities include a smartly appointed leisure club, a business centre, along with a good choice of formal and informal eating in two restaurants; Vespers is the fine dining option.

Rooms 125 (32 GF) S £140-£165; Facilities Spa FTV WiFi HL Gym Sauna Steam room Conf Class 196 Board 30 Thtr 255 Del £140* Services Lift Air con Parking 200 Notes LB Civ Wed 100

Holiday Inn Basingstoke
★★★ 80% HOTEL

tel: 0871 942 9004 **Grove Rd RG21 3EE**
email: reservations-basingstoke@ihg.com web: www.hibasingstokehotel.co.uk
dir: On A339 (Alton road) S of Basingstoke

Located conveniently on the southern approach to Basingstoke and close to the M3, this modern, comfortable hotel offers well-equipped, air-conditioned bedrooms. There is a busy Conference Academy on site. The staff are friendly throughout the hotel. Free parking is available.

Rooms 86 (1 fmly) (43 GF) Facilities STV FTV WiFi Complimentary passes available at nearby leisure centre Xmas New Year Conf Class 70 Board 70 Thtr 140 Services Air con Parking 150 Notes Civ Wed 140

BASINGSTOKE *continued*

B

Premier Inn Basingstoke Central

BUDGET HOTEL

tel: 0871 527 8062 **Basingstoke Leisure Park, Worting Rd RG22 6PG**
web: www.premierinn.com
dir: M3 junct 6, A339 towards Newbury. A340 follow brown Leisure Park signs. At next rdbt right onto B3400 (Churchill Way West). Right on next rdbt into Leisure Park. Hotel adjacent to Spruce Goose Beefeater

High quality, budget accommodation ideal for both families and business travellers. Spacious, en suite bedrooms feature tea and coffee making facilities, and Freeview TV in most hotels. Internet access and WiFi are available for a small fee. The adjacent family restaurant features a wide and varied menu. See also the Hotel Groups pages.

Rooms 71

BASLOW
Derbyshire

Map 16 SK27

Cavendish Hotel

★★★★ 80% @@ HOTEL

tel: 01246 582311 **DE45 1SP**
email: info@cavendish-hotel.net **web:** www.cavendish-hotel.net
dir: M1 junct 29/A617 W to Chesterfield & A619 to Baslow. Hotel in village centre, off main road

This stylish property, dating back to the 18th century, is delightfully situated on the outskirts of the Chatsworth Estate. Elegantly appointed bedrooms offer a host of thoughtful amenities, while comfortable public areas are furnished with period pieces and paintings. Guests have a choice of dining in either the informal conservatory Garden Room or the elegant Gallery Restaurant.

Rooms 24 (3 fmly) (2 GF) **S** £166-£196; **D** £227-£257 (incl. bkfst)* **Facilities** FTV WiFi ॐ Putt green Xmas New Year **Conf** Class 8 Board 18 Thtr 25 Del £205* **Parking** 50 **Notes** LB ⊗ RS 25 Dec evening

---

Fischer's Baslow Hall

★★★ @@@ HOTEL

tel: 01246 583259 **Calver Rd DE45 1RR**
email: reservations@fischers-baslowhall.co.uk **web:** www.fischers-baslowhall.co.uk
dir: On A623 between Baslow & Calver

Located at the end of a chestnut tree-lined drive on the edge of the Chatsworth Estate, in marvellous gardens, this beautiful Derbyshire manor house offers sumptuous accommodation and facilities. Staff provide very friendly and personally attentive service. There are two styles of bedroom available - traditional, individually-themed rooms in the main house and spacious, more contemporary-styled rooms with Italian marble bathrooms in the Garden House. The cuisine is excellent and may prove the highlight of any stay.

Rooms 11 (5 annexe) (4 GF) ╭ **S** £100-£145; **D** £150-£250 (incl. bkfst)*
Facilities FTV WiFi ॐ **Conf** Board 15 Thtr 20 Del from £225 to £245* **Parking** 40
Notes LB ⊗ No children 12 yrs Closed 25-26 Dec RS 31 Dec Civ Wed 38

BASSENTHWAITE
Cumbria

Map 18 NY23

Armathwaite Hall Country House & Spa

★★★★  COUNTRY HOUSE HOTEL

tel: 017687 76551 **CA12 4RE**
email: reservations@armathwaite-hall.com **web:** www.armathwaite-hall.com
dir: M6 junct 40/A66 to Keswick rdbt then A591 signed Carlisle. 8m to Castle Inn junct, turn left. Hotel 300yds

Enjoying fine views over Bassenthwaite Lake, this impressive mansion, dating from the 17th century, is situated amid 400 acres of deer park. The comfortably furnished bedrooms and well-appointed bathrooms are complemented by a choice of public rooms that have many original features. The spa is an outstanding asset to the leisure facilities; it offers an infinity pool, thermal suite, sauna, state-of-the-art gym, treatments, exercise classes and a hot tub overlooking the landscaped gardens.

Rooms 46 (8 fmly) (8 GF) **Facilities** Spa STV WiFi supervised Fishing Gym Archery Clay shooting Quad & mountain bikes Falconry Xmas New Year **Conf** Class 50 Board 60 Thtr 200 **Services** Lift **Parking** 100 **Notes** Civ Wed 150

BEST WESTERN PLUS Castle Inn

★★★★ 76% HOTEL

Best Western PLUS

tel: 017687 76401 **CA12 4RG**
email: reservations@castleinncumbria.co.uk **web:** www.castleinncumbria.co.uk
dir: A591 to Carlisle, pass Bassenthwaite village on right. Hotel on left of T-junct

Overlooking some of England's highest fells and Bassenthwaite Lake, this fine hotel is ideally situated for exploring Bassenthwaite, Keswick and the Lake District. The accommodation, extensive leisure facilities and friendly service are certainly strong points here. Ritson's Restaurant and Laker's Lounge offer a range of dishes using locally sourced meats from the fells; managed, sustainable fish stocks; and international and seasonal ingredients.

Rooms 42 (4 fmly) (9 GF) **S** £82-£280; **D** £92-£330 (incl. bkfst)* **Facilities** FTV WiFi Putt green Gym Sauna Steam room Xmas New Year **Conf** Class 108 Board 60 Thtr 200 Del from £120 to £160 **Parking** 120 **Notes** LB Civ Wed 180

The Pheasant

★★★ 86%  HOTEL

tel: 017687 76234 **CA13 9YE**
email: info@the-pheasant.co.uk **web:** www.the-pheasant.co.uk
dir: Midway between Keswick & Cockermouth, signed from A66

Enjoying a rural setting, within well-tended gardens, on the western side of Bassenthwaite Lake, this friendly 500-year-old inn is steeped in tradition. The attractive oak-panelled bar has seen few changes over the years, and features log fires and a great selection of malt whiskies. The individually decorated bedrooms are stylish and thoughtfully equipped.

Rooms 15 (2 annexe) (2 GF) **S** £95-£110; **D** £105-£190 (incl. bkfst)* **Facilities** FTV WiFi New Year **Parking** 40 **Notes** No children 12yrs Closed 25 Dec

Ravenstone Lodge

★★★ 81%  COUNTRY HOUSE HOTEL

tel: 01768 776629 & 07584 317120 **CA12 4QG**
email: enquiries@ravenstonelodge.co.uk **web:** www.ravenstonelodge.co.uk
dir: 5m N of Keswick on A591

Close to both Keswick and Bassenthwaite, set in rolling countryside, this small country house hotel offers warm, genuine hospitality along with high quality food. Bedrooms are well equipped and appointed, benefitting from a rolling refurbishment programme. Outside garden seating or the large conservatory offer unrestricted views of the picture postcard location.

Rooms 9 (1 fmly) (2 GF) **D** £70-£140 (incl. bkfst)* **Facilities** FTV WiFi **Parking** 15 **Notes** ⊗

Find out more about the AA's Hotel rating scheme on page 18

BATH	Map 4 ST76
Somerset	

See also Colerne & Hinton Charterhouse

Macdonald Bath Spa

★★★★★ 87% ◉◉ HOTEL

tel: 0844 879 9106 & 01225 444424 **Sydney Rd BA2 6JF**
email: sales.bathspa@macdonald-hotels.co.uk
web: www.macdonaldhotels.co.uk/bathspa
dir: A4, left onto A36 at 1st lights. Right at lights after pedestrian crossing left into Sydney Place. Hotel 200yds on right

A delightful Georgian mansion set amidst seven acres of pretty landscaped grounds, just a short walk from the many and varied delights of the city centre. A timeless elegance pervades the gracious public areas and bedrooms. Facilities include a popular leisure club, a choice of dining options and a number of meeting rooms.

Rooms 129 (3 fmly) (17 GF) ⌇ **D** £125–£320* **Facilities** Spa STV FTV WiFi ⌇ ⌇ ⌇ Gym Thermal suite Outdoor hydro pool Whirlpool Xmas New Year **Conf** Class 100 Board 50 Thtr 130 **Services** Lift Air con **Parking** 160 **Notes** ⊗ Civ Wed 130

The Royal Crescent Hotel

★★★★★ 85% ◉◉◉ HOTEL

tel: 01225 823333 **16 Royal Crescent BA1 2LS**
email: info@royalcrescent.co.uk **web:** www.royalcrescent.co.uk
dir: From A4, right at lights. 2nd left into Bennett St, into The Circus, 2nd exit into Brock St

The Royal Crescent Hotel is set in a number of houses in the famous Royal Crescent, and is one of the country's most interesting and historic places to stay. Bedrooms offer a range of suites and sizes, all with individual style and character, many have views across the city, and all are most comfortably appointed. Public rooms make the most of the character of the houses and are styled in keeping with the elegance of the period. The hotel has a superb spa and range of leisure facilities, as well as a number of meeting rooms and private dining venues. The bar and Dower House restaurant offer the very best of contemporary dining and are not to be missed. Ingredients are sourced locally where possible, and elegantly presented by Head Chef David Campbell and his team.

Rooms 45 (8 fmly) (7 GF) ⌇ **S** £239–£1170; **D** £264–£1195 (incl. bkfst)*
Facilities Spa STV FTV WiFi ⌇ ⌇ ⌇ Gym 1920s river launch Xmas New Year **Conf** Class 20 Board 20 Thtr 50 Del from £325 to £1191 **Services** Lift Air con **Parking** 27 **Notes** LB Civ Wed 50

The Bath Priory Hotel, Restaurant & Spa

★★★★★ 84% ◉◉◉ HOTEL

tel: 01225 331922 **Weston Rd BA1 2XT**
email: info@thebathpriory.co.uk **web:** www.thebathpriory.co.uk
dir: Adjacent to Victoria Park

The Bath Priory Hotel is a country house set in four acres of beautiful grounds. It features a luxury spa and an award-winning, multi-AA Rosetted restaurant. The Priory Restaurant is under the direction of Head Chef, Sam Moody. Sam and his team deliver food that is derived from modern European cuisine, created from the very finest local produce and seasonal fruit, vegetable and herbs from the property's own garden. Opening onto the leafy gardens, the Mediterranean-style spa features an indoor heated swimming pool with a pool-side sauna and modern steam pod. Luxury beauty treatments are also available by appointment. Luxurious bedrooms

have elegant decor and free WiFi access. All rooms feature period furniture and spacious en suite bathrooms with fluffy bathrobes and designer toiletries.

Rooms 33 (6 annexe) (2 fmly) (1 GF) ⌇ **S** £320–£1050; **D** £320–£1050 (incl. bkfst)*
Facilities Spa STV FTV WiFi ⌇ ⌇ ⌇ Gym Steam pod Sauna Xmas New Year **Conf** Class 24 Board 16 Thtr 24 Del £370* **Parking** 40 **Notes** Civ Wed 70

Combe Grove Manor Hotel

★★★★ 80% ◉◉ COUNTRY HOUSE HOTEL

tel: 01225 834644 **Brassknocker Hill, Monkton Combe BA2 7HS**
email: combegrovemanor@pumahotels.co.uk **web:** www.pumahotels.co.uk
dir: Exit A36 at Limpley Stoke onto Brassknocker Hill. Hotel 0.5m up hill on left

Set in over 80 acres of gardens, this Georgian mansion commands stunning views over Limpley Stoke Valley. Most bedrooms are in the Garden Lodge, a short walk from the main house. The superb range of indoor and outdoor leisure facilities includes a beauty clinic with holistic therapies, golf, tennis and two pools. The Eden Brasserie is in the cellar (please note that the narrow steps may prove a problem for less able guests).

Rooms 42 (33 annexe) (5 fmly) (8 GF) **Facilities** Spa FTV WiFi HL ⌇ ⌇ ⌇ Gym Driving range Xmas New Year **Conf** Class 60 Board 30 Thtr 90 **Parking** 150 **Notes** Civ Wed 50

Bailbrook House Hotel

★★★★ 80% HOTEL

tel: 01225 855100 **Eveleigh Av, London Road West BA1 7JD**
email: reception.bailbrook@handpicked.co.uk **web:** www.bailbrookhouse.co.uk
dir: M4 junct 18/A46, at bottom of long hill take slip road to city centre. At rdbt take 1st exit, London Rd. Hotel 200mtrs on left

This hotel has seen a dramatic rebuilding programme, an impressive transformation from its former presentation. The hotel now has superior accommodation, ideally situated on the edge of Bath and set in attractive grounds with ample parking, it is perfectly placed to avoid parking and driving in the city, but close enough to allow ease of access. Bedrooms are spacious and extremely well appointed. There are two dining options and a range of meeting and conference facilities.

Rooms 94 (81 annexe) (2 fmly) (27 GF) ⌇ **Facilities** STV FTV WiFi ⌇ Gym New Year **Conf** Class 72 Board 40 Thtr 160 Del from £150 to £210* **Services** Lift Air con **Parking** 120 **Notes** ⊗ Civ Wed 120

Francis Hotel Bath - MGallery

★★★★ 76% HOTEL

tel: 01225 424105 & 338970 **Queen Square BA1 2HH**
email: h6636@accor.com **web:** www.francishotel.com
dir: M4 junct 18/A46 to Bath junct. 3rd exit onto A4, right into George St, left into Gay St into Queen Sq. Hotel on left

Overlooking Queen Square in the centre of the city, this elegant Georgian hotel is within walking distance of Bath's many attractions. The public rooms provide a variety of areas where guests can eat, drink and relax - from the informal café-bar to a more formal restaurant, to the traditional lounge. Bedrooms have air conditioning.

Rooms 98 (17 fmly) ⌇ **S** £99–£239; **D** £99–£239* **Facilities** STV WiFi ⌇ HL Xmas New Year **Conf** Class 40 Board 30 Thtr 80 **Services** Lift Air con **Parking** 40 **Notes** ⊗ Civ Wed 100

INSPECTORS' CHOICE

The Queensberry Hotel

 ★★★ HOTEL

tel: 01225 447928 **Russel St BA1 2QF**
email: reservations@thequeensberry.co.uk **web:** www.thequeensberry.co.uk
dir: 100mtrs from the Assembly Rooms

This charming family-run hotel, situated in a quiet residential street near the city centre, consists of four delightful townhouses. The spacious bedrooms offer deep armchairs, marble bathrooms and a range of modern comforts. Sumptuously furnished sitting rooms add to The Queensberry's appeal and allow access to the very attractive and peaceful walled gardens. The Olive Tree is a stylish restaurant that combines Georgian opulence with contemporary simplicity. Innovative menus are based on best quality ingredients and competent cooking. The Olive Tree is the Winner of the AA Wine Award 2014-2015. Valet parking proves a useful service.

Rooms 29 (2 fmly) (2 GF) ⚫ **S** £125-£195; **D** £135-£255* **Facilities** FTV WiFi
Conf Class 12 Board 25 Thtr 35 Del from £195 to £265* **Services** Lift **Parking** 6
Notes ⊗

Haringtons Hotel

★★★ 80% METRO HOTEL

tel: 01225 461728 & 445883 **8-10 Queen St BA1 1HE**
email: post@haringtonshotel.co.uk **web:** www.haringtonshotel.co.uk
dir: A4 into George St, into Milsom St. 1st right into Quiet St, 1st left into Queen St

Dating back to the 18th century, this hotel is situated in the heart of the city and provides all the expected modern facilities and comforts. Although a full dinner in a restaurant is not offered, the comfortably furnished lounge is light and airy and open throughout the day for light snacks and refreshments. A warm welcome is assured from the proprietors and staff, making this a delightful place to stay.

Rooms 13 (3 fmly) ⚫ **Facilities** STV FTV WiFi **Conf** Class 10 Board 12 Thtr 18
Parking 11 **Notes** ⊗

Abbey Hotel

★★★ 79% ⚫⚫⚫ HOTEL

tel: 01225 461603 **1 North Pde BA1 1LF**
email: reservations@abbeyhotelbath.co.uk **web:** www.abbeyhotelbath.co.uk
dir: M 4 junct 18/A46 for approx 8m. At rdbt right onto A4 for 2m. Once past Morrissons stay in left lane & turn left at lights. Over bridge & right at lights. Over rdbt & right at lights. Hotel at end of road

Perfectly located in the heart of Bath and just a two minute stroll to the famous Abbey, this popular hotel offers a relaxing welcome with professional, helpful service in contemporary surroundings. The impressive Brasserie offers an excellent range of the highest quality dishes with something to suit all tastes. In the warmer months, outdoor seating on the front terrace is the ideal location for coffee or lunch.

Rooms 60 (7 fmly) (3 GF) ⚫ **S** fr £99; **D** fr £120* **Facilities** WiFi Xmas New Year
Conf Class 10 Board 16 Thtr 30 **Services** Lift **Notes** LB Civ Wed 60

Premier Inn Bath

BUDGET HOTEL

tel: 0871 527 9454 **James Street West BA1 2BX**
web: www.premierinn.com
dir: M4 junct 18, A46 towards city centre. In approx 7m 3rd exit A4 towards city centre. 1.5m left into Gay St, through Queen Sq, straight ahead into Charles St. At 2nd lights left into James St West. Hotel 200mtrs on right

High quality, budget accommodation ideal for both families and business travellers. Spacious, en suite bedrooms feature tea and coffee making facilities, and Freeview TV in most hotels. Internet access and WiFi are available for a small fee. The adjacent family restaurant features a wide and varied menu. See also the Hotel Groups pages.

Rooms 108

Milsoms Bath

RESTAURANT WITH ROOMS

tel: 01225 750128 📠 01225 750121 **24 Milsom St BA1 1DG**
email: bath@milsomshotel.co.uk **web:** www.milsomshotel.co.uk
dir: M4 junct 18, A46 (Bath), 3m, through Pennsylvania. 3rd exit at rdbt onto A420 (Bristol). 1st left signed Hamswell/Park & Ride, left at junct towards Lansdown. Right at next T-junct. 5th right into George St. 1st left into Milsom St

Located at the end of the main street in busy, central Bath, this stylish restaurant with rooms offers a range of comfortable, well-equipped accommodation. The ground-floor Loch Fyne Restaurant serves an excellent selection of dishes at both lunch and dinner, with an emphasis on freshest quality fish and shellfish. A good selection of hot and cold items is also available in the same restaurant at breakfast.

Rooms 9

B

BATTLE Map 7 TQ71
East Sussex

Powder Mills Hotel

★★★ 82% ◎◎ HOTEL

tel: 01424 775511 **Powdermill Ln TN33 OSP**
email: powdc@aol.com **web:** www.powdermillshotel.com
dir: M25 junct 5, A21 towards Hastings. At Johns Cross take A2100 to Battle. Pass Abbey on right, 1st right into Powdermill Ln. 1m, hotel on right

A delightful 18th-century country-house hotel set amidst 150 acres of landscaped grounds with lakes and woodland. The individually decorated bedrooms are tastefully furnished and thoughtfully equipped; some rooms have sun terraces with lovely views over the lake. Public rooms include a cosy lounge bar, music room, drawing room, library, restaurant and conservatory.

Rooms 40 (10 annexe) (5 GF) ⮑ **S** £90-£110; **D** £120-£350 (incl. bkfst)*
Facilities STV FTV WiFi ⮑ ⮎ 🦢 Fishing Jogging trails Woodland walks Clay pigeon shooting Archery Xmas New Year **Conf** Class 50 Board 16 Thtr 250 Del from £125 to £145* **Parking** 101 **Notes** LB Civ Wed 100

Brickwall Hotel

★★★ 78% HOTEL

tel: 01424 870253 & 870339 **The Green, Sedlescombe TN33 OQA**
email: info@brickwallhotel.com **web:** www.brickwallhotel.com
dir: A21 on B2244 at top of Sedlescombe Green

This is a well-maintained Tudor house, which is situated in the heart of a pretty village overlooking the green. The spacious public rooms feature a lovely wood-panelled restaurant with a wealth of oak beams, a choice of lounges and a smart bar. Bedrooms are pleasantly decorated and some have garden views.

Rooms 24 (2 fmly) (17 GF) ⮑ **S** £60-£80; **D** £80-£125 (incl. bkfst)* **Facilities** FTV WiFi ⮑ ⮎ Xmas New Year **Conf** Class 40 Board 30 Thtr 30 **Parking** 40

BEAMINSTER Map 4 ST40
Dorset

BridgeHouse

★★★ 81% ◎◎ HOTEL

tel: 01308 862200 **3 Prout Bridge DT8 3AY**
email: enquiries@bridge-house.co.uk **web:** www.bridge-house.co.uk
dir: A3066 to Beaminster, hotel 100yds from town square

Dating back to the 13th century, this property offers friendly and attentive service. The stylish bedrooms feature finest Italian cotton linens, flat-screen TVs and WiFi. There are five types of room to choose from, including four-poster and coach house rooms. Smartly presented public rooms include the Georgian dining room, a cosy bar and an adjacent lounge. There's also a breakfast room and the Beaminster Brasserie with its alfresco eating area under a canopy overlooking the attractive walled garden.

Rooms 13 (4 annexe) (2 fmly) (4 GF) ⮑ **S** £95-£170; **D** £125-£220 (incl. bkfst)
Facilities FTV WiFi ⮑ Xmas New Year **Conf** Class 14 Board 10 Thtr 24 Del from £195 to £245 **Parking** 20 **Notes** LB Civ Wed 100

BEANACRE Map 4 ST96
Wiltshire

Beechfield House Hotel, Restaurant & Gardens

★★★★ ◎ COUNTRY HOUSE HOTEL

tel: 01225 703700 **SN12 7PU**
email: reception@beechfieldhouse.co.uk **web:** www.beechfieldhouse.co.uk
dir: M4 junct 17, A350 S, bypass Chippenham, towards Melksham. Hotel on left in Beanacre

This is a charming, privately-owned hotel set within eight acres of beautiful grounds that has its own arboretum. Bedrooms are individually styled and include four-poster rooms, and ground-floor rooms in the coach house. Relaxing public areas are comfortably furnished and there is a beauty salon with a range of pampering treatments available. At dinner there is a very good selection of carefully prepared dishes with an emphasis on seasonal and local produce.

Rooms 24 (7 fmly) (4 GF) **S** £100-£160; **D** £125-£205 (incl. bkfst)* **Facilities** FTV WiFi ⮑ ⮎ 🦢 Beauty treatment room Xmas New Year **Conf** Class 60 Board 36 Thtr 80 Del from £165* **Parking** 70 **Notes** LB Civ Wed 70

BEAULIEU Map 5 SU30
Hampshire

The Montagu Arms Hotel

★★★★ 81% ◎◎◎ HOTEL

tel: 01590 612324 & 624467 **Palace Ln SO42 7ZL**
email: reservations@montaguarmshotel.co.uk **web:** www.montaguarmshotel.co.uk
dir: M27 junct 2, follow signs for Beaulieu. In Dibden Purlieu right at rdbt. Hotel on left in Beaulieu

Situated at the heart of this charming village and surrounded by glorious New Forest scenery, the Montagu Arms dates back to 1742, and still retains the character of a traditional country house. The individually designed bedrooms include some with four-posters. Public rooms include a choice of two dining options: the informal Monty's brasserie serving home-cooked classics, and the stylish, award-winning Terrace Restaurant. Much produce comes from the kitchen garden project which saw a derelict piece of land to the rear transformed to produce organic fruit, vegetables and herbs plus free-range eggs from the hens. In warmer weather there is a sheltered alfresco eating area overlooking the pretty terraced garden. Complimentary use of leisure and spa facilities is available to guests at a sister hotel six miles away.

Rooms 22 (3 fmly) ⮑ **S** £121.50-£149; **D** £143-£348 (incl. bkfst) **Facilities** FTV WiFi 🦢 Complimentary use of spa in Brockenhurst Xmas New Year **Conf** Class 45 Board 30 Thtr 60 Del from £175 **Parking** 86 **Notes** LB ⊗ Civ Wed 100

B

Beaulieu Hotel

★★★ 81% 🏵 HOTEL

tel: 023 8029 3344 & 0800 444441 **Beaulieu Rd SO42 7YQ**
email: beaulieu@newforesthotels.co.uk **web:** www.newforesthotels.co.uk
dir: M27 junct 1, A337 towards Lyndhurst. Left at lights, through Lyndhurst, right onto B3056, hotel in 3m

Located in the heart of the beautiful New Forest National Park and close to Beaulieu Road railway station, this popular, small hotel provides an ideal base for exploring the area. Once a coaching inn, the hotel now particularly welcomes families; children will delight in seeing the ponies on the doorstep. Bedrooms, all with free WiFi and flat-screen TVs, range from cosy Keeper rooms to Crown rooms which also have four-posters and iPod docking stations. The relaxing Exbury Restaurant has doors that lead out onto the patio area and the landscaped gardens, and alfresco eating is possible in the summer.

Rooms 28 (7 annexe) (5 fmly) (4 GF) 🐾 **Facilities** FTV WiFi ⅃ HL 🏊 Steam room Xmas New Year **Conf** Class 100 Board 100 Thtr 250 **Services** Lift **Parking** 60 **Notes** Civ Wed 200

The Master Builders at Bucklers Hard

★★★ 78% HOTEL

tel: 01590 616253 **Buckler's Hard SO42 7XB**
email: enquiries@themasterbuilders.co.uk **web:** www.themasterbuilders.co.uk
dir: M27 junct 2, follow Beaulieu signs. At T-junct left onto B3056, 1st left to Buckler's Hard. Hotel 2m on left before village

A tranquil historic riverside setting creates the backdrop for this delightful property. The main house bedrooms are full of historical features and are of individual design, and in addition there are some bedrooms in the newer wing. Public areas include a popular bar and guest lounge, whilst grounds are an ideal location for alfresco dining in the summer months. Award-winning cuisine is served in the stylish dining room.

Rooms 26 (18 annexe) (4 fmly) (8 GF) **S** £75-£225; **D** £85-£235 (incl. bkfst)*
Facilities FTV WiFi ⅃ Xmas New Year **Conf** Class 30 Board 20 Thtr 40 Del from £135 to £165* **Parking** 40 **Notes** LB Civ Wed 100

BECCLES
Suffolk

Map 13 TM48

Waveney House Hotel

★★★ 83% HOTEL

tel: 01502 712270 **Puddingmoor NR34 9PL**
email: enquiries@waveneyhousehotel.co.uk **web:** www.waveneyhousehotel.co.uk
dir: From A146 onto Common Lane North, left into Pound Rd, left into Ravensmere, right onto Smallgate, right onto Old Market, continue to Puddingmoor

An exceptionally well presented, privately owned hotel situated by the River Waveney on the edge of this busy little market town. The stylish public rooms include a smart lounge bar and a contemporary-style restaurant with views over the river. The spacious bedrooms are attractively decorated with co-ordinated fabrics and have many thoughtful touches.

Rooms 12 (3 fmly) **S** £98.50; **D** £98.50 (incl. bkfst)* **Facilities** FTV WiFi Xmas New Year **Conf** Class 100 Board 50 Thtr 160 **Parking** 45 **Notes** ⊗ Civ Wed 80

BEDFORD
Bedfordshire

Map 12 TL04

The Barns Hotel

★★★★ 76% 🏵 HOTEL

tel: 0844 855 9101 **Cardington Rd MK44 3SA**
email: foh@barnshotelbedford.co.uk **web:** www.barnshotelbedford.co.uk
dir: M1 junct 13, A421, approx 10m to A603 Sandy/Bedford exit, hotel on right at 2nd rdbt

A tranquil location on the outskirts of Bedford, friendly staff and well-equipped bedrooms all combine to make this a good choice. Cosy day rooms and two informal bars add to the hotel's appeal, while large windows in the restaurant make the most of the view over the river. The original barn houses the conference and function suite.

Rooms 49 (18 GF) 🐾 **Facilities** WiFi Free use of local leisure centre (1m) New Year **Conf** Class 40 Board 40 Thtr 120 **Parking** 90 **Notes** ⊗ Civ Wed 90

The Bedford Swan Hotel

★★★★ 74% 🏵 HOTEL

tel: 01234 346565 **The Embankment MK40 1RW**
email: info@bedfordswanhotel.co.uk **web:** www.bedfordswanhotel.co.uk
dir: Towards Bedford - A421 or A1M/A428

This historic hotel successfully combines original features with modern comforts. The bedrooms ooze style and quality; the needs of the modern traveller are catered for. The award-winning River Room Restaurant offers a varied choice of freshly prepared dishes. The hotel also offers meeting and function rooms, spa facilities and secure parking.

Rooms 113 (10 fmly) (12 smoking) **Facilities** Spa STV FTV WiFi ⅃ 🏊 Xmas New Year **Conf** Class 40 Board 60 Thtr 250 **Services** Lift Air con **Parking** 80 **Notes** Civ Wed 250

Woodland Manor Hotel

★★★ 72% HOTEL

tel: 01234 363281 **Green Ln, Clapham MK41 6EP**
email: reception@woodlandmanorhotel.co.uk **web:** www.woodlandmanorhotel.co.uk
dir: A6 towards Kettering. Clapham N of town centre. On entering village 1st right into Green Ln. Hotel 200mtrs on right

Sitting in acres of wooded grounds and gardens, this secluded Grade II listed, Victorian manor house offers a warm welcome. The hotel has spacious bedrooms and ample parking plus meeting rooms that are suitable for a variety of occasions. Public areas include a cosy bar and a smart restaurant, where traditional English dishes, with a hint of French flair, are served.

Rooms 34 (3 annexe) (6 fmly) (3 GF) 🐾 **S** £85; **D** £100* **Facilities** STV FTV WiFi ⅃ **Conf** Class 25 Board 22 Thtr 80 Del from £130 to £147* **Parking** 60 **Notes** ⊗ Civ Wed 80

B

BEDFORD *continued*

Premier Inn Bedford (Priory Marina)

BUDGET HOTEL

tel: 0871 527 8066 **Priory Country Park, Barkers Ln MK41 9DJ**
web: www.premierinn.com
dir: M1 junct 13, A421, A6, A428 signed Cambridge. Cross River Ouse, right at next rdbt into Barkers Lane. Follow Priory Country Park signs. Hotel adjacent to Priory Marina Beefeater

High quality, budget accommodation ideal for both families and business travellers. Spacious, en suite bedrooms feature tea and coffee making facilities, and Freeview TV in most hotels. Internet access and WiFi are available for a small fee. The adjacent family restaurant features a wide and varied menu. See also the Hotel Groups pages.

Rooms 57

Premier Inn Bedford South (A421)

BUDGET HOTEL

tel: 0871 527 9410 **Marsh Leys, Kempston MK42 7DN**
web: www.premierinn.com
dir: See website for detailed directions

Rooms 60

BELTON
Lincolnshire   Map 11 SK93

De Vere Belton Woods

★★★★ 77% HOTEL

tel: 01476 593200 **NG32 2LN**
email: belton.woods@devere-hotels.com **web:** www.devere.co.uk
dir: A1 to Gonerby Moor Services. B1174 towards Great Gonerby. At top of hill turn left towards Manthorpe/Belton. At T-junct turn left onto A607. Hotel 0.25m on left

Beautifully located amidst 475 acres of picturesque countryside, this is a destination venue for lovers of sport, especially golf, as well as a relaxing executive retreat for seminars. Comfortable and well-equipped accommodation complements the elegant and spacious public areas, which provide a good choice of drinking and dining options.

Rooms 136 (136 fmly) (68 GF) 🐾 **Facilities** Spa STV FTV WiFi ↘ HL 🕲 supervised ✦ 45 ⚘ Putt green 🏌 Gym Squash Outdoor activity centre 🎵 Xmas New Year **Conf** Class 180 Board 80 Thtr 270 **Services** Lift **Parking** 350 **Notes** Civ Wed 80

Visit theAA.com/shop
for the latest Pub, B&B and Restaurant Guides

BEMBRIDGE
Isle of Wight   Map 5 SZ68

Bembridge Coast Hotel

★★★ 80% HOTEL

tel: 01983 873931 **Fishermans Walk PO35 5TH**
web: www.warnerleisurehotels.co.uk
dir: A3055 Ryde to Sandown, approx 1.5m, left at lights into Carpenter's Rd to St Helens. At mini-rdb 2nd exit onto A3395 signed Bembridge. In Bembridge follow one-way system to right, left after bakery into Forelands Rd. 1m, left into Lane End Rd. Follow to end, right to hotel entrance

This hotel occupies a delightfully peaceful location on the east coast of the Isle of Wight in 23-acre grounds. The accommodation is comfortable, and there are a number of rooms with sea views for which a small supplementary charge applies. A full activities itinerary ensures that guests can make the most of what this hotel, and this beautiful island, has to offer. The helpful reservations team can also arrange ferry bookings from the UK mainland. Please note that this is an adults-only (over 21 years) hotel.

Rooms 258 (30 annexe) (76 GF) 🐾 **Facilities** Spa FTV WiFi HL 🕲 supervised ⚘ Putt green 🏌 Gym Tropicarium Solarium Archery Rifle shooting Crossbow Indoor & outdoor bowls 🎵 Xmas New Year **Services** Lift **Parking** 244 **Notes** ⊗ No children 21yrs

---

BERWICK-UPON-TWEED
Northumberland   Map 21 NT95

Queens Head

★★★ 78% SMALL HOTEL

tel: 01289 307852 **Sandgate TD15 1EP**
email: info@queensheadberwick.co.uk **web:** www.thequeensheadhotel.com
dir: A1 towards centre & town hall, into High St. Right at bottom to Hide Hill

The Queens Head is a small hotel situated in the town centre, close to the old walls of this former garrison town. Bedrooms provide many thoughtful extras as standard. Dining remains a strong aspect with a carte menu that offers an impressive choice of tasty, freshly prepared dishes served in the comfortable lounge or dining room.

Rooms 6 (1 fmly) 🐾 S £60-£75; D £80-£95 (incl. bkfst)* **Facilities** STV FTV WiFi ↘ **Notes** ⊗

BEVERLEY
East Riding of Yorkshire   Map 17 TA03

BEST WESTERN Lairgate Hotel

★★★ 72% HOTEL

tel: 01482 882141 **30/32 Lairgate HU17 8EP**
email: lairgate@bestwestern.co.uk
dir: A63 towards town centre. Hotel 220yds on left, follow one-way system

Located just off the market square, this pleasing Georgian hotel has been appointed to offer stylish accommodation. Bedrooms are elegant and well equipped, and public rooms include a comfortable lounge, a lounge bar, and restaurant with a popular sun terrace.

Rooms 30 (1 fmly) (8 GF) 🐾 S £81-£90; D £100-£135 (incl. bkfst)* **Facilities** FTV WiFi 🎵 New Year **Conf** Class 40 Board 30 Thtr 80 Del from £150 to £180* **Parking** 18 **Notes** LB ⊗ Closed 26 Dec & 1 Jan RS 25 Dec Civ Wed 70

B

BEWDLEY
Worcestershire
Map 10 S077

Mercure Kidderminster Hotel

★★★★ 71% HOTEL

tel: 0844 815 9033 **Habberley Rd DY12 1LA**
email: info@mercurekidderminster.co.uk **web:** www.jupiterhotels.co.uk
dir: A456 towards Kidderminster to ring road, follow signs to Bewdley. Pass Safari Park then exit A456/Town Centre, take sharp right after 200yds onto B4190, hotel 400yds on right

This 19th-century property is set in 20 acres of neat landscaped grounds in the Worcestershire countryside, close to West Midland Safari Park. The bedrooms are modern and well equipped; some rooms have great views of the grounds. Public rooms include a choice of lounges and the brasserie restaurant; the property also boasts great leisure facilities that include a coffee shop, hairdressers and a 25 meter swimming pool.

Rooms 44 (3 fmly) (17 GF) ♦ **Facilities** FTV WiFi ⌨ 🕹 supervised 🏊 Gym Beauty treatment room **Conf** Class 120 Board 60 Thtr 350 **Notes** ⊗ Civ Wed 250

BEXHILL
East Sussex
Map 6 TQ70

The Cooden Beach Hotel

★★★ 80% HOTEL

tel: 01424 842281 **Cooden Beach TN39 4TT**
email: rooms@thecoodenbeachhotel.co.uk **web:** www.thecoodenbeachhotel.co.uk
dir: A259 towards Bexhill. Signed at rdbt in Little Common Village. Hotel at end of road in Cooden, just past railway station

This privately owned hotel is situated in private gardens which have direct access to the beach. With a train station within walking distance the location is perfectly suited for both business and leisure guests. Bedrooms are comfortably appointed, and public areas include a spacious restaurant, lounge, bar and leisure centre with swimming pool.

Rooms 41 (8 annexe) (10 fmly) (4 GF) ♦ **Facilities** FTV WiFi ⌨ 🕹 Gym Sauna Steam room Spa bath Beauty treatment room Xmas New Year **Conf** Class 40 Board 40 Thtr 150 **Parking** 60 **Notes** Civ Wed 160

BEXLEY
Greater London
Map 6 TQ47

Holiday Inn London - Bexley

★★★ 78% HOTEL

tel: 0871 942 9006 & 01322 625513 **Black Prince Interchange, Southwold Rd DA5 1ND**
email: bexley@ihg.com **web:** www.hilondonbexleyhotel.co.uk
dir: M25 junct 2, A2 towards London. Exit at Black Prince Interchange (signed Bexley, Bexleyheath, A220, A223). Hotel on left

This hotel is within easy access of London and the Kent countryside; only 10 minutes from the famous Bluewater Shopping Centre and 15 minutes from Brands Hatch motor racing circuit. All bedrooms are air conditioned; suites are available. The hotel has a range of meeting rooms.

Rooms 107 (17 fmly) (33 GF) (8 smoking) **Facilities** STV FTV WiFi ⌨ Fitness room Xmas New Year **Conf** Class 42 Board 50 Thtr 120 **Services** Lift Air con **Parking** 200 **Notes** ⊗ Civ Wed 100

BIBURY
Gloucestershire
Map 5 SP10

Swan Hotel

★★★★ 75% 🌐 HOTEL

tel: 01285 740695 **GL7 5NW**
email: info@swanhotel.co.uk **web:** www.cotswold-inns-hotels.co.uk/swan
dir: 9m S of Burford A40 onto B4425. 6m N of Cirencester A4179 onto B4425

This hotel, built in the 17th century as a coaching inn, is set in peaceful and picturesque surroundings. It provides well-equipped and smartly presented accommodation, including four luxury cottage suites set just outside the main hotel. The elegant public areas are comfortable and have feature fireplaces. There is a choice of dining options to suit all tastes.

Rooms 22 (4 annexe) (1 fmly) ♦ **S** £150-£210; **D** £170-£210 (incl. bkfst)*
Facilities FTV WiFi Fishing Xmas New Year **Conf** Class 50 Board 32 Thtr 80 **Services** Lift **Parking** 22 **Notes** LB Civ Wed 110

BICESTER
Oxfordshire
Map 11 SP52

Premier Inn Bicester

BUDGET HOTEL

tel: 0871 527 9394 **Oxford Rd OX26 1BT**
web: www.premierinn.com
dir: M40 junct 9, A41 towards Bicester. 1.5m, hotel on left adjacent to Brewers Fayre

High quality, budget accommodation ideal for both families and business travellers. Spacious, en suite bedrooms feature tea and coffee making facilities, and Freeview TV in most hotels. Internet access and WiFi are available for a small fee. The adjacent family restaurant features a wide and varied menu. See also the Hotel Groups pages.

Rooms 84

B

BIDEFORD
Devon
Map 3 SS42

The Royal Hotel

Brend Hotels

★★★ 74% HOTEL

tel: 01237 472005 **Barnstaple St EX39 4AE**
email: reservations@royalbideford.co.uk **web:** www.royalbideford.co.uk
dir: At eastern end of old Bideford Bridge

A quiet and relaxing hotel, the Royal is set near the river within a five-minute walk of the busy town centre and the quay. The bright, well maintained public areas retain much of the charm and style of the hotel's 16th-century origins, particularly in the wood-panelled Kingsley Suite. Bedrooms are well equipped and comfortable. The meals at dinner and the lounge snacks are delicious.

Rooms 32 (2 fmly) (2 GF) ↟ **S** £57–£130; **D** £85–£150* **Facilities** FTV WiFi ♨ Xmas New Year **Conf** Class 100 Board 100 Thtr 100 **Services** Lift **Parking** 70 **Notes** LB ⊗ Civ Wed 130

Durrant House Hotel

★★★ Ⓐ HOTEL

tel: 01237 472361 **Heywood Rd, Northam EX39 3QB**
email: info@durranthousehotel.com **web:** www.durranthousehotel.com
dir: A39 to Bideford, over New Torridge Bridge, right at rdbt, hotel 500yds on right

This large hotel offers bedrooms with Italian-marble bathrooms, and the facilities include a hospitality tray, hairdryer, TV, clock radio and an iron with ironing board; superior rooms have wonderful views of the Torridge estuary and Taw Valley, plus rain showers, sofas and luxury toiletries. The fine dining, oak-panelled Olive Tree Restaurant offers dishes based on locally sourced produce.

Rooms 125 (25 fmly) (14 GF) ↟ **S** £40–£60; **D** £70–£160 (incl. bkfst)* **Facilities** Spa FTV WiFi HL ↘ Gym Sauna Sun shower ♫ Xmas New Year **Conf** Class 100 Board 80 Thtr 350 Del from £67.50 to £85* **Services** Lift **Parking** 200 **Notes** LB Civ Wed 100

BIGBURY-ON-SEA
Devon
Map 3 SX64

Henley Hotel

★★ 83% SMALL HOTEL

tel: 01548 810240 **TQ7 4AR**
email: thehenleyhotel@btconnect.com **web:** www.thehenleyhotel.co.uk
dir: Through Bigbury, past Golf Centre into Bigbury-on-Sea. Hotel on left

Henley Hotel is an Edwardian building complete with its own private cliff path to a sandy beach, and stunning views from an elevated position. Family run, it is a perfect choice for guests wishing to escape to a peaceful retreat. Personal service, friendly hospitality and food cooked with care using local, fresh produce combine to make this an uncomplicated and special place to stay.

Rooms 6 ↟ **S** £90; **D** £120–£150 (incl. bkfst)* **Facilities** FTV WiFi **Parking** 9 **Notes** LB No children 12yrs Closed Nov-Mar

---

BILDESTON
Suffolk
Map 13 TL94

The Bildeston Crown

★★★ ◉◉ HOTEL

tel: 01449 740510 **104 High St IP7 7EB**
email: reception@thebildestoncrown.co.uk **web:** www.thebildestoncrown.co.uk
dir: A12 junct 31, B1070 towards Hadleigh. At T-junct left onto A1141, right onto B1115. Hotel 0.5m

The Bildeston Crown is a charming Grade II former coaching inn situated in a peaceful village. Public areas feature beams, exposed brickwork and oak floors, with contemporary style décor. There is a choice of bars, a lounge and a restaurant. The individually designed bedrooms, including a romantic four-poster room, have lovely co-ordinated fabrics and modern facilities that include Musicast systems and internet access via WiFi and LAN. Food here is the real focus and certainly a draw; both the chef and the owner, who is a farmer, are very conscious of reducing 'food miles'; top quality produce such as Red Poll beef (from the owner's own farm), locally reared lamb, pork and seasonal game appear on the menus. Accomplished technical skills achieve award-winning results.

Rooms 12 ↟ **Facilities** STV FTV WiFi Xmas New Year **Conf** Class 25 Board 16 Thtr 40 **Services** Lift **Parking** 30 **Notes** Civ Wed 50

B

BILLINGHAM
County Durham   Map 19 NZ42

Wynyard Hall Hotel

★★★★ HOTEL

tel: 01740 644811 **Wynyard TS22 5NF**
email: enq@wynyardhall.co.uk **web:** www.wynyardhall.co.uk
dir: A19, A1027 towards Stockton. At rdbt take B1274 (Junction Rd). At next rdbt take A177 (Durham Rd). Right onto Wynyard Rd signed Wolviston. Left into estate

Drive though the gates, over the lion bridge, and Wynyard Hall will immediately impress with its grandeur and elegance. The opulent public areas are as much a feature of the property as are the grounds and gardens. The individually designed bedrooms and suites are stunning, with a combination of modern and period style furniture. The elegant, award-winning Duke of Wellington restaurant is also impressive, although as we go to press there has been a change of chef. The Rosette award has been suspended until such time as one of our inspectors can reasses the operation. The Essential Time Treatment Suite offers many relaxing therapies and beauty treatments. As a wedding venue the hall provides the option for a civil ceremony, or a religious service in the chapel, followed by a memorable reception.

Rooms 25 (9 annexe) (1 fmly) (9 GF) **Facilities** Spa FTV WiFi Clay pigeon shooting Archery Hawk walk Boot camp Xmas New Year **Conf** Class 240 Board 50 Thtr 300 **Services** Lift **Parking** 500 **Notes** Civ Wed 150

BILSBORROW
Lancashire   Map 18 SD53

Premier Inn Preston North

BUDGET HOTEL

tel: 0871 527 8912 **Garstang Rd PR3 0RN**
web: www.premierinn.com
dir: 4m from M6 junct 32 on A6 towards Garstang. 7m from Preston

High quality, budget accommodation ideal for both families and business travellers. Spacious, en suite bedrooms feature tea and coffee making facilities, and Freeview TV in most hotels. Internet access and WiFi are available for a small fee. The adjacent family restaurant features a wide and varied menu. See also the Hotel Groups pages.

Rooms 40

BINGLEY
West Yorkshire   Map 19 SE13

Five Rise Locks Hotel & Restaurant

★★★ 75% ◉ SMALL HOTEL

tel: 01274 565296 **Beck Ln BD16 4DD**
email: info@five-rise-locks.co.uk **web:** www.five-rise-locks.co.uk
dir: From Main St into Park Rd, in 0.5m left into Beck Ln

A warm welcome and comfortable accommodation awaits guests at this impressive Victorian building. Bedrooms are of a good size and feature homely extras. The restaurant offers imaginative dishes and the bright breakfast room overlooks open countryside.

Rooms 9 (2 GF) **S** £50-£69; **D** £70-£115 (incl. bkfst)* **Facilities** FTV WiFi
Conf Class 16 Board 18 Thtr 25 **Parking** 20 **Notes** LB

Mercure Bradford, Bankfield Hotel

★★★ 75% HOTEL

tel: 0844 815 9004 **Bradford Rd BD16 1TU**
email: info@mercurebradford.co.uk **web:** www.jupiterhotels.co.uk
dir: From M62 junct 26 onto M606, at rdbt follow signs for A650 Skipton/Keighley, hotel 2m from Shipley

This striking gothic style mansion house is set in landscaped gardens and is a short walk from the River Aire. The rural setting is peaceful yet the hotel is also convenient for Bradford and Leeds. The hotel is understandably a popular wedding venue and also caters well for corporate guests with extensive meeting facilities available in a designated conference centre. Free WiFi access is provided throughout the hotel.

Rooms 103 **Facilities** WiFi **Conf** Class 200 Board 80 Thtr 350 **Parking** 350 **Notes** Civ Wed 350

B

BIRCHANGER GREEN MOTORWAY SERVICE AREA (M11)   Map 6 TL52
Essex

Days Inn Bishop's Stortford - M11

BUDGET HOTEL

tel: 01279 656477 **CM23 5QZ**
email: birchanger.hotel@welcomebreak.co.uk **web:** www.welcomebreak.co.uk
dir: M11 junct 8

This modern building offers accommodation in smart, spacious and well-equipped bedrooms, suitable for families and business travellers, and all with en suite bathrooms. Continental breakfast is available and other refreshments may be taken at the nearby family restaurant. See also the Hotel Groups pages.

Rooms 60 (12 fmly) (29 GF) (8 smoking)

BIRKENHEAD   Map 15 SJ38
Merseyside

The RiverHill Hotel

★★★ 83% HOTEL

tel: 0151 653 3773 **Talbot Rd, Prenton CH43 2HJ**
email: reception@theriverhill.co.uk **web:** www.theriverhill.co.uk
dir: M53 junct 3, A552. Left onto B5151 at lights, hotel 0.5m on right

Pretty lawns and gardens provide the setting for this friendly, privately owned hotel. Its convenient location and attractive grounds make it a popular wedding venue. The comfortable bedrooms are equipped with a wealth of extras; ground floor, family, and four-poster rooms are available. Well-cooked meals and substantial breakfasts are served in the elegant restaurant overlooking the garden.

Rooms 14 (1 fmly) **Facilities** FTV WiFi Free use of local leisure facilities **Conf** Class 30 Board 52 Thtr 50 **Parking** 32 **Notes** ⊗ Civ Wed 40

Premier Inn Wirral (Greasby)

BUDGET HOTEL

tel: 0871 527 9176 **Greasby Rd, Greasby, Wirral CH49 2PP**
web: www.premierinn.com
dir: 9m from Liverpool city centre. 2m from M53 junct 2. Just off B5139

High quality, budget accommodation ideal for both families and business travellers. Spacious, en suite bedrooms feature tea and coffee making facilities, and Freeview TV in most hotels. Internet access and WiFi are available for a small fee. The adjacent family restaurant features a wide and varied menu. See also the Hotel Groups pages.

Rooms 30

BIRMINGHAM   Map 10 SP08
West Midlands

See also **Bromsgrove, Lea Marston, Oldbury & Sutton Coldfield**

Hotel du Vin Birmingham

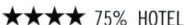

★★★★ 78% ◉◉ TOWN HOUSE HOTEL

tel: 0844 736 4250 **25 Church St B3 2NR**
email: info@birmingham.hotelduvin.com **web:** www.hotelduvin.com
dir: M6 junct 6/A38(M) to city centre, over flyover. Keep left & exit at St Chads Circus signed Jewellery Quarter. At lights & rdbt take 1st exit, follow signs for Colmore Row, opposite cathedral. Right into Church St, across Barwick St. Hotel on right

The former Birmingham Eye Hospital has become a chic and sophisticated hotel. The stylish, high-ceilinged rooms, all with a wine theme, are luxuriously appointed

---

and feature stunning bathrooms, sumptuous duvets and Egyptian cotton sheets. The Bistro offers relaxed dining and a top-notch wine list, while other attractions include a champagne bar, a wine boutique and a health club.

Rooms 66 ⟨ **Facilities** Spa STV FTV WiFi ⟳ Gym Steam room Sauna Plunge shower Xmas New Year **Conf** Class 40 Board 40 Thtr 84 **Services** Lift Air con
Notes Civ Wed 84

Macdonald Burlington Hotel

★★★★ 76% HOTEL

tel: 0844 879 9019 & 0121 643 9191 **Burlington Arcade, 126 New St B2 4JQ**
email: events.burlington@macdonald-hotels.co.uk
web: www.macdonaldhotels.co.uk/burlington
dir: M6 junct 6, A38, follow city centre signs

The Burlington's original Victorian grandeur - the marble and iron staircases and the high ceilings - blend seamlessly with modern facilities. Bedrooms are equipped to a good standard and public areas include a stylish bar and coffee lounge. The Berlioz Restaurant specialises in innovative dishes using fresh produce.

Rooms 114 (6 fmly) ⟨ **Facilities** STV WiFi ⟳ HL New Year **Conf** Class 200 Board 80 Thtr 500 **Services** Lift **Notes** Closed 24-26 Dec Civ Wed 400

Novotel Birmingham Centre

★★★★ 75% HOTEL

tel: 0121 643 2000 **70 Broad St B1 2HT**
email: h1077@accor.com **web:** www.novotel.com
dir: M6 junct 6, A38(M) (Aston Expressway), A456 towards Kidderminster

This large, modern, purpose-built hotel benefits from an excellent city centre location, with the bonus of secure parking. Bedrooms are spacious, modern and well equipped especially for business users; four rooms have facilities for less able guests. Public areas include the Garden Brasserie, function rooms and a fitness room.

Rooms 148 (148 fmly) ⟨ **Facilities** WiFi ⟳ Gym Fitness room Cardiovascular equipment Sauna Steam room New Year **Conf** Class 120 Board 90 Thtr 300 **Services** Lift **Parking** 53

Malmaison Birmingham

★★★★ 73% ◉ HOTEL

tel: 0844 693 0651 **1 Wharfside St, The Mailbox B1 1RD**
email: birmingham@malmaison.com **web:** www.malmaison.com
dir: M6 junct 6, A38 towards Birmingham. Hotel within The Mailbox, signed from A38

The 'Mailbox' development, of which this stylish and contemporary hotel is a part, incorporates the very best in fashionable shopping outlets, an array of restaurants and ample parking. The air-conditioned bedrooms are stylishly decorated and feature comprehensive facilities. Public rooms include a contemporary bar and brasserie which prove a hit with guests and locals alike. Gymtonic, and a Petit Spa offering rejuvenating treatments are also available.

Rooms 189 **Facilities** WiFi Gym **Conf** Class 40 Board 24 Thtr 50 **Services** Lift Air con

B

Menzies Hotels Birmingham City Strathallan

MenziesHotels

★★★★ 73% HOTEL

tel: 0121 455 9777 **225 Hagley Rd, Edgbaston B16 9RY**
email: strathallan@menzieshotels.co.uk **web:** www.menzies-hotels.co.uk
dir: From A38 follow signs for ICC into Broad St, towards Five Ways island, take
underpass to Hagley Rd. Hotel 0.5m

Located just a few minutes from the city's central attractions and with the benefit
of excellent parking, this hotel provides a range of comfortable and well-equipped
bedrooms. A modern lounge bar and contemporary restaurant offer a good range of
dining options.

Rooms 135 (36 fmly) ➠ **S** £45-£149; **D** £45-£149 **Facilities** STV FTV WiFi ⊳ Gym
Xmas New Year **Conf** Class 90 Board 50 Thtr 170 Del from £95 to £165 **Services** Lift
Parking 120 **Notes** LB ⊗ Civ Wed 100

Copthorne Hotel Birmingham

MILLENNIUM
HOTELS AND RESORTS
MILLENNIUM · COPTHORNE

★★★★ 71% HOTEL

tel: 0121 200 2727 **Paradise Circus B3 3HJ**
email: reservations.birmingham@millenniumhotels.co.uk
web: www.millenniumhotels.co.uk
dir: M6 junct 6, city centre A38(M). After Queensway Tunnel follow International
Convention Centre signs. At Paradise Circus island take right lane. Hotel in centre

This hotel is one of the few establishments in the city that benefits from its own car
park. Bedrooms are spacious and come in a choice of styles, all with excellent
facilities. Guests can choose to eat in the Bugis Street Brasserie which offers
traditional Chinese, Singaporean and Malay cuisine.

Rooms 211 **Facilities** FTV WiFi ⊳ HL Gym Xmas New Year **Conf** Class 120 Board 30
Thtr 200 **Services** Lift **Parking** 78 **Notes** ⊗ Civ Wed 150

BEST WESTERN Westley Hotel

Best
Western

★★★ 82% HOTEL

tel: 0121 706 4312 **80-90 Westley Rd, Acocks Green B27 7UJ**
email: reservations@westley-hotel.co.uk **web:** www.westley-hotel.co.uk
dir: A41 signed Birmingham on Solihull by-pass, to Acocks Green. At rdbt, 2nd exit B4146
(Westley Rd). Hotel 200yds on left

Situated in the city suburbs and conveniently located for the N.E.C. and the airport,
this friendly hotel provides well-equipped, smartly presented bedrooms. In addition
to the main restaurant, there is also a lively bar and brasserie together with a large
function room.

Rooms 37 (11 annexe) (3 fmly) (3 GF) **Facilities** STV WiFi ⊳ New Year **Conf** Class 80
Board 50 Thtr 200 **Parking** 150 **Notes** ⊗ Civ Wed 200

Holiday Inn Birmingham City

Holiday Inn

★★★ 81% HOTEL

tel: 0871 942 9008 & 0121 634 6202 **Smallbrook Queensway B5 4EW**
email: reservations@hibirmingham.co.uk **web:** www.holidayinn.co.uk/birminghamcity
dir: M6 junct 6, A38(M) to city centre, keep left after flyover & two underpasses. 2nd left
into Suffolk Place. 1st right into St Jude's Passage

This is a large hotel in the city centre with extensive meeting rooms and a business
centre. The lounge bar with a roof terrace is a popular meeting place. The Albany
Restaurant offers lunch and dinner, and room service is available.

Rooms 241 (8 fmly) ➠ **S** £49-£199; **D** £49-£199 **Facilities** FTV WiFi ⊳ HL
Conf Class 300 Board 150 Thtr 600 Del from £99 to £189* **Services** Lift Air con
Parking 8 **Notes** LB

Edgbaston Palace Hotel

★★★ 73% HOTEL

tel: 0121 452 1577 **198-200 Hagley Rd, Edgbaston B16 9PQ**
email: enquiries@edgbastonpalacehotel.com **web:** www.edgbastonpalacehotel.com
dir: M5 junct 3 N, A456 for 4.3m. Hotel on right

Dating back to the 19th century, this Grade II listed Victorian property has
bedrooms that are modern, well appointed and offer good comfort levels. The
hospitality is warm, personal and refreshing. Supervised children under 18 are
welcome.

Rooms 48 (21 annexe) (3 fmly) (16 GF) **Facilities** FTV WiFi **Conf** Class 70 Board 60
Thtr 200 **Parking** 70 **Notes** ⊗ Civ Wed

Great Barr Hotel & Conference Centre

★★★ 67% HOTEL

tel: 0121 357 1141 **Pear Tree Dr, Newton Rd, Great Barr B43 6HS**
email: sales@thegreatbarrhotel.com **web:** www.thegreatbarrhotel.com
dir: M6 junct 7, at Scott Arms x-rds right towards West Bromwich (A4010) Newton Rd.
Hotel 1m on right

This busy hotel, situated in a leafy residential area, is particularly popular with
business clients; the hotel has excellent, state-of-the-art training and seminar
facilities. There is a traditional oak-panelled bar and formal restaurant, and
bedrooms are appointed to a good standard with the expected amenities.

Rooms 92 (6 fmly) **Facilities** STV WiFi ⊳ **Conf** Class 90 Board 60 Thtr 200
Parking 200 **Notes** RS BH (restaurant may close) Civ Wed 200

Campanile Birmingham

Campanile
HOTEL RESTAURANT

BUDGET HOTEL

tel: 0121 359 3330 **Chester St, Aston B6 4BE**
email: birmingham@campanile.com **web:** www.campanile.com
dir: Adjacent to rdbt at junct of A4540 & A38

This modern building offers accommodation in smart, well-equipped bedrooms, all
with en suite bathrooms. Refreshments may be taken at the informal bistro. See
also the Hotel Groups pages.

Rooms 110 (5 fmly) **Conf** Class 100 Board 100 Thtr 250

Holiday Inn Express Birmingham - South A45

Holiday Inn
Express

BUDGET HOTEL

tel: 0121 289 3333 **1270 Coventry Rd, Yardley B25 8BS**
email: reservations@hiex-birmingham.co.uk **web:** www.hiexpressbirminghamsouth.co.uk
dir: A45 Coventry

A modern hotel ideal for families and business travellers. Fresh and uncomplicated,
the spacious rooms include Sky TV, power shower and tea and coffee-making
facilities. Continental buffet breakfast is included in the room rate; other meals
may be taken at the nearby family pub or restaurant. See also the Hotel Groups
pages.

Rooms 83 ➠ **Conf** Board 16 Thtr 24

BIRMINGHAM *continued*

Ibis Birmingham Bordesley Circus

BUDGET HOTEL

tel: 0121 506 2600 **1 Bordesley Park Rd, Bordesley B10 0PD**
email: H2178@accor.com **web:** www.ibishotel.com

Modern, budget hotel offering comfortable accommodation in bright and practical bedrooms. Breakfast is self-service and dinner is available in the restaurant. See also the Hotel Groups pages.

Rooms 87 (15 GF) 🐾

Ibis Birmingham City Centre

BUDGET HOTEL

tel: 0121 622 6010 **Arcadian Centre, Ladywell Walk B5 4ST**
email: h1459@accor-hotels.com **web:** www.ibishotel.com
dir: From motorways follow city centre signs. Then follow Bullring or Indoor Market signs. Hotel adjacent to market

Rooms 159 (5 fmly) **Conf** Class 60 Board 50 Thtr 120

Ibis Birmingham Holloway Circus

BUDGET HOTEL

tel: 0121 622 4925 **55 Irving St B1 1DH**
email: H2092@accor.com **web:** www.ibishotel.com
dir: From M6 take A38 (City Centre), left after 2nd tunnel. Right at rdbt, 4th left (Sutton St) into Irving St. Hotel on left

Rooms 51 (26 GF)

Premier Inn Birmingham Broad St Canal Side

BUDGET HOTEL

tel: 0871 527 8078 **20 Bridge St B1 2JH**
web: www.premierinn.com
dir: M6 junct 6, A38(M) towards city centre. Follow signs for city centre/ICC/A456 (Broad St). Left at Hyatt Hotel, hotel on right at bottom of Bridge St

High quality, budget accommodation ideal for both families and business travellers. Spacious, en suite bedrooms feature tea and coffee making facilities, and Freeview TV in most hotels. Internet access and WiFi are available for a small fee. The adjacent family restaurant features a wide and varied menu. See also the Hotel Groups pages.

Rooms 83

Premier Inn Birmingham Broad Street (Brindley Place)

BUDGET HOTEL

tel: 0871 527 8076 **80 Broad St B15 1AU**
web: www.premierinn.com
dir: M6 junct 6, A38(M) (Aston Expressway). Follow City Centre, ICC & NIA signs into Broad St. Right into Sheepcote St. 2nd left at rdbt into Essington St. Hotel on left. (NB for Sat Nav use B16 8AL)

Rooms 62

Premier Inn Birmingham Central East

BUDGET HOTEL

tel: 0871 527 8080 **Richard St, Aston, Waterlinks B7 4AA**
web: www.premierinn.com
dir: M6 junct 6, signed city centre. A38(M) signed A4540 (ring road). At rdbt 1st exit 50mtrs left into Richard St, hotel on left (barrier access to car park)

Rooms 61

Premier Inn Birmingham Central (Hagley Road)

BUDGET HOTEL

tel: 0871 527 8082 **Hagley Rd B16 9NY**
web: www.premierinn.com
dir: M6 junct 6, A38(M) (Aston Express Way). Follow city centre, ICC & NIA signs, into Broad St. From M5 junct 3, A456 for approx 3m, hotel on left

Rooms 62

Premier Inn Birmingham City Centre (New Street)

BUDGET HOTEL

tel: 0871 527 9442 **Birmingham Exchange Buildings, Stephenson Place B2 4NH**
web: www.premierinn.com
dir: M6 junct 6, A38 (Corporation St) keep right at fork. Exit towards New St, merge into Suffolk St Queensway. At rdbt 1st exit into Smallbrook Queensway, left into Hill St, right into Queen's Drive. Multi-storey parking at New St Station, The Pallasades or Bull Ring

Rooms 140

Premier Inn Birmingham City Centre (Waterloo Street)

BUDGET HOTEL

tel: 0871 527 8074 **3-6 Waterloo St B2 5PG**
web: www.premierinn.com
dir: M6 junct 6, A38 (Corporation St). Follow West Bromwich/A41 signs. Merge into St Chad's Queensway. 2nd exit for Great Charles St Queensway, becomes Livery St. Left into Waterloo St

Rooms 109

Premier Inn Birmingham (Great Barr/M6 Jct 7)

BUDGET HOTEL

tel: 0871 527 8072 **Birmingham Rd, Great Barr B43 7AG**
web: www.premierinn.com
dir: M6 junct 7, A34 towards Walsall. Hotel on left behind Beacon Harvester

Rooms 32

Premier Inn Birmingham South (Hall Green)

BUDGET HOTEL

tel: 0871 527 8092 **Stratford Rd, Hall Green B28 9ES**
web: www.premierinn.com
dir: M42 junct 4, A34 towards Shirley signed Birmingham. Straight on at 6 rdbts. At 7th rdbt 4th exit. Hotel on left

Rooms 51

B

Premier Inn Birmingham South (Longbridge St)

BUDGET HOTEL

tel: 0871 527 9434 **2 College St, Longbridge B31 2US**
web: www.premierinn.com
dir: M5 junct 4, A38 towards Birmingham. 3m (pass Morrisons & McDonald's) to rdbt. 1st exit towards A38 (B'ham).Right at 1st lights signed Longbridge train station. 1st right at Sainsburys, hotel on right. Please note for Sat Nav use postcode B31 2TW

Rooms 75

BIRMINGHAM AIRPORT	Map 10 SP08
West Midlands	

Novotel Birmingham Airport

★★★★ 73% HOTEL

tel: 0121 782 7000 & 782 4111 **B26 3QL**
email: H1158@accor.com **web:** www.novotel.com
dir: M42 junct 6, A45 to Birmingham, signed to airport. Hotel opposite main terminal

This smartly decorated hotel with air conditioning throughout its public areas and bedrooms benefits from being less than a minute's walk from the main terminal of Birmingham International Airport. Spacious bedrooms are comfortable and modern bathrooms are stylish with powerful showers. The Elements bar and restaurant provides a great atmosphere for meals and a fitness room is available on site. Long stay car parking packages can be arranged at this location.

Rooms 195 (24 fmly) 🐾 **Facilities** STV WiFi ⤡ Gym Fitness room **Conf** Class 10 Board 20 Thtr 35 **Services** Lift Air con

---

Ibis Birmingham Airport

BUDGET HOTEL

tel: 0121 780 5800 **Ambassador Rd, Bickenhill, Solihull B26 3AW**
email: H6359@accor.com **web:** www.ibishotel.com
dir: M42 junct 6, A45 follow signs to Birmingham Airport

Modern, budget hotel offering comfortable accommodation in bright and practical bedrooms. Breakfast is self-service and dinner is available in the restaurant. See also the Hotel Groups pages.

Rooms 162 (2 fmly) 🐾 **S** £69-£195; **D** £69-£195*

BIRMINGHAM (NATIONAL EXHIBITION CENTRE)	Map 10 SP18
West Midlands	

BEST WESTERN PREMIER Moor Hall Hotel & Spa

★★★★ 80% ❀ HOTEL

tel: 0121 308 3751 **Moor Hall Dr, Four Oaks B75 6LN**
email: mail@moorhallhotel.co.uk **web:** www.moorhallhotel.co.uk

(For full entry see Sutton Coldfield)

Nailcote Hall

★★★★ 76% ❀ HOTEL

tel: 024 7646 6174 **Nailcote Ln, Berkswell CV7 7DE**
email: info@nailcotehall.co.uk **web:** www.nailcotehall.co.uk

(For full entry see Balsall Common)

Crowne Plaza Birmingham NEC

★★★★ 76% HOTEL

tel: 0871 942 9160 **National Exhibition Centre, Pendigo Way B40 1PS**
email: necroomsales@ihg.com **web:** www.cpbirminghamnec.hotel.co.uk
dir: M42 junct 6, follow signs for NEC, take 2nd exit on left, South Way for hotel entrance 50mtrs on right

On the doorstep of the NEC and overlooking Pendigo Lake, this hotel has contemporary design and offers well-equipped bedrooms with air conditioning. Bedrooms have ample working space and high-speed internet access (for an additional charge). Eating options include the modern Pendigo Restaurant overlooking the lake, the bar and 24-hour room service.

Rooms 242 (13 fmly) **Facilities** STV WiFi HL Gym Sauna **Conf** Class 140 Board 56 Thtr 200 **Services** Lift Air con **Parking** 348 **Notes** ⊗

Arden Hotel & Leisure Club

★★★ 74% HOTEL

tel: 01675 443221 **Coventry Rd, Bickenhill B92 OEH**
email: enquiries@ardenhotel.co.uk **web:** www.ardenhotel.co.uk
dir: M42 junct 6, A45 towards Birmingham. Hotel 0.25m on right, just off Birmingham International railway island

This smart hotel neighbouring the NEC, offers modern rooms and well-equipped leisure facilities. After dinner in the formal restaurant, the place to relax is the spacious lounge area. A buffet breakfast is served in the bright and airy Meeting Place.

Rooms 216 (6 fmly) (6 GF) (12 smoking) **S** £50-£175; **D** £50-£175* **Facilities** Spa STV WiFi ⤡ 🕸 Gym Beautician ⫫ Xmas New Year **Conf** Class 40 Board 60 Thtr 200 Del from £99 to £175* **Services** Lift **Parking** 300 **Notes** LB Civ Wed 100

Premier Inn Birmingham NEC/Airport

BUDGET HOTEL

tel: 0871 527 8086 **Off Bickenhill Parkway, National Exhibition Centre B40 1QA**
web: www.premierinn.com
dir: M42 junct 6 signed NEC. Turn right towards North Way. Follow Premier Inn signs. Hotel on left at 5th rdbt

High quality, budget accommodation ideal for both families and business travellers. Spacious, en suite bedrooms feature tea and coffee making facilities, and Freeview TV in most hotels. Internet access and WiFi are available for a small fee. The adjacent family restaurant features a wide and varied menu. See also the Hotel Groups pages.

Rooms 199

BISHOP AUCKLAND
County Durham — Map 19 NZ22

Premier Inn Bishop Auckland

BUDGET HOTEL

tel: 0871 527 8096 **West Auckland Rd DL14 9AP**
web: www.premierinn.com
dir: From S: A1 junct 58, left onto A68 signed Corbridge/Bishop Auckland. At 1st rdbt 2nd exit onto A6072 signed Shildon. Straight on at 4 rdbts, follow Shildon/Bishop Auckland signs. Hotel approx 1m on left

High quality, budget accommodation ideal for both families and business travellers. Spacious, en suite bedrooms feature tea and coffee making facilities, and Freeview TV in most hotels. Internet access and WiFi are available for a small fee. The adjacent family restaurant features a wide and varied menu. See also the Hotel Groups pages.

Rooms 49

BISHOP'S STORTFORD
Hertfordshire — Map 6 TL42

Down Hall Country House Hotel

★★★★ 77% HOTEL

tel: 01279 731441 **Hatfield Heath CM22 7AS**
email: info@downhall.co.uk **web:** www.downhall.co.uk
dir: A1060, at Hatfield Heath keep left. Right into lane opposite Hunters Meet restaurant, left at end, follow signs

Imposing country house hotel set amidst 100 acres of mature grounds in a peaceful location just a short drive from Stansted Airport. Bedrooms are generally quite spacious; each one is pleasantly decorated, tastefully furnished and equipped with modern facilities. Public rooms include a choice of restaurants, a cocktail bar, two lounges and leisure facilities.

Rooms 99 (20 GF) **S** fr £89; **D** fr £99* **Facilities** FTV WiFi Gym Giant chess Whirlpool Sauna Snooker room Xmas New Year **Conf** Class 140 Board 68 Thtr 200 Del from £149* **Services** Lift **Parking** 150 **Notes** Civ Wed 150

The Legacy Great Hallingbury Manor Hotel

★★★ 80% HOTEL

tel: 08444 119068 & 0330 333 2868 **Tilekiln Green, Great Hallingbury CM22 7TJ**
email: info@greathallingburymanor.co.uk **web:** www.legacy-hotels.co.uk
dir: M11 junct 8 rdbt take exit to B1256, turn immediately right at petrol station. Under bridge, sharp left bend, continue for 500yds. Hotel on left

This Tudor-style Manor is set in lovely landscaped grounds and is surrounded by open countryside. It was completely refurbished a couple of years ago and now has a very contemporary feel throughout. The property is situated close to Stansted Airport, and the major road networks are within easy reach. Bedrooms are smartly appointed and have a range of thoughtful touches; public areas include a choice of lounges, a bar and an open-plan restaurant.

Rooms 45 (22 annexe) (3 fmly) (16 GF) **Facilities** FTV WiFi Xmas New Year **Conf** Class 80 Board 30 Thtr 170 **Parking** 80 **Notes** Civ Wed 170

Days Hotel London Stansted - M11

BUDGET HOTEL

tel: 01279 213900 **M11 Motorway, Junction 8, Old Dunmow Rd CM23 5QZ**
web: www.welcomebreak.co.uk
dir: Adjacent to M11 junct 8

This modern building offers accommodation in smart, spacious and well-equipped bedrooms, suitable for families and business travellers, and all with en suite bathrooms. There is an attractive lounge area and a dining room where breakfast is served and other refreshments may be taken. See also the Hotel Groups pages.

Rooms 77 (16 fmly) (16 GF) (8 smoking)

BISHOPSTEIGNTON
Devon — Map 3 SX97

Cockhaven Manor Hotel

THE INDEPENDENTS
HOTEL ASSOCIATION

★★ 74% HOTEL

tel: 01626 775252 **Cockhaven Rd TQ14 9RF**
email: cockhaven@btconnect.com **web:** www.cockhavenmanor.com
dir: A380 towards Torquay, A381 towards Teignmouth. Left at Metro Motors. Hotel 500yds on left

Cockhaven Manor is a friendly, family-run inn that dates back to the 16th century. Bedrooms are well equipped and many enjoy views across the beautiful Teign estuary. A choice of dining options is offered, and traditional and interesting dishes, along with locally caught fish, prove popular.

Rooms 12 (2 fmly) **S** £50-£65; **D** £75-£90 (incl. bkfst)* **Facilities** FTV WiFi Petanque **Conf** Class 50 Board 30 Thtr 50 Del from £80 to £100* **Parking** 50 **Notes** LB Closed 25-26 Dec Civ Wed 100

BLACKBURN
Lancashire — Map 18 SD62

See also Langho

Mercure Blackburn Foxfields Country Hotel

★★★ 74% HOTEL

tel: 01254 822556 **Whalley Rd, Billington, Clitheroe BB7 9HY**
email: enquiries@hotels-blackburn.com **web:** www.hotels-blackburn.com
dir: Just off A59

This modern hotel is easily accessible from major road networks. Bedrooms are comfortable and spacious, and include some suites and others with separate dressing areas. Facilities include a good-sized swimming pool, a small gym and conference suites. The hotel is also a popular wedding venue, and its traditional restaurant serves an interesting range of cuisine.

Rooms 44 (16 annexe) (27 fmly) (13 GF) (8 smoking) **S** £60-£100; **D** £60-£120* **Facilities** STV FTV WiFi Gym Sauna Steam room Xmas New Year **Conf** Class 60 Board 60 Thtr 140 Del from £85 to £145* **Parking** 194 **Notes** LB Civ Wed 200

Premier Inn Blackburn North West

BUDGET HOTEL

tel: 0871 527 8098 **Myerscough Rd, Balderstone BB2 7LE**
web: www.premierinn.com
dir: M6 junct 31, A59 towards Clitheroe. Hotel opposite British Aerospace, adjacent to Boddington Arms

High quality, budget accommodation ideal for both families and business travellers. Spacious, en suite bedrooms feature tea and coffee making facilities, and Freeview TV in most hotels. Internet access and WiFi are available for a small fee. The adjacent family restaurant features a wide and varied menu. See also the Hotel Groups pages.

Rooms 20

Premier Inn Blackburn South

BUDGET HOTEL

tel: 0871 527 8100 **Off Eccleshill Rd, Riversway Dr, Lower Darwen BB3 0SN**
web: www.premierinn.com
dir: At M65 junct 4

Rooms 43

BLACKPOOL	Map 18 SD33
Lancashire	

The Imperial Hotel

★★★★ 72% HOTEL

tel: 01253 623971 **North Promenade FY1 2HB**
email: imperialblackpool@pumahotels.co.uk **web:** www.pumahotels.co.uk
dir: M55 junct 2, A583 (North Shore), follow signs to North Promenade. Hotel on seafront, north of tower

Enjoying a prime seafront location, this grand Victorian hotel offers smartly appointed, well-equipped bedrooms and spacious, elegant public areas. Facilities include a smart leisure club, a comfortable lounge, the No 10 bar and an attractive split-level restaurant that overlooks the seafront. Conferences and functions are extremely well catered for.

Rooms 180 (16 fmly) ⌥ **S** £69-£152; **D** £79-£152* **Facilities** Spa STV WiFi ⌂⌥ supervised Gym Xmas New Year **Conf** Class 280 Board 70 Thtr 600 Del from £110 to £160* **Services** Lift **Parking** 150 **Notes** LB Civ Wed 200

Carousel Hotel

★★★ 77% HOTEL

tel: 01253 402642 **663-671 New South Prom FY4 1RN**
email: carousel.reservations@sleepwellhotels.com **web:** www.sleepwellhotels.com
dir: From M55 follow signs to airport, pass airport to lights. Turn right, hotel 100yds on right

This friendly seafront hotel, close to the Pleasure Beach, offers smart, contemporary accommodation. Bedrooms are comfortably appointed and have a modern, stylish feel to them. An airy restaurant and a spacious bar/lounge both overlook the Promenade. The hotel has good conference and meeting facilities and its own car park.

Rooms 92 (22 fmly) **Facilities** FTV WiFi ⌂ ♫ Xmas New Year **Conf** Class 30 Board 40 Thtr 100 **Services** Lift **Parking** 46 **Notes** ⊗ Civ Wed 150

The Claremont Hotel

★★ 78% HOTEL

tel: 0844 811 5570 **270 North Promenade FY1 1SA**
email: reservations@choice-hotels.co.uk **web:** www.choicehotels.co.uk
dir: M55 junct 3 follow sign for promenade. Hotel beyond North Pier

Conveniently situated, the Claremont is a popular family holiday hotel. Bedrooms are bright and attractively decorated, and extensive public areas include a spacious air-conditioned restaurant which offers a good choice of dishes. There is a well equipped, supervised children's play room, and entertainment is provided during the season.

Rooms 143 (50 fmly) ⌥ **S** £35-£60; **D** £69-£120 (incl. bkfst & dinner) **Facilities** FTV WiFi ⌂ Beauty treatments ♫ Xmas New Year **Conf** Class 140 Board 30 Thtr 380 Del from £82 to £103 **Services** Lift **Parking** 40 **Notes** LB ⊗

New Guilderoy Hotel

★★ 78% SMALL HOTEL

tel: 01253 351547 **57-59 Holmfield Rd, North Shore FY2 9RU**
email: simon_connelly@yahoo.com **web:** www.new-guilderoy-hotel-blackpool.co.uk
dir: M55 Blackpool. Follow signs North Shore. Located behind The Cliffs Hotel, Queens Promenade

This pleasant family-run hotel, sits in a quiet location, away from the hubbub of the town, yet is conveniently close to the attractions and sea. There is a relaxing lounge and a cosy bar; there is also a very good wine list to choose from. Home cooked food is a feature here and menus at both breakfast and dinner offer a good choice.

Rooms 15 (5 fmly) ⌥ **S** £20-£35; **D** £40-£75 (incl. bkfst) **Facilities** FTV WiFi Xmas New Year **Notes** LB ⊗ Closed 10 Nov-22 Dec RS 2 Jan-28 Feb

The Viking Hotel

★★ 76% HOTEL

tel: 0844 811 5570 **479 South Promenade FY4 1AX**
email: reservations@choice-hotels.co.uk **web:** www.choicehotels.co.uk
dir: M55 junct 3, follow Pleasure Beach signs

Located close to the centre of the South Promenade, this establishment offers well equipped accommodation and a warm welcome. Meals are served in the attractive sea view restaurant and entertainment is available in the renowned 'Talk of the Coast' night club. Leisure facilities at sister hotels are also available free of charge.

Rooms 100 (10 GF) ⌥ **S** £35-£89; **D** £66-£129 (incl. bkfst & dinner) **Facilities** FTV WiFi Cabaret club ♫ Xmas New Year **Services** Lift **Parking** 50 **Notes** LB ⊗ No children 18yrs

The Cliffs Hotel

★★ 74% HOTEL

tel: 0844 811 5570 & 01253 595559 **Queens Promenade FY2 9SG**
email: reservations@choice-hotels.co.uk **web:** www.choicehotels.co.uk
dir: M55 junct 3, follow Promenade signs. Hotel just after Gynn rdbt

This large, privately owned and extremely popular hotel is within easy reach of the town centre. The bedrooms, including spacious family rooms, vary in size. Public areas offer an all-day coffee shop, a smart restaurant and a family room where children are entertained.

Rooms 163 (47 fmly) ⌥ **Facilities** FTV WiFi ⌥ supervised Gym Beauty treatments Sauna ♫ Xmas New Year **Conf** Class 210 Board 50 Thtr 475 Del from £81* **Services** Lift **Parking** 30 **Notes** ⊗ Civ Wed 100

B

BLACKPOOL *continued*

Queens Hotel

★★ 74% HOTEL

Leisureplex

tel: 01253 342015 & 336980 **469-471 South Promendae FY4 1AY**
email: queens.blackpool@leisureplex.co.uk **web:** www.leisureplex.co.uk

Queens Hotel is situated on the South Promenade overlooking the Irish Sea, close to the South Pier and Pleasure Beach. The bedrooms are well equipped and some rooms have lovely sea views. The spacious public areas include a choice of lounges, a range of bars, a conservatory and a large dining room as well as a refurbished 300-seat theatre bar.

Rooms 110 (8 fmly) ◆ **Facilities** FTV WiFi HL ⊗ supervised ♫ Xmas New Year **Conf** Class 60 Board 60 Thtr 80 **Services** Lift **Parking** 55 **Notes** ⊗ Closed Jan-Feb

Hotel Sheraton

★★ 70% HOTEL

tel: 01253 352723 **54-62 Queens Promenade FY2 9RP**
email: email@hotelsheraton.co.uk **web:** www.hotelsheraton.co.uk
dir: 1m N from Blackpool Tower towards Fleetwood

This family-owned and run hotel is situated at the quieter, northern end of the promenade. Public areas include a choice of spacious lounges with sea views, a heated indoor swimming pool and a large function suite where popular dancing and cabaret evenings are held. The smartly appointed bedrooms come in a range of sizes and styles.

Rooms 104 (45 fmly) (15 smoking) **Facilities** ⊗ Table tennis Darts ♫ Xmas New Year **Conf** Class 100 Board 150 Thtr 200 **Services** Lift **Parking** 20 **Notes** ⊗

Headlands Hotel

★★ 69% HOTEL

tel: 01253 341179 **611-613 South Promenade FY4 1NJ**
email: info@theheadlandsblackpool.co.uk **web:** www.theheadlandsblackpool.co.uk
dir: From end of M55 follow South Promenade signs

This friendly, family-owned hotel stands on the South Promenade, close to the Pleasure Beach and many of the town's major attractions. Bedrooms are traditionally furnished and many enjoy sea views. There is a choice of lounges and live entertainment is provided regularly. Home-cooked food is served in the panelled dining room.

Rooms 41 (10 fmly) ◆ **Facilities** FTV WiFi Darts Games room Pool Snooker ♫ Xmas New Year **Services** Lift **Parking** 38 **Notes** Closed 2-15 Jan

Alumhurst Hotel

★★ 63% HOTEL

tel: 01253 620959 & 07746 191023 **13-15 Charnley Rd FY1 4PE**
email: alumhursthotel@btconnect.com **web:** www.alumhursthotel.com
dir: End of M55 take urban route to central parking area (red). Follow to end, right to exit, left into Central Drive. Follow round to Debenhams then right & 1st left

Close to the Winter Gardens and Blackpool's multiplicity of attractions, this personally-managed hotel has been in the Francis family for 40 years, and offers a range of room options. Premier and traditional rooms are comfortable and well presented, but it is the 'retro 70s' rooms that stand out. These offer the expected comfort along with clever nostalgic touches such as Goblin Teasmades, cabinet TVs, 70s magazines and décor, and wind-up alarm clocks. There's also a bar and

lounge with pool, darts, a jukebox, TV and fruit machines. The bar also has an area dedicated to 'Old Blackpool'.

Rooms 32 (9 fmly) (7 smoking) ◆ **S** £41; **D** £72-£90 (incl. bkfst)* **Facilities** FTV WiFi Child facilities **Services** Lift **Parking** 6 **Notes** ⊗ Closed mid Nov-Mar

The Craig-y-Don Hotel

★★ 63% SMALL HOTEL

tel: 01253 624249 **211-213 Central Promenade FY1 5DL**
email: craig-y-donhotel@btconnect.com **web:** www.craig-y-don.com
dir: On promenade, 2/3m past Blackpool Pleasure Beach

This hotel has a promenade location; many rooms enjoy sea views, and this is very much a holiday hotel. Freshly cooked dinner is available in the spacious dining room. Bedrooms are available in a range of sizes. The busy bar features cabaret and entertainment most nights.

Rooms 38 (28 fmly) (7 GF) ◆ **S** £35-£50; **D** £50-£80 (incl. bkfst)* **Facilities** FTV WiFi ♫ Xmas New Year **Services** Lift **Notes** LB ⊗ RS Nov-May wknds only

Lyndene Hotel

★★ Ⓐ HOTEL

tel: 01253 346779 **303/315 Promenade FY1 6AN**
email: enquiries@lyndenehotel.com **web:** www.lyndenehotel.com

Family run for over 20 years, this hotel is on the promenade and offers bedrooms with LCD flat-screen TVs, safes and hospitality trays; some rooms are on the ground floor. Public rooms include two air-conditioned lounges, two restaurants and an outside seating area and sun terrace. Entertainment is offered every evening.

Rooms 140 (60 fmly) (12 GF) (140 smoking) ◆ **Facilities** FTV WiFi ♫ Xmas New Year **Services** Lift **Parking** 70 **Notes** ⊗ No children 5yrs

Hotel Ibis Styles Blackpool

BUDGET HOTEL

tel: 01253 752478 **Talbot Square FY1 1ND**
email: H9148@accor.com **web:** www.focushotels.co.uk/hotels
dir: M55 junct 4, follow signs for A583 Blackpool North Shore, approx 4m to seafront. Property on right opposite North Pier entrance

Modern, budget hotel offering comfortable accommodation in bright and practical bedrooms. Breakfast is self-service and dinner is available in the restaurant. See also the Hotel Groups pages.

Rooms 90 (4 fmly)

Premier Inn Blackpool Airport

BUDGET HOTEL

tel: 0871 527 8106 **Squire Gate Ln FY4 2QS**
web: www.premierinn.com
dir: M55 junct 4, A5230, left at 1st rdbt towards airport. Hotel just before Squires Gate rail station

High quality, budget accommodation ideal for both families and business travellers. Spacious, en suite bedrooms feature tea and coffee making facilities, and Freeview TV in most hotels. Internet access and WiFi are available for a small fee. The adjacent family restaurant features a wide and varied menu. See also the Hotel Groups pages.

Rooms 39

Premier Inn Blackpool (Bispham)

BUDGET HOTEL

tel: 0871 527 8102 **Devonshire Rd, Bispham FY2 0AR**
web: www.premierinn.com
dir: M55 junct 4, A583. At 5th lights turn right (Whitegate Drive). Approx. 4.5m onto A587 (Devonshire Rd)

Rooms 40

Premier Inn Blackpool Central

BUDGET HOTEL

tel: 0871 527 8108 **Yeadon Way, South Shore FY1 6BF**
web: www.premierinn.com
dir: M55 junct 4 to Blackpool, straight on at last island onto Yeaden Way. Follow signs for Central Car Park/Coach Area. Left at Total garage

Rooms 82

Premier Inn Blackpool East (M55 Jct 4)

BUDGET HOTEL

tel: 0871 527 8110 **Whitehills Park, Preston New Rd FY4 5NZ**
web: www.premierinn.com
dir: Just off M55 junct 4. 1st left off rdbt. Hotel on right

Rooms 81

BLAKENEY
Norfolk

Map 13 TG04

B

Morston Hall

★★★★ HOTEL

tel: 01263 741041 & 740419 **Morston, Holt NR25 7AA**
email: reception@morstonhall.com **web:** www.morstonhall.com
dir: 1m W of Blakeney on A149 - King's Lynn to Cromer road
This delightful 17th-century country-house hotel enjoys a tranquil setting amid well-tended gardens. The comfortable public rooms offer a choice of attractive lounges and a sunny conservatory, while the elegant dining room is the perfect setting to enjoy Galton Blackiston's award-winning cuisine. The spacious bedrooms are individually decorated and stylishly furnished with modern opulence.

Rooms 13 (6 annexe) (7 GF) S £190-£240; D £360-£380 (incl. bkfst & dinner)*
Facilities STV FTV WiFi New Year **Conf** Class 20 Board 16 Del from £230 to £250*
Parking 40 **Notes** LB Closed 1 Jan-last Fri in Jan & 2 days Xmas

The Blakeney Hotel

★★★★ 78% HOTEL

tel: 01263 740797 **The Quay NR25 7NE**
email: reception@blakeneyhotel.co.uk **web:** www.blakeneyhotel.co.uk
dir: From A148 between Fakenham & Holt, take B1156 to Langham & Blakeney

A traditional, privately-owned hotel situated on the quayside with superb views across the estuary and the salt marshes to Blakeney Point. Public rooms feature an elegant restaurant, ground-floor lounge, a bar and a first-floor sun lounge overlooking the harbour. Bedrooms are smartly decorated and equipped with modern facilities. The leisure area is a real feature with pool, sauna, steam room and mini-gym.

Rooms 63 (16 annexe) (20 fmly) (17 GF) S £81-£157; D £162-£338 (incl. bkfst & dinner)* **Facilities** FTV WiFi HL Gym Billiards Snooker Table tennis Sauna Steam room Spa bath Xmas New Year **Conf** Class 100 Board 100 Thtr 150 Del £150*
Services Lift **Parking** 60 **Notes** LB

B

BLEADON	Map 4 ST35
Somerset	

Premier Inn Weston-Super-Mare

BUDGET HOTEL

tel: 0871 527 9154 **Bridgwater Rd, Lympsham BS24 OBP**
web: www.premierinn.com
dir: M5 junct 22, A38 (Bristol Rd) signed Weston-Super-Mare. At 1st rdbt take 1st exit into Bridgewater Rd (A370). Approx 2m to hotel

High quality, budget accommodation ideal for both families and business travellers. Spacious, en suite bedrooms feature tea and coffee making facilities, and Freeview TV in most hotels. Internet access and WiFi are available for a small fee. The adjacent family restaurant features a wide and varied menu. See also the Hotel Groups pages.

Rooms 24

BLETCHINGDON	Map 11 SP51
Oxfordshire	

The Oxfordshire Inn

★★★ 66% HOTEL

tel: 01869 351444 **Heathfield Village OX5 3DX**
email: staff@oxfordshireinn.co.uk **web:** www.oxfordshireinn.co.uk
dir: M40 junct 9, A34 towards Oxford, A4027 towards Bletchingdon. Hotel signed 0.7m on right

A converted farmhouse with additional outbuildings that is located close to major motorway networks. The accommodation is set around an open courtyard, and includes suites that have four-poster beds. There is a spacious bar and restaurant.

Rooms 28 (4 fmly) (15 GF) ✆ **Facilities** FTV WiFi Putt green Golf driving range Xmas New Year **Conf** Class 80 Board 30 Thtr 140 **Parking** 50

BODMIN	Map 2 SX06
Cornwall	

Trehellas House Hotel & Restaurant

★★★ 75% ❀ SMALL HOTEL

tel: 01208 72700 **Washaway PL30 3AD**
email: enquiries@trehellashouse.co.uk **web:** www.trehellashouse.co.uk
dir: A389 from Bodmin towards Wadebridge. Hotel on right 0.5m beyond road to Camelford

This 18th-century former posting inn retains many original features and provides comfortable accommodation. Bedrooms are located in both the main house and adjacent coach house - all provide the same high standards. An interesting choice of cuisine, with an emphasis on locally-sourced ingredients, is offered in the impressive slate-floored restaurant.

Rooms 12 (7 annexe) (2 fmly) (5 GF) **S** £50-£70; **D** £50-£175 (incl. bkfst)*
Facilities FTV WiFi ⚡ Xmas New Year **Conf** Board 20 Thtr 20 **Parking** 32 **Notes** LB No children 13yrs

Westberry Hotel

★★ 81% HOTEL

tel: 01208 72772 **Rhind St PL31 2EL**
email: westberry@btconnect.com **web:** www.westberryhotel.net
dir: On ring road off A30 & A38. St Petroc's Church on right, at mini rdbt turn right. Hotel on right

This popular hotel is conveniently located for both Bodmin town centre and the A30. The bedrooms are attractive and well equipped, and a spacious bar lounge and billiard room are also provided. The restaurant serves a variety of dishes, ranging from bar snacks to a more extensive carte menu.

Rooms 20 (8 annexe) (2 fmly) (6 GF) ✆ **S** £48-£78; **D** £68-£98 (incl. bkfst)*
Facilities STV FTV WiFi ⚡ **Conf** Class 80 Board 80 Thtr 100 **Parking** 30 **Notes** LB

Premier Inn Bodmin

BUDGET HOTEL

tel: 0871 527 8112 **Launceston Rd PL31 2AR**
web: www.premierinn.com
dir: From A30 S'bound exit onto A389, hotel 0.5m on right. N'bound exit onto A38, follow A389 signs. Left at T-junct

High quality, budget accommodation ideal for both families and business travellers. Spacious, en suite bedrooms feature tea and coffee making facilities, and Freeview TV in most hotels. Internet access and WiFi are available for a small fee. The adjacent family restaurant features a wide and varied menu. See also the Hotel Groups pages.

Rooms 44

BOGNOR REGIS	Map 6 SZ99
West Sussex	

The Russell Hotel

★★★ 73% HOTEL

tel: 01243 871300 **King's Pde PO21 2QP**
email: reservations.russell@visionhotels.co.uk **web:** www.visionhotels.co.uk
dir: A27 follow signs for town centre, hotel on seafront

Situated in a pleasant location close to the seafront, the Russell Hotel offers large and well-appointed bedrooms; some are fully accessible and many have sea views. This hotel also caters for visually impaired people, their families, friends and guide dogs, as well as offering a warm welcome to business and leisure guests. There are of course special facilities for the guide dogs. Leisure facilities are also available.

Rooms 40 (5 fmly) ✆ **S** £45-£150; **D** £49-£170 (incl. bkfst)* **Facilities** FTV ⚡ supervised Putt green Gym ♫ Xmas New Year **Conf** Class 60 Board 40 Thtr 100 **Services** Lift **Parking** 6 **Notes** Civ Wed 80

B

The Inglenook

★★★ 70% SMALL HOTEL

tel: 01243 262495 & 265411 **255 Pagham Rd, Nyetimber PO21 3QB**
email: reception@the-inglenook.com **web:** www.the-inglenook.com
dir: A27 into Vinnetrow Rd, left at Walnut Tree, hotel 2.5m on right

This 16th-century inn retains much of its original character, including exposed beams throughout. Bedrooms are individually decorated and vary in size. There is a cosy lounge, a well-kept garden and a bar that offers a popular evening menu and convivial atmosphere. The restaurant, overlooking the garden, also serves enjoyable cuisine.

Rooms 18 (1 fmly) (2 GF) ☞ **Facilities** STV FTV WiFi Xmas New Year **Conf** Class 50 Board 50 Thtr 100 Del from £90 to £120 **Parking** 35 **Notes** Civ Wed 80

The Royal Norfolk Hotel

★★ 76% HOTEL

tel: 01243 826222 **The Esplanade PO21 2LH**
email: royalnorfolk@leisureplex.co.uk **web:** www.leisureplex.co.uk
dir: From A259 follow Longford Rd through lights to Canada Grove to T-junct. Right, take 2nd exit at rdbt. Hotel on right

Located on the seafront, but set back behind well-tended lawns and gardens, is this fine Regency hotel. The bedrooms are traditionally furnished and provide guests with modern comforts. There are sea views from the bar and restaurant, as well as the lounges.

Rooms 60 (4 fmly) (7 GF) ☞ **S** £38-£58; **D** £62-£102 (incl. bkfst)* **Facilities** FTV WiFi ♫ Xmas New Year **Services** Lift **Parking** 35 **Notes** LB ⊗ Closed 2 Jan-14 Feb

Premier Inn Bognor Regis

BUDGET HOTEL

tel: 0871 527 8114 **Shripney Rd PO22 9PA**
web: www.premierinn.com
dir: From A27 & A29 rdbt junct follow Bognor Regis signs. Approx 4m, hotel on left

High quality, budget accommodation ideal for both families and business travellers. Spacious, en suite bedrooms feature tea and coffee making facilities, and Freeview TV in most hotels. Internet access and WiFi are available for a small fee. The adjacent family restaurant features a wide and varied menu. See also the Hotel Groups pages.

Rooms 24

BOLTON
Greater Manchester
Map 15 SD70

Egerton House Hotel

★★★ 78% ⚫ HOTEL

tel: 01204 307171 **Blackburn Rd, Egerton BL7 9SB**
email: reservation@egertonhouse.co.uk **web:** www.egertonhouse-hotel.co.uk
dir: M61, A666 (Bolton road), pass ASDA on right. Hotel 2m on just after war memorial on right

Peace and relaxation come as standard at this popular, privately owned hotel that sits in acres of well-tended woodland gardens. Public rooms are stylishly appointed and have an inviting, relaxing atmosphere. Many of the individually styled, attractive guest bedrooms enjoy delightful garden views. Conferences and meetings are well catered for.

Rooms 29 (7 fmly) **Facilities** FTV WiFi ☀ Xmas New Year **Conf** Class 90 Board 60 Thtr 150 **Parking** 135 **Notes** ⊗ Civ Wed 140

Mercure Bolton Georgian House Hotel

★★★ 75% HOTEL

tel: 0844 815 9029 **Manchester Rd, Blackrod BL6 5RU**
email: info@mercurebolton.co.uk **web:** www.jupiterhotels.co.uk
dir: M61 junct 6, follow Blackrod A6027 signs. 200mtrs turn right onto A6 signed Chorley. Hotel 0.5m on right

This hotel has a pleasant location and very good parking, convenient for corporate or leisure guests alike. Bedrooms are pleasantly appointed, and beds very comfortable. There is a range of meeting rooms and the hotel is popular for weddings. There is a choice of dining venues and a pleasant bar.

Rooms 91 **Facilities** WiFi ♨ 🏊 Gym Sauna Beauty treatments Dance studio **Conf** Class 60 Board 40 Thtr 275 **Parking** 300 **Notes** Civ Wed 275

Mercure Bolton Last Drop Village Hotel & Spa

★★★ 74% HOTEL

tel: 01204 591131 **Hospital Rd, Bromley Cross BL7 9PZ**
email: h6634@accor.com **web:** www.mercure.com
dir: 3m N of Bolton off B5472

MercureBolton Last Drop Village Hotel & Spa is a collection of 18th-century farmhouses set on cobbled streets with various shops and a local pub. Extensive self-contained conference rooms, a modern health and beauty spa and breathtaking views of the West Pennine Moors make this a popular choice with both corporate and leisure guests. The bedrooms are well equipped and spacious.

Rooms 128 (10 annexe) (29 fmly) (20 GF) **Facilities** Spa FTV WiFi 🏊 Gym Craft shops Thermal suite Rock sauna Steam bath Bio sauna Xmas New Year **Conf** Class 300 Board 95 Thtr 700 **Services** Lift **Parking** 400 **Notes** Civ Wed 500

Premier Inn Bolton (Reebok Stadium)

BUDGET HOTEL

tel: 0871 527 8116 **Arena Approach 3, Horwich BL6 6LB**
web: www.premierinn.com
dir: M61 junct 6, right at rdbt, left at 2nd rdbt

High quality, budget accommodation ideal for both families and business travellers. Spacious, en suite bedrooms feature tea and coffee making facilities, and Freeview TV in most hotels. Internet access and WiFi are available for a small fee. The adjacent family restaurant features a wide and varied menu. See also the Hotel Groups pages.

Rooms 74

Premier Inn Bolton West

BUDGET HOTEL

tel: 0871 527 8118 **991 Chorley New Rd, Horwich BL6 4BA**
web: www.premierinn.com
dir: M61 junct 6, follow dual carriageway signed Bolton/Horwich (Reebok Stadium on left). Hotel at 2nd rdbt

Rooms 60

B

BOLTON ABBEY	Map 19 SE05
North Yorkshire	

INSPECTORS' CHOICE

The Devonshire Arms Country House Hotel & Spa

★★★★ ●●● HOTEL

tel: 01756 710441 & 718111 **BD23 6AJ**
email: res@devonshirehotels.co.uk **web:** www.thedevonshirearms.co.uk
dir: On B6160, 250yds N of junct with A59

With stunning views of the Wharfedale countryside this beautiful hotel, owned by the Duke and Duchess of Devonshire, dates back to the 17th century. Bedrooms are elegantly furnished; those in the old part of the house are particularly spacious and have four-posters and fine antiques. The sitting rooms are delightfully cosy with log fires, and the dedicated staff deliver service with a blend of friendliness and professionalism. The Burlington Restaurant offers accomplished cuisine, while the Brasserie provides a lighter alternative.

Rooms 40 (1 fmly) (17 GF) ✎ **S** £205-£460; **D** £255-£570 (incl. bkfst)* **Facilities** Spa STV WiFi ❧ ⓣ supervised ⌆ Fishing ⛳ Gym Classic cars Falconry Laser pigeon shooting Fly fishing Cricket Xmas New Year **Conf** Class 80 Board 30 Thtr 90 **Parking** 150 **Notes** Civ Wed 90

BOREHAMWOOD	Map 6 TQ19
Hertfordshire	

Ibis London Elstree Borehamwood

BUDGET HOTEL

tel: 020 8736 2600 **Elstree Way WD6 1JY**
email: H6186@accor.com **web:** www.ibishotel.com
dir: M25 junct 23, A1, exit at Borehamwood, take A5135 (Elstree Way)

Modern, budget hotel offering comfortable accommodation in bright and practical bedrooms. Breakfast is self-service and dinner is available in the restaurant. See also the Hotel Groups pages.

Rooms 122 (16 fmly) (16 GF)

Premier Inn London Elstree/Borehamwood

BUDGET HOTEL

tel: 0871 527 8654 **Warwick Rd WD6 1US**
web: www.premierinn.com
dir: Exit A1 signed Borehamwood onto A5135 (Elstree Way). Pass BP Garage, left into Warwick Rd

High quality, budget accommodation ideal for both families and business travellers. Spacious, en suite bedrooms feature tea and coffee making facilities, and Freeview TV in most hotels. Internet access and WiFi are available for a small fee. The adjacent family restaurant features a wide and varied menu. See also the Hotel Groups pages.

Rooms 120

BOROUGHBRIDGE	Map 19 SE36
North Yorkshire	

BEST WESTERN Crown Hotel

★★★ 77% HOTEL

tel: 01423 322328 **Horsefair YO51 9LB**
email: sales@crownboroughbridge.co.uk **web:** www.crownboroughbridge.co.uk
dir: A1(M) junct 48 towards Boroughbridge. Hotel 1m

Situated in the centre of town but convenient for the A1(M), The Crown provides a full leisure complex, conference rooms and a secure car park. Bedrooms are well appointed. A wide range of well-prepared dishes can be enjoyed in both the restaurant and bar.

Rooms 37 (3 fmly) (2 GF) **S** £75-£95; **D** £89-£142* **Facilities** FTV WiFi ❧ HL ⓣ supervised Gym Xmas New Year **Conf** Class 80 Board 80 Thtr 150 Del from £128 to £145* **Parking** 60 **Notes** ⊗ Civ Wed 120

The Crown Inn

 RESTAURANT WITH ROOMS

tel: 01423 322300 📠 01423 322033 **Roecliffe YO51 9LY**
email: info@crowninnroecliffe.com **web:** www.crowninnroecliffe.com
dir: A1(M) junct 48, follow signs for Boroughbridge. At rdbt exit towards Roecliffe & brown tourist signs

The Crown is a 16th-century coaching inn providing an excellent combination of traditional charm and modern comforts. Service is friendly and professional and food is a highlight of any stay. The kitchen team use the finest of Yorkshire produce from the best local suppliers to create a weekly-changing seasonal menu. Bedrooms are attractively furnished with stylish en suite bathrooms.

Rooms 4 (1 fmly)

Grantham Arms

 RESTAURANT WITH ROOMS

tel: 01423 323980 **Milby YO51 9BW**
email: info@granthamarms.co.uk **web:** www.granthamarms.co.uk

The Grantham Arms is a real gem of a place, from the neat and tidy garden area at the front, to the flamboyant and extravagant design of the interior. The public areas are a real feature with mood lighting, contemporary design furniture and wooden floorings. Bedrooms are very well appointed with quality throughout. Food is a highlight of any visit with fresh seasonal and local produce being a feature on all menus. Dinner, lunch and afternoon tea are available. Staff have a wonderful friendly way and makes this quite an exceptional place to visit.

Rooms 8 (1 annexe) (1 fmly)

BORROWDALE	Map 18 NY21
Cumbria	

See also **Keswick & Rosthwaite**

Lodore Falls Hotel

LAKE DISTRICT
HOTELS

★★★★ 80% ⬡ HOTEL

tel: 017687 77285 & 0800 840 1246 **CA12 5UX**
email: lodorefalls@lakedistricthotels.net **web:** www.lakedistricthotels.net/lodorefalls
dir: M6 junct 40, A66 to Keswick, B5289 to Borrowdale. Hotel on left

This impressive hotel has an enviable location overlooking Derwentwater. The bedrooms, many with lake or fell views, are comfortably equipped; family rooms and suites are also available. The dining room, bar and lounge areas are appointed to a very high standard. One of the treatments in the hotel's Elemis Spa actually makes use of the Lodore Waterfall.

Rooms 69 (11 fmly) ⬧ **S** £55-£118; **D** £110-£496 (incl. bkfst) **Facilities** Spa STV FTV WiFi ⬧ ⬧ ⬧ Fishing Gym Sauna Xmas New Year **Conf** Class 90 Board 45 Thtr 200 Del from £138 to £174 **Services** Lift **Parking** 103 **Notes** LB Civ Wed 130

Borrowdale Gates Hotel

★★★★ 77% ⬡ COUNTRY HOUSE HOTEL

tel: 017687 77204 **CA12 5UQ**
email: hotel@borrowdale-gates.com **web:** www.borrowdale-gates.com
dir: From A66 follow B5289 for approx 4m. Turn right over bridge, hotel 0.25m beyond village

This friendly hotel is peacefully located in the Borrowdale Valley, close to the village but in its own three acres of wooded grounds. Public rooms include comfortable lounges and a restaurant with picture postcard views. Bedrooms and their en suites have benefited from investment and refurbishment with very good results.

Rooms 25 (2 fmly) (9 GF) ⬧ **S** £62-£72; **D** £124-£200 (incl. bkfst)* **Facilities** FTV WiFi ⬧ Xmas New Year **Services** Lift **Parking** 29 **Notes** Closed 5-31 Jan

See advert on page 82

Borrowdale Hotel

LAKE DISTRICT
HOTELS

★★★★ 75% HOTEL

tel: 017687 77224 **CA12 5UY**
email: borrowdale@lakedistricthotels.net **web:** www.lakedistricthotels.net
dir: 3m from Keswick, on B5289 at S end of Lake Derwentwater

Situated in the beautiful Borrowdale Valley overlooking Derwentwater, this traditionally styled hotel guarantees a friendly welcome. Extensive public areas include a choice of lounges, traditional dining room, lounge bar and popular conservatory which serves more informal meals. Bedrooms vary in style and size, including two that are suitable for less able guests.

Rooms 40 (2 fmly) (4 GF) ⬧ **S** £112-£118; **D** £189-£247 (incl. bkfst) **Facilities** STV FTV WiFi ⬧ Leisure facilities available at nearby sister hotel Xmas New Year **Conf** Class 30 Board 24 Thtr 80 **Parking** 30

Borrowdale Gates

Grange-in-Borrowdale, Borrowdale CA12 5UQ • **Tel:** 017687 77204 or 0845 833 2524
Website: www.borrowdale-gates.com • **Email:** hotel@borrowdale-gates.com

S et in the tranquil, stunning scenery of the Borrowdale Valley, described by Alfred Wainwright as the *"loveliest square mile in Lakeland"*, this private luxury 4 star hotel is a hidden gem for guests looking to relax and enjoy fine cuisine in a restaurant with panoramic views, log fires, Lakeland-inspired organic cooking and warm, comfortable bedrooms.

Rooms with views is the unique speciality here, where each room has been recently refurbished with attention to detail and designed for individual comfort and relaxation. Guests can be mesmerised by the scenery, whether enjoyed from private balconies or the panoramic windows in the restaurant and lounge, which look out onto dramatic fells, rolling fields and wildlife at the doorstep.

In addition, with an AA Rosette award-winning team of chefs, the hotel's kitchen one of the best in the North West, taking advantage of this region abundant with high quality produce so the dishes are sourced locally and responsibly, to give guests a true contemporary taste of Cumbria.

After a day of walking, touring or sightseeing, with the many attractions of Keswick nearby, guests enjoy a renowned friendly personal service in a peaceful setting, surrounded by fells in two acres of wooded grounds on the edge of the hamlet of Grange, close to the shores of Derwentwater.

Finally, the overall guest experience extends to partnerships with selected local companies, such as guiding or golf, to make the most of any visit so people wish to return to this "home-from-home."

RECOMMENDED IN THE AREA

- Keswick's Theatre by the Lake
- Honister Slate Mine
- Lakeside and Fell Walks
- Golf (Keswick 9.6 miles, Silloth on Solway 32.4 miles)
- Cycling (Whinlatter)
- Watersports

B

BORROWDALE *continued*

Leathes Head Hotel

★★★ 83% HOTEL

tel: 017687 77247 & 77650 **CA12 5UY**
email: reservations@leatheshead.co.uk **web:** www.leatheshead.co.uk
dir: 3.5m from Keswick on B5289 (Borrowdale road). Hotel on left 0.25m before Grange Bridge

A fine Edwardian building, with lovely gardens, set in the heart of the unspoilt Borrowdale Valley. The hospitality and customer care are really outstanding here. The bedrooms have commanding views and the award-winning food, including a wonderful Cumbrian breakfast, will not disappoint.

Rooms 11 (2 fmly) (3 GF) ⬤ **S** £132-£190; **D** £165-£245 (incl. bkfst & dinner)*
Facilities FTV WiFi **Parking** 16 **Notes** No children 15yrs Closed late Nov-mid Feb

BOSCASTLE
Cornwall
Map 2 SX09

The Wellington Hotel

★★★ 78% ⬤⬤ HOTEL

tel: 01840 250202 **The Harbour PL35 OAQ**
email: info@wellingtonhotelboscastle.com **web:** www.wellingtonhotelboscastle.com
dir: A30/A395 at Davidstowe follow Boscastle signs. B3266 to village. Right into Old Rd

This 16th-century coaching inn is very much a landmark in Boscastle and has been providing rest and relaxation for weary travellers for many years. There is character in abundance which adds to its engaging charm and personality. The Long Bar is popular with visitors and locals alike and features a delightful galleried area. The stylish bedrooms come in varying sizes, including the spacious Tower Rooms; all provide contemporary comforts and the expected necessities. In addition to the bar menus, The Waterloo Restaurant is the elegant setting for accomplished cuisine.

Rooms 14 (1 fmly) ⬤ **S** £45-£55; **D** £95-£125 (incl. bkfst)* **Facilities** FTV WiFi ⬤ Xmas New Year **Conf** Class 40 Board 24 Thtr 50 Del from £95 to £140* **Parking** 14 **Notes** LB

BOSHAM
West Sussex
Map 5 SU80

The Millstream Hotel & Restaurant

★★★ 85% ⬤⬤ HOTEL

tel: 01243 573234 **Bosham Ln PO18 8HL**
email: info@millstreamhotel.com **web:** www.millstreamhotel.com
dir: 4m W of Chichester on A259, left at Bosham rdbt. After 0.5m right at T-junct signed to church & quay. Hotel 0.5m on right

Lying in the idyllic village of Bosham, this attractive hotel provides comfortable, well-equipped and tastefully decorated bedrooms. Many guests regularly return here for the relaxed atmosphere created by the notably efficient and friendly staff. Public rooms include a cocktail bar that opens onto the garden, and a pleasant award-winning restaurant where varied and freshly prepared cuisine can be enjoyed. Markwick's Brasserie Restaurant is open all day for coffee, snacks, light lunches and dinners.

Rooms 35 (2 annexe) (2 fmly) (9 GF) **S** £99-£109; **D** £159-£229 (incl. bkfst)*
Facilities FTV WiFi Painting & Bridge breaks ♬ Xmas New Year **Conf** Class 20 Board 20 Thtr 45 Del from £150 to £170* **Parking** 44 **Notes** LB ⊗ Civ Wed 75

BOSTON
Lincolnshire
Map 12 TF34

Supreme Inns Boston

★★★ 78% HOTEL

tel: 01205 822804 **Donnington Rd, Bicker Bar Roundabout PE20 3AN**
email: enquiries@supremeinns.co.uk **web:** www.supremeinns.co.uk
dir: At rdbt junct of A52 & A17

Situated south west of Boston and surrounded by the Lincolnshire Fens, this modern, purpose-built hotel offers well equipped bedrooms that have flat-screen TVs and internet access. Food is available in the restaurant or all day in the relaxing bar area. Wedding, private dinner and conference facilities are all available.

Rooms 55 (27 GF) **Facilities** FTV WiFi ⬤ Xmas New Year **Conf** Board 35 Thtr 60 **Parking** 65 **Notes** ⊗ Civ Wed 60

BEST WESTERN White Hart Hotel and Eatery

★★★ 77% HOTEL

tel: 01205 311900 **1-5 High St, Bridge Foot PE21 8SH**
email: whitehartboston@bulldogmail.co.uk **web:** www.whitehartboston.com
dir: In town centre

The White Hart Hotel is well appointed and attractive, and is conveniently located in the centre of this market town with great views of the 700-year-old St Botolph's Church, known as the Boston Stump, from its riverside location. The hotel has spacious public areas including the Riverside Restaurant for evening meals, and the lively Courtyard Bar which is open for brunch, lunch and afternoon tea. There is a wonderful outside area for relaxing, eating and drinking. Conferences and weddings are catered for. Off-street parking in a private car park is also available.

Rooms 26 ⬤ **S** £65; **D** £95 **Facilities** FTV WiFi ⬤ HL Xmas New Year **Conf** Class 26 Board 26 Thtr 80 Del £129 **Parking** 35 **Notes** LB Civ Wed 80

Boston West Hotel

★★★ 73% HOTEL

tel: 01205 292969 & 290670 **Hubberts Bridge PE20 3QX**
email: info@bostonwesthotel.co.uk **web:** www.bostonwesthotel.co.uk
dir: A1121 signed Boston, hotel on left after speed camera

A modern, purpose-built hotel situated in a rural location on the outskirts of town. The smartly appointed bedrooms are spacious and thoughtfully equipped; some rooms have balconies with stunning countryside views. Public rooms include a restaurant and a large open-plan lounge bar which overlooks the golf course.

Rooms 24 (5 fmly) (12 GF) **S** £49-£60; **D** £49-£60* **Facilities** FTV WiFi ⬤ 18 Putt green Driving range New Year **Conf** Class 60 Board 40 Thtr 80 Del £95* **Services** Lift **Parking** 24 **Notes** ⊗ Civ Wed 110

B

BOSTON *continued*

Premier Inn Boston

BUDGET HOTEL

tel: 0871 527 8120 **Wainfleet Rd PE21 9RW**
web: www.premierinn.com
dir: A52, 300yds E of junct with A16 Boston/Grimsby road

High quality, budget accommodation ideal for both families and business travellers. Spacious, en suite bedrooms feature tea and coffee making facilities, and Freeview TV in most hotels. Internet access and WiFi are available for a small fee. The adjacent family restaurant features a wide and varied menu. See also the Hotel Groups pages.

Rooms 54

BOTLEY	Map 5 SU51
Hampshire	

Macdonald Botley Park, Golf & Spa

★★★★ 76%  COUNTRY HOUSE HOTEL

tel: 01489 780 888 & 0844 879 9034 **Winchester Rd, Boorley Green SO32 2UA**
email: general.botleypark@macdonald-hotels.co.uk
web: www.macdonald-hotels.co.uk/botleypark
dir: M27 junct 7, A334 towards Botley. At 1st rdbt left, pass M&S store, over at next 5 mini rdbts. At 6th mini rdbt turn right. In 0.5m hotel on left

This modern and spacious hotel sits peacefully in the midst of its own 176-acre parkland golf course. Bedrooms are comfortably appointed with a good range of extras, and extensive leisure facilities are on offer. Attractive public areas include a relaxing restaurant and the more informal Swing and Divot Bar.

Rooms 130 (30 fmly) (44 GF) ↻ **S** £79-£289; **D** £89-£299 **Facilities** Spa STV WiFi ↳ ⌘ ♨ 18 ♧ Putt green Gym Squash Dance studio Xmas New Year **Conf** Class 180 Board 100 Thtr 450 Del from £159 to £249 **Services** Air con **Parking** 250 **Notes** ⊛ Civ Wed 400

BOURNEMOUTH	Map 5 SZ19
Dorset	

See also **Christchurch**

Bournemouth Highcliff Marriott Hotel

★★★★ 80% ◎◎ HOTEL

tel: 01202 557702 **St Michaels Rd, West Cliff BH2 5DU**
email: mhrs.bohbm.ays@marriotthotels.co.uk
web: www.bournemouthhighcliffmarriott.co.uk
dir: A338 into Bournemouth then BIC signs to West Cliff Rd. 2nd right into St Michaels Rd. Hotel at end of road on left

Originally built as a row of coastguard cottages, this establishment has expanded over the years into a very elegant and charming hotel. Impeccably maintained throughout, many of the bedrooms have sea views. An excellent range of leisure, business and conference facilities are offered, as well as private dining and banqueting rooms. The hotel also has direct access to the Bournemouth International Centre.

Rooms 160 (19 annexe) (22 fmly) (4 GF) ↻ **Facilities** STV FTV WiFi ☺ ⚲ ♨ Gym Beautician Beauty treatment room ♫ Xmas New Year **Conf** Class 180 Board 90 Thtr 350 **Services** Lift Air con **Parking** 80 **Notes** ⊛ Civ Wed 250

The Green House

★★★★ 77% ◉ TOWN HOUSE HOTEL

tel: 01202 498900 **4 Grove Rd BH1 3AX**
email: reception@thegreenhousehotel.com **web:** www.thegreenhousehotel.com

This hotel has a clear commitment to the environment which goes beyond just energy efficient lighting; everything has been designed and built to be sympathetic to the environment. The beautifully appointed bedrooms and bathrooms demonstrate the 'green' principle from the locally-made 100% wool carpets and solid wood furniture to the wallpapers and paint that have been used. The ingredients used for the menus are locally sourced and organic.

Rooms 32 (3 fmly) (6 GF) ↻ **Facilities** FTV WiFi ↳ Xmas New Year **Conf** Class 40 Board 40 Thtr 100 **Services** Lift **Parking** 32 **Notes** ⊛ Civ Wed 100

Hotel Miramar

★★★★ 77% HOTEL

tel: 01202 556581 **East Overcliff Dr, East Cliff BH1 3AL**
email: sales@miramar-bournemouth.com **web:** www.miramar-bournemouth.com
dir: From Wessex Way rdbt into St Pauls Rd, right at next rdbt. 3rd exit at next rdbt, 2nd exit at next rdbt into Grove Rd. Hotel car park on right

Conveniently located on the East Cliff, this Edwardian hotel enjoys glorious sea views. The Miramar was a favoured destination of famed author JRR Tolkien, who often stayed here. The bedrooms are comfortable and well equipped, and there are spacious public areas and a choice of lounges. The friendly staff and a relaxing environment are noteworthy here.

Rooms 43 (6 fmly) ↻ **S** £57.50-£70; **D** £115-£200 (incl. bkfst)* **Facilities** FTV WiFi ↳ HL ♫ Xmas New Year **Conf** Class 50 Board 50 Thtr 200 Del from £90 to £130* **Services** Lift **Parking** 90 **Notes** LB Civ Wed 110

Menzies Hotels Bournemouth East Cliff Court

★★★★ 77% HOTEL

tel: 01202 554545 **East Overcliff Dr BH1 3AN**
email: eastcliff@menzieshotels.co.uk **web:** www.menzieshotels.co.uk
dir: From M3, M27 towards Bournemouth on A338 (leads onto Wessex Way), follow signs to East Cliff, hotel on seafront

Enjoying panoramic views across the bay, this popular hotel offers bedrooms that are modern and contemporary in style; they are appointed to a very high standard, and many have the benefit of balconies and sea views. Stylish public areas include a range of inviting lounges, a spacious restaurant and a selection of conference rooms.

Rooms 67 (15 fmly) (2 GF) (5 smoking) ↻ **S** £25-£233; **D** £45-£243* **Facilities** FTV WiFi ⚲ Full leisure facilities at adjacent Menzies Carlton Xmas New Year **Conf** Class 60 Board 40 Thtr 150 Del from £110 to £210* **Services** Lift **Parking** 45 **Notes** LB Civ Wed 250

Find out more about
the AA's awards for food
excellence on page 19

B

Park Central Hotel

★★★★ 76% HOTEL

tel: 01202 203600 **Exeter Rd BH2 5AJ**
email: reception@parkcentralhotel.co.uk **web:** www.parkcentralhotel.co.uk
dir: A338, A35 (St Pauls Rd). At rdbt 3rd exit onto B3066 (Holdenburst Rd). Straight on at 3 rdbts, hotel on right opposite Bournemouth International Centre

Located opposite Bournemouth International Centre, this modern, contemporary hotel is in a good location and has sea views. The bedrooms are comfortable and attractively furnished. The menu features creative modern ideas based on intuitive combinations of well-sourced raw materials featuring, of course a great deal of seafood. A pre-theatre menu is also available, but be sure to book as this can prove very popular.

Rooms 50 (6 fmly) (7 GF) ☏ **S** £58-£140; **D** £68-£160 (incl. bkfst)* **Facilities** FTV WiFi ☼ In-room spa ♫ Xmas New Year **Services** Lift **Parking** 29 **Notes** ⊗

BEST WESTERN The Connaught Hotel

★★★★ 75% HOTEL

tel: 01202 298020 **West Hill Rd, West Cliff BH2 5PH**
email: reception@theconnaught.co.uk **web:** www.theconnaught.co.uk
dir: Follow Town Centre West & BIC signs

Conveniently located on the West Cliff, close to the BIC, beaches and town centre, this privately-owned hotel offers well equipped, neatly decorated rooms, some with balconies. The hotel boasts a very well-equipped leisure complex with a large pool and gym. Breakfast and dinner offer imaginative dishes made with quality local ingredients.

Rooms 80 (26 annexe) ☏ **S** £55-£85; **D** £75-£135 (incl. bkfst) **Facilities** Spa FTV WiFi ☼ ☜ supervised Gym Sauna Steam room Beauty therapies Xmas New Year **Conf** Class 60 Board 35 Thtr 180 Del from £135 to £185* **Services** Lift **Parking** 66 **Notes** ⊗ Civ Wed 200

See advert below

Hermitage Hotel

★★★★ 75% HOTEL

tel: 01202 557363 **Exeter Rd BH2 5AH**
email: info@hermitage-hotel.co.uk **web:** www.hermitage-hotel.co.uk
dir: A338 (Ringwood), follow signs for BIC & pier. Hotel directly opposite

Occupying an impressive location overlooking the seafront, at the heart of the town centre, the Hermitage offers friendly and attentive service. The majority of the smart bedrooms are comfortably appointed and all are very well equipped; many rooms have sea views. The wood-panelled lounge provides an elegant and tranquil area, as does the restaurant where well-prepared and interesting dishes are served.

Rooms 74 (11 annexe) (9 fmly) (7 GF) ☏ **Facilities** FTV WiFi ☼ Xmas New Year **Conf** Class 60 Board 60 Thtr 180 **Services** Lift **Parking** 58 **Notes** ⊗

B

BOURNEMOUTH *continued*

Menzies Hotels Bournemouth / Carlton

★★★★ 75% HOTEL

MenziesHotels

tel: 01202 552011 **East Overcliff BH1 3DN**
email: carlton@menzieshotels.co.uk **web:** www.menzieshotels.co.uk
dir: From M3, M27 towards Bournemouth on A338 (leads onto Wessex Way), follow signs to East Cliff, hotel on seafront

Enjoying a prime location on the East Cliff, and with views of the Isle of Wight and Dorset coastline, the Carlton has attractive gardens and pool area. Most of the spacious bedrooms enjoy sea views. Leisure facilities include an indoor and outdoor pool as well as a gym. Guests can enjoy an interesting range of carefully prepared dishes in Frederick's restaurant. The conference and banqueting facilities are varied.

Rooms 76 (17 fmly) (8 GF) ✎ **S** £35–£280; **D** £55–£300 **Facilities** Spa FTV WiFi ⊗ ⊀ Gym Hair & beauty salon Xmas New Year **Conf** Class 110 Board 50 Thtr 200 Del from £110 to £210* **Services** Lift **Parking** 87 **Notes** LB Civ Wed 200

The Norfolk

★★★★ 74% HOTEL

PEEL HOTELS PLC

tel: 01202 551521 **Richmond Hill BH2 6EN**
email: gm@norfolkroyale-hotel-bournemouth.com **web:** www.peelhotels.co.uk
dir: A338 into Bournemouth take Richmond Hill exit to A347 Wimborne, turn left at top into Richmond Hill. Hotel on right

Easily recognisable by its wrought iron balconies, this Edwardian hotel is conveniently located for the centre of the town. Most of the bedrooms are contained in a modern wing at the side of the building, overlooking the pretty landscaped gardens. There is a car park at rear of the hotel.

Rooms 95 (23 fmly) (9 GF) ✎ **Facilities** Spa STV FTV WiFi ⊗ HL ⊗ Membership of nearby health club ♬ Xmas New Year **Conf** Class 50 Board 40 Thtr 150 **Services** Lift **Parking** 95 **Notes** ⊗ Civ Wed 150

Hallmark Bournemouth

★★★★ 73% HOTEL

hallmark

tel: 01202 751000 **Durley Chine Rd, West Cliff BH2 5JS**
email: bournemouth.sales@hallmarkhotels.co.uk
web: www.hallmarkhotels.co.uk/bournemouth
dir: A338 follow signs to West Cliff & BIC, hotel on right

This property is conveniently located and offers a friendly atmosphere and attentive service. The comfortable bedrooms are tastefully appointed and are suitable for both business and leisure guests. The restaurant and bar serve a good choice of dishes, and the well-appointed leisure area is popular with both residents and locals alike. There is also a good range of conference facilities and meeting rooms.

Rooms 83 (5 GF) ✎ **S** £49–£109; **D** £59–£179* **Facilities** Spa FTV WiFi ⊗ Gym Sauna Steam room Aromatherapy cave Relaxation room Xmas New Year **Conf** Class 80 Board 40 Thtr 250 Del from £99 to £179* **Services** Lift **Parking** 80 **Notes** LB Civ Wed 200

Cumberland Hotel

★★★ 88% HOTEL

tel: 01202 290722 & 298350 **East Overcliff Dr BH1 3AF**
email: info@cumberlandbournemouth.co.uk **web:** www.cumberlandbournemouth.co.uk
dir: A35 towards East Cliff & beaches, right onto Holdenhurst Rd, straight over 2 rdbts, left at junct to East Overcliff Drive, hotel on seafront

A purpose built, art deco hotel where many of the bedrooms are appointed in keeping with the hotel's original character. Front-facing bedrooms have balconies with superb sea views. The comfortable public areas are spacious and striking in their design. The Mirabelle Restaurant and the Ventana Bar offer cuisine prepared from local produce.

Rooms 102 (20 fmly) **S** £28–£69; **D** £59–£249 (incl. bkfst)* **Facilities** FTV WiFi ⊗ ⊗ ⊀ Gym Squash Oceana day spa at Cliffside Hotel (sister hotel next door) Xmas New Year **Conf** Class 180 Board 40 Thtr 250 Del from £65 to £125* **Services** Lift **Parking** 50 **Notes** LB Civ Wed 100

Langtry Manor - Lovenest of a King

★★★ 82% HOTEL

tel: 0844 3725 432 & 01202 553887 **Derby Rd, East Cliff BH1 3QB**
email: lillie@langtrymanor.com **web:** www.langtrymanor.co.uk
dir: A31/A338, 1st rdbt by rail station turn left. Over next rdbt, 1st left into Knyveton Rd. Hotel opposite

Retaining a stately air, this property was originally built in 1877 by Edward VII for his mistress Lillie Langtry. The individually furnished and decorated bedrooms include several with four-poster beds. Enjoyable cuisine is served in the magnificent dining hall that displays several large Tudor tapestries. There is an Edwardian banquet on Saturday evenings.

Rooms 20 (8 annexe) (2 fmly) (3 GF) **Facilities** FTV WiFi Free use of health club (200yds) ♬ Xmas New Year **Conf** Class 60 Board 40 Thtr 100 **Parking** 30 **Notes** Civ Wed 100

BEST WESTERN Hotel Royale

★★★ 81% HOTEL

Best Western

tel: 01202 554794 **16 Gervis Rd BH1 3EQ**
email: reservations@thehotelroyale.com **web:** www.thehotelroyale.com
dir: M27 junct 1, A31 onto A338 to Bournemouth, follow signs for East Cliff & seafront. Over 2 rdbts into Gervis Rd. Hotel on right

Located on the East Cliff, just a short walk from the seafront and local shops and amenities, is this privately owned hotel. Public areas are contemporary in style, and facilities include a small health club and spacious function rooms. Bedrooms are comfortable and well furnished.

Rooms 64 (8 annexe) (22 fmly) (8 GF) 🐾 **Facilities** STV FTV WiFi ⌇ 🐾 Xmas New Year **Conf** Class 60 Board 40 Thtr 100 **Services** Lift **Parking** 80 **Notes** ⊗

The Riviera Hotel

★★★ 81% HOTEL

tel: 01202 763653 **Burnaby Rd, Alum Chine BH4 8JF**
email: info@rivierabournemouth.co.uk **web:** www.rivierabournemouth.co.uk
dir: A338, follow signs to Alum Chine

The Riviera offers a range of comfortable, well-furnished bedrooms and bathrooms. Welcoming staff provide efficient service delivered in a friendly manner. In addition to a spacious lounge with regular entertainment, there are indoor and outdoor pools, all just a short walk from the beach.

Rooms 72 (4 annexe) (24 fmly) (11 GF) 🐾 **S** £25-£85; **D** £40-£210* **Facilities** FTV WiFi 🐾 🐾 Games room Sauna Spa bath Treatments available ♫ Xmas New Year **Conf** Class 120 Board 50 Thtr 180 Del from £75 to £175* **Services** Lift **Parking** 45 **Notes** LB Civ Wed 160

The Chine

★★★ 80% HOTEL

tel: 0845 337 1550 **Boscombe Spa Rd BH5 1AX**
email: reservations@fjbhotels.co.uk **web:** www.fjbcollection.co.uk
dir: Follow BIC signs, A338/Wessex Way to St Pauls rdbt. 1st exit, to next rdbt, 2nd exit signed Eastcliff, Boscombe, Southbourne. Next rdbt, 1st exit into Christchurch Rd. After 2nd lights, right into Boscombe Spa Rd

Benefiting from superb views, this popular hotel is set in delightful gardens with private access to the seafront and a sandy beach that stretches for miles; it is just a five-minute drive from the shops and entertainments of the town centre. The excellent range of facilities includes an indoor pool, a seasonal outdoor pool, jacuzzi, gym and sauna. There are also children's facilities and dedicated entertainers during the school holidays. The spacious bedrooms, some with balconies, are well appointed and thoughtfully equipped. The Seaview Restaurant and Gallery Brasserie are popular eating options.

Rooms 83 (23 annexe) (16 fmly) (8 GF) **Facilities** STV WiFi 🐾 supervised 🐾 supervised 🐾 Gym Games room Children's indoor play area Xmas New Year **Conf** Class 70 Board 40 Thtr 140 **Services** Lift **Parking** 55 **Notes** ⊗ Civ Wed 120

Elstead Hotel

★★★ 80% HOTEL

CLASSIC BRITISH HOTELS

tel: 01202 293071 📄 01202 293827 **Knyveton Rd BH1 3QP**
email: info@the-elstead.co.uk **web:** www.the-elstead.co.uk
dir: A338 (Wessex Way) to St Pauls rdbt, left & left again

Ideal as a base for business and leisure travellers, this popular hotel is conveniently located for the town centre, seafront and BIC. An impressive range of facilities is offered, including meeting rooms, an indoor leisure centre and comfortable lounges.

Rooms 50 (15 fmly) 🐾 **Facilities** FTV WiFi 🐾 supervised Gym Sauna Steam room Pool & snooker tables Xmas New Year **Conf** Class 70 Board 35 Thtr 80 **Services** Lift **Parking** 40 **Notes** Civ Wed 60

Royal Exeter Hotel

★★★ 80% HOTEL

tel: 01202 438000 **Exeter Rd BH2 5AG**
email: enquiries@royalexeterhotel.com **web:** www.royalexeterhotel.com
dir: Opposite Bournemouth International Centre

Ideally located opposite the Bournemouth International Centre, and convenient for the beach and town centre, this busy hotel caters for both business and leisure guests. Public areas are smart, and there's a modern open-plan lounge bar and restaurant, together with an exciting adjoining bar complex.

Rooms 54 (13 fmly) (12 smoking) **Facilities** FTV WiFi Gym ♫ **Conf** Class 40 Board 40 Thtr 100 **Services** Lift **Parking** 50 **Notes** ⊗

See advert on page 88

BOURNEMOUTH *continued*

Suncliff Hotel

★★★ 78% HOTEL

tel: 01202 291711 & 298350 **29 East Overcliff Dr BH1 3AG**
email: info@suncliffbournemouth.co.uk **web:** www.suncliffbournemouth.co.uk
dir: A338/A35 towards East Cliff & beaches, right into Holdenhurst Rd, straight over 2 rdbts, left at junct into East Overcliff Drive, hotel on seafront

Enjoying splendid views from the East Cliff and catering mainly for leisure guests, this friendly hotel offers a range of facilities and services. Bedrooms are well equipped and comfortable, and many have sea views. Public areas include a large conservatory, an attractive bar and pleasant lounges.

Rooms 97 (29 fmly) (14 GF) ☞ **S** £20-£60; **D** £40-£130 (incl. bkfst)* **Facilities** FTV WiFi ☍ ⏍ ⤳ Gym Squash Sauna Table tennis Oceana day spa at sister hotel ♫ Xmas New Year **Conf** Class 70 Board 60 Thtr 100 Del from £45 to £120* **Services** Lift **Parking** 62 **Notes** LB Civ Wed 80

Cliffeside Hotel

★★★ 77% HOTEL

tel: 01202 555724 & 298350 **East Overcliff Dr BH1 3AQ**
email: info@cliffsidebournemouth.co.uk **web:** www.cliffsidebournemouth.co.uk
dir: A35, A338 to East Cliff & beaches, right into Holdenhurst Rd, over next 2 rdbts, at junct left into East Overcliff Drive, hotel on left

Benefiting from an elevated position on the seafront and just a short walk from town, it's no wonder that this friendly hotel has many returning guests. Bedrooms and public areas are attractively appointed, many with sea views. The Atlantic Restaurant offers guests a fixed-price menu.

Rooms 62 (5 fmly) (2 GF) ☞ **Facilities** WiFi ⏍ ⤳ Gym Squash Sauna Beauty treatment room ♫ Xmas New Year **Conf** Class 70 Board 40 Thtr 120 **Services** Lift **Parking** 72 **Notes** Civ Wed 120

Hotel Piccadilly

★★★ 75% HOTEL

tel: 01202 298024 **25 Bath Rd BH1 2NN**
email: enquiries@hotelpiccadilly.co.uk **web:** www.hotelpiccadilly.co.uk
dir: From A338 take 1st exit rdbt, signed East Cliff. 3rd exit at next rdbt signed Lansdowne, 3rd exit at next rdbt into Bath Rd

This hotel offers a friendly welcome to guests, many of whom return on a regular basis, particularly for the superb ballroom dancing facilities and small break packages which are a feature here. Bedrooms are smartly decorated, well maintained and comfortable. Dining in the attractive restaurant is always popular and dishes are freshly prepared and appetising.

Rooms 45 (2 fmly) (5 GF) **Facilities** FTV WiFi Ballroom ♫ Xmas New Year **Conf** Class 50 Board 50 Thtr 140 **Services** Lift **Parking** 45 **Notes** ⊗ Civ Wed 200

Trouville Hotel

★★★ 75% HOTEL

tel: 01202 552262 **Priory Rd BH2 5DH**
email: reception@trouvillehotel.com **web:** www.trouvillehotel.com
dir: Follow Town Centre West signs. Exit at rdbt signed BIC/West Cliff/Beaches. 2nd exit at next rdbt, left at next rdbt. Hotel on left near end of Priory Rd

Located near Bournemouth International Centre, the seafront and the shops, this hotel has the advantage of indoor leisure facilities and a large car park. Bedrooms are generally a good size with comfortable furnishings, and there are plenty of family rooms. The air-conditioned restaurant offers a daily changing menu.

Rooms 99 (19 annexe) (21 fmly) (6 GF) ☞ **Facilities** FTV WiFi ☍ ⏍ Gym Sauna ♫ Xmas New Year **Conf** Class 100 Board 80 Thtr 250 **Services** Lift **Parking** 70 **Notes** Civ Wed 130

B

Mayfair Hotel

★★★ 74% HOTEL

tel: 01202 551983 **27 Bath Rd BH1 2NW**
email: info@themayfair.com **web:** www.themayfair.com
dir: Exit A338 at St Pauls Rd (Asda rdbt), right into Holdenhurst Rd, 3rd exit from Lansdowne rdbt

Occupying a central location in the heart of Bournemouth and within walking distance of both the town centre and the seafront, this hotel offers guests comfortable, modern accommodation. There is a spacious restaurant and bar area, plus a pleasant outdoor patio and function room.

Rooms 40 (6 fmly) (1 GF) **Facilities** WiFi Ballroom dancing programme on request Xmas New Year **Conf** Class 40 Board 30 Thtr 60 Del from £80 to £95 **Services** Lift **Parking** 30 **Notes** ⊗ Civ Wed 80

Hotel Collingwood

★★★ 71% HOTEL

tel: 01202 557575 **11 Priory Rd, West Cliff BH2 5DF**
email: info@hotel-collingwood.co.uk **web:** www.hotel-collingwood.co.uk
dir: A338 left at West Cliff sign, over 1st rdbt, left at 2nd rdbt. Hotel 500yds on left

This privately owned and managed hotel is situated close to the BIC. Bedrooms are airy, with the emphasis on comfort. An excellent range of leisure facilities is available and the public areas are spacious and welcoming. Pinks Restaurant offers carefully prepared cuisine and a fixed-price, five-course dinner.

Rooms 53 (16 fmly) (6 GF) **Facilities** FTV WiFi Gym Steam room Sauna Games room Snooker room Xmas New Year **Conf** Class 60 Board 20 Thtr 100 **Services** Lift **Parking** 55

Durley Dean Hotel

★★★ 70% HOTEL

tel: 01202 557711 **West Cliff Rd BH2 5HE**
email: reservations@durleydean.co.uk **web:** www.durleydean.co.uk
dir: Into Bournemouth, follow signs for Westcliff. Onto Durley Chine Rd South to next rdbt, hotel at 2nd exit on left

Situated close to the seafront on the West Cliff, this modern hotel has bedrooms which vary in size and style. There is a restaurant, a comfortable bar and several meeting rooms. Parking is also a bonus.

Rooms 117 (36 fmly) (6 GF) **Facilities** FTV WiFi Gym Sauna Xmas New Year **Conf** Class 40 Board 45 Thtr 150 **Services** Lift **Parking** 30 **Notes** ⊗ Civ Wed 120

Tower House Hotel

★★ 76% HOTEL

tel: 01202 290742 **West Cliff Gardens BH2 5HP**
email: towerhouse.hotel@btconnect.com **web:** www.towerhousehotelbournemouth.com

Tower House Hotel is a popular family-owned and run hotel on the West Cliff. The owners and their staff are friendly and helpful. The bedrooms are comfortable and well maintained, and the hotel provides good off-road parking.

Rooms 32 (12 fmly) (3 GF) **S** £20-£53; **D** £40-£106 (incl. bkfst)* **Facilities** FTV WiFi Xmas New Year **Services** Lift **Parking** 30 **Notes** Closed 2-31 Jan

Devon Towers Hotel

★★ 75% HOTEL

Leisureplex

tel: 01202 553863 **58-62 St Michael's Rd, West Cliff BH2 5ED**
email: devontowers@leisureplex.co.uk **web:** www.leisureplex.co.uk
dir: A338 into Bournemouth, follow signs for BIC. Left into St. Michaels Rd at top of hill. Hotel 100mtrs on left

Located in a quiet road within walking distance of the West Cliff and shops, this hotel appeals to the budget leisure market. The four-course menus offer plenty of choice and entertainment is featured most evenings. The bar and lobby area provide plenty of space for relaxing.

Rooms 60 (8 GF) **S** £37-£49; **D** £58-£82 (incl. bkfst)* **Facilities** FTV WiFi Xmas New Year **Services** Lift **Parking** 6 **Notes** ⊗ Closed Jan-mid Feb (ex Xmas) RS mid-end Feb, Mar & Nov

Durley Grange Hotel

★★ 75% HOTEL

tel: 01202 554473 **6 Durley Rd, West Cliff BH2 5JL**
email: reservations@durleygrange.com **web:** www.durleygrange.com
dir: A338/Bournemouth West rdbt. Over next rdbt, 1st left into Sommerville Rd & right into Durley Rd

Located in a quiet area, the town and beaches are all in walking distance of this welcoming, friendly hotel. Bedrooms are brightly decorated, comfortable and well equipped. There is an indoor pool and sauna for all-year round use, and enjoyable meals are served in the smart dining room. Parking is a plus.

Rooms 52 (8 fmly) (4 GF) **S** £30-£72; **D** £60-£144 (incl. bkfst & dinner)* **Facilities** WiFi Sauna Xmas New Year **Services** Lift **Parking** 35 **Notes** ⊗

BOURNEMOUTH *continued*

Ullswater Hotel

★★ 71% HOTEL

tel: 01202 555181 **West Cliff Gardens BH2 5HW**
email: enquiries@ullswater-hotel.co.uk **web:** www.ullswater-hotel.co.uk
dir: In Bournemouth follow signs to West Cliff. Hotel just off Westcliff Rd

Ullswater Hotel is a welcoming family-run establishment conveniently located for the city and the seafront. The well-equipped bedrooms vary in size, and the charming lounge bar and dining room are very smart. Cuisine is hearty and homemade, offering a good choice from the daily-changing menu.

Rooms 42 (8 fmly) (2 GF) ✱ **Facilities** FTV WiFi ➘ Snooker room Table tennis ♫ Xmas New Year **Conf** Class 30 Board 24 Thtr 40 **Services** Lift **Parking** 12

Premier Inn Bournemouth Central

BUDGET HOTEL

tel: 0871 527 8124 **Westover Rd BH1 2BZ**
web: www.premierinn.com
dir: M27 junct 1, A31. Left at Ashley Heath junct. A338 towards Bournemouth. At rdbt 1st exit. At next rdbt 3rd exit (Holdenhurst Rd). At next rdbt 3rd exit (Bath Rd). At next rdbt 3rd exit onto Bath Hill. At next rdbt into Westover Rd, right into Hinton Rd, hotel on right

High quality, budget accommodation ideal for both families and business travellers. Spacious, en suite bedrooms feature tea and coffee making facilities, and Freeview TV in most hotels. Internet access and WiFi are available for a small fee. The adjacent family restaurant features a wide and varied menu. See also the Hotel Groups pages.

Rooms 120

Premier Inn Bournemouth East

BUDGET HOTEL

tel: 0871 527 8126 **47 Christchurch Rd, Boscombe BH1 3PA**
web: www.premierinn.com
dir: M27 junct 1, A31, 9m, left at Ashley Heath junct, take A338 signed Bournemouth. At 1st rdbt take 1st exit into Saint Paul's Rd. At 2nd rdbt 1st exit onto Christchurch Rd. Hotel on right

Rooms 20

Premier Inn Bournemouth Westcliffe

BUDGET HOTEL

tel: 0871 527 8128 **Poole Rd BH2 5QU**
web: www.premierinn.com
dir: M27 junct 1, A31. At Ashley Heath junction, left. Take A338 signed Bournemouth. At Bournemouth West rdbt 1st exit signed Ring Road, West Cliff. At next rdbt (St Michael's) 3rd exit (signed Westbourne) into Poole Rd. Hotel on right

Rooms 101

Chester House Hotel

★★★ 74% SMALL HOTEL

tel: 01451 820286 **Victoria St GL54 2BU**
email: info@chesterhousehotel.com **web:** www.chesterhousehotel.com
dir: On A429 between Northleach & Stow-on-the-Wold

Chester House Hotel occupies a secluded but central location in this delightful Cotswold village. Bedrooms, some at ground floor level, are situated in the main house and adjoining coach house. The public areas are stylish, light and airy. Breakfast is taken in the main building whereas dinner is served in the attractive restaurant just a few yards away.

Rooms 22 (10 annexe) (3 fmly) (8 GF) ✱ **S** £80-£140; **D** £95-£140 (incl. bkfst)* **Facilities** FTV WiFi Beauty therapist New Year **Parking** 18 **Notes** Closed 7 Jan-1 Feb

See Windermere

Days Inn Cambridge - A1

BUDGET HOTEL

tel: 01954 267176 **Cambridge Extra Services, Junction A14/M11 CB23 4WU**
email: cambridge.hotel@welcomebreak.co.uk **web:** www.welcomebreak.co.uk
dir: A14/M11 Cambridge Extra Services

This modern, purpose built accommodation offers smartly appointed, well-equipped bedrooms, with good power showers. There is a choice of adjacent food outlets where guests may enjoy breakfast, snacks and meals. See also the Hotel Groups pages.

Rooms 82 (14 fmly) (40 GF) (19 smoking)

Coppid Beech

★★★★ 74% ◉ HOTEL

tel: 01344 303333 **John Nike Way RG12 8TF**
email: sales@coppidbeech.com **web:** www.coppidbeech.com
dir: M4 junct 10 take Wokingham/Bracknell onto A329. In 2m take B3408 to Binfield, at lights turn right. Hotel 200yds on right

This chalet designed hotel offers extensive facilities and includes a ski-slope, ice rink, nightclub, health club and Bier Keller. Bedrooms range from suites to standard rooms - all are impressively equipped. A choice of dining is offered; there's a full bistro menu available in the Keller, and for more formal dining, Rowan's restaurant provides award-winning cuisine.

Rooms 205 (6 fmly) (16 GF) **S** £80-£205; **D** £100-£295 (incl. bkfst) **Facilities** STV WiFi ❄ Gym Beauty treatment room Ice rink Dry ski slope Snow boarding Freestyle park ♫ New Year **Conf** Class 161 Board 24 Thtr 350 Del from £150 to £215 **Services** Lift Air con **Parking** 350 **Notes** LB ❀ Civ Wed 200

B

Stirrups Country House

★★★ 82% HOTEL

tel: 01344 882284 **Maidens Green RG42 6LD**
email: reception@stirrupshotel.co.uk **web:** www.stirrupshotel.co.uk
dir: 3m N on B3022 towards Windsor

Situated in a peaceful location between Maidenhead, Bracknell and Windsor, this hotel has high standards of comfort particularly in the bedrooms; some rooms have a small sitting room area. There is a popular bar, a restaurant, function rooms and delightful grounds.

Rooms 35 (5 annexe) (6 fmly) (2 GF) ✿ **S** £80–£94; **D** £80–£94* **Facilities** STV WiFi ⬧ New Year **Conf** Class 50 Board 40 Thtr 100 **Services** Lift **Parking** 100 **Notes** LB ⊗ Civ Wed 100

Premier Inn Bracknell Central

BUDGET HOTEL

tel: 0871 527 8132 **Wokingham Rd RG42 1NA**
web: www.premierinn.com
dir: M4 junct 10, A329(M) (Bracknell) to lights. 1st left, 3rd exit rdbt by Morrisons to town centre. Left at rdbt, left at next rdbt. Hotel on left

High quality, budget accommodation ideal for both families and business travellers. Spacious, en suite bedrooms feature tea and coffee making facilities, and Freeview TV in most hotels. Internet access and WiFi are available for a small fee. The adjacent family restaurant features a wide and varied menu. See also the Hotel Groups pages.

Rooms 60

Premier Inn Bracknell (Twin Bridges)

BUDGET HOTEL

tel: 0871 527 8130 **Downshire Way RG12 7AA**
web: www.premierinn.com
dir: M4 junct 10, A329(M) towards Bracknell. Straight on at mini rdbt. At Twin Bridges rdbt take 2nd exit. Hotel on right adjacent to Downshire Arms Beefeater

Rooms 28

BRADFORD   **Map 19 SE13**
West Yorkshire

See also **Gomersal**

BEST WESTERN PLUS Cedar Court Hotel

★★★★ 73% HOTEL

tel: 01274 406606 **Mayo Av, Off Rooley Ln BD5 8HW**
email: sales@cedarcourtbradford.co.uk **web:** www.cedarcourthotels.co.uk
dir: M62 junct 26, M606, to end of motorway, take 1st left

This purpose built, modern hotel is conveniently located just off the motorway and close to the city centre and the airport. The hotel boasts extensive function and conference facilities, a well-equipped leisure club and an elegant restaurant. Bedrooms are comfortably appointed for both business and leisure guests.

Rooms 131 (7 fmly) (23 GF) **S** £38–£75; **D** £38–£85* **Facilities** STV FTV WiFi ⬧ ⊞ Gym Steam room Sauna Solarium New Year **Conf** Class 300 Board 100 Thtr 800 Del £125* **Services** Lift **Parking** 350 **Notes** LB ⊗ Civ Wed 550

Midland Hotel

★★★ 78% HOTEL

tel: 01274 735735 **Forster Square BD1 4HU**
email: info@midland-hotel-bradford.com **web:** www.peelhotels.co.uk
dir: M62 junct 26, M606, past ASDA, left at rdbt onto A650. Through 2 rdbts & 2 lights. Follow A6181/Haworth signs. Up hill, next left into Manor Row. Hotel 400mtrs

Ideally situated in the heart of the city, this grand Victorian hotel provides modern, very well equipped accommodation and comfortable, spacious day rooms. Ample parking is available in what was once the city's railway station, and a Victorian walkway linking the hotel to the old platform can still be used today.

Rooms 90 (5 fmly) (10 smoking) ✿ **Facilities** STV FTV WiFi ⬧ New Year **Conf** Class 150 Board 100 Thtr 450 Del from £115 to £155 **Services** Lift **Parking** 60 **Notes** Civ Wed 450

BEST WESTERN Bradford Guide Post Hotel

★★★ 75% HOTEL

tel: 0844 332 0459 & 01274 607866 **Common Rd, Low Moor BD12 0ST**
email: sue.barnes@guideposthotel.net **web:** www.guideposthotel.net
dir: From M606 rdbt take 2nd exit. At next rdbt take 1st exit (Cleckheaton Rd). 0.5m, turn right at bollard into Common Rd

Situated south of the city, this hotel offers attractively styled, modern, comfortable bedrooms. The restaurant offers an extensive range of food using fresh, local produce; lighter snack meals are served in the bar. There is also a choice of well-equipped meeting and function rooms. There is disabled access to the hotel, restaurant and one function room.

Rooms 42 (10 fmly) (13 GF) ✿ **Facilities** FTV WiFi ⬧ Complimentary use of nearby swimming & gym facilities **Conf** Class 80 Board 60 Thtr 120 **Parking** 100 **Notes** Civ Wed 120

Campanile Bradford

★★★ 73% HOTEL

Campanile

tel: 01274 683683 **6 Roydsdale Way, Euroway Estate BD4 6SA**
email: bradford@campanile.com **web:** www.campanile.com
dir: M62 junct 26 into M606. Exit Euroway Estate East into Merrydale Rd, right onto Roydsdale Way

This modern building offers accommodation in smart, well-equipped bedrooms, all with en suite bathrooms. Refreshments may be taken at the informal bistro.

Rooms 130 (37 fmly) (22 GF) (8 smoking) **Facilities** STV FTV WiFi **Conf** Class 100 Board 100 Thtr 300 **Services** Lift **Parking** 200 **Notes** Civ Wed 170

Premier Inn Bradford Central

BUDGET HOTEL

tel: 0871 527 9306 **Vicar Ln BD1 5LD**
web: www.premierinn.com
dir: M62 junct 24, M606, at junct 3 take 4th exit into Rooley Ln (A6177) towards Ring Rd/A650/Leeds/A647. In 1m 1st exit into Wakefield Rd towards City Centre. Follow Wakefield Rd/A650 signs. Straight on a 2 rdbts, right into Vicar Ln

High quality, budget accommodation ideal for both families and business travellers. Spacious, en suite bedrooms feature tea and coffee making facilities, and Freeview TV in most hotels. Internet access and WiFi are available for a small fee. The adjacent family restaurant features a wide and varied menu. See also the Hotel Groups pages.

Rooms 118

B

BRADFORD-ON-AVON
Wiltshire

Map 4 ST86

Widbrook Grange

U HOTEL

tel: 01225 864750 & 863173 **Trowbridge Rd BA15 1UH**
email: stay@widbrookgrange.com **web:** www.widbrookgrange.com
dir: 1m SE from Bradford on A363, hotel diagonally opposite Bradford Marina & Arabian
Stud

Currently the rating for this establishment is not confirmed. This may be due to a
change of ownership or because it has only recently joined the AA rating scheme.
For further details please see the AA website: theAA.com

Rooms 20 (15 annexe) (6 fmly) (13 GF) ⚓ **Facilities** FTV WiFi ⌕ ⌕ Gym Children's
weekend play room Beauty treatments New Year **Conf** Class 35 Board 25 Thtr 50
Parking 50 **Notes** Closed 24-30 Dec Civ Wed 50

BRAINTREE
Essex

Map 7 TL72

White Hart Hotel

★★★ 76% HOTEL

tel: 01376 321401 **Bocking End CM7 9AB**
email: whitehart.braintree@greeneking.co.uk **web:** www.oldenglishinns.co.uk
dir: Exit A120 towards town centre. Hotel at B1256 & Bocking Causeway junct

This 18th-century former coaching inn is conveniently located in the heart of the
bustling town centre. The smartly appointed public rooms include a large lounge
bar, a restaurant and meeting rooms. The pleasantly decorated bedrooms have co-
ordinated fabrics and many thoughtful touches.

Rooms 32 (8 fmly) ⚓ **Facilities** FTV WiFi New Year **Conf** Class 8 Board 10 Thtr 16
Del from £99* **Parking** 40 **Notes** ⊗ Civ Wed 35

Premier Inn Braintree (A120)

BUDGET HOTEL

tel: 0871 527 8138 **Cressing Rd, Galley's Corner CM77 8GG**
web: www.premierinn.com
dir: On A120 (Stansted to Braintree link road). Adjacent to Mulberry Tree Brewers Fayre

High quality, budget accommodation ideal for both families and business
travellers. Spacious, en suite bedrooms feature tea and coffee making facilities,
and Freeview TV in most hotels. Internet access and WiFi are available for a small
fee. The adjacent family restaurant features a wide and varied menu. See also the
Hotel Groups pages.

Rooms 60

Premier Inn Braintree (Freeport Village)

BUDGET HOTEL

tel: 0871 527 8140 **Fowlers Farm, Cressing Rd CM77 8DH**
web: www.premierinn.com
dir: M11 junct 8, follow signs to A120 Colchester & Freeport Shopping Village. At Galley's
Corner rdbt, 4th exit, left into Wyevale Garden Centre. Hotel adjacent

Rooms 47

BRAITHWAITE
Cumbria

Map 18 NY22

The Cottage in the Wood

◉◉ RESTAURANT WITH ROOMS

tel: 017687 78409 **Whinlatter Pass CA12 5TW**
email: relax@thecottageinthewood.co.uk **web:** www.thecottageinthewood.co.uk
dir: M6 junct 40, A66 W. After Keswick exit for Braithwaite via Whinlatter Pass (B5292),
establishment at top of pass

This charming property sits on wooded hills with striking views of Skiddaw, and is
conveniently placed for Keswick. The owners provide excellent hospitality in a
relaxed manner. The award-winning food, freshly prepared and locally sourced, is
served in the bright and welcoming conservatory restaurant that has stunning
views. The comfortable bedrooms are well appointed and have many useful extras.

Rooms 9

BRAMPTON
Cumbria

Map 21 NY56

INSPECTORS' CHOICE

Farlam Hall Hotel

★★★ ◉◉ HOTEL

tel: 016977 46234 **CA8 2NG**
email: farlam@relaischateaux.com **web:** www.farlamhall.co.uk
dir: On A689 (Brampton to Alston). Hotel 2m on left - not in Farlam village

This delightful country house has a history dating back to 1428, although the
building today is very much the result of alterations carried out in the mid-19th
century. The hotel is run by a friendly family team and their enthusiastic staff,
and is set in beautifully landscaped Victorian gardens complete with an
ornamental lake and stream. Lovingly restored over many years, it provides very
high standards of comfort and hospitality. Gracious public rooms invite
relaxation, and much thought has gone into the beautiful bedrooms, many of
which are simply stunning. Nearby are Hadrian's Wall and the Northern Pennines
Area of Outstanding Natural Beauty, which both provide endless opportunities
for walking and sightseeing.

Rooms 12 (1 annexe) (2 GF) ⚓ **S** £165-£195; **D** £310-£370 (incl. bkfst & dinner)
Facilities FTV WiFi ⌕ ⌕ New Year **Conf** Class 24 Board 12 Thtr 24 Del from £195 to
£215 **Parking** 25 **Notes** LB No children 5yrs Closed 24-30 Dec & 4-17 Jan Civ Wed 45

BRANCASTER STAITHE
Norfolk   Map 13 TF74

The White Horse

★★★ 80% ◉◉ HOTEL

tel: 01485 210262 **PE31 8BY**
email: reception@whitehorsebrancaster.co.uk **web:** www.whitehorsebrancaster.co.uk
dir: On A149 (coast road) midway between Hunstanton & Wells-next-the-Sea

A charming hotel situated on the north Norfolk coast with contemporary bedrooms in two wings, some featuring an interesting cobbled fascia. Each room is attractively decorated and thoughtfully equipped. There is a large bar and a lounge area leading through to the conservatory restaurant, with stunning tidal marshland views across to Scolt Head Island.

Rooms 15 (8 annexe) (4 fmly) (8 GF) ☞ **Facilities** FTV WiFi ☼ Xmas New Year **Parking** 60

BRANDON
Warwickshire   Map 11 SP47

Mercure Coventry Brandon Hall Hotel & Spa

★★★★ 74% ◉ HOTEL

tel: 024 7654 6000 **Main St CV8 3FW**
email: h6625@accor.com **web:** www.mercure.com
dir: A45 towards Coventry S. After Peugeot-Citroen garage on left, at island take 5th exit to M1 South/London (back onto A45). After 200yds, immediately after Texaco garage, left into Brandon Ln, hotel after 2.5m

An impressive tree-lined avenue leads to this 17th-century property which sits in 17 acres of grounds. The hotel provides a peaceful and friendly sanctuary away from the hustle and bustle. Bedrooms provide comfortable facilities and a good range of extras for guest comfort. There is a Spa Naturel with health, beauty and fitness facilities in a separate building.

Rooms 120 (30 annexe) (10 fmly) (50 GF) ☞ **Facilities** Spa STV WiFi ⊗ Gym Steam room Sauna Xmas New Year **Conf** Class 120 Board 112 Thtr 280 **Services** Lift **Parking** 200 **Notes** Civ Wed 280

BRANKSOME

See Poole

BRANSCOMBE
Devon   Map 4 SY18

The Bulstone Hotel

★★ 72% HOTEL

tel: 01297 680446 **High Bulstone EX12 3BL**
email: bulstone@aol.com **web:** www.childfriendlyhotels.com
dir: A3052 (Exeter to Lyme Regis road) at Branscombe Cross follow brown hotel sign

Situated in a peaceful location close to the beautiful east Devon coast, this family-friendly hotel is ideally placed for a relaxing break with plenty of attractions within easy reach. All bedrooms consist of a main bedroom and separate children's room, each being practically furnished and equipped. Additional facilities include a playroom, a snug lounge, and the dining room where enjoyable home-cooked meals are offered. There is no charge for children under ten, and children's tea is at 5pm.

Rooms 7 (7 fmly) (4 GF) **Facilities** FTV WiFi Children's playroom Xmas New Year **Conf** Class 25 Board 25 **Services** Air con **Parking** 25 **Notes** ⊗

BRENTFORD
Greater London

Holiday Inn London Brentford Lock

★★★★ 73% HOTEL PLAN 1 C3

tel: 020 8232 2000 **Commerce Rd TW8 8GA**
email: info@holidayinnbrentford.co.uk **web:** www.holidayinnbrentford.co.uk
dir: M4 junct 2 onto A4. At rdbt take 4th exit onto A315, hotel on right

This modern contemporary hotel overlooking The Grand Union Canal is ideally suited for Kew Gardens, Brentford, Twickenham, the North Circular and the Bath Roads. Bedrooms are spacious, well equipped and suit business travellers and leisure guests alike. The ground floor areas have recently been refurbished and offer a homely stylish open-plan feel; small gym on site. There is chargeable car parking in lower ground floor area.

Rooms 134 **Facilities** STV WiFi Beauty treatments available **Conf** Class 200 Board 120 Thtr 700 **Services** Air con **Parking** 60 **Notes** Civ Wed 180

Premier Inn London Kew

BUDGET HOTEL PLAN 1 C3

tel: 0871 527 8670 **52 High St TW8 0BB**
web: www.premierinn.com
dir: At junct of A4 (M4), A205 & A406, Chiswick rdbt, take A205 towards Kew & Brentford. 200yds right fork onto A315 (High St), for 0.5m. Hotel on left

High quality, budget accommodation ideal for both families and business travellers. Spacious, en suite bedrooms feature tea and coffee making facilities, and Freeview TV in most hotels. Internet access and WiFi are available for a small fee. The adjacent family restaurant features a wide and varied menu. See also the Hotel Groups pages.

Rooms 141

BRENTWOOD
Essex   Map 6 TQ59

Marygreen Manor Hotel

★★★★ 71% ◉ HOTEL

tel: 01277 225252 **London Rd CM14 4NR**
email: info@marygreenmanor.co.uk **web:** www.marygreenmanor.co.uk
dir: M25 junct 28, onto A1023 over 2 sets of lights, hotel on right

This 16th-century house was built by Robert Wright, who named the house 'Manor of Mary Green' after his young bride. Public rooms exude character and have a wealth of original features that include exposed beams, carved panelling and the impressive Tudors Restaurant. Bedrooms are tastefully decorated and thoughtfully equipped.

Rooms 44 (40 annexe) (35 GF) ☞ **S** £85-£135; **D** £95-£145* **Facilities** STV FTV WiFi ☼ **Conf** Class 20 Board 25 Thtr 50 Del from £139 to £159* **Parking** 100 **Notes** ⊗ Civ Wed 60

B

BRENTFORD *continued*

De Rougemont Manor

★★★★ 71% HOTEL

tel: 01277 226418 & 220483 **Great Warley St CM13 3JP**
email: info@derougemontmanor.co.uk **web:** www.derougemontmanor.co.uk
dir: M25 junct 29, A127 to Southend then B186 towards Great Warley

Expect a warm welcome at this family-owned and managed hotel, situated on the outskirts of Brentwood just off the M25. The stylish bedrooms are divided between the main hotel and a bedroom wing; each one is tastefully appointed and well equipped. Public rooms include a smart lounge bar, restaurant and a choice of seating areas.

Rooms 74 (10 annexe) (8 fmly) (16 GF) ➘S £69-£129; **D** £69-£149 (incl. bkfst)*
Facilities FTV WiFi ➘ ⚘ ☻ Gym 3-acre nature reserve Xmas New Year **Conf** Class 60 Board 40 Thtr 250 Del from £160 to £180* **Services** Lift Air con **Parking** 200
Notes ⊗ Civ Wed 90

Premier Inn Brentwood

BUDGET HOTEL

tel: 0871 527 8142 **Brentwood House, 169 Kings Rd CM14 4EF**
web: www.premierinn.com
dir: From S: M25 junct 28 take A1023 (or from N: at Brook Street rdbt 2nd exit onto A1023). Right at lights into Kings Rd, at rdbt 2nd exit into Kings Rd

High quality, budget accommodation ideal for both families and business travellers. Spacious, en suite bedrooms feature tea and coffee making facilities, and Freeview TV in most hotels. Internet access and WiFi are available for a small fee. The adjacent family restaurant features a wide and varied menu. See also the Hotel Groups pages.

Rooms 122

BRIDGNORTH
Shropshire
Map 10 S079

The Old Vicarage Hotel

★★★ 83% ◉◉ SMALL HOTEL

tel: 01746 716497 **Worfield WV15 5JZ**
email: admin@oldvicarageworfield.com **web:** www.oldvicarageworfield.com
dir: Exit A454 approx 3.5m NE of Bridgnorth, 5m S of Telford's southern business area. Follow brown signs

This delightful property is set in acres of wooded farmland in a quiet and peaceful area of Shropshire. Service is friendly and helpful, and customer care is one of the many strengths of this charming small hotel. The well-equipped bedrooms are individually appointed, and thoughtfully and luxuriously furnished. The lounge and conservatory are the perfect places to enjoy a pre-dinner drink or the complimentary afternoon tea. The restaurant is a joy, serving award-winning modern British cuisine in elegant surroundings.

Rooms 14 (4 annexe) (1 fmly) (2 GF) **Facilities** FTV WiFi ➘ ⚘ New Year **Conf** Class 40 Board 30 Thtr 60 **Parking** 30 **Notes** Civ Wed 60

BRIDGWATER
Somerset
Map 4 ST23

Walnut Tree Hotel

★★★ 77% HOTEL

tel: 01278 662255 **North Petherton TA6 6QA**
email: reservations@walnuttreehotel.com **web:** www.walnuttreehotel.com
dir: M5 junct 24. Follow North Petherton signs. 1.3m. Hotel in village centre

Popular with both business and leisure guests, this 18th-century former coaching inn is conveniently located within easy reach of the M5. The spacious and smartly decorated bedrooms are well furnished to ensure a comfortable and relaxing stay. An extensive selection of dishes is offered in either the restaurant, or the more informal setting of the bistro.

Rooms 30 (3 fmly) (3 GF) ➘S £79-£119; **D** £98-£138 (incl. bkfst)* **Facilities** FTV WiFi ➘ Gym New Year **Conf** Class 60 Board 50 Thtr 100 Del from £115 to £138* **Parking** 70 **Notes** ⊗ Civ Wed 100

Apple Tree Hotel

★★★ 71% HOTEL

tel: 01278 733238 **Keenthorne TA5 1HZ**
email: reservations@appletreehotel.com **web:** www.appletreehotel.com

(For full entry see Nether Stowey)

Premier Inn Bridgwater

BUDGET HOTEL

tel: 0871 527 8148 **Express Park, Bristol Rd TA6 4RR**
web: www.premierinn.com
dir: M5 junct 23, A38 to Bridgwater. Hotel on right in 2m

High quality, budget accommodation ideal for both families and business travellers. Spacious, en suite bedrooms feature tea and coffee making facilities, and Freeview TV in most hotels. Internet access and WiFi are available for a small fee. The adjacent family restaurant features a wide and varied menu. See also the Hotel Groups pages.

Rooms 40

B

BRIDLINGTON	**Map 17 TA16**
East Riding of Yorkshire	

Expanse Hotel

★★★ 75% HOTEL

tel: 01262 675347 **North Marine Dr YO15 2LS**
email: reservations@expanse.co.uk **web:** www.expanse.co.uk
dir: Follow North Beach signs, pass under railway arch for North Marine Drive. Hotel at bottom of hill

This traditional seaside hotel overlooks the bay and has been in the same family's ownership for many years. Service is relaxed and friendly and the modern bedrooms are well equipped. Comfortable public areas include a conference suite, a choice of bars and an inviting lounge. Complimentary WiFi is available.

Rooms 45 (2 fmly) ♦ **S** £37.95-£68; **D** £75.90-£166 (incl. bkfst)* **Facilities** FTV WiFi ♪ ♬ Xmas New Year **Conf** Class 50 Board 50 Thtr 180 **Services** Lift **Parking** 17 **Notes** LB ⊗ Civ Wed 140

BRIDPORT	**Map 4 SY49**
Dorset	

Bridge House Hotel

THE INDEPENDENTS
HOTEL ASSOCIATION

★★★ 73% METRO HOTEL

tel: 01308 423371 **115 East St DT6 3LB**
email: info@bridgehousebridport.co.uk **web:** www.bridgehousebridport.co.uk
dir: From A35 follow town centre signs, hotel 200mtrs on right

A short stroll from the town centre, this 18th-century Grade II listed property offers well-equipped bedrooms that vary in size. In addition to the main lounge, there is a small bar-lounge, a separate breakfast room and wine bar. A range of dining options are within walking distance.

Rooms 10 (3 fmly) ♦ **S** fr £82; **D** £119-£130 (incl. bkfst)* **Facilities** FTV WiFi New Year **Conf** Class 20 Board 15 Thtr 36 **Parking** 13

Haddon House Hotel

★★★ 71% HOTEL

tel: 01308 423626 & 425323 **West Bay DT6 4EL**
email: info@haddonhousehotel.co.uk **web:** www.haddonhousehotel.co.uk
dir: At Crown Inn rdbt take B3157 (West Bay Rd), hotel 0.5m on right at mini-rdbt

This attractive, creeper-clad hotel offers good standards of accommodation and is situated a few minutes' walk from the seafront and the quay. A friendly and relaxed style of service is provided. An extensive range of dishes, from lighter bar snacks to main meals, is on offer in the Tudor-style restaurant.

Rooms 12 (2 fmly) (2 GF) **S** £79.50-£89.50; **D** £92.50-£130 (incl. bkfst)* **Facilities** FTV WiFi ♪ New Year **Conf** Class 20 Board 26 Thtr 60 **Parking** 40 **Notes** LB ⊗

BRIGHOUSE	**Map 16 SE12**
West Yorkshire	

Premier Inn Huddersfield North

Premier Inn

BUDGET HOTEL

tel: 0871 527 8530 **Wakefield Rd HD6 4HA**
web: www.premierinn.com
dir: M62 junct 25, A644 signed Huddersfield, Dewsbury & Wakefield. Hotel 500mtrs up hill on right

High quality, budget accommodation ideal for both families and business travellers. Spacious, en suite bedrooms feature tea and coffee making facilities, and Freeview TV in most hotels. Internet access and WiFi are available for a small fee. The adjacent family restaurant features a wide and varied menu. See also the Hotel Groups pages.

Rooms 71

BRIGHTON & HOVE
East Sussex

Map 6 TQ30

See also **Steyning**

Hotel du Vin Brighton

★★★★ 78% 🏵 TOWN HOUSE HOTEL

tel: 01273 718588 **2-6 Ship St BN1 1AD**
email: info@brighton.hotelduvin.com **web:** www.hotelduvin.com
dir: From A23 follow seafront/city centre signs. Right at seafront, right into Middle St. Follow to end bear right into Ship St. Hotel on right

This tastefully converted mock-Tudor building occupies a convenient location in a quiet side street close to the seafront. The individually designed bedrooms have a wine theme, and all are comprehensively equipped. Public areas offer a spacious split-level bar, an atmospheric and locally popular restaurant, plus useful private dining and meeting facilities.

Rooms 49 (2 fmly) (4 GF) **Facilities** STV WiFi 🎵 Xmas New Year **Conf** Class 50 Board 60 Thtr 80 **Services** Air con **Notes** Civ Wed 120

The Old Ship Hotel

★★★★ 73% HOTEL

tel: 01273 329001 **King's Rd BN1 1NR**
email: oldship@pumahotels.co.uk **web:** www.pumahotels.co.uk
dir: A23 to seafront, right at rdbt along Kings Rd. Hotel 200yds on right

This historic hotel enjoys a stunning seafront location and offers guests elegant surroundings to relax in. Bedrooms are well designed, with modern facilities ensuring comfort. Many original features have been retained, including the Paganini Ballroom. Facilities include a sleek bar, alfresco dining and a variety of conference rooms.

Rooms 154 🛌 **S** £80-£290; **D** £80-£450* **Facilities** FTV WiFi Gym Xmas New Year **Conf** Class 100 Board 35 Thtr 250 Del from £115 to £175* **Services** Lift **Parking** 40 **Notes** Civ Wed 150

Mercure Brighton Seafront Hotel

★★★★ 70% HOTEL

tel: 0844 815 9061 **149 Kings Rd BN1 2PP**
email: info@mercurebrighton.co.uk **web:** www.jupiterhotels.co.uk
dir: A23 follow signs for seafront. Right at Brighton Pier rdbt. Hotel on right, just after West Pier

Located right on the seafront in the heart of Brighton, this hotel offers uninterrupted sea views from all seafront-facing rooms and public areas. Brighton Pier, the Lanes and Town Centre are just a couple of minutes walk. The Hotel is spacious and offers comfortably appointed accommodation, all with complimentary WiFi access. Plenty of secure off road parking is available.

Rooms 117 **Facilities** WiFi 🅿 **Conf** Class 80 Board 60 Thtr 180 **Parking** 38 **Notes** Civ Wed 180

BEST WESTERN Princes Marine

★★★ 78% HOTEL

tel: 01273 207660 **153 Kingsway BN3 4GR**
email: princesmarine@bestwestern.co.uk **web:** www.princesmarinehotel.co.uk
dir: Right at Brighton Pier, follow seafront for 2m. Hotel 200yds from King Alfred leisure centre

This friendly hotel enjoys a seafront location and offers spacious, comfortable bedrooms equipped with a good range of facilities including free WiFi. There is a

stylish restaurant, modern bar and selection of roof-top meeting rooms with sea views. Limited parking is available at the rear.

Rooms 48 (4 fmly) 🛌 **Facilities** STV FTV WiFi 🅿 **Conf** Class 40 Board 40 Thtr 70 **Services** Lift **Parking** 30 **Notes** ⊗

BEST WESTERN Brighton Hotel

★★★ 76% METRO HOTEL

tel: 01273 820555 **143/145 King's Rd BN1 2PQ**
email: info@thebrightonhotel.com **web:** www.thebrightonhotel.co.uk
dir: M23 onto A23 to pier. Right at rdbt, hotel just past West Pier

This friendly hotel is well placed in a prime seafront location close to the historic West Pier. The contemporary bedrooms are spaciously appointed and well equipped. The lounge, bar and restaurant are sunny, bright and comfortable with great sea views. Dinner is not available in the restaurant but a 24-hour room service menu is in place, and restaurants are within easy walking distance. Parking facilities, though limited, are a real bonus in this area of town.

Rooms 55 (6 fmly) 🛌 **Facilities** FTV WiFi 🅿 HL **Conf** Class 30 Board 40 Thtr 70 **Services** Lift **Parking** 10 **Notes** ⊗ Civ Wed 140

The Kings Hotel

★★★ 72% METRO HOTEL

tel: 01273 820854 **139-141 Kings Rd BN1 2NA**
email: info@kingshotelbrighton.co.uk **web:** www.kingshotelbrighton.com
dir: Follow signs to seafront. At Brighton Pier rdbt take 3rd exit & drive west (seafront on left). Hotel adjacent to West Pier

Located on the seafront adjacent to West Pier, this Grade II listed, Regency building has been restored to offer contemporary accommodation. Although the hotel does not provide a full dinner service, light snacks are available throughout the day and evening in the public areas and also in the guests' bedrooms. There is limited parking space which is a bonus in Brighton.

Rooms 90 (3 fmly) (6 GF) 🛌 **S** £55-£95; **D** £75-£225 (incl. bkfst)* **Facilities** FTV WiFi 🅿 **Conf** Class 25 Board 30 Thtr 70 Del from £90 to £220* **Services** Lift **Parking** 11

Queens Hotel

★★★ 72% HOTEL

tel: 01273 321222 & 0800 970 7570 **1-3 King's Rd BN1 1NS**
email: info@queenshotelbrighton.com **web:** www.queenshotelbrighton.com
dir: A23 to Brighton town centre, follow signs for seafront. At Brighton Pier right onto seafront, hotel 500mtrs

This hotel has a fantastic location with views of the beach and pier. The modern bedrooms and bathrooms are spacious, and many benefit from uninterrupted sea views. All bedrooms have LCD TVs and free WiFi. There is a spacious bar and restaurant area plus fully equipped spa, gym and swimming pool.

Rooms 94 (28 fmly) **S** £59-£275; **D** £69-£300 (incl. bkfst)* **Facilities** Spa FTV WiFi 🅿 HL 🏊 supervised Gym Beauty salon **Conf** Class 50 Board 50 Thtr 150 Del from £120 to £195* **Services** Lift **Notes** ⊗ Civ Wed 120

B

Umi Brighton Hotel

★★★ 70% HOTEL

tel: 01273 323221 **64 King's Rd BN1 1NA**
email: reservations@umibrighton.co.uk **web:** www.umibrighton.co.uk
dir: On A259 adjacent to Brighton Centre

Umi Hotel is located right in the heart of Brighton on the seafront with just a short walk to the Pier, Station and City Centre. Bedrooms are modern in style and include free WiFi access, all seafront bedrooms benefit from excellent uninterrupted sea views. The little Bay Restaurant has a theatre-style theme and offers a good range of dishes at very affordable prices, both a cooked and continental breakfast is served here daily. There is a Coffee Republic on site.

Rooms 78 (20 fmly) (1 GF) **Facilities** FTV WiFi ↘ HL Free use of leisure centre in Queens Hotel **Conf** Class 20 Board 20 Thtr 20 **Services** Lift **Notes**

The Grand, Brighton

Ⓤ

tel: 01273 224300 **King's Rd BN1 2FW**
email: reservations@grandbrighton.co.uk **web:** www.devere.co.uk
dir: On A259 adjacent to Brighton Centre

Currently the rating for this establishment is not confirmed. We are working with the management / owners whilst works and changes take place to achieve an AA star rating. For further details please see the AA website: theAA.com

Rooms 201 (60 fmly) ✎ **S** £69-£219; **D** £89-£249 (incl. bkfst)* **Facilities** Spa FTV WiFi Gym ♬ Xmas New Year **Conf** Class 450 Board 60 Thtr 800 Del from £135* **Services** Lift **Parking** 50 **Notes** Civ Wed 800

Ibis Brighton City Centre

BUDGET HOTEL

tel: 01273 201000 **88-92 Queens Rd BN1 3XE**
email: h6444@accor.com **web:** www.ibishotel.com

Modern, budget hotel offering comfortable accommodation in bright and practical bedrooms. Breakfast is self-service and dinner is available in the restaurant. See also the Hotel Groups pages.

Rooms 140 (26 fmly) (8 GF) ✎

Premier Inn Brighton City Centre

BUDGET HOTEL

tel: 0871 527 8150 **144 North St BN1 1RE**
web: www.premierinn.com
dir: From A23 follow signs for city centre. Right at lights near Royal Pavilion, take road ahead on left (runs adjacent to Pavilion) into Church St, 1st left into New Rd leading North St

High quality, budget accommodation ideal for both families and business travellers. Spacious, en suite bedrooms feature tea and coffee making facilities, and Freeview TV in most hotels. Internet access and WiFi are available for a small fee. The adjacent family restaurant features a wide and varied menu. See also the Hotel Groups pages.

Rooms 160

BRISTOL **Map 4 ST57**
Bristol

Aztec Hotel & Spa

★★★★ 80% ◉ HOTEL

tel: 01454 201090 **Aztec West Business Park, Almondsbury BS32 4TS**
email: aztec@shirehotels.com **web:** www.aztechotelbristol.com
dir: Access via M5 junct 16 & M4

Situated close to Cribbs Causeway shopping centre and major motorway links, this stylish hotel offers comfortable, very well-equipped bedrooms and suites. Built in a Nordic style, public rooms boast log fires and vaulted ceilings. Leisure facilities include a popular gym and good size pool. The Quarter Jacks Restaurant Bar & Lounge offers relaxed informal dining with a focus on simply prepared, quality regional foods. The hotel has a spa with a gym, pool, children's pool, whirlpool, sauna, steam room and a range of treatments.

Rooms 128 (8 fmly) (29 GF) **S** £90-£200; **D** £90-£200* **Facilities** Spa STV WiFi ↘ HL Ⓐ Gym Steam room Sauna Children's splash pool Activity studio New Year **Conf** Class 120 Board 36 Thtr 200 Del from £145 to £185* **Services** Lift **Parking** 240 **Notes** LB ⊗ Civ Wed 120

Bristol Marriott City Centre

★★★★ 77% HOTEL

tel: 0117 929 4281 **Lower Castle St BS1 3AD**
web: www.bristolmarriottcitycentre.co.uk
dir: M32 follow signs to Broadmead, take slip road to large rdbt, take 3rd exit. Hotel on right

Situated at the foot of the picturesque Castle Park, this mainly business-orientated hotel is well placed for the city centre. Executive and deluxe bedrooms have high speed internet access. In addition to a coffee bar and lounge menu, the Mediterrano Restaurant offers an interesting selection of well-prepared dishes.

Rooms 300 (135 fmly) **Facilities** STV FTV WiFi ↘ Ⓐ Gym Steam room Sauna Spa pool Xmas New Year **Conf** Class 280 Board 40 Thtr 600 **Services** Lift Air con **Notes** ⊗ Civ Wed 700

Hotel du Vin Bristol

★★★★ 76% ◉ TOWN HOUSE HOTEL

tel: 0844 7364 252 **The Sugar House, Narrow Lewins Mead BS1 2NU**
email: info.bristol@hotelduvin.com **web:** www.hotelduvin.com
dir: From A4 follow city centre signs. After 400yds pass Rupert St NCP on right. Hotel on opposite carriageway

This hotel is part of one of Britain's most innovative hotel groups, offering high standards of hospitality and accommodation. Housed in a Grade II listed, converted 18th-century sugar refinery, it provides great facilities with a modern, minimalist design. The bedrooms are exceptionally well designed and the bistro offers an excellent menu and wine list.

Rooms 40 (10 fmly) ✎ **S** £109-£175; **D** £139-£375 (incl. bkfst)* **Facilities** STV FTV WiFi ↘ ♬ New Year **Conf** Class 36 Board 34 Thtr 72 Del from £175 to £275* **Services** Lift **Parking** 9 **Notes** LB Civ Wed 65

BRISTOL *continued*

DoubleTree by Hilton Bristol City Centre

★★★★ 75% HOTEL

tel: 0117 926 0041 **Redcliffe Way BS1 6NJ**
email: sales@focusbristol.co.uk **web:** doubletree3.hilton.com
dir: 1m from M32. 400yds from Temple Meads BR station, before church

This large modern hotel is situated in the heart of the city centre and offers spacious public areas and ample parking. Bedrooms are well equipped for both business and leisure guests. Dining options include a relaxed bar and a unique kiln restaurant where a good selection of freshly prepared dishes is available.

Rooms 201 ⟨ **S** £75-£209; **D** £75-£209* **Facilities** FTV WiFi ⬭ Gym New Year **Conf** Class 120 Board 75 Thtr 300 Del from £99 to £245* **Services** Lift Air con **Parking** 150 **Notes** LB ⊗ Civ Wed 250

Holiday Inn Bristol Filton

★★★★ 74% HOTEL

tel: 0871 942 9014 **Filton Rd, Hambrook BS16 1QX**
email: bristol@ihg.com **web:** www.hibristolfiltonhotel.co.uk
dir: M4 junct 19/M32 junct 1/A4174 towards Filton & Bristol. Hotel 800yds on left

With easy access of both the M4 and M5 this is, understandably, a popular hotel with business guests. Public areas are spacious and relaxing with a wide choice of comfortable seating options. There are two restaurants - Sampans with a selection of dishes from the Far East, and the more traditional Junction Restaurant. Bedrooms vary in size, but all are well furnished and well equipped. A large car park, leisure facilities and range of conference rooms are all available.

Rooms 211 (40 fmly) (70 GF) (2 smoking) **Facilities** STV FTV WiFi ⬭ 🐟 supervised Fishing Gym Beauty treatment room Sauna Xmas New Year **Conf** Class 180 Board 75 Thtr 250 **Services** Lift Air con **Parking** 250 **Notes** ⊗ Civ Wed 250

Mercure Brigstow Bristol

★★★★ 74% HOTEL

tel: 0117 929 1030 **5-7 Welsh Back BS1 4SP**
email: H6548@accor.com **web:** www.mercure.com
dir: From the centre follow Baldwin St then right into Queen Charlotte St

In a prime position on the river this handsome, purpose-built hotel is designed and finished with care. The shopping centre and theatres are within easy walking distance. The stylish bedrooms are extremely well equipped, including plasma TV screens in the bathrooms. There is an integrated state-of-the-art conference and meeting centre, and a smart restaurant and bar overlooking the harbour. Guests have complimentary use of a squash and health club, plus free internet access.

Rooms 116 ⟨ **Facilities** STV FTV WiFi ⬭ Gym Free access to nearby gym & squash courts New Year **Conf** Class 40 Board 30 Thtr 85 **Services** Lift Air con **Notes** Civ Wed 80

Mercure Bristol Holland House Hotel & Spa

★★★★ 74% HOTEL

tel: 0117 968 9900 **Redcliffe Hill BS1 6SQ**
email: h6698@accor.com **web:** www.mercure.com
dir: M4 junct 19 towards city centre, follow signs A4 then A370, take A38 Redcliffe Hill. Hotel opposite St Mary Redcliffe Church

This modern hotel, just a ten-minute walk from Bristol Temple Meads, has striking, contemporary style throughout, and offers some impressive facilities including a spa, a fitness suite and meeting rooms. The hotel has a green-bicycle service for guests. Bedrooms are stylishly designed with large plasma screen TVs, comfortable beds and free internet access. Dining is offered in the Phoenix Restaurant and bar.

Rooms 275 (59 fmly) (44 GF) ⟨ **S** £69-£129; **D** £79-£139* **Facilities** Spa FTV WiFi ⬭ HL 🏊 Gym Free bike rental Xmas New Year **Conf** Class 150 Board 80 Thtr 220 **Services** Lift Air con **Parking** 140 **Notes** LB ⊗ Civ Wed 220

Mercure Bristol North The Grange

★★★★ 74% COUNTRY HOUSE HOTEL

tel: 0844 815 9063 **Northwoods, Winterbourne BS36 1RP**
email: gm.mercurebristolnorthgrange@jupiterhotels.co.uk **web:** www.jupiterhotels.co.uk
dir: A38 towards Filton/Bristol. At rdbt 1st exit into Bradley Stoke Way, at lights 1st left into Woodlands Ln, at 2nd rdbt left into Tench Ln. In 1m left at T-junct, hotel 200yds on left

Built in the 19th century and surrounded by 18 acres of attractive grounds, this is a pleasant hotel situated only a short drive from the city centre. The bedrooms are spacious and well equipped; there is a leisure centre with a pool plus a range of meeting facilities. The conservatory bar has a terrace which makes a delightful place to enjoy a drink under the shade of a 200-year-old cedar tree. The hotel is popular as a wedding venue.

Rooms 68 (20 fmly) (22 GF) **S** £40-£200; **D** £40-£200 **Facilities** STV FTV WiFi 🏊 Gym Xmas New Year **Conf** Class 120 Board 134 Thtr 150 **Parking** 150 **Notes** LB Civ Wed 150

Novotel Bristol Centre

★★★★ 72% HOTEL

tel: 0117 976 9988 **Victoria St BS1 6HY**
email: H5622@accor.com **web:** www.novotel.com
dir: At end of M32 follow signs for Temple Meads station to rdbt. Final exit, hotel immediately on right

This city centre hotel provides smart, contemporary style accommodation. Most of the bedrooms demonstrate the Novotel 'Novation' style with unique swivel desk, internet access, air-conditioning and a host of extras. The hotel is convenient for the mainline railway station and also has its own car park.

Rooms 131 (34 fmly) ⟨ **Facilities** STV FTV WiFi ⬭ HL Gym Sauna Steam room **Conf** Class 70 Board 35 Thtr 210 **Services** Lift Air con **Parking** 100 **Notes** ⊗ Civ Wed 100

B

BEST WESTERN Henbury Lodge Hotel

★★★ 80%  HOTEL

tel: 0117 950 2615 **Station Rd, Henbury BS10 7QQ**
email: info@henburyhotel.com **web:** www.henburyhotel.com
dir: M5 junct 17/A4018 towards city centre, 3rd rdbt right into Crow Ln. At end turn right, hotel 200mtrs on right

This quietly located hotel is popular with both business and leisure guests. Bedrooms, in a wide range of shapes and sizes, are divided between the main house and a converted stable block; all are comfortably furnished and equipped. The small and friendly team offer a very personal welcome and many guests here are regulars. Dinner and breakfast are taken in the stylish restaurant where high quality local produce is used.

Rooms 20 (9 annexe) (4 fmly) (6 GF) **S** £88-£104; **D** £102-£118 (incl. bkfst)* **Facilities** FTV WiFi ♧ **Conf** Class 15 Board 20 Thtr 20 **Parking** 20 **Notes** LB ⊗ Closed 22 Dec-9 Jan

The Avon Gorge Hotel

★★★ 77% HOTEL

tel: 0117 973 8955 **Sion Hill, Clifton BS8 4LD**
email: rooms@theavongorge.com **web:** www.theavongorge.com
dir: From S: M5 junct 19, A369 to Clifton Toll, over suspension bridge, 1st right into Sion Hill. From N: M5 junct 18A, A4 to Bristol, under suspension bridge, follow signs to bridge, exit Sion Hill

This is a delightful terraced property overlooking the Clifton Suspension Bridge. It offers bedrooms of varying shapes and sizes with either views across the river or of Clifton village. Meals can be taken in the contemporary Bridge Café restaurant where a range of carefully prepared, tempting dishes is available. There is a limited amount of free parking space at the rear of the hotel or on-street (no restrictions) in the vicinity.

Rooms 75 (8 fmly) (4 GF) **Facilities** STV WiFi ♧ Xmas New Year **Conf** Class 40 Board 30 Thtr 100 Del from £155 to £195 **Services** Lift **Parking** 25 **Notes** Civ Wed 100

Rodney Hotel

★★★ 68% HOTEL

tel: 0117 973 5422 **4 Rodney Place, Clifton BS8 4HY**
email: rodney@cliftonhotels.com **web:** www.cliftonhotels.com/bristolhotels/rodney
dir: Off Clifton Down Rd

With easy access from the M5, this attractive, listed building in Clifton is conveniently close to the city centre. The individually decorated bedrooms provide a useful range of extra facilities for the business traveller; the public areas include a

smart bar and small restaurant offering enjoyable and carefully prepared dishes. A pleasant rear garden provides additional seating in the summer months.

Rooms 31 (1 fmly) (2 GF) ☎ **S** £44-£94; **D** £49-£113* **Facilities** FTV WiFi **Conf** Class 20 Board 20 Thtr 30 Del from £102 to £158 **Parking** 7 **Notes** Closed 22 Dec-3 Jan RS Sun Civ Wed 40

BEST WESTERN Victoria Square Hotel

★★ 79% HOTEL

tel: 0117 973 9058 **Victoria Square, Clifton BS8 4EW**
email: info@victoriasquarehotel.co.uk **web:** www.victoriasquarehotel.co.uk
dir: M5 junct 19, follow Clifton signs. Over suspension/toll bridge, right into Clifton Down Rd. Left into Merchants Rd then into Victoria Square

This welcoming hotel offers high quality, individual bedrooms and bathrooms in a variety of shapes and sizes. The hotel is just one mile from the city centre and a two-minute stroll from the heart of Clifton village. The atmosphere is relaxed, and guests have a choice of dining options - from lighter meals in the bar to a range of imaginative dishes in the main restaurant.

Rooms 41 (20 annexe) (3 fmly) (3 GF) ☎ **S** £50-£75; **D** £69-£119 (incl. bkfst)* **Facilities** FTV WiFi ♧ **Conf** Class 15 Board 20 Thtr 30 **Parking** 15 **Notes** ⊗

Clifton Hotel

★★ 78% HOTEL

tel: 0117 973 6882 **St Pauls Rd, Clifton BS8 1LX**
email: clifton@cliftonhotels.com **web:** www.cliftonhotels.com/bristolhotels/clifton
dir: M32 follow Bristol/Clifton signs, along Park St. Left at lights into St Pauls Rd

This popular hotel offers a relaxed, friendly service and very well equipped bedrooms. There is a welcoming lounge by the reception, and in summer months drinks and meals can be enjoyed on the terrace. Racks Bar and Restaurant offers an interesting selection of modern dishes in informal surroundings. There is some street parking, but for a small charge, secure garage parking is available.

Rooms 59 (2 fmly) (12 GF) ☎ **S** £83; **D** £101* **Facilities** STV FTV WiFi **Services** Lift **Parking** 12

Ibis Bristol Centre

BUDGET HOTEL

tel: 01173 199000 **Explore Ln BS1 5TY**
email: H5547@accor.com **web:** www.ibishotel.com
dir: Off A4 in harbourside district

Modern, budget hotel offering comfortable accommodation in bright and practical bedrooms. Breakfast is self-service and dinner is available in the restaurant. See also the Hotel Groups pages.

Rooms 182 (2 fmly)

Ibis Bristol Temple Meads

BUDGET HOTEL

tel: 0117 319 9001 **Avon St BS2 0PS**
email: H6593@accor.com **web:** www.ibis.com
dir: M4 junct 19, M32, follow Temple Meads train station signs. Left after underpass

Rooms 141 (7 fmly) ☎ **Conf** Class 12 Board 12 Thtr 12

B

BRISTOL *continued*

Premier Inn Bristol Airport (Sidcot)

BUDGET HOTEL

tel: 0871 527 8154 **Bridgwater Rd, Winscombe BS25 1NN**
web: www.premierinn.com
dir: Between M5 junct 21 & 22 (9m from Bristol Airport), onto A371 towards Banwell, Winscombe to A38. Right at lights, Hotel 300yds on left

High quality, budget accommodation ideal for both families and business travellers. Spacious, en suite bedrooms feature tea and coffee making facilities, and Freeview TV in most hotels. Internet access and WiFi are available for a small fee. The adjacent family restaurant features a wide and varied menu. See also the Hotel Groups pages.

Rooms 31

Premier Inn Bristol (Alveston)

BUDGET HOTEL

tel: 0871 527 8152 **Thornbury Rd, Alveston BS35 3LL**
web: www.premierinn.com
dir: Just off M5. From N: exit at junct 14 onto A38 towards Bristol. From S: exit at junct 16 onto A38 towards Gloucester

Rooms 75

Premier Inn Bristol City Centre (Haymarket)

BUDGET HOTEL

tel: 0871 527 8156 **The Haymarket BS1 3LR**
web: www.premierinn.com
dir: M4 junct 19, M32 towards city centre. Through 2 sets of lights, at 3rd lights turn right, to rdbt, take 2nd exit. Hotel on left

Rooms 224

Premier Inn Bristol City Centre King St

BUDGET HOTEL

tel: 0871 527 8158 **Llandoger Trow, King St BS1 4ER**
web: www.premierinn.com
dir: A38 into city centre. Left onto B4053 Baldwin St. Right into Queen Charlotte St, follow one-way system, bear right at river. Hotel on right

Rooms 60

Premier Inn Bristol Cribbs Causeway

BUDGET HOTEL

tel: 0871 527 8160 **Cribbs Causeway, Catbrain Ln BS10 7TQ**
web: www.premierinn.com
dir: M5 junct 17, A4018. 1st left at rdbt into Lysander Rd. Right into Catbrain Hill, leads to Catbrain Lane

Rooms 106

Premier Inn Bristol East (Emersons Green)

BUDGET HOTEL

tel: 0871 527 8162 **200/202 Westerleigh Rd, Emersons Green BS16 7AN**
web: www.premierinn.com
dir: M4 junct 19 onto M32 junct 1, left onto A4174 (Avon Ring Rd). Hotel at 3rd rdbt

Rooms 67

Premier Inn Bristol Filton

BUDGET HOTEL

tel: 0871 527 8164 **Shield Retail Park, Gloucester Road North, Filton BS34 7BR**
web: www.premierinn.com
dir: M5 junct 16, A38 signed Filton/Patchway. Pass airport & Royal Mail on right. Left at 2nd rdbt, 1st left into retail park

Rooms 62

Premier Inn Bristol South

BUDGET HOTEL

tel: 0871 527 8166 **Hengrove Leisure Park, Hengrove Way BS14 0HR**
web: www.premierinn.com
dir: From city centre take A37 to Wells & Shepton Mallet. Right onto A4174. Hotel at 3rd lights

Rooms 56

BRIXHAM   Map 3 SX95
Devon

Quayside Hotel

★★★ 75% ◉ HOTEL

tel: 01803 855751 **41-49 King St TQ5 9TJ**
email: reservations@quaysidehotel.co.uk **web:** www.quaysidehotel.co.uk
dir: A380, at 2nd rdbt at Kinkerswell towards Brixham on A3022

With views over the harbour and bay, this hotel was formerly six cottages, and the public rooms retain a certain cosiness and intimacy. These include the lounge, residents' bar and Ernie Lister's public bar. Freshly-landed fish features on the menus, alongside a number of creative and skilfully prepared dishes, served in the well-appointed restaurant. Good food is also available in the public bar. The owners and their team of local staff provide friendly and attentive service.

Rooms 29 (2 fmly) ⚑ **Facilities** FTV WiFi ⌂ ♬ Xmas New Year **Conf** Class 18 Board 18 Thtr 25 **Parking** 30

Berry Head Hotel

THE INDEPENDENTS
HOTEL ASSOCIATION

★★★ 75% HOTEL

tel: 01803 853225 **Berry Head Rd TQ5 9AJ**
email: stay@berryheadhotel.com **web:** www.berryheadhotel.com
dir: From marina, 1m, hotel on left

From its stunning cliff-top location, this imposing property dates back to 1809, and has spectacular views across Torbay. Public areas include two comfortable lounges, an outdoor terrace, and a swimming pool, together with a bar serving a range of popular dishes. Many of the bedrooms have the benefit of splendid sea views.

Rooms 32 (7 fmly) **S** £55-£70; **D** £110-£180 (incl. bkfst)* **Facilities** FTV WiFi ⚡ 🏊 Petanque Sailing Deep sea fishing Yacht charter 🎣 Xmas New Year **Conf** Class 250 Board 40 Thtr 300 Del from £75 to £135* **Services** Lift **Parking** 100 **Notes** LB Civ Wed 200

BROADWAY	
Worcestershire	Map 10 SP03

AA HOTEL OF THE YEAR FOR ENGLAND 2014–2015

Dormy House Hotel

★★★★ 87% ◎◎ HOTEL

tel: 01386 852711 **Willersey Hill WR12 7LF**
email: reservations@dormyhouse.co.uk. **web:** www.dormyhouse.co.uk
dir: 2m E of Broadway off A44, at top of Fish Hill turn for Saintbury/Picnic area. In 0.5m turn left, hotel on left

Dormy House is a converted 17th-century farmhouse set in 400-acre grounds on the Farncombe Estate, with stunning views over Broadway. The hotel recently underwent a multi-million pound refurbishment, part of which was a new luxury spa that offers a wide range of treatments, a swimming pool, a Veuve Clicquot

Champagne nail bar, gym and thermal suite. The best traditions are retained - customer care, real fires, comfortable sofas and afternoon teas. Dinner features an interesting choice of dishes created by a skilled kitchen brigade. Dormy House Hotel is the AA Hotel of the Year for England 2014-2015.

Rooms 40 (21 annexe) (8 fmly) (21 GF) 🐾 **S** £240-£500; **D** £250-£510 (incl. bkfst) **Facilities** Spa STV FTV WiFi ⚡ 🏊 Gym Nature & jogging trail Circular walks Champagne nail bar Xmas New Year **Parking** 90 **Notes** Civ Wed 80

See advert below

The Lygon Arms

★★★★ 82% ◎◎ HOTEL

PUMA HOTELS COLLECTION

tel: 01386 852255 **High St WR12 7DU**
email: thelygonarms@pumahotels.co.uk **web:** www.pumahotels.co.uk
dir: From Evesham take A44 signed Oxford, 5m. Follow Broadway signs. Hotel on left

A hotel with a wealth of historic charm and character, the Lygon Arms dates back to the 16th century. There is a choice of restaurants, a stylish cosy bar, an array of lounges and a smart spa and leisure club. Bedrooms vary in size and style, but all are thoughtfully equipped and include a number of contemporary rooms as well as a cottage in the grounds.

Rooms 78 (16 fmly) (17 GF) 🐾 **Facilities** Spa STV FTV WiFi ⚡ 🏊 supervised 🏊 🏊 Gym Beauty treatments Xmas New Year **Conf** Class 42 Board 30 Thtr 100 **Parking** 200 **Notes** Civ Wed 100

BROADWAY *continued*

B

The Broadway Hotel

★★★ 82% ⊛ HOTEL

tel: 01386 852401 **The Green, High St WR12 7AA**
email: info@broadwayhotel.info **web:** www.cotswold-inns-hotels.co.uk/broadway
dir: Follow signs to Evesham, then Broadway. Left onto Leamington Rd, hotel just off village green

The Broadway Hotel is a half-timbered Cotswold stone property, built in the 15th century as a retreat for the Abbots of Pershore. It combines modern, attractive decor with original charm and character. Bedrooms are tastefully furnished and well equipped while public rooms include a relaxing lounge, cosy bar and charming restaurant; alfresco all-day dining in summer months proves popular.

Rooms 19 (1 fmly) (3 GF) **S** £120-£160; **D** £160-£180 (incl. bkfst)* **Facilities** FTV WiFi Xmas New Year **Parking** 20 **Notes** LB

Russell's

⊛ RESTAURANT WITH ROOMS

tel: 01386 853555 📄 01386 853964 **20 High St WR12 7DT**
email: info@russellsofbroadway.co.uk **web:** www.russellsofbroadway.co.uk
dir: Opposite village green

Situated in the centre of picturesque Broadway, this restaurant with rooms makes a great base for exploring local attractions. The superbly appointed bedrooms, each with its own character, have air conditioning and a wide range of extras. The cuisine is a real draw here with freshly-prepared, local produce skilfully utilised.

Rooms 7 (3 annexe) (4 fmly)

BROCKENHURST
Hampshire

Map 5 SU30

INSPECTORS' CHOICE

Rhinefield House Hotel

HANDPICKED HOTELS
BUILT FOR PLEASURE

★★★★ ⊛⊛ HOTEL

tel: 01590 622922 & 0845 072 7516 **Rhinefield Rd SO42 7QB**
email: rhinefieldhouse@handpicked.co.uk
web: www.handpickedhotels.co.uk/rhinefieldhouse
dir: A35 towards Christchurch. 3m from Lyndhurst turn left to Rhinefield, 1.5m to hotel

This stunning 19th-century, mock-Elizabethan mansion is set in 40 acres of beautifully landscaped gardens and forest. Bedrooms are spacious and great consideration is given to guest comfort. The elegant and award-winning Armada Restaurant is richly furnished, and features a fireplace carving (nine years in

the making) that is worth taking time to admire. If the weather permits, the delightful terrace is just the place for enjoying alfresco eating.

Rooms 50 (10 fmly) (18 GF) **S** £144-£420; **D** £144-£440 (incl. bkfst)* **Facilities** Spa STV WiFi ↕ HL 🔄 🜂 🕭 🏊 Gym Hydrotherapy pool Plunge pool Steam room Sauna Xmas New Year **Conf** Class 72 Board 56 Thtr 160 Del from £165 to £210* **Services** Lift **Parking** 100 **Notes** LB ⊗ Civ Wed 130

Careys Manor Hotel & Senspa

★★★★ 84% ⊛⊛ HOTEL

tel: 01590 624467 **SO42 7RH**
email: stay@careysmanor.com **web:** www.careysmanor.com
dir: M27 junct 3, M271, A35 to Lyndhurst. A337 towards Brockenhurst. Hotel on left after Beaulieu sign

This smart property offers a host of facilities that include an Oriental-style spa and leisure suite with an excellent range of unusual treatments, and three contrasting restaurants that offer a choice of Thai, French or modern British cuisine. Many of the spacious and well appointed bedrooms have balconies overlooking the gardens. Extensive function and conference facilities are also available.

Rooms 79 (61 annexe) (31 GF) **Facilities** Spa FTV WiFi 🔄 🕭 🏊 Gym Steam room Beauty therapists Hydrotherapy pool Xmas New Year **Conf** Class 70 Board 40 Thtr 120 **Services** Lift **Parking** 180 **Notes** ⊗ No children 16yrs Civ Wed 100

The Balmer Lawn Hotel

★★★★ 82% ⊛ HOTEL

tel: 01590 623116 **Lyndhurst Rd SO42 7ZB**
email: info@balmerlawnhotel.com **web:** www.balmerlawnhotel.com
dir: Just off A337 from Brockenhurst towards Lymington

Situated in the heart of the New Forest, this peacefully located hotel provides comfortable public rooms and a wide range of bedrooms. A selection of carefully prepared and enjoyable dishes is offered in the spacious restaurant. The extensive function and leisure facilities make this popular with both families and conference delegates.

Rooms 50 (10 fmly) 🕊 **Facilities** FTV WiFi 🔄 🜂 🕭 Gym Squash Indoor leisure suite Beauty treatment room Sauna 🎵 Xmas New Year **Conf** Class 76 Board 48 Thtr 150 **Services** Lift **Parking** 100 **Notes** Civ Wed 120

B

THE PIG

★★★ ◉◉ ◎ COUNTRY HOUSE HOTEL

tel: 01590 622354 & 0845 077 9494 **Beaulieu Rd SO42 7QL**
email: info@thepighotel.com **web:** www.thepighotel.co.uk
dir: At Brockenhurst onto B3055 (Beaulieu Road). 1m on left up private road

A delightful country house where the focus is very much on the food, with the chef, gardener and forager working as a team to create menus of seasonal, locally sourced produce; all ingredients are found within a 15-mile radius. The result of such a policy is that menus change daily, and sometimes even more frequently! The stylish dining room is an authentically reproduced Victorian greenhouse, and alfresco eating is possible as there is a wood-fired oven in the courtyard. The bedrooms have eclectic furnishings, good beds and views of either the forest or the garden; two suites with private courtyards are available.

Rooms 26 (10 annexe) (2 fmly) (10 GF) ⚫ **Facilities** STV FTV WiFi ⌕ ☺ ☺ Beauty treatment room Xmas New Year **Conf** Board 14 **Parking** 20

Cloud Hotel

★★★ 78% SMALL HOTEL

tel: 01590 622165 & 622354 **Meerut Rd SO42 7TD**
email: enquiries@cloudhotel.co.uk **web:** www.cloudhotel.co.uk
dir: M27 junct 1 signed New Forest, A337 through Lyndhurst to Brockenhurst. On entering Brockenhurst 1st right. Hotel 300mtrs

This charming hotel enjoys a peaceful location on the edge of the village. The bedrooms are bright and comfortable with pine furnishings and smart en suite facilities. Public rooms include a selection of cosy lounges, a delightful rear garden with outdoor seating and a restaurant specialising in home-cooked, wholesome English food.

Rooms 18 (1 fmly) (2 GF) ⚫ **Facilities** FTV WiFi Xmas **Conf** Class 12 Board 12 Thtr 40 **Parking** 20 **Notes** ⊗ No children 12yrs Closed 27 Dec–11 Jan

Forest Park Hotel

★★★ 71% HOTEL

tel: 01590 622844 **Rhinefield Rd SO42 7ZG**
email: reservations@forestpark-hotel.co.uk **web:** www.forestpark-hotel.co.uk

Located in the heart of the beautiful New Forest National Park this popular, small hotel provides an ideal base for exploring this remarkable area. Accommodation offers 38 comfortable en suite rooms with WiFi available throughout. The hotel is very family friendly; children will delight in seeing the ponies on the doorstep. The recently refurbished restaurant has views of the landscaped gardens with cuisine to match. The bar offers a more relaxed atmosphere for lunch and evening meals.

Rooms 38 **Facilities** FTV **Conf** Class 15 Board 20 Thtr 40 **Notes** Civ Wed

Watersplash Hotel

★★ 65% HOTEL

tel: 01590 622344 **The Rise SO42 7ZP**
email: bookings@watersplash.co.uk **web:** www.watersplash.co.uk
dir: M3 junct 13/M27 junct 1/A337 S through Lyndhurst & Brockenhurst. The Rise on left, hotel on left

This popular, welcoming hotel that dates from Victorian times has been in the same family for over 40 years. It is in a great location close to the centre of Brockenhurst, and the delights of the New Forest are easily accessible. The bedrooms are pleasantly appointed and come in a range of sizes. The public rooms are spacious and comfortable, and include a pleasant bar. There is a well-tended garden, and good parking facilities.

Rooms 23 (6 fmly) (2 GF) ⚫ **Facilities** FTV WiFi ⌁ Beauty & massage therapist Xmas New Year **Conf** Class 20 Board 20 Thtr 80 **Parking** 29

The Cottage Hotel

★★ 64% HOTEL

tel: 01590 22296 **Sway Rd SO42 7SH**
email: enquiries@cottagelodge.co.uk **web:** www.cottagelodge.co.uk
dir: Exit A337 opposite Careys Manor Hotel into Grigg Ln, 0.25m over x-rds, cottage next to war memorial

Parts of this attractive small hotel date back over 300 years, and it has been skilfully modernised by the resident owners, Mr and Mrs Moore, to provide a choice of well furnished, bright bedrooms. There is a low-beamed lounge and a licensed restaurant which offers both table d'hôte and a varied à la carte menu. Light refreshments and cream teas are served on the terrace tea garden between Easter and October.

Rooms 15 (3 fmly) (7 GF) ⚫ **S** £50–£110; **D** £60–£160 (incl. bkfst)* **Facilities** FTV WiFi ⌕ **Parking** 15 **Notes** LB ⊗ Closed 1 wk at Xmas

B

BROMBOROUGH
Merseyside

Map 15 SJ38

Premier Inn Wirral (Bromborough)

BUDGET HOTEL

tel: 0871 527 9172 **High St, Bromborough Cross CH62 7EZ**
web: www.premierinn.com
dir: On A41 (New Chester Rd), 2m from M53 junct 5

High quality, budget accommodation ideal for both families and business travellers. Spacious, en suite bedrooms feature tea and coffee making facilities, and Freeview TV in most hotels. Internet access and WiFi are available for a small fee. The adjacent family restaurant features a wide and varied menu. See also the Hotel Groups pages.

Rooms 32

BROME
Suffolk

Map 13 TM17

BEST WESTERN Brome Grange Hotel

★★★ 77% ⊛ HOTEL

tel: 01379 870456 **Norwich Rd, Nr Diss IP23 8AP**
email: info@bromegrangehotel.co.uk **web:** www.bromegrange.co.uk
dir: Located on the A140 between Ipswich & Norwich in the village of Brome

Conveniently located between Ipswich and Norfolk the Best Western Brome Hotel has undergone major refurbishment under its new owners. Bedrooms are spacious, well equipped and attractively presented. The charming cosy bar has lots of character and the restaurant is very popular with locals and residents. A warm welcome is assured and ample secure parking is available for guests.

Rooms 26 (24 annexe) (2 fmly) (24 GF) ⟡ **S** £69-£105; **D** £79-£105 (incl. bkfst)*
Facilities FTV WiFi Xmas New Year **Conf** Class 60 Board 40 Thtr 150 Del from £99 to £119* **Parking** 100 **Notes** LB Civ Wed 110

BROMLEY
Greater London

BEST WESTERN Bromley Court Hotel

★★★ 77% HOTEL PLAN 1 H1

tel: 020 8461 8600 & 8461 8627 **Bromley Hill BR1 4JD**
email: enquiries@bromleycourthotel.co.uk **web:** www.bromleycourthotel.co.uk
dir: N of town centre, off A21. Private drive opposite Volkswagen garage on Bromley Hill

Set amid three acres of grounds, this smart hotel enjoys a peaceful location, in a residential area on the outskirts of town. Well maintained bedrooms are smartly appointed and thoughtfully equipped. The contemporary-style restaurant offers a good choice of meals in comfortable surroundings. Extensive facilities include a leisure club and a good range of meeting rooms.

Rooms 115 (4 fmly) ⟡ **S** £55-£108; **D** £65-£123* **Facilities** STV FTV WiFi ⟳ Gym Steam room Spa pool ♫ Xmas New Year **Conf** Class 70 Board 40 Thtr 150 Del from £155 to £165 **Services** Lift Air con **Parking** 86 **Notes** Civ Wed 180

BROMSGROVE
Worcestershire

Map 10 SO97

Holiday Inn Birmingham - Bromsgrove

★★★★ 75% HOTEL

tel: 01527 576600 & 0871 942 9142 **Kidderminster Rd B61 9AB**
email: info@hi-birminghambromsgrove.co.uk **web:** www.hi-birminghambromsgrove.co.uk
dir: From S: M5 junct 5, A38 to Bromsgrove 2m. At rdbt left, B4091,1.5m. Left at 2nd rdbt A448. Hotel 0.5m on left. From N: M5 junct 4, A38/Bromsgrove for 2m. Through lights, straight on at rdbt. Filter right at lights. Right at 2nd rdbt onto A448. Hotel 0.5m on left

Public areas in this striking building are comfortable and spacious. A selection of meeting rooms is available, along with function suites, a courtyard garden and plenty of natural light. Bedrooms come in a variety of styles - some are more compact than others but all offer an excellent working environment for the business guest. Leisure facilities include a steam room, sauna, pool and gym. There is an extensive car park.

Rooms 110 (11 fmly) (31 GF) **Facilities** Spa STV FTV WiFi ⟳ HL 🔾 Gym Sauna Steam room **Conf** Class 120 Board 50 Thtr 220 Del from £99 to £139 **Services** Lift Air con **Parking** 220 **Notes** ⊗ Civ Wed 180

Premier Inn Bromsgrove Central

BUDGET HOTEL

tel: 0871 527 8168 **Birmingham Rd B61 0BA**
web: www.premierinn.com
dir: M42 junct 1 (S'bound access only) or M5 junct 4 S'bound or M5 junct 5 N'bound onto A38 towards Bromsgrove. Hotel adjacent to Guild Brewers Fayre. (NB for Sat Nav use B60 1GJ)

High quality, budget accommodation ideal for both families and business travellers. Spacious, en suite bedrooms feature tea and coffee making facilities, and Freeview TV in most hotels. Internet access and WiFi are available for a small fee. The adjacent family restaurant features a wide and varied menu. See also the Hotel Groups pages.

Rooms 78

Premier Inn Bromsgrove South (Worcester Road)

BUDGET HOTEL

tel: 0871 527 8170 **Worcester Rd, Upton Warren B61 7ET**
web: www.premierinn.com
dir: M5 junct 5, A38 towards Bromsgrove, 1.2m. Or M42 junct 1, A38 S, cross over A448

Rooms 27

Symbols and abbreviations are explained on page 7

BROOK (NEAR CADNAM)	Map 5 SU21
Hampshire	

The Bell Inn

★★★ 75%  HOTEL

tel: 023 8081 2214 **SO43 7HE**
email: bell@bramshaw.co.uk **web:** www.bellinnbramshaw.co.uk
dir: M27 junct 1 onto B3079, hotel 1.5m on right

The inn is part of the Bramshaw Golf Club and has tailored its style to suit this market, but it is also an ideal base for visiting the New Forest. Bedrooms are comfortable and attractively furnished, and the public areas, particularly the welcoming bar, have a cosy and friendly atmosphere.

Rooms 27 (2 annexe) (1 fmly) (8 GF) **S** £59-£79; **D** £89-£169 (incl. bkfst)*
Facilities FTV WiFi ⅃ 36 Putt green Xmas New Year **Conf** Class 20 Board 30 Thtr 50
Del from £120* **Parking** 150 **Notes** LB ⊗ Civ Wed 50

BROXTON	Map 15 SJ45
Cheshire	

De Vere Carden Park

★★★★ 85%  HOTEL

tel: 0871 222 4682 **Carden Park CH3 9DQ**
email: reservations.carden@devere-hotels.com **web:** www.devere.co.uk
dir: M56 junct 15, M53 Chester. Take A41 signed Whitchurch. 8m. At Broxton rdbt right onto A534 (signed Wrexham). Hotel 1.5m on left

This impressive Cheshire estate dates back to the 17th century and consists of 1,000 acres of mature parkland. The hotel offers a choice of dining options along with superb leisure facilities that include golf courses, a fully equipped gym, a swimming pool and popular spa. Spacious, thoughtfully equipped bedrooms have excellent business and in-room entertainment facilities.

Rooms 196 (83 annexe) (24 fmly) (68 GF) **Facilities** Spa STV WiFi ❧ ❦ supervised ⅃ 36 ⚐ Putt green Gym Archery Quad bikes Mountain bike Laser clay shooting Sauna Steam room Xmas New Year **Conf** Class 240 Board 125 Thtr 350 **Services** Lift **Parking** 700 **Notes** Civ Wed 350

BRYHER	Map 2 SV81
Cornwall (Isles of Scilly)	

Hell Bay

★★★★ 82%  HOTEL

tel: 01720 422947 **TR23 0PR**
email: contactus@hellbay.co.uk **web:** www.hellbay.co.uk
dir: Access by boat from Penzance, plane from Exeter, Newquay or Land's End

Located on the smallest of the inhabited islands of the Scilly Isles on the edge of the Atlantic, this hotel makes a really special destination. The owners have filled the hotel with original works of art by artists who have connections with the islands, and the interior is decorated in cool blues and greens creating an extremely restful environment. The contemporary bedrooms are equally stylish, and many have garden access and stunning sea views. Eating here is a delight, and naturally seafood features strongly on the award-winning, daily-changing menus.

Rooms 25 (25 annexe) (3 fmly) (15 GF) ❧ **S** £168.75-£400; **D** £270-£640 (incl. bkfst & dinner)* **Facilities** STV FTV WiFi ❧ ❦ ⅃ 7 ⚐ ⛵ Gym Beauty treatment room **Conf** Class 36 Board 36 Thtr 36 **Notes** LB Closed Nov-Feb

BUCKHURST HILL	Map 6 TQ49
Essex	

Premier Inn Loughton/Buckhurst Hill

BUDGET HOTEL

tel: 0871 527 8686 **High Rd IG9 5HT**
web: www.premierinn.com
dir: M25 junct 26 towards Loughton. A121 into Buckhurst Hill (approx 5m), hotel on left

High quality, budget accommodation ideal for both families and business travellers. Spacious, en suite bedrooms feature tea and coffee making facilities, and Freeview TV in most hotels. Internet access and WiFi are available for a small fee. The adjacent family restaurant features a wide and varied menu. See also the Hotel Groups pages.

Rooms 49

BUCKINGHAM	Map 11 SP63
Buckinghamshire	

Villiers Hotel

★★★★ 73%  HOTEL

tel: 01280 822444 **3 Castle St MK18 1BS**
email: villiers@oxfordshire-hotels.co.uk **web:** www.oxfordshire-hotels.co.uk
dir: M1 junct 13 (N) or junct 15 (S) follow signs to Buckingham. Castle St by Old Town Hall

Guests can enjoy a town centre location with a high degree of comfort at this 400-year-old former coaching inn. Relaxing public areas feature flagstone floors, oak panelling and real fires whilst bedrooms are modern, spacious and equipped to a high level. Diners can unwind in the atmospheric bar before taking dinner in the award-winning restaurant.

Rooms 49 (4 fmly) (3 GF) **S** £75-£140; **D** £90-£180 (incl. bkfst)* **Facilities** STV FTV WiFi Xmas New Year **Conf** Class 120 Board 80 Thtr 250 Del from £120 to £180* **Services** Lift **Parking** 52 **Notes** LB ⊗ Civ Wed 180

B

BUCKINGHAM continued

BEST WESTERN Buckingham Hotel

★★★ 76% HOTEL

tel: 01280 822622 **Buckingham Ring Rd MK18 1RY**
email: info@thebuckinghamhotel.co.uk **web:** www.thebuckinghamhotel.co.uk
dir: A421 to Buckingham, take ring road S towards Brackley & Bicester. Hotel on left

A purpose-built hotel, which offers comfortable and spacious rooms with well designed working spaces for business travellers. There are also extensive conference facilities. The open-plan restaurant and bar offer a good range of dishes, and the well-equipped leisure suite is popular with guests.

Rooms 70 (6 fmly) (31 GF) **Facilities** STV FTV WiFi ⌦ ⌖ supervised Gym Sauna Steam room Xmas New Year **Conf** Class 60 Board 60 Thtr 200 **Parking** 200 **Notes** Civ Wed 120

BUCKLAND (NEAR BROADWAY)   Map 10 SP03
Gloucestershire

INSPECTORS CHOICE

Buckland Manor

★★★★ ◉◉◉ COUNTRY HOUSE HOTEL

tel: 01386 852626 **WR12 7LY**
email: info@bucklandmanor.co.uk **web:** www.bucklandmanor.co.uk
dir: 2m S of Broadway, off B4632

Buckland Manor is a grand 13th-century manor house, surrounded by well-kept and beautiful gardens that feature a stream and waterfall. Everything at this hotel is geared to encourage rest and relaxation. Spacious bedrooms and public areas are furnished with high quality pieces and decorated in keeping with the style of the manor; crackling log fires warm the wonderful lounges. The elegant dining room, with views over the rolling hills, is the perfect place to enjoy dishes that use excellent local produce.

Rooms 13 (1 fmly) (4 GF) ⌖ **S** £190-£555; **D** £210-£575 (incl. bkfst)* **Facilities** FTV WiFi ⌖ Putt green ⌖ Xmas New Year **Conf** Board 10 Thtr 30 **Parking** 20 **Notes** LB ⊗ No children 12yrs Civ Wed 40

BUDE   Map 2 SS20
Cornwall

Falcon Hotel

★★★ 80% HOTEL

tel: 01288 352005 **Breakwater Rd EX23 8SD**
email: reception@falconhotel.com **web:** www.falconhotel.com
dir: Exit A39 to Bude, then Widemouth Bay. Hotel on right over canal bridge

Dating back to 1798, this long-established hotel boasts delightful walled gardens, ideal for afternoon teas. Bedrooms offer high standards of comfort and quality; there is also a four-poster room complete with spa bath. A choice of menus is offered in the elegant restaurant and the friendly bar. The hotel has an impressive function room.

Rooms 29 (7 fmly) ⌖ **Facilities** STV FTV WiFi ⌦ ⌖ ♫ New Year **Conf** Class 50 Board 50 Thtr 200 **Services** Lift **Parking** 40 **Notes** ⊗ RS 25 Dec Civ Wed 160

The Cliff Hotel at Bude

★★ 76% HOTEL

tel: 01288 353110 **Maer Down, Crooklets Beach EX23 8NG**
email: cliff_hotel@btconnect.com **web:** www.cliffhotel.co.uk
dir: A39 through Bude, left at top of High St, pass Sainsburys, 1st right between golf course, over x-rds, premises at end on right

Overlooking the sea from a clifftop location, this friendly and efficient establishment provides spacious, well-equipped bedrooms. The various public areas include a bar and lounge, as well as an impressive range of leisure facilities. Delicious dinners and tasty breakfasts are available in the attractive dining room.

Rooms 15 (15 fmly) (8 GF) **Facilities** FTV WiFi ⌖ ⌖ Putt green Gym **Parking** 25 **Notes** Closed Nov-Mar

Hotel Penarvor

★★ 75% SMALL HOTEL

tel: 01288 352036 **Crooklets Beach EX23 8NE**
email: stay@hotelpenarvor.co.uk **web:** www.hotelpenarvor.co.uk
dir: A39 towards Bude for 1.5m. At 2nd rdbt turn right, pass shops. Top of hill, left signed Crooklets Beach

Adjacent to the golf course and overlooking Crooklets Beach, this family-owned hotel has a relaxed and friendly atmosphere. Bedrooms vary in size but are all equipped to a similar standard. An interesting selection of dishes, using fresh local produce is available in the restaurant, and bar meals are also provided.

Rooms 16 (6 fmly) (3 GF) ⌖ **Facilities** FTV WiFi **Parking** 20 **Notes** Closed 24-28 Dec

Find out more about Hotel Bathrooms in our feature on page 26

B

BURFORD
Oxfordshire
Map 5 SP21

The Bay Tree Hotel

COTSWOLD
INNS & HOTELS

★★★★ 73% HOTEL

tel: 01993 822791 **Sheep St OX18 4LW**
email: info@baytreehotel.info **web:** www.cotswold-inns-hotels.co.uk/bay-tree
dir: A40 or A361 to Burford. From High St turn into Sheep St, next to old market square. Hotel on right

The modern decorative style combines seamlessly with features from this delightful inn's long history. Bedrooms are tastefully furnished and some have four-poster or half-tester beds. Public areas consist of a character bar, a sophisticated airy restaurant, a selection of meeting rooms and an attractive walled garden.

Rooms 21 (13 annexe) (2 fmly) (3 GF) **S** £160-£170; **D** £180-£190 (incl. bkfst)*
Facilities WiFi ⛲ Xmas New Year **Conf** Class 12 Board 25 Thtr 40 **Parking** 50
Notes LB Civ Wed 90

The Lamb Inn

COTSWOLD
INNS & HOTELS

★★★ 87% SMALL HOTEL

tel: 01993 823155 **Sheep St OX18 4LR**
email: info@lambinn-burford.co.uk **web:** www.cotswold-inns-hotels.co.uk/lamb
dir: A40 into Burford, downhill, 1st left into Sheep St, hotel last on right

This enchanting old inn is just a short walk from the centre of this delightful Cotswold village. An abundance of character and charm is found in the cosy lounge with log fire, and intimate bar with flagged floors. An elegant restaurant offers locally sourced produce in carefully prepared dishes. Bedrooms, some with original features, are comfortable and well appointed.

Rooms 17 (1 fmly) (4 GF) **S** £150-£170; **D** £160-£180 (incl. bkfst)* **Facilities** WiFi Xmas New Year **Notes** LB

BURGESS HILL
West Sussex
Map 6 TQ31

Premier Inn Burgess Hill

Premier Inn

BUDGET HOTEL

tel: 0871 527 8172 **Charles Av RH15 9AG**
web: www.premierinn.com
dir: M25 junct 7, M23, A23. Left at Burgess Hill follow A2300 signs. At rdbt 2nd exit onto A2300. At next rdbt 4th exit onto A273, straight on at next 2 rdbts, at 3rd rdbt (Tesco) 1st left. Hotel 2nd left

High quality, budget accommodation ideal for both families and business travellers. Spacious, en suite bedrooms feature tea and coffee making facilities, and Freeview TV in most hotels. Internet access and WiFi are available for a small fee. The adjacent family restaurant features a wide and varied menu. See also the Hotel Groups pages.

Rooms 60

BURLEY
Hampshire
Map 5 SU20

Moorhill House Hotel

NEW FOREST HOTELS

★★★ 81% COUNTRY HOUSE HOTEL

tel: 01425 403285 & 0800 444 441 **BH24 4AH**
email: moorhill@newforesthotels.co.uk **web:** www.newforesthotels.co.uk
dir: M27, A31, follow signs to Burley, through village, up hill, right opposite school & cricket grounds

Situated deep in the heart of the New Forest and formerly a grand gentleman's residence, this charming hotel offers a relaxed and friendly environment. Bedrooms, which come in varying sizes, are smartly decorated. A range of facilities is provided and guests can relax by walking around the extensive grounds. Both dinner and breakfast offer a choice of interesting and freshly prepared dishes.

Rooms 31 (13 fmly) (3 GF) 🐾 **Facilities** FTV WiFi ⛲ HL ⛲ ⛲ Badminton (Apr-Sep) Sauna Xmas New Year **Conf** Class 60 Board 65 Thtr 120 **Parking** 50
Notes Civ Wed 90

BURNHAM
Buckinghamshire
Map 6 SU98

Burnham Beeches Hotel

corus hotels

★★★★ 76% HOTEL

tel: 0844 736 8603 **Grove Rd SL1 8DP**
email: sales.burnhambeeches@corushotels.com
web: www.corushotels.com/burnham-beeches
dir: M40 junct 2, A355 towards Slough, right at 2nd rdbt, 1st right to Grove Rd

Set in attractive mature grounds on the fringes of woodland, this extended Georgian manor house has spacious, comfortable and well-equipped bedrooms. Public rooms include a cosy lounge/bar offering all-day snacks and an elegant wood-panelled restaurant that serves interesting cuisine; there are also conference facilities, a fitness centre and pool.

Rooms 82 (22 fmly) (12 GF) 🐾 **Facilities** FTV WiFi ⛲ ⛲ ⛲ Gym Beauty treatment room Xmas New Year **Conf** Class 80 Board 60 Thtr 150 **Services** Lift **Parking** 150
Notes ⊗ Civ Wed 120

The Grovefield House Hotel

CLASSIC LODGES

★★★★ 73% HOTEL

tel: 08446 932960 **Taplow Common Rd SL1 8LP**
email: info.grovefield@classiclodges.co.uk
web: www.classiclodges.co.uk/Grovefield_House_Hotel_Windsor
dir: M4 junct 7, A4 towards Maidenhead. Next rdbt right under rail bridge. Straight over mini rdbt, garage on right. 1.5m, hotel on right

Set in its own spacious grounds, the Grovefield is conveniently located for Heathrow Airport as well as Slough and Maidenhead. Accommodation is spacious and well presented and most rooms have views over the attractive gardens. Public areas include a range of meeting rooms, a comfortable bar/lounge area and Hamilton's restaurant.

Rooms 40 (5 fmly) (7 GF) **Facilities** FTV WiFi ⛲ Putt green Fishing ⛲ Xmas New Year **Conf** Class 80 Board 80 Thtr 180 **Services** Lift **Parking** 155 **Notes** Civ Wed 150

BURNHAM MARKET
Norfolk   Map 13 TF84

The Hoste

★★★★ 79% ◉◉ HOTEL

tel: 01328 738777 **The Green PE31 8HD**
email: reservations@thehoste.com **web:** www.thehoste.com
dir: Signed on B1155, 5m W of Wells-next-the-Sea

A stylish, privately-owned inn situated in the heart of a bustling village close to the north Norfolk coast. The extensive public rooms feature a range of dining areas that include a conservatory with plush furniture, a sunny patio and a traditional pub. The tastefully furnished and thoughtfully equipped bedrooms are generally very spacious and offer a high degree of comfort.

Rooms 37 (7 GF) ⚡ **S** £110–£220; **D** £130–£240 (incl. bkfst)* **Facilities** Spa STV WiFi Beauty treatment rooms Xmas New Year **Conf** Class 40 Board 16 Thtr 25 **Services** Air con **Parking** 45 **Notes** RS 25 & 31 Dec

See advert on opposite page

BURNLEY
Lancashire   Map 18 SD83

Premier Inn Burnley

BUDGET HOTEL

tel: 0871 527 8174 **Queen Victoria Rd BB10 3EF**
web: www.premierinn.com
dir: M65 junct 12, 5th exit at rdbt, 1st exit at rdbt, keep in right lane at lights, 2nd exit at next rdbt, 3rd at next rdbt, under bridge, left before football ground

High quality, budget accommodation ideal for both families and business travellers. Spacious, en suite bedrooms feature tea and coffee making facilities, and Freeview TV in most hotels. Internet access and WiFi are available for a small fee. The adjacent family restaurant features a wide and varied menu. See also the Hotel Groups pages.

Rooms 43

BURNSALL
North Yorkshire   Map 19 SE06

The Devonshire Fell

◉◉ RESTAURANT WITH ROOMS

tel: 01756 729000 & 718111 📄 01756 729009 **BD23 6BT**
email: manager@devonshirefell.co.uk **web:** www.devonshirefell.co.uk
dir: On B6160, 6m from Bolton Abbey rdbt, A59 junct

Located on the edge of the attractive village of Burnsall, this establishment offers comfortable, well-equipped accommodation in a relaxing atmosphere. There is an extensive menu featuring local produce, and meals can be taken either in the bar area or the more formal restaurant. A function room with views over the valley is also available.

Rooms 12 (2 fmly)

BURRINGTON (NEAR PORTSMOUTH ARMS STATION)
Devon   Map 3 SS61

INSPECTORS' CHOICE

Northcote Manor

★★★ ◉◉ COUNTRY HOUSE HOTEL

tel: 01769 560501 **EX37 9LZ**
email: rest@northcotemanor.co.uk **web:** www.northcotemanor.co.uk
dir: From A377 opposite Portsmouth Arms, into hotel drive (NB do not enter Burrington village

A warm and friendly welcome is assured at this beautiful country-house hotel, built in 1716 and surrounded by 20 acres of grounds and woodlands. Guests can enjoy wonderful views over the Taw River Valley while relaxing in the delightful environment created by the attentive staff. A meal in either the intimate, more formal Manor House Restaurant or the Walled Garden Restaurant will prove a highlight; both offer menus of the finest local produce used in well-prepared dishes. Bedrooms, including some suites, are individually styled, spacious and well appointed.

Rooms 16 (2 fmly) (3 GF) ⚡ **S** £155–£215; **D** £260–£340 (incl. bkfst & dinner) **Facilities** FTV WiFi 🏊 ⛳ Xmas New Year **Conf** Class 50 Board 30 Thtr 80 Del £170 **Parking** 50 **Notes** Civ Wed 100

BURTON UPON TRENT
Staffordshire

Map 10 SK22

Mercure Burton Upon Trent Newton Park

★★★★ 71% COUNTRY HOUSE HOTEL

tel: 0844 815 9018 **Newton Solney DE15 0SS**
email: info@mercureburton.co.uk **web:** www.jupiterhotels.co.uk
dir: On B5008 past Repton to Newton Solney. Hotel on left

Standing in eight acres of grounds, this Grade II listed 18th-century Italian-style country house manor provides comfort in elegant surroundings. The well-equipped bedrooms are suitable for both business and leisure guests. The oak-panelled restaurant serves a good choice of dishes and overlooks the landscaped gardens. Eight fully-equipped meeting rooms are available.

Rooms 50 (3 fmly) (5 GF) ⟡ **Facilities** STV FTV WiFi ⟁ Gym **Conf** Class 70 Board 60 Thtr 100 Del from £110 to £175* **Services** Lift **Parking** 60 **Notes** Civ Wed 100

Holiday Inn Express Burton upon Trent

BUDGET HOTEL

tel: 01283 504300 **2nd Av, Centrum 100 DE14 2WF**
email: reservations@exhiburton.co.uk **web:** www.exhiburton.co.uk
dir: From A38 Branston exit take A5121 signed Town Centre. At McDonalds rdbt, turn left into 2nd Avenue. Hotel on left

A modern hotel ideal for families and business travellers. Fresh and uncomplicated, the spacious rooms include Sky TV, power shower and tea and coffee-making facilities. Continental buffet breakfast is included in the room rate; other meals may be taken at the nearby family pub or restaurant. See also the Hotel Groups pages.

Rooms 82 (47 fmly) (14 GF) ⟡ **S** £55-£99; **D** £55-£99 (incl. bkfst)* **Conf** Class 30 Board 25 Thtr 60 Del from £90 to £120*

Premier Inn Burton upon Trent Central

BUDGET HOTEL

tel: 0871 527 9280 **Wellington Rd DE14 2WD**
web: www.premierinn.com
dir: Exit A38 at Branston junction onto A5121 to Burton on Trent. Straight on at lights. At rdbt take 3rd exit, hotel on left

High quality, budget accommodation ideal for both families and business travellers. Spacious, en suite bedrooms feature tea and coffee making facilities, and Freeview TV in most hotels. Internet access and WiFi are available for a small fee. The adjacent family restaurant features a wide and varied menu. See also the Hotel Groups pages.

Rooms 64

Premier Inn Burton upon Trent East

BUDGET HOTEL

tel: 0871 527 8176 **Ashby Road East DE15 0PU**
web: www.premierinn.com
dir: 2m E of Burton upon Trent on A50

Rooms 34

BURY
Greater Manchester

Map 15 SD81

Red Hall Hotel

★★★ 80% HOTEL

tel: 01706 822476 **Manchester Rd, Walmersley BL9 5NA**
email: info@red-hall.co.uk **web:** www.red-hall.co.uk
dir: M66 junct 1, A56. Over motorway bridge, hotel approx 300mtrs on right

Originally a farmhouse, this hotel, located in the picturesque village of Warmersley on the outskirts of Ramsbottom, is just off the M66, making it ideal for business and leisure guests alike. Bedrooms are contemporary and well equipped. There is a restaurant and lounge bar, plus meeting and event facilities.

Rooms 37 (2 fmly) (18 GF) ⟡ **Facilities** STV WiFi Xmas New Year **Conf** Class 60 Board 30 Thtr 140 **Services** Lift **Parking** 100 **Notes** Civ Wed

B

BURY *continued*

Premier Inn Bury

BUDGET HOTEL

tel: 0871 527 9294 **5 Knowsley Place, Duke St BL9 0EJ**
web: www.premierinn.com
dir: M66 junct 2, A58 towards Bolton & Bury. At rdbt in Bury centre follow A58 (Angouleme Way). Left in Knowsley St, hotel on left

High quality, budget accommodation ideal for both families and business travellers. Spacious, en suite bedrooms feature tea and coffee making facilities, and Freeview TV in most hotels. Internet access and WiFi are available for a small fee. The adjacent family restaurant features a wide and varied menu. See also the Hotel Groups pages.

Rooms 115

BURY ST EDMUNDS
Suffolk   Map 13 TL86

The Angel Hotel

★★★★ 86% TOWN HOUSE HOTEL

tel: 01284 714000 **Angel Hill IP33 1LT**
email: staying@theangel.co.uk **web:** www.theangel.co.uk
dir: From A134, left at rdbt into Northgate St. Continue to lights, right into Mustow St, left into Angel Hill. Hotel on right

The Angel Hotel is an impressive building situated just a short walk from the town centre. One of the hotel's more notable guests over the last 400 years was Charles Dickens, who is reputed to have written part of *The Pickwick Papers* while in residence. The hotel offers a range of individually designed bedrooms that include a selection of four-poster rooms and a suite.

Rooms 78 (5 fmly) (22 GF) ✿ **S** £90–£325; **D** £110–£340 (incl. bkfst)* **Facilities** FTV WiFi **Conf** Class 16 Board 16 Thtr 22 Del £150* **Services** Lift **Parking** 20

BEST WESTERN Priory Hotel

★★★ 82% HOTEL

tel: 01284 766181 **Mildenhall Rd IP32 6EH**
email: reservations@prioryhotel.co.uk **web:** www.prioryhotel.co.uk
dir: From A14 (junct 43) take Bury St Edmunds W slip road. Follow signs to Brandon. At mini-rdbt turn right. Hotel 0.5m on left

Priory Hotel is an 18th-century Grade II listed building set in landscaped grounds on the outskirts of town. The attractively decorated, tastefully furnished and thoughtfully equipped bedrooms are split between the main house and garden wings, which have their own sun terraces. Public rooms feature a smart restaurant, a conservatory dining room and a lounge bar.

Rooms 36 (29 annexe) (1 fmly) (30 GF) ✿ **Facilities** FTV WiFi Xmas New Year **Conf** Class 24 Board 30 Thtr 75 Del from £138 to £142* **Parking** 60 **Notes** Civ Wed 75

The Grange Hotel

★★★ 77%  COUNTRY HOUSE HOTEL

tel: 01359 231260 **Barton Rd, Thurston IP31 3PQ**
email: info@grangecountryhotel.com **web:** www.grangecountryhousehotel.com
dir: A14 junct 45 towards Gt Barton, right at T-junct. At x-rds left into Barton Rd to Thurston. At rdbt, left after 0.5m, hotel on right

A Tudor-style country-house hotel situated on the outskirts of town. The individually decorated bedrooms have co-ordinated fabrics and many thoughtful touches; some

---

rooms have nice views of the gardens. Public areas include a smart lounge bar, two private dining rooms, the Garden Restaurant and banqueting facilities.

Rooms 18 (5 annexe) (1 fmly) (3 GF) ✿ **Facilities** FTV WiFi Beauty treatment room Xmas New Year **Conf** Class 40 Board 30 Thtr 135 Del from £102.50 to £142.50* **Parking** 100 **Notes** Civ Wed 150

BUXTON
Derbyshire   Map 16 SK07

The Palace Hotel

★★★★ 71% HOTEL

tel: 01298 22001 **Palace Rd SK17 6AG**
email: palace@pumahotels.co.uk **web:** www.pumahotels.co.uk
dir: M6 junct 20, follow M56/M60 signs to Stockport then A6 to Buxton, hotel adjacent to railway station

This impressive Victorian hotel is located on the hill overlooking the town. Public areas are traditional and elegant in style, and include chandeliers and decorative ceilings. The bedrooms are spacious and equipped with modern facilities, and The Dovedale Restaurant provides modern British cuisine. Good leisure facilities are available.

Rooms 122 (18 fmly) **S** £60–£130; **D** £60–£130* **Facilities** Spa WiFi ⊗ supervised Gym Beauty facilities Xmas New Year **Conf** Class 125 Board 80 Thtr 350 Del from £100 to £180* **Services** Lift **Parking** 180 **Notes** LB Civ Wed 100

BEST WESTERN Lee Wood Hotel

★★★ 82%  HOTEL

tel: 01298 23002 **The Park SK17 6TQ**
email: reservations@leewoodhotel.co.uk **web:** www.leewoodhotel.co.uk
dir: From town centre take A5004 NE, hotel 150mtrs beyond University of Derby (Buxton Campus)

This elegant Georgian hotel offers high standards of comfort and hospitality. The individually furnished bedrooms are generally spacious, with all of the expected modern conveniences. There is a choice of two comfortable lounges and a conservatory restaurant. The quality cooking, good service and fine hospitality are noteworthy.

Rooms 39 (5 annexe) (4 fmly) **Facilities** STV FTV WiFi ↘ Gym Serenity beauty & wellbeing New Year **Conf** Class 65 Board 40 Thtr 120 **Services** Lift **Parking** 50 **Notes** Civ Wed 120

CADNAM
Hampshire   Map 5 SU31

Bartley Lodge Hotel

★★★ 85%  HOTEL

tel: 023 8081 2248 & 0800 444 441 **Lyndhurst Rd SO40 2NR**
email: bartley@newforesthotels.co.uk **web:** www.newforesthotels.co.uk
dir: M27 junct 1 at 1st rdbt 1st exit, at 2nd rdbt 3rd exit onto A337. Hotel sign on left

This 18th-century former hunting lodge is very quietly situated, yet is just minutes from the M27. Bedrooms vary in size but all are well equipped. There is a selection of small lounge areas, a cosy bar and an indoor pool, together with a small fitness suite. The Crystal dining room offers a tempting choice of well prepared dishes.

Rooms 40 (15 fmly) (4 GF) ✿ **Facilities** FTV WiFi ↘ HL ⊗ ⟿ Sauna Xmas New Year **Conf** Class 60 Board 60 Thtr 120 **Services** Lift **Parking** 60 **Notes** Civ Wed 100

CAMBERLEY
Surrey   Map 6 SU86

See also **Yateley**

Macdonald Frimley Hall Hotel & Spa

★★★★ 80% HOTEL

tel: 0844 879 9110 **Lime Av GU15 2BG**
email: sales.frimleyhall@macdonald-hotels.co.uk
web: www.macdonaldhotels.co.uk/frimleyhall
dir: M3 junct 3, A321 follow Bagshot signs. Through lights, left onto A30 signed Camberley & Basingstoke. To rdbt, 2nd exit onto A325, take 5th right

The epitomé of classic English elegance, Macdonald Frimley Hall Hotel is an ivy-clad Victorian manor house set in two acres of immaculate grounds in the heart of Surrey. The bedrooms and public areas are smart and have a modern decorative theme. The hotel boasts an impressive health club and spa with treatment rooms, a fully equipped gym and heated indoor swimming pool.

Rooms 98 (15 fmly) **Facilities** Spa FTV WiFi HL Gym Technogym Sauna Steam room Relaxation room Xmas New Year **Conf** Class 100 Board 60 Thtr 250 **Parking** 150 **Notes** Civ Wed 220

Lakeside International

★★★ 73% HOTEL

tel: 01252 838000 **Wharf Rd, Frimley Green GU16 6JR**
email: info@lakesideinthotel.com **web:** www.lakesideinternationalhotel.com
dir: Exit A321 at mini-rdbt turn into Wharf Rd. Lakeside complex on right

This hotel, geared towards the business market, enjoys a lakeside location with noteworthy views. Bedrooms are modern, comfortable and with a range of facilities. Public areas are spacious and include a residents' lounge, bar, games room, a smart restaurant and an established health and leisure club.

Rooms 98 (1 fmly) (31 GF) **Facilities** FTV WiFi Gym Squash Sauna Steam room **Conf** Class 100 Board 40 Thtr 120 **Services** Lift **Parking** 250 **Notes** Civ Wed 100

The Ely

★★★ 71% HOTEL

tel: 01252 860444 **London Road (A30), Blackwater GU17 9LJ**
email: 5249@greeneking.co.uk **web:** www.oldenglish.co.uk
dir: M3 junct 4A, A327 towards Yateley. Right onto A30

This establishment benefits from being conveniently located close to Camberley and the M3. Bedrooms are particularly spacious and families are well catered for. A variety of enjoyable, substantial dishes is available throughout the day with the addition of a specials board in the evening. The range of options at breakfast is impressive. There is ample free parking on site and free WiFi throughout the hotel.

Rooms 35 **Facilities** WiFi **Conf** Class 30 Board 40 Thtr 80 **Parking** 50

Premier Inn Camberley

BUDGET HOTEL

tel: 0871 527 9322 **Park St GU15 3SG**
web: www.premierinn.com
dir: M3 junct 4, A331 towards Camberley. In 2m, at major junct into right lane, 4th exit signed A30. For parking, in 1m, right into Southern Rd for Atrium Car Park

High quality, budget accommodation ideal for both families and business travellers. Spacious, en suite bedrooms feature tea and coffee making facilities,

and Freeview TV in most hotels. Internet access and WiFi are available for a small fee. The adjacent family restaurant features a wide and varied menu. See also the Hotel Groups pages.

Rooms 95

Premier Inn Sandhurst

BUDGET HOTEL

tel: 0871 527 8958 **221 Yorktown Rd, College Town, Sandurst GU47 0RT**
web: www.premierinn.com
dir: M3 junct 4, A331 to Camberley. At large rdbt take A321 towards Bracknell. At 3rd lights, hotel on left

Rooms 40

CAMBORNE
Cornwall   Map 2 SW63

Premier Inn Camborne

BUDGET HOTEL

tel: 0871 527 9308 **Treswithian Rd TR14 7NF**
web: www.premierinn.com
dir: From M5 (S) junct 31, A30 to Bodmin, then to Redruth, follow signs to Camborne. Left onto A3047, to rdbt, 1st exit to hotel

High quality, budget accommodation ideal for both families and business travellers. Spacious, en suite bedrooms feature tea and coffee making facilities, and Freeview TV in most hotels. Internet access and WiFi are available for a small fee. The adjacent family restaurant features a wide and varied menu. See also the Hotel Groups pages.

Rooms 65

CAMBOURNE
Cambridgeshire   Map 12 TL35

The Cambridge Belfry

★★★★ 81% HOTEL

tel: 01954 714600 **Back St CB23 6BW**
email: cambridgebelfry@qhotels.co.uk **web:** www.qhotels.co.uk
dir: M11 junct 13, A428 towards Bedford, follow signs to Cambourne. Exit at Cambourne, keep left. Left at rdbt, hotel on left

This exciting hotel, built beside the water, is located at the gateway to Cambourne Village and Business Park. Contemporary in style throughout, the hotel boasts state-of-the-art leisure facilities, including Reflections Spa offering a range of therapies and treatments, and extensive conference and banqueting rooms. There are two eating options - the Bridge Restaurant and the Brooks Brasserie. Original artwork is displayed throughout the hotel. QHotels is the AA Hotel Group of the Year 2014-15.

Rooms 120 (30 GF) **Facilities** Spa FTV WiFi HL Gym Beauty treatments Fitness classes Xmas New Year **Conf** Class 70 Board 70 Thtr 250 Del from £135 to £165* **Services** Lift **Parking** 200 **Notes** Civ Wed 130

C

Hotel Felix

★★★★ 82% 🌹🌹 HOTEL

tel: 01223 277977 **Whitehouse Ln CB3 0LX**
email: help@hotelfelix.co.uk **web:** www.hotelfelix.co.uk
dir: M11 junct 13. From A1 N, take A14 onto A1307. At 'City of Cambridge' sign left into Whitehouse Ln

A beautiful Victorian mansion set amidst three acres of landscaped gardens, this property was originally built in 1852 for a surgeon from the famous Addenbrookes Hospital. The contemporary-style bedrooms have carefully chosen furniture and many thoughtful touches, whilst public rooms feature an open-plan bar, the adjacent Graffiti restaurant and a small quiet lounge.

Rooms 52 (5 fmly) (26 GF) 🐾 **Facilities** STV WiFi ↘ Xmas New Year **Conf** Class 36 Board 34 Thtr 60 **Services** Lift **Parking** 90 **Notes** Civ Wed 60

Hotel du Vin Cambridge

★★★★ 77% 🌹 TOWN HOUSE HOTEL

tel: 01223 227330 & 08447 364 253 **15-19 Trumpington St CB2 1QA**
email: info.cambridge@hotelduvin.com **web:** www.hotelduvin.com
dir: M11 junct 11 Cambridge S, pass Trumpington Park & Ride on left. Hotel 2m on right after double rdbt

This beautiful building, which dates back in part to medieval times, has been transformed to enhance its many quirky architectural features. The bedrooms and suites, some with private terraces, have the company's trademark monsoon showers and Egyptian linen. The French-style bistro has an open-style kitchen and the bar is set in the unusual labyrinth of vaulted cellar rooms. There is also a library, specialist wine tasting room and private dining room.

Rooms 41 (3 annexe) (6 GF) **D** £169-£419* **Facilities** STV WiFi Xmas New Year **Conf** Class 18 Board 18 Thtr 30 Del from £239 to £349* **Services** Lift Air con **Parking** 24

Menzies Hotels Cambridge

★★★★ 77% 🌹 HOTEL

tel: 01954 249988 **Bar Hill CB23 8EU**
email: cambridge@menzieshotels.co.uk **web:** www.menzieshotels.co.uk
dir: M11 junct 13, A14, follow signs for Huntingdon. Take B1050 (Bar Hill), hotel 1st exit on rdbt

The Menzies Cambridge Hotel is ideally situated amidst 200 acres of open countryside, just five miles from the university city of Cambridge. Public rooms include a brasserie restaurant and the popular Gallery Bar. The contemporary-style bedrooms are smartly decorated and equipped with a good range of useful facilities. The hotel also has a leisure club, swimming pool and golf course.

Rooms 136 (35 fmly) (68 GF) (4 smoking) **S** £69-£169; **D** £69-£169 **Facilities** STV FTV WiFi ↘ HL 🏊 ⚘ 18 ⛳ Putt green Gym Hair & beauty salon Steam room Sauna Xmas New Year **Conf** Class 90 Board 45 Thtr 220 Del from £99 to £219 **Services** Lift **Parking** 200 **Notes** LB Civ Wed 200

BEST WESTERN PLUS The Gonville Hotel

★★★★ 76% HOTEL

tel: 01223 366611 & 221111 **Gonville Place CB1 1LY**
email: all@gonvillehotel.co.uk **web:** www.gonvillehotel.co.uk
dir: M11 junct 11, on A1309 follow city centre signs. At 2nd mini rdbt right into Lensfield Rd, over junct with lights. Hotel 25yds on right

This is a well-established hotel situated on the inner ring road, a short walk across the green from the city centre. The air-conditioned public areas are cheerfully furnished, and include a lounge bar and brasserie. Bedrooms are well appointed and appealing, offering a good range of facilities for both corporate and leisure guests.

Rooms 84 (2 fmly) (8 GF) 🐾 **Facilities** FTV WiFi ↘ HL New Year **Conf** Class 30 Board 30 Thtr 50 **Services** Lift Air con **Parking** 80 **Notes** RS 24-29 Dec

The Varsity Hotel & Spa

★★★★ 75% HOTEL

tel: 01223 306030 **Thompson's Ln CB5 8AQ**
email: info@thevarsityhotel.co.uk **web:** www.thevarsityhotel.co.uk
dir: M11 junct 13, pass Park & Ride, next rdbt 1st left, right at next junct into Bridge St, right into Thompou's Lane

Situated close to the River Cam and occupying a central location, The Varsity Hotel is a stylish property. The bedrooms are smartly decorated and have all the expected facilities including power showers, CD players and free internet access. The River Bar, to the side of the hotel, has a buzzing atmosphere and offers a range of popular dishes. The hotel has a health club and spa, and a roof top bar.

Rooms 48 (2 fmly) 🐾 **D** £139-£750 (incl. bkfst)* **Facilities** Spa FTV WiFi ↘ Gym Sauna Steam room Valet parking New Year **Conf** Class 40 Board 30 Thtr 60 **Services** Lift Air con **Notes** Civ Wed 60

C

BEST WESTERN PLUS Cambridge Quy Mill Hotel

★★★ 84% HOTEL

tel: 01223 293383 & 378110 **Church Rd, Stow Cum Quy CB25 9AF**
email: info@cambridgequymill.co.uk **web:** www.cambridgequymill.co.uk
dir: Exit A14 at junct 35, E of Cambridge, onto B1102 for 50yds. Entrance opposite church

Set in open countryside, this 19th-century former watermill is conveniently situated for access to Cambridge. Bedroom styles differ, yet each room is smartly appointed and brightly decorated; superior, spacious courtyard rooms are noteworthy. Well-designed public areas include several spacious bar/lounges, with a choice of casual and formal eating areas; service is both friendly and helpful. There is a smart leisure club with state-of-the-art equipment, as well as a health spa.

Rooms 51 (30 annexe) (1 fmly) (24 GF) 🐾 **Facilities** Spa FTV WiFi ♙ HL 🐾 Gym New Year **Conf** Class 30 Board 24 Thtr 80 **Parking** 90 **Notes** Closed 24-25 Dec RS 26 Dec Civ Wed 80

Holiday Inn Cambridge

★★★ 80% HOTEL

tel: 0871 942 9015 **Lakeview, Bridge Rd, Impington CB24 9PH**
email: reservations-cambridge@ihg.com **web:** www.hicambridgehotel.co.uk
dir: 2.5m N, on N side of rdbt junct A14 & B1049

A modern, purpose-built hotel conveniently situated just off the A14 junction, a short drive from the city centre. Public areas include a popular bar, the Junction Restaurant and a large open-plan lounge. Bedrooms come in a variety of styles and are suited to both business and leisure guests alike.

Rooms 161 (14 fmly) (75 GF) **Facilities** Spa STV WiFi ♙ HL 🐾 supervised Gym **Conf** Class 40 Board 45 Thtr 120 **Services** Air con **Parking** 175 **Notes** ⊗ Civ Wed 100

Arundel House Hotel

★★★ 79% HOTEL

tel: 01223 367701 **Chesterton Rd CB4 3AN**
email: info@arundelhousehotels.co.uk **web:** www.arundelhousehotels.co.uk
dir: In city centre on A1303

Overlooking the River Cam and enjoying views of open parkland, this popular and smart hotel was originally a row of townhouses dating from Victorian times. Bedrooms are attractive and have a special character. The smart public areas feature a conservatory for informal snacks, a spacious bar and an elegant restaurant for more serious dining.

Rooms 103 (22 annexe) (7 fmly) (14 GF) **S** £75-£125; **D** £95-£150 (incl. bkfst)* **Facilities** FTV WiFi ♙ New Year **Conf** Class 24 Board 22 Thtr 50 Del £145* **Parking** 70 **Notes** LB ⊗ Closed 25-26 Dec

The Lensfield Hotel

★★★ 79% METRO HOTEL

tel: 01223 355017 **53-57 Lensfield Rd CB2 1EN**
email: reservations@lensfieldhotel.co.uk **web:** www.lensfieldhotel.co.uk
dir: M11 juncts 11,12 or 13, follow signs to city centre. Access via Silver St, Trumpington St, left into Lensfield Rd

Located close to all the city's attractions, this constantly improving hotel provides a range of attractive bedrooms, equipped with thoughtful extras. Comprehensive breakfasts are taken in an elegant dining room and a comfortable bar and cosy foyer lounge are also available.

Rooms 38 (3 fmly) (4 GF) **S** £72-£135; **D** £110-£289 (incl. bkfst)* **Facilities** Spa STV FTV WiFi ♙ HL Gym **Services** Air con **Parking** 5 **Notes** LB ⊗ Closed last 2 wks in Dec-4 Jan

Centennial Hotel

★★★ 71% HOTEL

tel: 01223 314652 **63-71 Hills Rd CB2 1PG**
email: reception@centennialhotel.co.uk **web:** www.centennialhotel.co.uk
dir: M11 junct 11, A1309 to Cambridge. Right Into Brooklands Ave to end. Left, hotel 100yds on right

This friendly hotel is convenient for the railway station and town centre. Well-presented public areas include a welcoming lounge, a relaxing bar and restaurant on the lower-ground level. Bedrooms are generally spacious, well maintained and thoughtfully equipped with a good range of facilities; several rooms are available on the ground floor.

Rooms 39 (1 fmly) (7 GF) 🐾 **Facilities** FTV WiFi ♙ **Conf** Class 25 Board 25 Thtr 25 **Parking** 28 **Notes** ⊗ Closed 23 Dec-1 Jan

Ashley Hotel

★★ 81% METRO HOTEL

tel: 01223 350059 & 367701 **74-76 Chesterton Rd CB4 1ER**
email: info@arundelhousehotels.co.uk
web: www.arundelhousehotels.co.uk/ashleyhotel.html
dir: On city centre ring road

Expect a warm welcome at this delightful Victorian property situated just a short walk from the River Cam. The smartly decorated bedrooms are generally quite spacious and equipped with a good range of useful extras. Breakfast is served at individual tables in the smart lower ground floor dining room.

Rooms 16 (5 fmly) (5 GF) **S** £65-£95; **D** £75-£95 (incl. bkfst)* **Facilities** FTV WiFi ♙ **Parking** 12 **Notes** ⊗ Closed 24-26 Dec

Helen Hotel

★★ 80% METRO HOTEL

tel: 01223 246465 **167-169 Hills Rd CB2 2RJ**
email: enquiries@helenhotel.co.uk **web:** www.helenhotel.co.uk
dir: On A1307, 1.25m from city centre (south side). At Cherry-Hinton Rd junct, opposite Homerton College

This extremely well maintained, privately owned hotel is situated close to the city centre and a range of popular eateries. Public areas include a smart lounge bar with plush sofas and a cosy breakfast room. Bedrooms are pleasantly decorated with co-ordinated fabrics and have many thoughtful touches.

Rooms 19 (2 fmly) (2 GF) 🐾 **S** £57-£68; **D** £85 (incl. bkfst)* **Facilities** FTV WiFi HL **Parking** 12 **Notes** ⊗ Closed Xmas & New Year

CAMBRIDGE *continued*

Premier Inn Cambridge (A14 Jct 32)

BUDGET HOTEL

tel: 0871 527 8186 **Ring Fort Rd CB4 2GW**
web: www.premierinn.com
dir: A14 junct 32, follow B1049/city centre signs. At 1st lights left into Kings Hedges Rd, 2nd left into Ring Fort Rd

High quality, budget accommodation ideal for both families and business travellers. Spacious, en suite bedrooms feature tea and coffee making facilities, and Freeview TV in most hotels. Internet access and WiFi are available for a small fee. The adjacent family restaurant features a wide and varied menu. See also the Hotel Groups pages.

Rooms 154

| CANNOCK | Map 10 SJ91 |
| Staffordshire | |

Premier Inn Cannock (Orbital)

BUDGET HOTEL

tel: 0871 527 8190 **Eastern Way WS11 8XR**
web: www.premierinn.com
dir: N'bound: M6 (Toll) junct 7, A5. At rdbt 1st exit (A5), 4th exit onto A460, 1st exit. S'bound: (no access from M6 Toll). M6 junct 11, A460 signed Cannock. At next 2 rdbts take 3rd exit. At next rdbt 1st exit onto service road. Hotel adjacent to Orbital Brewers Fayre

High quality, budget accommodation ideal for both families and business travellers. Spacious, en suite bedrooms feature tea and coffee making facilities, and Freeview TV in most hotels. Internet access and WiFi are available for a small fee. The adjacent family restaurant features a wide and varied menu. See also the Hotel Groups pages.

Rooms 21

Premier Inn Cannock South

BUDGET HOTEL

tel: 0871 527 8192 **Watling St WS11 1SJ**
web: www.premierinn.com
dir: At junct of A5 & A460, 2m from M6 juncts 11 & 12

Rooms 60

| CANTERBURY | Map 7 TR15 |
| Kent | |

ABode Canterbury

★★★★ 82% HOTEL

tel: 01227 766266 & 826678 **High St CT1 2RX**
email: reservations@abodecanterbury.co.uk **web:** www.abodecanterbury.co.uk
dir: M2 junct 7. Follow Canterbury signs onto ringroad. At Wincheap rdbt turn into city. Left into Rosemary Ln, into Stour St. Hotel at end

ABode Canterbury is a stylish hotel set on Canterbury's main street. A range of well appointed bedrooms and suites are available, many retaining original features, all boasting modern facilities and smart en suites. A choice of dining options and bars include The Michael Caines Restaurant, a smart Champagne Bar, and the more relaxed and hip Old Brewery Tavern.

Rooms 72 (10 fmly) ♠ ✦ **S** £99-£500; **D** £99-£500 (incl. bkfst) **Facilities** STV WiFi ◊ Gym New Year **Conf** Class 48 Board 20 Thtr 140 Del from £155 to £175 **Services** Lift Air con **Parking** 14 **Notes** Civ Wed 100

BEST WESTERN Abbots Barton Hotel

★★★ 79% HOTEL

tel: 01227 760341 **New Dover Rd CT1 3DU**
email: info@abbotsbartonhotel.com **web:** www.abbotsbartonhotel.com
dir: Please phone for directions

Abbots Barton Hotel is in a central location, just a 10-minute walk from the City Centre, and benefits from two acres of gardens and on-site parking. Bedrooms are comfortably appointed throughout, traditional in style yet with all modern amenities including free WiFi and digital TV. The bar and restaurant are open daily, and there are good function facilities with a private bar and patio ideal for conference and weddings.

Rooms 53 (3 fmly) (6 GF) **S** £60-£115; **D** £75-£135* **Facilities** FTV WiFi Xmas **Conf** Class 70 Board 70 Thtr 180 Del from £79 to £129* **Services** Lift Air con **Notes** LB Civ Wed 80

Castle House

★★★ 73% METRO HOTEL

tel: 01227 761897 **28 Castle St CT1 2PT**
dir: Next to Canterbury Castle

Conveniently located in the city centre opposite the imposing ruins of the ancient Norman castle; part of the building dates back to the 1730s. Bedrooms are spacious, all with en suite facilities and many useful extras, such as WiFi. There is a walled garden in which to relax during the warmer months.

Rooms 15

Premier Inn Canterbury City Centre

BUDGET HOTEL

tel: 0871 527 9408 **New Dover Rd CT1 1UP**
web: www.premierinn.com
dir: M2 junction 7. At Brenley Corner rdbt 4th exit onto A2. Left then merge onto A2050. At London Rd rdbt 2nd exit (A2050). At St Peters rdbt 3rd exit onto A290.At Wincheap rdbt 2nd exit onto A28. At St Georges rdbt 2nd exit onto A257. At lights right (A257). At lights right onto A2050. Hotel in view

High quality, budget accommodation ideal for both families and business travellers. Spacious, en suite bedrooms feature tea and coffee making facilities, and Freeview TV in most hotels. Internet access and WiFi are available for a small fee. The adjacent family restaurant features a wide and varied menu. See also the Hotel Groups pages.

Rooms 120

| CARBIS BAY |

See St Ives (Cornwall)

C

CARLISLE
Cumbria

Map 18 NY35

Crown Hotel

★★★★ 75%  HOTEL

tel: 01228 561888 **Station Rd, Wetheral CA4 8ES**
email: info@crownhotelwetheral.co.uk **web:** www.crownhotelwetheral.co.uk
dir: M6 junct 42, B6263 to Wetheral, right at village shop, car park at rear of hotel

Set in the attractive village of Wetheral, with landscaped gardens to the rear, this hotel is well suited to both business and leisure guests. Bedrooms vary in size and style and include two apartments in an adjacent house ideal for long stays. A choice of dining options is available, with the popular Waltons Bar an informal alternative to the main restaurant.

Rooms 51 (2 annexe) (10 fmly) (3 GF) ✎ **Facilities** Spa STV WiFi HL ⧖ supervised Gym Squash Children's splash pool Steam room Beauty room Sauna Dance studio Xmas New Year **Conf** Class 60 Board 65 Thtr 140 Del from £130 to £140 **Parking** 55 **Notes** Civ Wed 120

Hallmark Hotel Carlisle

★★★★ 74% HOTEL

tel: 01228 531951 & 633503 **Court Square CA1 1QY**
email: carlisle.reservations@hallmarkhotels.co.uk
web: www.hallmarkhotels.co.uk/carlisle
dir: M6 junct 43, to city centre, then follow road to left & railway station

This hotel is at the heart of the town, opposite the railway station. Most of the bedrooms have benefited from an investment programme, and the smart ground-floor areas include a popular bar and restaurant. A number of meeting rooms are available and at the rear of the hotel is a small car park.

Rooms 70 (3 fmly) ✎ **Facilities** FTV WiFi Xmas New Year **Conf** Class 100 Board 30 Thtr 240 **Services** Lift **Parking** 26 **Notes** ⊗ Civ Wed 200

The Crown & Mitre

★★★ 72% HOTEL

tel: 01228 525491 **4 English St CA3 8HZ**
email: info@crownandmitre-hotel-carlisle.com
web: www.crownandmitre-hotel-carlisle.com
dir: A6 to city centre, pass station on left. Turn left at end of English St, then immediate right onto Blackfriars St

Located in the heart of the city, this Edwardian hotel is close to the cathedral and a few minutes' walk from the castle. Bedrooms vary in size and style, from smart executive rooms to more functional standard rooms. Public rooms include a comfortable lounge area and the lovely bar with its feature stained-glass windows.

Rooms 95 (20 annexe) (4 fmly) ✎ **S** £60-£80; **D** £70-£105 (incl. bkfst)*
Facilities STV FTV WiFi ⧖ Xmas New Year **Conf** Class 250 Board 50 Thtr 400 Del from £99 to £130* **Services** Lift **Parking** 42 **Notes** Civ Wed 200

Ibis Carlisle

BUDGET HOTEL

tel: 01228 518000 **Portlands, Botchergate CA1 1RP**
email: H3443@accor.com **web:** www.ibis.com
dir: M6 junct 42/43 follow signs for city centre. Hotel on Botchergate

Modern, budget hotel offering comfortable accommodation in bright and practical bedrooms. Breakfast is self-service and dinner is available in the restaurant See also the Hotel Groups pages.

Rooms 102 (17 fmly) ✎

Premier Inn Carlisle Central

BUDGET HOTEL

tel: 0871 527 8210 **Warwick Rd CA1 2WF**
web: www.premierinn.com
dir: M6 junct 43, on A69

High quality, budget accommodation ideal for both families and business travellers. Spacious, en suite bedrooms feature tea and coffee making facilities, and Freeview TV in most hotels. Internet access and WiFi are available for a small fee. The adjacent family restaurant features a wide and varied menu. See also the Hotel Groups pages.

Rooms 44

Premier Inn Carlisle Central North

BUDGET HOTEL

tel: 0871 527 8212 **Kingstown Rd CA3 OAT**
web: www.premierinn.com
dir: M6 junct 44, A7 towards Carlisle, hotel 1m on left

Rooms 49

Premier Inn Carlisle (M6 Jct 42)

BUDGET HOTEL

tel: 0871 527 8206 **Carleton CA4 OAD**
web: www.premierinn.com
dir: Just off M6 junct 42, S of Carlisle

Rooms 61

CARLISLE *continued*

Premier Inn Carlisle (M6 Jct 44)

BUDGET HOTEL

tel: 0871 527 8208 **Parkhouse Rd CA3 0JR**
web: www.premierinn.com
dir: M6 junct 44, A7 signed Carlisle. Hotel on right at 1st set of lights

Rooms 127

CARTMEL	Map 18 SD37
Cumbria	

Aynsome Manor Hotel

★★★ 82% COUNTRY HOUSE HOTEL

tel: 015395 36653 **LA11 6HH**
email: aynsomemanor@btconnect.com **web:** www.aynsomemanorhotel.co.uk
dir: M6 junct 36, A590 signed Barrow-in-Furness towards Cartmel. Left at end of road, hotel before village

Dating back, in part, to the early 16th century, this manor house overlooks the fells and the nearby priory. Spacious bedrooms, including some courtyard rooms, are comfortably furnished. Dinner in the elegant restaurant features local produce whenever possible, and there is a choice of lounges to relax in.

Rooms 12 (2 annexe) (2 fmly) ⚓ **S** £80-£120; **D** £90-£125 (incl. bkfst) **Facilities** FTV WiFi New Year **Parking** 20 **Notes** LB Closed 2-31 Jan

---

INSPECTORS' CHOICE

L'enclume

⚜⚜⚜⚜⚜ RESTAURANT WITH ROOMS

tel: 015395 36362 **Cavendish St LA11 6PZ**
email: info@lenclume.co.uk **web:** www.lenclume.co.uk
dir: From A590 turn left for Cartmel before Newby Bridge

L'enclume is a delightful 13th-century property in the heart of a lovely village, and offers top notch 21st-century cooking that draws foodies from far and wide. Simon Rogan cooks imaginative and adventurous food in this stylish restaurant. Individually designed, modern, en suite rooms vary in size and style, and are either in the main property or dotted about the village only a few moments' walk from the restaurant.

Rooms 17 (11 annexe) (3 fmly)

CASTLE CARY	Map 4 ST63
Somerset	

The Pilgrims

⚜⚜ RESTAURANT WITH ROOMS

tel: 01963 240600 **Lovington BA7 7PT**
email: jools@thepilgrimsatlovington.co.uk **web:** www.thepilgrimsatlovington.co.uk
dir: On B3153, 1.5m E of lights on A37 at Lydford

The Pilgrims describes itself as 'the pub that thinks it's a restaurant', which is pretty accurate. With a real emphasis on fresh, local and carefully prepared produce, both dinner and breakfast are the focus of any stay here. In addition, the resident family proprietors provide a friendly and relaxed atmosphere. Comfortable and well-equipped bedrooms are available in the adjacent, converted cider barn.

Rooms 5 (5 annexe)

CASTLE COMBE	Map 4 ST87
Wiltshire	

The Manor House, an Exclusive Hotel & Golf Club

★★★★★ 83% COUNTRY HOUSE HOTEL

tel: 01249 782206 **SN14 7HR**
email: enquiries@manorhouse.co.uk **web:** www.manorhouse.co.uk
dir: M4 junct 17 follow Chippenham signs onto A420 Bristol, then right onto B4039. Through village, right after bridge. Useful to follow brown tourism signs to Castle Combe Racing Circuit

This delightful hotel is situated in a secluded valley adjacent to a picturesque village, where there have been no new buildings for 300 years. There are 365 acres of grounds to enjoy, complete with an Italian garden and an 18-hole golf course. Bedrooms, some in the main house and some in a row of stone cottages, have been superbly furnished, and public rooms include a number of cosy lounges with roaring fires. Service is a pleasing blend of professionalism and friendliness. The award-winning food utilises top quality local produce.

Rooms 48 (26 annexe) (8 fmly) (12 GF) ⚓ **S** £265-£650; **D** £265-£650 (incl. bkfst)* **Facilities** STV WiFi ⚒ 18 ⛳ Putt green Fishing 🚣 Jogging track Hot air ballooning Giant games on lawns Xmas New Year **Conf** Class 84 Board 40 Thtr 120 Del from £190* **Parking** 100 **Notes** LB Civ Wed 110

CASTLE DONINGTON	

See East Midlands Airport

CASTLEFORD	Map 16 SE42
West Yorkshire	

Premier Inn Castleford M62 Jct 31

BUDGET HOTEL

tel: 0871 527 8216 **Pioneer Way WF10 5TG**
web: www.premierinn.com
dir: M62 junct 31, A655 towards Castleford, right at 1st lights, then left

High quality, budget accommodation ideal for both families and business travellers. Spacious, en suite bedrooms feature tea and coffee making facilities, and Freeview TV in most hotels. Internet access and WiFi are available for a small fee. The adjacent family restaurant features a wide and varied menu. See also the Hotel Groups pages.

Rooms 62

C

Premier Inn Castleford M62 Jct 32

BUDGET HOTEL

tel: 0871 527 8218 **Colarado Way WF10 4TA**
web: www.premierinn.com
dir: M62 junct 32, follow signs for Xscape. Hotel adjacent to Xscape complex

Rooms 119

CAVENDISH	Map 13 TL84
Suffolk	

The George

◉◉ RESTAURANT WITH ROOMS

tel: 01787 280248 **The Green CO10 8BA**
email: thegeorgecavendish@gmail.com **web:** www.thecavendishgeorge.co.uk
dir: A1092 into Cavendish, The George next to village green

The George is situated in the heart of the pretty village of Cavendish and has five very stylish bedrooms. The front-facing rooms overlook the village; the comfortable, spacious bedrooms retain many of their original features. The award-winning restaurant is very well appointed and dinner should not be missed. Guests are guaranteed to receive a warm welcome, attentive friendly service and great food.

Rooms 5 (1 fmly)

CHADDESLEY CORBETT	Map 10 SO87
Worcestershire	

INSPECTORS' CHOICE

Brockencote Hall Country House Hotel

EDEN HOTEL COLLECTION

★★★★ ◉◉◉ COUNTRY HOUSE HOTEL

tel: 01562 777876 **DY10 4PY**
email: info@brockencotehall.com **web:** www.brockencotehall.com
dir: A38 to Bromsgrove, off A448 towards Kidderminster

Brockencote Hall Hotel is a Victorian country manor house hotel set in 70 acres of beautiful parkland, complete with a scenic lake, tennis courts and dovecote. It has been returned to its former glory with a sympathetic refurbishment. A fountain now adorns the approach, the terrace and gardens have been freshly landscaped and the new private dining rooms, restaurant and public areas are classically decorated in gentle greys, lavenders and damson velvets. Head Chef Adam Brown creates inspired dishes that revolve around the seasons and local suppliers, with a focus on the purity of flavours. Eden Hotel Collection is the AA Small Hotel Group of the Year 2014-15.

Rooms 21 (4 fmly) (5 GF) ↜ **S** £95-£345; (incl. bkfst) **Facilities** FTV WiFi ↺ ♨ Fishing ⌕ Xmas New Year **Conf** Class 35 Board 35 Thtr 80 Del from £195 to £215 **Parking** 60 **Notes** LB ⊗ Civ Wed 95

CHAGFORD	Map 3 SX78
Devon	

INSPECTORS' CHOICE

Gidleigh Park

GIDLEIGH COLLECTION

★★★★★ ◉◉◉◉◉ COUNTRY HOUSE HOTEL

tel: 01647 432367 **TQ13 8HH**
email: gidleighpark@gidleigh.co.uk **web:** www.gidleigh.com
dir: From Chagford, right at Lloyds Bank into Mill St. After 150yds fork right. 2m to end

Built in 1928 as a private residence for an Australian shipping magnate and set in 107 acres of lovingly tended grounds, this world-renowned hotel retains a timeless charm and a very endearing, homely atmosphere. The individually styled bedrooms are sumptuously furnished; some with separate seating areas, some with balconies and many enjoying panoramic views. There are spa suites, a loft suite which is ideal for families, and the stunning thatched Pavilion in the grounds. The latter has two bedrooms, two bathrooms, a lounge and kitchen diner. The spacious public areas feature antique furniture, beautiful flower arrangements and magnificent artwork. The award-winning cuisine created by Michael Caines, together with the top quality wine list, will make a stay here a truly memorable experience.

Rooms 24 (4 fmly) (4 GF) ↜ **S** £325-£1200; **D** £350-£1225 (incl. bkfst)*
Facilities STV FTV WiFi ♨ Putt green Fishing ⌕ Bowls Xmas New Year **Conf** Class 22 Board 18 Thtr 22 Del £500* **Parking** 45

C

CHARD
Somerset
Map 4 ST30

Cricket St Thomas Hotel
Warner Leisure Hotels
Life begins at Warner

★★★★ 75% COUNTRY HOUSE HOTEL

tel: 01460 30111 **TA20 4DD**
email: cricket.sales@bourne-leisure.co.uk **web:** www.warnerleisurehotels.co.uk
dir: M5 junct 25, A358 towards Chard, A30 to Crewkerne. Hotel 3m from Chard

This Grade II listed house has an interesting history including the fact that Lord Nelson and Lady Hamilton were frequent visitors. The hotel is set in splendid parkland, with colourful gardens, lakes, and a unique woodland area. Various holiday packages are available, and there are extensive leisure facilities, as well as live entertainment and various dining venues, including Fenocchi's, with an Italian-themed menu. The bedrooms are spacious and well appointed. Please note that this is an adults-only (over 21 years) hotel.

Rooms 239 (84 GF) **Facilities** Spa FTV WiFi HL Putt green Gym Rifle shooting Archery Xmas New Year **Conf** Class 50 Board 25 Thtr 80 **Services** Lift **Parking** 351 **Notes** No children 21yrs Civ Wed 80

Lordleaze Hotel
THE INDEPENDENTS
HOTEL ASSOCIATION

★★★ 77% HOTEL

tel: 01460 61066 **Henderson Dr, Forton Rd TA20 2HW**
email: info@lordleazehotel.com **web:** www.lordleazehotel.com
dir: A358 from Chard, left at St Mary's Church to Forton & Winsham on B3162. Follow signs to hotel

Conveniently and quietly located, this hotel is close to the Devon, Dorset and Somerset borders, and only minutes from Chard. All bedrooms are well equipped and comfortable. The friendly lounge bar has a wood-burning stove and serves tempting bar meals. The conservatory restaurant offers more formal dining.

Rooms 25 (2 fmly) (7 GF) S £79-£90; D £125-£135 (incl. bkfst)* **Facilities** FTV WiFi Xmas New Year **Conf** Class 60 Board 40 Thtr 180 Del £120* **Parking** 55 **Notes** LB Civ Wed 100

CHARINGWORTH
Gloucestershire
Map 10 SP13

Charingworth Manor Hotel
CLASSIC LODGES
the sign of a great hotel

★★★★ 75% COUNTRY HOUSE HOTEL

tel: 08446 932961 **Charingworth Manor GL55 6NS**
email: info.charingworthmanor@classiclodges.co.uk
web: www.classiclodges.co.uk/Charingworth_Manor_The_Cotswolds
dir: M40 exit at signs for A429/Stow. Follow signs for Moreton-in-Marsh. From Chipping Camden follow signs for Charingworth Manor

This 14th-century manor house retains many original features including flagstone floors, exposed beams and open fireplaces. The house has a beautiful setting in 50 acres of grounds and has been carefully extended to provide high quality accommodation and a delightful, small leisure facility. Spacious bedrooms are furnished with period pieces and modern amenities.

Rooms 26 (18 annexe) (2 fmly) (12 GF) **Facilities** WiFi Gym Sauna Steam room In-room beauty treatments Xmas New Year **Conf** Class 20 Board 40 Thtr 60 **Parking** 50 **Notes** Civ Wed 85

CHARMOUTH
Dorset
Map 4 SY39

Fernhill Hotel

★★★ 81% HOTEL

tel: 01297 560492 **Fernhill DT6 6BX**
email: mail@fernhill-hotel.co.uk **web:** www.fernhill-hotel.co.uk
dir: A35 onto A3052 to Lyme Regis. Hotel 0.25m on left

Fernhill is a small, friendly hotel in well-tended grounds on top of a hill. It boasts an outdoor pool and treatment rooms, together with elegant public areas. Each of the comfortable bedrooms is individually styled and many have views of the Char Valley and beyond. The menus are based on seasonal, locally sourced produce.

Rooms 10 (1 fmly) S £90-£140; D £120-£170 (incl. bkfst)* **Facilities** FTV WiFi Fishing Holistic treatment centre Massage baths Xmas **Conf** Class 20 Board 24 Thtr 100 **Parking** 48 **Notes** LB Closed 31 Dec-30 Jan Civ Wed 100

CHARNOCK RICHARD MOTORWAY SERVICE AREA (M6)
Lancashire
Map 15 SD51

Days Inn Charnock Richard - M6
Welcome Break

BUDGET HOTEL

tel: 01257 791746 **Welcome Break Service Area PR7 5LR**
email: charnockhotel@welcomebreak.co.uk **web:** www.welcomebreak.co.uk
dir: Between junct 27 & 28 of M6 N'bound. 500yds from Camelot Theme Park via Mill Lane

This modern building offers accommodation in smart, spacious and well-equipped bedrooms, suitable for families and business travellers, and all with en suite bathrooms. Continental breakfast is available and other refreshments may be taken at the nearby family restaurant. See also the Hotel Groups pages.

Rooms 100 (68 fmly) (32 GF) (20 smoking) **Conf** Class 16 Board 24 Thtr 40

CHATHAM
Kent
Map 7 TQ76

Bridgewood Manor
QHOTELS
INSPIRED BY YOU

★★★★ 79% HOTEL

tel: 01634 201333 **Bridgewood Roundabout, Walderslade Woods ME5 9AX**
email: bridgewoodmanor@qhotels.co.uk **web:** www.qhotels.co.uk
dir: Adjacent to Bridgewood rdbt on A229. Take 3rd exit signed Walderslade & Lordswood. Hotel 50mtrs on left

Bridgewood Manor is a modern, purpose-built hotel situated on the outskirts of Rochester. Bedrooms are pleasantly decorated, comfortably furnished and equipped with many thoughtful touches. The hotel has an excellent range of leisure and conference facilities. Guests can dine in the informal Terrace Bistro or experience fine dining in the more formal Squires restaurant, where the service is both attentive and friendly. QHotels is the AA Hotel Group of the Year 2014-15.

Rooms 100 (12 fmly) (26 GF) **Facilities** Spa FTV WiFi supervised Gym Beauty treatments Xmas New Year **Conf** Class 110 Board 80 Thtr 200 **Services** Lift **Parking** 170 **Notes** Civ Wed 130

C

Holiday Inn Rochester - Chatham

★★★ 78% HOTEL

tel: 0871 942 9069 **Maidstone Rd ME5 9SF**
web: www.hirochesterhotel.co.uk
dir: M2 junct 3 or M20 junct 6, then A229 for Chatham

A modern, well-equipped hotel close to Rochester, Canterbury and the historic Chatham Dockyards. Bedrooms, including family rooms, are comfortable and spacious; all have air conditioning and broadband access. Public facilities include a lounge, bar and modern restaurant. There is a gym, indoor pool, sauna, spa and an impressive self-contained conference centre.

Rooms 149 (29 fmly) (53 GF) (16 smoking) **Facilities** STV FTV WiFi ⌨ 🕸 supervised Gym Beauty treatment room Steam room Sauna Pilates Beauty evenings **Conf** Class 45 Board 45 Thtr 100 **Services** Lift Air con **Parking** 200 **Notes** ⊗ Civ Wed 100

Ramada Encore Chatham

★★★ 72% HOTEL

tel: 01634 891677 **Western Av, Chatham Historic Dockyard ME4 4NT**
email: operations@encorechatham.co.uk **web:** www.encorechatham.co.uk
dir: Follow signs for Chatham Historic Dockyard

Located in the historic dockyard and just minutes from the town centre, this hotel offers stylish, comfortable accommodation. The smart open-plan bar and restaurant are modern in design and provide a choice of seating areas; a full menu is on offer all day and in the evening. Free WiFi is available throughout the public areas, and there is a meeting room.

Rooms 90 (14 fmly) (8 smoking) ↖ **Facilities** STV FTV WiFi HL **Conf** Class 12 Board 12 Thtr 20 **Services** Lift Air con **Parking** 60 **Notes** ⊗

Follow us on twitter
@TheAA_Lifestyle

Follow us on Facebook
www.facebook.com/TheAAUK

CHATHILL
Northumberland

Map 21 NU12

INSPECTORS' CHOICE

Doxford Hall Hotel & Spa

★★★★ ◉◉ COUNTRY HOUSE HOTEL

tel: 01665 589700 & 589707 **NE67 5DN**
email: info@doxfordhall.com **web:** www.doxfordhall.com
dir: 8m N of Alnwick just off A1, signed Christon Bank & Seahouses. Take B6347 follow signs for hotel

A beautiful country-house hotel set in a private estate, surrounded by countryside and convenient for visiting nearby historic towns and attractions. Bedrooms are spacious and luxuriously furnished, each named after Northumbrian Castles. The dining room and lounges are very attractive. There is an impressive grand staircase and beautiful wood throughout the hotel. The spa adds to the range of facilities.

Rooms 31 (1 fmly) (11 GF) ↖ **S** £75-£200; **D** £99-£280 (incl. bkfst)* **Facilities** Spa FTV WiFi ⌨ HL 🕸 supervised Gym Sauna Steam room Spa bath Xmas New Year **Conf** Class 100 Board 22 Thtr 250 Del from £140 to £160* **Services** Lift **Parking** 100 **Notes** Civ Wed 250

CHEADLE
Greater Manchester

Map 16 SJ88

Premier Inn Manchester (Cheadle)

BUDGET HOTEL

tel: 0871 527 8728 **Royal Crescent SK8 3FE**
web: www.premierinn.com
dir: Exit A34 at Cheadle Royal rdbt behind TGI Friday's

High quality, budget accommodation ideal for both families and business travellers. Spacious, en suite bedrooms feature tea and coffee making facilities, and Freeview TV in most hotels. Internet access and WiFi are available for a small fee. The adjacent family restaurant features a wide and varied menu. See also the Hotel Groups pages.

Rooms 65

CHELMSFORD
Essex

Map 6 TL70

Pontlands Park

★★★ 83% HOTEL

tel: 01245 476444 **West Hanningfield Rd, Great Baddow CM2 8HR**
email: sales@pontlandsparkhotel.co.uk **web:** www.heritageleisure.co.uk
dir: A12, A130 , A1114 to Chelmsford. 1st exit at rdbt, 1st slip road on left. Left towards Great Baddow, 1st left into West Hanningfield Rd. Hotel 400yds on left

A Victorian country-house hotel situated in a peaceful rural location amidst attractive landscaped grounds. The stylishly furnished bedrooms are generally quite spacious; each is individually decorated and equipped with modern facilities. The elegant public rooms include a tastefully furnished sitting room, a cosy lounge bar, smart conservatory restaurant and an intimate dining room.

Rooms 35 (10 fmly) (11 GF) **Facilities** FTV WiFi ⚽ ⛱ Gym Beauty room
Conf Class 40 Board 40 Thtr 100 **Parking** 100 **Notes** ⊗ Closed 24-26 Dec
Civ Wed 100

County Hotel

★★★ 81% ⚘ HOTEL

tel: 01245 455700 **29 Rainsford Rd CM1 2PZ**
email: kloftus@countyhotelgroup.co.uk **web:** www.countyhotelgroup.co.uk
dir: From town centre, past rail & bus station. Hotel 300yds left beyond lights

This popular hotel is ideally situated within easy walking distance of the railway station, bus depot and town centre. Stylish bedrooms offer spacious comfort and plentiful extras including free WiFi. There are a smart restaurant, bar and lounge as well as sunny outdoor terraces for making the most of warm weather. The hotel also has a range of meeting rooms and banqueting facilities.

Rooms 50 🛏 **S** £50-£110; **D** £60-£150* **Facilities** FTV WiFi HL Xmas New Year
Conf Class 84 Board 64 Thtr 160 Del from £120 to £170* **Services** Lift **Parking** 80
Notes LB ⊗ Closed 27-30 Dec Civ Wed 80

BEST WESTERN Ivy Hill

★★★ 79% HOTEL

tel: 01277 353040 & 355111 **Writtle Rd, Margaretting CM4 0EH**
email: sales@ivyhillhotel.co.uk **web:** www.heritageleisure.co.uk
dir: Just off A12 junct 14. Hotel on left at top of slip road

A smartly appointed hotel conveniently situated just off the A12. The spacious bedrooms are tastefully decorated, have co-ordinated fabrics and all the expected facilities. Public rooms include a choice of lounges, a cosy bar, a smart conservatory and restaurant, as well as a range of conference and banqueting facilities.

Rooms 33 (5 fmly) (11 GF) **Facilities** FTV WiFi ⛱ **Conf** Class 80 Board 40 Thtr 180
Parking 200 **Notes** ⊗ Closed 24-26 Dec Civ Wed 100

BEST WESTERN Atlantic Hotel

★★★ 77% HOTEL

tel: 01245 268168 **New St CM1 1PP**
email: info@atlantichotel.co.uk **web:** www.atlantichotel.co.uk
dir: From Chelmsford rail station, left into Victoria Rd, left at lights into New St, hotel on right

Ideally situated just a short walk from the railway station with its quick links to London, this modern, purpose-built hotel has contemporary-style bedrooms

equipped with modern facilities. The open-plan public areas include Sapori Ristorante, an Italian restaurant, a lounge bar and a conservatory.

Rooms 59 (3 fmly) (27 GF) **S** £70-£105; **D** £80-£125 (incl. bkfst)* **Facilities** FTV WiFi
Gym Complimentary use of facilities at Fitness First 🎵 **Conf** Class 40 Board 10
Thtr 15 **Services** Air con **Parking** 60 **Notes** ⊗ Closed 23 Dec-3 Jan

Premier Inn Chelmsford (Boreham)

BUDGET HOTEL

tel: 0871 527 8220 **Main Rd, Boreham CM3 3HJ**
web: www.premierinn.com
dir: M25 junct 28, A12 to Colchester, B1137 to Boreham

High quality, budget accommodation ideal for both families and business travellers. Spacious, en suite bedrooms feature tea and coffee making facilities, and Freeview TV in most hotels. Internet access and WiFi are available for a small fee. The adjacent family restaurant features a wide and varied menu. See also the Hotel Groups pages.

Rooms 78

Premier Inn Chelmsford (Springfield)

BUDGET HOTEL

tel: 0871 527 8222 **Chelmsford Service Area, Colchester Rd, Springfield CM2 5PY**
web: www.premierinn.com
dir: At A12 junct 19, Chelmsford bypass, signed Chelmsford Service Area

Rooms 61

CHELTENHAM
Gloucestershire

Map 10 SO92

Ellenborough Park

★★★★★ 86% ⚘⚘⚘ COUNTRY HOUSE HOTEL

tel: 01242 545454 **Southam Rd GL52 3NH**
email: info@ellenboroughpark.com **web:** www.ellenboroughpark.com
dir: A46 right after 3m onto B4079, merges with A435, 4m, over 3 rdbts, left onto Southam Lane, right onto Old Road, right onto B4632, hotel on right

Set on the original Cheltenham Racecourse estate, this impressive hotel dates in part from the 16th century and has been beautifully restored. The Nina Campbell-designed bedrooms and suites are spread across the main house and adjacent buildings, and all feature superb beds, a great range of modern amenities, and luxurious bathrooms. The stylish Indian-themed spa has a gym and outdoor heated pool. There are two dining options; the modern Brasserie offers a country house

C

menu, while the elegant, oak-panelled Beaufort dining room is more formal and offers a high standard of classic cuisine.

Rooms 62 (44 annexe) (20 GF) ↖ **D** £230-£840 (incl. bkfst)* **Facilities** Spa STV FTV WiFi ↕ ➘ ➚ Gym Xmas New Year **Conf** Class 70 Board 40 Thtr 120 **Services** Lift Air con **Parking** 130 **Notes** LB Civ Wed 120

The Greenway Hotel & Spa

★★★★ 82% ◉◉ COUNTRY HOUSE HOTEL

tel: 01242 862352 **Shurdington GL51 4UG**
email: info@thegreenway.co.uk **web:** www.thegreenwayhotelandspa.com
dir: From Cheltenham centre 2.5m S on A46

This hotel, with a wealth of history, is peacefully located in a delightful setting within easy reach of the many attractions of the Cotswolds and also the M5. The Manor House bedrooms are luxuriously appointed - traditional in style yet with plasma TVs and internet access. The tranquil Coach House rooms, in the converted stable block, have direct access to the beautiful grounds. The attractive dining room overlooks the sunken garden and is the venue for excellent food, proudly served by dedicated and attentive staff. Eden Hotel Collection is the AA Small Hotel Group of the Year 2014-15.

Rooms 19 (6 annexe) (1 fmly) ↖ **S** £139-£209; **D** £149-£229 (incl. bkfst) **Facilities** Spa FTV WiFi ↕ ➚ Gym Xmas New Year **Conf** Board 18 Thtr 50 Del from £158 to £198 **Parking** 30 **Notes** LB Civ Wed 60

The Cheltenham Chase Hotel

★★★★ 80% HOTEL

tel: 01452 519988 **Shurdington Rd, Brockworth GL3 4PB**
email: cheltenhamreservations@qhotels.co.uk **web:** www.qhotels.co.uk
dir: M5 junct 11a onto A417 Cirencester. 1st exit A46 to Stroud, hotel 500yds on left.

Conveniently positioned for Cheltenham, Gloucester, and the M5, this hotel is set in landscaped grounds with ample parking. Bedrooms are spacious with attractive colour schemes and excellent facilities; executive rooms and suites benefit from air conditioning. Public areas include an open-plan bar/lounge, Hardy's restaurant, extensive meeting and functions rooms and a well-equipped leisure club. QHotels is the AA Hotel Group of the Year 2014-15.

Rooms 122 (19 fmly) (44 GF) ↖ **S** £89-£149; **D** £99-£159 (incl. bkfst)* **Facilities** Spa STV FTV WiFi ↕ ➚ Gym Steam room Sauna Xmas New Year **Conf** Class 160 Board 80 Thtr 350 Del from £129 to £165* **Services** Lift Air con **Parking** 240 **Notes** LB ⊗ Civ Wed 344

Cheltenham Park Hotel

★★★★ 79% ◉ HOTEL

tel: 01242 222021 **Cirencester Rd, Charlton Kings GL53 8EA**
email: cheltenhampark@pumahotels.co.uk **web:** www.pumahotels.co.uk
dir: On A435, 2m SE of Cheltenham near Lilley Brook Golf Course

Located south of Cheltenham, this attractive Georgian property is set in its own landscaped gardens, adjacent to Lilley Brook Golf Course. All the bedrooms, whether premium or standard, are spacious and well equipped for both business and leisure guests. The hotel has an impressive health and leisure club with the latest gym equipment, plus a pool, steam room and beauty salon; extensive meeting facilities are available. The Lakeside Restaurant serves carefully prepared cuisine.

Rooms 152 (119 annexe) ↖ **Facilities** Spa WiFi ➚ supervised Gym Beauty treatment rooms Spa pool Sauna Steam room Xmas New Year **Conf** Class 180 Board 110 Thtr 320 **Parking** 170 **Notes** Civ Wed 100

Hotel du Vin Cheltenham

★★★★ 77% ◉ HOTEL

tel: 0844 7364 254 **Parabola Rd GL50 3AQ**
email: info@cheltenham.hotelduvin.com **web:** www.hotelduvin.com
dir: M5 junct 11, follow signs for city centre. At rdbt opposite Morgan Estate Agents take 2nd left, 200mtrs to Parabola Rd

This hotel, in the Montpellier area of the town, has spacious public areas that are packed with stylish features. The pewter-topped bar has comfortable seating and the spacious restaurant has the Hotel du Vin trademark design; alfresco dining is possible on the extensive terrace area. Bedrooms are very comfortable, with Egyptian linen, deep baths and power showers. The spa is the ideal place to relax and unwind. Although parking is limited, it is a definite bonus. Service is friendly and attentive.

Rooms 49 (2 fmly) (5 GF) ↖ **Facilities** Spa STV WiFi **Conf** Class 24 Board 24 Thtr 30 **Services** Lift Air con **Parking** 26 **Notes** Civ Wed 60

Mercure Cheltenham Queen's Hotel

★★★★ 77% HOTEL

tel: 01242 514754 **The Promenade GL50 1NN**
email: h6632@accor.com **web:** www.mercure.com
dir: Follow town centre signs. Left at Montpellier Walk rdbt. Entrance 500mtrs right

With its spectacular position at the top of the main promenade, this landmark hotel is an ideal base from which to explore the charms of this Regency spa town and also the Cotswolds. Bedrooms are very comfortable and include two beautiful four-poster rooms. Smart public rooms include the popular Gold Cup bar and a choice of dining options.

Rooms 84 (15 fmly) ↖ **Facilities** STV WiFi HL Xmas New Year **Conf** Class 60 Board 40 Thtr 100 **Services** Lift Air con **Parking** 70 **Notes** Civ Wed 100

George Hotel

★★★ 80% ◉◉ HOTEL

tel: 01242 235751 **St Georges Rd GL50 3DZ**
email: hotel@stayatthegeorge.co.uk **web:** www.stayatthegeorge.co.uk
dir: M5 junct 11 follow town centre signs. At 2nd lights left into Gloucester Rd, past rail station over mini-rdbt. At lights right into St Georges Rd. Hotel 0.75m on left

A genuinely friendly, privately-owned hotel occupying part of a Regency terrace, just two-minutes walk from the town centre. The contemporary interior is elegant and stylish, and the well-equipped, modern bedrooms offer a relaxing haven; individually designed junior suites and deluxe double rooms are available. Lunch or dinner can be enjoyed in the lively atmosphere of Monty's Brasserie, perhaps followed by an evening in the vibrant cocktail bar which hosts live entertainment on Friday and Saturday evenings.

Rooms 31 (1 GF) ↖ **D** £90-£110 (incl. bkfst)* **Facilities** STV WiFi Complimentary membership to local health club Live music at wknds ♫ **Conf** Class 18 Board 24 Thtr 30 Del from £135* **Parking** 30 **Notes** LB ⊗ Closed 25-26 Dec RS 24 Dec

C

CHELMSFORD *continued*

BEST WESTERN Cheltenham Regency Hotel

★★★ 80% HOTEL

tel: 01452 713226 **Gloucester Rd, Staverton GL51 0ST**
email: info@cheltenhamregency.co.uk web: www.cheltenhamregency.co.uk
dir: M5 junct 11 onto A40 to Cheltenham. Left at rdbt, hotel 1m on left

This hotel provides high standards of quality and comfort. The bedrooms are large
and include several suites; all are very well equipped and ideal for both business
and leisure guests. A good selection of carefully prepared dishes is available from
either the extensive lounge/bar menu, or a more formal offering can be found in the
main restaurant.

Rooms 47 (2 fmly) (16 GF) ⌁ S £75-£105; D £85-£125 (incl. bkfst)* **Facilities** FTV
WiFi ⌁ Xmas New Year **Conf** Class 90 Board 80 Thtr 170 Del from £145 to £200*
Services Lift Air con **Parking** 120 **Notes** LB ⊗ Civ Wed 140

The Royal George Hotel

★★★ 68% HOTEL

tel: 01452 862506 **Birdlip GL4 8JH**
email: 6503@greeneking.co.uk web: www.oldenglish.co.uk
dir: M5 junct 11A take A417 towards Cirencester. At Air Balloon rdbt take 2nd exit then
1st right into Birdlip, hotel on right

This attractive property, built around a 17th-century Cotswold house, has been
sympathetically converted and extended to become a pleasant and friendly hotel.
The bedrooms, including a four-poster room, are spacious and comfortably
furnished with modern facilities. The public areas have been designed to create a
traditional English pub with the bar leading onto a terrace that overlooks extensive
lawns.

Rooms 34 (4 fmly) (12 GF) **Facilities** STV WiFi ⌗ Xmas **Conf** Class 60 Board 40
Thtr 90 **Notes** ⊗ Civ Wed 80

Premier Inn Cheltenham Central

BUDGET HOTEL

tel: 0871 527 8224 **374 Gloucester Rd GL51 7AY**
web: www.premierinn.com
dir: M5 junct 11, A40 (Cheltenham). Follow dual carriageway to end, straight on at 1st
rdbt, right at 2nd rdbt

High quality, budget accommodation ideal for both families and business
travellers. Spacious, en suite bedrooms feature tea and coffee making facilities,
and Freeview TV in most hotels. Internet access and WiFi are available for a small
fee. The adjacent family restaurant features a wide and varied menu. See also the
Hotel Groups pages.

Rooms 43

Premier Inn Cheltenham West

BUDGET HOTEL

tel: 0871 527 8226 **Tewkesbury Rd, Uckington GL51 9SL**
web: www.premierinn.com
dir: M5 junct 10 (S'bound exit only), A4019, hotel in 2m. Or M5 junct 11, A40 towards
Cheltenham. At Benhall Rdbt left onto A4103 (Princess Elizabeth Way) follow racecourse
signs. At rdbt left onto A4019 signed Tewkesbury/M5 North. Hotel opposite Sainsburys

Rooms 40

CHERTSEY	Map 6 TQ06
Surrey	

Hamilton's

◉ RESTAURANT WITH ROOMS

tel: 01932 560745 **23 Windsor St KT16 8AY**
email: bookings@hamiltons23.com web: www.hamiltons23.com
dir: M25 junct 11 St Peters Way (A317). At rdbt 1st exit, Chertsey Rd (A317), next rdbt 2nd
exit into Free Prae Rd, then Pound Rd. Left into London St, opposite church

Hamilton's is an intimate and attractive building close to the cricket ground. The en
suite rooms are beautifully appointed and equipped with all modern amenities. The
restaurant offers a fine dining menu from Wednesday to Saturday, while a freshly
cooked breakfast ensures a good start to the day. Free parking is available.

Rooms 5

CHESSINGTON	Map 6 TQ16
Greater London	

Premier Inn Chessington

BUDGET HOTEL

tel: 0871 527 8228 **Leatherhead Rd KT9 2NE**
web: www.premierinn.com
dir: M25 junct 9, A243 towards Kingston-upon-Thames for approx 2m. Hotel adjacent to
Chessington World of Adventures

High quality, budget accommodation ideal for both families and business
travellers. Spacious, en suite bedrooms feature tea and coffee making facilities,
and Freeview TV in most hotels. Internet access and WiFi are available for a small
fee. The adjacent family restaurant features a wide and varied menu. See also the
Hotel Groups pages.

Rooms 42

C

CHESTER
Cheshire

Map 15 SJ46

See also **Puddington**

The Chester Grosvenor
★★★★★  HOTEL

tel: 01244 324024 **Eastgate CH1 1LT**
email: reservations@chestergrosvenor.com **web:** www.chestergrosvenor.com
dir: A56 follow signs for city centre hotels. On Eastgate St next to the Eastgate clock

Located within the Roman walls of the city, this Grade II listed, half-timbered building is the essence of Englishness. Furnished with fine fabrics and queen or king-size beds, the suites and bedrooms are of the highest standard, each designed with guest comfort as a priority. The eating options are the art deco La Brasserie, a bustling venue awarded 2 AA Rosettes; the Arkle Bar and Lounge for morning coffee, light lunches, afternoon tea and drinks; plus the fine dining restaurant, Simon Radley at The Chester Grosvenor, which offers creative cuisine with flair and style, and has been awarded 4 AA Rosettes. The hotel has a luxury spa and small fitness centre.

Rooms 80 (7 fmly) ꟾ S fr £155; **D** fr £165 (incl. bkfst)* **Facilities** Spa STV FTV WiFi ꟾ HL Gym New Year **Conf** Class 100 Board 50 Thtr 250 Del from £162.50* **Services** Lift Air con **Notes** ⊗ Closed 25 Dec RS Sun & Mon Civ Wed 250

Rowton Hall Country House Hotel & Spa
★★★★ 81% ◉ HOTEL

tel: 01244 335262 **Whitchurch Rd, Rowton CH3 6AD**
email: reception@rowtonhallhotelandspa.co.uk **web:** www.rowtonhallhotel.co.uk
dir: M56 junct 12, A56 to Chester. At x-rds left onto A41 towards Whitchurch. Approx 1m, follow hotel signs

This delightful Georgian manor house, set in mature grounds, retains many original features such as a superb carved staircase and several eye-catching fireplaces. Bedrooms vary in size but all have been stylishly fitted and have impressive en suites. Public areas include a smart leisure centre, extensive function facilities and a striking restaurant that serves imaginative dishes.

Rooms 37 (4 fmly) (8 GF) ꟾ S £92.50–£500; **D** £92.50–£500 **Facilities** Spa FTV WiFi ◉ ☺ ☙ Gym Sauna Steam room Xmas New Year **Conf** Class 48 Board 50 Thtr 170 Del from £125 to £250 **Parking** 200 **Notes** Civ Wed 170

Grosvenor Pulford Hotel & Spa
★★★★ 80% ◉ HOTEL

tel: 01244 570560 **Wrexham Rd, Pulford CH4 9DG**
email: reservations@grosvenorpulfordhotel.co.uk **web:** www.grosvenorpulfordhotel.co.uk
dir: M53, A55 at junct signed A483 Chester/Wrexham & North Wales. Left onto B5445, hotel 2m on right

Set in a rural location, this modern, stylish hotel features a magnificent spa with a large Roman-style swimming pool. Among the range of bedrooms are several executive suites, and others that have spiral staircases leading to the bedroom sections. A smart brasserie restaurant and bar provides a wide range of imaginative dishes in a relaxed atmosphere.

Rooms 73 (10 fmly) (21 GF) ꟾ S £85–£195; **D** £105–£205 (incl. bkfst)* **Facilities** Spa STV FTV WiFi ꟾ HL ⊛ ☺ Gym Steam room Sauna Xmas New Year **Conf** Class 100 Board 60 Thtr 220 Del from £130 to £150* **Services** Lift **Parking** 200 **Notes** LB Civ Wed 200

ABode Chester
★★★★ 78% ◉◉ HOTEL

tel: 01244 347000 **Grosvenor Rd CH1 2DJ**
email: generalmanager@abodechester.co.uk **web:** www.abodechester.co.uk

This modern, glass-fronted property sits prominently in the centre of Chester overlooking the Castle and adjacent to the racecourse. Bedrooms are well designed and equipped for the modern traveller with a range of large spacious suites also available. Food is a highlight here, with a range of dining options and bars. The Michael Caines Restaurant crowns the top of the building with far-reaching views over Chester Racecourse and beyond. Additional facilities include secure parking, a gym and beauty treatments.

Rooms 84 ꟾ **Facilities** FTV WiFi ꟾ Gym Treatment room **Conf** Class 24 Board 36 Thtr 90 **Services** Lift Air con **Parking** 18 **Notes** ⊗ Civ Wed

BEST WESTERN PREMIER Queen Hotel
★★★★ 78% HOTEL

tel: 01244 305000 **City Rd CH1 3AH**
email: queenhotel@feathers.uk.com **web:** www.feathers.uk.com
dir: Follow signs for railway station, hotel opposite

This hotel is ideally located opposite the railway station and just a couple minutes' walk from the city. Public areas include a restaurant, small gym, waiting room bar, separate lounge and Roman-themed gardens. Bedrooms are generally spacious and reflect the hotel's Victorian heritage.

Rooms 218 (11 fmly) (12 GF) ꟾ **Facilities** STV FTV WiFi ꟾ HL Gym Beauty treatment room Table tennis ♫ Xmas New Year **Conf** Class 150 Board 60 Thtr 400 **Services** Lift **Parking** 150 **Notes** ⊗ Civ Wed 400

C

CHESTER *continued*

Macdonald New Blossoms Hotel

★★★★ 74% HOTEL

tel: 01244 323186 & 0844 8799113 **St John St CH1 1HL**
email: events.blossoms@macdonald-hotels.co.uk
web: www.macdonaldhotels.co.uk/blossoms
dir: M53 junct 12 follow city centre signs for Eastgate, through pedestrian zone, hotel on left

Ideally located to explore the historic city of Chester, this is a modern and contemporary hotel. Bedrooms range from executive to feature four-poster rooms, with many retaining the charm of the original Victorian building. A stylish brasserie restaurant and bar offer an informal dining experience.

Rooms 67 (1 fmly) 🐾 **Facilities** FTV WiFi ⚄ Xmas New Year **Conf** Class 50 Board 40 Thtr 90 Del from £130 to £150* **Services** Lift Air con **Notes** ⊗ Civ Wed 80

Mercure Chester Abbots Well Hotel

★★★★ 74% HOTEL

tel: 0844 815 9001 **Whitchurch Rd, Christleton CH3 5QL**
email: gm.mercurechester@jupiterhotels.co.uk **web:** www.jupiterhotels.co.uk
dir: A41 (Whitchurch) hotel on right in 200mtrs

This smart, modern hotel is located just a short drive from the city centre; with extensive meeting and function facilities, a well-equipped leisure club and ample parking, it is a popular conference venue. Bedrooms vary in size and style but all are well equipped for both business and leisure guests. Food is served in the airy restaurant and also in the large open-plan bar lounge.

Rooms 126 (6 fmly) (58 GF) 🐾 **Facilities** STV WiFi ⚄ 🔄 Gym Xmas New Year **Conf** Class 80 Board 60 Thtr 230 **Services** Lift **Parking** 160 **Notes** ⊗ Civ Wed 180

BEST WESTERN Westminster Hotel

★★★ 81% HOTEL

tel: 01244 317341 **City Rd CH1 3AF**
email: westminsterhotel@feathers.uk.com **web:** www.feathers.uk.com
dir: A56, 3m to city centre, left signed rail station. Hotel opposite station, on right

Situated close to the railway station and city centre, the Westminster is an established hotel. It has an attractive Tudor-style exterior, while bedrooms are brightly decorated with a modern theme; family rooms are available. There is a choice of bars and lounges, and the dining room serves a good range of dishes.

Rooms 75 (5 fmly) (5 GF) **Facilities** FTV WiFi Free gym facilities at sister hotel Xmas New Year **Conf** Class 60 Board 40 Thtr 150 **Services** Lift **Notes** ⊗ Civ Wed 100

Holiday Inn Chester South

★★★ 78% HOTEL

tel: 0871 942 9019 & 01244 688770 **Wrexham Rd CH4 9DL**
email: reservations-chester@ihg.com **web:** www.hichestersouthhotel.co.uk
dir: Near Wrexham junct on A483

Located close to the A55 and opposite the Park and Ride for the city centre, this hotel offers spacious and comfortable accommodation. Meals can be taken in the attractive bar or in the restaurant. There is also a well-equipped leisure club for residents, and extensive conference facilities are available.

Rooms 143 (21 fmly) (71 GF) **Facilities** STV FTV WiFi HL 🔄 supervised Gym Beauty treatment room Xmas New Year **Conf** Class 70 Board 70 Thtr 100 **Services** Lift Air con **Parking** 150 **Notes** ⊗ Civ Wed 50

Mill Hotel & Spa Destination

★★★ 77% HOTEL

tel: 01244 350035 **Milton St CH1 3NF**
email: reservations@millhotel.com **web:** www.millhotel.com
dir: M53 junct 12, A56, left at 2nd rdbt (A5268), 1st left, 2nd left

This hotel is a stylish conversion of an old corn mill, and enjoys an idyllic canalside location near to the inner ring road and close to the city centre. The bedrooms come in a variety of styles, and public rooms are spacious and comfortable. There are several dining options, and meals are often served on a broad-beam boat that cruises Chester's canal system, to and from the hotel. A well-equipped leisure centre is also provided.

PREMIER ROOM

Rooms 131 (49 annexe) (57 fmly) 🐾 **Facilities** Spa STV FTV WiFi HL 🔄 supervised Gym Aerobic studio Hairdresser Sauna Steam room Kinesis studio 🎵 Xmas New Year **Conf** Class 36 Board 30 Thtr 100 **Services** Lift **Parking** 120 **Notes** ⊗

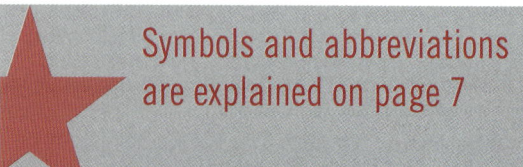

Symbols and abbreviations are explained on page 7

C

Brookside Hotel

★★★ 72% HOTEL

tel: 01244 381943 & 390898 **Brook Ln CH2 2AN**
email: info@brookside-hotel.co.uk **web:** www.brookside-hotel.co.uk
dir: M53 junct 12, A56 towards Chester, A41. 0.5m left signed Newton (Plas Newton Ln). 0.5m right into Brook Ln. Hotel 0.5m. Or from Chester inner ring road follow A5116/Ellesmere Port/Hospital signs (keep in right lane to take right fork). Immediately left. At mini-rdbt 2nd right

This hotel is conveniently located in a residential area just north of the city centre. The attractive public areas consist of a foyer lounge, a small bar and a split-level restaurant. The homely bedrooms are thoughtfully furnished and some feature four-poster beds.

Rooms 26 (9 fmly) (4 GF) **Facilities** WiFi **Conf** Class 20 Board 12 **Parking** 20 **Notes** ⊗ Closed 20 Dec-3 Jan

Premier Inn Chester Central (North)

BUDGET HOTEL

tel: 0871 527 8230 **76 Liverpool Rd CH2 1AU**
web: www.premierinn.com
dir: M53 junct 12, A56. At 2nd rdbt right signed A41 to Chester Zoo. At 1st lights left into Heath Rd, leads into Mill Ln. Under small rail bridge. Hotel at end on right

High quality, budget accommodation ideal for both families and business travellers. Spacious, en suite bedrooms feature tea and coffee making facilities, and Freeview TV in most hotels. Internet access and WiFi are available for a small fee. The adjacent family restaurant features a wide and varied menu. See also the Hotel Groups pages.

Rooms 31

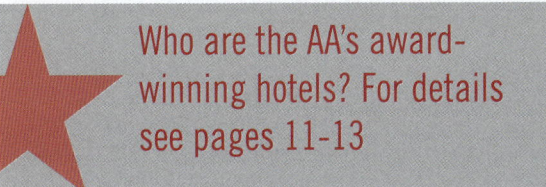

Who are the AA's award-winning hotels? For details see pages 11-13

Premier Inn Chester Central (South East)

BUDGET HOTEL

tel: 0871 527 8232 **Caldy Valley Rd, Boughton CH3 5PR**
web: www.premierinn.com
dir: M53 junct 12, A56 to Chester. At 1st lights onto A41 (Whitchurch). At 2nd rdbt rd exit into Caldy Valley Rd (Huntington). Hotel on right

Rooms 94

Premier Inn Chester City Centre

BUDGET HOTEL

tel: 0871 527 8234 **20-24 City Rd CH1 3AE**
web: www.premierinn.com
dir: M53 junct 12, follow A56/Chester City Centre signs. At rdbt 1st exit onto A5268 (St Oswalds Way) follow railway station signs. At Bar's Rdbt 1st exit. Hotel on right

Rooms 120

CHESTERFIELD	Map 16 SK37
Derbyshire	

Casa Hotel

★★★★ 82% 🏵🏵 HOTEL

tel: 01246 245999 **Lockoford Ln S41 7JB**
email: enquiries@casahotels.co.uk **web:** www.casahotels.co.uk
dir: M1 junct 29 to A617 Chesterfield/A61 Sheffield, 1st exit at rdbt, hotel on left

A luxurious hotel with a contemporary Spanish theme throughout. The stylish bedrooms feature air conditioning, Hypnos beds and bathrooms with rainshowers. Some also have jacuzzi baths and two have balconies with hot tubs. Cocina Restaurant offers appealing menus featuring ingredients from the hotel's own organic farm. The conference and events facilities are excellent and complimentary WiFi is offered.

Rooms 100 (6 fmly) ⌁ **S** £99-£125; **D** £109-£140 (incl. bkfst)* **Facilities** STV FTV WiFi ⅂ HL Gym New Year **Conf** Class 140 Board 50 Thtr 280 **Services** Lift Air con **Parking** 200 **Notes** LB ⊗ Civ Wed 280

C

CHESTERFIELD *continued*

Peak Edge Hotel at the Red Lion

★★★★ 82% ◉◉ HOTEL

tel: 01246 566142 **Darley Rd, Stone Edge S45 OLW**
email: sleep@peakedgehotel.co.uk **web:** www.peakedgehotel.co.uk
dir: M1 junct 29, A617 to Chesterfield. At rdbt take 1st exit onto A61, at next rdbt 2nd exit onto Whitecotes Ln, continue onto Matlock Rd (A632) then Darley Rd (B5057)

The Peak Edge Hotel is set in the heart of the Derbyshire countryside and surrounded by great views on all sides. The modern rooms are spacious, comfortable, and all benefit from high quality bathrooms. The Inn has a rustic ambiance of the 17th century with stone walls and wooden flooring. The staff are very friendly and well informed. Food is a highlight of any stay, with locally sourced produce put to good use.

Rooms 27 (2 fmly) (15 GF) ⟋ **S** £150-£300; **D** £150-£300 (incl. bkfst)* **Facilities** FTV WiFi ⌀ ♫ Xmas New Year **Conf** Class 120 Board 40 Thtr 140 **Services** Lift Air con **Parking** 70 **Notes** LB Civ Wed 140

Ringwood Hall Hotel

★★★ 86% HOTEL   THE INDEPENDENTS

tel: 01246 280077 **Brimington S43 1DQ**
email: reception@ringwoodhallhotel.com **web:** www.ringwoodhallhotel.com
dir: M1 junct 30, A619 to Chesterfield through Staveley. Hotel on left

A beautifully presented Georgian manor house set in 29 acres of peaceful grounds, between the M1 and Chesterfield. The stylish bedrooms include 'Feature Rooms' and three apartments within the grounds. Public areas include comfortable

lounges, the Markham Bar and a Cocktail Lounge. The health and fitness club has a pool, sauna, steam room and gym.

Rooms 74 (10 annexe) (32 fmly) (32 GF) ⟋ **S** £75-£105; **D** £98.50-£135 (incl. bkfst)* **Facilities** FTV WiFi ⌀ Gym Steam room Sauna Xmas New Year **Conf** Class 80 Board 60 Thtr 250 Del from £95 **Parking** 150 **Notes** LB Civ Wed 250

Sandpiper Hotel

★★★ 70% HOTEL   THE INDEPENDENTS

tel: 01246 450550 **Sheffield Rd, Sheepbridge S41 9EH**
email: sue@sandpiperhotel.co.uk **web:** www.sandpiperhotel.co.uk
dir: M1 junct 29, A617 to Chesterfield then A61 to Sheffield. 1st exit take Dronfield/Unstone sign. Hotel 0.5m on left

Conveniently situated for both the A61, the M1, and Chesterfield, this modern hotel offers comfortable and well-furnished bedrooms. Public areas are situated in a separate building across the car park, and include a cosy bar and open-plan restaurant, serving a range of interesting and popular dishes.

Rooms 40 (6 fmly) (11 GF) **S** £55; **D** £55-£60* **Facilities** FTV WiFi ⌀ New Year **Conf** Class 35 Board 35 Thtr 100 Del £110* **Services** Lift **Parking** 120 **Notes** ⊗ Civ Wed 90

Ibis Chesterfield

BUDGET HOTEL   ibis

tel: 01246 221333 **Lordsmill St S41 7RW**
email: h3160@accor.com **web:** www.ibishotel.com
dir: M1 junct 29/A617 to Chesterfield. 2nd exit at 1st rdbt. Hotel on right at 2nd rdbt

Modern, budget hotel offering comfortable accommodation in bright and practical bedrooms. Breakfast is self-service and dinner is available in the restaurant. See also the Hotel Groups pages.

Rooms 86 (21 fmly) (8 GF) **Conf** Board 12 Thtr 25

Premier Inn Chesterfield North

BUDGET HOTEL   Premier Inn

tel: 0871 527 8238 **Tapton Lock Hill, off Rotherway S41 7NJ**
web: www.premierinn.com
dir: Adjacent to Tesco, at A61 & A619 rdbt, 1m N of city centre

High quality, budget accommodation ideal for both families and business travellers. Spacious, en suite bedrooms feature tea and coffee making facilities, and Freeview TV in most hotels. Internet access and WiFi are available for a small fee. The adjacent family restaurant features a wide and varied menu. See also the Hotel Groups pages.

Rooms 60

Premier Inn Chesterfield West

BUDGET HOTEL

tel: 0871 527 8240 **Baslow Rd, Eastmoor S42 7DA**
web: www.premierinn.com
dir: M1 junct 29, A617. At next rdbt 2nd exit. At next rdbt 1st exit into Markham Rd. At next rdbt 2nd exit into Wheatbridge Rd, left into Chatsworth Rd. 2.5m to hotel

Rooms 23

C

CHESTER-LE-STREET
County Durham   Map 19 NZ25

Lumley Castle Hotel

★★★★ 75% HOTEL

tel: 0191 389 1111 **Lumley Castle DH3 4NX**
email: reservations@lumleycastle.com **web:** www.lumleycastle.com
dir: A1(M) junct 63, follow Chester-le-Street signs. Follow signs for Riverside then Lumley Castle

Dominating the Country Durham landscape for the past 600 years, Lumley Castle cannot help but impress. The place has a real sense of theatre and as a guest you are left in no doubt that you are in a proper castle. The magnificent state rooms along with other public areas are very well presented in accord with all expectations. Bedrooms differ in style, size and type and make good use of all available space. The staff are warm and welcoming, and quality food is served throughout.

Rooms 73 (47 annexe) (9 fmly) (27 GF) ✆ **S** £79-£99; **D** £119-£350 (incl. bkfst)*
Facilities FTV WiFi HL **Conf** Class 60 Board 50 Thtr 200 Del from £125 to £159*
Services Lift **Notes** LB ⊗ Closed 24-26 Dec & 1-2 Jan Civ Wed

CHICHESTER
West Sussex   Map 5 SU80

The Goodwood Hotel

★★★★ 81% ◉◉ HOTEL

tel: 01243 775537 **PO18 0QB**
email: reservations@goodwood.com **web:** www.goodwood.com

(For full entry see Goodwood)

The Ship Hotel

★★★★ 77% ◉ HOTEL

tel: 01243 778000 **57 North St PO19 1NH**
email: enquiries@theshiphotel.net **web:** www.theshiphotel.net
dir: From A27, onto inner ring road to Northgate. At Northgate rdbt left into North St, hotel on left

This well-presented Grade II listed, Georgian property occupies a prime position at the top of North Street. The stylish bedrooms have flat-screen TVs, Egyptian cotton linen and high-speed WiFi access. The bar and restaurant are contemporary venues for enjoying meals, and refreshments which are served all day. The hotel is just a few minutes' away from the famous Festival Theatre; and Goodwood, for motorsport and horse racing, is also close by.

Rooms 37 (1 annexe) (2 fmly) **S** £92.50-£125; **D** £125-£295 (incl. bkfst)*
Facilities FTV WiFi ♨ Xmas New Year **Conf** Class 50 Board 30 Thtr 50 Del from £160 to £330* **Services** Lift **Parking** 35 **Notes** LB ⊗ Civ Wed 70

The Millstream Hotel & Restaurant

★★★ 85% ◉◉ HOTEL

tel: 01243 573234 **Bosham Ln PO18 8HL**
email: info@millstreamhotel.com **web:** www.millstreamhotel.com

(For full entry see Bosham)

Crouchers Country Hotel & Restaurant

★★★ 80% ◉◉ HOTEL

tel: 01243 784995 **Birdham Rd PO20 7EH**
email: crouchers@btconnect.com **web:** www.croucherscountryhotel.com
dir: From A27 (Chichester bypass) onto A286 towards West Wittering, 2m, hotel on left between Chichester Marina & Dell Quay

This friendly, family-run hotel, situated in open countryside, is just a short drive from the harbour. The stylish and well-equipped bedrooms are situated in a separate barn, coach house and stable block, and include four-poster rooms and rooms with patios that overlook the fields. The modern oak-beamed restaurant, with country views, serves award-winning cuisine.

Rooms 26 (23 annexe) (2 fmly) (15 GF) **Facilities** STV FTV WiFi Xmas New Year **Conf** Class 80 Board 50 Thtr 80 **Parking** 80 **Notes** Civ Wed 70

Premier Inn Chichester

BUDGET HOTEL

tel: 0871 527 8242 **Chichester Gate Leisure Park, Terminus Rd PO19 8EL**
web: www.premierinn.com
dir: A27 towards city centre. Follow Terminus Road Industrial Estate signs. Left at 1st lights, left at next lights into Chichester Gate Leisure Park. Hotel on right

High quality, budget accommodation ideal for both families and business travellers. Spacious, en suite bedrooms feature tea and coffee making facilities, and Freeview TV in most hotels. Internet access and WiFi are available for a small fee. The adjacent family restaurant features a wide and varied menu. See also the Hotel Groups pages.

Rooms 83

CHIEVELEY
Berkshire   Map 5 SU47

The Crab at Chieveley

◉◉ RESTAURANT WITH ROOMS

tel: 01635 247550 🖹 01635 247440 **Wantage Rd RG20 8UE**
email: info@crabatchieveley.com **web:** www.crabatchieveley.com
dir: 1.5m W of Chieveley on B4494

The individually themed bedrooms at this former pub have been appointed to a very high standard and include a full range of modern amenities. Ground-floor rooms have a small private patio area complete with a hot tub. The warm and cosy restaurant offers an extensive and award-winning range of fish and seafood dishes.

Rooms 14 (5 annexe)

C

CHILDER THORNTON
Cheshire

Map 15 SJ37

Premier Inn Wirral (Childer Thornton)

BUDGET HOTEL

tel: 0871 527 9174 **New Chester Rd CH66 1QW**
web: www.premierinn.com
dir: M53 junct 5, A41 towards Chester. Hotel on right (same entrance as Burleydam Garden Centre)

High quality, budget accommodation ideal for both families and business travellers. Spacious, en suite bedrooms feature tea and coffee making facilities, and Freeview TV in most hotels. Internet access and WiFi are available for a small fee. The adjacent family restaurant features a wide and varied menu. See also the Hotel Groups pages.

Rooms 31

CHIPPENHAM
Wiltshire

Map 4 ST97

BEST WESTERN PLUS Angel Hotel

★★★ 80% HOTEL

tel: 01249 652615 **Market Place SN15 3HD**
email: reception@angelhotelchippenham.co.uk **web:** www.angelhotelchippenham.co.uk
dir: Follow tourist signs for Bowood House. Under railway arch, follow 'Borough Parade Parking' signs. Hotel adjacent to car park

Several impressive buildings combine to make this smart and comfortable hotel. The well-equipped bedrooms vary from those in the main house where character is the key, to the smart executive-style, courtyard rooms. The lounge and restaurant are bright and modern, and offer an imaginative carte and an all-day menu.

Rooms 50 (35 annexe) (3 fmly) (12 GF) **S** £81.85-£108.85; **D** £101.85-£118.85 **Facilities** STV FTV WiFi Gym **Conf** Class 50 Board 50 Thtr 100 Del from £155 to £175 **Parking** 50 **Notes** LB

Premier Inn Chippenham

BUDGET HOTEL

tel: 0871 527 8244 **Cepen Park, West Cepen Way SN14 6UZ**
web: www.premierinn.com
dir: M4 junct 17, A350 towards Chippenham. Hotel at 1st main rdbt

High quality, budget accommodation ideal for both families and business travellers. Spacious, en suite bedrooms feature tea and coffee making facilities, and Freeview TV in most hotels. Internet access and WiFi are available for a small fee. The adjacent family restaurant features a wide and varied menu. See also the Hotel Groups pages.

Rooms 79

CHIPPING CAMPDEN
Gloucestershire

Map 10 SP13

Three Ways House

★★★ 86% HOTEL

tel: 01386 438429 **Mickleton GL55 6SB**
email: reception@puddingclub.com **web:** www.threewayshousehotel.com
dir: In Mickleton centre, on B4632 Stratford-upon-Avon to Broadway road

Built in 1870, this charming hotel has welcomed guests for over 100 years and is home to the world famous Pudding Club, formed in 1985 to promote traditional English puddings. Individuality is a hallmark here, as reflected in a number of the bedrooms that have been designed around a pudding theme. Public areas are stylish and include the air-conditioned restaurant, lounges and meeting rooms.

Rooms 48 (7 fmly) (14 GF) ✆ **S** £88-£105; **D** £145-£250 (incl. bkfst)* **Facilities** FTV WiFi ⌁ ♪ Xmas New Year **Conf** Class 40 Board 35 Thtr 100 Del from £130* **Services** Lift **Parking** 37 **Notes** LB Civ Wed 100

The Kings

RESTAURANT WITH ROOMS

tel: 01386 840256 & 841056 📠 01386 841598 **The Square GL55 6AW**
email: info@kingscampden.co.uk **web:** www.kingscampden.co.uk
dir: In centre of town square

Located in the centre of this delightful Cotswold town, The Kings effortlessly blends a relaxed and friendly welcome with efficient service. Bedrooms and bathrooms come in a range of shapes and sizes and all are appointed to a high level of quality and comfort. Dining options, whether in the main restaurant or the comfortable bar area, serve a tempting menu to suit all tastes, from light salads and pasta, to meat and fish dishes.

Rooms 19 (5 annexe) (3 fmly)

CHIPPING NORTON
Oxfordshire
Map 10 SP32

Wild Thyme Restaurant with Rooms

 RESTAURANT WITH ROOMS

tel: 01608 645060 **10 New St OX7 5LJ**
email: enquiries@wildthymerestaurant.co.uk **web:** www.wildthymerestaurant.co.uk
dir: On A44 in town centre off market square

Set in the bustling Cotswold market town of Chipping Norton, this restaurant with rooms offers three en suite bedrooms that are individually designed, well equipped, and have many thoughtful extras. The restaurant serves exciting Modern British food that is presented with relaxed and friendly service.

Rooms 3

CHORLEY
Lancashire
Map 15 SD51

Premier Inn Chorley North

BUDGET HOTEL

tel: 0871 527 8246 **Malthouse Farm, Moss Ln, Whittle-le-Woods PR6 8AB**
web: www.premierinn.com
dir: M61 junct 8 onto A674 (Wheelton), 400yds on left into Moss Ln

High quality, budget accommodation ideal for both families and business travellers. Spacious, en suite bedrooms feature tea and coffee making facilities, and Freeview TV in most hotels. Internet access and WiFi are available for a small fee. The adjacent family restaurant features a wide and varied menu. See also the Hotel Groups pages.

Rooms 81

Premier Inn Chorley South

BUDGET HOTEL

tel: 0871 527 8248 **Bolton Rd PR7 4AB**
web: www.premierinn.com
dir: From N: M61 junct 8, A6 to Chorley. From S: M6 junct 27 follow Standish signs. Left onto A5106 to Chorley, A6 towards Preston. Hotel 0.5m on right

Rooms 29

CHRISTCHURCH
Dorset
Map 5 SZ19

Christchurch Harbour Hotel

★★★★ 83%  HOTEL

tel: 01202 483434 **95 Mudeford BH23 3NT**
email: christchurch@harbourhotels.co.uk **web:** www.christchurch-harbour-hotel.co.uk
dir: On A35 to Christchurch onto A337 to Highcliffe. Right at rdbt, hotel 1.5m on left

Delightfully situated on the side of Mudeford Quay close to sandy beaches, and conveniently located for Bournemouth Airport and the BIC, this hotel boasts an impressive spa and leisure facility. The bedrooms are particularly well appointed and stylishly finished; many have excellent views, and some have balconies. Guests can eat in the award-winning Jetty Restaurant, or the Upper Deck Bar and Restaurant.

Rooms 64 (2 fmly) (14 GF) **Facilities** Spa FTV WiFi Gym Steam room Sauna Exercise classes Hydrotherapy pool Xmas New Year **Conf** Class 20 Board 30 Thtr 100 **Services** Lift **Parking** 55 **Notes** Civ Wed 100

Captain's Club Hotel and Spa

★★★★ 81% HOTEL

tel: 01202 475111 **Wick Ferry, Wick Ln BH23 1HU**
email: enquiries@captainsclubhotel.com **web:** www.captainsclubhotel.com
dir: B3073 to Christchurch. On Fountain rdbt take 5th exit (Sopers Ln) 2nd left (St Margarets Ave) 1st right onto Wick Ln

The Captain's Club Hotel is situated in the heart of the town on the banks of the River Stour at Christchurch Quay, and only ten minutes from Bournemouth. All bedrooms, including the suites and apartments, have views overlooking the river. Guests can relax in the hydrotherapy pool, enjoy a spa treatment or sample the cuisine in Tides Restaurant.

Rooms 29 (12 fmly) **Facilities** Spa STV FTV WiFi Hydrotherapy pool Sauna Dry flotation **Conf** Class 72 Board 64 Thtr 140 Del from £195* **Services** Lift Air con **Parking** 41 **Notes** Civ Wed 100

Premier Inn Christchurch East

BUDGET HOTEL

tel: 0871 527 8250 **Somerford Rd BH23 3QG**
web: www.premierinn.com
dir: In Christchurch from A35 & B3059 rdbt junct take B3059 (Somerford Rd)

High quality, budget accommodation ideal for both families and business travellers. Spacious, en suite bedrooms feature tea and coffee making facilities, and Freeview TV in most hotels. Internet access and WiFi are available for a small fee. The adjacent family restaurant features a wide and varied menu. See also the Hotel Groups pages.

Rooms 102

Premier Inn Christchurch West

BUDGET HOTEL

tel: 0871 527 8252 **Barrack Rd BH23 2BN**
web: www.premierinn.com
dir: From A338 take A3060 towards Christchurch. Left onto A35. Hotel on right

Rooms 41

C

CHURT
Surrey

Map 5 SU83

BEST WESTERN Frensham Pond Hotel

★★★ 81% 🌸 HOTEL

tel: 01252 795161 **Bacon Ln GU10 2QB**
email: info@frenshampondhotel.co.uk **web:** www.frenshampondhotel.co.uk
dir: A3 onto A287. 4m left at 'Beware Horses' sign. Hotel 0.25m

This 15th-century house occupies a superb location on the edge of Frensham Pond. The bedrooms are mainly spacious, and the superior, garden annexe rooms have their own patio and air conditioning. The contemporary bar and lounge offers a range of snacks, and the leisure club has good facilities.

Rooms 51 (12 annexe) (14 fmly) (27 GF) **S** £60-£240; **D** £60-£240* **Facilities** STV FTV WiFi ♨ Gym Squash Xmas New Year **Conf** Class 45 Board 40 Thtr 120 Del from £75 to £110* **Parking** 120 **Notes** LB Civ Wed 130

CIRENCESTER
Gloucestershire

Map 5 SP00

Barnsley House

★★★★ 🌸🌸 COUNTRY HOUSE HOTEL

tel: 01285 740000 **Barnsley GL7 5EE**
email: info@barnsleyhouse.com **web:** www.barnsleyhouse.com
dir: 4m NE of Cirencester on B4425

This delightful Cotswold country house has been appointed to provide the highest levels of quality, comfort and relaxation. Individually styled bedrooms come in a range of shapes and sizes, from the large character rooms in the main house to the more contemporary-style stable rooms; all rooms have garden views and are packed with guest extras and little luxuries, including plasma TVs in the bathrooms. The delightful gardens, originally designed in the late 1950s by previous owner and award-winning gardener Rosemary Verey and her husband, include a fruit and vegetable area which is the home of much of the produce used in the delicious cuisine on offer in Potager Restaurant. In the grounds is the Garden Spa with treatment rooms, sauna, steam room and an outdoor hydrotherapy pool. The hotel also has a cinema.

Rooms 18 (12 annexe) (10 GF) **Facilities** Spa STV FTV WiFi ♨ 🛝 🏊 Cinema Bicycles Hydrotherapy pool Relaxation rooms Xmas New Year **Conf** Class 20 Board 18 Thtr 30 **Parking** 30 **Notes** ⊗ No children 14yrs Civ Wed 100

The Crown of Crucis

★★★ 77% HOTEL

tel: 01285 851806 **Ampney Crucis GL7 5RS**
email: reception@thecrownofcrucis.co.uk **web:** www.thecrownofcrucis.co.uk
dir: A417 to Fairford, hotel 2.5m on left

This delightful hotel consists of two buildings; one a 16th-century coaching inn, which houses the bar and restaurant, and a more modern bedroom block which surrounds a courtyard. Rooms are attractively appointed and offer modern facilities; the restaurant serves a range of imaginative dishes.

Rooms 25 (2 fmly) (13 GF) **S** £85-£105; **D** £115-£165 (incl. bkfst)* **Facilities** FTV WiFi ♨ New Year **Conf** Class 50 Board 40 Thtr 100 **Parking** 82 **Notes** LB RS 25-26 Dec Civ Wed 90

Corinium Hotel & Restaurant

★★★ 🅰 SMALL HOTEL

tel: 01285 659711 **12 Gloucester St GL7 2DG**
email: info@coriniumhotel.co.uk **web:** www.coriniumhotel.co.uk
dir: From A417/A419/A429 towards Cirencester. A435 at rdbt. After 500mtrs turn left at lights, then 1st right, car park on left

This delightful 16th-century small hotel is quietly situated just five minutes walk from town, and is an ideal base from which to explore the Cotswolds. The Corinium has a locally renowned restaurant offering Modern British cuisine, as well as a cosy bar full of Cotswold charm. Other benefits include free WiFi throughout hotel, an attractive secluded garden for alfresco dining and ample free parking.

Rooms 15 (2 fmly) (2 GF) **S** £55-£80; **D** £65-£120 (incl. bkfst)* **Facilities** FTV WiFi ♨ **Conf** Class 30 Board 34 Thtr 70 Del from £110 to £150* **Parking** 30 **Notes** LB

CLACTON-ON-SEA
Essex

Map 7 TM11

The Legacy Kingscliff Hotel

★★★ 77% HOTEL

tel: 0844 411 9492 & 0330 333 2992 **King's Pde, Holland on Sea CO15 5JB**
email: info@thekingscliffhotel.com **web:** www.legacy-hotels.co.uk
dir: A12 junct 29 onto A120, then A133, at Weeley rdbt take 3rd exit, turn onto Marine Parade East & continue onto Kings Parade

The Legacy Kingscliff Hotel enjoys a prominent position along the seafront and has recently undergone a major refurbishment. Bedrooms are all attractively presented, comfortable and very well equipped; some front-facing rooms enjoy wonderful sea views. There is a popular restaurant along with a stylish lounge bar for guests. Secure parking is available and free WiFi is available throughout the hotel. This hotel is a very popular wedding and conference venue.

Rooms 30 (2 fmly) (7 GF) 🐾 **Facilities** FTV WiFi ♨ Xmas New Year **Conf** Class 50 Board 30 Thtr 90 **Parking** 50 **Notes** Civ Wed

---

Premier Inn Clacton-on-Sea

BUDGET HOTEL

tel: 0871 527 8254 **Crown Green Roundabout, Colchester Rd, Trending CO16 9AA**
web: www.premierinn.com
dir: A12, A120 towards Harwich. In 4m take A133 to Clacton-on-Sea. Hotel off Weeley Rdbt

High quality, budget accommodation ideal for both families and business travellers. Spacious, en suite bedrooms feature tea and coffee making facilities, and Freeview TV in most hotels. Internet access and WiFi are available for a small fee. The adjacent family restaurant features a wide and varied menu. See also the Hotel Groups pages.

Rooms 40

CLAVERDON
Warwickshire   Map 10 SP16

Ardencote Manor Hotel & Spa

★★★★ 80%  HOTEL

tel: 01926 843111 **The Cumsey, Lye Green Rd, Claverdon CV35 8LT**
email: hotel@ardencote.com **web:** www.ardencote.com
dir: Telephone or see website for directions

Originally built as a gentleman's residence around 1860, this hotel is set in 83 acres of landscaped grounds. Public rooms include a choice of lounge areas, a cocktail bar and conservatory breakfast room. Main meals are served in the Lodge Restaurant, a separate building with a light contemporary style, which sits beside a small lake. An extensive range of leisure and conference facilities is provided and bedrooms are smartly decorated and tastefully furnished.

Rooms 110 (10 fmly) (30 GF) ♣ **S** £75-£110; **D** £95-£165 (incl. bkfst) **Facilities** Spa STV FTV WiFi ♭ HL 🏊 ✂ ⚓ 9 ⛳ Putt green 🏌 Gym Squash Sauna Steam room Dance studio Xmas New Year **Conf** Class 70 Board 50 Thtr 175 Del from £130 to £180 **Services** Lift Air con **Parking** 350 **Notes** LB ⊗ Civ Wed 150

CLEARWELL
Gloucestershire   Map 4 SO50

Tudor Farmhouse Hotel & Restaurant

★★★ 83% ●● HOTEL

tel: 01594 833046 **High St GL16 8JS**
email: info@tudorfarmhousehotel.co.uk **web:** www.tudorfarmhousehotel.co.uk
dir: A4136 onto B4228, through Coleford, right into Clearwell, hotel on right just before War Memorial Cross

Dating from the 13th century, this idyllic former farmhouse retains a host of original features including exposed stonework, oak beams, wall panelling and wonderful inglenook fireplaces. Bedrooms have great individuality and style and are located either in the main house or in converted buildings in the grounds. Creative menus offer quality cuisine, served in the intimate, candlelit restaurant.

Rooms 23 (18 annexe) (3 fmly) (10 GF) ♣ **Facilities** STV FTV WiFi ♭ HL Xmas New Year **Conf** Class 20 Board 12 Thtr 30 **Parking** 30 **Notes** Closed 2-5 Jan

The Wyndham Arms Hotel

★★★ 68% ● HOTEL

tel: 01594 833666 **GL16 8JT**
email: nigel@thewyndhamhotel.co.uk **web:** www.thewyndhamhotel.co.uk
dir: Exit B4228, in village centre on B4231

The history of this charming village inn can be traced back over 600 years. It has exposed stone walls, original beams and an impressive inglenook fireplace in the friendly bar. Most bedrooms are in a modern extension, while the other rooms, in the main house, are more traditional in style. A range of dishes is offered in the bar or restaurant.

Rooms 18 (12 annexe) (3 fmly) (6 GF) **S** £45-£65; **D** £75-£150 (incl. bkfst) **Facilities** FTV WiFi ♭ Xmas **Conf** Class 30 Board 22 Thtr 56 **Parking** 52 **Notes** LB Closed 1st wk Jan

CLECKHEATON
West Yorkshire   Map 19 SE12

Premier Inn Bradford South

BUDGET HOTEL

tel: 0871 527 8136 **Whitehall Rd, Dye House Dr BD19 6HG**
web: www.premierinn.com
dir: On A58 at intersection with M62 & M606

High quality, budget accommodation ideal for both families and business travellers. Spacious, en suite bedrooms feature tea and coffee making facilities, and Freeview TV in most hotels. Internet access and WiFi are available for a small fee. The adjacent family restaurant features a wide and varied menu. See also the Hotel Groups pages.

Rooms 40

CLEETHORPES
Lincolnshire   Map 17 TA30

Kingsway Hotel

★★★ 80% HOTEL

tel: 01472 601122 **Kingsway DN35 0AE**
email: reception@kingsway-hotel.com **web:** www.kingsway-hotel.com
dir: Exit A180 at Grimsby, to Cleethorpes seafront. Hotel at Kingsway & Queen Parade junct - A1098

This seafront hotel has been in the same family for four generations and continues to provide traditional comfort and friendly service. The lounges are comfortable and good food is served in the pleasant dining room. The bedrooms are bright and nicely furnished - most are comfortably proportioned.

Rooms 49 ♣ **S** £65-£79; **D** £96-£110 (incl. bkfst)* **Facilities** STV FTV WiFi **Conf** Board 18 Thtr 22 **Services** Lift **Parking** 50 **Notes** ⊗ No children 5yrs Closed 25-26 Dec

C

CLOVELLY
Devon
Map 3 SS32

Red Lion Hotel

★★ 78% HOTEL

tel: 01237 431237 **The Quay EX39 5TF**
email: redlion@clovelly.co.uk **web:** www.clovelly.co.uk
dir: Exit A39 at Clovelly Cross onto B3237. Pass visitor centre, 1st left by white rails to harbour

'Idyllic' is the only word to describe the harbour-side setting of this charming 18th-century inn, with the famous fishing village forming a spectacular backdrop. Bedrooms are stylish and enjoy delightful views. The inn's relaxed atmosphere is conducive to switching off from the pressures of modern life, even when the harbour comes alive with the activities of the local fishermen during the day.

Rooms 17 (6 annexe) (5 fmly) (2 GF) 🐾 **S** £70-£108; **D** £140-£180 (incl. bkfst)* **Facilities** FTV WiFi Sea fishing Diving, tennis & spa treatments can be arranged Xmas New Year **Parking** 11 **Notes** LB Civ Wed 70

New Inn

★★ 72% HOTEL

tel: 01237 431303 **High St EX39 5TQ**
email: newinn@clovelly.co.uk **web:** www.clovelly.co.uk
dir: At Clovelly Cross, exit A39 onto B3237. Follow down hill for 1.5m. Right at sign 'All vehicles for Clovelly'

Famed for its cobbled descent to the harbour, this fascinating fishing village is a traffic-free zone. Consequently, luggage is conveyed by sledge or donkey to this much-photographed hotel. Carefully renovated bedrooms and public areas are smartly presented with quality, locally-made furnishings. Meals may be taken in the elegant restaurant or the popular Upalong bar.

Rooms 8 (1 fmly) (1 GF) 🐾 **Facilities** FTV WiFi Sea fishing Diving & tennis can be arranged Xmas New Year **Notes** Civ Wed 50

CLOWNE
Derbyshire
Map 16 SK47

Hotel Van Dyk

★★★★ 76% 🏵 SMALL HOTEL

tel: 01246 810219 **Worksop Rd S43 4TD**
email: info@hotelvandyk.co.uk **web:** www.vandykhotel.co.uk
dir: M1 junct 30, 2nd right towards Worksop, 2nd rdbt 1st exit, 3rd rdbt straight over. Through lights, hotel 100yds on right

A sympathetic renovation has resulted in a small vibrant boutique-style hotel where staff are always on hand to offer friendly and welcoming service. Accommodation is luxurious and equipped with many thoughtful extras. Bowdens Restaurant offers fine dining and makes the ideal setting for a memorable evening; alternatively there's Southgate Grill for those looking for a more casual eating option.

Rooms 15 (4 fmly) 🐾 **Facilities** FTV WiFi 🎵 Xmas New Year **Conf** Class 50 Board 60 Thtr 200 **Parking** 78 **Notes** ⊗ Civ Wed 250

COBHAM
Surrey
Map 6 TQ16

Premier Inn Cobham

BUDGET HOTEL

tel: 0871 527 8256 **Portsmouth Rd, Fairmile KT11 1BW**
web: www.premierinn.com
dir: M25 junct 10, A3 towards London, A245 towards Cobham. In Cobham town centre left onto A307 (Portsmouth Rd). Hotel on left

High quality, budget accommodation ideal for both families and business travellers. Spacious, en suite bedrooms feature tea and coffee making facilities, and Freeview TV in most hotels. Internet access and WiFi are available for a small fee. The adjacent family restaurant features a wide and varied menu. See also the Hotel Groups pages.

Rooms 48

COCKERMOUTH
Cumbria
Map 18 NY13

The Trout Hotel

★★★★ 79% HOTEL

tel: 01900 823591 **Crown St CA13 0EJ**
email: reservations@trouthotel.co.uk **web:** www.trouthotel.co.uk
dir: Adjacent to Wordsworth House

Dating back to 1670, this privately owned hotel has an enviable setting on the banks of the River Derwent. The well-equipped bedrooms, some contained in a wing overlooking the river, are comfortable and mostly spacious. The Terrace Bar & Bistro, serving food all day, has a sheltered patio area. There is also a cosy bar, a choice of lounge areas and an attractive, traditional-style dining room that offers a good choice of set-price dishes.

Rooms 49 (4 fmly) (15 GF) 🐾 **S** £121; **D** £125 (incl. bkfst)* **Facilities** STV FTV WiFi ⌕ Fishing Xmas New Year **Conf** Class 20 Board 20 Thtr 25 **Parking** 40 **Notes** LB Civ Wed 60

Shepherds Hotel

★★★ 75% HOTEL

tel: 0845 459 9770 **Lakeland Sheep & Wool Centre, Egremont Rd CA13 0QX**
email: info@argyllholidays.com **web:** www.shepherdshotel.co.uk
dir: At junct of A66 & A5086 S of Cockermouth, entrance off A5086, 200mtrs from rdbt

This hotel is modern in style and offers thoughtfully equipped accommodation. It is well situated for the Northern Lakes area and has good road links. The restaurant, open all day, serves a wide variety of meals and snacks; the Black Rock dishes are recommended. Free WiFi is available in the bedrooms.

Rooms 26 (4 fmly) (13 GF) **S** £58-£70; **D** £69-£120 (incl. bkfst)* **Facilities** STV FTV WiFi ↷ Pool table Small children's play area **Conf** Class 30 Board 30 Thtr 40 **Services** Lift **Parking** 100 **Notes** LB Closed 25-26 Dec

COGGESHALL	Map 7 TL82
Essex	

White Hart Hotel

★★★ 73% HOTEL

OldEngl sh

tel: 01376 561654 **Market End CO6 1NH**
email: 6529@greeneking.co.uk **web:** www.oldenglish.co.uk
dir: From A12 through Kelvedon & onto B1024 to Coggeshall

The White Hart Hotel is a delightful inn situated in the centre of this bustling market town. Bedrooms vary in size and style; each one offers good quality and comfort with extras such as CD players, fruit and mineral water. The heavily beamed public areas include a popular bar serving a varied menu, a large restaurant offering European style cuisine and a cosy residents' lounge.

Rooms 18 (1 fmly) (18 smoking) **Facilities** STV FTV ♬ Xmas **Conf** Class 10 Board 22 Thtr 30 **Parking** 47

COLCHESTER	Map 13 TL92
Essex	

Wivenhoe House Hotel

★★★★ 81% HOTEL

tel: 01206 863666 **Wivenhoe Park CO4 3SQ**
email: info@wivenhoehouse.co.uk **web:** www.wivenhoehouse.co.uk
dir: From A12 take exit signed Colchester. Follow A133 towards Clacton. Take B1027 for Wivenhoe, right on Boundry Rd, right on Park Rd, signed

A superb building which forms part of Essex University, the property has been totally refurbished. The bedrooms are split between the main building and the more contemporary extension; each one has been individually decorated, furnished to a very high standard and has modern technology. Public rooms include the Signatures fine dining restaurant and a modern brasserie; there is also a choice of lounges with plush furnishings.

Rooms 40 (6 fmly) ↰ **Facilities** STV FTV WiFi ↷ Xmas New Year **Conf** Class 81 Board 20 Thtr 140 **Services** Lift **Parking** 40 **Notes** Civ Wed

Crowne Plaza Resort Colchester - Five Lakes

★★★★ 78% ⬡ HOTEL

tel: 01621 868888 **Colchester Rd CM9 8HX**
email: enquiries@cpcolchester.co.uk **web:** www.cpcolchester.co.uk

(For full entry see Tolleshunt Knights)

Stoke by Nayland Hotel, Golf & Spa

★★★★ 75% ⬡⬡ HOTEL

tel: 01206 262836 & 265835 **Keepers Ln, Leavenheath CO6 4PZ**
email: sales@stokebynayland.com **web:** www.stokebynayland.com
dir: Exit A134 at Leavenheath onto B1068, hotel 0.75m on right

This hotel is situated on the edge of Dedham Vale, an Area of Outstanding Natural Beauty, in 300 acres of undulating countryside with lakes and two golf courses. The spacious bedrooms are attractively decorated and equipped with modern facilities, including ISDN lines. Free WiFi is available throughout. Public rooms include the Spikes bar, a conservatory, a lounge, a smart restaurant, conference and banqueting suites. The superb Peake Spa and Fitness Centre offers extensive facilities including health and beauty treatments.

Rooms 80 (4 fmly) (26 GF) **Facilities** Spa STV FTV WiFi ↷ ⊛ supervised ⚓ 36 Putt green Fishing Gym Squash Driving range Snooker tables ♬ Xmas New Year **Conf** Class 300 Board 60 Thtr 450 **Services** Lift **Parking** 335 **Notes** ⊗ Civ Wed 200

BEST WESTERN Marks Tey Hotel

★★★★ 70% HOTEL

tel: 01206 210001 **London Rd, Marks Tey CO6 1DU**
email: info@marksteyhotel.co.uk **web:** www.marksteyhotel.co.uk
dir: Off A12/A120 junct signed Marks Tey/Stansted. At rdbt follow Stanway signs. Follow over A12, at next rdbt take 1st exit. Hotel on left

Best Western Marks Tey Hotel is a purpose-built hotel situated just off the A12 on the outskirts of Colchester. Public rooms include a brasserie restaurant, a choice of lounges, a bar and a conservatory. Bedrooms come in a variety of styles; each one is smartly furnished and equipped with modern facilities. The hotel also has conference and leisure facilities.

Rooms 110 (57 GF) ↰ **S** £65-£95; **D** £65-£115 (incl. bkfst) **Facilities** FTV WiFi ↷ ⊛ supervised ⟲ Gym Steam room Beauty treatment room Sauna Xmas New Year **Conf** Class 100 Board 60 Thtr 200 Del from £130 to £190 **Services** Lift **Parking** 200 **Notes** LB ⊗ Civ Wed 160

Holiday Inn Colchester

★★★ 83% HOTEL

tel: 0871 942 9020 **Abbotts Ln, Eight Ash Green CO6 3QL**
email: colchester@ihg.com **web:** www.hicolchesterhotel.co.uk
dir: Exit A12 at junct with A1124, follow Halstead signs. 0.25m, hotel at rdbt on left

This hotel is situated three miles from Colchester and is ideally located just off the A12 in a quiet village setting. All bedrooms are air conditioned and have high-speed internet access. Trader's bar and grill offers a relaxed and informal environment; a range of conference rooms can cater for meetings and weddings.

Rooms 110 (25 fmly) (54 GF) **S** fr £59; **D** fr £59* **Facilities** Spa STV FTV WiFi ↷ HL ⊛ supervised Gym Health club Hair & beauty salon Personal training Exercise classes Xmas New Year **Conf** Class 60 Board 50 Thtr 120 Del from £125* **Services** Air con **Parking** 130 **Notes** LB ⊗ Civ Wed 100

COLCHESTER *continued*

The North Hill Hotel

★★★ 82% HOTEL

tel: 01206 574001 **51 North Hill CO1 1PY**
email: info@northhillhotel.com **web:** www.northhillhotel.com
dir: Follow directions for town centre, down North Hill, hotel on left

The North Hill Hotel is situated in the centre of this historic town. The contemporary open-plan public areas include a small lounge bar and the Green Room restaurant. The smartly appointed bedrooms are modern and well equipped with large flat-screen TVs and many thoughtful touches.

Rooms 17 (3 fmly) (1 GF) ⌇ **S** £64.50-£99.50; **D** £89.50-£109.50 (incl. bkfst)*
Facilities FTV WiFi Xmas New Year **Conf** Class 25 Board 20 Thtr 30 Del from £110 to £125* **Notes** ⊗

BEST WESTERN The Rose & Crown Hotel

★★★ 80% HOTEL

tel: 01206 866677 **East St CO1 2TZ**
email: info@rose-and-crown.com **web:** www.rose-and-crown.com
dir: From A12 follow Rollerworld signs, hotel by level crossing

This delightful 14th-century coaching inn is situated close to the shops and is full of charm and character. Public areas feature a wealth of exposed beams and timbered walls, and includes the contemporary East St Grill. Although the bedrooms vary in size, all are stylishly decorated and equipped with many thoughtful extras suitable for both business and leisure guests; luxury executive rooms are available.

Rooms 39 (3 fmly) (12 GF) **Facilities** WiFi **Conf** Class 50 Board 45 Thtr 100
Services Lift **Parking** 50 **Notes** ⊗ Civ Wed 80

Premier Inn Colchester (A12)

BUDGET HOTEL

tel: 0871 527 8260 **Ipswich Rd CO4 9WP**
web: www.premierinn.com
dir: From A12 exit at Colchester Nrth/A1232 junct off towards Colchester. Hotel on right, 200yds from rdbt. (NB for Sat Nav use CO4 9TD)

High quality, budget accommodation ideal for both families and business travellers. Spacious, en suite bedrooms feature tea and coffee making facilities, and Freeview TV in most hotels. Internet access and WiFi are available for a small fee. The adjacent family restaurant features a wide and varied menu. See also the Hotel Groups pages.

Rooms 60

Premier Inn Colchester Central

BUDGET HOTEL

tel: 0871 527 8258 **Cowdray Av CO1 1UT**
web: www.premierinn.com
dir: From Ipswich A12 junct 29. At rdbt onto A1232 (Ipswich road). At 2nd rdbt 2nd exit onto A133 (Cowdray Ave). Hotel approx 0.5m on right

Rooms 20

COLEFORD   Map 4 SO51
Gloucestershire

Bells Hotel & The Forest of Dean Golf Club

★★★ 71% HOTEL

tel: 01594 832583 **Lords Hill GL16 8BE**
email: enquiries@bells-hotel.co.uk **web:** www.bells-hotel.co.uk
dir: 0.25m from Coleford. Off B4228

Set in its own grounds, with an 18-hole golf course, this purpose-built establishment offers a range of facilities. Bedrooms vary in style and space, and a number are on the ground floor. There is a small gym, and a comfortable bar and lounge which is available until late. The hotel's club house, just yards away, has a bar with all-day meals and snacks, a restaurant, a games/TV room and conference and function rooms.

Rooms 53 (12 fmly) (36 GF) (5 smoking) ⌇ **Facilities** FTV WiFi ⌗ 18 Putt green Bowling green Short mat bowling room ♫ Xmas New Year **Conf** Class 250 Board 100 Thtr 350 **Parking** 100 **Notes** ⊗ Civ Wed 150

COLERNE   Map 4 ST87
Wiltshire

Lucknam Park Hotel & Spa

★★★★★  COUNTRY HOUSE HOTEL

tel: 01225 742777 **SN14 8AZ**
email: reservations@lucknampark.co.uk **web:** www.lucknampark.co.uk
dir: M4 junct 17, A350 towards Chippenham, then A420 towards Bristol for 3m. At Ford left to Colerne, 3m, right at x-rds, entrance on right

Approaching this Palladian mansion along a magnificent mile-long avenue of beech and lime trees, builds a wonderful sense of anticipation. Surrounded by 500 acres of parkland and beautiful gardens, the hotel offers a wealth of choices ranging from pampered relaxation within the indulgent spa, complete with an innovative new Well-Being centre, to more energetic equestrian pursuits. Elegant bedrooms and suites are split between the main building and adjacent courtyard, all of which exude quality, individuality and comfort. Dining options range from the informal Brasserie (awarded 1 AA Rosette), to the formal and very accomplished main restaurant, The Park (with 3 AA Rosettes), where skilled, sincere and engaging staff contribute to a memorable experience. For anyone with a passion for food, the recently opened Cookery School is also worth investigating.

Rooms 42 (18 annexe) (16 GF) ⌇ **S** £360-£1230; **D** £360-£1230* **Facilities** Spa STV FTV WiFi ⌗ 🎣 ⌗ ⌗ Gym Cross country course Mountain bikes Equestrian centre Cookery school Xmas New Year **Conf** Class 24 Board 24 Thtr 60 Del £415* **Parking** 80
Notes LB ⊗ Civ Wed 110

COLESHILL
Warwickshire   Map 10 SP18

Grimstock Country House Hotel

★★★ 74% COUNTRY HOUSE HOTEL

tel: 01675 462121 **Gilson Rd, Gilson B46 1LJ**
email: enquiries@grimstockhotel.co.uk **web:** www.grimstockhotel.co.uk
dir: Exit A446 at rdbt onto B4117 to Gilson, hotel 100yds on right

This privately owned hotel is convenient for Birmingham International Airport and the NEC, and benefits from a peaceful rural setting. Bedrooms are spacious and comfortable. Public rooms include two restaurants, a wood-panelled bar, good conference facilities and a gym featuring the latest cardiovascular equipment.

Rooms 44 (1 fmly) (13 GF) **Facilities** FTV WiFi ⮶ Gym Xmas New Year **Conf** Class 60 Board 50 Thtr 100 **Parking** 100 **Notes** Civ Wed 100

COLTISHALL
Norfolk   Map 13 TG21

Norfolk Mead Hotel

★★★★ 78% ⊚ COUNTRY HOUSE HOTEL

tel: 01603 737531 **Church Loke NR12 7DN**
email: info@norfolkmead.co.uk **web:** www.norfolkmead.co.uk
dir: Coltishall village, go right with petrol station on left, 200 yds church on right, go down driveway

This beautiful hotel enjoys a peaceful location and is set in its own extensive grounds, while still being a short walk to the pretty village of Coltishall. A major renovation was completed in 2013, bedrooms are all beautifully designed, and the public areas are very well appointed. Afternoon tea can be enjoyed in the walled garden on finer days and the cosy bar is very comfortable. There is an award-winning restaurant, which benefits from garden and river views.

Rooms 13 (2 annexe) (2 fmly) (1 GF) ⮕ **S** £120-£175; **D** £130-£185 (incl. bkfst)*
Facilities FTV WiFi ⮶ ⮶ Xmas New Year **Conf** Class 20 Board 20 Thtr 200 Del from £175 to £250* **Parking** 40 **Notes** LB ⊗ Civ Wed 40

COLYFORD
Devon   Map 4 SY29

Swallows Eaves Hotel

★★ 85% SMALL HOTEL

tel: 01297 553184 **Swan Hill Rd EX24 6QJ**
email: info@swallowseaves.co.uk **web:** www.swallowseaves.co.uk
dir: On A3052 between Lyme Regis & Sidmouth, in village centre, opposite post office store

Close to the Devon and Dorset border, this intimate and welcoming hotel is ideally located for exploring this beautiful area. The relaxed atmosphere is matched with attentive service. Comfortable bedrooms come complete with Egyptian cotton bedding and large fluffy towels. Local produce features on the menu which is offered in the stylish Reeds restaurant.

Rooms 7 (1 GF) ⮕ **S** £75-£85; **D** £95-£135 (incl. bkfst)* **Facilities** FTV WiFi **Conf** Thtr 20 **Parking** 18 **Notes** LB ⊗ No children 14yrs

COPTHORNE

See Gatwick Airport

CORBY
Northamptonshire   Map 11 SP88

Premier Inn Corby

BUDGET HOTEL

tel: 0871 527 8264 **1 Little Colliers Field NN18 8TJ**
web: www.premierinn.com
dir: M1 junct 19, A14 E'bound. Exit at junct 7, left at rdbt onto A43. At next rdbt left onto A6003. Hotel at next rdbt (NB for Sat Nav use NN18 9EX)

High quality, budget accommodation ideal for both families and business travellers. Spacious, en suite bedrooms feature tea and coffee making facilities, and Freeview TV in most hotels. Internet access and WiFi are available for a small fee. The adjacent family restaurant features a wide and varied menu. See also the Hotel Groups pages.

Rooms 56

CORFE CASTLE
Dorset   Map 4 SY98

Mortons House Hotel

★★★ 87% ⊚⊚ HOTEL

tel: 01929 480988 **49 East St BH20 5EE**
email: stay@mortonshouse.co.uk **web:** www.mortonshouse.co.uk
dir: On A351 between Wareham & Swanage

Set in delightful gardens and grounds with excellent views of Corfe Castle, this impressive building dates back to Tudor times. The oak-panelled drawing room has a roaring log fire in cooler months, and an interesting range of enjoyable cuisine is available in the well-appointed dining room. Bedrooms, many with views of the castle, are comfortable and well equipped.

Rooms 21 (7 annexe) (2 fmly) (7 GF) ⮕ **S** £80-£120; **D** £100-£160 (incl. bkfst)*
Facilities FTV WiFi HL Xmas New Year **Conf** Class 45 Board 20 Thtr 45 Del from £135 to £155* **Parking** 40 **Notes** LB ⊗ Civ Wed 60

CORLEY MOTORWAY SERVICE AREA (M6)
Warwickshire   Map 10 SP38

Days Inn Corley - NEC - M6

BUDGET HOTEL

tel: 01676 543800 **Junction 3-4, M6 North, Corley CV7 8NR**
email: corley.hotel@welcomebreak.co.uk **web:** www.welcomebreak.co.uk
dir: On M6 between juncts 3 & 4 N'bound

This modern building offers accommodation in smart, spacious and well-equipped bedrooms, suitable for families and business travellers, and all with en suite bathrooms. Continental breakfast is available and other refreshments may be taken at the nearby family restaurant. See also the Hotel Groups pages.

Rooms 50 (13 fmly) (24 GF) (8 smoking) ⮕

C

CORNHILL-ON-TWEED
Northumberland — Map 21 NT83

Tillmouth Park Country House Hotel

★★★ 87% COUNTRY HOUSE HOTEL

tel: 01890 882255 **TD12 4UU**
email: reception@tillmouthpark.f9.co.uk **web:** www.tillmouthpark.co.uk
dir: Exit A1(M) at East Ord rdbt at Berwick-upon-Tweed. Take A698 signed Cornhill & Coldstream. Hotel 9m on left

Tillmouth Park is an imposing mansion set in landscaped grounds by the River Till. Gracious public rooms include a stunning galleried lounge with a drawing room adjacent. The quiet, elegant dining room overlooks the gardens, whilst lunches and early dinners are available in the bistro. Bedrooms retain much traditional character and include several magnificent master rooms.

Rooms 14 (2 annexe) (2 fmly) (2 GF) (4 smoking) **S** £79-£145; **D** £175-£249 (incl. bkfst) **Facilities** FTV WiFi Game shooting Fishing New Year **Conf** Class 20 Board 20 Thtr 50 Del from £200 to £210 **Parking** 50 **Notes** LB Closed 3 Jan-1 Apr Civ Wed 50

CORSE LAWN
Gloucestershire — Map 10 SO83

INSPECTORS' CHOICE

Corse Lawn House Hotel

★★★ ◉◉ HOTEL

tel: 01452 780771 **GL19 4LZ**
email: enquiries@corselawn.com **web:** www.corselawn.com
dir: On B4211 5m SW of Tewkesbury

This gracious Grade II listed Queen Anne house, in 12 acres of grounds, has been home to the Hine family for more than thirty years. Aided by an enthusiastic and committed team, the family continues to preside over all aspects of the hotel, creating a wonderfully relaxed environment. Bedrooms offer a reassuring mix of comfort and quality, and include four-poster rooms. In both The Restaurant and The Bistro the impressive cuisine is based on excellent produce, much of it locally sourced.

Rooms 18 (3 fmly) (5 GF) ⌑ **S** £70-£100; **D** £90-£120 (incl. bkfst)* **Facilities** STV FTV WiFi ⌑ ⌑ ⌑ ⌑ Badminton Table tennis New Year **Conf** Class 30 Board 25 Thtr 50 Del from £135 to £150* **Parking** 62 **Notes** LB Closed 24-26 Dec Civ Wed 70

CORSHAM
Wiltshire — Map 4 ST87

Guyers House Hotel

★★★ 79% ◉◉ HOTEL

tel: 01249 713399 **Pickwick SN13 0PS**
web: www.guyershouse.com
dir: A4 between Pickwick & Corsham

This privately owned hotel retains the charm and ambiance of a country house. The bedrooms are well appointed in keeping with the style of the house, and equipped with all modern amenities. The award-winning restaurant is the ideal place for an intimate dinner or a family gathering; alfresco dining is possible when the weather is favourable. The gardens are a feature and are open to the public on certain days under the National Garden Scheme. The hotel is conveniently located for easy access to Bath.

Rooms 37 (13 GF) ⌑ **S** £95-£130; **D** £130-£160 (incl. bkfst)* **Facilities** FTV WiFi ⌑ ⌑ ⌑ Gym Xmas **Conf** Class 34 Board 24 Thtr 75 Del from £135* **Parking** 60 **Notes** ⊗ Closed 30 Dec-3 Jan Civ Wed 100

COVENTRY
West Midlands — Map 10 SP37

See also **Meriden & Nuneaton**

BEST WESTERN PLUS Windmill Village Hotel

★★★★ 77% HOTEL

tel: 02476 404040 **Birmingham Rd, Allesley CV5 9AL**
email: reservations@windmillvillagehotel.co.uk **web:** www.windmillvillagehotel.co.uk
dir: A45, close to Coventry City Centre

This modern hotel is conveniently located on the outskirts of Coventry and is a short drive from Birmingham and the NEC. Bedrooms are all very attractively presented and most rooms have views over the hotel's challenging golf course. The leisure facilities are first rate and include a very well-equipped gym and a swimming pool. Business guests are well catered for with a range of conference facilities including business suites, and free WiFi is available throughout the hotel.

Rooms 105 (35 annexe) (10 fmly) (39 GF) ⌑ **Facilities** Spa FTV WiFi ⌑ ⌑ supervised ⌑ 18 Putt green Gym Xmas New Year **Conf** Class 140 Board 60 Thtr 400 **Services** Lift **Parking** 400 **Notes** Civ Wed 100

Holiday Inn Coventry

★★★ 79% HOTEL

tel: 0871 942 9021 & 024 7658 7420 **Hinckley Rd CV2 2HP**
email: reservations-coventrym6@ihg.com **web:** www.holidayinn.co.uk
dir: M6 junct 2. Hotel on A4600

Situated close to the city centre and major motorway networks, this hotel offers comfortable and modern accommodation. Facilities include the Spirit Leisure Suite, Traders Restaurant, spacious lounges where food is served all day, and extensive conference services.

Rooms 158 (11 fmly) (64 GF) (16 smoking) **D** £69-£139* **Facilities** STV WiFi HL ⌑ supervised Gym Steam room Sauna Aqua-aerobic classes Zumba classes New Year **Conf** Class 120 Board 105 Thtr 350 Del from £80 to £130* **Services** Lift Air con **Parking** 246 **Notes** Civ Wed 200

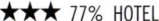

Novotel Coventry

★★★ 77% HOTEL

tel: 024 7636 5000 **Wilsons Ln CV6 6HL**
email: h0506@accor-hotels.com **web:** www.novotel.com
dir: M6 junct 3. Follow signs for B4113 towards Longford & Bedworth. 3rd exit on large rdbt

Novotel Coventry is a modern hotel convenient for Birmingham, Coventry and the motorway network, offering spacious, well-equipped accommodation. The bright brasserie has extended dining hours, alternatively there is an extensive room-service menu. Family rooms and a play area make this a child-friendly hotel, and there is also a selection of meeting rooms.

Rooms 98 (25 GF) **Facilities** STV WiFi **Conf** Class 100 Board 40 Thtr 200 **Services** Lift **Parking** 120 **Notes** Civ Wed 50

Ibis Coventry Centre

BUDGET HOTEL

tel: 024 7625 0500 **Mile Ln, St John's Ringway CV1 2LN**
email: H2793@accor.com **web:** www.ibishotel.com
dir: A45, A4114 signed Jaguar Assembly Plant. At inner ring road towards ring road S. Exit junct 5 for Mile Lane

Modern, budget hotel offering comfortable accommodation in bright and practical bedrooms. Breakfast is self-service and dinner is available in the restaurant. See also the Hotel Groups pages.

Rooms 89 (5 fmly) (25 GF)

Ibis Coventry South

BUDGET HOTEL

tel: 024 7663 9922 **Abbey Rd, Whitley CV3 4LF**
email: H2094@accor.com **web:** www.ibishotel.com
dir: Signed from A46/A423 rdbt. Take A423 towards A45. Follow signs for Racquets Health Club & Jaguar Engineering Plant. 1st exit from Jaguar rdbt, hotel at end of lane by The Virgin sports centre

Rooms 52 (52 annexe) (1 fmly) (25 GF) **Conf** Class 20 Board 16 Thtr 20 Del from £65 to £85

Premier Inn Coventry (Binley/A46)

BUDGET HOTEL

tel: 0871 527 8268 **Rugby Rd, Binley Woods CV3 2TA**
web: www.premierinn.com
dir: M6 junct 2 follow Warwick, A46 & M40 signs. Follow 'All traffic' signs, under bridge onto A46. Left at 1st rdbt to Binley. Hotel on right at next rdbt

High quality, budget accommodation ideal for both families and business travellers. Spacious, en suite bedrooms feature tea and coffee making facilities, and Freeview TV in most hotels. Internet access and WiFi are available for a small fee. The adjacent family restaurant features a wide and varied menu. See also the Hotel Groups pages.

Rooms 76

Premier Inn Coventry City Centre

BUDGET HOTEL

tel: 0871 527 8272 **Belgrade Plaza, Bond St CV1 4AH**
web: www.premierinn.com
dir: A4053 (ring road) junct 9, follow Belgrade Plaza car park signs. Hotel in same complex

Rooms 119

Premier Inn Coventry City Centre (Earlsdon Park)

BUDGET HOTEL

tel: 0871 527 9318 **Earlsdon Park CV1 3BH**
web: www.premierinn.com
dir: From Coventry ring road follow Ikea signs. Hotel adjacent to Coventry RFC on Butts Rd. Parking in multi storey adjacent

Rooms 100

Premier Inn Coventry East (Ansty)

BUDGET HOTEL

tel: 0871 527 8274 **Coombe Fields Rd, Ansty CV7 9JP**
web: www.premierinn.com
dir: M6 junct 2, B4065 towards Ansty. After village right onto B4029 signed Brinklow. Right into Coombe Fields Rd, hotel on right

Rooms 27

Premier Inn Coventry (M6 Jct 2)

BUDGET HOTEL

tel: 0871 527 8266 **Gielgud Way, Cross Point Business Park CV2 2SZ**
web: www.premierinn.com
dir: M6 junct 2 towards Coventry onto A4600 (Hinckley road). At rdbt 1st exit into Parkway, left at next rdbt into Olivier Way. At next rdbt straight on into retail park towards cinema, hotel on right

Rooms 48

Premier Inn Coventry South (A45)

BUDGET HOTEL

tel: 0871 527 8270 **Kenpas Highway CV3 6PB**
web: www.premierinn.com
dir: M6 junct 2, A46. Follow A45 towards Birmingham

Rooms 37

C

COWES
Isle of Wight

Map 5 SZ49

BEST WESTERN New Holmwood Hotel

★★★ 78% HOTEL

tel: 01983 292508 **Queens Rd, Egypt Point PO31 8BW**
email: reception@newholmwoodhotel.co.uk **web:** www.newholmwoodhotel.co.uk
dir: From A3020 at Northwood Garage lights, left & follow to rdbt. 1st left then sharp right into Baring Rd, 4th left into Egypt Hill. At bottom turn right, hotel on right

Just by the Esplanade, this hotel has an enviable outlook. Bedrooms are comfortable and very well equipped, and the light and airy, glass-fronted restaurant looks out to sea and serves a range of interesting meals. The sun terrace is delightful in the summer and there is a small pool area.

Rooms 26 (1 fmly) (9 GF) ⌔ **Facilities** STV FTV WiFi ⌔ Xmas New Year **Conf** Class 60 Board 50 Thtr 100 Del from £102.50 to £120* **Parking** 20 **Notes** Civ Wed 50

CRAMLINGTON
Northumberland

Map 21 NZ27

Premier Inn Newcastle Gosforth/Cramlington

BUDGET HOTEL

tel: 0871 527 8788 **Moor Farm Roundabout, Off Front St, Annitsford NE23 7QA**
web: www.premierinn.com
dir: At rdbt junct of A19 & A189, S of Cramlington

High quality, budget accommodation ideal for both families and business travellers. Spacious, en suite bedrooms feature tea and coffee making facilities, and Freeview TV in most hotels. Internet access and WiFi are available for a small fee. The adjacent family restaurant features a wide and varied menu. See also the Hotel Groups pages.

Rooms 40

CRAWLEY

See Gatwick Airport

CREWE
Cheshire

Map 15 SJ75

Crewe Hall

INSPIRED BY YOU

★★★★ 81% ⊛ HOTEL

tel: 01270 253333 **Weston Rd CW1 6UZ**
email: crewehall@qhotels.co.uk **web:** www.qhotels.co.uk
dir: M6 junct 16, A500 to Crewe. Take A5020. 1st exit at next rdbt to Crewe. Hotel 150yds on right

Standing in 500 acres of mature grounds, this historic hall dates back to the 17th century, yet retains an elaborate interior with Victorian-style architecture. Bedrooms are spacious, well equipped and comfortable with traditionally styled suites in the main hall and modern rooms in the west wing. Afternoon tea is served in The Sheridan Lounge, while The Brasserie Restaurant and Bar is contemporary and has a relaxed atmosphere. The health and beauty spa ensure that the hotel is a popular choice with both corporate and leisure guests. QHotels is the AA Hotel Group of the Year 2014-15.

Rooms 117 (91 annexe) (5 fmly) (35 GF) **Facilities** Spa STV WiFi ⌔ 🕸 ⌔ Gym Enclosed events field **Conf** Class 172 Board 96 Thtr 364 **Services** Lift **Parking** 500 **Notes** Civ Wed 180

Hunters Lodge Hotel

★★★ 66% HOTEL

tel: 01270 539100 **Sydney Rd, Sydney CW1 5LU**
email: info@hunterslodge.co.uk **web:** www.hunterslodge.co.uk
dir: M6 junct 16. 1m from Crewe station, off A534

Dating back to the 18th century, the hotel has been extended and modernised over the years. Accommodation, mainly located in adjacent well-equipped bedroom wings, includes family and four-poster rooms. Imaginative dishes are served in the popular bar which also offers open fires and friendly and efficient service.

Rooms 57 (4 fmly) (31 GF) (2 smoking) **S** £36.50-£55; **D** £56.50-£97 (incl. bkfst)* **Facilities** STV FTV WiFi ⌔ Gym **Conf** Class 100 Board 80 Thtr 160 Del from £118.80 to £136.35* **Parking** 240 **Notes** ⊗ RS Sun eve Civ Wed 130

Premier Inn Crewe Central

BUDGET HOTEL

tel: 0871 527 8276 **Weston Rd CW1 6FX**
web: www.premierinn.com
dir: M6 junct 16, A500, at rdbt 3rd exit onto A5020 (Old Park Rd). At next rdbt 2nd exit into Western Rd, at next rdbt 3rd exit, hotel on left

High quality, budget accommodation ideal for both families and business travellers. Spacious, en suite bedrooms feature tea and coffee making facilities, and Freeview TV in most hotels. Internet access and WiFi are available for a small fee. The adjacent family restaurant features a wide and varied menu. See also the Hotel Groups pages.

Rooms 20

Premier Inn Crewe West

BUDGET HOTEL

tel: 0871 527 8278 **Coppenhall Ln, Woolstanwood CW2 8SD**
web: www.premierinn.com
dir: At junct of A530 & A532, 9m from M6 junct 16 N'bound

Rooms 42

CRICK
Northamptonshire

Map 11 SP57

Holiday Inn Rugby - Northampton

★★★ 74% HOTEL

tel: 0871 942 9059 & 01788 824800 **M1 Junction 18 NN6 7XR**
email: rugbyhi@ihg.com **web:** www.hirugbyhotel.co.uk
dir: 0.5m from M1 junct 18

Situated in pleasant surroundings, located just off the M1, this modern hotel offers well-equipped and comfortable bedrooms. Public areas include the popular Traders restaurant and a lounge where an all-day menu is available. The Spirit Health Club provides indoor swimming and a good fitness facility.

Rooms 90 (19 fmly) (42 GF) (12 smoking) **Facilities** STV WiFi 🕸 Gym New Year **Conf** Class 90 Board 64 Thtr 170 **Services** Lift Air con **Parking** 250 **Notes** Civ Wed

Ibis Rugby

BUDGET HOTEL

tel: 01788 824331 **Parklands NN6 7EX**
email: H3588@accor.com **web:** www.ibishotel.com
dir: M1 junct 18, follow Daventry/Rugby A5 signs. At rdbt 3rd exit signed DIRFT East. Hotel on right

Modern, budget hotel offering comfortable accommodation in bright and practical bedrooms. Breakfast is self-service and dinner is available in the restaurant. See also the Hotel Groups pages.

Rooms 111 (47 fmly) (12 GF) **Conf** Class 25 Board 25 Thtr 30

CRICKLADE	**Map 5 SU09**
Wiltshire	

Cricklade House

★★★ 80% HOTEL

tel: 01793 750751 **Common Hill SN6 6HA**
email: reception@cricklade hotel.co.uk **web:** www.crickladehotel.co.uk
dir: A419 onto B4040. Left at clock tower. Right at rdbt. Hotel 0.5m up hill on left

A haven of peace and tranquillity with spectacular views, this hotel is set in over 30 acres of beautiful countryside. Bedrooms vary in size and style; there are main building rooms and courtyard rooms - all offer high levels of comfort and quality. Public areas include an elegant lounge, dining room and a Victorian-style conservatory that runs the full length of the building. The extensive leisure facilities include a 9-hole golf course, an indoor pool and a gym.

Rooms 47 (21 annexe) (2 fmly) (5 GF) **S** £74.50-£140; **D** £94.50-£190 (incl. bkfst)*
Facilities STV FTV WiFi ⌂ 🕲 ⅃ 9 ☺ Gym Aromatherapy Beautician Xmas New Year
Conf Class 60 Board 42 Thtr 120 Del from £120 to £156* **Parking** 100
Notes Civ Wed 120

CROMER	**Map 13 TG24**
Norfolk	

Sea Marge Hotel

★★★ 87% HOTEL

tel: 01263 579579 **16 High St, Overstrand NR27 0AB**
email: seamarge@mackenziehotels.com **web:** www.mackenziehotels.com
dir: A140 from Norwich then A149 to Cromer, B1159 to Overstrand. Hotel in village centre

An elegant Grade II listed Edwardian mansion perched on the clifftop amidst pretty landscaped gardens which lead down to the beach. Bedrooms are tastefully decorated and thoughtfully equipped; many have superb sea views. Public rooms offer a wide choice of areas in which to relax, including Frazer's restaurant and a smart lounge bar.

Rooms 25 (6 annexe) (6 fmly) (2 GF) ⓝ **S** £79-£119; **D** £158-£203 (incl. bkfst)*
Facilities FTV WiFi ☺ Xmas New Year **Conf** Class 55 Board 30 Thtr 70
Del from £140* **Services** Lift **Parking** 50 **Notes** LB

The Cliftonville Hotel

★★★ 78% HOTEL

tel: 01263 512543 **Seafront NR27 9AS**
email: reservations@cliftonvillehotel.co.uk **web:** www.cliftonvillehotel.co.uk
dir: From A149 (coast road), 500yds from town centre, N'bound on clifftop by sunken gardens

The Cliftonville Hotel is an imposing Edwardian hotel situated on the main coast road with stunning views of the sea. Public areas feature a magnificent staircase, minstrels' gallery, coffee shop, lounge bar, a further residents' lounge, Boltons Bistro and an additional restaurant. The pleasantly decorated bedrooms are generally quite spacious and have lovely sea views.

Rooms 30 (2 fmly) **S** £60-£95; **D** £120-£190 (incl. bkfst)* **Facilities** FTV WiFi Xmas New Year **Conf** Class 100 Board 60 Thtr 150 **Services** Lift **Parking** 20 **Notes** LB

Hotel de Paris

★★ 74% HOTEL

tel: 01263 513141 **High St NR27 9HG**
email: deparis.cromer@alfatravel.co.uk **web:** www.leisureplex.co.uk
dir: Enter Church St (one way) after lights left straight into Jetty St, car park at end on left

An imposing, traditional-style resort hotel, situated in a prominent position overlooking the pier and beach. The bedrooms are pleasantly decorated and equipped with a good range of useful extras; many rooms have lovely sea views. The spacious public areas include a large lounge bar, restaurant, games room and a further lounge.

Rooms 63 (8 fmly) ⓝ **S** £39-£59; **D** £62-£102 (incl. bkfst)* **Facilities** FTV WiFi Games room ♫ Xmas New Year **Services** Lift **Parking** 14 **Notes** LB ⊗ Closed Jan-Feb RS Mar, Nov & Dec

C

CROOKLANDS
Cumbria

Map 18 SD58

Crooklands Hotel

★★★ 78% HOTEL

tel: 015395 67432 **LA7 7NW**
email: reception@crooklands.com **web:** www.crooklands.com
dir: M6 junct 36 onto A65. Left at rdbt. Hotel 1.5m on right past garage

Although only a stone's throw from the M6, this hotel enjoys a peaceful rural location. Housed in a converted 200-year-old farmhouse, the restaurant retains many original features such as the beams and stone walls. Bedrooms are a mix of modern and traditional and vary in size. The hotel is a popular stop-over for both leisure and corporate guests travelling between England and Scotland.

Rooms 30 (3 fmly) (14 GF) ✿ **S** £75-£95; **D** £90-£130 (incl. bkfst) **Facilities** FTV WiFi New Year **Conf** Class 50 Board 40 Thtr 80 Del from £120 to £140 **Services** Lift **Parking** 80 **Notes** LB ⊗ Closed 24-28 Dec

CROYDON
Greater London

Map 6 TQ36

Croydon Park Hotel

★★★★ 73% HOTEL

tel: 020 8680 9200 **7 Altyre Rd CR9 5AA**
email: info@croydonparkhotel.com **web:** www.croydonparkhotel.com
dir: 3 min walk from East Croydon Station

This hotel is located in the heart of the town centre, a 3-minute walk to East Croydon train station and with easy access to both Gatwick Airport and central London. Bedrooms vary in style, but all are comfortably appointed. The two dining options are Whistlers Bar with a menu available throughout the day, and Oscars Brasserie with a daily buffet and carte menu. Conference and leisure facilities are available.

Rooms 211 (36 fmly) (6 GF) (15 smoking) **Facilities** FTV WiFi ☝ ☝ supervised Gym Squash Sauna Xmas New Year **Conf** Class 100 Board 30 Thtr 220 **Services** Lift Air con **Parking** 91 **Notes** ⊗ Civ Wed 220

Hallmark Hotel Croydon

★★★★ 73% HOTEL

tel: 020 8680 1999 **Purley Way CR9 4LT**
email: croydon.reservations@hallmarkhotels.co.uk
web: www.hallmarkhotels.co.uk/croydon
dir: Follow A23 & Central London signs. Hotel on left adjacent to Airport House

This hotel (formerly the Aerodrome Hotel) sits in a prime location and offers comfortably appointed bedrooms, all with LCD TVs and free WiFi throughout. Following a refurbishment programme, public areas are stylish and modern in their design and include a spacious open-plan bar and brasserie. Ideal for both the leisure and corporate market, there are a number of fully-equipped meeting and conference facilities.

Rooms 110 (10 fmly) ✿ **S** £54-£82; **D** £59-£118* **Facilities** STV FTV WiFi ☝ Xmas New Year **Conf** Class 60 Board 36 Thtr 170 Del from £125 to £155* **Services** Lift **Parking** 79 **Notes** LB ⊗ Civ Wed 150

Selsdon Park Hotel & Golf Club

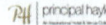

★★★★ 71% HOTEL

tel: 020 8657 8811 **Addington Rd, Sanderstead CR2 8YA**
email: selsdonpark.reception@principal-hayley.com **web:** www.principal-hayley.com
dir: 3m SE of Croydon, off A2022

Surrounded by 200 acres of mature parkland with its own 18-hole golf course, this imposing Jacobean mansion is less than 20 minutes from central London. The hotel's impressive range of conference rooms along with the spectacular views of the North Downs countryside, make this a popular venue for both weddings and meetings. The leisure facilities are impressive.

Rooms 199 (19 fmly) (33 GF) **Facilities** Spa STV WiFi ☝ ☝ ⅃ 18 ☝ Putt green ☝ Gym Squash Xmas **Conf** Class 250 Board 100 Thtr 350 **Services** Lift **Parking** 300 **Notes** ⊗ Civ Wed 350

Holiday Inn Express London - Croydon

BUDGET HOTEL

tel: 020 8253 1200 **1 Priddys Yard, Off Frith Rd CRO 1TS**
email: gm@exhicroydon.com **web:** www.hiexpress.com/london-croydon
dir: From A235 into Lower Coombe St, at rdbt 1st exit, at next rdbt 2nd exit onto dual carriageway, right to Centrale Shopping Centre, under car park, follow to right, 1st left

A modern hotel ideal for families and business travellers. Fresh and uncomplicated, the spacious rooms include Sky TV, power shower and tea and coffee-making facilities. Continental buffet breakfast is included in the room rate; other meals may be taken at the nearby family pub or restaurant. See also the Hotel Groups pages.

Rooms 156 (62 fmly) ✿ **Conf** Class 30 Board 30 Thtr 60

Premier Inn Croydon South

BUDGET HOTEL

tel: 0871 527 8280 **104 Coombe Rd CRO 5RB**
web: www.premierinn.com
dir: M25 junct 7, A23 to Purley, A235 to Croydon. Pass Tree House pub on left. Right at lights onto A212

High quality, budget accommodation ideal for both families and business travellers. Spacious, en suite bedrooms feature tea and coffee making facilities, and Freeview TV in most hotels. Internet access and WiFi are available for a small fee. The adjacent family restaurant features a wide and varied menu. See also the Hotel Groups pages.

Rooms 39

Premier Inn Croydon Town Centre

BUDGET HOTEL

tel: 0871 527 9438 **Philips House, Lansdowne Rd CRO 2BX**
web: www.premierinn.com

Rooms 168

Premier Inn Croydon West

BUDGET HOTEL

tel: 0871 527 8282 **The Colonnades Leisure Park, 619 Purley Way CRO 4RQ**
web: www.premierinn.com
dir: From N: M1, M25, A23 towards Croydon. From S: M25 junct 7, A23 towards Purley Way, 8m, hotel close to junct with Waddon Way

Rooms 84

CULLOMPTON
Devon
Map 3 ST00

Padbrook Park

★★★ 78% HOTEL

tel: 01884 836100 **EX15 1RU**
email: info@padbrookpark.co.uk **web:** www.padbrookpark.co.uk
dir: 1m from M5 junct 28, follow brown signs

This purpose-built hotel is part of a golf and leisure complex located in the Culm Valley, just one mile from the M5. Set in 100 acres of parkland with an 18-hole golf course, Padbrook Park has a friendly, relaxed atmosphere and a contemporary feel. A variety of room types is available, including family, inter-connecting, superior and deluxe rooms.

Rooms 40 (4 fmly) (11 GF) ❀ **S** £40–£80; **D** £60–£95* **Facilities** STV FTV WiFi ❧ HL ♨ 18 Putt green Fishing Gym 3 rink bowling centre Crazy golf Beauty treatment room ♫ Xmas New Year **Conf** Class 150 Board 50 Thtr 200 Del from £95* **Services** Lift **Parking** 250 **Notes** LB ⊗ Civ Wed 200

DAGENHAM
Greater London
Map 6 TQ48

Premier Inn London Dagenham

BUDGET HOTEL

tel: 0871 527 9364 **Chequers Corner, 2 New Rd RM9 6YS**
web: www.premierinn.com
dir: M25 junct 30/A13 signed Barking. Continue on A13 through underpass then flyover, following directions to Central London, Barking & Docklands. Left off A13 - Dagenham East. At rdbt 4th exit, then left at traffic signals onto A1306 Dagenham. Continue at traffic signals. Inn on left

High quality, budget accommodation ideal for both families and business travellers. Spacious, en suite bedrooms feature tea and coffee making facilities, and Freeview TV in most hotels. Internet access and WiFi are available for a small fee. The adjacent family restaurant features a wide and varied menu. See also the Hotel Groups pages.

Rooms 80

DARLINGTON
County Durham
Map 19 NZ21

Rockliffe Hall

★★★★★ ❀❀ HOTEL

tel: 01325 729999 **Rockliffe Park, Hurworth-on-Tees DL2 2DU**
email: enquiries@rockliffehall.com **web:** www.rockliffehall.com
dir: A66 towards Darlington, A167, through Hurworth-on-Tees. In Croft-on-Tees left into Hurworth Rd

This impressive hotel enjoys a peaceful setting on a restored 18th-century estate by the banks of the River Tees. Luxurious, spacious bedrooms, contemporary in style, are split between the original old hall, the new hall and Tiplady Lodge. Dining options include The Orangery, The Clubhouse and The Brasserie. A state-of-the-art spa and championship golf course, with a first-class club house, complete the picture.

Rooms 61 (5 fmly) (17 GF) ❀ **Facilities** Spa STV FTV WiFi ❧ ⊛ ♨ 18 Putt green Fishing Gym Nordic walking ♫ Xmas New Year **Conf** Class 100 Board 30 Thtr 180 **Services** Lift **Parking** 200 **Notes** ⊗ Civ Wed 180

See advert on page 142

DARLINGTON *continued*

Headlam Hall

★★★★ 80% @@ HOTEL

tel: 01325 730238 **Headlam, Gainford DL2 3HA**
email: admin@headlamhall.co.uk **web:** www.headlamhall.co.uk
dir: 2m N of A67 between Piercebridge & Gainford

This impressive Jacobean hall lies in farmland north-east of Piercebridge and has its own 9-hole golf course. The main house retains many historical features, including flagstone floors and a pillared hall. Bedrooms are well proportioned and traditionally styled; a converted coach house contains the more modern rooms. There are extensive conference facilities, and the hotel is popular as a wedding venue. Further facilities include a stunning spa complex with a 14-metre pool, an outdoor hot spa, drench shower, sauna and steam room, as well as a gym with the latest cardio and resistance equipment, and five treatment rooms offering a range of therapies and beauty treatments.

Rooms 39 (22 annexe) (4 fmly) (9 GF) ↖ **S** £100-£135; **D** £125-£165 (incl. bkfst)*
Facilities Spa STV FTV WiFi ↘ ⊛ ⅃ 9 ⚘ Putt green Fishing ↯ Gym New Year
Conf Class 40 Board 40 Thtr 120 Del from £145* **Services** Lift **Parking** 80 **Notes** LB Closed 24-26 Dec Civ Wed 150

Bannatyne Hotel Darlington

★★★★ 75% HOTEL

tel: 01325 365858 **Southend Av DL3 7HZ**
email: enquiries.darlingtonhotel@bannatyne.co.uk **web:** www.bannatyne.co.uk
dir: From S: A1(M) junct 57, A66(M) signed Darlington. 2nd rdbt 2nd exit into Grange Rd. 3rd left into Southend Ave. From N: A1(M) junct 58, A68 signed Darlington, left at 1st rdbt, 2nd rdbt 2nd exit into Carmel Rd N, into Carmel Rd S. Left at 4th rdbt into Grange Rd, 3rd left

This hotel, with excellent parking, is close to the town centre and provides well-equipped accommodation with WiFi in all areas. Public areas include the brasserie-style bar and restaurant, Maxine's, plus good function, conference and wedding facilities. Free use of Bannatyne's Spa and gym (just five minutes away) is also available to guests. Very friendly hospitality is assured from the young and enthusiastic team at this hotel.

Rooms 60 (4 fmly) (11 GF) ↖ **Facilities** FTV WiFi ↘ Xmas New Year **Conf** Class 60 Board 60 Thtr 120 **Services** Lift **Parking** 50 **Notes** ⊗ Civ Wed 120

D

Hall Garth Hotel, Golf and Country Club

★★★ 79% HOTEL

tel: 01325 300400 **Coatham Mundeville DL1 3LU**
email: gm@hallgarthdarlignton.co.uk **web:** www.hallgarthdarlington.co.uk
dir: A1(M) junct 59, A167 towards Darlington. After 600yds left at top of hill, hotel on right

Peacefully situated in grounds that feature a golf course, this hotel is just a few minutes from the motorway network. The well-equipped bedrooms come in various styles - it's worth asking for one of the trendy, modern rooms. Public rooms include relaxing lounges, a fine-dining restaurant and a separate pub. The extensive leisure and conference facilities are an important focus here.

Rooms 56 (16 annexe) (3 fmly) (1 GF) **Facilities** Spa STV FTV WiFi ↘ ⊗ supervised ⚓ 9 Putt green Gym Steam room Beauty salon Sauna Spa Xmas New Year **Conf** Class 160 Board 80 Thtr 250 Del from £115 to £148* **Parking** 150 **Notes** Civ Wed 170

BEST WESTERN Walworth Castle Hotel

★★★ 75% HOTEL

tel: 01325 485470 **Walworth DL2 2LY**
email: enquiries@walworthcastle.co.uk **web:** www.walworthcastle.co.uk
dir: A1(M) junct 58 follow signs to Corbridge. Left at The Dog pub. Hotel on left after 2m

This 12th-century castle is privately owned and has been tastefully converted. Accommodation is offered in a range of styles, including an impressive suite and more compact rooms in an adjoining wing. Dinner can be taken in the fine dining Hansards Restaurant or the more relaxed Farmer's Bar. This is a popular venue for conferences and weddings.

Rooms 32 (14 annexe) (4 fmly) (8 GF) ⌧ **Facilities** Spa FTV WiFi ↘ ⊗ Beauty rooms Hair salon Xmas New Year **Conf** Class 60 Board 40 Thtr 120 **Parking** 100 **Notes** ⊗ Civ Wed 100

Premier Inn Darlington

BUDGET HOTEL

tel: 0871 527 8286 **Morton Park Way, Morton Park DL1 4PJ**
web: www.premierinn.com
dir: A1(M) junct 57, A66(M), A66 towards Teeside. At 3rd rdbt left onto B6280. Hotel on right. From N: A1(M) junct 57 onto A167, A1150, A66 towards Darlington, right onto B6280. Hotel on right

High quality, budget accommodation ideal for both families and business travellers. Spacious, en suite bedrooms feature tea and coffee making facilities, and Freeview TV in most hotels. Internet access and WiFi are available for a small fee. The adjacent family restaurant features a wide and varied menu. See also the Hotel Groups pages.

Rooms 58

DARTFORD　　　　　　　　　　　　　　　**Map 6 TQ57**
Kent

Rowhill Grange Hotel & Utopia Spa

★★★★ 81% ⊛⊛ HOTEL

tel: 01322 615136 **Wilmington DA2 7QH**
email: admin@rowhillgrange.co.uk **web:** www.rowhillgrange.co.uk
dir: M25 junct 3 take B2173 to Swanley, then B258 to Hextable

Set in nine acres of mature woodland this hotel enjoys a tranquil setting, yet is accessible to road networks. Bedrooms are stylishly and individually decorated;

many have four-poster or sleigh beds. The elegant lounge is popular for afternoon teas, and the leisure and conference facilities are impressive. There is a smart, conservatory restaurant and also a more informal brasserie.

Rooms 38 (8 annexe) (4 fmly) (3 GF) ⌧ **Facilities** Spa STV FTV WiFi ↘ ⊗ ⚓ Gym Beauty treatment Hair salon Aerobic studio Japanese therapy pool Xmas New Year **Conf** Class 64 Board 34 Thtr 160 Del from £155 to £175* **Services** Lift **Parking** 150 **Notes** ⊗ Civ Wed 150

Campanile Dartford

BUDGET HOTEL

tel: 01322 278925 **1 Clipper Boulevard West, Crossways Business Park DA2 6QN**
email: dartford@campanile.com **web:** www.campanile.com
dir: Follow signs for Ferry Terminal from Dartford Bridge

This modern building offers accommodation in smart, well-equipped bedrooms, all with en suite bathrooms. Refreshments may be taken at the informal bistro. See also the Hotel Groups pages.

Rooms 125 (14 fmly) (39 GF) ⌧ **Conf** Class 30 Board 30 Thtr 40

Premier Inn Dartford

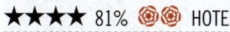

BUDGET HOTEL

tel: 0871 527 9328 **Halcrow Av DA1 5FX**
web: www.premierinn.com
dir: M25 junct 1A , A206 towards Erith. At next rdbt right to Bridge Business Park. At next rdbt left towards Power Station. Hotel 300yds on left

High quality, budget accommodation ideal for both families and business travellers. Spacious, en suite bedrooms feature tea and coffee making facilities, and Freeview TV in most hotels. Internet access and WiFi are available for a small fee. The adjacent family restaurant features a wide and varied menu. See also the Hotel Groups pages.

Rooms 60

DARTMOUTH　　　　　　　　　　　　　　　**Map 3 SX85**
Devon

The Dart Marina Hotel

★★★★ 79% ⊛ HOTEL

tel: 01803 832580 & 837120 **Sandquay Rd TQ6 9PH**
email: reservations@dartmarina.com **web:** www.dartmarina.com
dir: A3122 from Totnes to Dartmouth. Follow road which becomes College Way, before Higher Ferry. Hotel sharp left in Sandquay Rd

Boasting a stunning riverside location with its own marina, this is a very special place to stay. Bedrooms vary in style, all have wonderful views, and some have private balconies where you can sit and soak up the atmosphere. The stylish public areas take full advantage of the waterside setting with opportunities to dine alfresco. In addition to the Wildfire Bar & Bistro, the River Restaurant is the venue for accomplished cooking.

Rooms 51 (4 annexe) (4 fmly) (4 GF) ⌧ **S** £95-£155; **D** £160-£230 (incl. bkfst)* **Facilities** Spa WiFi ⊗ Gym Xmas New Year **Services** Lift **Parking** 50 **Notes** LB

D

DARTMOUTH *continued*

Royal Castle Hotel

★★★ 81% HOTEL

tel: 01803 833033 **11 The Quay TQ6 9PS**
email: enquiry@royalcastle.co.uk **web:** www.royalcastle.co.uk
dir: In centre of town, overlooking Inner Harbour

At the edge of the harbour, this imposing 17th-century former coaching inn is filled with charm and character. Bedrooms are well equipped and comfortable, and many have harbour views. A choice of quiet seating areas is offered in addition to both the traditional and contemporary bars. A variety of eating options is available, including the main restaurant which has lovely views.

Rooms 25 (3 fmly) **Facilities** FTV WiFi ♫ Xmas New Year **Conf** Class 30 Board 20 Thtr 50 **Parking** 15 **Notes** Civ Wed 80

Stoke Lodge Hotel

★★★ 73% HOTEL

tel: 01803 770523 **Stoke Fleming TQ6 0RA**
email: mail@stokelodge.co.uk **web:** www.stokelodge.co.uk
dir: 2m S A379

This family-run hotel continues to attract returning guests and is set in three acres of gardens and grounds with lovely views across to the sea. A range of leisure facilities is offered including both indoor and outdoor pools, along with a choice of comfortable lounges. Bedrooms are pleasantly appointed. The restaurant offers a choice of menus and an impressive wine list.

Rooms 25 (5 fmly) (7 GF) **S** £74-£77; **D** £99.50-£114 (incl. bkfst)* **Facilities** FTV WiFi ⌖ ⌖ ⌖ Putt green Table tennis Pool & Snooker tables Sauna Xmas New Year **Conf** Class 60 Board 30 Thtr 80 Del from £95* **Parking** 50 **Notes** LB

DAVENTRY	Map 11 SP56
Northamptonshire	

Fawsley Hall

★★★★ ⨳⨳ HOTEL

tel: 01327 892000 **Fawsley NN11 3BA**
email: reservations@fawsleyhall.com **web:** www.fawsleyhall.com
dir: A361 S of Daventry, between Badby & Charwelton, hotel signed single track lane

Dating back to the 15th century, this delightful hotel is peacefully located in beautiful gardens designed by 'Capability' Brown. Spacious, individually designed bedrooms and stylish public areas are beautifully furnished with antique and period pieces. The different wings of the house - Tudor, Georgian and Victorian - all have their distinct identity. For a true sense of the past, why not stay in the Queen's Suite, where Elizabeth I is documented to have slept in 1575. Afternoon tea is served in the impressive Great Hall, and dinner is available in the award-winning fine-dining restaurant, with its original beams and stonework, an impressive inglenook fireplace, and candlelit tables dressed in fine white linen. The hotel has its own cinema and The Grayshot Spa features an ozone pool, treatment rooms and fitness studio.

Rooms 58 (14 annexe) (2 GF) **Facilities** Spa STV WiFi ⌖ ⌖ ⌖ Gym Health & beauty treatment rooms Fitness studio 29-seat cinema Xmas New Year **Conf** Class 64 Board 40 Thtr 120 **Parking** 140 **Notes** Civ Wed 120

Daventry Court Hotel

PUMA HOTELS
COLLECTION

★★★★ 74% HOTEL

tel: 01327 307000 **Sedgemoor Way NN11 0SG**
email: daventry@pumahotels.co.uk **web:** www.pumahotels.co.uk
dir: M1 junct 16, A45 to Daventry, at 1st rdbt turn right signed Kilsby/M1(N). Hotel on right in 1m

This modern, striking hotel overlooking Drayton Water boasts spacious public areas that include a good range of banqueting, meeting and leisure facilities. It is a popular venue for conferences. Bedrooms are suitable for both business and leisure guests.

Rooms 155 (17 fmly) **Facilities** Spa FTV WiFi HL ⌖ supervised Gym Steam room Sauna Health & beauty salon New Year **Conf** Class 200 Board 100 Thtr 600 **Services** Lift **Parking** 350 **Notes** Civ Wed 280

Premier Inn Daventry

Premier Inn

BUDGET HOTEL

tel: 0871 527 8288 **High St, Weedon NN7 4PX**
web: www.premierinn.com
dir: M1 junct 16, A45 towards Daventry. Through Upper Heyford & Flore. Hotel on left before Weedon & A5 junct

High quality, budget accommodation ideal for both families and business travellers. Spacious, en suite bedrooms feature tea and coffee making facilities, and Freeview TV in most hotels. Internet access and WiFi are available for a small fee. The adjacent family restaurant features a wide and varied menu. See also the Hotel Groups pages.

Rooms 47

DAWLISH	Map 3 SX97
Devon	

Langstone Cliff Hotel

THE INDEPENDENTS

★★★ 79% HOTEL

tel: 01626 868000 **Dawlish Warren EX7 ONA**
email: reception@langstone-hotel.co.uk **web:** www.langstone-hotel.co.uk
dir: 1.5m NE off A379 - Exeter Rd to Dawlish Warren

A family-owned and run hotel, the Langstone Cliff Hotel offers a range of leisure, conference and function facilities. Bedrooms, many with sea views and balconies, are spacious, comfortable and well equipped. The hotel has a number of attractive lounges and a well-stocked bar. Dinner is served, often carvery style, in the restaurant.

Rooms 64 (2 annexe) (52 fmly) (10 GF) ⚡ **S** £45-£95; **D** £90-£204 (incl. bkfst)*
Facilities STV FTV WiFi ⚡ ⚡ ⚡ Gym Table tennis Golf practice area Hair & beauty salon Therapy room Ballroom ♫ Xmas New Year Child facilities
Conf Class 200 Board 80 Thtr 400 Del £112.50* **Services** Lift **Parking** 200 **Notes** LB Civ Wed 400

DEAL	Map 7 TR35
Kent	

Dunkerleys Hotel & Restaurant

★★★ 79% ⚜⚜ HOTEL

tel: 01304 375016 **19 Beach St CT14 7AH**
email: info@dunkerleys.co.uk **web:** www.dunkerleys.co.uk
dir: From M20 or M2 follow signs for A258 Deal. Hotel close to Pier

This hotel is centrally located and on the seafront. Bedrooms are furnished to a high standard with a good range of amenities. The restaurant and bar offer a comfortable and attractive environment in which to relax and to enjoy the cuisine that makes the best use of local ingredients. Service throughout is friendly and attentive.

Rooms 16 (2 fmly) **S** £80-£100; **D** £120-£150 (incl. bkfst) **Facilities** FTV WiFi Xmas New Year **Notes** LB ⊗ RS Sun eve & Mon

DEDDINGTON	Map 11 SP43
Oxfordshire	

Deddington Arms

★★★ 75% ⚜ HOTEL

tel: 01869 338364 **Horsefair OX15 0SH**
email: deddarms@oxfordshire-hotels.co.uk **web:** www.oxfordshire-hotels.co.uk
dir: From S: M40 junct 10/A43. 1st rdbt left to Aynho (B4100) & left to Deddington (B4031). From N: M40 junct 11 to hospital & Adderbury on A4260, then to Deddington

This charming and friendly old inn is conveniently located off the market square. The well-equipped bedrooms are comfortably appointed and situated either in the main building or a purpose-built courtyard wing. The bar is full of character, and the delightful restaurant enjoys a well-deserved reputation locally.

Rooms 27 (4 fmly) (10 GF) (2 smoking) **Facilities** STV FTV WiFi ⚡ Xmas New Year **Conf** Class 20 Board 25 Thtr 40 **Parking** 36 **Notes** ⊗

DEDHAM	Map 13 TM03
Essex	

Maison Talbooth

PRIDE OF BRITAIN HOTELS

★★★ ⚜⚜ COUNTRY HOUSE HOTEL

tel: 01206 322367 **Stratford Rd CO7 6HN**
email: maison@milsomhotels.co.uk **web:** www.milsomhotels.com
dir: A12 towards Ipswich, 1st turn signed Dedham, follow to left bend, turn right. Hotel 1m on right

Warm hospitality and quality service are to be expected at this Victorian country-house hotel, which is situated in a peaceful rural location amidst pretty landscaped grounds overlooking the Stour River Valley. Public areas include a comfortable drawing room where guests may take afternoon tea or snacks. Residents are chauffeured to the popular Le Talbooth Restaurant just a mile away for dinner. The spacious bedrooms are individually decorated and tastefully furnished with lovely co-ordinated fabrics and many thoughtful touches.

Rooms 12 (1 fmly) (5 GF) ⚡ **D** £220-£440 (incl. bkfst)* **Facilities** Spa STV WiFi ⚡ ⚡ ⚡ Xmas **Conf** Class 20 Board 16 Thtr 30 **Parking** 40 **Notes** LB Civ Wed 50

D

DEDHAM *continued*

milsoms

★★★ 82% SMALL HOTEL

tel: 01206 322795 **Stratford Rd CO7 6HW**
email: milsoms@milsomhotels.com web: www.milsomhotels.com
dir: 6m N of Colchester off A12, follow Stratford St Mary/Dedham signs. Turn right over A12, hotel on left

Situated in the Dedham Vale, an Area of Outstanding Natural Beauty, this is the perfect base to explore the countryside on the Essex/Suffolk border. This establishment is styled along the lines of a contemporary 'gastro bar' combining good food served in an informal atmosphere, with stylish and well-appointed accommodation.

Rooms 15 (3 fmly) (4 GF) **D** £125-£210 (incl. bkfst)* **Facilities** STV WiFi Use of spa at nearby sister hotel Maison Talbooth ♫ Xmas **Conf** Board 24 Del from £155* **Parking** 90 **Notes** LB

DELPH	Map 16 SD90
Greater Manchester	

The Saddleworth Hotel

★★★★ 84% COUNTRY HOUSE HOTEL

tel: 01457 871888 **Huddersfield Rd OL3 5LX**
email: enquiries@thesaddleworthhotel.co.uk web: www.thesaddleworthhotel.co.uk
dir: M62 junct 21, A640 towards Huddersfield. At Junction Inn take A6052 towards Delph; at White Lion left onto unclassified road; in 0.5m left on A62 towards Huddersfield. Hotel 0.5m on right

Situated in nine acres of landscaped gardens and woodlands in the Castleshaw Valley, this lovingly restored 17th-century building, once a coaching station, has stunning views. The hotel offers comfort and opulence together with a team of staff who provide delightful customer care. Antique pieces have been acquired from far and wide, and no expense has been spared to provide guests with the latest up-to-date facilities. The restaurant, with black table linen and crystal glassware, offers an award-winning, fashionably understated, modern European menu.

Rooms 16 (8 annexe) (4 fmly) (4 GF) **Facilities** FTV WiFi ♭ ➔ Gym Xmas New Year **Conf** Class 40 Board 40 Thtr 150 **Parking** 140 **Notes** ⊗ Civ Wed 250

DERBY	Map 11 SK33
Derbyshire	

See also **Morley**

Hallmark Derby

★★★★ 79% HOTEL

tel: 01332 345894 **Midland Rd DE1 2SQ**
email: derby.reservations@hallmarkhotels.co.uk web: www.hallmarkhotels.co.uk/derby
dir: Opposite rail station

This early Victorian hotel situated opposite Derby Midland Station provides very comfortable accommodation. The executive rooms are ideal for business travellers as they are equipped with writing desks and high speed internet access. Public rooms include a comfortable lounge and a popular restaurant. Service is skilled, attentive and friendly. There is also a walled garden and private parking.

Rooms 102 (6 fmly) **D** fr £59* **Facilities** FTV WiFi ♫ Xmas New Year **Conf** Class 50 Board 35 Thtr 150 Del from £129* **Services** Lift **Parking** 70 **Notes** LB Civ Wed 150

Menzies Hotels Derby - Mickleover Court

★★★★ 78% HOTEL

tel: 01332 521234 **Etwall Rd, Mickleover DE3 0XX**
email: mickleovercourt@menzieshotels.co.uk web: www.menzieshotels.co.uk
dir: A50 towards Derby, exit at junct 5. A516 towards Derby, take exit signed Mickleover

Located close to Derby, this modern hotel is well suited to both the conference and leisure markets. Bedrooms are spacious, air conditioned, well equipped and include some smart executive rooms and suites. The well presented leisure facilities are amongst the best in the region.

Rooms 99 (20 fmly) (5 smoking) ♠ **S** £49-£159; **D** £49-£159 **Facilities** STV FTV WiFi ♭ ⊛ Gym Beauty salon Steam room Xmas New Year **Conf** Class 106 Board 45 Thtr 200 Del from £115 to £165* **Services** Lift Air con **Parking** 225 **Notes** LB Civ Wed 200

Holiday Inn Derby Riverlights

★★★★ 72% HOTEL

tel: 01332 412644 & 412533 **Derby Riverlights, Morledge DE1 2AY**
email: reservations@hiderby.co.uk web: www.holidayinn.com/derbyriver
dir: M1 junct 25, A52 to Derby. Follow signs to City Centre/Westfield Shopping Centre. Hotel on Morledge on right by bus station

With a central location adjacent to the Westfield Shopping Centre, this hotel is ideal for business and leisure guests. The lobby area is a four storey atrium. The stylish bedrooms are well equipped, and there is air conditioning and free WIFI throughout. The contemporary restaurant, Stresa, on the 4th floor boasts the highest views of Derby, offering a relaxed environment, and a variety of dishes, specially prepared with locally sourced ingredients. Discounted rates for guests are offered at the Westfield Riverside car park.

Rooms 105 (11 smoking) ♠ **S** £79-£169; **D** £79-£169* **Facilities** FTV WiFi ♭ HL Gym **Conf** Class 60 Board 50 Thtr 130 **Services** Lift Air con **Notes** LB Civ Wed 120

Ramada Encore Derby

★★★ 75% HOTEL

tel: 0844 801 3680 **Locomotive Way, Pride Park DE24 8PU**
email: admin@encorederby.co.uk **web:** www.encorederby.co.uk
dir: M1 junct 25, A52 towards Derby. Telephone for detailed directions

This hotel offers stylish and comfortable accommodation. The Hub is a smart, modern, open-plan bar and restaurant with a choice of seating areas - it offers an extensive menu throughout the day. Secure on-site parking is available, and the hotel is within walking distance of Derby railway station.

Rooms 112 (6 fmly) ⚡ **Facilities** STV WiFi HL Gym Sauna **Conf** Class 40 Board 20 Thtr 60 **Services** Lift Air con **Parking** 110 **Notes** ⊗

Hallmark Inn

★★★ 74% METRO HOTEL

tel: 01332 292000 **Midland Rd DE1 2SL**
email: europeanreception@hallmarkhotels.co.uk **web:** www.hallmarkhotels.co.uk
dir: City centre, 200yds from railway station

This is a contemporary hotel, offering quality accommodation plus a lounge bar, free WiFi and free parking. Situated just 100 metres from the railway station and not far from the city centre.

Rooms 87 (18 fmly) **D** fr £49* **Facilities** FTV WiFi **Conf** Class 20 Board 30 Thtr 60 Del from £99* **Services** Lift **Parking** 90 **Notes** ⊗

Premier Inn Derby East

BUDGET HOTEL

tel: 0871 527 8292 **The Wyvern, Stanier Way DE21 6BF**
web: www.premierinn.com
dir: M1 junct 25, A52 towards Derby. After 6.5m exit for Wyvern/Pride Park. 1st exit at rdbt (A52 Nottingham), straight on at next rdbt. Hotel on left

High quality, budget accommodation ideal for both families and business travellers. Spacious, en suite bedrooms feature tea and coffee making facilities, and Freeview TV in most hotels. Internet access and WiFi are available for a small fee. The adjacent family restaurant features a wide and varied menu. See also the Hotel Groups pages.

Rooms 83

Premier Inn Derby North West

BUDGET HOTEL

tel: 0871 527 8294 **95 Ashbourne Rd, Mackworth DE22 4LZ**
web: www.premierinn.com
dir: Exit M1 junct 25 onto A52 towards Derby. At Pentagon Island straight ahead towards city centre. Follow A52/Ashbourne signs into Mackworth

Rooms 22

Premier Inn Derby South

BUDGET HOTEL

tel: 0871 527 8296 **Foresters Leisure Park, Osmaston Park Rd DE23 8AG**
web: www.premierinn.com
dir: M1 junct 24, A6 towards Derby. Left onto A5111 (ring road), hotel in 2m

Rooms 27

Premier Inn Derby West

BUDGET HOTEL

tel: 0871 527 8298 **Manor Park Way, Uttoxeter New Rd DE22 3HN**
web: www.premierinn.com
dir: M1 junct 25, A38 W towards Burton upon Trent (approx 15m). Left at island (city hospital), right at lights, 3rd exit at city hospital island

Rooms 66

DERBY SERVICE AREA (A50) Map 11 SK42
Derbyshire

Days Inn Donington - A50

BUDGET HOTEL

tel: 01332 799666 **Welcome Break Services, A50 Westbound DE72 2WA**
email: derby.hotel@welcomebreak.co.uk **web:** www.welcomebreak.co.uk
dir: M1 junct 24/24a, onto A50 towards Stoke/Derby. Hotel between juncts 1 & 2

This modern building offers accommodation in smart, spacious and well-equipped bedrooms, suitable for families and business travellers, and all with en suite bathrooms. Continental breakfast is available and other refreshments may be taken at the nearby family restaurant. See also the Hotel Groups pages.

Rooms 47 (38 fmly) (17 GF) (9 smoking) **Conf** Class 20 Board 40 Thtr 40

DEVIZES Map 4 SU06
Wiltshire

The Bear Hotel

★★★ 75% HOTEL

tel: 01380 722444 **Market Place SN10 1HS**
email: info@thebearhotel.net **web:** www.thebearhotel.net
dir: In town centre, follow Market Place signs

Tracing its history back over three centuries, this friendly establishment occupies a prominent position in a bustling town. Staff and management are keen to please and offer friendly and hospitable service. Bedrooms are pleasantly appointed and have flat-screen TVs and broadband connection. The hotel has two restaurants - Lambtons Restaurant for fine dining and The Bear Grill Bistro. In summer there is a courtyard for alfresco dining. The hotel is a popular venue for conferences and weddings. Please note that there is restricted service on Christmas Day and Boxing Day - accommodation is not available.

Rooms 25 (5 fmly) ⚡ **Facilities** WiFi ♫ **Conf** Class 55 Board 48 Thtr 110 **Services** Lift **Parking** 14 **Notes** ⊗ RS 25-26 Dec Civ Wed 100

DIDCOT Map 5 SU59
Oxfordshire

Premier Inn Oxford South (Didcot)

BUDGET HOTEL

tel: 0871 527 8868 **Milton Heights, Milton OX14 4TX**
web: www.premierinn.com
dir: On A4130. Just off A34 at Milton interchange, between Oxford & Newbury

High quality, budget accommodation ideal for both families and business travellers. Spacious, en suite bedrooms feature tea and coffee making facilities, and Freeview TV in most hotels. Internet access and WiFi are available for a small fee. The adjacent family restaurant features a wide and varied menu. See also the Hotel Groups pages.

Rooms 83

D

DOGMERSFIELD
Hampshire

Map 5 SU75

INSPECTORS' CHOICE

Four Seasons Hotel Hampshire

★★★★★ @@ COUNTRY HOUSE HOTEL

tel: 01252 853000 **Dogmersfield Park, Chalky Ln RG27 8TD**
email: reservations.ham@fourseasons.com **web:** www.fourseasons.com/hampshire
dir: M3 junct 5 onto A287 Farnham. After 1.5m left for Dogmersfield, hotel 0.6m on left

This Georgian manor house, set in 500 acres of rolling grounds and English Heritage listed gardens, offers the upmost in luxury and relaxation, just an hour from London. The spacious and stylish bedrooms are particularly well appointed and offer up-to-date technology. Fitness and spa facilities include nearly every conceivable indoor and outdoor activity, in addition to luxurious pampering. An elegant restaurant, a healthy eating spa café and a trendy bar are popular venues.

Rooms 133 (23 GF) 🐾 **Facilities** Spa STV WiFi 🐦 🎣 Fishing 🏌 Gym Clay pigeon shooting Bikes Canal boat Falconry Horse riding Jogging trails 🎵 Xmas New Year **Conf** Class 110 Board 60 Thtr 260 **Services** Lift Air con **Parking** 165 **Notes** Civ Wed 200

DONCASTER
South Yorkshire

Map 16 SE50

BEST WESTERN PREMIER Mount Pleasant Hotel

★★★★ 80% @ HOTEL

tel: 01302 868696 & 868219 **Great North Rd DN11 0HW**
email: reception@mountpleasant.co.uk **web:** www.mountpleasant.co.uk

(For full entry see Rossington)

Ramada Encore Doncaster Airport

★★★ 74% HOTEL

tel: 01302 718520 **Robin Hood Airport DN9 3RH**
email: reception@encoredoncaster.co.uk **web:** www.encoredoncaster.co.uk
dir: M180 junct 3, follow signs for airport

Conveniently situated only a few minutes' walk from the main terminal at Robin Hood Airport, this purpose-built hotel is a good base for both the business and the leisure traveller. The air-conditioned bedrooms are spacious and bright, with power showers in the bathrooms. Public areas include the Hub Bar and Lounge. Secure parking is available on site.

Rooms 102 (36 fmly) (3 GF) (8 smoking) 🐾 **Facilities** STV FTV WiFi ◊ HL **Conf** Class 20 Board 20 Thtr 40 **Services** Lift Air con **Parking** 144 **Notes** ⊗

Campanile Doncaster

BUDGET HOTEL

tel: 01302 370770 **Doncaster Leisure Park, Bawtry Rd DN4 7PD**
email: doncaster@campanile.com **web:** www.campanile.com
dir: Follow signs to Doncaster Leisure Centre, left at rdbt before Dome complex

This modern building offers accommodation in smart, well-equipped bedrooms, all with en suite bathrooms. Refreshments may be taken at the informal bistro. See also the Hotel Groups pages.

Rooms 50 (25 GF) **S** £29-£70; **D** £29-£70* **Conf** Class 15 Board 15 Thtr 25 Del £65*

Premier Inn Doncaster Central

BUDGET HOTEL

tel: 0871 527 8302 **High Fishergate DN1 1QZ**
web: www.premierinn.com
dir: Off A630 (Church Way)

High quality, budget accommodation ideal for both families and business travellers. Spacious, en suite bedrooms feature tea and coffee making facilities, and Freeview TV in most hotels. Internet access and WiFi are available for a small fee. The adjacent family restaurant features a wide and varied menu. See also the Hotel Groups pages.

Rooms 140

Premier Inn Doncaster Central East

BUDGET HOTEL

tel: 0871 527 8304 **Doncaster Leisure Park, Herten Way DN4 7NW**
web: www.premierinn.com
dir: M18 junct 3, signed Doncaster racecourse. Left into Whiterose Way (B&Q on left). Straight on at rdbt into Wilmington Dr, right at next rdbt into Lakeside Boulevard. At next rdbt 2nd exit. Straight on at next rdbt, hotel ahead

Rooms 47

Premier Inn Doncaster (Lakeside)

BUDGET HOTEL

tel: 0871 527 8300 **Wilmington Dr, Doncaster Carr DN4 5PJ**
web: www.premierinn.com
dir: M18 junct 3, A6182. Hotel near junct with access road

Rooms 42

DORCHESTER
Dorset

Map 4 SY69

BEST WESTERN Kings Arms Hotel

★★★ 75% HOTEL

tel: 01305 265353 **30 High East St DT1 1HF**
email: info@kingsarmshoteldorchester.com **web:** www.kingsarmsdorchester.com
dir: In town centre

Previous guests at this 18th-century hotel, set in the very heart of Dorchester, have included Queen Victoria and John Lennon. Built in 1720, the hotel has been substantially refurbished in recent years but still retains many Georgian features, including age-darkened beams in the cosy bar. Guests can dine in the bar/bistro which offers a range of interesting dishes. Bedrooms offer character and comfort and include a number with four-posters.

Rooms 37 (3 GF) **Facilities** FTV WiFi ⌕ Xmas New Year **Conf** Class 80 Board 80 Thtr 80 **Services** Lift **Parking** 37 **Notes** Civ Wed 80

The Wessex Royale Hotel

THE INDEPENDENTS
HOTEL ASSOCIATION

★★★ 75% HOTEL

tel: 01305 262660 **High West St DT1 1UP**
email: info@wessexroyalehotel.co.uk **web:** www.wessexroyalehotel.co.uk
dir: From A35 follow town centre signs. Straight on, hotel at top of hill on left

This centrally situated Georgian townhouse dates from 1756 and successfully combines historic charm with modern comforts. The restaurant is a relaxed location for enjoying innovative food, and the hotel offers the benefit of a smart conservatory, ideal for functions. Limited courtyard parking is available.

Rooms 27 (2 annexe) (3 fmly) (2 GF) ✆ **S** £59-£89; **D** £69-£115 (incl. bkfst)*
Facilities STV FTV WiFi ⌕ **Conf** Class 40 Board 40 Thtr 80 **Parking** 11 **Notes** LB ⊗ Closed 23-30 Dec

Premier Inn Dorchester

BUDGET HOTEL

Premier Inn

tel: 0871 527 9376 **21 Weymouth Avene DT1 1QT**
web: www.premierinn.com
dir: On A35 follow Dorchester & Weymouth signs. At rdbt take B3150 (Stinsford Hill) left into Kings Rd. At rdbt 2nd exit into Prince of Wales Rd (B3144). Left into Weymouth Ave. Left into Brewery Sq

High quality, budget accommodation ideal for both families and business travellers. Spacious, en suite bedrooms feature tea and coffee making facilities, and Freeview TV in most hotels. Internet access and WiFi are available for a small fee. The adjacent family restaurant features a wide and varied menu. See also the Hotel Groups pages.

Rooms 76

DORCHESTER (ON THAMES)	Map 5 SU59
Oxfordshire	

White Hart Hotel

★★★ 74% HOTEL

tel: 01865 340074 **High St OX10 7HN**
email: whitehart@oxfordshire-hotels.co.uk **web:** www.oxfordshire-hotels.co.uk
dir: M40 junct 6, take B4009 through Watlington & Benson to A4074. Follow signs to Dorchester. Hotel on right

Period charm and character are plentiful throughout this 17th-century coaching inn, which is situated in the heart of a picturesque village. The spacious bedrooms are individually decorated and thoughtfully equipped. Public rooms include a cosy bar, a choice of lounges and an atmospheric restaurant, complete with vaulted timber ceiling.

Rooms 28 (4 annexe) (2 fmly) (9 GF) ✆ **Facilities** FTV WiFi ⌕ Xmas New Year **Conf** Class 20 Board 18 Thtr 30 **Parking** 36 **Notes** ⊗

George Hotel

★★★ 67% HOTEL

tel: 01865 340404 **25 High St OX10 7HH**
email: georgedorchester@relaxinnz.co.uk **web:** www.thegeorgedorchester.co.uk
dir: M40 junct 6 onto B4009 through Watlington & Benson. Take A4074 at BP petrol station, follow Dorchester signs. Hotel on left

Located on the quaint High Street, The George is directly opposite the stunning abbey. Once a coaching inn, this historic property provides comfortable accommodation in the main house and also in a separate building which was once the stable. The food is freshly prepared and can be enjoyed in the formal beamed restaurant, in the more relaxed Potboys Bar with open fires, or in the garden in warmer months. Complimentary WiFi is available throughout.

Rooms 24 (15 annexe) (1 fmly) (10 GF) ✆ **Facilities** FTV WiFi Beauty treatment room Xmas New Year **Conf** Class 20 Board 24 Thtr 40 **Parking** 50 **Notes** ⊗

DORKING	Map 6 TQ14
Surrey	

Mercure Boxhill Burford Bridge Hotel

Mercure
HOTELS

★★★★ 76% ⊛⊛ HOTEL

tel: 01306 884561 **Burford Bridge, Box Hill RH5 6BX**
email: h6635@accor.com **web:** www.mercure.com
dir: M25 junct 9, A245 towards Dorking. Hotel approx 5m on A24

Steeped in history, this hotel was reputedly where Lord Nelson and Lady Hamilton met for the last time, and it is said that the landscape around the hotel has inspired many poets. The hotel has a contemporary feel throughout. The grounds, running down to the River Mole, are extensive, and there are good transport links to major centres, including London. The elegant Emlyn Restaurant offers a modern award-winning menu.

Rooms 57 (22 fmly) (3 GF) **Facilities** WiFi ⌕ ♫ Xmas New Year **Conf** Class 80 Board 60 Thtr 120 **Parking** 130 **Notes** ⊗ Civ Wed 200

Mercure Dorking White Horse Hotel

Mercure
HOTELS

★★★ 74% HOTEL

tel: 01306 881138 **High St RH4 1BE**
email: h6637@accor.com **web:** www.mercure.com
dir: M25 junct 9, A24 S towards Dorking. Hotel in town centre

The hotel was first established as an inn in 1750, although parts of the building date back as far as the 15th century. Its town centre location and Dickensian charm have long made this a popular destination for travellers. There are beamed ceilings, open fires and four-poster beds; more contemporary rooms can be found in the garden wing.

Rooms 78 (41 annexe) (2 fmly) (5 GF) **Facilities** FTV WiFi Discount at local leisure centre Xmas New Year **Conf** Class 30 Board 30 Thtr 50 **Parking** 73

D

Hogarths Hotel

★★★★ 76% HOTEL

tel: 01564 779988 **Four Ashes Rd B93 8QE**
email: reception@hogarths.co.uk **web:** www.hogarths.co.uk
dir: M42 Junct 4, 1st exit to A3400. Left to Gate Ln. Left onto Four Ashes Rd. Hotel 300 mtrs on left

Hogarths Hotel with its contemporary interior design and panoramic views of the gardens from the open-plan and airy Brasserie, is a stunning property. The relaxed style of service is in keeping and effective. Bedrooms meet all modern day requirements, and many have their own balcony or outside area. The young team deliver high quality and friendly service throughout. The lake area for weddings and conferences events has recently been restored, and is a stunning attraction in the well-kept and managed gardens.

Rooms 49 (5 annexe) (9 fmly) (15 GF) ⌀ **S** £105-£145; **D** £135-£165 (incl. bkfst)*
Facilities FTV WiFi ♨ ♫ Xmas New Year **Conf** Class 60 Board 46 Thtr 120 Del from £115* **Services** Lift **Parking** 120 **Notes** LB Civ Wed 120

BEST WESTERN PLUS Dover Marina Hotel

★★★★ 75% HOTEL

tel: 01304 203633 **Dover Waterfront CT17 9BP**
email: reservations@dovermarinahotel.co.uk **web:** www.dovermarinahotel.co.uk
dir: M20 junct 13, A20 to Dover, straight on at 2 rdbts, at 3rd take 2nd exit into Union St. Cross swing bridge, next left into Marine Pde/Waterloo Cres. Hotel 200yds on left

An attractive terraced waterfront hotel overlooking the harbour that offers a wide range of facilities including meeting rooms, health club, hairdresser and beauty treatments. Some of the tastefully decorated bedrooms have balconies, some have broadband access and many of the rooms have superb sea views. Public rooms include a large, open-plan lounge bar and a smart bistro restaurant.

Rooms 81 (5 fmly) ⌀ **Facilities** Spa STV FTV WiFi Gym Xmas New Year **Conf** Class 60 Board 50 Thtr 110 **Services** Lift **Notes** ⊗ Civ Wed 100

Wallett's Court Country House Hotel & Spa

★★★★ 71% HOTEL

tel: 01304 852424 & 0800 035 1628 **West Cliffe, St Margarets-at-Cliffe CT15 6EW**
email: wc@wallettscourt.com **web:** www.wallettscourt.com
dir: From Dover take A258 towards Deal. 1st right to St Margarets-at-Cliffe & West Cliffe, 1m on right opposite West Cliffe church

Wallett's Court is a lovely Jacobean manor situated in a peaceful location on the outskirts of town. Bedrooms in the original house are traditionally furnished whereas the rooms in the courtyard buildings are more modern; all are equipped to a high standard. Public rooms include a smart bar, a lounge and a restaurant that utilises local organic produce. An impressive spa facility is housed in converted barn buildings in the grounds.

Rooms 16 (13 annexe) (2 fmly) (7 GF) **Facilities** Spa FTV WiFi ⊛ ♨ Putt green ♨ Gym Treatment suite Aromatherapy massage Beauty therapy Golf pitching range Xmas New Year **Conf** Class 25 Board 16 Thtr 25 Del £149* **Parking** 30 **Notes** Civ Wed 40

Ramada Hotel Dover

 RAMADA.

★★★★ 70% HOTEL

tel: 01304 821230 **Singledge Ln, Whitfield CT16 3EL**
email: reservations@ramadadover.co.uk **web:** www.ramadadover.co.uk
dir: From M20 follow signs to A2 towards Canterbury. Turn right after Whitfield rdbt. From A2 towards Dover, turn left before Whitfield rdbt

A modern purpose-built hotel situated in a quiet location between Dover and Canterbury, close to the ferry port and seaside. The open-plan public areas are contemporary in style and include a lounge, a bar and The Olive Tree Restaurant. The stylish bedrooms are simply decorated with co-ordinated soft furnishings and many thoughtful extras.

Rooms 68 (19 fmly) (68 GF) ⌀ **Facilities** STV FTV WiFi ♨ HL Gym Xmas New Year **Conf** Class 25 Board 20 Thtr 400 **Parking** 110 **Notes** ⊗ Civ Wed

Premier Inn Dover (A20)

BUDGET HOTEL

tel: 0871 527 8310 **Folkestone Rd CT15 7AB**
web: www.premierinn.com
dir: A20 to Dover. Through tunnel, take 2nd exit onto B2011. 1st left at rdbt. In 1m hotel on left

High quality, budget accommodation ideal for both families and business travellers. Spacious, en suite bedrooms feature tea and coffee making facilities, and Freeview TV in most hotels. Internet access and WiFi are available for a small fee. The adjacent family restaurant features a wide and varied menu. See also the Hotel Groups pages.

Rooms 64

Premier Inn Dover East

BUDGET HOTEL

tel: 0871 527 8308 **Jubilee Way, Guston Wood CT15 5FD**
web: www.premierinn.com
dir: At rdbt junct of A2 & A258

Rooms 40

Premier Inn Dover (Eastern Ferry Terminal)

BUDGET HOTEL

tel: 0871 527 8306 **Marine Court, Marine Pde CT16 1LW**
web: www.premierinn.com
dir: In town centre adjacent to ferry terminal. M20 junct 13 onto A20 for 8.2m

Rooms 100

D

The Marquis at Alkham

 RESTAURANT WITH ROOMS

tel: 01304 873410 & 822945 01304 873418 **Alkham Valley Rd, Alkham CT15 7DF**
email: info@themarquisatalkham.co.uk **web:** www.themarquisatalkham.co.uk
dir: A256 from Dover, at rdbt 1st exit into London Rd, left into Alkham Rd, Alkham Valley Rd. Establishment 1.5m after sharp bend

Located between Dover and Folkestone, this modern, contemporary restaurant with rooms offers luxury accommodation with modern features - flat-screen TVs, WiFi, power showers and bathrobes to name but a few. All the stylish bedrooms are individually designed and have fantastic views of the Kent Downs. The award-winning restaurant, open for lunch and dinner, specialises in modern British cuisine guided by Head Chef Charlie Lakin. Both continental and a choice of cooked breakfasts are offered.

Rooms 10 (3 fmly)

DRIFFIELD (GREAT)
East Riding of Yorkshire

Map 17 TA05

BEST WESTERN Bell Hotel

★★★ 80% HOTEL

tel: 01377 256661 **46 Market Place YO25 6AN**
email: bell@bestwestern.co.uk **web:** www.bw-bellhotel.co.uk
dir: From A164, right at lights. Car park 50yds on left behind black railings

This 250-year-old hotel incorporates the old corn exchange and town hall. It is furnished with antique and period pieces, and contains many items of local historical interest. The bedrooms vary in size, but all offer modern facilities and some have their own sitting rooms. The hotel has a relaxed and very friendly atmosphere. In the separate leisure club there is an impressive range of facilities including a pool, gym and a spa, which boasts a wide range of treatments and features a hydrotherapy pool, a saunarium, a Rasul chamber and a flotation chamber. Spa packages and pamper days are available.

Rooms 16 (3 GF) **Facilities** Spa FTV WiFi Gym Squash Masseur Snooker New Year **Conf** Class 100 Board 40 Thtr 150 **Services** Lift **Parking** 18 **Notes** No children 16yrs Closed 25 Dec & 1 Jan RS 24 & 26 Dec Civ Wed 120

Follow us on Facebook
www.facebook.com/TheAAUK

DROITWICH
Worcestershire

Map 10 SO86

St Andrews Town Hotel

★★★ 83% HOTEL

tel: 01905 779677 **St Andrews Dr WR9 8AL**
email: enquiries@st-andrewshotel.com **web:** www.st-andrewshotel.com
dir: From N: M5 junct 5, right onto A38, left onto B4065 Bromsgrove Rd, Queen St, B4090 Worcester Rd, right into St Andrews Drive. From S: M5 junct 6, right onto A4538, right onto A38, B4090 Worcester Rd, left into St Andrews Drive after Methodist Church

Ideally located in the heart of Droitwich and only minutes from both the town centre and motorway links, this elegant Georgian hotel has recently benefited from part refurbishment and guests can enjoy a comfortable stay in attractively designed bedrooms. Classic British dishes are served in the restaurant, with good use made of locally sourced, seasonal ingredients. The tranquil gardens make an ideal location for weddings and special occasions.

Rooms 31 (4 fmly) (6 GF) **S** £50-£65; **D** £65-£125 (incl. bkfst)* **Facilities** FTV WiFi **Conf** Class 30 Board 30 Thtr 90 Del £125* **Parking** 60 **Notes** Civ Wed 80

See advert on page 152

D

DUDLEY	Map 10 SO99
West Midlands	

Copthorne Hotel Merry Hill - Dudley

★★★★ 73% HOTEL

MILLENNIUM
HOTELS AND RESORTS
MILLENNIUM • COPTHORNE

tel: 01384 482882 **The Waterfront, Level St, Brierley Hill DY5 1UR**
email: reservations.merryhill@millenniumhotels.co.uk
web: www.millenniumhotels.co.uk/copthornedudley
dir: Follow signs for Merry Hill Centre

This hotel enjoys a waterfront location and is close to the Merry Hill Shopping Mall. Polished marble floors, rich fabrics and striking interior design are all in evidence in the stylish public areas. Bedrooms are spacious and some have Connoisseur status, which includes the use of a private lounge. A modern leisure centre with pool occupies the lower level.

Rooms 138 (14 fmly) **S** £43-£170; **D** £43-£170* **Facilities** Spa STV WiFi ⌷ HL ☍ supervised Gym Aerobics Beauty/massage therapists Steam room Sauna Dance studio ♫ Xmas New Year **Conf** Class 240 Board 60 Thtr 570 **Services** Lift **Parking** 100 **Notes** LB ⊗ Civ Wed 400

Premier Inn Dudley Town Centre

BUDGET HOTEL

Premier Inn

tel: 0871 527 9420 **Castlegate Business Park, Castlegate Way DY1 4TA**
web: www.premierinn.com
dir: From N: M5 junct 2, A4123 signed Dudley. At rdbt onto A4123. 4th exit into Wolverhampton Rd (A4123). Left into Birmingham Rd (A461). At rdb 4th exit into Castlegate Way. At next rdbt 3rd exit

High quality, budget accommodation ideal for both families and business travellers. Spacious, en suite bedrooms feature tea and coffee making facilities, and Freeview TV in most hotels. Internet access and WiFi are available for a small fee. The adjacent family restaurant features a wide and varied menu. See also the Hotel Groups pages.

Rooms 63

DUMBLETON	Map 10 SP03
Gloucestershire	

Dumbleton Hall Hotel

★★★ 79% COUNTRY HOUSE HOTEL

tel: 01386 881240 **WR11 7TS**
email: dh@pofr.co.uk **web:** www.dumbletonhall.co.uk
dir: M5 junct 9/A46. 2nd exit at rdbt signed Evesham. Through Beckford for 1m, turn right signed Dumbleton. Hotel at S end of village

Standing on the site of a 16th-century building also known as Dumbleton Hall, the current mansion, surrounded by 19 acres of landscaped gardens and parkland, was built in the mid-18th century. Panoramic views of the Vale of Evesham can be seen from every window, and the spacious public rooms make this an ideal venue for weddings, conferences or just as a hideaway retreat. The individually designed bedrooms vary in size and layout; one room is adapted for less able guests.

Rooms 34 (9 fmly) **Facilities** WiFi ⌷ Xmas New Year **Conf** Class 60 Board 60 Thtr 100 **Services** Lift **Parking** 60 **Notes** Civ Wed 100

DUNSTABLE	Map 11 TL02
Bedfordshire	

Premier Inn Dunstable/Luton

BUDGET HOTEL

Premier Inn

tel: 0871 527 8330 **350 Luton Rd LU5 4LL**
web: www.premierinn.com
dir: M1 junct 11, follow Dunstable signs. At 1st rdbt turn right. Hotel on left on A505

High quality, budget accommodation ideal for both families and business travellers. Spacious, en suite bedrooms feature tea and coffee making facilities, and Freeview TV in most hotels. Internet access and WiFi are available for a small fee. The adjacent family restaurant features a wide and varied menu. See also the Hotel Groups pages.

Rooms 42

D

Premier Inn Dunstable South (A5)

BUDGET HOTEL

tel: 0871 527 8332 **Watling St, Kensworth LU6 3QP**
web: www.premierinn.com
dir: M1 junct 9 towards Dunstable on A5, hotel on right after Packhorse pub

Rooms 40

DUNWICH	Map 13 TM47
Suffolk	

The Ship at Dunwich

★★ 82% ◉ SMALL HOTEL

tel: 01728 648219 & 07921 061060 **St James St IP17 3DT**
email: info@shipatdunwich.co.uk **web:** www.shipatdunwich.co.uk
dir: From N: A12, exit at Blythburgh onto B1125, then left to village. Inn at end of road. From S: A12, turn right to Westleton. Follow signs for Dunwich

A delightful inn situated in the heart of this quiet village, surrounded by nature reserves and heathland, and just a short walk from the beach. Public rooms feature a smart lounge bar with an open fire and real ales on tap. The comfortable bedrooms are traditionally furnished; some rooms have lovely views across the sea or marshes.

Rooms 15 (4 annexe) (4 fmly) (4 GF) **S** £95-£97.50; **D** £97.50-£112.50 (incl. bkfst)*
Facilities FTV WiFi Xmas New Year **Parking** 15

DURHAM	Map 19 NZ24
County Durham	

Ramside Hall Hotel

★★★★ 80% ◉ HOTEL

CLASSIC
BRITISH HOTELS

tel: 0191 386 5282 **Carrville DH1 1TD**
email: mail@ramsidehallhotel.co.uk **web:** www.ramsidehallhotel.co.uk
dir: A1(M) junct 62, A690 to Sunderland. Straight on at lights. 200mtrs after rail bridge turn right

With its proximity to the motorway and delightful parkland setting, this establishment combines the best of both worlds - convenience and tranquillity. The hotel boasts 27 holes of golf, a choice of lounges, two eating options and two bars. Bedrooms are furnished and decorated to a very high standard and include two very impressive presidential suites.

Rooms 80 (10 fmly) (28 GF) **Facilities** STV WiFi ☇ 27 Putt green Steam room Sauna Golf academy Driving range ♫ Xmas New Year **Conf** Class 160 Board 40 Thtr 500 **Services** Lift **Parking** 500 **Notes** Civ Wed 500

Honest Lawyer Hotel

★★★ 82% ◉ HOTEL

tel: 0191 378 3780 **Croxdale Bridge, Croxdale DH1 3SP**
email: enquiries@honestlawyerhotel.com **web:** www.honestlawyerhotel.com
dir: A1(M) junct 61, A688 towards Bishops Auckland. Right at rdbt (continue on A688), right at next rdbt onto A167 towards Durham. In 2.5m hotel on right

This hotel offers a mixture of smart motel-style bedrooms along with six junior suites in the main building that have four-poster beds. 40" LCD TVs, power showers and complimentary WiFi are provided as standard. Facilities also include a beauty treatment room and a boutique offering ladies fashion, jewellery and gifts. Bailey's Bar & Restaurant, with its open kitchen, offers a seasonally changing menu and friendly service. There is also a terrace and modern event facilities. There are good transportation links to Durham and the motorway.

Rooms 46 (40 annexe) (6 fmly) (40 GF) **Facilities** FTV WiFi ☇ ♫ Xmas New Year **Conf** Class 27 Board 24 Thtr 50 **Services** Air con **Parking** 150 **Notes** Civ Wed 40

Premier Inn Durham City Centre

BUDGET HOTEL

tel: 0871 527 8338 **Freemans Place, Walkergate DH1 1SQ**
web: www.premierinn.com
dir: A1(M) junct 62, A690 (Leazes Rd) towards city centre. In Durham follow Watergate signs, under bridge immediately left into Walkergate (one way). Back under A690, hotel on right

High quality, budget accommodation ideal for both families and business travellers. Spacious, en suite bedrooms feature tea and coffee making facilities, and Freeview TV in most hotels. Internet access and WiFi are available for a small fee. The adjacent family restaurant features a wide and varied menu. See also the Hotel Groups pages.

Rooms 103

Premier Inn Durham East

BUDGET HOTEL

tel: 0871 527 8340 **Broomside Park, Belmont Industrial Estate DH1 1GG**
web: www.premierinn.com
dir: A1(M) junct 62, A690 W towards Durham. In 1m left. Hotel on left

Rooms 40

Premier Inn Durham North

BUDGET HOTEL

tel: 0871 527 8342 **adj. Arnison Retail Centre, Pity Me DH1 5GB**
web: www.premierinn.com
dir: A1 junct 63, A167 to Durham. Straight on at 5 rbts, left at 6th rbt. Hotel on right after 200yds

Rooms 60

DUXFORD	Map 12 TL44
Cambridgeshire	

Duxford Lodge Hotel

THE INDEPENDENTS
HOTEL ASSOCIATION

★★★ 78% HOTEL

tel: 01223 836444 **Ickleton Rd CB22 4RT**
email: admin@duxfordlodgehotel.co.uk **web:** www.duxfordlodgehotel.co.uk
dir: M11 junct 10, onto A505 to Duxford. 1st right at rdbt, hotel 0.75m on left

A warm welcome is assured at this attractive red-brick hotel in the heart of a delightful village. Public areas include a cosy relaxing bar, separate lounge, and an attractive restaurant, where an excellent and imaginative menu is offered. The bedrooms are well appointed, comfortable and smartly furnished.

Rooms 15 (4 annexe) (2 fmly) (4 GF) ☇ **Facilities** FTV WiFi **Conf** Class 20 Board 20 Thtr 45 Del from £140* **Parking** 34 **Notes** ⊗ Closed 25 Dec-2 Jan Civ Wed 50

E

EASINGTON
North Yorkshire   Map 19 NZ71

The Grinkle Park Hotel

★★★★ 74% COUNTRY HOUSE HOTEL

tel: 08446 932965 **TS13 4UB**
email: info.grinklepark@classiclodges.co.uk
web: www.classiclodges.co.uk/Grinkle_Park_Hotel_Cleveland
dir: Take A171 from Guisborough towards Whitby. Hotel signed on left

Grinkle Park Hotel is a 19th-century baronial hall situated between the North Yorkshire Moors and the coast, and surrounded by 35 acres of parkland, and gardens where peacocks roam. It retains many original features including fine wood panelling, and the bedrooms are individually designed. The comfortable lounge and bar have welcoming log fires, while the Camelia Room is ideal for smaller weddings and private dining.

Rooms 20 (1 fmly) **Facilities** WiFi ⌨ ♨ ⭁ Xmas New Year **Conf** Class 80 Board 60 Thtr 180 **Parking** 150 **Notes** ⊗ Civ Wed 150

EASINGWOLD
North Yorkshire   Map 19 SE56

George Hotel

THE CIRCLE

★★ 78% SMALL HOTEL

tel: 01347 821698 **Market Place YO61 3AD**
email: info@the-george-hotel.co.uk **web:** www.the-george-hotel.co.uk
dir: From A19 midway between York & Thirsk, into Easingwold

A friendly welcome awaits at this former coaching inn that faces the Georgian market square. Bedrooms are very comfortably furnished and well equipped, and the mews rooms have their own external access. An extensive range of well-produced food is available both in the bar and restaurant. There are two comfortable lounges and complimentary use of a local fitness centre.

Rooms 15 (2 fmly) (6 GF) ⌨ **S** £75-£100; **D** £90-£120 (incl. bkfst)* **Facilities** FTV WiFi Complimentry use of local fitness centre New Year **Conf** Board 12 Del from £120 to £180* **Parking** 10 **Notes** LB ⊗

EAST GRINSTEAD
West Sussex   Map 6 TQ33

Gravetye Manor Hotel

RELAIS & CHATEAUX

★★★★ COUNTRY HOUSE HOTEL

tel: 01342 810567 **Vowels Ln, West Hoathly RH19 4LJ**
email: info@gravetyemanor.co.uk **web:** www.gravetyemanor.co.uk
dir: B2028 to Haywards Heath. 1m after Turners Hill fork left towards Sharpthorne, 1st left into Vowels Lane

Gravetye Manor is a beautiful Elizabethan mansion, built in 1598 and enjoying a tranquil setting. One of the first country house hotels in Britain, it remains an excellent example of its type. Bedrooms and bathrooms have been sympathetically refurbished with style and luxurious finishing touches. The day rooms, each with oak panelling, fresh flower arrangements and open fires, create a relaxing atmosphere. Cuisine is excellent and makes use of local suppliers and producers. Guests should take time to explore the impressive gardens and grounds; a perfect spot for afternoon tea.

Rooms 17 ⌨ **S** £160-£210; **D** £240-£455 (incl. bkfst)* **Facilities** FTV WiFi ⌨ Fishing ⭁ Deer stalking Xmas New Year **Conf** Board 15 Del from £320 to £395* **Parking** 20 **Notes** ⊗ No children 7yrs Civ Wed 60

The Felbridge Hotel & Spa

★★★★ 86% 🌹🌹 HOTEL

tel: 01342 337700 **London Rd RH19 2BH**
email: sales@felbridgehotel.co.uk **web:** www.felbridgehotel.co.uk
dir: From W: M23 junct 10, follow signs to A22. From N: M25 junct 6. Hotel on A22 at Felbridge

This hotel is within easy reach of the M25 and Gatwick as well as Eastbourne and the glorious south coast. All bedrooms are beautifully styled and offer a wealth of amenities. Diners can choose from the Bay Tree Brasserie, Anise Fine Dining Restaurant or contemporary QUBE Bar. Facilities include a selection of modern meeting rooms, the luxurious Chakra Spa and swimming pool.

Rooms 120 (16 fmly) (53 GF) 🐾 **S** £81-£200; **D** £91-£210* **Facilities** Spa STV FTV WiFi 🏃 🏊 Gym Sauna Steam room Hairdresser Nail bar Xmas New Year **Conf** Class 120 Board 100 Thtr 500 Del from £150 to £250* **Services** Air con **Parking** 300 **Notes** LB ⊗ Civ Wed 150

See advert on opposite page

Premier Inn East Grinstead

BUDGET HOTEL

tel: 0871 527 8348 **London Rd, Felbridge RH19 2QR**
web: www.premierinn.com
dir: M25 junct 6. Hotel at junction of A22 & A264

High quality, budget accommodation ideal for both families and business travellers. Spacious, en suite bedrooms feature tea and coffee making facilities, and Freeview TV in most hotels. Internet access and WiFi are available for a small fee. The adjacent family restaurant features a wide and varied menu. See also the Hotel Groups pages.

Rooms 41

EAST HORSLEY   Map 6 TQ05
Surrey

The Legacy Thatcher's Hotel

★★★ 78% HOTEL

tel: 0844 411 9043 & 0330 333 2843 **Guildford Rd KT24 6TB**
email: reception@thatchershotel.co.uk **web:** www.legacy-hotels.co.uk
dir: M25 junct 10/A3 exit to London/Guildford/Kingston. At rdbt take 3rd exit onto A3 for 0.5m, turn left onto Old Lane, 2.3m turn right onto Hirsham Road, at end turn left

This Tudor-style property sits within its own garden in the tranquil Surrey countryside, and is the ideal base to visit Thorpe Park. The hotel offers a choice of comfortable accommodation, meeting rooms for all occasions, free parking and a well-appointed restaurant overlooking the garden. Traditional afternoon tea is served in the Club Bar, together with a range of beverages. Free WiFi is offered throughout the hotel.

Rooms 87 (12 fmly) (20 GF) 🐾 **Facilities** FTV WiFi 🏃 Xmas New Year **Conf** Class 70 Board 66 Thtr 170 **Services** Lift **Parking** 140 **Notes** Civ Wed

---

EAST MIDLANDS AIRPORT   Map 11 SK42
Leicestershire

BEST WESTERN PREMIER Yew Lodge Hotel & Spa

★★★★ 78% 🌹🌹 HOTEL

tel: 01509 672518 **Packington Hill DE74 2DF**
email: info@yewlodgehotel.co.uk **web:** www.yewlodgehotel.co.uk
dir: M1 junct 24. Follow signs to Loughborough & Kegworth on A6. On entering village, 1st right, after 400yds hotel on right

This smart, family-owned hotel is close to both the motorway and airport, yet is peacefully located. Modern, stylish bedrooms and public areas are thoughtfully appointed and smartly presented. The restaurant serves interesting dishes, while lounge service and extensive conference facilities are available. A very well equipped spa and leisure centre complete the picture.

Rooms 103 (22 fmly) 🐾 **Facilities** Spa STV FTV WiFi 🏃 HL ⊙ Gym Beauty therapy suite Steam room Sauna Power plate Xmas New Year **Conf** Class 150 Board 84 Thtr 330 **Services** Lift **Parking** 180 **Notes** Civ Wed 260

The Priest House Hotel

★★★★ 78% 🌹🌹 HOTEL

tel: 01332 810649 **Kings Mills DE74 2RR**
email: thepriesthouse@handpicked.co.uk
web: www.handpickedhotels.co.uk/thepriesthouse
dir: M1 junct 24, A50, take 1st slip road signed Castle Donington. Right at lights, hotel in 2m

A historic hotel peacefully situated in a picturesque riverside setting. Public areas include a fine dining restaurant, a modern brasserie and conference rooms. Bedrooms are situated in both the main building and converted cottages, and the executive rooms feature state-of-the-art technology.

Rooms 42 (18 annexe) (5 fmly) (16 GF) 🐾 **Facilities** STV FTV WiFi 🏃 HL Fishing Xmas New Year **Conf** Class 40 Board 40 Thtr 120 **Parking** 200 **Notes** ⊗ Civ Wed 120

EAST MIDLANDS AIRPORT *continued*

Premier Inn East Midlands Airport

BUDGET HOTEL

tel: 0871 527 8350 **Pegasus Business Park, Herald Way DE74 2TQ**
web: www.premierinn.com
dir: From S: M1 junct 23a, A453 signed to airport. From N: M1 junct 24, A456 signed to airport. Hotel on Pegasus Business Park

High quality, budget accommodation ideal for both families and business travellers. Spacious, en suite bedrooms feature tea and coffee making facilities, and Freeview TV in most hotels. Internet access and WiFi are available for a small fee. The adjacent family restaurant features a wide and varied menu. See also the Hotel Groups pages.

Rooms 80

| **EASTBOURNE** | Map 6 TV69 |
| East Sussex | |

The Grand Hotel

★★★★★ 85% ◉◉ HOTEL

tel: 01323 412345 **King Edward's Pde BN21 4EQ**
email: reservations@grandeastbourne.com **web:** www.grandeastbourne.com
dir: On seafront W of Eastbourne, 1m from railway station

This famous Victorian hotel offers high standards of service and hospitality, and is in close proximity to both the beach and the South Downs National Park. The extensive public rooms feature a magnificent Great Hall, with marble columns and high ceilings, where guests can relax and enjoy afternoon tea. The spacious bedrooms provide high levels of comfort; many with stunning sea views and a number with private balconies. Guests can choose fine dining in The Mirabelle, or

Follow us on twitter
@TheAA_Lifestyle

the Garden Restaurant, and there are bars as well as superb spa and leisure facilities.

Rooms 152 (20 fmly) (4 GF) ⌇ **D** £195-£440 (incl. bkfst)* **Facilities** Spa STV WiFi ⌇ HL ⌘ supervised ⌇ supervised Putt green Gym Snooker table ♫ Xmas New Year Child facilities **Conf** Class 200 Board 40 Thtr 350 Del £195* **Services** Lift **Parking** 80 **Notes** LB Civ Wed 300

Langham Hotel

★★★★ 72% ◉ HOTEL

tel: 01323 731451 **Royal Pde BN22 7AH**
web: www.langhamhotel.co.uk
dir: Follow seafront signs. Hotel 0.5m E of pier

This popular hotel is situated in a prominent position with superb views of the sea and pier. Bedrooms are pleasantly decorated, and equipped with modern facilities. Superior rooms, some with four-poster beds are stylish and offer sea views. The spacious public rooms include the Grand Parade bar, a lounge and a fine dining conservatory restaurant. The hotel has 40 additional secure, charged-for parking spaces within 350 yards on Fridays, Saturdays and Sundays.

Rooms 80 (2 fmly) ⌇ **S** £49.50-£77; **D** £99-£145 (incl. bkfst)* **Facilities** STV FTV WiFi ⌇ ♫ Xmas New Year **Conf** Class 40 Board 30 Thtr 80 Del from £105 to £125 **Services** Lift **Parking** 5 **Notes** LB ⊗ Civ Wed 140

Hydro Hotel

★★★ 82% HOTEL

tel: 01323 720643 **Mount Rd BN20 7HZ**
email: sales@hydrohotel.com **web:** www.hydrohotel.com
dir: From pier/seafront, right along Grand Parade. At Grand Hotel follow Hydro Hotel sign. Into South Cliff, 200mtrs

This well-managed and popular hotel enjoys an elevated position with views of attractive gardens and the sea beyond. The spacious bedrooms are attractive and well equipped. In addition to the comfortable lounges, guests also have access to fitness facilities and a hairdressing salon. Service is both professional and efficient throughout.

Rooms 83 (3 fmly) (3 GF) ⌇ **S** £65-£100; **D** £99-£225 (incl. bkfst)* **Facilities** FTV WiFi ⌇ Putt green ⌇ Beauty room Hair salon Xmas New Year **Conf** Class 90 Board 40 Thtr 140 Del from £140* **Services** Lift **Parking** 40 **Notes** LB RS 24-28 & 30-31 Dec Civ Wed 120

E

The Devonshire Park Hotel

★★★ 79% HOTEL

tel: 01323 728144 **27-29 Carlisle Rd BN21 4JR**
email: info@devonshire-park-hotel.co.uk **web:** www.devonshire-park-hotel.co.uk
dir: Follow signs to seafront, exit at Wish Tower. Hotel opposite Congress Theatre

A handsome family-run hotel handily placed for the seafront and theatres. Attractively furnished rooms are spacious and comfortable; many boast king-size beds and all are equipped with WiFi and satellite TV. Guests can relax in the well presented lounges, the cosy bar or, when the weather's fine, on the garden terrace.

Rooms 35 (8 GF) ✿ **Facilities** STV WiFi Xmas New Year **Services** Lift **Parking** 25 **Notes** ⊗ No children 12yrs

BEST WESTERN Lansdowne Hotel

★★★ 78% HOTEL

tel: 01323 725174 & 745483 **King Edward's Pde BN21 4EE**
email: reception@lansdowne-hotel.co.uk **web:** www.bw-lansdownehotel.co.uk
dir: At W end of seafront opposite Western Lawns, 1m from railway station

Enjoying an enviable position at the quieter end of the parade, this hotel overlooks the Western Lawns and Wish Tower, and is just a few minutes' walk from many of the town's attractions. Public rooms include a variety of lounges, a range of meeting rooms, and games rooms. Bedrooms are attractively decorated and many offer sea views. The hotel has a wheelchair lift near the front entrance that operates between the pavement and one of the ground-floor public rooms.

Rooms 102 (10 fmly) (7 smoking) ✿ **S** £60-£80; **D** £99-£149 (incl. bkfst) **Facilities** FTV WiFi ♨ HL Table tennis Pool table 2 Snooker tables Xmas New Year **Conf** Class 40 Board 40 Thtr 80 Del from £99 to £135 **Services** Lift **Parking** 22 **Notes** LB Civ Wed 60

New Wilmington Hotel

★★★ 77% HOTEL

tel: 01323 721219 **25-27 Compton St BN21 4DU**
email: info@new-wilmington-hotel.co.uk **web:** www.new-wilmington-hotel.co.uk
dir: A22 to Eastbourne seafront. Right along promenade to Wish Tower. Right, then left at end of road, hotel 2nd on left

This friendly, family-run hotel is conveniently located close to the seafront, the Congress Theatre and Winter Gardens. Public rooms are well presented and include a cosy bar, a small comfortable lounge and a spacious restaurant. Bedrooms are comfortably appointed and tastefully decorated; family and superior bedrooms are available.

Rooms 40 (14 fmly) (3 GF) ✿ **Facilities** STV FTV WiFi ♨ ♫ Xmas New Year **Conf** Class 20 Board 20 Thtr 40 **Services** Lift **Parking** 3 **Notes** Closed 3 Jan-mid Feb

Chatsworth Hotel

★★★ 74% HOTEL

tel: 01323 411016 & 748700 **Grand Pde BN21 3YR**
email: chatsworth@lionhotelsltd.com **web:** www.lionhotelsltd.com
dir: M23 then A27 to Polegate. A2270 into Eastbourne, follow seafront signs. Hotel near pier

Within minutes of the town centre and pier, this attractive Edwardian hotel is located on the seafront. The public areas consist of the Chatsworth Bar, a cosy lounge and the Devonshire Restaurant. Bedrooms, many with sea views, are traditional in style and have a range of facilities. Service is friendly and helpful throughout.

Rooms 45 (2 fmly) ✿ **S** £50-£65; **D** £90-£130 (incl. bkfst)* **Facilities** Spa STV FTV WiFi HL Gym Hairdresser Sauna Massage Beauty treatments ♫ Xmas New Year **Conf** Class 60 Board 40 Thtr 100 Del from £110 to £140* **Services** Lift **Notes** LB ⊗ Civ Wed 140

Albany Lions Hotel

★★★ 67% HOTEL

tel: 01323 722788 & 748700 **Grand Pde BN21 4DJ**
email: albany@lionhotelsltd.com **web:** www.lionhotelsltd.com
dir: From town centre follow Seafront/Pier signs

This hotel, close to the bandstand, has a seafront location that is within walking distance of the main town centre. A carvery dinner is served in the restaurant, which has great sea views from most tables, and a relaxing drink or afternoon tea can be enjoyed in the sun lounge.

Rooms 61 (5 fmly) ✿ **S** £45-£60; **D** £90-£120 (incl. bkfst)* **Facilities** STV FTV WiFi HL Hairdresser Massage ♫ Xmas New Year **Conf** Class 60 Board 40 Thtr 120 Del from £110 to £140* **Services** Lift **Notes** LB ⊗

Courtlands Hotel

★★★ 67% HOTEL

tel: 01323 723737 **3-5 Wilmington Gardens BN21 4JN**
email: bookings@courtlandseastbourne.com **web:** www.courtlandseastbourne.co
dir: Exit Grand Parade at Carlisle Rd

Situated opposite the Congress Theatre, this hotel is just a short walk from both the seafront and Devonshire Park. Bedrooms are comfortably furnished and pleasantly decorated. Public areas are smartly appointed and include a cosy bar, a separate lounge and an attractive dining room.

Rooms 45 (4 fmly) (3 GF) **Facilities** STV FTV ♨ ♫ Xmas New Year **Conf** Class 20 Board 18 Thtr 55 **Services** Lift **Parking** 36 **Notes** Civ Wed 100

Mansion Lions Hotel

★★★ 66% HOTEL

tel: 01323 727411 & 748700 **Grand Pde BN21 3YS**
email: mansion@lionhotelsltd.com **web:** www.lionhotelsltd.com
dir: From town centre follow Seafront/Pier signs. Hotel on seafront

Directly overlooking the beach, this Victorian hotel is only two minutes' walk from the magnificent pier, the shopping centre and bandstand. The well-equipped bedrooms are spacious, comfortably furnished and some have sea views. An enjoyable four-course evening meal and a filling breakfast are served in the stylish Hartington Restaurant. There is an attractive lounge, and a pretty garden can be found at the back of the hotel.

Rooms 108 (6 fmly) (4 GF) ✿ **S** £45-£60; **D** £90-£120 (incl. bkfst)* **Facilities** STV WiFi HL ♫ Xmas New Year **Conf** Class 80 Board 40 Thtr 150 Del from £110 to £140* **Services** Lift **Notes** LB ⊗ Closed 2-31 Jan Civ Wed 150

E

EASTBOURNE *continued*

Queens Hotel

★★ 76% HOTEL

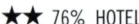

Leisureplex

tel: 01323 722822 **Marine Pde BN21 3DY**
email: queens.eastbourne@alfatravel.co.uk **web:** www.leisureplex.co.uk
dir: Follow signs for seafront, hotel opposite pier

Popular with tour groups, this long-established hotel enjoys a central, prominent seafront location overlooking the pier. Spacious public areas include a choice of lounges, and regular entertainment is also provided. Bedrooms are suitably appointed and equipped.

Rooms 122 (5 fmly) ↟ **Facilities** FTV WiFi Snooker ♫ Xmas New Year **Services** Lift **Parking** 50 **Notes** ⊗ Closed Jan (ex New Year) RS Nov, Feb-Mar

Congress Hotel

★★ 75% HOTEL

tel: 01323 732118 **31-41 Carlisle Rd BN21 4JS**
email: reservations@congresshotel.co.uk **web:** www.congresshotel.co.uk
dir: From Eastbourne seafront W towards Beachy Head. Right at Wishtower into Wilmington Sq, cross Compton St, hotel on left

An attractive Victorian property ideally located close to the seafront, Wish Tower and Congress Theatre. The bedrooms are bright and spacious. Family rooms are available plus there are facilities for less mobile guests. Entertainment is provided in a large dining room that has a dance floor and bar.

Rooms 62 (6 fmly) (8 GF) ↟ **S** £33-£48; **D** £66-£96 (incl. bkfst) **Facilities** FTV WiFi HL Games room ♫ Xmas New Year **Services** Lift **Parking** 12 **Notes** LB RS Jan-Feb

The Palm Court

★★ 75% HOTEL

tel: 01323 725811 **15 Burlington Place BN21 4AR**
email: thepalmcourt@btconnect.com **web:** www.thepalmcourthotel.co.uk
dir: From pier, W along seafront, Burlington Place 5th right

This family-run hotel is ideally situated close to the seafront and local theatres. The well appointed public areas include the lounge, spacious bar and stylish restaurant. Bedrooms vary in size but all offer plenty of handy accessories, comfortable furnishings and bright modern bathrooms. Good mobility facilities are provided.

Rooms 38 (5 GF) ↟ **S** £40-£48; **D** £80-£96 (incl. bkfst)* **Facilities** FTV WiFi Xmas New Year **Services** Lift **Notes** LB ⊗

Alexandra Hotel

★★ 70% HOTEL

tel: 01323 720131 **King Edwards Pde BN21 4DR**
email: alexandrahotel@mistral.co.uk **web:** www.alexandrahotel.mistral.co.uk
dir: On seafront at junct of Carlisle Road & King Edward Parade

Located at the west end of the town, opposite the Wishing Tower, this hotel boasts panoramic views of the sea from many rooms. Bedrooms vary in size but are comfortable with good facilities for guests. A warm welcome is guaranteed at this long-standing, family-run establishment.

Rooms 38 (2 fmly) (3 GF) ↟ **Facilities** FTV WiFi ♫ Xmas New Year **Services** Lift **Notes** ⊗ Closed Jan & Feb RS Mar

The Afton Hotel

★★ 69% HOTEL

tel: 01323 733162 **2-8 Cavendish Place BN21 3EJ**
email: info@aftonhotel.com **web:** www.aftonhotel.co.uk
dir: From A22, A27 or A259, follow seafront signs. Hotel by pier

This friendly family-run hotel is ideally located in the centre of town, opposite the pier and close to the shopping centre. Bedrooms vary in size but are all comfortable and well co-ordinated. The spacious restaurant serves traditional home cooking. A full programme of entertainment is provided.

Rooms 54 (3 fmly) (2 GF) ↟ **S** £30-£40; **D** £50-£80 (incl. bkfst)* **Facilities** WiFi ♫ Xmas New Year **Conf** Class 50 Board 50 Thtr 100 **Services** Lift **Notes** LB

Savoy Court Hotel

★★ 62% HOTEL

tel: 01323 723132 **11-15 Cavendish Place BN21 3EJ**
email: info@savoycourthotel.co.uk **web:** www.savoycourthotel.co.uk
dir: M25 junct 6, A22 to Eastbourne. Hotel 50mtrs from pier

Located close to the pier and within easy walking distance of the beaches and open-air bandstand this hotel offers bedrooms that are pleasantly decorated and furnished. The public areas include a cosy lounge and spacious bar/lounge for relaxing at the end of the day.

Rooms 29 (3 fmly) (5 GF) **S** £30-£55; **D** £38-£90* **Facilities** FTV WiFi Xmas New Year **Conf** Class 40 Board 30 Thtr 60 **Services** Lift **Notes** ⊗

Premier Inn Eastbourne

BUDGET HOTEL

Premier Inn

tel: 0871 527 8352 **Willingdon Dr BN23 8AL**
web: www.premierinn.com
dir: From A22 or A27 at Polegate, take bypass signed Eastbourne (A22). Continue to Shinewater rdbt. Left towards Langney. Hotel 0.25m on left

High quality, budget accommodation ideal for both families and business travellers. Spacious, en suite bedrooms feature tea and coffee making facilities, and Freeview TV in most hotels. Internet access and WiFi are available for a small fee. The adjacent family restaurant features a wide and varied menu. See also the Hotel Groups pages.

Rooms 47

Premier Inn Eastbourne (Polegate)

BUDGET HOTEL

tel: 0871 527 8354 **Hailsham Rd, Polegate BN26 6QL**
web: www.premierinn.com
dir: At rdbt junct of A22 & A27

Rooms 40

EASTLEIGH	**Map 5 SU41**
Hampshire	

Holiday Inn Southampton - Eastleigh M3 Jct 13

★★★ 82% HOTEL

tel: 0871 942 9075 **Leigh Rd SO50 9PG**
email: reservations-eastleigh@ihg.com **web:** www.hisouthamptoneastleighhotel.co.uk
dir: M3 junct 13, right at lights, follow signs to Eastleigh, hotel on right

Located close to the M3 and convenient for Southampton Airport and the New Forest, this hotel is suitable for both the business and leisure traveller. All bedrooms have air conditioning and work desks as standard, but there are also executive rooms and suites with extra facilities. Junction Restaurant serves international dishes and there is a cocktail lounge. The popular leisure area includes a swimming pool, jacuzzi, aerobics studio, steam room, sauna and beauty treatments.

Rooms 129 (41 fmly) (27 GF) **Facilities** Spa FTV WiFi ⓈⓀ HL ⓈⓀ Gym Whirlpool spa Steam room Sauna Personal trainer Studio **Conf** Class 60 Board 50 Thtr 120 **Services** Lift Air con **Parking** 175 **Notes** ⓈⓀ Civ Wed 100

Premier Inn Southampton (Eastleigh)

BUDGET HOTEL

tel: 0871 527 8994 **Leigh Rd SO50 9YX**
web: www.premierinn.com
dir: M3 junct 13, A335 towards Eastleigh. Hotel on right

High quality, budget accommodation ideal for both families and business travellers. Spacious, en suite bedrooms feature tea and coffee making facilities, and Freeview TV in most hotels. Internet access and WiFi are available for a small fee. The adjacent family restaurant features a wide and varied menu. See also the Hotel Groups pages.

Rooms 60

EDGWARE	**Map 6 TQ19**
Greater London	

Premier Inn London Edgware

BUDGET HOTEL

tel: 0871 527 8652 **435 Burnt Oak Broadway HA8 5AQ**
web: www.premierinn.com
dir: M1 junct 4, A41, A5 towards Edgware. 3m to hotel

High quality, budget accommodation ideal for both families and business travellers. Spacious, en suite bedrooms feature tea and coffee making facilities, and Freeview TV in most hotels. Internet access and WiFi are available for a small fee. The adjacent family restaurant features a wide and varied menu. See also the Hotel Groups pages.

Rooms 111

EGHAM	**Map 6 TQ07**
Surrey	

Great Fosters

★★★★ 84% ◉◉ HOTEL

tel: 01784 433822 **Stroude Rd TW20 9UR**
email: reception@greatfosters.co.uk **web:** www.greatfosters.co.uk
dir: From A30 (Bagshot to Staines), right at lights by Wheatsheaf pub into Christchurch Rd. Straight on at rdbt (pass 2 shop parades on right). Left at lights into Stroude Rd. Hotel 0.75m on right

This Grade II listed mansion dates back to the 16th century. The main house rooms are very much in keeping with the house's original style but are, of course, up-to-date with modern amenities. The stables and cloisters provide particularly stylish and luxurious accommodation. A stimulating range of award-winning cuisine can be enjoyed in The Estate Grill and The Tudor Room. The beautiful public rooms, including the Terrace during the summer months, provide the perfect setting for afternoon tea and cocktails. A host of meeting and event facilities provide the setting for a range of individual events.

Rooms 43 (22 annexe) (1 fmly) (13 GF) ⓈⓀ **S** £140; **D** £180-£495 **Facilities** STV WiFi ⓈⓀ ⓈⓀ ⓈⓀ Xmas New Year **Conf** Class 72 Board 50 Thtr 150 Del from £255 to £350 **Parking** 200 **Notes** LB ⓈⓀ Civ Wed 180

the runnymede-on-thames

★★★★ 83% HOTEL

tel: 01784 220600 **Windsor Rd TW20 OAG**
email: info@therunnymede.co.uk **web:** www.therunnymede.com
dir: M25 junct 13, onto A308 towards Windsor

Enjoying a peaceful location beside the River Thames, this large modern hotel, with its excellent range of facilities, balances both leisure and corporate business. The extensive function suites, together with spacious lounges and stylish, well laid-out bedrooms are impressive. Superb spa facilities are available, and the good food and beverage venues offer wonderful river views.

Rooms 181 (19 fmly) ⓈⓀ **S** £132-£338; **D** £169-£376 (incl. bkfst)* **Facilities** Spa STV WiFi ⓈⓀ HL ⓈⓀ supervised ⓈⓀ supervised ⓈⓀ Gym Dance studio Boat hire Group treatment suite Gym trail ⓈⓀ Xmas New Year Child facilities **Conf** Class 250 Board 76 Thtr 300 Del from £199 to £326* **Services** Lift Air con **Parking** 300 **Notes** LB ⓈⓀ Civ Wed 140

ELLESMERE PORT	**Map 15 SJ47**
Cheshire	

Mercure Chester North Woodhey House Hotel

★★★ 73% HOTEL

tel: 0151 339 5121 **Berwick Road West / Welsh Rd, Little Sutton CH66 4PS**
email: enquiries@woodheyhouse-hotel-chester.com **web:** www.mercure.com
dir: A41 S, right at 2nd set of lights onto A550 towards Queensferry. Hotel 1m on left

Located in a quiet rural setting, yet within easy reach of the M53, this hotel is an ideal stop-off for both business and leisure guests. All bedrooms are well equipped, and the day rooms are stylishly appointed. They include a bar, restaurant and a very good range of meeting and conference facilities. The hotel also has an indoor pool, gym and steam room.

Rooms 75 (8 fmly) (23 GF) ⓈⓀ **Facilities** FTV WiFi ⓈⓀ Gym Sauna Steam room Xmas New Year **Conf** Class 120 Board 80 Thtr 250 **Services** Lift **Parking** 150 **Notes** Civ Wed 100

E

E

Langdale Hotel & Spa

★★★★ 81% ◉◉ COUNTRY HOUSE HOTEL

tel: 015394 38014 & 38012 **LA22 9JD**
email: info@langdale.co.uk **web:** www.langdale.co.uk
dir: In Langdale Valley W of Ambleside

Founded on the site of an abandoned 19th-century gunpowder works, this modern hotel is set in 35 acres of woodland and waterways. Comfortable bedrooms, many with spa baths, vary in size. Extensive public areas include a choice of stylish restaurants, conference and leisure facilities and an elegant bar with an interesting selection of snuff. There is also a traditional pub run by the hotel just along the main road.

Rooms 56 (51 annexe) (4 fmly) (25 GF) ⬥ **Facilities** Spa STV FTV WiFi ⬥ supervised ⬥ Fishing Gym Steam room Solarium Aerobics studio Health & beauty salon Cycle hire Xmas New Year **Conf** Class 40 Board 35 Thtr 80 Del from £135 to £155 **Parking** 65 **Notes** ⊗ Civ Wed 65

New Dungeon Ghyll Hotel

★★★ 75% HOTEL

tel: 015394 37213 **Great Langdale, Ambleside LA22 9JX**
email: enquiries@dungeon-ghyll.com **web:** www.dungeon-ghyll.com
dir: From Ambleside follow A593 towards Coniston for 3m, at Skelwith Bridge right onto B5343 towards 'The Langdales'

This friendly hotel enjoys a tranquil, idyllic position at the head of the valley, set among the impressive peaks of Langdale. Bedrooms vary in size and style, but all the rooms are brightly decorated and smartly furnished. Bar meals are served all day, and dinner can be enjoyed in the restaurant overlooking the landscaped gardens; there is also a cosy lounge/bar.

Rooms 22 (1 fmly) (4 GF) ⬥ **Facilities** FTV WiFi ⬥ Xmas New Year **Parking** 30 **Notes** ⊗

Lamb Hotel

OldEngl☘sh

★★★ Ⓐ HOTEL

tel: 01353 663574 **2 Lynn Rd CB7 4EJ**
email: lamb.ely@oldenglishinns.co.uk **web:** www.oldenglish.co.uk
dir: From A10 into Ely, hotel in town centre

The Lamb Hotel is a 15th-century former coaching inn situated in the heart of this popular market town. The hotel offers a combination of light, modern and traditional public rooms, while the bedrooms provide contemporary standards of accommodation. Food is available throughout the hotel - the same menu is provided in the bar and restaurant areas.

Rooms 31 (4 fmly) **Facilities** FTV WiFi HL Xmas New Year **Conf** Class 30 Board 30 Thtr 70 **Parking** 14

Dunstanburgh Castle Hotel

★★ 85% HOTEL

tel: 01665 576111 **NE66 3UN**
email: stay@dunstanburghcastlehotel.co.uk **web:** www.dunstanburghcastlehotel.co.uk
dir: From A1 take B1340 to Denwick past Rennington & Masons Arms. Right signed Embleton

The focal point of the village, this friendly, family-run hotel has a dining room and grill room that offer different menus, plus a cosy bar and two lounges. In addition to the main bedrooms, a barn conversion houses three stunning suites, each with a lounge and gallery bedroom above.

Rooms 32 (12 annexe) (6 fmly) ⬥ **Facilities** WiFi **Parking** 33 **Notes** Closed Dec-Jan

Brookfield Hotel

★★★ 80% HOTEL

tel: 01243 373363 **Havant Rd PO10 7LF**
email: bookings@brookfieldhotel.co.uk **web:** www.brookfieldhotel.co.uk
dir: From A27 onto A259 towards Emsworth. Hotel 0.5m on left

This well-established family-run hotel has spacious public areas with popular conference and banqueting facilities. Bedrooms are in a modern style, and comfortably furnished. The popular Hermitage Restaurant offers a seasonally changing menu and an interesting wine list.

Rooms 39 (6 fmly) (12 GF) ⬥ **S** £75-£180; **D** £115-£240* **Facilities** STV FTV WiFi ⬥ Xmas New Year **Conf** Class 50 Board 50 Thtr 100 Del from £136 to £184 **Parking** 80 **Notes** ⊗ Civ Wed 100

36 on the Quay

◉◉◉ RESTAURANT WITH ROOMS

tel: 01243 375592 & 372257 **47 South St PO10 7EG**
web: www.36onthequay.co.uk
dir: Last building on right in South St, which runs from square in centre of Emsworth

Occupying a prime position with far-reaching views over the estuary, this 16th-century house is the scene for some accomplished and exciting cuisine. The elegant restaurant occupies centre stage with peaceful pastel shades, local art and crisp napery together with glimpses of the bustling harbour outside. The contemporary bedrooms offer style, comfort and thoughtful extras.

Rooms 7 (2 annexe)

Royal Chace Hotel

★★★★ 78% ◉ HOTEL

tel: 020 8884 8181 **The Ridgeway EN2 8AR**
email: reservations@royalchacehotel.co.uk **web:** www.royal-chace.com
dir: M25 junct 24, A1005 towards Enfield. Hotel 3m on right

This professionally run, privately owned hotel enjoys a peaceful location with open fields to the rear. Public rooms are smartly appointed; the ground-floor Kings

Restaurant is particularly appealing with its warm colour schemes and friendly service. Bedrooms are well presented and thoughtfully equipped.

Rooms 92 (5 fmly) (32 GF) 🐾 **Facilities** FTV WiFi 🎿 Gym New Year **Conf** Class 100 Board 40 Thtr 250 **Parking** 200 **Notes** ⊗ RS Sun eve Civ Wed 220

Premier Inn Enfield

BUDGET HOTEL

tel: 0871 527 8374 **Innova Park, Corner of Solar Way EN3 7XY**
web: www.premierinn.com
dir: M25 junct 25, A10 towards London, left into Bullsmoor Lane & Mollison Ave. Over rdbt, right at lights into Innova Science Park

High quality, budget accommodation ideal for both families and business travellers. Spacious, en suite bedrooms feature tea and coffee making facilities, and Freeview TV in most hotels. Internet access and WiFi are available for a small fee. The adjacent family restaurant features a wide and varied menu. See also the Hotel Groups pages.

Rooms 160

EPPING
Essex   Map 6 TL40

BEST WESTERN The Bell Hotel

★★★ 75% HOTEL

tel: 01992 573138 **High Rd, Bell Common CM16 4DG**
email: reservations@bellhotelepping.com **web:** www.bellhotelepping.com
dir: M11 junct 7, B1393 to Epping. Hotel on right past town centre

This hotel enjoys a convenient location on the outskirts of the town centre, close to the M25 and M1. The nearby tube station allows for quick access to London. There is a range of bedroom styles, all attractively presented and featuring LCD TVs and free WiFi. Public areas include a cosy bar and a popular restaurant, along with well-equipped conference facilities.

Rooms 79 (5 fmly) (38 GF) (10 smoking) **Facilities** FTV WiFi ☕ Xmas New Year **Conf** Class 50 Board 50 Thtr 85 **Parking** 80 **Notes** ⊗ Civ Wed 60

EPSOM
Surrey   Map 6 TQ26

Premier Inn Epsom Central

BUDGET HOTEL

tel: 0871 527 8376 **2-4 St Margarets Dr, off Dorking Rd KT18 7LB**
web: www.premierinn.com
dir: M25 junct 9, A24 towards Epsom, hotel on left, just before town centre

High quality, budget accommodation ideal for both families and business travellers. Spacious, en suite bedrooms feature tea and coffee making facilities, and Freeview TV in most hotels. Internet access and WiFi are available for a small fee. The adjacent family restaurant features a wide and varied menu. See also the Hotel Groups pages.

Rooms 58

Premier Inn Epsom North

BUDGET HOTEL

tel: 0871 527 8380 **272 Kingston Rd, Ewell KT19 0SH**
web: www.premierinn.com
dir: M25 junct 8, A217 towards Sutton. A240 towards Ewell. At Beggars Hill rdbt 2nd exit into Kingston Rd

Rooms 29

ERMINGTON
Devon   Map 3 SX65

Plantation House

 RESTAURANT WITH ROOMS

tel: 01548 831100 & 830741 **Totnes Rd PL21 9NS**
email: info@plantationhousehotel.co.uk **web:** www.plantationhousehotel.co.uk

Peacefully situated within the picturesque South Hams, this former parish rectory now provides an intimate and relaxing base from which to explore the area. Quality, comfort and individuality are hallmarks throughout, with bedrooms offering impressive standards and a host of thoughtful extras. The stylish bathrooms come equipped with cosseting towels, robes and under-floor heating. A drink beside the crackling log fire is the ideal prelude to dinner, where skill and passion underpin menus focusing upon wonderful local produce. Breakfast is equally enjoyable, with superb eggs provided by the resident hens.

Rooms 8

ESCRICK
North Yorkshire   Map 16 SE64

The Parsonage Country House Hotel

★★★ 79% COUNTRY HOUSE HOTEL

tel: 01904 728111 **York Rd YO19 6LF**
email: reservations@parsonagehotel.co.uk **web:** www.parsonagehotel.co.uk
dir: A64 onto A19 (Selby), Follow to Escrick. Hotel by St Helens Church

This 19th-century, former parsonage has been carefully restored and extended, and is situated in six acres of gardens. Bedrooms are smartly appointed and well equipped for both business and leisure guests. Public areas include an elegant restaurant, conference facilities and a choice of attractive lounges. Cloisters Spa is located in the formal gardens and includes a swimming pool, jacuzzi, sauna, steam room, aromatherapy salt room and an excellent gym. Please note that the Spa and Health Club is for adults aged 18+ only.

Rooms 50 (13 annexe) (4 fmly) (9 GF) 🐾 **S** £85-£105; **D** £100-£160 (incl. bkfst)*
Facilities Spa FTV WiFi 🏊 Putt green Gym Sauna Steam room Aromatherapy room Salt room Xmas New Year **Conf** Class 80 Board 50 Thtr 150 Del from £120 to £140*
Services Lift **Parking** 120 **Notes** LB ⊗ Civ Wed 150

EVERSHOT
Dorset

Map 4 ST50

Summer Lodge Country House Hotel, Restaurant & Spa

★★★★ ✿✿✿ COUNTRY HOUSE HOTEL

tel: 01935 482000 **DT2 0JR**
email: summer@relaischateaux.com **web:** www.summerlodgehotel.co.uk
dir: 1m W of A37 halfway between Dorchester & Yeovil

This picturesque hotel is situated in the heart of Dorset and is the ideal retreat for getting 'away from it all', and it's worth arriving in time for the excellent afternoon tea. Bedrooms are appointed to a very high standard; each is individually designed, with upholstered walls and a wealth of luxurious facilities. Expect plasma screen TVs, DVD players, radios, air conditioning and WiFi access, plus little touches such as homemade shortbread, fresh fruit and scented candles. The delightful public areas include a sumptuous lounge complete with an open fire, and the elegant restaurant where the cuisine continues to be the high point of any stay.

Rooms 25 (15 annexe) (6 fmly) (2 GF) ⚭ **S** £235-£650; **D** £235-£650 (incl. bkfst)*
Facilities Spa STV FTV WiFi ⬙ ⬙ ⬙ ⬙ Gym Sauna Xmas New Year **Conf** Class 16 Board 16 Thtr 24 Del from £300 to £715* **Services** Air con **Parking** 41 **Notes** LB Civ Wed 30

George Albert Hotel

★★★ 81% ✿ HOTEL

tel: 01935 483430 **Wardon Hill DT2 9PW**
email: enquiries@gahotel.co.uk **web:** www.gahotel.co.uk
dir: On A37 (between Yeovil & Dorchester). Adjacent to Southern Counties Shooting Ground

Situated mid-way between Dorchester and Yeovil, this hotel has much to offer for both business and leisure guests. The bedrooms offer impressive levels of comfort and many also have wonderful views across the Dorset countryside. Stylish public areas include extensive function rooms, a relaxing lounge, and a choice of dining options. Additional facilities include a karting track and clay pigeon shooting.

Rooms 39 (3 fmly) ⚭ **Facilities** FTV WiFi ⬙ Shooting Clay pigeon Kart track Xmas New Year **Conf** Class 60 Board 90 Thtr 250 **Services** Lift Air con **Parking** 200 **Notes** ⊗ Civ Wed 405

EVESHAM
Worcestershire

Map 10 SP04

Dumbleton Hall Hotel

★★★ 79% COUNTRY HOUSE HOTEL

tel: 01386 881240 **WR11 7TS**
email: dh@pofr.co.uk **web:** www.dumbletonhall.co.uk

(For full entry see Dumbleton)

The Evesham Hotel

★★★ 77% HOTEL

tel: 01386 765566 **Coopers Ln, Off Waterside WR11 1DA**
email: reception@eveshamhotel.com **web:** www.eveshamhotel.com
dir: M5 junct 9, A46 to Evesham. At rdbt on entering Evesham, take B4184 towards town, right at new bridge lights, 800yds, right into Coopers Ln

Dating from 1540 and set in extensive grounds, this delightful hotel has well-equipped accommodation that includes a selection of quirkily themed rooms, including Alice in Wonderland, Egyptian, and Aquarium (which has a tropical fish tank in the bathroom). A reputation for food is well deserved, with a particularly strong choice for vegetarians. Children are welcome and toys are always available.

Rooms 39 (2 fmly) (11 GF) ⚭ **S** £85-£120; **D** £115-£170 (incl. bkfst)* **Facilities** FTV WiFi ⬙ Putt green ⬙ Xmas New Year **Conf** Class 18 Board 22 Thtr 24 Del from £144 to £164* **Parking** 50

Premier Inn Evesham

BUDGET HOTEL

tel: 0871 527 8384 **Evesham Country Park, A46 Trunk Rd, Twyford WR11 4TP**
web: www.premierinn.com
dir: At rdbt junct of A46(T) & A4184 at N end of Evesham bypass. Adjacent to Evesham Country Park

High quality, budget accommodation ideal for both families and business travellers. Spacious, en suite bedrooms feature tea and coffee making facilities, and Freeview TV in most hotels. Internet access and WiFi are available for a small fee. The adjacent family restaurant features a wide and varied menu. See also the Hotel Groups pages.

Rooms 40

EXETER
Devon

Map 3 SX99

ABode Exeter

★★★★ 80% ✿✿ HOTEL

tel: 01392 319955 **Cathedral Yard EX1 1HD**
email: reservationsexeter@abodehotels.co.uk **web:** www.abodeexeter.co.uk
dir: M5 junct 30 towards A379. Follow city centre signs. Hotel opposite cathedral behind High St

ABode Exeter enjoys a central location in the heart of the city's Cathedral Yard. Steeped in history, this property, formerly The Royal Clarence, is reported to have been the very first hotel in England. A range of well-appointed bedrooms and suites, many retaining original features, all boast modern facilities and smart en suites. A choice of dining options and bars includes The Michael Caines Restaurant, the all-day Cafe Bar & Grill, and the more relaxed Well House Tavern.

Rooms 53 (3 fmly) ⚭ **S** £79-£130; **D** £79-£320* **Facilities** STV FTV WiFi ⬙ Gym Xmas New Year **Conf** Class 70 Board 50 Thtr 150 Del from £145 to £175* **Services** Lift Air con **Notes** LB ⊗ Civ Wed 150

E

Mercure Exeter Southgate Hotel & Spa

★★★★ 73% HOTEL

tel: 01392 412812 **Southernhay East EX1 1QF**
email: h6624@accor.com **web:** www.mercure.com
dir: M5 junct 30, 3rd exit (Exeter), 2nd left towards city centre, 3rd exit at next rdbt, hotel 2m on right

Centrally located and with excellent parking, The Southgate offers a diverse range of leisure and business facilities. Public areas are pleasantly spacious with comfortable seating in the bar and lounge; there is also a terrace. The bedrooms, in differing sizes, are well equipped and have modern facilities.

Rooms 154 (6 fmly) (23 GF) ♠ **Facilities** FTV WiFi ♦ 🏊 supervised Gym Sauna Spa bath New Year **Conf** Class 70 Board 50 Thtr 150 **Services** Lift **Parking** 101 **Notes** ⊗ Civ Wed 80

BEST WESTERN Lord Haldon Country Hotel

★★★ 77% HOTEL

tel: 01392 832483 **Dunchideock EX6 7YF**
email: enquiries@lordhaldonhotel.co.uk **web:** www.lordhaldonhotel.co.uk
dir: M5 junct 31, A30, 1st exit, follow signs through Ide to Dunchideock

Set in rural tranquillity, this is an attractive country house where guests are assured of a warm welcome from the professional team of staff. The well-equipped bedrooms are comfortable, and many have stunning views. The daily-changing menu features skilfully cooked dishes, with most of the produce sourced locally.

Rooms 25 (3 fmly) ♠ **Facilities** FTV WiFi ♦ Xmas New Year **Conf** Class 100 Board 40 Thtr 250 Del £129.95* **Parking** 120 **Notes** Civ Wed 120

The Devon Hotel

★★★ 77% HOTEL

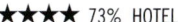

tel: 01392 259268 **Exeter Bypass, Matford EX2 8XU**
email: reservations@devonhotel.co.uk **web:** www.devonhotel.co.uk
dir: M5 junct 30 follow Marsh Barton Ind Est signs on A379. Hotel on Marsh Barton rdbt

Within easy access of the city centre, the M5 and the city's business parks, this smart Georgian hotel offers modern, comfortable accommodation. The Carriages Bar and Brasserie is popular with guests and locals alike, offering a wide range of dishes as well as a carvery at both lunch and dinner. Service is friendly and attentive, and extensive meeting and business facilities are available.

Rooms 40 (40 annexe) (2 fmly) (11 GF) ♠ **S** £65-£95; **D** £80-£100* **Facilities** FTV WiFi ♦ Xmas New Year **Conf** Class 80 Board 40 Thtr 150 **Parking** 250 **Notes** LB ⊗ Civ Wed 100

Queens Court Hotel

★★★ 74% ⚜⚜ HOTEL

tel: 01392 272709 **6-8 Bystock Ter EX4 4HY**
email: enquiries@queenscourt-hotel.co.uk **web:** www.queenscourt-hotel.co.uk
dir: Exit dual carriageway at junct 30 onto B5132 (Topsham Rd) towards city centre. Hotel 200yds from Central Station

Quietly located within walking distance of the city centre, this privately owned hotel is a listed, early Victorian property that provides friendly hospitality. The smart public areas and contemporary bedrooms are tastefully furnished, and the stylish and attractive Olive Tree restaurant offers an award-winning selection of dishes. Rooms are available for conferences, meetings, weddings and parties. Complimentary parking is available in a public car park directly opposite the hotel entrance.

Rooms 18 (1 fmly) **Facilities** FTV WiFi **Conf** Class 30 Board 30 Thtr 60 **Services** Lift **Notes** ⊗ Closed Xmas & New Year RS 25-30 Dec Civ Wed 60

Gipsy Hill Hotel

★★★ 73% HOTEL

tel: 01392 465252 **Gipsy Hill Ln, Monkerton EX1 3RN**
email: stay@gipsyhillhotel.co.uk **web:** www.gipsyhillhotel.co.uk
dir: M5 junct 29 towards Exeter. Right at 1st rdbt, right again at next rdbt, turn left onto Pinn Lane, right onto Gipsy Hill Lane

Located on the edge of the city, with easy access to the M5 and the airport, this popular hotel is set in attractive, well-tended gardens and boasts far-reaching country views. The hotel offers a range of conference and function rooms, comfortable bedrooms and modern facilities. An intimate bar and lounge are adjacent to the elegant restaurant.

Rooms 37 (17 annexe) (4 fmly) (12 GF) ♠ **S** £49-£79; **D** £59-£99 (incl. bkfst)* **Facilities** FTV WiFi ♦ Xmas New Year **Conf** Class 80 Board 80 Thtr 300 **Parking** 60 **Notes** LB ⊗ Civ Wed 160

Barton Cross Hotel & Restaurant

★★★ 71% ⚜ HOTEL

tel: 01392 841245 **Huxham, Stoke Canon EX5 4EJ**
email: bartonxhuxham@aol.com **web:** www.thebartoncrosshotel.co.uk
dir: From A396, 0.5m to Stoke Canon, 3m N of Exeter

17th-century charm combined with 21st-century luxury perfectly sums up the appeal of this lovely country hotel. The bedrooms are spacious, tastefully decorated and well maintained. Public areas include the cosy first-floor lounge and the lounge/bar with its warming log fire. The restaurant offers a seasonally changing menu of consistently enjoyable cuisine.

Rooms 9 (2 fmly) (2 GF) (2 smoking) ♠ **Facilities** STV FTV WiFi ♦ Xmas New Year **Conf** Class 20 Board 20 Thtr 20 **Parking** 35

E

EVESHAM *continued*

Premier Inn Exeter Central St Davids

BUDGET HOTEL

tel: 0871 527 9278 **Bonhay Rd EX4 4BG**
web: www.premierinn.com
dir: M5 junct 31, A30 towards Bodmin & Oakehampton. Exit onto A377 towards Exeter & Crediton. Hotel on left

High quality, budget accommodation ideal for both families and business travellers. Spacious, en suite bedrooms feature tea and coffee making facilities, and Freeview TV in most hotels. Internet access and WiFi are available for a small fee. The adjacent family restaurant features a wide and varied menu. See also the Hotel Groups pages.

Rooms 102

Premier Inn Exeter (Countess Wear)

BUDGET HOTEL

tel: 0871 527 8386 **398 Topsham Rd EX2 6HE**
web: www.premierinn.com
dir: 2m from M5 junct 30/A30 junct 29. Follow signs for Exeter & Dawlish (A379). On dual carriageway take 2nd slip road on left at Countess Wear rdbt. Hotel adjacent to Beefeater

Rooms 44

Premier Inn Exeter M5 Jct 29

BUDGET HOTEL

tel: 0871 527 9468 **Fitzroy Rd EX1 3LJ**
web: www.premierinn.com
dir: M5 junct 29., A3015 towards city centre. Straight on at 1st rdbt. 2nd right (at lights) into Fitzroy Rd

Rooms 102

Chi Restaurant & Bar with Accommodation

RESTAURANT WITH ROOMS

tel: 01626 890213 📠 01626 891678 **Fore St, Kenton EX6 8LD**
email: enquiries@chi-restaurant.co.uk **web:** www.chi-restaurant.co.uk
dir: 5m S of Exeter. M5 junct 30, A379 towards Dawlish, in village centre

This former pub has been spectacularly transformed into a chic and contemporary bar, allied with a stylish Chinese restaurant. Dishes are beautifully presented with an emphasis on quality produce and authenticity, resulting in a memorable dining experience. Bedrooms are well equipped and all provide good levels of space and comfort, along with modern bathrooms.

Rooms 5 (1 fmly)

EXFORD	Map 3 SS83
Somerset	

Crown Hotel

★★★ 79% ❀ HOTEL

tel: 01643 831554 **TA24 7PP**
email: info@crownhotelexmoor.co.uk **web:** www.crownhotelexmoor.co.uk
dir: M5 junct 25, follow Taunton signs. Take A358 from Taunton, then B3224 via Wheddon Cross to Exford

Guest comfort is of utmost importance here at the Crown Hotel. Afternoon tea is served in the lounge beside a roaring fire, and tempting menus in the bar and restaurant are all part of the charm of this delightful old coaching inn, that specialises in breaks for shooting and other country sports. Bedrooms retain a traditional style yet offer a range of modern comforts and facilities. Many have views of this pretty moorland village.

Rooms 16 (3 fmly) 🐾 **S** £60–£79; **D** £100–£159 (incl. bkfst)* **Facilities** FTV WiFi ⚐ Xmas New Year **Conf** Board 15 **Parking** 30 **Notes** LB

EXMOUTH
Devon

Map 3 SY08

Royal Beacon Hotel

★★★ 78% HOTEL

tel: 01395 264886 **The Beacon EX8 2AF**
email: info@royalbeacon.co.uk **web:** www.royalbeaconhotel.co.uk
dir: From M5 onto A376 & Marine Way. Follow seafront signs. On Imperial Rd left at T-junct then 1st right. Hotel 100yds on left

This elegant Georgian property sits in an elevated position overlooking the town and has fine views of the estuary towards the sea. Bedrooms are individually styled and many have sea views. Public areas include a well stocked bar, a cosy lounge, an impressive function suite, and a choice of restaurants where freshly prepared and enjoyable cuisine is offered.

Rooms 52 (17 annexe) (2 fmly) (8 GF) ⌁ **S** £65; **D** £75-£125 (incl. bkfst)*
Facilities FTV WiFi ⌂ Xmas New Year **Conf** Class 100 Board 60 Thtr 160 Del £130*
Services Lift **Parking** 28 **Notes** LB ⊗ Civ Wed 160

Cavendish Hotel

★★ 74% HOTEL

tel: 01395 272528 **11 Morton Crescent, The Esplanade EX8 1BE**
email: cavendish.exmouth@alfatravel.co.uk **web:** www.leisureplex.co.uk
dir: Follow seafront signs, hotel in centre of large crescent

Situated on the seafront, this terraced hotel attracts many groups from around the country. With fine views out to sea, the hotel is within walking distance of the town centre. The bedrooms are neatly presented, and front-facing rooms are always popular. Entertainment is provided on most evenings during the summer.

Rooms 78 (3 fmly) (21 GF) ⌁ **S** £39-£51; **D** £62-£98 (incl. bkfst)* **Facilities** FTV WiFi Snooker ♫ Xmas New Year **Services** Lift **Parking** 25 **Notes** LB ⊗ Closed Dec-Jan (ex Xmas) RS Nov & Feb-Mar

FALFIELD
Gloucestershire

Map 4 ST69

BEST WESTERN The Gables Hotel

★★★ 74% HOTEL

tel: 01454 260502 **Bristol Rd GL12 8DL**
email: mail@thegablesbristol.co.uk **web:** www.thegablesbristol.co.uk
dir: M5 junct 14 N'bound. Left at end of sliproad. Right onto A38, hotel 300yds on right

Conveniently located, just a few minutes from the motorway this establishment is ideally suited to both business and leisure guests, with easy access to Cheltenham, Gloucester, Bristol and Bath. Bedrooms are spacious and well equipped. Relaxing public areas consist of a light and airy bar and restaurant where meals and all-day snacks are available; a more formal restaurant is open for dinner. There is also a range of meeting rooms.

Rooms 46 (4 fmly) (18 GF) **S** £59-£99; **D** £69-£129 (incl. bkfst)* **Facilities** FTV WiFi ⌂ New Year **Conf** Class 90 Board 50 Thtr 200 **Parking** 104 **Notes** LB ⊗ Civ Wed 150

FALMOUTH
Cornwall

Map 2 SW83

See also **Mawnan Smith**

The Royal Duchy Hotel

★★★★ 79% ⊛⊛ HOTEL

tel: 01326 313042 **Cliff Rd TR11 4NX**
email: reservations@royalduchy.com **web:** www.royalduchy.com
dir: On Cliff Rd, along Falmouth seafront

Staff at this hotel, which looks out over the sea and towards Pendennis Castle, create a very friendly environment. The comfortable lounge and cocktail bar are well appointed and just the place for a light lunch. Leisure facilities include a beauty salon, and meeting rooms are also available. The award-winning Terrace Restaurant serves carefully prepared dishes, and guests can sit on the sea-facing terrace in warmer weather. The bedrooms vary in size and aspect, and many have sea views. Babysitting is happily arranged for families with small children and babies.

Rooms 43 (6 fmly) (1 GF) **S** £80-£112; **D** £140-£344 (incl. bkfst)* **Facilities** FTV WiFi ⌂ ⌖ Games room Sauna Hot stone therapy beds Beauty treatment room ♫ Xmas New Year **Child facilities Conf** Thtr 50 **Services** Lift **Parking** 50 **Notes** LB ⊗ Civ Wed 100

See advert on opposite page

FALMOUTH *continued*

The Greenbank Hotel

★★★★ 76% ◉◉ HOTEL

tel: 01326 312440 **Harbourside TR11 2SR**
email: reception@greenbank-hotel.co.uk **web:** www.greenbank-hotel.co.uk
dir: A39 to Falmouth, left at Ponsharden rdbt onto North Parade. 500yds past Falmouth
Marina on the Harbourfront

Located by the marina, and with its own private quay dating from the 17th century,
The Greenbank Hotel has a strong maritime theme throughout. Set at the water's
edge, the lounge, restaurant and many bedrooms all benefit from harbour views.
The restaurant provides a choice of interesting and enjoyable dishes.

Rooms 60 (5 fmly) ✎ **S** £99-£109; **D** £155-£245 (incl. bkfst)* **Facilities** FTV WiFi ⌕
Private beach & quay Xmas New Year **Conf** Class 30 Board 50 Thtr 90
Del from £140* **Services** Lift **Parking** 68 **Notes** LB ⊗ Civ Wed 90

St Michael's Hotel and Spa

★★★★ 76% ◉ HOTEL

tel: 01326 312707 **Gyllyngvase Beach, Seafront TR11 4NB**
email: info@stmichaelshotel.co.uk **web:** www.stmichaelshotel.co.uk
dir: A39 into Falmouth, follow beach signs, at 2nd mini-rdbt into Pennance Rd. Take 2nd
left & 2nd left again

Overlooking the bay, this hotel is in an excellent position and commands lovely
views. It is appointed in a fresh, contemporary style that reflects its location by the
sea. The Flying Fish restaurant has a great atmosphere and a real buzz about it.
The light and bright bedrooms, some with balconies, are well equipped. There are
excellent leisure facilities including a fitness and health club together with a spa
offering many treatments. The attractive gardens also provide a place to relax and
unwind.

Rooms 61 (8 annexe) (7 fmly) (12 GF) ✎ **Facilities** Spa FTV WiFi ⌕ ⊗ ⌒ Gym Sauna
Steam room Aqua aerobics Fitness classes Xmas New Year **Conf** Class 150 Board 50
Thtr 200 **Parking** 60 **Notes** ⊗ Civ Wed 80

Falmouth Hotel

★★★ 79% ◉ HOTEL

tel: 01326 312671 & 0800 019 3121 **Castle Beach TR11 4NZ**
email: reservations@falmouthhotel.com **web:** www.falmouthhotel.com
dir: A30 to Truro then A390 to Falmouth. Follow signs for beaches, hotel on seafront near
Pendennis Castle

This spectacular beach-front Victorian property affords wonderful sea views from
many of its comfortable bedrooms, some of which have their own balconies.
Spacious public areas include a number of inviting lounges, a choice of dining
options and an impressive range of leisure facilities.

Rooms 71 (16 fmly) ✎ **Facilities** Spa FTV WiFi ⌕ Putt green Gym Beauty salon &
Therapeutic rooms Xmas New Year **Conf** Class 150 Board 100 Thtr 250 **Services** Lift
Parking 120 **Notes** Civ Wed 250

BEST WESTERN Penmere Manor Hotel

★★★ 79% HOTEL

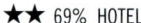

tel: 01326 211411 **Mongleath Rd TR11 4PN**
email: reservations@penmere.co.uk **web:** www.penmere.co.uk
dir: Exit A39 at Hillhead rdbt, over double mini rdbt. After 0.75m left into Mongleath Rd

Set in five acres on the outskirts of town, this Georgian manor house was originally
built for a ship's captain. Now a family-owned hotel it provides friendly service and

a good range of facilities. Bedrooms vary in size and are located in the manor house
and the garden wing. Various menus are available in the bar and the smart
restaurant. There is a health and beauty centre offering a wide range of treatments
and the water in the indoor pool is UV filtered.

Rooms 37 (12 fmly) (13 GF) ✎ **Facilities** FTV WiFi ⌕ ⌁ Gym Sauna New Year
Conf Class 20 Board 30 Thtr 60 **Parking** 50 **Notes** Closed 22-27 Dec

Penmorvah Manor

★★★ 73% HOTEL

tel: 01326 250277 **Budock Water TR11 5ED**
email: reception@penmorvah.co.uk **web:** www.penmorvah.co.uk
dir: A39 to Hillhead rdbt, take 2nd exit. Right at Falmouth Football Club, through Budock.
Hotel opposite Penjerrick Gardens

Situated within two miles of central Falmouth, this extended Victorian manor house
is a peaceful hideaway, set in six acres of private woodland and gardens.
Penmorvah is well positioned for visiting the local gardens, and offers many
garden-tour breaks. Dinner features locally sourced, quality ingredients such as
Cornish cheeses, meat, fish and game.

Rooms 27 (1 fmly) (10 GF) ✎ **S** £59-£65; **D** £99-£169 (incl. bkfst)* **Facilities** FTV
WiFi ⌕ Xmas New Year **Conf** Class 100 Board 50 Thtr 200 Del from £99 to £109*
Parking 100 **Notes** LB Civ Wed 120

Membly Hall Hotel

★★ 71% HOTEL

tel: 01326 312869 **Sea Front, Cliff Rd TR11 4NT**
email: memblyhallhotel@tiscali.co.uk **web:** www.memblyhallhotel.co.uk
dir: A39 to Falmouth. Follow seafront & beaches signs

Located conveniently on the seafront and enjoying splendid views, this family-run
hotel offers friendly service. Bedrooms are pleasantly spacious and well equipped.
Carefully prepared and enjoyable meals are served in the spacious dining room.
Live entertainment is provided on some evenings and there is also a sauna and spa
pool.

Rooms 35 (3 fmly) (6 GF) ✎ **S** £38-£49; (incl. bkfst)* **Facilities** FTV WiFi Gym Indoor
short bowls Table tennis Pool table Sauna Spa pool ♪ New Year **Conf** Class 130
Board 60 Thtr 150 **Services** Lift **Parking** 30 **Notes** LB ⊗ Closed Xmas week RS Dec-
Jan

Madeira Hotel

★★ 69% HOTEL

tel: 01326 313531 **Cliff Rd TR11 4NY**
email: madeira.falmouth@alfatravel.co.uk **web:** www.leisureplex.co.uk
dir: A39 (Truro to Falmouth), follow tourist 'Hotels' signs to seafront

This popular hotel offers splendid sea views and a pleasant, convenient location,
which is close to the town. Extensive sun lounges are popular haunts from which to
enjoy the views, while additional facilities include an oak-panelled cocktail bar.
Bedrooms, many with sea views, are available in a range of sizes.

Rooms 50 (8 fmly) (7 GF) **Facilities** FTV ♪ Xmas New Year **Services** Lift **Parking** 11
Notes ⊗ Closed Dec-Feb (ex Xmas) RS Nov & Mar

FAREHAM
Hampshire   Map 5 SU50

Solent Hotel & Spa

★★★★ 80% HOTEL

tel: 01489 880000 **Rookery Av, Whiteley PO15 7AJ**
email: solent@shirehotels.com **web:** www.solenthotel.com
dir: M27 junct 9, hotel on Solent Business Park

Close to the M27 with easy access to Portsmouth, the New Forest and other attractions, this smart, purpose-built hotel enjoys a peaceful location. Bedrooms are spacious and very well appointed and there is a well-equipped spa with health and beauty facilities.

Rooms 115 (9 fmly) (39 GF) **S** £90–£200; **D** £90–£200* **Facilities** Spa STV WiFi ⌂ HL ⌖ ⌘ Gym Steam room Sauna Children's splash pool Activity studio Xmas New Year **Conf** Class 100 Board 80 Thtr 200 Del from £145 to £185* **Services** Lift **Parking** 200 **Notes** ⊗ Civ Wed 160

Lysses House Hotel

★★★ 75% HOTEL

tel: 01329 822622 **51 High St PO16 7BQ**
email: lysses@lysses.co.uk **web:** www.lysses.co.uk
dir: M27 junct 11 follow Fareham signs, stay in left lane to Delme rdbt. At rdbt 3rd exit into East St, follow into High St. Hotel at top on right

This attractive Georgian hotel is situated on the edge of the town in a quiet location and provides spacious and well-equipped accommodation. There are conference facilities, and a lounge bar serving a range of snacks together with the Richmond Restaurant that offers imaginative cuisine.

Rooms 21 (2 fmly) (7 GF) **S** £65–£92; **D** £95–£115 (incl. bkfst)* **Facilities** FTV WiFi Free entry to nearby LA Fitness (5 mins walk away) **Conf** Class 42 Board 28 Thtr 95 Del from £122 to £140.50* **Services** Lift **Parking** 30 **Notes** ⊗ Closed 25 Dec-1 Jan RS 24 Dec & BHs Civ Wed 100

Red Lion Hotel

★★★ 70% HOTEL

tel: 01329 822640 **East St PO16 0BP**
email: 9200@greeneking.co.uk **web:** www.oldenglish.co.uk
dir: M27 junct 11. Take slip road down hill, towards Fareham. 3rd exit at rdbt (East Street). Hotel 0.25m on left

This hotel, which was formerly a coaching inn, is conveniently located within a few moments' walk of the market town of Fareham. An array of substantial hot and cold meals is served throughout the day in the bright informal restaurant and bar area. Bedrooms provide good comfort levels, and the hotel has pretty gardens and benefits from barrier operated parking.

Rooms 46 **Conf** Class 40 Board 40 Thtr 85 **Parking** 100

Premier Inn Fareham

BUDGET HOTEL

tel: 0871 527 8396 **Southampton Rd, Park Gate SO31 6AF**
web: www.premierinn.com
dir: M27 junct 9, follow Fareham West, A27 signs. (NB for Sat Nav use SO31 6BZ)

High quality, budget accommodation ideal for both families and business travellers. Spacious, en suite bedrooms feature tea and coffee making facilities, and Freeview TV in most hotels. Internet access and WiFi are available for a small fee. The adjacent family restaurant features a wide and varied menu. See also the Hotel Groups pages.

Rooms 41

FARNBOROUGH
Hampshire   Map 5 SU85

Aviator

★★★★ 81% HOTEL

tel: 01252 555890 **Farnborough Rd GU14 6EL**
email: enquiries@aviatorbytag.com **web:** www.aviatorbytag.com
dir: A325 to Aldershot, 3m, hotel on right

Aviator is a striking property with a modern, sleek interior overlooking Farnborough airfield and located close to the main transport networks. This hotel is suitable for both the business and leisure travellers. The bedrooms are well designed and provide complimentary WiFi. Both the Brasserie and the Deli source local ingredients for their menus.

Rooms 169 ⌂ **S** £135-£245; **D** £135-£245* **Facilities** STV WiFi ⌂ Gym Exercise studio Theraputic, holistic & beauty treatments Xmas New Year **Conf** Class 30 Board 40 Thtr 110 Del from £240 to £280* **Services** Lift Air con **Parking** 169 **Notes** ⊗ Civ Wed 150

Holiday Inn Farnborough

★★★ 81% HOTEL

tel: 0871 942 9029 & 01252 894300 **Lynchford Rd GU14 6AZ**
email: reservations-farnborough@ihg.com **web:** www.hifarnboroughhotel.co.uk
dir: M3 junct 4, A325 through Farnborough towards Aldershot. Hotel on left at The Queen's rdbt

This hotel occupies a perfect location for events in Aldershot and Farnborough with ample parking on site and easy access to the M3. Modern bedrooms provide good comfort levels, and internet access is provided throughout. Leisure facilities comprise a swimming pool, gym and beauty treatment rooms. Smart meeting rooms are also available.

Rooms 142 (31 fmly) (35 GF) **S** £49-£199; **D** £59-£245* **Facilities** Spa STV WiFi ⌂ HL ⌖ supervised Gym Sauna Steam room Beauty room ♬ Xmas New Year **Conf** Class 80 Board 60 Thtr 180 Del from £135 to £240* **Services** Air con **Parking** 170 **Notes** LB Civ Wed 180

Premier Inn Farnborough

BUDGET HOTEL

tel: 0871 527 8398 **Ively Rd, Southwood GU14 0JP**
web: www.premierinn.com
dir: M3 junct 4a, A327 to Farnborough. Hotel on left at 5th rdbt (Monkey Puzzle Rdbt)

High quality, budget accommodation ideal for both families and business travellers. Spacious, en suite bedrooms feature tea and coffee making facilities, and Freeview TV in most hotels. Internet access and WiFi are available for a small fee. The adjacent family restaurant features a wide and varied menu. See also the Hotel Groups pages.

Rooms 62

FARNHAM
Surrey
Map 5 SU84

BEST WESTERN Frensham Pond Hotel

★★★ 81%  HOTEL

tel: 01252 795161 **Bacon Ln GU10 2QB**
email: info@frenshampondhotel.co.uk **web:** www.frenshampondhotel.co.uk

(For full entry see Churt)

Mercure Farnham Bush Hotel

★★★ 78% HOTEL

tel: 01252 234800 **The Borough GU9 7NN**
email: H6621@accor.com **web:** www.mercure.com
dir: M3 junct 4, A31, follow town centre signs. At East Street lights turn left, hotel on right

Dating back to the 17th century, this extended former coaching inn is attractively presented and has a courtyard and a lawned garden. The bedrooms are well appointed, with quality fabrics and good facilities. The public areas include the panelled Oak Lounge, a smart cocktail bar and a conference facility in an adjoining building.

Rooms 94 (3 fmly) (27 GF) **Facilities** FTV WiFi Xmas **Conf** Class 80 Board 30 Thtr 140 **Parking** 70 **Notes** Civ Wed 100

The Legacy Farnham Hog's Back Hotel

★★★ 77% HOTEL

tel: 0844 411 9041 & 0330 333 2841 **Hog's Back, Seale GU10 1EX**
email: res@farnhamhogsbackhotel.co.uk **web:** www.legacy-hotels.co.uk
dir: On A31 Hogs Back Road 15 mins from Farnham & Guildford

The Legacy Farnham Hog's Back Hotel offers a convenient location, plenty of free parking, comfortable rooms with all the required amenities, including free WiFi, and the extensive Active Life Health Club. There is also a choice of two event suites, one of which has its own exclusive entrance, designed to host a range of different occasions such as business meetings, weddings or civil partnerships.

Rooms 96 (17 fmly) (24 GF) **S** £69-£139; **D** £79-£149* **Facilities** Spa STV WiFi HL Gym Steam room Sauna Xmas New Year **Conf** Class 120 Board 40 Thtr 180 Del from £115 to £145* **Parking** 150 **Notes** LB Civ Wed 150

FAWKHAM GREEN
Kent
Map 6 TQ56

Brandshatch Place Hotel & Spa

★★★★ 80% HOTEL

tel: 01474 875000 & 0845 072 7395 **Brands Hatch Rd, Fawkham Green DA3 8NQ**
email: brandshatchplace@handpicked.co.uk
web: www.handpickedhotels.co.uk/brandshatchplace
dir: M25 junct 3, A20 West Kingsdown. Left at paddock entrance/Fawkham Green sign. 3rd left signed Fawkham Rd. Hotel 500mtrs on right

This charming 18th-century Georgian country house close to the famous racing circuit offers stylish and elegant rooms. Bedrooms are appointed to a very high standard, offering impressive facilities and excellent levels of comfort and quality. The hotel also features a comprehensive leisure club with substantial crèche facilities.

Rooms 38 (12 annexe) (1 fmly) (6 GF) **S** £114-£214; **D** £114-£314 (incl. bkfst)*
Facilities Spa FTV WiFi Gym Squash Aerobic dance studio Sauna Steam room Xmas New Year **Conf** Class 60 Board 50 Thtr 160 Del from £140 to £165* **Services** Lift **Parking** 100 **Notes** LB Civ Wed 110

FELIXSTOWE
Suffolk
Map 13 TM33

The Brook Hotel

★★★ 77% HOTEL

tel: 01394 278441 **Orwell Rd IP11 7PF**
email: welcome@brookhotel.com **web:** www.brookhotel.com

The Brook Hotel is a modern, well furnished building ideally situated in a residential area close to the town centre and the sea. Public areas include a lounge bar, a large open-plan restaurant with a bar area and a residents' lounge. Bedrooms are generally quite spacious; each one is pleasantly decorated and equipped with modern facilities.

Rooms 25 (5 fmly) (3 GF) **Facilities** FTV WiFi Xmas New Year **Conf** Class 60 Board 60 Thtr 100 **Parking** 20 **Notes** Civ Wed 150

Marlborough Hotel

★★ 72% HOTEL

tel: 01394 285621 **Sea Front IP11 2BJ**
email: hsm@marlborough-hotel-felix.com **web:** www.marlborough-hotel-felix.com
dir: From A14 follow 'Docks' signs. Over Dock rdbt, rail crossing & lights. Left at T-junct. Hotel 400mtrs on left

Situated on the seafront, overlooking the beach and just a short stroll from the pier and town centre, this traditional resort hotel offers a good range of facilities including the smart Rattan Restaurant, Flying Boat Bar and L'Aperitif lounge. The pleasantly decorated bedrooms come in a variety of styles; some have lovely sea views.

Rooms 48 (1 fmly) **Facilities** STV WiFi Pool table Xmas New Year **Conf** Class 60 Board 40 Thtr 80 **Services** Lift **Parking** 16 **Notes**

FERNDOWN
Dorset
Map 5 SU00

Premier Inn Bournemouth/Ferndown

BUDGET HOTEL

tel: 0871 527 8122 **Ringwood Rd, Tricketts Cross BH22 9BB**
web: www.premierinn.com
dir: Off A348 just before Tricketts Cross rdbt

High quality, budget accommodation ideal for both families and business travellers. Spacious, en suite bedrooms feature tea and coffee making facilities, and Freeview TV in most hotels. Internet access and WiFi are available for a small fee. The adjacent family restaurant features a wide and varied menu. See also the Hotel Groups pages.

Rooms 32

FLAMBOROUGH
East Riding of Yorkshire
Map 17 TA27

North Star Hotel

★★ 80% SMALL HOTEL

tel: 01262 850379 **North Marine Dr YO15 1BL**
email: thenorthstarhotel@live.co.uk **web:** www.thenorthstarhotel.co.uk
dir: B1229 or B1255 to Flamborough. Follow signs for North Landing along North Marine Dr. Hotel 100yds from sea

Standing close to the North Landing of Flamborough Head, this family-run hotel overlooks delightful countryside, and provides excellent accommodation and caring hospitality. A good range of fresh local food, especially fish, is available in both the bar and the dining room.

Rooms 7 ⟡ **S** £55-£65; **D** £90-£100 (incl. bkfst)* **Facilities** FTV **Parking** 60 **Notes** LB ⊗ Closed Xmas RS Nov-Etr

FLEET
Hampshire   Map 5 SU85

The Lismoyne Hotel

★★★★ 75% HOTEL

tel: 01252 628555 **45 Church Rd GU51 4NE**
email: info@lismoynehotel.com **web:** www.lismoynehotel.com
dir: M3 junct 4a follow signs for Fleet. Pass railway station over lights into shopping area. Right into Church Rd, hotel on left

A new lease of life has been given to The Lismoyne Hotel following sympathetic refurbishments in the last couple of years. The hotel is set in its own grounds with ample parking available. There is a choice of comfortable rooms, equipped to a very good standard. The hotel also boasts the largest banqueting suite in the area, which is ideal for a range of events.

Rooms 62 (4 fmly) (28 GF) ⟡ **S** £50-£175; **D** £65-£275 **Facilities** STV FTV WiFi ⟲ Xmas New Year **Conf** Class 46 Board 60 Thtr 145 Del from £75 to £165 **Parking** 100 **Notes** LB Civ Wed 145

Premier Inn Fleet

BUDGET HOTEL

tel: 0871 527 9446 **Waterfront Business Park, 7-11 Fleet Rd GU51 3QT**
web: www.premierinn.com
dir: On A3013

High quality, budget accommodation ideal for both families and business travellers. Spacious, en suite bedrooms feature tea and coffee making facilities, and Freeview TV in most hotels. Internet access and WiFi are available for a small fee. The adjacent family restaurant features a wide and varied menu. See also the Hotel Groups pages.

Rooms 70

FLEET MOTORWAY SERVICE AREA (M3)
Hampshire   Map 5 SU75

Days Inn Fleet - M3

BUDGET HOTEL

tel: 01252 815587 **Fleet Services GU51 1AA**
email: fleet.hotel@welcomebreak.co.uk **web:** www.welcomebreak.co.uk
dir: Between junct 4a & 5 southbound on M3

This modern building offers accommodation in smart, spacious and well-equipped bedrooms, suitable for families and business travellers, and all with en suite bathrooms. Continental breakfast is available and other refreshments may be taken at the nearby family restaurant. See also the Hotel Groups pages.

Rooms 59 (46 fmly) (5 smoking)

FLITWICK
Bedfordshire   Map 11 TL03

Menzies Hotels Woburn Flitwick Manor

MenziesHotels

★★★★ 75% ⚜ COUNTRY HOUSE HOTEL

tel: 01525 712242 **Church Rd MK45 1AE**
email: flitwick@menzieshotels.co.uk **web:** www.menzieshotels.co.uk
dir: M1 junct 12, follow signs for Flitwick, turn left into Church Rd, hotel on left

With its picturesque setting in acres of gardens and parkland, yet only minutes from the motorway, this lovely Georgian house combines the best of both worlds, being both accessible and peaceful. Bedrooms are individually decorated and furnished with period pieces; some are air conditioned. Cosy and intimate, the lounge and restaurant give the hotel a home-from-home feel.

Rooms 18 (1 fmly) (5 GF) (1 smoking) ⟡ **S** £64-£114; **D** £89-£139 **Facilities** STV FTV WiFi ⟲ ⛳ Putt green ⛳ Xmas New Year **Conf** Class 30 Board 22 Thtr 50 Del from £145* **Parking** 18 **Notes** LB Civ Wed 58

FOLKESTONE
Kent   Map 7 TR23

The Southcliff Hotel

★★ 66% HOTEL

tel: 01303 850075 **22-26 The Leas CT20 2DY**
email: sales@thesouthcliff.co.uk **web:** www.thesouthcliff.co.uk
dir: M20 junct 13, follow signs for The Leas. Left at rdbt onto Sandgate Rd, right onto Shakespeare Terrace, right at end of road, hotel on right

Located on the town's panoramic promenade with a bird's eye view of the sea, this historical Victorian hotel is perfectly located for cross channel connections and is only minutes from the town centre. The bedrooms are spacious and airy with some boasting balconies and sea views. Enjoy dinner in the spacious restaurant or relax in the contemporary bar. Parking is available by arrangement.

Rooms 68 ⟡ **Facilities** FTV WiFi ♫ Xmas New Year **Conf** Class 120 Board 50 Thtr 200 **Services** Lift **Notes** ⊗

F

FOLKESTONE *continued*

Premier Inn Folkestone (Channel Tunnel)

BUDGET HOTEL

tel: 0871 527 8400 **Cherry Garden Ln CT19 4AP**
web: www.premierinn.com
dir: M20 junct 13. Follow Folkestone, A20 signs. At lights turn right, hotel on right

High quality, budget accommodation ideal for both families and business travellers. Spacious, en suite bedrooms feature tea and coffee making facilities, and Freeview TV in most hotels. Internet access and WiFi are available for a small fee. The adjacent family restaurant features a wide and varied menu. See also the Hotel Groups pages.

Rooms 79

Rocksalt Rooms

 RESTAURANT WITH ROOMS

tel: 01303 212070 **2 Back St CT19 6NN**
email: info@rocksaltfolkestone.co.uk **web:** www.rocksaltfolkestone.co.uk
dir: M20 junct 13 follow signs to harbour (A259). At harbour left onto Fish Market

Overlooking the busy harbour, often crowded with small leisure boats, and having wonderful sea views, Rocksalt enjoys a great location in Folkestone. Bedrooms are stylish, well appointed with original antique beds and equipped with a host of thoughtful little extras. Continental breakfasts are delivered promptly to the guests' rooms each morning, and dinner is served in the award-winning restaurant that is also blessed with panoramic views.

Rooms 4 (1 fmly)

FOREST ROW
East Sussex
Map 6 TQ43

INSPECTORS' CHOICE

Ashdown Park Hotel & Country Club

★★★★ ◉◉ HOTEL

tel: 01342 824988 **Wych Cross RH18 5JR**
email: reservations@ashdownpark.com **web:** www.ashdownpark.com
dir: A264 to East Grinstead, then A22 to Eastbourne. 2m S of Forest Row at Wych Cross lights. Left to Hartfield, hotel on right 0.75m

Situated in 186 acres of landscaped gardens and parkland, this impressive country house enjoys a peaceful countryside setting in the heart of the Ashdown Forest. Bedrooms are individually styled and decorated. Public rooms include a restored 18th-century chapel, ideal for exclusive meetings and wedding parties,

---

plus three drawing rooms, a cocktail bar and the award-winning Anderida Restaurant. The extensive indoor and outdoor leisure facilities include the Country Club and Spa plus an 18-hole, par 3 golf course and driving range.

Rooms 106 (12 fmly) (16 GF) ⟅ **D** £230-£510 (incl. bkfst)* **Facilities** Spa FTV WiFi ⟅ HL ⟅ ⟅ 18 ⟅ Putt green ⟅ Gym Aerobics Snooker Clay pigeon Archery Falconry Cycling Xmas New Year **Conf** Class 70 Board 40 Thtr 160 Del from £200 to £320 **Parking** 200 **Notes** LB Civ Wed 150

FORMBY
Merseyside
Map 15 SD30

Formby Hall Golf Resort & Spa

★★★★ 77% HOTEL

tel: 01704 875699 **Southport Old Rd L37 OAB**
email: gm@formbyhallgolfresort.co.uk **web:** www.formbyhallgolfresort.co.uk
dir: A565 to 2nd rdbt, follow brown signs

This hotel offers modern, boutique-style bedrooms with state-of-the-art facilities, some with excellent views over the championship golf course. The lavish spa offers peace and tranquillity along with a superbly equipped gym. Two golf courses and a driving range also add to the hotel's outstanding facilities. The Brasserie is an informal eating option and guests can enjoy a relaxing drink in the 19th Hole bar.

Rooms 62 (10 fmly) (29 GF) ⟅ **Facilities** Spa STV FTV WiFi ⟅ HL ⟅ ⟅ 18 Putt green Gym Kinesis studio Driving range Short ball area ⟅ Xmas New Year **Conf** Class 60 Board 40 Thtr 300 **Services** Lift Air con **Parking** 457 **Notes** ⊗ Civ Wed 100

FOWEY
Cornwall
Map 2 SX15

The Fowey Hotel

RICHARDSON HOTELS

★★★★ 75% ◉ HOTEL

tel: 01726 832551 **The Esplanade PL23 1HX**
email: reservations@thefoweyhotel.co.uk **web:** www.thefoweyhotel.co.uk
dir: A30 to Okehampton, continue to Bodmin. Then B3269 to Fowey for 1m, on right bend left junct then right into Dagands Rd. Hotel 200mtrs

This attractive hotel stands proudly above the estuary, with marvellous views of the river from the public areas and the majority of the bedrooms. High standards are evident throughout, augmented by a relaxed and welcoming atmosphere. There is a spacious bar, an elegant restaurant and a smart drawing room. Imaginative dinners make good use of quality local ingredients.

Rooms 37 (2 fmly) ⟅ **S** £85-£260; **D** £99-£269 (incl. bkfst) **Facilities** FTV WiFi ⟅ Xmas New Year **Conf** Class 60 Board 20 Thtr 100 Del from £175 to £250 **Services** Lift **Parking** 17 **Notes** LB Civ Wed 120

FRADDON
Cornwall
Map 2 SW95

Premier Inn Newquay (A30/Fraddon)

BUDGET HOTEL

tel: 0871 527 8816 **Penhale Round TR9 6NA**
web: www.premierinn.com
dir: On A30, 2m S of Indian Queens

High quality, budget accommodation ideal for both families and business travellers. Spacious, en suite bedrooms feature tea and coffee making facilities, and Freeview TV in most hotels. Internet access and WiFi are available for a small fee. The adjacent family restaurant features a wide and varied menu. See also the Hotel Groups pages.

Rooms 40

FRANKBY
Merseyside
Map 15 SJ28

Hillbark Hotel & Spa

★★★★★ 86% ◉◉◉ HOTEL

tel: 0151 625 2400 **Royden Park CH48 1NP**
email: enquiries@hillbarkhotel.co.uk **web:** www.hillbarkhotel.co.uk
dir: M53 junct 3, A552 (Upton), right onto A551 (Arrowe Park Rd). 0.6m at lights left into Arrowe Brook Rd. 0.5m on left

Originally built in 1891 on Bidston Hill, this Elizabethan-style mansion was actually moved, brick by brick, to its current site in 1931. The house now sits in a 250-acre woodland estate and enjoys delightful views towards the River Dee and to hills in North Wales. Bedrooms are luxuriously furnished and well equipped, while elegant day rooms are richly styled. There is a choice of eating options including the fine dining restaurant and a spa.

Rooms 18 (1 fmly) ☏ **S** £190-£260; **D** £210-£280 (incl. bkfst)* **Facilities** Spa STV FTV WiFi ↻ ♨ Gym Cinema Library Games room Children's play area Xmas New Year **Conf** Class 300 Board 60 Thtr 750 Del £265* **Services** Lift **Parking** 160 **Notes** LB ⊗ Civ Wed 500

FRESHWATER
Isle of Wight
Map 5 SZ38

Albion Hotel

★★★ 71% HOTEL

tel: 01983 755755 **PO40 9RA**
email: enquiries@albionhotel.info **web:** www.sandringhamhotel.co.uk/albion

In an idyllic location on the island's southern heritage coast, the Albion Hotel is right on the seafront with stunning views of Freshwater Bay. The bedrooms and bathrooms are spacious and offer guests modern, comfortable accommodation; many rooms have balconies. Breakfast and dinner are served in the traditionally styled restaurant that also enjoys the lovely views.

Rooms 40 **Facilities** ☺ Xmas **Conf** Class 30 Board 40 Thtr 60 **Parking** 30

FROME
Somerset
Map 4 ST74

Premier Inn Frome

BUDGET HOTEL

tel: 9871 527 8404 **Commerce Park, Jenson Av BA11 2LD**
web: www.premierinn.com
dir: M4 junct 18, A46 follow Warminster & Frome signs. Hotel off A361 (Frome bypass) in Commerce Park

High quality, budget accommodation ideal for both families and business travellers. Spacious, en suite bedrooms feature tea and coffee making facilities, and Freeview TV in most hotels. Internet access and WiFi are available for a small fee. The adjacent family restaurant features a wide and varied menu. See also the Hotel Groups pages.

Rooms 40

GARFORTH
West Yorkshire
Map 16 SE43

BEST WESTERN PLUS Milford Hotel

★★★ 83% HOTEL

tel: 01977 681800 **A1 Great North Rd, Peckfield LS25 5LQ**
email: enquiries@mlh.co.uk **web:** www.mlh.co.uk
dir: On A63, 1.5m W of A1(M) junct 42 & 4.5m E of M1 junct 46

This friendly, family-owned and run hotel is conveniently situated, and provides very comfortable, modern accommodation. The air-conditioned bedrooms are particularly spacious and well equipped, and ten boutique-style superior rooms are available. Public areas include a relaxing lounge area, the contemporary Watermill Restaurant, and lounge bar, which has a working waterwheel.

Rooms 46 (13 GF) ☏ **S** £39-£109; **D** £39-£109* **Facilities** FTV WiFi ↻ Xmas New Year **Conf** Class 35 Board 30 Thtr 60 Del from £90 to £98* **Services** Air con **Parking** 80 **Notes** LB Civ Wed 80

GARSTANG
Lancashire
Map 18 SD44

BEST WESTERN Garstang Country Hotel & Golf Centre

★★★ 79% HOTEL

tel: 01995 600100 **Garstang Rd, Bowgreave PR3 1YE**
email: reception@garstanghotelandgolf.com **web:** www.garstanghotelandgolf.com
dir: M6 junct 32 take 1st right after Shell garage on A6 onto B6430. 1m, hotel on left

This smart, purpose-built hotel enjoys a peaceful location alongside its own 18-hole golf course. Comfortable and spacious bedrooms are well equipped for both business and leisure guests, while inviting public areas include a restaurant and a choice of bars - one serving food.

Rooms 32 (16 GF) ☏ **Facilities** STV FTV WiFi ↥ 18 Putt green Golf driving range Xmas New Year **Conf** Class 150 Board 80 Thtr 250 **Services** Lift **Parking** 172 **Notes** ⊗ Civ Wed 200

G

GATESHEAD
Tyne & Wear

Map 21 NZ26

Newcastle Gateshead Marriott Hotel MetroCentre

★★★★ 76% HOTEL

tel: 0191 493 2233 **MetroCentre NE11 9XF**
email: reservations.newcastle.england.metrocentre@marriotthotels.co.uk
web: www.newcastlemarriottmetrocentre.co.uk
dir: From N exit A1 at MetroCentre exit, take 'Other Routes'. From S exit A1 at MetroCentre exit, turn right

Set just off the A1 and on the doorstep of the popular Metro shopping centre, this stylish purpose-built hotel provides modern amenities including a leisure centre, conference facilities and an informal stylish restaurant. All bedrooms are smartly laid out and thoughtfully equipped to suit both the business traveller and the leisure guest.

Rooms 150 (147 fmly) **Facilities** Spa STV FTV WiFi ↘ HL ⊗ Gym Health & beauty clinic Dance studio Hairdresser Spinning studio Sauna Steam room **Conf** Class 172 Board 48 Thtr 400 **Services** Lift Air con **Parking** 300 **Notes** ⊗ Civ Wed 100

Eslington Villa Hotel

★★★ 82% ⊛ HOTEL

tel: 0191 487 6017 & 420 0666 **8 Station Rd, Low Fell NE9 6DR**
email: home@eslingtonvilla.co.uk **web:** www.eslingtonvilla.co.uk
dir: From A1(M) exit for Team Valley Trading Estate. Right at 2nd rdbt along Eastern Av. Left at car show room, hotel 100yds on left

Set in a residential area, this smart hotel combines a bright, contemporary atmosphere with the period style of a fine Victorian villa. The overall ambience is relaxed and inviting. Chunky sofas grace the cocktail lounge, while tempting dishes can be enjoyed in either the classical dining room or modern conservatory overlooking the Team Valley.

Rooms 17 (2 fmly) (3 GF) ⟋ **S** £74.50-£84.50; **D** £89.50-£99.50 (incl. bkfst)*
Facilities FTV WiFi **Conf** Class 30 Board 25 Thtr 36 Del from £110 to £120*
Parking 28 **Notes** ⊗ Closed 25-26 Dec & 1 Jan

Ramada Encore Newcastle - Gateshead

★★★ 79% HOTEL

tel: 0191 481 3600 **Hawks Rd, Gateshead Quays NE8 3AD**
web: www.encorenewcastlegateshead.co.uk
dir: Located Gateshead Quays

This modern, purpose-built hotel is located at the Gateshead Quays. Bedrooms are well appointed and comfortable with well-presented en suites. Public areas are open-plan with a relaxed all-day menu serving food in all locations. A small gym and off-road parking are added benefits.

Rooms 200 (75 fmly) ⟋ **Facilities** FTV WiFi ↘ HL Gym **Conf** Class 14 Board 18 Thtr 20 Del from £67 to £117.50* **Services** Lift **Parking** 70 **Notes** ⊗

Premier Inn Newcastle (Metro Centre)

BUDGET HOTEL

tel: 0871 527 8792 **Derwent Haugh Rd, Swalwell NE16 3BL**
web: www.premierinn.com
dir: From A1 & A694 junct into Derwent Haugh Rd. 1m N of Metro Centre

High quality, budget accommodation ideal for both families and business travellers. Spacious, en suite bedrooms feature tea and coffee making facilities,

and Freeview TV in most hotels. Internet access and WiFi are available for a small fee. The adjacent family restaurant features a wide and varied menu. See also the Hotel Groups pages.

Rooms 69

Premier Inn Newcastle South

BUDGET HOTEL

tel: 0871 527 8806 **Lobley Hill Rd NE11 9NA**
web: www.premierinn.com
dir: A1 onto A692

Rooms 42

Premier Inn Newcastle (Team Valley)

BUDGET HOTEL

tel: 0871 527 8794 **Maingate, Kingsway North, Team Valley NE11 0BE**
web: www.premierinn.com
dir: A1 onto B1426 signed Team Valley (S'bound) or Teams/Consett (N'bound). Take Gateshead exit at rdbt. At bottom of hill straight on at rdbt. Hotel opposite

Rooms 115

GATWICK AIRPORT (LONDON)
West Sussex

Map 6 TQ24

See also **Dorking, East Grinstead & Reigate**

INSPECTORS' CHOICE

Langshott Manor

★★★★ ⊛⊛⊛ COUNTRY HOUSE HOTEL

tel: 01293 786680 **Langshott Ln RH6 9LN**
email: admin@langshottmanor.com **web:** www.langshottmanor.com
dir: From A23 take Ladbroke Rd, off Chequers rdbt to Langshott, after 0.75m hotel on right

On the outskirts of town this charming timber-framed Tudor manor house is set amidst beautifully landscaped grounds with an ancient moat. The stylish public areas feature a choice of inviting lounges with polished oak panelling, exposed beams and crackling log fires. Each bedroom - whether in the manor itself or in one of three mews buildings in the grounds - has been designed with flair and imagination. Expect sumptuous furnishings, Egyptian linens, flat-screen TVs and bathrooms with deep baths and power showers. The Mulberry restaurant overlooks a picturesque pond and offers an imaginative menu.

G

Rooms 22 (15 annexe) (2 fmly) (8 GF) ⟟ **S** £99-£199; **D** £99-£399* **Facilities** FTV WiFi ⟟ Xmas New Year **Conf** Class 20 Board 22 Thtr 40 Del from £190 to £245* **Parking** 25 **Notes** ⊗ Civ Wed 60

Sofitel London Gatwick

 SOFITEL

★★★★ 78% ◎◎ HOTEL

tel: 01293 567070 & 555000 **North Terminal RH6 OPH**
email: h6204-re@accor.com **web:** www.sofitelgatwick.com
dir: M23 junct 9, follow to 2nd rdbt. Hotel straight ahead

One of the closest hotels to the airport, this modern, purpose-built hotel is located only minutes from the terminals. Bedrooms are contemporary and all are air conditioned. Guests have a choice of eating options including a French-style café, a brasserie and an oriental restaurant.

Rooms 518 (19 fmly) **Facilities** FTV WiFi ⟟ Gym **Conf** Class 150 Board 90 Thtr 300 **Services** Lift Air con **Parking** 565 **Notes** ⊗

Holiday Inn London Gatwick Worth

★★★★ 72% HOTEL

tel: 01293 884806 **Crabbet Park, Turners Hill Rd, Worth RH10 4SS**
email: info@higatwickworth.co.uk **web:** www.higatwickworth.co.uk
dir: M23 junct 10/A264 Copthorne Way at rdbt last exit towards Three Bridges. 1st left along Old Hollow, right at end of lane then 1st right into Crabbet Park

This purpose-built hotel is ideally placed for access to Gatwick Airport. The bedrooms are spacious and suitably appointed with good facilities. Public areas consist of a light and airy bar area and a brasserie-style restaurant offering good value meals. Guests have use of the superb leisure club next door.

Rooms 118 (39 fmly) (56 GF) ⟟ **S** £50-£250; **D** £50-£250 **Facilities** FTV WiFi ⟟ HL Use of gym & pool next door (chargeable) Xmas New Year **Conf** Class 80 Board 80 Thtr 250 Del from £123 to £175 **Services** Lift Air con **Parking** 150 **Notes** LB ⊗ Civ Wed 60

Copthorne Hotel Effingham Gatwick

 MILLENNIUM

★★★★ 71% HOTEL

tel: 01342 714994 **West Park Rd RH10 3EU**
email: sales.effingham@millenniumhotels.co.uk **web:** www.millenniumhotels.co.uk
dir: M23 junct 10, A264 towards East Grinstead. Over rdbt, at 2nd rdbt left onto B2028. Effingham Park on right

A former stately home, set in 40 acres of grounds, this hotel is popular for conference and weekend functions. The main restaurant is an open-plan brasserie serving modern continental cuisine, and snacks are also available in the bar. Bedrooms are spacious and well equipped. Facilities include a golf course and a leisure club.

Rooms 122 (9 fmly) (20 GF) ⟟ **Facilities** Spa STV WiFi ⟟ ⟟ 9 ⟟ Putt green ⟟ Gym Aerobic & Dance studios Xmas New Year **Conf** Class 450 Board 250 Thtr 800 **Services** Lift **Parking** 500 **Notes** ⊗ Civ Wed 600

Copthorne Hotel London Gatwick

MILLENNIUM

★★★★ 71% HOTEL

tel: 01342 348800 & 348888 **Copthorne Way RH10 3PG**
email: sales.gatwick@millenniumhotels.co.uk **web:** www.millenniumhotels.co.uk
dir: On A264, 2m E of A264/B2036 rdbt

Situated in a tranquil position, the Copthorne is set in 100 acres of wooded, landscaped gardens containing jogging tracks, a putting green and a petanque pit. The sprawling building is built around a 16th-century farmhouse and has

comfortable bedrooms; many are air conditioned. There are three dining options, ranging from the informal bar and carvery to the more formal Lion d'Or.

Rooms 227 (10 fmly) (122 GF) **Facilities** STV WiFi ⟟ HL ⟟ ⟟ ⟟ Gym Squash Aerobic studio Jogging trail Xmas New Year **Conf** Class 60 Board 48 Thtr 155 **Parking** 300 **Notes** ⊗ Civ Wed 100

Stanhill Court Hotel

★★★ 82% HOTEL

tel: 01293 862166 **Stanhill Rd, Charlwood RH6 OEP**
email: enquiries@stanhillcourthotel.co.uk **web:** www.stanhillcourthotel.co.uk
dir: N of Charlwood towards Newdigate

This hotel dates back to 1881 and enjoys a secluded location of 35 acres of well-tended grounds with views over the Downs. Bedrooms are individually furnished and decorated, and many have four-poster beds. Public areas include a library, a bright Spanish-style bar and a traditional wood-panelled restaurant. Extensive and varied function facilities make this a popular wedding venue.

Rooms 34 (2 fmly) (1 GF) ⟟ **Facilities** FTV WiFi ⟟ ⟟ Xmas New Year **Conf** Class 100 Board 70 Thtr 300 Del from £135 to £149* **Parking** 150 **Notes** ⊗ Civ Wed 300

Holiday Inn London - Gatwick Airport

★★★ 77% HOTEL

tel: 0871 942 9030 & 01293 787648 **Povey Cross Rd RH6 OBA**
web: www.higatwickairporthotel.co.uk
dir: M23 junct 9, follow Gatwick, then Reigate signs. Hotel on left after 3rd rdbt

Situated close to the airport, this modern hotel provides air conditioned, smart accommodation with facilities suiting both the business and leisure guest. There is a restaurant and bar, and a variety of conference rooms plus a supporting business centre. Park and Fly stays are popular.

Rooms 216 (13 fmly) (37 GF) (22 smoking) **Facilities** STV WiFi ⟟ HL **Conf** Class 100 Board 70 Thtr 210 **Services** Lift Air con **Parking** 600

Ibis London Gatwick Airport

 ibis

BUDGET HOTEL

tel: 01293 590300 **London Rd, County Oak RH10 9GY**
email: H1889@accor.com **web:** www.ibis.com
dir: M23 junct 10, A2011 towards Crawley. Onto A23 left towards Crawley/Brighton. Hotel on left

Modern, budget hotel offering comfortable accommodation in bright and practical bedrooms. Breakfast is self-service and dinner is available in the restaurant. See also the Hotel Groups pages.

Rooms 141

Premier Inn Crawley East

 Premier Inn

BUDGET HOTEL

tel: 0871 527 8412 **Crawley Av, Gossops Green RH10 8BA**
web: www.premierinn.com
dir: M23 junct 11, A23 towards Crawley & Gatwick Airport

High quality, budget accommodation ideal for both families and business travellers. Spacious, en suite bedrooms feature tea and coffee making facilities, and Freeview TV in most hotels. Internet access and WiFi are available for a small fee. The adjacent family restaurant features a wide and varied menu. See also the Hotel Groups pages.

Rooms 83

GATWICK AIRPORT (LONDON) *continued*

Premier Inn Crawley (Pound Hill)

BUDGET HOTEL

tel: 0871 527 8410 **Balcombe Rd, Worth RH10 3NL**
web: www.premierinn.com
dir: M23 junct 10, B2036 S towards Crawley

Rooms 41

Premier Inn Crawley South (Goffs Park)

BUDGET HOTEL

tel: 0871 527 8414 **45 Goffs Park Rd RH11 8AX**
web: www.premierinn.com
dir: M23 junct 11, A23 towards Crawley. At 2nd rdbt take 3rd exit for town centre, then 2nd right into Goffs Park Rd

Rooms 49

Premier Inn Gatwick Airport Central

BUDGET HOTEL

tel: 0871 527 8406 **Longbridge Way, North Terminal RH6 0NX**
web: www.premierinn.com
dir: M23 junct 9/9A towards North Terminal, at rdbt take 3rd exit, hotel on right

Rooms 219

Premier Inn Gatwick Airport North

BUDGET HOTEL

tel: 0871 527 9354 **Crossway, Gatwick North Terminal RH6 0PH**
web: www.premierinn.com
dir: M23 junct 9. Follow signs for Gatwick North Terminal, at North Terminal rdbt enter at Arrivals Road (2nd exit), turn right onto Northway (Drop Off point), hotel is on right.

Rooms 630

Premier Inn Gatwick Airport South

BUDGET HOTEL

tel: 0871 527 8408 **London Rd, Lowfield Heath RH10 9ST**
web: www.premierinn.com
dir: M23 junct 9a towards North Terminal rdbt. Follow A23 & Crawley signs. Hotel in 2m

Rooms 102

Premier Inn Gatwick Manor Royal

BUDGET HOTEL

tel: 0871 527 9214 **Crawley Business Quarter, Fleming Way RH10 9DF**
web: www.premierinn.com
dir: M23 junct 10, A2011 (Crawley Ave). At rdbt 4th exit onto A23 (London Rd), at rdbt right into Fleming Way. Hotel 300yds on left

Rooms 180

GERRARDS CROSS	**Map 6 TQ08**
Buckinghamshire	

The Bull Hotel

★★★★ 76% ⚜ HOTEL

tel: 01753 885995 **Oxford Rd SL9 7PA**
email: bull@sarova.com **web:** www.sarova.com
dir: M40 junct 2 follow Beaconsfield on A355. After 0.5m 2nd exit at rdbt signed A40 Gerrards Cross for 2m. The Bull on right

Dating from the 17th-century, this former inn has been extensively refurbished to provide smart, well-equipped bedrooms. Public areas include the popular bar and Beeches Restaurant, serving a wide variety of dishes to suit all tastes. In addition there is the informal Jack Shrimpton bar offering snacks and bar meals. Attractive gardens and a good range of function rooms make this a popular wedding and events venue.

Rooms 150 (15 fmly) (19 GF) 🛏 **S** £80-£285; **D** £90-£295 (incl. bkfst)* **Facilities** FTV WiFi ↻ Use of private leisure facilities Xmas New Year **Conf** Class 108 Board 40 Thtr 180 Del £365* **Services** Lift **Parking** 150 **Notes** LB Civ Wed 114

GILLINGHAM	**Map 7 TQ76**
Kent	

Premier Inn Gillingham Business Park

BUDGET HOTEL

tel: 0871 527 8416 **Will Adams Way ME8 6BY**
web: www.premierinn.com
dir: M2 junct 44, A278 to A2. Left at Tesco. Hotel at next rdbt

High quality, budget accommodation ideal for both families and business travellers. Spacious, en suite bedrooms feature tea and coffee making facilities, and Freeview TV in most hotels. Internet access and WiFi are available for a small fee. The adjacent family restaurant features a wide and varied menu. See also the Hotel Groups pages.

Rooms 46

Premier Inn Gillingham/Rainham

BUDGET HOTEL

tel: 0871 527 9268 **High St, Rainham ME8 7JE**
web: www.premierinn.com
dir: M25 junct 2 (Canterbury/Dover/A2), A2 to M2 (Dover). Exit at junct 4 (Rainham/ Medway Tunnel), straight on at 2 rdbts. At 3rd rdbt take 3rd exit (Rainham High St). Hotel on right at 3rd lights

Rooms 26

G

GIRTON
Cambridgeshire

Map 12 TL46

Premier Inn Cambridge North (Girton)

BUDGET HOTEL

tel: 0871 527 8188 **Huntingdon Rd CB3 0DR**
web: www.premierinn.com
dir: A14 junct 31 follow signs towards Cambridge. Pass BP garage, next right. Hotel adjacent to Traveller's Rest Beefeater

High quality, budget accommodation ideal for both families and business travellers. Spacious, en suite bedrooms feature tea and coffee making facilities, and Freeview TV in most hotels. Internet access and WiFi are available for a small fee. The adjacent family restaurant features a wide and varied menu. See also the Hotel Groups pages.

Rooms 20

GISBURN
Lancashire

Map 18 SD84

Stirk House Hotel

★★★ 82% HOTEL

tel: 01200 445581 **BB7 4LJ**
email: reservations@stirkhouse.co.uk **web:** www.stirkhouse.co.uk
dir: W of village, on A59. Hotel 0.5m on left

This delightful historic hotel enjoys a peaceful location in its own grounds, amid rolling countryside. Extensive public areas include excellent conference and banqueting facilities, a leisure centre and an elegant restaurant. The stylish bedrooms and suites vary in size and style but all are comfortable and well equipped. Hospitality is warm and friendly, and service attentive.

Rooms 32 (11 annexe) (2 fmly) (10 GF) ⚑ **S** £87-£116; **D** £112-£116 (incl. bkfst)*
Facilities STV WiFi ⚒ supervised Gym Beauty treatment room Aromatherapy Personal training Kick boxing New Year **Conf** Class 150 Board 45 Thtr 200 Del from £98.50 to £120* **Parking** 100 **Notes** LB Civ Wed 95

GLASTONBURY
Somerset

Map 4 ST53

Premier Inn Glastonbury

BUDGET HOTEL

tel: 0871 527 9398 **Morland Rd BA6 9FW**
web: www.premierinn.com
dir: From A361 & A39 rdbt junct (SW of Glastonbury) take A39 towards Street. Right at lights into Morlands Enterprise Park. Left at 1st rdbt

High quality, budget accommodation ideal for both families and business travellers. Spacious, en suite bedrooms feature tea and coffee making facilities, and Freeview TV in most hotels. Internet access and WiFi are available for a small fee. The adjacent family restaurant features a wide and varied menu. See also the Hotel Groups pages.

Rooms 60

GLENRIDDING
Cumbria

Map 18 NY31

The Inn on the Lake

LAKE DISTRICT HOTELS

★★★★ 79% HOTEL

tel: 017684 82444 & 0800 840 1245 **Lake Ullswater CA11 0PE**
email: innonthelake@lakedistricthotels.net **web:** www.lakedistricthotels.net/innonthelake
dir: M6 junct 40, A66 to Keswick. At rdbt take A592 to Ullswater Lake. Along lake to Glenridding. Hotel on left on entering village

In a picturesque lakeside setting, this restored Victorian hotel is a popular leisure destination as well as catering for weddings and conferences. Superb views can be enjoyed from the bedrooms and from the garden terrace where afternoon teas are served during warmer months. There is a popular pub in the grounds, and moorings for yachts are available to guests. Sailing tuition can be arranged.

Rooms 47 (20 fmly) (1 GF) ⚑ **S** fr £120; **D** fr £197 (incl. bkfst & dinner)
Facilities FTV WiFi ⚒ Putt green ⚑ Gym Sauna 9 hole pitch & putt course Xmas New Year **Conf** Class 42 Board 30 Thtr 100 Del from £150 **Services** Lift **Parking** 100 **Notes** LB Civ Wed 110

BEST WESTERN Glenridding Hotel

★★★ 81% HOTEL

tel: 01768 482289 **CA11 0PB**
email: glenridding@bestwestern.co.uk **web:** www.bw-glenriddinghotel.co.uk
dir: N'bound M6 junct 36, A591 Windermere then A592, for 14m. S'bound M6 junct 40, A592 for 13m

This friendly hotel benefits from a picturesque location in the village centre, and many rooms have fine views of the lake and fells. Public areas are extensive and include a choice of dining options including Ratchers Restaurant and a café. Leisure facilities are available along with a conference room and a garden function room.

Rooms 36 (7 fmly) (8 GF) **Facilities** STV WiFi ⚒ Spa bath Sauna Snooker Table tennis Xmas New Year **Conf** Class 30 Board 24 Thtr 30 **Services** Lift **Parking** 30 **Notes** Civ Wed 120

GLOSSOP	Map 16 SK09
Derbyshire	

Wind in the Willows Hotel

★★ 85% COUNTRY HOUSE HOTEL

tel: 01457 868001 **Derbyshire Level SK13 7PT**
email: info@windinthewillows.co.uk **web:** www.windinthewillows.co.uk
dir: 1m E of Glossop on A57, turn right opposite Royal Oak, hotel 400yds on right

This impressive house sits in peaceful grounds with lovely views of the Peak District National Park. Individually furnished bedrooms are in keeping with the Victorian style of the house. Beautiful original oak panelling and crackling log fires add to the charm of the lounges and dining room. There is also a conference suite that is perfect for meetings, private dining or special occasions.

Rooms 12 ♦ **S** £75-£125; **D** £145-£195 (incl. bkfst)* **Facilities** FTV WiFi ♭ Xmas New Year **Conf** Class 12 Board 16 Thtr 40 **Parking** 16 **Notes** LB ⊗ No children 10yrs

GLOUCESTER	Map 10 SO81
Gloucestershire	

Hallmark Hotel Gloucester

★★★★ 74% HOTEL

tel: 01452 525653 **Matson Ln, Robinswood Hill GL4 6EA**
email: gloucester.reservations@hallmarkhotels.co.uk
web: www.hallmarkhotels.co.uk/gloucester
dir: A40 towards Gloucester onto A38. 1st exit at 4th rdbt (Painswick Rd). Right onto Matson Lane

Ideally located for exploring the Cotswolds and Gloucester, this hotel offers well-appointed bedrooms and relaxing public areas. The large leisure club has a well-equipped gym, squash courts and pool. Complimentary WiFi is available throughout.

Rooms 95 ♦ **Facilities** FTV WiFi ♭ ⊛ supervised ☉ Gym Squash Beauty salon Xmas New Year **Conf** Class 150 Board 18 Thtr 220 **Parking** 150 **Notes** Civ Wed 120

Mercure Gloucester, Bowden Hall Hotel

★★★★ 70% HOTEL

tel: 0844 815 9077 **Bondend Ln, Upton St Leonards GL4 8ED**
email: info@mercuregloucester.co.uk **web:** www.jupiterhotels.co.uk
dir: A417/A38/Gloucester. At rdbt take 2nd exit. At 2nd lights left onto Abbeymead Ave (becomes Metz Way). 1.5m, 3rd left onto Upton Lane, left into Bondend Rd, then left into Bondend Lane. Hotel at end

Conveniently located a short distance from the M5, the hotel is set in delightful grounds and is an ideal venue for weddings, banquets and meetings, or for a quiet break. Bedrooms are spacious and nicely appointed and many have lovely views of the grounds. Guests can choose to dine in the restaurant or bar.

Rooms 72 ♦ **S** £62-£109; **D** £62-£119* **Facilities** STV WiFi ♭ HL ♬ Xmas New Year **Conf** Class 70 Board 30 Thtr 120 **Parking** 130 **Notes** Civ Wed 120

Hatton Court

★★★ 82% HOTEL

tel: 01452 617412 **Upton Hill, Upton St Leonards GL4 8DE**
email: res@hatton-court.co.uk **web:** www.hatton-court.co.uk
dir: From Gloucester on B4073 (Painswick road). Hotel at top of hill on right

Built in the style of a 17th-century Cotswold manor house and set in seven acres of well-kept gardens, this hotel is popular with both business and leisure guests. It stands at the top of Upton Hill and commands truly spectacular views of the Severn Valley. The bedrooms, including a four-poster room, are comfortable and tastefully furnished with many extra facilities. The elegant Tara Restaurant offers varied menus, and outdoor seating in summer; there is also a bar and foyer lounge.

Rooms 45 (28 annexe) (6 fmly) ♦ **S** £50-£100; **D** £60-£190 (incl. bkfst)* **Facilities** FTV WiFi HL ⚘ Gym Xmas New Year **Conf** Class 100 Board 60 Thtr 200 **Del from** £99 to £159* **Parking** 80 **Notes** LB Civ Wed 120

Holiday Inn Gloucester - Cheltenham

★★★ 80% HOTEL

tel: 0871 942 9034 **Crest Way, Barnwood GL4 3RX**
email: reservations-gloucester@ihg.com **web:** www.higloucesterhotel.co.uk
dir: A40 to Gloucester. At rdbt take 2nd exit signed A417/Cirencester. At next rdbt take 2nd exit then 1st left

This hotel is conveniently located close to the M5, and within easy driving distance of both Gloucester and Cheltenham. Bedrooms vary in size from the larger, well-equipped executive rooms to smaller style standard doubles. A good selection of dining options is available in either the lounge/bar, the relaxing restaurant or via room service. Guests can also enjoy the well-equipped leisure facilities.

Rooms 125 (25 fmly) (61 GF) (6 smoking) **Facilities** Spa STV FTV WiFi ♭ HL ⊛ Gym Dance studio New Year **Conf** Class 50 Board 60 Thtr 140 **Services** Air con **Parking** 200 **Notes** ⊗ Civ Wed 120

Hatherley Manor

★★★ 79% HOTEL

CLASSIC
BRITISH HOTELS

tel: 01452 730217 **Down Hatherley Ln GL2 9QA**
email: reservations@hatherleymanor.com **web:** www.hatherleymanor.com
dir: A38 into Down Hatherley Lane, signed. Hotel 600yds on left

Within easy striking distance of the M5, Gloucester, Cheltenham and the Cotswolds, this stylish 17th-century manor, set in attractive grounds, remains popular with both business and leisure guests. Bedrooms are well appointed and offer contemporary comforts. A particularly impressive range of meeting and function rooms is available.

Rooms 50 (5 fmly) (18 GF) **Facilities** FTV WiFi Xmas New Year **Conf** Class 90 Board 75 Thtr 400 **Parking** 250 **Notes** Civ Wed 300

Premier Inn Gloucester (Barnwood)

BUDGET HOTEL

Premier Inn

tel: 0871 527 8456 **Barnwood GL4 3HR**
web: www.premierinn.com
dir: M5 junct 11, A40 towards Gloucester. At 1st rdbt A417 towards Cirencester, at next rdbt take 4th exit

High quality, budget accommodation ideal for both families and business travellers. Spacious, en suite bedrooms feature tea and coffee making facilities, and Freeview TV in most hotels. Internet access and WiFi are available for a small fee. The adjacent family restaurant features a wide and varied menu. See also the Hotel Groups pages.

Rooms 83

Premier Inn Gloucester Business Park

BUDGET HOTEL

tel: 0871 527 8462 **Gloucester Business Park, Brockworth GL3 4AJ**
web: www.premierinn.com
dir: M5 junct 11a, A417 towards Cirencester. At Brockworth Rdbt follow Gloucester Business Park signs, onto dual carriageway (Valiant Way). At next rdbt left into Delta Way. Hotel adjacent to Tesco

Rooms 48

Premier Inn Gloucester (Little Witcombe)

BUDGET HOTEL

tel: 0871 527 8458 **Witcombe GL3 4SS**
web: www.premierinn.com
dir: M5 junct 11a, A417 signed Cirencester. At 1st exit turn right onto A46 towards Stroud & Witcombe. Left at next rdbt by Crosshands pub

Rooms 39

Premier Inn Gloucester (Longford)

BUDGET HOTEL

tel: 0871 527 8460 **Tewkesbury Rd, Longford GL2 9BE**
web: www.premierinn.com
dir: M5 junct 11, A40 towards Gloucester & Ross-on-Wye. Hotel on A38 towards Gloucester

Rooms 60

Premier Inn Gloucester North

BUDGET HOTEL

tel: 0871 527 8464 **Tewkesbury Rd, Twigworth GL2 9PG**
web: www.premierinn.com
dir: On A38, 1m N from junct with A40

Rooms 50

The Wharf House Restaurant with Rooms

 RESTAURANT WITH ROOMS

tel: 01452 332900 ⬛ 01452 332901 **Over GL2 8DB**
email: thewharfhouse@yahoo.co.uk **web:** www.thewharfhouse.co.uk
dir: From A40 between Gloucester & Highnam exit at lights for Over. Establishment signed

The Wharf House was built to replace the old lock cottage and, as the name suggests, it is located at the very edge of the river; it has pleasant views and an outdoor terrace. The bedrooms and bathrooms have been finished to a high standard, and there are plenty of guest extras. Seasonal, local produce can be enjoyed both at breakfast and dinner in the delightful AA Rosetted restaurant.

Rooms 7 (1 fmly)

GODALMING	Map 6 SU94
Surrey	

Premier Inn Godalming

BUDGET HOTEL

tel: 0871 527 8466 **Guildford Rd GU7 3BX**
web: www.premierinn.com
dir: Exit A3 onto A3000 signed Godalming. 1m to rdbt, turn right into Guildford Rd towards Godalming. Hotel on left in 500yds

High quality, budget accommodation ideal for both families and business travellers. Spacious, en suite bedrooms feature tea and coffee making facilities, and Freeview TV in most hotels. Internet access and WiFi are available for a small fee. The adjacent family restaurant features a wide and varied menu. See also the Hotel Groups pages.

Rooms 17

GOLANT	Map 2 SX15
Cornwall	

Cormorant Hotel & Restaurant

★★★ 81% 🏵🏵 HOTEL

tel: 01726 833426 **PL23 1LL**
email: relax@cormoranthotel.co.uk **web:** www.cormoranthotel.co.uk
dir: A390 onto B3269 signed Fowey. In 3m left to Golant, through village to end of road, hotel on right

This hotel focuses on traditional hospitality, attentive service and good food. All the bedrooms enjoy views of the river, and guests can expect goose and down duvets, flat-screen digital TVs and free WiFi access. Breakfast and lunch may be taken on the terrace which overlooks the river.

Rooms 14 (4 GF) ☛ **S** £80-£245; **D** £90-£245 (incl. bkfst) **Facilities** FTV WiFi ⇘ ☒ Xmas New Year **Parking** 20 **Notes** LB ☒ No children 16yrs

GOMERSAL	Map 19 SE22
West Yorkshire	

Gomersal Park Hotel

★★★ 79% HOTEL

tel: 01274 869386 **Moor Ln BD19 4LJ**
email: enquiries@gomersalparkhotel.com **web:** www.gomersalparkhotel.com
dir: A62 to Huddersfield. At junct with A65, by Greyhound Pub right, after 1m take 1st right after Oakwell Hall

Constructed around a 19th-century house, this stylish, modern hotel enjoys a peaceful location and pleasant grounds. Deep sofas ensure comfort in the open-plan lounge and the Massimo Italian Restaurant offers a wide choice of freshly prepared meals. The well-equipped bedrooms are contemporary and comfortable. Extensive public areas include a well-equipped leisure complex and pool, and a wide variety of air-conditioned conference rooms.

Rooms 100 (3 fmly) (32 GF) **Facilities** FTV WiFi ⇘ ☒ supervised Gym Sauna, Solarium **Conf** Class 130 Board 60 Thtr 250 **Services** Lift **Parking** 150 **Notes** Civ Wed 200

GOODRINGTON

See Paignton

GOODWOOD
West Sussex   Map 6 SU81

The Goodwood Hotel

★★★★ 81% HOTEL

tel: 01243 775537 **PO18 0QB**
email: reservations@goodwood.com **web:** www.goodwood.com
dir: Off A285, 3m NE of Chichester

Set at the centre of the 12,000-acre Goodwood Estate, this attractive hotel boasts extensive indoor and outdoor leisure facilities, along with a range of meeting rooms plus conference and banqueting facilities. Bedrooms are furnished to a consistently high standard, including a luxury suite located in the old coaching inn, and Executive rooms, each with a patio. Eating options include the Richmond Arms which sources produce extensively from the estate farm; The Richmond Arms Bar, and the Goodwood Bar and Grill. Overnight guests can also choose to dine in The Kennels, a private members' clubhouse.

Rooms 91 (15 fmly) (31 GF) S £145-£330; **D** £145-£330 (incl. bkfst)*
Facilities Spa STV FTV WiFi ⚽ ⚽ ♨ 18 ⚑ Putt green Gym Golf driving range Sauna Steam room Fitness studio Xmas New Year **Conf** Class 60 Board 50 Thtr 150 Del from £160* **Parking** 150 **Notes** Civ Wed 120

GOOLE
East Riding of Yorkshire   Map 17 SE72

The Lowther Hotel

★★★ 82% HOTEL

tel: 01405 767999 **Aire St DN14 5QW**
web: www.lowtherhotel.co.uk
dir: M62 junct 36, A614, follow town centre signs. At clock tower rdbt right into Aire St. Hotel at end on left

A beautifully restored, Georgian Grade II* listed building that combines historic features with contemporary design, set in a unique location, overlooking the port. Bedrooms are stylish, well equipped and have free WiFi. Public areas include Bar

Absolut and The Burlington Restaurant. The impressive Mural Rooms are perfect for weddings, conferences and meetings. Private parking is also available.

Rooms 14 (1 fmly) **Facilities** FTV WiFi ♬ Xmas New Year **Conf** Class 36 Board 36 Thtr 100 **Parking** 30 **Notes** ⊗ Civ Wed 60

Premier Inn Goole

BUDGET HOTEL

tel: 0871 527 8468 **Rawcliffe Rd, Airmyn DN14 8JS**
web: www.premierinn.com
dir: M62 junct 36, A614 signed Rawcliffe. Hotel immediately on left

High quality, budget accommodation ideal for both families and business travellers. Spacious, en suite bedrooms feature tea and coffee making facilities, and Freeview TV in most hotels. Internet access and WiFi are available for a small fee. The adjacent family restaurant features a wide and varied menu. See also the Hotel Groups pages.

Rooms 41

GORDANO SERVICE AREA (M5)
Somerset   Map 4 ST57

Days Inn Bristol West - M5

BUDGET HOTEL

tel: 01275 373709 & 373624 **BS20 7XG**
email: gordano.hotel@welcomebreak.co.uk **web:** www.welcomebreak.co.uk
dir: M5 junct 19, follow signs for Gordano Services

This modern building offers accommodation in smart, spacious and well-equipped bedrooms, suitable for families and business travellers, and all with en suite bathrooms. Continental breakfast is available and other refreshments may be taken at the nearby family restaurant. See also the Hotel Groups pages.

Rooms 60 (52 fmly) (29 GF) (8 smoking) S £46-£76; **D** £56-£85 **Conf** Board 10 Del £100*

G

GORLESTON ON SEA
Norfolk   Map 13 TG50

The Pier Hotel

★★★ 85% HOTEL

tel: 01493 662631 **Harbourmouth, South Pier NR31 6PL**
email: bookings@pierhotelgorleston.co.uk **web:** www.pierhotelgorleston.co.uk
dir: From A47 W of Great Yarmouth take A12 signed Lowestoft. At 3rd rdbt 1st left (Beccles Rd) signed Gorleston. At rdbt 2nd left (Church Rd). Next rdbt 1st left (Baker St). Right into Pier Plain, then Pier Walk to Pier Gdns

Ideally situated on the seafront this hotel offers smartly appointed bedrooms that are thoughtfully equipped and have a good range of useful extras; some rooms have superb sea views. The public areas include a large restaurant and a conservatory, which leads to a terrace and bar.

Rooms 21 (1 fmly) ❦ **S** £65-£78; **D** £80-£150 (incl. bkfst)* **Facilities** STV FTV WiFi ⌕ ♫ New Year **Parking** 14 **Notes** ⊗

GOSFORTH
Cumbria   Map 18 NY00

Westlakes Hotel

★★★ 81% HOTEL

tel: 019467 25221 **CA20 1HP**
email: info@westlakeshotel.co.uk **web:** www.westlakeshotel.co.uk
dir: From A595 take B5344 signed Seascale. Hotel entrance 1st right

Located amid the stunning scenery of the western lakes and within easy striking distance of a whole array of visitor attractions, Westlakes Hotel offers accommodation of a high standard, with many thoughtful extras provided. High quality food is served in the restaurant with relaxed and friendly service led by the hands-on owners and their team. There are excellent walking opportunities from this hotel.

Rooms 10 (4 annexe) (1 GF) ❦ **S** £65-£92; **D** £80-£115.50* **Facilities** FTV WiFi **Conf** Class 30 Board 30 Thtr 50 Del £134* **Parking** 50 **Notes** ⊗

GOSPORT
Hampshire   Map 5 SZ69

Premier Inn Gosport

BUDGET HOTEL

tel: 0871 527 9436 **Fareham Rd PO13 0ZX**
web: www.premierinn.com
dir: M27 junct 11 (Wbound exit), at Wallington rdbt 1st exit onto A27 (Fareham Central Gosport & A32). At Quay St rdbt left onto A32. At rdbt 2nd exit onto A32. Left at one-way system signed Gosport. Right at lights into Forrest Way, left into Holbrook, & Gosport Leisure Centre

High quality, budget accommodation ideal for both families and business travellers. Spacious, en suite bedrooms feature tea and coffee making facilities, and Freeview TV in most hotels. Internet access and WiFi are available for a small fee. The adjacent family restaurant features a wide and varied menu. See also the Hotel Groups pages.

Rooms 63

GRANGE-OVER-SANDS
Cumbria   Map 18 SD47

Netherwood Hotel

★★★ 78% HOTEL

tel: 015395 32552 **Lindale Rd LA11 6ET**
email: enquiries@netherwood-hotel.co.uk **web:** www.netherwood-hotel.co.uk
dir: On B5277 before station

This imposing hotel stands in terraced grounds, enjoys fine views of Morecambe Bay, and is also popular as a conference and wedding venue. Good levels of hospitality and service ensure all guests are well looked after. Bedrooms vary in size but all are well furnished and have smart modern bathrooms. Magnificent woodwork is a feature of the public areas.

Rooms 34 (5 fmly) ❦ **Facilities** Spa FTV WiFi ⌕ supervised ⬇ Gym Beauty salon Steam room Fitness centre New Year **Conf** Class 150 Board 60 Thtr 150 **Services** Lift **Parking** 100 **Notes** Civ Wed 200

Cumbria Grand Hotel

★★★ 70% HOTEL

tel: 015395 32331 **LA11 6EN**
email: salescumbria@strathmorehotels.com **web:** www.strathmorehotels.com
dir: M6 junct 36, A590 & follow Grange-over-Sands signs

Set within extensive grounds, this large hotel offers fine views over Morecambe Bay and caters well for a mixed market. Public areas are pure nostalgia, and include a grand dining room and fine ballroom. Bedrooms are comfortably equipped and some have views of the bay.

Rooms 122 (10 fmly) (25 GF) ❦ **Facilities** STV WiFi ⬈ Putt green Snooker & pool table Table tennis ♫ Xmas New Year **Conf** Class 80 Board 36 Thtr 160 Del from £75 to £95 **Services** Lift **Parking** 75

See advert on page 501

GRANGE-OVER-SANDS *continued*

G

INSPECTORS' CHOICE

Clare House

★★ ⚜ HOTEL

tel: 015395 33026 & 34253 **Park Rd LA11 7HQ**
email: info@clarehousehotel.co.uk **web:** www.clarehousehotel.co.uk
dir: A590 onto B5277, through Lindale into Grange, keep left, hotel 0.5m on left past Crown Hill & St Paul's Church

A warm, genuine welcome awaits guests at this delightful hotel, proudly run by the Read family for over 40 years. Situated in its own secluded gardens, it provides a relaxed haven in which to enjoy the panoramic views across Morecambe Bay. The stylish bedrooms and public areas are comfortable and attractively furnished. Skilfully prepared dinners and hearty breakfasts are served in the elegant dining room.

Rooms 18 (4 GF) 🐾 **S** £91-£95; **D** £182-£190 (incl. bkfst & dinner)* **Facilities** FTV WiFi 🏊 **Parking** 18 **Notes** LB ⊗ Closed mid Dec-late Mar

---

GRANTHAM
Lincolnshire   Map 11 SK93

Ramada Grantham

★★★★ 72% HOTEL

ⓡ RAMADA.

tel: 01476 593000 **Swingbridge Rd NG31 7XT**
email: info@ramadagrantham.co.uk **web:** www.ramadagrantham.co.uk
dir: Exit A1 at Grantham/Melton Mowbray junct onto A607. From N: 1st exit at mini rdbt, hotel on right. From S: at rdbt 2nd exit. Next left at T-junct. At mini rdbt 2nd exit. Hotel on right

A modern, purpose-built hotel ideally placed for touring the area. Bedrooms are spacious, smartly decorated and equipped with modern facilities. Public rooms include a large open-plan lounge/bar area with comfortable seating and an intimate restaurant as well as conference and banqueting facilities. The property also has smart leisure facilities.

Rooms 89 (44 GF) (2 smoking) **S** £79-£155; **D** £79-£155 (incl. bkfst)* **Facilities** FTV WiFi 🏊 ⓧ Gym Steam room Sauna Xmas New Year **Conf** Class 90 Board 60 Thtr 200 Del from £100 to £150* **Parking** 102 **Notes** ⊗ Civ Wed 200

Premier Inn Grantham

BUDGET HOTEL

Premier Inn

tel: 0871 527 8470 **A1/607 Junction, Harlaxton Rd NG31 7UA**
web: www.premierinn.com
dir: A1 onto A607. N'bound: hotel on right. S'bound: under A1, hotel on left

High quality, budget accommodation ideal for both families and business travellers. Spacious, en suite bedrooms feature tea and coffee making facilities, and Freeview TV in most hotels. Internet access and WiFi are available for a small fee. The adjacent family restaurant features a wide and varied menu. See also the Hotel Groups pages.

Rooms 59

GRASMERE
Cumbria   Map 18 NY30

Daffodil Hotel

★★★★ 83% HOTEL

tel: 015394 63550 **Keswick Rd LA22 9PR**
email: stay@daffodilhotel.com **web:** www.daffodilhotel.com
dir: M6 junct 36 then A591, past Windermere & Ambleside. Hotel on left on entering Grasmere

Daffodil Hotel provides very high levels of service, comfort and luxury in a beautiful location on the edge of Grasmere, within easy walking distance of the village. Most rooms have either a lake or a valley view, several with private balconies, and are equipped to very high standards.

Rooms 78 (11 fmly) 🐾 **S** £65-£400; **D** £79-£420 (incl. bkfst)* **Facilities** Spa FTV WiFi 🏊 HL Sauna Steam room Tepidarium Xmas New Year **Conf** Class 160 Board 42 Thtr 200 **Services** Lift Air con **Parking** 96 **Notes** Civ Wed 200

Wordsworth Hotel & Spa

★★★★ 81% HOTEL

tel: 015394 35592 **Stock Ln LA22 9SW**
email: enquiry@thewordsworthhotel.co.uk **web:** www.thewordsworthhotel.co.uk
dir: Off A591. In centre of village adjacent to St Oswald's Church

This historic hotel, ideally situated in the heart of Grasmere provides high levels of style and luxury. The bedrooms are equipped with smart furnishings, comfortable beds with Egyptian cotton linens, and quality accessories. Guests can enjoy fine dining in the modernised Signature Restaurant which boasts stylish and elegant decor, and for a less formal dining experience, light meals and fine ales are offered in the Dove Bistro. The hotel has a heated swimming pool, and the sauna and spa make the ideal place for relaxation.

Rooms 40 (2 fmly) (3 GF) ↖ **S** £109-£199; **D** £138-£300 (incl. bkfst)* **Facilities** Spa FTV WiFi ↕ 🏊 Gym Beauty treatment room Mixed sauna Nail bar Xmas New Year **Conf** Class 50 Board 40 Thtr 100 Del from £169 to £209* **Services** Lift **Parking** 60 **Notes** LB Civ Wed 100

Grasmere Hotel

★★★ 82% HOTEL

tel: 015394 35277 **Broadgate LA22 9TA**
email: info@grasmerehotel.co.uk **web:** www.grasmerehotel.co.uk
dir: Located at northern end of Grasmere Village

Grasmere Hotel is a small luxury Victorian period hotel situated on the edge of the lake, providing stylish accommodation and contemporary comfort. Breakfast and dinner are served in the conservatory restaurant overlooking secluded gardens and the river Rothay. Expect a warm welcome and personal hospitality. Private car parking available.

Rooms 11 (2 GF) ↖ **S** £61-£66; **D** £112-£142 (incl. bkfst) **Facilities** FTV WiFi ↕ Xmas New Year **Parking** 12 **Notes** LB No children 10yrs Closed 4-29 Jan

Oak Bank Hotel

★★★ 81% HOTEL

tel: 015394 35217 **Broadgate LA22 9TA**
email: info@lakedistricthotel.co.uk **web:** www.lakedistricthotel.co.uk
dir: N'bound: M6 junct 36 onto A591 to Windermere, Ambleside, then Grasmere. S'bound: M6 junct 40 onto A66 to Keswick, A591 to Grasmere

Privately owned and personally run by friendly proprietors, Oak Bank is a Victorian house in the charming village of Grasmere. Bedrooms are well-equipped and include one with a four-poster bed, as well as a suite with jacuzzi bath. In colder weather, welcoming log fires burn in the comfortable lounges. The restaurant has a conservatory extension overlooking the garden, and there is also a pleasant bar.

Rooms 14 (1 GF) ↖ **S** £88.50-£142; **D** £109-£215 (incl. bkfst & dinner) **Facilities** FTV WiFi Use of nearby leisure facilities New Year **Parking** 14 **Notes** LB Closed 2-22 Jan, 7-20 Aug, 21-26 Dec

Macdonald Swan Hotel

★★★ 80% HOTEL

tel: 0844 879 9120 **LA22 9RF**
email: sales/oldengland@macdonald-hotels.co.uk **web:** www.macdonaldhotels.co.uk
dir: M6 junct 36, A591 towards Kendal, A590 to Keswick through Ambleside. Hotel on right on entering village

Close to Dove Cottage and occupying a prominent position on the edge of the village, this 300-year-old inn is mentioned in Wordsworth's poem, *The Waggoner*. Attractive public areas are spacious and comfortable, and bedrooms are equally stylish. A modern bar and grill menu is available, while the elegant restaurant offers more formal dining.

Rooms 37 (2 fmly) (21 GF) ↖ **Facilities** FTV WiFi HL Xmas New Year **Conf** Class 20 Board 30 Thtr 40 **Parking** 45 **Notes** Civ Wed 60

Gold Rill Country House Hotel

★★★ 79% HOTEL

tel: 015394 35486 **Red Bank Rd LA22 9PU**
email: reception@goldrill.co.uk **web:** www. goldrill.co.uk
dir: A591 into village centre, turn into road opposite St Oswald's Church. Hotel 300yds on left after public carpark

This popular hotel enjoys a fine location on the edge of the village with spectacular views of the lake and surrounding fells. Attractive bedrooms - some with balconies - are tastefully decorated and many have separate, comfortable seating areas. The hotel boasts a private pier, an outdoor heated pool and a putting green. Public areas include a well-appointed restaurant and choice of lounges.

Rooms 32 (7 annexe) (2 fmly) (11 GF) ↖ **S** £61-£166; **D** £122-£206 (incl. bkfst & dinner) **Facilities** FTV WiFi ↘ Putt green New Year **Parking** 35 **Notes** ⊗ Closed mid Dec-mid Jan (ex New Year)

GRASSINGTON	Map 19 SE06
North Yorkshire	

Grassington House

 RESTAURANT WITH ROOMS

tel: 01756 752406 ▤ 01756 752050 **5 The Square BD23 5AQ**
email: bookings@grassingtonhousehotel.co.uk **web:** www.grassingtonhousehotel.co.uk
dir: A59 into Grassington, in town square opposite post office

Located in the square of the popular village of Grassington, this beautifully converted Georgian house is personally run by owners John and Sue. Delicious food, individually designed bedrooms and warm hospitality ensure an enjoyable stay. There is a stylish lounge bar looking out to the square and the restaurant is split between two rooms; here guests will find the emphasis is on fresh, local ingredients and attentive, yet friendly service.

Rooms 9 (2 fmly)

G

GRAVESEND　　　　　　　　　　　　　　Map 6 TQ67
Kent

Premier Inn Gravesend (A2/Singlewell)

BUDGET HOTEL

tel: 0871 527 8472 **Hevercourt Rd, Singlewell DA12 5UQ**
web: www.premierinn.com
dir: At Gravesend East exit on A2

High quality, budget accommodation ideal for both families and business travellers. Spacious, en suite bedrooms feature tea and coffee making facilities, and Freeview TV in most hotels. Internet access and WiFi are available for a small fee. The adjacent family restaurant features a wide and varied menu. See also the Hotel Groups pages.

Rooms 31

Premier Inn Gravesend Central

BUDGET HOTEL

tel: 0871 527 8474 **Wrotham Rd DA11 7LF**
web: www.premierinn.com
dir: A2 onto A227 towards town centre, 1m to hotel

Rooms 36

GREAT BIRCHAM　　　　　　　　　　　　Map 13 TF73
Norfolk

The Kings Head Hotel

★★★ 86% ❀ HOTEL

tel: 01485 578265 & 572846 **PE31 6RJ**
email: info@thekingsheadhotel.co.uk **web:** www.the-kings-head-bircham.co.uk
dir: A148 to Hillington through village, 1st left Bircham

A delightful family-run hotel situated in the heart of this north Norfolk village close to Royal Sandringham. The property is very contemporary, yet still retains much of its original character. The spacious bedrooms are tastefully appointed and equipped with modern facilities. Public rooms inlude a lounge, bar, restaurant and further dining room.

Rooms 12 🕯 **D** £90–£160 (incl. bkfst)* **Facilities** FTV WiFi ⬧ Xmas New Year **Conf** Class 30 Board 20 Thtr 40 **Parking** 30 **Notes** LB Civ Wed 80

GREAT CHESTERFORD　　　　　　　　　Map 12 TL54
Essex

The Crown House

★★★ 76% HOTEL

tel: 01799 530515 & 530257 **CB10 1NY**
email: reservations@crownhousehotel.com **web:** www.crownhousehotel.com
dir: From N: M11 at junct 9 (from S junct 10) follow signs for Saffron Walden, then Great Chesterford B1383

This Georgian coaching inn, situated in a peaceful village close to the M11, has been sympathetically restored and retains much original character. The bedrooms are well equipped and individually decorated; some rooms have delightful four-poster beds. Public rooms include an attractive lounge bar, an elegant oak-panelled restaurant and an airy conservatory.

Rooms 18 (10 annexe) (1 fmly) (5 GF) **Facilities** FTV WiFi ⬧ New Year **Conf** Class 14 Board 12 Thtr 30 **Parking** 30 **Notes** Closed 27-30 Dec Civ Wed 60

G

G

INSPECTORS' CHOICE

Belmond Le Manoir aux Quat' Saisons

★★★★★ @@@@@ HOTEL

tel: 01844 278881 **Church Rd OX44 7PD**
email: lemanoir@blanc.co.uk **web:** www.manoir.com
dir: From A329 2nd right to Great Milton Manor, hotel 200yds on right

Even though Le Manoir is now very much part of the British scene, its iconic chef patron, Raymond Blanc, still fizzes with new ideas and projects. His first loves are his kitchen and his garden and the vital link between them. The fascinating grounds feature a Japanese tea garden and two acres of vegetables and herbs that supply the kitchen with an almost never-ending supply of top-notch produce. Even the car park has a stunning artichoke sculpture. The kitchen is the epicentre, with outstanding cooking highlighting freshness and seasonality. Bedrooms in this idyllic 'grand house on a small scale' are either in the main house or around an outside courtyard; all offer the highest levels of comfort and quality, have magnificent marble bathrooms and are equipped with a host of thoughtful extra touches. For something really special there is the 15th-century dovecot with a stunning upper-floor bedroom and a bathroom below. La Belle Epoque is the private dining room, ideal for weddings, celebrations and corporate events.

Rooms 32 (23 annexe) (13 GF) **Facilities** STV FTV WiFi ♨ Cookery school Water gardens Bikes Spa treatment Xmas New Year **Conf** Board 20 Thtr 24 **Parking** 60 **Notes** ⊗ Civ Wed 50

The Bull at Great Totham

@@ RESTAURANT WITH ROOMS

tel: 01621 893385 & 894020 📠 01621 894029 **2 Maldon Rd CM9 8NH**
email: reservations@thebullatgreattotham.co.uk **web:** www.thebullatgreattotham.co.uk
dir: Exit A12 at Witham junct to Great Totham

A 16th-century coaching inn located in the village of Great Totham, The Bull is now a very stylish restaurant with rooms that offers en suite bedrooms with satellite TVs with Freeview; WiFi is available throughout. Guests can enjoy dinner in the gastro-pub or in the award-winning, fine dining restaurant, The Willow Room.

Rooms 4

Imperial Hotel

THE INDEPENDENTS
HOTEL ASSOCIATION

★★★★ 75% @ HOTEL

tel: 01493 842000 **North Dr NR30 1EQ**
email: reservations@imperialhotel.co.uk **web:** www.imperialhotel.co.uk
dir: Follow signs to seafront, turn left. Hotel opposite Waterways

This friendly, family-run hotel is situated at the quieter end of the seafront within easy walking distance of the town centre. Bedrooms are attractively decorated with co-ordinated soft furnishings and many thoughtful touches; most rooms have superb sea views. Public areas include the smart Bar Fizz and the Café Cru restaurant.

Rooms 39 (4 fmly) ⟲ **S** £90–£140; **D** £100–£160 (incl. bkfst) **Facilities** FTV WiFi ❧ New Year **Conf** Class 40 Board 30 Thtr 140 **Services** Lift **Parking** 40 **Notes** LB Civ Wed 140

Furzedown Hotel

★★★ 79% HOTEL

tel: 01493 844138 **19-20 North Dr NR30 4EW**
email: paul@furzedownhotel.co.uk **web:** www.furzedownhotel.co.uk
dir: At end of A47 or A12, towards seafront, left, hotel opposite Waterways

Expect a warm welcome at this family-run hotel situated at the northern end of the seafront overlooking the town's Venetian Waterways. Bedrooms are pleasantly decorated and thoughtfully equipped; many rooms have superb sea views. The stylish public areas include a comfortable lounge bar, a smartly appointed restaurant and a cosy TV room.

Rooms 20 (11 fmly) **Facilities** FTV WiFi New Year **Conf** Class 80 Board 40 Thtr 75 **Parking** 30

GREAT YARMOUTH *continued*

G

The Cliff Hotel

★★★ 78% HOTEL

tel: 01493 662179 **Cliff Hill, Gorleston NR31 6DH**
email: reception@thecliffhotel.co.uk **web:** www.thecliffhotel.co.uk
dir: A47 Acle new road rdbt 3rd exit, continue A12 3rd rdbt, 1st exit onto Victoria Rd, 3rd right onto Avondale Rd, follow round

Having undergone a major refurbishment in 2013, the Cliff Hotel offers an extensive choice of stylish, very well appointed bedrooms. Overlooking the harbour and Gorleston Beach, the hotel enjoys a prominent position in the town. Ample secure parking is available and the modern terrace along with the contemporary lounge is very popular with guests.

Rooms 37 (4 fmly) ♦ **S** £88-£99; **D** £99-£115 (incl. bkfst)* **Facilities** FTV WiFi Children's play area Xmas New Year **Conf** Class 60 Board 45 Thtr 160 Del from £103 to £423* **Parking** 30 **Notes** ⊗ Civ Wed 80

Andover House

★★★ 77% ⊛⊛ SMALL HOTEL

tel: 01493 843490 **28-30 Camperdown NR30 3JB**
email: bookings@andoverhouse.co.uk **web:** www.andoverhouse.co.uk
dir: Opposite Wellington Pier turn into Shadingfield Close, right into Kimberley Terrace, follow into Camperdown. Property on left

This charming Victorian building enjoys a peaceful location on a tree-lined avenue close to the town centre and the beach, making it an ideal base from which to explore the Norfolk Broads. Andover House offers a range of individually styled comfortable bedrooms along with a modern bar and well-appointed lounge areas. The award-winning brasserie-style restaurant offers an extensive choice of imaginative dishes and there is a smart sun terrace available for guests.

Rooms 20 **S** £59-£79; **D** £59-£99 (incl. bkfst)* **Facilities** STV WiFi ⇘ **Conf** Class 20 Board 20 Thtr 36 **Notes** ⊗ No children 13yrs

Burlington Palm Hotel

★★★ 75% HOTEL

tel: 01493 844568 **11 North Dr NR30 1EG**
email: enquiries@burlington-hotel.co.uk **web:** www.burlington-hotel.co.uk
dir: A12 to seafront, left at Marine Lodge. Hotel near tennis courts

This privately owned hotel is situated at the quiet end of the resort, overlooking the sea. Bedrooms come in a variety of sizes and styles; they are pleasantly decorated and well equipped, and many have lovely sea views. The spacious public rooms

include a range of seating areas, a choice of dining rooms, two bars and a heated indoor swimming pool.

Rooms 69 (9 fmly) (1 GF) ♦ **S** £60-£110; **D** £80-£160 (incl. bkfst) **Facilities** FTV WiFi ⛄ Xmas **Conf** Class 60 Board 30 Thtr 120 Del from £70 to £120 **Services** Lift **Parking** 70 **Notes** LB ⊗ Closed 28 Dec-2 Jan

See advert on opposite page

Comfort Hotel Great Yarmouth

★★★ 75% HOTEL

tel: 01493 855070 & 850044 **Albert Square NR30 3JH**
email: sales@comfortgreatyarmouth.co.uk **web:** www.comfortgreatyarmouth.co.uk
dir: From seafront left at Wellington Pier into Kimberley Terr. Left into Albert Sq, hotel on left

A large hotel situated in the quieter end of town, just off the seafront and within easy walking distance of the town centre. The pleasantly decorated, well-equipped bedrooms are generally quite spacious and include WiFi. Public rooms include a comfortable lounge, a bar and smart brasserie-style restaurant.

Rooms 50 (12 fmly) (3 GF) **S** £39-£79; **D** £49-£119 (incl. bkfst) **Facilities** FTV WiFi ⇘ Xmas **Conf** Class 50 Board 30 Thtr 120 Del from £75 to £82.50* **Parking** 15 **Notes** LB ⊗ Civ Wed 120

The Prom Hotel

★★★ 75% HOTEL

tel: 01493 842308 **77 Marine Pde NR30 2DH**
email: info@promhotel.co.uk **web:** www.promhotel.co.uk

The Prom Hotel is ideally situated on the seafront close to the bright lights and attractions of Marine Parade. The open-plan public areas include a smart lounge bar with views of the sea, and a relaxed restaurant; guests also have the use of a further quieter lounge bar with plush seating. The modern contemporary bedrooms are smartly appointed and have many thoughtful touches; many rooms have lovely sea views.

Rooms 33 (1 fmly) ♦ **S** £75-£90; **D** £90-£115 (incl. bkfst)* **Facilities** STV FTV WiFi ⇘ Xmas **Parking** 30

Knights Court Hotel

★★★ 72% HOTEL

tel: 01493 843089 & 07748 501009 **22 North Dr NR30 4EW**
email: enquiries@knights-court.co.uk
dir: From A12 & A47 rdbt, A149 to seafront

Knights Court is a small privately-owned hotel situated on the seafront overlooking the beach. The smartly appointed bedrooms are comfortable and well equipped;

many of the rooms have lovely sea views. Breakfast and dinner are served in the stylish dining room and there is a cosy lounge bar with views of the beach.

Rooms 20 (5 fmly) ✿ **Facilities** STV FTV WiFi ♨ **Conf** Class 40 Board 20 Thtr 40 **Parking** 22 **Notes** ⊗

The Waverley Hotel

★★★ 68% HOTEL

tel: 01493 853388 **32-34 Princes Rd NR30 2DG**
email: thewaverleyhotel.gy@gmail.com **web:** www.thewaverleyhotelgy.com
dir: Follow A47 from London to Great Yarmouth or A143 from Haverhill. Hotel opposite Britannia Pier at Princes Rd

The Waverley is situated in a side road adjacent to the seafront and close to the local amenities. The property has been totally refurbished by the current owner to a very good standard. Public rooms include a large lounge bar, foyer and spacious restaurant. Bedrooms are contemporary in style and have a good range of extra facilities.

Rooms 47 (2 fmly) ✿ **S** £35-£50; **D** £60-£75 (incl. bkfst)* **Facilities** FTV WiFi Library ♫ Xmas New Year **Conf** Class 60 Board 60 Thtr 60 Del from £75 to £120* **Services** Lift **Notes** LB ⊗

The Nelson Hotel

★★★ 66% HOTEL

tel: 01493 855551 **1 Marine Pde NR30 3AG**
email: johnrushworth@theukholidaygroup.com **web:** www.grandukhotels.co.uk
dir: On right of Marine Parade, opposite Sealife Centre

The Nelson Hotel is ideally situated overlooking the sea, close to the pier and just a short stroll from the town centre and local amenities. It is ideal for both business and leisure guests, and all of the bedrooms are well equipped, while some rooms have lovely sea views. Public areas include a lounge with plush sofas, a bar and a separate dining room.

Rooms 50 (10 fmly) ✿ **S** £20-£70; **D** £40-£120 (incl. bkfst)* **Facilities** FTV WiFi ♫ Xmas New Year **Conf** Class 60 Board 60 Thtr 100 **Services** Lift **Notes** ⊗ Closed 2 Jan-end Feb

New Beach Hotel

★★ 71% HOTEL

tel: 01493 332300 **67 Marine Pde NR30 2EJ**
email: newbeach.gtyarmouth@alfatravel.co.uk **web:** www.leisureplex.co.uk
dir: Follow signs to seafront. Hotel facing Britannia Pier

This Victorian building is centrally located on the seafront, overlooking Britannia Pier and the sandy beach. Bedrooms are pleasantly decorated and equipped with modern facilities; many have lovely sea views. Dinner is taken in the restaurant which doubles as the ballroom, and guests can also relax in the bar or sunny lounge.

Rooms 77 (4 fmly) **S** £36-£47; **D** £56-£78 (incl. bkfst)* **Facilities** FTV WiFi ♫ Xmas New Year **Services** Lift **Notes** ⊗ Closed Dec-Feb (ex Xmas) RS Nov & Mar

GREAT YELDHAM	**Map 13 TL73**
Essex	

The White Hart

 RESTAURANT WITH ROOMS

tel: 01787 237250 📠 01787 238044 **Poole St CO9 4HJ**
email: mjwmason@yahoo.co.uk **web:** www.whitehartyeldham.com
dir: On A1017 in village

The White Hart is a large timber-framed character building that includes the main restaurant and bar areas while the bedrooms are located in the converted coach house; all are smartly appointed and well equipped with many thoughtful extras. The comfortable lounge and bar and the beautifully landscaped gardens provide areas for relaxation. Locally sourced produce is used on menus in the main house restaurant which is popular with local residents and guests alike.

Rooms 11 (2 fmly)

G

GREENFORD
Greater London

Premier Inn London Greenford

BUDGET HOTEL PLAN 1 C4

tel: 0871 527 8658 **Western Av UB6 8TE**
web: www.premierinn.com
dir: From A40 (Western Avenue) E'bound, exit at Perivale. Right, left at 2nd lights. Hotel opposite Hoover Building

High quality, budget accommodation ideal for both families and business travellers. Spacious, en suite bedrooms feature tea and coffee making facilities, and Freeview TV in most hotels. Internet access and WiFi are available for a small fee. The adjacent family restaurant features a wide and varied menu. See also the Hotel Groups pages.

Rooms 39

GREETHAM
Rutland   Map 11 SK91

Greetham Valley

★★★ 75% HOTEL

tel: 01780 460444 **Wood Ln LE15 7SN**
email: info@greethamvalley.co.uk **web:** www.greethamvalley.co.uk
dir: A1/B668. Left towards Greetham, Cottesmore & Oakham. Left at x-rds after 0.5m, follow brown signs to golf club entrance

Spacious bedrooms with storage facilities designed for golfers, offer high levels of comfort and many have superb views over the two golf courses. Meals are taken in the clubhouse restaurants with a choice of informal or more formal styles. A beauty suite and extensive conference facilities are ideal for both large and small groups.

Rooms 35 (17 GF) ✆ **S** £55-£115; **D** £55-£115 (incl. bkfst)* **Facilities** FTV WiFi ♨ 45 Putt green Fishing Gym 4x4 off-road course Archery centre Bowls green Driving range Petanque New Year **Conf** Class 150 Board 80 Thtr 280 Del from £105 to £117 **Services** Lift **Parking** 300 **Notes** LB ⊗ Civ Wed 200

GRIMSBY
Lincolnshire   Map 17 TA21

Millfields Hotel

THE INDEPENDENTS
HOTEL ASSOCIATION

★★★ ⬛ HOTEL

tel: 01472 356068 **53 Bargate DN34 5AD**
email: info@millfieldshotel.co.uk **web:** www.millfieldshotel.co.uk
dir: A180, right at KFC rdbt then left at next rdbt. Right at 2nd lights & right onto Bargate, hotel 0.5m on left after Wheatsheaf pub

Dating from 1879 this hotel is surrounded by its own grounds and caters for both leisure and business guests. The bedrooms are individually designed and there is a four-poster room. The contemporary Orangery Restaurant offers both carte and traditional bar menus. The hotel has extensive leisure facilities.

Rooms 27 (4 annexe) (7 fmly) (13 GF) ✆ **Facilities** FTV WiFi Gym Squash Sauna Steam room Hairdresser Beauty salon Aromatherapist **Conf** Class 25 Board 25 Thtr 50 **Parking** 75 **Notes** ⊗ Civ Wed 50

Premier Inn Grimsby

BUDGET HOTEL

tel: 0871 527 8478 **Europa Park, Appian Way, off Gilbey Rd DN31 2UT**
web: www.premierinn.com
dir: M180 junct 5, A180 towards town centre. At 1st rdbt take 2nd exit. 1st left, left at mini rdbt into Appian Way

High quality, budget accommodation ideal for both families and business travellers. Spacious, en suite bedrooms feature tea and coffee making facilities, and Freeview TV in most hotels. Internet access and WiFi are available for a small fee. The adjacent family restaurant features a wide and varied menu. See also the Hotel Groups pages.

Rooms 40

GRIMSTON
Norfolk   Map 12 TF72

INSPECTORS' CHOICE

Congham Hall Country House Hotel

★★★ ⓜⓜ COUNTRY HOUSE HOTEL

tel: 01485 600250 **Lynn Rd PE32 1AH**
email: info@conghamhallhotel.co.uk **web:** www.conghamhallhotel.co.uk
dir: At A149/A148 junct, NE of King's Lynn, take A148 towards Fakenham for 100yds. Right to Grimston, hotel 2.5m on left

An elegant 18th-century Georgian manor set amid 30 acres of mature landscaped grounds and surrounded by parkland. The inviting public rooms provide a range of tastefully furnished areas in which to sit and relax. Imaginative cuisine is served in the Orangery Restaurant which has an intimate atmosphere and panoramic views of the gardens. The bedrooms, tastefully furnished with period pieces, have modern facilities and many thoughtful touches.

Rooms 26 (6 annexe) (12 GF) ✿ **Facilities** WiFi 🌀 🏌 Putt green ⛳ Xmas New Year **Conf** Class 12 Board 28 Thtr 50 **Parking** 50 **Notes** Civ Wed 100

GRINDLEFORD
Derbyshire   Map 16 SK27

The Maynard

★★★ 81% 🏵🏵 HOTEL

tel: 01433 630321 **Main Rd S32 2HE**
email: info@themaynard.co.uk **web:** www.themaynard.co.uk
dir: A625 from Sheffield to Castleton. Left into Grindleford on B6521. Hotel on left after Fox House Hotel

This building, dating back over 100 years, is situated in a beautiful and tranquil location yet within easy reach of Sheffield and the M1. The bedrooms are contemporary in style and offer a wealth of accessories. The Peak District views from the restaurant and garden are stunning.

Rooms 10 (1 fmly) ✿ **S** £80-£135; **D** £85-£140 (incl. bkfst)* **Facilities** FTV WiFi **Conf** Class 60 Board 40 Thtr 120 Del from £125 to £145* **Parking** 60 **Notes** Civ Wed 120

Find out more about the AA's Hotel rating scheme on page 18

GUILDFORD
Surrey   Map 6 SU94

The Mandolay Hotel

★★★★ 77% HOTEL

tel: 01483 303030 **36-40 London Rd GU1 2AE**
email: info@guildford.com **web:** www.guildford.com
dir: M25 junct 10, follow A3 (S) for 7m. Take 3rd exit at 1st rdbt onto London Rd for 1m

Situated close to the heart of the town centre of Guildford, The Mandolay Hotel offers 72 comfortable bedrooms. Extensive meeting facilities provide for business visitors with off-street parking available. Free unrestricted WiFi is available throughout the hotel and there are over 900 international TV channels free of charge. A range of dining options, from coffee shop and bar menu to full restaurant service, are on offer.

Rooms 72 (4 fmly) (13 GF) ✿ **S** £79-£129; **D** £89-£139 **Facilities** STV FTV WiFi ⌕ Xmas New Year **Conf** Class 200 Board 100 Thtr 700 Del from £120 to £160 **Services** Lift **Parking** 41 **Notes** LB ⊗ Civ Wed 120

G

GUILDFORD *continued*

Holiday Inn Guildford

★★★★ 74% HOTEL

tel: 0871 942 9036 **Egerton Rd GU2 7XZ**
email: reservations-guildford@ihg.com **web:** www.higuildfordhotel.co.uk
dir: A3 to Guildford. Exit at sign for Research Park/Onslow Village. 3rd exit at 1st rdbt, 2nd exit at 2nd rdbt

This hotel is in a convenient location just off the A3 and within a 25 minute-drive of the M25. Public areas are stylish, and on-site facilities include a swimming pool and gym. The accommodation is spacious and comfortable and caters well for both the business and leisure markets. A number of well-equipped meeting rooms is available. There is ample free parking.

Rooms 168 (89 fmly) (66 GF) **Facilities** Spa STV FTV WiFi HL Gym Fitness studio Beauty treatments **Conf** Class 100 Board 60 Thtr 180 **Services** Air con **Parking** 230 **Notes** Civ Wed 180

Premier Inn Guildford Central

BUDGET HOTEL

tel: 0871 527 8482 **Parkway GU1 1UP**
web: www.premierinn.com
dir: M25 junct 10, follow Portsmouth (A3) signs. Exit for Guildford Centre/Leisure Complex (A322/A320/A25). Turn left, hotel on left

High quality, budget accommodation ideal for both families and business travellers. Spacious, en suite bedrooms feature tea and coffee making facilities, and Freeview TV in most hotels. Internet access and WiFi are available for a small fee. The adjacent family restaurant features a wide and varied menu. See also the Hotel Groups pages.

Rooms 87

GUISBOROUGH
North Yorkshire
Map 19 NZ61

Gisborough Hall

★★★★ 80% HOTEL

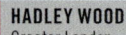

tel: 0844 879 9149 & 01287 611500 **Whitby Ln TS14 6PT**
email: general.gisboroughhall@macdonald-hotels.co.uk
web: www.macdonald-hotels.co.uk/Gisborough
dir: A171, follow signs for Whitby to Waterfall rdbt, 3rd exit into Whitby Ln, hotel 500yds on right

Dating back to the mid-19th century, this elegant country house provides a pleasing combination of original features and modern facilities. Bedrooms, including four-poster and family rooms, are richly furnished. The elegant Drawing Room is welcoming and has an open fire, whilst the opulent G Bar & Bistro provides a contemporary alternative. Excellent food is served in Chaloner's Restaurant.

Rooms 71 (2 fmly) (12 GF) **S** £89-£169; **D** £99-£189 (incl. bkfst)* **Facilities** Spa STV FTV WiFi HL Sauna Xmas New Year **Conf** Class 150 Board 32 Thtr 400 Del from £135 to £165* **Services** Lift **Parking** 180 **Notes** LB Civ Wed 250

Premier Inn Middlesborough South (Guisborough)

BUDGET HOTEL

tel: 0871 527 8772 **Middlesbrough Rd, Upsall TS14 6RW**
web: www.premierinn.com
dir: Off A171 towards Whitby

High quality, budget accommodation ideal for both families and business travellers. Spacious, en suite bedrooms feature tea and coffee making facilities, and Freeview TV in most hotels. Internet access and WiFi are available for a small fee. The adjacent family restaurant features a wide and varied menu. See also the Hotel Groups pages.

Rooms 20

HADLEY WOOD
Greater London
Map 6 TQ29

West Lodge Park Hotel

★★★★ 80% HOTEL

tel: 020 8216 3900 & 8216 3903 **Cockfosters Rd EN4 0PY**
email: westlodgepark@bealeshotels.co.uk **web:** www.bealeshotels.co.uk
dir: On A111, 1m S of M25 junct 24

A stylish country house set in stunning parkland and gardens, yet only 12 miles from central London and a few miles from the M25. Bedrooms are individually decorated in traditional style and offer excellent facilities. Annexe rooms feature air-conditioning and have access to an outdoor patio area. Public rooms include the award-winning Cedar Restaurant, cosy bar area and separate lounge.

Rooms 59 (13 annexe) (1 fmly) (11 GF) **Facilities** STV FTV WiFi Putt green Free use of nearby leisure club New Year **Conf** Class 30 Board 30 Thtr 64 **Services** Lift **Parking** 200 **Notes** Civ Wed 72

HADLOW
Kent
Map 6 TQ65

Hadlow Manor Hotel

★★★ 75% HOTEL

tel: 01732 851442 **Goose Green TN11 0JH**
email: hotel@hadlowmanor.co.uk **web:** www.hadlowmanor.co.uk
dir: On A26 (Maidstone to Tonbridge road). 1m E of Hadlow

This is a friendly, independently owned country-house hotel, ideally situated between Maidstone and Tonbridge. Traditionally styled bedrooms are spacious and attractively furnished with many amenities. Public areas include a sunny restaurant, bar and lounge. The gardens are delightful and there's a seated area ideal for relaxation in warmer weather. Meeting and banqueting facilities are available.

Rooms 29 (2 fmly) (8 GF) **S** fr £64; **Facilities** STV FTV WiFi Xmas New Year **Conf** Class 90 Board 103 Thtr 200 Del from £125* **Parking** 120 **Notes** LB Civ Wed 200

H

HADNALL
Shropshire Map 15 SJ52

Saracens at Hadnall

 RESTAURANT WITH ROOMS

tel: 01939 210877 01939 210877 **Shrewsbury Rd SY4 4AG**
email: reception@saracensathadnall.co.uk **web:** www.saracensathadnall.co.uk
dir: M54 onto A5 towards Shrewsbury, take A49 towards Whitchurch. In Hadnall, property diagonally opposite church

This Georgian Grade II listed former farmhouse and village pub has been tastefully converted into a very smart restaurant with rooms, without any loss of original charm and character. The bedrooms are thoughtfully equipped. Skilfully prepared meals are served in either the elegant dining room or the adjacent conservatory, where there is a glass-topped well.

Rooms 5

HAGLEY
Worcestershire Map 10 SO98

Premier Inn Hagley

BUDGET HOTEL

tel: 0871 527 8484 **Birmingham Rd DY9 9JS**
web: www.premierinn.com
dir: M5 junct 3, A456 towards Kidderminster (dual carriageway). Hotel visible on opposite side of road. At next rdbt double back follow A456 Birmingham signs. Hotel on left

High quality, budget accommodation ideal for both families and business travellers. Spacious, en suite bedrooms feature tea and coffee making facilities, and Freeview TV in most hotels. Internet access and WiFi are available for a small fee. The adjacent family restaurant features a wide and varied menu. See also the Hotel Groups pages.

Rooms 40

HALIFAX
West Yorkshire Map 19 SE02

Holdsworth House Hotel

★★★★ 75%  HOTEL

tel: 01422 240024 **Holdsworth HX2 9TG**
email: info@holdsworthhouse.co.uk **web:** www.holdsworthhouse.co.uk
dir: From town centre take A629 towards Keighley. 1.5m right at garage, into Shay Ln. Hotel on right after 1m

This delightful 17th-century Jacobean manor house, set in well-tended gardens, offers individually decorated, thoughtfully equipped bedrooms. Public rooms, adorned with beautiful paintings and antique pieces, include a choice of inviting lounges and superb conference and function facilities. Dinner provides the highlight of any stay and is served in the elegant restaurant by friendly, attentive staff.

Rooms 40 (2 fmly) (15 GF) ↑ **S** £79-£175; **D** £115-£250* **Facilities** FTV WiFi New Year **Conf** Class 75 Board 50 Thtr 150 Del from £155 to £195* **Parking** 60 **Notes** Civ Wed 120

The White Swan Hotel

★★★ 74% HOTEL

tel: 01422 355541 **Princess St HX1 1TS**
email: info@whiteswanhalifax.com **web:** www.whiteswanhalifax.com
dir: Adjacent to Town Hall

The White Swan is a well established hotel noted for its friendly staff. Located in the heart of the town it offers comfortable, well-equipped bedrooms plus conference and function facilities. The lounge area is ideal for relaxing, and for the more energetic guest there is a small fitness room.

Rooms 40 (2 fmly) ↑ **S** £45-£79; **D** £45-£89* **Facilities** STV FTV WiFi Gym **Conf** Class 35 Board 35 Thtr 80 **Services** Lift **Parking** 9 **Notes** Closed 24-26 Dec

Premier Inn Halifax

BUDGET HOTEL

tel: 0871 527 8486 **Salterhebble Hill, Huddersfield Rd HX3 0QT**
web: www.premierinn.com
dir: Just off M62 junct 24 on A629 towards Halifax

High quality, budget accommodation ideal for both families and business travellers. Spacious, en suite bedrooms feature tea and coffee making facilities, and Freeview TV in most hotels. Internet access and WiFi are available for a small fee. The adjacent family restaurant features a wide and varied menu. See also the Hotel Groups pages.

Rooms 31

Premier Inn Halifax Town Centre

BUDGET HOTEL

tel: 0871 527 9348 **Broad Street Plaza HX1 1YA**
web: www.premierinn.com

Rooms 100

HAMPTON COURT
Greater London

The Carlton Mitre Hotel

★★★★ 74% HOTEL PLAN 1 B1

tel: 020 8979 9988 & 8783 3505 **Hampton Court Rd KT8 9BN**
email: info@carltonhotels.co.uk **web:** www.carltonhotels.co.uk/mitre
dir: M3 junct 1 follow signs to Sunbury & Hampton Court Palace. At Hampton Court Palace rdbt right, hotel on right

This hotel, dating back in parts to 1655, enjoys an enviable setting on the banks of the River Thames opposite Hampton Court Palace. The riverside restaurant and Edge bar/brasserie command wonderful views as well as spacious terraces for alfresco dining. Bedrooms are spacious and elegant with excellent facilities. Parking is limited.

Rooms 36 (2 fmly) (12 GF) **D** £125-£165* **Facilities** FTV WiFi ↻ Xmas New Year **Conf** Class 60 Board 40 Thtr 120 **Services** Lift Air con **Parking** 13 **Notes** LB ⊗ Civ Wed 100

H

HANDFORTH

See Manchester Airport

HARPENDEN
Hertfordshire

Map 6 TL11

Harpenden House Hotel

★★★★ 74% HOTEL

tel: 01582 449955 **18 Southdown Rd AL5 1PE**
email: reservations@harpendenhouse.co.uk **web:** www.harpendenhouse.co.uk
dir: M1 junct 10 left at rdbt. Next rdbt right onto A1081 to Harpenden. Over 2 mini rdbts, through town centre. Next rdbt left, hotel 200yds on left

This attractive Grade II listed Georgian building overlooks East Common. The hotel gardens are particularly attractive and the public areas are stylishly decorated, including the restaurant which has an impressive ceiling. Some of the bedrooms and a large suite are located in the original house but most of the accommodation is in the annexe.

Rooms 78 (61 annexe) (13 fmly) (2 GF) ⬧ **Facilities** WiFi Complimentary use of local leisure centre **Conf** Class 60 Board 60 Thtr 150 **Parking** 80 **Notes** ⊗ RS wknds & BHs Civ Wed 120

HARROGATE
North Yorkshire

Map 19 SE35

See also **Knaresborough**

Rudding Park Hotel, Spa & Golf

★★★★ ◉◉ HOTEL

tel: 01423 871350 **Rudding Park, Follifoot HG3 1JH**
email: reservations@ruddingpark.com **web:** www.ruddingpark.co.uk
dir: From A61 at rdbt with A658 take York exit, follow signs to Rudding Park

Set in beautiful parkland, Rudding Park dates from the early 19th century. Interiors are stylishly contemporary and elegant, with luxurious bedrooms; the new Follifoot wing features stunning suites and bedrooms with spas. Carefully prepared meals and Yorkshire tapas are served in the contemporary Clocktower, which has a striking pink chandelier. The stylish bar and conservatory lead to a generous terrace which is perfect for eating alfresco. The grandeur of the mansion house and grounds make this a popular wedding venue. The hotel has

an impressive spa, gym, private cinema and extensive conference facilities, plus an adjoining 18-hole, par 72 golf course and driving range.

Rooms 90 (15 fmly) (38 GF) ⬧ **Facilities** Spa STV FTV WiFi ⬧ HL ⬧ supervised ⬧ 18 Putt green Gym Driving range Jogging trail Sauna Hammam ♫ Xmas New Year **Conf** Class 150 Board 40 Thtr 300 **Services** Lift **Parking** 350 **Notes** ⊗ Civ Wed 300

Nidd Hall Hotel

Warner Leisure Hotels
Life begins at Warner

★★★★ 78% ◉◉ COUNTRY HOUSE HOTEL

tel: 01423 771598 **Nidd HG3 3BN**
web: www.warnerleisurehotels.co.uk
dir: A59 through Knaresborough, follow signs for Ripley. Hotel on right

This fine hotel is set in 45 acres of Victorian and Edwardian gardens. Bedrooms are spacious and appointed to a high standard, while public areas are delightful and retain many original features. Leisure and spa facilities are available along with a variety of outdoor activities. This is an adults-only (above 21 years old) hotel.

Rooms 183 (47 GF) ⬧ **S** £112; **D** £224 (incl. bkfst & dinner)* **Facilities** Spa FTV WiFi HL ⬧ supervised ⬧ Putt green Fishing ⬧ Gym ♫ Xmas New Year **Conf** Class 40 Board 30 Thtr 60 **Services** Lift **Parking** 200 **Notes** LB ⊗ No children 21yrs

The White Hart Hotel

★★★★ 78% ◉◉ HOTEL

tel: 01423 505681 **2 Cold Bath Rd HG2 0NF**
email: reception@whitehart.net **web:** www.whitehart.net
dir: A59 to Harrogate. A661 3rd exit on rdbt to Harrogate. Left at rdbt onto A6040 for 1m. Right onto A61. Bear left down Montpellier Hill

The White Hart Hotel has an excellent location in Harrogate and has been welcoming guests for over 200 years. The bedrooms, including executive rooms with four-posters and views over the Montpellier Quarter, are attractively designed. The Tea Rooms serve from early morning until late afternoon, and the hotel has introduced a pub concept called the Fat Badger, with real ales, an extensive wine list and high quality food. Alfresco eating and drinking are possible in good weather. Secure parking is available and there is WiFi throughout.

Rooms 53 (1 fmly) ❧ **Facilities** FTV WiFi ⟁ Gym Xmas New Year **Conf** Class 40 Board 30 Thtr 80 **Services** Lift **Parking** 80 **Notes** ⊗ Civ Wed 80

Hotel du Vin Harrogate

★★★★ 78% TOWN HOUSE HOTEL

tel: 0844 736 4257 **Prospect Place HG1 1LB**
email: info@harrogate.hotelduvin.com **web:** www.hotelduvin.com
dir: A1(M) junct 47, A59 to Harrogate, follow town centre signs to Prince of Wales rdbt, 3rd exit, remain in right lane. Right at lights into Albert St, right into Prospect Place

This town house was created from eight Georgian-style properties and overlooks The Stray. The spacious, open-plan lobby has seating, a bar and the reception desk. Hidden downstairs is a cosy snug cellar. The French-influenced bistro offers high quality cooking and a great choice of wines. Bedrooms face front and back, and are smart and modern, with excellent 'deluge' showers.

Rooms 48 (4 GF) ❧ **S** £85-£440; **D** £95-£450 (incl. bkfst)* **Facilities** Spa STV FTV WiFi ⟁ New Year **Conf** Class 20 Board 30 Thtr 60 Del from £145 to £225* **Services** Lift **Parking** 30 **Notes** Civ Wed 90

Studley Hotel

★★★★ 76% HOTEL

tel: 01423 560425 **Swan Rd HG1 2SE**
email: info@studleyhotel.co.uk **web:** www.studleyhotel.co.uk
dir: Adjacent to Valley Gardens, opposite Mercer Gallery

This friendly, well-established hotel, close to the town centre and Valley Gardens, is well known for its Orchid Restaurant, which provides a dynamic and authentic approach to Pacific Rim and Asian cuisine. Bedrooms are modern and come in a variety of styles and sizes, while the stylish bar lounge provides an excellent place for relaxing. A PC is available for guests' use.

Rooms 28 (1 fmly) ❧ **S** £82-£120; **D** £114-£154 (incl. bkfst)* **Facilities** STV WiFi ⟁ Free use of facilities at local Health Club **Conf** Class 15 Board 12 Thtr 15 **Services** Lift **Parking** 15 **Notes** LB ⊗ Closed 22-30 Dec

BEST WESTERN PLUS Cedar Court Hotel

★★★★ 76% HOTEL

tel: 01423 858585 & 858595 (Res) **Queens Buildings, Park Pde HG1 5AH**
email: cedarcourt@bestwestern.co.uk **web:** www.cedarcourthotels.co.uk
dir: From A1(M) follow signs to Harrogate on A661 past Sainsburys. At rdbt left onto A6040. Hotel right after church

This Grade II listed building was Harrogate's first hotel and enjoys a peaceful location in landscaped grounds, close to the town centre. It provides spacious, well-equipped accommodation. Public areas include a brasserie-style restaurant, a small gym and an open-plan lounge and bar. Functions and conferences are particularly well catered for.

Rooms 100 (8 fmly) (7 GF) **S** £79-£149; **D** £89-£159 (incl. bkfst)* **Facilities** FTV WiFi ⟁ Gym Xmas New Year **Conf** Class 80 Board 70 Thtr 320 Del from £99 to £169* **Services** Lift **Parking** 150 **Notes** LB ⊗ Civ Wed 320

The Majestic Hotel

★★★★ 76% HOTEL

tel: 01423 700300 **Ripon Rd HG1 2HU**
email: majestic@pumahotels.co.uk **web:** www.pumahotels.co.uk
dir: M1 onto A1(M) at Wetherby. Take A661 to Harrogate. Hotel in town centre adjacent to Royal Hall

Popular for conferences and functions, this grand Victorian hotel is set in 12 acres of landscaped grounds that is within walking distance of the town centre. It benefits from spacious public areas, and the comfortable bedrooms, including some spacious suites, come in a variety of sizes.

Rooms 170 (8 fmly) **S** £59-£129; **D** £69-£169 **Facilities** Spa FTV WiFi ⟁ HL ⟁ ⟁ Gym Xmas New Year **Conf** Class 260 Board 70 Thtr 500 Del from £99 to £179* **Services** Lift **Parking** 250 **Notes** LB Civ Wed 200

H

HARROGATE *continued*

Old Swan Hotel

★★★★ 76% HOTEL

tel: 08446 932964 **Swan Rd HG1 2SR**
email: info.oldswan@classiclodges.co.uk
web: www.classiclodges.co.uk/The_Old_Swan_Hotel_Harrogate
dir: From A1, A59 Ripon, left Empress rdbt, keep left, right at Prince of Wales rdbt. Straight across lights, left into Swan Rd

In the heart of Harrogate and within walking distance of the Harrogate International Centre and Valley Gardens, this hotel is famed as being Agatha Christie's hiding place during her disappearance in 1926. The bedrooms are stylishly furnished, and the public areas include the Library Restaurant, the Wedgwood Room and the lounge bar. Extensive conference and banqueting facilities are available. There is also a beautiful wedding pavilion set within the private gardens.

Rooms 136 **Facilities** STV WiFi 🕊 Xmas New Year **Conf** Class 200 Board 100 Thtr 450 **Services** Lift **Parking** 175 **Notes** ⊗ Civ Wed 350

Cairn Hotel

★★★ 68% HOTEL

tel: 01423 504005 **Ripon Rd HG1 2JD**
email: salescairn@strathmorehotels.com **web:** www.strathmorehotels.com

This large Victorian hotel is just a short walk from the town centre and also benefits from free on-site parking. Many of the original features have been retained and the spacious foyer lounge and bar areas are perfect for relaxing. Bedrooms are comfortable, with Club Rooms offering extra accessories and luxury touches. Complimentary WiFi is also provided in public areas and there is a fitness room with a mini gym.

Rooms 135 (7 fmly) 🐾 **S** £45-£95; **D** £69-£145 (incl. bkfst)* **Facilities** WiFi Gym Xmas New Year **Conf** Class 170 Board 100 Thtr 400 Del from £89 to £145* **Services** Lift **Parking** 150 **Notes** LB Civ Wed 150

See advert on page 501

Premier Inn Harrogate

BUDGET HOTEL

tel: 0871 527 8490 **Hornbeam Park Av HG2 8RA**
web: www.premierinn.com
dir: A1(M) junct 46 W, A661 to Harrogate. In 2m left at The Woodlands lights. 1.5m left into Hornbeam Park Ave

High quality, budget accommodation ideal for both families and business travellers. Spacious, en suite bedrooms feature tea and coffee making facilities, and Freeview TV in most hotels. Internet access and WiFi are available for a small fee. The adjacent family restaurant features a wide and varied menu. See also the Hotel Groups pages.

Rooms 50

HARROW
Greater London

BEST WESTERN Cumberland Hotel

★★★ 72% METRO HOTEL PLAN 1 C5

tel: 020 8863 4111 **1 St Johns Rd HA1 2EF**
email: reservations@cumberlandhotel.co.uk **web:** www.cumberlandhotel.co.uk
dir: Into Harrow via Station or Sheepcote Rd, into Gayton Rd, then Lyon Rd which becomes St Johns Rd

Situated within walking distance of the town centre, this hotel is ideally located for all local attractions and amenities. Bedrooms provide good levels of comfort and are practically equipped to meet the requirements of all travellers. The public areas comprise a well-stocked pub-style bar, which serves homemade food. Parking is located at the rear of the building.

Rooms 85 (54 annexe) (6 fmly) (15 GF) **Facilities** FTV WiFi Xmas New Year **Conf** Class 70 Board 62 Thtr 130 **Parking** 67 **Notes** ⊗ Civ Wed 150

HARROW WEALD
Greater London

BEST WESTERN PLUS Grim's Dyke Hotel

★★★★ 73% ⊛ HOTEL PLAN 1 B5

tel: 020 8385 3100 & 8954 4227 **Old Redding HA3 6SH**
email: reservations@grimsdyke.com **web:** www.grimsdyke.com
dir: A410 onto A409 north towards Bushey, at top of hill at lights turn left into Old Redding, opposite 'The Viewpoint'

Once home to Sir William Gilbert, this Grade II mansion contains many references to well-known Gilbert and Sullivan productions. The house is set in over 40 acres of beautiful parkland and gardens. Bedrooms in the main house are elegant and traditional, while those in the adjacent lodge are aimed more at the business guest.

Rooms 46 (37 annexe) (4 fmly) (17 GF) 🐾 **Facilities** STV FTV WiFi ↕ 🕊 Gilbert & Sullivan opera dinner Murder mystery & Sabrage evenings ♫ Xmas New Year **Conf** Class 60 Board 32 Thtr 90 **Parking** 97 **Notes** RS 24-31 Dec Civ Wed 90

HARTLEPOOL
County Durham · Map 19 NZ53

BEST WESTERN Grand Hotel

★★★ 78% HOTEL

tel: 01429 266345 **Swainson St TS24 8AA**
email: grandhotel@tavistockleisure.com **web:** www.tavistockleisure.com
dir: A689 into town centre. Left onto Victoria Rd, hotel on right

This hotel retains many original features and the public areas include a grand ballroom and a lively open-plan lounge bar. The modern, vibrant, basement restaurant is called Grand Central and serves a wide choice of freshly-made Italian-American food. The bedrooms are modern in design and have high spec fixtures and fittings. The staff provide attentive and friendly service.

Rooms 48 (1 fmly) 🐾 **Facilities** STV FTV WiFi Affiliation with local gym Beauty treatment room ♫ New Year **Conf** Class 200 Board 60 Thtr 250 **Services** Lift **Parking** 50 **Notes** ⊗ Civ Wed 200

Premier Inn Hartlepool Marina

BUDGET HOTEL

tel: 0871 527 8492 **Maritime Av, Hartlepool Marina TS24 OXZ**
web: www.premierinn.com
dir: Approx 1m from A689/A179 junct. On marina

High quality, budget accommodation ideal for both families and business travellers. Spacious, en suite bedrooms feature tea and coffee making facilities, and Freeview TV in most hotels. Internet access and WiFi are available for a small fee. The adjacent family restaurant features a wide and varied menu. See also the Hotel Groups pages.

Rooms 60

HARTLEY WINTNEY
Hampshire — Map 5 SU75

The Elvetham Hotel

★★★ 80% HOTEL

tel: 01252 844871 **RG27 8AR**
email: enq@elvethamhotel.co.uk **web:** www.elvethamhotel.co.uk
dir: M3 junct 4A W, junct 5 E (or M4 junct 11, A33, B3011). Hotel signed from A323 between Hartley Wintney & Fleet

The Elvetham Hotel is a spectacular 19th-century mansion set in 35 acres of grounds with an arboretum. All bedrooms are individually styled and many have views of the manicured gardens. A popular venue for weddings and conferences, the hotel lends itself to team building events and outdoor pursuits.

Rooms 72 (29 annexe) (10 fmly) (15 GF) ☏ S £65-£98; **D** £95-£150 (incl. bkfst)
Facilities STV FTV WiFi ⟲ ☺ Putt green ⚓ Gym Badminton Boules Volleyball New Year **Conf** Class 70 Board 48 Thtr 110 Del from £145 to £235 **Parking** 200
Notes Closed 24-27 Dec Civ Wed 200

HARTSHEAD MOOR MOTORWAY SERVICE AREA (M62)
West Yorkshire — Map 19 SE12

Days Inn Bradford - M62

BUDGET HOTEL

tel: 01274 851706 **Hartshead Moor Service Area, Clifton HD6 4JX**
email: hartshead.hotel@welcomebreak.co.uk **web:** www.welcomebreak.co.uk
dir: M62 between junct 25 & 26

This modern building offers accommodation in smart, spacious and well-equipped bedrooms, suitable for families and business travellers, and all with en suite bathrooms. Continental breakfast is available and other refreshments may be taken at the nearby family restaurant. See also the Hotel Groups pages.

Rooms 38 (33 fmly) (17 GF) **Conf** Board 10

HARWICH
Essex — Map 13 TM23

The Pier at Harwich

★★★★ 79% ❀❀ SMALL HOTEL

tel: 01255 241212 **The Quay CO12 3HH**
email: pier@milsomhotels.com **web:** www.milsomhotels.com/thepier
dir: From A12 take A120 to Quay. Hotel opposite lifeboat station

The Pier is situated on the quay, overlooking the ports of Harwich and Felixstowe. The bedrooms are tastefully decorated, thoughtfully equipped, and furnished in a contemporary style; many rooms have superb sea views. The public rooms include the informal Ha'Penny Bistro, the first-floor Harbourside Restaurant, a smart lounge bar and a plush residents' lounge.

Rooms 14 (7 annexe) (5 fmly) (1 GF) ☏ **D** £115-£165 (incl. bkfst)* **Facilities** STV WiFi Day cruises on yachts Golf breaks arranged with nearby course Sea bass fishing Xmas **Conf** Board 16 **Parking** 12 **Notes** LB Civ Wed 50

HARWICH *continued*

Tower Hotel

★★★ 78% HOTEL

tel: 01255 504952 **Dovercourt CO12 3PJ**
email: reception@tower-hotel-harwich.co.uk **web:** www.tower-hotel-harwich.co.uk
dir: Follow main road into Harwich. Past BP garage on left

The Tower Hotel is an impressive late 17th-century Italian-style building, with a
wealth of ornamental ceiling cornices, beautiful architraves and an impressive
balustrade. Bedrooms, many named after prominent people from Harwich's past,
are spacious and furnished to a very high standard. Evening meals and breakfast
are served in the decorative dining rooms, and Rigby's bar offers tempting meals
and a wide range of refreshments.

Rooms 13 (2 fmly) (2 GF) **S** £48-£68; **D** £63-£95* **Facilities** WiFi **Conf** Class 30
Board 30 Thtr 30 **Parking** 30 **Notes** ⊗ Civ Wed 40

Cliff Hotel

★★ 67% HOTEL

tel: 01255 503345 & 507373 **Marine Pde, Dovercourt CO12 3RE**
email: reception@cliffhotelharwich.fsnet.co.uk **web:** www.cliffhotelharwich.co.uk
dir: From A120 at rdbt into Parkeston Rd. At mini rdbt left onto B1325 signed Harwich. At
lights in Dovercourt right into Kingsway, to seafront. Right into Marine Parade

The Cliff Hotel is conveniently situated on the seafront close to the railway station
and ferry terminal. Public rooms are smartly appointed and include the Shade Bar,
a comfortable lounge, a restaurant, and the Marine Bar with views of Dovercourt
Bay. The pleasantly decorated bedrooms have co-ordinated soft furnishings and
modern facilities; many have sea views.

Rooms 26 (3 fmly) **D** £50-£70* **Facilities** STV WiFi New Year **Conf** Class 150
Board 40 Thtr 200 Del from £80* **Parking** 50 **Notes** LB ⊗ RS Xmas & New Year
Civ Wed 100

Premier Inn Harwich

BUDGET HOTEL

tel: 0871 527 8494 **Parkstone Rd, Dovercourt CO12 4NX**
web: www.premierinn.com
dir: A120 to Harwich, hotel opposite Morrisons. Right at rdbt. Hotel entrance through Lidl
car park

High quality, budget accommodation ideal for both families and business
travellers. Spacious, en suite bedrooms feature tea and coffee making facilities,
and Freeview TV in most hotels. Internet access and WiFi are available for a small
fee. The adjacent family restaurant features a wide and varied menu. See also the
Hotel Groups pages.

Rooms 45

Lythe Hill Hotel & Spa

★★★★ 76% ◉◉ HOTEL

tel: 01428 651251 **Petworth Rd GU27 3BQ**
email: lythe@lythehill.co.uk **web:** www.lythehill.co.uk
dir: From High St onto B2131. Hotel 1.25m on right

This privately-owned hotel sits in 22 acres of attractive parkland. It has been
described as a hamlet of character buildings, each furnished in a style that
complements the age of the property; the oldest one dating back to 1475. The
restaurant offers interesting, quality dishes, and is also the venue for breakfast
and afternoon tea. The bedrooms are split between a number of 15th-century
buildings, and vary in size. The stylish Armana spa includes a 16-metre swimming
pool, as well as various ESPA treatments and therapies, spa bath, sauna and a fully
equipped gym.

Rooms 44 (9 fmly) (19 GF) ✿ **Facilities** Spa FTV WiFi ⓢ ♨ ♒ Gym Boules Giant
chess ♫ Xmas New Year **Conf** Class 40 Board 30 Thtr 128 **Parking** 120
Notes Civ Wed 128

Bannatyne Spa Hotel Hastings

★★★★ 80% HOTEL

tel: 0844 248 3836 **Battle Rd TN38 8EA**
email: enquiries.hastingshotel@bannatyne.co.uk **web:** www.bannatyne.co.uk
dir: M25 junct 5, A21 (Hastings). At 5th rdbt 2nd exit (Hastings/Filmwell). After 2 rdbts
right (Folkestone/A259/Battle/A2100). Left at A2100/The Ridge Way. At 2nd rdbt right to
hotel

This hotel offers a range of facilities that will appeal to both leisure and business
travellers. The well-appointed accommodation is available in a range of types and
sizes from small doubles to superior rooms, while the public areas are a tasteful
blend of contemporary design and period features. The Conservatory Restaurant
has attractive views over the formal garden. There is a spa and health club plus
meeting facilities. Free WiFi is available.

Rooms 38 (7 fmly) (4 GF) ✿ **S** £95-£220; **D** £95-£220 (incl. bkfst)* **Facilities** Spa
FTV WiFi ♭ ⓢ supervised ♨ Gym Xmas New Year **Conf** Class 300 Board 50 Thtr 500
Services Lift **Parking** 150 **Notes** ⊗ Civ Wed 300

BEST WESTERN Royal Victoria Hotel

★★★ 74% HOTEL

tel: 01424 445544 **Marina, St Leonards-on-Sea TN38 0BD**
email: reception@royalvichotel.co.uk **web:** www.royalvichotel.co.uk
dir: On A259 (seafront road) 1m W of Hastings pier

This imposing 18th-century property is situated in a prominent position overlooking the sea. A superb marble staircase leads up from the lobby to the main public areas on the first floor which has panoramic views of the sea. The spacious bedrooms are pleasantly decorated and well equipped, and include duplex and family suites.

Rooms 50 (15 fmly) **Facilities** STV WiFi ᐅ Xmas New Year **Conf** Class 40 Board 40 Thtr 100 **Services** Lift **Parking** 6 **Notes** Civ Wed 50

The Chatsworth Hotel

★★★ 68% HOTEL

tel: 01424 720188 **Carlisle Pde TN34 1JG**
email: info@chatsworthhotel.com **web:** www.chatsworthhotel.com
dir: A21 to town centre. At seafront turn right before next lights

Enjoying a central position on the seafront, close to the pier, this hotel is a short walk from the old town and within easy reach of the county's many attractions. Bedrooms are smartly decorated, equipped with a range of extras, and many rooms enjoy splendid sea views. Guests can also enjoy an exciting Indian meal in the contemporary restaurant.

Rooms 52 (5 fmly) ᐟ **S** £45-£85; **D** £55-£125* **Facilities** FTV WiFi Xmas New Year **Conf** Class 20 Board 20 Thtr 40 Del from £85 to £125* **Services** Lift **Parking** 8 **Notes** LB ⊗

Premier Inn Hastings

BUDGET HOTEL

tel: 0871 527 8496 **1 John Macadam Way, St Leonards on Sea TN37 7DB**
web: www.premierinn.com
dir: A21 into Hastings. Hotel on right after junct with A2100 - Battle road

High quality, budget accommodation ideal for both families and business travellers. Spacious, en suite bedrooms feature tea and coffee making facilities, and Freeview TV in most hotels. Internet access and WiFi are available for a small fee. The adjacent family restaurant features a wide and varied menu. See also the Hotel Groups pages.

Rooms 44

HATFIELD Map 6 TL20
Hertfordshire

Beales Hotel

★★★★ 79% ◉◉ HOTEL

tel: 01707 288500 **Comet Way AL10 9NG**
email: hatfield@bealeshotels.co.uk **web:** www.bealeshotels.co.uk
dir: On A1001 opposite Galleria Shopping Mall - follow signs for Galleria

Beales Hotel is a stunning contemporary property. Within easy access of the M25, its striking exterior incorporates giant glass panels and cedar wood slats. Bedrooms have luxurious beds, flat-screen TVs and smart bathrooms. Public areas include a small bar and attractive restaurant, which opens throughout the day. The hotel is fully air-conditioned and free wired broadband is available in bedrooms, conference and banqueting rooms.

Rooms 53 (3 fmly) (21 GF) ᐟ **Facilities** STV WiFi Free use of nearby leisure club Xmas New Year **Conf** Class 124 Board 64 Thtr 300 **Services** Lift Air con **Parking** 126 **Notes** ⊗ RS 27-30 Dec Civ Wed 300

Mercure Hatfield Oak Hotel

★★★ 74% HOTEL

tel: 01707 275701 **Roehyde Way AL10 9AF**
email: enquiries@hotels-hatfield.com **web:** www.hotels-hatfield.com
dir: M25 junct 23 between juncts 2 & 3 of A1(M). Roehyde Way runs parallel to A1(M)

This hotel enjoys an enviable location for both leisure and business guests, it is within easy reach of major roads and central London. In addition, the University of Hertfordshire is situated nearby. The accommodation has been appointed to a good standard with flat-screen TVs and WiFi, among other facilities. The hotel also caters for conference and banqueting.

Rooms 76 (5 fmly) (36 GF) ᐟ **Facilities** FTV WiFi ᐅ **Conf** Class 50 Board 50 Thtr 100 **Parking** 85 **Notes** ⊗ Civ Wed 120

Premier Inn Hatfield

BUDGET HOTEL

tel: 0871 527 8498 **Lemsford Rd AL10 0DZ**
web: www.premierinn.com
dir: From A1(M) junct 4, A1001 towards Hatfield. At rbt take 2nd exit, 1st right

High quality, budget accommodation ideal for both families and business travellers. Spacious, en suite bedrooms feature tea and coffee making facilities, and Freeview TV in most hotels. Internet access and WiFi are available for a small fee. The adjacent family restaurant features a wide and varied menu. See also the Hotel Groups pages.

Rooms 40

H

HATHERSAGE
Derbyshire   Map 16 SK28

George Hotel

★★★ 83%  HOTEL

tel: 01433 650436 **Main Rd S32 1BB**
email: info@george-hotel.net **web:** www.george-hotel.net
dir: In village centre on A6187, SW of Sheffield

The George is a relaxing 500-year-old hostelry in the heart of this picturesque town. The beamed bar lounge has great character and traditional comfort, and the restaurant is light, modern and spacious with original artworks. Upstairs the decor is simpler with lots of light hues; the split-level and four-poster rooms are especially appealing. The quality cooking is a key feature of the hotel.

Rooms 24 (2 fmly) (5 GF) ✆ S £70-£164; **D** £80-£198 (incl. bkfst)* **Facilities** FTV WiFi Xmas New Year **Conf** Class 20 Board 36 Thtr 80 Del £148* **Parking** 40 **Notes** LB ⊗ Civ Wed 70

HAVANT
Hampshire   Map 5 SU70

Premier Inn Portsmouth (Havant)

BUDGET HOTEL

tel: 0871 527 8900 **65 Bedhampton Hill, Bedhampton PO9 3JN**
web: www.premierinn.com
dir: At rdbt just off A3(M) junct 5 towards Bedhampton

High quality, budget accommodation ideal for both families and business travellers. Spacious, en suite bedrooms feature tea and coffee making facilities, and Freeview TV in most hotels. Internet access and WiFi are available for a small fee. The adjacent family restaurant features a wide and varied menu. See also the Hotel Groups pages.

Rooms 37

HAVERHILL
Suffolk   Map 12 TL64

Days Inn Haverhill

BUDGET HOTEL

tel: 01440 716950 **Phoenix Road & Bumpstead Rd, Haverhill Business Park CB9 7AE**
email: info@daysinnhaverhill.co.uk **web:** www.haverhilldaysinn.co.uk
dir: A1017 (Haverhill bypass). Hotel on 5th rdbt

This modern building offers accommodation in smart, spacious and well-equipped bedrooms, suitable for families and business travellers, and all with en suite bathrooms. Continental breakfast is available and other refreshments may be taken at the nearby family restaurant. See also the Hotel Groups pages.

Rooms 80 (8 fmly) (14 GF) ✆ **Conf** Class 28 Board 24 Thtr 60

HAWES
North Yorkshire   Map 18 SD88

Simonstone Hall Hotel

★★★ 77% HOTEL

tel: 01969 667255 **Simonstone DL8 3LY**
email: enquiries@simonstonehall.com **web:** www.simonstonehall.com
dir: 1.5m N of Hawes on road signed Muker & Buttertubs

This former hunting lodge provides professional, friendly service and a relaxed atmosphere. There is an inviting drawing room, stylish fine dining restaurant, a bar and a conservatory. The generally spacious bedrooms are elegantly designed to reflect the style of the house, and many offer spectacular views of the countryside.

Rooms 18 (10 fmly) (2 GF) ✆ **Facilities** FTV WiFi Xmas New Year **Conf** Class 20 Board 20 Thtr 50 **Parking** 40 **Notes** Civ Wed 70

HAYDOCK
Merseyside   Map 15 SJ59

Premier Inn Haydock

BUDGET HOTEL

tel: 0871 527 8500 **Yew Tree Way, Golbourne WA3 3JD**
web: www.premierinn.com
dir: M6 junct 23, A580 towards Manchester. Approx 2m. Straight on at major rdbt. Hotel on left

High quality, budget accommodation ideal for both families and business travellers. Spacious, en suite bedrooms feature tea and coffee making facilities, and Freeview TV in most hotels. Internet access and WiFi are available for a small fee. The adjacent family restaurant features a wide and varied menu. See also the Hotel Groups pages.

Rooms 60

HAYLE
Cornwall
Map 2 SW53

Premier Inn Hayle

BUDGET HOTEL

tel: 0871 527 8506 **Carwin Rise, Loggans TR27 4PN**
web: www.premierinn.com
dir: On A30 at Loggans Moor rdbt exit into Carwin Rise. Hotel on right

High quality, budget accommodation ideal for both families and business travellers. Spacious, en suite bedrooms feature tea and coffee making facilities, and Freeview TV in most hotels. Internet access and WiFi are available for a small fee. The adjacent family restaurant features a wide and varied menu. See also the Hotel Groups pages.

Rooms 56

Rosewarne Manor

 RESTAURANT WITH ROOMS

tel: 01209 610414 & 07966 090341 **20 Gwinear Rd TR27 5JQ**
email: enquiries@rosewarnemanor.co.uk **web:** www.rosewarnemanor.co.uk
dir: A30 Camborne West towards Connor Downs, left into Gwinear Rd. 0.75m to Rosewarne Manor

Rosewarne Manor offers a flexible suite, which can be booked for bed and breakfast or self catering; it is well appointed and well equipped. The award-winning restaurant, overlooking the garden, offers menus that are created from fresh, local produce. The Manor can also be booked for a range of functions. Parking is available.

Rooms 1 (1 annexe)

HAYLING ISLAND
Hampshire
Map 5 SU70

Langstone Hotel

★★★★ 73%  HOTEL

tel: 023 9246 5011 **Northney Rd PO11 0NQ**
email: info@langstonehotel.co.uk **web:** www.langstonehotel.co.uk
dir: From A27 take A3023 signed Havant/Hayling Island. Over bridge onto Hayling Island, sharp left after bridge

This hotel is located on the north shore of Hayling Island, yet is only minutes from the M27 with easy access to Fareham, Havant and Chichester. All the smartly designed, air-conditioned bedrooms, including 45 superior rooms, have views over Langstone harbour. The Brasserie offers a good choice of dishes and overlooks the harbour. A gym, indoor pool, sauna, steam, beauty salon and fitness club are also available.

Rooms 148 (40 fmly) (60 GF) (5 smoking) ☝ **S** £69-£199; **D** £69-£199*
Facilities Spa STV FTV WiFi ↘ HL ⚡ supervised Gym Sauna Steam room Fitness classes Xmas New Year **Conf** Class 80 Board 50 Thtr 180 Del from £118 to £155*
Services Lift **Parking** 150 **Notes** Civ Wed 150

Sinah Warren Hotel

 Warner Leisure Hotels
Life begins at Warner

★★★ 80% HOTEL

tel: 023 9246 6421 **Ferry Rd PO11 0BZ**
email: sinahwarren2@bourne-leisure.co.uk **web:** www.warnerleisurehotels.co.uk
dir: A27 at Havant junct, take A3023 to Hayling Island, 2nd exit at rdbt towards Manor Rd, 3rd exit at next rdbt into Ferry Rd. Hotel 1.5m on right

Located in a beautiful part of Hampshire, this hotel offers a great range of leisure facilities and numerous daily in-house and external activities catering for all. The accommodation is spacious, and some rooms have sea views. The packages range from a minimum two-night, half board stay. Please note that this is an adults-only (over 21 years) hotel.

Rooms 280 (34 annexe) (116 GF) ☝ **Facilities** Spa FTV WiFi HL ⚡ ↘ supervised ♨ ☕ Gym 𝄞 Xmas New Year **Conf** Class 300 Board 250 Thtr 500 **Services** Lift **Parking** 260 **Notes** ⊗ No children 21yrs

HAYWARDS HEATH
West Sussex
Map 6 TQ32

BEST WESTERN The Birch Hotel

★★★ 78% HOTEL

tel: 01444 451565 **Lewes Rd RH17 7SF**
email: info@birchhotel.co.uk **web:** www.birchhotel.co.uk
dir: On A272 opposite Princess Royal Hospital & behind Shell Garage

Originally the home of an eminent Harley Street surgeon, this attractive Victorian property has been extended to combine modern facilities with the charm of its original period. Public rooms include the conservatory-style Pavilion Restaurant, along with an open-plan lounge and brasserie-style bar serving a range of light meals.

Rooms 51 (3 fmly) (12 GF) ☝ **S** £80-£100; **D** £80-£110 (incl. bkfst)* **Facilities** STV FTV WiFi **Conf** Class 30 Board 26 Thtr 50 Del from £115 to £135* **Parking** 60 **Notes** Civ Wed 60

H

H

HEACHAM
Norfolk

Map 12 TF63

Heacham Manor Hotel

★★★ 85% 🏵 HOTEL

tel: 01485 536030 & 579800 **Hunstanton Rd PE31 7JX**
email: info@heacham-manor.co.uk **web:** www.heacham-manor.co.uk
dir: On A149 between Heacham & Hunstanton. Near Hunstanton rdbt with water tower

This delightful 16th-century, Grade II listed house has been beautifully restored. The property is approached via a winding driveway through landscaped grounds to the front of the hotel. Public areas include a smart dining room, a sunny conservatory and a cosy bar which leads out onto a terrace. The bedrooms are very stylish and have modern facilities.

Rooms 45 (32 annexe) (10 fmly) (12 GF) **Facilities** FTV WiFi ↧ 18 Swimming pools & leisure facilities available at sister resort Xmas New Year **Conf** Class 35 Board 20 Thtr 40 **Parking** 55 **Notes** ⊗ Civ Wed 100

HEATHROW AIRPORT (LONDON)
Greater London

See also **Slough & Staines-upon-Thames**

Sheraton Skyline Hotel

★★★★ 81% HOTEL PLAN 1 A3

tel: 020 8759 2535 **Bath Rd UB3 5BP**
email: res268_skyline@sheraton.com **web:** www.sheraton.com/skyline
dir: M4 junct 4 for Heathrow, follow Terminal 1, 2 & 3 signs. Before airport entrance take slip road to left for 0.25m signed A4/Central London

Within easy reach of all terminals this hotel offers well appointed and comfortable bedrooms with air conditioning. The extensive, contemporary public areas are light and spacious, and include a wide range of eating and drinking options, function rooms, club lounge and a gym.

Rooms 350 (59 fmly) 🐾 **Facilities** STV FTV WiFi ↧ ⓧ supervised Gym 24hr Fitness centre Xmas New Year **Conf** Class 320 Board 100 Thtr 500 **Services** Lift Air con **Parking** 336 **Notes** Civ Wed 100

Crowne Plaza London - Heathrow

CROWNE PLAZA
HOTELS & RESORTS

★★★★ 77% HOTEL PLAN 1 A3

tel: 0871 942 9140 **Stockley Rd UB7 9NA**
email: lonha.reservations@ihg.com **web:** www.cpheathrowairporthotel.co.uk
dir: M4 junct 4 follow signs to Uxbridge on A408, hotel 400yds on left

This smart hotel is conveniently located for access to Heathrow Airport and the motorway network. Excellent facilities include versatile conference and meeting rooms, a spa and a leisure complex. Guests have the choice of two bars, both serving food, plus two restaurants. Air-conditioned bedrooms are furnished and decorated to a high standard and feature a comprehensive range of extra facilities.

Rooms 465 (204 fmly) (37 GF) 🐾 **Facilities** STV WiFi ↧ HL ⓧ supervised ↧ 9 Putt green Gym Steam room Sauna Physiotherapy **Conf** Class 120 Board 75 Thtr 200 **Services** Lift Air con **Parking** 800 **Notes** ⊗

BEST WESTERN PLUS Park Grand London Heathrow

Best Western
PLUS

★★★★ 74% HOTEL PLAN 1 B3

tel: 020 7479 2255 & 3118 9600 **449 Great West Rd TW5 0BY**
email: john@montcalm.co.uk **web:** www.parkgrandheathrow.co.uk
dir: From A4 Great Western Rd, turn into Jersey Rd, 3rd exit at rdbt, turn left. Hotel on the left

This modern hotel is in a convenient location just five miles from London Heathrow Airport and with easy access to Central London. The hotel is modern in style with spacious open-plan public areas including a stylish bar and restaurant. Bedrooms are also modern in style and are very comfortable, all fully air-conditioned and benefit from digital TV and complimentary WiFi. Parking is available on site.

Rooms 124 (14 fmly) 🐾 **S** £45-£200; **D** £55-£250* **Facilities** STV FTV WiFi ↧ HL Gym **Conf** Class 60 Board 40 Thtr 70 **Services** Lift Air con **Parking** 30 **Notes** LB ⊗ Civ Wed 80

DoubleTree by Hilton London Heathrow Airport

fOCUShotels
management limited

★★★★ 74% HOTEL PLAN 1 A3

tel: 0208 564 4450 & 564 4458 **Bath Rd, Cranford TW5 9QE**
email: reservations@doubletree-heathrow.com **web:** www.focushotels.co.uk/hotels
dir: M4 junct 3 follow signs to Heathrow Terminals 1, 2 & 3. Hotel on right of A4 Bath Rd

This well presented hotel is conveniently situated just three miles from Heathrow Airport. Bedrooms are located in a smart block and all are well appointed for both business and leisure guests; each has a flat-screen TV, climate control and good lighting. Arts Bar and Brasserie lead from a contemporary open-plan reception area. Chargeable car park on site.

Rooms 200 (18 fmly) (37 GF) 🐾 **S** £59-£250; **D** £59-£250* **Facilities** FTV WiFi ↧ **Conf** Class 35 Board 30 Thtr 70 Del from £169 to £269* **Services** Lift Air con **Parking** 65 **Notes** LB ⊗ Civ Wed 65

Holiday Inn London - Heathrow

★★★★ 74% HOTEL PLAN 1 A3

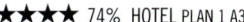

tel: 020 8990 0000 **Bath Rd, Corner Sipson Way UB7 0DP**
email: enquiries@hiheathrow.co.uk **web:** www.hiheathrow.co.uk
dir: Exit airport via main tunnel, at end left towards A4/Other Routes, follow signs for A4. At main lights (hotel visable) turn right, 1st left into Sipson Way

A property close to the terminals, with a frequent bus service to the airport. Public areas include a large brasserie-style restaurant and bar plus shop, mini gym and parking. Bedrooms are spacious and air conditioned, with facilities to suit the business traveller; there are a number of executive rooms available.

Rooms 230 (15 fmly) (58 GF) ⌨ **Facilities** FTV WiFi ⬧ HL Gym Xmas New Year **Conf** Class 60 Board 50 Thtr 130 Del from £149 to £220 **Services** Lift Air con **Parking** 94 **Notes** Civ Wed 80

Holiday Inn London Heathrow M4 Jct 4

★★★★ 74% HOTEL PLAN 1 A3

tel: 0871 942 9095 **Sipson Rd UB7 0JU**
email: reservations-heathrowm4@ihg.com **web:** www.holidayinn.co.uk
dir: M4 junct 4, keep left, 1st left into Holloway Lane, left at mini rdbt then left. For detailed directions contact hotel

This landmark hotel can be seen for miles when travelling on the M4 and is situated close to Heathrow Airport; it is an ideal base for the airport and for families visiting local attractions. The bedrooms are air conditioned and well equipped. There are two restaurants, a small gym and ample parking.

Rooms 616 (120 fmly) (25 smoking) ⌨ **Facilities** STV WiFi ⬧ HL Gym Xmas New Year **Conf** Class 80 Board 80 Thtr 180 **Services** Lift Air con **Parking** 450 **Notes** ⊗

Novotel London Heathrow

★★★★ 73% HOTEL PLAN 1 A3

tel: 01895 431431 **Cherry Ln UB7 9HB**
email: H1551-gm@accor.com **web:** www.novotel.com
dir: M4 junct 4, follow Uxbridge signs on A408. Keep left, take 2nd exit off traffic island into Cherry Ln signed West Drayton. Hotel on left

Conveniently located for Heathrow Airport and the motorway network, this modern hotel provides comfortable accommodation. The large, airy indoor atrium creates a sense of space in the public areas, which include an all-day restaurant and bar, meeting rooms, fitness centre and swimming pool. Ample secure parking is available.

Rooms 178 (178 fmly) (10 GF) **Facilities** STV WiFi ⬧ HL ⬧ Gym **Conf** Class 100 Board 90 Thtr 250 **Services** Lift Air con **Parking** 100 **Notes** Civ Wed 160

The Continental Hotel

★★★ 81% ⬛ HOTEL PLAN 1 B2

tel: 020 8572 3131 & 8538 5883 **29-31 Lampton Rd TW3 1JA**
email: reservations@thecontinental-hotel.com **web:** www.thecontinental-hotel.com
dir: A4, right onto A3006, left onto A3005 then left onto Lampton Rd

This hotel enjoys a prime location just a few minutes walk from Hounslow Central Line; central London can be reached in 40 minutes. The bedrooms are air conditioned, and complimentary broadband is available. The bedroom en suites are marble-clad wet rooms with power showers. The on-site Golds Gym has a 21-metre indoor pool, a state-of-the-art fitness centre and beauty treatment rooms.

Rooms 70 (8 fmly) ⌨ **S** £85-£149; **D** £105-£169* **Facilities** Spa STV FTV WiFi ⬧ Gym ⬧ Xmas New Year **Services** Lift Air con **Parking** 70 **Notes** LB ⊗

Days Hotel Hounslow

★★★ 74% HOTEL PLAN 1 B2

tel: 020 8538 1230 **8-10 Lampton Rd TW3 1JL**
email: gm@dhhounslow.com **web:** www.dhhounslow.com
dir: A4 (Bath Rd), A3006, into Lampton Rd - A3005

A purpose-built hotel situated in the centre of Hounslow, within walking distance of the tube station and with easy access to the motorway network. The accommodation is comfortable and offers a range of amenities. The public areas are light and airy, and parking is available.

Rooms 96 (11 fmly) (4 GF) **S** £69-£99; **D** £79-£119 (incl. bkfst) **Facilities** FTV WiFi ⬧ Xmas New Year **Conf** Class 50 Board 60 Thtr 100 Del from £129 to £159 **Services** Lift Air con **Parking** 20 **Notes** ⊗

Ibis London Heathrow Airport

BUDGET HOTEL PLAN 1 A3

tel: 020 8759 4888 **112/114 Bath Rd UB3 5AL**
email: H0794@accor.com **web:** www.ibishotel.com/heathrow
dir: Follow Heathrow Terminals 1, 2 & 3 signs, then onto spur road, exit at sign for A4/Central London. Hotel 0.5m on left

Modern, budget hotel offering comfortable accommodation in bright and practical bedrooms. Breakfast is self-service and dinner is available in the restaurant. See also the Hotel Groups pages.

Rooms 351 (24 fmly) (39 GF) **Conf** Class 16 Board 16 Thtr 20

Premier Inn Hayes Heathrow

BUDGET HOTEL PLAN 1 A4

tel: 0871 527 8504 **362 Uxbridge Rd UB4 0HF**
web: www.premierinn.com
dir: M4 junct 3, A312 N straight across next rdbt onto dual carriageway, at A4020 junct turn left, hotel 100yds on right

High quality, budget accommodation ideal for both families and business travellers. Spacious, en suite bedrooms feature tea and coffee making facilities, and Freeview TV in most hotels. Internet access and WiFi are available for a small fee. The adjacent family restaurant features a wide and varied menu. See also the Hotel Groups pages.

Rooms 62

Premier Inn Heathrow Airport (Bath Road)

BUDGET HOTEL PLAN 1 A3

tel: 0871 527 8508 **15 Bath Rd TW6 2AB**
web: www.premierinn.com
dir: M4 junct 4, follow signs for Heathrow Terminals 1, 2 & 3. Left onto Bath Rd signed A4/London. Hotel on right after 0.5m

Rooms 590

Premier Inn Heathrow Airport (M4 Jct 4)

BUDGET HOTEL PLAN 1 A3

tel: 0871 527 8510 **Shepiston Ln, Heathrow Airport UB3 1RW**
web: www.premierinn.com
dir: M4 junct 4 take 3rd exit off rdbt. Hotel on right

Rooms 134

H

Premier Inn Heathrow Longford House

BUDGET HOTEL PLAN 1 A3

tel: 0871 527 9344 **Bath Rd, Hillingdon UB7 0EB**
web: www.premierinn.com
dir: M25 junct 14, follow A3113/Heathrow T4 & Cargo signs. At rdbt 1st left onto A3044, at next rdbt 3rd exit signed Longford. Hotel approx 250yds on left

Rooms 400

Sofitel London Heathrow

SOFITEL
LUXURY HOTELS

AA Advertised ⚙⚙⚙ PLAN 1 A3

tel: 020 8757 7777 & 8757 7725 **Terminal 5, Wentworth Dr, London Heathrow Airport TW6 2GD**
email: slh@sofitelheathrow.com **web:** www.sofitelheathrow.com
dir: M25, junct 14. At rdbt take 2nd exit, after 80m turn left. Hotel on right

This is the only Heathrow Airport hotel with direct access to Terminal 5 via a covered walkway and Terminals 1, 2, 3 and 4 via courtesy of the Heathrow Express/Connect rail connection. It is only 21 minutes from Central London by train. Sofitel London Heathrow boasts 605 non-smoking bedrooms including 27 suites, 45 meeting rooms, 2 restaurants, 2 bars and a tea salon as well as private dining options. The hotel also offers a hair salon, a state-of-the-art health spa and gym as well as on-site car park.

Rooms 605 (38 GF) ☏ **S** £169-£289; **D** £169-£289 **Facilities** Spa STV FTV WiFi Gym
Conf Class 820 Board 80 Thtr 1200 Del from £199 to £309 **Services** Lift Air con
Parking 360 **Notes** ⊗ Civ Wed 220

Renaissance London Heathrow Hotel

R
RENAISSANCE
LONDON HEATHROW HOTEL

AA Advertised

tel: 020 8897 6363 **Bath Rd TW6 2AQ**
email: re3@renaissanceheathrow.co.uk **web:** www.renaissancelondonheathrow.co.uk
dir: M4 junct 4 take spur road towards airport, then 2nd left. At rdbt, 2nd exit signed 'Renaissance Hotel'. Hotel adjacent to Customs House

This spacious hotel is located on the perimeter of Heathrow Airport with spectacular views of the main runway, and is within easy reach of Windsor and motorway and rail networks to London. The hotel has excellent conference and leisure facilities.

Rooms 649 (56 GF) ☏ **Facilities** STV WiFi ⚑ Gym Steam room Solarium Fitness studio Beauty & massage treatment Personal trainer **Conf** Class 300 Board 80 Thtr 450
Services Lift Air con **Parking** 700 **Notes** ⊗ Civ Wed 150

HELLIDON
Northamptonshire
Map 11 SP55

Hellidon Lakes Golf & Spa Hotel

QHOTELS
INSPIRED BY YOU

★★★★ 77% HOTEL

tel: 01327 262550 **NN11 6GG**
email: hellidonlakes@qhotels.co.uk **web:** www.qhotels.co.uk
dir: Off A361 between Daventry & Banbury, signed

Some 220 acres of beautiful countryside, which include 27 holes of golf and 12 lakes, combine to form a rather spectacular backdrop to this impressive hotel. Bedroom styles vary, from ultra smart, modern rooms through to those in the original wing that offer superb views. There is an extensive range of facilities available, from meeting rooms to a swimming pool, gym and ten-pin bowling. Golfers of all levels can try some of the world's most challenging courses on the indoor golf simulator. QHotels is the AA Hotel Group of the Year 2014-15.

Rooms 110 (5 fmly) ☏ **S** £65-£165; **D** £65-£165* **Facilities** Spa FTV WiFi ⚑ HL ⏱ ♨
27 ⛳ Putt green Fishing ⚓ Gym Beauty therapist Indoor smart golf 10-pin bowling
Steam room Coarse fishing lake Xmas New Year **Conf** Class 150 Board 80 Thtr 300
Del from £109 to £165* **Services** Lift **Parking** 200 **Notes** LB Civ Wed 220

HELMSLEY
North Yorkshire
Map 19 SE68

INSPECTORS' CHOICE

Feversham Arms Hotel & Verbena Spa

★★★★ ⚙⚙ HOTEL

tel: 01439 770766 **1 High St YO62 5AG**
email: info@fevershamarmshotel.com **web:** www.fevershamarmshotel.com
dir: A168 (signed Thirsk) A1, A170 or A64 (signed York) from A1 to York North, B1363 to Helmsley. Hotel 125mtrs from Market Place

This long established hotel lies just round the corner from the main square, and under caring ownership proves to be a refined operation, yet without airs and graces. There are several lounge areas and a high-ceilinged conservatory restaurant where menus are created with skill and minimal fuss from good local ingredients. The bedrooms, including four air-conditioned poolside suites (some with wood-burners) and spa suites with balconies or French balconies, all have their own individual character and decor. Expect Egyptian cotton sheets, duck down duvets and Bang and Olufsen TVs with DVD and CD player. The spa offers a comprehensive range of pampering treatments.

Rooms 33 (9 fmly) (8 GF) ☏ **S** £105-£250; **D** £110-£400 (incl. bkfst)* **Facilities** Spa
STV FTV WiFi ⚑ Sauna Saunarium Xmas New Year **Conf** Class 20 Board 24 Thtr 35
Del from £200 to £350* **Services** Lift **Parking** 50 **Notes** LB Civ Wed 50

H

Black Swan Hotel

★★★★ 78% ❀❀❀ HOTEL

tel: 01439 770466 **Market Place YO62 5BJ**
email: enquiries@blackswan-helmsley.co.uk **web:** www.blackswan-helmsley.co.uk
dir: A1 junct 49, A168, A170 east, hotel 14m from Thirsk

People have been visiting this establishment for over 200 years and it has become a landmark that dominates the market square. The hotel is renowned for its hospitality and friendliness; many of the staff are long-serving and dedicated. The bedrooms are stylish and include a junior suite and feature rooms. Dinner in the award-winning restaurant is the highlight of any stay. The hotel has a Tearoom and Patisserie that is open daily.

Rooms 45 (4 fmly) 🐾 **Facilities** STV FTV WiFi Xmas New Year **Conf** Class 30 Board 26 Thtr 50 Del from £145 to £165* **Parking** 50 **Notes** Civ Wed 130

The Pheasant Hotel

★★★ 87% ❀❀ COUNTRY HOUSE HOTEL

tel: 01439 771241 **Mill St, Harome YO62 5JG**
email: reservations@thepheasanthotel.com **web:** www.thepheasanthotel.com
dir: Leave A1M at Thirsk, follow A170 E towards Helmsley/Scarborough & then through Helmsley. Right after 0.5m to Harome, follow road for 2.5m

The Pheasant Hotel sits in a delightful small North Yorkshire village, overlooking the village pond. The public areas are delightful in a very country house style, with ample outside seating areas that are ideal for the delightful afternoon tea. The rooms are spacious, very well appointed and have a luxury feel to them. The small heated pool is easily accessible and the hotel has ample parking. Food is the highlight of the stay with the menu boasting local produce and inventive cooking.

Rooms 16 (2 fmly) (3 GF) 🐾 **S** £80–£165; **D** £155–£255 (incl. bkfst)* **Facilities** FTV WiFi ⌕ ⚐ Xmas New Year **Conf** Class 30 Board 20 Thtr 30 Del from £182.50 to £225* **Parking** 16 **Notes** LB Civ Wed 60

HELSTON
Cornwall

Map 2 SW62

Premier Inn Helston

BUDGET HOTEL

tel: 0871 527 8512 **Clodgey Ln TR13 8FZ**
web: www.premierinn.com
dir: A39 towards Falmouth. Right onto A394 towards Helston, 8m. At rdbt 1st exit (Helston bypass) signed Penzance (A394)/Lizard. Hotel at next rdbt on left. NB for Sat Nav use TR13 0QD

High quality, budget accommodation ideal for both families and business travellers. Spacious, en suite bedrooms feature tea and coffee making facilities, and Freeview TV in most hotels. Internet access and WiFi are available for a small fee. The adjacent family restaurant features a wide and varied menu. See also the Hotel Groups pages.

Rooms 50

HEMEL HEMPSTEAD
Hertfordshire

Map 6 TL00

Holiday Inn Hemel Hempstead

★★★ 79% HOTEL

tel: 0871 942 9041 **Breakspear Way HP2 4UA**
email: reservations-hemelhempsteadm1@ihg.com
web: www.holidayinn.co.uk/hemelhempstead
dir: M1 junct 8, over rdbt, 1st left after BP garage

A modern, purpose-built hotel that is convenient for the motorway networks. Bedrooms are spacious and well suited to the business traveller. Executive rooms and public areas are particularly well styled. Other facilities include a leisure club and a range of meeting rooms.

Rooms 144 (43 fmly) (42 GF) **Facilities** Spa STV WiFi ⓑ 🏊 supervised Gym Physiotherapy by appointment **Conf** Class 22 Board 30 Thtr 80 **Services** Lift Air con **Parking** 200 **Notes** ⊗ Civ Wed 60

BEST WESTERN The Watermill

★★★ 74% HOTEL

tel: 01442 349955 **London Rd, Bourne End HP1 2RJ**
email: info@hotelwatermill.co.uk **web:** www.hotelwatermill.co.uk
dir: From M25 & M1 follow signs to Aylesbury on A41, A4251 to Bourne End. Hotel 0.25m on right

In the heart of the county this modern hotel has been built around an old flour mill on the banks of the River Bulbourne with water meadows adjacent. The thoughtfully equipped, contemporary bedrooms are located in three annexes situated around the complex. A good range of air-conditioned conference and meeting rooms complement the lounge bar and restaurant.

Rooms 71 (71 annexe) (10 fmly) (35 GF) (8 smoking) 🐾 **Facilities** STV FTV WiFi Fishing Xmas New Year **Conf** Class 150 Board 125 Thtr 200 **Parking** 100 **Notes** ⊗ Civ Wed 180

The Bobsleigh Hotel

★★★ 74% HOTEL

tel: 0844 879 9033 **Hempstead Rd, Bovingdon HP3 0DS**
email: bobsleigh@macdonald-hotels.co.uk **web:** www.macdonaldhotels.co.uk
dir: M1 junct 8, A414 signed Hemel Hempstead. At Plough Rdbt follow railway station signs. Pass rail station on left, straight on at rdbt, under 2 bridges. Left onto B4505 (Box Lane) signed Chesham. Hotel 1.5m on left

Located just outside the town, the hotel enjoys a pleasant rural setting, yet is within easy reach of local transport links and the motorway network. Bedrooms vary in size; all are modern in style. There is an open-plan lobby, a bar area and an attractive dining room with views over the garden.

Rooms 46 (14 annexe) (6 fmly) (30 GF) 🐾 **Facilities** FTV WiFi New Year **Conf** Class 50 Board 40 Thtr 150 Del from £110 to £165* **Parking** 60 **Notes** Civ Wed 100

Premier Inn Hemel Hempstead Central

BUDGET HOTEL

tel: 0871 527 8514 **Moor End Rd HP1 1DL**
web: www.premierinn.com
dir: M1 junct 8, A414, follow town centre signs. Right at 1st mini rdbt, right at 2nd mini rdbt into Seldon Hill Rd, follow Riverside car park signs (footbridge to hotel from floor 3). (NB for Sat Nav use HP1 1BT)

High quality, budget accommodation ideal for both families and business travellers. Spacious, en suite bedrooms feature tea and coffee making facilities, and Freeview TV in most hotels. Internet access and WiFi are available for a small fee. The adjacent family restaurant features a wide and varied menu. See also the Hotel Groups pages.

Rooms 113

Premier Inn Hemel Hempstead West

BUDGET HOTEL

tel: 0871 527 8516 **A41 Service Area, Bourne End HP1 2SB**
web: www.premierinn.com
dir: M25 junct 20, A41 exit at services. Or from M1 junct 8, A414, A41, exit at services

Rooms 61

HENLEY-ON-THAMES
Oxfordshire

Map 5 SU78

Hotel du Vin Henley-on-Thames

★★★★ 76% ⑩⑩ TOWN HOUSE HOTEL

tel: 01491 848400 & 0844 736 4258 **New St RG9 2BP**
email: info.henley@hotelduvin.com **web:** www.hotelduvin.com
dir: M4 junct 8/9 signed High Wycombe, 2nd exit onto A404 in 2m. A4130 to Henley, over bridge, through lights, into Hart St, right into Bell St, right into New St, hotel on right

Situated just 50 yards from the water's edge, this hotel retains the character and much of the architecture of its former life as a brewery. Food, and naturally wine, take on a strong focus here and guests will find an interesting mix of dishes to choose from; there are three private dining rooms where the fermentation room and old malt house once were; alfresco dining is popular when the weather permits. Bedrooms provide comfort, style and a good range of facilities including power showers. Parking is available and there is a drop-off point in the courtyard.

Rooms 43 (4 fmly) (4 GF) 🐾 **D** £125-£225* **Facilities** STV FTV WiFi ⓑ Xmas New Year **Conf** Class 20 Board 36 Thtr 56 Del from £230 to £300* **Services** Air con **Parking** 46 **Notes** Civ Wed 60

Milsoms Henley-on-Thames

RESTAURANT WITH ROOMS

tel: 01491 845780 & 845789 **20 Market Place RG9 2AH**
email: henley@milsomshotel.co.uk **web:** www.milsomshotel.co.uk
dir: In centre of town, close to town hall

The seven en suite bedrooms are located in a listed building above the Loch Fyne Restaurant in Henley's Market Place. Each bedroom is individually appointed and equipped to meet the needs of the modern traveller; particular care has been taken to incorporate original features into the contemporary design. The restaurant has a commitment to offer ethically sourced seafood.

Rooms 7 (2 fmly)

HEREFORD	Map 10 SO54
Herefordshire	

See also **Leominster**

Holme Lacy House Hotel

Warner Leisure Hotels
Life begins at Warner

★★★★ 72% ◉◉ COUNTRY HOUSE HOTEL

tel: 01432 870870 **Holme Lacy HR2 6LP**
web: www.warnerleisurehotels.co.uk
dir: B4399 at Holme Lacy, take lane opposite college. Hotel 500mtrs on right

This is a grand Grade I listed mansion with a rich history, just a short drive from Hereford and in a peaceful location, set in twenty acres of superb parkland in the heart of the Wye Valley. The well-appointed bedrooms are comfortable and vary in size and style. There's plenty to do here, with a full daily entertainment programmes, an indoor pool, and health and beauty treatments. The three restaurants provide carefully selected menus of quality cuisine. Exclusively for adults (above 21 years old).

Rooms 180 (150 annexe) (53 GF) ⌂ **Facilities** Spa FTV WiFi HL ⊗ ⌘ Putt green Fishing ⌘ Gym Archery Rifle shooting Aquafit Yoga Fencing ♬ Xmas New Year **Services** Lift **Parking** 200 **Notes** ⊗ No children 21yrs

Castle House

★★★ 86% ◉◉ HOTEL

tel: 01432 356321 **Castle St HR1 2NW**
email: info@castlehse.co.uk **web:** www.castlehse.co.uk
dir: Follow signs to City Centre East. At junct of Commercial Rd & Union St follow hotel signs

Enjoying a prime city centre location, with a terraced garden leading to the castle moat, this delightful Grade II-listed Georgian mansion is the epitome of elegance and sophistication. The character bedrooms are equipped with every luxury to

ensure a memorable stay and are complemented perfectly by the well-proportioned and restful lounge and bar, together with the elegant topiary-themed restaurant where award-winning modern British cuisine is served.

Rooms 24 (8 annexe) (4 GF) ⌂ **Facilities** STV FTV WiFi ⌇ Free membership at local spa Xmas New Year **Services** Lift **Parking** 12 **Notes** ⊗ Civ Wed 50

See advert on page 204

Three Counties Hotel

★★★ 78% HOTEL

tel: 01432 299955 **Belmont Rd HR2 7BP**
email: enquiries@threecountieshotel.co.uk **web:** www.threecountieshotel.co.uk
dir: On A465 (Abergavenny road)

Just a mile west of the city centre, this large, privately owned, modern complex has well-equipped, spacious bedrooms; many are located in separate single-storey buildings around the extensive car park. There is a spacious, comfortable lounge, a traditional bar and an attractive restaurant.

Rooms 60 (32 annexe) (4 fmly) (46 GF) **S** £65-£73; **D** £88-£98 (incl. bkfst)*
Facilities STV FTV WiFi **Conf** Class 200 Board 120 Thtr 450 Del from £94 to £104*
Parking 250 **Notes** LB Civ Wed 350

Premier Inn Hereford

BUDGET HOTEL

tel: 0871 527 8518 **Holmer Rd, Holmer HR4 9RS**
web: www.premierinn.com
dir: From N: M5 junct 7, A4103 to Worcester. M50 junct 4, A49 (Leominster road). Hotel 800yds on left

High quality, budget accommodation ideal for both families and business travellers. Spacious, en suite bedrooms feature tea and coffee making facilities, and Freeview TV in most hotels. Internet access and WiFi are available for a small fee. The adjacent family restaurant features a wide and varied menu. See also the Hotel Groups pages.

Rooms 81

HERNE BAY
Kent
Map 7 TR16

Premier Inn Canterbury North/Herne Bay

BUDGET HOTEL

tel: 0871 527 8520 **Blacksole Farm, Margate Rd CT6 6LA**
web: www.premierinn.com
dir: From M2 junct 7 follow Canterbury signs, A299 signed Ramsgate/Margate. Exit at Broomfield & Beltinge. Hotel just off rdbt

High quality, budget accommodation ideal for both families and business travellers. Spacious, en suite bedrooms feature tea and coffee making facilities, and Freeview TV in most hotels. Internet access and WiFi are available for a small fee. The adjacent family restaurant features a wide and varied menu. See also the Hotel Groups pages.

Rooms 50

HERTFORD
Hertfordshire
Map 6 TL31

White Horse Hotel

★★★ 78% HOTEL

tel: 01992 586791 **Hertingfordbury Rd, Hertingfordbury SG14 2LB**
email: gmewhhh.co.uk web: www.fairviewhotels.com
dir: From A10 follow A414 signs. From Hertford under rail bridge, over rdbt, left at next rdbt, hotel 300yds on right

The Georgian façade of this former coaching inn belies a much older interior with oak beams dating back 400 years. Many of the spacious bedrooms overlook the picturesque gardens. Public rooms include a beamed bar with its open fireplace and a spacious conservatory restaurant.

Rooms 44 (2 annexe) (4 fmly) (2 GF) ⚑ S £45-£85; D £50-£110 (incl. bkfst)*
Facilities FTV WiFi Xmas New Year Conf Class 30 Board 26 Thtr 60 Del from £100 to £145* Services Air con Parking 50 Notes LB ⊗ Civ Wed 95

HESWALL
Merseyside
Map 15 SJ28

Premier Inn Wirral (Heswall)

BUDGET HOTEL

tel: 0871 527 9178 **Chester Rd, Gayton CH60 3SD**
web: www.premierinn.com
dir: M53 junct 4, A5137 signed Heswall. In 3m left at next rdbt, hotel on left

High quality, budget accommodation ideal for both families and business travellers. Spacious, en suite bedrooms feature tea and coffee making facilities, and Freeview TV in most hotels. Internet access and WiFi are available for a small fee. The adjacent family restaurant features a wide and varied menu. See also the Hotel Groups pages.

Rooms 37

HETHERSETT	Map 13 TG10
Norfolk	

Park Farm Hotel

★★★★ 77% HOTEL

tel: 01603 810264 **NR9 3DL**
email: enq@parkfarm-hotel.co.uk **web:** www.parkfarm-hotel.co.uk
dir: 5m S of Norwich, exit A11 onto B1172

An elegant Georgian farmhouse set in landscaped grounds surrounded by open countryside. The property has been owned and run by the Gowing family since 1958. Bedrooms are pleasantly decorated and tastefully furnished; some rooms have patio doors with a sun terrace. Public rooms include a stylish conservatory, a lounge bar, a smart restaurant and superb leisure facilities.

Rooms 53 (16 annexe) (15 fmly) (26 GF) **Facilities** Spa FTV WiFi supervised Gym Beauty salon Hairdressing Xmas New Year **Conf** Class 50 Board 50 Thtr 120 **Parking** 150 **Notes** Civ Wed 100

HETTON	Map 18 SD95
North Yorkshire	

INSPECTORS CHOICE

The Angel Inn

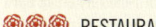 RESTAURANT WITH ROOMS

tel: 01756 730263 01756 730363 **BD23 6LT**
email: info@angelhetton.co.uk **web:** www.angelhetton.co.uk
dir: B6265 from Skipton towards Grassington. At Rylstone turn left by pond, follow signs to Hetton

This roadside inn is steeped in history; parts of the building go back more than 500 years. The restaurant and bar are in the main building, which has ivy and green canopies at the front. Food is a highlight of any stay, offering excellent ingredients, skilfully prepared and carefully presented. The large and stylish bedrooms are across the road in a converted barn which has great views of the Dales, its own wine cave and private parking.

Rooms 9

Read all about
Visiting the Northeast in our feature on page 22

HEXHAM	Map 21 NY96
Northumberland	

Langley Castle Hotel

★★★★ 81% HOTEL

tel: 01434 688888 **Langley NE47 5LU**
email: manager@langleycastle.com **web:** www.langleycastle.com
dir: From A69 S on A686 for 2m. Hotel on right

Langley is a magnificent 14th-century fortified castle, with its own chapel, set in ten acres of parkland. There is an award-winning restaurant, a comfortable drawing room and a cosy bar. Bedrooms are furnished with period pieces and most feature window seats. Restored buildings in the grounds have been converted into very stylish Castle View bedrooms.

Rooms 27 (18 annexe) (8 fmly) (9 GF) **S** £119.50-£209.50; **D** £155-£279 (incl. bkfst)* **Facilities** STV WiFi HL Xmas **Conf** Class 60 Board 40 Thtr 120 Del from £185 to £235* **Services** Air con **Parking** 70 **Notes** LB Civ Wed 120

H

HEXHAM *continued*

De Vere Slaley Hall

★★★★ 80% ⊛ HOTEL

tel: 0871 222 4688 **Slaley NE47 OBX**
email: slaley.hall@devere-hotels.com **web:** www.devere.co.uk
dir: A1 from S to A68 link road follow signs for Slaley Hall

One thousand acres of Northumbrian forest and parkland, two championship golf courses and indoor leisure facilities can all be found here. Spacious bedrooms are fully air conditioned, equipped with a range of extras and the deluxe rooms offer excellent standards. Public rooms include a number of lounges and dining options, including the fine-dining Dukes Grill, informal Claret Jug and the impressive main restaurant that overlooks the golf course.

Rooms 142 (18 fmly) (37 GF) ♙ **Facilities** Spa FTV WiFi ⊛ supervised ⚒ 36 Putt green Gym Quad bikes Archery Clay pigeon shooting 4x4 driving Xmas New Year **Conf** Class 220 Board 150 Thtr 300 **Services** Lift Air con **Parking** 500 **Notes** Civ Wed 250

BEST WESTERN Beaumont Hotel

★★★ 81% HOTEL

tel: 01434 602331 **Beaumont St NE46 3LT**
email: reservations@beaumonthotelhexham.co.uk **web:** www.bw-beaumonthotel.co.uk
dir: A69 towards town centre

In a region steeped in history, this family-run hotel is located in the centre of Hexham, overlooking the park and 7th-century abbey. The hotel has two bars, a comfortable reception lounge and a first-floor restaurant. Bedrooms are a mix of traditional and contemporary; the South Wing rooms are spacious with a more contemporary feel and have flat-screen TVs.

Rooms 34 (3 fmly) ♙ **S** £82-£90; **D** £140-£180 (incl. bkfst)* **Facilities** FTV WiFi ⊠ Xmas New Year **Conf** Class 60 Board 40 Thtr 100 **Services** Lift **Parking** 16 **Notes** LB ⊗ Civ Wed 50

Who are the AA's award-winning hotels? For details see pages 11-13

see pages 11-13

HIGHAM   Map 16 SK35
Derbyshire

Santo's Higham Farm Hotel

★★★ 77% ⊛ HOTEL

tel: 01773 833812 **Main Rd DE55 6EH**
email: reception@santoshighamfarm.co.uk **web:** www.santoshighamfarm.co.uk
dir: M1 junct 28, A38 towards Derby, then A61 towards Chesterfield. Onto B6013 towards Belper, hotel 300yds on right

With panoramic views across the rolling Amber Valley, this 15th-century crook barn and farmhouse has been expertly restored and extended. There's an Italian wing and an international wing of themed bedrooms and mini suites. Freshly prepared dishes, especially fish, are available in Guiseppe's restaurant. This hotel makes an ideal romantic hideaway.

Rooms 31 (3 fmly) (7 GF) ♙ **Facilities** FTV WiFi ⊠ Xmas New Year **Conf** Class 40 Board 34 Thtr 100 Del from £105 to £110* **Parking** 100 **Notes** ⊗ Civ Wed 100

HIGHBRIDGE   Map 4 ST34
Somerset

Laburnum House Lodge Hotel

★★ 65% HOTEL

tel: 01278 781830 **Sloway Ln, West Huntspill TA9 3RJ**
email: laburnumhh@aol.com **web:** www.laburnumhousehotel.co.uk
dir: M5 junct 22. W on A38 approx 5m, right at Crossways Inn. 300yds & left into Sloway Ln, 300yds to hotel

This hotel is in an excellent rural location, set in its own grounds, and offers an impressive range of facilities. Bedrooms (all individual lodge accommodation with their own access) are spacious, and many are suitable for families. The hotel also offers a range of meeting rooms and leisure facilities. Dogs are welcome here.

Rooms 68 (9 fmly) (68 GF) ♙ **S** £58-£80; **D** £68-£94* **Facilities** STV FTV WiFi ⊠ HL ⊛ ♨ Gym **Conf** Class 60 Board 40 Thtr 100 Del from £90 to £110* **Services** Lift **Parking** 100 **Notes** LB Civ Wed

HIGHCLIFFE
Dorset
Map 5 SZ29

Premier Inn Christchurch/Highcliffe

BUDGET HOTEL

tel: 0871 527 9276 **266 Lymington Rd BH23 5ET**
web: www.premierinn.com
dir: From A35 (Christchurch rdbt) onto A337 towards New Milton & Lymington. Approx 2m hotel on left

High quality, budget accommodation ideal for both families and business travellers. Spacious, en suite bedrooms feature tea and coffee making facilities, and Freeview TV in most hotels. Internet access and WiFi are available for a small fee. The adjacent family restaurant features a wide and varied menu. See also the Hotel Groups pages.

Rooms 62

HIGH WYCOMBE
Buckinghamshire
Map 5 SU89

Fox Country Inn
★★★ 67% HOTEL

tel: 0845 643 9933 & 01491638814 **Ibstone HP14 3XT**
email: info@foxcountryinn.co.uk **web:** www.foxcountryinn.co.uk
dir: M40 junct 5 follow signs to Ibstone, hotel 1.5m on left

This stylish modern hotel enjoys a peaceful rural location on the outskirts of High Wycombe. The modern bedrooms are all attractively presented and have a host of thoughtful little extras. Free WiFi is available throughout the hotel. The bar and restaurant have a contemporary open-plan style and food is served throughout the day in the bar and on the terrace.

Rooms 18 (2 fmly) (10 GF) **S** £55-£79; **D** £70-£89 **Facilities** FTV WiFi Xmas New Year **Conf** Class 40 Board 24 Thtr 40 Del from £115 to £135 **Parking** 23 **Notes** Civ Wed 50

Premier Inn High Wycombe

BUDGET HOTEL

tel: 0871 527 8522 **Thanstead Farm, London Rd, Loudwater HP10 9YL**
web: www.premierinn.com
dir: M40 junct 3, A40 towards High Wycombe

High quality, budget accommodation ideal for both families and business travellers. Spacious, en suite bedrooms feature tea and coffee making facilities, and Freeview TV in most hotels. Internet access and WiFi are available for a small fee. The adjacent family restaurant features a wide and varied menu. See also the Hotel Groups pages.

Rooms 108

Premier Inn High Wycombe Central

BUDGET HOTEL

tel: 0871 527 9326 **Arch Way HP13 5HL**
web: www.premierinn.com
dir: M4, junct 8/9, A404M signed Marlow & Wycombe. Exit for High Wycombe, right at rdbt (town centre) via Marlow Hill. Left at 1st mini rdbt, right at next rdbt, left signed Dovecot. Right at next junct into Arch Way, (Sainsburys on left) 1st left, left to hotel (NB for Sat Nav use HP11 2DN)

Rooms 120

HINCKLEY
Leicestershire
Map 11 SP49

Sketchley Grange Hotel
★★★★ 78% HOTEL

tel: 01455 251133 **Sketchley Ln, Burbage LE10 3HU**
email: info@sketchleygrange.co.uk **web:** www.sketchleygrange.co.uk
dir: M69 junct 1, B4109 towards Hinkley. Left at 2nd rdbt. Into Sketchley Ln, 1st right (also Sketchley Ln)

Close to motorway connections, this hotel is peacefully set in its own grounds, and enjoys open country views. Extensive leisure facilities include a stylish health and leisure spa. Modern meeting facilities, a choice of bars, and two dining options, together with comfortable bedrooms furnished with many extras, make this a special hotel.

Rooms 95 (9 fmly) (6 GF) **Facilities** Spa STV FTV WiFi Gym Steam room Sauna Xmas New Year **Conf** Class 150 Board 30 Thtr 300 **Services** Lift **Parking** 270 **Notes** Civ Wed 120

Puma Hinckley Island Hotel

★★★★ 76% HOTEL

tel: 01455 631122 **Watling Street (A5) LE10 3JA**
email: hinckleyisland@pumahotels.co.uk **web:** www.pumahotels.co.uk
dir: On A5, S of junct 1 on M69

Puma Hinckley Island Hotel is a large, constantly improving establishment offering good facilities for both leisure and business guests. Bedrooms are well equipped, with the Club Floors providing high levels of comfort and good workspace. A choice of dining styles is available in the Brasserie or Conservatory restaurants, and the Triumph Bar is a must for motorcycle enthusiasts. The modern leisure club also offers a range of spa treatments.

Rooms 362 (14 GF) **Facilities** STV WiFi supervised Gym Steam room **Conf** Class 240 Board 40 Thtr 400 **Services** Lift Air con **Parking** 600 **Notes** Civ Wed 350

Premier Inn Hinckley

BUDGET HOTEL

tel: 0871 527 8524 **Coventry Rd LE10 0NB**
web: www.premierinn.com
dir: M69 junct 1, A5 towards Nuneaton. In 2.5m right at rdbt onto B4666 signed Hinckley Town Centre. Hotel on right (entrance via Total petrol station)

High quality, budget accommodation ideal for both families and business travellers. Spacious, en suite bedrooms feature tea and coffee making facilities, and Freeview TV in most hotels. Internet access and WiFi are available for a small fee. The adjacent family restaurant features a wide and varied menu. See also the Hotel Groups pages.

Rooms 53

HINTLESHAM
Suffolk   Map 13 TM04

INSPECTORS' CHOICE

Hintlesham Hall Hotel

★★★★ @@ HOTEL

tel: 01473 652334 **George St IP8 3NS**
email: reservations@hintleshamhall.com **web:** www.hintleshamhall.com
dir: 4m W of Ipswich on A1071 to Hadleigh & Sudbury

Hospitality and service are key features at this imposing Grade I listed country-house hotel, situated in 175 acres of grounds and landscaped gardens. Originally a manor house dating from the Elizabethan era, the building was extended in the 17th and 18th centuries. It was a Red Cross hospital in World War II and has been a hotel for nearly forty years. Individually decorated bedrooms offer a high degree of comfort; each one is tastefully furnished and equipped with many thoughtful touches. The spacious public rooms include a series of comfortable lounges, and an elegant restaurant which serves fine classical cuisine based on top-notch ingredients. WiFi is available throughout.

Rooms 33 (10 GF) **D** £189–£489 (incl. bkfst)* **Facilities** FTV WiFi 18 Putt green Health & Beauty services Clay pigeon shooting Xmas New Year **Conf** Class 50 Board 32 Thtr 80 **Parking** 60 **Notes** LB Civ Wed 110

HINTON CHARTERHOUSE
Somerset   Map 4 ST75

Homewood Park Hotel & Spa

★★★★ 82% @@ HOTEL

tel: 01225 723731 **BA2 7TB**
email: info@homewoodpark.co.uk **web:** www.homewoodpark.co.uk
dir: 6m SE of Bath on A36, left at 2nd sign for Freshford

This hotel has a delightful location in attractive parkland, close to Bath and the Longleat estate. Bedrooms are stylishly and comfortably appointed, and many enjoy splendid countryside views. The spa and leisure facilities are notable, and a meal in the restaurant should not be missed.

Rooms 21 (2 annexe) (3 fmly) (2 GF) **Facilities** Spa FTV WiFi Sauna Steam room Nail bar Xmas New Year **Conf** Class 30 Board 25 Thtr 40 **Parking** 40 **Notes** Civ Wed 100

HOCKLEY HEATH
West Midlands   Map 10 SP17

Nuthurst Grange Hotel

★★★★ 79% @@ HOTEL

tel: 01564 783972 **Nuthurst Grange Ln B94 5NL**
email: info@nuthurst-grange.co.uk **web:** www.nuthurst-grange.co.uk
dir: Exit A3400, 0.5m south of Hockley Heath. Turn at sign into Nuthurst Grange Lane

A stunning avenue is the approach to this country-house hotel, set amid several acres of well-tended gardens and mature grounds, with views over rolling countryside. The spacious bedrooms and bathrooms offer considerable luxury and comfort, and public areas include restful lounges, meeting rooms and a sunny restaurant. The kitchen brigade produces highly imaginative British and French cuisine, complemented by very attentive, professional restaurant service.

Rooms 19 (7 fmly) (2 GF) **Facilities** STV FTV WiFi **Conf** Class 50 Board 35 Thtr 100 **Parking** 80 **Notes** RS 24-26 Dec Civ Wed 100

HOLLINGBOURNE
Kent   Map 7 TQ85

Mercure Maidstone, Great Danes Hotel

★★★★ 72% HOTEL

Mercure
HOTELS

tel: 0844 815 9045 **ME17 1RE**
email: info@mercuremaidstone.co.uk **web:** www.jupiterhotels.co.uk
dir: M20 junct 8, follow Leeds Castle signs, at 2nd rdbt turn right

The property is set within 26 acres of private grounds just a few minutes from junction 8 of the M20 and close to the channel ports and Eurotunnel. The smartly appointed bedrooms are well equipped and suitable for business and leisure guests. Public rooms include Art's Bar and Grill as well as an indoor pool, fitness centre and a 9-hole golf course.

Rooms 126 **Facilities** WiFi Gym Steam room Beauty treatments **Conf** Class 220 Board 60 Thtr 650 **Parking** 500 **Notes** Civ Wed 650

HOLT
Norfolk

Map 13 TG03

The Pheasant Hotel & Restaurant

★★★★ 80% HOTEL

tel: 01263 588382 & 588540 **Coast Rd, Kelling NR25 7EG**
email: enquiries@pheasanthotelnorfolk.co.uk **web:** www.pheasanthotelnorfolk.co.uk
dir: On A149 coast road, mid-way between Sheringham & Blakeney

The Pheasant is a charming country house hotel set in its own extensive grounds, enjoying a peaceful rural location in the small village of Kelling, making it an ideal base from which to explore the beautiful North Norfolk coast and the surrounding villages of Cley and Blakeney. The hotel has undergone a major refurbishment and all bedrooms are beautifully presented and most comfortable. Afternoon tea is served on the terrace on warmer days and the lounge bar is cosy.

Rooms 32 (1 fmly) (32 GF) ♠ **S** £85-£110; **D** £136-£180 (incl. bkfst & dinner)*
Facilities FTV WiFi ♦ Xmas New Year **Conf** Class 50 Thtr 100 Del from £100 to £130*
Notes Civ Wed 200

The Lawns Wine Bar

 RESTAURANT WITH ROOMS

tel: 01263 713390 **26 Station Rd NR25 6BS**
email: info@lawnshotelholt.co.uk **web:** www.lawnshotelholt.co.uk
dir: A148 (Cromer road). 0.25m from Holt rdbt, turn left, 400yds along Station Rd

The Lawns is a superb Georgian house situated in the centre of this delightful north Norfolk market town. The open-plan public areas include a large wine bar, a conservatory and a smart restaurant. The spacious bedrooms are tastefully appointed with co-ordinated soft furnishings and have many thoughtful touches.

Rooms 10 (2 annexe)

HONITON
Devon

Map 4 ST10

The Deer Park Country House Hotel

★★★ 78% HOTEL

tel: 01404 41266 **Weston EX14 3PG**
email: admin@deerparkcountryhotel.co.uk **web:** www.deerparkcountryhotel.co.uk
dir: A30, take slip road into Honiton signed Turks Head. Next right then next left into Heathpark Industrial Estate. Hotel approx 1.6m

This country manor hotel is set in 80 acres of gardens, which includes an alfresco dining area with wood-burning oven and a walled kitchen garden. The hotel is just a short drive to Honiton and has easy access to the A30. The spacious accommodation is located in both the main house and separate recently refurbished garden rooms. Deer Park is ideal for both business and leisure guests, and its picturesque setting makes it ideal for weddings and events. The hotel also boasts the Priory Collection, the largest collection of sporting memorabilia in the country.

Rooms 32 (17 annexe) (2 fmly) (4 GF) ♠ **Facilities** FTV WiFi Fishing ♨ Beauty treatment room Clay shooting Archery Xmas New Year **Conf** Class 20 Board 20 Thtr 250 Del from £120 to £160* **Parking** 70 **Notes** Civ Wed 350

HOOK
Hampshire

Map 5 SU75

Raven Hotel

★★★ 67% HOTEL

tel: 01256 762541 **Station Rd RG27 9HS**
email: raven.hook@greeneking.co.uk **web:** www.oldenglish.co.uk
dir: From M3 junct 5, take 2nd exit at rdbt (B3349). Hotel 0.6m on the right, next to Hook railway station

This former coaching inn, conveniently located close to Hook railway station and a short distance from the M3, has been tastefully converted into a hotel. Bedrooms are comfortable and well appointed and have free WiFi. The popular restaurant offers an inviting menu of freshly prepared dishes plus daily-changing specials. Function rooms are available as is parking.

Rooms 41 (2 fmly) (5 GF) **S** £40-£90; **D** £50-£120 (incl. bkfst)* **Facilities** FTV WiFi ♦ New Year **Conf** Class 60 Board 70 Thtr 100 Del from £99 to £103* **Parking** 60 **Notes** ⊗

HOPE
Derbyshire

Map 16 SK18

Losehill House Hotel & Spa

★★★★ 78% HOTEL

tel: 01433 621219 **Lose Hill Ln, Edale Rd S33 6AF**
email: info@losehillhouse.co.uk **web:** www.losehillhouse.co.uk
dir: A6187 into Hope. Into Edale Rd opposite church. 1m, left & follow signs to hotel

Situated down a quiet leafy lane, this hotel occupies a secluded spot in the Peak District National Park. Bedrooms are comfortable and beautifully appointed. The outdoor hot tub, with stunning views over the valley, is a real indulgence; a heated swimming pool, sauna and spa treatments are also on offer. The views from the Orangery Restaurant are a real delight.

Rooms 24 (3 annexe) (4 fmly) (3 GF) ♠ **Facilities** Spa FTV WiFi ⊗ ♫ Xmas New Year **Conf** Class 20 Board 15 Thtr 30 Del from £175 to £265* **Services** Lift **Parking** 25 **Notes** ⊗ Civ Wed 100

HORLEY

Hotels are listed under Gatwick Airport

HORNCASTLE
Lincolnshire

Map 17 TF26

BEST WESTERN Admiral Rodney Hotel

★★★ 78% HOTEL

tel: 01507 523131 **North St LN9 5DX**
email: admiralrodney@bulldogmail.co.uk **web:** www.admiralrodney.com

The Admiral Rodney, a former coaching inn, is located in the picturesque town of Horncastle. Public areas are mostly open plan with a large lounge and bar area to relax in. The spacious bedrooms are well appointed and include up-to-date technology; free WiFi is also available throughout the hotel. A brasserie-style menu is served throughout the day and evening, and guests can eat in either the Courtyard Restaurant or alfresco when the weather's warmer. Large function rooms and extensive parking are all available. The staff are very welcoming.

Rooms 31 (4 fmly) (7 GF) **Facilities** STV FTV WiFi ♦ HL Xmas **Conf** Class 60 Board 40 Thtr 140 **Services** Lift **Parking** 60 **Notes** Civ Wed 100

HORSHAM
West Sussex   Map 6 TQ13

Premier Inn Horsham

BUDGET HOTEL

tel: 0871 527 8526 **57 North St RH12 1RB**
web: www.premierinn.com
dir: Opposite railway station, 5m from M23 junct 11

High quality, budget accommodation ideal for both families and business travellers. Spacious, en suite bedrooms feature tea and coffee making facilities, and Freeview TV in most hotels. Internet access and WiFi are available for a small fee. The adjacent family restaurant features a wide and varied menu. See also the Hotel Groups pages.

Rooms 40

HORSLEY
Derbyshire   Map 11 SK34

Horsley Lodge Hotel & Golf Club

★★★ 81% HOTEL

tel: 01332 780838 **Smalley Mill Rd DE21 5BL**
email: reception@horsleylodge.co.uk **web:** www.horsleylodge.co.uk
dir: M1 junct 25 (from the S) or junct 28 (from the N). Off A38 Coxbench / Little Eaton exit

This family-run hotel is full of character. Situated equidistant from Derby and Nottingham, it is ideal for exploring the Peak District. Bedrooms and bathrooms have stylish decor, beautiful fabrics and quality furnishings. Barn Cottage offers even greater luxury and is tucked away not far from the main building. The Brasserie overlooks the 18-hole golf course.

Rooms 14 (3 annexe) (2 fmly) (1 GF) ⓕ **S** £120-£140; **D** £130-£195 (incl. bkfst)*
Facilities FTV WiFi ⇘ ⚒ 18 Putt green Fishing Golf driving range Xmas New Year
Conf Class 70 Board 50 Thtr 100 **Parking** 100 **Notes** Civ Wed 100

HOUGHTON-LE-SPRING
Tyne & Wear   Map 19 NZ34

Chilton Country Pub & Hotel

★★★ 74% HOTEL

tel: 0191 385 2694 **Black Boy Rd, Chilton Moor, Fencehouses DH4 6PY**
email: reception@chiltoncountrypub.co.uk **web:** www.chiltoncountrypubandhotel.co.uk
dir: A1(M) junct 62, onto A690 towards Sunderland. Left at Rainton Bridge & Fencehouses sign, right at rdbt, next rdbt straight over, next left. At next junct left, hotel on right

This country pub and hotel has been extended from the original farm cottages. Bedrooms are modern and comfortable and some rooms are particularly spacious. This hotel is popular for weddings and functions; there is also a well stocked bar, and a wide range of dishes is served in the Orangery and restaurant.

Rooms 25 (7 fmly) (11 GF) ⓕ **S** £50-£70; **D** £55-£97 **Facilities** STV FTV WiFi ⇘ ⚒
Xmas **Conf** Class 50 Board 30 Thtr 150 Del £88 **Parking** 100 **Notes** LB ⊗

HOVE

See Brighton & Hove

HOWTOWN (NEAR POOLEY BRIDGE)
Cumbria   Map 18 NY41

INSPECTORS' CHOICE

Sharrow Bay Country House Hotel

★★★ ◉◉ ⬡ COUNTRY HOUSE HOTEL

tel: 017684 86301 **Sharrow Bay CA10 2LZ**
email: info@sharrowbay.co.uk **web:** www.sharrowbay.co.uk
dir: M6 junct 40. From Pooley Bridge right fork by church towards Howtown. Right at x-rds right, follow lakeside road for 2m

Enjoying breathtaking views and an idyllic location on the shores of Lake Ullswater, Sharrow Bay is often described as the first country-house hotel. Individually styled bedrooms, all with a host of thoughtful extras, are situated either in the main house, in delightful buildings in the grounds or at Bank House - an Elizabethan farmhouse complete with lounges and breakfast room. Opulently furnished public areas include a choice of inviting lounges and two elegant dining rooms.

Rooms 17 (10 annexe) (9 fmly) (8 GF) ⓕ **S** £130-£430; **D** £180-£480 (incl. bkfst)*
Facilities FTV WiFi ⚒ Xmas New Year **Conf** Class 15 Board 20 Thtr 40 Del from £330 to £580* **Parking** 28 **Notes** LB No children 8yrs Civ Wed 50

HOYLAKE
Merseyside   Map 15 SJ28

Holiday Inn Express Liverpool - Hoylake

BUDGET HOTEL

tel: 0151 632 2073 **The Kings Gap CH47 1HE**
email: info@hiexpresshoylake.com **web:** www.hiexpresshoylake.co.uk
dir: M53 towards Liverpool junct 2, then A551 towards Hoylake, at rdbt turn right onto The King's Gap. Hotel on right

A modern hotel ideal for families and business travellers. Fresh and uncomplicated, the spacious rooms include Sky TV, power shower and tea and coffee-making facilities. Continental buffet breakfast is included in the room rate; other meals may be taken at the nearby family pub or restaurant. See also the Hotel Groups pages.

Rooms 56 (24 fmly) (10 GF) ⓕ **Conf** Class 40 Board 40 Thtr 100

HUCKNALL
Nottinghamshire
Map 16 SK54

Premier Inn Nottingham North West (Hucknall)

BUDGET HOTEL

tel: 0871 527 8852 **Nottingham Rd NG15 7PY**
web: www.premierinn.com
dir: A611, A6002, straight on at 2 rdbts. Hotel 500yds on right

High quality, budget accommodation ideal for both families and business travellers. Spacious, en suite bedrooms feature tea and coffee making facilities, and Freeview TV in most hotels. Internet access and WiFi are available for a small fee. The adjacent family restaurant features a wide and varied menu. See also the Hotel Groups pages.

Rooms 35

HUDDERSFIELD
West Yorkshire
Map 16 SE11

Cedar Court Hotel

★★★★ 72% HOTEL

tel: 01422 375431 & 314001 **Ainley Top HD3 3RH**
email: sales@cedar-court-huddersfield.co.uk **web:** www.cedarcourthotels.co.uk
dir: 500yds from M62 junct 24

Sitting adjacent to the M62, this hotel is an ideal location for business travellers and for those touring the West Yorkshire area. Bedrooms are comfortably appointed; there is a busy lounge with snacks available all day, as well as a modern restaurant and a fully equipped leisure centre. In addition, the hotel has extensive meeting and banqueting facilities.

Rooms 113 (6 fmly) (9 GF) **S** £39-£129; **D** £39-£129* **Facilities** STV FTV WiFi ⅃ ☜ supervised Gym Steam room Sauna Xmas New Year **Conf** Class 150 Board 100 Thtr 500 Del from £89 to £199* **Services** Lift **Parking** 250 **Notes** LB Civ Wed 400

The Huddersfield Central Lodge

★★★ 74% METRO HOTEL

tel: 01484 515551 **11/15 Beast Market HD1 1QF**
email: joe@centrallodge.com **web:** www.centrallodge.com
dir: Off main town centre ring road, take turning for Kirkgate, town centre, 1st right & 1st right again. Hotel on left

This friendly, family-run Metro Hotel offers smart, spacious bedrooms, all en suite. Across a private courtyard from the main building are more rooms, many with kitchenettes. Public rooms include a fully licensed bar and lounge, a 40 square metre conservatory and an outdoor covered and heated smoking area. Large screen TVs are in all of these areas. Many recommended restaurants with a wide variety of cuisine are within a 5 to 10 minute walk from the Central Lodge. On site secure free parking is available to all guests along with free WiFi throughout.

Rooms 23 (4 fmly) (1 GF) (6 smoking) ☜ **S** £57-£65; **D** £66-£76 (incl. bkfst)* **Facilities** FTV WiFi ⅃ **Parking** 50

Premier Inn Huddersfield Central

BUDGET HOTEL

tel: 0871 527 8528 **St Andrews Way HD1 3AQ**
web: www.premierinn.com
dir: Telephone or see website for detailed directions

High quality, budget accommodation ideal for both families and business travellers. Spacious, en suite bedrooms feature tea and coffee making facilities, and Freeview TV in most hotels. Internet access and WiFi are available for a small fee. The adjacent family restaurant features a wide and varied menu. See also the Hotel Groups pages.

Rooms 52

Premier Inn Huddersfield West

BUDGET HOTEL

tel: 0871 527 8532 **New Hey Rd, Ainley Top HD2 2EA**
web: www.premierinn.com
dir: Just off M62 junct 24. From M62 take Brighouse exit from rdbt (A643). 1st left into Grimescar Rd, right into New Hey Rd

Rooms 42

315 Bar and Restaurant

◉ RESTAURANT WITH ROOMS

tel: 01484 602613 **315 Wakefield Rd, Lepton HD8 0LX**
email: info@315barandrestaurant.co.uk **web:** www.315barandrestaurant.co.uk
dir: M1 junct 38, A637 towards Huddersfield. At rdbt take A642 towards Huddersfield. Establishment on right in Lepton

In a wonderful setting, 315 Bar and Restaurant is very well presented and benefits from countryside views from the well-appointed dining room and conservatory areas. The interior is modern with open fires that add character and ambiance, while the chef's table gives a real insight into the working of the kitchen. Bedrooms are well-appointed and modern, and most have feature bathrooms. Staff are friendly and attentive, and there are excellent parking facilities.

Rooms 10 (3 fmly)

HUNGERFORD
Berkshire
Map 5 SU36

Littlecote House Hotel

Warner Leisure Hotels
Life begins at Warner

★★★★ 78% ◉◉ COUNTRY HOUSE HOTEL

tel: 01488 682509 **RG17 0SU**
email: marie.jones@bourne-leisure.co.uk **web:** www.warnerleisurehotels.co.uk
dir: M4 junct 14, A338, right onto A4, right onto B4192, left into Littlecote Road, hotel 0.5m on right at top of hill

This hotel provides comfortable, spacious accommodation and is located in stunning grounds close to the Cotswolds, only a 10-minute drive from Hungerford. There are traditional-style bedrooms in the ornate Grade I listed Tudor building and more contemporary rooms in the main building. Facilities include a regular programme of entertainment, beauty treatments and a choice of dining locations in either Oliver's Bistro or Pophams Restaurant. This is an adults-only (over 21 years) hotel.

Rooms 201 (12 annexe) (55 GF) ☜ **Facilities** Spa FTV WiFi HL ☜ ☻ Putt green ⅃ Gym ♫ Xmas New Year **Conf** Class 70 Board 30 Thtr 70 **Services** Lift **Parking** 520 **Notes** No children 21yrs Civ Wed 120

HUNGERFORD *continued*

Three Swans Hotel

★★★ 71% HOTEL

tel: 01488 682721 **117 High St RG17 0LZ**
email: info@threeswans.net **web:** www.threeswans.net
dir: M4 junct 14 follow signs to Hungerford. Hotel in High St on left

Centrally located in the bustling market town of Hungerford, this charming former inn, dating back some 700 years, has been renovated in a fresh and airy style. Visitors will still see the original arch under which the horse-drawn carriages once passed. There is a wood-panelled bar, a spacious lounge and attractive rear garden to relax in. The informal restaurant is decorated with artwork by local artists. Bedrooms are well appointed and comfortable.

Rooms 26 (10 annexe) (2 fmly) (5 GF) (3 smoking) ☏ **S** £85-£95; **D** £90-£100 (incl. bkfst)* **Facilities** FTV WiFi Access to local private gym Xmas New Year **Conf** Class 40 Board 30 Thtr 55 **Parking** 30

HUNSTANTON	Map 12 TF64
Norfolk	

BEST WESTERN Le Strange Arms Hotel

★★★★ 75% HOTEL

tel: 01485 534411 **Golf Course Rd, Old Hunstanton PE36 6JJ**
email: reception@lestrangearms.co.uk **web:** www.abacushotels.co.uk
dir: Off A149 1m N of Hunstanton. Left at sharp right bend by pitch & putt course

Le Strange Arms is an impressive hotel with superb views from the wide lawns down to the sandy beach and across The Wash. Bedrooms in the main house are individually decorated. Public rooms include the comfortable Oak House and lounge, open for meals from midday, and a conference and banqueting suite. There is a choice of dining options - The Le Strange Bistro, or the Ancient Mariner, a traditional inn adjacent to the hotel, serving good food and real ales.

Rooms 43 (7 annexe) (2 fmly) ☏ **Facilities** STV WiFi ☒ Xmas New Year **Conf** Class 150 Board 50 Thtr 180 **Services** Lift **Parking** 80 **Notes** ⊗ Civ Wed 70

Caley Hall Hotel

★★★ 85% ◉ HOTEL

tel: 01485 533486 **Old Hunstanton Rd PE36 6HH**
email: mail@caleyhallhotel.co.uk **web:** www.caleyhallhotel.co.uk
dir: 1m from Hunstanton, on A149

Situated within easy walking distance of the seafront, Caley Hall Hotel offers tastefully decorated bedrooms in a series of converted outbuildings. Each is smartly furnished and thoughtfully equipped. Public rooms feature a large open-plan lounge/bar with plush leather seating, and a restaurant offering an interesting choice of dishes.

Rooms 39 (20 fmly) (30 GF) ☏ **Facilities** STV FTV WiFi New Year **Parking** 50 **Notes** Closed 23-27 Dec & 4-17 Jan

The Neptune Restaurant with Rooms

 RESTAURANT WITH ROOMS

tel: 01485 532122 **85 Old Hunstanton Rd, Old Hunstanton PE36 6HZ**
email: reservations@theneptune.co.uk **web:** www.theneptune.co.uk
dir: On A149, past Hunstanton, 200mtrs on left after post office

This charming 18th-century coaching inn, now a restaurant with rooms, is ideally situated for touring the Norfolk coastline. The smartly appointed bedrooms are brightly finished with co-ordinated fabrics and hand-made New England furniture. Public rooms feature white clapboard walls, polished dark wood floors, fresh flowers and Lloyd Loom furniture. Obviously, the food is very much a draw here with the carefully prepared, award-winning cuisine utilising excellent local produce, from oysters and mussels from Thornham to quinces grown on a neighbouring farm.

Rooms 6

HUNTINGDON	Map 12 TL27
Cambridgeshire	

The Old Bridge Hotel

★★★ 87% ◉◉ HOTEL

tel: 01480 424300 **1 High St PE29 3TQ**
email: oldbridge@huntsbridge.co.uk **web:** www.huntsbridge.com
dir: From A14 or A1 follow Huntingdon signs. Hotel visible from inner ring road

The Old Bridge Hotel is an imposing 18th-century building situated close to shops and amenities. On offer is superb accommodation in stylish and individually decorated bedrooms that include many useful extras. Guests can choose from the same menu whether dining in the open-plan terrace, or the more formal restaurant with its bold colour scheme. There is also an excellent business centre.

Rooms 24 (2 fmly) (2 GF) ✿ **S** £89-£130; **D** £120-£230 (incl. bkfst) **Facilities** STV FTV WiFi ↻ Fishing Private mooring for boats Xmas New Year **Conf** Class 50 Board 30 Thtr 60 Del from £165 to £195* **Services** Air con **Parking** 50 **Notes** LB Civ Wed 100

The George

★★★ 73% HOTEL

 OldEnglish

tel: 01480 432444 **George St PE29 3AB**
email: 6457@greeneking.co.uk **web:** www.oldenglish.co.uk
dir: Exit A14 for Huntingdon racecourse. 3m to junct with ring road. Hotel opposite

This former coaching inn is ideally situated in the centre of town and was once the home of Oliver Cromwell's grandfather. The public rooms include a spacious lounge bar with plush seating, and a smart brasserie offering an interesting choice of dishes. Bedrooms are pleasantly decorated and equipped with modern facilities.

Rooms 26 (3 fmly) **Facilities** WiFi ↻ ♫ Xmas **Conf** Class 40 Board 40 Thtr 120 **Parking** 50 **Notes** Civ Wed 90

Premier Inn Huntingdon (A1/A14)

BUDGET HOTEL

 Premier Inn

tel: 0871 527 8540 **Great North Rd, Brampton PE28 4NQ**
web: www.premierinn.com
dir: At junct of A1 & A14. (NB from N do not use junct 14. Take exit for Huntingdon & Brampton). Access to hotel via Services

High quality, budget accommodation ideal for both families and business travellers. Spacious, en suite bedrooms feature tea and coffee making facilities, and Freeview TV in most hotels. Internet access and WiFi are available for a small fee. The adjacent family restaurant features a wide and varied menu. See also the Hotel Groups pages.

Rooms 80

HYDE
Greater Manchester

Map 16 SJ99

Premier Inn Manchester (Hyde)

BUDGET HOTEL

Premier Inn

tel: 0871 527 8712 **Stockport Rd, Mottram SK14 3AU**
web: www.premierinn.com
dir: At end of M67 between A57 & A560

High quality, budget accommodation ideal for both families and business travellers. Spacious, en suite bedrooms feature tea and coffee making facilities, and Freeview TV in most hotels. Internet access and WiFi are available for a small fee. The adjacent family restaurant features a wide and varied menu. See also the Hotel Groups pages.

Rooms 83

HYTHE
Kent

Map 7 TR13

Mercure Hythe Imperial

★★★★ 73% HOTEL

Mercure HOTELS

tel: 01303 267441 **Princes Pde CT21 6AE**
email: h6862@accor.com **web:** www.mercure.com
dir: M20, junct 11 onto A261. In Hythe follow Folkestone signs. Right into Twiss Rd to hotel

This imposing seafront hotel is enhanced by impressive grounds including a 13-green golf course, tennis court and extensive gardens. Bedrooms are varied in style but all offer modern facilities, and many enjoy stunning sea views. The elegant restaurant, bar and lounges are traditional in style and retain many original features. The leisure club includes a gym, a squash court, an indoor pool, and a spa offering a range of luxury treatments.

Rooms 100 (11 fmly) (6 GF) ✿ **Facilities** Spa FTV WiFi ↻ ⓢ ⌕ 13 ⌣ Putt green Gym Squash Snooker & pool table Aerobic studio Table tennis Sauna Steam room ♫ Xmas New Year **Conf** Class 120 Board 80 Thtr 220 **Services** Lift **Parking** 207 **Notes** Civ Wed 120

ILFORD
Greater London

Premier Inn Ilford

BUDGET HOTEL PLAN 1 H5

Premier Inn

tel: 0871 527 8542 **Redbridge Lane East IG4 5BG**
web: www.premierinn.com
dir: At end of M11 follow London East, A12 & Chelmsford signs onto A12, hotel on left at bottom of slip road

High quality, budget accommodation ideal for both families and business travellers. Spacious, en suite bedrooms feature tea and coffee making facilities, and Freeview TV in most hotels. Internet access and WiFi are available for a small fee. The adjacent family restaurant features a wide and varied menu. See also the Hotel Groups pages.

Rooms 44

ILFRACOMBE
Devon

Map 3 SS54

Sandy Cove Hotel

★★★ 75% ◉ HOTEL

tel: 01271 882 243 **Old Coast Rd, Combe Martin Bay, Berrynarbor EX34 9SR**
email: info@sandycove-hotel.co.uk **web:** www.sandycove-hotel.co.uk
dir: A339 to Combe Martin, through village towards Ilfracombe for approx 1m. Turn right just over brow of hill marked Sandy Cove

This hotel enjoys a truly spectacular position, with front-facing bedrooms that benefit from uninterrupted views of the north Devon coastline. In addition, guests can relax on the sea decks or in the terraced garden, and really appreciate the peace and tranquillity. Locally sourced produce is a feature of the menus offered in the dining room, which makes the perfect setting for a romantic dinner or a family gathering.

Rooms 36 (15 fmly) (7 GF) ✿ **S** £70-£95; **D** £90-£200 (incl. bkfst & dinner)* **Facilities** WiFi ↻ ⓢ ⌕ Sauna Steam room Heated relaxation loungers Xmas New Year **Conf** Class 20 Board 30 Thtr 30 **Parking** 45 **Notes** LB Civ Wed 150

ILFRACOMBE *continued*

Darnley Hotel

★★ 78% HOTEL

tel: 01271 863955 **3 Belmont Rd EX34 8DR**
email: darnleyhotel@yahoo.co.uk **web:** www.darnleyhotel.co.uk
dir: A361 to Barnstaple & Ilfracombe. Left at Church Hill, 1st left into Belmont Rd. 3rd entrance on left under walled arch

Standing in award-winning, mature gardens, with a wooded path to the High Street and the beach (about a five minute stroll away), this former Victorian gentleman's residence offers friendly, informal service. The individually furnished and decorated bedrooms vary in size. Dinners feature honest home cooking, with 'old fashioned puddings' always proving popular.

Rooms 8 (2 fmly) (2 GF) 🐾 **S** £40-£45; **D** £70-£86 (incl. bkfst) **Facilities** FTV WiFi Xmas **Parking** 10 **Notes** No children 3yrs

Imperial Hotel

★★ 72% HOTEL

tel: 01271 862536 **Wilder Rd EX34 9AL**
email: imperial.ilfracombe@alfatravel.co.uk **web:** www.leisureplex.co.uk
dir: Opposite Landmark Theatre

This popular hotel is just a short walk from the shops and harbour, overlooking gardens and the sea. Public areas include the spacious sun lounge, where guests can relax and enjoy the excellent views. Comfortable bedrooms are well equipped, with several having the added bonus of sea views.

Rooms 104 (6 fmly) 🐾 **Facilities** FTV WiFi 🎵 Xmas New Year **Services** Lift **Parking** 7 **Notes** ⊗ Closed Dec-Feb (ex Xmas) RS Mar & Nov

ILKLEY
West Yorkshire
Map 19 SE14

The Craiglands Hotel

★★★ 70% HOTEL

tel: 01943 430001 & 886450 **Cowpasture Rd LS29 8RQ**
email: reservations@craiglands.co.uk **web:** www.craiglands.co.uk
dir: A65 into Ilkley. Left at T-junct. Past rail station, fork right into Cowpasture Rd. Hotel opposite school

This grand Victorian hotel is situated close to the town centre. Spacious public areas and a good range of services are ideal for business or leisure. Extensive conference facilities are available along with an elegant restaurant and traditionally styled bar and lounge. Bedrooms, varying in size and style, are comfortably furnished and well equipped.

Rooms 62 (4 fmly) 🐾 **S** £59-£119; **D** £69-£129 (incl. bkfst)* **Facilities** FTV WiFi 🛁 Xmas New Year **Conf** Class 200 Board 100 Thtr 500 Del from £84* **Services** Lift **Parking** 200 **Notes** LB ⊗ Civ Wed 500

ILSINGTON
Devon
Map 3 SX77

Ilsington Country House Hotel

★★★ 86% ◎◎ COUNTRY HOUSE HOTEL

tel: 01364 661452 **Ilsington Village TQ13 9RR**
email: hotel@ilsington.co.uk **web:** www.ilsington.co.uk
dir: M5 onto A38 to Plymouth. Exit at Bovey Tracey. 3rd exit from rdbt to 'Ilsington', then 1st right. Hotel in 5m by Post Office

This friendly, family-owned hotel, offers tranquillity and far-reaching views from its elevated position on the southern slopes of Dartmoor. The stylish suites and bedrooms, some on the ground floor, are individually furnished. The restaurant provides a stunning backdrop for the innovative, daily-changing menus which feature local fish, meat and game. Additional facilities include an indoor pool and the Blue Tiger Inn, where a pint, a bite to eat and convivial banter can all be enjoyed.

Rooms 25 (4 fmly) (6 GF) 🐾 **S** £90-£110; **D** £110-£220 (incl. bkfst)* **Facilities** FTV WiFi ⊗ supervised 🏊 Gym Steam room Sauna Beauty treatment rooms Xmas New Year **Conf** Class 60 Board 40 Thtr 100 Del from £140 to £155* **Services** Lift **Parking** 100 **Notes** LB Civ Wed 120

INSTOW
Devon
Map 3 SS43

Commodore Hotel

★★★ 82% HOTEL

tel: 01271 860347 **Marine Pde EX39 4JN**
email: admin@commodore-instow.co.uk **web:** www.commodore-instow.co.uk
dir: M5 junct 27 follow N Devon link road to Bideford. Right before bridge, hotel in 3m

Maintaining its links with the local maritime and rural communities, The Commodore provides an interesting place to stay. Situated at the mouth of the Taw and Torridge rivers and overlooking a sandy beach, it offers well-equipped bedrooms, many with balconies. There are five ground-floor suites. Eating options include the restaurant, the Quarterdeck bar, or the terrace in the warmer months.

Rooms 25 (1 fmly) (5 GF) 🐾 **S** £69-£100; **D** £140-£240 (incl. bkfst & dinner)* **Facilities** FTV WiFi 🛁 Xmas New Year **Parking** 200 **Notes** LB ⊗ No children 3yrs

IPSWICH
Suffolk
Map 13 TM14

Hintlesham Hall Hotel

★★★★ ◎◎ HOTEL

tel: 01473 652334 **George St IP8 3NS**
email: reservations@hintleshamhall.com **web:** www.hintleshamhall.com

(For full entry see Hintlesham)

Salthouse Harbour Hotel

★★★★ ◉◉ TOWN HOUSE HOTEL

tel: 01473 226789 **No 1 Neptune Quay IP4 1AX**
email: staying@salthouseharbour.co.uk **web:** www.salthouseharbour.co.uk
dir: From A14 junct 56 follow signs for town centre, then Salthouse signs

Situated just a short walk from the town centre, this waterfront warehouse conversion is a clever mix of contemporary styles and original features. The hotel is stylishly designed throughout with modern art, sculptures, interesting artefacts and striking colours. The spacious bedrooms provide luxurious comfort; some have feature bathrooms and some have balconies. Two air-conditioned penthouse suites, with stunning views, have extras such as state-of-the-art sound systems and telescopes. Award-winning food is served in the busy, ground-floor brasserie, and alfresco eating is possible in warmer weather.

Rooms 70 (6 fmly) ☊ **Facilities** FTV WiFi **Services** Lift **Parking** 30

milsoms Kesgrave Hall

★★★★ 77% ◉ HOTEL

tel: 01473 333741 **Hall Rd, Kesgrave IP5 2PU**
email: reception@kesgravehall.com **web:** www.milsomshotels.com/kesgravehall
dir: A12 N of Ipswich, left at Ipswich/Woodbridge rdbt onto A1214. Right after 0.5m into Hall Rd. Hotel 200yds on left

Kesgrave Hall is a superb 18th-century, Grade II listed Georgian mansion set amidst 38 acres of mature grounds. Appointed in a contemporary style, the large

open-plan public areas include a smart bar, a lounge with plush sofas, and a restaurant where guests can watch the chefs in action. Bedrooms are tastefully appointed and thoughtfully equipped.

Rooms 23 (8 annexe) (3 fmly) (8 GF) ☊ **D** £130-£305 (incl. bkfst)* **Facilities** STV FTV WiFi ⇘ ⚘ Xmas **Conf** Class 200 Board 24 Thtr 600 Del £165* **Parking** 100 **Notes** LB Civ Wed

Novotel Ipswich Centre

★★★★ 73% HOTEL

tel: 01473 232400 **Greyfriars Rd IP1 1UP**
email: h0995@accor.com **web:** www.novotel.com
dir: From A14 towards Felixstowe. Left onto A137, 2m into town centre. Hotel on double rdbt by Stoke Bridge

This modern, red brick hotel is perfectly placed in the centre of town close to shops, bars and restaurants. The open-plan public areas include a Mediterranean-style restaurant and a bar with a small games area. The bedrooms are smartly appointed and have many thoughtful touches; three rooms are suitable for less mobile guests.

Rooms 101 (8 fmly) ☊ **S** £49-£115; **D** £49-£115* **Facilities** STV FTV WiFi ⇘ HL Gym Xmas New Year **Conf** Class 100 Board 45 Thtr 180 Del from £135 to £160* **Services** Lift Air con **Parking** 53 **Notes** Civ Wed 150

BEST WESTERN Claydon Country House Hotel

★★★ 81% ◉ HOTEL

tel: 01473 830382 **16-18 Ipswich Rd, Claydon IP6 0AR**
email: enquiries@hotelsipswich.com **web:** www.hotelsipswich.com
dir: From A14, NW of Ipswich. After 4m take Great Blakenham Rd (B1113) to Claydon, hotel on left

A delightful hotel situated just off the A14, within easy driving distance of the town centre. The pleasantly decorated bedrooms are thoughtfully equipped and one room has a lovely four-poster bed. An interesting choice of freshly prepared dishes is available in the smart restaurant, and guests have the use of a relaxing lounge bar.

Rooms 36 (3 fmly) (12 GF) ☊ **Facilities** FTV WiFi ⇘ Xmas New Year **Conf** Class 50 Board 40 Thtr 80 Del from £120 to £135* **Services** Air con **Parking** 85 **Notes** ⊗ Civ Wed 75

IPSWICH *continued*

BEST WESTERN Gatehouse Hotel

★★★ 80% HOTEL

tel: 01473 741897 **799 Old Norwich Rd IP1 6LH**
email: enquiries@gatehousehotel.com **web:** www.gatehousehotel.com
dir: A14 junct 53, A1156 signed Ipswich, left at lights into Norwich Rd, hotel on left

A Regency-style property set amidst three acres of landscaped grounds, on the outskirts of town in a quiet road just a short drive from the A14. The spacious bedrooms have co-ordinated soft furnishings and many thoughtful touches. Public rooms include a smart lounge bar, an intimate restaurant and a cosy drawing room with plush leather sofas.

Rooms 15 (4 annexe) (1 fmly) (6 GF) ⋒ **Facilities** STV FTV WiFi ⇗ Xmas **Parking** 25 **Notes** ⊗

Ramada Encore Ipswich

★★★ 78% HOTEL

tel: 01473 694600 **Ranelagh Rd IP2 0AD**
email: reservations@encoreipswich.co.uk **web:** www.encoreipswich.co.uk
dir: A14/A1214. Hotel 0.3m from Ipswich rail station

A modern purpose-built hotel situated close to the railway station and within easy walking distance of Ipswich Town FC. The contemporary open-plan public areas feature a smart lounge bar which leads through to the bright and airy restaurant. The smart bedrooms are very well equipped and have interactive flat-screen TVs with internet access. The hotel also has a small gym.

Rooms 126 (9 fmly) (16 GF) ⋒ **Facilities** WiFi HL Gym **Conf** Class 16 Board 20 Thtr 35 **Services** Lift Air con **Parking** 24 **Notes** ⊗

Premier Inn Ipswich (Chantry Park)

BUDGET HOTEL

tel: 0871 527 8548 **Old Hadleigh Rd IP8 3AR**
web: www.premierinn.com
dir: From A12/A14 junct take A1214 to Ipswich town centre. Left at lights by Holiday Inn, left onto A1071. At mini rdbt turn right. Hotel on right

High quality, budget accommodation ideal for both families and business travellers. Spacious, en suite bedrooms feature tea and coffee making facilities, and Freeview TV in most hotels. Internet access and WiFi are available for a small fee. The adjacent family restaurant features a wide and varied menu. See also the Hotel Groups pages.

Rooms 49

Premier Inn Ipswich North

BUDGET HOTEL

tel: 0871 527 8550 **Paper Mill Ln, Claydon IP6 0BE**
web: www.premierinn.com
dir: A14 junct 52. At rdbt exit onto Paper Mill Lane. Hotel 1st left

Rooms 59

Premier Inn Ipswich South

BUDGET HOTEL

tel: 0871 527 8552 **Bourne Hill, Wherstead IP2 8ND**
web: www.premierinn.com
dir: From A14 follow Ipswich Central A137 signs, then Ipswich Central & Docks signs. At bottom of hill at rdbt 2nd exit. Hotel on right

Rooms 40

Premier Inn Ipswich South East

BUDGET HOTEL

tel: 0871 527 8554 **Augusta Close, Ransomes Euro Park IP3 9SS**
web: www.premierinn.com
dir: A14 junct 57, stay in right lane. At rdbt 2nd exit, then 1st left. Hotel adjacent to Swallow Restaurant

Rooms 20

Premier Inn Ipswich Town Centre (Quayside)

BUDGET HOTEL

tel: 0871 527 9388 **33 Key St IP4 1BZ**
web: www.premierinn.com

Rooms 85

IREBY	Map 18 NY23
Cumbria	

Overwater Hall

★★★ 87% ◉◉ COUNTRY HOUSE HOTEL

tel: 017687 76566 **CA7 1HH**
email: welcome@overwaterhall.co.uk **web:** www.overwaterhall.co.uk
dir: From A591 take turn to Ireby at Castle Inn. Hotel signed after 2m on right

This privately owned country house dates back to 1811 and is set in lovely gardens surrounded by woodland. The owners have lovingly restored this Georgian property over the years paying great attention to the authenticity of the original design; guests will receive warm hospitality and attentive service in a relaxed manner. The elegant and well appointed bedrooms include the more spacious Superior Rooms and the Garden Room; all bedrooms have WiFi. Creative dishes are served in the traditional-style dining room.

Rooms 11 (2 fmly) (1 GF) ⋒ **S** £100-£175; **D** £200-£290 (incl. bkfst & dinner)*
Facilities FTV WiFi ⇗ Xmas New Year **Parking** 20 **Notes** LB Closed 2-16 Jan Civ Wed 30

KEGWORTH

See East Midlands Airport

KEIGHLEY
West Yorkshire
Map 19 SE04

Dalesgate Hotel

★★ 70% HOTEL

tel: 01535 664930 **406 Skipton Rd, Utley BD20 6HP**
email: info@dalesgate.co.uk **web:** www.dalesgate.co.uk
dir: In town centre follow A629 over rdbt onto B6265. Right after 0.75m into St. John's Rd. 1st right into hotel car park

Originally the residence of a local chapel minister, this modern, well-established hotel provides well-equipped, comfortable bedrooms. It also boasts a cosy bar and pleasant restaurant, serving an imaginative range of dishes. A large car park is provided to the rear.

Rooms 20 (2 fmly) (3 GF) **Parking** 25 **Notes** RS 22 Dec-4 Jan

Premier Inn Bradford North (Bingley)

BUDGET HOTEL

tel: 0871 527 8134 **502 Bradford Rd, Sandbeds BD20 5NG**
web: www.premierinn.com
dir: M62 juncts 26 or 27 follow A650/Keighley & Skipton signs. From Bingley Bypass (A650 Cottingley) right at 1st rdbt signed Crossflatts & Micklethwaite. Hotel 50yds on left. (NB for Sat Nav use BD20 5NH)

High quality, budget accommodation ideal for both families and business travellers. Spacious, en suite bedrooms feature tea and coffee making facilities, and Freeview TV in most hotels. Internet access and WiFi are available for a small fee. The adjacent family restaurant features a wide and varied menu. See also the Hotel Groups pages.

Rooms 40

KENDAL
Cumbria
Map 18 SD59

See also **Crooklands**

BEST WESTERN PLUS Castle Green Hotel in Kendal

★★★★ 77% ◉◉ HOTEL

tel: 01539 734000 **LA9 6RG**
email: reception@castlegreen.co.uk **web:** www.castlegreen.co.uk
dir: M6 junct 37, A684 towards Kendal. Hotel on right in 5m

This smart, modern hotel enjoys a peaceful location and is conveniently situated for access to both the town centre and the M6. Stylish bedrooms are thoughtfully equipped for both the business and leisure guest. The Greenhouse Restaurant provides imaginative dishes and boasts a theatre kitchen; alternatively Alexander's

Pub serves food all day. The hotel has a fully equipped business centre and leisure club.

Rooms 99 (3 fmly) (25 GF) ⚓ **Facilities** Spa FTV WiFi ⓑ ⓒ Gym Steam room Aerobics Yoga Beauty salon Xmas New Year **Conf** Class 120 Board 100 Thtr 300 Del from £135 to £155* **Services** Lift **Parking** 200 **Notes** ⊗ Civ Wed 250

Stonecross Manor Hotel

★★★ 72% HOTEL

tel: 01539 733559 **Milnthorpe Rd LA9 5HP**
email: info@stonecrossmanor.co.uk **web:** www.stonecrossmanor.co.uk
dir: M6 junct 36, A590, follow signs to Windermere, take exit for Kendal South. Hotel just past 30mph sign on left

Located on the edge of Kendal, this smart hotel offers a good combination of traditional style and modern facilities. Bedrooms are comfortable, well equipped and some feature four-poster beds. Guests can relax in the lounges or bar and enjoy an extensive choice of home cooked meals in the pleasant restaurant. Facilities also include a swimming pool.

Rooms 30 (4 fmly) **S** £85-£158; **D** £99-£169 (incl. bkfst)* **Facilities** FTV WiFi ⓑ HL ⓒ Xmas New Year **Conf** Class 80 Board 40 Thtr 140 Del from £110 to £130* **Services** Lift **Parking** 55 **Notes** LB Civ Wed 130

Premier Inn Kendal Central

BUDGET HOTEL

tel: 0871 527 8562 **Maude St LA9 4QD**
web: www.premierinn.com
dir: M6 junct 36, A591 to Kendal. (NB ignore exit for Kendal South). At Plumbgarm Rdbt take 3rd exit, 0.5m to Kendal. Hotel on right

High quality, budget accommodation ideal for both families and business travellers. Spacious, en suite bedrooms feature tea and coffee making facilities, and Freeview TV in most hotels. Internet access and WiFi are available for a small fee. The adjacent family restaurant features a wide and varied menu. See also the Hotel Groups pages.

Rooms 55

K

KENILWORTH
Warwickshire
Map 10 SP27

Chesford Grange

QHOTELS
INSPIRED BY YOU

★★★★ 77% HOTEL

tel: 01926 859331 **Chesford Bridge CV8 2LD**
email: chesfordreservations@qhotels.co.uk **web:** www.qhotels.co.uk
dir: 0.5m SE of junct A46/A452. At rdbt turn right signed Leamington Spa, follow signs to hotel

This much-extended hotel set in 17 acres of private grounds is well situated for Birmingham International Airport, the NEC and major routes. Bedrooms range from traditional style to contemporary rooms featuring state-of-the-art technology. Public areas include a leisure club and extensive conference and banqueting facilities. QHotels is the AA Hotel Group of the Year 2014-15.

Rooms 205 (20 fmly) (43 GF) 🐾 **Facilities** Spa STV WiFi 🦢 🛞 supervised Gym Steam room Solarium Xmas New Year **Conf** Class 350 Board 50 Thtr 710 **Services** Lift **Parking** 650 **Notes** Civ Wed 700

KENTISBURY
Devon
Map 3 SS64

Kentisbury Grange

★★★★ 76% 🏵🏵 HOTEL

tel: 01271 882295 **EX31 4NL**
email: reception@kentisburygrange.co.uk **web:** www.kentisburygrange.com
dir: From Barnstaple take A3125. At rdbt take 2nd exit onto A39 to Burrington through Shirwell and Arlington. After Kentisbury Ford, follow signposts for hotel for approx 0.75m.

High quality and comfort are in generous supply at this proud Victorian country house. Total refurbishment has resulted in an impressive blend of traditional elegance and contemporary luxury. Bedrooms and bathrooms offer the pampering touches which make all the difference, thus ensuring a relaxing and rewarding stay. The Coach House restaurant is the venue for dining, where a skilled kitchen team maximise the benefits of excellent local produce. Surrounded by the stunning North Devon countryside and a short drive from the superb beaches, this is a great base from which to explore all the area has to offer.

Rooms 16 (5 annexe) (9 GF) 🐾 **S** £125-£260; **D** £125-£260 (incl. bkfst)*
Facilities FTV WiFi 🦢 Xmas New Year **Conf** Del £188* **Services** Air con **Notes** LB 🛞 Civ Wed

---

KENTON
Greater London

Premier Inn London Harrow

Premier Inn

BUDGET HOTEL PLAN 1 C5

tel: 0871 527 8664 **Kenton Rd HA3 8AT**
web: www.premierinn.com
dir: M1 junct 5, follow Harrow & Kenton signs. Hotel between Harrow & Wembley on A4006 opposite Kenton railway station

High quality, budget accommodation ideal for both families and business travellers. Spacious, en suite bedrooms feature tea and coffee making facilities, and Freeview TV in most hotels. Internet access and WiFi are available for a small fee. The adjacent family restaurant features a wide and varied menu. See also the Hotel Groups pages.

Rooms 101

KESWICK
Cumbria
Map 18 NY22

Dale Head Hall Lakeside Hotel

★★★ 82% COUNTRY HOUSE HOTEL

tel: 017687 72478 **Lake Thirlmere CA12 4TN**
email: onthelakeside@daleheadhall.co.uk **web:** www.daleheadhall.co.uk
dir: Between Keswick & Grasmere. Exit A591 onto private drive

Set in attractive, tranquil grounds on the shores of Lake Thirlmere, this historic lakeside residence dates from the 16th century. Comfortable and inviting public areas include a choice of lounges and a traditionally furnished restaurant featuring a daily-changing menu. Most bedrooms are spacious and have views of the lake or surrounding mountains.

Rooms 12 (1 fmly) (2 GF) 🐾 **S** £105-£125; **D** £140-£350 (incl. bkfst) **Facilities** STV WiFi 🐟 Fishing 🎣 Fishing permits Boating Xmas New Year **Conf** Class 20 Board 20 Thtr 20 Del from £165 to £185 **Parking** 34 **Notes** LB 🛞 Closed 3-30 Jan Civ Wed 50

Skiddaw Hotel

LAKE DISTRICT ▪▪▪▪▪ HOTELS

★★★ 80% HOTEL

tel: 017687 72071 **Main St CA12 5BN**
email: info@skiddawhotel.co.uk **web:** www.lakedistricthotels.net/skiddawhotel
dir: A66 to Keswick, follow town centre signs. Hotel in market square

Occupying a central position overlooking the market square, this hotel provides smartly furnished bedrooms that include several family suites and a room with a four-poster bed. In addition to the restaurant, food is served all day in the bar and in the conservatory. There is also a quiet residents' lounge and two conference rooms.

Rooms 43 (7 fmly) ✦ **S** fr £94; **D** fr £187 (incl. bkfst) **Facilities** STV WiFi Use of leisure facilities at sister hotels (3m) ♫ Xmas New Year **Conf** Class 60 Board 40 Thtr 70 Del from £115 **Services** Lift **Parking** 35 **Notes** Civ Wed 90

Keswick Country House Hotel

★★★ 77% HOTEL

tel: 0844 811 5580 **Station Rd CA12 4NQ**
email: reservations@choicehotels.co.uk **web:** www.thekeswickhotel.co.uk
dir: M6 junct 40, A66, 1st slip road into Keswick, then follow signs for leisure pool

This impressive Victorian hotel is set amid attractive gardens close to the town centre. Eight superior bedrooms are available in the Station Wing, which is accessed through a conservatory. The attractively appointed main house rooms are modern in style and offer a good range of amenities. Public areas include a well-stocked bar, a spacious and relaxing lounge, and a restaurant serving interesting dinners.

Rooms 70 (6 fmly) (4 GF) ✦ **S** £45-£120; **D** £84-£188 (incl. bkfst & dinner) **Facilities** FTV WiFi Putt green ⛳ Xmas New Year **Conf** Class 70 Board 60 Thtr 110 Del from £97.50 to £128.50 **Services** Lift **Parking** 70 **Notes** LB ⊗ Civ Wed 100

Kings Arms Hotel

LAKE DISTRICT HOTELS

★★★ 71% HOTEL

tel: 017687 72083 **27 Main St CA12 5BL**
email: kingsarms@lakedistricthotels.net **web:** www.lakedistricthotels.net/kingsarms

Located in the heart of Keswick, the Kings Arms Hotel offers modern, tastefully refurbished bedrooms and en suites, alongside intimate public areas and a choice of two restaurants. The bar offers some great local real ales and changing guest beers. The small hands-on team offer friendly and relaxed service.

Rooms 13 ✦ **D** fr £137 (incl. bkfst) **Facilities** FTV WiFi Complimentary leisure club membership at sister hotel Xmas

Swinside Lodge Country House Hotel

★★ 85% COUNTRY HOUSE HOTEL

tel: 017687 72948 **Grange Rd, Newlands CA12 5UE**
email: info@swinsidelodge-hotel.co.uk **web:** www.swinsidelodge-hotel.co.uk
dir: A66, left at Portinscale to Grange, 2m (NB ignore signs to Swinside). Hotel on right

Surrounded by fells, this beautifully maintained Georgian property is situated at the foot of Cat Bells and is only a five-minute stroll from the shores of Derwentwater.

Guests are made to feel genuinely welcome, with the friendly proprietors on hand to provide attentive service. The elegantly furnished lounges are an ideal place to relax before dinner. The four-course set dinner menu is creative, featuring high quality ingredients and beautifully presented dishes.

Rooms 7 (7 fmly) ✦ **S** £128-£144; **D** £212-£304 (incl. bkfst & dinner)* **Facilities** WiFi **Parking** 12 **Notes** LB No children 12yrs Closed 9 Dec-1 Feb

KETTERING Map 11 SP87
Northamptonshire

INSPECTORS' CHOICE

Rushton Hall Hotel and Spa

★★★★ COUNTRY HOUSE HOTEL

tel: 01536 713001 **NN14 1RR**
email: enquiries@rushtonhall.com **web:** www.rushtonhall.com
dir: A14 junct 7, A43 to Corby then A6003 to Rushton, turn after bridge

Rushton Hall is an elegant country house hotel set amidst 30 acres of parkland and surrounded by open countryside. The stylish public rooms include a library, a superb open-plan lounge bar with a magnificent vaulted ceiling and plush sofas, and an oak-panelled dining hall, where Adrian Coulthard oversees a very high quality operation. The tastefully appointed bedrooms have co-ordinated fabrics and many thoughtful touches.

Rooms 46 (5 fmly) (2 GF) ✦ **S** £160-£390; **D** £160-£390 (incl. bkfst)* **Facilities** Spa FTV WiFi ❄ Gym Billiard table Sauna Steam room Xmas New Year **Conf** Class 100 Board 40 Thtr 200 Del from £180 to £220* **Services** Lift **Parking** 140 **Notes** ⊗ Civ Wed 160

Kettering Park Hotel & Spa

shire

★★★★ 80% HOTEL

tel: 01536 416666 **Kettering Parkway NN15 6XT**
email: kpark@shirehotels.com **web:** www.ketteringparkhotel.com
dir: Exit A14 junct 9 (M1 to A1 link road), hotel in Kettering Venture Park

Expect a warm welcome at this stylish hotel situated just off the A14. The spacious, smartly decorated bedrooms are well equipped and meticulously maintained. Guests can choose from classical or contemporary dishes in the restaurant and lighter meals that are served in the bar. The extensive leisure facilities are impressive.

Rooms 119 (29 fmly) (35 GF) **S** £90-£200; **D** £90-£200* **Facilities** STV FTV WiFi ❄ HL ❄ Gym Steam room Sauna Beauty treatment room Children's splash pool Activity studio New Year **Conf** Class 120 Board 40 Thtr 260 Del from £145 to £185* **Services** Lift Air con **Parking** 200 **Notes** LB ⊗ Civ Wed 120

KETTERING *continued*

Barton Hall Hotel

★★★ 82% HOTEL

tel: 01536 515505 **Barton Rd, Barton Seagrave NN15 6SG**
email: enquiries@bartonhall.com **web:** www.bartonhall.com
dir: From A14 take junct 10 onto Barton Rd. Hotel on the right approx 0.5m

Barton Hall Hotel has benefited from recent refurbishment and now offers modern and comfortable accommodation to suit both business and leisure guests. All of the rooms include 40" Smart TVs with complementary WiFi throughout. Dinner can be enjoyed in Vines Brasserie, which serves a traditional menu in a relaxing and friendly environment.

Rooms 18 (3 fmly) (3 GF) ⟑ S £100-£120; **D** £100-£220 (incl. bkfst)* **Facilities** FTV WiFi ⇗ **Conf** Class 150 Board 60 Thtr 300 Del £145* **Parking** 80 **Notes** ⊗ Civ Wed 160

Naseby Hotel

★★★ 72% HOTEL

tel: 01536 734736 **Sheep St NN16 0AN**
email: nasebyhotel@yahoo.co.uk **web:** www.nasebyhotel.co.uk
dir: A14 junct 8, left at rdbt, follow road to set of lights. At rdbt take middle lane, straight over & left at lights. Hotel on left

Situated in the heart of Kettering, and originally built in the 16th century, this hotel has a sleek modern interior along with some lovely original features. There is a good range of stylish, modern bedrooms. Secure parking is available, as is free WiFi.

Rooms 41 (1 fmly) (3 GF) **Facilities** FTV WiFi ⇗ Xmas New Year **Conf** Class 100 Board 80 Thtr 200 **Services** Air con **Parking** 15 **Notes** ⊗

Premier Inn Kettering

BUDGET HOTEL

tel: 0871 527 8564 **Rothwell Rd NN16 8XF**
web: www.premierinn.com
dir: Off A14 junct 7

High quality, budget accommodation ideal for both families and business travellers. Spacious, en suite bedrooms feature tea and coffee making facilities, and Freeview TV in most hotels. Internet access and WiFi are available for a small fee. The adjacent family restaurant features a wide and varied menu. See also the Hotel Groups pages.

Rooms 59

KIDDERMINSTER   Map 10 SO87
Worcestershire

BEST WESTERN Stone Manor Hotel

★★★★ 72% ⊛ HOTEL

tel: 01562 777555 **Stone DY10 4PJ**
email: enquiries@stonemanorhotel.co.uk **web:** www.stonemanorhotel.co.uk
dir: 2.5m from Kidderminster on A448, on right

This converted, much extended former manor house stands in 25 acres of impressive grounds and gardens. The well-equipped accommodation includes rooms with four-poster beds and luxuriously appointed annexe bedrooms. Quality furnishing and decor styles throughout the public areas highlight the intrinsic charm of the interior; the hotel is a popular venue for wedding receptions.

Rooms 57 (5 annexe) (7 GF) **Facilities** STV WiFi ⇗ ↘ ☃ ⤴ Pool table Complimentary use of local leisure centre **Conf** Class 48 Board 60 Thtr 150 **Parking** 400 **Notes** ⊗ Civ Wed 150

The Granary Hotel & Restaurant

★★★ 80% ⊛⊛ HOTEL

tel: 01562 777535 **Heath Ln, Shenstone DY10 4BS**
email: info@granary-hotel.co.uk **web:** www.granary-hotel.co.uk
dir: On A450 between Stourbridge & Worcester, 1m from Kidderminster

This modern hotel offers spacious, well-equipped accommodation with many rooms enjoying views towards Great Witley and the Amberley Hills. Public areas include a bar and a residents' lounge. The attractive, modern restaurant serves dishes created from locally sourced produce that is cooked with flair and imagination. There are also extensive conference facilities, and the hotel is popular as a wedding venue.

Rooms 18 (1 fmly) (18 GF) ⟑ S £60-£85; **D** £80-£105 (incl. bkfst)* **Facilities** FTV WiFi **Conf** Class 80 Board 70 Thtr 200 **Parking** 96 **Notes** LB Civ Wed 120

Gainsborough House Hotel

★★★ 78% HOTEL

THE INDEPENDENTS
HOTEL ASSOCIATION

tel: 01562 820041 **Bewdley Hill DY11 6BS**
email: reservations@gainsboroughhousehotel.com
web: www.gainsboroughhousehotel.com
dir: Follow A456 to Kidderminster (West Midlands Safari Park), pass hospital, hotel 500yds on left

This listed Georgian hotel provides a wide range of thoughtfully furnished bedrooms that have smart modern bathrooms. The contemporary decor and furnishing throughout the public areas highlights the many retained period features. A large function suite and several meeting rooms are available.

Rooms 42 (16 fmly) (12 GF) **S** £56-£89; **D** £56-£89* **Facilities** STV FTV WiFi ⓠ Xmas New Year **Conf** Class 70 Board 60 Thtr 250 Del from £95 to £120* **Services** Air con **Parking** 90 **Notes** LB ⊗ Civ Wed 250

Premier Inn Kidderminster

BUDGET HOTEL

tel: 0871 527 9350 **Slingfield Mill, Weavers Wharf DY10 1AA**
web: www.premierinn.com
dir: M5 junct 3 , A456 towards Kidderminster, 5.5m. Straight on at 1st rdbt, left into Lower Mill St. Straight on into Crown Ln

High quality, budget accommodation ideal for both families and business travellers. Spacious, en suite bedrooms feature tea and coffee making facilities, and Freeview TV in most hotels. Internet access and WiFi are available for a small fee. The adjacent family restaurant features a wide and varied menu. See also the Hotel Groups pages.

Rooms 56

KINGSBRIDGE
Devon — Map 3 SX74

Buckland-Tout-Saints

★★★ 81% ⊛ COUNTRY HOUSE HOTEL

tel: 01548 853055 **Goveton TQ7 2DS**
email: enquiries@bucklandtoutsaints.co.uk **web:** www.tout-saints.co.uk
dir: Turn off A381 to Goveton. Follow brown tourist signs to St Peter's Church. Hotel 2nd right after church

It is well worth navigating the winding country lanes to dine at this delightful Queen Anne manor house that has been host to many famous guests over the years. Set in over four acres of gardens the hotel is a peaceful retreat. Bedrooms are tastefully furnished and attractively decorated; the majority are very spacious. Local produce is used with care and imagination to create the dishes offered. This is a popular choice for weddings. Eden Hotel Collection is the AA Small Hotel Group of the Year 2014-15.

Rooms 16 (6 fmly) ⓡ **S** £79-£159; **D** £89-£269 (incl. bkfst)* **Facilities** STV WiFi ⓠ ⌣ Xmas New Year **Conf** Class 40 Board 26 Thtr 80 Del from £149 to £199* **Parking** 16 **Notes** LB Closed 2-16 Jan Civ Wed 120

KINGSCLERE
Hampshire — Map 5 SU55

Sandford Springs Hotel and Golf Club

★★★★ 77% HOTEL

tel: 01635 291500 & 291501 **RG26 5RT**
email: info@sandfordsprings.co.uk **web:** www.sandfordsprings.co.uk
dir: M3 junct 6, A339 for 9m, hotel on right; M4 junct 13, A34 to Newbury then A339 for 11 miles, hotel on left

This modern hotel is located in a lovely country location and offers a super range of facilities with three 9 hole golf courses; the parks, woods and lakes. In addition there are also conference and meeting facilities. The bedrooms are spacious and have good facilities. A choice of restaurants, the Dining Room in the hotel and the Kingsclere, which overlooks the golf course, providing all day dining.

Rooms 40 (4 fmly) (21 GF) ⓡ **S** £79-£159; **D** £89-£169 (incl. bkfst) **Facilities** FTV WiFi ⓠ ⌁ 27 Putt green New Year **Conf** Class 50 Board 40 Thtr 80 Del from £140 to £180 **Services** Lift Air con **Parking** 150 **Notes** LB ⊗ Civ Wed 100

KING'S LANGLEY
Hertfordshire — Map 6 TL00

Premier Inn King's Langley

BUDGET HOTEL

tel: 0871 527 8568 **Hempstead Rd WD4 8BR**
web: www.premierinn.com
dir: 1m from M25 junct 20 on A4251 after King's Langley

High quality, budget accommodation ideal for both families and business travellers. Spacious, en suite bedrooms feature tea and coffee making facilities, and Freeview TV in most hotels. Internet access and WiFi are available for a small fee. The adjacent family restaurant features a wide and varied menu. See also the Hotel Groups pages.

Rooms 60

KING'S LYNN
Norfolk — Map 12 TF62

The Legacy Duke's Head Hotel

★★★★ 77% HOTEL

tel: 08444 119484 & 0330 333 2984 **5-6 Tuesday Market Place PE30 1JS**
email: reception@dukesheadhotel.com **web:** www.legacy-hotels.co.uk

Occupying a central location and overlooking the market square, this hotel is a beautiful property. The bedrooms are smartly decorated, and include wide-screen TVs, free WiFi and bathrooms with walk-in showers. Parking is also available.

Rooms 78 (6 fmly) ⓡ **Facilities** FTV WiFi ⓠ Xmas New Year **Conf** Class 80 Board 100 Thtr 220 **Services** Lift **Parking** 40 **Notes** ⊗ Civ Wed 200

BEST WESTERN PLUS Knights Hill Hotel and Spa

★★★★ 72% HOTEL

tel: 01553 675566 **Knights Hill Village, South Wootton PE30 3HQ**
email: reception@knightshill.co.uk **web:** www.abacushotels.co.uk
dir: At junct A148 & A149

This hotel village complex is set on a 16th-century site on the outskirts of King's Lynn. The smartly decorated, well-equipped bedrooms are situated in extensions of the original hunting lodge. Public areas have a wealth of historic charm including the Garden Bistro & Bar and the Farmers Arms Inn, which serves good food and real ales. The hotel also has conference and leisure facilities, including the Imagine Spa.

Rooms 79 (12 annexe) (1 fmly) (38 GF) ⓡ **Facilities** Spa STV WiFi ⓠ ⓣ ⌣ ⌁ Gym Xmas New Year **Conf** Class 150 Board 30 Thtr 200 **Parking** 350 **Notes** Civ Wed 90

KING'S LYNN *continued*

Congham Hall Country House Hotel

★★★ ◎◎ COUNTRY HOUSE HOTEL

tel: 01485 600250 **Lynn Rd PE32 1AH**
email: info@conghamhallhotel.co.uk **web:** www.conghamhallhotel.co.uk

(For full entry see Grimston)

Bank House Hotel

★★★ 83% ◎ HOTEL

tel: 01553 660492 **King's Staithe Square PE30 1RD**
email: info@thebankhouse.co.uk **web:** www.thebankhouse.co.uk
dir: In King's Lynn Old Town follow quay, through floodgates, hotel on right opposite Custom House

This Grade II listed, 18th-century town house is situated on the quay side in the heart of King's Lynn's historical quarter. Bedrooms are individually decorated and have high quality fabrics and furnishings along with a range of useful facilities. Public rooms include the Counting House coffee shop, a wine bar and brasserie restaurant, as well as a residents' lounge.

Rooms 11 (5 fmly) ⚓ **S** £80-£110; **D** £110-£150 (incl. bkfst)* **Facilities** FTV WiFi ⤵ Xmas New Year **Conf** Class 20 Board 15 Thtr 30 Del from £150* **Notes** LB ⊗

Stuart House Hotel

★★★ 72% HOTEL

tel: 01553 772169 **35 Goodwins Rd PE30 5QX**
email: reception@stuarthousehotel.co.uk **web:** www.stuarthousehotel.co.uk
dir: At A47/A10/A149 rdbt follow signs to town centre. Under Southgate Arch, right into Guanock Terrace, right into Goodwins Rd

This small privately-owned hotel is situated in a peaceful residential area just a short walk from the town centre. Bedrooms come in a variety of styles and sizes; all are pleasantly decorated and thoughtfully equipped. There is a choice of eating options with informal dining in the bar and a daily-changing menu in the elegant restaurant.

Rooms 18 (2 fmly) (3 GF) ⚓ **S** £75-£90; **D** £98-£180 (incl. bkfst)* **Facilities** FTV WiFi ⤵ **Conf** Class 30 Board 20 Thtr 50 **Parking** 30 **Notes** LB ⊗ RS 25-26 Dec & 1 Jan Civ Wed 60

Grange Hotel

★★ 72% HOTEL

tel: 01553 673777 & 671222 **Willow Park, South Wootton Ln PE30 3BP**
email: info@thegrangehotelkingslynn.co.uk **web:** www.thegrangehotelkingslynn.co.uk
dir: A148 towards King's Lynn for 1.5m. At lights left into Wootton Rd, 400yds, on right into South Wootton Ln. Hotel 1st on left

Expect a warm welcome at this Edwardian house which is situated in a quiet residential area in its own grounds. Public rooms include a smart lounge bar and a cosy restaurant. The spacious bedrooms are pleasantly decorated and equipped with many thoughtful touches; some are located in an adjacent wing.

Rooms 9 (4 annexe) (2 fmly) (4 GF) **Facilities** WiFi Xmas **Conf** Class 15 Board 12 Thtr 20 **Parking** 15

Premier Inn King's Lynn

BUDGET HOTEL

tel: 0871 527 8570 **Clenchwarton Rd, West Lynn PE34 3LJ**
web: www.premierinn.com
dir: At junct of A47 & A17

High quality, budget accommodation ideal for both families and business travellers. Spacious, en suite bedrooms feature tea and coffee making facilities, and Freeview TV in most hotels. Internet access and WiFi are available for a small fee. The adjacent family restaurant features a wide and varied menu. See also the Hotel Groups pages.

Rooms 61

Fallowfields Hotel and Restaurant

★★★ 80% ◎◎◎ HOTEL

tel: 01865 820416 **Faringdon Rd OX13 5BH**
email: stay@fallowfields.com **web:** www.fallowfields.com
dir: A34 (Oxford Ring Rd) take A420 towards Swindon. At junct with A415 left, 100yds, exit at mini rdbt. Hotel on left after 1m

Located in rural Oxfordshire just ten miles from Oxford city centre, this small family-run hotel offers the personal touch. Bedrooms are generous in size and some have delightful views over the croquet lawn. The grounds are home to several breeds of cattle, pigs and chickens, and the kitchen garden is the source of much of the produce used on the menus. The cooking here is a real feature, delivering great, refined dishes.

Rooms 10 (2 fmly) ⚓ **Facilities** FTV WiFi ⤵ Falconry Archery Xmas New Year **Conf** Class 25 Board 20 Thtr 60 **Parking** 50 **Notes** Civ Wed 100

BEST WESTERN Willerby Manor Hotel

★★★ 83% ◎ HOTEL

tel: 01482 652616 **Well Ln HU10 6ER**
email: willerbymanor@bestwestern.co.uk **web:** www.willerbymanor.co.uk

(For full entry see Willerby)

Holiday Inn Hull Marina

★★★ 82% HOTEL

tel: 0871 942 9043 & 01482 386300 **The Marina, Castle St HU1 2BX**
email: reservations-hull@ihg.com **web:** www.holidayinn.co.uk
dir: M62 junct 38, A63 to Hull. Follow Marina & Ice Arena signs. Hotel on left adjacent to Ice Arena

Situated overlooking the marina just off the A63, Holiday Inn Hull Marina offers well-equipped accommodation including executive rooms. Public areas are attractively designed and include meeting rooms and a leisure club. The Junction Restaurant serves contemporary cuisine, and guests can eat alfresco on the patio if the weather permits.

Rooms 100 (10 fmly) **Facilities** FTV WiFi ⤵ ⊗ supervised Gym New Year **Conf** Class 70 Board 50 Thtr 120 **Services** Lift Air con **Parking** 151 **Notes** ⊗ Civ Wed 120

K

Mercure Hull Royal Hotel

★★★ 77% HOTEL

tel: 01482 325087 **170 Ferensway HU1 3UF**
email: reservations@hotels-hull.co.uk **web:** www. hotels-hull.com
dir: A63 to city centre. Follow signs to railway station, hotel connected

A railway hotel in Victorian times, this impressive building has been modernised in recent years. The stunning central lounge area is the focal point and there are extensive conference and banqueting facilities, with complimentary parking and WiFi access also provided. The contemporary bedrooms have bold colour schemes with good facilities including flat-screen TVs; many have air conditioning. There is a leisure club adjacent to the hotel.

Rooms 155 (29 fmly) **Facilities** FTV WiFi Xmas New Year **Conf** Class 150 Board 70 Thtr 400 **Services** Lift **Parking** 84 **Notes** Civ Wed 400

Campanile Hull

BUDGET HOTEL

tel: 01482 325530 **Beverley Rd, Freetown Way (City Centre) HU2 9AN**
email: hull@campanile.com **web:** www.campanile.com
dir: M62 junct 38, A63 to Hull, pass Humber Bridge on right. Over flyover, follow railway station signs onto A1079. Hotel at bottom of Ferensway

This modern building offers accommodation in smart, well-equipped bedrooms, all with en suite bathrooms. Refreshments may be taken at the informal bistro. See also the Hotel Groups pages.

Rooms 48 (48 annexe) (24 GF) **S** £29-£60; **D** £29-£60* **Conf** Class 15 Board 15 Thtr 25

Ibis Hull

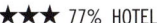

BUDGET HOTEL

tel: 01482 387500 **Osborne St HU1 2NL**
email: h3479@accor.com **web:** www.ibishotel.com
dir: M62/A63 straight across at rdbt, follow signs for Princes Quay onto Myton St. Hotel on corner of Osborne St & Ferensway

Modern, budget hotel offering comfortable accommodation in bright and practical bedrooms. Breakfast is self-service and dinner is available in the restaurant. See also the Hotel Groups pages.

Rooms 106 (19 GF)

Premier Inn Hull City Centre

BUDGET HOTEL

tel: 0871 527 8534 **Tower St HU9 1TQ**
web: www.premierinn.com
dir: M62, A63 into Hull city centre. At rdbt left onto A1165 (Great Union St), left into Citadel Way. Hotel at end on right

High quality, budget accommodation ideal for both families and business travellers. Spacious, en suite bedrooms feature tea and coffee making facilities, and Freeview TV in most hotels. Internet access and WiFi are available for a small fee. The adjacent family restaurant features a wide and varied menu. See also the Hotel Groups pages.

Rooms 136

Premier Inn Hull North

BUDGET HOTEL

tel: 0871 527 8536 **Ashcombe Rd, Kingswood Park HU7 3DD**
web: www.premierinn.com
dir: A63 to town centre, take A1079 N for approx 5m. Right at rdbt onto A1033. Hotel at 2nd rdbt in New Kingswood Park

Rooms 42

Premier Inn Hull West

BUDGET HOTEL

tel: 0871 527 8538 **Ferriby Rd, Hessle HU13 0JA**
web: www.premierinn.com
dir: A63 onto A15 to Humber Bridge (Beverley & Hessle Viewpoint). Hotel at 1st rdbt

Rooms 61

KINGSWINFORD Map 10 S088
West Midlands

Premier Inn Dudley (Kingswinford)

BUDGET HOTEL

tel: 0871 527 8314 **Dudley Rd DY6 8WT**
web: www.premierinn.com
dir: A4123 to Dudley, A461 follow signs for Russell's Hall Hospital. On A4101 to Kingswinford, hotel opposite Pensnett Trading Estate

High quality, budget accommodation ideal for both families and business travellers. Spacious, en suite bedrooms feature tea and coffee making facilities, and Freeview TV in most hotels. Internet access and WiFi are available for a small fee. The adjacent family restaurant features a wide and varied menu. See also the Hotel Groups pages.

Rooms 45

KINGTON Map 9 S025
Herefordshire

Burton Hotel

★★★ 78% HOTEL

tel: 01544 230323 **Mill St HR5 3BQ**
email: info@burtonhotel.co.uk **web:** www.burtonhotel.co.uk
dir: At A44 & A411 rdbt junct follow Town Centre signs

Situated in the town centre, this friendly, privately-owned hotel offers spacious, pleasantly proportioned and well-equipped bedrooms. Smartly presented public areas include a lounge bar, and leisure facilities including a well-equipped gym, spa and swimming pool. Outside there is a small, flood-lit golf-putting area laid with astro turf. The attractive restaurant offers carefully prepared cuisine. There are function and meeting facilities in a purpose-built, modern wing. Well spaced parking is located to the rear of the hotel.

Rooms 16 (5 fmly) **S** £56-£66; **D** £96-£114 (incl. bkfst)* **Facilities** Spa FTV WiFi supervised Putt green Gym Steam room Sauna Therapy rooms **Conf** Class 100 Board 20 Thtr 150 **Services** Lift **Parking** 50 **Notes** LB Civ Wed 120

K

KIRKBY FLEETHAM
North Yorkshire   Map 19 SE29

The Black Horse

 RESTAURANT WITH ROOMS

tel: 01609 749010 & 749011 📠 01423 507836 **Lumley Ln DL7 OSH**
email: gm@blackhorsekirkbyfleetham.com **web:** www.blackhorsekirkbyfleetham.com
dir: A1 onto A648 towards Northallerton. Left into Ham Hall Ln, through Scruton. At T-junct left into Fleetham Ln. Through Great Fencote to Kirkby Fleetham, into Lumley Ln, inn on left past post office

Set in a small village, The Black Horse provides everything needed for a getaway break including award-winning food. The spacious bedrooms, named after famous racehorses, are beautifully designed in New England-French style with pastel colours, co-ordinating fabrics and excellent beds; many of the superb bathrooms feature slipper or roll-top baths. There is a large dining room and bar that attracts locals as well as visitors from further afield.

Rooms 7 (1 fmly)

KIRKBY LONSDALE
Cumbria   Map 18 SD67

The Whoop Hall

★★ 74% HOTEL

tel: 015242 71284 **Burrow with Burrow LA6 2HP**
email: info@whoophall.co.uk **web:** www.whoophall.co.uk
dir: On A65, 1m SE of Kirkby Lonsdale

This popular inn combines traditional charm with modern facilities, that include a very well-equipped leisure complex. Bedrooms, some with four-poster beds, and some housed in converted barns, are appointed to a smart, stylish standard. A fire warms the bar on chillier days, and an interesting choice of dishes is available in both the bar and galleried restaurant throughout the day and evening.

Rooms 24 (4 fmly) (2 GF) 🐾 **Facilities** FTV WiFi ⏱ supervised Gym Beauty treatment room Sauna 🎵 Xmas New Year **Conf** Class 72 Board 56 Thtr 169 **Parking** 100 **Notes** ⊗ Civ Wed 120

Hipping Hall

 RESTAURANT WITH ROOMS

tel: 015242 71187 📠 015242 72452 **Cowan Bridge LA6 2JJ**
email: info@hippinghall.com **web:** www.hippinghall.com
dir: M6 junct 36, A65 through Kirkby Lonsdale towards Skipton. On right after Cowan Bridge

Close to the market town of Kirkby Lonsdale, Hipping Hall offers spacious bedrooms, designed using soft shades with sumptuous textures and fabrics; the bathrooms use natural stone, slate and limestone to great effect. There are also three spacious cottage suites that create a real hideaway experience. The sitting room, with large, comfortable sofas has a traditional feel. The 3 AA Rosette-worthy restaurant is a 15th-century hall with tapestries and a minstrels' gallery that is as impressive as it is intimate.

Rooms 9 (3 annexe)

The Sun Inn

RESTAURANT WITH ROOMS

tel: 015242 71965 📠 015242 72485 **6 Market St LA6 2AU**
email: email@sun-inn.info **web:** www.sun-inn.info
dir: From A65 follow signs to town centre. Inn on main street

The Sun is a 17th-century inn situated in a historic market town, overlooking St Mary's Church. The atmospheric bar features stone walls, wooden beams and log fires with real ales available. Delicious meals are served in the bar or the more formal, modern restaurant. Traditional and modern styles are blended together in the beautifully appointed rooms with excellent en suites.

Rooms 11 (1 fmly)

Plato's

RESTAURANT WITH ROOMS

tel: 015242 74180 **2 Mill Brow LA6 2AT**
email: hello@platoskirkby.co.uk **web:** www.platoskirkbylonsdale.co.uk
dir: M6 junct 36, A65 Kirkby Lonsdale, after 5m at rdbt take 1st exit, onto one-way system

Tucked away in the heart of the popular market town, Plato's is steeped in history. Sumptuous bedrooms have a wealth of thoughtful extras, and imaginative food is available in the elegant restaurant with its open-plan kitchen. The lounge bar is more rustic in style with fires to relax by. A warm welcome and professional service is assured. The Pop Shop offers Plato's cuisine to take away.

Rooms 8

KNARESBOROUGH
North Yorkshire   Map 19 SE35

General Tarleton Inn

RESTAURANT WITH ROOMS

tel: 01423 340284 📠 01423 340288 **Boroughbridge Rd, Ferrensby HG5 OPZ**
email: gti@generaltarleton.co.uk **web:** www.generaltarleton.co.uk
dir: A1(M) junct 48 at Boroughbridge, take A6055 to Knaresborough. 4m on right

This 18th-century coaching inn is both beautiful and stylish. Though the physical aspects are impressive, the emphasis here is on food with high-quality, skilfully prepared dishes served in the smart bar-brasserie and in the Orangery. There is also a richly furnished cocktail lounge with a galleried private dining room above it. Bedrooms are very comfortable and business guests are also well catered for.

Rooms 13

KNIPTON
Leicestershire   Map 11 SK83

The Manners Arms

RESTAURANT WITH ROOMS

tel: 01476 879222 📠 01476 879228 **Croxton Rd NG32 1RH**
email: info@mannersarms.com **web:** www.mannersarms.com
dir: From A607 follow signs to Knipton; from A52 follow signs to Belvoir Castle

Part of the Rutland Estate and built as a hunting lodge for the 6th Duke, The Manners Arms offers thoughtfully furnished bedrooms designed by the present Duchess. Public areas include the intimate Beater's Bar and attractive Red Coats Restaurant, popular for its imaginative menus.

Rooms 10 (1 fmly)

KNOWSLEY
Merseyside   Map 15 SJ49

Suites Hotel Knowsley

THE INDEPENDENTS

★★★★ 76% HOTEL

tel: 0151 549 2222 **Ribblers Ln L34 9HA**
email: enquiries@suiteshotelgroup.com **web:** www.suiteshotelgroup.com
dir: M57 junct 4. Telephone for detailed directions

Located close to the M57, this hotel is just a 10-minute drive from Liverpool's city centre. It offers superior, well-equipped accommodation and there is a choice of lounges plus Handley's Restaurant. Guests have the use of the impressive leisure centre, and there are extensive conference facilities.

Rooms 99 (39 fmly) (16 GF) ➧ **Facilities** Spa STV WiFi ↝ HL ⊠ supervised Gym Xmas New Year **Conf** Class 60 Board 50 Thtr 240 **Services** Lift Air con **Parking** 200 **Notes** ⊗ Civ Wed 140

KNUTSFORD
Cheshire   Map 15 SJ77

The Mere Golf Resort & Spa

★★★★ 84% ⊛⊛ HOTEL

tel: 01565 830155 **WA16 6LJ**
web: www.themereresort.co.uk
dir: M6 junct 19 or M56 junct 7

This hotel sits alongside Mere Lake and is close to the picturesque town of Knutsford; there are excellent transport links with Manchester International Airport being only ten minutes away. The resort's historic main Victorian building conveys the classic charm of that era, and offers stylish, luxury accommodation. The championship golf course designed by James Braid is both beautiful and challenging. The spa features an extensive range of treatments and facilities

including a Thermal Zone. The staff are professional and very friendly, offering personal service.

Rooms 81 **Conf** Class 350 Board 40 Thtr 700

Cottons Hotel & Spa

shire

★★★★ 79% ⊛ HOTEL

tel: 01565 650333 **Manchester Rd WA16 0SU**
email: cottons@shirehotels.com **web:** www.cottonshotel.com
dir: On A50, 1m from M6 junct 19

The superb leisure facilities and quiet location are great attractions at this hotel, which is just a short distance from Manchester Airport. Bedrooms are smartly appointed in various styles, and executive rooms have very good working areas. The hotel has spacious lounge areas and an excellent leisure centre.

Rooms 109 (14 fmly) (38 GF) ➧ **S** £90-£200; **D** £90-£200* **Facilities** Spa STV WiFi ↝ ⊠ ⌇ Gym Steam room Activity studio for exercise classes Sauna Children's splash pool Xmas New Year **Conf** Class 100 Board 36 Thtr 200 **Del** from £145 to £185* **Services** Lift Air con **Parking** 180 **Notes** LB ⊗ Civ Wed 120

Mere Court Hotel & Conference Centre

★★★★ 73% ⊛ HOTEL

tel: 01565 831000 **Warrington Rd, Mere WA16 0RW**
email: sales@merecourt.co.uk **web:** www.merecourt.co.uk
dir: A50, 1m W of junct with A556, on right

This is a smart and attractive hotel, set in extensive, well-tended gardens. The elegant and spacious bedrooms are individually styled and offer a host of thoughtful extras. Conference facilities are particularly impressive and there is a large, self contained, conservatory function suite. Dining is available in the fine dining Arboreum Restaurant.

Rooms 34 (24 fmly) (12 GF) **Facilities** STV FTV WiFi Xmas New Year **Conf** Class 75 Board 50 Thtr 200 **Del** from £130 to £155* **Services** Lift **Parking** 150 **Notes** ⊗ Civ Wed 150

The Longview Hotel & Stuffed Olive Restaurant

★★ 82% HOTEL

tel: 01565 632119 & 632244 **55 Manchester Rd WA16 0LX**
email: enquiries@longviewhotel.com **web:** www.longviewhotel.com
dir: M6 junct 19 take A556 W towards Chester. Left at lights onto A5033, 1.5m to rdbt then left. Hotel 200yds on right

This friendly Victorian hotel offers high standards of hospitality and service. Attractive public areas include a cellar bar and foyer lounge area. The restaurant has a traditional feel and offers an imaginative selection of dishes. Bedrooms, some located in a superb renovation of nearby houses, are individually styled and offer a good range of thoughtful amenities, including broadband internet access.

Rooms 32 (19 annexe) (1 fmly) (5 GF) **Facilities** FTV WiFi **Conf** Class 20 Board 20 **Parking** 20 **Notes** Closed 21 Dec-6 Jan

KNUTSFORD *continued*

Premier Inn Knutsford (Bucklow Hill)

BUDGET HOTEL

tel: 0871 527 8572 **Bucklow Hill WA16 6RD**
web: www.premierinn.com
dir: M6 junct 19, A556 towards Manchester Airport & Stockport

High quality, budget accommodation ideal for both families and business travellers. Spacious, en suite bedrooms feature tea and coffee making facilities, and Freeview TV in most hotels. Internet access and WiFi are available for a small fee. The adjacent family restaurant features a wide and varied menu. See also the Hotel Groups pages.

Rooms 69

Premier Inn Knutsford (Mere)

BUDGET HOTEL

tel: 0871 527 8574 **Warrington Rd, Hoo Green, Mere WA16 OPZ**
web: www.premierinn.com
dir: M6 junct 19, A556, follow Manchester signs. At 1st lights left onto A50 towards Warrington. Hotel 1m on right

Rooms 28

LACEBY	Map 17 TA20
Lincolnshire	

BEST WESTERN Oaklands Hall Hotel

★★★ 80% ⊛ HOTEL

tel: 01472 872248 **Barton St DN37 7LF**
email: reception@oaklandshallhotel.co.uk **web:** www.oaklandshallhotel.co.uk
dir: At junct of A46 & A18 at Laceby, on edge of Grimsby

This attractive 19th-century property is located on a private estate in five acres of parkland. It has been refurbished with a contemporary style while retaining beautiful period features. The Comfy Duck restaurant is stylish, and food is a highlight of any stay, with a strong emphasis on local produce. Bedrooms are comfortable and complimentary WiFi is provided.

Rooms 46 (4 fmly) (10 GF) ⚡ **Facilities** FTV WiFi ↕ Xmas New Year **Conf** Class 150 Board 50 Thtr 180 Del from £105 to £145 **Parking** 80 **Notes** ⊗ Civ Wed 200

LANCASTER	Map 18 SD46
Lancashire	

Lancaster House

English Lakes
Hotels Resorts & Venues

★★★★ 78% ⊛ HOTEL

tel: 01524 844822 **Green Ln, Ellel LA1 4GJ**
email: lancasterhouse@englishlakes.co.uk **web:** www.englishlakes.co.uk
dir: M6 junct 33 N towards Lancaster. Through Galgate into Green Ln. Hotel before university on right

This modern hotel enjoys a rural setting south of the city and close to the university. The attractive open-plan reception and lounge boast a roaring log fire in colder months. Bedrooms are spacious, and include 19 rooms that are particularly well equipped for business guests. There are leisure facilities with a hot tub and a function suite.

Rooms 99 (29 fmly) (44 GF) ⚡ S £79-£158; D £88-£176 (incl. bkfst)* **Facilities** Spa STV WiFi ↕ HL ⚡ supervised Gym Beauty salon Xmas New Year **Conf** Class 60 Board 48 Thtr 250 Del from £99* **Parking** 120 **Notes** LB Civ Wed 140

Premier Inn Lancaster

BUDGET HOTEL

tel: 0871 527 8576 **Lancaster Business Park, Caton Rd LA1 3PE**
web: www.premierinn.com
dir: M6 junct 34, A683 towards Lancaster. Hotel 0.25m on left at entrance to Business Park

High quality, budget accommodation ideal for both families and business travellers. Spacious, en suite bedrooms feature tea and coffee making facilities, and Freeview TV in most hotels. Internet access and WiFi are available for a small fee. The adjacent family restaurant features a wide and varied menu. See also the Hotel Groups pages.

Rooms 85

LAND'S END	Map 2 SW32
Cornwall	

The Land's End Hotel

★★★ 71% HOTEL

tel: 01736 871844 **TR19 7AA**
email: reservations@landsendhotel.co.uk **web:** www.landsendhotel.co.uk
dir: From Penzance take A30, follow Land's End signs. After Sennen 1m to Land's End

This famous location provides a memorable setting for The Land's End Hotel. Bedrooms, many with stunning views of the Atlantic, are pleasantly decorated and comfortable. Refurbished public areas provide plenty of style and comfort with a relaxing lounge and convivial bar. The restaurant is equally impressive with accomplished cuisine complementing the amazing views out to sea.

Rooms 30 (4 fmly) **Facilities** FTV WiFi Free entry to Land's End Visitor Centre & Attractions Xmas **Conf** Class 50 Board 30 Thtr 100 **Parking** 100 **Notes** ⊗ Civ Wed 120

LANGAR	Map 11 SK73
Nottinghamshire	

Langar Hall

★★★ 81% ⊛⊛ HOTEL

tel: 01949 860559 **NG13 9HG**
email: info@langarhall.co.uk **web:** www.langarhall.com
dir: Via Bingham from A52 or Cropwell Bishop from A46, both signed. Hotel behind church

This delightful hotel enjoys a picturesque rural location, yet is only a short drive from Nottingham. Individually styled bedrooms are furnished with fine period pieces and benefit from some thoughtful extras. There is a choice of lounges, warmed by real fires, and a snug little bar. Imaginative food is served in the dining room, while the garden conservatory provides a lighter menu.

Rooms 12 (1 fmly) (1 GF) **S** £100-£140; **D** £130-£189 (incl. bkfst)* **Facilities** FTV WiFi Fishing 🎣 Xmas New Year Child facilities **Conf** Class 16 Board 12 Thtr 16 Del £175 **Parking** 20 **Notes** Civ Wed 50

LANGHO	Map 18 SD73
Lancashire	

Northcote

★★★★ ◉◉◉◉ SMALL HOTEL

tel: 01254 240555 **Northcote Rd BB6 8BE**
email: reception@northcote.com **web:** www.northcote.com
dir: M6 junct 31, 9m to Northcote. Follow Clitheroe (A59) signs, Hotel on left before rdbt

In the last year or so, Northcote has undergone a major transformation. The house has been renovated, the gardens re-landscaped, and the kitchen rebuilt. There is also a cookery school, which takes up to eight students, and transforms into a chef's table for up to 12 guests. This is a gastronomic haven where guests return to sample the delights provided by Nigel Haworth and Lisa Allen, Chef Patron and Head Chef respectively, alongside an efficient and imaginative kitchen brigade. The outstanding cooking includes Lancashire's finest fare, and fruit and herbs from the hotel's own beautifully laid out organic gardens. Drinks can be enjoyed in the newly re-designed and elegantly furnished lounges and bar. Each of the luxury bedrooms has its own identity with sumptuous fabrics and soft furnishings, sophisticated lighting and ultra modern bathrooms; some have a garden patio. There are also garden rooms being built adjacent to the main building, and these should be available from December 2014.

Rooms 18 (2 fmly) (4 GF) ✎ **S** £240-£265; **D** £275-£300 (incl. bkfst)* **Facilities** STV FTV WiFi 🦢 Xmas New Year **Conf** Class 40 Board 20 Thtr 40 **Parking** 50 **Notes** LB ⊗ Civ Wed 60

BEST WESTERN Mytton Fold Hotel and Golf Club

★★★ ◭ HOTEL

tel: 01254 240662 & 245392 **Whalley Rd BB6 8AB**
email: reception@myttonfold.co.uk **web:** www.bw-myttonfoldhotel.co.uk
dir: At large rdbt on A59, follow signs for Whalley, exit into Whalley Road. Hotel on right

Set in pretty and well maintained grounds that are a riot of colour in the summer, this hotel has views over the golf course to Pendle Hill beyond. The bedrooms are smart and include two with four-posters. This is a popular wedding venue.

Rooms 43 (12 fmly) (10 GF) ✎ **S** £70-£95; **D** £80-£120 (incl. bkfst)* **Facilities** STV WiFi ⚲ 18 Putt green Xmas **Conf** Class 60 Board 40 Thtr 290 **Services** Lift **Parking** 300 **Notes** LB Closed 1 Jan Civ Wed 250

LASTINGHAM	Map 19 SE79
North Yorkshire	

Lastingham Grange Hotel

★★★ 81% HOTEL

tel: 01751 417345 & 417402 **YO62 6TH**
email: reservations@lastinghamgrange.com **web:** www.lastinghamgrange.com
dir: From A170 follow signs for Appleton-le-Moors, continue into Lastingham, pass church on left, right, then left up hill. Hotel on right

A warm welcome and sincere hospitality have been the hallmarks of this hotel for over 50 years. Antique furniture is plentiful, and the lounge and the dining room both look out onto the terrace and sunken rose garden below. There is a large play area for older children and the moorland views are breathtaking.

Rooms 12 (2 fmly) **S** £99-£140; **D** £130-£199 (incl. bkfst)* **Facilities** FTV WiFi 🦢 Large adventure playground **Parking** 30 **Notes** LB Closed Dec-Feb

---

LAVENHAM	Map 13 TL94
Suffolk	

The Swan

T|A HOTEL COLLECTION

★★★★ ◉◉ HOTEL

tel: 01787 247477 **High St CO10 9QA**
email: info@theswanatlavenham.co.uk **web:** www.theswanatlavenham.co.uk
dir: From Bury St Edmunds take A134 (S), then A1141 to Lavenham

The Swan is a delightful collection of listed buildings, dating back to the 14th century, lovingly restored to retain their original charm. Public rooms include comfortable lounge areas, a charming rustic bar, an informal brasserie and a fine-dining restaurant. Bedrooms are tastefully furnished and equipped with many thoughtful touches. The friendly staff are helpful, attentive and offer professional service.

Rooms 45 (7 fmly) (9 GF) ✎ **S** £105-£155; **D** £195-£350 (incl. bkfst)* **Facilities** FTV WiFi ⚲ Spa & treatments from Dec 2014 Xmas New Year **Conf** Class 36 Board 30 Thtr 50 Del from £198* **Parking** 30 **Notes** LB Civ Wed 100

L

LAVENHAM *continued*

INSPECTORS' CHOICE

Lavenham Great House 'Restaurant With Rooms'

 RESTAURANT WITH ROOMS

tel: 01787 247431 📄 01787 248007 **Market Place CO10 9QZ**
email: info@greathouse.co.uk **web:** www.greathouse.co.uk
dir: Exit A1141 into Market Ln, behind cross on Market Place

The 18th-century frontage on Market Place conceals a 15th-century timber-framed building that is now a restaurant with rooms. Lavenham Great House remains a pocket of France offering high-quality rural cuisine served by French staff. The spacious bedrooms are individually decorated and thoughtfully equipped with many useful extras; some rooms have a separate lounge area.

Rooms 5 (1 fmly)

| LEA MARSTON | Map 10 SP29 |
Warwickshire

Lea Marston Hotel & Spa

★★★★ 76% ◉◉ HOTEL

CLASSIC
BRITISH HOTELS

tel: 01675 470468 **Haunch Ln B76 OBY**
email: info@leamarstonhotel.co.uk **web:** www.leamarstonhotel.co.uk
dir: M42 junct 9, A4097 to Kingsbury. Hotel signed 1.5m on right

Excellent access to the motorway network and a good range of sports facilities make this hotel a popular choice for conferences and leisure breaks. Bedrooms are mostly set around an attractive quadrangle and are generously equipped. Diners can choose between the popular Sportsman's Lounge Bar and the elegant Adderley Restaurant.

Rooms 88 (18 fmly) (49 GF) 🐾 **Facilities** Spa FTV WiFi 🏊 ⚓ 9 ⛳ Putt green Gym Golf driving range Golf simulator Sauna Steam room Rasul Hydrotherapy bath Xmas New Year **Conf** Class 50 Board 30 Thtr 140 Del from £135 to £170* **Services** Lift **Parking** 200 **Notes** ⊗ Civ Wed 100

| LEAMINGTON SPA (ROYAL) | Map 10 SP36 |
Warwickshire

INSPECTORS' CHOICE

Mallory Court Hotel

★★★ ◉◉◉ HOTEL

EDEN HOTEL COLLECTION

tel: 01926 330214 **Harbury Ln, Bishop's Tachbrook CV33 9QB**
email: reception@mallory.co.uk **web:** www.mallory.co.uk
dir: M40 junct 13 N'bound left, left again towards Bishops Tachbrook, right into Harbury Ln after 0.5m. M40 junct 14 S'bound A452 to Leamington, at 2nd rdbt left into Harbury Ln

Mallory Court Hotel is part of the Eden Hotel Collection and with its tranquil rural setting, this elegant Lutyens-style country house is an idyllic retreat, set in ten acres of landscaped gardens with immaculate lawns and an orchard. Relaxation is easy in the two sumptuous lounges, drawing room or conservatory. Dining is a treat in either the elegant restaurant or the brasserie. Simon Haigh heads up a team of expert chefs producing dishes that continue to delight. Bedrooms in the main house are luxuriously decorated and most have wonderful views. Those in the Knights Suite are more contemporary and have their own access via a smart conference and banqueting facility. Eden Hotel Collection is the AA Small Hotel Group of the Year 2014-15.

Rooms 31 (11 annexe) (2 fmly) (5 GF) 🐾 **S** £125-£450; **D** £165-£495 (incl. bkfst)* **Facilities** FTV WiFi 🏊 ⛱ Use of nearby club facilities Xmas New Year **Conf** Class 160 Board 50 Thtr 200 Del from £189 to £240* **Services** Lift **Parking** 100 **Notes** ⊗ Civ Wed 160

Angel Hotel

★★★ 75% HOTEL

tel: 01926 881296 **143 Regent St CV32 4NZ**
email: angelhotel143@hotmail.com **web:** www.angelhotelleamington.co.uk
dir: In town centre at junct of Regent St & Holly Walk

This centrally located hotel is divided into two parts: the original inn, and a more modern extension. Public rooms include a comfortable foyer lounge area, a smart restaurant and an informal bar. Bedrooms are individual in style, and, whether modern or traditional, all have the expected facilities.

Rooms 48 (3 fmly) (3 GF) **S** £65-£85; **D** £85-£105 (incl. bkfst)* **Facilities** STV FTV WiFi **Conf** Class 40 Board 40 Thtr 70 **Services** Lift **Parking** 38 **Notes** LB ⊗

BEST WESTERN Falstaff Hotel

★★★ 73% HOTEL

tel: 01926 312044 **16-20 Warwick New Rd CV32 5JQ**
email: sales@falstaffhotel.com **web:** www.falstaffhotel.com
dir: M40 junct 13 or 14, follow Leamington Spa signs. Over 4 rdbts, under bridge. Left into Princes Dr, right at mini-rdbt

Bedrooms at this hotel come in a variety of sizes and styles and are well equipped, with many thoughtful extras. Snacks can be taken in the relaxing lounge bar, and an interesting selection of English and continental dishes is offered in the restaurant; 24-hour room service is also available. Conference and banqueting facilities are extensive.

Rooms 59 (3 fmly) (16 GF) ↖ **S** £65-£95; **D** £75-£105 (incl. bkfst) **Facilities** FTV WiFi ↘ Arrangement with local health club Xmas New Year **Conf** Class 30 Board 30 Thtr 70 Del from £100 to £150 **Parking** 40 **Notes** LB

Premier Inn Leamington Spa Town Centre

BUDGET HOTEL

tel: 0871 527 9380 **Regency Arcade, The Parade CV32 4BQ**
web: www.premierinn.com
dir: From N, M40 junct 15/A452. Through 4 rdbts. At next rdbt take 4th exit, at final rdbt, take 1st exit A452 (Adelaide Road). Right onto Dormer Place & left onto St Peters Road into St Peters car park. Follow directional signage to Premier Inn. From S, M40 junct 13 then follow directions as above

High quality, budget accommodation ideal for both families and business travellers. Spacious, en suite bedrooms feature tea and coffee making facilities, and Freeview TV in most hotels. Internet access and WiFi are available for a small fee. The adjacent family restaurant features a wide and varied menu. See also the Hotel Groups pages.

Rooms 82

LEDBURY
Herefordshire   Map 10 SO73

Feathers Hotel

★★★ 81% HOTEL

tel: 01531 635266 & 638950 **High St HR8 1DS**
email: mary@feathers-ledbury.co.uk **web:** www.feathers-ledbury.co.uk
dir: S from Worcester on A449, E from Hereford on A438, N from Gloucester on A417. Hotel in town centre

A wealth of authentic features can be found at this historic timber-framed hotel, situated in the middle of town. The comfortably equipped bedrooms are tastefully decorated; there is also Eve's Cottage, in the grounds, and Lanark House, a two-bedroom apartment that is ideal for families and self-catering use. Well-prepared meals can be taken in Fuggles Brasserie with its adjoining bar, and breakfast is served in Quills Restaurant.

Rooms 22 (3 annexe) (2 fmly) ↖ **S** £95-£125; **D** £145-£235 (incl. bkfst)* **Facilities** STV FTV WiFi ↘ Gym Steam room New Year **Conf** Class 80 Board 40 Thtr 140 Del £137.50* **Parking** 30 **Notes** LB Civ Wed 100

Leadon House Hotel

★★ SMALL HOTEL

tel: 01531 631199 **Ross Rd HR8 2LP**
email: leadon.house@btconnect.com **web:** www.leadonhouse.com
dir: M5 junct 8/M50/A417 exit Ledbury. Left at 1st rdbt then take A449. Hotel 400yds on right by Ledbury Rugby Club

Enjoy a relaxing break at this family-run hotel, which has been tastefully refurbished in an Edwardian style, offering an idyllic environment and a peaceful night's stay. Many interesting architectural features add to the unique charm and elegance. All rooms are en suite and finished to a high standard, with plenty of attention paid to detail. Also available is the Coach House two bedroom apartment.

Rooms 8 (2 annexe) (1 fmly) (1 GF) **Facilities** FTV WiFi **Parking** 10 **Notes** ⊗

LEEDS
West Yorkshire   Map 19 SE23

See also **Gomersal & Wakefield**

Thorpe Park Hotel & Spa

shire

★★★★ 84% HOTEL

tel: 0113 264 1000 **Century Way, Thorpe Park LS15 8ZB**
email: thorpepark@shirehotels.com **web:** www.thorpeparkhotel.com
dir: M1 junct 46, follow signs for Thorpe Park

Conveniently close to the M1, this hotel offers bedrooms that are modern in both style and facilities. The terrace and courtyard offer all-day casual dining and refreshments, and the restaurant features a Mediterranean-themed menu. There is also a state-of-the-art spa and leisure facility.

Rooms 111 (3 fmly) (25 GF) ↖ **S** £90-£200; **D** £90-£200* **Facilities** Spa STV WiFi ↘ HL Gym Activity studio Steam room Sauna New Year **Conf** Class 100 Board 50 Thtr 200 Del from £145 to £185* **Services** Lift Air con **Parking** 200 **Notes** LB ⊗ Civ Wed 150

De Vere Oulton Hall

★★★★ 83% HOTEL

tel: 0113 282 1000 **Rothwell Ln, Oulton LS26 8HN**
email: oulton.hall@devere-hotels.com **web:** www.devere.co.uk
dir: 2m from M62 junct 30, follow Rothwell signs, then 'Oulton 1m' sign. 1st exit at next 2 rdbts. Hotel on left. Or 1m from M1 junct 44, follow Castleford & Pontefract sign on A639

Surrounded by the beautiful Yorkshire Dales, yet only 15 minutes from the city centre, this elegant 19th-century house offers the best of both worlds. Impressive features include stylish, opulent day rooms and delightful formal gardens, which have been restored to their original design. The hotel boasts a choice of dining options, and extensive leisure facilities. Golfers can book preferential tee times at the adjacent golf club.

Rooms 152 **Facilities** Spa STV FTV WiFi HL 27 Gym Beauty therapy Aerobics Xmas New Year **Conf** Class 150 Board 40 Thtr 350 **Services** Lift Air con **Parking** 260 **Notes** ⊗ Civ Wed 200

LEEDS *continued*

The New Ellington

★★★★ 83%  TOWN HOUSE HOTEL

tel: 0113 204 2150 **23-25 York Place LS1 2EY**
email: info@thenewellington.com **web:** www.thenewellington.com

Near the central railway station and the civic and business quarters, this hotel, with an art deco and a musical theme in part, offers guests modern amenities. Bedrooms are air-conditioned, offer free WiFi, high quality bed linen and Nespresso coffee machines; some have quiet balconies too. The ground floor atrium Gin Bar lounge leads to the lower ground floor restaurant that serves a range of interesting dishes. Limited on-site chargeable parking is available on a first-come first-served basis.

Rooms 34 (3 GF) ♦ **Facilities** FTV WiFi ♦ **Conf** Class 15 Board 16 Thtr 30 **Services** Lift Air con **Parking** 6 **Notes** ⊗ Closed 24-27 Dec

The Queens

★★★★ 81% HOTEL

INSPIRED BY YOU

tel: 0113 243 1323 **City Square LS1 1PJ**
email: queensreservations@qhotels.co.uk **web:** www.qhotels.co.uk
dir: M621, M1 & M62 follow signs for city centre & rail station, along Neville St towards City Square. Under rail bridge, at lights left into slip road in front of hotel

A legacy from the golden age of railways and located in the heart of Leeds, overlooking City Square, this grand Victorian hotel retains much of its original splendour. Public rooms include the spacious lounge bar, a range of conference and function rooms along with the grand ballroom. Bedrooms vary in size but all are very well equipped, and there is a choice of suites available. QHotels is the AA Hotel Group of the Year 2014-15.

Rooms 215 (16 fmly) ♦ **Facilities** STV WiFi ♦ Xmas New Year **Conf** Class 255 Board 80 Thtr 500 **Services** Lift Air con **Parking** 80 **Notes** ⊗ Civ Wed 600

Park Plaza Leeds

★★★★ 75% HOTEL

Park Plaza
Hotels & Resorts

tel: 0844 415 6720 **Boar Ln LS1 5NS**
email: pplinfo@pphe.com **web:** www.parkplaza.com
dir: Follow signs for city centre

Chic, stylish, ultra modern, city-centre hotel located just opposite City Square. Chino Latino, located on the first floor, is a fusion Far East and modern Japanese restaurant with a Latino bar. Stylish, air-conditioned bedrooms are spacious and have a range of modern facilities, including high-speed internet connection.

Rooms 187 ♦ **Facilities** STV WiFi ♦ Gym Xmas New Year **Conf** Class 70 Board 60 Thtr 220 **Services** Lift Air con **Parking** 6 **Notes** Civ Wed 120

Novotel Leeds Centre

★★★★ 74% HOTEL

NOVOTEL

tel: 0113 242 6446 **4 Whitehall, Whitehall Quay LS1 4HR**
email: H3270@accor.com **web:** www.novotel.com
dir: M621 junct 3, follow signs to rail station. Into Aire St & left at lights

With a minimalist style, this contemporary hotel provides a quality experience close to the city centre and within walking distance of the train station. Spacious, climate-controlled bedrooms are provided, whilst public areas are smartly presented and there is complimentary WiFi throughout the hotel. The bar is modern

and airy, while Elements Restaurant offers an informal brasserie style. Facilities also include a fitness suite and a sauna.

Rooms 196 (50 fmly) ♦ **Facilities** STV FTV WiFi ♦ HL Gym Steam room Sauna Xmas **Conf** Class 50 Board 50 Thtr 100 **Services** Lift **Parking** 80

The Met

★★★★ 73% HOTEL

 principal hayley

tel: 0113 245 0841 **King St LS1 2HQ**
email: metropole.sales@principal-hotels.com **web:** www.principal-hayley.com
dir: From M1, M62 & M621 follow city centre signs. A65 into Wellington St. At 1st traffic island right into King St, hotel on right

Said to be the best example of this type of building in the city, this splendid terracotta-fronted hotel is centrally located and convenient for the railway station. All bedrooms are appointed to suit the business traveller, with hi-speed internet access and a working area. The Restaurant and the Tempest Bar make convenient dining options. There are also impressive conference and banqueting facilities. Some parking space is available.

Rooms 120 **Facilities** STV FTV WiFi ♦ **Conf** Class 120 Board 100 Thtr 250 **Services** Lift **Parking** 30 **Notes** ⊗ RS 24 Dec-1 Jan Civ Wed 200

BEST WESTERN PLUS Milford Hotel

★★★ 83% HOTEL

Best Western
PLUS

tel: 01977 681800 **A1 Great North Rd, Peckfield LS25 5LQ**
email: enquiries@mlh.co.uk **web:** www.mlh.co.uk

(For full entry see Garforth)

The Cosmopolitan

★★★ 81% HOTEL

 PEEL HOTELS PLC

tel: 0113 243 6454 **2 Lower Briggate LS1 4AE**
email: info@cosmopolitan-hotel-leeds.com **web:** www.cosmopolitan-hotel-leeds.com
dir: M621 junct 3. Keep in right lane. Follow until road splits into 4 lanes. Keep right, right at lights. (ASDA House on left). Left at lights. Over bridge, left, hotel opposite. Parking in 150mtrs

This smartly presented, Victorian building is located on the south side of the city. The well-equipped bedrooms offer a choice of standard or executive grades. Staff are friendly and helpful ensuring a warm and welcoming atmosphere. Discounted overnight parking is provided in the adjacent 24-hour car park.

Rooms 89 (5 fmly) (14 smoking) ♦ **S** £49-£139; **D** £59-£159* **Facilities** STV FTV WiFi ♦ Xmas New Year **Conf** Class 45 Board 40 Thtr 120 Del from £100* **Services** Lift **Notes** LB

Chevin Country Park Hotel & Spa

★★★ 77%  HOTEL

tel: 01943 467818 **Yorkgate LS21 3NU**
email: chevin@crerarhotels.com **web:** www.crerarhotels.com

(For full entry see Otley)

Bewleys Hotel Leeds

★★★ 77% HOTEL

tel: 0113 234 2340 **City Walk, Sweet St LS11 9AT**
email: leeds@bewleyshotels.com **web:** www.bewleyshotels.com
dir: M621 junct 3, at 2nd lights left into Sweet St, right & right again

Located on the edge of the city centre, this hotel has the added advantage of secure underground parking. Bedrooms are spacious and comfortable with an extensive room service menu. Downstairs, the light and airy bar lounge leads into a brasserie where a wide selection of popular dishes is offered. High quality meeting rooms are also available.

Rooms 334 (73 fmly) (27 smoking) ⟁ **Facilities** STV FTV WiFi New Year **Conf** Class 44 Board 30 Thtr 70 **Services** Lift **Parking** 160 **Notes** ⊗ Closed 24-29 Dec Civ Wed 60

Malmaison Leeds

★★★ 75% ⚙ HOTEL

tel: 0844 693 0654 **1 Swinegate LS1 4AG**
email: leeds@malmaison.com **web:** www.malmaison.com
dir: M621/M1 junct 3, follow city centre signs. At KPMG building, right into Sovereign Street. Hotel at end on right

Close to the waterfront, this stylish property offers striking bedrooms with CD players and air conditioning. The popular bar and brasserie feature vaulted ceilings, intimate lighting and offer a choice of a full three-course meal or a substantial snack. Service is both willing and friendly. A small fitness centre and impressive meeting rooms complete the package.

Rooms 100 (4 fmly) ⟁ **Facilities** STV WiFi ➹ Gym Xmas New Year **Conf** Class 30 Board 30 Thtr 80 **Services** Lift Air con **Notes** Civ Wed 70

Mercure Leeds Parkway Hotel

★★★ 73% HOTEL

tel: 0844 815 9020 **Otley Rd LS16 8AG**
email: info@mercureleeds.co.uk **web:** www.mercureleeds.co.uk
dir: From A1 take A58 towards Leeds, then right onto A6120. At A660 turn right towards Airport/Skipton. Hotel 2m on right

This hotel is conveniently located and caters well for both business and leisure guests. It is close to Leeds yet has a quiet spot near to the Yorkshire Dales. The lovely gardens lead on to wildlife walks that can be followed directly into Golden Acre Park (a beautiful 179 acre park and wildlife sanctuary). The hotel is a popular wedding venue and also has extensive conference facilities in the adjacent Summit Centre. A leisure club with indoor pool and fitness centre is also available and the hotel offers complimentary WiFi.

Rooms 118 (4 fmly) (18 GF) ⟁ **S** £65-£125; **D** £65-£125* **Facilities** STV FTV WiFi ➹ ⚡ Gym Beauty facilities Xmas New Year **Conf** Class 120 Board 40 Thtr 300 Del from £100 to £130* **Services** Lift **Parking** 300 **Notes** LB Civ Wed 250

Holiday Inn Express Leeds - East

BUDGET HOTEL

tel: 0845 112 6039 & 0113 288 0574 **Aberford Rd, Oulton LS26 8EJ**
email: reservations@hiexpressleedseast.co.uk **web:** www.hiexpressleedseast.co.uk
dir: M62 junct 29, E towards Pontefract. Exit at junct 30, A642 signed Rothwell. Hotel opposite at 1st rdbt

A modern hotel ideal for families and business travellers. Fresh and uncomplicated, the spacious rooms include Sky TV, power shower and tea and coffee-making facilities. Continental buffet breakfast is included in the room rate; other meals

may be taken at the nearby family pub or restaurant. See also the Hotel Groups pages.

Rooms 77 (50 fmly) (32 GF) ⟁ **S** £39-£89; **D** £39-£89 (incl. bkfst)* **Conf** Class 20 Board 20 Thtr 25

Ibis Leeds Centre

BUDGET HOTEL

tel: 0113 396 9000 **Marlborough St LS1 4PB**
email: H3652@accor.com **web:** www.ibis.com
dir: M1 junct 43 or M62 junct 2 take A643 & follow city centre signs. Left on slip road opposite Yorkshire Post. Hotel opposite TGI Fridays restaurant

Modern, budget hotel offering comfortable accommodation in bright and practical bedrooms. Breakfast is self-service and dinner is available in the restaurant See also the Hotel Groups pages.

Rooms 168 (14 fmly) ⟁ **S** £45-£185; **D** £45-£185*

Premier Inn Leeds/Bradford Airport

BUDGET HOTEL

tel: 0871 527 8578 **Victoria Av, Yeadon LS19 7AW**
web: www.premierinn.com
dir: On A658, near Leeds/Bradford Airport

High quality, budget accommodation ideal for both families and business travellers. Spacious, en suite bedrooms feature tea and coffee making facilities, and Freeview TV in most hotels. Internet access and WiFi are available for a small fee. The adjacent family restaurant features a wide and varied menu. See also the Hotel Groups pages.

Rooms 60

Premier Inn Leeds/Bradford (South)

BUDGET HOTEL

tel: 0871 527 8580 **Wakefield Rd, Drighlington BD11 1EA**
web: www.premierinn.com
dir: On Drighlington bypass, adjacent to M62 junct 27. Take A650, right to Drighlington, right, hotel on left

Rooms 42

Premier Inn Leeds City Centre

BUDGET HOTEL

tel: 0871 527 8582 **Citygate, Wellington St LS3 1LW**
web: www.premierinn.com
dir: At A65 & A58 junct

Rooms 140

Premier Inn Leeds City Centre (Leeds Arena)

BUDGET HOTEL

tel: 0871 527 9356 **Hepworth Point, Claypit Ln LS2 8BQ**
web: www.premierinn.com
dir: On foot from Leeds rail station cross road into Park Row, continue into Cookridge St to Clay Pit Ln. Hotel on left at top of lane

Rooms 131

L

LEEDS *continued*

Premier Inn Leeds City West

BUDGET HOTEL

tel: 0871 527 8584 **City West One Office Park, Gelderd Rd LS12 6LX**
web: www.premierinn.com
dir: M621 junct 1 take ring road towards Leeds. At 1st lights right into Gelderd Rd, right at rdbt

Rooms 126

Premier Inn Leeds East

BUDGET HOTEL

tel: 0871 527 8586 **Selby Rd, Whitkirk LS15 7AY**
web: www.premierinn.com
dir: M1 junct 46 towards Leeds. At 2nd rdbt follow Temple Newsam signs. Hotel 500mtrs on right

Rooms 87

Three Horseshoes Inn & Country Hotel

★★★ 79% ❀❀ HOTEL

tel: 01538 300296 **Buxton Rd, Blackshaw Moor ST13 8TW**
email: enquires@threeshoesinn.co.uk **web:** www.threeshoesinn.co.uk
dir: 2m N of Leek on A53

This traditional, family-owned hostelry provides stylish, individually designed, modern bedrooms, including several four-poster rooms. The smart brasserie, with an open kitchen and countryside views, offers modern English and Thai dishes, and there is also a pub and carvery; the award-winning gardens and grounds are ideal for alfresco dining. The staff are attentive and friendly.

Rooms 26 (2 fmly) (10 GF) ➦ **S** £82.50-£120; **D** £92.50-£170 (incl. bkfst)*
Facilities FTV WiFi ◊ **Conf** Class 50 Board 25 Thtr 60 Del from £140* **Services** Lift
Parking 80 **Notes** LB ⊗ Closed 24 Dec-1 Jan Civ Wed 120

See also **Rothley**

Hotel Maiyango

★★★★ 75% ❀ SMALL HOTEL

tel: 0116 251 8898 **13-21 St Nicholas Place LE1 4LD**
email: reservations@maiyango.com **web:** www.maiyango.com
dir: B4114 (Narborough Rd) to city centre, right onto A47 (Hinkley Rd), keep right into St Nicholas Place

Hotel Maiyango is a boutique hotel offering a warm welcome and professional service. Access to the public areas is via a discreet foyer adjacent to a Middle Eastern-themed restaurant (under the same ownership), where imaginative food is sure to be a memorable experience. Spacious bedrooms, decorated in minimalist style are enhanced by quality modern art, fine furnishings and superb bathrooms. Parking is available close by.

Rooms 14 ➦ **S** £90-£150; **D** £90-£150 (incl. bkfst)* **Facilities** FTV WiFi ◊ ♫ Xmas
New Year **Conf** Class 50 Board 30 Thtr 70 Del from £145* **Services** Lift Air con
Notes LB ⊗ Closed 25 Dec & 1 Jan

Mercure Leicester The Grand Hotel

★★★★ 72% HOTEL

Mercure HOTELS

tel: 0844 815 9012 **Granby St LE1 6ES**
email: info@mercureleicester.co.uk **web:** www.jupiterhotels.co.uk
dir: A5460 into city. Follow Leicester Central Station signs. Left off St Georges Way, A594 onto Charles St. 1st left onto Northampton St, right onto Granby St. Hotel on left

Located in the heart of Leicester city centre, this hotel offers well appointed bedrooms and spacious public areas. Conferences and weddings are catered for. On site parking is a plus. Free WiFi is available throughout.

Rooms 104 ➦ **S** £69-£159; **D** £79-£169 (incl. bkfst)* **Facilities** FTV WiFi ◊ Xmas New
Year **Conf** Class 200 Board 35 Thtr 450 Del from £130 to £155* **Services** Lift
Parking 110 **Notes** Civ Wed 120

Belmont Hotel

★★★ 83% HOTEL

CLASSIC BRITISH HOTELS

tel: 0116 254 4773 **De Montfort St LE1 7GR**
email: info@belmonthotel.co.uk **web:** www.belmonthotel.co.uk
dir: From A6 take 1st right after rail station. Hotel 200yds on left

This well-established hotel, under the same family ownership, has been welcoming guests for over 70 years. It is conveniently situated within easy walking distance of the railway station and city centre though it sits in a quiet leafy residential area. Extensive public rooms are smartly appointed and include the informal Bowie's Bistro, Jamie's Bar with its relaxed atmosphere, and the more formal Cherry Restaurant.

Rooms 75 (7 fmly) (9 GF) (2 smoking) **Facilities** FTV WiFi ◊ Gym **Conf** Class 75
Board 65 Thtr 175 **Services** Lift **Parking** 70 **Notes** Closed 25-26 Dec Civ Wed 100

L

Campanile Leicester

BUDGET HOTEL

tel: 0116 261 6600 **St Matthew's Way, 1 Bedford Street North LE1 3JE**
email: leicester@campanile.com **web:** www.campanile.com
dir: A5460. Right at end of road, left at rdbt on A594. Follow Vaughan Way, Burleys Way then St. Matthew's Way. Hotel on left

This modern building offers accommodation in smart, well-equipped bedrooms, all with en suite bathrooms. Refreshments may be taken at the informal bistro. See also the Hotel Groups pages.

Rooms 93 ⬧ **Conf** Class 30 Board 30 Thtr 40

Ibis Leicester

BUDGET HOTEL

tel: 0116 248 7200 **St Georges Way, Constitution Hill LE1 1PL**
email: H3061@accor.com **web:** www.ibishotel.com
dir: From M1/M69 junct 21, follow town centre signs, central ring road (A594)/railway station, hotel opposite Leicester Mercury

Modern, budget hotel offering comfortable accommodation in bright and practical bedrooms. Breakfast is self-service and dinner is available in the restaurant. See also the Hotel Groups pages.

Rooms 94 (15 fmly)

Premier Inn Leicester (Braunstone)

BUDGET HOTEL

tel: 0871 527 8590 **Meridian Business Park, Thorpe Astley, Braunstone LE19 1LU**
web: www.premierinn.com
dir: M1 junct 21, follow A563 (outer ring road) signs W to Thorpe Astley. At slip road after Texaco garage. Hotel on left

High quality, budget accommodation ideal for both families and business travellers. Spacious, en suite bedrooms feature tea and coffee making facilities, and Freeview TV in most hotels. Internet access and WiFi are available for a small fee. The adjacent family restaurant features a wide and varied menu. See also the Hotel Groups pages.

Rooms 51

Premier Inn Leicester (Braunstone South)

BUDGET HOTEL

tel: 0871 527 8588 **Braunstone Lane East LE3 2FW**
web: www.premierinn.com
dir: M1 junct 21, at M69 junct take A5460 towards city. After 1m right at lights to hotel

Rooms 170

Premier Inn Leicester Central (A50)

BUDGET HOTEL

tel: 0871 527 8594 **Heathley Park, Groby Rd LE3 9QE**
web: www.premierinn.com
dir: Off A50, city centre side of County Hall & Glenfield General Hospital

Rooms 76

Premier Inn Leicester City Centre

BUDGET HOTEL

tel: 0871 527 8596 **1 St Georges Way LE1 1AA**
web: www.premierinn.com
dir: Telephone for detailed directions

Rooms 135

Premier Inn Leicester (Forest East)

BUDGET HOTEL

tel: 0871 527 8592 **Hinckley Rd, Leicester Forest East LE3 3GD**
web: www.premierinn.com
dir: M1 junct 21, A5460. At major junct (Holiday Inn on right), left into Braunstone Lane. In 2m left onto A47 towards Hinkley. Hotel 400yds on left

Rooms 40

Premier Inn Leicester North West

BUDGET HOTEL

tel: 0871 527 8598 **Leicester Rd, Glenfield LE3 8HB**
web: www.premierinn.com
dir: M1 junct 21a N'bound, A46. Onto A50 for Glenfield & County Hall. Or M1 junct 22 S'bound onto A50 towards Glenfield. Into County Hall. Hotel on left adjacent to Gynsills

Rooms 43

Premier Inn Leicester South (Oadby)

BUDGET HOTEL

tel: 0871 527 8600 **Glen Rise, Oadby LE2 4RG**
web: www.premierinn.com
dir: M1 junct 21, A563 signed South. Right at Leicester racecourse. Follow Market Harborough signs. Dual carriageway, straight on at rdbt. Into single lane, hotel on right

Rooms 30

LEICESTER FOREST MOTORWAY SERVICE AREA (M1) Map 11 SK50
Leicestershire

Days Inn Leicester Forest East - M1

BUDGET HOTEL

tel: 0116 239 0534 **Leicester Forest East, M1 Junct 21 LE3 3GB**
email: leicester.hotel@welcomebreak.co.uk **web:** www.welcomebreak.co.uk
dir: On M1 N'bound between junct 21 & 21A

This modern building offers accommodation in smart, spacious and well-equipped bedrooms, suitable for families and business travellers, and all with en suite bathrooms. Continental breakfast is available, and other refreshments may be taken at the nearby family restaurant. See also the Hotel Groups pages.

Rooms 86 (71 fmly) (10 smoking) **Conf** Board 10

LEINTWARDINE Herefordshire	Map 9 SO47

The Lion

⚜ RESTAURANT WITH ROOMS

tel: 01547 540203 & 540747 📄 01547 540747 **High St SY7 0JZ**
email: enquiries@thelionleintwardine.co.uk **web:** www.thelionleintwardine.co.uk
dir: Beside bridge on A4113 (Ludlow to Knighton road) in Leintwardine

This quiet country restaurant with rooms in the picturesque village of Leintwardine, set beside the River Teme, is just a short distance from Ludlow and Craven Arms. The interior is stylish and all the contemporary bedrooms are en suite. Dining is taken seriously here and the modern, imaginative food uses the freshest local ingredients. The well-stocked bar offers a selection of real ales and lagers and there is a separate drinkers' bar too. The Lion is particularly popular with families as the garden has a secure children's play area, and in warmer months guests can eat alfresco. The friendly staff help to make any visit memorable.

Rooms 8 (1 fmly)

LENHAM Kent	Map 7 TQ85

L

INSPECTORS' CHOICE

Chilston Park Hotel

★★★★  HOTEL

Hand PICKED
HOTELS
BUILT FOR PLEASURE

tel: 01622 859803 **Sandway ME17 2BE**
email: chilstonpark@handpicked.co.uk
web: www.handpickedhotels.co.uk/chilstonpark
dir: Exit A20 to Lenham, right into High St, pass station on right, 1st left, over x-roads, hotel 0.25m on left

This elegant Grade I listed country house is set in 23 acres of immaculately landscaped gardens and parkland. An impressive collection of original paintings and antiques creates a unique environment. The sunken Venetian-style restaurant serves modern British food with French influences. Bedrooms are individual in design, some have four-poster beds and many have garden views.

Rooms 53 (23 annexe) (2 fmly) (3 GF) ⏶ **S** £104-£328; **D** £104-£328 (incl. bkfst) **Facilities** STV FTV WiFi ⇘ HL Fishing ⛳ Xmas New Year **Conf** Class 60 Board 50 Thtr 100 Del from £130 to £155* **Services** Lift **Parking** 100 **Notes** LB ⊗ Civ Wed 90

LEOMINSTER Herefordshire	Map 10 SO45

BEST WESTERN Talbot Hotel

★★★ 75% HOTEL

Best Western

tel: 01568 616347 **West St HR6 8EP**
email: talbot@bestwestern.co.uk **web:** www.bw-talbothotel.co.uk
dir: From A49, A44 or A4112, hotel in town centre

This charming former coaching inn is located in the town centre and makes an ideal base for exploring the area. Public areas feature original beams and antique furniture, and include an atmospheric bar and elegant restaurant. The bedrooms vary in size, but all are comfortably furnished and equipped. Facilities are available for private functions and conferences.

Rooms 28 (3 fmly) (2 GF) **S** £63.50-£80; **D** £75-£91.50 **Facilities** FTV WiFi **Conf** Class 60 Board 30 Thtr 130 Del from £95 to £101 **Parking** 26 **Notes** LB ⊗

LEWDOWN Devon	Map 3 SX48

INSPECTORS' CHOICE

Lewtrenchard Manor

★★★  HOTEL

tel: 01566 783222 **EX20 4PN**
email: info@lewtrenchard.co.uk **web:** www.lewtrenchard.co.uk
dir: A30 from Exeter to Plymouth/Tavistock road. At T-junct turn right, then left onto old A30 (Lewdown road). Left in 6m signed Lewtrenchard

This Jacobean mansion was built in the 1600s, and is surrounded by its own idyllic grounds in a quiet valley close to the northern edge of Dartmoor. Public rooms include a fine gallery, as well as magnificent carvings and oak panelling. Imaginative and carefully prepared dishes are created using the best Devon produce, much from the hotel's kitchen garden, and is served either in the dining room or at the chef's table, the Purple Carrot. Bedrooms, varying in style and including courtyard suites, are comfortably furnished and spacious. There are a variety of leisure activities including falconry, horse riding, fishing, cycling and clay pigeon shooting on offer.

Rooms 14 (2 fmly) (3 GF) ⏶ **S** £140-£200; **D** £165-£235 (incl. bkfst)* **Facilities** FTV WiFi ⇘ Fishing ⛳ Clay pigeon shooting Falconry Beauty therapies Xmas New Year **Conf** Class 40 Board 30 Thtr 60 Del £187* **Parking** 50 **Notes** LB Civ Wed 100

L

LEYLAND
Lancashire
Map 15 SD52

BEST WESTERN PREMIER Leyland Hotel

★★★★ 76% HOTEL

tel: 01772 422922 **Leyland Way PR25 4JX**
email: leylandhotel@feathers.uk.com **web:** www.feathers.uk.com
dir: M6 junct 28, left at end of slip road, hotel 100mtrs on left

This purpose-built hotel enjoys a convenient location, just off the M6, within easy reach of Preston and Blackpool. Spacious public areas include extensive conference and banqueting facilities as well as a smart leisure club.

Rooms 93 (4 fmly) (31 GF) ⚓ **S** £49-£129; **D** £49-£129 **Facilities** FTV WiFi ↘ HL 🏊 supervised Gym Xmas New Year **Conf** Class 100 Board 40 Thtr 220 **Parking** 150 **Notes** LB ⊗ Civ Wed 200

Farington Lodge Hotel

★★★★ 75% HOTEL

tel: 01772 421321 **Stanifield Ln, Farington PR25 4QR**
email: info.farington@classiclodges.co.uk
web: www.classiclodges.co.uk/Farington_Lodge_Hotel_Preston
dir: Left at rdbt at end of M65, left at next rdbt. Entrance 1m on right after lights

This Grade II listed Georgian house, ideally located close to the M6, M61 and M65, is set in three acres of quiet, mature gardens and offers a romantic getaway. The choice of bedroom styles range from classic and traditional rooms in the original house to the contemporary, purpose-built executive rooms; all are stylishly decorated to a very high standard. This hotel is a popular venue for weddings, private dining and other special occasions.

Rooms 27 (3 fmly) (6 GF) ⚓ **Facilities** FTV WiFi ↘ Xmas New Year **Conf** Class 80 Board 60 Thtr 180 Del from £139.95* **Parking** 90 **Notes** ⊗ Civ Wed 150

LICHFIELD
Staffordshire
Map 10 SK10

INSPECTORS' CHOICE

Swinfen Hall Hotel

★★★★ ⚜⚜ HOTEL

tel: 01543 481494 **Swinfen WS14 9RE**
email: info@swinfenhallhotel.co.uk **web:** www.swinfenhallhotel.co.uk
dir: Set back from A38, 2.5m outside Lichfield, towards Birmingham

Dating from 1757, this lavishly decorated mansion has been painstakingly restored by the present owners. It is set in 100 acres of parkland which includes a deer park. Public rooms are particularly stylish, with intricately carved ceilings and impressive oil portraits. Bedrooms on the first floor boast period features and tall sash windows; those on the second floor (the former servants' quarters) are smaller and more contemporary by comparison. Service in the award-winning restaurant is both professional and attentive.

Rooms 17 (5 fmly) ⚓ **Facilities** STV FTV WiFi ↘ 🎣 Fishing ↘ Jogging trail 100 acre park New Year **Conf** Class 50 Board 50 Thtr 160 Del from £180* **Parking** 80 **Notes** ⊗ Civ Wed 120

BEST WESTERN The George Hotel

★★★ 81% HOTEL

tel: 01543 414822 **12-14 Bird St WS13 6PR**
email: mail@thegeorgelichfield.co.uk **web:** www.thegeorgelichfield.co.uk
dir: From Bowling Green Island on A461 take Lichfield exit. Left at next island into Swan Rd, as road bears left, turn right into Bird St for hotel car park

Situated in the city centre, this privately owned hotel provides good quality, well-equipped accommodation which includes a room with a four-poster bed. Facilities here include a large ballroom, plus several other rooms for meetings and functions.

Rooms 45 (5 fmly) **S** £45-£105; **D** £60-£125 (incl. bkfst) **Facilities** FTV WiFi ↘ HL Gym **Conf** Class 60 Board 40 Thtr 110 Del from £120 to £140 **Services** Lift **Parking** 45 **Notes** LB ⊗ Civ Wed 110

Cathedral Lodge Hotel

★★★ 73% HOTEL

tel: 01543 414500 **62 Beacon St WS13 7AR**
email: enquiries@cathedrallodgehotel.com **web:** www.cathedrallodgehotel.com
dir: From Birmingham, A38 to Lichfield. Hotel in city centre

This hotel is within easy walking distance of the famous cathedral and just a short drive from the NEC, Belfry Golf Course and many other attractions. The accommodation is modern, spacious and comfortable, and each room has a large, flat-screen TV with Sky. There is a large function suite together with conference facilities.

Rooms 36 (2 fmly) (6 smoking) **Facilities** FTV WiFi ↘ Xmas New Year **Conf** Class 80 Board 70 Thtr 80 **Notes** ⊗

Premier Inn Lichfield

BUDGET HOTEL

tel: 0871 527 8602 **Fine Ln, Fradley WS13 8RD**
web: www.premierinn.com
dir: On A38, 3 NE of Lichfield

High quality, budget accommodation ideal for both families and business travellers. Spacious, en suite bedrooms feature tea and coffee making facilities, and Freeview TV in most hotels. Internet access and WiFi are available for a small fee. The adjacent family restaurant features a wide and varied menu. See also the Hotel Groups pages.

Rooms 30

LINCOLN
Lincolnshire
Map 17 SK97

Washingborough Hall Hotel

★★★ 86% ◎◎ COUNTRY HOUSE HOTEL

tel: 01522 790340 **Church Hill, Washingborough LN4 1BE**
email: enquiries@washingboroughhall.com **web:** www.washingboroughhall.com
dir: B1190 into Washingborough. Right at rdbt, hotel 500yds on left

This Georgian manor stands on the edge of the quiet village of Washingborough and is set in attractive gardens. Public rooms are pleasantly furnished and comfortable, while the restaurant offers interesting menus. Bedrooms are individually designed and most have views out over the grounds to the countryside beyond.

Rooms 12 (3 fmly) ⟡ **Facilities** FTV WiFi ⟡ ⟡ Bicycles for hire New Year **Conf** Class 30 Board 26 Thtr 50 **Parking** 40 **Notes** Civ Wed 70

BEST WESTERN PLUS Bentley Hotel & Spa

★★★ 85% HOTEL

tel: 01522 878000 **Newark Rd, South Hykeham LN6 9NH**
email: info@bentleyhotellincoln.co.uk **web:** www.bentleyhotellincoln.co.uk
dir: A1 onto A46 E towards Lincoln for 10m. Over 1st rdbt on Lincoln Bypass to hotel 50yds on left

This modern hotel is on a ring road, so it is conveniently located for all local attractions. Attractive bedrooms, most with air conditioning, are well equipped and spacious. The hotel has a leisure suite with gym and large pool (with a hoist for the less able). Spa facilities include a hairdresser, treatment rooms and thermal suite. Extensive conference facilities are available.

Rooms 80 (5 fmly) (26 GF) ⟡ **S** £98-£108; **D** £113-£149 (incl. bkfst)* **Facilities** Spa STV FTV WiFi ⟡ HL ⟡ Gym Steam room Sauna New Year **Conf** Class 150 Board 30 Thtr 300 Del from £120* **Services** Lift Air con **Parking** 170 **Notes** LB ⊗ Civ Wed 120

The Lincoln Hotel

★★★ 80% ◎ HOTEL

tel: 01522 520348 **Eastgate LN2 1PN**
email: reservations@thelincolnhotel.com **web:** www.thelincolnhotel.com
dir: Adjacent to cathedral

This privately owned modern hotel enjoys superb uninterrupted views of Lincoln Cathedral. There are ruins of the Roman wall and Eastgate in the grounds. Bedrooms are contemporary with up-to-the-minute facilities. An airy restaurant and bar, a cellar bar, plus a comfortable lounge are provided. There are substantial conference and meeting facilities.

Rooms 71 (4 fmly) (8 GF) **S** £80-£115; **D** £86-£141 (incl. bkfst)* **Facilities** FTV WiFi Gym **Conf** Class 50 Board 40 Thtr 120 Del from £139 to £159* **Services** Lift **Parking** 120 **Notes** LB ⊗ Civ Wed 150

The White Hart

★★★ 80% HOTEL

tel: 01522 526222 & 563293 **Bailgate LN1 3AR**
email: info@whitehart-lincoln.co.uk **web:** www.whitehart-lincoln.co.uk
dir: A46 onto B1226, through Newport Arch. Hotel 0.5m on left as road bends left

Lying in the shadow of Lincoln's magnificent cathedral, this hotel is perfectly positioned for exploring the shops and sights of this medieval city. The attractive bedrooms are furnished and decorated in a traditional style and many have views of the cathedral. Given the hotel's central location, parking is a real benefit.

Rooms 50 (3 fmly) **Facilities** FTV WiFi ⟡ **Conf** Class 80 Board 103 Thtr 160 **Services** Lift **Parking** 50 **Notes** Civ Wed 120

Branston Hall Hotel

★★★ 75% ◎◎ COUNTRY HOUSE HOTEL

tel: 01522 793305 **Branston Park, Branston LN4 1PD**
email: info@branstonhall.com **web:** www.branstonhall.com
dir: On B1188, 3m SE of Lincoln

Dating back to 1885 this country house sits in 88 acres of beautiful grounds complete with a lake. There is an elegant restaurant, a spacious bar and a beautiful lounge in addition to impressive conference and leisure facilities. Individually styled bedrooms vary in size and include several with four-poster beds. The hotel is a popular wedding venue.

Rooms 50 (7 annexe) (3 fmly) (4 GF) **Facilities** Spa STV FTV WiFi ⟡ Gym Jogging circuit Xmas New Year **Conf** Class 54 Board 40 Thtr 200 **Services** Lift **Parking** 100 **Notes** ⊗ Civ Wed 160

See advert on opposite page

Tower Hotel

★★★ 72% HOTEL

tel: 01522 529999 **38 Westgate LN1 3BD**
email: tower.hotel@btclick.com **web:** www.lincolntowerhotel.com
dir: From A46 follow signs to Lincoln N then to Bailgate area. Through arch, 2nd right

This hotel faces the Norman castle wall and is in a very convenient location for the city. The relaxed and friendly atmosphere is very noticeable here. There's a modern conservatory bar and a stylish restaurant where contemporary dishes are available throughout the day.

Rooms 15 (1 fmly) ⟡ **S** £70; **D** £95 (incl. bkfst)* **Facilities** STV FTV WiFi
Conf Class 24 Board 16 Thtr 24 **Notes** Closed 24-27 Dec & 1 Jan

Ibis Lincoln

BUDGET HOTEL

tel: 01522 698333 **Runcorn Rd (A46), off Whisby Rd LN6 3QZ**
email: H3161@accor-hotels.com **web:** www.ibishotel.com
dir: Exit A46 (ring road) into Whisby Rd. 1st left

Modern, budget hotel offering comfortable accommodation in bright and practical bedrooms. Breakfast is self-service and dinner is available in the restaurant See also the Hotel Groups pages.

Rooms 86 (19 fmly) (8 GF) ⟡ **S** £38-£70; **D** £38-£70* **Conf** Class 12 Board 20 Thtr 35

Premier Inn Lincoln

BUDGET HOTEL

tel: 0871 527 8604 **Lincoln Rd, Canwick Hill LN4 2RF**
web: www.premierinn.com
dir: Approx 1m S of city centre at junction of B1188 & B1131

High quality, budget accommodation ideal for both families and business travellers. Spacious, en suite bedrooms feature tea and coffee making facilities, and Freeview TV in most hotels. Internet access and WiFi are available for a small fee. The adjacent family restaurant features a wide and varied menu. See also the Hotel Groups pages.

Rooms 60

Premier Inn Lincoln City Centre

BUDGET HOTEL

tel: 0871 527 9418 **Broadgate LN2 5AQ**
web: www.premierinn.com
dir: From N: from A57 left into Mint St (B1003). Right into Broadgate (A15). From S: on A46 to A1434/Newark Rd rdbt. Straight on next rdbt into St Catherines (A15), straight on at next rdbt. Left into St Swithins Sq. Right into Silver St (B1003). Right into Broadgate (A15)

Rooms 131

The Old Bakery

⟡⟡ RESTAURANT WITH ROOMS

tel: 01522 576057 & 07949 035554 **26/28 Burton Rd LN1 3LB**
email: enquiries@theold-bakery.co.uk **web:** www.theold-bakery.co.uk
dir: Exit A46 at Lincoln North follow signs for cathedral. 3rd exit at 1st rdbt, 1st exit at next rdbt

Situated close to the castle at the top of the town, this converted bakery offers well-equipped bedrooms and a delightful dining operation. The cooking has gained two AA Rosettes, and uses much local produce. Expect good friendly service from the dedicated staff.

Rooms 4 (1 fmly)

L

LIPHOOK
Hampshire

Map 5 SU83

Old Thorns Manor Hotel Golf & Country Estate

★★★★ 72% HOTEL

tel: 01428 724555 & 725844 **Griggs Green GU30 7PE**
email: reservations@oldthorns.com **web:** www.oldthorns.com
dir: At Griggs Green exit A3, hotel 0.5m

Old Thorns is a modern relaxed and welcoming hotel, set in 400 acres of the peaceful Hampshire countryside, which includes a championship golf course. The bedrooms are spacious and stylish and offer high levels of comfort. The leisure facilities are extensive and include a health club, wellness centre and spa; in addition there is also a sports bar, champagne and cocktail bar, Kings Restaurant and all-day dining is also available.

Rooms 175 (2 fmly) (64 GF) **Facilities** Spa STV FTV WiFi 18 Putt green Gym Xmas New Year **Conf** Class 100 Board 30 Thtr 300 Del £149* **Services** Lift **Parking** 278 **Notes** Civ Wed 250

LISKEARD
Cornwall

Map 2 SX26

Premier Inn Liskeard

BUDGET HOTEL

tel: 0871 527 8608 **Liskeard Retail Park, Haviland Rd PL14 3FG**
web: www.premierinn.com
dir: Off A38, on A390 SW of Liskeard

High quality, budget accommodation ideal for both families and business travellers. Spacious, en suite bedrooms feature tea and coffee making facilities, and Freeview TV in most hotels. Internet access and WiFi are available for a small fee. The adjacent family restaurant features a wide and varied menu. See also the Hotel Groups pages.

Rooms 51

LITTLEHAMPTON
West Sussex

Map 6 TQ00

Premier Inn Littlehampton

BUDGET HOTEL

tel: 0871 527 8610 **Roundstone Ln, East Preston BN16 1EB**
web: www.premierinn.com
dir: A27 onto A280 signed Littlehampton/Rustington & Angmering. At next rdbt follow Littlehampton, Rustington/A259 signs. At next rdbt 1st exit signed East Preston. Hotel on left

High quality, budget accommodation ideal for both families and business travellers. Spacious, en suite bedrooms feature tea and coffee making facilities, and Freeview TV in most hotels. Internet access and WiFi are available for a small fee. The adjacent family restaurant features a wide and varied menu. See also the Hotel Groups pages.

Rooms 20

LIVERPOOL
Merseyside

Map 15 SJ39

Thornton Hall Hotel and Spa

★★★★ 79% HOTEL

tel: 0151 336 3938 & 353 3717 **Neston Rd CH63 1JF**
email: reservations@thorntonhallhotel.com **web:** www.thorntonhallhotel.com

(For full entry see Thornton Hough)

Hope Street Hotel

★★★★ 76% HOTEL

tel: 0151 709 3000 **40 Hope St L1 9DA**
email: sleep@hopestreethotel.co.uk **web:** www.hopestreethotel.co.uk
dir: Follow Cathedral & University signs on entering city. Telephone for detailed directions

This stylish property is located within easy walking distance of the city's cathedrals, theatres, major shops and attractions. Stylish bedrooms and suites are appointed with flat-screen TVs, DVD players, internet access and comfy beds with Egyptian cotton sheets; the bathrooms have rain showers and deep tubs. The London Carriage Works Restaurant specialises in local, seasonal produce and the adjacent lounge bar offers lighter all-day dining and wonderful cocktails.

Rooms 89 (16 fmly) (5 GF) **D** £114-£190* **Facilities** STV FTV WiFi Gym Massage & beauty therapists Xmas New Year **Conf** Class 40 Board 30 Thtr 70 Del from £200* **Services** Lift Air con **Parking** 10 **Notes** LB Civ Wed 70

L

Malmaison Liverpool

★★★★ 75%  HOTEL

tel: 0844 693 0655 **7 William Jessop Way, Princes Dock L3 1QZ**
email: liverpool@malmaison.com **web:** www.malmaison.com
dir: A5080 follow signs for Pier Head/Southport/Bootle. Into Baln St to rdbt, 1st exit at rdbt, immediately left onto William Jessop Way

This is a purpose-built hotel with cutting edge and contemporary style. 'Mal' Liverpool, as its known, has a stunning location, alongside the river and docks, and in the heart of the city's regeneration. Bedrooms are stylish and comfortable and are provided with lots of extra facilities. The public areas are packed with fun and style, and there is a number of meeting rooms as well as private dining, including a chef's table.

Rooms 130 ✆ **Facilities** STV WiFi Gym **Conf** Class 28 Board 22 Thtr 50 **Services** Lift Air con

Novotel Liverpool

★★★★ 75% HOTEL

tel: 0151 603 2801 **40 Hanover St L1 4LN**
email: h6495@accor.com **web:** www.novotel.com

This attractive and stylish city centre hotel is convenient for Liverpool Echo Arena, Liverpool One shopping centre and the Albert Dock; it is adjacent to a town centre car park. The hotel has a range of conference and leisure facilities which include an indoor heated pool and fitness suite. The restaurant offers a contemporary style menu. The bedrooms are comfortable and stylishly designed.

Rooms 209 (127 fmly) ✆ **S** £70-£250; **D** £70-£250 **Facilities** FTV WiFi ⅃ ⊗ Gym Steam room **Conf** Class 60 Board 50 Thtr 90 Del from £115 to £290 **Services** Lift **Notes** LB

BEST WESTERN Alicia Hotel

★★★ 78% HOTEL

tel: 0151 727 4411 **3 Aigburth Dr, Sefton Park L17 3AA**
email: aliciahotel@feathers.uk.com **web:** www.feathers.uk.com
dir: From end of M62 take A5058 to Sefton Park, then left, follow park around

This stylish and friendly hotel overlooks Sefton Park and is just a few minutes' drive from both the city centre and John Lennon Airport. Bedrooms are well equipped and comfortable. Day rooms include a striking modern restaurant and bar. Extensive, stylish function facilities make this a popular wedding venue.

Rooms 41 (8 fmly) ✆ **Facilities** STV WiFi HL Xmas New Year **Conf** Class 80 Board 40 Thtr 120 Del from £110 to £160 **Services** Lift **Parking** 40 **Notes** ⊗ Civ Wed 120

BEST WESTERN Feathers Liverpool Hotel

★★★ 77% HOTEL

tel: 0151 709 9655 ▤ 0151 709 3838 **115-125 Mount Pleasant L3 5TF**
email: feathershotel@feathers.uk.com **web:** www.feathers.uk.com/feathers-hotel
dir: Located in the city centre

This stylish and friendly hotel has a prime city centre location close to both cathedrals, universities and is just a few minutes' walk from shopping areas. Bedrooms come in a variety of distinctive styles and are well equipped and comfortable. Public rooms include a striking modern restaurant and bar.

Rooms 81 **Facilities** FTV WiFi **Conf** Board 12 **Parking** 24 **Notes** Civ Wed

Jurys Inn Liverpool

★★★ 75% HOTEL

tel: 0151 244 3777 **No 31 Keel Wharf L3 4FN**
email: jurysinnliverpool@jurysinns.com **web:** www.jurysinns.com
dir: Follow City Centre & Albert Dock signs. Hotel at Kings Waterfront adjacent to Albert Dock, opposite BT Convention Centre & Echo Arena

Located on the Kings Waterfront adjacent to the BT Convention Centre, Echo Arena, Albert Dock complex and a short walk from the very popular shopping district of Liverpool One, this hotel offers contemporary and spacious bedrooms. Guests have a choice of dining options - the Innfusion restaurant and the Inntro bar. There are ten dedicated meeting rooms and WiFi is available throughout. There is ample secure parking nearby.

Rooms 310 (58 fmly) **Facilities** FTV WiFi ⅃ **Conf** Class 50 Board 40 Thtr 100 **Services** Lift Air con **Notes** ⊗ Civ Wed 100

Campanile Liverpool

BUDGET HOTEL

tel: 0151 709 8104 **Chaloner St, Queens Dock L3 4AJ**
email: liverpool@campanile.com **web:** www.campanile.com
dir: Follow tourist signs marked Albert Dock. Hotel on waterfront

This modern building offers accommodation in smart, well-equipped bedrooms, all with en suite bathrooms. Refreshments may be taken at the informal bistro. See also the Hotel Groups pages.

Rooms 100 (4 fmly) (33 GF) **Conf** Class 18 Board 24 Thtr 35

Ibis Liverpool Centre Albert Dock

BUDGET HOTEL

tel: 0151 706 9800 **27 Wapping L1 8LY**
email: H3140@accor.com **web:** www.ibishotel.com
dir: From M62 follow Albert Dock signs. Opposite Dock entrance

Modern, budget hotel offering comfortable accommodation in bright and practical bedrooms. Breakfast is self-service and dinner is available in the restaurant. See also the Hotel Groups pages.

Rooms 127 (15 fmly) (23 GF) ✆

Premier Inn Liverpool (Aintree)

BUDGET HOTEL

tel: 0871 527 8612 **Ormskirk Rd, Aintree L9 5AS**
web: www.premierinn.com
dir: M58, A57, A59 towards Liverpool. Pass Aintree Retail Park, left at lights into Aintree Racecourse. Hotel on left

High quality, budget accommodation ideal for both families and business travellers. Spacious, en suite bedrooms feature tea and coffee making facilities, and Freeview TV in most hotels. Internet access and WiFi are available for a small fee. The adjacent family restaurant features a wide and varied menu. See also the Hotel Groups pages.

Rooms 40

LIVERPOOL *continued*

Premier Inn Liverpool Airport

BUDGET HOTEL

tel: 0871 527 8626 **57 Speke Hall Av L24 1YQ**
web: www.premierinn.com
dir: A561 towards Liverpool follow 'Liverpool John Lennon Airport' signs into Seake Hall Ave, at 1st rdbt take 2nd left. Hotel 300mtrs on left

Rooms 10

Premier Inn Liverpool Albert Dock

BUDGET HOTEL

tel: 0871 527 8622 **East Britannia Building, Albert Dock L3 4AD**
web: www.premierinn.com
dir: Follow signs for Liverpool City Centre & Albert Dock

Rooms 130

Premier Inn Liverpool City Centre (Liverpool One)

BUDGET HOTEL

tel: 0871 527 9382 **48 Hanover St L1 4AF**
web: www.premierinn.com
dir: A5047 follow signs for city centre. At lights left onto A5048, at next lights right onto A5047. Head for A5038 signed Toxteth, Airport. Right into Renshaw Street & right onto Ranelagh Street. Premier Inn on left opposite BBC Radio Merseyside

Rooms 183

Premier Inn Liverpool City Centre (Moorfields)

BUDGET HOTEL

tel: 0871 527 8624 **Vernon St L2 2AY**
web: www.premierinn.com
dir: From M62 follow Liverpool City Centre & Birkenhead Tunnel signs. At rdbt 3rd exit into Dale St, right into Vernon St. Hotel on left

Rooms 165

Premier Inn Liverpool North

BUDGET HOTEL

tel: 0871 527 8628 **Northern Perimeter Rd L30 7PT**
web: www.premierinn.com
dir: 0.25m from end of M58/M5, on A5207

Rooms 63

Premier Inn Liverpool (Roby)

BUDGET HOTEL

tel: 0871 527 8616 **Roby Rd, Huyton L36 4HD**
web: www.premierinn.com
dir: Just off M62 junct 5 on A5080

Rooms 53

Premier Inn Liverpool (Tarbock)

BUDGET HOTEL

tel: 0871 527 8618 **Wilson Rd, Tarbock L36 6AD**
web: www.premierinn.com
dir: At M62 & M57 junct. M62 junct 6, take A5080 (Huyton).1st right into Wilson Rd

Rooms 41

Premier Inn Liverpool (West Derby)

BUDGET HOTEL

tel: 0871 527 8620 **Queens Dr, West Derby L13 0DL**
web: www.premierinn.com
dir: At end of M62 right under flyover onto A5058 (follow football stadium signs). Hotel 1.5m on left, just past Esso garage

Rooms 84

| LIVERSEDGE | Map 16 SE12 |
| West Yorkshire | |

Healds Hall Hotel & Restaurant

THE INDEPENDENTS
HOTEL ASSOCIATION

★★★ 78% ◉ HOTEL

tel: 01924 409112 **Leeds Rd WF15 6JA**
email: enquire@healdshall.co.uk **web:** www.healdshall.co.uk
dir: On A62 between Leeds & Huddersfield. 50yds on left after lights at Swan Pub

This 18th-century house, in the heart of West Yorkshire, provides comfortable and well-equipped accommodation and excellent hospitality. The hotel has earned a good local reputation for the quality of its food and offers a choice of casual or more formal dining styles, from a wide range of dishes on the various menus.

Rooms 24 (3 fmly) (3 GF) ↖ **S** £55-£95; **D** £65-£110 (incl. bkfst) **Facilities** FTV WiFi ↳ **Conf** Class 60 Board 45 Thtr 100 Del from £100 to £150 **Parking** 90 **Notes** LB Closed 1 Jan & BH Mon RS Sun eve Civ Wed 100

| LIZARD | Map 2 SW71 |
| Cornwall | |

Housel Bay Hotel

★★★ 72% ◉ HOTEL

tel: 01326 290417 & 290917 **Housel Cove TR12 7PG**
email: info@houselbay.com **web:** www.houselbay.com
dir: A39 or A394 to Helston, then A3083. At Lizard sign turn left, left at school, down lane to hotel

This long-established hotel has stunning views across the Western Approaches, equally enjoyable from the lounge and many of the bedrooms. Good cuisine is available in the stylish dining room, from where guests might enjoy a stroll to the end of the garden, which leads directly onto the Cornwall coastal path.

Rooms 20 (1 fmly) ↖ **S** £60-£70; **D** £95-£105 (incl. bkfst)* **Facilities** FTV WiFi ↳ Xmas New Year **Services** Lift **Parking** 35 **Notes** LB ⊗

London

Index of London Hotels

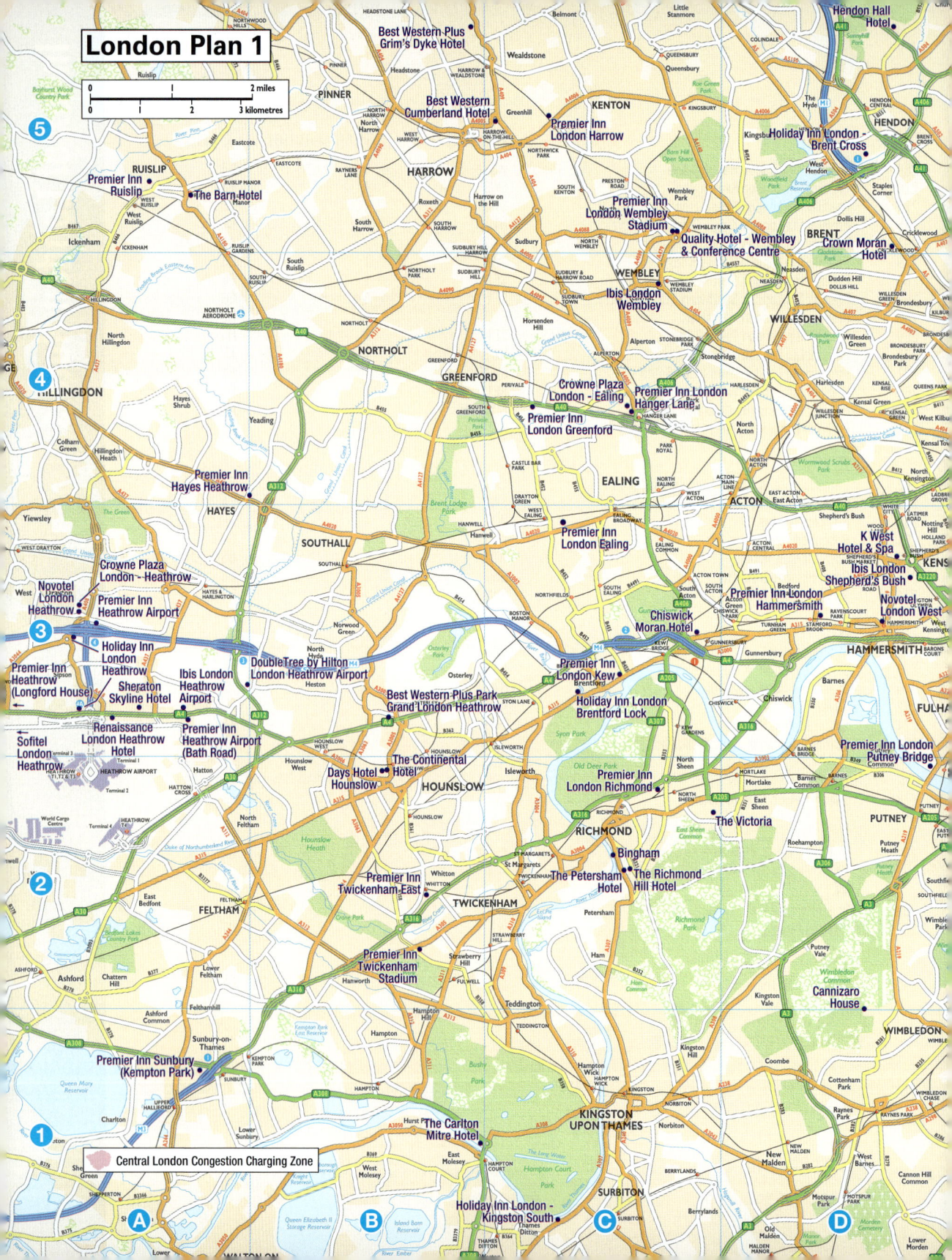

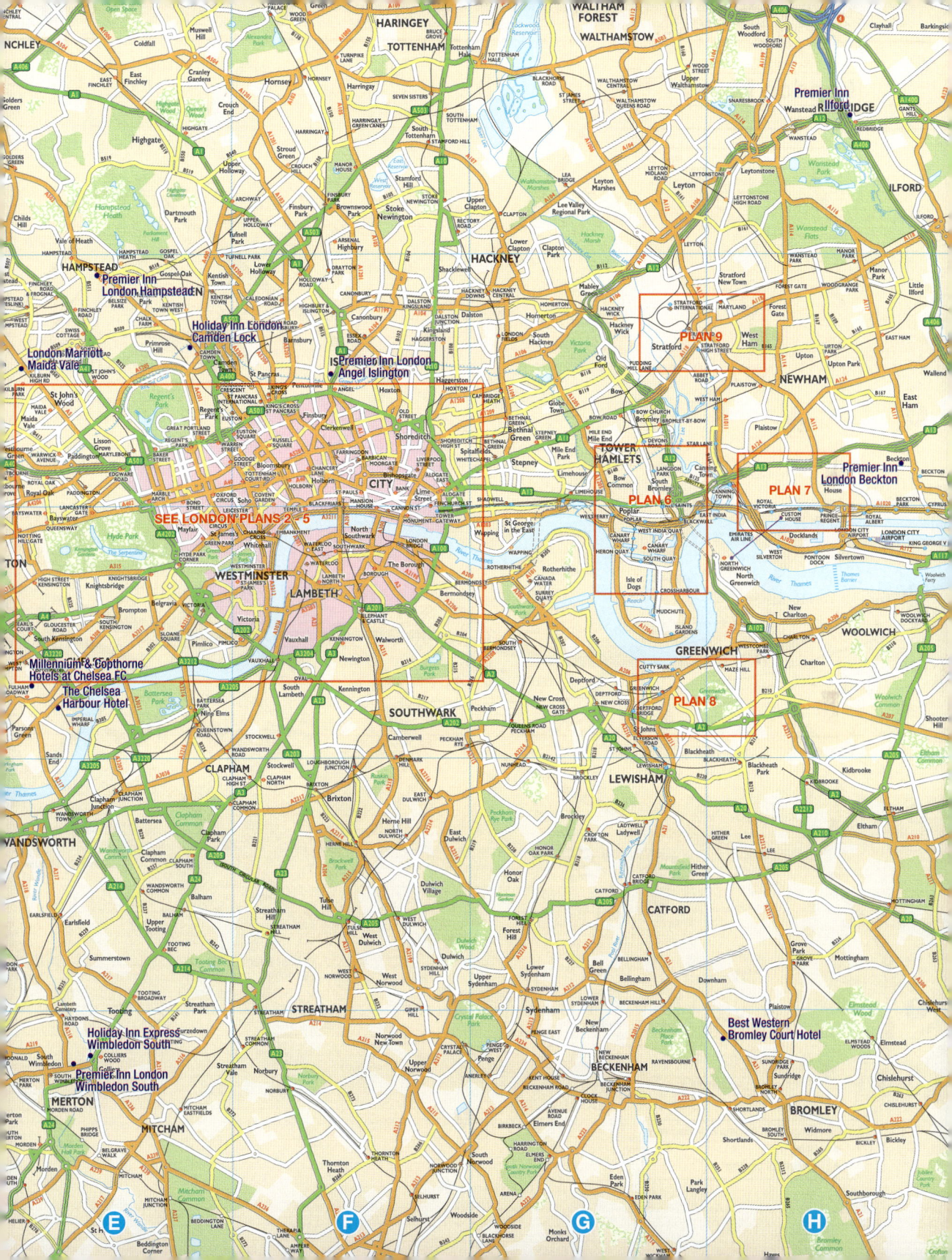

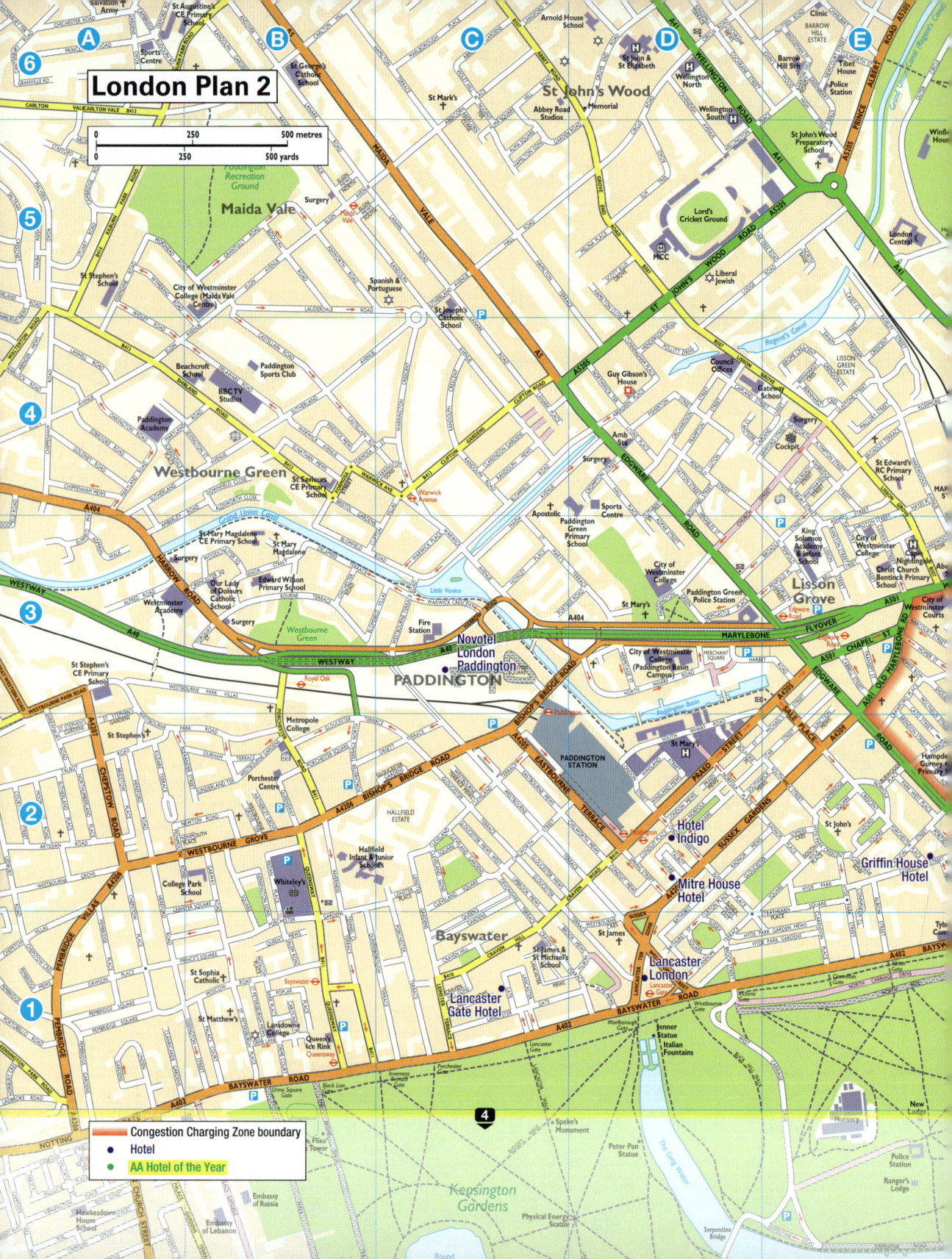

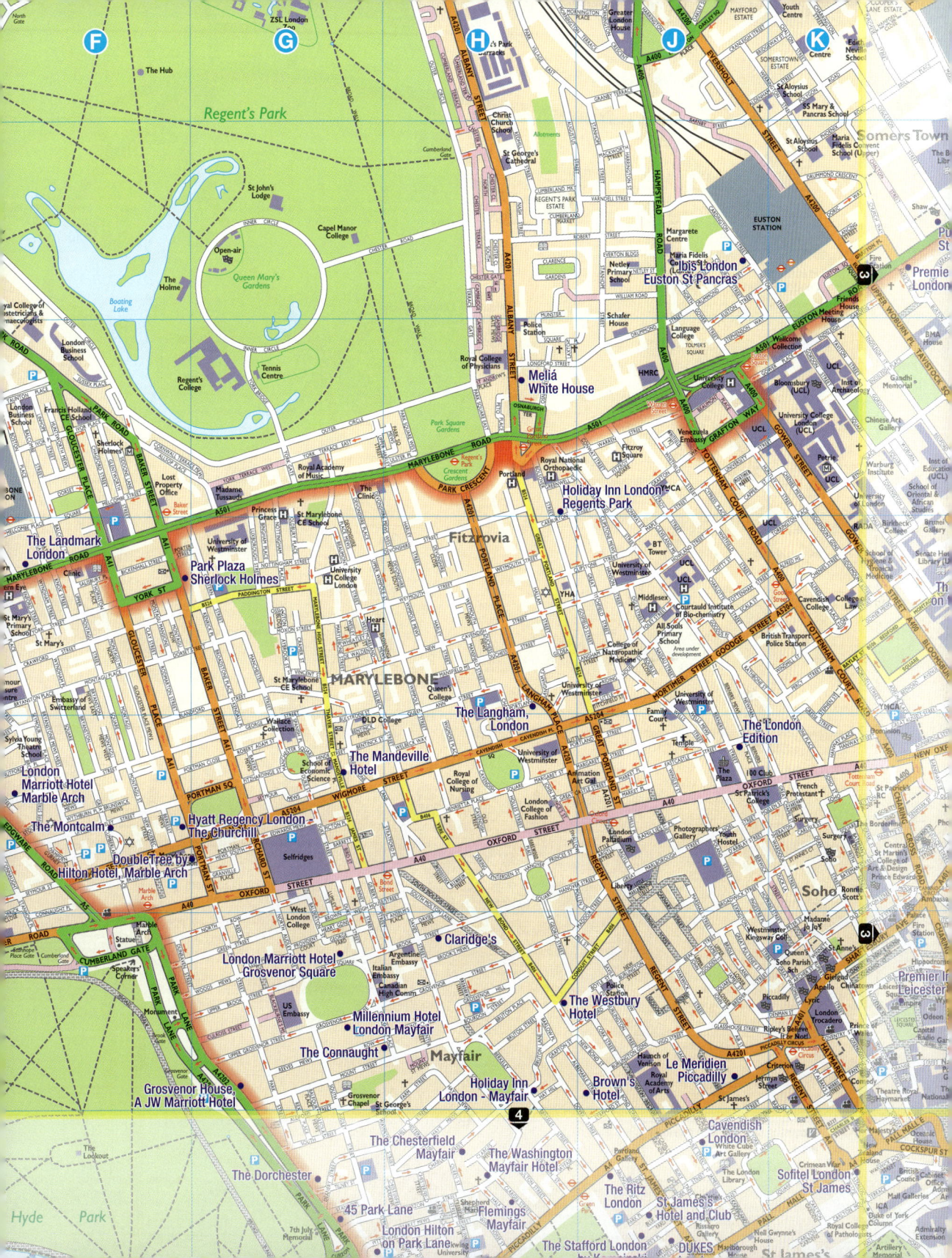

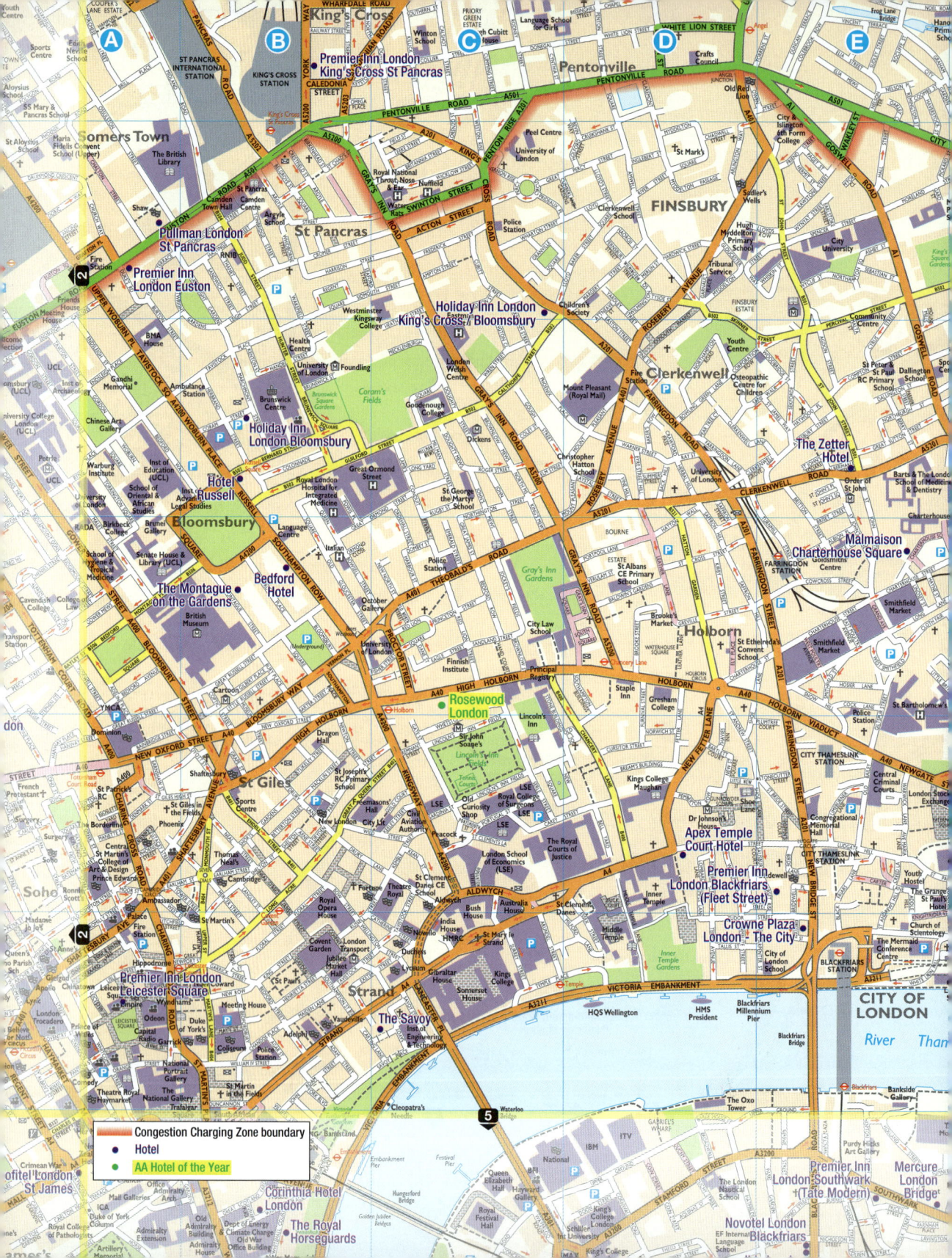

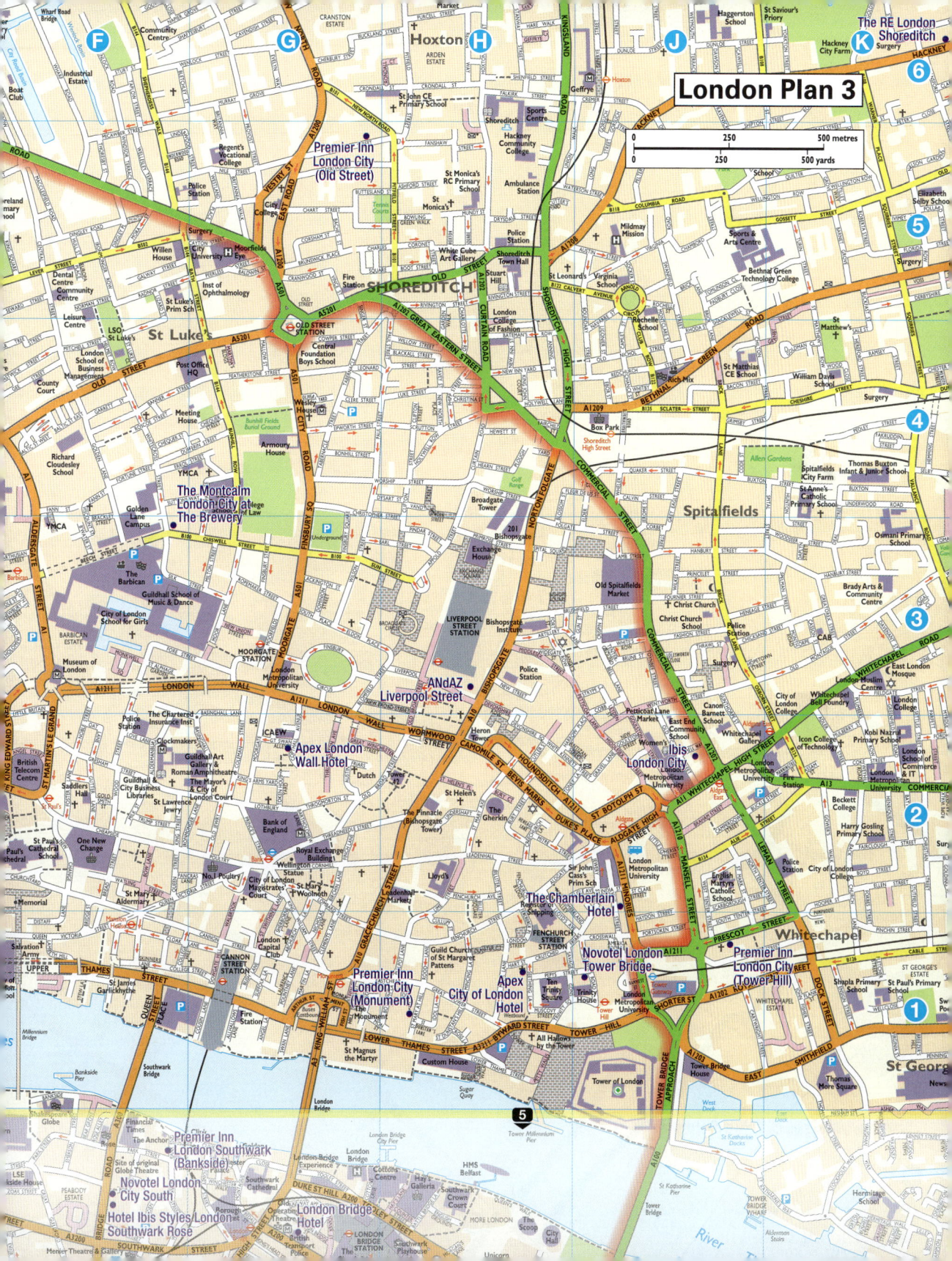

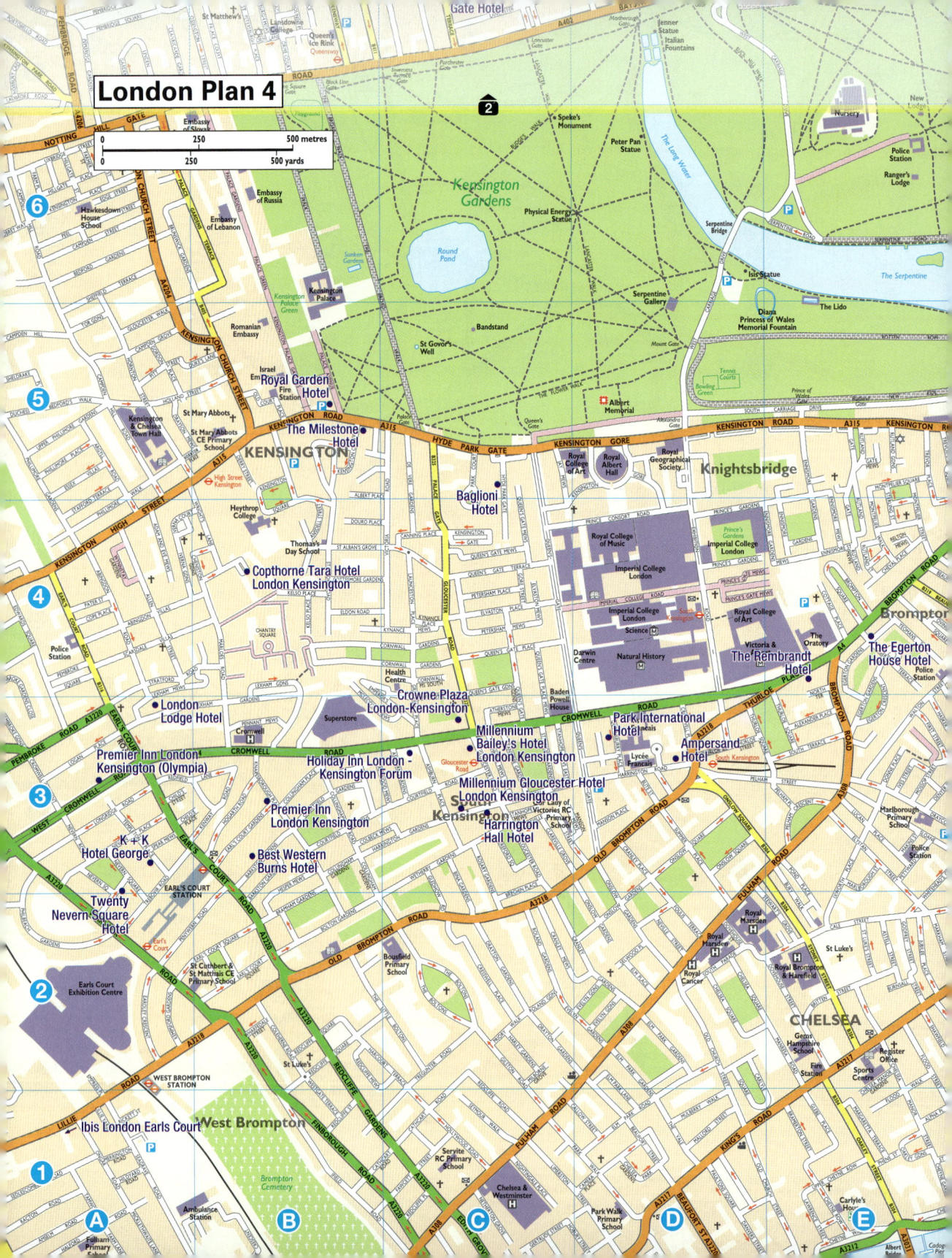

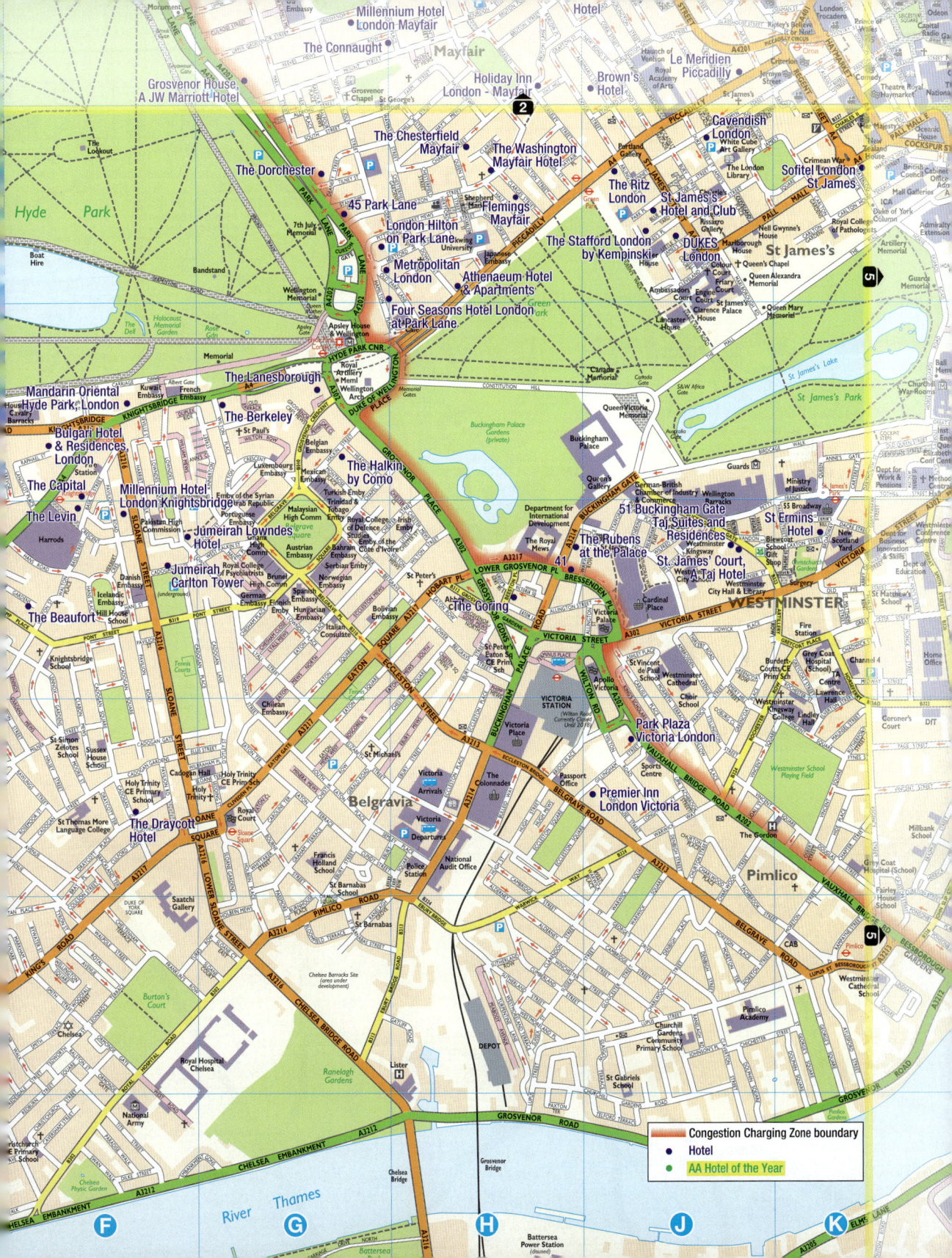

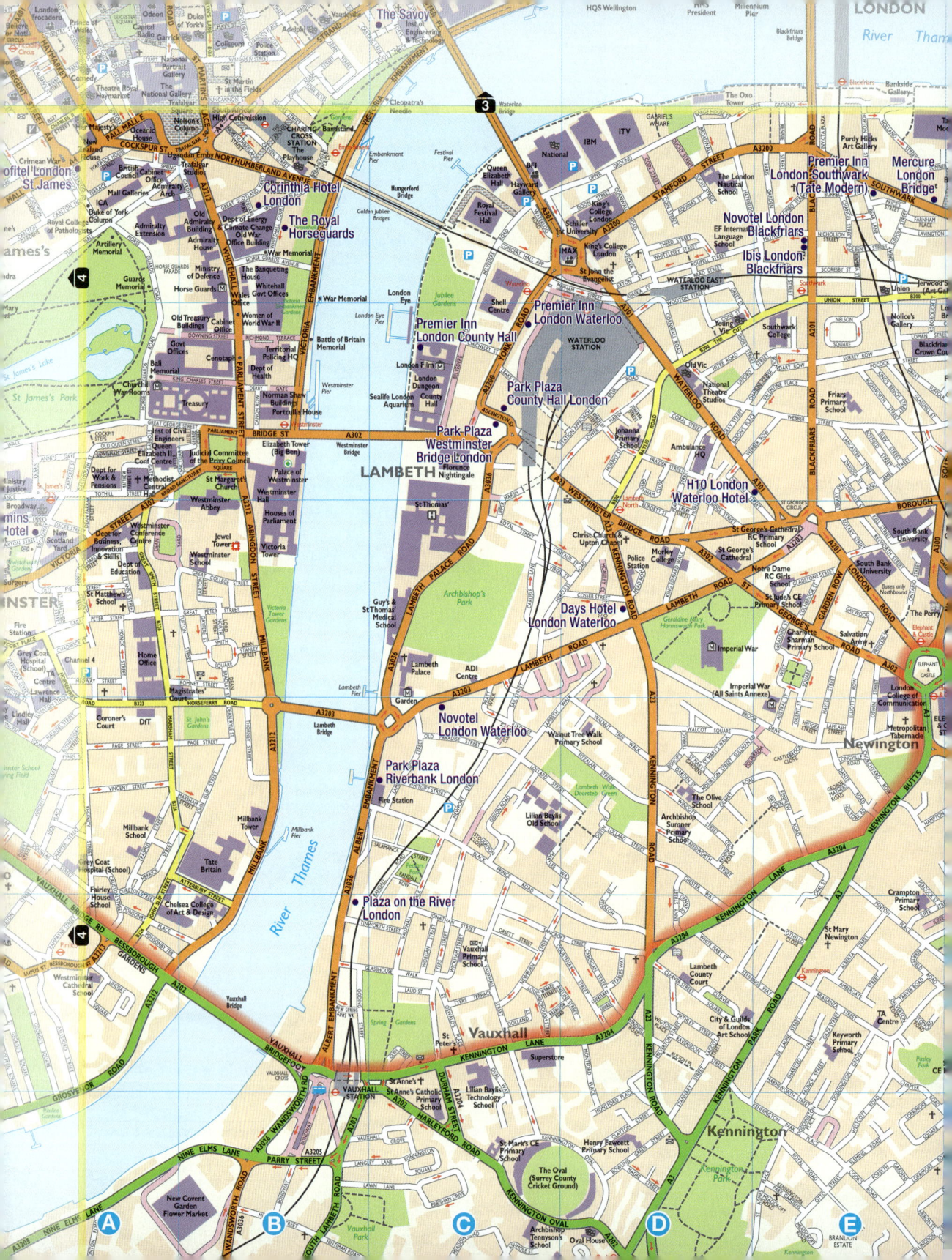

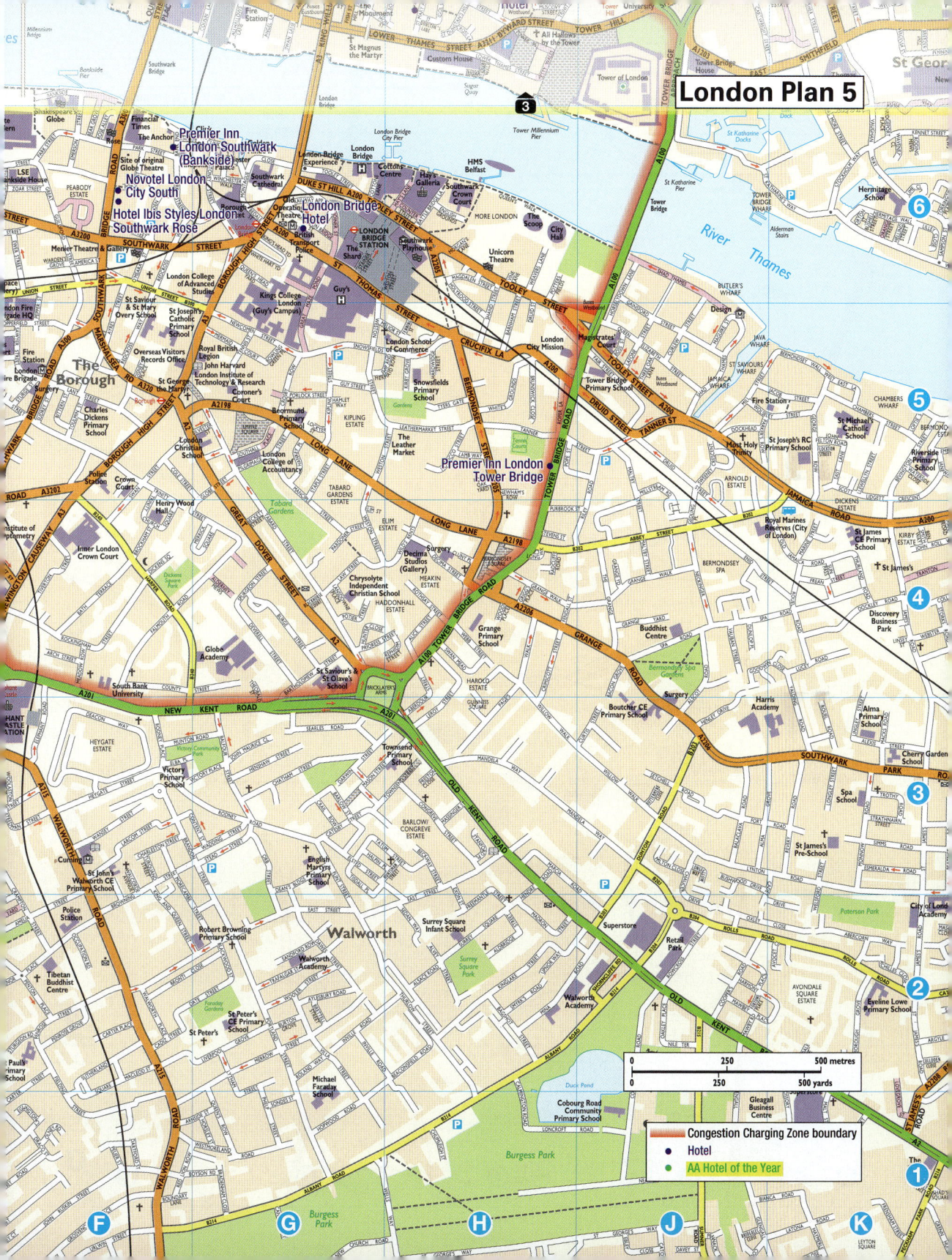

London Plan 5

Congestion Charging Zone boundary
● **Hotel**
● **AA Hotel of the Year**

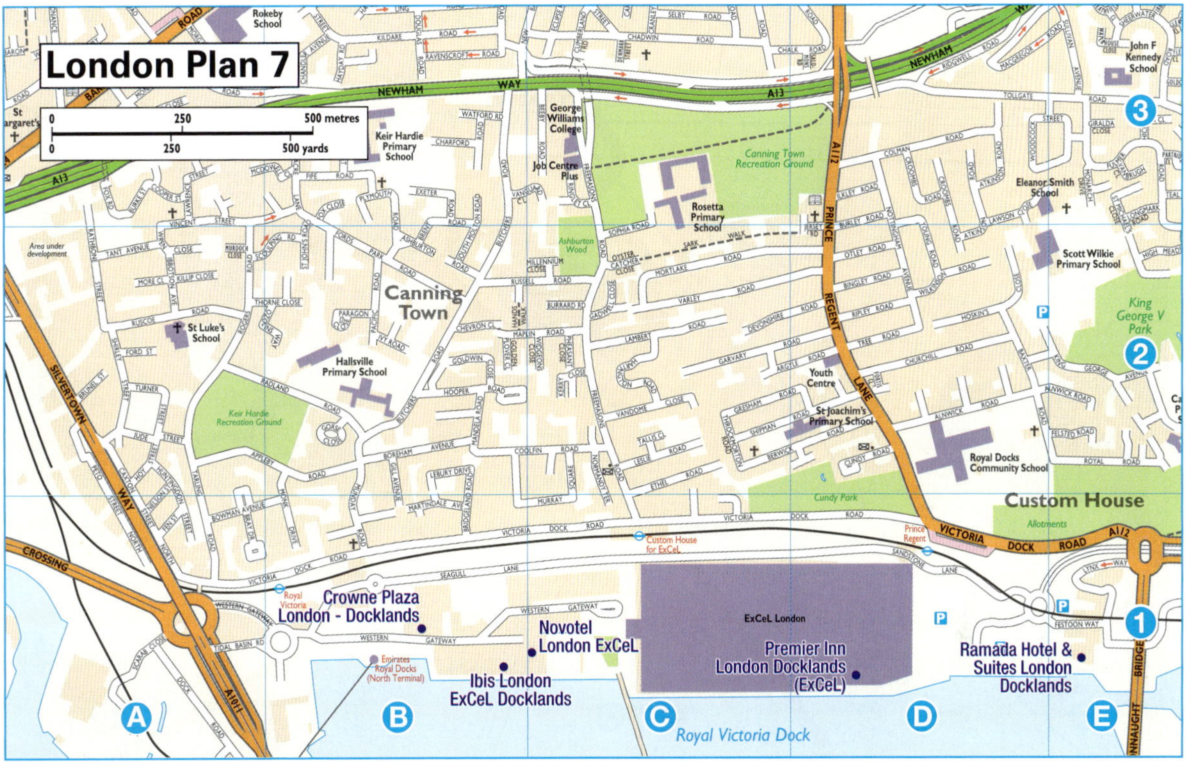

London Plan 7

0 250 500 metres
0 250 500 yards

Rokeby School
Keir Hardie Primary School
George Williams College
Job Centre Plus
Canning Town Recreation Ground
Rosetta Primary School
John F Kennedy School
Eleanor Smith School
Scott Wilkie Primary School
King George V Park
Ashburton Wood

St Margaret's
Area under development
St Luke's School
Canning Town
Hallsville Primary School
Keir Hardie Recreation Ground
Youth Centre
St Joachim's Primary School
Royal Docks Community School

Candy Park
Custom House
Allotments
Custom House for ExCeL
Royal Victoria
Crowne Plaza London - Docklands
Novotel London ExCeL
Ibis London ExCeL Docklands
Emirates Royal Docks (North Terminal)
ExCeL London
Premier Inn London Docklands (ExCeL)
Ramada Hotel & Suites London Docklands
Royal Victoria Dock

A B C D E
1 2 3

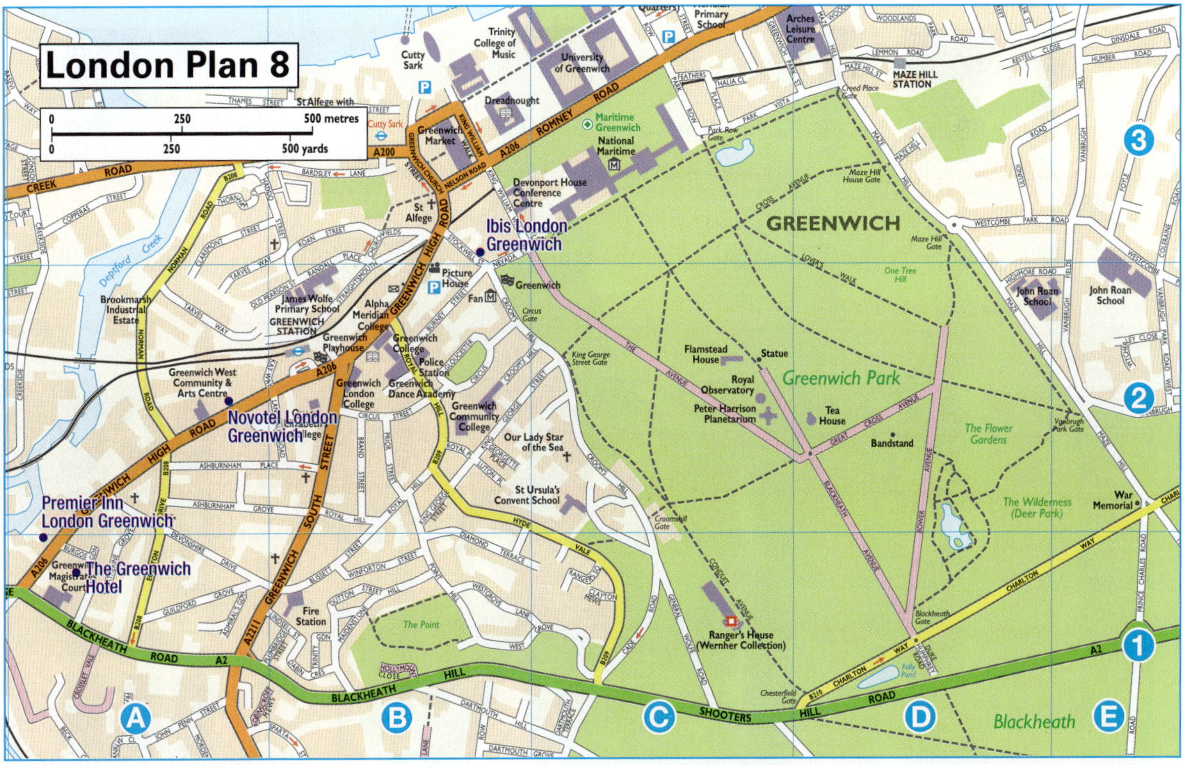

London Plan 8

0 250 500 metres
0 250 500 yards

Cutty Sark
Trinity College of Music
University of Greenwich
Primary School
Arches Leisure Centre
MAZE HILL STATION

St Alfege with
Cutty Sark
Greenwich Market
Dreadnought
Maritime Greenwich
National Maritime
Devonport House Conference Centre
St Alfege
Ibis London Greenwich
Picture House
Fan
Greenwich
Circus Gate
Maze Hill House Gate
John Roan School
John Roan School
GREENWICH
Westcombe Park
One Tree Hill

Brookmarsh Industrial Estate
James Wolfe Primary School
Alpha Meridian College
GREENWICH STATION
Greenwich Playhouse
Greenwich West Community & Arts Centre
Greenwich College
Greenwich London College
Police Station
Greenwich Dance Academy
Greenwich Community College
Our Lady Star of the Sea
St Ursula's Convent School
King George Street Gate
Flamstead House
Statue
Royal Observatory
Peter Harrison Planetarium
Tea House
Bandstand
Greenwich Park
The Flower Gardens
Vanbrugh Park Gate
Novotel London Greenwich
The Wilderness (Deer Park)

Premier Inn London Greenwich
Greenwich Magistrates Court
The Greenwich Hotel
Fire Station
The Point
Croom's Hill Gate
Ranger's House (Werner Collection)
Blackheath Gate
War Memorial
Chesterfield Gate
BLACKHEATH ROAD
SHOOTERS HILL ROAD
Folly Pond
Blackheath

A B C D E
1 2 3

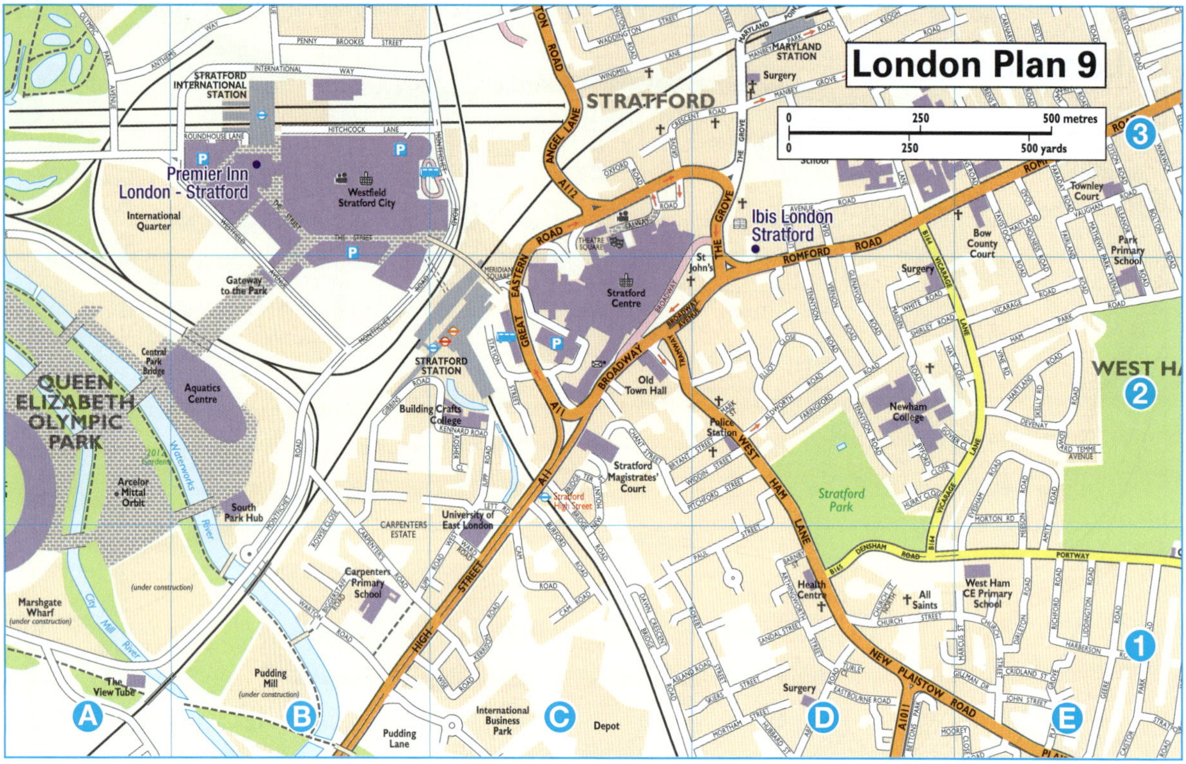

STRATFORD

MARYLAND STATION

Surgery

STRATFORD INTERNATIONAL STATION

P

Premier Inn London - Stratford

Westfield Stratford City

International Quarter

Gateway to the Park

P

Ibis London Stratford

Bow County Court

Townley Court

Park Primary School

ROMFORD ROAD

Surgery

WEST HA

St John's

Theatre Square

Stratford Centre

Central Park Bridge

QUEEN ELIZABETH OLYMPIC PARK

Aquatics Centre

STRATFORD STATION

Newham College

Arcelor Mittal Orbit

South Park Hub

Building Crafts College

Old Town Hall

Stratford Park

Police Station

Marshgate Wharf
(under construction)

University of East London

CARPENTERS ESTATE

Carpenters Primary School

Stratford Magistrates' Court

Stratford High Street

Health Centre

All Saints

West Ham CE Primary School

The View Tube

Pudding Mill
(under construction)

International Business Park

Depot

Surgery

NEW PLAISTOW ROAD

PORTWAY

Pudding Lane

A B C D E

1 2 3

0   250   500 metres
0   250   500 yards

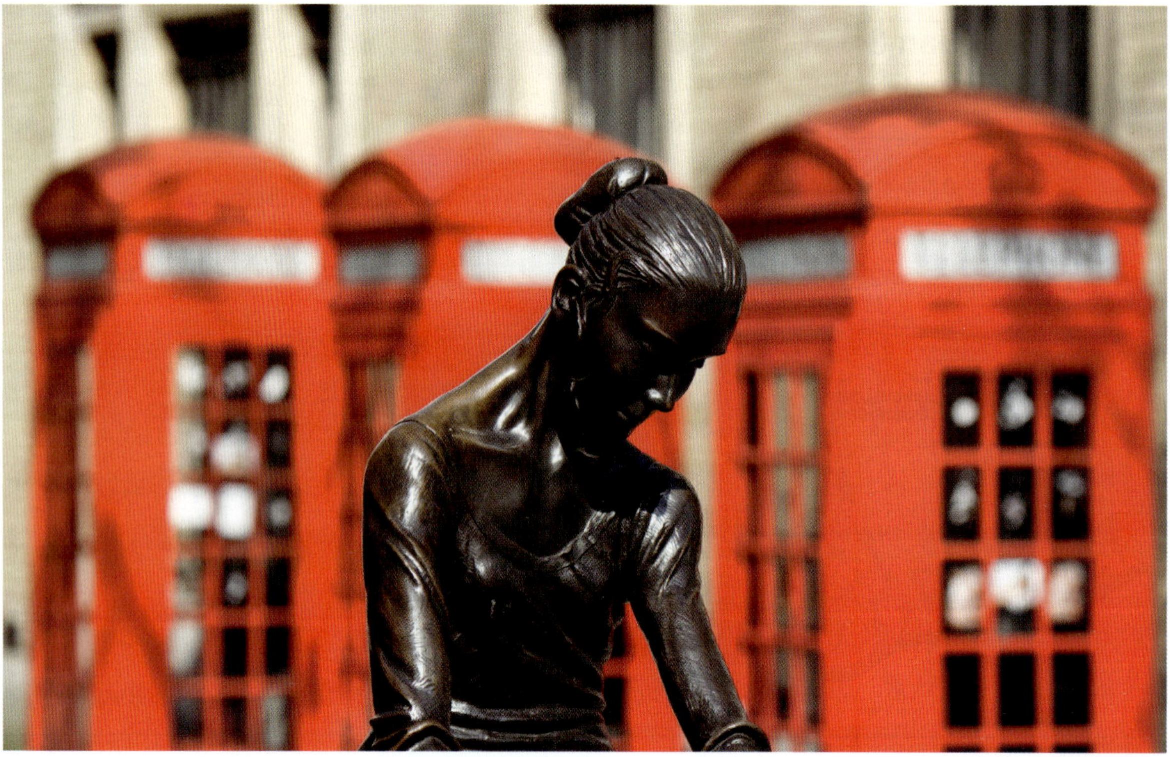

LONDON

LONDON

Greater London Plans 1-9, pages 248-260. (Small scale maps 6 & 7 at back of book.) Hotels are listed below in postal district order, commencing East, then North, South and West, with a brief indication of the area covered. Detailed plans 2-9 show the locations of AA-appointed hotels within the Central London postal districts. If you do not know the postal district of the hotel you want, please refer to the index preceding the street plans for the entry and map pages. The plan reference for each AA-appointed hotel also appears within its directory entry.

E1 STEPNEY AND EAST OF THE TOWER OF LONDON

Ibis London City

BUDGET HOTEL PLAN 3 J2

tel: 020 7422 8400 **5 Commercial St E1 6BF**
email: H5011@accor.com **web:** www.ibis.com
dir: M25 junct 30, A13, follow The City signs, then Aldgate signs

Modern, budget hotel offering comfortable accommodation in bright and practical bedrooms. Breakfast is self-service and dinner is available in the restaurant. See also the Hotel Groups pages.

Rooms 348 🐾

Premier Inn London City (Tower Hill)

BUDGET HOTEL PLAN 3 J1

tel: 0871 527 8646 **22-24 Prescott St, Tower Hill E1 8BB**
web: www.premierinn.com
dir: Nearest tube: Tower Hill. 3 mins walk from Docklands Light Rail (DLR)

High quality, budget accommodation ideal for both families and business travellers. Spacious, en suite bedrooms feature tea and coffee making facilities, and Freeview TV in most hotels. Internet access and WiFi are available for a small fee. The adjacent family restaurant features a wide and varied menu. See also the Hotel Groups pages.

Rooms 165

E4 CHINGFORD | Map 6 TQ39

Premier Inn Chingford

BUDGET HOTEL

tel: 0871 527 9836 **Rangers Rd, Chingford E4 7QH**
web: www.premierinn.com
dir: M25 junct 26, A121 (Loughton) At next rdbt 1st exit (A121). At Wake Arms rdbt 2nd exit onto A104 (Woodford). Right onto A1069 (Rangers Rd). 1m, hotel on right

High quality, budget accommodation ideal for both families and business travellers. Spacious, en suite bedrooms feature tea and coffee making facilities, and Freeview TV in most hotels. Internet access and WiFi are available for a small fee. The adjacent family restaurant features a wide and varied menu. See also the Hotel Groups pages.

Rooms 24

E6 EAST HAM

Premier Inn London Beckton

BUDGET HOTEL PLAN 1 H4

tel: 0871 527 8644 **1 Woolwich Manor Way, Beckton E6 5NT**
web: www.premierinn.com
dir: A13 onto A117 (Woolwich Manor Way) towards City Airport, hotel on left after 1st rdbt

High quality, budget accommodation ideal for both families and business travellers. Spacious, en suite bedrooms feature tea and coffee making facilities, and Freeview TV in most hotels. Internet access and WiFi are available for a small fee. The adjacent family restaurant features a wide and varied menu. See also the Hotel Groups pages.

Rooms 90

E14 CANARY WHARF & LIMEHOUSE

INSPECTORS' CHOICE

Four Seasons Hotel London at Canary Wharf

★★★★★ ◉ HOTEL PLAN 6 A3

tel: 020 7510 1999 **Westferry Circus, Canary Wharf E14 8RS**
email: reservations.caw@fourseasons.com **web:** www.fourseasons.com/canarywharf
dir: From A13 follow Canary Wharf, Isle of Dogs & Westferry Circus signs. Hotel off 3rd exit of Westferry Circus rdbt

With superb views over the London skyline and the Thames, this stylish modern hotel enjoys a delightful riverside location. Spacious contemporary bedrooms are particularly thoughtfully equipped. Public areas include the Italian Quadrato Bar and Restaurant, an impressive business centre and a gym. Guests also have complimentary use of the impressive Virgin Active Health Club adjacent to the hotel. Welcoming staff provide exemplary levels of service and hospitality.

Rooms 142 🐾 **Facilities** STV FTV WiFi ৬ HL ⑭ supervised ⬙ Gym Fitness centre Beauty treatment room Xmas New Year **Conf** Class 120 Board 56 Thtr 200 **Services** Lift Air con **Parking** 33 **Notes** Civ Wed 200

LONDON

E14 CANARY WHARF & LIMEHOUSE *continued*

London Marriott West India Quay

★★★★★ 85%  HOTEL PLAN 6 B4

tel: 020 7093 1000 **22 Hertsmere Rd, Canary Wharf E14 4ED**
email: mhrs.loncw.ays@marriotthotels.com **web:** www.londonmarriottwestindiaquay.co.uk
dir: Exit Aspen Way at Hertsmere Rd. Hotel opposite, adjacent to Canary Wharf

This spectacular skyscraper with curved glass façade is located at the heart of the docklands, adjacent to Canary Wharf and overlooking the water. The hotel is modern, but not pretentiously trendy; eye-catching floral displays add warmth to the public areas. Bedrooms, many of which overlook the quay, provide every modern convenience, including broadband and air conditioning. Curve Restaurant offers good quality cooking focusing on fresh fish.

Rooms 301 (22 fmly) 🐾 **Facilities** STV WiFi ⌂ Gym Xmas New Year **Conf** Class 132 Board 27 Thtr 290 **Services** Lift Air con **Notes** ⊗ Civ Wed 290

Ibis London Docklands

BUDGET HOTEL PLAN 6 D4

tel: 020 7517 1100 **1 Baffin Way E14 9PE**
email: H2177@accor.com **web:** www.ibishotel.com
dir: From Tower Bridge follow City Airport and Royal Docks signs, exit for 'Isle of Dogs'. Hotel on 1st left opposite McDonalds

Modern, budget hotel offering comfortable accommodation in bright and practical bedrooms. Breakfast is self-service and dinner is available in the restaurant. See also the Hotel Groups pages.

Rooms 87 (15 GF)

E15 STRATFORD

Ibis London Stratford

BUDGET HOTEL PLAN 9 D3

tel: 020 8536 3700 **1A Romford Rd, Stratford E15 4LJ**
email: h3099@accor.com **web:** www.ibishotel.com

Modern, budget hotel offering comfortable accommodation in bright and practical bedrooms. Breakfast is self-service and dinner is available in the restaurant. See also the Hotel Groups pages.

Rooms 108 🐾

Premier Inn London - Stratford

BUDGET HOTEL PLAN 9 B3

tel: 0871 527 9286 **International Square, Westfield Stratfield City, Montfichet Road, Olympic Park E15 1AZ**
web: www.premierinn.com
dir: From A11 or A12 follow signs for Westfield Shopping City & Stratford International & Car Park A

High quality, budget accommodation ideal for both families and business travellers. Spacious, en suite bedrooms feature tea and coffee making facilities, and Freeview TV in most hotels. Internet access and WiFi are available for a small fee. The adjacent family restaurant features a wide and varied menu. See also the Hotel Groups pages.

Rooms 267

E16 SILVERTOWN

Novotel London ExCeL

★★★★ 79% HOTEL PLAN 7 C1

tel: 020 7540 9700 **7 Western Gateway, Royal Victoria Docks E16 1AA**
email: H3656@accor.com **web:** www.novotel.com/3656
dir: M25 junct 30, A13 follow City signs, exit at Canning Town. Follow ExCeL West signs. Hotel adjacent

This hotel is situated adjacent to the ExCeL exhibition centre and overlooks the Royal Victoria Dock. Design throughout the hotel is contemporary and stylish. Public rooms include a range of meeting rooms, a modern coffee station, indoor leisure facilities and a smart bar and restaurant, both with a terrace overlooking the dock. Bedrooms feature modern decor, a bathroom with separate bath and shower, and an extensive range of extras.

Rooms 257 (176 fmly) 🐾 **Facilities** STV FTV WiFi ⌂ Gym Sauna Steam room Relaxation room with massage bed **Conf** Class 55 Board 30 Thtr 70 **Services** Lift Air con **Parking** 80 **Notes** Civ Wed 50

Crowne Plaza London - Docklands

★★★★ 77% HOTEL PLAN 7 B1

tel: 020 7055 2000 **Royal Victoria Dock, Western Gateway E16 1AL**
email: sales@crowneplazadocklands.co.uk **web:** www.cpdocklands.co.uk
dir: A1020 towards ExCeL. Follow signs for ExCeL West. Hotel on left 400mtrs before ExCeL

Ideally located for the ExCeL exhibition centre, Canary Wharf and London City airport, this unique, contemporary hotel overlooking Royal Victoria Dock, offers accommodation suitable for both leisure and business travellers. Rooms are spacious and equipped with all modern facilities. The hotel has a busy bar, a contemporary restaurant and health and fitness facilities with an indoor pool, jacuzzi and sauna.

Rooms 210 (10 fmly) (4 smoking) 🐾 **Facilities** Spa STV WiFi ⌂ HL supervised Gym Beauty treatment room Sauna Steam room Fitness studios Xmas New Year **Conf** Class 140 Board 62 Thtr 250 Del from £265* **Services** Lift Air con **Parking** 75 **Notes** ⊗ Civ Wed 250

Ramada Hotel & Suites London Docklands

★★★★ 72% HOTEL PLAN 7 E1

tel: 020 7540 4820 **Excel 2 Festoon Way, Royal Victoria Dock E16 1RH**
email: reservations@ramadadocklands.co.uk **web:** www.ramadadocklands.co.uk
dir: Follow signs for ExCeL East & London City Airport. Over Connaught Bridge then immediately left at rdbt

This hotel benefits from a stunning waterfront location and is close to the events venue, ExCeL, the O2 Arena, Canary Wharf and London City Airport. The accommodation comprises a mix of spacious bedrooms and suites. The relaxed public areas consist of a modern restaurant and informal lounge area. Parking, a fitness room and meeting rooms are available on site. Free WiFi is available.

Rooms 224 (71 fmly) (23 smoking) 🐾 **S** £300; **D** £320 **Facilities** FTV WiFi Gym **Conf** Class 20 Board 25 Thtr 30 Del £385 **Services** Lift Air con **Parking** 60 **Notes** LB Civ Wed 120

LONDON

Ibis London ExCeL Docklands

BUDGET HOTEL PLAN 7 B1

tel: 020 7055 2300 **9 Western Gateway, Royal Victoria Docks E16 1AB**
email: H3655@accor.com **web:** www.ibishotel.com
dir: M25, A13 to London, City Airport, ExCeL East

Modern, budget hotel offering comfortable accommodation in bright and practical bedrooms. Breakfast is self-service and dinner is available in the restaurant See also the Hotel Groups pages.

Rooms 278 (33 fmly) ⚓

Premier Inn London Docklands (ExCeL)

BUDGET HOTEL PLAN 7 D1

tel: 0871 527 8650 **Excel East, Royal Victoria Dock E16 1SL**
web: www.premierinn.com
dir: A13 onto A1020. At Connaught rdbt take 2nd exit into Connaught Rd. Hotel on right

High quality, budget accommodation ideal for both families and business travellers. Spacious, en suite bedrooms feature tea and coffee making facilities, and Freeview TV in most hotels. Internet access and WiFi are available for a small fee. The adjacent family restaurant features a wide and varied menu. See also the Hotel Groups pages.

Rooms 202

EC1 CITY OF LONDON

The Zetter Hotel

★★★★ 80%  HOTEL PLAN 3 E4

tel: 020 7324 4444 & 7324 4567 **St John's Square, 86-88 Clerkenwell Rd EC1M 5RJ**
email: info@thezetter.com **web:** www.thezetter.com
dir: From West A401, Clerkenwell Rd A5201. Hotel 200mtrs on left

This iconic hotel offers individually styled bedrooms with an impressive array of amenities, including the latest in-room entertainment. The Roof Top Studio rooms, some with a private patio, have amazing views over London's historic Clerkenwell and beyond. The Bistrot Bruno Loubet offers award-winning, imaginative and modern French cuisine, and the Atrium Bar and Lounge is the place to meet for coffee, have a light lunch or enjoy a drink. Two stylish rooms are available for private events.

Rooms 59 ⚓ **Facilities** STV WiFi Complimentary use of local gym **Conf** Class 28 Board 32 Thtr 50 **Services** Lift Air con **Parking** 1 **Notes** ⊗

Malmaison Charterhouse Square

★★★★ 78%  HOTEL PLAN 3 E3

tel: 0844 693 0656 **18-21 Charterhouse Square, Clerkenwell EC1M 6AH**
email: london@malmaison.com **web:** www.malmaison.com
dir: Exit Barbican Station turn left, take 1st left. Hotel on far left corner of Charterhouse Square

Situated in a leafy and peaceful square, Malmaison Charterhouse maintains the same focus on quality service and food as the other hotels in the group. The bedrooms, stylishly decorated in calming tones, have all the expected facilities including power showers, CD players and free internet access. The brasserie and bar at the hotel's centre has a buzzing atmosphere and offers traditional French cuisine.

Rooms 97 (5 GF) **Facilities** STV WiFi ♨ Gym **Conf** Class 18 Board 16 Thtr 30 **Services** Lift Air con

The Montcalm London City at The Brewery

Ⓤ PLAN 3 F3

tel: 020 7614 0100 **52 Chiswell St EC1Y 4SB**
dir: From Gatwick M23 N to M25 signed Heathrow Airport/Central London to M4. From Heathrow M4 E 9m

Currently the rating for this establishment is not confirmed. This may be due to a change of ownership or because it has only recently joined the AA rating scheme. For further details please see the AA website: theAA.com

Rooms 235 ⚓ **D** £216-£600* **Facilities** STV FTV WiFi ♨ HL Gym Xmas New Year **Conf** Class 40 Board 40 Thtr 60 **Services** Lift Air con **Notes** LB ⊗ Civ Wed

EC2

ANdAZ Liverpool Street

★★★★★ 86% ◉◉◉ HOTEL PLAN 3 H3

tel: 020 7961 1234 **40 Liverpool St EC2M 7QN**
email: guestservices.londonliv@andaz.com **web:** www.london.liverpoolstreet.andaz.com
dir: On corner of Liverpool St & Bishopsgate, attached to Liverpool St station

ANdAZ is an exciting and contemporary place to stay - no reception desk here so guests are checked-in by staff with laptops. Bedrooms are stylish, and designed very much with the executive in mind, with iPods and WiFi as well as a mini bar stocked with healthy choices. The dining options are varied and many - 1 Rosette Miyako restaurant for Japanese cuisine, 3 Rosette 1901 Restaurant and Wine Bar, St Georges pub, 1 Rosette Catch and Champagne bar, and the Eastway brasserie. There are also rooms for private dining and other events.

Rooms 267 ⚓ **Facilities** STV FTV WiFi ♨ Gym Steam room Beauty treatment rooms ♬ New Year **Conf** Class 120 Board 60 Thtr 250 **Services** Lift Air con **Notes** ⊗ Civ Wed 230

Apex London Wall Hotel

★★★★ 80% HOTEL PLAN 3 G2

tel: 0845 365 0000 & 020 7562 3030 **7-9 Copthall Av EC2R 7NJ**
email: london.reservations@apexhotels.co.uk **web:** www.apexhotels.co.uk
dir: Near Moorgate & Bank stations

A sister property to the nearby City of London Hotel. This hotel is situated in the heart of London's financial district and is close to many places of interest. This 'boutique' property offers contemporary accommodation for both business and leisure travellers. Bedrooms and bathrooms have been fitted to a very high standard and feature some great guest comforts. Off the Wall restaurant offers informal dining with a modern British menu.

Rooms 89 ⚓ **Facilities** FTV WiFi ♨ Gym Xmas New Year **Services** Lift Air con **Notes** ⊗ No children

Find out more about Hotel Bathrooms in our feature on page 26

Apex City of London Hotel

★★★★ 81%  HOTEL PLAN 3 H1

tel: 0845 365 0000 & 020 7702 2020 **1 Seething Ln EC3N 4AX**
email: london.reservations@apexhotels.co.uk **web:** www.apexhotels.co.uk
dir: Opposite Tower of London

Situated close to Tower Bridge, this hotel is in the heart of the business district. Bedrooms are appointed to a high standard and have walk-in power showers in the en suites. The gym has the most up-to-date equipment. The Addendum Restaurant offers a good dining option.

Rooms 179 (5 GF) (6 smoking) 🐾 **Facilities** STV FTV WiFi ⃰ Gym **Conf** Class 36 Board 30 Thtr 80 Del from £215 to £330* **Services** Lift Air con **Notes** ⊗

The Chamberlain Hotel

★★★★ 78% HOTEL PLAN 3 J2

tel: 020 7680 1500 **130-135 Minories EC3N 1NU**
email: thechamberlain@fullers.co.uk **web:** www.thechamberlainhotel.com
dir: M25 junct 30, A13 W towards London. Follow into Aldgate, left after bus station. Hotel halfway down Minories

This smart hotel is ideally situated for the City, Tower Bridge, plus both Aldgate and Tower underground stations. The impressive bedrooms are stylish, well equipped and comfortable, and the modern bathrooms are fitted with TVs to watch from the bath. Informal day rooms include a popular pub, a lounge and an attractive restaurant.

Rooms 64 🐾 **Facilities** STV WiFi ⃰ **Conf** Class 20 Board 22 Thtr 40 Del from £225 to £275* **Services** Lift Air con **Notes** ⊗ Closed 24-28 Dec

Novotel London Tower Bridge

★★★★ 74% HOTEL PLAN 3 J1

tel: 020 7265 6000 & 7265 6002 **10 Pepys St EC3N 2NR**
email: H3107@accor.com **web:** www.novotel.com

Located near the Tower of London, this smart hotel is convenient for Docklands, the City, Heathrow and London City airports. Air-conditioned bedrooms are spacious, modern, and offer a great range of facilities. There is a smart bar and restaurant, a small gym, children's play area and extensive meeting and conference facilities.

Rooms 203 (130 fmly) 🐾 **Facilities** STV FTV WiFi ⃰ Gym Steam room Sauna Fitness room Xmas New Year **Conf** Class 56 Board 25 Thtr 100 **Services** Lift

Premier Inn London City (Monument)

BUDGET HOTEL PLAN 3 H1

tel: 0871 527 9452 **20 St Mary at Hill EC3R 8EE**
web: www.premierinn.com
dir: Nearest tube stations: Monument & Bank

High quality, budget accommodation ideal for both families and business travellers. Spacious, en suite bedrooms feature tea and coffee making facilities, and Freeview TV in most hotels. Internet access and WiFi are available for a small fee. The adjacent family restaurant features a wide and varied menu. See also the Hotel Groups pages.

Rooms 184

Crowne Plaza London - The City

★★★★ 80%  HOTEL PLAN 3 E1

tel: 0871 942 9190 & 020 7438 8000 **19 New Bridge St EC4V 6DB**
email: loncy.info@ihg.com **web:** www.cplondoncityhotel.co.uk
dir: Opposite Blackfriars station

This hotel has a 1919 façade, but is modern and bright inside; it is situated close to the north bank of the River Thames and also to Blackfriars station. Bedrooms are modern and well equipped. There is a small gym and valet parking is available. Booking for dinner is required.

Rooms 203 (60 fmly) (7 smoking) **Facilities** STV WiFi ⃰ HL Gym Xmas New Year **Conf** Class 100 Board 50 Thtr 160 **Services** Lift Air con **Notes** ⊗ Civ Wed 160

Apex Temple Court Hotel

★★★★ 78% HOTEL PLAN 3 D2

tel: 0845 365 0000 & 020 7353 4113 **1-2 Serjeants' Inn, Fleet St EC4Y 1LL**
email: london.reservations@apexhotels.co.uk **web:** www.apexhotels.co.uk
dir: Within Inner Temple, off Fleet St

This property, located just off Fleet Street and a moment's walk from the Inner Temple, has a traditional appearance and a contemporary interior. Bedrooms, incorporating up-to-date technology, are stylish and furnished with guest comfort in mind; some benefit from city skyline views. The cuisine is a highlight with brasserie-style dining in Chambers Restaurant and Bar, plus there are excellent breakfasts to look forward to. The hotel also has a gym.

Rooms 184 🐾 **Facilities** STV FTV WiFi ⃰ HL Gym Xmas New Year **Services** Lift Air con **Notes** ⊗

Premier Inn London Blackfriars (Fleet Street)

BUDGET HOTEL PLAN 3 E2

tel: 0871 527 9362 **1-2 Dorset Rise EC4Y 8EN**
web: www.premierinn.com
dir: Please telephone for detailed directions

High quality, budget accommodation ideal for both families and business travellers. Spacious, en suite bedrooms feature tea and coffee making facilities, and Freeview TV in most hotels. Internet access and WiFi are available for a small fee. The adjacent family restaurant features a wide and varied menu. See also the Hotel Groups pages.

Rooms 256

See LONDON plan 1 F4

Premier Inn London Angel Islington

BUDGET HOTEL

tel: 0871 527 8558 **Parkfield St, Islington N1 OPS**
web: www.premierinn.com
dir: From A1 (Islington High St) into Berners Rd bear left into Parkfield St. N1 car park opposite hotel

High quality, budget accommodation ideal for both families and business travellers. Spacious, en suite bedrooms feature tea and coffee making facilities, and Freeview TV in most hotels. Internet access and WiFi are available for a small fee. The adjacent family restaurant features a wide and varied menu. See also the Hotel Groups pages.

Rooms 95

Premier Inn London City (Old Street)

BUDGET HOTEL PLAN 3 G5

tel: 0871 527 9312 **1 Silicon Way N1 6AT**
web: www.premierinn.com
dir: From Old Street tube station exit 1 (on foot) onto A501 (City Rd). Right into East St. 2nd right into Brunswick Place (Three Crowns pub on corner), 1st left into Corsham St

Rooms 251

Premier Inn London King's Cross St Pancras

BUDGET HOTEL PLAN 3 B6

tel: 0871 527 8672 **26-30 York Way, Kings Cross N1 9AA**
web: www.premierinn.com
dir: M25 junct 16 onto M40 (becomes A40). Follow City signs, exit at Euston Rd, follow one-way system to York Way

Rooms 276

NW1 REGENT'S PARK & CAMDEN TOWN

INSPECTORS' CHOICE

The Landmark London

★★★★★ ◉◉ HOTEL PLAN 2 F3

tel: 020 7631 8000 **222 Marylebone Rd NW1 6JQ**
email: reservations@thelandmark.co.uk **web:** www.landmarklondon.co.uk
dir: Adjacent to Marylebone Station. Hotel on Marylebone Rd

Once one of the last truly grand railway hotels, The Landmark boasts a number of stunning features, the most spectacular being the naturally lit central atrium forming the hotel's focal point. When it comes to eating and drinking there are a number of choices, including the Cellars bar for cocktails and upmarket bar meals, the Mirror Bar, and The Gazebo - ideal for a business meeting or a quick snack. The Winter Garden Restaurant has the centre stage in the atrium and is a great place to watch the world go by; and the twotwentytwo restaurant and bar is a relaxing place to meet, eat and drink. The air-conditioned bedrooms are luxurious and have large, stylish bathrooms. The health club offers a complete wellbeing experience.

Rooms 300 (71 fmly) (52 smoking) 🐾 **S** fr £252; **D** fr £252* **Facilities** Spa STV FTV WiFi ♨ 🏊 Gym Beauty treatments & massages 🎵 Xmas New Year **Conf** Class 364 Board 50 Thtr 568 **Services** Lift Air con **Parking** 80 **Notes** ⊗ Civ Wed 300

Meliá White House

★★★★ 80% ◉◉ HOTEL PLAN 2 H4

tel: 020 7391 3000 **Albany St, Regents Park NW1 3UP**
email: melia.white.house@melia.com **web:** www.melia-whitehouse.com
dir: Opposite Gt Portland St underground station & next to Regents Park/Warren Street underground

Owned by the Spanish Solmelia company, this impressive art deco property is located opposite Great Portland Street tube station. Spacious public areas offer a high degree of comfort and include an elegant cocktail bar, a fine dining restaurant and a more informal brasserie. Stylish bedrooms come in a variety of sizes, but all offer high levels of comfort and are thoughtfully equipped.

Rooms 581 (7 fmly) 🐾 **Facilities** STV FTV WiFi ♨ HL Gym 🎵 Xmas New Year **Conf** Class 80 Board 60 Thtr 140 **Services** Lift Air con **Notes** ⊗ Civ Wed 140

Pullman London St Pancras

pullman

★★★★ 78% ◉ HOTEL PLAN 3 A5

tel: 020 7666 9000 & 7666 9010 **100-110 Euston Rd NW1 2AJ**
email: H5309@accor.com **web:** www.accorhotels.com/5309
dir: Between St Pancras & Euston stations, entrance opposite British Library

This hotel enjoys a central location adjacent to the British Library and close to some of London's main transport hubs. The style is modern and contemporary throughout. Bedrooms vary in size but are all very well equipped and many have views over the city. Open-plan public areas include a leisure suite and extensive conference facilities including the Shaw Theatre. Free WiFi is available.

Rooms 312 🐾 **Facilities** WiFi ♨ HL Gym Sauna Xmas **Conf** Class 220 Board 80 Thtr 446 **Services** Lift Air con **Notes** ⊗

Holiday Inn London Camden Lock

★★★★ 73% HOTEL PLAN 1 E4

tel: 020 7485 4343 **30 Jamestown Rd, Camden Lock NW1 7BY**
email: info@hicamdenlock.co.uk **web:** www.holidayinncamden.co.uk
dir: From Camden Town tube station take left fork. Jamestown Rd 2nd on left

Located in the heart of trendy Camden and overlooking Regent's Canal, this contemporary hotel offers a range of accommodation to meet the needs of a discerning clientele, and it is the perfect base for exploring the many attractions that London has to offer. The new Open Lobby Concept is a relaxing environment where you can catch up on emails or relax over a coffee or cocktail. In any case, friendly Camdeners are at hand to ensure a memorable experience.

Rooms 130 **Facilities** STV WiFi ♨ **Conf** Class 60 Board 60 Thtr 200 **Notes** ⊗ Civ Wed 220

Ibis London Euston St Pancras

ibis

BUDGET HOTEL PLAN 2 J5

tel: 020 7388 7777 **3 Cardington St NW1 2LW**
email: H0921@accor-hotels.com **web:** www.ibishotel.com
dir: From Euston Rd or station, right to Melton St & into Cardington St

Modern, budget hotel offering comfortable accommodation in bright and practical bedrooms. Breakfast is self-service and dinner is available in the restaurant. See also the Hotel Groups pages.

Rooms 380 🐾 **Conf** Class 40 Board 40 Thtr 100

LONDON

LONDON

NW2 BRENT CROSS & CRICKLEWOOD

Crown Moran Hotel

★★★★ 76% HOTEL PLAN 1 D5

tel: 020 8452 4175 **142-152 Cricklewood Broadway, Cricklewood NW2 3ED**
email: crownres@moranhotels.com **web:** www.moranhotels.com
dir: M1 junct 1 follow signs onto North Circular (W) A406. Junct with A5 (Staples Corner).
At rdbt take 1st exit onto A5 to Cricklewood

This striking hotel is connected by an impressive glass atrium to the popular Crown
Pub. Features include excellent function and conference facilities, a leisure club, a
choice of stylish lounges and bars and a contemporary restaurant. The air-
conditioned bedrooms are appointed to a high standard and include a number of
trendy suites.

Rooms 152 (63 fmly) (35 GF) ◖ **Facilities** STV WiFi ⬙ ⊛ **Gym** ♫ Xmas New Year
Conf Class 150 Board 80 Thtr 300 **Services** Lift Air con **Parking** 39 **Notes** ⊛
Civ Wed 300

Holiday Inn London - Brent Cross

★★★ 78% HOTEL PLAN 1 D5

tel: 0871 942 9112 & 020 8967 6359 **Tilling Rd, Brent Cross NW2 1LP**
web: www.holidayinn.co.uk
dir: At M1 junct 1. At rdbt after bridge turn left into Tilling Rd

Ideally located beside the M1 on the A406 North Circular, just a few minutes' walk
from Brent Cross Shopping Centre and four miles from Wembley Stadium. The hotel
offers well-appointed bedrooms with air conditioning and high-speed internet
access; WiFi is available in the public areas. Conference rooms and a contemporary
restaurant are available, plus there is ample parking.

Rooms 154 (87 fmly) (16 smoking) **Facilities** STV FTV WiFi HL New Year
Conf Class 40 Board 32 Thtr 80 **Services** Lift Air con **Parking** 150 **Notes** ⊛

NW3 HAMPSTEAD AND SWISS COTTAGE

Premier Inn London Hampstead

BUDGET HOTEL PLAN 1 E4

tel: 0871 527 8662 **215 Haverstock Hill, Hampstead NW3 4RB**
web: www.premierinn.com
dir: A41 to Swiss Cottage. Before junct take feeder road left into Buckland Cresent into
Belsize Ave. Left into Haverstock Hill

High quality, budget accommodation ideal for both families and business
travellers. Spacious, en suite bedrooms feature tea and coffee making facilities,
and Freeview TV in most hotels. Internet access and WiFi are available for a small
fee. The adjacent family restaurant features a wide and varied menu. See also the
Hotel Groups pages.

Rooms 143

NW4 HENDON

Hendon Hall Hotel

★★★★ 76% ⊛⊛ HOTEL PLAN 1 D5

tel: 020 8457 2500 **Ashley Ln, Hendon NW4 1HF**
email: hendonhall@handpicked.co.uk **web:** www.handpickedhotels.co.uk/hendonhall
dir: M1 junct 2 follow A406. Right at lights into Parson St, right into Ashley Ln. Hotel on
right

This impressive property was originally built in the 16th century when it was known
as Hendon Manor, and is now a stylish hotel boasting smart, well-equipped,

comfortable bedrooms with luxury toiletries, free WiFi and well-appointed en suites.
Public areas include meeting and conference facilities, a contemporary cocktail bar
and a richly decorated restaurant that opens onto a garden terrace. Staff are
friendly and attentive.

Rooms 57 ◖ **Facilities** STV FTV WiFi ⬙ ☙ Xmas New Year **Conf** Class 130 Board 76
Thtr 200 **Services** Lift Air con **Parking** 70 **Notes** ⊛ Civ Wed 120

NW6 MAIDA VALE

London Marriott Maida Vale

★★★★ 77% HOTEL PLAN 1 E4

tel: 020 7543 6000 **Plaza Pde, Maida Vale NW6 5RP**
email: reservations.london.england.maidavale@marriotthotels.com
web: www.londonmarriottmaidavale.co.uk
dir: From M1 take A5 S'bound for 3m. Hotel on left. From Marble Arch take A5 N'bound.
Hotel on right

This smart, modern hotel is conveniently located just north of central London. Air-
conditioned bedrooms are tastefully decorated and provide a range of extras. The
hotel also boasts extensive function facilities as well as an indoor leisure centre
which has a swimming pool, gym and health and beauty salon.

Rooms 237 (40 fmly) **Facilities** STV WiFi ⬙ ⊛ **Gym** Hair & beauty salon Beauty
treatment rooms Exercise studio & classes Xmas **Conf** Class 70 Board 30 Thtr 200
Del from £219 to £329* **Services** Lift Air con **Parking** 28 **Notes** ⊛ Civ Wed 100

SE1 SOUTHWARK AND WATERLOO

Plaza on the River London

★★★★★ 82% TOWN HOUSE HOTEL PLAN 5 B2

tel: 0844 854 5295 **18 Albert Embankment SE1 7TJ**
email: guestrelations@plazaontheriver.co.uk **web:** www.plazaontheriver.co.uk
dir: From Houses of Parliament turn into Millbank, at rdbt left into Lambeth Bridge. At
rdbt 3rd exit into Albert Embankment

This is a superb modern townhouse overlooking London from the south bank of the
Thames, with outstanding views of the capital's landmarks. The bedrooms are large
and many are full suites with state-of-the-art technology and kitchen facilities; all
are decorated in an elegant modern style. Service includes a full range of in-room
dining options; additionally, the bar and restaurant in the adjacent Park Plaza are
available to guests.

Rooms 65 (65 fmly) (65 smoking) ◖ **S** £199-£464; **Facilities** STV FTV WiFi ⬙ HL Gym
Xmas New Year **Conf** Class 450 Board 40 Thtr 650 Del from £309 to £609
Services Lift Air con **Notes** LB Civ Wed 600

Park Plaza Westminster Bridge London

★★★★ 81% ⊛ HOTEL PLAN 5 C5

tel: 0844 415 6790 **SE1 7UT**
email: ppwlres@pphe.com **web:** www.parkplaza.com

A very smart hotel located in the city, close to Waterloo Station, featuring eye-
catching, contemporary decor, a state-of-the-art indoor leisure facility and
extensive conference and banqueting facilities. There is the awarding wining Joel
brasserie as well as Ichi, the popular sushi bar. The bedrooms are also up-to-the-
minute in style and feature a host of extras including a mini bar, a safe and modem
points.

Rooms 1019 (420 fmly) ◖ **Facilities** Spa STV FTV WiFi ⬙ HL ⊛ **Gym** ♫ Xmas New
Year **Conf** Class 800 Board 50 Thtr 1400 **Services** Lift Air con **Notes** ⊛
Civ Wed 1400

London Bridge Hotel

★★★★ 81% HOTEL PLAN 5 G6

tel: 020 7855 2200 **8-18 London Bridge St SE1 9SG**
email: sales@londonbridgehotel.com **web:** www.londonbridgehotel.com
dir: Access through London Bridge Station, past taxi rank, towards Shard into London Bridge St (one way). Hotel on left

This elegant, independently owned hotel enjoys a prime location on the edge of the city, adjacent to London Bridge station. Smartly appointed, well-equipped bedrooms include a number of spacious deluxe rooms and suites. Free WiFi is available throughout. The Quarter Bar & Lounge is the ideal place for light bites, old favourites and cocktails. The Londinium restaurant offers a seasonal British menu.

Rooms 138 (10 fmly) (5 smoking) **Facilities** STV FTV WiFi ♿ Gym **Conf** Class 36 Board 36 Thtr 80 **Services** Lift Air con **Notes** ⊗

Park Plaza County Hall London

★★★★ 79% ⚫ HOTEL PLAN 5 C5

tel: 0844 415 6760 **1 Addington St SE1 7RY**
email: ppchinfo@pphe.com **web:** www.parkplazacountyhall.com
dir: From Houses of Parliament cross Westminster Bridge (A302). At rdbt take 4th right at dedicated lights

This hotel is located just south of Westminster Bridge near Waterloo International Rail Station. This contemporary design-led, air-conditioned establishment features studios and suites, most with kitchenettes and seating areas with a flat-screen TV. There are six meeting rooms, an executive lounge, a restaurant and bar plus a fully-equipped gym with sauna and steam room. WiFi is available.

Rooms 398 (303 fmly) **Facilities** STV FTV WiFi ♿ HL Gym Sauna Steam room Beauty therapy room Xmas New Year **Conf** Class 60 Board 40 Thtr 100 **Services** Lift Air con **Notes** ⊗

Park Plaza Riverbank London

★★★★ 77% ⚫⚫ HOTEL PLAN 5 C3

tel: 0844 854 5290 **18 Albert Embankment SE1 7SP**
email: rppres@pphe.com **web:** www.parkplazariverbank.com
dir: From Houses of Parliament turn onto Millbank, at rdbt left onto Lambeth Bridge. At rdbt take 3rd exit onto Albert Embankment

Situated on the south side of the River Thames, this hotel offers guests the convenience of a central London location and high levels of comfort. Contemporary design coupled with a host of up-to-date facilities, the hotel is home to the Chino Latino brasserie. The air-conditioned bedrooms have flat-screen TVs and large work desks; some rooms and suites have stunning views of the Houses of Parliament. Other facilities include WiFi throughout, high-tech conference rooms, a business centre, and a fitness centre with cardiovascular equipment.

Rooms 394 **Facilities** STV FTV WiFi ♿ HL Gym **Conf** Class 405 Board 40 Thtr 700 **Services** Lift Air con **Notes** ⊗ Civ Wed 150

Novotel London City South

★★★★ 77% HOTEL PLAN 5 F6

tel: 020 7089 0400 **Southwark Bridge Rd SE1 9HH**
email: H3269@accor.com **web:** www.novotel.com
dir: At junct at Thrale St, off Southwark St

Conveniently located for both business and leisure guests, with The City just across the Thames; other major attractions are also easily accessible. The hotel is contemporary in design with smart, modern bedrooms and spacious public rooms. There is a gym, sauna and steam room on the 6th floor, and limited parking is available at the rear of the hotel.

Rooms 182 (139 fmly) **Facilities** STV FTV WiFi ♿ HL Gym Steam room Sauna **Conf** Class 45 Board 40 Thtr 100 **Services** Lift Air con **Parking** 50

Mercure London Bridge

★★★★ 76% HOTEL PLAN 5 E6

tel: 020 7902 0800 **71-79 Southwark St SE1 0JA**
email: H2814@accor.com **web:** www.mercure.com
dir: A200 to London Bridge. Left into Southwark St

This smart, contemporary hotel forms part of the rejuvenation of the South Bank. With the City of London just over the river and a number of tourist attractions within easy reach, the hotel is well located for business and leisure visitors alike. Facilities include spacious air-cooled bedrooms, a modern bar and the stylish Loft Restaurant.

Rooms 144 (15 fmly) (5 GF) **S** £99-£350; **D** £109-£450* **Facilities** STV FTV WiFi ♿ HL Gym Xmas **Conf** Class 40 Board 30 Thtr 60 Del from £250 to £750* **Services** Lift Air con

H10 London Waterloo Hotel

★★★★ 75% ⚫ HOTEL PLAN 5 E5

tel: 020 7928 4062 **284-302 Waterloo Rd SE1 8RQ**
email: h10.london.waterloo@h10hotels.com **web:** www.hotelh10londonwaterloo.com
dir: 450mtrs from Waterloo Station, 300mtrs from Lambeth North

This hotel, conveniently situated for the South Bank and Waterloo Station, has a host of features. Bedrooms are stylish and designed with the international traveller in mind. The bar provides a useful internet facility and the stylish restaurant offers fresh and interesting dishes. The staff are friendly and efficient.

Rooms 177 **S** £139-£159; **D** £259-£279* **Facilities** STV FTV WiFi ♿ Gym Beauty treatment room Xmas New Year **Conf** Class 45 Board 24 Thtr 70 **Services** Lift Air con **Notes** ⊗

SE1 SOUTHWARK AND WATERLOO *continued*

Novotel London Blackfriars

★★★★ 74% HOTEL PLAN 5 E6

tel: 020 7660 0834 **46 Blackfriars Rd SE1 8NZ**
email: H7942@accor.com **web:** www.novotel.com

This latest generation Novotel is just south of the Thames and was opened in late 2012, utilising the latest in hotel and bedroom technology. There are media hubs in each bedroom, as well as air conditioning and glass walls to the bathroom that "steam-over" in an instant for privacy if desired. There are also a swimming pool, gym and sauna in the basement, and a bar and restaurant on the ground floor.

Rooms 182 (39 fmly) ↴ **S** £115-£395; **D** £125-£415* **Facilities** FTV WiFi HL 🔄 Gym Saunarium **Conf** Class 50 Board 40 Thtr 90 **Services** Lift Air con **Notes** LB

Novotel London Waterloo

★★★★ 74% HOTEL PLAN 5 C3

tel: 020 7793 1010 **113 Lambeth Rd SE1 7LS**
email: h1785@accor.com **web:** www.novotel.com/1785
dir: Opposite Houses of Parliament on S bank of River Thames

This hotel is in an excellent location, with Lambeth Palace, the Houses of Parliament and Waterloo Station all within a short walk. The bedrooms are spacious and benefit from air conditioning. The open-plan public areas include the Elements bar and restaurant, and also a children's play area. There are also a fitness room, well-equipped conference facilities and secure parking.

Rooms 187 (80 fmly) ↴ **Facilities** STV WiFi ↕ HL Gym Steam room Sauna **Conf** Class 24 Board 24 Thtr 40 **Services** Lift Air con **Parking** 40

Days Hotel London Waterloo

BUDGET HOTEL PLAN 5 D4

tel: 020 7922 1331 **54 Kennington Rd SE1 7BJ**
email: book@hotelwaterloo.com **web:** www.hotelwaterloo.com
dir: On corner of Kennington Rd & Lambeth Rd. Opposite Imperial War Museum

This modern building offers accommodation in smart, spacious and well-equipped bedrooms, suitable for families and business travellers, and all with en suite bathrooms. Continental breakfast is available and other refreshments may be taken at the nearby family restaurant. See also the Hotel Groups pages.

Rooms 162 (15 fmly) (13 GF) ↴

Hotel Ibis Styles London Southwark Rose

BUDGET HOTEL PLAN 5 F6

tel: 020 7015 1480 **Southwark Rose, 47 Southwark Bridge Rd SE1 9HH**
email: h7465@accor.com **web:** www.ibis.com
dir: From Westminster Bridge, into Stamford Rd, continue to Southwark St, left into Southwark Bridge Rd

Conveniently located just south of the River Thames on Southwark Bridge, this modern hotel offers well equipped air-conditioned bedrooms, internet and ample work space. There is a pleasant restaurant, bar lounge and business area on the 6th floor offering breakfast and dinner. The staff are friendly and welcoming. A limited amount of parking is available at the rear of the hotel. See also the Hotel Groups pages.

Rooms 114 (6 fmly) **Conf** Class 50 Board 26 Thtr 60

Ibis London Blackfriars

BUDGET HOTEL PLAN 5 E6

tel: 020 7633 2720 **49 Blackfriars Rd SE1 8NZ**
email: H7943@accor.com **web:** www.ibis.com/7943
dir: Next to Southwark and Blackfriars underground stations

Modern, budget hotel offering comfortable accommodation in bright and practical bedrooms. Breakfast is self-service and dinner is available in the restaurant. See also the Hotel Groups pages.

Rooms 297 (10 fmly) ↴ **S** £109-£209; **D** £109-£209*

Premier Inn London County Hall

BUDGET HOTEL PLAN 5 C5

tel: 0871 527 8648 **Belvedere Rd, Westminster SE1 7PB**
web: www.premierinn.com
dir: In County Hall building. Nearest tube: Waterloo

High quality, budget accommodation ideal for both families and business travellers. Spacious, en suite bedrooms feature tea and coffee making facilities, and Freeview TV in most hotels. Internet access and WiFi are available for a small fee. The adjacent family restaurant features a wide and varied menu. See also the Hotel Groups pages.

Rooms 313

Premier Inn London Greenwich

BUDGET HOTEL PLAN 8 A1

tel: 0871 527 9208 **43-81 Greenwich High Rd, Greenwich SE10 8JL**
web: www.premierinn.com
dir: Telephone for detailed directions

Rooms 150

Premier Inn London Southwark

BUDGET HOTEL PLAN 5 F6

tel: 0871 527 8676 **Bankside, 34 Park St SE1 9EF**
web: www.premierinn.com
dir: A3200 onto A300 (Southwark Bridge Rd), 1st left into Sumner St, right into Park St. From S: M3, A3 follow Central London signs

Rooms 59

Premier Inn London Southwark (Tate Modern)

BUDGET HOTEL PLAN 5 E6

tel: 0871 527 9332 **15A Great Suffolk St, Southwark SE1 0FL**
web: www.premierinn.com
dir: Please telephone for detailed directions

Rooms 122

Premier Inn London Tower Bridge

BUDGET HOTEL PLAN 5 H5

tel: 0871 527 8678 **159 Tower Bridge Rd SE1 3LP**
web: www.premierinn.com
dir: S of Tower Bridge on A100

Rooms 196

Premier Inn London Waterloo

BUDGET HOTEL PLAN 5 C5

tel: 0871 527 9412 **York Rd, Waterloo SE1 7NY**
web: www.premierinn.com
dir: Nearest station: Waterloo

Rooms 234

SE10 GREENWICH

The Greenwich Hotel

★★★★ 75% HOTEL PLAN 8 A1

tel: 0208 4694440 **Catherine Grove SE10 8FR**
email: info@the-greenwich.co.uk **web:** www.thegreenwichlondon.com
dir: S from Central London across Waterloo Bridge. Continue to Elephant & Castle jct towards New Cross & follow A1 to Greenwich. From M25 head for A2 Central London

The Greenwich Hotel is a stylish and attractive boutique-style hotel with a very contemporary feel. Bedrooms vary in size, have state-of-the-art TVs, air conditioning and very comfortable beds. The Restaurant offers modern international cuisine, and the cocktail bar is always popular. There are also meeting facilities, a fitness room and limited secure parking is a bonus.

Rooms 144 (6 fmly) (19 GF) ☞ D £109-£249* **Facilities** FTV WiFi ⬧ Gym Xmas New Year **Conf** Class 35 Board 24 Thtr 60 Del from £155 to £259* **Services** Lift Air con **Parking** 16 **Notes** LB ⊗

Novotel London Greenwich

★★★★ 74% HOTEL PLAN 8 A2

tel: 020 8312 6800 **173-185 Greenwich High Rd, Greenwich SE10 8JA**
email: H3476@accor.com **web:** www.novotel.com
dir: Adjacent to Greenwich Station

This purpose-built hotel is conveniently located for rail and DLR stations, as well as major attractions such as the Royal Maritime Museum and the Royal Observatory. Air-conditioned bedrooms are spacious and equipped with a host of extras, and public areas include a small gym, contemporary lounge bar and restaurant.

Rooms 151 (34 fmly) ☞ **Facilities** STV FTV WiFi ⬧ HL Gym Steam room Xmas **Conf** Class 40 Board 32 Thtr 92 **Services** Lift Air con **Parking** 30

Ibis London Greenwich

BUDGET HOTEL PLAN 8 B3

tel: 020 8305 1177 **30 Stockwell St, Greenwich SE10 9JN**
email: H0975@accor.com **web:** www.ibishotel.com
dir: From Waterloo Bridge, Elephant & Castle, A2 to Greenwich

Modern, budget hotel offering comfortable accommodation in bright and practical bedrooms. Breakfast is self-service and dinner is available in the restaurant. See also the Hotel Groups pages.

Rooms 120 (10 fmly) (12 GF) ☞

SW1 WESTMINSTER

INSPECTORS' CHOICE

The Berkeley

★★★★★ ❀❀❀❀❀ HOTEL PLAN 4 G5

MAYBOURNE HOTEL GROUP

tel: 020 7235 6000 **Wilton Place, Knightsbridge SW1X 7RL**
email: info@the-berkeley.co.uk **web:** www.the-berkeley.co.uk
dir: 300mtrs from Hyde Park Corner along Knightsbridge

This stylish hotel, just off Knightsbridge, boasts an excellent range of bedrooms, each furnished with care and a host of thoughtful extras. Newer rooms feature trendy, spacious glass and marble bathrooms and some of the private suites have their own roof terrace. The striking Blue Bar enhances the reception rooms, all of which are adorned with magnificent flower arrangements. Various eating options include the Caramel Room for breakfast, an all-day menu from 11am, and afternoon tea. Marcus Wareing at The Berkeley has attained 5 AA Rosettes for stunning French cuisine, and here guests can also book the chef's table. The health spa offers a range of treatment rooms and includes a stunning open-air, roof-top pool.

Rooms 210 ☞ **Facilities** Spa STV FTV WiFi ⬧ ⊗ Gym Beauty/therapy treatments Xmas **Conf** Class 80 Board 54 Thtr 180 **Services** Lift Air con **Notes** ⊗ Civ Wed 160

Find out more about
the AA's awards for food
excellence on page 19

SW1 WESTMINSTER *continued*

St James's Hotel and Club

★★★★★ ◉◉◉◉ TOWN HOUSE HOTEL PLAN 4 J6

tel: 020 7316 1600 **7-8 Park Place SW1A 1LP**
email: info@stjameshotelandclub.com **web:** www.stjameshotelandclub.com
dir: On A4 near Picadilly Circus & St James's St

Dating back to 1857, this elegant property with its distinctive neo-Gothic exterior is discreetly set in the heart of St James. Inside there is impressive decor created by interior designer Anne Maria Jagdfeld. Air-conditioned bedrooms are appointed to a very high standard and feature luxurious beds and a range of modern facilities. Stylish open-plan public areas offer a smart bar/lounge and the fine dining restaurant, Seven Park Place by William Drabble, which serves modern French dishes based on primarily British ingredients.

Rooms 60 (8 fmly) (15 GF) ✏ **D** £260–£3000* **Facilities** STV FTV WiFi **Conf** Class 30 Board 25 Thtr 40 **Services** Lift Air con **Notes** ⊗ Civ Wed 40

DUKES London

★★★★★ ◉◉◉ HOTEL PLAN 4 J6

tel: 020 7491 4840 **35 St James's Place SW1A 1NY**
email: bookings@dukeshotel.com **web:** www.dukeshotel.com
dir: From Pall Mall into St James's St. 2nd left into St James's Place. Hotel in courtyard on left

Discreetly tucked away in St James's, Dukes is over 100 years old. Its style is understated, with smart, well-equipped bedrooms and public areas. The

Penthouse Suite has its own balcony with views over Green Park. Facilities include a gym, marble steam room and body-care treatments. The award-winning restaurant, Thirty Six by Nigel Mendham, offers British cuisine based on the very best ingredients. A smart lounge and a sophisticated and buzzing cocktail bar add to guests' enjoyment, and Martinis are a must!

Rooms 90 (40 fmly) (4 GF) ✏ **Facilities** STV FTV WiFi ⌁ Gym Steam room Health club Personal training Beauty treatment room Xmas New Year **Conf** Class 30 Board 30 Thtr 70 **Services** Lift Air con **Notes** ⊗ Civ Wed 60

The Halkin by Como

★★★★★ ◉◉◉ TOWN HOUSE HOTEL PLAN 4 G5

tel: 020 7333 1000 **Halkin St, Belgravia SW1X 7DJ**
email: res.thehalkin@comohotel.com **web:** www.comohotels.com/thehalkin
dir: Between Belgrave Sq & Grosvenor Place. Via Chapel St into Headfort Place, left into Halkin St

This smart, contemporary hotel has an enviable and peaceful position just a short stroll from both Hyde Park and the designer shops of Knightsbridge. Service is attentive, friendly and very personalised. The stylish bedrooms and suites are equipped to the highest standard with white marble bathrooms and every conceivable extra. Each floor is discreetly designed following the themes of water, air, fire, earth and sky. There is the airy Halkin Bar that offers all-day eating including an afternoon tea menu, and a stylish restaurant serving award-winning dishes.

Rooms 41 ✏ **S** £318–£834; **D** £318–£834 **Facilities** STV FTV WiFi ⌁ Gym Complimentary use of spa at sister hotel **Conf** Class 20 Board 26 Thtr 40 **Services** Lift Air con **Notes** ⊗

INSPECTORS' CHOICE

Jumeirah Carlton Tower

★★★★★ ◉◉◉ HOTEL PLAN 4 F4

tel: 020 7235 1234 **Cadogan Place SW1X 9PY**
email: jctinfo@jumeirah.com **web:** www.jumeirah.com
dir: A4 towards Knightsbridge, right onto Sloane St. Hotel on left before Cadogan Place

This impressive hotel enjoys an enviable position in the heart of Knightsbridge, overlooking Cadogan Gardens. The stunningly designed bedrooms, including a number of suites, vary in size and style. Many have wonderful city views and all have free WiFi. Leisure facilities include a glass-roofed swimming pool, a well-equipped gym and a number of treatment rooms. The renowned Rib Room Bar & Restaurant provides excellent dining, together with the other options of the Club Room, and Chinoiserie.

Rooms 216 (76 smoking) ⌂ **Facilities** Spa STV FTV WiFi ⌂ ⊗ Gym Golf simulator (50 courses) ♫ **Conf** Class 250 Board 90 Thtr 400 **Services** Lift Air con **Parking** 30 **Notes** ⊗ Civ Wed 400

INSPECTORS' CHOICE

The Lanesborough

★★★★★ ◉◉◉ HOTEL PLAN 4 G5

tel: 020 7259 5599 **Hyde Park Corner SW1X 7TA**
email: pmccolgan@lanesborough.com **web:** www.lanesborough.com
dir: At Hyde Park corner

Currently this elegant and iconic hotel is undergoing a major refurbishment. Highest of international standards of comfort, quality and security are unlikely to change and bedrooms will reflect the historic nature of the property, offering high levels of comfort and a superb range of complimentary facilities.

Rooms 93 (7 fmly) (6 GF) (38 smoking) ⌂ **Facilities** Spa STV FTV WiFi ⌂ Gym ♫ **Conf** Class 48 Board 52 Thtr 100 **Services** Lift Air con **Parking** 48 **Notes** Civ Wed 100

Find out more about the AA's Hotel rating scheme on page 18

Find out more about the AA Hotel Groups of the Year see pages 15 & 16

SW1 WESTMINSTER *continued*

INSPECTORS' CHOICE

Mandarin Oriental Hyde Park, London

★★★★★ ⊛⊛⊛ HOTEL PLAN 4 F5

tel: 020 7235 2000 **66 Knightsbridge SW1X 7LA**
email: molon-reservations@mohg.com **web:** www.mandarinoriental.com/london
dir: Harrods 400mtrs on right & Harvey Nichols directly opposite hotel

Situated in fashionable Knightsbridge and overlooking Hyde Park, this iconic venue is a popular destination for highfliers, celebrities and the young and fashionable. Bedrooms, many with park views, are appointed to the highest standards with luxurious features such as the finest Irish linen and goose down pillows. Guests have a choice of dining options - Bar Boulud (with 2 AA Rosettes) offering a contemporary bistro menu of seasonal, rustic French dishes; and Dinner by Heston Blumenthal where the dishes are based on recipes dating as far back as the 14th century, but with Heston's legendary modern twist. The Mandarin Bar serves light snacks and cocktails. The stylish spa is a destination in its own right and offers a range of innovative treatments.

Rooms 198 ✎ **S** fr £371.70; **D** fr £371.70* **Facilities** Spa STV FTV WiFi ⬇ 🏊 Gym Sanarium Steam room Vitality pool Zen colour therapy Relaxation area Xmas New Year **Conf** Class 120 Board 60 Thtr 250 **Services** Lift Air con **Parking** 25 **Notes** LB ⊗ Civ Wed 250

INSPECTORS' CHOICE

The Goring

★★★★★ ⊛⊛ HOTEL PLAN 4 H4

tel: 020 7396 9000 **Beeston Place SW1W 0JW**
email: reception@thegoring.com **web:** www.thegoring.com
dir: Off Lower Grosvenor Place, just prior to Royal Mews

This icon of British hospitality for over 100 years is centrally located and within walking distance of the Royal Parks and principal shopping areas. Spacious bedrooms and suites, - some contemporary in style with state-of-the-art technology and others more classically furnished - all boast high levels of comfort and quality. The Duchess of Cambridge stayed in the newly created Royal Suite on the night before her wedding in 2011. Elegant day rooms include the Garden Bar and the drawing room, both popular for afternoon tea and cocktails. The stylish airy restaurant offers a popular menu of contemporary British cuisine, and delightful private dining rooms are available. Guests will experience a personalised service from the attentive and friendly team.

Rooms 69 (9 fmly) ✎ **S** £360-£575; **D** £395-£675* **Facilities** STV WiFi ⬇ Free membership of nearby health club Xmas New Year **Conf** Class 30 Board 25 Thtr 50 **Services** Lift Air con **Parking** 16 **Notes** ⊗ Civ Wed 50

INSPECTORS' CHOICE

The Stafford London by Kempinski

★★★★★ ⊛ HOTEL PLAN 4 J6

tel: 020 7493 0111 & 518 1119 **16-18 St James's Place SW1A 1NJ**
email: reservation.london@kempinski.com **web:** www.kempinski.com/en/london
dir: Exit Pall Mall into St James's St. 2nd left into St James's Place

Tucked away in a quiet corner of St James's, this classically styled boutique hotel retains an air of understated luxury. The American Bar is a fabulous venue in its own right, festooned with an eccentric array of celebrity photos, caps and ties. Also, afternoon tea is a long established tradition here. From the pristine, tastefully decorated and air-conditioned bedrooms, to the highly professional, yet friendly service, this exclusive hotel maintains the highest standards. 26 stunning mews suites are available.

Rooms 105 (38 annexe) (8 GF) (2 smoking) ✆ **Facilities** STV WiFi ⓈGym Use of fitness club nearby Xmas New Year **Conf** Class 20 Board 24 Thtr 60 **Services** Lift Air con **Notes** ⊗ Civ Wed 44

41

THE
RED CARNATION
HOTEL COLLECTION

★★★★★ TOWN HOUSE HOTEL PLAN 4 H4

tel: 020 7300 0041 **41 Buckingham Palace Rd SW1W OPS**
email: book41@rchmail.com **web:** www.41hotel.com
dir: Opposite Buckingham Palace Mews entrance

Small, intimate and very private, this stunning town house is located opposite the Royal Mews. Decorated in stylish black and white, bedrooms successfully combine comfort with state-of-the-art technology such as iPod docking stations, interactive TV and free high-speed internet access. Thoughtful touches such as fresh fruit, flowers and scented candles add to the very welcoming atmosphere. The large lounge is the focal point; food and drinks are available as are magazines and newspapers from around the world plus internet access. Attentive personal service and a host of thoughtful extra touches make 41 really special.

Rooms 30 (2 fmly) ✆ **S** £323-£443; **D** £347-£467* **Facilities** STV WiFi Ⓢ Local health club Beauty treatments In-room spa Xmas New Year **Conf** Board 8 **Services** Lift Air con

---

51 Buckingham Gate, Taj Suites and Residences

★★★★★ TOWN HOUSE HOTEL PLAN 4 J4

tel: 020 7769 7766 **SW1E 6AF**
email: info@51-buckinghamgate.co.uk **web:** www.51-buckinghamgate.com
dir: From Buckingham Palace onto Buckingham Gate, 100mtrs, hotel on right

This all-suites hotel is a favourite with those who desire a quiet, sophisticated environment. Each of the suites has its own butler on hand plus a kitchen, and most have large lounge areas furnished in a contemporary style with modern accessories. There are one, two, three and four bedroom suites to choose from, which include the stunning Jaguar Suite and the spectacular brand new Cinema Suite. The hotel has a spa and a well-equipped gym.

Rooms 86 (86 fmly) (4 GF) ✆ **Facilities** Spa STV WiFi Ⓢ HL Gym Sauna Steam room Xmas New Year **Conf** Class 90 Board 60 Thtr 180 **Services** Lift Air con **Notes** ⊗ Civ Wed 150

Corinthia Hotel London

SOFITEL
LUXURY HOTELS

★★★★★ 87% ◉◉ HOTEL PLAN 5 B6

tel: 020 7930 8181 **Whitehall Place SW1A 2BD**
email: london@corinthia.com **web:** www.corinthia.com/london
dir: M4 onto A4, follow Central London signs. Pass Green Park, right into Coventry St, 1st right into Haymarket, left into Pall Mall East, right into Trafalgar Sq, 3rd exit into Whitehall Place

This refurbished hotel is steeped in history and is reputed to be one of London's earliest hotels having opened in 1885. After a very high quality refurbishment, the hotel has emerged with exceptional style. The team are welcoming and friendly and all requests are met with aplomb. Bedrooms, including suites and penthouses, are equipped to very high standards and offer all modern amenities. The eating options are The Northall with British cuisine and The Massimo Restaurant offering Mediterranean seafood. The Bassoon Bar is the place for cocktails and its worth noting the counter which is actually an elongated piano. The Espa Spa offers world class facilities. Valet parking is available.

Rooms 294 (10 fmly) (46 smoking) ✆ **Facilities** Spa STV WiFi Ⓢ Ⓡ Gym Vitality pool Nail studio Hair salon Relaxation sleep pod Xmas New Year **Conf** Class 120 Board 50 Thtr 250 **Services** Lift Air con **Notes** ⊗ Civ Wed 250

SW1 WESTMINSTER *continued*

Sofitel London St James

SOFITEL
LUXURY HOTELS

★★★★★ 87% ⊙ HOTEL PLAN 4 K6

tel: 020 7747 2200 **6 Waterloo Place SW1Y 4AN**
email: H3144@sofitel.com **web:** www.sofitelstjames.com
dir: 3 mins' walk from Piccadilly Circus & Trafalgar Square

Located in the exclusive area of St James's, this Grade II listed, former bank is convenient for most of the city's attractions, theatres and the financial district. The modern bedrooms are equipped to a high standard and feature luxurious beds, while more traditional public areas, including the French restaurant, provide a taste of classical charm.

Rooms 183 (102 fmly) ✍ **Facilities** Spa STV WiFi ⌦ Gym Gym So FIT, So SPA & Live entertainment ♫ Xmas New Year **Conf** Class 120 Board 44 Thtr 170 **Services** Lift Air con **Notes** Civ Wed 140

The Royal Horseguards

★★★★★ 81% ⊛⊛ HOTEL PLAN 5 B6

tel: 0871 376 9033 **2 Whitehall Court SW1A 2EJ**
email: royalhorseguards@guoman.co.uk **web:** www.theroyalhorseguards.com
dir: Trafalgar Sq to Whitehall, left to Whitehall Pl, turn right

This majestic hotel in the heart of Whitehall sits beside the Thames and enjoys unrivalled views of the London Eye and the city skyline. Bedrooms, appointed to a high standard, are well equipped and some of the luxurious bathrooms are finished in marble. Impressive public areas and outstanding meeting facilities are also available.

Rooms 282 (7 fmly) ✍ **Facilities** STV WiFi Gym ♫ Xmas New Year **Conf** Class 180 Board 84 Thtr 240 **Services** Lift Air con **Notes** ⊗ Civ Wed 228

The Rubens at the Palace

THE
RED CARNATION
HOTEL COLLECTION

★★★★ 84% ⊛⊛ HOTEL PLAN 4 H4

tel: 020 7834 6600 **39 Buckingham Palace Rd SW1W 0PS**
email: bookrb@rchmail.com **web:** www.rubenshotel.com
dir: Opposite Royal Mews, 100mtrs from Buckingham Palace

This hotel enjoys an enviable location close to Buckingham Palace. Stylish, air-conditioned bedrooms include the pinstripe-walled Savile Row rooms, which follow a tailoring theme, and the opulent Royal rooms, named after different monarchs. Public rooms include The Library fine dining restaurant, and a comfortable stylish cocktail bar and lounge. The team here pride themselves on their warmth and friendliness.

Rooms 161 (13 fmly) ✍ **S** £191-£311; **D** £203-£323* **Facilities** STV WiFi ⌦ Health club & beauty treatment available nearby ♫ Xmas New Year **Conf** Class 50 Board 30 Thtr 90 **Services** Lift Air con **Notes** LB Civ Wed 80

St Ermins Hotel

★★★★ 84% ⊙⊙⊙ HOTEL PLAN 4 K4

tel: 020 7222 7888 & 0800 635 0438 **2 Caxton St, St James Park, Westminster SW1H 0QW**
email: reservations@sterminshotel.co.uk **web:** www.sterminshotel.co.uk
dir: Just off Victoria St, directly opposite New Scotland Yard

Located in an enviable London location, the delightful courtyard offers a sanctuary from the hustle and bustle of the city. Following an impressive refurbishment the property boasts day rooms with quality finishes - no detail has been overlooked. The results are fresh, modern and innovative, with a respectful nod to the hotel's former character. Award-winning cuisine is served in the popular Caxton Grill. Limited valet parking is available by arrangement.

Rooms 331 (18 fmly) (12 GF) ✍ **S** £325-£705; **D** £325-£705* **Facilities** STV FTV WiFi ⌦ HL Gym Xmas New Year **Conf** Class 80 Board 60 Thtr 160 **Services** Lift Air con **Parking** 5 **Notes** Civ Wed 160

Cavendish London

★★★★ 81% ⊙⊙ HOTEL PLAN 4 J6

tel: 020 7930 2111 **81 Jermyn St SW1Y 6JF**
email: info@thecavendishlondon.com **web:** www.thecavendishlondon.com
dir: From Piccadilly, pass The Ritz, 1st right into Dukes St before Fortnum & Mason

This smart, stylish hotel enjoys an enviable location in the prestigious St James's area, just a short walk from Green Park and Piccadilly. Bedrooms have a fresh, contemporary feel, and there are a number of spacious executive rooms, studios and suites. Elegant public areas include a spacious first-floor lounge and well-appointed conference and function facilities. The popular Petrichor restaurant is committed to sourcing sustainable ingredients, especially from British producers. A good value, pre-theatre menu is available.

Rooms 230 (12 fmly) ✍ **Facilities** STV WiFi HL **Conf** Class 50 Board 40 Thtr 80 **Services** Lift Air con **Parking** 50 **Notes** ⊗

Park Plaza Victoria London

Park Plaza
Hotels & Resorts

★★★★ 78% ⊙ HOTEL PLAN 4 J3

tel: 0844 854 5290 & 7769 9800 **239 Vauxhall Bridge Rd SW1V 1EQ**
email: info@victoriaparkplaza.com **web:** www.parkplaza.com
dir: Turn right from Victoria Station

This smart modern hotel close to Victoria station is well located for all of central London's major attractions. Air-conditioned bedrooms are tastefully appointed and thoughtfully equipped for both business and leisure guests. Airy, stylish public areas include an elegant bar and restaurant, a popular coffee bar and extensive conference facilities complete with a business centre.

Rooms 299 ✍ **Facilities** Spa STV FTV WiFi ⌦ Gym Sauna Steam room Xmas **Conf** Class 240 Board 45 Thtr 550 **Services** Lift Air con **Parking** 36 **Notes** ⊗ Civ Wed 500

St. James' Court , A Taj Hotel

★★★★ 77% HOTEL PLAN 4 J4

tel: 020 7834 6655 & 7963 8308 **Buckingham Gate SW1E 6AF**
email: info.london@tajhotels.com **web:** www.stjamescourthotel.co.uk
dir: Facing Buckingham Palace, turn left onto Buckingham Gate. Hotel 100mtrs on the right

Enjoying a prestigious location, this elegant Victorian hotel is a few minutes' walk from Buckingham Palace. Air-conditioned bedrooms are smartly appointed and superbly equipped. Public areas include a choice of three restaurants - Bank, Bistro 51 and Quilon, - two bars, conference and business facilities and a fitness club with Sodashi Spa. Service is attentive and friendly.

Rooms 338 (17 smoking) ✆ **S** £199-£540; **D** £199-£540* **Facilities** Spa STV FTV WiFi ↻ HL Gym Steam room Sauna ♫ Xmas New Year **Conf** Class 90 Board 60 Thtr 180 **Services** Lift Air con **Notes** ⊗ Civ Wed 180

Millennium Hotel London Knightsbridge

★★★★ 75%  HOTEL PLAN 4 F4

MILLENNIUM
HOTELS AND RESORTS
MILLENNIUM • COPTHORNE

tel: 020 7235 4377 **17 Sloane St, Knightsbridge SW1X 9NU**
email: reservations.knightsbridge@millenniumhotels.co.uk
web: www.millennium.co.uk
dir: From Knightsbridge tube station towards Sloane St. Hotel 70mtrs on right

This fashionable hotel boasts an enviable location in Knightsbridge's chic shopping district. Air-conditioned, thoughtfully equipped bedrooms are complemented by a popular lobby lounge and MU Restaurant and Lounge where the cuisine is French with Asian influences. Valet parking is available if pre-booked.

Rooms 222 (41 fmly) (19 smoking) **Facilities** STV FTV WiFi ↻ HL Xmas New Year **Conf** Class 80 Board 50 Thtr 120 **Services** Lift Air con **Parking** 11 **Notes** ⊗

Jumeirah Lowndes Hotel

Ⓤ PLAN 4 F4

tel: 020 7823 1234 **21 Lowndes St SW1X 9ES**
email: jlhinfo@jumeirah.com **web:** www.jumeirah.com
dir: M4 onto A4 into London. Left from Brompton Rd into Sloane St. Left into Pont St, Lowndes St next left. Hotel on right

This chic, contemporary hotel is a smart modern townhouse set in timelessly stylish Belgravia. Guests can enjoy a meal in the international bistro Lowndes Bar &

Kitchen, or relax outside on The Terrace with an open-air barbeque. The recently refurbished bedrooms and suites all have a contemporary style with high-spec facilities such as iPads and WiFi. There are also extensive leisure facilities at the nearby Jumeirah Carlton Tower, which includes access to The Peak Health Club & Spa. For further details please see the AA website: theAA.com

Rooms 88 (12 fmly) **Facilities** Spa STV FTV WiFi ↻ ❄ supervised Gym **Conf** Class 15 Board 18 Thtr 25 **Services** Lift Air con **Notes** ⊗

Premier Inn London Victoria

BUDGET HOTEL PLAN 4 J3

Premier Inn

tel: 0871 527 8680 **82-83 Eccleston Square, Victoria SW1V 1PS**
web: www.premierinn.com
dir: From Victoria Station, right into Wilton Rd, 3rd right into Gillingham St, hotel 150mtrs

High quality, budget accommodation ideal for both families and business travellers. Spacious, en suite bedrooms feature tea and coffee making facilities, and Freeview TV in most hotels. Internet access and WiFi are available for a small fee. The adjacent family restaurant features a wide and varied menu. See also the Hotel Groups pages.

Rooms 110

SW3 CHELSEA, BROMPTON

INSPECTORS' CHOICE

The Capital

★★★★★ ◉◉◉ TOWN HOUSE HOTEL PLAN 4 F5

tel: 020 7589 5171 **Basil St, Knightsbridge SW3 1AT**
email: reservations@capitalhotel.co.uk **web:** www.capitalhotel.co.uk
dir: 20yds from Harrods, & Knightsbridge tube station

Personal service is assured at this small, family-owned hotel set in the heart of Knightsbridge. Beautifully designed bedrooms come in a number of styles, but all rooms feature antique furniture, a marble bathroom and a thoughtful range of extras including complimentary WiFi. Cocktails are a speciality in the delightful, stylish bar, whilst afternoon tea in the elegant, bijou lounge is a must.

Rooms 49 **S** £228-£345; **D** £290-£445 (incl. bkfst)* **Facilities** STV FTV WiFi ↻ Xmas New Year **Conf** Class 24 Board 24 Thtr 30 **Services** Lift Air con **Parking** 12 **Notes** ⊗

SW3 CHELSEA, BROMPTON *continued*

INSPECTORS' CHOICE

The Egerton House Hotel

THE RED CARNATION HOTEL COLLECTION

★★★★★ TOWN HOUSE HOTEL PLAN 4 E4

tel: 020 7589 2412 **17 Egerton Ter, Knightsbridge SW3 2BX**
email: bookeg@rchmail.com **web:** www.egertonhousehotel.com
dir: Just off Brompton Rd, between Harrods & Victoria & Albert Museum, opposite Brompton Oratory

This delightful town house enjoys a prestigious Knightsbridge location, a short walk from Harrods and close to the Victoria & Albert Museum. Air-conditioned bedrooms and public rooms are appointed to the highest standards, with luxurious furnishings and quality antique pieces; an exceptional range of facilities include iPods, safes, mini bars and flat-screen TVs. Staff offer the highest levels of personalised, attentive service.

Rooms 28 (5 fmly) (2 GF) ✿ **D** £295-£1500* **Facilities** STV WiFi Xmas New Year **Conf** Class 12 Board 10 Thtr 14 **Services** Lift Air con

The Draycott Hotel

★★★★★ 83% TOWN HOUSE HOTEL PLAN 4 F3

tel: 020 7730 6466 **26 Cadogan Gardens SW3 2RP**
email: reservations@draycotthotel.com **web:** www.draycotthotel.com
dir: From Sloane Sq station towards Peter Jones, keep to left. At Kings Rd take 1st right into Cadogan Gdns, 2nd right, hotel on left corner

Enjoying a prime location just yards from Sloane Square, this town house provides an ideal base in one of the most fashionable areas of London. Many regular guests regard this as their London residence and staff pride themselves on their hospitality. Beautifully appointed bedrooms include a number of very spacious suites and all are equipped to a high standard. Attractive day rooms, furnished with antique and period pieces, include a choice of lounges, one with access to a lovely sheltered garden.

Rooms 35 (9 fmly) (2 GF) ✿ **S** £156-£199; **D** £264-£378 **Facilities** STV FTV WiFi Beauty treatments Massage **Services** Lift Air con **Notes** LB

INSPECTORS' CHOICE

The Levin

★★★★ TOWN HOUSE HOTEL PLAN 4 F4

tel: 020 7589 6286 **28 Basil St, Knightsbridge SW3 1AS**
email: reservations@thelevinhotel.co.uk **web:** www.thelevinhotel.co.uk
dir: 20yds from Harrods, & Knightsbridge tube station

This sophisticated town house is the sister property to the adjacent Capital Hotel and enjoys a prime location on the doorstep of Knightsbridge's stylish department and designer stores. Bedrooms and en suites offer stylish elegance alongside a host of up-to-date modern comforts; extra touches include champagne bars and state-of-the-art audio-visual systems and complimentary WiFi. Guests can enjoy all-day dining in the stylish, popular, lower ground-floor Metro Restaurant.

Rooms 12 (1 GF) **S** £240-£355; **D** £260-£379 (incl. bkfst) **Facilities** STV FTV WiFi ☟ Xmas New Year **Services** Lift Air con **Parking** 8 **Notes** ⊗

SW3 CHELSEA, BROMPTON *continued*

The Beaufort

★★★★ 80% TOWN HOUSE HOTEL PLAN 4 F4

tel: 020 7584 5252 **33 Beaufort Gardens SW3 1PP**
email: reservations@thebeaufort.co.uk **web:** www.thebeaufort.co.uk
dir: 100yds past Harrods on left of Brompton Rd

This friendly, attractive town house enjoys a peaceful location in a tree-lined cul-de-sac just a few minutes' walk from Knightsbridge. Air-conditioned bedrooms are thoughtfully furnished and equipped with CD players, movie channel access, safe and free WiFi. Guests are offered complimentary drinks and afternoon cream tea with home-made scones and clotted cream. A good continental breakfast is served in bedrooms.

Rooms 29 (3 GF) **S** £180-£216; **D** £240-£312* **Facilities** STV FTV WiFi **Conf** Thtr 10 **Services** Lift Air con **Notes** ⊗

SW5 EARL'S COURT

K + K Hotel George

★★★★ 77% HOTEL PLAN 4 A3

tel: 020 7598 8700 & 7598 8707 **1-15 Templeton Place, Earl's Court SW5 9NB**
email: hotelgeorge@kkhotels.co.uk **web:** www.kkhotels.com/george
dir: Earls Court Rd (A3220), right into Trebovir Rd, right into Templeton Place

This smart hotel enjoys a central location, just a few minutes' walk from Earls Court and with easy access to London's central attractions. Stylish public areas include a bar/bistro, an executive lounge and meeting facilities, and a restaurant that overlooks the attractive rear garden. Bedrooms are particularly well equipped with a host of useful extras including free, high-speed internet access.

Rooms 154 (38 fmly) (8 GF) (7 smoking) 🛏 **S** £150-£330; **D** £180-£405 (incl. bkfst)* **Facilities** STV FTV WiFi ⇘ HL Gym Wellness area with exercise machines Sauna **Conf** Class 14 Board 18 Thtr 35 Del from £180 to £270* **Services** Lift Air con **Parking** 20 **Notes** LB

Twenty Nevern Square Hotel

★★★★ 71% TOWN HOUSE HOTEL PLAN 4 A3

tel: 020 7565 9555 & 7370 4934 **20 Nevern Square, Earls Court SW5 9PD**
email: hotel@twentynevernsquare.co.uk **web:** www.twentynevernsquare.co.uk
dir: From station take Warwick Rd exit, right, 2nd right into Nevern Sq. Hotel 30yds on right

This smart boutique-style town house hotel is discreetly located in Nevern Square and is ideally situated for both Earls Court and Olympia. The stylish, individually furnished bedrooms, which vary in shape and size, are appointed to a high standard and are well equipped. Public areas include a delightful lounge and Café Twenty where breakfast and light meals are served.

Rooms 20 (3 GF) **Facilities** FTV WiFi **Conf** Class 20 Board 20 Thtr 20 **Services** Lift **Parking** 4 **Notes** ⊗

See advert on page 277

BEST WESTERN Burns Hotel

★★★ 73% METRO HOTEL PLAN 4 B3

tel: 020 7373 3151 **18-26 Barkston Gardens, Kensington SW5 0EN**
email: info@burnshotel.co.uk **web:** www.burnshotel.co.uk
dir: From A4, right to Earls Court Rd (A3220), 2nd left

This friendly Victorian hotel overlooks a leafy garden in a quiet residential area not far from the Earls Court exhibition centre and tube station. Bedrooms are attractively appointed, with modern facilities. Public areas, although not extensive, are stylish.

Rooms 105 (10 fmly) **Facilities** STV WiFi ⇘ **Services** Lift **Notes** ⊗

Premier Inn London Kensington

BUDGET HOTEL PLAN 4 B3

tel: 0871 527 8666 **11 Knaresborough Place, Kensington SW5 0TJ**
web: www.premierinn.com
dir: Just off A4 (Cromwell Rd). Nearest tube: Earls Court

High quality, budget accommodation ideal for both families and business travellers. Spacious, en suite bedrooms feature tea and coffee making facilities, and Freeview TV in most hotels. Internet access and WiFi are available for a small fee. The adjacent family restaurant features a wide and varied menu. See also the Hotel Groups pages.

Rooms 184

Premier Inn London Kensington (Olympia)

BUDGET HOTEL PLAN 4 A3

tel: 0871 527 8668 **22-32 West Cromwell Rd, Kensington SW5 9QJ**
web: www.premierinn.com
dir: On N side of West Cromwell Rd, between juncts of Cromwell Rd, Earls Court Rd & Warwick Rd

Rooms 86

SW6 FULHAM

Millennium & Copthorne Hotels at Chelsea FC

★★★★ 77% HOTEL PLAN 1 E3

tel: 020 7565 1400 **Stamford Bridge, Fulham Rd SW6 1HS**
email: reservations@chelseafc.com **web:** www.millenniumhotels.co.uk
dir: 4 mins walk from Fulham Broadway tube station

A unique destination in a fashionable area of the city. Situated at Chelsea's famous Stamford Bridge ground, the accommodation offered here is very up-to-the-minute. Bedroom facilities include flat-screen LCD TVs, video on demand, broadband, WiFi and good-sized desk space; larger Club rooms have additional features. For eating there's a brasserie, the Bridge Bar and sports bar, and for corporate guests a flexible arrangement of meeting and event rooms is available.

Rooms 281 (64 fmly) ♙ **Facilities** STV FTV WiFi ⌂ Stadium tours **Conf** Class 600 Board 30 Thtr 950 **Services** Lift Air con **Notes** ⊗ Civ Wed 50

Ibis London Earls Court

★★★ 70% HOTEL PLAN 4 A1

tel: 020 7610 0880 **47 Lillie Rd SW6 1UD**
email: h5623@accor.com **web:** www.ibishotel.com
dir: From Hammersmith flyover towards London, keep in right lane, right at Kings pub on Talgarth Rd to join North End Rd. At mini-rdbt turn right. Hotel on left

Situated opposite the Earls Court Exhibition Centre, this large, modern hotel is popular with business and leisure guests. Bedrooms are comfortable and well equipped. There is a café bar open all day, and a restaurant that serves evening meals. There are also extensive conference facilities and an underground car park.

Rooms 504 (20 fmly) **Facilities** FTV WiFi ⌂ **Conf** Class 750 Board 25 Thtr 1200 **Services** Lift **Parking** 114

Premier Inn London Putney Bridge

BUDGET HOTEL PLAN 1 D3

tel: 0871 527 8674 **3 Putney Bridge Approach SW6 3JD**
web: www.premierinn.com
dir: Nearest tube: Putney Bridge. Hotel on A219, N of River Thames

High quality, budget accommodation ideal for both families and business travellers. Spacious, en suite bedrooms feature tea and coffee making facilities, and Freeview TV in most hotels. Internet access and WiFi are available for a small fee. The adjacent family restaurant features a wide and varied menu. See also the Hotel Groups pages.

Rooms 154

SW7 SOUTH KENSINGTON

INSPECTORS' CHOICE

Bulgari Hotel & Residences, London

★★★★★ ◉◉ HOTEL PLAN 4 F5

tel: 020 7151 1010 & 7151 1082 **171 Knightsbridge SW7 1DW**
email: london-info@bulgarihouse.com **web:** www.bulgarihotels.com/london
dir: Almost opposite Hyde Park

This striking, contemporary hotel is in the heart of Knightsbridge and becomes the third Bulgari property, after Milan and Bali. Luxury accommodation is stylish and deeply comfortable, complete with Bulgari trunks mini-bar and beverage facility. Bathrooms are equally lavish with deep baths and rain showers. Spacious public areas include a stunning spa complete with a 25m swimming pool, separate vitality pool and range of treatment rooms. A unique, hammered silver, oval bar provides the focal point of the bar with a sweeping staircase taking guests down to the restaurant which at the time of going to press is being taken over by Alain Ducasse and his protégé Damien Leroux, and rebranded as London Rivea. Immaculately attired staff offer high standards of service and hospitality.

Rooms 85 (17 smoking) ♙ **S** £528-£828; **D** £528-£828* **Facilities** Spa WiFi ⌂ HL ⊗ Gym The Screening Room cinema Xmas New Year **Conf** Class 80 Board 40 Thtr 100 **Services** Lift Air con **Parking** 6

SW7 SOUTH KENSINGTON *continued*

INSPECTORS' CHOICE

Baglioni Hotel

★★★★★ ⊛ HOTEL PLAN 4 C5

tel: 020 7368 5700 **60 Hyde Park Gate, Kensington Rd, Kensington SW7 5BB**
email: info.london@baglionihotels.com web: www.baglionihotels.com
dir: On corner of Hyde Park Gate & De Vere Gardens

Located in the heart of Kensington and overlooking Hyde Park, this small hotel buzzes with Italian style and chic. Bedrooms, mostly suites, are generously sized and designed in bold dark colours; they have espresso machines, interactive plasma-screen TVs and a host of other excellent touches. Service is both professional and friendly, with personal butlers for the bedrooms. Public areas include the main open-plan space with bar, lounge and Brunello Restaurant, all merging together with great elan; there is a spa with four treatment rooms and a techno-gym, and a fashionable private club bar downstairs.

Rooms 67 (7 fmly) (30 smoking) ⌁ **Facilities** Spa STV FTV WiFi ⌁ Gym Xmas New Year **Conf** Class 33 Board 34 Thtr 60 **Services** Lift Air con **Parking** 2 **Notes** Civ Wed 60

Millennium Bailey's Hotel London Kensington

★★★★ 76% ⊛ HOTEL PLAN 4 C3

MILLENNIUM
HOTELS AND RESORTS
MILLENNIUM · COPTHORNE

tel: 020 7373 6000 **140 Gloucester Rd SW7 4QH**
email: reservations.baileys@millenniumhotels.co.uk web: www.millenniumhotels.co.uk
dir: From A4, at Cromwell Hospital, into Knaresborough Place, to Courtfield Rd to corner of Gloucester Rd, hotel opposite tube station

This elegant hotel has a town house feel and enjoys a prime location. Air-conditioned bedrooms are smartly appointed and thoughtfully equipped, particularly the club rooms which benefit from DVD players. Public areas include a stylish contemporary restaurant and bar. Guests may also use the facilities at the larger sister hotel which is adjacent.

Rooms 211 (3 smoking) ⌁ **Facilities** STV WiFi ⌁ Gym New Year **Services** Lift Air con **Parking** 120 **Notes** ⊗

Crowne Plaza London-Kensington

★★★★ 76% HOTEL PLAN 4 C3

CROWNE PLAZA
HOTELS & RESORTS

tel: 020 7373 2222 & 7341 2340 **100 Cromwell Rd SW7 4ER**
email: lonke.reservations@ihg.com web: www.cplondonkensingtonhotel.co.uk
dir: Opposite Gloucester Road tube station. From M4 follow Central London signs. At Cromwell Rd hotel is visible on left

A boutique hotel with a grand Victorian townhouse façade and a one-acre landscaped garden, offering contemporary accommodation. Facilities include a state-of-the-art fitness suite, and sauna. The ground-floor Streetside Restaurant offers a relaxed atmosphere.

Rooms 162 (74 fmly) ⌁ **S** £149-£600; **D** £159-£610 (incl. bkfst)* **Facilities** STV FTV WiFi ⌁ Gym **Conf** Class 64 Board 60 Thtr 150 **Services** Lift Air con **Notes** ⊗

Millennium Gloucester Hotel London Kensington

★★★★ 76% HOTEL PLAN 4 C3

MILLENNIUM
HOTELS AND RESORTS
MILLENNIUM · COPTHORNE

tel: 020 7373 6030 **4-18 Harrington Gardens SW7 4LH**
email: reservations.gloucester@millenniumhotels.co.uk web: www.millenniumhotels.co.uk
dir: Opposite Gloucester Rd tube station

This spacious, stylish hotel is centrally located, close to The Victoria & Albert Museum and Gloucester Road tube station. Air-conditioned bedrooms are furnished in a variety of contemporary styles and Clubrooms benefit from a dedicated club lounge with complimentary breakfast and snacks. A wide range of eating options includes Singaporean and Mediterranean cuisine.

Rooms 610 (8 fmly) (37 smoking) **Facilities** STV WiFi Gym **Conf** Class 300 Board 100 Thtr 500 **Services** Lift Air con **Parking** 110 **Notes** ⊗ Civ Wed 500

Harrington Hall Hotel

★★★★ 75% HOTEL PLAN 4 C3

tel: 020 7396 9696 **5-25 Harrington Gardens SW7 4JW**
email: nhharringtonhall@nh-hotels.com web: www.nh-hotels.com
dir: 2 mins walk from Gloucester Road tube station

This splendid period property is centrally located just a stone's throw from Gloucester Road tube station and is convenient for visiting the museums and for shopping in Knightsbridge. Spacious bedrooms are smartly appointed and boast a host of extra touches. The public areas include extensive meeting facilities, a lounge bar and a restaurant.

Rooms 200 (17 fmly) ⌁ **Facilities** STV FTV WiFi ⌁ HL Gym Sauna Xmas New Year **Conf** Class 100 Board 50 Thtr 240 **Services** Lift Air con **Notes** ⊗ Civ Wed 200

Holiday Inn London - Kensington Forum

★★★★ 74% HOTEL PLAN 4 C3

Holiday Inn

tel: 0871 942 9100 **97 Cromwell Rd SW7 4DN**
email: hikensingtonforum@ihg.com web: www.holidayinn.co.uk
dir: From S Circular onto N Circular at Chiswick Flyover. Onto A4 (Cromwell Rd) to Gloucester Rd

This hotel is ideally situated within a few minutes' walk from the Gloucester Road underground station and close to many of London's attractions, such as the Natural History Museum, Science Museum, Kensington High Street and the West End. The bedrooms and bathrooms are well appointed and vary in size. The ground-floor areas include a gym and a stylish business lounge.

Rooms 906 (26 fmly) (46 smoking) **S** £105-£450; **D** £105-£450* **Facilities** STV FTV WiFi ⌁ HL Gym Fitness room Xmas New Year **Conf** Class 150 Board 50 Thtr 300 **Services** Lift Air con **Parking** 76 **Notes** LB ⊗ Civ Wed 250

The Rembrandt Hotel

★★★★ 74% HOTEL PLAN 4 E4

SAROVA HOTELS

tel: 020 7589 8100 **11 Thurloe Place, Knightsbridge SW7 2RS**
email: rembrandt@sarova.co.uk **web:** www.sarova.com
dir: M4 onto A4 (Cromwell Rd) into central London. Hotel opposite Victoria & Albert Museum

This attractive hotel is conveniently situated opposite the Victoria & Albert Museum, a stone's throw from Harrods. Smart, well-appointed bedrooms are thoughtfully equipped and public areas include a restaurant and an attractive bar lounge and conservatory. Guests also benefit from concessions at the adjacent Roman-styled health and leisure suite.

Rooms 193 S £169-£480; D £179-£490 (incl. bkfst)* **Facilities** Spa STV FTV WiFi Gym **Conf** Class 84 Board 80 Thtr 200 Del from £230 to £580* **Services** Lift **Notes** Civ Wed 200

Park International Hotel

★★★★ 73% HOTEL PLAN 4 D3

tel: 020 7370 5711 **117-129 Cromwell Rd SW7 4DS**

The Park International Hotel is within easy reach of all major attractions in Kensington and Chelsea, and the underground network. The hotel offers a range of newly designed rooms to meet the needs of the modern traveller, and the Heritage Suites, individually styled for that extra bit of opulence. Afternoon tea is served in the Checkmate Bar, cocktails are served in the Piano Bar and breakfast in the Orchid Room. The menu offers a blend of carefully chosen Thai and Modern British dishes.

Rooms 172 **Conf** Class 20 Board 18 Thtr 30

Ampersand Hotel

U PLAN 4 D3

tel: 020 7589 5895 **10 Harrington Rd SW7 3ER**
email: info@ampersandhotel.com **web:** www.ampersandhotel.com
dir: A minute's walk from South Kensington tube station

Currently the rating for this establishment is not confirmed. This may be due to a change of ownership or because it has only recently joined the AA rating scheme. For further details please see the AA website: theAA.com

Rooms 111 (13 GF) (16 smoking) S £155-£170; D £162-£216* **Facilities** STV FTV WiFi Gym **Conf** Class 20 Board 20 Thtr 26 Del from £237 to £291* **Services** Lift Air con

SW10 WEST BROMPTON

The Chelsea Harbour Hotel

★★★★★ 86% HOTEL PLAN 1 E3

CHELSEA HARBOUR HOTEL

tel: 020 7823 3000 **Chelsea Harbour SW10 0XG**
email: reservations.chelseaharbour@millenniumhotels.com
web: www.thechelseaharbourhotel.co.uk
dir: A4 to Earls Court Rd S towards river. Right into Kings Rd, left into Lots Rd

Against the picturesque backdrop of Chelsea Harbour's small marina, this modern hotel offers spacious, comfortable accommodation. All rooms are suites, which are superbly equipped; many enjoy splendid views of the marina. In addition, there are also several luxurious penthouse suites. Public areas include a modern bar and

restaurant, excellent leisure facilities (including a spa) and extensive meeting and function rooms.

Rooms 158 (158 fmly) S fr £220; D fr £220* **Facilities** Spa STV FTV WiFi Gym Sauna Steam room Xmas New Year **Conf** Class 115 Board 40 Thtr 600 **Services** Lift Air con **Parking** 2000 **Notes** Civ Wed 450

SW14 EAST SHEEN

The Victoria

RESTAURANT WITH ROOMS PLAN 1 C2

tel: 020 8876 4238 020 8878 3464 **10 West Temple Sheen SW14 7RT**
email: bookings@thevictoria.net **web:** www.thevictoria.net
dir: Off Upper Richmond Rd West into Derby Rd, then into West Temple Sheen

The Victoria is in a quiet residential area close to Richmond Park. The bedrooms are refreshingly stylish and thoughtfully equipped. The public areas consist of a small contemporary seating area, a modern bar, and an award-winning restaurant that serves imaginative and well sourced dishes. Al fresco dining is also an option.

Rooms 7 (2 fmly)

SW19 WIMBLEDON

Cannizaro House

★★★★ 76% COUNTRY HOUSE HOTEL PLAN 1 D2

tel: 020 8879 1464 **West Side, Wimbledon Common SW19 4UE**
email: info@cannizarohouse.com **web:** www.cannizarohouse.com
dir: From A3 follow A219 signed Wimbledon into Parkside, right into Cannizaro Rd, sharp right into West Side

This unique, elegant 18th-century house has a long tradition of hosting the rich and famous of London society. A few miles from the city centre, the landscaped grounds provide a peaceful escape and a country-house ambience; fine art, murals and stunning fireplaces feature throughout. Spacious bedrooms are individually furnished and equipped to a high standard. The award-winning restaurant menus proudly herald locally sourced, organic ingredients.

Rooms 46 (10 fmly) (5 GF) S £155-£625; D £155-£625 (incl. bkfst)* **Facilities** STV FTV WiFi **Conf** Class 50 Board 40 Thtr 120 Del from £245 to £350* **Services** Lift **Parking** 95 **Notes** LB Civ Wed 200

SW19 WIMBLEDON *continued*

Holiday Inn Express Wimbledon South

BUDGET HOTEL PLAN 1 E1

tel: 020 8545 7300 **Miller's Meadhouse, 200 High St, Colliers Wood SW19 2BH**
email: reservations@exhiwimbledon.co.uk web: www.exhiwimbledon.co.uk
dir: A238 Kingston Road, at lights into Merton High St, signed Colliers Wood. Hotel directly opposite Colliers Wood underground station

A modern hotel ideal for families and business travellers. Fresh and uncomplicated, the spacious rooms include Sky TV, power shower and tea and coffee-making facilities. Continental buffet breakfast is included in the room rate; other meals may be taken at the nearby family pub or restaurant. See also the Hotel Groups pages.

Rooms 139 (92 fmly) (12 GF) **Conf** Class 12 Board 12 Thtr 20

Premier Inn London Wimbledon South

BUDGET HOTEL PLAN 1 E1

tel: 0871 527 8684 **27 Chapter Way, Off Merantun Way, Wimbledon SW19 2RF**
web: www.premierinn.com
dir: M25 junct 10, A3 towards London. Exit A298 (Wimbledon) onto A238. Right onto A219, left onto A24 (Merantun Way). At rdbt 3rd exit signed Merton Abbey Mills

High quality, budget accommodation ideal for both families and business travellers. Spacious, en suite bedrooms feature tea and coffee making facilities, and Freeview TV in most hotels. Internet access and WiFi are available for a small fee. The adjacent family restaurant features a wide and varied menu. See also the Hotel Groups pages.

Rooms 132

W1 WEST END

The Connaught

MAYBOURNE
HOTEL GROUP

★★★★★ ◉◉◉◉ HOTEL PLAN 2 G1

tel: 020 7499 7070 **Carlos Place W1K 2AL**
email: info@the-connaught.co.uk web: www.the-connaught.com
dir: Between Grosvenor Sq & Berkeley Sq

This iconic hotel is truly spectacular, with stunning interior design. There are sumptuous day rooms and stylish bedrooms with state-of-the-art facilities and marble en suites with deep tubs, TV screens and power showers. Butlers are available at the touch of a button and guests are pampered by friendly, attentive staff offering intuitive service. There is a choice of bars and restaurants including the Espelette bistro, and the award-winning cuisine of Hélène Darroze which is imaginative, inspired and truly memorable. The excellent Aman Spa at the hotel offers health and beauty treatments, a swimming pool and fitness centre.

Rooms 123 (17 smoking) ✆ **Facilities** Spa STV FTV WiFi 🕙 Gym **Conf** Class 70 Board 60 Thtr 120 **Services** Lift Air con **Notes** ⊗ Civ Wed 200

45 Park Lane

★★★★★ ◉◉◉ HOTEL PLAN 4 G6

tel: 0207 493 4545 **45 Park Ln W1K 1BJ**
email: info45parklane@dorchestercollection.com web: www.45parklane.com
dir: Park Lane, near The Dorchester

This hotel offers luxurious and contemporary interiors. The bedrooms, including ten suites, all have a view of Hyde Park; the Penthouse Suite has its own roof terrace. A striking central staircase leads to a mezzanine featuring Bar 45, a library and a private media room. Other public areas include a lounge area and CUT at 45 Park Lane, a modern American steak restaurant.

Rooms 45

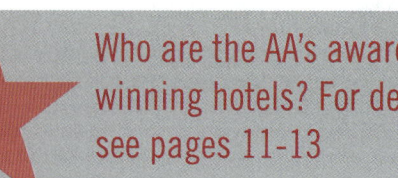

Who are the AA's award-winning hotels? For details see pages 11-13

The Ritz London

★★★★★ ◎◎◎ HOTEL PLAN 4 J6

tel: 020 7493 8181 **150 Piccadilly W1J 9BR**
email: enquire@theritzlondon.com **web:** www.theritzlondon.com
dir: From Hyde Park Corner E on Piccadilly. Hotel on right after Green Park

This renowned, stylish hotel offers guests the ultimate in sophistication while still managing to retain all its former historic glory. Bedrooms and suites are exquisitely furnished in Louis XVI style, with fine marble bathrooms and every imaginable comfort. Elegant reception rooms include the Palm Court with its legendary afternoon teas, the beautiful fashionable Rivoli Bar and the sumptuous Ritz Restaurant, complete with gold chandeliers and extraordinary trompe-l'oeil decoration.

Rooms 133 (65 fmly) (24 smoking) 🐾 **S** fr £315; **D** fr £315* **Facilities** STV FTV WiFi 🏊 Gym The Ritz Club & Casino The Ritz Salon 🎵 Xmas New Year **Conf** Class 40 Board 30 Thtr 70 **Services** Lift Air con **Parking** 10 **Notes** LB ⊗ Civ Wed 60

Athenaeum Hotel & Apartments

★★★★★ ◎◎ HOTEL PLAN 4 H6

tel: 020 7499 3464 **116 Piccadilly W1J 7BJ**
email: info@athenaeumhotel.com **web:** www.athenaeumhotel.com
dir: On Piccadilly, overlooking Green Park

With a discreet address in Mayfair, this well-loved hotel offers bedrooms appointed to the highest levels of comfort; all include Bose iPod speakers, a pillow menu and WiFi, and several boast views over Green Park. The hotel also has suites, and for the ultimate luxury there's a roof-top suite with a private balcony. The hotel has a whisky bar, the Garden Lounge for award-winning afternoon teas, and even a pudding parlour open in the evenings. The stylish restaurant serves British cuisine which will appeals to all ages. A range of spacious and well-appointed apartments can be found in a row of Edwardian townhouses adjacent to the hotel. There is an extensive range of beauty treatments available along with conference and meeting facilities.

Rooms 156 (8 smoking) **Facilities** STV WiFi Gym Steam rooms Sauna Hairdressing salon Free bike hire Xmas New Year **Conf** Class 35 Board 36 Thtr 55 **Services** Lift Air con **Notes** ⊗ Civ Wed 80

Brown's Hotel

★★★★★ ◎◎ HOTEL PLAN 2 J1

ℛF
THE ROCCO FORTE COLLECTION

tel: 020 7493 6020 **Albemarle St, Mayfair W1S 4BP**
email: reservations.browns@roccofortehotels.com **web:** www.roccofortehotels.com
dir: A short walk from Green Park, Bond St, Piccadilly & Buckingham Palace

Brown's is a London hospitality icon that maintains its charm through the successful balance of traditional and contemporary. Bedrooms are luxurious, furnished to the highest standard and come with all the modern comforts expected of such a grand Mayfair hotel. The hotel has 29 suites including two Royal Suites and two Presidential Suites. The elegant, yet informal, HIX Mayfair serves a traditional selection of popular British dishes that are created with great skill, and it is also home to a collection of works by leading British artists. The English Tea Room proves a great meeting place for afternoon tea.

Rooms 117 (12 smoking) 🐾 **Facilities** Spa STV WiFi Gym 🎵 Xmas New Year **Conf** Class 30 Board 30 Thtr 70 **Services** Lift Air con **Notes** ⊗ Civ Wed 70

W1 WEST END *continued*

The Dorchester

★★★★★ ◉◉ HOTEL PLAN 4 G6

tel: 020 7629 8888 **Park Ln W1K 1QA**
email: information.tdl@dorchestercollection.com **web:** www.thedorchester.com
dir: Halfway along Park Ln between Hyde Park Corner & Marble Arch

One of London's finest, The Dorchester remains one of the best-loved hotels in the country and always delivers. The spacious bedrooms and suites are beautifully appointed and feature fabulous marble bathrooms. Leading off from the foyer, The Promenade is the perfect setting for afternoon tea or drinks. In the evening guests can relax to the sound of live jazz, while enjoying a cocktail in the stylish bar. Dining options include the sophisticated Chinese restaurant, China Tang; Alain Ducasse at The Dorchester from the world renowned French chef of the same name; and of course, The Grill.

Rooms 250 ☎ **S** £355-£985; **D** £415-£1045* **Facilities** Spa STV FTV WiFi ↘ HL Gym Steam rooms Fitness suite ♫ Xmas New Year **Conf** Class 300 Board 42 Thtr 500 **Services** Lift Air con **Parking** 20 **Notes** LB ⊗ Civ Wed 432

Four Seasons Hotel London at Park Lane

★★★★★ ◉◉ HOTEL PLAN 4 G6

tel: 020 7499 0888 **Hamilton Place, Park Ln W1J 7DR**
email: reservations@fourseasons.com **web:** www.fourseasons.com/london
dir: From Piccadilly into Old Park Ln, into Hamilton Place

This long-established popular hotel is discreetly located near Hyde Park Corner, in the heart of Mayfair. It successfully combines modern efficiencies with

traditional luxury. Guest care is consistently of the highest order, even down to the smallest detail of the personalised wake-up call. The bedrooms are elegant and spacious, and the unique conservatory rooms are particularly special. Spacious public areas include extensive conference and banqueting facilities, Lane's bar and fine-dining restaurant and an elegant lounge where wonderful afternoon teas are served.

Rooms 193 (49 smoking) ☎ **S** £370-£800; **D** £370-£800* **Facilities** Spa STV FTV WiFi ↘ Gym Fitness Centre ♫ Xmas New Year **Conf** Class 174 Board 108 Thtr 375 **Services** Lift Air con **Parking** 10 **Notes** Civ Wed 350

Claridge's

MAYBOURNE
HOTEL GROUP

★★★★★ HOTEL PLAN 2 H1

tel: 020 7629 8860 **Brook St W1K 4HR**
email: info@claridges.co.uk **web:** www.claridges.co.uk
dir: 1st turn after Green Park tube station to Berkeley Sq & 4th exit into Davies St. 3rd right into Brook St

Once renowned as the resort of kings and princes, Claridge's today continues to set the standards by which other hotels are judged. The sumptuous, air-conditioned bedrooms are elegantly themed to reflect the Victorian or art deco architecture of the building. Fera at Claridge's, overseen by chef Simon Rogan, is currently establishing itself, and the stylish cocktail bar is a hit with residents and non-residents alike. Service throughout is punctilious and thoroughly professional.

Rooms 203 (144 fmly) ☎ **S** £420-£810; **D** £420-£810* **Facilities** Spa STV WiFi Gym Beauty & health treatments Use of sister hotel's swimming pool ♫ Xmas New Year **Conf** Class 130 Board 60 Thtr 250 Del from £535 to £925* **Services** Lift Air con **Notes** LB ⊗ Civ Wed 200

LONDON

Metropolitan London

★★★★★ 86% ◉◉ HOTEL PLAN 4 G6

tel: 020 7447 1000 **Old Park Ln W1K 1LB**
email: res.met.lon@comohotels.com **web:** www.comohotels.com/metropolitanlondon
dir: On corner of Old Park Ln & Hertford St

Overlooking Hyde Park this hotel is located within easy reach of the fashionable stores of Knightsbridge and Mayfair. The hotel's contemporary style allows freedom and space to relax. Understated luxury is the key here with bedrooms enjoying great natural light. There is also a Shambhala Spa, steam room and fully equipped gym. For those seeking a culinary experience, Nobu offers innovative Japanese cuisine with an upbeat atmosphere.

Rooms 144 (23 smoking) ✆ **S** £249-£3150; **D** £249-£3150* **Facilities** Spa STV FTV WiFi ⬙ Gym Steam rooms ♫ **Conf** Class 25 Board 30 Thtr 80 **Services** Lift Air con **Parking** 8 **Notes** LB Civ Wed 80

The Langham, London

★★★★★ 85% ◉◉ HOTEL PLAN 2 H3

tel: 020 7636 1000 **Portland Place W1B 1JA**
email: lon.info@langhamhotels.com **web:** www.langhamlondon.com
dir: N of Regent St, left opposite All Soul's Church

This hotel has a grand entrance which leads into restored interior elegance. Dating back to 1865 the building displays a contemporary, luxurious style. Situated near Regent Street it is ideally located for both theatreland and the principal shopping areas. Bedrooms are delightfully appointed and many have excellent views. The Landau restaurant and Artesian bar offer high standards of service, delivered by a friendly team. Palm Court is a great place for afternoon tea or a glass of champagne. There is also an extensive health club complete with a 16-metre pool.

Rooms 378 (9 fmly) (15 smoking) **Facilities** Spa STV WiFi ⬙ ⌨ supervised Gym Health club Sauna Steam room ♫ Xmas New Year **Conf** Class 148 Board 80 Thtr 300 **Services** Lift Air con **Notes** ⊗ Civ Wed 280

The London Edition

★★★★★ 84% ◉◉ HOTEL PLAN 2 J2

tel: 020 7781 0000 🖨 020 7781 0100 **1O Berners St W1T 3NP**
web: www.edition-hotels.marriott.com/london

The London Edition is the latest from the EDITION portfolio, transforming this landmark building with innovation and truly great design. Excellent dining is provided in the Berners Tavern, under direction of award-winning chef Jason Atherton. The reservations only Punch Room is a great place to unwind, with a traditional punch bowl. Service is personal and friendly with a modern twist, ensuring a flawless and memorable guest experience. A dynamic fusion of past and present makes the best use of space with stunning public areas and artwork. Bedrooms are finished in either light oak or dark walnut creating a cosy, cabin like feel; akin to that of a private yacht. Berners Tavern is the AA Restaurant of the Year for London 2014-2015.

Rooms 173 ✆ **D** fr £355* **Facilities** FTV WiFi Gym **Conf** Class 36 Board 14 Thtr 60 **Notes** ⊗

Hyatt Regency London - The Churchill

★★★★★ 83% ◉◉◉ HOTEL PLAN 2 F2

tel: 020 7486 5800 **3O Portman Square W1H 7BH**
email: london.churchill@hyatt.com **web:** www.london.churchill.hyatt.com
dir: From Marble Arch rdbt, follow signs for Oxford Circus into Oxford St. Left after 2nd lights into Portman St. Hotel on left

This smart hotel enjoys a central location overlooking Portman Square. Excellent conference and in-room facilities, plus a fitness room make this the ideal choice for both corporate and leisure guests. To set the style, guests are greeted by stunning floral displays in the sophisticated lobby. The Montagu restaurant offers contemporary dining, plus the option to sit at the Chef's Table for a front row seat to watch all the action in the kitchen.

Rooms 434 ✆ **S** £240-£660; **D** £240-£660 **Facilities** STV FTV WiFi ⬙ ⌨ Gym Jogging track ♫ Xmas New Year **Conf** Class 160 Board 68 Thtr 250 **Services** Lift Air con **Parking** 48 **Notes** ⊗ Civ Wed 250

Grosvenor House, A JW Marriott Hotel

★★★★★ 83% ◉ HOTEL PLAN 2 G1

tel: 020 7499 6363 & 7399 8400 **Park Ln W1K 7TN**
email: grosvenor.house@marriotthotels.com **web:** www.londongrosvenorhouse.co.uk
dir: Centrally located on Park Ln, between Hyde Park Corner & Oxford St

This quintessentially British hotel, overlooking Hyde Park offers luxurious accommodation, warm hospitality and exemplary service that epitomises the fine hotel culture of London. The property boasts the largest ballroom in Europe, and there is a steakhouse and a cocktail bar. The Park Room and The Library make perfect settings for afternoon tea.

Rooms 494 (10 fmly) (111 smoking) **Facilities** STV WiFi ⬙ Gym Fitness centre Xmas New Year **Conf** Class 800 Board 140 Thtr 1500 **Services** Lift Air con **Parking** 48 **Notes** ⊗ Civ Wed 1500

LONDON

W1 WEST END *continued*

London Hilton on Park Lane

★★★★★ 83% HOTEL PLAN 4 G6

tel: 020 7493 8000 **22 Park Ln W1K 1BE**
email: reservations.parklane@hilton.com **web:** www.parklanehilton.com
dir: From N: M1/A41 towards central London & West End. W along Oxford St, into Park
Lane. From S: A23 for central London & West End, cross Vauxhall Bridge (A202) & into
Park Lane

Located in the heart of Park Lane, this landmark hotel offers a luxury environment
overlooking Hyde Park and the city. A dedicated team of staff is available to meet
their guests' every need. Having undergone a full refurbishment, the bedrooms are
designed with quality appointments and luxury fabrics. Several eating options are
available - from the renowned Galvin at Windows to the all-day dining of Podium,
which also serves a splendid afternoon tea.

Rooms 453 (52 smoking) 🛏 **S** £269-£719; **D** £269-£719* **Facilities** Spa STV FTV WiFi
⤢ Gym 🎵 Xmas New Year **Conf** Class 600 Board 60 Thtr 1100 **Services** Lift Air con
Parking 242 **Notes** ⊗ Civ Wed 1000

Le Meridien Piccadilly

★★★★★ 82% ◉ HOTEL PLAN 2 J1

tel: 020 7734 8000 **21 Piccadilly W1J 0BH**
email: reservations.piccadilly@lemeridien.com **web:** www.lemeridien.com/piccadilly
dir: 100mtrs from Piccadilly Circus

Situated in the heart of Piccadilly, this well established hotel is ideally located for
the West End and Theatreland. The well-equipped, air-conditioned bedrooms,
varying in shape and size, are modern and contemporary in style. Public areas
include extensive leisure facilities, with a state-of-the-art gym, pool and sauna, the
trendy Longitude 0° 8' cocktail bar, and the popular Terrace Restaurant which
overlooks Piccadilly.

Rooms 280 🛏 **Facilities** Spa STV WiFi ⤢ ⊗ supervised Gym Squash **Conf** Class 160
Board 80 Thtr 250 **Services** Lift Air con **Notes** ⊗ Civ Wed 200

The Montcalm

★★★★★ 81% ◉◉◉ HOTEL PLAN 2 F2

tel: 020 7402 4288 **Great Cumberland Place W1H 7TW**
email: reservations@montcalm.co.uk **web:** www.montcalm.co.uk
dir: 2 mins' walk N from Marble Arch station

The Montcalm is ideally situated in the heart of London, just a short walk from
Marble Arch, Oxford Street, Park Lane, Mayfair, Hyde Park and Theatreland. The
elegantly decorated bedrooms are tastefully appointed and have many thoughtful
touches. Public areas include a contemporary lounge bar and The Crescent
restaurant which serves modern European cuisine, while the three AA Rosette-
worthy Sixtyone Restaurant is overseen by Chef Patron, Arnaud Stevens. The hotel
has a range of private rooms and conference suites, as well as spa, sauna, steam
room, gym and exercise pool.

Rooms 143 (17 fmly) (7 GF) 🛏 **Facilities** Spa STV WiFi ⊗ Gym **Conf** Class 250
Board 250 Thtr 500 **Services** Lift Air con **Notes** ⊗ Civ Wed 60

The Westbury Hotel

★★★★★ 80% ◉◉◉ HOTEL PLAN 2 H1

tel: 020 7629 7755 **Bond St W1S 2YF**
email: reservations@westburymayfair.com **web:** www.westburymayfair.com
dir: From Oxford Circus S down Regent St, right onto Conduit St, hotel at junct of Conduit
St & Bond St

A well-known favourite with an international clientele, The Westbury is located at
the heart of London's finest shopping district and provides a calm atmosphere away
from the hubbub. The standards of accommodation are high throughout and
bedrooms have panoramic views; the options include a variety of suites and a two-
bedroom penthouse suite. Reception rooms offer a good choice for both relaxing and
eating and include the stylish Polo Bar, The Westbury lounge, the Tsukiji Sushi
Restaurant and the fine-dining option in award-winning Alyn Williams at the
Westbury. Private dining is also available.

Rooms 246 (80 fmly) 🛏 **Facilities** STV FTV WiFi ⤢ Gym Fitness centre Steam room
Sauna Xmas New Year **Conf** Class 170 Board 36 Thtr 250 **Services** Lift Air con
Notes ⊗ Civ Wed 80

The Chesterfield Mayfair

★★★★ ◉◉ HOTEL PLAN 4 H6

THE RED CARNATION HOTEL COLLECTION

tel: 020 7491 2622 **35 Charles St, Mayfair W1J 5EB**
email: bookch@rchmail.com **web:** www.chesterfieldmayfair.com
dir: Hyde Park Corner along Piccadilly, left into Half Moon St. At end left & 1st right
into Queens St, then right into Charles St

Quiet elegance and an atmosphere of exclusivity characterise this stylish
Mayfair hotel where attentive, friendly service is paramount. The bedrooms, each
with a marble-clad bathroom, have contemporary styles - perhaps with floral
fabric walls, an African theme or with Savile Row stripes. In addition to these
deluxe bedrooms there are 13 individually designed suites; some with four-
poster beds and some with jacuzzis. The Butler's Restaurant is the fine dining
option, and The Conservatory, with views over the garden, is just the place for
cocktails, light lunches and afternoon teas. The hotel is air-conditioned
throughout.

Rooms 107 🛏 **S** £195-£390; **D** £220-£1470* **Facilities** STV WiFi ⤢ 🎵 **Conf** Class 45
Board 45 Thtr 100 Del from £285 to £635* **Services** Lift Air con **Notes** LB Civ Wed 120

LONDON

London Marriott Hotel Grosvenor Square

★★★★ 84% 🏵🏵 HOTEL PLAN 2 G1

tel: 020 7493 1232 **Grosvenor Square W1K 6JP**
email: dann.davies@marriotthotels.com **web:** www.londonmarriottgrosvenorsquare.co.uk
dir: M4 E to Cromwell Rd through Knightsbridge to Hyde Park Corner. Into Park Lane, right at Brook Gate into Upper Brook St to Grosvenor Sq

Situated adjacent to Grosvenor Square in the heart of Mayfair, this hotel boasts convenient access to the city, West End and some of London's most exclusive shops. Bedrooms and public areas are furnished and decorated to a high standard and retain the traditional elegance for which the area is known. The hotel's eating options include Maze Grill which has two AA Rosettes.

Rooms 237 (26 fmly) **Facilities** WiFi Gym Exercise & fitness centre Xmas **Conf** Class 500 Board 120 Thtr 900 **Services** Lift Air con **Notes** ⊗ Civ Wed 600

Flemings Mayfair

★★★★ 82% 🏵 HOTEL PLAN 4 H6

tel: 020 7499 0000 **Half Moon St, Mayfair W1J 7BH**
email: guest@flemings.co.uk **web:** www.flemings-mayfair.co.uk
dir: On quiet residential street off Piccadilly, 3 mins walk from Green Park

The second oldest hotel in London offers modern décor with a cosy atmosphere and friendly, personal service. While public areas are compact, high quality is apparent with chandeliers and feature fireplaces. Bedrooms vary in size but have recently been upgraded and are equipped with an excellent range of facilities.

Rooms 129 (24 fmly) (24 GF) 🐾 **S** £150-£450; **D** £190-£495* **Facilities** STV FTV WiFi ⌂ Gym Xmas New Year **Conf** Board 22 **Services** Lift Air con **Notes** LB

The Mandeville Hotel

★★★★ 82% 🏵 HOTEL PLAN 2 G2

tel: 020 7935 5599 **Mandeville Place W1U 2BE**
email: sales@mandeville.co.uk **web:** www.mandeville.co.uk
dir: 3 mins walk from Bond St tube station

This is a stylish and attractive boutique-style hotel with a very contemporary feel. Bedrooms are high in quality, are air conditioned and large, and have very comfortable beds. One of the suites, The Penthouse, has a patio with views over London. The Reform Social & Grill Restaurant offers award-winning modern British cuisine, and the cocktail bar is always popular.

Rooms 142 (6 fmly) 🐾 **Facilities** STV FTV WiFi ⌂ Xmas New Year **Conf** Class 20 Board 20 Thtr 40 **Services** Lift Air con **Notes** ⊗

London Marriott Hotel Marble Arch

★★★★ 80% HOTEL PLAN 2 F2

tel: 020 7723 1277 **134 George St W1H 5DN**
email: mhrs.lonma.sales.marketing.coordinator@marriotthotels.com
web: www.londonmarriottmarblearch.co.uk
dir: From Marble Arch turn into Edgware Rd, then 4th right into George St. Left into Dorset St for entrance

Situated just off the Edgware Road and close to the Oxford Street shops, this friendly hotel offers smart, well-equipped, air-conditioned bedrooms. Public areas are stylish, and include a smart indoor leisure club and an Italian-themed restaurant. Secure underground parking is available.

Rooms 240 (100 fmly) 🐾 **Facilities** STV FTV WiFi HL 🔲 supervised Gym Xmas New Year **Conf** Class 90 Board 60 Thtr 170 **Services** Lift Air con **Parking** 83 **Notes** ⊗ Civ Wed 150

Millennium Hotel London Mayfair

★★★★ 79% 🏵🏵 HOTEL PLAN 2 G1

tel: 020 7629 9400 **Grosvenor Square W1K 2HP**
email: reservations@millenniumhotels.co.uk **web:** www.millenniumhotels.co.uk
dir: S side of Grosvenor Square, 5 mins walk from Oxford St & Bond St stations

This hotel benefits from a prestigious location in the heart of Mayfair, close to Bond Street. Smart bedrooms are generally spacious and club-floor rooms have exclusive use of their own lounge with complimentary refreshments. A choice of bars and dining options is available along with conference facilities and a fitness room.

Rooms 336 🐾 **S** £228-£660; **D** £240-£690 **Facilities** STV FTV WiFi ⌂ HL Gym Fitness suite 🎵 Xmas New Year **Conf** Class 250 Board 70 Thtr 500 Del from £319 to £831 **Services** Lift Air con **Notes** LB ⊗ Civ Wed 250

DoubleTree by Hilton Hotel, Marble Arch

★★★★ 77% 🏵🏵🏵🏵 HOTEL PLAN 2 F2

tel: 020 7935 2361 **4 Bryanston St W1H 7BY**
email: lonma.res@hilton.com **web:** www.londonmarblearch.doubletreebyhilton.com
dir: Walking distance from Oxford St, Marble Arch & Hyde Park

This hotel is a well located, historic property. The bedrooms, including executive and deluxe club floor rooms, vary in size but all are smartly equipped, boast bright trendy soft furnishings and are air conditioned; the en suites are equally modern and stylish. The public areas include a cocktail bar/lounge, Fire & Spice all-day dining concept, and the acclaimed Texture Restaurant which delivers impressive, modern cooking. The hotel offers free WiFi throughout.

Rooms 122 (12 fmly) (5 GF) 🐾 **S** £170-£360; **D** £190-£360 (incl. bkfst)* **Facilities** STV FTV WiFi ⌂ HL Gym **Conf** Class 60 Board 50 Thtr 130 Del from £250 to £380* **Services** Lift Air con **Notes** LB ⊗

Park Plaza Sherlock Holmes

★★★★ 76% 🏵 HOTEL PLAN 2 F3

tel: 0844 415 6740 **108 Baker St W1U 6LJ**
email: info@sherlockholmeshotel.com **web:** www.sherlockholmeshotel.com
dir: From Marylebone Flyover into Marylebone Rd. At Baker St turn right for hotel on left

Chic and modern, this boutique-style hotel is near a number of London underground and rail stations. Public rooms include a popular bar, sited just inside the main entrance, and Sherlock's Grill, where the mesquite-wood burning stove is a feature of the cooking. The hotel also features an indoor health suite and a relaxing lounge.

Rooms 119 (20 fmly) 🐾 **Facilities** STV WiFi Gym Beauty treatment room 🎵 Xmas **Conf** Class 35 Board 30 Thtr 80 **Services** Lift Air con **Notes** ⊗ Civ Wed 80

W1 WEST END *continued*

The Washington Mayfair Hotel

★★★★ 75% HOTEL PLAN 4 H6

tel: 020 7499 7000 **5-7 Curzon St, Mayfair W1J 5HE**
email: sales@washington-mayfair.co.uk **web:** www.washington-mayfair.co.uk
dir: From Green Park station take Piccadilly exit & turn right. 4th right into Curzon St

Situated in the heart of Mayfair, this stylish, independently owned hotel offers a very high standard of accommodation. The personalised, friendly service is noteworthy. Bedrooms are attractively furnished and provide high levels of comfort. The hotel is also a popular venue for afternoon tea and refreshments, served in the marbled and wood-panelled lounge.

Rooms 171 (32 smoking) ↑ **S** £200-£500; **D** £200-£1000* **Facilities** FTV WiFi ↘ Gym Xmas New Year **Conf** Class 40 Board 36 Thtr 110 Del from £280 to £450*
Services Lift Air con **Notes** LB ⊗

Holiday Inn London - Mayfair

★★★★ 74% HOTEL PLAN 2 H1

tel: 0871 942 9110 **3 Berkeley St W1J 8NE**
email: himayfair-reservations@ihg.com **web:** www.hilondonmayfairhotel.co.uk
dir: At corner of Berkeley St & Piccadilly

Located in the heart of Mayfair and just minutes from Green Park tube station, this busy hotel has the benefit of well-proportioned, attractive bedrooms and elegant public areas. Options for dining include the graceful Nightingales Restaurant or choices from a substantial snack menu in the lounge bar.

Rooms 196 (63 fmly) **Facilities** STV WiFi ↘ Use of local gym Xmas New Year **Conf** Class 32 Board 32 Thtr 65 **Services** Lift Air con **Parking** 18 **Notes** ⊗

Holiday Inn London - Regents Park

★★★★ 70% HOTEL PLAN 2 H4

tel: 0871 942 9111 & 020 7388 2302 **Carburton St, Regents Park W1W 5EE**
email: reservations-londonregentspark@ihg.com
web: www.hilondonregentsparkhotel.co.uk
dir: From E: from King's Cross, A50, left into Bolsover St. From W: A40 onto A501 (Regent's Park Station on right). Left into Albany St, 1st right to cross Euston Rd. Pass Gt Portland St tube station to Bolsover St. Hotel on left

Well located and with the benefit of an adjacent public car park, this popular modern hotel provides a range of comfortable bedrooms equipped for both business and leisure guests. The attractive Junction Restaurant is the setting for brasserie-style eating and a comprehensive buffet breakfast provides a good start to the day. The hotel also provides excellent conference facilities within The Academy Centre.

Rooms 332 (2 fmly) **D** £70-£400* **Facilities** STV FTV WiFi ↘ HL **Conf** Class 200 Board 50 Thtr 350 Del from £150 to £300* **Services** Lift Air con **Notes** LB ⊗

W2 BAYSWATER, PADDINGTON

Lancaster London

★★★★ 85% ⊛⊛ HOTEL PLAN 2 D1

tel: 020 7551 6000 **Lancaster Ter W2 2TY**
email: book@lancasterlondon.com **web:** www.lancasterlondon.com
dir: Adjacent to Lancaster Gate tube station, 1m from Paddington Heathrow Express, 1m from A40, opposite Hyde Park

Located adjacent to Hyde Park, this large hotel offers a wide range of facilities. There are many room types; higher floors have excellent panoramic views of the city and park, and the suites are truly impressive. The hotel also offers two contrasting award-winning restaurants - the contemporary Island Restaurant & Bar, and Nipa restaurant with authentic Thai cuisine. There are spacious state-of-the-art, flexible conference and banqueting facilities, a 24-hour business centre and secure parking. This is an environmentally conscious hotel which has instigated many initiatives including a honey farm on the roof.

Rooms 416 (40 fmly) (28 smoking) ↑ **S** £139-£429; **D** £139-£429* **Facilities** STV FTV WiFi ↘ Gym Xmas New Year **Conf** Class 550 Board 46 Thtr 1000 Del from £291.60 to £399.60* **Services** Lift Air con **Parking** 40 **Notes** LB ⊗ Civ Wed 1000

Novotel London Paddington

★★★★ 76% HOTEL PLAN 2 C3

tel: 020 7266 6000 **3 Kingdom St, Paddington W2 6BD**
email: h6455@accor.com **web:** www.novotel.com
dir: Easy access from Westway A40 & Bishops Bridge Rd A4206

Located in the Paddington Central area, this hotel is easily accessible by road, and is only a few minutes walk from Paddington Station. Ideal for business or leisure guests. The facilities include the Elements Restaurant, a bar, conference facilities, a swimming pool, sauna, plus steam and fitness rooms. An NCP car park is a 5-minute walk away.

Rooms 206 (24 fmly) **Facilities** STV WiFi ↘ ⚑ Gym Steam room Sauna **Conf** Class 70 Board 40 Thtr 150 **Services** Lift

Hotel Indigo

★★★★ 74% HOTEL PLAN 2 D2

tel: 020 7706 4444 **16 London St, Paddington W2 1HL**
email: malcolm@lth-hotels.com **web:** www.indigopaddington.com

This smart hotel is located within a stone's throw of Paddington Station. Contemporary and stylish, bedrooms are equipped with all modern extras; they boast high quality comfy beds ensuring a great night's sleep and en suites with power showers and quality toiletries. Delightful public areas include a restaurant, bar and a coffee shop offering tempting cakes.

Rooms 64 ↑ **Facilities** STV FTV WiFi HL Gym **Services** Lift Air con **Notes** ⊗

Lancaster Gate Hotel

★★★ 74% HOTEL PLAN 2 C1

tel: 020 7479 2500 & 7262 5090 **66 Lancaster Gate W2 3NA**
email: info@lghhydepark.co.uk **web:** www.lancastergatehotelhydepark.co.uk
dir: Just off Bayswater Rd

This hotel offers a convenient location between Oxford Street and Knightsbridge and is also close to Hyde Park and Kensington Gardens. Bedrooms are well equipped with broadband and safes, as well as TVs with a wide range of channels. There is a comfortable bar and stylish restaurant, and the hotel also has a range of meeting rooms.

Rooms 188 (3 fmly) (13 GF) (4 smoking) **S** £79-£250; **D** £79-£280* **Facilities** STV FTV WiFi Off site leisure facilities available **Conf** Class 24 Board 22 Thtr 50 Del from £135 to £270* **Services** Lift Air con **Notes** LB

LONDON

Mitre House Hotel

★★ 72% METRO HOTEL PLAN 2 D2

tel: 020 7723 8040 & 7402 5695 **178-184 Sussex Gardens, Hyde Park W2 1TU**
email: reservations@mitrehousehotel.com **web:** www.mitrehousehotel.com
dir: Parallel to Bayswater Rd & one block from Paddington Station

This family-run hotel continues to offers a warm welcome and attentive service. It is ideally located, close to Paddington station and near the West End and major attractions. Bedrooms include a number of family suites and there is a lounge bar. Limited parking is available.

Rooms 69 (7 fmly) (7 GF) (69 smoking) **S** fr £75; **D** fr £95 (incl. bkfst)* **Facilities** STV WiFi **Services** Lift **Parking** 20 **Notes** ⊗

Griffin House Hotel

Ⓤ PLAN 2 E2

tel: 020 77236532 **10 Connaught St, Marble Arch W2 2AH**
email: info@griffinhousehotel.co.uk **web:** www.griffinhousehotel.co.uk
dir: Close to Hyde Park and Marble Arch

Currently the rating for this establishment is not confirmed. This may be due to a change of ownership or because it has only recently joined the AA rating scheme. For further details please see the AA website: theAA.com

Rooms 15 **S** £79-£109; **D** £99-£129 (incl. bkfst)* **Facilities** WiFi ⇗ **Notes** ⊗

W4 CHISWICK

Chiswick Moran Hotel

★★★★ 75% HOTEL PLAN 1 C3

tel: 020 8996 5200 **626 Chiswick High Rd W4 5RY**
email: chiswickres@moranhotels.com **web:** www.moranhotels.com
dir: 200yds from M4 junct 2

This stylish, modern hotel is conveniently located for Heathrow and central London, with Gunnersby tube station just a few minutes' walk away. Airy, spacious public areas include a modern restaurant, a popular bar and excellent meeting facilities. Fully air-conditioned bedrooms are stylish and extremely well appointed with broadband, laptop safes and flat-screen TVs. All boast spacious, modern bathrooms, many with walk-in rain showers.

Rooms 123 (10 fmly) ♪ **Facilities** STV FTV WiFi ⇗ Gym Xmas New Year **Conf** Class 45 Board 40 Thtr 90 **Services** Lift Air con **Parking** 40 **Notes** ⊗ Civ Wed 80

W5 EALING

Crowne Plaza London - Ealing

★★★★ 77% HOTEL PLAN 1 C4

tel: 0208 233 3200 **Western Av, Hanger Ln, Ealing W5 1HG**
email: info@cp-londonealing.co.uk **web:** www.cp-londonealing.co.uk
dir: A40 from central London towards M40. Exit at Ealing & North Circular A406 sign. At rdbt take 2nd exit signed A40. Hotel on left

Appointed to a high standard, this hotel occupies a prime position on the A40 and North Circular at Hangar Lane; Wembley Stadium is easily accessible. Modern, well-equipped, air-conditioned and sound-proofed bedrooms offer good facilities. There is a smart gym and a steam room, together with meeting facilities and the West 5 Brasserie. On-site parking is available.

Rooms 131 (17 GF) (15 smoking) **Facilities** FTV WiFi ⇗ Gym Steam room Xmas New Year **Conf** Class 30 Board 36 Thtr 80 **Services** Lift Air con **Parking** 85 **Notes** ⊗

Premier Inn London Ealing

BUDGET HOTEL PLAN 1 C3

tel: 0871 527 9368 **22-24 Uxbridge Rd, Ealing W5 2SR**
web: www.premierinn.com
dir: M4 junct 1, A406 (signed North Circular & M1). Left onto A4020 (signed Ealing & Southall). Hotel on right after Ealing Broadway tube station

High quality, budget accommodation ideal for both families and business travellers. Spacious, en suite bedrooms feature tea and coffee making facilities, and Freeview TV in most hotels. Internet access and WiFi are available for a small fee. The adjacent family restaurant features a wide and varied menu. See also the Hotel Groups pages.

Rooms 165

Premier Inn London Hanger Lane

BUDGET HOTEL PLAN 1 C4

tel: 0871 527 8346 **1-6 Ritz Pde, Ealing W5 3RA**
web: www.premierinn.com
dir: M4 junct 2, A4 follow North Circular/A406 signs, for 0.5m. Take A406 for approx 2.5m. Right into Ashbourne Rd, immediately left into Ashbourne Parade, right into Ritz Parade. Hotel on right

Rooms 59

W6 HAMMERSMITH

Novotel London West

★★★★ 74% ◉ HOTEL PLAN 1 D3

tel: 020 8741 1555 **1 Shortlands W6 8DR**
email: H0737@accor.com **web:** www.novotellondonwest.co.uk
dir: M4 (A4) & A316 junct at Hogarth rdbt. Along Great West Rd, left for Hammersmith before flyover. On Hammersmith Bridge Rd to rdbt, take 5th exit. 1st left into Shortlands, 1st left to hotel main entrance

A Hammersmith landmark, this substantial hotel is a popular base for both business and leisure travellers. Spacious, air-conditioned bedrooms have a good range of extras and many have additional beds, making them suitable for families. The hotel also has its own car park, business centre and shop, and boasts one of the largest convention centres in Europe.

Rooms 630 (148 fmly) **Facilities** STV WiFi Gym **Conf** Class 540 Board 75 Thtr 1000 **Services** Lift Air con **Parking** 240

Premier Inn London Hammersmith

BUDGET HOTEL PLAN 1 D3

tel: 0871 527 8660 **255 King St, Hammersmith W6 9LU**
web: www.premierinn.com
dir: From central London on A4 to Hammersmith, follow A315 towards Chiswick

High quality, budget accommodation ideal for both families and business travellers. Spacious, en suite bedrooms feature tea and coffee making facilities, and Freeview TV in most hotels. Internet access and WiFi are available for a small fee. The adjacent family restaurant features a wide and varied menu. See also the Hotel Groups pages.

Rooms 106

W8 KENSINGTON

INSPECTORS' CHOICE

Royal Garden Hotel

★★★★★ ◉◉◉ HOTEL PLAN 4 B5

tel: 020 7937 8000 **2-24 Kensington High St W8 4PT**
email: reservations@royalgardenhotel.co.uk **web:** www.royalgardenhotel.co.uk
dir: Adjacent to Kensington Palace

This landmark hotel, just a short walk from the Royal Albert Hall, has airy, stylish public rooms that include the Park Terrace Restaurant, Lounge and Bar; Bertie's cocktail bar and the contemporary 10th-floor Min Jiang Restaurant. The latter offers authentic Chinese cuisine and enjoys breathtaking views of the city. The stylish and contemporary bedrooms are equipped with up-to-date facilities and include a number of spacious, air-conditioned rooms and suites with super views over Kensington Gardens. All rooms have iPod docking stations, flat-screen TVs and triple-glazed windows as standard. Guests have complimentary use of the Soma Spa gym, sauna and steam room.

Rooms 394 (41 fmly) (37 smoking) 🛰 **S** £160-£440; **D** £210-£490* **Facilities** Spa STV FTV WiFi ⬧ HL Gym Health club Sauna Steam room 🎵 Xmas New Year **Conf** Class 320 Board 100 Thtr 550 Del from £320 to £625* **Services** Lift Air con **Parking** 200 **Notes** ⊗ Civ Wed 400

INSPECTORS' CHOICE

The Milestone Hotel

★★★★★ ◉◉ HOTEL PLAN 4 B5

 THE RED CARNATION HOTEL COLLECTION

tel: 020 7917 1000 **1 Kensington Court W8 5DL**
email: bookms@rchmail.com **web:** www.milestonehotel.com
dir: From Warwick Rd right into Kensington High St. Hotel 400yds past Kensington tube station. Adjacent to Kensington Palace

This delightful town house enjoys a wonderful location opposite Kensington Palace and is near the elegant shops. The individually themed bedrooms include a selection of stunning suites that are equipped with every conceivable extra - fruit, cookies, chocolates, complimentary newspapers and even the next day's weather forecast. Up-to-the-minute technology includes high speed WiFi and interactive TV. Public areas include the luxurious Park Lounge where afternoon tea is served, the delightful split-level Stables Bar, a conservatory, the sumptuous Cheneston's restaurant and a fully equipped small gym, resistance pool and a spa treatment room.

Rooms 62 (9 fmly) (1 GF) (5 smoking) 🛰 **S** £342-£504; **D** £378-£540* **Facilities** STV FTV WiFi ⬧ HL 🔆 Gym Health club Beauty treatment room 🎵 Xmas New Year Child facilities **Conf** Class 20 Board 20 Thtr 50 Del from £475 to £595* **Services** Lift Air con **Parking** 1 **Notes** LB Civ Wed 30

Copthorne Tara Hotel London Kensington

★★★★ 72% HOTEL PLAN 4 B4

 MILLENNIUM HOTELS AND RESORTS MILLENNIUM · COPTHORNE

tel: 020 7937 7211 & 7872 2000 **Scarsdale Place, Wrights Ln W8 5SR**
email: reservations.tara@millenniumhotels.co.uk **web:** www.millenniumhotels.co.uk
dir: From Kensington High St into Wrights Ln (NB for Sat Nav use W8 5SY)

This expansive hotel is ideally placed for Kensington High Street shops and tube station. Smart public areas include a trendy coffee shop, a gym, a stylish brasserie and bar, plus extensive conference facilities. Bedrooms include several well-equipped rooms for less mobile guests, in addition to a number of Connoisseur rooms that have the use of a club lounge as one of its many complimentary facilities.

Rooms 833 (3 fmly) 🛰 **S** £100-£360; **D** £110-£370 (incl. bkfst)* **Facilities** FTV WiFi ⬧ HL Fitness room Xmas New Year **Conf** Class 160 Board 90 Thtr 280 **Services** Lift Air con **Parking** 126 **Notes** LB ⊗ Civ Wed 280

London Lodge Hotel

[U] PLAN 4 A3

tel: 020 7244 8444 020 73736661 **134-136 Lexham Gardens, kensington W8 6JE**
email: info@londonlodgehotel.com **web:** www.londonlodgehotel.com
dir: Located in the heart of Kensington, close to Earls Court & Olympia exhibition centres

Currently the rating for this establishment is not confirmed. This may be due to a change of ownership or because it has only recently joined the AA rating scheme. For further details please see the AA website: theAA.com

Rooms 28 **Facilities** STV WiFi ⟳

W14 WEST KENSINGTON

K West Hotel & Spa

★★★★ 77% HOTEL PLAN 1 D3

tel: 020 8008 6600 **Richmond Way W14 0AX**
email: info@k-west.co.uk **web:** www.k-west.co.uk
dir: From A40(M) take Shepherd's Bush exit. At Holland Park rdbt 3rd exit. 1st left & left again. Hotel straight ahead

This stylish, contemporary hotel is conveniently located for Notting Hill, the exhibition halls and the BBC; Bond Street is only a 10-minute tube journey away. Funky, minimalist public areas include a trendy lobby bar and mezzanine-style restaurant. Spacious bedrooms and suites are extremely well appointed and offer luxurious bedding and a host of thoughtful extras such as CD and DVD players. WiFi is available throughout. The spa offers a comprehensive range of health, beauty and relaxation treatments.

Rooms 220 (31 GF) **Facilities** Spa STV FTV WiFi ⟳ Gym Hydrotherapy pool Sauna Steam room Snow room Solarium 🎵 New Year **Conf** Class 20 Board 25 Thtr 55 **Services** Lift Air con **Parking** 100 **Notes** ⊗

Ibis London Shepherd's Bush

BUDGET HOTEL PLAN 1 D3

tel: 020 7348 2020 **3-5 Rockley Rd W14 0DJ**
email: H7813@accor.com **web:** www.ibis.com/7813
dir: Walking distance from Shepherd's Bush Market & Shepherd's Bush Central Tube Station

Modern, budget hotel offering comfortable accommodation in bright and practical bedrooms. Breakfast is self-service and dinner is available in the restaurant. See also the Hotel Groups pages.

Rooms 128 📞

WC1 BLOOMSBURY, HOLBORN

AA HOTEL OF THE YEAR FOR LONDON 2014-2015

Rosewood London

★★★★★ 88% ⊚⊚ HOTEL PLAN 3 C3

tel: 020 7781 8888 **252 High Holborn WC1V 7EN**
email: london@rosewoodhotels.com **web:** www.rosewoodhotels.com/london
dir: 200mtrs E from Holborn underground station

Situated in the heart of Holborn, this impressive hotel was original built in 1912, and designed by H. Percy Monckton in a flamboyant Edwardian style. Interior design by Tony Chi is striking, stylish, and unconventional in parts, and so combines a London residential feel which is wholly sympathetic to its many heritage features. Spacious public areas include the very popular Scarfes Bar, Holborn Dining Room and the elegant Mirror Room salon, complete with stunning flower displays, where afternoon tea is served. Modern contemporary accommodation is luxurious with many super touches, and includes an impressive range of suites.

Rooms 306 (24 fmly) (10 smoking) 📞 **S** £300-£600; **D** £300-£600* **Facilities** Spa STV FTV WiFi ⟳ Gym 🎵 **Conf** Class 240 Board 90 Thtr 430 **Services** Lift Air con **Notes** LB Civ Wed 300

The Montague on the Gardens

THE RED CARNATION HOTEL COLLECTION

★★★★ 85% ⊚ HOTEL PLAN 3 B3

tel: 020 7637 1001 **15 Montague St, Bloomsbury WC1B 5BJ**
email: bookmt@rchmail.com **web:** www.montaguehotel.com
dir: Just off Russell Square, adjacent to British Museum

This stylish hotel is situated right next to the British Museum. A special feature is the alfresco terrace overlooking a delightful garden. Other public rooms include the Blue Door Bistro and Chef's Table, a bar, a lounge and a conservatory where traditional afternoon teas are served. The bedrooms are beautifully appointed and range from split-level suites to more compact rooms.

Rooms 100 (10 fmly) (19 GF) 📞 **S** £174-£330; **D** £192-£348* **Facilities** STV WiFi ⟳ HL Gym 🎵 Xmas New Year **Conf** Class 50 Board 50 Thtr 120 Del from £257 to £448* **Services** Lift Air con **Notes** LB Civ Wed 90

LONDON

WC1 BLOOMSBURY, HOLBORN *continued*

Hotel Russell

★★★★ 76% HOTEL PLAN 3 B4

tel: 020 7837 6470 **Russell Square WC1B 5BE**
email: russell.reservations@principal-hayley.com **web:** www.principal-hayley.com
dir: From A501 into Woburn Place. Hotel 500mtrs on left

This landmark Grade II, Victorian hotel is located on Russell Square, within walking distance of the West End and theatre district. Many bedrooms are stylish and state-of-the-art in design, while others are more traditional. Spacious public areas include the impressive foyer with a restored mosaic floor, a choice of lounges and an elegant restaurant.

Rooms 373 (2 fmly) ⚫ **Facilities** STV FTV WiFi **Conf** Class 200 Board 75 Thtr 450 **Services** Lift Air con **Notes** ⊗ Civ Wed 300

Holiday Inn London Kings Cross/Bloomsbury

★★★★ 69% HOTEL PLAN 3 C5

tel: 020 7833 3900 & 7698 4030 **1 Kings Cross Rd WC1X 9HX**
email: sales@holidayinnlondon.com **web:** www.holidayinn.co.uk
dir: On corner of King Cross Rd & Calthorpe St

Conveniently located for Kings Cross station and The City, this modern hotel offers smart, spacious air-conditioned accommodation with a wide range of facilities. There are versatile meeting rooms, a bar, a well-equipped fitness centre and a choice of restaurants including one serving Indian cuisine.

Rooms 405 (163 fmly) (126 smoking) ⚫ **Facilities** Spa STV FTV WiFi HL ⊙ Gym **Conf** Class 120 Board 30 Thtr 220 Del from £200 to £300 **Services** Lift Air con **Parking** 14 **Notes** ⊗

Holiday Inn London Bloomsbury

★★★ 81% HOTEL PLAN 3 B4

tel: 0871 942 9222 **Coram St WC1N 1HT**
email: bloomsbury@ihg.com **web:** www.holidayinn.co.uk
dir: Off Upper Woburn Place

Centrally located, this modern and stylish hotel is within easy reach of many of London's tourist attractions and close to St Pancras International Rail Station. The bedrooms boast a pillow menu, air-conditioning and high-speed internet access. The Junction restaurant offers a modern menu, while Callaghans is a traditional Irish pub featuring the best Irish beers. The meeting rooms can cater for many different events.

Rooms 314 (30 fmly) **Facilities** STV WiFi ⬡ HL ♬ **Conf** Class 180 Board 80 Thtr 350 **Services** Lift Air con **Notes** ⊗

Bedford Hotel

★★★ 73% HOTEL PLAN 3 B3

tel: 020 7636 7822 & 7692 3620 **83-93 Southampton Row WC1B 4HD**
email: info@imperialhotels.co.uk **web:** www.imperialhotels.co.uk

Just off Russell Square, this intimate hotel is ideal for visits to the British Museum and Covent Garden. The bedrooms are well equipped with all the expected facilities including modem points if requested. The ground floor has a lounge, a bar and restaurant plus there's a delightful secret rear garden. The underground car park is a bonus.

Rooms 184 (1 fmly) **S** £93; **D** £124 (incl. bkfst)* **Facilities** FTV WiFi Xmas New Year **Conf** Board 12 **Services** Lift **Parking** 50 **Notes** LB ⊗

Premier Inn London Euston

BUDGET HOTEL PLAN 3 A5

tel: 0871 527 8656 **1 Duke's Rd, Euston WC1H 9PJ**
web: www.premierinn.com
dir: On corner of Euston Road & Duke's Road, between Kings Cross/St Pancras & Euston stations

High quality, budget accommodation ideal for both families and business travellers. Spacious, en suite bedrooms feature tea and coffee making facilities, and Freeview TV in most hotels. Internet access and WiFi are available for a small fee. The adjacent family restaurant features a wide and varied menu. See also the Hotel Groups pages.

Rooms 220

WC2 SOHO, STRAND

INSPECTORS' CHOICE

The Savoy

★★★★★ ◎◎ HOTEL PLAN 3 C1

tel: 020 7836 4343 **Strand WC2R 0EU**
email: savoy@fairmont.com **web:** www.fairmont.com/savoy
dir: Halfway along The Strand between Trafalgar Sq & Aldwych

The Savoy Hotel has been at the forefront of the London hotel scene since it opened in 1889. The hotel has been lovingly restored in recent years, with much of its art deco and Edwardian heritage kept intact. The bedrooms, including an extensive range of stunning suites, vary in style and size, and many overlook the River Thames. The famous River Restaurant, Savoy Grill and American Bar remain as well-loved favourites; the Thames Foyer is well known for its afternoon teas; and the Beaufort Bar offers a comprehensive range of champagnes. Immaculately presented staff offer excellent standards of hospitality and service.

Rooms 268 (5 fmly) (10 smoking) ⚫ **S** £354-£1626; **D** £354-£1626* **Facilities** Spa STV FTV WiFi ⬡ ⊙ supervised Gym Fitness gallery Health & beauty treatments Personal training ♬ Xmas New Year **Conf** Class 300 Board 60 Thtr 500 **Services** Lift Air con **Parking** 65 **Notes** Civ Wed 300

Premier Inn London Leicester Square

BUDGET HOTEL PLAN 3 A1

tel: 0871 527 9334 **1 Leicester Place, Leicester Square WC2H 7BP**
web: www.premierinn.com
dir: Nearest tube station: Leicester Sq. From Cranbourne St into Leicester Sq. Hotel on right (Leicester Pl). (Car parks: China Town & Witcombe St, approx 10 mins walk)

High quality, budget accommodation ideal for both families and business travellers. Spacious, en suite bedrooms feature tea and coffee making facilities, and Freeview TV in most hotels. Internet access and WiFi are available for a small fee. The adjacent family restaurant features a wide and varied menu. See also the Hotel Groups pages.

Rooms 83

LONDON GATEWAY MOTORWAY SERVICE AREA (M1)   Map 6 TQ19

Ramada London North - M1

★★★ 73% HOTEL

tel: 020 8906 7000 **Welcome Break Service Area NW7 3HU**
email: lgw.hotel@welcomebreak.co.uk **web:** www.welcomebreak.co.uk
dir: On M1 between junct 2/4 N'bound & S'bound

This modern building offers accommodation in smart, spacious and well-equipped bedrooms, suitable for families and business travellers, and all with en suite bathrooms. Continental breakfast is available and other refreshments may be taken at the nearby family restaurant.

Rooms 200 (190 fmly) (80 GF) (20 smoking) **D** £85-£125 **Facilities** FTV WiFi ⬆ Gym **Conf** Class 30 Board 50 Thtr 70 Del from £165 to £190 **Services** Lift Air con **Parking** 160 **Notes** LB Civ Wed 80

LONG EATON   Map 11 SK43
Derbyshire

Novotel Nottingham East Midlands

NOVOTEL

★★★ 71% HOTEL

tel: 0115 946 5111 **Bostock Ln NG10 4EP**
email: H0507@accor.com **web:** www.novotel.com
dir: M1 junct 25 onto B6002 to Long Eaton. Hotel 400yds on left

In close proximity to the M1, this purpose-built hotel has much to offer. All bedrooms are spacious, have sofa beds and provide exceptional desk space. Public rooms include a bright brasserie, which is open all day and provides extended dining until midnight. There is a comprehensive range of meeting rooms.

Rooms 108 (40 fmly) (20 GF) **S** £45-£95; **D** £45-£95* **Facilities** WiFi ⬆ HL ⬇ **Conf** Class 130 Board 100 Thtr 250 Del from £105 to £125 **Services** Lift **Parking** 220 **Notes** LB Civ Wed 80

LONGHORSLEY   Map 21 NZ19
Northumberland

Macdonald Linden Hall, Golf & Country Club

MACDONALD
HOTELS & RESORTS

★★★★ 79% ◉◉ HOTEL

tel: 01670 500000 & 0844 879 9084 **NE65 8XF**
email: lindenhall@macdonald-hotels.co.uk **web:** www.macdonaldhotels.co.uk
dir: N'bound on A1 take A697 towards Coldstream. Hotel 1m N of Longhorsley

This impressive Georgian mansion lies in 400 acres of parkland and offers extensive indoor and outdoor leisure facilities including a golf course. The Dobson

Restaurant provides a fine dining experience, or guests can eat in the more informal Linden Tree pub. The good-sized bedrooms have a restrained modern style. The team of staff are enthusiastic and professional.

Rooms 50 (3 fmly) (16 GF) ⬆ **Facilities** Spa STV FTV WiFi ⬆ ⬇ supervised ⬆ 18 ⬆ Putt green ⬆ Gym Steam room Sauna Xmas New Year **Conf** Class 120 Board 50 Thtr 300 Del from £120 to £165* **Services** Lift **Parking** 300 **Notes** LB Civ Wed 120

LONG MELFORD   Map 13 TL84
Suffolk

The Bull

★★★ 74% HOTEL

tel: 01787 378494 **Hall St CO10 9JG**
email: bull.longmelford@greeneking.co.uk **web:** www.oldenglish.co.uk
dir: 3m N of Sudbury on A134

The public areas of this delightful 14th-century property feature a wealth of charm and character, including exposed beams, carvings, heraldic markings and huge open fireplaces. Bedrooms are smartly decorated, thoughtfully equipped and retain many original features. Snacks or light lunches are served in the bar, or guests can choose to dine in the more formal restaurant.

Rooms 25 (4 fmly) ⬆ **S** £65-£80; **D** £75-£110 (incl. bkfst) **Facilities** FTV WiFi Xmas New Year **Conf** Class 40 Board 30 Thtr 100 Del from £99 to £135 **Parking** 35 **Notes** ⊗ Civ Wed 100

LOOE   Map 2 SX25
Cornwall

Trelaske Hotel & Restaurant

★★★ 79% ◉◉ HOTEL

tel: 01503 262159 **Polperro Rd PL13 2JS**
email: info@trelaske.co.uk **web:** www.trelaske.co.uk
dir: B252 signed Looe. Over Looe bridge signed Polperro. 1.9m, hotel signed on left, turn right

This small and welcoming hotel offers comfortable accommodation, professional and friendly service plus award-winning food. Set in its own very well-tended and pretty grounds, it is only two miles from Polperro and Looe.

Rooms 7 (4 annexe) (2 fmly) (2 GF) ⬆ **S** £105-£125; **D** £115-£125 (incl. bkfst) **Facilities** FTV WiFi **Conf** Class 30 Board 40 Thtr 100 Del from £150 to £175 **Parking** 50 **Notes** LB Closed 2 Jan-12 Feb

---

Hannafore Point Hotel

THE INDEPENDENTS

★★★ 73% HOTEL

tel: 01503 263273 **Marine Dr, West Looe PL13 2DG**
email: stay@hannaforepointhotel.com **web:** www.hannaforepointhotel.com
dir: A38, left onto A385 to Looe. Over bridge turn left. Hotel 0.5m on left

With panoramic coastal views of St George's Island around to Rame Head, this popular hotel provides a warm welcome. The wonderful view is certainly a feature of the spacious restaurant and bar, creating a scenic backdrop for both dinners and breakfasts. Additional facilities include a heated indoor pool and a gym.

Rooms 37 (5 fmly) **S** £50-£70; **D** £100-£160 (incl. bkfst)* **Facilities** FTV WiFi ⬆ ⬇ Gym Spa pool Steam room Sauna ⬆ Xmas New Year **Conf** Class 80 Board 40 Thtr 120 Del from £75 to £130* **Services** Lift **Parking** 32 **Notes** LB Civ Wed 150

L

L

LOSTWITHIEL
Cornwall

Map 2 SX15

BEST WESTERN Restormel Lodge Hotel

★★★ 75% HOTEL

tel: 01208 872223 **Castle Hill PL22 0DD**
email: bookings@restormellodgehotel.co.uk **web:** www.bw-restormellodgehotel.co.uk
dir: On A390 in Lostwithiel town centre

A short drive from the Eden Project, this popular hotel offers a friendly welcome to all visitors and is ideally situated for exploring the area. The older building houses the bar, restaurant and lounges, with original features adding to the character. Bedrooms are comfortably furnished, with a number overlooking the secluded outdoor pool.

Rooms 36 (12 annexe) (12 fmly) (9 GF) ⬠ **S** £39-£69; **D** £49-£119 (incl. bkfst)*
Facilities FTV WiFi ⬠ ⬠ Xmas New Year **Conf** Class 12 Board 12 Thtr 12
Del from £69 to £99* **Parking** 60 **Notes** LB

LOUGHBOROUGH
Leicestershire

Map 11 SK51

Quorn Country Hotel

★★★★ 76% ⬠ HOTEL

PRIMA

tel: 01509 415050 & 415061 **Charnwood House, 66 Leicester Rd LE12 8BB**
email: reservations@quorncountryhotel.co.uk **web:** www.primahotels.co.uk/quorn

(For full entry see Quorn)

Follow us on twitter
@TheAA_Lifestyle

Link Hotel

★★★ 81% HOTEL

tel: 01509 211800 **New Ashby Rd LE11 4EX**
email: info@linkhotel.co.uk **web:** www.linkhotelloughborough.co.uk
dir: M1 junct 23, follow A512 signed Loughborough. Continue on A512, turn left onto slip road to reach hotel

Ideally located, close to Loughborough University, and only half a mile away from J23 on the M1, this hotel offers modern and stylish accommodation, with warm hospitality at the forefront. A modern restaurant, bar and lounge area are available. A small gym is also on site.

Rooms 94 (12 fmly) (47 GF) ⬠ **Facilities** FTV WiFi ⬠ Gym Xmas New Year
Conf Class 40 Board 30 Thtr 180 **Services** Air con **Parking** 164 **Notes** ⬠ Civ Wed

Premier Inn Loughborough

BUDGET HOTEL

tel: 0871 527 9314 **Southfields Rd LE11 9SA**
web: www.premierinn.com
dir: M1 junct 23, A512 towards Loughborough. Left into Greenclose Ln. Right onto A6, Right into Southfield Rd, hotel on left

High quality, budget accommodation ideal for both families and business travellers. Spacious, en suite bedrooms feature tea and coffee making facilities, and Freeview TV in most hotels. Internet access and WiFi are available for a small fee. The adjacent family restaurant features a wide and varied menu. See also the Hotel Groups pages.

Rooms 112

LOUTH
Lincolnshire
Map 17 TF38

Brackenborough Hotel

★★★ 88% HOTEL

tel: 01507 609169 **Cordeaux Corner, Brackenborough LN11 0SZ**
email: reception@brackenborough.co.uk **web:** www.oakridgehotels.co.uk
dir: On A16, Louth to Grimsby road, 1m from Louth

In an idyllic setting amid well-tended gardens, this hotel offers attractive bedrooms, each individually decorated with co-ordinated furnishings and many extras. The award-winning bistro offers informal dining and the menu is based on locally sourced produce. The hotel specialises in weddings, events and private functions and has excellent conference facilities. Free WiFi is available. Guests have free access to state-of-the-art leisure facilities (less than half a mile away) that includes a swimming pool, tennis courts and a gym.

Rooms 24 (2 fmly) (6 GF) **Facilities** FTV WiFi ⇩ Gym ♬ Xmas New Year **Conf** Class 150 Board 50 Thtr 300 **Services** Air con **Parking** 90 **Notes** ⊗ Civ Wed 220

BEST WESTERN Kenwick Park Hotel

★★★ 77% HOTEL

tel: 01507 608806 **Kenwick Park Estate LN11 8NR**
email: enquiries@kenwick-park.co.uk **web:** www.kenwick-park.co.uk
dir: A16 from Grimsby, then A157 Mablethorpe/Manby Rd. Hotel 400mtrs down hill on right

This elegant Georgian house is situated on the 320-acre Kenwick Park estate, overlooking its own golf course. Bedrooms are spacious, comfortable and provide modern facilities. Public areas include a restaurant and a conservatory bar that overlook the grounds. There is also an extensive leisure centre and state-of-the-art conference and banqueting facilities.

Rooms 34 (5 annexe) (10 fmly) (11 GF) **Facilities** Spa FTV WiFi ⊗ supervised ↕ 18 ⛳ Putt green Gym Squash Health & beauty centre Xmas New Year **Conf** Class 40 Board 90 Thtr 250 Del from £75* **Parking** 100 **Notes** Civ Wed 200

LOWER BARTLE
Lancashire
Map 18 SD43

Bartle Hall Hotel

★★★★ 71% HOTEL

tel: 01772 690506 **Lea Ln PR4 0HA**
email: info@bartlehall.co.uk **web:** www.bartlehall.co.uk
dir: M6 junct 32 into Tom Benson Way, follow signs for Woodplumpton

Ideally situated between Preston and Blackpool, Bartle Hall is within easy access of the M6 and the Lake District. Set in its own extensive grounds the hotel offers comfortable, well-equipped and renovated accommodation. The restaurant cuisine uses local produce and there is a large comfortable bar and lounge. There are also extensive conference facilities, and this hotel is a popular wedding venue.

Rooms 15 (2 annexe) (2 fmly) (2 GF) **S** £75-£95; **D** £80-£125 (incl. bkfst) **Facilities** FTV WiFi ⇩ HL Xmas New Year **Conf** Class 50 Board 40 Thtr 200 **Parking** 150 **Notes** LB Civ Wed 130

LOWER BEEDING
West Sussex
Map 6 TQ22

South Lodge, an Exclusive Hotel

SOUTH LODGE
AN EXCLUSIVE HOTEL

★★★★★ 84% ⊕⊕⊕⊕ COUNTRY HOUSE HOTEL

tel: 01403 891711 **Brighton Rd RH13 6PS**
email: enquiries@southlodgehotel.co.uk **web:** www.southlodgehotel.co.uk
dir: A23, onto B2110. Right, through Handcross to A281 junct. Left, hotel on right

This impeccably presented 19th-century lodge with stunning views of the rolling South Downs is an ideal retreat. There is the traditional and elegant Camellia Restaurant, offering memorable, seasonal dishes, and The Pass Restaurant, which is an innovative take on the chef's table concept - a mini-restaurant within the kitchen itself. Guests can take a tour of the restored Victorian wine cellar, either with a sommelier or on their own. The elegant lounge is popular for afternoon teas. Bedrooms are individually designed with character and quality throughout. The conference facilities are impressive.

Rooms 89 (11 fmly) (19 GF) **S** £275-£695; **D** £275-£695 (incl. bkfst)* **Facilities** STV WiFi ⇩ ↕ 36 ⛳ Putt green Fishing ⊰ Gym Mountain bikes Archery Clay pigeon shooting Xmas New Year **Conf** Class 100 Board 50 Thtr 170 Del from £0* **Services** Lift **Parking** 200 **Notes** LB Civ Wed 130

L

L

LOWER SLAUGHTER
Gloucestershire   Map 10 SP12

INSPECTORS' CHOICE

Lower Slaughter Manor

★★★★ ◉◉◉ COUNTRY HOUSE HOTEL

tel: 01451 820456 **GL54 2HP**
email: info@lowerslaughter.co.uk **web:** www.lowerslaughter.co.uk
dir: Exit A429 signed 'The Slaughters'. Manor 0.5m on right on entering village

There is a timeless elegance about this wonderful manor, which dates back to the 17th century. Its imposing presence makes it very much the centrepiece of this famous Cotswold village. Inside, the levels of comfort and quality are immediately evident, with crackling log fires warming the many sumptuous lounges. Spacious and tastefully furnished bedrooms are either in the main building or in the adjacent coach house. Fine dining at the hotel is in the award-winning Sixteen58 Restaurant where the menus are based on local, seasonal produce; special dietary needs can be catered for.

Rooms 19 (8 annexe) (5 fmly) (4 GF) ✎ **S** £165-£810; **D** £185-£830 (incl. bkfst)*
Facilities STV FTV WiFi ⌕ ☃ ⚘ Xmas New Year **Conf** Class 40 Board 30 Thtr 70
Del from £225 to £255* **Parking** 20 **Notes** LB Civ Wed 74

Symbols and abbreviations are explained on page 7

LOWESTOFT
Suffolk   Map 13 TM59

Ivy House Country Hotel

★★★ 83% ◉◉ HOTEL

tel: 01502 501353 & 588144 **Ivy Ln, Beccles Rd, Oulton Broad NR33 8HY**
email: aa@ivyhousecountryhotel.co.uk **web:** www.ivyhousecountryhotel.co.uk
dir: On A146 SW of Oulton Broad turn into Ivy Ln beside Esso petrol station. Over railway bridge, follow private drive

A peacefully located, family-run hotel set in three acres of mature landscaped grounds and just a short walk from Oulton Broad. Public rooms include an 18th-century thatched barn restaurant where an interesting choice of dishes is served. The attractively decorated bedrooms are housed in garden wings, and many have lovely views of the grounds to the countryside beyond.

Rooms 20 (20 annexe) (1 fmly) (17 GF) ✎ **Facilities** FTV WiFi **Conf** Board 22 Thtr 55 **Parking** 50 **Notes** Closed 15 Dec-4 Jan Civ Wed 80

Premier Inn Lowestoft

BUDGET HOTEL

tel: 0871 527 8688 **249 Yarmouth Rd NR32 4AA**
web: www.premierinn.com
dir: On A12, 2m N of Lowestoft

High quality, budget accommodation ideal for both families and business travellers. Spacious, en suite bedrooms feature tea and coffee making facilities, and Freeview TV in most hotels. Internet access and WiFi are available for a small fee. The adjacent family restaurant features a wide and varied menu. See also the Hotel Groups pages.

Rooms 60

Corton Coastal Village

Warner Leisure Hotels
Life begins at Warner

AA Advertised

tel: 01502 730 226 **The Street, Corton NR32 5HR**
web: www.warnerleisurehotels.co.uk
dir: From A1(M)/M1, follow A47 towards Great Yarmouth. Take A12 south approx 8m. At end of dual carriage way left into Corton Long Lane. At end of Corton Long Lane left into The Street, Corton on right

Deckchairs, dancing and seaside fun is what Corton is all about. All breaks at this popular cliff top chalet resort include breakfast and dinner, a range of daytime activities and nightly entertainment.

Rooms 182 (112 GF) ✎ **S** £40-£63; **D** £80-£152 (incl. bkfst)* **Facilities** STV FTV WiFi ⚐ Putt green Gym Snooker Wii Table Tennis Shuffleboard Archery Rifle shooting ♪ Xmas New Year **Services** Air con **Parking** 180 **Notes** LB ⊗ No children 21yrs

LUDLOW
Shropshire

Map 10 SO57

INSPECTORS' CHOICE

Fishmore Hall

★★★ ◉◉◉ SMALL HOTEL

tel: 01584 875148 **Fishmore Rd SY8 3DP**
email: reception@fishmorehall.co.uk **web:** www.fishmorehall.co.uk
dir: A49 into Henley Rd. 1st right, Weyman Rd, at bottom of hill right into Fishmore Rd

Located in a rural area within easy reach of the town centre, this Palladian-style Georgian house has been sympathetically renovated and extended to provide high standards of comfort and facilities. The contemporary interior highlights many period features, and public areas include a comfortable lounge and restaurant, the setting for award-winning imaginative cooking.

Rooms 15 (1 GF) ↙ **S** £110-£210; **D** £150-£250 (incl. bkfst)* **Facilities** FTV WiFi ⌘ ⚴ Treatment cabin offering beauty treatments & massage Xmas New Year **Conf** Class 60 Board 40 Thtr 130 Del from £165* **Services** Lift **Parking** 48 **Notes** LB Civ Wed 130

Overton Grange Hotel and Restaurant

★★★ 86% ◉◉ HOTEL

tel: 01584 873500 & 0845 476 1000 **Old Hereford Rd SY8 4AD**
email: info@overtongrangehotel.com **web:** www.overtongrangehotel.com
dir: A49, B4361 to Ludlow. Hotel 200yds on left

This is a traditional country-house hotel with stylish, comfortable bedrooms, and high standards of guest care. Food is an important part of what the hotel has to offer and the restaurant serves classically based, French-style cuisine, using locally sourced produce whenever possible. Meeting and conference rooms are available.

Rooms 14 ↙ **S** £95-£145; **D** £145-£195 (incl. bkfst) **Facilities** Spa FTV WiFi ⌘ Xmas **Conf** Class 50 Board 30 Thtr 100 Del from £129.50 to £159.50 **Parking** 45 **Notes** LB ⊗ No children 7yrs Civ Wed 100

The Feathers Hotel

★★★ 82% ◉ HOTEL

tel: 01584 875261 **The Bull Ring SY8 1AA**
email: enquiries@feathersatludlow.co.uk **web:** www.feathersatludlow.co.uk
dir: From A49 follow town centre signs to centre. Hotel on left

Famous for the carved woodwork outside and in, this picture-postcard 17th-century hotel is one of the town's best-known landmarks and is in an excellent location. Bedrooms are traditional both in style and decor. The public areas have retained much of the traditional charm, and the first-floor lounge is particularly stunning. Modern British menus are offered in the smart restaurant which has wooden beams and exposed brickwork.

Rooms 40 (3 fmly) **S** £85-£95; **D** £120-£130 (incl. bkfst)* **Facilities** STV FTV WiFi ⌘ Xmas New Year **Conf** Class 40 Board 40 Thtr 80 Del £139* **Services** Lift **Parking** 33 **Notes** LB

Dinham Hall Hotel

★★★ 80% ◉◉ HOTEL

tel: 01584 876464 **By The Castle SY8 1EJ**
email: info@dinhamhall.com **web:** www.dinhamhall.com
dir: In town centre, opposite castle

Built in 1792, this lovely house stands in attractive gardens immediately opposite Ludlow Castle, and it has a well-deserved reputation for warm hospitality. The well-equipped bedrooms include two in a converted cottage, and some rooms have four-poster beds. The comfortable public rooms are elegantly appointed. Dishes served in the brasserie-style restaurant are based on good, seasonal produce.

Rooms 13 (2 annexe) (2 fmly) (2 GF) **S** £95-£145; **D** £125-£195 (incl. bkfst) **Facilities** FTV WiFi Xmas New Year **Conf** Class 20 Board 26 Thtr 40 Del from £129.50 to £159.50 **Parking** 16 **Notes** LB No children 7yrs

The Clive Bar & Restaurant with Rooms

◉◉ RESTAURANT WITH ROOMS

tel: 01584 856565 & 856665 📠 01584 856661 **Bromfield SY8 2JR**
email: info@theclive.co.uk **web:** www.theclive.co.uk
dir: 2m N of Ludlow on A49 in Bromfield

The Clive is just two miles from the busy town of Ludlow and is a convenient base for visiting the local attractions or for business. The bedrooms, located in an annexe, are spacious and very well equipped; some are suitable for families and many are on the ground-floor level. Meals are available in the well-known Clive Restaurant or in the bar areas. The property also has a small meeting room.

Rooms 15 (15 annexe) (9 fmly)

L

Luton Hoo Hotel, Golf and Spa

★★★★★ 87% ◉◉ HOTEL

tel: 01582 734437 & 698888 **The Mansion House LU1 3TQ**
email: reservations@lutonhoo.com **web:** www.lutonhoo.com
dir: M1 junct 10a, 3rd exit onto A1081 towards Harpenden & St Albans. Hotel approx 1m on left

A luxury hotel in more than 1,000 acres of 'Capability' Brown designed parkland and formal gardens, with an 18-hole, par 73 golf course and the River Lea meandering through. The centrepiece is the Grade I listed Mansion House that has architectural influences by many famous architects including Robert Adams. There are three sumptuous lounges where guests can enjoy afternoon tea and pre-dinner drinks, and two eating options - The Wernher Restaurant and the Adams Brasserie. The spacious bedrooms and impressive suites combine historic character with modern amenities. The Robert Adams Club House is the perfect place for relaxation, with the brasserie, a spa, golf, pool and gym together with two bars, and Warren Weir, at the foot of the estate, on the river bank is an exclusive retreat for weddings and meetings.

Rooms 228 (50 fmly) (65 GF) ✎ **D** £280-£1100 (incl. bkfst) **Facilities** Spa FTV WiFi ⇗ HL 🏊 ♨ 18 ⛳ Putt green Fishing 🎣 Gym Bird watching Clay pigeon shooting Archery Falconry Cycling Snooker ♫ Xmas New Year **Conf** Class 220 Board 60 Thtr 388 Del from £225* **Services** Lift **Parking** 316 **Notes** LB Civ Wed 380

Icon Hotel

★★★ 83% HOTEL

tel: 01582 722123 **15 Stuart St LU1 2SA**
email: reservations@iconhotelluton.com **web:** www.iconhotelluton.com
dir: M1 junct 10 & 10A, A1081 signed Luton, left follow Luton Retail Park & station signs. Left at next rdbt, left at next rdbt onto A505 (Park Viaduct). Straight on at next rdbt, left into Hastings St

This modern, purpose-built hotel occupies a prominent position close to the town centre and is a short drive from the international airport. The contemporary, open-plan bar is very comfortable and Capello's Restaurant offers a modern Mediterranean menu. The bedrooms are attractively presented and feature the latest technology along with large LCD TVs and complimentary WiFi. There is a range of business suites and a well-equipped gym.

Rooms 60 (7 fmly) (5 GF) ✎ **S** £49-£169; **D** £49-£229* **Facilities** FTV WiFi ⇗ Gym Therapy treatments by prior arrangement ♫ Xmas New Year **Conf** Class 30 Board 25 Thtr 60 Del from £125 to £165* **Services** Lift Air con **Parking** 18 **Notes** ⊗

Premier Inn Luton Town Centre

BUDGET HOTEL

tel: 0871 527 9542 **Regent St LU1 5FA**
web: www.premierinn.com
dir: M1 junct 10 (sbound), A1081 (Luton Airport). At 1st rdbt left onto London Rd (A1081). Into Castle St, left into Windsor St. 1st right into Chapel St. 1st left into Regent St. Hotel on left

High quality, budget accommodation ideal for both families and business travellers. Spacious, en suite bedrooms feature tea and coffee making facilities, and Freeview TV in most hotels. Internet access and WiFi are available for a small fee. The adjacent family restaurant features a wide and varied menu. See also the Hotel Groups pages.

Rooms 120

Ibis London Luton Airport

BUDGET HOTEL

tel: 01582 424488 **Spittlesea Rd LU2 9NH**
email: H1040@accor.com **web:** www.ibishotel.com
dir: M1 junct 10, follow signs to Luton Airport. Hotel 600mtrs from airport

Modern, budget hotel offering comfortable accommodation in bright and practical bedrooms. Breakfast is self-service and dinner is available in the restaurant. See also the Hotel Groups pages.

Rooms 162 (8 fmly) ✎ **Conf** Class 18 Board 30 Thtr 60

Premier Inn Luton Airport

BUDGET HOTEL

tel: 0871 527 8690 **Osborne Rd LU1 3HJ**
web: www.premierinn.com
dir: M1 junct 10, A1081 follow signs for Luton, at 3rd rdbt left into Gypsy Lane, left at next rdbt

High quality, budget accommodation ideal for both families and business travellers. Spacious, en suite bedrooms feature tea and coffee making facilities, and Freeview TV in most hotels. Internet access and WiFi are available for a small fee. The adjacent family restaurant features a wide and varied menu. See also the Hotel Groups pages.

Rooms 129

LYME REGIS
Dorset
Map 4 SY39

Royal Lion Hotel

 ★★★ 74% HOTEL

tel: 01297 445622 **Broad St DT7 3QF**
email: enquiries@royallionhotel.com **web:** www.royallionhotel.com
dir: From W on A35 take A3052, or from E take B3165 to Lyme Regis. Hotel in town centre, opposite The Fossil Shop

This 17th-century, former coaching inn is full of character and charm, and is just a short walk from the seafront. Bedrooms vary in size; those in the newer wing are more spacious and some have balconies, sea views or a private terrace. In addition to the elegant dining room and guest lounges, a heated pool, jacuzzi, sauna and small gym are available. A good selection of enjoyable, well-prepared dishes is offered in either the bar or main restaurant. There is a car park at the rear.

Rooms 33 (8 fmly) (4 GF) ⚓ **S** £79; **D** £110-£120 (incl. bkfst)* **Facilities** FTV WiFi ⚒ Sauna Games room Snooker tables Table tennis Xmas New Year **Conf** Class 20 Board 20 Thtr 50 **Parking** 33 **Notes** LB

Swallows Eaves Hotel

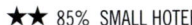 ★★ 85% SMALL HOTEL

tel: 01297 553184 **Swan Hill Rd EX24 6QJ**
email: info@swallowseaves.co.uk **web:** www.swallowseaves.co.uk

(For full entry see Colyford, Devon)

LYMINGTON
Hampshire
Map 5 SZ39

Stanwell House Hotel

★★★ 88% ⧇⧇ HOTEL

tel: 01590 677123 **14-15 High St SO41 9AA**
email: enquiries@stanwellhouse.com **web:** www.stanwellhouse.com
dir: M27 junct 1, follow signs to Lyndhurst then Lymington

Stanwell House Hotel is a privately owned Georgian building situated on the wide high street only a few minutes from the marina, and a short drive from the New Forest. Styling itself as a boutique hotel, the bedrooms are individually designed; there are Terrace rooms with garden access, four-poster rooms, and Georgian rooms in the older part of the building. The four suites include two with their own roof terrace. Dining options include the informal bistro and the intimate Seafood Restaurant. Service is friendly and attentive. A meeting room is available.

Rooms 29 (7 fmly) (7 GF) ⚓ **Facilities** FTV WiFi Xmas New Year **Conf** Class 35 Board 30 Thtr 70 Del from £150 to £175 **Parking** 12 **Notes** Civ Wed 100

Macdonald Elmers Court Hotel & Resort

★★★ 82% HOTEL

tel: 0844 879 9060 **South Baddesley Rd SO41 5ZB**
email: elmerscourt@macdonald-hotels.co.uk **web:** www.macdonaldhotels.co.uk
dir: M27 junct 1, through Lyndhurst, Brockenhurst to Lymington, hotel 200yds right after Lymington ferry terminal

Originally known as The Elms, this Tudor manor house dates back to the 1820s. Ideally located at the edge of the New Forest and overlooking The Solent with views towards the Isle of Wight, the hotel offers suites and self-catering accommodation in the grounds, along with a host of leisure facilities.

Rooms 42 (42 annexe) (8 fmly) (22 GF) ⚓ **S** £89-£245; **D** £89-£245* **Facilities** Spa FTV WiFi ⚒ ⚒ supervised ⚒ Putt green ⚒ Gym Squash Steam room Aerobics classes Sauna Table tennis Xmas New Year **Conf** Class 70 Board 40 Thtr 120 Del from £150 to £200* **Parking** 100 **Notes** LB ⊗ Civ Wed 120

Premier Inn Lymington (New Forest Hordle)

BUDGET HOTEL

tel: 0871 527 8692 **Silver St, Hordle SO41 0FN**
web: www.premierinn.com
dir: M27 junct 1, A337. 3.5m, left into High St (A35) right into Gosport Ln. Left into Clay Hill (A337). Right into Grigg Ln (B3055). Approx 8m, left into Barrows Ln, right into Silver St

High quality, budget accommodation ideal for both families and business travellers. Spacious, en suite bedrooms feature tea and coffee making facilities, and Freeview TV in most hotels. Internet access and WiFi are available for a small fee. The adjacent family restaurant features a wide and varied menu. See also the Hotel Groups pages.

Rooms 20

LYMM
Cheshire
Map 15 SJ68

The Lymm Hotel

★★★ 73% HOTEL

tel: 01925 752233 **Whitbarrow Rd WA13 9AQ**
email: general.lymm@macdonald-hotels.co.uk **web:** www.macdonaldhotels.co.uk/lymm
dir: M6 junct 20, B5158 to Lymm. Left at junct, 1st right, left at mini-rdbt, into Brookfield Rd, 3rd left into Whitbarrow Rd

In a peaceful residential area, this hotel benefits from both a quiet setting and convenient access to local motorway networks. It offers comfortable bedrooms equipped for both the business and leisure guest. Public areas include an attractive bar and an elegant restaurant. There is also extensive parking.

Rooms 62 (38 annexe) (5 fmly) (11 GF) ⚓ **Facilities** STV WiFi Xmas New Year **Conf** Class 60 Board 40 Thtr 120 Del from £95 to £125* **Parking** 75 **Notes** Civ Wed 100

<table>
<tr><td>

LYNDHURST
Hampshire

Map 5 SU30

</td></tr>
</table>

INSPECTORS' CHOICE

Lime Wood

★★★★★ ⚙⚙⚙ COUNTRY HOUSE HOTEL

tel: 023 8028 7177 **Beaulieu Rd SO43 7FZ**
email: info@limewood.co.uk **web:** www.limewood.co.uk
dir: Exit A35 onto B3056 towards Beaulieu, hotel 1m on right

This meticulously restored country house situated deep in the New Forest, provides a wealth of facilities and much opulence. The hotel prides itself on its relaxed, friendly and attentive service, and has lots to interest and captivate. The luxurious bedrooms are notable; some are in the pavilion and some in the main house. The last couple of years have seen the end of The Dining Room and The Scullery and the creation of a single restaurant, Hartnett Holder & Co which will be headed up by current head Chef Luke Holder, and Angela Hartnett. The Herb House spa offers a hydrotherapy pool and many other excellent facilities along with a gym and steam room.

Rooms 32 (16 annexe) (7 fmly) (5 GF) ✆ **D** £225-£950* **Facilities** Spa STV FTV WiFi ⚐ 🏊 Gym Xmas New Year **Conf** Board 30 Thtr 50 **Services** Lift **Parking** 60 **Notes** LB Civ Wed 60

See advert on opposite page

BEST WESTERN Forest Lodge Hotel

NEW FOREST HOTELS

★★★ 83% ⚙⚙ HOTEL

tel: 023 8028 3677 & 0800 444 441 **Pikes Hill, Romsey Rd SO43 7AS**
email: forest@newforesthotels.co.uk **web:** www.newforesthotels.co.uk
dir: M27 junct 1, A337 towards Lyndhurst. In village, with police station & courts on right, take 1st right into Pikes Hill

Situated on the edge of Lyndhurst, this hotel is set well back from the main road. The smart, contemporary bedrooms include four-poster rooms and family rooms; children are very welcome here. The eating options are the Forest Restaurant and the fine-dining Glasshouse Restaurant. There is an indoor swimming pool and Nordic sauna.

Rooms 36 (11 fmly) (10 GF) ✆ **Facilities** FTV WiFi ⚐ HL 🏊 Xmas New Year **Conf** Class 70 Board 60 Thtr 120 **Parking** 50 **Notes** Civ Wed 90

The Bell Inn

★★★ 75% ⚙ HOTEL

tel: 023 8081 2214 **SO43 7HE**
email: bell@bramshaw.co.uk **web:** www.bellinnbramshaw.co.uk

(For full entry see Brook (Near Cadnam))

Penny Farthing Hotel

★★★ 75% METRO HOTEL

tel: 023 8028 4422 **Romsey Rd SO43 7AA**
email: stay@pennyfarthinghotel.co.uk **web:** www.pennyfarthinghotel.co.uk
dir: M27 junct 1, A337 to Lyndhurst. Hotel on left after White Rabbit Inn

This friendly, well-appointed establishment situated just off Lyndhurst High street is suitable for business or for exploring the New Forest area. The attractive bedrooms are well-equipped with free WiFi available throughout. There is a spacious breakfast room, a comfortable lounge bar and a cycle store.

Rooms 19 (1 fmly) (1 GF) ✆ **S** £59-£78; **D** £88-£136 (incl. bkfst) **Facilities** FTV WiFi ⚐ **Parking** 26 **Notes** LB ⊗ Closed Xmas week

Ormonde House Hotel

★★★ 71% METRO HOTEL

tel: 023 8028 2806 **Southampton Rd SO43 7BT**
email: enquiries@ormondehouse.co.uk **web:** www.ormondehouse.co.uk
dir: M27/M271/A35 E through Ashurst, hotel on right on entering Lyndhurst

Ormonde House is located on the edge of Lyndhurst village in the heart of the New Forest, and provides comfortable en suite accommodation, with breakfast served in the dining room and conservatory. It is dog friendly with ample off-street parking. The ideal location for all New Forest activities and attractions.

Rooms 22 (4 annexe) (2 fmly) (7 GF) ✆ **Facilities** FTV WiFi New Year **Parking** 22 **Notes** Closed 13-27 Dec

HARTNETT HOLDER & CO

Hartnett Holder & Co is a relaxed, stylish and comfortable upscale restaurant - full of character, yet unpretentious. Angela Hartnett and Lime Wood's Luke Holder, with their team, create locally sourced English dishes with a respectful nod to the seasons and to Italian culinary ideologies. This collaboration is reflected in their fresh, confident approach ensuring that this is "fun dining, not fine dining".

Hartnett and Holder's food is out-and-out British yet comes with the much loved Italian approach to eating - where sharing and provenance is everything. Expect a menu of Italian influenced forest dishes with English classics, pulling together both chef's much admired signature styles. Sample dishes include pizzetta with quail egg, taleggio and spinach, whole wild turbot (for two) with fennel, basil & preserved lemon or gnocchi with veal bolognaise.

Lime Wood, Beaulieu Road, Lyndhurst, Hampshire SO43 7FZ
Tel: 02380 287177   Website: www.hhandco.co.uk   Email: info@hhandco.co.uk

L

LYNMOUTH
Devon

Map 3 SS74

Tors Hotel

★★★ 79% ⊚ HOTEL

tel: 01598 753236 **EX35 6NA**
email: info@torshotellynmouth.co.uk **web:** www.torslynmouth.co.uk
dir: Adjacent to A39 on Countisbury Hill just before entering Lynmouth from Minehead

In an elevated position overlooking Lynmouth Bay, this friendly hotel is set in five acres of woodland and has recently undergone a transformation. Stylish public areas showcase an eclectic collection of objets d'art and antiques, interspersed with lovely comfy sofas. The hotel even has its own cinema and superb outdoor terraces with unrivalled views of the bay. The majority of the bedrooms also benefit from the wonderful outlook with a variety of options available. In the AA rosetted restaurant you will find a relaxed atmosphere with superb quality food, an excellent wine list and probably the best views in the village. The whole family will find a warm welcome in the restaurant and as much care will be taken with your little one's ice cream as with your carefully prepared main meal.

Rooms 28 (5 fmly) **Facilities** STV FTV WiFi Xmas New Year **Conf** Class 40 Board 25 Thtr 60 **Services** Lift **Parking** 40 **Notes** Closed 7 Nov-7 Dec Civ Wed 70

Rising Sun Hotel

★★ 81% ⊚ HOTEL

tel: 01598 753223 **Harbourside EX35 6EG**
email: reception@risingsunlynmouth.co.uk **web:** www.risingsunlynmouth.co.uk
dir: M5 junct 23, A39 to Minehead. Hotel on harbour

The Rising Sun is a delightful thatched establishment, once a smugglers' inn, that sits on the harbour front. Popular with locals and guests alike, there is the option of eating in either the convivial bar or the restaurant; a comfortable, quiet lounge is also available. Bedrooms, located in the inn and adjoining cottages, are individually designed and have modern facilities.

Rooms 14 (1 fmly) (1 GF) **Facilities** Xmas

Bath Hotel

★★ 74% HOTEL

tel: 01598 752238 **Sea Front EX35 6EL**
email: info@bathhotellynmouth.co.uk **web:** www.bathhotellynmouth.co.uk
dir: M5 junct 25, A39 to Lynmouth

Bath Hotel is a well established, friendly hotel, situated near the harbour, offering lovely views from the attractive, sea-facing bedrooms and providing an excellent starting point for scenic walks. There are two lounges and a sun lounge. The restaurant menu is extensive, and features daily-changing specials that make good use of fresh produce and local fish.

Rooms 22 (9 fmly) **S** £45-£65; **D** £78-£130 (incl. bkfst)* **Facilities** FTV WiFi **Parking** 12 **Notes** Closed Dec & Jan RS Nov & Feb

---

LYTHAM ST ANNES
Lancashire

Map 18 SD32

Clifton Arms Hotel

★★★★ 79% ⊚⊚ HOTEL

tel: 01253 739898 **West Beach, Lytham FY8 5QJ**
email: welcome@cliftonarms-lytham.com **web:** www.cliftonarms-lytham.com
dir: On A584 along seafront

This well established hotel occupies a prime position overlooking Lytham Green and the Ribble Estuary beyond. Bedrooms vary in size and are appointed to a high standard; front-facing rooms are particularly spacious and enjoy splendid views. There is an elegant restaurant, a stylish open-plan lounge and cocktail bar, as well as function and conference facilities.

Rooms 48 (2 fmly) ⌕ **S** £88-£118; **D** £125-£205 (incl. bkfst)* **Facilities** STV FTV WiFi ⌕ Xmas New Year **Conf** Class 100 Board 60 Thtr 150 Del from £150 to £180 **Services** Lift **Parking** 40 **Notes** LB ⊗ Civ Wed 100

Bedford Hotel

★★★ 82% ⊚ HOTEL

tel: 01253 724636 **307-313 Clifton Drive South FY8 1HN**
email: reservations@bedford-hotel.com **web:** www.bedford-hotel.com
dir: From M55 follow signs for airport to last lights. Left through 2 sets of lights. Hotel 300yds on left

This popular family-run hotel is close to the town centre and the seafront. Bedrooms vary in size and style and include superior and club class rooms. The newer bedrooms are particularly elegant and tastefully appointed. Spacious public areas include a choice of lounges, a coffee shop, fitness facilities and an impressive function suite.

Rooms 44 (6 GF) ⌕ **S** £65-£70; **D** £85-£120 (incl. bkfst)* **Facilities** FTV WiFi ⌕ Gym Hydrotherapy spa bath Xmas New Year **Conf** Class 140 Board 60 Thtr 200 **Services** Lift **Parking** 25 **Notes** LB ⊗

BEST WESTERN Glendower Promenade Hotel

★★★ 80% HOTEL

tel: 01253 723241 **North Promenade FY8 2NQ**
email: recp@theglendowerhotel.co.uk **web:** www.theglendowerhotel.co.uk
dir: M55 follow airport signs. Left at Promenade to St Annes. Hotel 500yds from pier

Located on the seafront and with easy access to the town centre, this popular, friendly hotel offers comfortably furnished, well-equipped accommodation. Bedrooms vary in size and style, and include four-poster rooms and very popular family suites. Public areas feature a choice of smart, comfortable lounges, a bright, modern leisure club and function facilities.

Rooms 60 (17 fmly) **Facilities** FTV WiFi ⌕ Gym Nintendo Wii play area Snooker table ♫ Xmas New Year **Conf** Class 120 Board 50 Thtr 150 **Services** Lift **Parking** 45 **Notes** Civ Wed 150

Chadwick Hotel

★★★ 74% HOTEL

tel: 01253 720061 **South Promenade FY8 1NP**
email: info@thechadwickhotel.com **web:** www.thechadwickhotel.com
dir: M6 junct 32, M55 to Blackpool, A5230 to South Shore. Follow signs for St Annes, hotel on Promenade's south end

This popular, comfortable and traditional hotel enjoys a seafront location. Bedrooms vary in size and style, but all are very thoughtfully equipped; those at the front boast panoramic sea views. Public rooms are spacious and comfortably furnished and the smart bar is stocked with some 200 malt whiskies. The hotel has a well-equipped, air-conditioned gym and indoor pool.

Rooms 72 (28 fmly) (13 GF) ⋔ **Facilities** FTV WiFi ⓢ Gym Turkish bath Games room Soft play adventure area Wii room Sauna ♫ Xmas New Year **Conf** Class 24 Board 28 Thtr 70 Del from £115 to £130* **Services** Lift **Parking** 40 **Notes** ⊗

MACCLESFIELD
Cheshire   Map 16 SJ97

Shrigley Hall Hotel, Golf & Country Club

★★★★ 77% ⬤ HOTEL

PUMA HOTELS COLLECTION

tel: 01625 575757 **Shrigley Park, Pott Shrigley SK10 5SB**
email: shrigleyhall@pumahotels.co.uk **web:** www.pumahotels.co.uk
dir: Exit A523 at Legh Arms towards Pott Shrigley. Hotel 2m on left before village

Originally built in 1825, Shrigley Hall is an impressive hotel set in 262 acres of mature parkland, commanding stunning views of the countryside. Features include a championship golf course. There is a wide choice of bedroom sizes and styles. The public areas are spacious, combining traditional and contemporary decor, and include a well-equipped gym.

Rooms 148 (11 fmly) ⋔ **Facilities** Spa STV WiFi ⓢ supervised ⛳ 18 ⛳ Putt green Fishing Gym Beauty salon Hydro centre ♫ Xmas New Year **Conf** Class 110 Board 42 Thtr 180 **Services** Lift **Parking** 300 **Notes** Civ Wed 150

Premier Inn Macclesfield North

BUDGET HOTEL

tel: 0871 527 8694 **Tytherington Business Park, Springwood Way, Tytherington SK10 2XA**
web: www.premierinn.com
dir: On A523 in Tytherington Business Park

High quality, budget accommodation ideal for both families and business travellers. Spacious, en suite bedrooms feature tea and coffee making facilities,

and Freeview TV in most hotels. Internet access and WiFi are available for a small fee. The adjacent family restaurant features a wide and varied menu. See also the Hotel Groups pages.

Rooms 41

Premier Inn Macclesfield South West

BUDGET HOTEL

tel: 0871 527 8696 **Congleton Rd, Gawsworth SK11 7XD**
web: www.premierinn.com
dir: M6 junct 17, A534 towards Congleton, A536 towards Macclesfield to Gawsworth. Hotel on left

Rooms 28

MAIDENCOMBE

See Torquay

MAIDENHEAD
Berkshire   Map 6 SU88

Holiday Inn Maidenhead/Windsor

Holiday Inn

★★★★ 74% HOTEL

tel: 0871 942 9053 & 01628 506000 **Manor Ln SL6 2RA**
email: reservations-maidenhead@ihg.com **web:** www.himaidenheadhotel.co.uk
dir: A404 towards High Wycombe. Exit at junct 9A. Left at mini rdbt. Hotel on right

Located close to Maidenhead town centre with transport links to Windsor and the M4, this well sited hotel is suitable for both the business and leisure traveller. Public areas include a spacious lounge bar, brasserie-style restaurant and extensive conference facilities. The popular leisure club includes swimming pool and a full gym.

Rooms 197 (23 fmly) (56 GF) ⋔ **Facilities** STV WiFi ⅃ HL ⓢ supervised Gym Steam room Sauna Beauty treatment room New Year **Conf** Class 200 Board 100 Thtr 400 **Services** Lift Air con **Parking** 250 **Notes** ⊗ Civ Wed 400

MAIDSTONE
Kent   Map 7 TQ75

Tudor Park, A Marriott Hotel & Country Club

TUDOR PARK

★★★★ 77% HOTEL

tel: 01622 734334 & 632004 **Ashford Rd, Bearsted ME14 4NQ**
email: mhrs.tdmgs.frontdesk@marriotthotels.com **web:** www.marriotttudorpark.co.uk
dir: M20 junct 8 to Lenham. At rdbt follow Bearsted & Maidstone signs on A20. Hotel 1m on left

Located on the outskirts of Maidstone in a wooded valley below Leeds Castle, this fine country hotel is set in 220 acres of parkland. Spacious bedrooms provide good levels of comfort and a comprehensive range of extras. Facilities include a championship golf course, a fully equipped gym and two dining options.

Rooms 120 (48 fmly) (60 GF) **S** £85-£160; **D** £85-£160 **Facilities** Spa WiFi ⓢ ⛳ 18 ⛳ Putt green Gym Driving range Beauty salon Steam room Xmas New Year **Conf** Class 100 Board 60 Thtr 250 Del from £135 to £180 **Services** Lift **Parking** 250 **Notes** ⊗ Civ Wed 160

M

MAIDSTONE *continued*

Grange Moor Hotel

★★★ 🅰

tel: 01622 677623 **4-8 St Michael's Rd ME16 8BS**
email: reservations@grangemoor.co.uk **web:** www.grangemoor.co.uk
dir: From town centre towards A26 (Tonbridge road). Hotel 0.25m on left, just after church

This establishment is easily recognised by the colourful hanging baskets in summer. It offers 50 well-appointed bedrooms that have TV, radio alarm clock, hairdryer, and tea- and coffee-making facilities. There is a guest lounge area and a Tudor-style bar and restaurant.

Rooms 50 (11 annexe) (5 fmly) (7 GF) 🐾 **S** £54-£65; **D** £59-£85 (incl. bkfst)
Facilities FTV WiFi **Conf** Class 60 Board 40 Thtr 100 Del from £55 to £90 **Parking** 75
Notes LB ⊗ Closed 23-30 Dec Civ Wed

Premier Inn Maidstone (A26/Wateringbury)

BUDGET HOTEL

tel: 0871 527 8706 **103 Tonbridge Rd, Wateringbury ME18 5NS**
web: www.premierinn.com
dir: M25 junct 3 onto M20. Exit at junct 4 onto A228 towards West Malling. A26 towards Maidstone, approx 3m

High quality, budget accommodation ideal for both families and business travellers. Spacious, en suite bedrooms feature tea and coffee making facilities, and Freeview TV in most hotels. Internet access and WiFi are available for a small fee. The adjacent family restaurant features a wide and varied menu. See also the Hotel Groups pages.

Rooms 40

Premier Inn Maidstone (Allington)

BUDGET HOTEL

tel: 0871 527 8698 **London Rd ME16 0HG**
web: www.premierinn.com
dir: M20 junct 5, 0.5m on London Rd towards Maidstone

Rooms 40

Premier Inn Maidstone (Leybourne)

BUDGET HOTEL

tel: 0871 527 8702 **Castle Way, Leybourne, West Malling ME19 5TR**
web: www.premierinn.com
dir: M20 junct 4, A228, hotel on left

Rooms 40

Premier Inn Maidstone (Sandling)

BUDGET HOTEL

tel: 0871 527 8704 **Allington Lock, Sandling ME14 3AS**
web: www.premierinn.com
dir: M20 junct 6, follow Museum of Kent Life signs

Rooms 40

Premier Inn Maidstone Town Centre

BUDGET HOTEL

tel: 0871 527 9392 **5-11 London Rd ME16 8HR**
web: www.premierinn.com
dir: M20 junct 5, A20 signed Maidstone (West) & Aylesford .At next rdbt 1st exit (Maidstone). Straight on at next rdbt

Rooms 99

MALMESBURY	Map 4 ST98
Wiltshire	

INSPECTORS' CHOICE

Whatley Manor Hotel and Spa

★★★★★ ◎◎◎◎ HOTEL

tel: 01666 822888 **Easton Grey SN16 0RB**
email: reservations@whatleymanor.com **web:** www.whatleymanor.com
dir: M4 junct 17, follow signs to Malmesbury, continue over 2 rdbts. Follow B4040 & signs for Sherston, hotel 2m on left

Sitting in 12 acres of beautiful countryside, this impressive country house provides the most luxurious surroundings. Spacious bedrooms, most with views over the attractive gardens, are individually decorated with splendid features such as Bang & Olufsen sound and vision systems and unique works of art. Several eating options are available: Le Mazot, a Swiss-style brasserie, The Dining Room that serves classical French cuisine with a contemporary twist via carte and tasting menus, plus the Kitchen Garden Terrace for alfresco breakfasts, lunches and dinners. Guests might even like to take a hamper and a picnic rug and find a quiet spot in the grounds. The old Loggia Barn is ideal for wedding ceremonies, and the Aquarius Spa is magnificent.

Rooms 23 (4 GF) ✎ **D** £305-£865 (incl. bkfst)* **Facilities** Spa STV FTV WiFi ◊ Fishing Gym Cinema Hydro pool (indoor/outdoor) Xmas New Year **Conf** Class 20 Board 24 Thtr 60 Del £325* **Services** Lift **Parking** 100 **Notes** LB No children 12yrs Civ Wed 120

Old Bell Hotel

★★★ 78% ◉◉ HOTEL

tel: 01666 822344 **Abbey Row SN16 0BW**
email: info@oldbellhotel.com **web:** www.oldbellhotel.com
dir: M4 junct 17, A429 N. Left at 1st rdbt. Left at T-junct. Hotel adjacent to Abbey

Dating back to 1220, the wisteria-clad Old Bell is reputed to be the oldest purpose-built hotel in England. Bedrooms vary in size and style; those in the main house tend to be more spacious and are traditionally furnished with antiques, while the newer bedrooms in the coach house have a contemporary feel. Guests have a choice of comfortable sitting areas and dining options, including the main restaurant where the award-winning cuisine is based on high quality ingredients.

Rooms 33 (15 annexe) (7 GF) ✎ **S** £89.50; **D** £115-£275 (incl. bkfst) **Facilities** FTV WiFi Xmas New Year **Conf** Class 32 Board 32 Thtr 60 **Parking** 33 **Notes** Civ Wed 90

BEST WESTERN Mayfield House Hotel

★★★ 74% HOTEL

tel: 01666 577409 **Crudwell SN16 9EW**
email: reception@mayfieldhousehotel.co.uk **web:** www.mayfieldhousehotel.co.uk
dir: M4 junct 17, A429 to Cirencester. 2m N of Malmesbury on left in Crudwell village

This popular hotel is in an ideal location for exploring the many attractions that Wiltshire and The Cotswolds have to offer. Bedrooms come in a range of shapes and

sizes, and include some on the ground-floor level in a cottage adjacent to the main building. In addition to outdoor seating, guests can relax with a drink in the comfortable lounge area where orders are taken for the carefully prepared dinner to follow.

Rooms 28 (8 annexe) (4 fmly) (8 GF) ✎ **S** £64-£78; **D** £88-£108 (incl. bkfst)* **Facilities** FTV WiFi ◊ ⚓ Xmas New Year **Conf** Class 30 Board 25 Thtr 40 **Parking** 50 **Notes** LB

MALTON   **Map 19 SE77**
North Yorkshire

The Talbot Hotel

★★★★ 85% ◉◉ HOTEL

tel: 01653 639096 **Yorkersgate YO17 7AJ**
email: info@talbotmalton.co.uk **web:** www.talbotmalton.co.uk
dir: From York take A64, exit at Malton sign. Hotel on right

This hotel is owned by the Fitzwilliam Estate and is set in its own beautifully landscaped grounds close to the historic market town. The interior features individually decorated bedrooms, including two luxurious suites. Each of the guest rooms has its own distinct personality. The restaurant has elegant furniture, crisp white linen and fine silver cutlery, and with James Martin as executive chef the best of Yorkshire produce is sure to be on offer. Elegant public areas can be found throughout this stunning hotel.

Rooms 26 (3 GF) ✎ **D** £99-£199 (incl. bkfst)* **Facilities** FTV WiFi HL Xmas New Year **Conf** Class 30 Board 24 Thtr 60 Del from £165 to £295* **Parking** 35 **Notes** LB Civ Wed 60

M

MALVERN
Worcestershire

Map 10 SO74

The Malvern

★★★★ 74% 🏵 HOTEL

tel: 01684 898290 **Grovewood Rd WR14 1GD**
email: enquiries@themalvernspa.com **web:** www.themalvernspa.com
dir: A4440 to Malvern. Over 2 rdbts, at 3rd rdbt turn left. 6m, left at rdbt, over 1st rdbt, hotel on right

This modern, friendly hotel is set on the outskirts of the famous spa town. The bedrooms are contemporary with sumptuous beds, and many guest extras are provided; the bathrooms have quality fixtures and fittings. There is a brasserie restaurant which offers quality seasonal menus that include healthy options and vegetarian dishes. The Malvern Spa, designed exclusively for adults, includes a hydrotherapy pool which goes from inside to outside, heat experiences, a range of saunas, crystal steam room, salt grotto, adventure showers along with a host of treatments. There is also a 50-station gym with state-of-the-art equipment. There is ample parking around the hotel.

Rooms 33 🐾 **Facilities** Spa FTV WiFi ⃝ 🏊 ⃛ Gym Exercise classes Xmas New Year **Conf** Class 40 Board 20 Thtr 80 **Services** Lift Air con **Parking** 82 **Notes** ⊗ No children 18yrs

The Abbey Hotel

★★★★ 74% HOTEL

SAROVA HOTELS

tel: 01684 892332 & 897897 **Abbey Rd WR14 3ET**
email: abbey@sarova.co.uk **web:** www.sarova.com
dir: In Great Malvern town centre, opposite theatres

This large, impressive, ivy-clad hotel stands in the centre of Great Malvern, at the foot of the Malvern Hills, next to the Abbey and close to the theatre. It provides well-equipped modern accommodation equally suitable for business guests and tourists. Facilities include a good range of function rooms making the hotel a popular venue for meetings and events.

Rooms 103 (11 fmly) (23 GF) **S** £80-£185; **D** £90-£195 (incl. bkfst)* **Facilities** STV FTV WiFi ⃝ Xmas New Year **Conf** Class 120 Board 40 Thtr 300 Del from £105 to £155* **Services** Lift **Parking** 85 **Notes** LB Civ Wed 300

The Cottage in the Wood Hotel

★★★ 86% 🏵🏵 HOTEL

tel: 01684 588860 **Holywell Rd, Malvern Wells WR14 4LG**
email: reception@cottageinthewood.co.uk **web:** www.cottageinthewood.co.uk
dir: 3m S of Great Malvern off A449, 500yds N of B4209, on opposite side of road

Sitting high up on a wooded hillside, this delightful, family-run hotel boasts stunning views over the Severn Valley. The bedrooms are divided between the main house, Beech Cottage and the Pinnacles. The public areas are very stylishly decorated, and imaginative food is served in an elegant dining room, overlooking the immaculate grounds.

Rooms 30 (23 annexe) (10 GF) 🐾 **S** £79-£121; **D** £99-£198 (incl. bkfst)* **Facilities** FTV WiFi Xmas New Year **Conf** Board 14 Thtr 20 Del £155* **Parking** 40 **Notes** LB

Colwall Park Hotel

★★★ 83% @@ HOTEL

tel: 01684 540000 **Walwyn Rd, Colwall WR13 6QG**
email: hotel@colwall.com **web:** www.colwall.co.uk
dir: Between Malvern & Ledbury in centre of Colwall on B4218

Standing in extensive gardens, this hotel was purpose built in the early 20th century to serve the local racetrack. Today the proprietors and loyal staff provide high levels of hospitality and service. The Seasons Restaurant has a well-deserved reputation for its cuisine. Bedrooms are tastefully appointed and public areas help to create a fine country-house atmosphere.

Rooms 22 (1 fmly) ↑ **S** £80-£135; **D** £110-£200 (incl. bkfst)* **Facilities** FTV WiFi ↕ ❧ Boules Xmas New Year **Conf** Class 80 Board 50 Thtr 150 Del £150* **Parking** 40 **Notes** LB ⊗

The Cotford Hotel & L'Amuse Bouche Restaurant

★★★ 79% @@ HOTEL

tel: 01684 572427 **51 Graham Rd WR14 2HU**
email: reservations@cotfordhotel.co.uk **web:** www.cotfordhotel.co.uk
dir: From Worcester follow signs to Malvern on A449. Left into Graham Rd signed town centre, hotel on right

This delightful house, built in 1851, reputedly for the Bishop of Worcester, stands in attractive gardens with stunning views of The Malverns. Bedrooms have been authentically renovated, retaining many of the original features and with a good selection of welcome extras. Food, service and hospitality are all major strengths.

Rooms 15 (3 fmly) (1 GF) ↑ **S** £69.50-£85; **D** £125-£140 (incl. bkfst) **Facilities** STV FTV WiFi ↕ ❧ **Conf** Class 26 Board 12 Thtr 26 **Parking** 15 **Notes** LB

See advert on opposite page

Mount Pleasant Hotel

★★★ 70% HOTEL

tel: 01684 561837 **Belle Vue Ter WR14 4PZ**
email: reception@mountpleasanthotel.co.uk **web:** www.mountpleasanthotel.co.uk
dir: On A449, in town centre opposite Priory Church

Mount Pleasant is an attractive Georgian house in the town centre that occupies an elevated position, and overlooks Priory Church and the picturesque Severn Plain. This family-run hotel, with a relaxed atmosphere, offers spacious, fully equipped bedrooms, and the Spring Bar and Restaurant serves home-made classic British cuisine as well as tea, coffee, cakes and biscuits. In winter guests can sit beside real log fires, and in warmer months the garden makes a delightful place to relax.

Rooms 14 (1 fmly) ↑ **Facilities** FTV WiFi Hair salon Complementary therapists Xmas New Year **Conf** Class 40 Board 50 Thtr 90 **Parking** 20 **Notes** ⊗

Holdfast Cottage Hotel

★★ 81% HOTEL

tel: 01684 310288 **Marlbank Rd, Welland WR13 6NA**
email: enquiries@holdfast-cottage.co.uk **web:** www.holdfast-cottage.co.uk
dir: M50 junct 1, follow Upton Three Counties/A38 signs, onto A4104 to Welland

At the base of the Malvern Hills this delightful wisteria-covered hotel sits in attractive manicured grounds. Charming public areas include an intimate bar, a log fire enhanced lounge and an elegant dining room. Bedrooms vary in size but all are comfortable and well appointed. Fresh local and seasonal produce are the basis for the cuisine.

Rooms 8 (1 fmly) **Facilities** FTV WiFi ↕ Xmas New Year **Conf** Class 30 Board 30 Thtr 26 **Parking** 16 **Notes** ⊗ Civ Wed 50

The Great Malvern Hotel

★★ 74% HOTEL

tel: 01684 563411 **Graham Rd WR14 2HN**
email: sutton@great-malvern-hotel.co.uk **web:** www.great-malvern-hotel.co.uk
dir: From Worcester on A449, left after fire station into Graham Rd. Hotel at end on right

Close to the town centre this privately owned and managed hotel is ideally situated for many of Malvern's attractions. The accommodation is spacious and well equipped. Public areas include quiet lounge areas, and a cosy bar which is popular with locals.

Rooms 13 (1 fmly) **S** £55-£70; **D** £75-£90 (incl. bkfst)* **Facilities** STV FTV WiFi ↕ ♫ **Conf** Class 20 Board 20 Thtr 20 **Services** Lift **Parking** 9

M

M

MANCHESTER
Greater Manchester

Map 16 SJ89

See also **Manchester Airport & Sale**

The Lowry Hotel

★★★★★ 86% HOTEL

tel: 0161 827 4000 **50 Dearmans Place, Chapel Wharf, Salford M3 5LH**
email: enquiries.lowry@roccofortehotels.com **web:** www.roccofortehotels.com
dir: M6 junct 19, A556/M56/A5103 for 4.5m. At rdbt take A57(M) to lights, right onto Water St. Left to New Quay St/Trinity Way. At 1st lights right into Chapel St for hotel

This modern, contemporary hotel, set beside the River Irwell in the centre of the city, offers spacious bedrooms equipped to meet the needs of business and leisure visitors alike. Many of the rooms look out over the river, as do the sumptuous suites. The River Room restaurant produces good brasserie cooking. Extensive business and function facilities are available, together with a spa to provide extra pampering.

Rooms 165 (7 fmly) ✆ **S** £139-£589; **D** £139-£589* **Facilities** **Spa** STV FTV WiFi ⇨ HL Gym Swimming facilities available nearby ♫ Xmas New Year **Conf** Class 250 Board 60 Thtr 400 Del from £175 to £350* **Services** Lift Air con **Parking** 100 **Notes** LB Civ Wed 400

The Midland

★★★★ 86% HOTEL

tel: 0161 236 3333 **Peter St M60 2DS**
email: midlandsales@qhotels.co.uk **web:** www.qhotels.co.uk
dir: M602 junct 3, follow Manchester Central Convention Complex signs, hotel opposite

This much loved, centrally located, well-established Edwardian-style hotel (Grade II listed) offers stylish, thoughtfully equipped bedrooms that have a contemporary feel. Elegant public areas are equally impressive and facilities include extensive function and meeting rooms. Eating options include the Octogan Lounge and Simon Rogan's award-winning classical French Restaurant, the Wyvern Restaurant. QHotels is the AA Hotel Group of the Year 2014-15.

Rooms 312 (13 fmly) ✆ **S** £129-£599; **D** £129-£599* **Facilities** STV WiFi ⇨ HL Gym Squash Hair & beauty salon ♫ **Conf** Class 300 Board 120 Thtr 600 Del from £169 to £239* **Services** Lift Air con **Notes** ⊗ Civ Wed 600

ABode Manchester

★★★★ 80% HOTEL

tel: 0161 247 7744 **107 Piccadilly M1 2DB**
email: reservationsmanchester@abodehotels.co.uk **web:** www.abodehotels.co.uk
dir: M62/M602 follow signs for city centre/Piccadilly

Located in the heart on Piccadilly, this grade II listed former wholesale textile warehouse has embraced its industrial heritage. Exposed steel beams and structural iron columns together with an ornate wrought iron and walnut staircase are striking features. Beds are low and comfortable, feature walls, a tuck box filled with regional food and drink, and complimentary WiFi can be found in all rooms. A choice of dining options include Café Bow for relaxed informal dining, or Michael Caines fine dining experience and Champagne bar in the basement.

Rooms 61 **Facilities** STV WiFi ⇨ **Conf** Board 26 Thtr 30 **Services** Lift Air con **Notes** ⊗ RS 25 Dec-2 Jan

Macdonald Manchester Hotel

★★★★ 79% HOTEL

tel: 0844 879 9088 & 0161 272 3200 **London Rd M1 2PG**
email: general.manchester@macdonald-hotels.co.uk **web:** www.macdonaldhotels.co.uk
dir: Opposite Piccadilly Station

Ideally situated just a short walk from Piccadilly Station, this hotel provides a handy location for both business and leisure travellers. Stylish, modern rooms have plasma TVs and iPod docking stations and the bathrooms offer walk-in power showers and luxury baths. The first-floor restaurant serves skilfully prepared dinners and hearty breakfasts. Staff throughout are cheerful and keen to please.

Rooms 338 (14 fmly) ✆ **S** £77-£245; **D** £77-£245* **Facilities** **Spa** FTV WiFi ⇨ HL Gym Sauna New Year **Conf** Class 150 Board 80 Thtr 250 Del from £115 to £220* **Services** Lift Air con **Parking** 85 **Notes** ⊗ Civ Wed 200

Holiday Inn Manchester - MediaCityUK

★★★★ 77% HOTEL

tel: 0161 813 1040 **Media City UK, Salford M50 2HT**
web: www.holidayinn.com/mediacity
dir: M602 junct 2 onto A576 to Salford Quays signed MediaCityUK

Located in the heart of the exciting media district on Salford Quays, this hotel is adjacent to the main production studios and only minutes from Old Trafford and The Lowry Centre. The stylish Hub Bar features TV-themed murals and the attractive Green Room Restaurant is on the mezzanine floor. Bedrooms are well equipped with safes and mini-bars, and many have views of the Manchester Shipping Canal. There's complimentary WiFi throughout, and a mini-gym is available to guests.

Rooms 218 (10 fmly) ✆ **S** £109-£209; **D** £109-£209* **Facilities** STV FTV WiFi ⇨ HL Gym Xmas New Year **Conf** Class 25 Board 30 Thtr 44 Del from £155 to £195* **Services** Lift Air con **Parking** 5000 **Notes** LB Civ Wed 70

Novotel Manchester Centre

★★★★ 75% HOTEL

tel: 0161 235 2200 **21 Dickinson St M1 4LX**
email: H3145@accor.com **web:** www.novotel.com
dir: From Oxford St into Portland St, left into Dickinson St. Hotel on right

This smart, modern property enjoys a central location convenient for theatres, shops, China Town and Manchester's business district. Spacious bedrooms are thoughtfully equipped and brightly decorated. Open-plan, contemporary public areas include an all-day restaurant and a stylish bar. Extensive conference and meeting facilities are available.

Rooms 164 (15 fmly) ✆ **Facilities** STV FTV WiFi ⇨ HL Gym Steam room Sauna Aromatherapy **Conf** Class 50 Board 36 Thtr 90 **Services** Lift Air con

The Palace Hotel

★★★★ 75% HOTEL

tel: 0161 288 1111 **Oxford St M60 7HA**
email: richard.grove@principal-hayley.com **web:** www.principal-hayley.com
dir: Opposite Manchester Oxford Road rail station

Formerly the offices of the Refuge Life Assurance Company, this impressive neo-Gothic building occupies a central location. There is a vast lobby, spacious open-plan bar lounge and restaurant, and extensive conference and function facilities. Bedrooms vary in size and style but are all spacious and well equipped.

Rooms 275 (59 fmly) ✆ **Facilities** STV WiFi **Conf** Class 650 Board 200 Thtr 1000 **Services** Lift **Notes** ⊗ Civ Wed 600

Arora Hotel

★★★★ 74% HOTEL

tel: 0161 236 8999 **18-24 Princess St M1 4LY**
email: manchesterreservations@arorahotels.com **web:** www.manchester.arorahotels.com
dir: Telephone for detailed directions

Conveniently located close to the city centre and ideal for both shopping and Theatres, the Arora provides comfortable accommodation. The hotel also has meeting room facilities, a small gym and a contemporary dining room in 24 Bar and Grill.

Rooms 141 (32 fmly) (15 GF) ⁂ **Facilities** FTV WiFi Gym **Conf** Class 40 Board 45 Thtr 100 **Services** Lift **Notes** ⊗ Civ Wed 60

Copthorne Hotel Manchester

★★★★ 74% HOTEL

tel: 0161 873 7321 **Clippers Quay, Salford Quays M50 3SN**
email: reservations.manchester@millenniumhotels.co.uk
web: www.millenniumhotels.co.uk
dir: From M602 follow signs for Salford Quays & Trafford Park on A5063. Hotel 0.75m on right

This smart hotel enjoys a convenient location on the redeveloped Salford Quays close to Old Trafford, The Lowry Centre and The Imperial War Museum. Bedrooms are comfortably appointed and well equipped for both business and leisure guests. The informal Quay Chop House Restaurant serves a wide range of modern dishes.

Rooms 166 (6 fmly) (23 GF) ⁂ **Facilities** STV WiFi ₆ HL **Conf** Class 80 Board 70 Thtr 160 **Services** Lift **Parking** 120 **Notes** ⊗ Civ Wed 160

Macdonald Townhouse Manchester

★★★★ 74% TOWN HOUSE HOTEL

tel: 0161 236 5122 **101 Portland St M1 6DF**
email: gm.townhouse@macdonald-hotels.co.uk
web: www.macdonaldhotels.co.uk/our-hotels/macdonald-townhouse-hotel
dir: From Piccadilly Station, along Piccadilly. Left into Portland St, hotel at junct with Princess St

This hotel, a former cotton warehouse and now a Grade II listed building, is ideally located for exploring the City of Manchester. There are comfortable and well-appointed bedrooms, a stylish bar and a lounge with a restaurant that is open for pre-theatre meals.

Rooms 85 (24 fmly) ⁂ S £89-£245; D £89-£245* **Facilities** FTV WiFi ₆ **Conf** Class 26 Board 30 Thtr 48 Del from £135 to £200* **Services** Lift Air con **Notes** LB ⊗

Mercure Manchester Piccadilly Hotel

★★★★ 73% HOTEL

tel: 0844 815 9024 **Portland St M1 4PH**
email: info@mercuremanchester.co.uk **web:** www.jupiterhotels.co.uk
dir: Opposite Piccadilly Gardens

Overlooking Picadilly Gardens and views of the city, this hotel is located within the heart of Manchester. Bedrooms and bathrooms are tastefully appointed, with a range of rooms for both leisure guests and the modern business traveller. Contemporary dining can be enjoyed within the Brasserie and popular bar areas. A range of spacious meetings and events space is also available. Free WiFi across the hotel is a plus. Parking available for car users.

Rooms 280 ⁂ **Facilities** FTV WiFi ₆ **Conf** Class 420 Board 30 Thtr 800 **Services** Lift Air con **Parking** 80 **Notes** ⊗ Civ Wed

Malmaison Manchester

★★★ 85% ⊛ HOTEL

tel: 0844 693 0657 **Piccadilly M1 3AQ**
email: manchester@malmaison.com **web:** www.malmaison.com
dir: Follow city centre signs, then signs to Piccadilly station. Hotel at bottom of station approach

Stylish and chic, Malmaison Manchester offers the best of contemporary hotel-keeping in a relaxed and comfortable environment. Converted from a former warehouse, it offers a range of bright meeting rooms, a gym and treatment rooms. The new Smoak Bar & Grill is impressive and understandably popular. Air-conditioned suites combine comfort with stunning design. Expect the unusual in some of the rooms, for instance the Cinema Suites have a private screening room with 52" screen and surround-sound.

Rooms 167 ⁂ **Facilities** STV WiFi ₆ HL Gym Sauna Spa Relaxation area Solarium Massage chairs Xmas New Year **Conf** Class 48 Board 30 Thtr 100 **Services** Lift Air con **Notes** Civ Wed 100

BEST WESTERN Willow Bank Hotel

★★★ 77% HOTEL

tel: 0161 224 0461 **340-342 Wilmslow Rd, Fallowfield M14 6AF**
email: gm-willowbank@feathers.uk.com
web: www.feathers.uk.com
dir: M60 junct 5, A5103, left onto B5093. Hotel 2.5m on left

This popular hotel is conveniently located three miles from the city centre, close to the universities. Bedrooms vary in size and style but all are appointed to impressively high standards; they are well equipped and many rooms benefit from CD players and PlayStations. Spacious, elegant public areas include a bar, a restaurant and meeting rooms.

Rooms 116 (4 fmly) **S** £49-£144; **D** £69-£169 (incl. bkfst)* **Facilities** FTV WiFi Xmas New Year **Conf** Class 50 Board 60 Thtr 120 **Parking** 100 **Notes** LB Civ Wed 125

Jurys Inn Manchester

★★★ 77% HOTEL

tel: 0161 953 8888 **56 Great Bridgewater St M1 5LE**
email: manchester_inn@jurysinns.com **web:** www.jurysinns.com
dir: In city centre adjacent to Manchester Central & Bridgewater Hall

Enjoying a prime city centre location, this hotel offers good value, air-conditioned accommodation, ideal for both business travellers and families. Public areas include a smart, spacious lobby, the Inn Pub and the Infusion Restaurant. There are several conveniently located car parks with special rates available.

Rooms 265 (11 fmly) (16 GF) **Facilities** FTV WiFi ₆ **Conf** Class 25 Board 25 Thtr 50 **Services** Lift Air con **Notes** ⊗

Chancellors Hotel & Conference Centre

★★★ 74% HOTEL

tel: 0161 907 7414 **Moseley Rd, Fallowfield M14 6NN**
email: chancellors@manchester.ac.uk **web:** www.chancellorshotel.co.uk
dir: Telephone for detailed directions

A Grade II listed manor house set in five acres of landscaped gardens hidden in the heart of Fallowfield, well located for the city's shopping, business and commercial centres. Bedrooms offer modern facilities and the cuisine is enjoyable. WiFi and secure parking are available.

Rooms 70 (4 fmly) (16 GF) **S** fr £30; **D** fr £40* **Facilities** FTV WiFi ₆ HL **Conf** Class 100 Board 50 Thtr 125 Del from £95* **Services** Lift **Parking** 70 **Notes** ⊗ Civ Wed 125

M

MANCHESTER *continued*

Novotel Manchester West

★★★ 74% HOTEL

tel: 0161 799 3535 **Worsley Brow M28 2YA**
email: H0907@accor.com **web:** www.novotel.com

(For full entry see Worsley)

Campanile Manchester

BUDGET HOTEL

tel: 0161 833 1845 **55 Ordsall Ln, Regent Rd, Salford M5 4RS**
email: manchester@campanile.com **web:** www.campanile.com
dir: M602 to Manchester, then A57. After large rdbt with Sainsbury's on left, left at next lights. Hotel on right

This modern building offers accommodation in smart, well-equipped bedrooms, all with en suite bathrooms. Refreshments may be taken at the informal bistro. See also the Hotel Groups pages.

Rooms 104 (25 GF) **Conf** Class 40 Board 30 Thtr 50

Ibis Manchester Centre Portland Street

BUDGET HOTEL

tel: 0161 6199 000 **96 Portland St M1 4JY**
email: H3142@accor.com **web:** www.ibishotel.com
dir: In city centre, between Princess St & Oxford St

Modern, budget hotel offering comfortable accommodation in bright and practical bedrooms. Breakfast is self-service and dinner is available in the restaurant. See also the Hotel Groups pages.

Rooms 127 (16 fmly) 🐾

Ibis Manchester Princess Street

BUDGET HOTEL

tel: 0161 272 5000 **Charles St, Princess St M1 7DL**
email: H3143@accor.com **web:** www.ibishotel.com
dir: M62, M602 towards Manchester Centre, follow signs for UMIST(A34)

Rooms 126 🐾

Premier Inn Manchester Central

BUDGET HOTEL

tel: 0871 527 8742 **Bishopsgate, 7-11 Lower Mosley St M2 3DW**
web: www.premierinn.com
dir: M56 to end, A5103 towards city. Right at 2nd lights. At next lights left into Oxford Rd, left at junct of St Peters Sq. Hotel on left

High quality, budget accommodation ideal for both families and business travellers. Spacious, en suite bedrooms feature tea and coffee making facilities, and Freeview TV in most hotels. Internet access and WiFi are available for a small fee. The adjacent family restaurant features a wide and varied menu. See also the Hotel Groups pages.

Rooms 147

Premier Inn Manchester City Centre

BUDGET HOTEL

tel: 0871 527 9390 **72 Dale St M1 2HR**
web: www.premierinn.com
dir: Please telephone for detailed directions

Rooms 193

Premier Inn Manchester City Centre (Deansgate)

BUDGET HOTEL

tel: 0871 527 8740 **Medlock St M15 5FJ**
web: www.premierinn.com
dir: M60 junct 24, A57(M) (Mancunian Way) towards city centre. Hotel adjacent, on A5103 (Medlock St)

Rooms 200

Premier Inn Manchester City Centre (Portland Street)

BUDGET HOTEL

tel: 0871 527 8746 **The Circus, 112-114 Portland St M1 4WB**
web: www.premierinn.com
dir: M6 junct 19, A556. M56, exit junct 3 onto A5103 to Medlock St, right into Whitworth St, left into Oxford St, right into Portland St

Rooms 225

Premier Inn Manchester City MEN/Printworks

BUDGET HOTEL

tel: 0871 527 8744 **North Tower, Victoria Bridge St, Salford M3 5AS**
web: www.premierinn.com
dir: M602 to city centre, A57(M) towards GMEX. 2nd exit follow A56 city centre signs. Left before MEN arena onto A6, 1st left

Rooms 170

Premier Inn Manchester (Denton)

BUDGET HOTEL

tel: 0871 527 8708 **Alphagate Dr, Manchester Rd South, Denton M34 3SH**
web: www.premierinn.com
dir: M60 junct 24, A57 signed Denton. 1st right at lights, right at next lights, hotel on left

Rooms 40

Premier Inn Manchester (Heaton Park)

BUDGET HOTEL

tel: 0871 527 8710 **Middleton Rd, Crumpsall M8 4NB**
web: www.premierinn.com
dir: M60 junct 19, A576 towards Manchester, through 2 sets of lights. Hotel on left

Rooms 45

Premier Inn Manchester Old Trafford

BUDGET HOTEL

tel: 0871 527 8750 **Waters Reach, Trafford Park M17 1WS**
web: www.premierinn.com
dir: M6 junct 19, A556 towards Altrincham. Follow Stretford & Manchester City Centre signs (road becomes A56). Follow Manchester United Football Stadium signs. At stadium left at lights. Into Sir Matt Busby Way, after 1st lights hotel on right

Rooms 160

Premier Inn Manchester (Salford Quays)

BUDGET HOTEL

tel: 0871 527 8718 **11 The Quays, Salford Quays, Salford M50 3SQ**
web: www.premierinn.com
dir: M602 junct 3, A5063, on Salford Quays

Rooms 52

Premier Inn Manchester Trafford Centre North

BUDGET HOTEL

tel: 0871 527 8752 **18-20 Trafford Boulevard,, Urmston M41 7JE**
web: www.premierinn.com
dir: M6, onto M62 at junct 21a, towards Manchester. M62 junct 1, M60 towards south. M60 junct 10, take B5214. Hotel on left just before Ellesmere Circle

Rooms 42

Premier Inn Manchester Trafford Centre South

BUDGET HOTEL

tel: 0871 527 8754 **Wilderspool Wood, Trafford Centre M17 8WW**
web: www.premierinn.com
dir: M6 onto M62 junct 21a towards Manchester. Or M62 junct 1 onto M60 S. Or M60 junct 10, B5124 towards Trafford Park. At 1st rdbt take last exit for Trafford Centre parking. At 2nd rdbt straight on. Hotel on left

Rooms 59

Premier Inn Manchester Trafford Centre West

BUDGET HOTEL

tel: 0871 527 8756 **Old Park Ln M17 8PG**
web: www.premierinn.com
dir: M60 junct 10 towards The Trafford Centre

Rooms 161

Premier Inn Manchester (West Didsbury)

BUDGET HOTEL

tel: 0871 527 8722 **Christies Field Office Park, Derwent Ave, Didsbury M21 7QS**
web: www.premierinn.com
dir: M60 junct 5, A5103 (Princess Parkway) towards Manchester on A5103. Hotel approx 1m

Rooms 80

MANCHESTER AIRPORT Map 15 SJ88
Greater Manchester

See also **Altrincham**

Stanneylands Hotel

★★★★ 78% ◉◉ HOTEL

tel: 01625 525225 **Stanneylands Rd SK9 4EY**
email: reservations@stanneylandshotel.co.uk **web:** www.stanneylandshotel.co.uk
dir: From M56 at airport exit, follow signs to Wilmslow. Left towards Handforth. Left at lights into Stanneylands Rd, hotel on left

This traditional country house hotel, just three miles from Manchester Airport, offers well-equipped bedrooms that include suites, prestige and executive rooms together with delightful, comfortable day rooms. The cuisine in the restaurant is of a high standard, and ranges from traditional favourites to more imaginative contemporary dishes. There is also the contemporary Calico café bar in a conservatory setting offering all-day menus, including afternoon tea, and live music played on the baby grand piano. The hotel makes an ideal wedding venue and is licensed to hold civil weddings. The staff throughout are friendly and obliging.

Rooms 56 (2 fmly) (10 GF) ♠ **Facilities** STV FTV WiFi ⅃ ♫ Xmas New Year
Conf Class 50 Board 40 Thtr 120 **Services** Lift **Parking** 108 **Notes** ⊗ Civ Wed 100

Hallmark Hotel Manchester

★★★★ 77% HOTEL

tel: 0161 437 0511 **Stanley Rd SK9 3LD**
email: linda.gregory@hallmarkhotels.co.uk **web:** www.hallmarkhotels.co.uk/manchester
dir: M60 junct 3/A34 signed Cheadle/Wilmslow. Right at 3rd rdbt into Stanley Rd (B5094). Hotel on left

Ideally located for Manchester Airport and just a few miles from both the Trafford Centre and the city's many shops, the Hallmark Hotel offers well appointed bedrooms. Guests can relax and unwind in the hotel's 20-metre pool, jacuzzi and steam rooms. The brasserie is open for both lunch and dinner, and offers a range of international dishes.

Rooms 88 (12 fmly) (12 GF) **Facilities** Spa FTV WiFi ⅃ ⛹ Gym Steam room Sauna Hair salon New Year **Conf** Class 250 Board 60 Thtr 500 **Services** Lift **Notes** ⊗ Civ Wed 300

M

MANCHESTER AIRPORT *continued*

Crowne Plaza Manchester Airport

★★★★ 76% HOTEL

tel: 0871 942 9055 **Ringway Rd M90 3NS**
email: reservations-manchesterairport@ihg.com
web: www.cpmanchesterairporthotel.co.uk
dir: M56 junct 5 signed Manchester Airport. At airport, follow signs to Terminal 1 & 3. Hotel adjacent to Terminal 3. Long stay car park on left

Located by Terminal 3 this smart, modern hotel offers well-equipped, comfortable bedrooms, all with air-conditioning and effective double-glazing. A choice of dining options and bars is available, and the hotel has spacious leisure facilities and ample on-site parking. The hospitality is friendly, with several long-serving staff members who greet regular customers as friends.

Rooms 294 (100 fmly) (51 GF) **Facilities** STV WiFi ⚲ HL Gym Saunas **Conf** Class 25 Board 20 Thtr 30 **Services** Lift Air con **Parking** 300 **Notes** ⊗

BEST WESTERN PLUS Pinewood on Wilmslow

★★★★ 73% HOTEL

tel: 01625 529211 **180 Wilmslow Rd SK9 3LF**
email: pinewood.res@pinewood-hotel.co.uk **web:** www.pinewood-hotel.co.uk
dir: Telephone for detailed directions

This stylish hotel is conveniently situated for the M60, Trafford Park, Trafford Centre and Manchester Airport. Bedrooms provide very good quality accommodation, comfortable beds, and a wealth of extras for the modern traveller. Well cooked meals and hearty breakfasts are served overlooking the gardens.

Rooms 70 (3 fmly) ⚲ **Facilities** FTV WiFi Use of nearby Total Fitness Club Xmas New Year **Conf** Class 60 Board 60 Thtr 120 **Services** Lift **Parking** 120 **Notes** ⊗ Civ Wed 120

Etrop Grange Hotel

★★★★ 71% ❀ HOTEL

tel: 0161 499 0500 **Thorley Ln M90 4EG**
email: gm@etrophotel.co.uk **web:** www.etrophotel.co.uk
dir: Off M56 junct 5. Follow signs to Terminal 2, take 1st left (Thorley Ln), 200yds on right

This Grade II listed Georgian mansion house is close to Terminal 2 but no-one would ever know once inside. Comfortable bedrooms provide modern comforts and good business facilities. Elegant day rooms include the Wine Glass restaurant serving creative dishes. Complimentary airport transfers are available to guests.

Rooms 64 (5 fmly) (15 GF) ⚲ **S** £69-£149; **D** £69-£149* **Facilities** FTV WiFi ⚲ Xmas New Year **Conf** Class 90 Board 40 Thtr 120 Del from £120 to £190* **Services** Air con **Parking** 90 **Notes** LB Civ Wed 100

Bewleys Hotel Manchester Airport

★★★ 78% HOTEL

tel: 0161 498 0333 & 498 1390 **Outwood Ln M90 4HL**
email: man@bewleyshotels.com **web:** www.bewleyshotels.com
dir: At Manchester Airport. Follow signs to Manchester Airport Terminal 3. Hotel on left on Terminal 3 rdbt

Located adjacent to the airport this modern, stylish hotel provides an ideal stop-off for air travellers and business guests alike. All bedrooms are spacious and well equipped and include a wing of superior rooms. Spacious, open-plan day rooms are stylishly appointed and include a large bar and restaurant along with a good range of meeting and conference facilities.

Rooms 365 (110 fmly) (24 GF) ⚲ **Facilities** WiFi ⚲ Gym **Conf** Class 40 Board 30 Thtr 100 **Services** Lift **Parking** 300 **Notes** ⊗

Premier Inn Manchester Airport

BUDGET HOTEL

tel: 0871 527 8726 **Runger Ln, Wilmslow Rd M90 5DL**
web: www.premierinn.com
dir: M56 junct 6, follow Wilmslow & Hale signs. Merge onto M56 signed Warrington, Macclesfield & Hale. Left into Runger Ln (signed Freight Terminal)

High quality, budget accommodation ideal for both families and business travellers. Spacious, en suite bedrooms feature tea and coffee making facilities, and Freeview TV in most hotels. Internet access and WiFi are available for a small fee. The adjacent family restaurant features a wide and varied menu. See also the Hotel Groups pages.

Rooms 195

Premier Inn Manchester Airport (FT)

BUDGET HOTEL

tel: 0871 527 8730 **Runger Ln, Wilmslow Rd M90 5DL**
web: www.premierinn.com
dir: M56 junct 6, follow Airport signs. 2nd exit at rdbt. Hotel on left. Through Travelodge car park. Hotel on right

Rooms 166

Premier Inn Manchester (Handforth)

BUDGET HOTEL

tel: 0871 527 8732 **30 Wilmslow Rd SK9 3EW**
web: www.premierinn.com
dir: M56 junct 6, A538 towards Wilmslow. At main junct into town centre bear left. In 2m hotel at top of hill on right just after Wilmslow Garden Centre

Rooms 35

Premier Inn Manchester (Wilmslow)

BUDGET HOTEL

tel: 0871 527 8736 **Racecourse Rd, Wilmslow SK9 5LR**
web: www.premierinn.com
dir: M6 junct 19 to Knutsford, follow Wilmslow signs. Left at 1st & 2nd lights towards Wilmslow. Through Mobberley, left just before Bird in Hand pub. At T-junct, right. Hotel 150yds on right

Rooms 37

MARAZION	Map 2 SW53
Cornwall	

Mount Haven Hotel & Restaurant

★★★ 85% ❀❀ HOTEL

tel: 01736 710249 **Turnpike Rd TR17 0DQ**
email: reception@mounthaven.co.uk **web:** www.mounthaven.co.uk
dir: From A30 towards Penzance. At rdbt take exit for Helston onto A394. Next rdbt right into Marazion, hotel on left

This hotel enjoys spectacular views across the sea towards St Michaels Mount. All rooms have spacious balconies from where the views can be enjoyed - sunrises and sunsets can be spectacular. Bedrooms are contemporarily styled and have

M

comfortable beds and exotic fabrics. Dining is a highlight with the freshest local seafood and fish used to create interesting menus. A range of holistic therapies is available, and the attentive and friendly service helps make a relaxing and enchanting environment throughout.

Rooms 18 (1 fmly) (6 GF) ⌕ **S** £90-£120; **D** £120-£200 (incl. bkfst)* **Facilities** FTV WiFi Aromatherapy Reflexology Massage Reiki Hot rocks Beauty treatment room Xmas New Year **Parking** 30 **Notes** ⊗

MARGATE
Kent   Map 7 TR37

Premier Inn Margate

BUDGET HOTEL

tel: 0871 527 8762 **Station Green, Station Rd CT9 5AF**
web: www.premierinn.com
dir: M2, A299, A28 to Margate seafront. Hotel adjacent to Margate station

High quality, budget accommodation ideal for both families and business travellers. Spacious, en suite bedrooms feature tea and coffee making facilities, and Freeview TV in most hotels. Internet access and WiFi are available for a small fee. The adjacent family restaurant features a wide and varied menu. See also the Hotel Groups pages.

Rooms 44

MARKET DRAYTON
Shropshire   Map 15 SJ63

Goldstone Hall

★★★ 88% HOTEL

tel: 01630 661202 **Goldstone TF9 2NA**
email: enquiries@goldstonehall.com **web:** www.goldstonehall.com
dir: 4m S of Market Drayton, 4m N of Newport. Hotel signed from A529 & A41

Situated in extensive grounds, this sympathetically refurbished period property is a family-run hotel. It provides traditionally furnished, well-equipped accommodation with outstanding en suite bathrooms and lots of thoughtful extras. Public rooms are extensive and include a choice of lounges, a snooker room and a conservatory. The kitchen has a well deserved reputation for good food that utilises home-grown produce, and a warm welcome is assured.

Rooms 12 (2 GF) ⌕ **S** £90-£110; **D** £140-£170 (incl. bkfst)* **Facilities** STV FTV WiFi ⤷ ⤹ Snooker table New Year **Conf** Class 30 Board 30 Thtr 50 Del from £130 **Parking** 60 **Notes** LB ⊗ Civ Wed 100

Ternhill Farm House & The Cottage Restaurant

 RESTAURANT WITH ROOMS

tel: 01630 638984 ▦ 01630 638752 **Ternhill TF9 3PX**
email: info@ternhillfarm.co.uk **web:** www.ternhillfarm.co.uk
dir: On junct A53 & A41, archway off A53 to back of property

This elegant Grade II listed, Georgian farmhouse stands in a large pleasant garden offers quality accommodation. There is a choice of comfortable lounges, and The Cottage Restaurant features imaginative dishes using local produce. Dinner is served Tuesday to Saturday. Secure parking is an additional benefit.

Rooms 7

MARKET HARBOROUGH
Leicestershire   Map 11 SP78

BEST WESTERN Three Swans Hotel

★★★ 79% HOTEL

tel: 01858 466644 **21 High St LE16 7NJ**
email: threeswans@bulldogmail.co.uk **web:** www.threeswans.co.uk
dir: M1 junct 20, A304 to Market Harborough. Through town centre on A6 from Leicester, hotel on right

Public areas in this former coaching inn include an elegant fine dining restaurant and cocktail bar, a smart foyer lounge and popular public bar areas. Bedroom styles and sizes vary, but are very well appointed and equipped. Those in the wing are particularly impressive, offering high quality and spacious accommodation.

Rooms 61 (48 annexe) (10 fmly) (20 GF) ⌕ **S** £45-£100; **D** £55-£150 **Facilities** STV FTV WiFi ⤷ Xmas New Year **Conf** Class 90 Board 50 Thtr 250 Del from £99 to £160 **Services** Lift **Parking** 100 **Notes** LB Civ Wed 140

Premier Inn Market Harborough

BUDGET HOTEL

tel: 0871 527 8764 **Melton Rd, East Langton LE16 7TG**
web: www.premierinn.com
dir: On A6, N of Market Harborough. Hotel on rdbt junct of A6 & B6047

High quality, budget accommodation ideal for both families and business travellers. Spacious, en suite bedrooms feature tea and coffee making facilities, and Freeview TV in most hotels. Internet access and WiFi are available for a small fee. The adjacent family restaurant features a wide and varied menu. See also the Hotel Groups pages.

Rooms 40

MARKET RASEN
Lincolnshire   Map 17 TF18

The Advocate Arms

 RESTAURANT WITH ROOMS

tel: 01673 842364 **2 Queen St LN8 3EH**
email: info@advocatearms.co.uk **web:** www.advocatearms.co.uk
dir: In town centre

Appointed to a high standard, this 18th-century property is located in the heart of Market Rasen and combines historic character with contemporary design. The operation centres around the stylish restaurant where service is friendly yet professional and the food is a highlight. The attractive bedrooms are very well equipped and feature luxury bathrooms.

Rooms 10 (2 fmly)

M

MARKFIELD
Leicestershire — Map 11 SK40

Field Head Hotel

★★★ 67% HOTEL

tel: 01530 245454 **Markfield Ln LE67 9PS**
email: 9160@greeneking.co.uk **web:** www.oldenglish.co.uk
dir: M1 junct 22, towards Leicester. At rdbt turn left, then right

This conveniently situated hotel dates back to the 17th century when it was a farmhouse; it has been considerably extended over the years. Within the public areas, the bar and lounge are the focal point for residents and non-residents alike, while meals can be taken either in the bar or the dining room. Bedrooms are modern and well furnished, and offer good all-round comforts and facilities. Four large feature bedrooms are available.

Rooms 28 (1 fmly) (13 GF) **Facilities** FTV WiFi ⬧ 🎵 Xmas New Year **Conf** Class 30 Board 36 Thtr 60 **Parking** 65 **Notes** Civ Wed 54

MARLBOROUGH
Wiltshire — Map 5 SU16

The Castle & Ball

★★★ 73% HOTEL

tel: 01672 515201 **High St SN8 1LZ**
email: castleandballmarlboroughreservations@greeneking.co.uk
web: www.oldenglish.co.uk
dir: From either A4 or A346 into town centre

This traditional coaching inn in the town centre offers contemporary and very well equipped bedrooms. Open-plan public areas include a comfortable bar/lounge area and a smartly appointed restaurant, which serves food all day. Meeting rooms are also available.

Rooms 37 (3 annexe) (5 fmly) (3 GF) 🐾 **Facilities** WiFi Xmas New Year **Parking** 48

MARLOW
Buckinghamshire — Map 5 SU88

Macdonald Compleat Angler

★★★★ ❀❀ HOTEL

tel: 01628 484444 **Marlow Bridge SL7 1RG**
email: compleatangler@macdonald-hotels.co.uk
web: www.macdonaldhotels.co.uk/compleatangler
dir: M4 junct 8/9 or M40 junct 4, A404(M) to rdbt, Bisham exit, 1m to Marlow Bridge, hotel on right

This well-established hotel enjoys an idyllic location overlooking the River Thames and the delightful Marlow weir. The bedrooms, which differ in size and style, are all individually decorated and are equipped with flat-screen satellite TVs, high-speed internet and air-conditioning. Some rooms have balconies with views of the weir and some have four-posters. The Riverside serves British dishes and has gained two AA rosettes. In summer guests can use two boats that the hotel has moored on the river and fishing is, of course, a popular activity - a ghillie can accompany guests if arranged in advance. Staff throughout are keen to please and nothing is too much trouble.

Rooms 64 (6 fmly) (6 GF) **S** £130-£290; **D** £140-£310 (incl. bkfst)* **Facilities** FTV WiFi ⬧ HL Fly & coarse fishing River trips (Apr-Sep) Xmas New Year **Conf** Class 65 Board 36 Thtr 150 Del from £220 to £295* **Services** Lift **Parking** 100 **Notes** LB Civ Wed 120

M

Danesfield House Hotel & Spa

★★★★ 86% HOTEL

tel: 01628 891010 **Henley Rd SL7 2EY**
email: reservations@danesfieldhouse.co.uk **web:** www.danesfieldhouse.co.uk
dir: 2m from Marlow on A4155 towards Henley

Set in 65 acres of elevated grounds just 45 minutes from central London and 30 minutes from Heathrow, this hotel enjoys spectacular views across the River Thames. Impressive public rooms include the cathedral-like Great Hall, an impressive spa, and The Orangery for informal dining. The beautiful Oak Room restaurant is an ideal setting to enjoy superb, imaginative fine dining. Some bedrooms have balconies and stunning views. Nothing is too much trouble for the team of committed staff.

Rooms 78 (3 fmly) (27 GF) ⌇ **S** £139-£164; **D** £179-£374 (incl. bkfst)*
Facilities Spa STV WiFi ⓢ ⓢ Putt green ⌇ Gym Jogging trail Steam room Hydrotherapy room Sauna Xmas New Year **Conf** Class 60 Board 50 Thtr 100 Del from £255 to £370* **Services** Lift **Parking** 100 **Notes** ⊗ Civ Wed 100

See advert on opposite page

Crowne Plaza Marlow

★★★★ 81% HOTEL

tel: 01628 496800 **Field House Ln SL7 1GJ**
email: enquiries@cpmarlow.co.uk **web:** www.cpmarlow.co.uk
dir: A404 exit to Marlow, left at mini rdbt, left into Field House Lane

This hotel is in the Thames Valley not far from Windsor, Henley-on-Thames and the motorway. The public areas are air conditioned and include the Agua Café and Bar and Glaze Restaurant. Leisure facilities include an up-to-the-minute gym and large pool. The bedrooms, including six contemporary suites, enjoy plenty of natural light and have excellent workstations; the Club Rooms have European and US power points

Rooms 168 (47 fmly) (56 GF) (11 smoking) ⌇ **Facilities** Spa STV FTV WiFi HL ⓢ ⌇ Gym Sauna Steam room Dance studio Xmas New Year **Conf** Class 180 Board 30 Thtr 450 **Services** Lift Air con **Parking** 300 **Notes** ⊗ Civ Wed 300

Premier Inn Marlow

BUDGET HOTEL

tel: 0871 527 8766 **The Causeway SL7 2AA**
web: www.premierinn.com
dir: M40 junct 4, A404 signed Marlow/Maidenhead. Left, follow A4155 signs to Marlow. At 3rd rdbt 1st exit into High St, signed Bisham. Straight on at mini rdbt. Hotel on left

High quality, budget accommodation ideal for both families and business travellers. Spacious, en suite bedrooms feature tea and coffee making facilities, and Freeview TV in most hotels. Internet access and WiFi are available for a small fee. The adjacent family restaurant features a wide and varied menu. See also the Hotel Groups pages.

Rooms 17

MARSTON	Map 11 SK84
Lincolnshire	

The Olde Barn Hotel

★★★ 70% HOTEL

tel: 01400 250909 **Toll Bar Rd NG32 2HT**
email: reservations@theoldebarnhotel.co.uk **web:** www.theoldebarnhotel.co.uk
dir: From A1 N: left to Marston adjacent to petrol station. From A1 S: 1st right after Allington/Belton exit

Located in the countryside one mile from the A1, this sympathetically renovated and extended former period barn provides a range of thoughtfully furnished bedrooms, ideal for both business and leisure customers. Imaginative food is offered in the attractive beamed restaurant, and extensive leisure facilities include a swimming pool, sauna, steam room and a well-equipped gym.

Rooms 101 (11 fmly) (51 GF) ⌇ **Facilities** Spa STV FTV WiFi ⓢ ⓢ Gym Xmas New Year **Conf** Class 180 Board 100 Thtr 300 Del from £95 to £150* **Services** Lift **Parking** 280 **Notes** Civ Wed 250

M

MASHAM	Map 19 SE28
North Yorkshire	

INSPECTORS' CHOICE

Swinton Park

★★★★ ◉◉◉ HOTEL

tel: 01765 680900 **HG4 4JH**
email: reservations@swintonpark.com **web:** www.swintonpark.com
dir: Please telephone for detailed directions

Although extended during the Victorian and Edwardian eras, the original part of this welcoming castle dates from the 17th century. Bedrooms are luxuriously furnished and come with a host of thoughtful extras. Samuel's restaurant (built by the current owner's great-great-great grandfather) is very elegant and serves imaginative dishes using local produce. The majority of the food is sourced from the 20,000-acre Swinton Estate, as the hotel, winner of several green awards, is committed to keeping the 'food miles' to a minimum. The gardens, including a four-acre walled garden, have been gradually restored. The Deerhouse is the venue for the hotel's alfresco food festivals, summer BBQs and weddings.

Rooms 31 (6 fmly) ⬥ **D** £195–£460 (incl. bkfst)* **Facilities** Spa FTV WiFi ⬥ ⬥ 9 Putt green Fishing ⬥ Gym Shooting Falconry Pony trekking Cookery school Off-road driving Xmas New Year **Conf** Class 60 Board 40 Thtr 110 **Services** Lift **Parking** 50 **Notes** LB Civ Wed 120

MATFEN	Map 21 NZ07
Northumberland	

Matfen Hall

★★★★ 81% ◉◉ HOTEL

tel: 01661 886500 & 855708 **NE20 0RH**
email: info@matfenhall.com **web:** www.matfenhall.com
dir: A69 onto B6318. Hotel just before village

Matfen Hall is a luxurious and elegant stately home set in 300 acres of beautiful Northumbrian countryside. The hotel offers individually decorated bedrooms in both traditional and contemporary styles. The estate boasts impressive public rooms including the Library Restaurant, the Print Room, and the Conservatory Bar, all surrounding the Great Hall, which is perfect for weddings and private dining. The golf estate includes a 27-hole course, a 3 par course and a driving range. Relax in the stylish spa, leisure and conference facilities.

Rooms 53 (11 fmly) ⬥ **Facilities** Spa STV FTV WiFi ⬥ HL ⬥ supervised ⬥ 27 Putt green Gym Sauna Steam room Salt grotto Ice fountain Aerobics Driving range Golf academy Xmas New Year **Conf** Class 46 Board 40 Thtr 120 **Services** Lift **Parking** 150 **Notes** Civ Wed 120

MAWGAN PORTH	Map 2 SW86
Cornwall	

The Scarlet Hotel

★★★★ 82% ◉◉ HOTEL

tel: 01637 861800 **Tredragon Rd TR8 4DQ**
email: stay@scarlethotel.co.uk **web:** www.scarlethotel.co.uk
dir: A39, A30 towards Truro. At Trekenning rdbt take A3059, follow Newquay Airport signs. Right after garage signed St Mawgan & Airport. Right after airport, at T-junct signed Padstow (B3276). At Mawgan Porth left. Hotel 250yds

Built as an eco hotel, this strikingly modern property has a stunning cliff-top location with magnificent views and offers something a little different. The very stylish and well-equipped bedrooms are categorised in five types: Just Right, Generous, Unique, Spacious and Indulgent. The Ayurvedic spa is exceptional and encompasses the rejuvenation of the whole body and mind; relaxation is the key here. Cuisine is equally important, and in tune with the hotel's environment policies, daily-changing menus feature fresh, seasonal and local produce. The team of 'hosts' offer a high level of hospitality and service.

Rooms 37 (5 GF) ⬥ **S** £175–£445; **D** £195–£465 (incl. bkfst)* **Facilities** Spa FTV WiFi ⬥ ⬥ ⬥ Yoga ♫ Xmas New Year **Conf** Board 16 **Services** Lift **Parking** 37 **Notes** No children 16yrs Closed 2-6 Feb Civ Wed 74

Bedruthan Hotel and Spa

★★★★ 78% HOTEL

tel: 01637 861200 & 860860 **TR8 4BU**
email: stay@bedruthan.com **web:** www.bedruthan.com
dir: From A39 or A30 follow signs to Newquay Airport. Pass airport, right at T-junct to Mawgan Porth. Hotel at top of hill on left

With stunning views over Mawgan Porth Bay from the public rooms and the majority of the bedrooms, this is a child-friendly hotel. Children's clubs for various ages are provided in addition to children's dining areas and appropriate meals and times. A homage to architecture of the 1970s, with a comfortable, contemporary feel, this hotel also has conference facilities. A choice of dining options is available with the relaxed vibe of the Wild Café, or alternatively The Herring which offers a creative and innovative menu, utilising excellent Cornish produce.

Rooms 101 (60 fmly) (1 GF) ⚓ **S** £65-£140; **D** £105-£295 (incl. bkfst)*
Facilities Spa FTV WiFi ⚗ 🎾 ⚡ ♨ Gym Jungle tumble ball pool Sauna Steam room Hydro pool Pool table Snooker room ♫ New Year Child facilities **Conf** Class 60 Board 40 Thtr 180 **Services** Lift **Parking** 100 **Notes** Closed 21-27 Dec Civ Wed 150

MAWNAN SMITH	Map 2 SW72
Cornwall	

Budock Vean - The Hotel on the River

★★★★ 79% ◉ COUNTRY HOUSE HOTEL

tel: 01326 252100 & 0800 833927 **TR11 5LG**
email: relax@budockvean.co.uk **web:** www.budockvean.co.uk
dir: From A39 follow tourist signs to Trebah Gardens. 0.5m to hotel

Set in 65 acres of attractive, well-tended grounds, this peaceful hotel offers an impressive range of facilities. It is convenient for visiting the Helford River estuary and many local gardens, or simply as a tranquil venue for a leisure break. The bedrooms are spacious and come in a choice of styles; some overlook the grounds and the golf course.

Rooms 57 (2 fmly) ⚓ **S** £88-£146; **D** £176-£292 (incl. bkfst & dinner)*
Facilities Spa FTV WiFi ⚗ 🎾 ♨ 9 ♨ Putt green ⚓ Private river boat & foreshore ♫ Xmas New Year **Conf** Class 40 Board 30 Thtr 60 Del from £124.50 to £182.50*
Services Lift **Parking** 100 **Notes** Closed 3 wks Jan Civ Wed 80

Meudon Hotel

★★★ 83% COUNTRY HOUSE HOTEL

tel: 01326 250541 **TR11 5HT**
email: wecare@meudon.co.uk **web:** www.meudon.co.uk
dir: From Truro A39 towards Falmouth at Hillhead (Anchor & Cannons) rdbt, follow signs to Mabe then Mawnan Smith, left at Red Lion, hotel on right

This charming late Victorian mansion is a relaxing place to stay, with friendly hospitality and attentive service. It sits in impressive 9-acre gardens that lead down to a private beach. The spacious and comfortable bedrooms are situated in a more modern building. The cuisine features the best of local Cornish produce and is served in the conservatory restaurant.

Rooms 29 (2 fmly) (15 GF) ⚓ **S** £104-£131; **D** £160-£304 (incl. bkfst & dinner)*
Facilities FTV WiFi ⚗ Fishing Private beach Hair salon Yacht for skippered charter Xmas **Conf** Class 30 Board 30 Thtr 30 Del from £140 to £170* **Services** Lift **Parking** 50 **Notes** LB Closed 28 Dec-Jan

Trelawne Hotel

★★★ 79% HOTEL

tel: 01326 250226 **TR11 5HS**
email: info@trelawnehotel.co.uk **web:** www.trelawnehotel.co.uk
dir: A39 to Falmouth, right at Hillhead rdbt signed Maenporth. Past beach, up hill, hotel on left

This hotel is surrounded by attractive lawns and gardens, and enjoys superb coastal views. An informal atmosphere prevails, and many guests return year after year. Bedrooms, many with sea views, are of varying sizes, but all are well equipped. Dinner features quality local produce used in imaginative dishes.

Rooms 14 (2 fmly) (4 GF) ⚓ **Facilities** FTV WiFi Xmas **Parking** 20

MELBOURN	Map 12 TL34
Cambridgeshire	

The Sheene Mill

RESTAURANT WITH ROOMS

tel: 01763 261393 **39 Station Rd SG8 6DX**
email: enquiries@thesheenemill.com **web:** www.thesheenemill.com
dir: M11 junct 10 onto A505 towards Royston. Right to Melbourn, pass church on right, on left before old bridge

This 16th-century watermill is ideally situated just off the A10, a short drive from both Cambridge and Royston. The bedrooms are individually decorated and well equipped; some rooms overlook the mill pond and terrace. Public rooms include a comfortable lounge, a bar, conservatory and a delightful restaurant overlooking the pond.

Rooms 9 (3 fmly)

MELKSHAM	Map 4 ST96
Wiltshire	

Shaw Country Hotel

★★ 76% SMALL HOTEL

tel: 01225 702836 & 790321 **Bath Rd, Shaw SN12 8EF**
email: info@shawcountryhotel.com **web:** www.shawcountryhotel.com
dir: 1m from Melksham, 9m from Bath on A365

Located within easy reach of both Bath and the M4, this relaxed and friendly hotel sits in its own gardens and includes a patio area ideal for enjoying a drink during the summer months. The house boasts very well-appointed bedrooms, a comfortable lounge and bar, and the Mulberry Restaurant, where a wide selection of innovative dishes make up both carte and set menus. A spacious function room is a useful addition.

Rooms 13 (2 fmly) ⚓ **S** £63-£88; **D** £88-£108 (incl. bkfst) **Facilities** FTV WiFi **Conf** Class 40 Board 20 Thtr 60 **Parking** 30 **Notes** RS 26-27 Dec & 1 Jan Civ Wed 90

M

MELTON MOWBRAY   Map 11 SK71
Leicestershire

Stapleford Park

★★★★ ◎◎ COUNTRY HOUSE HOTEL

tel: 01572 787000 **Stapleford LE14 2EF**
email: reservations@stapleford.co.uk **web:** www.staplefordpark.com
dir: 1m SW of B676, 4m E of Melton Mowbray & 9m W of Colsterworth

This stunning mansion, dating back to the 14th century, sits in over 500 acres of beautiful grounds. Spacious, sumptuous public rooms include a choice of lounges and an elegant restaurant. An additional brasserie-style restaurant is located in the golf complex. The hotel also boasts a spa with health and beauty treatments and gym, plus horse riding and many other country pursuits. Bedrooms are individually styled and furnished to a high standard. Attentive service is delivered with a relaxed yet professional style. Dinner, in the impressive dining room, is a highlight of any stay.

Rooms 55 (7 annexe) (10 fmly) 🐾 **Facilities** Spa STV FTV WiFi ⓘ ⓧ ⌀ 18 ⚑ Putt green Fishing ⚓ Gym Archery Croquet Falconry Horse riding Petanque Shooting Billiards ♫ Xmas New Year **Conf** Class 140 Board 80 Thtr 200 **Services** Lift **Parking** 120 **Notes** Civ Wed 150

Sysonby Knoll Hotel

★★★ 79% HOTEL

tel: 01664 563563 **Asfordby Rd LE13 0HP**
email: reception@sysonby.com **web:** www.sysonby.com
dir: 0.5m from town centre on A6006

This well established hotel sits on the edge of Melton Mowbray and is set in attractive gardens with ample parking. The hotel has been run by the same family since 1965 and continues to provide friendly, attentive service. The lounges are comfortable and WiFi is available throughout. Freshly prepared dishes are served in the restaurant which overlooks the attractive gardens. The bedrooms are spacious and of a high quality and include four-poster rooms in the main building and executive rooms in an annexe.

Rooms 30 (7 annexe) (1 fmly) (7 GF) 🐾 **Facilities** FTV WiFi ⓘ Fishing ⚓ **Conf** Class 25 Board 34 Thtr 50 **Parking** 48 **Notes** Closed 25 Dec-1 Jan

Quorn Lodge Hotel

★★★ 71% HOTEL

tel: 01664 566660 **46 Asfordby Rd LE13 0HR**
email: quornlodge@aol.com **web:** www.quornlodge.co.uk
dir: From town centre take A6006. Hotel 300yds from junct of A606/A607 on right

Centrally located, this smart privately owned and managed hotel offers a comfortable and welcoming atmosphere. Bedrooms are individually decorated and thoughtfully designed. The public rooms consist of a bright restaurant overlooking the garden, a cosy lounge bar and a modern function suite. High standards are maintained throughout and parking is a bonus.

Rooms 21 (4 fmly) (3 GF) 🐾 **S** £59-£69; **D** £79-£89 (incl. bkfst)* **Facilities** STV FTV WiFi ⓘ Gym **Conf** Class 70 Board 80 Thtr 100 Del from £125 to £145* **Parking** 38 **Notes** LB ⓧ Civ Wed 80

MEMBURY MOTORWAY SERVICE AREA (M4)   Map 5 SU37
Berkshire

Days Inn Membury - M4

BUDGET HOTEL

tel: 01488 72336 **Membury Service Area RG17 7TZ**
email: membury.hotel@welcomebreak.co.uk **web:** www.welcomebreak.co.uk
dir: M4 between junct 14 & 15

This modern building offers accommodation in smart, spacious and well-equipped bedrooms, suitable for families and business travellers, and all with en suite bathrooms. Continental breakfast is available and other refreshments may be taken at the nearby family restaurant. See also the Hotel Groups pages.

Rooms 38 (32 fmly) (17 GF) (5 smoking) **Conf** Board 10

M

MERIDEN
West Midlands

Map 10 SP28

Forest of Arden, A Marriott Hotel & Country Club

★★★★ 82% @ HOTEL

tel: 01676 522335 **Maxstoke Ln CV7 7HR**
web: www.marriottforestofarden.co.uk
dir: M42 junct 6 onto A45 towards Coventry, over Stonebridge flyover. After 0.75m left into Shepherds Ln. Left at T-junct. Hotel 1.5m on left

The ancient oaks, rolling hills and natural lakes of the 10,000 acre Forest of Arden estate provide an idyllic backdrop for this modern hotel and country club. The hotel boasts an excellent range of leisure facilities and is regarded as one of the finest golfing destinations in the UK. Bedrooms provide every modern convenience and a full range of facilities.

Rooms 214 (65 GF) ↟ **Facilities** Spa WiFi ⓣ ⚲ 18 ⛳ Putt green Fishing ⬥ Gym Floodlit golf academy New Year **Conf** Class 180 Board 40 Thtr 300 **Services** Lift **Parking** 300 **Notes** ⊗ Civ Wed 250

BEST WESTERN PLUS Manor NEC Birmingham

★★★★ 76% @@ HOTEL

tel: 01676 522735 **Main Rd CV7 7NH**
email: reservations@manorhotelmeriden.co.uk **web:** www.manorhotelmeriden.co.uk
dir: M42 junct 6, A45 towards Coventry then A452 signed Leamington. At rdbt take B4102 signed Meriden, hotel on left

This sympathetically extended Georgian manor in the heart of a sleepy village is just a few minutes away from the M6, M42 and National Exhibition Centre. The Regency Restaurant offers modern dishes, while Houston's serves lighter meals and snacks. The bedrooms are smart and well equipped.

Rooms 112 (15 fmly) (20 GF) **Facilities** FTV WiFi ⌖ Xmas New Year **Conf** Class 150 Board 60 Thtr 250 **Services** Lift **Parking** 190 **Notes** Civ Wed 200

MEVAGISSEY
Cornwall

Map 2 SX04

Tremarne Hotel

★★★ 84% HOTEL

tel: 01726 842213 **Polkirt PL26 6UY**
email: info@tremarne-hotel.co.uk **web:** www.tremarne-hotel.co.uk
dir: From A390 at St Austell take B3273 to Mevagissey. Follow Portmellon signs through Mevagissey. At top of Polkirt Hill 1st right into Higherwell Park. Hotel drive facing

A very popular hotel, set in landscaped gardens with a swimming pool, that has superb views towards Mevagissey. The friendliness of Michael, Fitz and the team cannot be bettered. The hotel offers comfortable, individually styled bedrooms that either have views of the sea or the countryside. Guests can expect good service and freshly-cooked food on a daily-changing menu.

Rooms 13 (2 fmly) ↟ **S** £83-£98; **D** £90-£166 (incl. bkfst)* **Facilities** FTV WiFi ⬥ New Year **Parking** 14 **Notes** LB ⊗ No children 6yrs Closed Jan

Trevalsa Court Hotel

★★★ 80% @ HOTEL

tel: 01726 842468 **School Hill, Polstreath PL26 6TH**
email: stay@trevalsa-hotel.co.uk **web:** www.trevalsa-hotel.co.uk
dir: From St Austell take B3273 to Mevagissey. Pass sign to Pentewan. At top of hill left at x-rds. Hotel signed

Very well located above the town of Mevagissey, with easy access to nearby attractions, this establishment is an Arts & Crafts style property appointed to a high standard throughout with lots of original features. Bedrooms, many with sea views, are comfortable and well presented; there is also a stylish guests' sitting room with views across the bay.

Rooms 14 (1 annexe) (1 fmly) (4 GF) ↟ **Facilities** FTV WiFi **Parking** 20 **Notes** Closed Dec & Jan

---

MEXBOROUGH
South Yorkshire

Map 16 SE40

BEST WESTERN Pastures Hotel

★★★ 82% HOTEL

tel: 01709 577707 **Pastures Rd S64 0JJ**
email: info@pastureshotel.co.uk **web:** www.pastureshotel.co.uk
dir: 0.5m from town centre on A6023, left by CLS Mot, signed Denaby Ings & Cadeby. Hotel on right

This private hotel is in a rural setting beside a working canal with view of Conisbro Castle in the distance, and is convenient for Doncaster or the Dearne Valley with its nature reserves and leisure centre. Guests can dine in the Pastures Lodge pub and family restaurant situated opposite the hotel, or in Reeds fine dining restaurant in the hotel (open Tuesday-Saturday). Bedrooms, in a modern, purpose-built block, are quiet, comfortable and equipped with many modern facilities.

Rooms 60 (5 fmly) (28 GF) ↟ **S** fr £60; **D** fr £70 (incl. bkfst)* **Facilities** STV WiFi ⬥ Xmas New Year **Conf** Class 170 Board 100 Thtr 250 Del from £118* **Services** Lift **Parking** 179 **Notes** ⊗ Civ Wed 200

MICHAELWOOD MOTORWAY SERVICE AREA (M5)
Gloucestershire

Map 4 ST79

Days Inn Michaelwood - M5

BUDGET HOTEL

tel: 01454 261513 **Michaelwood Service Area, Lower Wick GL11 6DD**
email: michaelwood.hotel@welcomebreak.co.uk **web:** www.welcomebreak.co.uk
dir: M5 N'bound between junct 13 & 14

This modern building offers accommodation in smart, spacious and well-equipped bedrooms, suitable for families and business travellers, and all with en suite bathrooms. Continental breakfast is available and other refreshments may be taken at the nearby family restaurant. See also the Hotel Groups pages.

Rooms 38 (15 fmly) (7 smoking) **Conf** Board 10

M

M

MIDDLESBROUGH
North Yorkshire
Map 19 NZ41

Premier Inn Middlesbrough Central South

BUDGET HOTEL

tel: 0871 527 8770 **Marton Way TS4 3BS**
web: www.premierinn.com
dir: Off A172 opposite South Cleveland Hospital complex

High quality, budget accommodation ideal for both families and business travellers. Spacious, en suite bedrooms feature tea and coffee making facilities, and Freeview TV in most hotels. Internet access and WiFi are available for a small fee. The adjacent family restaurant features a wide and varied menu. See also the Hotel Groups pages.

Rooms 74

MIDDLETON-IN-TEESDALE
County Durham
Map 18 NY92

The Teesdale Hotel

★★ 71% HOTEL

tel: 01833 640264 **Market Place DL12 0QG**
email: enquiries@teesdalehotel.co.uk **web:** www.teesdalehotel.co.uk
dir: From Barnard Castle take B6278, follow signs for Middleton-in-Teesdale & Highforce. Hotel in town centre

Located in the heart of this popular village, The Teesdale Hotel is a family-run establishment that offers a relaxed and friendly atmosphere. Bedrooms and bathrooms are well equipped and offer a good standard of quality and comfort. Public areas include a residents' lounge on the first floor, a spacious restaurant and a lounge bar which is popular with locals.

Rooms 14 (1 fmly)  **Facilities** WiFi **Conf** Class 20 Board 20 Thtr 40 **Parking** 20

MIDDLETON STONEY
Oxfordshire
Map 11 SP52

BEST WESTERN The Jersey Arms

★★ 76% HOTEL

tel: 01869 343234 & 343270 **OX25 4AD**
email: jerseyarms@bestwestern.co.uk **web:** www.jerseyarms.co.uk
dir: 3m from A34, on B430, 10m N of Oxford, between junct 9 & 10 of M40

With a history dating back to the 13th century, the Jersey Arms combines old-fashioned charm with contemporary style and elegance. The individually designed bedrooms are well equipped and comfortable. The lounge has an open fire, and the smart and spacious restaurant provides a calm atmosphere in which to enjoy the popular cuisine.

Rooms 20 (14 annexe) (3 fmly) (9 GF) **S** £75; **D** £95-£135 (incl. bkfst)* **Facilities** FTV WiFi ᐃ Xmas New Year **Conf** Class 20 Board 20 Thtr 20 Del from £125 to £150* **Parking** 55 **Notes** LB ⊗

MIDSOMER NORTON
Somerset
Map 4 ST65

BEST WESTERN PLUS Centurion Hotel

★★★★ 78% ⊛ HOTEL

tel: 01761 417711 & 412214 **Charlton Ln BA3 4BD**
email: enquiries@centurionhotel.co.uk **web:** www.centurionhotel.co.uk
dir: Just off A367, 10m S of Bath. Once in Radstock follow signs at mini rdbt for Shepton Mallet/Wells, follow for 2m, left at small rdbt

Centurion Hotel is located just nine miles from Bath in a peaceful area with surrounding grounds and a nine hole golf course. Bedrooms and bathrooms have been recently completely refurbished and offer good levels of quality and comfort. In addition to the relaxing public areas a range of leisure facilities are available, including gym, swimming pool and the new Green Apple spa. Dinner may be taken in the more relaxed Jays bar or in the stylish Cubros Restaurant with the option of dining in the relaxing conservatory area.

Rooms 45 (2 fmly) (18 GF) **S** £87.50-£120; **D** £100-£155 (incl. bkfst)* **Facilities** Spa FTV WiFi ᐃ ⊗ ♿ 9 Putt green Gym Spa pool Sauna Steam room New Year **Conf** Class 50 Board 50 Thtr 180 **Parking** 100 **Notes** LB ⊗ Closed 24-26 Dec Civ Wed 110

MILTON COMMON
Oxfordshire
Map 5 SP60

The Oxfordshire

★★★★ 81% ⊛ HOTEL

tel: 01844 278300 **Rycote Ln OX9 2PU**
email: gm@theoxfordshire.com **web:** www.theoxfordshire.com
dir: M40 junct 7 N'bound (junct 8 S'bound), A329 towards Thame

Located within easy reach of the M40, this hotel is at the championship golf course, The Oxfordshire, in the heart of the beautiful Chilterns. The accommodation offers impressive levels of comfort and quality, and all rooms are air-conditioned and have access onto a balcony. The Tempus Spa includes a 15-metre pool, modern gym and three treatment rooms. This resort makes an ideal location for a relaxing break, especially for golf enthusiasts.

Rooms 50 (18 GF) **Facilities** Spa FTV WiFi ᐃ ⊗ ♿ 18 Putt green Gym Sauna Steam room New Year **Conf** Class 66 Board 54 Thtr 180 **Services** Lift Air con **Parking** 150 **Notes** ⊗ Civ Wed

The Oxford Belfry

★★★★ 79% HOTEL

tel: 01844 279381 **OX9 2JW**
email: oxfordbelfry@qhotels.co.uk **web:** www.qhotels.co.uk
dir: M40 junct 7 onto A329 to Thame. Left onto A40, hotel 300yds on right

This modern hotel has a relatively rural location and enjoys lovely views of the countryside to the rear. The hotel is built around two very attractive courtyards and has a number of lounges and conference rooms, as well as indoor leisure facilities and outdoor tennis courts. Bedrooms are large and feature a range of extras. QHotels is the AA Hotel Group of the Year 2014-15.

Rooms 154 (20 fmly) (66 GF) **S** £81-£157; **D** £105-£169 (incl. bkfst)* **Facilities** Spa FTV WiFi ᐃ HL ⊗ ♿ ⛲ Gym Steam room Sauna Aerobics studio Xmas New Year **Conf** Class 180 Board 100 Thtr 450 Del from £130 to £160 **Services** Lift **Parking** 350 **Notes** LB Civ Wed 300

MILTON KEYNES
Buckinghamshire

Map 11 SP83

See also **Aspley Guise**

Mercure Milton Keynes Parkside Hotel

★★★★ 74% ◉ HOTEL

tel: 01908 661919 **Newport Rd, Woughton on the Green MK6 3LR**
email: H6627-gm@accor.com **web:** www.mercure.com
dir: M1 junct 14, A509 towards Milton Keynes. 2nd exit on H6 follow signs to Woughton on the Green

Situated in five acres of landscaped grounds in a peaceful village setting, this hotel is only five minutes' drive from the hustle and bustle of the town centre. Bedrooms are divided between executive rooms in the main house and standard rooms in the adjacent coach house. Public rooms include a range of meeting rooms, and Strollers bar. The Lanes Restaurant provides a relaxing venue where eclectic modern dishes are offered.

Rooms 49 (1 fmly) (19 GF) ⚘ **Facilities** STV WiFi HL Free entry to health & fitness club (approx 2m) Xmas New Year **Conf** Class 60 Board 50 Thtr 150 **Parking** 75 **Notes** Civ Wed 120

Holiday Inn Milton Keynes

★★★★ 74% HOTEL

tel: 01908 698541 & 0871 942 9057 **500 Saxon Gate West MK9 2HQ**
email: reservations-miltonkeynes@ihg.com **web:** www.himiltonkeyneshotel.com
dir: M1 junct 14. Straight on at 7 rdbts. At 8th (Saxon South) turn right. Hotel after lights on left

Ideally located to explore central England, with both Oxford and Cambridge within an hour's drive, and central London just 40 minutes away by train. The hotel is a spacious, purpose-built, city-centre property offering a range of well-appointed bedrooms, conference rooms and a fully-equipped health club. The Junction restaurant offers a contemporary dining experience in a relaxing environment.

Rooms 166 (17 fmly) **S** £30–£250; **D** £30–£250* **Facilities** STV WiFi HL 🕓 supervised Gym Sauna Beauty room Xmas New Year **Conf** Class 48 Board 48 Thtr 100 Del from £125 to £155* **Services** Lift Air con **Parking** 85 **Notes** LB ⊗ Civ Wed 70

Novotel Milton Keynes

★★★ 75% HOTEL

tel: 01908 322212 **Saxon St, Layburn Court, Heelands MK13 7RA**
email: H3272@accor.com **web:** www.novotel.com
dir: M1 junct 14, follow Childsway signs towards city centre. Right into Saxon Way, straight across all rdbts, hotel on left

Contemporary in style, this purpose-built hotel is situated on the outskirts of the town, just a few minutes' drive from the centre and mainline railway station. Bedrooms provide ample workspace and a good range of facilities for the modern traveller, and public rooms include a children's play area and indoor leisure centre.

Rooms 124 (40 fmly) (33 GF) ⚘ **Facilities** FTV WiFi ⏱ 🕓 Gym Steam room Sauna **Conf** Class 75 Board 40 Thtr 120 **Services** Lift **Parking** 130 **Notes** Civ Wed 100

Ramada Encore Milton Keynes

★★★ 75% HOTEL

tel: 01908 545500 **312 Midsummer Boulevard MK9 2EA**
email: enquiries@encoremiltonkeynes.co.uk **web:** www.encoremiltonkeynes.co.uk

This hotel is located in the heart of the town centre, close to the central railway station. The accommodation is stylish, contemporary and has all the modern comforts such as air conditioning and WiFi. There are two meeting rooms as well as an attractive bar and restaurant. Limited on-site parking is available, charged at a daily rate.

Rooms 159 (28 fmly) (16 smoking) ⚘ **Facilities** STV WiFi Xmas New Year **Conf** Class 30 Board 30 Thtr 64 **Services** Lift Air con **Parking** 50 **Notes** ⊗

Broughton Hotel

BUDGET HOTEL

tel: 01908 667726 **Broughton MK10 9AA**
email: 6418@greeneking.co.uk **web:** www.hungryhorse.co.uk
dir: M1 junct 14, at 1st rdbt A5130 signed Woburn, 600yds. Right for Broughton, hotel on left

This hotel is within easy reach of road networks and offers modern accommodation. Day rooms are dominated by an open-plan lounge bar and the Hungry Horse food concept, which proves particularly popular with young families. See also the Hotel Groups pages.

Rooms 30 (2 fmly) (14 GF) **Conf** Class 30 Board 30 Thtr 80

Campanile Milton Keynes

BUDGET HOTEL

tel: 01908 649819 **40 Penn Road (off Watling St), Fenny Stratford, Bletchley MK2 2AU**
email: miltonkeynes@campanile.com **web:** www.campanile.com
dir: M1 junct 14, A4146 to A5. S'bound on A5. 4th exit at 1st rdbt to Fenny Stratford. Hotel 500yds on left

This modern building offers accommodation in smart, well-equipped bedrooms, all with en suite bathrooms. Refreshments may be taken at the informal bistro. See also the Hotel Groups pages.

Rooms 80 (26 GF) ⚘ **Conf** Class 30 Board 30 Thtr 40

Premier Inn Milton Keynes Central

BUDGET HOTEL

tel: 0871 527 8774 **Secklow Gate West MK9 3BZ**
web: www.premierinn.com
dir: M1 junct 14 follow H6 route over 6 rdbts, at 7th (South Secklow) turn right, hotel on left

High quality, budget accommodation ideal for both families and business travellers. Spacious, en suite bedrooms feature tea and coffee making facilities, and Freeview TV in most hotels. Internet access and WiFi are available for a small fee. The adjacent family restaurant features a wide and varied menu. See also the Hotel Groups pages.

Rooms 38

Premier Inn Milton Keynes East (Willen Lake)

BUDGET HOTEL

tel: 0871 527 8778 **Brickhill St, Willen Lake MK15 9HQ**
web: www.premierinn.com
dir: M1 junct 14 , H6 (Childsway). Right at 3rd rdbt into Brickhill St. Right at 1st mini rdbt, hotel 1st left

Rooms 41

M

MILTON KEYNES *continued*

Premier Inn Milton Keynes South

BUDGET HOTEL

tel: 0871 527 8780 **Lakeside Grove, Bletcham Way, Caldecotte MK7 8HP**
web: www.premierinn.com
dir: M1 junct 14, towards Milton Keynes on H6 (Childs Way). Straight on at 2 rdbts. Left at 3rd onto V10 (Brickhill St). Straight on at 5 rdbts, at 6th right onto H10 (Bletcham Way)

Rooms 41

Premier Inn Milton Keynes South West (Furzton Lake)

BUDGET HOTEL

tel: 0871 527 8776 **Shirwell Crescent, Furzton MK4 1GA**
web: www.premierinn.com
dir: M1 junct 14, A509 to Milton Keynes. Straight on at 8 rdbts, at 9th rdbt (North Grafton) left onto V6. Right at next onto H7. Over The Bowl rdbt, hotel on left

Rooms 120

MINEHEAD	Map 3 SS94
Somerset	

Channel House Hotel

★★★ 81% SMALL HOTEL

tel: 01643 703229 **Church Path TA24 5QG**
email: channelhouse@btconnect.com **web:** www.channelhouse.co.uk
dir: From A39 right at rdbt to seafront, left onto promenade. 1st right, 1st left into Blenheim Gdns,1st right into Northfield Rd

This family-run hotel offers relaxing surroundings, yet is only a short walk from the town centre. The South West Coastal Path starts from the hotel's two-acre gardens. Many of the exceptionally well-equipped bedrooms benefit from wonderful views. Imaginative menus are created from the best local produce. The hotel is totally non-smoking.

Rooms 8 ℮ **S** £103-£121; **D** £166-£202 (incl. bkfst & dinner)* **Facilities** FTV WiFi **Services** Air con **Parking** 10 **Notes** LB ⊗ No children 15yrs Closed Nov & 29 Dec-15 Mar

Northfield Hotel

★★★ 77% HOTEL

tel: 01643 705155 **Northfield Rd TA24 5PU**
email: res@nfhotel.co.uk **web:** www.northfield-hotel.co.uk
dir: M5 junct 23, follow A38 to Bridgwater then A39 to Minehead

Dating back to the Edwardian era, this hotel was originally a private house. From its elevated position, it enjoys lovely views out over the town and the Bristol Channel. The peaceful setting makes it an ideal location for exploring both locally and further afield, with the stunning expanse of Exmoor just a short drive away. Bedrooms offer good levels of comfort and quality, likewise the spacious and elegant public areas with a choice of lounges available. The attractive wood-panelled dining room is the venue for enjoyable cuisine with a range of dishes to suit all tastes. Additional facilities include a lovely garden and indoor swimming pool.

Rooms 30 (4 fmly) (4 GF) ℮ **S** £63-£83; **D** £118-£170 (incl. bkfst) **Facilities** FTV WiFi ⊗ Putt green Gym Xmas New Year **Conf** Class 30 Board 20 Thtr 40 Del from £140 to £190 **Services** Lift **Parking** 30 **Notes** LB

MINSTER	Map 7 TR36
Kent	

Premier Inn Ramsgate

BUDGET HOTEL

tel: 0871 527 9270 **Tothill St CT12 4HY**
web: www.premierinn.com
dir: M25 onto A2 (signed Dover) merge onto M2 (signed Canterbury). Onto A299 (signed Margate/Ramsgate). Hotel at Minister rdbt

High quality, budget accommodation ideal for both families and business travellers. Spacious, en suite bedrooms feature tea and coffee making facilities, and Freeview TV in most hotels. Internet access and WiFi are available for a small fee. The adjacent family restaurant features a wide and varied menu. See also the Hotel Groups pages.

Rooms 71

MONK FRYSTON	Map 16 SE52
North Yorkshire	

Monk Fryston Hall Hotel

★★★ 81% COUNTRY HOUSE HOTEL

tel: 01977 682369 **LS25 5DU**
email: reception@monkfrystonhallhotel.co.uk **web:** www.monkfrystonhallhotel.co.uk
dir: A1(M) junct 42, A63 towards Selby. Monk Fryston 2m, hotel on left

This delightful 16th-century mansion house enjoys a peaceful location in 30 acres of grounds, yet is only minutes' drive from the A1. Many original features have been retained and the public rooms are furnished with antique and period pieces. Bedrooms are individually styled and thoughtfully equipped for both business and leisure guests.

Rooms 29 (2 fmly) (5 GF) ℮ **Facilities** STV FTV WiFi ⊗ ⊗ Xmas New Year **Conf** Class 30 Board 25 Thtr 70 **Parking** 80 **Notes** Civ Wed 72

MORECAMBE	Map 18 SD46
Lancashire	

The Midland

English Lakes
Hotels Resorts & Venues

★★★★ 75% ⊛ HOTEL

tel: 01524 424000 **Marine Road West LA4 4BU**
email: themidland@englishlakes.co.uk **web:** www.englishlakes.co.uk/hotels/midland
dir: A589 towards Morecambe, follow seafront signs, left on B5321 (Lancaster Rd) then Easton Rd, left into Central Drive. Right at rdbt on seafront. Left to hotel entrance

This art deco hotel sits on the seafront and commands stunning views across Morecambe Bay to the mountains of the Lake District. Stylish and modern accommodation is provided in the well-appointed bedrooms. Spa facilities are available on site, and guests can use the leisure club at the nearby sister hotel.

Rooms 44 ℮ **S** £77-£204; **D** £94-£348 (incl. bkfst)* **Facilities** FTV WiFi ⊗ Xmas New Year **Conf** Class 30 Board 48 Thtr 140 Del £155* **Services** Lift **Parking** 70 **Notes** Civ Wed 140

Clarendon Hotel

★★★ 72% HOTEL

tel: 01524 410180 **76 Marine Road West, West End Promenade LA4 4EP**
email: clarendon@mitchellshotels.co.uk **web:** www.mitchells.co.uk
dir: M6 junct 34 follow Morecambe signs. At rdbt (with 'Toby Carvery' on corner) 1st exit to Westgate, follow to seafront. Right at lights, hotel 3rd block

This traditional seafront hotel offers views over Morecambe Bay, modern facilities and convenient parking. An extensive fish and grill menu is offered in the contemporary Waterfront Restaurant and guests can relax in the comfortable lounge bar. Davy Jones Locker in the basement has a more traditional pub atmosphere and offers cask ales and regular live entertainment.

Rooms 29 (3 fmly) ✷ **S** £45-£60; **D** £75-£90 (incl. bkfst)* **Facilities** STV WiFi HL Xmas New Year **Conf** Class 40 Board 40 Thtr 90 **Services** Lift **Parking** 22 **Notes** LB Civ Wed 60

Lothersdale Hotel

★★★ 🅰 HOTEL

tel: 01524 416404 **320-323 Marine Rd LA4 5AA**
email: mail@bfhotels.com **web:** www.bfhotels.com
dir: M6 junct 34 follow signs for Morecambe & Heysham. Straight over 3 rdbts following sign for Promenade. At seafront turn left, hotel 0.5m on left

The Lothersdale Hotel is on the Promenade with breathtaking views of Morecambe Bay and the Lakeland Fells, and these same views are enjoyed by the Superior bedrooms. The Bury family and their staff are keenly interested in the comfort of their visitors. The hotel is close to the start of the 'Way of the Roses', and is an ideal base for those venturing across country on this popular route. The lounge and bar are attractively furnished and decorated, and there is a weekly program of entertainment.

Rooms 45 (1 fmly) (6 GF) ✷ **S** £25-£50; **D** £49-£150 (incl. bkfst)* **Facilities** FTV WiFi ⊳ ♫ Xmas New Year **Conf** Class 100 Board 50 Thtr 150 Del from £39 to £110* **Services** Lift **Parking** 21 **Notes** LB ⊗ Civ Wed 45

MORETONHAMPSTEAD   Map 3 SX78
Devon

The White Hart Hotel

★★★ 80% HOTEL

tel: 01647 440500 **The Square TQ13 8NQ**
email: enquiries@whitehartdartmoor.co.uk **web:** www.whitehartdartmoor.co.uk
dir: A30 towards Okehampton. At Whiddon Down take A382 for Moretonhampstead

Dating back to the 1700s, this former coaching inn is located on the edge of Dartmoor. A relaxed and friendly atmosphere prevails, with the staff providing attentive service. Comfortable bedrooms have a blend of traditional and contemporary styles with thoughtful extras provided. Dining is in either the brasserie restaurant or more informally in the bar, where quality cuisine is served.

Rooms 28 (8 annexe) (3 fmly) (4 GF) ✷ **Facilities** FTV WiFi ⊳ Xmas New Year **Conf** Class 30 Board 20 Thtr 50 **Notes** Civ Wed 60

Bovey Castle

Ⓤ

EDEN HOTEL COLLECTION

tel: 0844 474 0077 & 01647 445 000 **Dartmoor National Park, North Bovey TQ13 8RE**
email: enquiries@boveycastle.com **web:** www.boveycastle.com
dir: A382 from A30 to Moretonhampstead, take B3212 signed Postbridge. Hotel 2m outside Moretonhampstead on left

At the time of going to print, this establishment was undergoing a change of ownership, and is now owned and managed by the Eden Hotel collection. With a fascinating history this country manor, set in 400 acres, became known as Bovey Castle in 2003. Since then it has been restored to its former glory and offers guests elegance, charm and a chance to 'get away from it all'. A number of country pursuits are available at the property, including a championship golf course. Each bedroom is unique in design and range from classic or castle rooms to state room and grand state rooms. In addition, within the grounds there are lodges, each with three en suite bedrooms. The spa has a superb pool and many therapeutic treatments. Eden Hotel Collection is the AA Small Hotel Group of the Year 2014-2015.

Rooms 64 **Facilities** WiFi ⅃ 18 ³ Fishing ⅃ Gym Falconry Archery Horse riding Clay pigeon Game shooting Trampoline Table Tennis **Conf** Class 64 Board 50 Thtr 120 Del from £219* **Notes** Civ Wed 150

MORETON-IN-MARSH   Map 10 SP23
Gloucestershire

Manor House Hotel

★★★★ 81% ⊚⊚ HOTEL

COTSWOLD
Inns & Hotels

tel: 01608 650501 **High St GL56 0LJ**
email: info@manorhousehotel.info **web:** www.cotswold-inns-hotels.co.uk/manor
dir: Off A429 at south end of town. Take East St off High St, hotel car park 3rd right

Dating back to the 16th century, this charming Cotswold coaching inn retains much of its original character with stone walls, impressive fireplaces and a relaxed, country-house atmosphere. Bedrooms vary in size and reflect the individuality of the building; all are well equipped and some are particularly opulent. Comfortable public areas include a popular bar, a brasserie and the stylish Mulberry Restaurant where the chance to enjoy an evening meal should not be missed.

Rooms 35 (1 annexe) (3 fmly) (1 GF) ✷ **S** £138-£178; **D** £158-£198 (incl. bkfst)* **Facilities** FTV WiFi Xmas New Year **Conf** Class 48 Board 54 Thtr 120 **Services** Lift **Parking** 24 **Notes** LB Civ Wed 120

White Hart Royal Hotel

★★★ 80% ⊚ HOTEL

tel: 01608 650731 **High St GL56 0BA**
email: whr@bulldogmail.co.uk **web:** www.whitehartroyal.co.uk
dir: On High St at junct with Oxford Rd

This historic hotel has been providing accommodation for hundreds of years and today offers high standards of quality and comfort. Public areas are full of character, and the bedrooms, in a wide range of shapes and sizes, include several very spacious and luxurious rooms situated adjacent to the main building. A varied range of well prepared dishes is available throughout the day and evening in the main bar and the relaxing restaurant.

Rooms 28 (8 annexe) (2 fmly) (9 GF) ✷ **Facilities** FTV WiFi ⊳ HL Xmas New Year **Conf** Class 40 Board 20 Thtr 55 **Parking** 6 **Notes** Civ Wed 50

M

MORETON-IN-MARSH *continued*

Redesdale Arms

★★★ 79% 🏵 HOTEL

tel: 01608 650308 **High St GL56 0AW**
email: info@redesdalearms.com **web:** www.redesdalearms.com
dir: On A429, 0.5m from rail station

This fine old inn has played a central role in the town for centuries. Traditional features combine successfully with contemporary comforts; bedrooms are located in the main building and in an annexe. Guests can choose from an imaginative menu in either the stylish restaurant or the conservatory.

Rooms 34 (26 annexe) (4 fmly) (16 GF) 🐾 **S** £69-£130; **D** £89-£200 (incl. bkfst)
Facilities STV FTV WiFi ⮧ Xmas New Year **Parking** 17 **Notes** ⊗

MORLEY	Map 11 SK34
Derbyshire	

The Morley Hayes Hotel

★★★★ 78% 🏵🏵 HOTEL

tel: 01332 780480 **Main Rd DE7 6DG**
email: hotel@morleyhayes.com **web:** www.morleyhayes.com
dir: 4m N of Derby on A608

Located in rolling countryside this modern golfing destination provides extremely comfortable, stylish bedrooms with wide-ranging facilities, plasma TVs, and state-of-the-art bathrooms; the plush suites are particularly eye-catching. Creative cuisine is offered in the Dovecote Restaurant, and both Roosters and the Spikes sports bar provide informal eating options.

Rooms 32 (4 fmly) (15 GF) 🐾 **S** £82.50-£135; **D** £125-£160 (incl. bkfst)*
Facilities STV FTV WiFi ⮧ HL ⚓ 27 Putt green Golf driving range **Conf** Class 50
Board 40 Thtr 120 Del from £139.95 to £147* **Services** Lift Air con **Parking** 245
Notes LB ⊗ Civ Wed 90

MORPETH	Map 21 NZ28
Northumberland	

Eshott Hall

★★★★ 76% 🏵🏵 COUNTRY HOUSE HOTEL

tel: 01670 787454 **Eshott NE65 9EN**
email: info@eshotthall.co.uk **web:** www.eshotthall.co.uk
dir: A1 Northbound from Morpeth 5m / A1 Southbound from Alnwick 15m

Eshott Hall dates back to the 16th century and is set behind walled gardens in the heart of Nortahumberland, just a few miles from the A1. Bedrooms are extremely comfortable and very well appointed, in keeping with the style and character of the house. Award-winning food uses the best from the local larder with public areas offering a real 'wow' factor.

Rooms 16 (5 annexe) (2 fmly) 🐾 **S** £99-£129; **D** £99-£220 (incl. bkfst)*
Facilities FTV WiFi Fishing ⚓ Football pitch Xmas New Year **Conf** Class 60
Board 50 Thtr 120 **Notes** Civ Wed 100

MOTTRAM ST ANDREW	Map 16 SJ87
Cheshire	

De Vere Mottram Hall

★★★★ 81% HOTEL

tel: 01625 828135 **Wilmslow Rd SK10 4QT**
email: dmh.sales@devere-hotels.com **web:** www.devere.co.uk
dir: M6 junct 18 from S, M6 junct 20 from N, M56 junct 6, A538 Prestbury

Set in 272 acres of some of Cheshire's most beautiful parkland, this 18th-century Georgian country house is certainly an idyllic retreat. The hotel boasts extensive leisure facilities, including a championship golf course, swimming pool, gym and spa. Bedrooms are well equipped and elegantly furnished, and include a number of four-poster rooms and suites.

Rooms 120 (37 fmly) (28 GF) 🐾 **Facilities** Spa STV WiFi ⮧ ⊛ supervised ⚓ 18 ⚓
Putt green Fishing Gym FA approved football pitch Xmas New Year **Conf** Class 120
Board 60 Thtr 180 **Services** Lift **Parking** 300 **Notes** ⊗ Civ Wed 160

MUCH WENLOCK	Map 10 SO69
Shropshire	

Raven Hotel

★★★ 78% 🏵🏵 HOTEL

tel: 01952 727251 **30 Barrow St TF13 6EN**
email: enquiry@ravenhotel.com **web:** www.ravenhotel.com
dir: M54 junct 4 or 5, take A442 S, then A4169 to Much Wenlock

This town-centre hotel spreads across several historic buildings with a 17th-century coaching inn at its centre. The accommodation is well furnished and equipped to offer modern comfort; some ground-floor rooms are available. Public areas feature an interesting collection of prints and memorabilia connected with the modern-day Olympic Games - an idea which was, interestingly, born in Much Wenlock.

Rooms 20 (13 annexe) (5 GF) **Facilities** FTV WiFi ⮧ New Year **Conf** Board 16 Thtr 16
Parking 30 **Notes** ⊗ Closed 25-26 Dec

Gaskell Arms

★★★ 75% SMALL HOTEL

tel: 01952 727212 **Bourton Rd TF13 6AQ**
email: maxine@gaskellarms.co.uk **web:** www.gaskellarms.co.uk
dir: M6 junct 10A onto M54, exit at junct 4, follow signs for Ironbridge/Much Wenlock & A4169

This 17th-century former coaching inn has exposed beams and log fires in the public areas, and much original charm and character is retained throughout. In addition to the lounge bar and restaurant offering a wide range of meals and snacks, there is a small bar which is popular with locals. Well-equipped bedrooms, some located in stylishly renovated stables, provide good standards of comfort.

Rooms 16 (3 fmly) (5 GF) **S** £75-£95; **D** £95-£120 (incl. bkfst)* **Facilities** FTV WiFi ⮧
Conf Class 30 Board 20 Thtr 30 **Parking** 40 **Notes** LB ⊗

MUDEFORD

See Christchurch

MULLION
Cornwall — Map 2 SW61

Mullion Cove Hotel

★★★ 86% ⊛ HOTEL

tel: 01326 240328 **TR12 7EP**
email: enquiries@mullion-cove.co.uk **web:** www.mullion-cove.co.uk
dir: A3083 towards The Lizard. Through Mullion towards Mullion Cove. Hotel in approx 1m

Built at the turn of the last century and set high above the working harbour of Mullion, this hotel has spectacular views of the rugged coastline; seaward facing rooms are always popular. The elegant restaurant offers some carefully prepared dishes using local produce, while an alternative option is to eat less formally in the stylish bistro. After dinner, guests might like to relax in one of the charming lounges.

Rooms 30 (3 fmly) (3 GF) ⚲ **S** £85–£330; **D** £90–£330 (incl. bkfst)* **Facilities** FTV WiFi ⚡ Xmas New Year **Conf** Class 20 Board 30 Thtr 50 Del from £150 to £375* **Services** Lift **Parking** 60 **Notes** LB

NAILSWORTH
Gloucestershire — Map 4 ST89

Wild Garlic Restaurant and Rooms

⊛⊛ RESTAURANT WITH ROOMS

tel: 01453 832615 **3 Cossack Square GL6 ODB**
email: info@wild-garlic.co.uk **web:** www.wild-garlic.co.uk
dir: M4 junct 18, A46 towards Stroud. Enter Nailsworth, left at rdbt, immediately left. Establishment opposite Britannia pub

Situated in a quiet corner of charming Nailsworth, this restaurant with rooms offers a delightful combination of welcoming, relaxed hospitality and serious cuisine. The spacious and well-equipped bedrooms are situated above the restaurant. The small and friendly team of staff ensure guests are very well looked after throughout their stay.

Rooms 3 (2 fmly)

NANTWICH
Cheshire — Map 15 SJ65

Rookery Hall Hotel & Spa

★★★★ ⊛⊛ HOTEL

tel: 01270 610016 & 0845 072 7533 **Main Rd, Worleston CW5 6DQ**
email: rookeryhall@handpicked.co.uk **web:** www.handpickedhotels.co.uk/rookeryhall
dir: From A51 N of Nantwich take B5074(Winsford) signed Rookery Hall. Hotel 1.5m on right

This fine 19th-century mansion is set in 38 acres of gardens, pasture and parkland. Bedrooms are spacious and appointed to a high standard with wide-screen plasma TVs and DVD players; many rooms have separate walk-in showers as well as deep tubs. Public areas are delightful and retain many original features. There is an extensive, state-of-the art spa and leisure complex.

Rooms 70 (39 annexe) (6 fmly) (23 GF) ⚲ **S** £98–£294; **D** £107–£304 (incl. bkfst)* **Facilities Spa** STV FTV WiFi ⚡ HL ⚡ ⚡ Gym Sauna Crystal steam room Hydrotherapy pool ♫ Xmas New Year **Conf** Class 90 Board 46 Thtr 200 Del from £139 to £159* **Services** Lift **Parking** 120 **Notes** ⊗ Civ Wed 160

Alvaston Hall Hotel

Warner Leisure Hotels
Life begins at Warner

★★★ 77% HOTEL

tel: 01270 624341 **Middlewich Rd CW5 6PD**
web: www.warnerleisurehotels.co.uk

Alvaston Hall Hotel is a Grade-II listed Victorian property located in the delightful Cheshire countryside and set in extensive grounds. Bedrooms vary in size and style; some have spacious seating areas and some have outdoor terraces. Outdoor and indoor leisure facilities include a 9-hole golf course, hair and beauty treatments, and a great range of entertainment and activities. Please note that this is an adults-only (over 21) hotel.

Rooms 168 (52 annexe) (96 GF) ⚲ **Facilities Spa** FTV WiFi ⚡ supervised ⚡ 9 Putt green ⚡ Gym Archery Bowling green Floodlit driving range ♫ Xmas New Year **Conf** Class 24 Board 16 Thtr 30 **Services** Lift **Parking** 108 **Notes** ⊗ No children 21yrs

N

NANTWICH *continued*

Premier Inn Crewe/Nantwich

BUDGET HOTEL

tel: 0871 527 8782 **221 Crewe Rd CW5 6NE**
web: www.premierinn.com
dir: M6 junct 16, A500 towards Chester, A534 towards Nantwich. Hotel approx 100yds on right

High quality, budget accommodation ideal for both families and business travellers. Spacious, en suite bedrooms feature tea and coffee making facilities, and Freeview TV in most hotels. Internet access and WiFi are available for a small fee. The adjacent family restaurant features a wide and varied menu. See also the Hotel Groups pages.

Rooms 37

| **NETHER STOWEY** | Map 4 ST13 |
| Somerset | |

Apple Tree Hotel

★★★ 71% HOTEL

tel: 01278 733238 **Keenthorne TA5 1HZ**
email: reservations@appletreehotel.com **web:** www.appletreehotel.com
dir: A39 from Bridgwater towards Minehead. Hotel on left, 2m past Cannington

Once a farm cottage, dating back over 300 years, this popular hotel now provides a perfect base from which to explore the many and varied places of interest in the locale, including the unspoilt beauty of the Quantock Hills. Whether choosing to stay for business or leisure, the warmth of welcome is always the same, with the owners ensuring guests are well looked after. Bedrooms provide all the expected contemporary comforts, with rooms offered in both the main building and adjacent garden rooms. Dinner is served in the conservatory restaurant, perhaps preceded with a relaxing drink in the bar or library lounge.

Rooms 16 (2 fmly) (7 GF) 🐾 **S** £73-£82; **D** £101-£110 (incl. bkfst)* **Facilities** FTV WiFi ↕ **Conf** Class 12 Board 12 Thtr 20 **Parking** 30 **Notes** ⊗

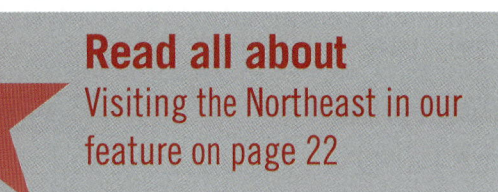

Read all about
Visiting the Northeast in our
feature on page 22

| **NEW ALRESFORD** | Map 5 SU53 |
| Hampshire | |

Swan Hotel

THE INDEPENDENTS

★★★ 74% HOTEL

tel: 01962 732302 & 734427 **11 West St SO24 9AD**
email: swanhotel@btinternet.com **web:** www.swanhotelalresford.com
dir: Exit A31 onto B3047

This former coaching inn dates back to the 18th century and remains a busy and popular destination for travellers and locals alike. Bedrooms are situated in both the main building and the more modern wing. The lounge bar and adjacent restaurant are open all day; for more traditional dining there is another restaurant which overlooks the busy village street.

Rooms 23 (12 annexe) (3 fmly) (5 GF) 🐾 **S** £65-£95; **D** £95 (incl. bkfst)* **Facilities** FTV WiFi ↕ New Year **Conf** Class 60 Board 40 Thtr 90 Del from £100 to £105* **Parking** 25 **Notes** LB RS 25 Dec

---

| **NEWARK-ON-TRENT** | Map 17 SK75 |
| Nottinghamshire | |

Kelham House Country Manor Hotel

U

tel: 01636 705266 **Main St, Kelham NG23 5QP**
email: enquiries@kelhamhouse.co.uk **web:** www.kelhamhouse.co.uk

Currently the rating for this establishment is not confirmed. This may be a due to a change of ownership or because it has only recently joined the AA rating scheme. For further details please see the AA website: the AA.com

Rooms 12 (5 annexe) (3 fmly) (5 GF) 🐾 **S** £65-£120; **D** £85-£160 (incl. bkfst)* **Facilities** FTV WiFi ↕ Xmas New Year **Conf** Class 80 Board 40 Thtr 200 Del from £125 to £155* **Parking** 100 **Notes** LB Civ Wed 100

Premier Inn Newark

BUDGET HOTEL

tel: 0871 527 8784 **Lincoln Rd NG24 2DB**
web: www.premierinn.com
dir: At junct of A1 & A46 & A17, follow B6166 signs

High quality, budget accommodation ideal for both families and business travellers. Spacious, en suite bedrooms feature tea and coffee making facilities, and Freeview TV in most hotels. Internet access and WiFi are available for a small fee. The adjacent family restaurant features a wide and varied menu. See also the Hotel Groups pages.

Rooms 40

Berkshire

Map 5 SU46

See also **Andover**

INSPECTORS' CHOICE

The Vineyard

★★★★★ 🌸🌸 HOTEL

tel: 01635 528770 **Stockcross RG20 8JU**
email: general@the-vineyard.co.uk **web:** www.the-vineyard.co.uk
dir: From M4 junct 13, A34 towards Newbury, exit at 3rd junct for Speen. Right at rdbt then right again at 2nd rdbt

A haven of style in the Berkshire countryside, this hotel prides itself on a superb art collection, which can be seen throughout the building. Bedrooms come in a variety of styles, including many split-level suites that are exceptionally well equipped. Comfortable lounges lead into the stylish restaurant, which serves the imaginative and precise contemporary French cuisine created by Daniel Galmiche, complemented by an equally impressive selection of wines from California and around the world; the cellar holds over 30,000 wines including bottles from the award-winning estate of owner Sir Peter Michael. The welcome throughout the hotel is warm and sincere, the service professional yet relaxed.

Rooms 49 (18 GF) 🐾 **D** £235-£694 (incl. bkfst)* **Facilities Spa** STV WiFi ↳ ⊛ Gym ♫ Xmas New Year **Conf** Class 70 Board 30 Thtr 140 Del from £250 to £395 **Services** Lift Air con **Parking** 100 **Notes** ⊗ Civ Wed 100

Donnington Valley Hotel & Spa

★★★★ 86% 🌸🌸 HOTEL

tel: 01635 551199 **Old Oxford Rd, Donnington RG14 3AG**
email: general@donningtonvalley.co.uk **web:** www.donningtonvalley.co.uk
dir: M4 junct 13, A34 signed Newbury. Take exit signed Donnington/Services, at rdbt 2nd exit signed Donnington. Left at next rdbt. Hotel 2m on right

In its own grounds complete with an 18-hole golf course, this stylish hotel boasts excellent facilities for both corporate and leisure guests; from the state-of-the-art spa offering excellent treatments, to an extensive range of meeting and function rooms. Air-conditioned bedrooms are stylish, spacious and particularly well equipped with fridges, lap-top safes and internet access. The Wine Press restaurant offers imaginative food complemented by a superb wine list.

N

Rooms 111 (4 fmly) (36 GF) 🐾 **S** £116-£191; **D** £132-£206 (incl. bkfst)*
Facilities Spa STV WiFi ↳ ⊛ ⅃ 18 Putt green Gym Aromatherapy Sauna Steam room Studio Xmas New Year **Conf** Class 50 Board 65 Thtr 160 Del from £180 to £224*
Services Lift Air con **Parking** 150 **Notes** LB Civ Wed 85

N

NEWBURY *continued*

Regency Park Hotel

★★★★ 75% ❀ HOTEL

tel: 01635 871555 **Bowling Green Rd, Thatcham RG18 3RP**
email: info@regencyparkhotel.co.uk **web:** www.regencyparkhotel.co.uk
dir: From Newbury take A4 signed Thatcham & Reading. 2nd rdbt exit signed Cold Ash. Hotel 1m on left

This smart, stylish hotel is ideal for both business and leisure guests. Spacious, well-equipped bedrooms include a number of contemporary, tasteful executive rooms. Smart, airy public areas include a state-of-the-art spa and leisure club, plus the Watermark Restaurant which offers appealing cuisine.

Rooms 108 (10 fmly) (9 GF) **Facilities** Spa STV FTV WiFi ⓈⓍ Gym Beauty treatments Sauna Steam room Xmas New Year **Conf** Class 80 Board 70 Thtr 200 Del from £160 to £235 **Services** Lift **Parking** 200 **Notes** ⊗ Civ Wed 100

Mercure Newbury Elcot Park

★★★★ 72% HOTEL

tel: 0844 815 9060 **Elcot RG20 8NJ**
email: gm.mercurenewburyelcotpark@jupiterhotels.co.uk **web:** www.jupiterhotels.co.uk
dir: M4 junct 13, A338 to Hungerford, A4 to Newbury. Hotel 4m from Hungerford

Enjoying a peaceful location yet within easy reach of both the A4 and M4, this country-house hotel is set in 16 acres of gardens and woodland. Bedrooms are comfortably appointed and include some located in an adjacent mews. Public areas include the Orangery Restaurant which enjoys views over the Kennet Valley and a range of conference rooms.

Rooms 73 (17 annexe) (4 fmly) (25 GF) **Facilities** FTV WiFi Ⓢ⛵ Gym New Year **Conf** Class 45 Board 35 Thtr 110 **Services** Lift **Parking** 130 **Notes** Civ Wed 120

BEST WESTERN West Grange Hotel

★★★★ 71% HOTEL

tel: 01635 273074 **Cox's Ln, Bath Rd, Midgham RG7 5UP**
email: reservations@westgrangehotel.co.uk **web:** www.westgrangehotel.co.uk
dir: M4 junct 12, A4 (Bath Rd), follow Newbury signs. Through Woolhampton, hotel on right in approx 2m

Conveniently situated between Reading and Newbury this modern hotel has well-appointed, spacious bedrooms; executive rooms are beautifully presented and have a host of additional features. The contemporary open-plan lounge and restaurant area serves an extensive choice of British cuisine. There is a range of business suites along with a larger conference room. Gardens are a real feature and the central courtyard is popular with guests.

Rooms 62 **Conf** Class 25 Board 30 Thtr 50

Newbury Manor Hotel

★★★ 77% ❀❀ HOTEL

tel: 01635 528838 **London Rd RG14 2BY**
email: enquiries@newbury-manor-hotel.co.uk **web:** www.newbury-manor-hotel.co.uk
dir: On A4 between Newbury & Thatcham

This former Georgian watermill, which still features the original millrace, is situated beside the River Kennet in well tended grounds. The character bedrooms vary in style and size and offer many accessories. Guests can dine in the award-winning River Bar Restaurant.

Rooms 34 (4 fmly) (11 GF) 🐾 **Facilities** FTV WiFi Ⓢ Fishing Xmas New Year **Conf** Class 90 Board 50 Thtr 190 **Parking** 100 **Notes** ⊗ Civ Wed 180

Donnington Grove Country Club

★★★ 73% HOTEL

tel: 01635 581000 **Grove Rd, Donnington RG14 2LA**
email: enquiries@donnington-grove.com **web:** www.donnington-grove.com

Situated on the outskirts of Newbury, overlooked by historic Donnington Castle, this hotel offers comfortable accommodation across the varied room categories. Once a splendid manor house, accommodation has been tastefully added to meet the needs of the leisure and business traveller. The estate comprises of some 550 acres featuring a popular championship golf course designed by Dave Thomas in 1991.

Rooms 34 **S** £71-£155; **D** £81-£175* **Facilities** FTV WiFi ⛳ 18 Putt green Fishing **Notes** Civ Wed 100

The Chequers Hotel

★★★ 72% HOTEL

tel: 01635 38000 **6-8 Oxford St RG14 1JB**
email: info@chequershotelnewbury.co.uk **web:** www.chequershotelnewbury.co.uk
dir: M4 junct 13, A34 S, A339 to Newbury. At 2nd rdbt right to town centre. At clock tower rdbt right, hotel on right

Situated just at the top of the main shopping street in Newbury and convenient for fast road connections, this 18th-century former coaching inn retains original features along with contemporary touches. The bedrooms come in a range of sizes and JP's Bistro is a popular eaterie. The hotel has ample parking which is a definite advantage in this town.

Rooms 56 (2 fmly) (6 GF) **Facilities** FTV WiFi Ⓢ **Conf** Class 36 Board 40 Thtr 160 Del from £100 to £145 **Parking** 60 **Notes** ⊗ Civ Wed 120

Premier Inn Newbury/Thatcham

BUDGET HOTEL

tel: 0871 527 8786 **Bath Rd, Midgham RG7 5UX**
web: www.premierinn.com
dir: M4 junct 12, A4 towards Newbury. Hotel 7m on right

High quality, budget accommodation ideal for both families and business travellers. Spacious, en suite bedrooms feature tea and coffee making facilities, and Freeview TV in most hotels. Internet access and WiFi are available for a small fee. The adjacent family restaurant features a wide and varied menu. See also the Hotel Groups pages.

Rooms 49

NEWBY BRIDGE
Cumbria   Map 18 SD38

Lakeside Hotel Lake Windermere

★★★★ 86% ❀❀ HOTEL

tel: 015395 30001 **Lakeside LA12 8AT**
email: sales@lakesidehotel.co.uk **web:** www.lakesidehotel.co.uk
dir: M6 junct 36, A590 to Barrow, follow signs to Newby Bridge. Right over bridge, hotel 1m on right

This impressive hotel enjoys an enviable location on the southern edge of Lake Windermere and has easy access to the Lakeside & Haverthwaite Steam Railway, and the ferry terminal. Bedrooms are individually styled, and many enjoy delightful lake views. Spacious lounges and a choice of restaurants are available. The state-of-the-art spa is exclusive to residents and provides a range of treatment suites. Staff throughout are friendly and nothing is too much trouble.

Rooms 74 (8 fmly) (8 GF) ✿ S £139-£309; D £159-£330 (incl. bkfst)* Facilities Spa
STV WiFi 🏊 Fishing Gym Private jetty Rowing boats ♫ Xmas New Year
Conf Class 50 Board 40 Thtr 100 Services Lift Parking 200 Notes LB ⊗ Civ Wed 70

The Swan Hotel & Spa

★★★★ 81% HOTEL

tel: 015395 31681 **LA12 8NB**
email: enquiries@swanhotel.com web: www.swanhotel.com
dir: M6 junct 36, A591, merge onto A590. At rdbts follow A590, left at Newby Bridge rdbt,
1st right for hotel

Set in idyllic surroundings, this hotel offers something to suit every taste, from a
gym and spa therapies for adults to a dedicated children's lounge. The well-
equipped bedrooms are thoroughly modern, but each has a vintage touch. Good
quality meals are served in the River Room; in good weather guests can eat on the
riverside terrace.

Rooms 51 (8 fmly) (14 GF) ✿ S £129-£199; D £129-£199 (incl. bkfst)*
Facilities Spa FTV WiFi 🏊 Gym Sauna Steam room Xmas New Year Conf Class 60
Board 40 Thtr 100 Del £175* Services Lift Air con Parking 100 Notes ⊗
Civ Wed 100

Whitewater Hotel

★★★★ 74% HOTEL

tel: 015395 31133 **The Lakeland Village LA12 8PX**
email: enquiries@whitewater-hotel.co.uk web: www.whitewater-hotel.co.uk
dir: M6 junct 36, follow signs for A590 Barrow, 1m, through Newby Bridge. Right at sign
for Lakeland Village, hotel on left

This tasteful conversion of an old mill on the River Leven is close to the southern
end of Lake Windermere. Bedrooms, many with lovely river views, are spacious and
comfortable. Public areas include a luxurious, well-equipped spa, squash courts,
and a choice of comfortable lounges. The Dolly Blue bar overlooks the river and is a
vibrant informal alternative to the fine dining restaurant.

Rooms 38 (10 fmly) (2 GF) ✿ Facilities Spa STV FTV WiFi ⌗ 🏊 supervised 🏊 Gym
Squash Table tennis Xmas New Year Conf Class 32 Board 40 Thtr 80 Services Lift
Parking 50 Notes ⊗ Civ Wed 110

Premier Inn Newcastle-under-Lyme

BUDGET HOTEL

tel: 0871 527 8808 **Talke Rd, Chesterton ST5 7AL**
web: www.premierinn.com
dir: M6 junct 12, A500, A34 to Newcastle-under-Lyme. Hotel 0.5m on right

High quality, budget accommodation ideal for both families and business
travellers. Spacious, en suite bedrooms feature tea and coffee making facilities,
and Freeview TV in most hotels. Internet access and WiFi are available for a small
fee. The adjacent family restaurant features a wide and varied menu. See also the
Hotel Groups pages.

Rooms 83

INSPECTORS' CHOICE

Jesmond Dene House

★★★★ ◉◉◉ HOTEL

tel: 0191 212 3000 **Jesmond Dene Rd NE2 2EY**
email: info@jesmonddenehouse.co.uk web: www.jesmonddenehouse.co.uk
dir: A167 N to A184. Right, right again into Jesmond Dene Rd, hotel on left

This grand house, overlooking the wooded valley of Jesmond Dene, yet just five
minutes from the centre of town, has been sympathetically converted into a
stylish, contemporary hotel destination. The bedrooms are beautifully designed
and boast flat-screen TVs, sumptuous beds with Egyptian cotton linen, digital
radios, well-stocked mini bars, free broadband, desk space and safes. Equally
eye-catching bathrooms with underfloor heating are equipped with high quality
bespoke amenities. The stylish restaurant is the venue for innovative cooking
which will prove a highlight of any stay.

Rooms 40 (8 annexe) (1 fmly) (4 GF) ✿ S £136-£241; D £172-£382 (incl. bkfst)*
Facilities STV FTV WiFi ⌗ HL Conf Class 80 Board 44 Thtr 125 Del from £206 to £246*
Services Lift Parking 64 Notes LB ⊗ Civ Wed 100

Hotel du Vin Newcastle

★★★★ 79% ◉◉ TOWN HOUSE HOTEL

tel: 0191 229 2200 **Allan House, City Rd NE1 2BE**
email: reception.newcastle@hotelduvin.com web: www.hotelduvin.com
dir: A1 junct 65 onto A184 Gateshead/Newcastle, Quayside to City Rd

The former maintenance depot of the Tyne Tees Shipping Company, this is a
landmark building on the Tyne. It has been transformed into a modern and stylish
hotel. Bedrooms are well equipped and deeply comfortable with all the Hotel du Vin
trademark items such as Egyptian cotton sheets, plasma TVs, DVD players and
monsoon showers. Guests can dine in the bistro or alfresco if the weather allows in
the courtyard.

Rooms 42 (6 GF) ✿ Facilities STV WiFi Conf Board 20 Thtr 26 Services Lift Air con
Parking 10 Notes Civ Wed 40

NEWCASTLE UPON TYNE *continued*

Hotel Indigo Newcastle

★★★★ 79% HOTEL

tel: 0191 300 9222 **2-8 Fenkle St NE1 5XU**
email: reception@hotelindigonewcastle.com **web:** www.hotelindigonewcastle.com
dir: Tyne Bridge, take 1st right St Nicholas St, 1st left Westgate Rd, right Scotswood Rd, continue onto Clayton St, hotel on right

This modern contemporary hotel is set in the heart of Newcastle in the historic Grainger Quarter. The bedrooms are spacious and comfortable, and some of them have their own balconies. Award-winning food in the Marco Pierre White Steakhouse Bar & Grill is high quality and locally sourced where possible. This vibrant hotel delivers professional but friendly service.

Rooms 148 ↖ **Facilities** STV FTV WiFi ↘ HL Gym ♫ Xmas New Year **Services** Lift Air con **Parking** 80 **Notes** ⊗

Holiday Inn Newcastle Jesmond

★★★★ 76% HOTEL

tel: 0191 281 5511 & 0785 4590612 **Jesmond Rd NE2 1PR**
web: www.hinewcastle.co.uk

Holiday Inn Newcastle Jesmond is located next to the Metro Station and benefits from off-road parking. The interior is modern, and there is a vibrant restaurant and bar operation. This is a great location for enjoying the café culture of Jesmond or the upbeat pace of the city centre.

Rooms 116 ↖ **Facilities** STV FTV WiFi ↘ HL Gym ♫ New Year **Conf** Class 160 Board 46 Thtr 250 Del £145* **Services** Lift Air con **Parking** 80 **Notes** ⊗ Civ Wed

Newcastle Gateshead Marriott Hotel MetroCentre

★★★★ 76% HOTEL

tel: 0191 493 2233 **MetroCentre NE11 9XF**
email: reservations.newcastle.england.metrocentre@marriotthotels.co.uk
web: www.newcastlemarriottmetrocentre.co.uk

(For full entry see Gateshead)

The Vermont Hotel

★★★★ 75% HOTEL

tel: 0191 233 1010 **Castle Garth NE1 1RQ**
email: info@vermonthotel.co.uk **web:** www.vermont-hotel.com

This iconic building offers some great views of the city. Centrally located and benefiting from some off-road car parking, The Vermont Hotel is accessible from both the Quayside and from the castle. There is an ongoing refurbishment programme throughout the bedrooms and public areas.

Rooms 101 ↖ **S** £70-£210; **D** £80-£220 (incl. bkfst) **Facilities** FTV WiFi ↘ Gym Sauna Steam room ♫ Xmas New Year **Conf** Class 80 Board 60 Thtr 220 Del from £120 to £290 **Services** Lift **Notes** LB ⊗ Civ Wed 220

Copthorne Hotel Newcastle

★★★★ 74% HOTEL

tel: 0191 222 0333 **The Close, Quayside NE1 3RT**
email: sales.newcastle@millenniumhotels.co.uk **web:** www.millenniumhotels.co.uk
dir: Follow signs to Newcastle city centre. Take B1600 Quayside exit, hotel on right

Set on the banks of the River Tyne close to the city centre, this stylish purpose-built hotel provides modern amenities including a leisure centre, conference facilities and a choice of restaurants for dinner. Bedrooms overlook the river, and there is a floor of 'Connoisseur' rooms that have their own dedicated exclusive lounge and business support services.

Rooms 156 (4 fmly) **S** £64-£299; **D** £64-£299 **Facilities** STV WiFi HL Gym Xmas New Year **Conf** Class 90 Board 60 Thtr 220 Del from £130 to £230 **Services** Lift **Parking** 180 **Notes** LB ⊗ Civ Wed 150

Malmaison Newcastle

★★★ 88% HOTEL

tel: 0844 693 0658 **Quayside NE1 3DX**
email: newcastle@malmaison.com **web:** www.malmaison.com
dir: Follow signs for city centre, then for Quayside/Law Courts. Hotel 100yds past Law Courts

Overlooking the river and the Millennium Bridge, the hotel has a prime position in the very popular quayside district. Bedrooms have striking decor, CD/DVD players, mini-bars and a number of individual touches. Food and drink are an integral part of the operation here, with a stylish brasserie-style restaurant and café bar, plus the Café Mal, a deli-style café next door to the main entrance.

Rooms 122 (10 fmly) ↖ **Facilities** Spa STV FTV WiFi Gym **Conf** Class 50 Board 30 Thtr 80 **Services** Lift Air con **Parking** 50 **Notes** ⊗ Civ Wed 80

Eslington Villa Hotel

★★★ 82%  HOTEL

tel: 0191 487 6017 & 420 0666 **8 Station Rd, Low Fell NE9 6DR**
email: home@eslingtonvilla.co.uk **web:** www.eslingtonvilla.co.uk

(For full entry see Gateshead)

Horton Grange Country House Hotel

★★★ 80% HOTEL

tel: 01661 860686 **Berwick Hill, Ponteland NE13 6BU**
email: info@hortongrange.co.uk **web:** www.hortongrange.co.uk
dir: A1/A19 junct at Seaton Burn take 1st exit at 1st rdbt, after 1m, left signed Ponteland/Dinnington. Hotel on right approx 2m

A Grade II listed building set in its own grounds just a short distance from Newcastle Airport and Ponteland. The main house has traditionally styled executive bedrooms, and in addition there are four contemporary garden rooms that are elegant and spacious. All bedrooms have flat-screen TVs, digital radios and broadband access. Food is served in the light and airy restaurant and the lounge that both overlook the gardens.

Rooms 9 (4 annexe) (1 fmly) (4 GF) **S** £70-£110; **D** £80-£135 (incl. bkfst)* **Facilities** FTV WiFi Xmas New Year **Conf** Class 40 Board 30 Thtr 120 Del from £133 to £138* **Parking** 50 **Notes** LB ⊗ Civ Wed 120

N

The Caledonian Hotel, Newcastle

★★★ 78% HOTEL

tel: 0191 281 7881 **64 Osborne Rd, Jesmond NE2 2AT**
email: info@caledonian-hotel-newcastle.com **web:** www.peelhotels.co.uk
dir: From A1 follow signs to Newcastle City, cross Tyne Bridge to Tynemouth. Left at lights at Osborne Rd, hotel on right

This hotel is located in the Jesmond area of the city, and offers comfortable bedrooms that are well equipped. The public areas include the trendy Billabong Bar and Bistro which serves food all day, and the terrace where a cosmopolitan atmosphere prevails. Alfresco dining is available.

Rooms 90 (6 fmly) (7 GF) (7 smoking) 🐾 **Facilities** WiFi Xmas New Year **Conf** Class 50 Board 50 Thtr 100 **Services** Lift **Parking** 35 **Notes** ⊗ Civ Wed 70

BEST WESTERN New Kent Hotel

★★★ 75% HOTEL

tel: 0191 281 7711 **127 Osborne Rd NE2 2TB**
email: reservations@newkenthotel.co.uk **web:** www.newkenthotel.co.uk
dir: On B1600, opposite St Georges Church

This popular business hotel offers relaxed service and typical Geordie hospitality. The bright modern bedrooms are well equipped and the modern bar is an ideal meeting place. A range of generous, good value dishes is served in the restaurant, which doubles as a wedding venue.

Rooms 32 (4 fmly) **S** £55-£71.50; **D** £91.50 (incl. bkfst)* **Facilities** STV FTV WiFi Xmas New Year **Conf** Class 30 Board 40 Thtr 60 **Parking** 22 **Notes** Civ Wed 90

Newgate Hotel

★★★ 64% METRO HOTEL

tel: 0191 232 6570 **Newgate St NE1 5SX**
email: enquiries@hotels-newcastle.com **web:** www.hotels-newcastle.com
dir: A184, A189 over bridge, right at 2nd lights, left at lights into Clayton St. 1st right to Fenkle St, 1st left to car park at end

Ideally located right in the heart of Newcastle, this hotel makes the perfect base for exploring the city. Bedrooms offer comfortable beds and free WiFi. Breakfast is served in the sixth-floor restaurant that has great views of the city.

Rooms 93 (8 fmly) **S** £50-£145; **D** £50-£145* **Facilities** STV WiFi **Conf** Board 12 Thtr 14 Del from £85 to £105* **Services** Lift **Parking** 120 **Notes** LB Closed 24-27 Dec

Premier Inn Newcastle Central

BUDGET HOTEL

tel: 0871 527 8802 **New Bridge Street West NE1 8BS**
web: www.premierinn.com
dir: Follow Gateshead & Newcastle signs on A167(M), over Tyne Bridge. A193 signed Wallsend & city centre, left to Carliol Square, hotel on corner

High quality, budget accommodation ideal for both families and business travellers. Spacious, en suite bedrooms feature tea and coffee making facilities, and Freeview TV in most hotels. Internet access and WiFi are available for a small fee. The adjacent family restaurant features a wide and varied menu. See also the Hotel Groups pages.

Rooms 172

Premier Inn Newcastle City Centre (Millennium Bridge)

BUDGET HOTEL

tel: 0871 527 8800 **City Rd, Quayside NE1 2AN**
web: www.premierinn.com
dir: At corner of City Rd (A186) & Crawhall Rd

Rooms 81

Premier Inn Newcastle (Holystone)

BUDGET HOTEL

tel: 0871 527 8790 **The Stonebrook, Edmund Rd, Holystone NE27 0UN**
web: www.premierinn.com
dir: 3m N of Tyne Tunnel. From A19 take A191 signed Gosforth. Hotel on left

Rooms 40

Premier Inn Newcastle Quayside

BUDGET HOTEL

tel: 0871 527 8804 **The Quayside NE1 3AE**
web: www.premierinn.com
dir: S'bound: A1, A167(M), A186 signed Walker & Wallsend follow B1600 Quayside signs. N'bound: A1, A184, A189 (cross river). 1st exit, follow B1600 Quayside signs. Hotel at foot of Tyne Bridge in Exchange building

Rooms 152

NEWCASTLE UPON TYNE AIRPORT Map 21 NZ17
Tyne & Wear

N

Novotel Newcastle Airport

★★★ 79% HOTEL

tel: 0284 345 2800 **Ponteland Rd, Kenton NE3 3HZ**
email: H1118@accor.com **web:** www.novotel.com
dir: A1(M) airport junct onto A696, take Kingston Park exit

This modern, well-proportioned hotel lies just off the bypass and is a five minute drive from the airport. The hotel has a scheduled shuttle service and flight information screens for air passengers. Bedrooms are spacious with a range of extras. The Elements Restaurant offers a flexible dining option and is open until late. There is a contemporary lounge bar and also a small leisure centre for the more energetic guests. Secure parking is available.

Rooms 126 (36 fmly) (11 smoking) **Facilities** STV WiFi 🏊 🎾 Gym Sauna **Conf** Class 150 Board 100 Thtr 200 **Services** Lift **Parking** 260 **Notes** Civ Wed 200

Premier Inn Newcastle Airport

BUDGET HOTEL

tel: 0871 527 8796 **Newcastle Int Airport, Ponteland Rd, Prestwick NE20 9DB**
web: www.premierinn.com
dir: A1 onto A696, follow Airport signs. At rdbt take turn immediately after airport exit

High quality, budget accommodation ideal for both families and business travellers. Spacious, en suite bedrooms feature tea and coffee making facilities, and Freeview TV in most hotels. Internet access and WiFi are available for a small fee. The adjacent family restaurant features a wide and varied menu. See also the Hotel Groups pages.

Rooms 88

NEWCASTE UPON TYNE AIRPORT *continued*

Premier Inn Newcastle Airport (South)

BUDGET HOTEL

tel: 0871 527 8798 **Callerton Lane Ends, Woolsington NE13 8DF**
web: www.premierinn.com
dir: Just off A696 on B6918, 0.3m from airport

Rooms 53

NEWENT	Map 10 SO72
Gloucestershire	

Three Choirs Vineyards

RESTAURANT WITH ROOMS

tel: 01531 890223 01531 890877 **GL18 1LS**
email: info@threechoirs.com **web:** www.threechoirs.com
dir: On B4215 N of Newent, follow brown tourist signs

This thriving vineyard continues to go from strength to strength and provides a wonderfully different place to stay. The restaurant, which overlooks the 100-acre estate, enjoys a popular following thanks to well-executed dishes that make good use of local produce. Spacious, high quality bedrooms are equipped with many extras, and each opens onto a private patio area which has wonderful views.

Rooms 11 (11 annexe) (1 fmly)

NEWHAVEN	Map 6 TQ40
East Sussex	

Premier Inn Newhaven

BUDGET HOTEL

tel: 0871 527 8810 **Avis Rd BN9 0AG**
web: www.premierinn.com
dir: From A26 (New Rd) through Drove Industrial Estate, left after underpass. Hotel in same complex as Sainsbury's

High quality, budget accommodation ideal for both families and business travellers. Spacious, en suite bedrooms feature tea and coffee making facilities, and Freeview TV in most hotels. Internet access and WiFi are available for a small fee. The adjacent family restaurant features a wide and varied menu. See also the Hotel Groups pages.

Rooms 70

Find out more about
Hotel Bathrooms in our
feature on page 26

NEWMARKET	Map 12 TL66
Suffolk	

Bedford Lodge Hotel & Spa

★★★★ ◉◉ HOTEL

tel: 01638 663175 **Bury Rd CB8 7BX**
email: info@bedfordlodgehotel.co.uk **web:** www.bedfordlodgehotel.co.uk
dir: From town centre take A1304 towards Bury St Edmunds, hotel 0.5m on left

Bedford Lodge Hotel is an imposing 18th-century Georgian hunting lodge with more modern additions, set in three acres of secluded landscaped gardens. Public rooms feature the newly refurbished and re-named Squires restaurant, Roxana Bar and a small lounge. The hotel also features superb leisure facilities including the Eden Health and Fitness Club, as well as self-contained conference and banqueting suites. Contemporary bedrooms have a light, airy feel, and each is tastefully furnished and well equipped.

Rooms 77 (6 fmly) (21 GF) (3 smoking) **S** £109-£149; **D** £120-£185 (incl. bkfst)*
Facilities Spa FTV WiFi Gym Steam room Sauna Spa bath Hydrotherapy pool Rasul Dry floatation Xmas New Year **Conf** Class 80 Board 50 Thtr 180 Del from £159 to £190* **Services** Lift Air con **Parking** 120 **Notes** ® RS Sat lunch Civ Wed 150

Tuddenham Mill

★★★★ 81% ◉◉ HOTEL

tel: 01638 713552 **High St, Tuddenham St Mary IP28 6SQ**
email: info@tuddenhammill.co.uk **web:** www.tuddenhammill.co.uk
dir: M11 junct 9, merge A14. Left lane junct 38 towards Thetford/Norwich. Signed Tuddenham

A beautifully converted old watermill set amidst landscaped grounds between Newmarket and Bury St Edmunds. The contemporary style bedrooms are situated in separate buildings adjacent to the main building, and each one is tastefully appointed with co-ordinated fabrics and soft furnishings. The public areas have a wealth of original features such as the water wheel and exposed beams; they include a lounge bar, a smart restaurant, a meeting room and choice of terraces.

Rooms 15 (12 annexe) (8 GF) **Facilities** STV FTV WiFi Xmas New Year **Conf** Class 16 Board 16 Thtr 40 **Parking** 40 **Notes** Civ Wed 60

BEST WESTERN Heath Court Hotel

★★★ 73% HOTEL

tel: 01638 667171 **Moulton Rd CB8 8DY**
email: quality@heathcourthotel.com **web:** www.heathcourthotel.com

Heath Court Hotel enjoys a very convenient location close to the town centre and overlooks the Newmarket gallops. Bedrooms are all well equipped and spacious, and free WiFi is available throughout the hotel. Ample secure parking is available and there is a popular restaurant and bar. At the time of going to press, parts of the hotel will be undergoing refurbishment. Contact the Heath Court for details.

Rooms 43 (2 fmly) **S** £51-£86; **D** £61-£102* **Facilities** FTV WiFi New Year
Conf Class 45 Board 40 Thtr 130 Del from £100 to £115* **Services** Lift **Parking** 50
Notes LB Civ Wed 120

Premier Inn Newmarket

BUDGET HOTEL

tel: 0871 527 9296 **Fred Archer Way CB8 7XN**
web: www.premierinn.com
dir: A14 junct 37, A142 (Fordham Rd). 2.3m, straight on at 2 rdbts. At end of Fordham Rd, into right lane, turn right. Hotel on right

High quality, budget accommodation ideal for both families and business travellers. Spacious, en suite bedrooms feature tea and coffee making facilities, and Freeview TV in most hotels. Internet access and WiFi are available for a small fee. The adjacent family restaurant features a wide and varied menu. See also the Hotel Groups pages.

Rooms 75

NEW MILTON	Map 5 SZ29
Hampshire	

INSPECTORS' CHOICE

Chewton Glen Hotel & Spa

★★★★★ ◉◉ COUNTRY HOUSE HOTEL

tel: 01425 275341 **Christchurch Rd BH25 6QS**
email: reservations@chewtonglen.com **web:** www.chewtonglen.com
dir: A35 from Lyndhurst for 10m, left at staggered junct. Follow tourist sign for hotel through Walkford, take 2nd left

Chewton has had a revitalisation in the last few years; the eco-friendly tree-houses are a recent development, and point the hotel in a fresh and exciting direction. Developments in the extensive grounds, which already boast so much, including golf and croquet, include a walled garden, which provides for the hotel kitchen, but is a feature in its own right. Bedrooms are luxurious and delightfully

appointed, while public areas are stylish and comfortable, the perfect place for traditional afternoon tea. Cuisine as ever, is at the forefront, and the Vetiver restaurant has something for every diner.

Rooms 70 (12 annexe) (11 GF) 🐾 **S** £325-£1595; **D** £325-£1595* **Facilities** Spa STV FTV WiFi 🏊 🌀 🎾 ♨ 9 ⛳ Putt green 🏌 Gym Hydrotherapy spa Dance studio Cycling & jogging trail Clay shooting Archery 🎵 Xmas New Year Child facilities **Conf** Class 70 Board 40 Thtr 150 **Services** Air con **Parking** 150 **Notes** LB ⊗ Civ Wed 140

NEWPORT	Map 5 SZ58
Isle of Wight	

Premier Inn Isle of Wight (Newport)

BUDGET HOTEL

tel: 0871 527 8556 **Seaclose, Fairlee Rd PO30 2DN**
web: www.premierinn.com
dir: From Newport take A3054 signed Ryde. In 0.75m at Seaclose lights, turn left. Hotel adjacent to council offices

High quality, budget accommodation ideal for both families and business travellers. Spacious, en suite bedrooms feature tea and coffee making facilities, and Freeview TV in most hotels. Internet access and WiFi are available for a small fee. The adjacent family restaurant features a wide and varied menu. See also the Hotel Groups pages.

Rooms 68

NEWPORT	Map 15 SJ71
Shropshire	

Premier Inn Newport / Telford

BUDGET HOTEL

tel: 0871 527 8808 **Stafford Rd TF10 9BY**
web: www.premierinn.com
dir: From A41 E of Newport take A518 towards Stafford. Hotel on right adjacent to Mere Park Garden Centre

High quality, budget accommodation ideal for both families and business travellers. Spacious, en suite bedrooms feature tea and coffee making facilities, and Freeview TV in most hotels. Internet access and WiFi are available for a small fee. The adjacent family restaurant features a wide and varied menu. See also the Hotel Groups pages.

Rooms 50

NEWQUAY
Cornwall

Map 2 SW86

Headland Hotel

★★★★ 82% HOTEL

tel: 01637 872211 **Fistral Beach TR7 1EW**
email: reception@headlandhotel.co.uk **web:** www.headlandhotel.co.uk
dir: A30 onto A392 at Indian Queens, approaching Newquay follow signs for Fistral Beach, hotel adjacent

This Victorian hotel enjoys a stunning location overlooking the sea on three sides, so views can be enjoyed from most of the windows. Bedrooms are comfortable and spacious. The grand public areas, with impressive floral displays, include various lounges and as a complement to the formal dining room, The Terrace offers a relaxed alternative. Recent additions include the spa, gym and leisure facilities including relaxation pool, steam room, aromatherapy showers and sauna. Self-catering cottages are available, and guests staying in these are welcome to use the hotel facilities.

Rooms 96 (25 fmly) S £65-£165; D £85-£405 (incl. bkfst)* **Facilities** Spa STV FTV WiFi 9 Putt green Gym Boules Outdoor activities Surf school Xmas New Year Child facilities **Conf** Class 120 Board 40 Thtr 250 Del from £99 to 300* **Services** Lift **Parking** 300 **Notes** LB Civ Wed 250

Atlantic Hotel

★★★ 79% HOTEL

tel: 01637 872244 **Dane Rd TR7 1EN**
email: info@atlantichotelnewquay.co.uk **web:** www.atlantichotelnewquay.co.uk
dir: A30 onto A392 to Indian Queens, approaching Newquay. Follow signs for Fistral Beach, hotel on hill overlooking sea & harbour

Located on a cliff top with stunning views of Newquay and the Atlantic seascape, this imposing property dominates the skyline and offers traditional hotel keeping

with modern comforts. All bedrooms are appointed to a high standard; balcony suites are available. Silks restaurant is popular with locals and residents alike.

Rooms 55 (10 fmly) S £61-£126; D £96-£192 (incl. bkfst)* **Facilities** STV FTV WiFi Xmas New Year **Conf** Class 350 Board 150 Thtr 350 Del £124.95* **Services** Lift **Parking** 55 **Notes** LB Civ Wed 360

See advert on opposite page

BEST WESTERN Hotel Bristol

★★★ 79% HOTEL

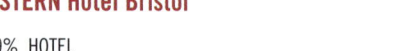

tel: 01637 875181 **Narrowcliff TR7 2PQ**
email: info@hotelbristol.co.uk **web:** www.hotelbristol.co.uk
dir: A30 onto A392, then A3058. Hotel 2.5m on left

This hotel is conveniently situated, and many of the bedrooms enjoy fine sea views. Staff are friendly and provide a professional and attentive service. There is a range of comfortable lounges, ideal for relaxing prior to eating in the elegant dining room. There are also leisure and conference facilities.

Rooms 74 (23 fmly) S £55-£102; D £78-£164 (incl. bkfst)* **Facilities** FTV WiFi HL Table tennis Xmas New Year Child facilities **Conf** Class 80 Board 30 Thtr 200 Del from £111 to £185* **Services** Lift **Parking** 105 **Notes** LB Closed 4-15 Jan Civ Wed 300

Porth Veor Manor

★★★ 79% HOTEL

tel: 01637 873274 & 839542 **Porth Way, Porth TR7 3LW**
email: enquiries@porthveormanor.com **web:** www.porthveormanor.com
dir: From A3058 at main rdbt onto B3276, hotel 0.5m on left

Overlooking Porth Beach and in a quiet location, this pleasant mid 19th-century manor house offers a relaxed and friendly atmosphere. The spacious bedrooms have satellite TVs, and many have views of the beach; superior rooms are available. The hotel has a fine dining restaurant, a lounge/bar, and an outdoor heated pool. There is direct access via a private path from the hotel grounds to the beach, and the coastal paths are just a short walk away.

Rooms 18 (6 fmly) **Facilities** STV FTV WiFi ↘ ⚹ Putt green ⚑ Xmas New Year **Conf** Class 50 Board 30 Thtr 60 **Parking** 36 **Notes** ⊗ No children 5yrs Civ Wed 80

Trebarwith Hotel

★★★ 79% HOTEL

tel: 01637 872288 & 0800 387520 **Trebarwith Crescent TR7 1BZ**
email: enquiry@trebarwith-hotel.co.uk **web:** www.trebarwith-hotel.co.uk
dir: From A3058 into Mount Wise Rd. 3rd right into Marcus Hill, across East St into Trebarwith Cres. Hotel at end

With breathtaking views of the rugged coastline and a path leading to the beach, this friendly, family-run hotel is set in its own grounds close to the town centre. The public rooms include a lounge, ballroom, restaurant and cinema. The comfortable bedrooms include four-poster and family rooms, and many benefit from the sea views.

Rooms 41 (8 fmly) (1 GF) ↘ **S** £39-£65; **D** £78-£130 (incl. bkfst)* **Facilities** FTV WiFi ↘ ⊗ Fishing Video theatre Games room Surf school Padi/SSI scuba diving centre ♫ **Conf** Class 30 Board 18 Thtr 45 **Parking** 41 **Notes** LB ⊗ Closed Nov-5 Apr

The Legacy Hotel Victoria

★★★ 77% HOTEL

tel: 08444 119 025 & 0330 3332825 **East St TR7 1DB**
email: bookings@hotel-victoria.co.uk **web:** www.legacy-hotels.co.uk
dir: A30 towards Bodmin following signs to Newquay. Hotel next to Newquay's main post office

Standing on the cliffs, overlooking Newquay Bay, the hotel is situated at the centre of this vibrant town. The spacious lounges and bar areas all benefit from glorious views. Varied menus, using the best of local produce, are offered in the restaurant. Bedrooms vary from spacious superior rooms and suites to standard inland-facing rooms. Berties pub, a nightclub, and indoor leisure facilities are also available.

Rooms 71 (23 fmly) (1 GF) (5 smoking) ↘ **Facilities** FTV WiFi ⊗ Gym Beauty treatment room Xmas New Year **Conf** Class 130 Board 50 Thtr 200 **Services** Lift **Parking** 50 **Notes** Civ Wed 90

N

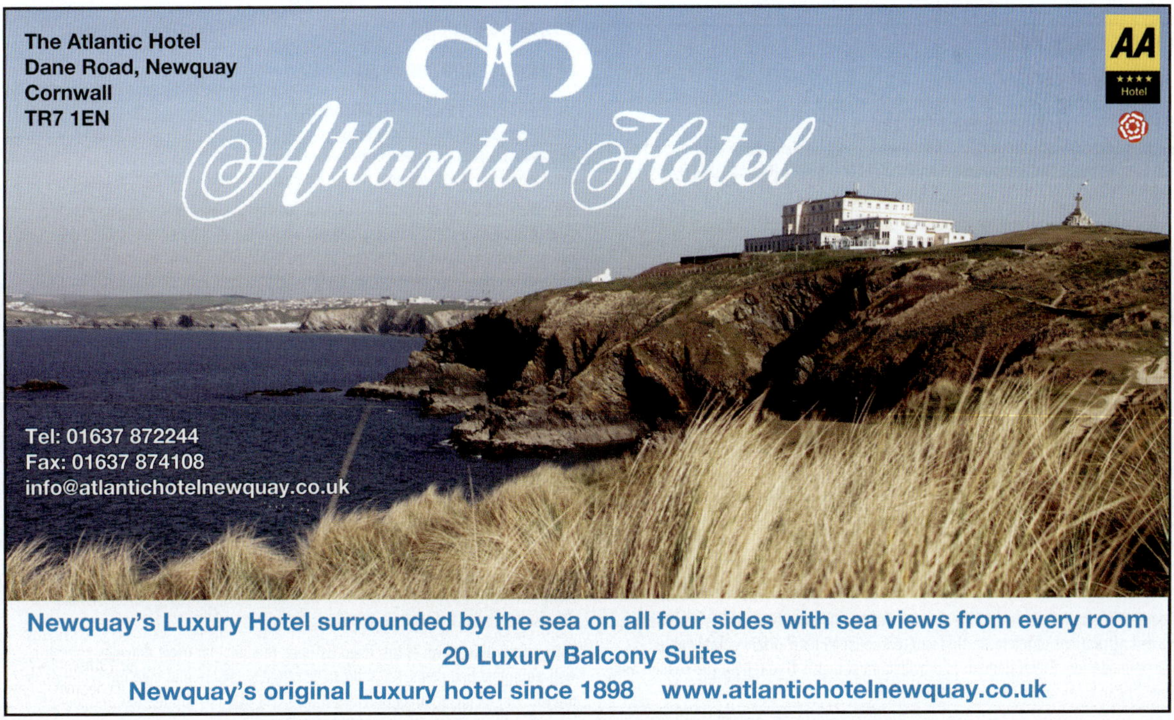

NEWQUAY *continued*

Hotel California

★★★ 68% HOTEL

tel: 01637 879292 & 872798 **Pentire Crescent TR7 1PU**
email: info@hotel-california.co.uk **web:** www.hotel-california.co.uk
dir: A392 to Newquay, follow signs for Pentire Hotels & Guest Houses

This hotel is tucked away in a delightful location, close to Fistral Beach and adjacent to the River Gannel. Many bedrooms have views across the river towards the sea, and some have balconies. There is an impressive range of leisure facilities, including ten-pin bowling and both indoor and outdoor pools. The cuisine is enjoyable and menus offer a range of interesting dishes.

Rooms 70 (27 fmly) (13 GF) **S** £38-£63; **D** £80-£113 (incl. bkfst)* **Facilities** FTV WiFi HL ⓧ ↘ Squash 4-lane American bowling alley Hairdresser Snooker & pool room Sauna Solarium ♬ Xmas New Year Child facilities **Conf** Class 100 Board 30 Thtr 100 Del from £50 to £65 **Services** Lift **Parking** 66 **Notes** Closed 3-25 Jan Civ Wed 150

Priory Lodge Hotel

★★ 76% HOTEL

tel: 01637 874111 **30 Mount Wise TR7 2BN**
email: fionapocklington@tiscali.co.uk **web:** www.priorylodgehotel.co.uk
dir: From lights in town centre onto Berry Rd, right onto B3282 (Mount Wise), 0.5m on right

This hotel enjoys a central location close to the town centre, the harbour and the local beaches. Secure parking is available at the hotel along with a range of leisure facilities including a heated pool, sauna, games room and hot tub. Attractively decorated bedrooms vary in size and style - many have sea views over Towan Beach.

Rooms 28 (6 annexe) (13 fmly) (1 GF) **S** £40-£50; **D** £60-£90 (incl. bkfst)* **Facilities** FTV WiFi ↘ ♬ **Parking** 30 **Notes** ⊗ Closed Dec-end Mar

Eliot Hotel

★★ 71% HOTEL

Leisureplex

tel: 01637 878177 **Edgcumbe Av TR7 2NH**
email: eliot.newquay@alfatravel.co.uk **web:** www.leisureplex.co.uk
dir: A30 onto A392 towards Quintrell Downs. Right at rdbt onto A3058. 4m to Newquay, left at amusements onto Edgcumbe Ave. Hotel on left

Located in a quiet residential area just a short walk from the beaches and the varied attractions of the town, this long-established hotel offers comfortable accommodation. Entertainment is provided most nights throughout the season and guests can relax in the spacious public areas.

Rooms 76 (10 fmly) ⓐ **S** £35-£47; **D** £56-£80 (incl. bkfst)* **Facilities** FTV ↘ ↘ Pool table Table tennis ♬ Xmas New Year **Services** Lift **Parking** 20 **Notes** ⊗ Closed Dec-Jan (ex Xmas) RS Feb-Mar

Glendorgal Resort

Ⓤ

tel: 01637 874937 & 859981 **Lusty Glaze Rd, Porth TR7 3AD**
email: info@glendorgal.co.uk **web:** www.glendorgal.co.uk
dir: A30 onto A392, 2nd rdbt, right onto A3058, at mini rdbt straight on, right into Lusty Glaze Rd, follow signs for Glendorgal

Currently the rating for this establishment is not confirmed. This may be due to a change of ownership or because it has only recently joined the AA rating scheme. For further details please see the AA website: theAA.com

Rooms 26 (8 fmly) **Facilities** WiFi ↘ ⓧ Gym Steam room Sauna **Conf** Class 80 Board 60 Thtr 90 **Parking** 70 **Notes** Civ Wed 150

Premier Inn Quintrell Downs

BUDGET HOTEL

Premier Inn

tel: 0871 527 8818 **Quintrell Downs TR8 4LE**
web: www.premierinn.com
dir: From A30 take A39. At rdbt 2nd exit signed Newquay A392. 4m, in Quintrell Downs take 1st exit at rdbt. Hotel on left

High quality, budget accommodation ideal for both families and business travellers. Spacious, en suite bedrooms feature tea and coffee making facilities, and Freeview TV in most hotels. Internet access and WiFi are available for a small fee. The adjacent family restaurant features a wide and varied menu. See also the Hotel Groups pages.

Rooms 75

Lewinnick Lodge

RESTAURANT WITH ROOMS

tel: 01637 878117 **Pentire Headland TR7 1QD**
email: thelodge@hospitalitycornwall.com
web: www.hospitalitycornwall.com/lewinnicklodge
dir: From A392, at rdbt exit into Pentire Rd then Pentire Ave. Turn right to Lewinnick Lodge

Set above the cliffs of Pentire Headland, looking out across the mighty Atlantic, guests are guaranteed amazing coastal views. Ten of the bedrooms were designed by Guy Bostock; these are modern, spacious, and offer many thoughtful extras, some with open-plan bathrooms. Modern British food with an emphasis on fresh fish is served all day.

Rooms 10

NEWTON ABBOT	Map 3 SX87
Devon	

See also Ilsington

BEST WESTERN Passage House Hotel

★★★ 74% HOTEL

Best Western

tel: 01626 355515 **Hackney Ln, Kingsteignton TQ12 3QH**
email: mail@passagehousegroup.co.uk **web:** www.passagehousegroup.co.uk/hotel
dir: A380 onto A381, follow racecourse signs

With memorable views of the Teign Estuary, this popular hotel provides spacious, well-equipped bedrooms. An impressive range of leisure and meeting facilities is offered and a conservatory provides a pleasant extension to the bar and lounge. A choice of eating options is available, either in the main restaurant, or the adjacent Passage House Inn for less formal dining.

Rooms 90 (52 annexe) (64 fmly) (26 GF) **Facilities** Spa WiFi ↳ 🐾 supervised Gym **Conf** Class 50 Board 40 Thtr 120 Del from £115 to £125* **Services** Lift **Parking** 300 **Notes** ⊗ RS 24-27 Dec Civ Wed 75

Premier Inn Newton Abbot

BUDGET HOTEL

tel: 0871 527 9300 **Newton Abbott Racecourse, Newton Rd TQ12 3AF**
web: www.premierinn.com
dir: A380 exit at Ware Barton signed A383/Ashburton, follow brown signs for Newton Abbot Racecourse through Kingsteignton. Then follow Officials Entrance sign to hotel

High quality, budget accommodation ideal for both families and business travellers. Spacious, en suite bedrooms feature tea and coffee making facilities, and Freeview TV in most hotels. Internet access and WiFi are available for a small fee. The adjacent family restaurant features a wide and varied menu. See also the Hotel Groups pages.

Rooms 60

NEWTON AYCLIFFE	Map 19 NZ22
County Durham	

Premier Inn Durham (Newton Aycliffe)

BUDGET HOTEL

tel: 0871 527 8336 **Ricknall Ln, Great North Rd DL5 6JG**
web: www.premierinn.com
dir: On A167 E of Newton Aycliffe, 3m from A1(M)

High quality, budget accommodation ideal for both families and business travellers. Spacious, en suite bedrooms feature tea and coffee making facilities, and Freeview TV in most hotels. Internet access and WiFi are available for a small fee. The adjacent family restaurant features a wide and varied menu. See also the Hotel Groups pages.

Rooms 44

NEWTON-LE-WILLOWS	Map 15 SJ59
Merseyside	

Holiday Inn Haydock M6 Jct 23

★★★ 79% HOTEL

tel: 0871 942 9039 **Lodge Ln WA12 0JG**
email: haydock@ihg.com **web:** www.hihaydockm6j23hotel.co.uk
dir: M6 junct 23, A49 to Ashton-in-Makerfield. Hotel 0.25m on right by racecourse

This hotel has an ideal location adjacent to Haydock Racecourse and within easy reach of north-west cities and attractions. A variety of bedrooms is available and public areas include extensive meeting and conference facilities, a smart Spirit health and leisure club and a spacious bar and restaurant.

Rooms 136 (12 fmly) (23 GF) (12 smoking) **Facilities** STV WiFi HL 🐾 Gym Xmas New Year **Conf** Class 70 Board 60 Thtr 180 **Services** Lift Air con **Parking** 204 **Notes** Civ Wed 120

NORMAN CROSS	Map 12 TL19
Cambridgeshire	

Premier Inn Peterborough A1(M) Jct 16

BUDGET HOTEL

tel: 0871 527 8870 **Norman Cross, A1(M) Junction 16 PE7 3TB**
web: www.premierinn.com
dir: A1(M) junct 16, A15 towards Yaxley, hotel in 100yds

High quality, budget accommodation ideal for both families and business travellers. Spacious, en suite bedrooms feature tea and coffee making facilities, and Freeview TV in most hotels. Internet access and WiFi are available for a small fee. The adjacent family restaurant features a wide and varied menu. See also the Hotel Groups pages.

Rooms 95

NORMANTON	Map 11 SK90
Rutland	

BEST WESTERN Normanton Park Hotel

★★★ 71% HOTEL

tel: 01780 720315 **Oakham LE15 8RP**
email: info@normantonpark.co.uk **web:** www.bw-normantonparkhotel.co.uk
dir: From A1 follow A606 towards Oakham, 5m. Turn left, 1.5m. Hotel on right

This hotel offers some of Rutland Water's best views over the south shore. The comfortable bedrooms are located in the main house and the courtyard. Public rooms include a conservatory dining room overlooking the water, and a cosy lounge is available for guests to relax in.

Rooms 30 (7 annexe) (6 fmly) (11 GF) 🐾 **Facilities** FTV WiFi Xmas New Year **Conf** Class 60 Board 80 Thtr 200 **Parking** 100 **Notes** Civ Wed 100

NORTHALLERTON	Map 19 SE39
North Yorkshire	

Solberge Hall

★★★ 85% ⚜ HOTEL

tel: 01609 779191 **Newby Wiske DL7 9ER**
email: reservations@solbergehall.co.uk **web:** www.solbergehall.co.uk
dir: A1(M) junct 51, follow A684 to Northallerton. After village of Ainderby Steeple turn right (signed Solberge Hall) for 2m

This charming Georgian manor house has a peaceful countryside setting between the Yorkshire Dales and the Vale of York. Solberge Hall has benefitted from complete refurbishment recently, retaining many period features combined with modern facilities, all ensuring a comfortable stay. Food is a highlight with fine dining offered in the elegant dining room, while the lounge bar is more informal. A range of meeting rooms are also available, and the country house style and stunning views make it an ideal wedding venue.

Rooms 24 (2 fmly) (3 GF) 🐾 **Facilities** FTV WiFi ↳ **Conf** Class 60 Board 50 Thtr 180 Del from £130 to £165 **Parking** 95 **Notes** ⊗ Civ Wed 150

N

NORTHAMPTON
Northamptonshire

Map 11 SP76

Campanile Northampton

Campanile

★★★ 74% HOTEL

tel: 01604 662599 **Cheaney Dr, Grange Park NN4 5FB**
email: northampton@campanile.com **web:** www.campanile.com
dir: M1 junct 15, A508 towards Northampton. 2nd exit at 1st rdbt, 2nd exit at 2nd rdbt into Grange Park

This modern building offers accommodation in smart, well-equipped bedrooms, all with en suite bathrooms. Refreshments may be taken at the informal bistro.

Rooms 87 (18 fmly) **Facilities** STV FTV WiFi Xmas New Year **Conf** Class 60 Board 60 Thtr 150 **Services** Lift Air con **Parking** 100

Westone Manor Hotel

★★★ 70% HOTEL

tel: 01604 739955 **Ashley Way, Weston Favell NN3 3EA**
email: enquiries@hotels-northampton.com **web:** www.hotels-northampton.com
dir: A43 Kettering for 0.5m. Then A4500 for Town Centre/Earls Barton/Weston Favell.Left at lights onto A4500 for 100yds. 1st right at sign Westone Manor Hotel Northampton, over small rdbt, hotel on left

Built in 1914 as the home of the local shoe manufacturer William Sears, this property has since been expanded, and now offers comfortable accommodation to the rear. A lounge, bar, and conservatory restaurant are available for the enjoyment of a range of meals. Free WiFi is available throughout the hotel.

Rooms 69 (38 annexe) (2 fmly) (19 GF) **Facilities** FTV WiFi Xmas New Year **Conf** Class 60 Board 60 Thtr 120 **Services** Lift **Parking** 70 **Notes** ⊗ Civ Wed 120

Ibis Northampton Centre

BUDGET HOTEL

tel: 01604 608900 **Sol Central, Marefair NN1 1SR**
email: H3657@accor.com **web:** www.ibishotel.com
dir: M1 junct 15/15a & city centre towards railway station

Modern, budget hotel offering comfortable accommodation in bright and practical bedrooms. Breakfast is self-service and dinner is available in the restaurant. See also the Hotel Groups pages.

Rooms 151 (14 fmly) ⋒ **Conf** Board 10

Premier Inn Northampton Bedford Road/A428

BUDGET HOTEL

tel: 0871 527 8822 **The Lakes, Bedford Rd NN4 7YD**
web: www.premierinn.com
dir: M1 junct 15, follow A508 (A45) signs to Northampton. A428 at rdbt take 4th exit (signed Bedford). Left at next rdbt. Hotel on right

High quality, budget accommodation ideal for both families and business travellers. Spacious, en suite bedrooms feature tea and coffee making facilities, and Freeview TV in most hotels. Internet access and WiFi are available for a small fee. The adjacent family restaurant features a wide and varied menu. See also the Hotel Groups pages.

Rooms 44

Premier Inn Northampton Great Billing/A45

BUDGET HOTEL

tel: 0871 527 8824 **Crow Ln, Great Billing NN3 9DA**
web: www.premierinn.com
dir: M1 junct 15, A508, A45 follow Billing Aquadrome signs

Rooms 60

Premier Inn Northampton South (Wootton)

BUDGET HOTEL

tel: 0871 527 8826 **Newport Pagnell Road West, Wootton NN4 7JJ**
web: www.premierinn.com
dir: M1 junct 15, A508 towards Northampton, exit at junct with A45. At rdbt take B526. Hotel on right

Rooms 45

Premier Inn Northampton West (Harpole)

BUDGET HOTEL

tel: 0871 527 8828 **Harpole Turn, Weedon Rd, Harpole NN7 4DD**
web: www.premierinn.com
dir: M1 junct 16, A45 towards Northampton. In 1m left into Harpole Turn. Hotel on left

Rooms 51

NORTH FERRIBY
East Riding of Yorkshire

Map 17 SE92

Hallmark Hotel Hull

★★★★ 73% HOTEL

tel: 01482 645212 **Ferriby High Rd HU14 3LG**
web: www.hallmarkhotels.co.uk/hull
dir: M62 onto A63 towards Hull. Exit at Humber Bridge signage. Follow North Ferriby signs, hotel 0.5m on left

This property is situated just outside Hull city centre, with breathtaking views of the Humber Bridge. Service is attentive with a friendly atmosphere. The comfortable bedrooms are tastefully appointed and are suitable for both business and leisure guests. The restaurant and bar serve a good choice of dishes. Conference facilities are available along with free WiFi and private parking.

Rooms 95 (3 fmly) (16 GF) ⋒ **Facilities** STV FTV WiFi ⟂ Xmas New Year **Conf** Class 85 Board 86 Thtr 200 **Parking** 150 **Notes** Civ Wed 200

NORTH KILWORTH Leicestershire	Map 11 SP68

Kilworth House Hotel & Theatre

★★★★ ◎◎ HOTEL

tel: 01858 880058 **Lutterworth Rd LE17 6JE**
email: info@kilworthhouse.co.uk **web:** www.kilworthhouse.co.uk
dir: A4304 towards Market Harborough, after Walcote, hotel 1.5m on right

Kilworth House Hotel is a restored Victorian country house located in 38 acres of private grounds offering state-of-the-art conference rooms. The gracious public areas feature many period pieces and original art works. The bedrooms are very comfortable and well equipped, and the large Orangery is now used for informal dining, while the opulent Wordsworth Restaurant has a more formal air. Close to the lake an open-air theatre which seats 540 has been built; professional productions are performed, and picnics can be arranged, or dinner back at the hotel is also an option.

Rooms 44 (2 fmly) (13 GF) ✆ **S** £140-£190; **D** £150-£200 (incl. bkfst)* **Facilities** FTV WiFi ⒔ Fishing ⒔ Gym Beauty therapy rooms Xmas **Conf** Class 30 Board 30 Thtr 80 Del from £180 to £234* **Services** Lift **Parking** 140 **Notes** LB ⊗ Civ Wed 180

NORTH SHIELDS Tyne & Wear	Map 21 NZ36

Premier Inn North Shields

BUDGET HOTEL

tel: 0871 527 8818 **Coble Dene Rd NE29 6DL**
web: www.premierinn.com
dir: From all directions follow signs for Royal Quays (Outlet Centre) & International Ferry Terminal. From A187 take Coble Dene Rd. At 3rd rdbt right, 1st right at mini rdbt

High quality, budget accommodation ideal for both families and business travellers. Spacious, en suite bedrooms feature tea and coffee making facilities, and Freeview TV in most hotels. Internet access and WiFi are available for a small fee. The adjacent family restaurant features a wide and varied menu. See also the Hotel Groups pages.

Rooms 50

NORTH WALSHAM Norfolk	Map 13 TG23

Beechwood Hotel

★★★ ◎◎ HOTEL

tel: 01692 403231 **Cromer Rd NR28 OHD**
email: info@beechwood-hotel.co.uk **web:** www.beechwood-hotel.co.uk
dir: B1150 from Norwich. At North Walsham left at 1st lights, then right at next

Expect a warm welcome at this elegant 18th-century house, situated just a short walk from the town centre. The individually styled bedrooms are tastefully furnished with well chosen antique pieces, attractive co-ordinated soft fabrics and many thoughtful touches. The spacious public areas include a lounge bar with plush furnishings, a further lounge and a smartly appointed restaurant.

Rooms 17 (4 GF) ✆ **Facilities** FTV WiFi ⒔ New Year **Conf** Class 20 Board 20 Thtr 20 **Parking** 20 **Notes** No children 10yrs

NORTH WALTHAM Hampshire	Map 5 SU54

Premier Inn Basingstoke South

BUDGET HOTEL

tel: 0871 527 8064 **RG25 2BB**
web: www.premierinn.com
dir: M3 junct 7, A30 follow signs for Kingsworthy and crematorium. Hotel 2m on right, adjacent to Wheatsheaf

High quality, budget accommodation ideal for both families and business travellers. Spacious, en suite bedrooms feature tea and coffee making facilities, and Freeview TV in most hotels. Internet access and WiFi are available for a small fee. The adjacent family restaurant features a wide and varied menu. See also the Hotel Groups pages.

Rooms 28

N

NORTHWICH
Cheshire
Map 15 SJ67

Premier Inn Northwich (Sandiway)

BUDGET HOTEL

tel: 0871 527 8830 **520 Chester Rd, Sandiway CW8 2DN**
web: www.premierinn.com
dir: M6 junct 19, A556 towards Chester. Hotel in 11m

High quality, budget accommodation ideal for both families and business travellers. Spacious, en suite bedrooms feature tea and coffee making facilities, and Freeview TV in most hotels. Internet access and WiFi are available for a small fee. The adjacent family restaurant features a wide and varied menu. See also the Hotel Groups pages.

Rooms 42

Premier Inn Northwich South

BUDGET HOTEL

tel: 0871 527 8832 **London Rd, Leftwich CW9 8EG**
web: www.premierinn.com
dir: Just off M6 junct 19. Follow A556 towards Chester. Right at sign for Northwich & Davenham

Rooms 33

NORWICH
Norfolk
Map 13 TG20

St Giles House Hotel

★★★★ 81%  HOTEL

tel: 01603 275180 **41-45 St Giles St NR2 1JR**
email: reception@stgileshousehotel.com **web:** www.stgileshousehotel.com
dir: A11 into central Norwich. Left at rdbt (Chapelfield Shopping Centre). 3rd exit at next rdbt. Left onto St Giles St. Hotel on left

St Giles House Hotel is a stylish 19th-century, Grade II listed building situated in the heart of the city. The property has a wealth of magnificent original features such as wood-panelling, ornamental plasterwork and marble floors. Public areas include an open-plan lounge bar/restaurant, a smart lounge with plush sofas and a Parisian-style terrace. The spacious, contemporary bedrooms are individually designed and have many thoughtful touches.

Rooms 24 (3 GF) 🦢 **Facilities** Spa FTV WiFi Xmas New Year **Conf** Class 20 Board 24 Thtr 45 **Services** Lift **Parking** 30 **Notes** ⊗ Civ Wed 60

Barnham Broom

★★★★ 78% ◉◉ HOTEL

tel: 01603 759393 **NR9 4DD**
web: www.barnham-broom.co.uk

(For full entry see Barnham Broom)

Park Farm Hotel

★★★★ 77% ◉ HOTEL

CLASSIC
BRITISH HOTELS

tel: 01603 810264 **NR9 3DL**
email: enq@parkfarm-hotel.co.uk **web:** www.parkfarm-hotel.co.uk

(For full entry see Hethersett)

De Vere Dunston Hall

★★★★ 77% HOTEL

tel: 01508 470444 **Ipswich Rd NR14 8PQ**
email: dhreception@devere-hotels.com **web:** www.devere.co.uk
dir: From A47 take A140 (Ipswich road). 0.25m, hotel on left

De Vere Dunston Hall is an imposing Grade II listed building set amidst 170 acres of landscaped grounds just a short drive from the city centre. The spacious bedrooms are smartly decorated, tastefully furnished and equipped to a high standard. The attractively appointed public rooms offer a wide choice of areas in which to relax, and the hotel also boasts a superb range of leisure facilities including an 18-hole PGA golf course, floodlit tennis courts and a football pitch.

Rooms 169 (16 fmly) (16 GF) (2 smoking) **Facilities** Spa WiFi ⓣ ♨ 18 Putt green Gym Floodlit driving range Xmas New Year **Conf** Class 140 Board 80 Thtr 300 **Services** Lift **Parking** 500 **Notes** Civ Wed 90

Sprowston Manor, A Marriott Hotel & Country Club

★★★★ 76% ◉ HOTEL

tel: 01603 410871 **Sprowston Park, Wroxham Rd, Sprowston NR7 8RP**
email: mhrs.nwigs.frontdesk@marriotthotels.com
web: www.marriottsprowstonmanor.co.uk
dir: NE of Norwich take A1151 (Wroxham road). 2m, follow signs to Sprowston Park

Surrounded by open parkland, this imposing property is set in attractively landscaped grounds and is just a short drive from the city centre. Bedrooms are spacious and feature a variety of decorative styles. The hotel also has extensive conference, banqueting and leisure facilities. Other public rooms include an array of seating areas and the elegant Manor Restaurant.

Rooms 94 (31 fmly) (5 GF) (8 smoking) **S** £130-£150; **D** £130-£150* **Facilities** Spa FTV WiFi ⓣ ♨ 18 Putt green Gym Steam room Sauna Xmas New Year **Conf** Class 100 Board 80 Thtr 500 **Del** from £135 to £145* **Services** Lift **Parking** 150 **Notes** LB ⊗ Civ Wed 300

The Maids Head Hotel

★★★★ 75% ◉ HOTEL

CLASSIC
BRITISH HOTELS

tel: 01603 209955 **Tombland NR3 1LB**
email: gm@maidsheadhotel.co.uk **web:** www.maidsheadhotel.co.uk
dir: In city centre. Telephone or see website for detailed directions

The Maids Head Hotel is an impressive 13th-century building situated close to the impressive Norman cathedral, and within easy walking distance of the city centre. The bedrooms are pleasantly decorated and thoughtfully equipped; some rooms have original oak beams. The spacious public rooms include a Jacobean bar, a range of seating areas and the Courtyard Restaurant.

Rooms 84 (10 fmly) **Facilities** FTV WiFi ♖ Beauty treatment room Use of nearby gym Xmas New Year **Conf** Class 30 Board 50 Thtr 100 **Services** Lift **Parking** 83 **Notes** ⊗ Civ Wed 100

Mercure Norwich Hotel

Mercure
HOTELS

★★★★ 71% HOTEL

tel: 0844 815 9036 **121-131 Boundary Rd NR3 2BA**
email: info@mercurenorwich.co.uk **web:** www.jupiterhotels.co.uk
dir: Approx 2m from airport on A140 Norwich ring road

Purpose-built property situated on the outer ring road within easy striking distance of the city centre. Bedrooms are spacious and well equipped with modern facilities.

Public rooms include an open-plan lounge bar and a smart restaurant. The hotel has leisure facilities, meeting rooms and a banqueting suite.

Rooms 107 **Facilities** WiFi ⌖ Gym Sauna Steam room **Conf** Class 160 Board 80 Thtr 400 **Parking** 225 **Notes** Civ Wed 400

BEST WESTERN Annesley House Hotel

★★★ 88% ◉◉ HOTEL

tel: 01603 624553 **6 Newmarket Rd NR2 2LA**
email: annesleyhouse@bestwestern.co.uk **web:** www.bw-annesleyhouse.co.uk
dir: On A11, 0.5m before city centre

Delightful Georgian property set in three acres of landscaped gardens close to the city centre. Bedrooms are split between three separate houses, two of which are linked by a glass walkway. Each is attractively decorated, tastefully furnished and thoughtfully equipped. Public rooms include a comfortable lounge/bar and a smart conservatory restaurant which overlooks the gardens.

Rooms 30 (12 annexe) (1 fmly) (9 GF) ⌖ **Facilities** FTV WiFi ⌖ **Parking** 28 **Notes** ⊗ Closed 24 Dec-2 Jan

Holiday Inn Norwich

★★★ 81% HOTEL

tel: 0871 942 9060 & 0800 405060 **Ipswich Rd NR4 6EP**
email: reservations-norwich@ihg.com **web:** www.holidayinn.co.uk
dir: A47 (Great Yarmouth) then A140 (Norwich). 1m, hotel on right

A modern, purpose-built hotel situated just off the A140, a short drive from the city centre. Public areas include a popular bar, the Junction Restaurant and a large open-plan lounge. Bedrooms come in a variety of styles and are suited to the needs of both the business and leisure guest alike.

Rooms 119 (41 fmly) (39 GF) **Facilities** STV FTV WiFi ⌖ HL ⌖ supervised Gym Sauna Steam room Beauty treatment room Xmas New Year **Conf** Class 48 Board 40 Thtr 150 **Services** Air con **Parking** 250 **Notes** ⊗ Civ Wed 120

Stower Grange

★★★ 80% ◉ COUNTRY HOUSE HOTEL

tel: 01603 860210 **School Rd, Drayton NR8 6EF**
email: enquiries@stowergrange.co.uk **web:** www.stowergrange.co.uk
dir: Norwich ring road N to Asda supermarket. Take A1067 (Fakenham road) at Drayton, right at lights into School Rd. Hotel 150yds on right

Expect a warm welcome at this 17th-century, ivy-clad property situated in a peaceful residential area close to the city centre and airport. The individually decorated bedrooms are generally quite spacious; each is tastefully furnished and equipped with many thoughtful touches. Public rooms include a smart open-plan lounge bar and an elegant restaurant.

Rooms 11 (1 fmly) ⌖ **Facilities** FTV WiFi ⌖ New Year **Conf** Class 45 Board 30 Thtr 100 **Parking** 40 **Notes** Civ Wed 100

BEST WESTERN George Hotel

★★★ 74% ◉ HOTEL

tel: 01603 617841 **10 Arlington Ln, Newmarket Rd NR2 2DA**
email: reservations@georgehotel.co.uk **web:** www.arlingtonhotelgroup.co.uk
dir: From A11 follow city centre signs, becomes Newmarket Rd. Hotel on left

Within just 10 minutes' walk of the town centre, this friendly, family-run hotel is well placed for guests wishing to explore the many sights of this historic city. The hotel occupies three adjacent buildings; the restaurant, bar and most bedrooms are located in the main building, while the adjacent cottages have been converted into comfortable and modern guest bedrooms.

Rooms 43 (5 annexe) (4 fmly) (19 GF) **Facilities** FTV WiFi Beauty therapist Holistic treatments Xmas New Year **Conf** Class 30 Board 30 Thtr 70 **Parking** 40 **Notes** ⊗

BEST WESTERN Brook Hotel Norwich

★★★ 73% HOTEL

tel: 01603 741161 **2 Barnard Rd, Bowthorpe NR5 9JB**
email: welcome@brookhotelnorwich.com **web:** www.brookhotelnorwich.com
dir: A47 towards Swaffham then A1074. Over double rdbt, to next rdbt, hotel on last exit

A modern, purpose-built hotel situated to the west of the city centre, just off the A47. The open-plan public areas include a lounge bar with TV, a foyer with plush sofas and a large dining room. The spacious bedrooms are equipped for both leisure and business guest alike.

Rooms 81 (13 fmly) (40 GF) **S** £70-£100; **D** £80-£110 (incl. bkfst)* **Facilities** FTV WiFi Gym Xmas New Year **Conf** Class 90 Board 60 Thtr 200 Del from £92.95* **Services** Air con **Parking** 100 **Notes** LB Civ Wed 200

The Old Rectory

★★ ◉◉ SMALL HOTEL

tel: 01603 700772 **103 Yarmouth Rd, Thorpe St Andrew NR7 0HF**
email: enquiries@oldrectorynorwich.com **web:** www.oldrectorynorwich.com
dir: From A47 southern bypass onto A1042 towards Norwich N & E. Left at mini rdbt onto A1242. After 0.3m through lights. Hotel 100mtrs on right

This delightful Grade II listed Georgian property is ideally located in a peaceful area overlooking the River Yare, just a few minutes' drive from the city centre. Spacious bedrooms are individually designed with carefully chosen soft fabrics, plush furniture and many thoughtful touches; many of the rooms overlook the swimming pool and landscaped gardens. Accomplished cooking is offered via an interesting daily-changing menu, which features skilfully prepared local produce.

Rooms 8 (3 annexe) ⌖ **S** £95-£170; **D** £130-£170 (incl. bkfst)* **Facilities** FTV WiFi ⌖ ⌖ **Conf** Class 12 Board 16 Thtr 25 **Parking** 15 **Notes** LB ⊗ Closed 23 Dec-3 Jan

NORWICH *continued*

Premier Inn Norwich Airport

BUDGET HOTEL

tel: 0871 527 8836 **Delft Way NR6 6BB**
web: www.premierinn.com
dir: From Norwich take A140 signed Cromer & Airport. Right at lights into Amsterdam Way. At mini-rdbt turn right. Hotel on right

High quality, budget accommodation ideal for both families and business travellers. Spacious, en suite bedrooms feature tea and coffee making facilities, and Freeview TV in most hotels. Internet access and WiFi are available for a small fee. The adjacent family restaurant features a wide and varied menu. See also the Hotel Groups pages.

Rooms 40

Premier Inn Norwich Central South

BUDGET HOTEL

tel: 0871 527 8838 **Broadlands Business Park, Old Chapel Way NR7 0WG**
web: www.premierinn.com
dir: A47 onto A1042, 3m E of city centre

Rooms 92

Premier Inn Norwich City Centre (Duke Street)

BUDGET HOTEL

tel: 0871 527 8840 **Duke St NR3 3AP**
web: www.premierinn.com
dir: From A1074, straight on at lights (Toys'R'Us) into St Benedict's St (or from A147 (A140, A11) right at lights. At next lights into Duke St (car park in St Andrews multi-storey on right - free to guests)

Rooms 117

Premier Inn Norwich Nelson City Centre

BUDGET HOTEL

tel: 0871 527 8842 **Prince of Wales Rd NR1 1DX**
web: www.premierinn.com
dir: Follow city centre, football ground & railway station signs. Hotel opposite station

Rooms 160

Premier Inn Norwich (Showground A47)

BUDGET HOTEL

tel: 0871 527 8834 **Longwater Interchange, Dereham Rd, New Costessey NR5 0TP**
web: www.premierinn.com
dir: A47 towards Dereham, take A1074 to City Centre. At rdbt 2nd exit, hotel on right. From N: A47 through Dereham. Straight on at 1st rdbt, at 2nd rdbt take 3rd exit. Hotel on left

Rooms 40

Brasteds

 RESTAURANT WITH ROOMS

tel: 01508 491112 📠 01508 491113 **Manor Farm Barns, Framingham Pigot NR14 7PZ**
email: enquiries@brasteds.co.uk **web:** www.brasteds.co.uk
dir: A11 onto A47 towards Great Yarmouth, then A146. 0.5m, right into Fox Rd, 0.5m on left

Brasteds is a lovely detached property set in 20 acres of mature, landscaped parkland on the outskirts of Norwich. The tastefully appointed bedrooms have beautiful soft furnishings and fabrics along with comfortable seating and many thoughtful touches. Public rooms include a cosy snug with plush sofas, and a smart dining room where breakfast is served. Dinner is available in Brasteds Restaurant, which can be found in an adjacent building.

Rooms 6 (1 fmly)

NOTTINGHAM   Map 11 SK53
Nottinghamshire

See also **Langar**

Hart's Hotel

★★★★ 80% HOTEL

tel: 0115 988 1900 **Standard Hill, Park Row NG1 6GN**
email: reception@hartsnottingham.co.uk **web:** www.hartsnottingham.co.uk
dir: At junct of Park Row & Ropewalk

This outstanding modern building stands on the site of the ramparts of the medieval castle, overlooking the city. Many of the bedrooms enjoy splendid views; all are well appointed and stylish. The Park Bar is the focal point of the public areas. Service is professional and caring and fine dining is offered at nearby Hart's Restaurant. Secure parking and private gardens are an added bonus.

Rooms 32 (1 fmly) (7 GF) 🐾 **D** £125-£265* **Facilities** STV FTV WiFi 🏊 Small unsupervised exercise room Beauty treatments Xmas New Year **Conf** Class 75 Board 30 Thtr 100 Del from £190* **Services** Lift **Parking** 16 **Notes** LB Civ Wed 100

The Nottingham Belfry

★★★★ 79% HOTEL

tel: 0115 973 9393 **Mellor's Way, Off Woodhouse Way NG8 6PY**
email: nottinghambelfry@qhotels.co.uk **web:** www.qhotels.co.uk
dir: From M1 junct 26 take A610 towards Nottingham. A6002 to Stapleford/Strelley. 0.75m, last exit at rdbt, hotel on right

Set conveniently close to the motorway links, yet not far from the city centre attractions, this modern hotel has a stylish and impressive interior. Bedrooms and bathrooms are spaciously appointed and very comfortable. There are two restaurants and two bars that offer interesting and satisfying cuisine. Staff are friendly and helpful. QHotels is the AA Hotel Group of the Year 2014-15.

Rooms 120 (20 fmly) (36 GF) ♠ **Facilities** Spa STV FTV WiFi ⌔ HL ⌘ Gym Sauna Steam room Aerobic studio Xmas New Year **Conf** Class 360 Board 60 Thtr 700 **Services** Lift **Parking** 250 **Notes** Civ Wed 150

Park Plaza Nottingham

★★★★ 73% ⊛ HOTEL

tel: 0844 415 6730 **41 Maid Marian Way NG1 6GD**
email: ppnsales@pphe.com **web:** www.parkplaza.com/nottinghamuk
dir: A6200 (Derby Rd) into Wollaton St. 2nd exit into Maid Marian Way. Hotel on left

This modern hotel is located in the centre of the city within walking distance of retail, commercial and tourist attractions. Bedrooms are spacious and comfortable, with many extras, including laptop safes and air conditioning. Service is discreetly attentive in the foyer lounge and the Chino Latino restaurant, where Pan-Asian cooking is a feature.

Rooms 178 (10 fmly) (16 smoking) **Facilities** STV FTV WiFi ⌔ Gym Complimentary fitness suite **Conf** Class 100 Board 54 Thtr 200 Del from £105 to £155* **Services** Lift Air con **Notes** ⊗ Civ Wed 180

BEST WESTERN Bestwood Lodge

★★★ 71% HOTEL

tel: 0115 920 3011 **Bestwood Country Park, Arnold NG5 8NE**
email: enquiries@bestwoodlodgehotel.co.uk **web:** www.bw-bestwoodlodge.co.uk
dir: From Nottingham take A60, left at lights into Oxclose Ln, right at next lights into Queens Bower Rd. 1st right. Keep right at fork in road

Set in 700 acres of parkland this Victorian building, once a hunting lodge, has stunning architecture that includes Gothic features and high vaulted ceilings. Bedrooms include all the modern comforts, suitable for both business and leisure guests, and the popular restaurant serves an extensive menu.

Rooms 39 (5 fmly) **Facilities** FTV WiFi ⌇ Guided walks Xmas **Conf** Class 65 Board 50 Thtr 200 **Parking** 120 **Notes** RS 25 Dec & 1 Jan Civ Wed 80

The Strathdon

★★ 71% HOTEL

tel: 0115 941 8501 **Derby Rd NG1 5FT**
email: info@strathdon-hotel-nottingham.com **web:** www.peelhotels.co.uk
dir: From M1 follow city centre signs. At Canning Circus into one-way system into Wollaton St, keep right, next right to hotel

This city-centre hotel has modern facilities and is very convenient for all city attractions. A popular themed bar has a large-screen TV and serves an extensive range of popular fresh food, while more formal dining is available in Bobbins Restaurant on certain evenings.

Rooms 68 (4 fmly) (16 smoking) **S** £50-£75; **D** £70-£95 (incl. bkfst)* **Facilities** FTV WiFi ⌇ Xmas New Year **Conf** Class 60 Board 40 Thtr 150 Del from £85 to £100* **Services** Lift **Notes** LB Civ Wed 85

Ibis Nottingham Centre

BUDGET HOTEL

tel: 0115 985 3600 **16 Fletcher Gate NG1 2FS**
email: h6160@accor.com **web:** www.ibishotel.com
dir: In Lace Market area of city centre

Modern, budget hotel offering comfortable accommodation in bright and practical bedrooms. Breakfast is self-service and dinner is available in the restaurant. See also the Hotel Groups pages.

Rooms 142 (33 fmly) ♠

Premier Inn Nottingham Arena (London Rd)

BUDGET HOTEL

tel: 0871 527 8848 **Island Site, London Rd NG2 4UU**
web: www.premierinn.com
dir: M1 junct 25, A52 into city centre. Follow signs for A60 to Loughborough. Hotel adjacent to BBC building

High quality, budget accommodation ideal for both families and business travellers. Spacious, en suite bedrooms feature tea and coffee making facilities, and Freeview TV in most hotels. Internet access and WiFi are available for a small fee. The adjacent family restaurant features a wide and varied menu. See also the Hotel Groups pages.

Rooms 87

Premier Inn Nottingham Castle Marina

BUDGET HOTEL

tel: 0871 527 8844 **Castle Marina Park, Castle Bridge Rd NG7 1GX**
web: www.premierinn.com
dir: M1 junct 24, A453. Follow ring road & signs for Queen's Drive Industrial Estate. After Homebase left into Castle Bridge Rd, opposite Pizza Hut restaurant. Hotel adjacent to Boathouse Beefeater

Rooms 39

Premier Inn Nottingham City Centre (Goldsmith Street)

BUDGET HOTEL

tel: 0871 527 8846 **Goldsmith St NG1 5LT**
web: www.premierinn.com
dir: A610 to city centre. Follow signs for Nottingham Trent University into Talbot St. 1st left into Clarendon St. Right at lights. Hotel on right

Rooms 161

Premier Inn Nottingham North (Daybrook)

BUDGET HOTEL

tel: 0871 527 8850 **101 Mansfield Rd, Daybrook NG5 6BH**
web: www.premierinn.com
dir: M1 junct 26, A610 towards Nottingham. Left onto A6514. Left onto A60 towards Mansfield. Hotel 0.25m on left

Rooms 64

N

NOTTINGHAM *continued*

Premier Inn Nottingham South

BUDGET HOTEL

tel: 0871 527 8854 **Loughborough Rd, Ruddington NG11 6LS**
web: www.premierinn.com
dir: M1 junct 24, follow A453 signs to Nottingham, A52 to Grantham. Hotel at 1st rdbt on left

Rooms 42

Premier Inn Nottingham West

BUDGET HOTEL

tel: 0871 527 8856 **The Phoenix Centre, Millennium Way West NG8 6AS**
web: www.premierinn.com
dir: M1 junct 26, 1m on A610 towards Nottingham

Rooms 86

INSPECTORS' CHOICE

Restaurant Sat Bains with Rooms

◉◉◉◉◉ RESTAURANT WITH ROOMS

tel: 0115 986 6566 📄 0115 986 0343 **Trentside, Lenton Ln NG7 2SA**
email: info@restaurantsatbains.net **web:** www.restaurantsatbains.com
dir: M1 junct 24, A453 Nottingham S. Over River Trent into central lane to rdbt. Left, left again towards river. Establishment on left after bend

This charming restaurant with rooms, a stylish conversion of Victorian farm buildings, is situated on the river and close to the industrial area of Nottingham. The bedrooms create a warm atmosphere by using quality soft furnishings together with antique and period furniture; suites and four-poster rooms are available. Public areas are chic and cosy, and the delightful restaurant complements the truly outstanding, much acclaimed cuisine.

Rooms 8 (4 annexe)

Cockliffe Country House

◉◉ RESTAURANT WITH ROOMS

tel: 0115 968 0179 📄 0115 968 0623 **Burntstump Country Park, Burntstump Hill, Arnold NG5 8PQ**
email: enquiries@cockliffehouse.co.uk **web:** www.cockliffehouse.co.uk
dir: M1 junct 27, follow signs to Hucknall (A611), then B6011, right at T-junct, follow signs for Cockliffe House

Expect a warm welcome at this delightful property situated in a peaceful rural location amid neat landscaped grounds, close to Sherwood Forest. Public areas include a smart breakfast room, a tastefully appointed restaurant and a cosy lounge bar. The individually decorated bedrooms have co-ordinated soft furnishings and many thoughtful touches.

Rooms 11 (4 annexe)

| **NUNEATON** | Map 11 SP39 |
Warwickshire

BEST WESTERN Weston Hall Hotel

★★★ 74% HOTEL

tel: 024 7631 2989 **Weston Ln, Bulkington CV12 9RU**
email: info@westonhallhotel.co.uk **web:** www.bw-westonhallhotel.co.uk
dir: M6 junct 2, B4065 through Ansty. Left in Shilton, from Bulkington follow Nuneaton signs, into Weston Ln at 30mph sign

This Grade II listed hotel, with origins dating back to the reign of Elizabeth I, sits within seven acres of peaceful grounds. The original three-gabled building retains many original features, such as the carved wooden fireplace in the library. Friendly service is provided; and the bedrooms, that vary in size, are thoughtfully equipped.

Rooms 38 (1 fmly) (14 GF) **Facilities** FTV WiFi ⬇ New Year **Conf** Class 100 Board 60 Thtr 200 **Parking** 250 **Notes** Civ Wed 200

Premier Inn Nuneaton/Coventry

BUDGET HOTEL

tel: 0871 527 8858 **Coventry Rd CV10 7PJ**
web: www.premierinn.com
dir: M6 junct 3, A444 towards Nuneaton. Hotel on B4113 on right, just off Griff Rdbt towards Bedworth

High quality, budget accommodation ideal for both families and business travellers. Spacious, en suite bedrooms feature tea and coffee making facilities, and Freeview TV in most hotels. Internet access and WiFi are available for a small fee. The adjacent family restaurant features a wide and varied menu. See also the Hotel Groups pages.

Rooms 48

| **OAKHAM** | Map 11 SK80 |
Rutland

INSPECTORS' CHOICE

Hambleton Hall

★★★★ ◉◉◉◉ COUNTRY HOUSE HOTEL

tel: 01572 756991 **Hambleton LE15 8TH**
email: hotel@hambletonhall.com **web:** www.hambletonhall.com
dir: 3m E off A606

Established over 30 years ago by Tim and Stefa Hart this delightful country house enjoys tranquil and spectacular views over Rutland Water. The beautifully manicured grounds are a delight to walk in. The bedrooms in the main house are stylish, individually decorated, and equipped with a range of thoughtful extras. A two-bedroom folly, with its own sitting and breakfast room, is only a short walk away. Day rooms include a cosy bar and a sumptuous drawing room, both featuring open fires. The elegant restaurant serves very accomplished, award-winning cuisine with menus highlighting locally sourced, seasonal produce - some of which is grown in the hotel's own grounds.

Rooms 17 (2 annexe) ⬩ **S** £195-£220; **D** £265-£460 (incl. bkfst)* **Facilities** STV FTV WiFi ⬩ ⬩ ⬩ Private access to lake Xmas New Year **Conf** Board 24 Thtr 40 Del from £300 to £330* **Services** Lift **Parking** 40 **Notes** LB Civ Wed 64

Barnsdale Lodge Hotel

★★★ 78% ⬡ HOTEL

tel: 01572 724678 **The Avenue, Rutland Water, North Shore LE15 8AH**
email: enquiries@barnsdalelodge.co.uk **web:** www.barnsdalelodge.co.uk
dir: A1 onto A606. Hotel 5m on right, 2m E of Oakham

A popular and interesting hotel converted from a farmstead overlooking Rutland Water. The public areas are dominated by a successful food operation with a good range of appealing meals on offer for either formal or informal dining. Bedrooms are comfortably appointed with excellent beds enhanced by contemporary soft furnishings and thoughtful extras.

Rooms 45 (2 fmly) (16 GF) ⬩ **S** £80-£95; **D** £95-£130 (incl. bkfst)* **Facilities** FTV WiFi ⬩ Fishing ⬩ Archery Beauty treatment room Golf Sailing Shooting Xmas New Year **Conf** Class 120 Board 76 Thtr 330 Del £135* **Parking** 200 **Notes** LB Civ Wed 200

OKEHAMPTON	Map 3 SX59
Devon	

Ashbury Hotel

★★ 74% HOTEL

tel: 01837 55453 **Higher Maddaford, Southcott EX20 4NL**
web: www.ashburygolfhotel.co.uk
dir: Exit A30 at Sourton Cross onto A386. Left onto A3079 to Bude at Fowley Cross. After 1m right to Ashbury. Hotel 0.5m on right

With no less than five courses and a clubhouse with lounge, bar and dining facilities, The Ashbury is a golfers' paradise. The majority of the well-equipped bedrooms are located in the farmhouse and the courtyard-style development around the putting green. Guests can enjoy the many on-site leisure facilities or join the activities available at the nearby sister hotel.

Rooms 222 (115 fmly) (89 GF) ⬩ **Facilities** Spa FTV WiFi ⬩ ⬩ 99 ⬩ Putt green Fishing Gym Badminton Shooting ranges Ten-pin bowling Indoor bowls 5-a-side Craft centre New Year **Conf** Thtr 250 Del from £60* **Parking** 200 **Notes** ⬩

Manor House Hotel

★★ 74% HOTEL

tel: 01837 53053 **Fowley Cross EX20 4NA**
email: reception@manorhousehotel.co.uk **web:** www.manorhousehotel.co.uk
dir: Exit A30 at Sourton Cross flyover, right onto A386. Hotel 1.5m on right

Enjoying views to Dartmoor in the distance, this hotel specialises in short breaks and is set in 17 acres of grounds, close to the A30. The superb range of sporting and craft facilities has been enhanced by an impressive swimming pool and relaxation spa; golf is also offered at the adjacent sister hotel. Bedrooms, many located on the ground floor, are comfortable and well equipped.

Rooms 200 (91 fmly) (90 GF) ⬩ **Facilities** Spa FTV WiFi ⬩ ⬩ 99 ⬩ Putt green Fishing ⬩ Gym Squash Craft centre Indoor bowls Shooting ranges Indoor tennis Exercise classes Xmas New Year **Parking** 200 **Notes** ⬩

White Hart Hotel

★★ 72% HOTEL

tel: 01837 52730 & 54514 **Fore St EX20 1HD**
email: enquiry@thewhitehart-hotel.com **web:** www.thewhitehart-hotel.com
dir: In town centre, adjacent to lights, car park at rear of hotel

Dating back to the 17th century and situated on the edge of the Dartmoor National Park, the White Hart offers modern facilities. Bedrooms are well equipped and spacious. Locally sourced, home-cooked food is on offer in the bars and the Courtney Restaurant; or guests can choose to eat in Vines Pizzeria. WiFi is available in public areas.

Rooms 19 (2 fmly) **Facilities** FTV WiFi ⬩ Xmas **Conf** Class 30 Board 40 Thtr 100 **Parking** 20

O

OLDBURY
West Midlands
Map 10 SO98

Premier Inn Birmingham Oldbury M5 Jct 2

BUDGET HOTEL

tel: 0871 527 8090 **Wolverhampton Rd B69 2BH**
web: www.premierinn.com
dir: M5 junct 2, A4123 (Wolverhampton Rd) N towards Dudley

High quality, budget accommodation ideal for both families and business travellers. Spacious, en suite bedrooms feature tea and coffee making facilities, and Freeview TV in most hotels. Internet access and WiFi are available for a small fee. The adjacent family restaurant features a wide and varied menu. See also the Hotel Groups pages.

Rooms 60

OLDHAM
Greater Manchester
Map 16 SD90

BEST WESTERN Hotel Smokies Park

★★★ 80% HOTEL

tel: 0161 785 5000 **Ashton Rd, Bardsley OL8 3HX**
email: sales@smokies.co.uk **web:** www.smokies.co.uk
dir: On A627 between Oldham & Ashton-under-Lyne

This modern, stylish hotel offers smart, comfortable bedrooms and suites. A wide range of Italian and English dishes is offered in the Mediterranean-style restaurant and there is a welcoming lounge bar with live entertainment at weekends. Also available are a small yet well equipped, residents-only fitness centre and extensive function facilities.

Rooms 73 (2 fmly) (22 GF) ↖ **S** £50-£80; **D** £50-£80* **Facilities** FTV WiFi ☼ Xmas New Year **Conf** Class 100 Board 40 Thtr 400 Del from £110 to £135* **Services** Lift **Parking** 120 **Notes** ⊗ RS 25 Dec-3 Jan Civ Wed 400

Premier Inn Oldham (Broadway)

BUDGET HOTEL

tel: 0871 527 8860 **Broadway/Hollinwood Av, Chadderton OL9 8DW**
web: www.premierinn.com
dir: M60 (anti-clockwise) junct 21, signed Manchester city centre. Take A663, hotel 400yds on left

High quality, budget accommodation ideal for both families and business travellers. Spacious, en suite bedrooms feature tea and coffee making facilities, and Freeview TV in most hotels. Internet access and WiFi are available for a small fee. The adjacent family restaurant features a wide and varied menu. See also the Hotel Groups pages.

Rooms 40

Premier Inn Oldham Central

BUDGET HOTEL

tel: 0871 527 8862 **Westwood Park, Chadderton Way, Chadderton OL1 2NA**
web: www.premierinn.com
dir: M62 junct 20, A627(M) to Oldham. Take A627 (Chadderton Way). Hotel on left opposite B&Q Depot

Rooms 40

OLD HARLOW
Essex
Map 6 TL41

Premier Inn Harlow

BUDGET HOTEL

tel: 0871 527 8488 **Cambridge Rd CM20 2EP**
web: www.premierinn.com
dir: M11 junct 7, A414, A1184 (Sawbridgeworth to Bishop's Stortford road)

High quality, budget accommodation ideal for both families and business travellers. Spacious, en suite bedrooms feature tea and coffee making facilities, and Freeview TV in most hotels. Internet access and WiFi are available for a small fee. The adjacent family restaurant features a wide and varied menu. See also the Hotel Groups pages.

Rooms 61

OLDSTEAD
North Yorkshire
Map 19 SE57

INSPECTORS' CHOICE

The Black Swan at Oldstead

◉◉◉ RESTAURANT WITH ROOMS

tel: 01347 868387 **YO61 4BL**
email: enquiries@blackswanoldstead.co.uk **web:** www.blackswanoldstead.co.uk
dir: Exit A19, 3m S Thirsk for Coxwold, left in Coxwold, left at Byland Abbey for Oldstead

The Black Swan is set amidst the stunning scenery of the North Yorkshire National Park, and parts of the building date back to the 16th century. Well appointed, very comfortable bedrooms and bathrooms provide the perfect get-away. Open fires, a traditional bar and a restaurant, serving award-winning food, is the icing on the cake for this little gem of a property.

Rooms 4

OLLERTON
Nottinghamshire
Map 16 SK66

Thoresby Hall Hotel

Warner Leisure Hotels
Life begins at Warner

★★★★ 78% ◉◉ COUNTRY HOUSE HOTEL

tel: 01623 821000 & 821033 **Thoresby Park NG22 9WH**
email: reception.thoresbyhall@bourne-leisure.co.uk **web:** www.warnerleisurehotels.co.uk

This hotel is set in acres of rolling parklands on the edge of Sherwood Forest. Thoresby Hall is a magnificent Grade I Victorian country house. Guests can choose to relax in the spa, stroll around the beautiful gardens or just sit and relax in the Great Hall. Bedrooms vary in style and size. This is an adults only (over 21 years) hotel.

Rooms 221 (168 annexe) (72 GF) **Facilities** Spa WiFi HL ⊕ supervised ⌘ Putt green Fishing ⊌ Gym Rifle shooting Archery Outdoor bowls Fencing Laser clay Yoga Tai chi ♫ Xmas New Year **Conf** Class 200 Board 30 Thtr 400 **Services** Lift **Parking** 140 **Notes** ⊗ No children 21yrs

ORFORD
Suffolk   Map 13 TM45

The Crown & Castle

★★★ 87% ◉◉ HOTEL

tel: 01394 450205 **IP12 2LJ**
email: info@crownandcastle.co.uk **web:** www.crownandcastle.co.uk
dir: Turn right from B1084 on entering village, towards castle

The Crown & Castle is a delightful inn situated adjacent to the Norman castle keep. Contemporary style bedrooms are spilt between the main house and the garden wing; the latter are more spacious and have patios with access to the garden. The restaurant has an informal atmosphere with polished tables and local artwork; the menu features quality, locally sourced produce.

Rooms 21 (14 annexe) (2 fmly) (13 GF) ⬧ **D** £135-£215 (incl. bkfst)* **Facilities** FTV WiFi ⬧ HL Xmas New Year **Parking** 17 **Notes** LB No children 8yrs

ORMSKIRK
Lancashire   Map 15 SD40

Premier Inn Southport (Ormskirk)

BUDGET HOTEL

tel: 0871 527 9010 **544 Southport Rd, Scarisbrick L40 9RG**
web: www.premierinn.com
dir: From Southport follow Ormskirk/A570 signs. Hotel on right of A570 (Southport Rd) at 1st lights (entrance just after lights)

High quality, budget accommodation ideal for both families and business travellers. Spacious, en suite bedrooms feature tea and coffee making facilities, and Freeview TV in most hotels. Internet access and WiFi are available for a small fee. The adjacent family restaurant features a wide and varied menu. See also the Hotel Groups pages.

Rooms 20

ORSETT
Essex   Map 6 TQ68

Orsett Hall Banqueting & Conference Centre

★★★★ 77% ◉◉ COUNTRY HOUSE HOTEL

tel: 01375 891402 **Prince Charles Av RM16 3HS**
email: reception@orsetthall.co.uk
dir: M25 junct 29, A127 Southend, A128 Hotel 3m on right

This beautiful country house hotel, conveniently located for the M25, is set in 12 acres of landscaped gardens, and has individually designed, luxurious bedrooms. The award-winning Garden restaurant is a fabulous dining venue and the stylish modern bar is popular with guests for afternoon tea. Orsett Hall has a first rate spa, and a very well equipped gym along with a range of business suites. Free WiFi is available throughout.

Rooms 41 (8 annexe) (3 fmly) (7 GF) ⬧ **Facilities** Spa FTV WiFi ⬧ Gym Hairdressers Xmas New Year **Conf** Class 200 Board 50 Thtr 450 **Services** Lift Air con **Parking** 250 **Notes** ⊗ Civ Wed 400

OSMOTHERLEY
North Yorkshire   Map 19 SE49

Cleveland Tontine

◉ RESTAURANT WITH ROOMS

tel: 01609 882671 ▤ 01609 882660 **Staddlebridge DL6 3JB**
email: bookings@theclevelandtontine.co.uk **web:** www.theclevelandtontine.co.uk
dir: Just off A172 junct on A19 Nbound

This iconic destination restaurant with rooms is a stunning place. Contemporary public areas sit alongside a traditional restaurant with open fires, tiled flooring and great food. Afternoon tea can be taken in the conservatory overlooking the gardens. Bedrooms are individually designed, with modern furniture and feature bathrooms. The service is friendly and relaxed, there is ample parking and major road links are close by.

Rooms 7 (4 fmly)

OSWESTRY
Shropshire   Map 15 SJ22

Wynnstay Hotel

★★★★ 77% ◉ HOTEL

tel: 01691 655261 **Church St SY11 2SZ**
email: info@wynnstayhotel.com **web:** www.wynnstayhotel.com
dir: B4083 to town, fork left at Honda Garage, right at lights. Hotel opposite church

This Georgian property was once a coaching inn and posting house and surrounds a unique 200-year-old Crown Bowling Green. Elegant public areas include a health, leisure and beauty centre, which is housed in a former coach house. Well-equipped bedrooms are individually styled and include several suites, four-poster rooms and a self-catering apartment. The Four Seasons Restaurant has a well deserved reputation for its food, and the adjacent Wilsons café/bar is a stylish, informal alternative.

Rooms 34 (5 fmly) ⬧ **Facilities** Spa FTV WiFi ⬧ supervised Gym Crown bowling green Beauty suite ♫ New Year **Conf** Class 150 Board 50 Thtr 290 **Parking** 80 **Notes** ⊗ Civ Wed 90

Lion Quays Waterside Resort

★★★★ 77% HOTEL

tel: 01691 684300 **Moreton, Weston Rhyn SY11 3EN**
email: reservations@lionquays.com **web:** www.lionquays.com
dir: On A5, 3m N of Oswestry

This resort is situated beside the Llangollen Canal which is in a convenient location for visiting Chester to the north and the Snowdonia region to the west. The comfortable bedrooms have views over the countryside or the magnificent grounds and gardens. Guests can dine either in the Waterside Bar or the Country Club which has a stunning 25-metre swimming pool, a state-of-the-art gym plus spa facilities. Extensive conference and meeting facilities are also available.

Rooms 82 (3 fmly) (25 GF) ⬧ **Facilities** Spa FTV WiFi ⬧ supervised ⬧ Gym Sauna Steam room Bowling green Fitness classes Xmas New Year **Conf** Class 200 Board 150 Thtr 600 **Services** Lift **Parking** 400 **Notes** ⊗ Civ Wed 600

O

OSWESTRY *continued*

Pen-y-Dyffryn Country Hotel

★★★ 85% ◉◉ ◉ COUNTRY HOUSE HOTEL

tel: 01691 653700 **Rhydycroesau SY10 7JD**
email: stay@peny.co.uk **web:** www.peny.co.uk
dir: A5 into town centre. Follow signs to Llansilin on B4580, hotel 3m W of Oswestry before Rhydycroesau

Peacefully situated in five acres of grounds, this charming old house dates back to around 1840, when it was built as a rectory. The tastefully appointed public rooms have real fires, lit in colder weather, and the accommodation includes several mini-cottages, each with its own patio. Many guests are attracted to this hotel for the excellent food and attentive, friendly service.

Rooms 12 (4 annexe) (1 fmly) (1 GF) ✆ **S** £90-£110; **D** £130-£190 (incl. bkfst) **Facilities** STV FTV WiFi ⬥ Guided walks New Year **Parking** 18 **Notes** LB No children 3yrs Closed 18 Dec-19 Jan

Premier Inn Oswestry

BUDGET HOTEL

tel: 0871 527 8864 **SY10 8NN**
web: www.premierinn.com
dir: From rdbt junct of A483 & A5 (SE of Oswestry) take A5 signed Oswestry B4579. Hotel 500yds

High quality, budget accommodation ideal for both families and business travellers. Spacious, en suite bedrooms feature tea and coffee making facilities, and Freeview TV in most hotels. Internet access and WiFi are available for a small fee. The adjacent family restaurant features a wide and varied menu. See also the Hotel Groups pages.

Rooms 59

Sebastians

◉◉ ◉ RESTAURANT WITH ROOMS

tel: 01691 655444 📠 01691 653452 **45 Willow St SY11 1AQ**
email: sebastians.rest@virgin.net **web:** www.sebastians-hotel.co.uk
dir: From town centre, take turn signed Selattyn into Willow St. 400yds from junct on left opposite Willow Street Gallery

Sebastians is an intrinsic part of the leisure scene in Oswestry and has built up a loyal local following. Meals feature French influences, with a multi-choice set menu as well as a simpler Market menu. Rooms are set around the pretty terrace courtyard, and provide very comfortable accommodation with all the comforts of home.

Rooms 5 (4 annexe) (4 fmly)

OTLEY	Map 19 SE24
West Yorkshire	

Chevin Country Park Hotel & Spa

★★★ 77% ◉ HOTEL

tel: 01943 467818 **Yorkgate LS21 3NU**
email: chevin@crerarhotels.com **web:** www.crerarhotels.com
dir: From Leeds/Bradford Airport rdbt take A658 N towards Harrogate, 0.75m to lights. Left, 2nd left into Yorkgate. Hotel 0.5m on left

Chevin Country Park Hotel is peacefully located in its own woodland yet is convenient for major road links and the airport. Bedrooms are split between the original main building and chalet-style accommodation in the extensive grounds. Public areas include a bar and several lounges. The Lakeside Restaurant provides views over the small lake, and good leisure facilities are available.

Rooms 49 (30 annexe) (7 fmly) (45 GF) **Facilities** Spa FTV WiFi ⏲ ⬥ Fishing Gym Steam room Xmas New Year **Conf** Class 90 Board 50 Thtr 120 **Parking** 100 **Notes** Civ Wed 100

OTTERSHAW	Map 6 TQ06
Surrey	

Foxhills Club and Resort

★★★★ 84% ◉ HOTEL

tel: 01932 872050 & 704500 **Stonehill Rd KT16 0EL**
email: reservations@foxhills.co.uk **web:** www.foxhills.co.uk
dir: M25 junct 11, A320 to Woking. 2nd rdbt last exit into Chobham Rd. Right into Foxhills Rd, left into Stonehill Rd

This 19th-century mansion hotel enjoys a peaceful setting in extensive grounds, not far from the M25 and Heathrow. Spacious well-appointed bedrooms are provided in a choice of annexes situated a short walk from the main house. Golf, tennis, three pools and impressive indoor leisure facilities are available. There is a superb spa offering a range of treatments and therapies plus a health club with all the latest fitness equipment. The eating options are the Manor Restaurant, in the former music room, and the Summerhouse Brasserie.

Rooms 70 (8 fmly) (39 GF) ✆ **Facilities** Spa STV FTV WiFi ⬥ ⏲ ⬩ ⬩ 45 ⬩ Putt green ⬩ Gym Squash Children's adventure playground Country pursuits Off-road course Hairdresser ♫ Xmas New Year **Conf** Class 62 Board 56 Thtr 100 **Parking** 500 **Notes** ⊗ Civ Wed 75

OTTERY ST MARY	Map 3 SY19
Devon	

Tumbling Weir Hotel

★★ 79% SMALL HOTEL

tel: 01404 812752 **Canaan Way EX11 1AQ**
email: reception@tumblingweirhotel.com **web:** www.tumblingweirhotel.co.uk
dir: A30 onto B3177 into Ottery St Mary, hotel signed from Mill St, access through old mill

Quietly located between the River Otter and its millstream, and set in well-tended gardens, this family-run hotel offers friendly and attentive service. Bedrooms are attractively presented and equipped with modern comforts. In the dining room, where a selection of carefully prepared dishes makes up the carte menu, beams and subtle lighting help to create an intimate atmosphere.

Rooms 10 (1 fmly) ✆ **S** £60-£70; **D** £95-£110 (incl. bkfst) **Facilities** FTV WiFi ⬥ ⬩ **Conf** Class 60 Board 50 Thtr 90 Del from £95 to £110 **Parking** 10 **Notes** LB ⊗ Closed 22 Dec-7 Jan

OUNDLE
Northamptonshire

Map 11 TL08

The Talbot Hotel

★★★ 78%  HOTEL

tel: 01832 273621 **New St PE8 4EA**
email: talbot@bulldogmail.co.uk **web:** www.thetalbot-oundle.com
dir: A605 Northampton/Oundle at rdbt exit Oundle A427 - Station Road turn onto New Street

This Grade I listed property is steeped in history and is reputed to house the staircase that Mary Queen of Scots walked down to her execution in 1587. Following extensive refurbishment, the hotel offers an open-plan eatery and coffee shop for relaxed dining. Accommodation offers a mix of traditional and contemporary, but all provide up-to-date amenities for guest comfort.

Rooms 34 (2 fmly) (12 GF) ❧ **Facilities** FTV WiFi Xmas New Year **Conf** Class 50 Board 30 Thtr 100 Del from £110 to £150 **Parking** 30 **Notes** Civ Wed 80

OXFORD
Oxfordshire

Map 5 SP50

INSPECTORS' CHOICE

Belmond Le Manoir aux Quat' Saisons
★★★★★ ◉◉◉◉◉ HOTEL

tel: 01844 278881 **Church Rd OX44 7PD**
email: lemanoir@blanc.co.uk **web:** www.manoir.com

(For full entry see Great Milton)

Macdonald Randolph Hotel

★★★★★ 81% ◉◉◉ HOTEL

tel: 01865 256400 **Beaumont St OX1 2LN**
email: randolph@macdonald-hotels.co.uk **web:** www.macdonaldhotels.co.uk
dir: M40 junct 8, A40 signed Oxford/Cheltenham, 5m, at lights to ring road rdbt. Right signed Kidlington/North Oxford. At next rdbt left towards city centre (A4165/ Banbury Rd). Through Summertown to lights at end of St Giles. Hotel on right

Superbly located near the city centre, The Randolph boasts impressive neo-Gothic architecture and tasteful decor. The spacious and traditional restaurant, complete with picture windows, is the ideal place to watch the world go by while enjoying freshly prepared, modern dishes. Bedrooms include a mix of classical and contemporary wing rooms, which have been appointed to a high standard. Parking is a real bonus.

Rooms 151 ❧ **S** £134-£241; **D** £144-£251* **Facilities** Spa STV FTV WiFi Gym Beauty treatment rooms Thermal suite Mini gym ♫ Xmas New Year **Conf** Class 130 Board 60 Thtr 300 Del from £145* **Services** Lift **Parking** 60 **Notes** LB Civ Wed 120

Old Parsonage Hotel

★★★★ 83% TOWN HOUSE HOTEL

tel: 01865 310210 **1 Banbury Rd OX2 6NN**
email: reception@oldparsonage-hotel.co.uk **web:** www.oldparsonage-hotel.co.uk
dir: From Oxford ring road to city centre via Summertown. Hotel last building on right before entering St Giles

The Old Parsonage is reopening after a major refurbishment. Dating back in parts to the 16th century, this stylish hotel offers great character and charm and is conveniently located at the northern edge of the city centre. The focal point of the operation is the busy all-day bar and restaurant which has a clubby, bohemian atmosphere; the small garden areas and terraces prove popular in summer months. The Pike Room is available for private lunches and dinners, weddings and meetings. Liveried bicycles are available for guests to explore the city.

Rooms 35 (4 fmly) (10 GF) ❧ **D** £195-£305* **Facilities** STV FTV WiFi ❧ In room beauty treatments Nearby fitness club House bikes Walking tours Library Xmas New Year **Conf** Class 8 Board 12 Thtr 20 Del from £275 to £500* **Services** Air con **Parking** 14 **Notes** LB Civ Wed 20

The Old Bank Hotel

★★★★ 79% TOWN HOUSE HOTEL

tel: 01865 799599 **92-94 High St OX1 4BJ**
email: reception@oldbank-hotel.co.uk **web:** www.oldbank-hotel.co.uk
dir: From Magdalen Bridge onto High St, hotel 50yds on left

Located close to the city centre and the colleges, this former bank benefits from an excellent location. An eclectic collection of modern pictures and photographs, many by well-known artists, are on display. Bedrooms are smart with excellent business facilities plus the benefit of air conditioning. Public areas include the vibrant all-day Quod Bar and Restaurant. The hotel has its own car park - a definite advantage in this busy city.

Rooms 42 (4 fmly) (1 GF) ❧ **D** £145-£320* **Facilities** STV FTV WiFi ❧ Beauty treatment room Bicycles Free use of nearby gym Bicycle & Walking tours ♫ Xmas **Conf** Board 30 Thtr 50 Del from £200 to £400* **Services** Lift Air con **Parking** 40 **Notes** ⊗

Oxford Spires Four Pillars Hotel

★★★★ 77% HOTEL

tel: 0800 374692 & 01865 324324 **Abingdon Rd OX1 4PS**
email: spires@four-pillars.co.uk **web:** www.four-pillars.co.uk/spires
dir: M40 junct 8 towards Oxford. Left towards Cowley. At 3rd rdbt follow city centre signs. Hotel in 1m

This purpose-built hotel is surrounded by extensive parkland, yet is only a short walk from the city centre. Bedrooms are attractively furnished, well equipped and include several apartments. Public areas include a spacious restaurant, open-plan bar/lounge, leisure club and extensive conference facilities.

Rooms 174 (10 annexe) (1 fmly) (54 GF) ❧ **S** £110-£250; **D** £120-£280 **Facilities** FTV WiFi ❧ ❧ Gym Beauty treatments Steam room Sauna Xmas New Year **Conf** Class 96 Board 76 Thtr 266 Del from £140 to £199 **Services** Lift **Parking** 95 **Notes** LB ⊗ Civ Wed 200

O

OXFORD *continued*

Malmaison Oxford

★★★★ 76%  HOTEL

hotels that dare to be different

tel: 0844 693 0659 **3 Oxford Castle, New Rd OX1 1AY**
email: oxford@malmaison.com **web:** www.malmaison.com
dir: M40 junct 9, A34 N to Botley interchange. Follow city centre & rail station signs. At rail station straight ahead to 2nd lights. Turn right, at next lights left into Park End St. Straight on at next lights, hotel 2nd left

Once the city's prison, this is definitely a hotel with a difference. Many of the rooms are actually converted from the old cells. Not to worry though as there have been many improvements since the prisoners left. Exceedingly comfortable beds and luxury bathrooms are just two of the changes. The hotel has a popular brasserie with quality and value much in evidence. Limited parking space is available.

Rooms 95 (5 GF) ⌇ **S** £125-£250; **Facilities** STV FTV WiFi Xmas New Year **Conf** Class 40 Board 40 Thtr 80 Del from £195 to £320* **Services** Lift **Parking** 30 **Notes** LB ⊗ Civ Wed 80

The Oxford Hotel

★★★★ 76%  HOTEL

PUMA HOTELS
COLLECTION

tel: 01865 489988 **Godstow Rd, Wolvercote Roundabout OX2 8AL**
email: oxford@pumahotels.co.uk **web:** www.pumahotels.co.uk
dir: Adjacent to A34/A40, 2m from city centre

Conveniently located on the northern edge of the city centre, this purpose-built hotel offers bedrooms that are bright, modern and well equipped. Guests can eat in the Medio Restaurant or try the Cappuccino Lounge menu. There is also the option to eat alfresco on the Patio Terrace when the weather is fine. The hotel offers impressive conference, business and leisure facilities.

Rooms 168 (11 fmly) (89 GF) **Facilities** Spa STV WiFi ⊛ supervised Gym Squash Steam room Beauty treatments New Year **Conf** Class 130 Board 110 Thtr 320 **Parking** 250 **Notes** Civ Wed 250

Oxford Thames Four Pillars Hotel

★★★★ 76% HOTEL

FOUR PILLARS HOTELS

tel: 0800 374692 & 01865 334444 **Henley Rd, Sandford-on-Thames OX4 4GX**
email: thames@four-pillars.co.uk **web:** www.four-pillars.co.uk/thames
dir: M40 junct 8 towards Oxford, follow ring road. Left at rdbt towards Cowley. At rdbt with lights turn left to Littlemore, hotel approx 1m on right

Set in 30 acres of beautiful grounds beside the river, this mellow stone property provides a quiet retreat, yet is close to the city. The spacious and traditional River Room Restaurant has superb views of the hotel's own boat moored on the river. The gardens can be enjoyed from the patios or balconies in the newer bedroom wings. Public rooms include a beamed bar and lounge area with minstrels' gallery, and Jerome's Leisure Club. The hotel is popular as a wedding venue.

Rooms 84 (5 fmly) (39 GF) ⌇ **S** £125-£250; **D** £125-£250 **Facilities** FTV WiFi ⊿ ⊛ ⊛ Gym Steam room Sauna Beauty treatment room Xmas New Year **Conf** Class 80 Board 40 Thtr 120 Del from £130 to £199 **Parking** 130 **Notes** LB ⊗ Civ Wed 100

Cotswold Lodge Hotel

★★★★ 73% HOTEL

CLASSIC
BRITISH HOTELS

tel: 01865 512121 **66a Banbury Rd OX2 6JP**
email: info@cotswoldlodgehotel.co.uk **web:** www.cotswoldlodgehotel.co.uk
dir: A40 (Oxford ring road) onto A4165 (Banbury road) signed city centre/Summertown. Hotel 2m on left

This Victorian property is located close to the centre of Oxford and offers smart, comfortable accommodation. Stylish bedrooms and suites are attractively presented and some have balconies. The public areas have an elegant country-house feel. The hotel is popular with business guests and caters for conferences and banquets.

Rooms 49 (14 GF) ⌇ **S** £65-£155; **D** £85-£200 **Facilities** STV FTV WiFi ⊿ Xmas New Year **Conf** Class 45 Board 40 Thtr 100 Del from £140 to £195* **Parking** 40 **Notes** LB ⊗ Civ Wed 100

Hawkwell House

★★★ 83% HOTEL

tel: 01865 749988 **Church Way, Iffley Village OX4 4DZ**
email: reservations@hawkwellhouse.co.uk **web:** www.hawkwellhouse.co.uk
dir: A34 follow signs to Cowley. At Littlemore rdbt A4158 exit into Iffley Rd. After lights left to Iffley

Set in a peaceful residential location, Hawkwell House is just a few minutes' drive from the Oxford ring road. The spacious rooms are modern, attractively decorated and well equipped. Public areas are tastefully appointed and the conservatory-style restaurant offers an interesting choice of dishes. The hotel also has a range of conference and function facilities.

Rooms 77 (15 annexe) (10 fmly) (15 GF) ⌇ **Facilities** STV FTV WiFi ⊿ ⊌ Xmas New Year **Conf** Class 100 Board 80 Thtr 200 **Services** Lift **Parking** 120 **Notes** ⊗ Civ Wed 150

Mercure Oxford Eastgate Hotel

★★★ 82%  HOTEL

Mercure
HOTELS

tel: 01865 248332 **73 High St OX1 4BE**
email: h6668@accor.com **web:** www.mercure.com
dir: A40 follow signs to Headington & Oxford city centre, over Magdalen Bridge, stay in left lane, through lights, left into Merton St, entrance to car park on left

Just a short stroll from the city centre, this hotel, as its name suggests, occupies the site of the city's medieval East Gate and boasts its own car park. Bedrooms are appointed and equipped to a high standard. Stylish public areas include the all-day Town House Brasserie and Bar.

Rooms 64 (3 fmly) (4 GF) ⌇ **Facilities** WiFi Xmas New Year **Services** Lift Air con **Parking** 40 **Notes** ⊗

O

Manor House Hotel

★★ 71% METRO HOTEL

tel: 01865 727627 & 458177 **250 Iffley Rd OX4 1SE**
email: manorhousehotel@hotmail.com **web:** www.manorhouseoxford.com
dir: On A4158, 1m from city centre

This family run establishment is easily accessible from the city centre and all major road links. The hotel provides informal but friendly and attentive service. The comfortably furnished bedrooms are well equipped. The hotel has a bar but there is a selection of restaurants and popular pubs within easy walking distance. Limited private parking is available.

Rooms 8 (2 fmly) **S** £69-£99; **D** £89-£99 (incl. bkfst)* **Facilities** STV FTV WiFi ⌑
Parking 6 **Notes** ⊗ Closed 20 Dec-20 Jan

Bath Place Hotel

★★ 68% METRO HOTEL

tel: 01865 791812 **4-5 Bath Place, Holywell St OX1 3SU**
email: info@bathplace.co.uk **web:** www.bathplace.co.uk
dir: On S side of Holywell St, parallel to High St

The hotel has been created from a group of 17th-century cottages originally built by Flemish weavers who were permitted to settle outside the city walls. This lovely hotel is very much at the heart of the city today and offers individually designed bedrooms, including some with four-posters.

Rooms 16 (3 fmly) (5 GF) ⌕ **S** £90-£105; **D** £110-£160 (incl. bkfst)* **Facilities** FTV
WiFi **Parking** 16

The Balkan Lodge Hotel

★★ 67% METRO HOTEL

tel: 01865 244524 **315 Iffley Rd OX4 4AG**
email: info@balkanlodgeoxford.co.uk **web:** www.balkanlodgeoxford.co.uk
dir: From M40, A40 take eastern bypass, into city on A4158

Conveniently located for the city centre and the ring road, this family operated metro hotel offers a comfortable stay. Bedrooms are attractive and well equipped. Public areas include a lounge and bar. A secure private car park is located to the rear of the building.

Rooms 12 **Facilities** WiFi **Parking** 12 **Notes** ⊗

Premier Inn Oxford

BUDGET HOTEL

tel: 0871 527 8866 **Oxford Business Park, Garsington Rd OX4 2JZ**
web: www.premierinn.com
dir: On Oxford Business Park, just off A4142 & B480 junct

High quality, budget accommodation ideal for both families and business travellers. Spacious, en suite bedrooms feature tea and coffee making facilities, and Freeview TV in most hotels. Internet access and WiFi are available for a small fee. The adjacent family restaurant features a wide and varied menu. See also the Hotel Groups pages.

Rooms 121

OXFORD MOTORWAY SERVICE AREA (M40) Map 5 SP60
Oxfordshire

Days Inn Oxford - M40

BUDGET HOTEL

tel: 01865 877000 **M40 junction 8A, Waterstock OX33 1LJ**
email: oxford.hotel@welcomebreak.co.uk **web:** www.welcomebreak.co.uk
dir: M40 junct 8a, at Welcome Break service area

This modern building offers accommodation in smart, spacious and well-equipped bedrooms, suitable for families and business travellers, and all with en suite bathrooms. Continental breakfast is available and other refreshments may be taken at the nearby family restaurant. See also the Hotel Groups pages.

Rooms 59 (56 fmly) (25 GF) (10 smoking)

PADSTOW Map 2 SW97
Cornwall

Treglos Hotel

★★★★ 84% ◉ HOTEL

tel: 01841 520727 **Constantine Bay PL28 8JH**
email: stay@tregloshotel.com **web:** www.tregloshotel.com
dir: From Oakhampton A30, follow A39 towards Wadebridge, then B3274 to Padstow. After 2m turn left to St Merryn. After 3m, at St Merryn x-rd/s turn left. Take next right to Treglos. After 1m turn right after Constantine Bay Stores. Hotel is on left

This long-established hotel is situated on the edge of the stunning Cornish coast with breathtaking views. The atmosphere is all about sophistication and elegance. Bedrooms are soundly appointed and well equipped, and there is a contemporary dining room with enjoyable cuisine and wonderful views over the coast. Guests will find a superb bar and lounges to relax and unwind in. On-site parking is a bonus.

Rooms 42 **S** £72-£110; **D** £144-£220 (incl. bkfst)* **Facilities** FTV WiFi ⌑ ⊛ ⌁ 18
Beauty treatments Infrared cabin Games room Childrens play ground **Services** Lift

The Metropole

★★★★ 75% ◉ HOTEL

RICHARDSON HOTELS

tel: 01841 532486 **Station Rd PL28 8DB**
email: reservations@the-metropole.co.uk **web:** www.the-metropole.co.uk
dir: M5/A30 pass Launceston, follow Wadebridge & N Cornwall signs. Take A39, follow Padstow signs

This long-established hotel first opened its doors to guests back in 1904, and it still retains an air of the sophistication and elegance of a bygone age. Bedrooms are soundly appointed and well equipped; dining options include the informal Met Café Bar, and the main restaurant with its enjoyable cuisine and wonderful views over the Camel estuary.

Rooms 58 (3 fmly) (2 GF) ⌕ **S** £59.50-£119.50; **D** £69-£189 (incl. bkfst)*
Facilities Spa FTV WiFi ⌁ Swimming pool open Jul & Aug only Xmas New Year
Conf Class 20 Board 20 Thtr 40 **Services** Lift **Parking** 36 **Notes** LB Civ Wed 110

PADSTOW *continued*

St Petroc's Hotel and Bistro

★★ 85% SMALL HOTEL

tel: 01841 532700 **4 New St PL28 8EA**
email: reservations@rickstein.com **web:** www.rickstein.com
dir: A39 onto A389, follow signs to town centre. Follow one-way system, hotel on right on leaving town

One of the oldest buildings in town, this charming establishment is just up the hill from the picturesque harbour. Style, comfort and individuality are all great strengths here, particularly so in the impressively equipped bedrooms. Breakfast, lunch and dinner all reflect a serious approach to cuisine, and the popular restaurant has a relaxed, bistro style. Comfortable lounges, a reading room and lovely gardens complete the picture.

Rooms 14 (4 annexe) (3 fmly) (3 GF) ⬢ **S** £160-£270; **D** £160-£270 (incl. bkfst)* **Facilities** FTV WiFi Cookery school New Year **Parking** 8 **Notes** LB Closed 25-26 Dec RS 24 Dec eve

The Old Ship Hotel

★★ 78% HOTEL

tel: 01841 532357 **Mill Square PL28 8AE**
email: stay@oldshiphotel-padstow.co.uk **web:** www.oldshiphotel-padstow.co.uk
dir: From M5 take A30 to Bodmin then A389 to Padstow, follow brown tourist signs to car park

This attractive inn is situated in the heart of the old town's quaint and winding streets, just a short walk from the harbour. A warm welcome is assured, accommodation is pleasant and comfortable, and public areas offer plenty of character. Freshly-caught fish features on both the bar and restaurant menus. On-site parking is a bonus.

Rooms 14 (4 fmly) **S** £60-£70; **D** £90-£130 (incl. bkfst)* **Facilities** STV FTV WiFi ♬ Xmas New Year **Parking** 20 **Notes** LB

INSPECTORS' CHOICE

The Seafood Restaurant

❀❀❀ RESTAURANT WITH ROOMS

tel: 01841 532700 📠 01841 532942 **Riverside PL28 8BY**
email: reservations@rickstein.com **web:** www.rickstein.com
dir: Into town centre down hill, follow round sharp bend, restaurant on left

Food lovers continue to beat a well-trodden path to this well-known restaurant. Situated on the edge of the harbour, just a stone's throw from the shops, The Seafood Restaurant offers chic and comfortable bedrooms that boast numerous thoughtful extras; some have views of the estuary and a couple have private balconies with stunning sea views. Service is relaxed and friendly; booking is essential for both accommodation and a table in the restaurant.

Rooms 20 (6 annexe) (6 fmly)

PAIGNTON	Map 3 SX86
Devon	

Redcliffe Hotel

★★★ 79% HOTEL

tel: 01803 526397 **Marine Dr TQ3 2NL**
email: redclfe@aol.com **web:** www.redcliffehotel.co.uk
dir: On seafront at Torquay end of Paignton Green

Set at the water's edge in three acres of well-tended grounds, this popular hotel enjoys uninterrupted views across Tor Bay. On offer is a diverse range of facilities including a leisure complex, beauty treatments and lots of outdoor family activities in the summer. Bedrooms are pleasantly appointed and comfortably furnished, while public areas offer ample space for rest and relaxation.

Rooms 68 (8 fmly) (3 GF) ⬢ **S** £55-£69; **D** £110-£138 (incl. bkfst)* **Facilities** Spa FTV WiFi ⊗ supervised ⬥ Putt green Fishing Gym Table tennis Carpet bowls Xmas New Year **Conf** Class 50 Board 50 Thtr 150 Del from £85 to £110* **Services** Lift **Parking** 80 **Notes** LB ⊗ Civ Wed 150

Premier Inn (Goodrington Sands)

BUDGET HOTEL

tel: 0871 527 9206 **Tanners Rd, Goodrington TQ4 6LP**
web: www.premierinn.com
dir: From Newton Abbot take A380 S. Left into A3022 (Totnes Rd), right at Hayes Rd into Penwill Way, right at B3199 into Dartmouth Rd, at lights left into Tanners Rd

High quality, budget accommodation ideal for both families and business travellers. Spacious, en suite bedrooms feature tea and coffee making facilities, and Freeview TV in most hotels. Internet access and WiFi are available for a small fee. The adjacent family restaurant features a wide and varied menu. See also the Hotel Groups pages.

Rooms 33

Premier Inn Paignton South (Brixham Road)

BUDGET HOTEL

tel: 0871 527 9324 **White Rock, Long Road South TQ4 7AZ**
web: www.premierinn.com
dir: From A3022 (Brixham Rd) between Tweenaway & Galmpton Warborough, right into Long Rd

Rooms 61

PAINSWICK
Gloucestershire   Map 4 SO80

INSPECTORS' CHOICE

Cotswolds88Hotel

★★★★ @@@ SMALL HOTEL

tel: 01452 813688 **Kemps Ln GL6 6YB**
email: reservations@cotswolds88hotel.com **web:** www.cotswolds88hotel.com
dir: From Stroud towards Cheltenham on A46, in Painswick centre right at St Marys Church into Victoria St. Left into St Marys St, right into Tibbiwell St, right into Kemps Lane

In the heart of a pretty village, this 18th-century house offers a range of beautifully presented and individually styled bedrooms. Most of the rooms have stunning countryside views and all are equipped to the highest standard. Residents have access to the private lounge with balcony and the cosy library. The modern restaurant has a well deserved reputation, and the dishes feature the finest locally sourced and organic produce.

Rooms 17 (8 annexe) (2 fmly) ↟ **Facilities** STV FTV WiFi ↷ HL Beauty treatment room Xmas New Year **Conf** Class 34 Board 30 Thtr 60 **Parking** 17 **Notes** Closed 1-14 Jan Civ Wed 120

PALTERTON
Derbyshire   Map 16 SK46

Twin Oaks Hotel

★★★ 75% HOTEL

tel: 01246 855455 **Church Ln S44 6UZ**
email: book@twinoakshotel.co.uk **web:** www.twinoakshotel.co.uk
dir: M1 junct 29, take Palterton turn, hotel 100mtrs down road on left

This hotel began life as a picturesque row of colliery cottages, but it has been meticulously redesigned and configured to meet the expectations of the modern business and leisure traveller. The bedrooms provide contemporary accommodation and the attractive public areas include a brasserie and bistro providing a range of dining options. The hotel is a popular wedding destination and enjoys very good transport links as it is near the M1.

Rooms 26 (4 annexe) (4 fmly) (14 GF) **D** £75-£105* **Facilities** FTV WiFi ↷ **Conf** Class 25 Board 25 Thtr 40 **Parking** 80 **Notes** ⊗ Civ Wed 80

PANGBOURNE
Berkshire   Map 5 SU67

The Elephant at Pangbourne

★★★ 80% @ HOTEL

tel: 0118 984 2244 **Church Rd RG8 7AR**
email: matt@elephanthotel.co.uk **web:** www.elephanthotel.co.uk
dir: M4 junct 12, A4 signed Theale/Newbury, right at 2nd rdbt signed Pangbourne. Hotel in village centre on left

Centrally located in this bustling village, just a short drive from Reading. Bedrooms are individual in style but identical in the attention to detail, with handcrafted Indian furniture and rich oriental rugs. Guests can enjoy award-winning cuisine in the restaurant, or there is bistro-style dining in the bar area.

Rooms 22 (8 annexe) (2 fmly) (4 GF) **Facilities** FTV WiFi ↘ Xmas New Year **Conf** Class 40 Board 30 Thtr 60 **Parking** 10 **Notes** Civ Wed 120

PATTERDALE
Cumbria   Map 18 NY31

Patterdale Hotel

★★ 75% HOTEL

tel: 0844 811 5580 & 017684 82231 **CA11 0NN**
email: reservations@choice-hotels.co.uk **web:** www.patterdalehotel.co.uk
dir: M6 junct 40, A592 towards Ullswater. 10m to Patterdale

Patterdale is a real tourist destination and this hotel makes a good base for those taking part in the many activity pursuits available in this area. The hotel enjoys delightful views of the valley and fells, being located at the southern end of Ullswater. The modern bedrooms vary in style. In busier periods accommodation is let for a minimum period of two nights.

Rooms 57 (15 fmly) (6 GF) ↟ **S** £39-£64; **D** £74-£128 (incl. bkfst & dinner) **Facilities** FTV WiFi ↘ Xmas New Year **Services** Lift **Parking** 30 **Notes** LB ⊗

PECKFORTON
Cheshire   Map 15 SJ55

Peckforton Castle

★★★★ 85% @@@ HOTEL

tel: 01829 260930 **Stone House Ln CW6 9TN**
email: info@peckfortoncastle.co.uk **web:** www.peckfortoncastle.co.uk
dir: A49. At Beeston Castle pub right signed Peckforton Castle. Approx 2m, entrance on right

Built in the mid-19th century by parliamentarian and landowner Lord John Tollemache, and now lovingly cared for by The Naylor Family, this Grade I medieval-style castle has been sympathetically renovated to provide high standards of comfort without losing original charm and character. Bedrooms and public areas retain many period features, and dining in the 1851 Restaurant is a memorable experience. Head Chef Mark Ellis is passionate about using only the finest ingredients, sourced locally where possible. There is a falconry centre at the castle.

Rooms 48 (7 fmly) (2 GF) ↟ **Facilities** Spa FTV WiFi HL ↘ Falconry Outdoor pursuits Land Rover experience Abseiling Beauty salon Xmas New Year **Conf** Class 80 Board 40 Thtr 180 **Services** Lift **Parking** 400 **Notes** ⊗ Civ Wed 165

P

PENDLEBURY	Map 15 SD70
Greater Manchester	

Premier Inn Manchester (Swinton)

BUDGET HOTEL

tel: 0871 527 8720 **219 Bolton Rd M27 8TG**
web: www.premierinn.com
dir: M60 junct 13 towards A572, at rdbt take 3rd exit towards Swinton. At next rdbt take A572. In 2m right onto A580. After 2nd lights A666 Kearsley, 1st left at rdbt. Pass fire station on right, 1st right

High quality, budget accommodation ideal for both families and business travellers. Spacious, en suite bedrooms feature tea and coffee making facilities, and Freeview TV in most hotels. Internet access and WiFi are available for a small fee. The adjacent family restaurant features a wide and varied menu. See also the Hotel Groups pages.

Rooms 31

PENKRIDGE	Map 10 SJ91
Staffordshire	

Mercure Stafford South Hatherton House Hotel

★★★ 71% HOTEL

tel: 01785 712459 **Pinfold Ln ST19 5QP**
email: enquiries@hotels-stafford.com **web:** www.hotels-stafford.com
dir: A449 to Wolverhampton. In Penkridge turn right into Pinfold Ln. Hotel on left in 300yds

The hotel offers comfortable accommodation to both leisure and business guests. The leisure facilities consist of a pool, steam room and jacuzzi with a well-equipped gym and two squash courts. Conference facilities are also available. There is free parking and easy access to the city and countryside.

Rooms 51 (4 fmly) (18 GF) **Facilities** FTV WiFi 🐾 Gym Squash Sauna Steam room Xmas New Year **Conf** Class 160 Board 120 Thtr 260 Del £138 **Parking** 200
Notes Civ Wed 200

PENRITH	Map 18 NY53
Cumbria	

See also **Glenridding and Shap**

North Lakes Hotel & Spa

shire

★★★★ 78% 🌸 HOTEL

tel: 01768 868111 **Ullswater Rd CA11 8QT**
email: nlakes@shirehotels.com **web:** www.northlakeshotel.com
dir: M6 junct 40 at junct with A66

With a great location, it's no wonder that this modern hotel is perpetually busy. Amenities include a good range of meeting and function rooms and excellent health and leisure facilities including a full spa. Themed public areas have a contemporary, Scandinavian country style and offer plenty of space and comfort. High standards of service are provided by a friendly team of staff.

Rooms 84 (6 fmly) (22 GF) **S** £90-£200; **D** £90-£200* **Facilities** Spa STV WiFi ⓑ 🐾 Gym Children's splash pool Steam room Activity & wellness studios Sauna New Year **Conf** Class 140 Board 30 Thtr 200 Del from £145 to £185* **Services** Lift **Parking** 150 **Notes** LB ⊗ Civ Wed 200

Temple Sowerby House Hotel & Restaurant

★★★ 88% 🎖🎖 COUNTRY HOUSE HOTEL

tel: 017683 61578 **CA10 1RZ**
email: stay@templesowerby.com **web:** www.templesowerby.com

(For full entry see Temple Sowerby)

The George Hotel

LAKE DISTRICT ▪▪▪▪ HOTELS

★★★ 82% HOTEL

tel: 01768 862696 & 0800 840 1242 **Devonshire St CA11 7SU**
email: georgehotel@lakedistricthotels.net **web:** www.lakedistricthotels.net
dir: M6 junct 40, 1m to town centre. From A6/A66 to Penrith

This inviting and popular hotel was once visited by 'Bonnie' Prince Charlie. Extended over the years, it currently offers well equipped bedrooms, and spacious public areas that retain a timeless charm. There is a choice of lounge areas that make ideal places for morning coffee and afternoon tea.

Rooms 35 (4 fmly) **S** fr £86; **D** £154-£235 (incl. bkfst) **Facilities** FTV WiFi ⓑ Xmas New Year **Conf** Class 80 Board 50 Thtr 120 Del from £115 **Parking** 40
Notes Civ Wed 120

Westmorland Hotel

★★★ 82% HOTEL

tel: 015396 24351 **Westmorland Place, Orton CA10 3SB**
email: reservations@westmorlandhotel.com **web:** www.westmorlandhotel.com

(For full entry see Tebay)

PENZANCE	Map 2 SW43
Cornwall	

Hotel Penzance

★★★★ 78% 🎖🎖 TOWN HOUSE HOTEL

tel: 01736 363117 **Britons Hill TR18 3AE**
email: reception@hotelpenzance.com **web:** www.hotelpenzance.com
dir: from A30, left at last rdbt for town centre. 3rd right onto Britons Hill. Restaurant on right

This Edwardian house has been tastefully redesigned, particularly in the contemporary Bay Restaurant. The focus on style is not only limited to the decor, but is also apparent in the award-winning cuisine that is based on fresh Cornish produce. Bedrooms have been appointed to modern standards and are particularly well equipped; many have views across Mounts Bay.

Rooms 25 (2 GF) 🪑 **S** £79-£95; **D** £145-£205 (incl. bkfst)* **Facilities** FTV WiFi 🌹 Xmas New Year **Conf** Class 50 Board 25 Thtr 80 **Parking** 12 **Notes** LB Civ Wed 80

Queens Hotel

★★★ 72% HOTEL

tel: 01736 362371 **The Promenade TR18 4HG**
email: enquiries@queens-hotel.com **web:** www.queens-hotel.com
dir: A30 to Penzance, follow signs for seafront pass harbour onto promenade, hotel on right

With views across Mount's Bay towards Newlyn, this impressive Victorian hotel has a long and distinguished history. Comfortable public areas are filled with interesting pictures and artefacts, and in the dining room guests can choose from the daily-changing menu. Bedrooms, many with sea views, vary in style and size.

Rooms 70 (10 fmly) 🪑 **S** £35-£99; **D** £70-£198 (incl. bkfst)* **Facilities** FTV WiFi 🕯 Hair & beauty salon Xmas New Year **Conf** Class 200 Board 120 Thtr 200 Del from £85 to £136* **Services** Lift **Parking** 50 **Notes** LB Civ Wed 250

PETERBOROUGH	Map 12 TL19
Cambridgeshire	

Bull Hotel

★★★★ 77% HOTEL

tel: 01733 561364 **Westgate PE1 1RB**
email: rooms@bull-hotel-peterborough.com **web:** www.peelhotels.co.uk
dir: From A1 follow city centre signs. Hotel opposite Queensgate shopping centre. Car park on Broadway adjacent to library

This pleasant city-centre hotel offers well-equipped, modern accommodation, which includes several wings of deluxe bedrooms. Public rooms include a popular bar and a brasserie-style restaurant serving a flexible range of dishes, with further informal dining available in the lounge. There is a good range of meeting rooms and conference facilities.

Rooms 118 (2 fmly) (5 GF) (4 smoking) 🪑 **S** £70-£135; **D** £80-£150* **Facilities** STV WiFi Xmas New Year **Conf** Class 120 Board 40 Thtr 200 Del from £130 to £160* **Parking** 100 **Notes** LB ⊗ Civ Wed 200

BEST WESTERN PLUS Orton Hall Hotel

★★★★ 72% HOTEL

tel: 01733 391111 **Orton Longueville PE2 7DN**
email: reception@ortonhall.co.uk **web:** www.abacushotels.co.uk
dir: Off A605 E, opposite Orton Mere

An impressive country-house hotel set in 20 acres of woodland on the outskirts of town and with easy access to the A1. The spacious and relaxing public areas

include the baronial Great Room and the Orton Suite for banqueting and for meetings, and the oak-panelled, award-winning Huntly Restaurant. The on-site pub, Ramblewood Inn, is an alternative, informal dining option.

Rooms 70 (2 fmly) (15 GF) 🪑 **Facilities Spa** FTV WiFi 🕯 🏊 Gym Sauna Steam room Xmas New Year **Conf** Class 70 Board 60 Thtr 160 **Parking** 200 **Notes** Civ Wed 150

Bell Inn Hotel

★★★ 81% 🏵 HOTEL

tel: 01733 241066 **Great North Rd PE7 3RA**
email: reception@thebellstilton.co.uk **web:** www.thebellstilton.co.uk

(For full entry see Stilton)

Days Inn Peterborough - A1

BUDGET HOTEL

tel: 01733 371540 **Peterborough Extra Services, A1 Junction 17, Great North Road, Haddon PE7 3UQ**
email: peterborough.hotel@welcomebreak.co.uk **web:** www.welcomebreak.co.uk
dir: A1(M) junct 17

This modern, purpose-built accommodation offers smartly appointed, particularly well-equipped bedrooms with good power showers. There is a choice of adjacent food outlets where guests can enjoy breakfast, snacks and meals. See also the Hotel Groups pages.

Rooms 82 (16 fmly) (40 GF) (11 smoking) 🪑

Premier Inn Peterborough (Ferry Meadows)

BUDGET HOTEL

tel: 0871 527 8872 **Ham Ln, Orton Meadows, Nene Park PE2 5UU**
web: www.premierinn.com
dir: A1(M) S junct 16, A15 through Yaxley, left at rdbt. A1(M) N junct 17, A1139 junct 3 right to Yaxley, right at 2nd rdbt

High quality, budget accommodation ideal for both families and business travellers. Spacious, en suite bedrooms feature tea and coffee making facilities, and Freeview TV in most hotels. Internet access and WiFi are available for a small fee. The adjacent family restaurant features a wide and varied menu. See also the Hotel Groups pages.

Rooms 40

Premier Inn Peterborough (Hampton)

BUDGET HOTEL

tel: 0871 527 8874 **Ashbourne Rd, off London Rd, Hampton PE7 8BT**
web: www.premierinn.com
dir: A1(M) S junct 16, A15 through Yaxley, hotel on left at 1st rdbt. Or A1(M) N junct 17, A1139, 2nd exit junct 3 follow Yaxley signs. Hotel on right at 2nd rdbt

Rooms 83

PETERBOROUGH *continued*

Premier Inn Peterborough North

BUDGET HOTEL

tel: 0871 527 8876 **1023 Lincoln Rd, Walton PE4 6AH**
web: www.premierinn.com
dir: A1, A47 towards Peterborough. In 7m exit at junct 17 signed city centre. At rdbt (bottom of slip road) straight on signed city centre. At next rdbt left onto dual carriageway. At next rdbt double back, follow signs for city centre. Hotel in 200mtrs

Rooms 40

PETERSFIELD	Map 5 SU72
Hampshire	

Langrish House

★★★ 80% ❀❀ HOTEL

tel: 01730 266941 **Langrish GU32 1RN**
email: frontdesk@langrishhouse.co.uk **web:** www.langrishhouse.co.uk
dir: A3 onto A272 towards Winchester. Hotel signed, 2.5m on left

Langrish House has been in the same family for seven generations. It is located in an extremely peaceful area just a few minutes' drive from Petersfield, halfway between Guildford and Portsmouth. Bedrooms are comfortable and well equipped with stunning views across the gardens to the hills. Guests can eat in the intimate Frederick's Restaurant with views over the lawn, or in the Old Vaults which have an interesting history dating back to 1644. The hotel is licensed for civil ceremonies and various themed events take place throughout the year.

Rooms 13 (1 fmly) (3 GF) ⚓ **S** £89-£109; **D** £119-£179 (incl. bkfst)* **Facilities** FTV WiFi 🦢 Xmas New Year **Conf** Class 18 Board 25 Thtr 60 Del £140* **Parking** 80 **Notes** Closed Early Jan Civ Wed 80

Premier Inn Petersfield

BUDGET HOTEL

tel: 0871 527 8878 **Winchester Rd GU32 3BS**
web: www.premierinn.com
dir: At junct of A3 & A272 W'bound signed Services

High quality, budget accommodation ideal for both families and business travellers. Spacious, en suite bedrooms feature tea and coffee making facilities, and Freeview TV in most hotels. Internet access and WiFi are available for a small fee. The adjacent family restaurant features a wide and varied menu. See also the Hotel Groups pages.

Rooms 51

PETWORTH	Map 6 SU92
West Sussex	

The Angel Inn

★★ 78% HOTEL

tel: 01798 344445 & 342153 **Angel St GU28 0BG**
email: reception@angelinnpetworth.co.uk **web:** www.angelinnpetworth.co.uk
dir: From Petworth Centre tak A283 towards Pulborough. 100yds on left

Located in the heart of the historic town of Petworth, the Angel has stylish yet traditionally decorated bedrooms and modern bathrooms. Guests can enjoy meals in the bar and restaurant area and there is a large walled garden for alfresco

dining in the warmer months. The hotel is just a two-minute walk away from the town centre.

Rooms 6 ⚓ **S** £90-£120; **D** £100-£160 (incl. bkfst)* **Facilities** STV WiFi New Year **Parking** 16

PICKERING	Map 19 SE78
North Yorkshire	

The White Swan Inn

★★★ 83% ❀❀ HOTEL

tel: 01751 472288 **Market Place YO18 7AA**
email: welcome@white-swan.co.uk **web:** www.white-swan.co.uk
dir: In town, between church & steam railway station

This 16th-century coaching inn offers well-equipped, comfortable bedrooms, including suites, either of a more traditional style in the main building or modern in the annexe. Service is friendly and attentive. Good food is served in the attractive restaurant, in the cosy bar and in the lounge, where a log fire burns in cooler months. A private dining room is also available. The comprehensive wine list focuses on many fine vintages.

Rooms 21 (9 annexe) (3 fmly) (8 GF) ⚓ **S** £119-£189; **D** £149-£249 (incl. bkfst)* **Facilities** FTV WiFi Xmas New Year **Conf** Class 18 Board 25 Thtr 35 Del from £165 to £185* **Parking** 45 **Notes** LB

BEST WESTERN Forest & Vale Hotel

★★★ 80% HOTEL

tel: 01751 472722 **Malton Rd YO18 7DL**
email: forestvale@bestwestern.co.uk **web:** www.bw-forestandvalehotel.co.uk
dir: On A169 towards York at rdbt on outskirts of Pickering

This lovely 18th-century manor house hotel makes an excellent base from which to explore the east coast resorts and the North Yorkshire Moors National Park, one of England's most beautiful areas. A dedicated approach to upgrading means that the hotel is particularly well maintained, inside and out. In addition to standard bedrooms there are more spacious deluxe, superior and executive rooms; they are more traditional in the main house while the ones in the wing are contemporary; one has a four-poster bed.

Rooms 22 (5 annexe) (7 fmly) (5 GF) ⚓ **S** £88-£133; **D** £88-£143* **Facilities** FTV WiFi ♧ **Conf** Class 40 Board 30 Thtr 100 Del from £150 to £175 **Parking** 40 **Notes** LB ⊗ Closed 24-26 Dec Civ Wed 90

The Beansheaf Hotel

★★ 71% HOTEL

tel: 01653 668614 **Malton Rd YO17 6UE**
email: enquiries@beansheafhotel.com **web:** www.beansheafhotel.com
dir: On A169 between Malton & Pickering at the Flamingo Land turning

This modern hotel is conveniently located on the A169 between Pickering and Malton. It is close to the A64 and ideal for exploring the North York Moors or visiting Flamingo Land. Leisure and business guests are equally well catered for with complimentary WiFi provided and there are dedicated meeting rooms. A range of bedrooms are available including singles, doubles, twins and family rooms. Ground floor rooms are also available. A wide range of homemade meals are served in the bar and restaurant.

Rooms 18 (8 GF) ⚓ **S** £54-£59; **D** £75-£85 (incl. bkfst)* **Facilities** FTV WiFi ♧ **Conf** Class 50 Board 25 Thtr 60 Del from £109 to £149* **Parking** 35

PIERCEBRIDGE
County Durham

Map 19 NZ21

George Hotel

★★★ 77% HOTEL

tel: 01325 374576 **DL2 3SW**
email: george@bulldogmail.co.uk **web:** www.george-ontees.co.uk
dir: A1 junct 56, left at rdbt, 5m down B2675

This well appointed and attractive hotel, once a coaching inn, is located in the rural village of Piercebridge and backs onto the River Tees; it has great countryside views. The hotel has well-appointed, traditionally styled bedrooms, inviting, spacious public areas with roaring fires in winter, and extensive function rooms. Guests can enjoy an evening meal in the restaurant that overlooks the river, and choose to relax outside for lunch, afternoon tea or just a drink. The riverside ballroom makes an ideal venue for wedding receptions. Off-street parking is also available.

Rooms 29 (7 fmly) (13 GF) ↖ **S** £39-£89; **D** £49-£109* **Facilities** FTV WiFi ↘ Fishing Xmas New Year **Conf** Class 120 Board 180 Thtr 200 Del from £85 to £105* **Parking** 100 **Notes** LB Civ Wed 200

PLYMOUTH
Devon

Map 3 SX45

Langdon Court Hotel & Restaurant

★★★★ 76% ◉◉ COUNTRY HOUSE HOTEL

tel: 01752 862358 **Adams Ln, Down Thomas PL9 0DY**
email: enquiries@langdoncourt.com **web:** www.langdoncourt.com
dir: From Plymouth follow Kingsbridge signs Elberton rdbt. Signs to Langdon Court

Langdon Court Hotel has a super location, set in seven acres of grounds and away from the traffic and hubbub of the city; a Grade II listed building, this Tudor Mansion in steeped in history and is very stylish. There are some excellent gardens and the hotel management is developing their own vineyard. Bedrooms are stylishly appointed, and comfortably furnished. The restaurant and bar areas offer enjoyable dining featuring fresh and local produce.

Rooms 18 (3 fmly) ↖ **S** £109-£129; **D** £129-£229 (incl. bkfst) **Facilities** STV FTV WiFi ↘ Xmas New Year **Conf** Class 20 Board 20 Thtr 60 Del £159 **Parking** 60 **Notes** LB ⊗ Civ Wed 100

BEST WESTERN Duke of Cornwall Hotel

★★★ 80% ◉ HOTEL

tel: 01752 275850 & 275855 **Millbay Rd PL1 3LG**
email: enquiries@thedukeofcornwall.co.uk **web:** www.thedukeofcornwall.co.uk
dir: Follow city centre, then Plymouth Pavilions Conference & Leisure Centre signs. Hotel opposite Plymouth Pavilions

A historic landmark, this city centre hotel is conveniently located. The spacious public areas include a popular bar, comfortable lounge and multi-functional ballroom. Bedrooms, many with far-reaching views, are individually styled and comfortably appointed. The range of dining options includes meals in the bar, or the elegant dining room for a more formal atmosphere.

Rooms 71 (4 fmly) (10 smoking) ↖ **S** £45-£109; **D** £50-£120 (incl. bkfst)* **Facilities** STV FTV WiFi ↘ Xmas New Year **Conf** Class 125 Board 84 Thtr 300 **Services** Lift **Parking** 25 **Notes** Civ Wed 300

Invicta Hotel

★★★ 78% HOTEL

tel: 01752 664997 **11-12 Osborne Place, Lockyer St, The Hoe PL1 2PU**
email: invictahotel@btconnect.com **web:** www.invictahotel.co.uk
dir: A38 to Plymouth, follow city centre signs, then signs to The Hoe & Barbican. Hotel opposite Hoe Park on Lockyer St at junct with Citadel Rd

Just a short stroll from the city centre, this elegant Victorian establishment stands opposite the famous bowling green. The atmosphere is relaxed and friendly and bedrooms are neatly presented, well-equipped and attractively decorated. Eating options include meals in the bar or in the more formal setting of the dining room.

Rooms 23 (4 fmly) (1 GF) ↖ **S** £57.50-£75; **D** £80-£110 (incl. bkfst) **Facilities** FTV WiFi Xmas **Conf** Class 30 Board 45 Thtr 45 Del from £150 to £220 **Parking** 14 **Notes** LB

New Continental Hotel

★★★ 77% HOTEL

tel: 01752 220782 & 276798 **Millbay Rd PL1 3LD**
email: reservations@newcontinental.co.uk **web:** www.newcontinental.co.uk
dir: A38, follow city centre signs for Continental Ferryport. Hotel before ferryport, adjacent to Plymouth Pavilions Conference Centre

Within easy reach of the city centre and The Hoe, this privately owned hotel continues to offer high standards of service and hospitality. A variety of bedroom sizes and styles is available, all with the same levels of equipment and comfort. The hotel is a popular choice for conferences and functions.

Rooms 99 (20 fmly) **Facilities** FTV WiFi ❄ supervised Gym Sauna Steam room **Conf** Class 100 Board 70 Thtr 350 **Services** Lift **Parking** 100 **Notes** ⊗ Closed 24 Dec-2 Jan Civ Wed 140

Copthorne Hotel Plymouth

★★★ 75% HOTEL

MILLENNIUM
MILLENNIUM · COPTHORNE

tel: 01752 224161 **Armada Way PL1 1AR**
email: sales.plymouth@millenniumhotels.co.uk **web:** www.millenniumhotels.co.uk
dir: From M5 follow A38 to Plymouth city centre. Follow ferryport signs over 2 rdbts. Hotel on 1st exit left before 4th rdbt

This hotel is conveniently located near the city's main attractions and the business area, and is also well situated for the theatre and The Hoe. The bedrooms offer a good range of facilities and are available in a range of sizes. The restaurant provides enjoyable dining and there is an all-day lounge and bar service. The secure parking is an asset.

Rooms 135 **Facilities** STV WiFi HL Gym New Year **Conf** Class 60 Board 60 Thtr 140 Del from £99 to £150* **Services** Lift **Parking** 50 **Notes** ⊗ Civ Wed 100

Ibis Hotel Plymouth

ibis

BUDGET HOTEL

tel: 01752 601087 **Marsh Mills, Longbridge Rd, Forder Valley PL6 8LD**
email: H2093@accor.com **web:** www.ibishotel.com
dir: A38 to Plymouth, 1st exit after flyover towards Estover, Leigham & Parkway Industrial Est. At rdbt, hotel at 4th exit

Modern, budget hotel offering comfortable accommodation in bright and practical bedrooms. Breakfast is self-service and dinner is available in the restaurant. See also the Hotel Groups pages.

Rooms 52 (1 fmly) (26 GF) ↖

P

PLYMOUTH *continued*

Premier Inn Plymouth Centre (Sutton Harbour)

BUDGET HOTEL

tel: 0871 527 8882 **Sutton Rd, Shepherds Wharf PL4 OHX**
web: www.premierinn.com
dir: A38, A374 towards Plymouth. Follow Coxside & National Marine Aquarium signs. Right at lights after leisure park. Hotel adjacent to Lockyers Quay. NB there are 2 Premier Inns on this site, this hotel is the larger

High quality, budget accommodation ideal for both families and business travellers. Spacious, en suite bedrooms feature tea and coffee making facilities, and Freeview TV in most hotels. Internet access and WiFi are available for a small fee. The adjacent family restaurant features a wide and varied menu. See also the Hotel Groups pages.

Rooms 107

Premier Inn Plymouth City Centre (Lockyers Quay)

BUDGET HOTEL

tel: 0871 527 8880 **1 Lockyers Quay, Coxside PL4 ODX**
web: www.premierinn.com
dir: From A38 (Marsh Mills rdbt) take A374 into Plymouth. Follow Coxside & National Marine Aquarium signs

Rooms 62

Premier Inn Plymouth East

BUDGET HOTEL

tel: 0871 527 8884 **300 Plymouth Rd, Crabtree PL3 6RW**
web: www.premierinn.com
dir: From E: Exit A38 at Marsh Mill junct. Straight on at rdbt, exit slip road 100mtrs on left. From W: Exit A38 at Plympton junct, at rdbt exit slip road adjacent to A38

Rooms 41

POCKLINGTON
East Riding of Yorkshire
Map 17 SE84

Feathers Hotel

★★ 71% HOTEL

tel: 01759 303155 **56 Market Place YO42 2AH**
email: info@thefeathers-hotel.co.uk **web:** www.thefeathers-hotel.co.uk
dir: From York, B1246 signed Pocklington. Hotel just off A1079

This busy, traditional inn provides comfortable, well-equipped and spacious accommodation. Public areas are smartly presented. Enjoyable meals are served in the bar and the conservatory restaurant; the wide choice of dishes makes excellent use of local and seasonal produce.

Rooms 16 (10 annexe) (2 fmly) (10 GF) ↰ **S** £50-£52; **D** £55-£65 (incl. bkfst)*
Facilities FTV WiFi **Parking** 25 **Notes** ⊗

POLPERRO
Cornwall
Map 2 SX25

Talland Bay Hotel

★★★ 87% ◉◉ COUNTRY HOUSE HOTEL

tel: 01503 272667 **Porthallow PL13 2JB**
email: info@tallandbayhotel.co.uk **web:** www.tallandbayhotel.co.uk
dir: From Looe over bridge towards Polperro on A387, 2nd turn to hotel

This hotel has the benefit of a wonderful location with far-reaching views, situated in its own extensive gardens that run down almost to the cliff edge. A warm and friendly atmosphere prevails. The bedrooms come in a range of styles - classic twins and doubles, and rooms and suites with sea views. There is also cottage accommodation, and one is particularly suitable for families or those with dogs. The public areas of the hotel are impressive and stylish. Eating options include a Brasserie and the Terrace Restaurant, where guests will find accomplished cooking, with an emphasis on carefully prepared local produce.

Rooms 20 (2 fmly) (5 GF) ↰ **S** £90-£210; **D** £100-£225 (incl. bkfst)* **Facilities** FTV WiFi ↰ ⚘ Xmas New Year **Conf** Class 20 Board 20 Thtr 20 **Parking** 20 **Notes** LB Civ Wed 65

PONTEFRACT
West Yorkshire
Map 16 SE42

Wentbridge House Hotel

★★★★ 80% ◉◉ HOTEL

tel: 01977 620444 **Wentbridge WF8 3JJ**
email: info@wentbridgehouse.co.uk **web:** www.wentbridgehouse.co.uk
dir: M62 junct 33 onto A1 S, hotel in 4m

This well-established hotel sits in 20 acres of landscaped gardens, offering spacious, well-equipped bedrooms and a choice of dining styles. Service in the Fleur de Lys restaurant is polished and friendly, and a varied menu offers a good choice of interesting dishes. The Brasserie has a more relaxed style of modern dining.

Rooms 41 (4 annexe) (4 fmly) (4 GF) ↰ **S** £110-£190; **D** £140-£220 (incl. bkfst)* **Facilities** FTV WiFi Xmas New Year **Conf** Class 100 Board 60 Thtr 130 Del from £110 to £150* **Services** Lift **Parking** 100 **Notes** LB ⊗ Civ Wed 130

Premier Inn Pontefract North

BUDGET HOTEL

tel: 0871 527 8886 **Pontefract Rd, Knottingley WF11 OBU**
web: www.premierinn.com
dir: M62 junct 33 onto A1 N. Exit at Pontefract junct (A645) to T-junct, right towards Pontefract. Hotel on right

High quality, budget accommodation ideal for both families and business travellers. Spacious, en suite bedrooms feature tea and coffee making facilities, and Freeview TV in most hotels. Internet access and WiFi are available for a small fee. The adjacent family restaurant features a wide and varied menu. See also the Hotel Groups pages.

Rooms 41

Premier Inn Pontefract South

BUDGET HOTEL

tel: 0871 527 8888 **Great North Rd, Darrington WF8 3BL**
web: www.premierinn.com
dir: Just off A1, 2m S of M62 junct 33

Rooms 28

POOLE	Map 4 SZ09
Dorset	

Hotel du Vin Poole

★★★★ 77%  HOTEL

tel: 0844 748 9265 **Thames St BH15 1JN**
email: info.poole@hotelduvin.com **web:** www.hotelduvin.com
dir: A31 to Poole, follow channel ferry signs. Left at Poole bridge onto Poole Quay, 1st left into Thames St. Hotel opposite St James Church

Offering a fresh approach to the well-established company style, this property boasts some delightful rooms packed with comfort and all the expected Hotel du Vin features. Situated near the harbour the hotel offers nautically-themed bedrooms and suites that have plasma TVs, DVD players and bathrooms with power showers. The public rooms are light, open spaces, and as with the other hotels in this group, the bar and restaurant form centre stage.

Rooms 38 (4 GF) **Facilities** STV WiFi Xmas New Year **Conf** Class 20 Board 20 Thtr 60 **Services** Air con **Parking** 50 **Notes** Civ Wed 100

Harbour Heights Hotel

★★★★ 76% ◎◎ HOTEL

tel: 0845 337 1550 **73 Haven Rd, Sandbanks BH13 7LW**
email: reservations@fjbhotels.co.uk **web:** www.fjbhotels.co.uk
dir: Follow signs for Sandbanks, hotel on left after Canford Cliffs

Enjoying stunning panoramic outlooks across the Sandbanks Peninsula and Poole Harbour, The Harbour Heights is an unassuming yet stylish and innovative boutique hotel. Attention to detail is very apparent, as state-of-the-art facilities blend with traditional comforts. The Harbar Brasserie is at the heart of Harbour Heights, offering excellent cuisine complemented by a fine and diverse wine cellar. The south-facing sun deck is the perfect setting for watching the cross-channel ferries come and go.

Rooms 38 **Facilities** STV WiFi Spa bath in all rooms ♫ Xmas New Year **Conf** Class 36 Board 22 Thtr 70 **Services** Lift Air con **Parking** 50 **Notes** ⊗ Civ Wed 100

The Haven

★★★★ 76% ◎◎ HOTEL

tel: 01202 707333 & 0845 337 1550 **Banks Rd, Sandbanks BH13 7QL**
email: reservations@fjbhotels.co.uk **web:** www.fjbcollection.co.uk
dir: B3965 towards Poole Bay, left onto the Peninsula. Hotel 1.5m on left adjacent to Swanage Toll Ferry

Enjoying an enviable location at the water's edge with views of Poole Bay, this well established hotel was once the home of radio pioneer, Guglielmo Marconi. A friendly team of staff provide good levels of customer care. Bedrooms vary in size and style; many have balconies and wonderful sea or harbour views. The leisure facilities are noteworthy - the Harmony at the Haven is where guests can find spa treatments, a fully equipped gym, indoor and outdoor heated pools and an all-weather tennis court. The hotel is a popular venue for conferences and weddings.

Rooms 84 (4 fmly) **S** £65-£109; **D** £119-£194 (incl. bkfst)* **Facilities** Spa FTV WiFi ⌇ 🏊 supervised ⌁ supervised ≋ Gym Dance studio Health & Beauty suite Sauna Steam room ♫ Xmas New Year **Conf** Class 70 Board 50 Thtr 160 Del from £130 to £165* **Services** Lift **Parking** 160 **Notes** LB ⊗ Civ Wed 80

The Sandbanks

★★★★ 74% HOTEL

tel: 01202 707377 & 0845 337 1550 **15 Banks Rd, Sandbanks BH13 7PS**
email: reservations@fjbhotels.co.uk **web:** www.fjbhotels.co.uk
dir: A338 from Bournemouth onto Wessex Way, to Liverpool Victoria rdbt. Left, then 2nd exit onto B3965. Follow beach signs. Hotel on left

Set on the delightful Sandbanks Peninsula, this well-loved hotel has direct access to the seven-mile blue flag beach and has stunning views across Poole Harbour and the sea. Most of the spacious bedrooms have sea views; some are air conditioned. There is an extensive range of leisure facilities, including an on-site watersports academy. The Sandbanks is a family-friendly hotel.

Rooms 108 (31 fmly) **Facilities** STV FTV WiFi 🏊 supervised Gym Sailing Mountain bikes Children's play area Watersports academy ♫ Xmas New Year **Conf** Class 50 Board 80 Thtr 150 **Services** Lift **Parking** 120 **Notes** ⊗ Civ Wed 100

Arndale Court Hotel

★★★ 71% HOTEL

tel: 01202 683746 **62/66 Wimborne Rd BH15 2BY**
email: info@arndalecourthotel.com **web:** www.arndalecourthotel.com
dir: On A349, opposite Poole Stadium

Ideally situated for the town centre and ferry terminal, this is a small, privately owned hotel. Bedrooms are well equipped, spacious and comfortable. Particularly well suited to business guests, this hotel has a pleasant range of stylish public areas and good parking.

Rooms 39 (7 fmly) (14 GF) **Facilities** STV FTV WiFi **Conf** Class 20 Board 30 Thtr 50 **Parking** 40 **Notes** RS 23 Dec-2 Jan

P

POOLE *continued*

Premier Inn Poole Centre (Holes Bay)

BUDGET HOTEL

tel: 0871 527 8892 **Holes Bay Rd BH15 2BD**
web: www.premierinn.com
dir: S of A35 & A349 on A350 (dual carriageway). Follow Poole Channel Ferry signs

High quality, budget accommodation ideal for both families and business travellers. Spacious, en suite bedrooms feature tea and coffee making facilities, and Freeview TV in most hotels. Internet access and WiFi are available for a small fee. The adjacent family restaurant features a wide and varied menu. See also the Hotel Groups pages.

Rooms 83

Premier Inn Poole North

BUDGET HOTEL

tel: 0871 527 8894 **Cabot Ln BH17 7DA**
web: www.premierinn.com
dir: Follow Poole/Channel Ferries signs. At Darby's Corner rdbt take 2nd exit. At 2nd lights right into Cabot Ln. Hotel on right

Rooms 126

Milsoms Poole

RESTAURANT WITH ROOMS

tel: 01202 609000 **47 Haven Rd, Canford Cliffs BH13 7LH**
email: poole@milsomshotel.co.uk **web:** www.milsomshotel.co.uk

Milsoms Poole is located in the Canford Cliffs area, moments from some of the country's best beaches and the picturesque Purbeck Hills. Comfortable and stylish en suite accommodation is situated above the popular seafood Loch Fyne Restaurant. The friendly and helpful team provide a warm welcome. Limited on-site parking is available.

Rooms 8

P

Visit theAA.com/shop
for the latest Pub, B&B and Restaurant Guides

PORLOCK
Somerset
Map 3 SS84

The Oaks Hotel

★★★ ⦿ HOTEL

tel: 01643 862265 **TA24 8ES**
email: info@oakshotel.co.uk **web:** www.oakshotel.co.uk
dir: From E of A39, enter village (road narrows to single track) then follow hotel sign. From W: down Porlock Hill, through village, hotel sign on right

A relaxing atmosphere is found at this charming Edwardian house, located near to the setting of R D Blackmore's novel, *Lorna Doone*. Quietly located and set in attractive grounds, the hotel enjoys elevated views across the village towards the sea. Bedrooms are thoughtfully furnished and comfortable, and the public rooms include a charming bar and a peaceful drawing room. In the dining room, guests can choose from the daily-changing menu, which features fresh, quality local produce.

Rooms 8 ⦿ **S** fr £170; **D** £230-£255 (incl. bkfst & dinner)* **Facilities** FTV WiFi ⦿ Xmas New Year **Parking** 12 **Notes** ⦿ No children 8yrs Closed Nov-Mar (ex Xmas & New Year)

PORTHLEVEN
Cornwall
Map 2 SW62

Kota Restaurant with Rooms

⦿ ⦿ RESTAURANT WITH ROOMS

tel: 01326 562407 01326 562407 **Harbour Head TR13 9JA**
email: info@kotakai.co.uk **web:** www.kotarestaurant.co.uk
dir: B3304 from Helston into Porthleven. Kota on harbour opposite slipway

Overlooking the water, this 300-year-old building is the home of Kota Restaurant ('kota' being the Maori word for 'shellfish'). The bedrooms are approached from a granite stairway to the side of the building. The family room is spacious and has the benefit of harbour views, while the smaller, double room is at the rear of the property. The enthusiastic young owners ensure guests enjoy their stay here, and a meal in the restaurant should not be missed. Breakfast features the best local produce.

Rooms 2 (2 annexe) (1 fmly)

PORTISHEAD
Somerset

Map 4 ST47

Premier Inn Portishead

BUDGET HOTEL

tel: 0871 527 8898 **Wyndham Way BS20 7GA**
web: www.premierinn.com
dir: M5 junct 19, A369 towards Portishead. Over 1st rdbt, hotel at next rdbt

High quality, budget accommodation ideal for both families and business travellers. Spacious, en suite bedrooms feature tea and coffee making facilities, and Freeview TV in most hotels. Internet access and WiFi are available for a small fee. The adjacent family restaurant features a wide and varied menu. See also the Hotel Groups pages.

Rooms 58

PORTSCATHO
Cornwall

Map 2 SW83

INSPECTORS' CHOICE

Driftwood

★★★ ◉◉◉ HOTEL

tel: 01872 580644 **Rosevine TR2 5EW**
email: info@driftwoodhotel.co.uk **web:** www.driftwoodhotel.co.uk
dir: A390 towards St Mawes. On A3078 turn left to Rosevine at Trewithian

Poised on the cliff side with panoramic views, this contemporary hotel has a peaceful and secluded location. A warm welcome is guaranteed here, where professional standards of service are provided in an effortless and relaxed manner. Cuisine is at the heart of any stay, with quality local produce used in a sympathetic and highly skilled manner. The extremely comfortable and elegant bedrooms are decorated in soft shades reminiscent of the seashore. There is a sheltered terraced garden that has a large deck for sunbathing.

Rooms 15 (1 annexe) (3 fmly) (3 GF) **S** £153-£225; **D** £190-£265 (incl. bkfst)* **Facilities** FTV WiFi ⅍ Private beach Beauty treatments on request **Parking** 20 **Notes** ⊗ Closed 7 Dec-5 Feb RS Xmas & New Year

PORTSMOUTH & SOUTHSEA
Hampshire

Map 5 SU60

Portsmouth Marriott Hotel

★★★★ 79% ◉ HOTEL

tel: 0870 400 7285 & 023 9238 3151 **Southampton Rd PO6 4SH**
web: www.portsmouthmarriott.co.uk
dir: M27 junct 12, keep left off slip road, exit Cosham. Hotel on left at lights

Close to the motorway and ferry port, this hotel is well suited to the business trade. The comfortable and well laid-out bedrooms provide a comprehensive range of facilities including up-to-date workstations. The leisure club offers a pool, a gym, and a health and beauty salon.

Rooms 174 (77 fmly) **S** £99-£215; **D** £99-£215* **Facilities** STV FTV WiFi ⅍ HL supervised Gym Exercise studio Beauty salon & treatment room Xmas New Year **Conf** Class 180 Board 30 Thtr 350 Del from £152 to £238* **Services** Lift Air con **Parking** 196 **Notes** LB Civ Wed 350

BEST WESTERN Royal Beach Hotel

★★★ 79% HOTEL

tel: 023 9273 1281 **South Pde, Southsea PO4 0RN**
email: enquiries@royalbeachhotel.co.uk **web:** www.royalbeachhotel.co.uk
dir: M27 to M275, follow signs to seafront. Hotel on seafront

This former Victorian seafront hotel is a smart and comfortable venue suitable for leisure and business guests alike. Bedrooms and public areas are well presented and generally spacious, and the smart Coast Bar is an ideal venue for a relaxing drink.

Rooms 124 (12 fmly) ☏ **S** £45-£75; **D** £70-£115 (incl. bkfst) **Facilities** STV FTV WiFi ⅍ Xmas New Year **Conf** Class 180 Board 40 Thtr 280 Del from £99 to £135 **Services** Lift **Parking** 50 **Notes** LB Civ Wed 85

The Farmhouse & Innlodge Hotel

BUDGET HOTEL

tel: 023 9265 0510 **Burrfields Rd PO3 5HH**
email: farmhouse.portsmouth@greeneking.co.uk **web:** www.oldenglish.co.uk
dir: A3(M)/M27 onto A27. Take Southsea exit, follow A2030. 3rd lights right into Burrfields Rd. Hotel 2nd car park on left

Located on the eastern fringe of the city, this purpose-built hotel is conveniently located for all major routes. The spacious, modern bedrooms are well equipped and include ground floor and family rooms. The Farmhouse Hungry Horse Pub offers a wide range of eating options, and there is an ActionZone adventure area. See also the Hotel Groups pages.

Rooms 74 (6 fmly) (33 GF) **Conf** Class 64 Board 40 Thtr 150

Ibis Portsmouth Centre

BUDGET HOTEL

tel: 023 9264 0000 **Winston Churchill Av PO1 2LX**
email: h1461@accor.com **web:** www.ibishotel.com
dir: M27 junct 12 onto M275. Follow signs for city centre, Sealife Centre & Guildhall. Right at rdbt into Winston Churchill Ave

Modern, budget hotel offering comfortable accommodation in bright and practical bedrooms. Breakfast is self-service and dinner is available in the restaurant. See also the Hotel Groups pages.

Rooms 144 ☏ **Conf** Class 20 Board 20 Thtr 30

P

PORTSMOUTH & SOUTHSEA *continued*

Premier Inn Portsmouth (Horndean)

BUDGET HOTEL

tel: 0871 527 8902 **2 Havant Rd PO8 ODT**
web: www.premierinn.com
dir: A3(M) junct 2, take B2149 signed Emsworth, Horndean. At rdbt left onto B2149, follow Horndean signs. At next rdbt left onto A3 towards Waterlooville. Hotel on left behind Red Lion

High quality, budget accommodation ideal for both families and business travellers. Spacious, en suite bedrooms feature tea and coffee making facilities, and Freeview TV in most hotels. Internet access and WiFi are available for a small fee. The adjacent family restaurant features a wide and varied menu. See also the Hotel Groups pages.

Rooms 25

Premier Inn Portsmouth (Port Solent)

BUDGET HOTEL

tel: 0871 527 8906 **Binnacle Way PO6 4FB**
web: www.premierinn.com
dir: M27 junct 12, left at lights onto Southampton Rd. Left after 200mtrs at lights onto Compass Rd. At mini-rdbt right onto Binnacle Way, hotel on right

Rooms 108

Premier Inn Portsmouth (Port Solent East)

BUDGET HOTEL

tel: 0871 527 8904 **1 Southampton Rd, North Harbour PO6 4SA**
web: www.premierinn.com
dir: M27 junct 12, A3, left onto A27. Hotel on left

Rooms 64

Premier Inn Southsea

BUDGET HOTEL

tel: 0871 527 9014 **Long Curtain Rd, Southsea PO5 3AA**
web: www.premierinn.com
dir: M1 junct 24, A453. Follow ring road & Queen's Drive Industrial Estate signs. After Homebase left into Castle Bridge Rd, hotel opposite Pizza Hut restaurant

Rooms 40

PORT SUNLIGHT	Map 15 SJ38
Merseyside	

Leverhulme Hotel

★★★★ 83% ⚜⚜ HOTEL

tel: 0151 644 6655 & 644 5555 **Central Rd CH62 5EZ**
email: enquiries@leverhulmehotel.co.uk **web:** www.leverhulmehotel.co.uk
dir: From Chester: M53 junct 5, A41 (Birkenhead) in approx 4m left into Bolton Rd, on at rdbt, 0.1m right into Church Drive. 0.2m hotel on right. From Liverpool: A41 (Chester), 2.7m, 3rd exit at 3rd rdbt into Bolton Rd (follow directions as above

Built in 1907, this Grade II listed, former cottage hospital is set in the picturesque garden village of Port Sunlight, which was created by Lord Leverhulme for his soap-factory workers in the late 19th century. Following an extensive restoration project, this art deco hotel has stylish bedrooms, appointed to a very high standard; all have impressive facilities including bathrooms with separate showers and LCD TVs;

the suites have roof-top terraces and hot tubs. The hotel also features a range of day rooms and an ultra-modern, award-winning restaurant.

Rooms 19 (4 annexe) (1 fmly) (4 GF) ☎ **S** £145-£190; **D** £165-£210 (incl. bkfst)*
Facilities STV FTV WiFi ⌕ HL 🏊 Gym Games room Children's play area Xmas New Year **Conf** Class 140 Board 30 Thtr 300 Del £265* **Parking** 73 **Notes** LB ⊗ Civ Wed 240

PRESTON	Map 18 SD52
Lancashire	

See also **Garstang**

Barton Grange Hotel

★★★★ 79% HOTEL

tel: 01772 862551 **Garstang Rd PR3 5AA**
email: stay@bartongrangehotel.com **web:** www.bartongrangehotel.co.uk

(For full entry see Barton)

Macdonald Tickled Trout

★★★★ 74% HOTEL

tel: 0844 8799053 **Preston New Rd, Samlesbury PR5 0UJ**
email: general.tickledtrout@macdonald-hotels.co.uk **web:** www.macdonaldhotels.co.uk
dir: M6 junct 31. A59 towards Preston

On the banks of the River Ribble, this hotel is conveniently located for the motorway, making it a popular venue for both business and leisure guests. Smartly appointed bedrooms are all tastefully decorated and equipped with a thoughtful range of extras. The hotel boasts a stylish wing of meeting rooms.

Rooms 98 (6 fmly) (10 GF) ☎ **Facilities** FTV WiFi ⌕ Fishing ♫ Xmas New Year **Conf** Class 60 Board 50 Thtr 120 **Services** Lift **Parking** 180 **Notes** Civ Wed 90

The Pines Hotel

★★★ 79% HOTEL

tel: 01772 338551 **570 Preston Rd, Clayton-Le-Woods, Chorley PR6 7EB**
email: mail@thepineshotel.co.uk **web:** www.thepineshotel.co.uk
dir: Exit M6 junct 28 N'bound towards Blackburn for 2.5m to hotel. M6 junct 2 S'bound towards Chorley for 1m. On A6

This unique and stylish hotel sits in four acres of mature grounds just a short drive from the motorway. Elegant bedrooms are individually designed and offer high levels of comfort and facilities. Day rooms include a smart bar and the aptly named Rosette Restaurant, while extensive function rooms make this hotel a popular venue for weddings.

Rooms 35 (2 fmly) (14 GF) ☎ **Facilities** FTV WiFi ⌕ ♫ Xmas New Year **Conf** Class 250 Board 100 Thtr 400 **Parking** 120 **Notes** ⊗ Civ Wed 250

The Park Hotel

★★★ 78% SMALL HOTEL

tel: 01772 726250 & 728096 **209 Tulketh Rd, Ashton-On-Ribble PR2 1ES**
email: info@parkhotelpreston.co.uk **web:** www.parkhotelpreston.co.uk
dir: A59 then A5085 Blackpool Road 2.4m, left into Tulketh Road, A5072, hotel 200yds on right

This Edwardian mansion house provides quality and comfort in keeping with its history. Original features including tall ceilings, tiled floors and stained glass windows are a real bonus. The main bedrooms and bathrooms are spacious and well equipped. Public areas include the homely bar for pre-dinner drinks and the well appointed dining room. Ample off-road car parking is available.

Rooms 18 (10 annexe) (1 fmly) (8 GF) 🐾 **Facilities** FTV WiFi ↻ **Conf** Class 15 Board 15 Thtr 20 Del from £95 to £125 **Parking** 14 **Notes** ⊗ RS 20 Dec-5 Jan

The Legacy Preston International Hotel

★★★ 74% HOTEL

tel: 08444 119 028 & 0330 333 2828 **Marsh Ln PR1 2YF**
email: res-prestoninternational@legacy-hotels.co.uk **web:** www.legacy-hotels.co.uk
dir: M6 junct 31 or 32, A59 (ring road). Hotel in approx 3.5m on one way system

This hotel is ideally located close to the town centre and the M6 making it a popular choice with both business and leisure guests. The contemporary bedrooms are very comfortable and well equipped, and free WiFi is available. The public areas include a light-filled lounge, and the menu in the restaurant offers a wide choice to suit most tastes. The hotel has secure parking.

Rooms 75 (12 fmly) 🐾 **Facilities** FTV WiFi ↻ **Conf** Class 20 Board 20 Thtr 40 **Services** Lift **Parking** 40 **Notes** ⊗

Ibis Preston North

BUDGET HOTEL

tel: 01772 861800 **Garstang Rd, Broughton PR3 5JE**
email: H3162@accor.com **web:** www.ibishotel.com
dir: M6 junct 32, then M55 junct 1. Left lane onto A6. Left at slip road, left again at mini-rdbt. 2nd turn, hotel on right past pub

Modern, budget hotel offering comfortable accommodation in bright and practical bedrooms. Breakfast is self-service and dinner is available in the restaurant. See also the Hotel Groups pages.

Rooms 82 (27 fmly) (16 GF) **Conf** Class 20 Board 20 Thtr 35

Premier Inn Preston Central

BUDGET HOTEL

tel: 0871 527 8908 **Fox St PR1 2AB**
web: www.premierinn.com
dir: Off Ridgway (A59). Telephone for detailed directions

High quality, budget accommodation ideal for both families and business travellers. Spacious, en suite bedrooms feature tea and coffee making facilities, and Freeview TV in most hotels. Internet access and WiFi are available for a small fee. The adjacent family restaurant features a wide and varied menu. See also the Hotel Groups pages.

Rooms 110

Premier Inn Preston East

BUDGET HOTEL

tel: 0871 527 8910 **Bluebell Way, Preston East Link Rd, Fulwood PR2 5PZ**
web: www.premierinn.com
dir: M6 junct 31a, follow ring road under motorway, hotel on left. (NB no exit for S'bound traffic - exit at M6 junct 31, join M6 N'bound, exit at junct 31a)

Rooms 65

Premier Inn Preston South (Craven Drive)

BUDGET HOTEL

tel: 0871 527 8914 **Lostock Ln, Bamber Bridge PR5 6BZ**
web: www.premierinn.com
dir: M6 junct 29, A582 (Lostock Ln). Straight on at 1st lights, into left lane, hotel on left adjacent to B&Q

Rooms 74

Premier Inn Preston South (Cuerden Way)

BUDGET HOTEL

tel: 0871 527 8916 **Lostock Ln, Bamber Bridge PR5 6BA**
web: www.premierinn.com
dir: Off M65 junct 1 (0.5m from M6 junct 29) close to rdbt junct of A582 & A6

Rooms 42

Premier Inn Preston West

BUDGET HOTEL

tel: 0871 527 8918 **Blackpool Rd, Lea PR4 0XB**
web: www.premierinn.com
dir: Off A583, opposite Texaco garage

Rooms 38

PRESTWICH	Map 15 SD80
Greater Manchester	

Premier Inn Manchester (Prestwich)

BUDGET HOTEL

tel: 0871 527 8714 **Bury New Rd M25 3AJ**
web: www.premierinn.com
dir: M60 junct 17, A56 signed Manchseter City Centre, Prestwich & Whitefield. Hotel on left

High quality, budget accommodation ideal for both families and business travellers. Spacious, en suite bedrooms feature tea and coffee making facilities, and Freeview TV in most hotels. Internet access and WiFi are available for a small fee. The adjacent family restaurant features a wide and varied menu. See also the Hotel Groups pages.

Rooms 60

P

PUDDINGTON
Cheshire

Map 15 SJ37

Macdonald Craxton Wood Hotel

★★★★ 77% ◉◉ HOTEL

tel: 0844 879 9038 **Parkgate Rd, Ledsham CH66 9PB**
email: craxton@macdonald-hotels.co.uk **web:** www.macdonaldhotels.co.uk
dir: From M6 take M56 towards N Wales, then A5117/A540 to Hoylake. Hotel on left 200yds past lights

Set in extensive grounds, this hotel offers a variety of spacious and comfortable rooms, well equipped with modern amenities. The restaurant features a range of dishes including signature grills and locally sourced ingredients. An extensive spa facility and a choice of function suites complete the package.

Rooms 72 (8 fmly) (30 GF) ✦ **Facilities** Spa FTV WiFi ⌇ HL ⊕ Gym Sauna & Steam room, Thermal Spa incl Rasul Xmas New Year **Conf** Class 200 Board 160 Thtr 300 Del from £125 **Services** Lift **Parking** 220 **Notes** ⊗ Civ Wed 350

Premier Inn Wirral (Two Mills)

BUDGET HOTEL

tel: 0871 527 9180 **Parkgate Rd, Two Mills CH66 9PD**
web: www.premierinn.com
dir: 5m from M56 junct 16 & M53 junct 5. On x-rds of A550 & A540

High quality, budget accommodation ideal for both families and business travellers. Spacious, en suite bedrooms feature tea and coffee making facilities, and Freeview TV in most hotels. Internet access and WiFi are available for a small fee. The adjacent family restaurant features a wide and varied menu. See also the Hotel Groups pages.

Rooms 31

PURTON
Wiltshire

Map 5 SU08

The Pear Tree at Purton

★★★ 81% ◉◉ HOTEL

tel: 01793 772100 **Church End SN5 4ED**
email: stay@peartreepurton.co.uk **web:** www.peartreepurton.co.uk
dir: M4 junct 16 follow signs to Purton, at Hartford House Stores turn right. Hotel 0.25m on left

A charming 15th-century, former vicarage set amidst extensive landscaped gardens in a peaceful location in the Vale of the White Horse near the Saxon village of Purton. The resident proprietors and staff provide efficient, dedicated service and friendly hospitality. The spacious bedrooms are individually decorated and have a good range of thoughtful extras such as fresh fruit, sherry and shortbread. Fresh ingredients feature on the award-winning menus.

Rooms 17 (2 fmly) (6 GF) ✦ **Facilities** STV FTV WiFi ⌇ ⤴ Outdoor giant chess & jenga Vineyard New Year **Conf** Class 30 Board 30 Thtr 60 Del £179.50* **Parking** 60 **Notes** Closed 26 Dec Civ Wed 50

QUORN
Leicestershire

Map 11 SK51

Quorn Country Hotel

★★★★ 76% ◉ HOTEL

tel: 01509 415050 & 415061 **Charnwood House, 66 Leicester Rd LE12 8BB**
email: reservations@quorncountryhotel.co.uk **web:** www.primahotels.co.uk/quorn
dir: M1 junct 23 onto A512 into Loughborough. Follow A6 signs. At 1st rdbt towards Quorn, through lights, hotel 500yds from 2nd rdbt

Professional service is one of the key strengths of this pleasing hotel, which sits beside the river in four acres of landscaped gardens and grounds. The smart modern conference centre and function suites are popular for both corporate functions and weddings. Public rooms include a smart comfortable lounge and bar, and guests have the choice of two dining options: the formal Shires restaurant and the informal conservatory-style Orangery.

Rooms 36 (2 fmly) (11 GF) **Facilities** WiFi ⌇ Fishing New Year **Conf** Class 162 Board 40 Thtr 300 Del from £125 to £145* **Services** Lift **Parking** 100 **Notes** ⊗ Civ Wed 200

RADLETT
Hertfordshire

Map 6 TL10

Premier Inn St Albans/Bricket Wood

BUDGET HOTEL

tel: 0871 527 9016 **Smug Oak Ln, Bricketwood AL2 3PN**
web: www.premierinn.com
dir: M1 junct 6 (or M25 junct 21a) follow Watford signs, left at lights signed M1/Bricket Wood. 2nd left into Mount Pleasant Ln, straight on at 2 mini rdbts, right at The Gate pub. Hotel at end

High quality, budget accommodation ideal for both families and business travellers. Spacious, en suite bedrooms feature tea and coffee making facilities, and Freeview TV in most hotels. Internet access and WiFi are available for a small fee. The adjacent family restaurant features a wide and varied menu. See also the Hotel Groups pages.

Rooms 56

RAINHAM Map 6 TQ58
Greater London

The Manor Hotel & Restaurant

★★★ 78% HOTEL

tel: 01708 555586 **Berwick Pond Rd RM13 9EL**
email: info@themanoressex.co.uk **web:** www.themanoressex.co.uk
dir: M25 junct 30/31, A13, 1st exit signed Wennington, right, at main lights right onto Upminster Rd North, left into Berwick Pond Rd

Located in countryside, the former Berwick Manor has been lovingly restored, and offers well-appointed, contemporary accommodation. The rooms are equipped with a good range of amenities including complimentary WiFi. Lunch and dinner are served in the attractive restaurant whilst alfresco dining is possible on the terrace. Two function suites provide the ideal events venue.

Rooms 15 (1 fmly) ↖ **Facilities** STV FTV WiFi Xmas New Year **Conf** Class 60 Board 40 Thtr 100 **Services** Lift **Parking** 60 **Notes** ⊗ Civ Wed 60

Premier Inn Rainham

BUDGET HOTEL

tel: 0871 527 8920 **New Rd, Wennington RM13 9ED**
web: www.premierinn.com
dir: M25 junct 30/31, A13 for Dagenham/Rainham, A1306 towards Wennington, Aveley, & Rainham. Hotel 0.5m on right

High quality, budget accommodation ideal for both families and business travellers. Spacious, en suite bedrooms feature tea and coffee making facilities, and Freeview TV in most hotels. Internet access and WiFi are available for a small fee. The adjacent family restaurant features a wide and varied menu. See also the Hotel Groups pages.

Rooms 61

RAINHILL Map 15 SJ49
Merseyside

Premier Inn Liverpool (Rainhill)

BUDGET HOTEL

tel: 0871 527 8614 **804 Warrington Rd L35 6PE**
web: www.premierinn.com
dir: Just off M62 junct 7, A57 towards Rainhill

High quality, budget accommodation ideal for both families and business travellers. Spacious, en suite bedrooms feature tea and coffee making facilities, and Freeview TV in most hotels. Internet access and WiFi are available for a small fee. The adjacent family restaurant features a wide and varied menu. See also the Hotel Groups pages.

Rooms 34

RAMSGATE Map 7 TR36
Kent

The Pegwell Bay Hotel

★★★ 78% HOTEL

tel: 01843 599590 **81 Pegwell Rd, Pegwell CT11 ONJ**
email: reception@pegwellbayhotel.co.uk **web:** www.pegwellbayhotel.co.uk
dir: Telephone for detailed directions

Boasting stunning views over The Channel, this historic cliff-top hotel is suitable for guests staying either on business or for leisure. Spacious, comfortable bedrooms are well equipped and include WiFi. A modern lounge, majestic dining room and traditional pub offer a variety of options for eating and for relaxation.

Rooms 42 (1 fmly) (6 GF) **Facilities** FTV WiFi Xmas New Year **Conf** Class 65 Board 65 Thtr 100 **Services** Lift **Parking** 80 **Notes** ⊗ Civ Wed 70

Comfort Inn Ramsgate

★★★ 71% HOTEL

tel: 01843 592345 **Victoria Pde, East Cliff CT11 8DT**
email: reservations@comfortinnramsgate.co.uk **web:** www.comfortinnramsgate.co.uk
dir: From M2 take A299 signed Ramsgate, B2054 to Victoria Parade, follow sign to harbour

This Victorian hotel stands on the seafront, close to the ferry terminal and the town. Bedrooms, some with balconies, are generously sized and well equipped. Guests can relax in the modern bar and lounge or be pampered in the beauty treatment room. The popular restaurant serves a particularly wide choice of dishes ranging from traditional British cuisine to Indian favourites.

Rooms 44 (8 fmly) ↖ **S** £40-£60; **D** £50-£120 (incl. bkfst) **Facilities** STV FTV WiFi ⇗ Gym Beauty salon Sauna Xmas New Year **Conf** Class 30 Board 30 Thtr 50 Del from £60 to £130 **Services** Lift Air con **Parking** 10 **Notes** LB ⊗

R

RAMSGATE *continued*

The Oak Hotel

★★ 84% HOTEL

tel: 01843 583686 & 581582 **66 Harbour Pde CT11 8LN**
email: reception@oakhotel.co.uk **web:** www.oakhotel.co.uk
dir: Follow road around harbour, right into Harbour Parade

Located within easy reach of the railway station, ferry terminal and the town centre's shops, this unpretentious hotel enjoys spectacular views of the marina and harbour. The comfortable bedrooms are attractively presented and very well equipped. The Restaurant Sixty-Six, Caffe Roma and The Lounge Bar offer a variety of dining options along a selection of wines, beers and spirits.

Rooms 34 (9 fmly) ⫩ **S** £54.50-£100; **D** £71.50-£110 (incl. bkfst)* **Facilities** FTV WiFi **Conf** Class 60 Board 50 Thtr 100 Del from £80* **Notes** ⊗

Royal Harbour Hotel

★★ 79% METRO HOTEL

tel: 01843 591514 **10-11 Nelson Crescent CT11 9JF**
email: info@royalharbourhotel.co.uk **web:** www.royalharbourhotel.co.uk
dir: A253 to Ramsgate. Follow signs to seafront. At Churchill Tavern, 1st left into Nelson Crescent

Dating back to 1799, this hotel is made up of adjoining Georgian Grade II listed townhouses, and occupies a prime position in the town's well known historic garden crescent. Many of the bedrooms boast magnificent views over the 'Royal Harbour', the yacht marina and the English Channel. The atmosphere is relaxed, the service is attentive and the breakfast is superb.

Rooms 19 (3 fmly) (1 GF) ⫩ **Facilities** FTV WiFi **Conf** Class 30 Board 25 Thtr 30 **Parking** 4

RAVENGLASS | Map 18 SD09
Cumbria

The Pennington Hotel

★★★ 82% ⊛ HOTEL

tel: 01229 717222 & 0845 450 6445 **CA18 1SD**
email: info@penningtonhotels.com **web:** www.penningtonhotels.com
dir: In village centre

This hotel has a very relaxed atmosphere throughout and the public areas are open plan with high quality fabrics and artwork. The bedrooms are modern in design and have high spec fixtures and fittings in the bathrooms. Honest cooking, based on local and fine quality ingredients, is offered on the seasonal menus. Staff show exceptional customer awareness and provide very attentive and friendly service.

Rooms 21 (3 annexe) (6 fmly) (5 GF) ⫩ **S** £90-£125; **D** £100-£150 (incl. bkfst)* **Facilities** FTV WiFi ⥄ Xmas New Year **Conf** Class 40 Board 40 Thtr 80 Del from £110 to £150* **Parking** 53 **Notes** LB

RAVENSCAR | Map 19 NZ90
North Yorkshire

Raven Hall Country House Hotel

★★★ 79% HOTEL

tel: 01723 870353 **YO13 OET**
email: enquiries@ravenhall.co.uk **web:** www.ravenhall.co.uk
dir: A171 towards Whitby. At Cloughton turn right onto unclassified road to Ravenscar

This impressive cliff top mansion enjoys breathtaking views over Robin Hood's Bay. Extensive well-kept grounds include tennis courts, putting green, swimming pools and historic battlements. The bedrooms vary in size but all are comfortably equipped, and many offer panoramic views. There are also eight environmentally-friendly Finnish lodges that have been furnished to a high standard.

Rooms 60 (8 annexe) (20 fmly) (5 GF) ⫩ **S** £52-£80; **D** £104-£162 (incl. bkfst)* **Facilities** FTV WiFi ⬚ ⌇ 9 ⚑ Putt green ⚐ Bowls Table tennis Xmas New Year **Conf** Class 80 Board 40 Thtr 100 Del from £90 to £140* **Services** Lift **Parking** 200 **Notes** LB Civ Wed 100

RAYLEIGH | Map 7 TQ89
Essex

Premier Inn Basildon (Rayleigh)

BUDGET HOTEL

tel: 0871 527 8058 **Rayleigh Weir, Arterial Road (A127) SS6 7XJ**
web: www.premierinn.com
dir: M25 junct 29, A127 towards Southend. Approx 13m exit at Rayleigh Weir junct onto A129 to Rayleigh. Straight on at 2 lights, 1st left (NB Sat Nav use code SS6 7XJ)

High quality, budget accommodation ideal for both families and business travellers. Spacious, en suite bedrooms feature tea and coffee making facilities, and Freeview TV in most hotels. Internet access and WiFi are available for a small fee. The adjacent family restaurant features a wide and varied menu. See also the Hotel Groups pages.

Rooms 49

READING | Map 5 SU77
Berkshire

The Forbury

★★★★★ 83% ⊛⊛ HOTEL

tel: 0118 952 7770 **26 The Forbury RG1 3EJ**
email: reception@theforburyhotel.co.uk **web:** www.theforburyhotel.co.uk
dir: Telephone for detailed directions

The imposing exterior of this hotel belies the caring approach of the staff who provide helpful service with a smile. The up-to-the-minute bedrooms have very appealing designs and sensory appeal. For film buffs, a 30-seater cinema is also available, complete with refreshments! Cerise is the convivial and stylish venue for award-winning cuisine.

Rooms 23 ⫩ **S** £138-£246; **D** £138-£246 (incl. bkfst)* **Facilities** FTV WiFi ⥄ ♫ Xmas New Year **Conf** Class 24 Board 24 Thtr 35 Del from £180 to £220 **Services** Lift **Parking** 20 **Notes** LB ⊗ Civ Wed 50

Holiday Inn Reading M4 Jct 10

★★★★ 80% ◉◉ HOTEL

tel: 0118 944 0444 **Wharfedale Rd, Winnersh Triangle RG41 5TS**
email: reservations@hireadinghotel.com **web:** www.hireadinghotel.com
dir: M4 junct 10/A329(M) towards Reading (E), 1st exit signed Winnersh/Woodley/A329, left at lights into Wharfedale Rd. Hotel on left

Situated in the Winnersh Triangle within close proximity of the M4, Reading, Bracknell and Wokingham, this hotel offers a range of air-conditioned, contemporary and stylish bedrooms, eight state-of-the-art meeting rooms and the Esprit Fitness and Spa with extensive leisure facilities including a 19-metre indoor pool and Dermalogica Spa. The Caprice Restaurant offers relaxed dining throughout the day. Complimentary underground parking is provided.

Rooms 174 (23 fmly) ✆ **S** £50-£254; **D** £50-£254* **Facilities** Spa FTV WiFi ᴥ HL ⓣ Gym Sauna Steam room ♬ Xmas New Year **Conf** Class 160 Board 64 Thtr 260 Del from £120 to £249* **Services** Lift Air con **Parking** 120 **Notes** LB Civ Wed 260

Millennium Madejski Hotel Reading

★★★★ 80% ◉◉ HOTEL

tel: 0118 925 3500 **Madejski Stadium RG2 0FL**
email: sales.reading@millenniumhotels.co.uk **web:** www.millenniumhotels.co.uk
dir: M4 junct 11 onto A33, follow signs for Madejski Stadium Complex

A stylish hotel, that features an atrium lobby with specially commissioned water sculpture, is part of the Madejski stadium complex, home to both Reading FC and the London Irish rugby team. Bedrooms are appointed with spacious workstations and plenty of amenities; there is also a choice of suites and a club floor with its own lounge. The hotel also has a fine dining restaurant.

Rooms 201 (39 fmly) (19 smoking) **Facilities** Spa STV WiFi ⓣ supervised Gym **Conf** Class 36 Board 30 Thtr 66 **Services** Lift Air con **Parking** 250 **Notes** RS Xmas & New Year

Crowne Plaza Reading

★★★★ 79% HOTEL

tel: 0118 925 9988 **Caversham Bridge, Richfield Av RG1 8BD**
email: info@cp-reading.co.uk **web:** www.cp-reading.co.uk
dir: A33 to Reading. Follow signs for Caversham & Henley. Take 1st exit at rdbt onto Caversham Rd. Left at rdbt & entrance on right

The Crowne Plaza Reading is ideally located in the city centre with good links to London or Heathrow Airport by train. In a fantastic location on the River Thames, guests can choose between stylish standard rooms, executive Club rooms and luxury executive suites. A range of dishes can be enjoyed at dinner, and in summer the dining area opens onto the terrace overlooking the river. Revive Health Club and Spa offers a superb health and fitness suite, with infinity-effect pool, sauna and luxury treatment rooms.

Rooms 122 (9 fmly) ✆ **Facilities** Spa STV FTV WiFi ᴥ HL ⓣ Gym Sauna Steam room **Conf** Class 110 Board 60 Thtr 200 **Services** Lift Air con **Parking** 200 **Notes** ⊗ Civ Wed 180

Novotel Reading Centre

★★★★ 78% HOTEL

tel: 0118 952 2600 **25b Friar St RG1 1DP**
email: h5432@accor.com **web:** www.novotel.com
dir: M4 junct 11 or A33 towards Reading, left for Garrard St car park, at rdbt 3rd exit on Friar St

This attractive and stylish city centre hotel is convenient for Reading's business and shopping centre; it is adjacent to a town centre car park, and has a range of conference facilities and excellent leisure options. The restaurant offers a contemporary style menu and a good wine list too. Bedrooms are comfortable and stylishly designed.

Rooms 178 (154 fmly) **Facilities** STV FTV WiFi HL ⓣ Gym Steam room Sauna **Conf** Class 50 Board 36 Thtr 90 Del from £120 to £190* **Services** Lift Air con **Parking** 15

Malmaison Reading

★★★★ 74% ◉ HOTEL

tel: 0844 693 0660 & 0118 956 2300 **Great Western House, 18-20 Station Rd RG1 1JX**
email: reading@malmaison.com **web:** www.malmaison.com
dir: Opposite rail station

This historic hotel has been transformed into the funky Malmaison style which reflects its proximity and long-standing relationship with the railway. Public areas feature rail memorabilia and excellent pictures, and include a Café Mal and a meeting room. Bedrooms here have all the amenities a modern executive would expect, plus comfort and quality in abundance. Dining is interesting too, with a menu that features home-grown and local produce accompanied by an impressive wine list.

Rooms 75 (6 fmly) (4 GF) ✆ **S** £69-£380; **D** £69-£380* **Facilities** FTV WiFi ᴥ HL Xmas New Year **Conf** Class 18 Board 22 Thtr 30 Del from £180 to £480* **Services** Lift Air con **Notes** LB ⊗ Civ Wed 20

Holiday Inn Reading South M4 Jct 11

★★★ 79% HOTEL

tel: 0871 702 9067 **Basingstoke Rd RG2 0SL**
email: reading@ihg.com **web:** www.hireadingsouthhotel.co.uk
dir: A33 to Reading. 1st rdbt right onto Imperial Way. Hotel on left

This bright hotel provides modern accommodation and the addition of leisure facilities which are a bonus at the end of a busy day. Meals are served in Traders restaurant, or snacks are available in the lounge. Callaghans, an Irish-style pub, offers live sports coverage. The business centre has a good range of conference and meeting rooms.

Rooms 202 (60 fmly) (99 GF) **Facilities** FTV WiFi ᴥ HL ⓣ supervised Gym Health & fitness centre **Conf** Class 45 Board 50 Thtr 100 **Services** Air con **Parking** 300 **Notes** ⊗ Civ Wed 100

R

READING *continued*

BEST WESTERN Calcot Hotel

★★★ 74% HOTEL

tel: 0118 941 6423 **98 Bath Rd, Calcot RG31 7QN**
email: enquiries@calcothotel.net **web:** www.calcothotel.co.uk
dir: M4 junct 12, A4 towards Reading, hotel in 0.5m

This hotel is conveniently located in a residential area just off the motorway. Bedrooms are well equipped with good business facilities, such as data ports and good workspace. There are attractive public rooms and function suites, and the informal restaurant offers enjoyable food in welcoming surroundings.

Rooms 78 (3 fmly) (6 GF) **Facilities** FTV WiFi New Year **Conf** Class 35 Board 35 Thtr 120 Del from £125 to £145* **Parking** 130 **Notes** Closed 25-30 Dec RS 2 Dec-6 Jan Civ Wed 200

Ibis Reading Centre

BUDGET HOTEL

tel: 0118 953 3500 **25A Friar St RG1 1DP**
email: H5431@accor.com **web:** www.ibishotel.com
dir: A329 into Friar St. Hotel near central railway station. Access by car in Garrard St

Modern, budget hotel offering comfortable accommodation in bright and practical bedrooms. Breakfast is self-service and dinner is available in the restaurant. See also the Hotel Groups pages.

Rooms 182

Premier Inn Reading (Caversham Bridge)

BUDGET HOTEL

tel: 0871 527 8922 **Richfield Av RG1 8EQ**
web: www.premierinn.com
dir: M4 junct 11, A33 to Reading. A329 towards Caversham. Left at TGI Friday's. Left at Crowne Plaza. Hotel 200yds on right

High quality, budget accommodation ideal for both families and business travellers. Spacious, en suite bedrooms feature tea and coffee making facilities, and Freeview TV in most hotels. Internet access and WiFi are available for a small fee. The adjacent family restaurant features a wide and varied menu. See also the Hotel Groups pages.

Rooms 74

Premier Inn Reading Central

BUDGET HOTEL

tel: 0871 527 8924 **Letcombe St RG1 2HN**
web: www.premierinn.com
dir: M4 junct 11, A33 towards town centre, straight on at 3 rdbts (approx 3.5m). Right onto A329 signed The Oracle, Riverside Shopping Centre. Branch immediately left, hotel opposite The Oracle shopping centre

Rooms 151

Premier Inn Reading South

BUDGET HOTEL

tel: 0871 527 8926 **Goring Ln, Grazeley Green RG7 1LS**
web: www.premierinn.com
dir: M4 junct 11, A33 towards Basingstoke. At rdbt take exit towards Burghfield & Mortimer. 3rd right into Grazeley Green. Under rail bridge turn left. Hotel on left

Rooms 32

The French Horn

 RESTAURANT WITH ROOMS

tel: 0118 969 2204 0118 944 2210 **Sonning RG4 6TN**
email: info@thefrenchhorn.co.uk **web:** www.thefrenchhorn.co.uk
dir: From A4 into Sonning, follow B478 through village over bridge, on right, car park on left

This long established Thames-side establishment has a lovely village setting and retains the traditions of classic hospitality. The restaurant is a particular attraction and provides attentive service. Bedrooms, including four cottage suites, are spacious and comfortable; many offer stunning views over the river. A private boardroom is available for corporate guests.

Rooms 20 (8 annexe)

| REDDITCH | Map 10 SP06 |
| Worcestershire | |

Abbey Hotel Golf & Spa

★★★★ 78% HOTEL

tel: 01527 406600 **Hither Green Ln, Dagnell End Rd, Bordesley B98 9BE**
email: info@theabbeyhotel.co.uk **web:** www.theabbeyhotel.co.uk
dir: M42 junct 2, A441 to Redditch. End of carriageway turn left (A441), Dagnell End Rd on left. Hotel 600yds on right

With convenient access to the motorway and a proximity to many attractions, this modern hotel is popular with both business and leisure travellers. Bedrooms are well equipped and attractively decorated; the executive corner rooms are especially spacious. Facilities include an 18-hole golf course, pro shop, large indoor pool and extensive conference facilities.

Rooms 99 (20 fmly) (23 GF) **S** £69-£149; **D** £79-£159 (incl. bkfst)* **Facilities** Spa FTV WiFi 18 Putt green Gym Flood lit golf driving range Xmas New Year **Conf** Class 60 Board 30 Thtr 170 Del from £140 to £170* **Services** Lift **Parking** 200 **Notes** LB Civ Wed 100

Holiday Inn Express Birmingham - Redditch

BUDGET HOTEL

tel: 01527 584658 & 587910 **2 Hewell Rd, Enfield B97 6AE**
email: reservations@express.gb.com **web:** www.hieredditchhotel.com
dir: M42 junct 2. 1st exit from rdbt to A44. 1st exit from rdbt to Bordesleigh. 4th exit from rdbt to Middelhouse Lane. Left at lights into B/ham Rd. 1st right into Clive Road. 1st exit from rdbt to Hewell Rd. 1st right into Gloucester Close

This modern town centre hotel, adjacent to the station, is ideal for families and business travellers. The spacious tranquil rooms include flat screen TVs with Freeview channels, and bathrooms with power showers. Complimentary hot buffet breakfast and free Wi-fi are included in the room rate. Freshly prepared meals are served in the GR Restaurant daily from 6pm-10pm. There are two air-conditioned meeting rooms, with natural light, available. See also the Hotel Groups pages.

Rooms 100 (75 fmly) (10 GF) (4 smoking) ⌇ **S** £50-£69; **D** £50-£69 (incl. bkfst)*
Conf Class 26 Board 20 Thtr 50 Del from £99 to £109*

Premier Inn Redditch

BUDGET HOTEL

tel: 0871 527 8928 **Birchfield Rd B97 6PX**
web: www.premierinn.com
dir: M5 junct 4, A38 towards Bromsgrove. At rdbt take A448 to Redditch. 1st exit for Webheath. At next rdbt 3rd exit, 1st right into Birchfield Rd

High quality, budget accommodation ideal for both families and business travellers. Spacious, en suite bedrooms feature tea and coffee making facilities, and Freeview TV in most hotels. Internet access and WiFi are available for a small fee. The adjacent family restaurant features a wide and varied menu. See also the Hotel Groups pages.

Rooms 33

Premier Inn Redditch North (A441)

BUDGET HOTEL

tel: 0871 527 9372 **Bordesley Ln B97 6AQ**
web: www.premierinn.com
dir: M42 junct 3, A435 (Alcester road). In 3m take A4023 towards Redditch & Bromsgrove. Exit 1st rdbt towards Birmingham (A441). At next rdbt 3rd exit onto Alvechurch Highway (A441). At next rdbt 4th exit into Millrace Rd, left into Bordesley Ln. Please note for Sat Nav use B97 6RR

Rooms 60

REDHILL	Map 6 TQ25
Surrey	

Nutfield Priory Hotel & Spa

★★★★ 83% ◉◉ HOTEL

tel: 01737 824400 & 0845 072 7485 **Nutfield RH1 4EL**
email: nutfieldpriory@handpicked.co.uk **web:** www.handpickedhotels.co.uk/nutfieldpriory
dir: M25 junct 6, follow Redhill signs via Godstone on A25. Hotel 1m on left after Nutfield Village. Or M25 junct 8, A25 through Reigate & Redhill. Hotel on right 1.5m after rail bridge

This Victorian country house dates back to 1872 and is set in 40 acres of grounds with stunning views over the Surrey countryside. Bedrooms are individually decorated and equipped with an excellent range of facilities. Public areas include the impressive grand hall, Cloisters Restaurant, the library, and a cosy lounge bar area.

Rooms 60 (4 fmly) ⌇ **D** £149-£309 (incl. bkfst)* **Facilities** Spa STV FTV WiFi ⌇ HL ⌖ Gym Squash Steam room Beauty therapy Aerobic & Step classes Saunas Xmas New Year **Conf** Class 50 Board 42 Thtr 90 Del from £195 to £274* **Services** Lift Air con **Parking** 130 **Notes** ⊗ Civ Wed 90

Premier Inn Redhill

BUDGET HOTEL

tel: 0871 527 8930 **Brighton Rd, Salfords RH1 5BT**
web: www.premierinn.com
dir: On A23, 2m S of Redhill; 3m N of Gatwick Airport

High quality, budget accommodation ideal for both families and business travellers. Spacious, en suite bedrooms feature tea and coffee making facilities, and Freeview TV in most hotels. Internet access and WiFi are available for a small fee. The adjacent family restaurant features a wide and varied menu. See also the Hotel Groups pages.

Rooms 48

REDRUTH	Map 2 SW64
Cornwall	

Penventon Park Hotel

★★★ 80% HOTEL

tel: 01209 203000 **TR15 1TE**
email: enquiries@penventon.com **web:** www.penventon.co.uk
dir: Exit A30 at Redruth. Follow signs for Redruth West, hotel 1m S

Set in attractive parkland, this Georgian mansion is ideal for both business and leisure guests, and is well placed for visiting the glorious Cornish coastal areas. The smart bedrooms include 20 Garden Suites with patio doors that give access to a decking area and the garden beyond. The menus offer a wide choice of Cornish, British, Italian and French dishes. Leisure facilities include a pool, fitness suite, and health spa with beauty and holistic therapies, as well as function rooms and bars.

Rooms 63 (3 fmly) (24 GF) ⌇ **S** £69-£199; **D** £99-£219 (incl. bkfst)* **Facilities** Spa FTV WiFi ⌇ ⌖ supervised Gym Sauna Pool table Solarium Personal trainer ♫ Xmas New Year **Conf** Class 100 Board 60 Thtr 200 Del from £123 to £158* **Parking** 100 **Notes** LB Civ Wed 150

REDWORTH	Map 19 NZ22
County Durham	

Redworth Hall Hotel

★★★★ 79% ◉ COUNTRY HOUSE HOTEL

tel: 01388 770600 **DL5 6NL**
email: redworthhall@pumahotels.co.uk **web:** www.pumahotels.co.uk
dir: From A1(M) junct 58, A68 signed Corbridge. Follow hotel signs

This imposing Georgian building includes a health club with state-of-the-art equipment and impressive conference facilities, making this hotel a popular destination for business travellers. There are several spacious lounges to relax in along with the Conservatory Restaurant. Bedrooms are very comfortable and well equipped.

Rooms 143 (12 fmly) ⌇ **Facilities** STV WiFi ⌇ HL ⌖ ⌖ ⌖ Gym Bodysense Health & Leisure Club Xmas New Year **Conf** Class 144 Board 90 Thtr 300 **Services** Lift **Parking** 300 **Notes** Civ Wed 240

R

REIGATE
Surrey   Map 6 TQ25

BEST WESTERN Reigate Manor Hotel

★★★ 73% HOTEL

tel: 01737 240125 **Reigate Hill RH2 9PF**
email: hotel@reigatemanor.co.uk **web:** www.reigatemanor.co.uk
dir: On A217, 1m S of M25 junct 8

On the slopes of Reigate Hill, the hotel is ideally located for access to the town and for motorway links. A range of public rooms is provided along with a variety of function rooms. Bedrooms are either traditional in style in the old house or of contemporary design in the wing.

Rooms 50 (1 fmly) ⚡ **S** £60-£95; **Facilities** FTV WiFi ⌧ **Conf** Class 80 Board 50 Thtr 200 Del from £150* **Parking** 130 **Notes** LB ⊗ Civ Wed 200

RENISHAW
Derbyshire   Map 16 SK47

Sitwell Arms Hotel

★★★ 73% HOTEL

tel: 01246 435226 **Station Rd S21 3WF**
email: info@sitwellarms.com **web:** www.sitwellarms.co.uk
dir: On A6135 to Sheffield, W of M1 junct 30

Parts of this attractive stone building date from the 18th century when it was a coaching inn. It has been extended to provide spacious comfortable bedrooms with modern facilities. A wide range of meals is served in the Wild Boar Restaurant; there is also a cocktail bar, informal lounge bar and a smart beer garden with patio and children's play area. The hotel has a gym and a hair and beauty salon.

Rooms 31 (8 fmly) (9 GF) **S** £32-£73.50; **D** £57.50-£110 (incl. bkfst)* **Facilities** FTV WiFi Gym Fitness studio Hair & beauty salon Xmas New Year **Conf** Class 60 Board 60 Thtr 160 **Services** Lift **Parking** 150 **Notes** ⊗ Civ Wed 150

RETFORD
Nottinghamshire   Map 17 SK78

Ye Olde Bell Hotel & Restaurant

★★★★ 79% HOTEL

tel: 01777 705121 **DN22 8QS**
email: enquiries@yeoldebell-hotel.co.uk **web:** www.yeoldebell-hotel.co.uk

(For full entry see Barnby Moor)

BEST WESTERN PLUS West Retford Hotel

★★★ 80% HOTEL

tel: 01777 706333 **24 North Rd DN22 7XG**
email: reservations@westretfordhotel.co.uk **web:** www.westretfordhotel.co.uk
dir: From A1 take A620 to Ranby/Retford. Left at rdbt into North Rd (A638). Hotel on right

Stylishly appointed throughout, and set in very attractive gardens close to the town centre, this 18th-century manor house offers a good range of well-equipped meeting rooms. The spacious, well-laid out bedrooms and suites are located in separate buildings and all offer modern facilities and comforts.

Rooms 63 (15 fmly) (32 GF) ⚡ **S** £65-£98; **D** £65-£111 **Facilities** FTV WiFi Xmas New Year **Conf** Class 80 Board 40 Thtr 150 Del from £110 to £140 **Parking** 150 **Notes** ⊗ Civ Wed 150

RICCALL
North Yorkshire   Map 16 SE63

Per Bacco at The Park View

RESTAURANT WITH ROOMS

tel: 01757 249146 **20 Main St YO19 6PX**
email: gianlucasechi@hotmail.co.uk **web:** www.per-bacco.co.uk
dir: A19 from Selby, left for Riccall by water tower, house 100yds on right

This spacious detached property is located in a quiet residential area and is convenient for York. The ground floor has been converted into an authentic Italian restaurant and there is a wide choice of fresh, home-made dishes and a friendly atmosphere. The restaurant is the main part of the business but there is also a range of comfortable en suite bedrooms. Ample parking is available.

Rooms 4 (2 fmly)

RICHMOND (UPON THAMES)
Greater London

The Petersham Hotel

★★★★ 80% ◉◉ HOTEL PLAN 1 C2

tel: 020 8940 7471 & 8939 1010 **Nightingale Ln TW10 6UZ**
email: enq@petershamhotel.co.uk **web:** www.petershamhotel.co.uk
dir: From Richmond Bridge rdbt A316 follow Ham & Petersham signs. Hotel in Nightingale Ln on left off Petersham Rd

Managed by the same family for over 25 years, this attractive hotel is located on a hill overlooking water meadows and a sweep of the River Thames. Bedrooms and suites are comfortably furnished, whilst public areas combine elegance and some fine architectural features. High quality produce features in dishes offered in the restaurant that looks out over the Thames below.

Rooms 58 (6 fmly) (3 GF) ⚡ **Facilities** STV FTV WiFi ⌧ Xmas New Year **Conf** Board 25 Thtr 35 **Services** Lift **Parking** 60 **Notes** ⊗ Civ Wed 40

The Richmond Hill Hotel

★★★★ 73% HOTEL PLAN 1 C2

tel: 0208 940 2247 **Richmond Hill TW10 6RW**
email: info.richmond@kewgreen.co.uk **web:** www.richmondhill-hotel.co.uk
dir: A316 for Richmond, hotel at top of Richmond Hill

This attractive Georgian manor is situated on Richmond Hill, enjoying elevated views over the Thames, and the town and the park are within walking distance. Bedrooms vary in size and style but all are comfortable and contemporary in style. There is a well-designed heath club, and extensive conference and banqueting facilities.

Rooms 149 (1 fmly) (15 GF) **Facilities** Spa STV FTV WiFi Gym Steam room Health & beauty suite Sauna Xmas New Year **Conf** Class 80 Board 50 Thtr 180 **Services** Lift Air con **Parking** 97 **Notes** Civ Wed 182

INSPECTORS' CHOICE

Bingham

★★★ TOWN HOUSE HOTEL PLAN 1 C2

tel: 020 8940 0902 **61-63 Petersham Rd TW10 6UT**
email: info@thebingham.co.uk **web:** www.thebingham.co.uk
dir: On A307

This Georgian building, dating back to 1740, overlooks the River Thames and is within easy reach of the town centre, Kew Gardens and Hampton Court. The contemporary bedrooms feature bespoke art deco style furniture and up-to-the-minute facilities such as WiFi, a digital music library, flat-screen TVs and 'rain dance' showers. Public rooms have views of the pretty garden and river. Guests can choose from a selection of meals that range from light snacks to two or three-course dinners.

Rooms 15 (2 fmly) **S** £160-£195; **D** £185-£210* **Facilities** FTV WiFi In room beauty treatments Xmas New Year **Conf** Class 70 Board 40 Thtr 100 **Services** Lift Air con **Parking** 8 **Notes** LB RS Sunday eve Civ Wed 90

Premier Inn London Richmond

BUDGET HOTEL PLAN 1 C2

tel: 0871 527 9346 **136-138 Lower Mortlake Rd, Richmond TW9 2JZ**
web: www.premierinn.com
dir: Please telephone for directions

High quality, budget accommodation ideal for both families and business travellers. Spacious, en suite bedrooms feature tea and coffee making facilities, and Freeview TV in most hotels. Internet access and WiFi are available for a small

fee. The adjacent family restaurant features a wide and varied menu. See also the Hotel Groups pages.

Rooms 92

RICKMANSWORTH Map 6 TQ09
Hertfordshire

INSPECTORS' CHOICE

The Grove

★★★★★ HOTEL

tel: 01923 807807 **Chandler's Cross WD3 4TG**
email: info@thegrove.co.uk **web:** www.thegrove.co.uk
dir: M25 junct 19, A411 towards Watford. Hotel on right

Set amid 300 acres of rolling countryside, much of which is golf course, the hotel combines historic features with cutting-edge, modern design. The spacious bedrooms have the latest in temperature control, lighting technology and flat-screen TVs; many have balconies. Suites in the original mansion are particularly stunning. Championship golf, a world-class spa and three dining options are just a few of the treasures to sample here. The hotel also has extensive crèche facilities. The hotel has three dining options - Collette's with 3 AA Rosettes that offers fine dining, and a more relaxed style in the Glasshouse and Stables restaurants. The walled garden is also well worth exploring.

Rooms 217 (69 fmly) (35 GF) **S** fr £285; **D** £310-£1000 (incl. bkfst)* **Facilities** Spa STV FTV WiFi supervised supervised 18 Putt green Gym Walk & cycle trails Giant chess Driving range Kids club Games room Xmas New Year **Conf** Class 300 Board 78 Thtr 450 Del from £306 to £450* **Services** Lift Air con **Parking** 400 **Notes** LB Civ Wed 450

R

RICKMANSWORTH *continued*

Long Island Hotel

★★ 🅰 HOTEL

tel: 01923 779466 **2 Victoria Close WD3 4EQ**
email: 5342@greeneking.co.uk **web:** www.oldenglish.co.uk
dir: M25 junct 18, A404, 1.5m. Left at rdbt into Nightingale Rd, 1st left

Located opposite Rickmansworth train station and 25 minutes from both Heathrow and Luton airports, this modern hotel provides comfortable accommodation for business or leisure guests. Evening meals and breakfasts are served in the American-themed Exchange Bar & Grill.

Rooms 50 (3 fmly) (12 GF) **Facilities** STV WiFi 🎵 **Conf** Class 15 Board 8 Thtr 12 **Parking** 120 **Notes** ⊗

RINGWOOD	Map 5 SU10
Hampshire	

Tyrrells Ford Country House Hotel

★★★ 72% SMALL HOTEL

tel: 01425 672646 **Avon BH23 7BH**
email: info@tyrrellsford.co.uk **web:** www.tyrrellsford.co.uk
dir: From A31 to Ringwood take B3347. Hotel 3m S on left

Set in the New Forest, this delightful family-run hotel has much to offer. Most bedrooms have views over the open country. Diners may eat in the formal restaurant, or sample the wide range of bar meals; all dishes are prepared using fresh local produce. The Gallery Lounge offers guests a peaceful area in which to relax.

Rooms 14 **Facilities** WiFi **Conf** Class 20 Board 20 Thtr 40 **Parking** 100 **Notes** ⊗ Civ Wed 150

RIPLEY	Map 16 SK35
Derbyshire	

Premier Inn Ripley

BUDGET HOTEL

tel: 0871 527 8935 **Nottingham Rd DE5 3QP**
web: www.premierinn.com
dir: From S: M1 junct 26, A610 towards Ripley. Hotel off rdbt adjacent to Butterley Park. From N: M1 junct 28, A38, A610 towards Nottingham. Hotel on right at rdbt

High quality, budget accommodation ideal for both families and business travellers. Spacious, en suite bedrooms feature tea and coffee making facilities, and Freeview TV in most hotels. Internet access and WiFi are available for a small fee. The adjacent family restaurant features a wide and varied menu. See also the Hotel Groups pages.

Rooms 60

ROCHDALE	Map 16 SD81
Greater Manchester	

Mercure Manchester Norton Grange Hotel & Spa

★★★★ 75% HOTEL

tel: 0870 194 2119 & 01706 630788 **Manchester Rd, Castleton OL11 2XZ**
email: h6631@accor.com **web:** www.mercure.com
dir: M62 junct 20, follow A664/Castleton signs. Right at next 2 rdbts. Hotel 0.5m on left

Standing in nine acres of grounds and mature gardens, this Victorian house provides comfort in elegant surroundings. The well-equipped bedrooms provide a host of extras for both the business and leisure guest. Public areas include the Pickwick bistro and smart Grange Restaurant, both offering a good choice of dishes. There is also an impressive leisure centre.

Rooms 81 (17 fmly) (10 GF) 🪶 **S** £64-£124; **D** £74-£144* **Facilities** Spa STV WiFi 🌀 Gym Leisure centre Indoor/Outdoor hydrotherapy pool Thermal suite Rock sauna Xmas New Year **Conf** Class 120 Board 70 Thtr 220 Del from £99 to £149* **Services** Lift **Parking** 150 **Notes** LB Civ Wed 150

BEST WESTERN Broadfield Park Hotel

★★★ 74% HOTEL

tel: 01706 639000 **Sparrow Hill OL16 1AF**
email: reception@broadfieldparkhotel.co.uk **web:** www.broadfieldparkhotel.co.uk
dir: M60 junct 20, follow signs for Rochdale & town centre. A640 into Drake St, hotel signed 0.5m on left

Broadfield Park Hotel overlooks historic Broadfield Park and the town centre and is only minutes away from the M60 and M62. Bedrooms are comfortably furnished and attractively decorated. The hotel offers a range of carefully prepared meals and snacks in either the formal restaurant, or the lounge bar. Service is friendly and attentive.

Rooms 29 (4 fmly) 🪶 **S** £40-£55; **D** £55-£85* **Facilities** FTV WiFi Xmas New Year **Conf** Class 120 Board 80 Thtr 200 **Parking** 30 **Notes** Civ Wed 200

Premier Inn Rochdale

BUDGET HOTEL

tel: 0871 527 8936 **Newhey Rd, Milnrow OL16 4JF**
web: www.premierinn.com
dir: M62 junct 21, at rdbt right towards Shaw, under motorway bridge, & 1st left

High quality, budget accommodation ideal for both families and business travellers. Spacious, en suite bedrooms feature tea and coffee making facilities, and Freeview TV in most hotels. Internet access and WiFi are available for a small fee. The adjacent family restaurant features a wide and varied menu. See also the Hotel Groups pages.

Rooms 40

ROCHESTER
Kent
Map 6 TQ76

Premier Inn Rochester

BUDGET HOTEL

tel: 0871 527 8938 **Medway Valley Leisure Park, Chariot Way, Strood ME2 2SS**
web: www.premierinn.com
dir: M2 junct 2, follow Rochester & West Malling signs. At rdbt onto A228 signed Rochester & Strood. At next rdbt 2nd exit into Roman Way signed Medway Valley Park. At next rdbt 1st exit into Chariot Way, hotel in 100mtrs

High quality, budget accommodation ideal for both families and business travellers. Spacious, en suite bedrooms feature tea and coffee making facilities, and Freeview TV in most hotels. Internet access and WiFi are available for a small fee. The adjacent family restaurant features a wide and varied menu. See also the Hotel Groups pages.

Rooms 121

ROMALDKIRK
County Durham
Map 19 NY92

INSPECTORS' CHOICE

The Rose & Crown

★★★ ◉◉ HOTEL

tel: 01833 650213 **DL12 9EB**
email: hotel@rose-and-crown.co.uk **web:** www.rose-and-crown.co.uk
dir: 6m NW from Barnard Castle on B6277

This charming 18th-century country inn is located in the heart of the village, overlooking fine dale scenery. The attractively furnished bedrooms, including suites, are split between the main house and the rear courtyard. Guests might like to have a drink in the cosy bar with its log fire, after returning from a long walk. Good local produce features extensively on the menus that can be enjoyed

in the oak-panelled restaurant, or in the brasserie and bar. Service is both friendly and attentive.

Rooms 14 (7 annexe) (2 fmly) (5 GF) ☎ **S** £95-£125; **D** £115-£200 (incl. bkfst)*
Facilities FTV WiFi ☼ Spa & golf available at nearby Headlam Hall New Year
Conf Board 12 **Parking** 20 **Notes** LB Closed 23-27 Dec

ROMFORD
Greater London
Map 6 TQ58

Premier Inn Romford Central

BUDGET HOTEL

tel: 0871 527 8940 **Mercury Gardens RM1 3EN**
web: www.premierinn.com
dir: M25 junct 28, A12 to Gallows Corner. Take A118 to next rdbt, turn left

High quality, budget accommodation ideal for both families and business travellers. Spacious, en suite bedrooms feature tea and coffee making facilities, and Freeview TV in most hotels. Internet access and WiFi are available for a small fee. The adjacent family restaurant features a wide and varied menu. See also the Hotel Groups pages.

Rooms 64

Premier Inn Romford West

BUDGET HOTEL

tel: 0871 527 8942 **Whalebone Lane North, Chadwell Heath RM6 6QU**
web: www.premierinn.com
dir: 6m from M25 junct 28 on A12 at junct with A1112

Rooms 42

R

ROMSEY	Map 5 SU32
Hampshire	

The White Horse Hotel & Brasserie

★★★★ 75% ⑨⑨ HOTEL

tel: 01794 512431 **19 Market Place SO51 8ZJ**
email: thewhitehorsesales@silkshotels.com **web:** www.silkshotels.com
dir: M27 junct 3, follow signs for Romsey, right at Broadlands. In Town centre

This family friendly hotel is located overlooking the market square of this historic town. This traditional, former coaching inn provides very comfortable and very stylish, individually designed bedrooms, including Loft Suites and a Penthouse. Public areas boast relaxing day rooms and an elegant contemporary bar. The Brasserie offers award-winning cuisine, with alfresco dining a possibility during the warmer summer months. Public car parks can be found close by, although the property does operate a valet parking service.

Rooms 31 (4 fmly) ⟨S £85-£95; **D** £115-£235 **Facilities** FTV WiFi ⟨ Xmas New Year **Conf** Class 40 Board 30 Thtr 30 Del from £145 to £165 **Notes** LB Civ Wed 65

See advert on opposite page

Potters Heron Hotel

★★★ 80% HOTEL

tel: 023 8027 7800 **Winchester Rd, Ampfield SO51 9ZF**
email: thepottersheron@pebblehotels.com **web:** www.pebblehotels.com
dir: M3 junct 12 follow Chandler's Ford signs. 2nd exit at 3rd rdbt follow Ampfield signs, over x-rds. Hotel on left in 1m

This distinctive thatched hotel retains many original features. In a convenient location with access to Winchester, Southampton and the M3, Potters Heron Hotel has modern accommodation and stylish, spacious public areas. Most of the

bedrooms have their own balcony or terrace. The pub and restaurant both offer an interesting range of dishes that will suit a variety of tastes.

Rooms 53 (1 fmly) (29 GF) ⟨S £69-£105; **D** £74-£120 (incl. bkfst)* **Facilities** WiFi ⟨ Xmas New Year **Conf** Class 40 Board 30 Thtr 100 Del from £135 **Services** Lift **Parking** 120 **Notes** ⊗ Civ Wed 100

Premier Inn Southampton West

BUDGET HOTEL

tel: 0871 527 9004 **Romsey Rd, Ower SO51 6ZJ**
web: www.premierinn.com
dir: Just off M27 junct 2. Take A36 towards Salisbury. Follow brown tourist signs 'Vine Inn'

High quality, budget accommodation ideal for both families and business travellers. Spacious, en suite bedrooms feature tea and coffee making facilities, and Freeview TV in most hotels. Internet access and WiFi are available for a small fee. The adjacent family restaurant features a wide and varied menu. See also the Hotel Groups pages.

Rooms 67

The Cromwell Arms Country Pub With Rooms

RESTAURANT WITH ROOMS

tel: 01794 519515 📄 01794 519516 **Mainstone SO51 8HG**
email: info@thecromwellarms.com **web:** www.thecromwellarms.com
dir: M27 junct 2 onto A3090 to Mainstone, on left

This charming country pub has a popular restaurant serving food all day and every day. In addition, there are luxury bedrooms, which are spacious, beautifully styled and come with a host of extras. Bathrooms are modern equipped with high quality towels and toiletries. The grounds are well kept, there is ample parking and also great access to major roads.

Rooms 10 (10 fmly)

ROSSINGTON	Map 16 SK69
South Yorkshire	

BEST WESTERN PREMIER Mount Pleasant Hotel

★★★★ 80% ⑨ HOTEL

tel: 01302 868696 & 868219 **Great North Rd DN11 0HW**
email: reception@mountpleasant.co.uk **web:** www.mountpleasant.co.uk
dir: On A638 (Great North Road) between Bawtry & Doncaster

This charming 18th-century house stands in 100 acres of wooded parkland between Doncaster and Bawtry, near Robin Hood Airport. Spacious public areas include well furnished lounges and the elegant Garden Restaurant. There are also a health and wellbeing centre, modern conference facilities and beautiful grounds, ideal for weddings. Bedrooms are individually designed; some have four-poster beds and the spa suites are even more impressive with luxurious bathrooms.

Rooms 56 (18 fmly) (27 GF) ⟨S £79-£129; **D** £99-£199 (incl. bkfst)* **Facilities** Spa STV WiFi ⟨ Beauty salon **Conf** Class 70 Board 70 Thtr 200 Del from £140* **Services** Lift **Parking** 140 **Notes** LB ⊗ Closed 25 Dec RS 24 Dec Civ Wed 180

R

The Chase Hotel

★★★ 82%  HOTEL

tel: 01989 763161 & 760644 **Gloucester Rd HR9 5LH**
email: res@chasehotel.co.uk **web:** www.chasehotel.co.uk
dir: M50 junct 4, 1st left exit towards rdbt, left at rdbt towards A40. Right at 2nd rdbt towards town centre, hotel 0.5m on left

This attractive Georgian mansion sits in its own landscaped grounds and is only a short walk from the town centre. Bedrooms, including two four-poster rooms, vary in size and character; all rooms are appointed to impressive standards. There is a light and spacious bar, and also Harry's restaurant which offers an excellent selection of enjoyable dishes.

Rooms 38 (2 fmly) ↖ **S** £65-£105; **D** £95-£210 (incl. bkfst) **Facilities** STV FTV WiFi ↘ New Year **Conf** Class 100 Board 80 Thtr 300 Del from £139* **Parking** 75 **Notes** LB ⊗ Closed 24-27 Dec Civ Wed 150

Glewstone Court Country House Hotel

★★★ 74%  COUNTRY HOUSE HOTEL

tel: 01989 770367 **Glewstone HR9 6AW**
email: info@glewstonecourt.com **web:** www.glewstonecourt.com
dir: From Ross-on-Wye market place follow A40/A49 Monmouth/Hereford signs, over Wilton Bridge to rdbt, left onto A40 towards Monmouth, in 1m right for hotel

This charming hotel enjoys an elevated position with views over Ross-on-Wye, and is set in well-tended gardens. Informal service is delivered with great enthusiasm by Bill Reeve-Tucker, whilst the kitchen is the domain of Christine Reeve-Tucker who offers an extensive menu of well executed dishes. Bedrooms come in a variety of sizes and are tastefully furnished and well equipped.

Rooms 8 (2 fmly) (1 GF) **S** £75-£110; **D** £135-£160 (incl. bkfst)* **Facilities** FTV WiFi ⛵ New Year **Conf** Class 18 Board 12 Thtr 24 Del from £136* **Parking** 25 **Notes** LB Closed 25-27 Dec Civ Wed 72

King's Head Hotel

★★★ 74% HOTEL

tel: 01989 763174 **8 High St HR9 5HL**
email: enquiries@kingshead.co.uk **web:** www.kingshead.co.uk
dir: In town centre, past market building on right

This establishment dates back to the 14th century and has a wealth of charm and character. Bedrooms are well equipped and comfortable with thoughtful guest extras provided; both four-poster and family rooms are available. The restaurant offers menus and a specials board that reflect a varied selection of local produce including fresh fish, free range beef and lamb. There is also a well-stocked bar serving hand-pulled, real ales.

Rooms 15 (1 fmly) ↖ **S** £56-£95; **D** £85-£110 (incl. bkfst)* **Facilities** FTV WiFi **Parking** 15

Pengethley Manor

★★★ 74% HOTEL

tel: 01989 730211 **Pengethley Park HR9 6LL**
email: reservations@pengethleymanor.co.uk **web:** www.pengethleymanor.co.uk
dir: 4m N on A49 (Hereford Rd), from Ross-on-Wye

Delightfully located with views in all directions over the countryside, this traditional manor-style hotel has plenty of character and comfort throughout. The bedrooms are divided between the main house and a more modern adjacent annexe. A good selection of dishes is offered both at lunch and dinner. A number of country walks start from the front door of the hotel.

Rooms 19 (8 annexe) (2 GF) ↖ **S** £50-£60; **D** £80-£120 (incl. bkfst)* **Facilities** FTV WiFi ↘ ⛵ supervised Xmas New Year **Conf** Class 20 Board 20 Thtr 20 **Parking** 30 **Notes** Civ Wed 80

The Royal Hotel

★★★ 71% HOTEL

tel: 01989 565105 **Palace Pound HR9 5HZ**
email: 6504@greeneking.co.uk **web:** www.oldenglish.co.uk
dir: At end of M50 take A40 signed Monmouth. At 3rd rdbt, left to Ross-on-Wye, over bridge, follow The Royal Hotel sign

Close to the town centre, this imposing hotel enjoys panoramic views from its prominent hilltop position. Reputedly visited by Charles Dickens in 1867, the establishment has been sympathetically furnished to combine the ambience of a bygone era with the comforts of today. In addition to the bar and dining areas, there are function rooms, an elegant restaurant and an attractive garden.

Rooms 42 (1 fmly) ↖ **Facilities** FTV WiFi ↘ Xmas New Year **Conf** Class 20 Board 28 Thtr 85 **Parking** 38 **Notes** Civ Wed 75

Premier Inn Ross-on-Wye

BUDGET HOTEL

tel: 0871 527 8424 **Ledbury Rd HR9 7QJ**
web: www.premierinn.com
dir: M50 junct 4, 1m from town centre

High quality, budget accommodation ideal for both families and business travellers. Spacious, en suite bedrooms feature tea and coffee making facilities, and Freeview TV in most hotels. Internet access and WiFi are available for a small fee. The adjacent family restaurant features a wide and varied menu. See also the Hotel Groups pages.

Rooms 43

Wilton Court Restaurant with Rooms

 RESTAURANT WITH ROOMS

tel: 01989 562569 📠 01989 768460 **Wilton Ln HR9 6AQ**
email: info@wiltoncourthotel.com **web:** www.wiltoncourthotel.com
dir: M50 junct 4, A40 towards Monmouth at 3rd rdbt left signed Ross-on-Wye, 1st right, on right

Dating back to the 16th century, Wilton Court has great charm and a wealth of character. Standing on the banks of the River Wye, just a short walk from the town centre, there is a genuinely relaxed, friendly and unhurried atmosphere created by hosts Roger and Helen Wynn and their reliable team. Bedrooms are tastefully furnished and well equipped, while public areas include a comfortable lounge, traditional bar and pleasant restaurant with a conservatory extension overlooking the garden. High standards of food, using fresh, locally sourced ingredients, are offered.

Rooms 10 (1 fmly)

R

ROSTHWAITE
Cumbria   Map 18 NY21

See also **Borrowdale**

Scafell Hotel

★★★ 79% HOTEL

tel: 017687 77208 **CA12 5XB**
email: info@scafell.co.uk **web:** www.scafell.co.uk
dir: M6 junct 40 to Keswick on A66. Take B5289 to Rosthwaite

Scafell Hotel is a friendly establishment, which enjoys a peaceful location, and is popular with walkers. Bedrooms have been tastefully appointed in a warm country house style with a contemporary twist; some have traditional antique furniture. Public areas include a residents' cocktail bar, lounge and spacious restaurant as well as the popular Riverside Inn, offering all-day menus in summer months.

Rooms 23 (2 fmly) (8 GF) ✆ **S** £50-£90; **D** £100-£180 (incl. bkfst)* **Facilities** FTV WiFi Guided walks Xmas New Year **Parking** 50 **Notes** LB Civ Wed 75

ROTHERHAM
South Yorkshire   Map 16 SK49

Hellaby Hall Hotel

★★★★ 76% 🌸 HOTEL

tel: 01709 702701 **Old Hellaby Ln, Hellaby S66 8SN**
email: reservations@hellabyhallhotel.co.uk **web:** www.primahotels.co.uk/hellaby
dir: 0.5m off M18 junct 1, onto A631 towards Maltby. Hotel in Hellaby - NB do not use postcode for Sat Nav

This 17th-century house was built to a Flemish design with high, beamed ceilings, staircases which lead off to private meeting rooms and a series of oak-panelled lounges. Bedrooms are elegant and well equipped, and guests can dine in the

formal Attic Restaurant. There are extensive leisure facilities and conference areas, and the hotel holds a licence for civil weddings.

Rooms 90 (6 fmly) (17 GF) **S** £65-£130; **D** £65-£130* **Facilities** Spa STV FTV WiFi ⌕ 🏊 Gym Beauty salon Exercise studio Spinning bike studio Xmas New Year **Conf** Class 300 Board 150 Thtr 500 Del from £125 to £150* **Services** Lift **Parking** 250 **Notes** LB Civ Wed 200

Carlton Park Hotel

★★★ 79% HOTEL

tel: 01709 849955 **102/104 Moorgate Rd S60 2BG**
email: reservations@carltonparkhotel.com **web:** www.carltonparkhotel.com
dir: M1 junct 33, onto A631, then A618. Hotel 800yds past District General Hospital

This modern hotel is situated in a pleasant residential area of the town, close to the hospital, yet within minutes of the M1. Bedrooms and bathrooms offer very modern facilities; three have separate sitting rooms. The restaurant and bar provide a lively atmosphere and there is a pool and leisure centre.

Rooms 80 (20 fmly) (16 GF) (6 smoking) **S** £49-£99; **D** £53-£99 (incl. bkfst)* **Facilities** STV FTV WiFi 🏊 Gym ♫ Xmas New Year **Conf** Class 120 Board 60 Thtr 300 Del from £125 to £145* **Services** Lift **Parking** 120 **Notes** ⊗ Civ Wed 150

Ibis Rotherham East

BUDGET HOTEL

tel: 01709 730333 **Moorhead Way, Bramley S66 1YY**
email: H3163@accor-hotels.com **web:** www.ibishotel.com
dir: M18 junct 1, left at rdbt, left at 1st lights. Hotel adjacent to supermarket

Modern, budget hotel offering comfortable accommodation in bright and practical bedrooms. Breakfast is self-service and dinner is available in the restaurant. See also the Hotel Groups pages.

Rooms 86 (22 fmly) (8 GF) ✆ **Conf** Class 20 Board 20 Thtr 30

Premier Inn Rotherham

BUDGET HOTEL

tel: 0871 527 8946 **Bawtry Rd S65 3JB**
web: www.premierinn.com
dir: On A631 towards Wickersley, between M18 junct 1 & M1 junct 33

High quality, budget accommodation ideal for both families and business travellers. Spacious, en suite bedrooms feature tea and coffee making facilities, and Freeview TV in most hotels. Internet access and WiFi are available for a small fee. The adjacent family restaurant features a wide and varied menu. See also the Hotel Groups pages.

Rooms 37

R

ROTHERWICK
Hampshire
Map 5 SU75

Tylney Hall Hotel

★★★★ @@ HOTEL

tel: 01256 764881 **RG27 9AZ**
email: sales@tylneyhall.com **web:** www.tylneyhall.com
dir: M3 junct 5, A287 to Basingstoke, over junct with A30, over rail bridge, towards Newnham. Right at Newnham Green. Hotel 1m on left

A grand Victorian country house set in 66 acres of beautiful parkland. The hotel offers high standards of comfort in relaxed yet elegant surroundings, featuring magnificently restored water gardens, originally laid out by the famous gardener, Gertrude Jekyll. Spacious public rooms include Italian and Wedgwood styled drawing rooms and the panelled Oak Room Restaurant that offers cuisine based on locally sourced ingredients. The spacious bedrooms are traditionally furnished and offer individual style and high degrees of comfort. The excellent leisure facilities include indoor and outdoor swimming pools, tennis courts, jogging trails, croquet lawns and a spa.

Rooms 112 (77 annexe) (1 fmly) (40 GF) 🐾 **D** £250-£530 (incl. bkfst)* **Facilities** Spa STV FTV WiFi 🕸 ⚲ ♨ 🏊 Gym Clay pigeon shooting Archery Falconry Balloon rides Laser shooting Jogging trail Xmas New Year **Conf** Class 70 Board 40 Thtr 120 **Parking** 120 **Notes** LB Civ Wed 120

ROTHLEY
Leicestershire
Map 11 SK51

Rothley Court

★★★ 73% HOTEL

tel: 0116 237 4141 **Westfield Ln LE7 7LG**
email: 6501@greeneking.co.uk **web:** www.oldenglish.co.uk
dir: On B5328

Mentioned in the Domesday Book, and complete with its own chapel, this historic property sits in seven acres of well-tended grounds. Public areas retain much of their original character and include an oak-panelled restaurant and a choice of function and meeting rooms. Bedrooms, some located in an adjacent stable block, are individually styled.

Rooms 30 (18 annexe) (3 fmly) (6 GF) 🐾 **Facilities** WiFi Xmas **Conf** Class 35 Board 35 Thtr 100 **Parking** 100 **Notes** ⊗ Civ Wed 85

ROWDE
Wiltshire
Map 4 ST96

The George & Dragon

@@ RESTAURANT WITH ROOMS

tel: 01380 723053 **High St SN10 2PN**
email: thegandd@tiscali.co.uk **web:** www.thegeorgeanddragonrowde.co.uk
dir: 1.5m from Devizes on A350 towards Chippenham

The George & Dragon dates back to the 14th century when it was a meeting house. Exposed beams, wooden floors, antique rugs and open fires create a warm atmosphere in the bar and restaurant. Bedrooms and bathrooms are very well decorated and equipped with some welcome extras. Dining in the bar or restaurant should not be missed, as local produce and fresh fish deliveries from Cornwall are offered on the daily-changing blackboard menu.

Rooms 3 (1 fmly)

ROWSLEY
Derbyshire

Map 16 SK26

The Peacock at Rowsley
★★★ ◉◉◉ HOTEL

tel: 01629 733518 **Bakewell Rd DE4 2EB**
email: reception@thepeacockatrowsley.com web: www.thepeacockatrowsley.com
dir: A6, 3m before Bakewell, 6m from Matlock towards Bakewell

Owned by Lord Manners of Haddon Hall, this hotel combines stylish
contemporary design by India Mahdavi with original period and antique
features. Bedrooms are individually designed and boast DVD players,
complimentary WiFi and smart marble bathrooms. Two rooms are particularly
special - one with a four-poster and one with an antique bed originating from
Belvoir Castle in Leicestershire. Imaginative cuisine, using local, seasonal
produce, is a highlight. Guests are warmly welcomed and service is attentive. Fly
fishing is popular in this area and the hotel has its own fishing rights on seven
miles of the Rivers Wye and Derwent.

Rooms 15 (6 fmly) ☎ **S** £90-£135; **D** £170-£300 (incl. bkfst)* **Facilities** WiFi ▷
Fishing ⟆ Free use of Woodlands Fitness Centre Free membership to Bakewell Golf
Club ♫ New Year **Conf** Class 8 Board 16 Del from £175 to £200* **Parking** 25
Notes No children 10yrs Civ Wed 20

See advert below

RUBERY
West Midlands

Map 10 SO97

Premier Inn Birmingham South (Rubery)

BUDGET HOTEL

tel: 0871 527 8094 **Birmingham Great Park, Ashbrook Dr, Parkway B45 9FP**
web: www.premierinn.com
dir: M5 junct 4, A38 towards Birmingham. Left at lights before Morrisons signed Great
Park. Right at rdbt. Right at next rdbt, hotel on right

High quality, budget accommodation ideal for both families and business
travellers. Spacious, en suite bedrooms feature tea and coffee making facilities,
and Freeview TV in most hotels. Internet access and WiFi are available for a small
fee. The adjacent family restaurant features a wide and varied menu. See also the
Hotel Groups pages.

Rooms 62

R

RUGBY
Warwickshire
Map 11 SP57

Brownsover Hall Hotel
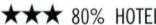

★★★ 80% HOTEL

tel: 01788 546100 & 555362 **Brownsover Ln, Old Brownsover CV21 1HU**
email: reservations@brownsoverhall.co.uk **web:** www.brownsoverhall.co.uk
dir: M6 junct 1, A426 to Rugby. After 0.5m at rdbt follow Brownsover signs, right into Brownsover Rd, right again into Brownsover Ln. Hotel 250yds on left

Brownsover Hall is a Grade II listed, Victorian Gothic building designed by Sir Gilbert Scott, set in seven acres of wooded parkland. Bedrooms vary in size and style, including spacious and contemporary rooms in the converted stable block. The former chapel makes a stylish restaurant, and for a less formal meal or a relaxing drink, the Whittle Bar is popular.

Rooms 47 (20 annexe) (3 fmly) (11 GF) **Facilities** STV FTV WiFi ♫ Xmas New Year **Conf** Class 36 Board 40 Thtr 70 **Parking** 100 **Notes** ⊗ Civ Wed 56

Premier Inn Rugby North M6 Jct 1

BUDGET HOTEL

tel: 0871 527 8948 **Central Park Dr, Central Park CV23 0WE**
web: www.premierinn.com
dir: M6 junct 1, S'bound onto A426. Hotel approx 1m on left at rdbt

High quality, budget accommodation ideal for both families and business travellers. Spacious, en suite bedrooms feature tea and coffee making facilities, and Freeview TV in most hotels. Internet access and WiFi are available for a small fee. The adjacent family restaurant features a wide and varied menu. See also the Hotel Groups pages.

Rooms 58

Premier Inn Rugby North (Newbold)

BUDGET HOTEL

tel: 0871 527 8950 **Brownsover Rd CV21 1HL**
web: www.premierinn.com
dir: M6 junct 1, A426 follow Rugby signs. Straight on at 2 rdbts. At 3rd rdbt, hotel on right. (NB for Sat Nav use CV21 1NX)

Rooms 49

RUGELEY
Staffordshire
Map 10 SK01

Premier Inn Rugeley

BUDGET HOTEL

tel: 0871 527 9272 **Tower Business Park WS15 2HJ**
web: www.premierinn.com
dir: M6 junct 14, A5013 towards Stafford. At rdbt 2nd exit onto A34. Take A513 signed Rugeley. At rdbt take 2nd exit onto A51. Left into Wolsley Rd, left into Powerstation Rd. Hotel off rdbt. (NB for Sat Nav use WS15 1PR)

High quality, budget accommodation ideal for both families and business travellers. Spacious, en suite bedrooms feature tea and coffee making facilities, and Freeview TV in most hotels. Internet access and WiFi are available for a small fee. The adjacent family restaurant features a wide and varied menu. See also the Hotel Groups pages.

Rooms 50

RUISLIP
Greater London

The Barn Hotel

★★★ 79% ⊛⊛ HOTEL PLAN 1 A5

tel: 01895 636057 **West End Rd HA4 6JB**
email: info@thebarnhotel.co.uk **web:** www.thebarnhotel.co.uk
dir: A40 onto A4180 (Polish War Memorial) exit to Ruislip. 2m to hotel entrance at mini-rdbt before Ruislip tube station

A mix of old and new, with parts dating back to the 17th century, this impressive property sits in three acres of gardens. Bedrooms vary in style, from contemporary to traditional with oak beams; all are comfortable and well appointed. The public areas provide a high level of quality and luxury.

Rooms 73 (3 fmly) (33 GF) (20 smoking) **Facilities** FTV WiFi ♫ Xmas New Year **Conf** Class 50 Board 30 Thtr 80 **Parking** 42 **Notes** ⊗ Civ Wed 74

Premier Inn Ruislip

BUDGET HOTEL PLAN 1 A5

tel: 0871 527 8952 **Ickenham Rd HA4 7DR**
web: www.premierinn.com
dir: From Ruislip High St into Ickenham Rd (B466). At mini rdbt 1st exit (The Orchard on left)

High quality, budget accommodation ideal for both families and business travellers. Spacious, en suite bedrooms feature tea and coffee making facilities, and Freeview TV in most hotels. Internet access and WiFi are available for a small fee. The adjacent family restaurant features a wide and varied menu. See also the Hotel Groups pages.

Rooms 20

RUNCORN
Cheshire
Map 15 SJ58

Holiday Inn Runcorn

★★★ 74% HOTEL

tel: 0871 942 9070 **Wood Ln, Beechwood WA7 3HA**
email: jonathan.huglin@ihg.com **web:** www.holidayinn.co.uk
dir: M56 junct 12, left at rdbt, 100yds on left into Halton Station Rd under rail bridge, into Wood Ln

This modern hotel offers extensive conference, meeting and leisure facilities. The bedrooms are well equipped and the spacious restaurant is open for lunch and dinner with an all-day menu provided in the lounge and bar. There is also a well equipped leisure centre and extensive conference facilities available.

Rooms 153 (149 fmly) (31 GF) **Facilities** STV WiFi HL ⊛ supervised Gym Xmas New Year **Conf** Class 250 Board 60 Thtr 500 **Services** Lift Air con **Parking** 250 **Notes** Civ Wed 500

Campanile Runcorn

BUDGET HOTEL

tel: 01928 581771 **Lowlands Rd WA7 5TP**
email: runcorn@campanile.com **web:** www.campanile.com
dir: M56 junct 12, A557, follow signs for Runcorn rail station/Runcorn College

This modern building offers accommodation in smart, well-equipped bedrooms, all with en suite bathrooms. Refreshments may be taken at the informal bistro. See also the Hotel Groups pages.

Rooms 53 (18 GF) **Conf** Class 24 Board 24 Thtr 35 Del £86*

R

Premier Inn Runcorn

BUDGET HOTEL

tel: 0871 527 8954 **Chester Rd, Preston Brook WA7 3BB**
web: www.premierinn.com
dir: 1m from M56 junct 11, at Preston Brook

High quality, budget accommodation ideal for both families and business travellers. Spacious, en suite bedrooms feature tea and coffee making facilities, and Freeview TV in most hotels. Internet access and WiFi are available for a small fee. The adjacent family restaurant features a wide and varied menu. See also the Hotel Groups pages.

Rooms 43

RUSPER
West Sussex   Map 6 TQ23

Ghyll Manor

★★★ 83%  COUNTRY HOUSE HOTEL

tel: 0845 345 3426 & 01293 871571 **High St RH12 4PX**
email: enquiries@ghyllmanor.co.uk **web:** www.ghyllmanor.co.uk
dir: A24 onto A264. Exit at Faygate, follow signs for Rusper, 2m to village

Located in the quiet village of Rusper, this traditional mansion house is set in 45 acres of idyllic, peaceful grounds. Accommodation is in either the main house or a range of courtyard-style cottages. A pre-dinner drink can be taken beside the fire, followed by an imaginative meal in the charming restaurant.

Rooms 29 (20 annexe) (7 fmly) (21 GF) ₹ **S** £135-£165; **D** £160-£190 (incl. bkfst & dinner)* **Facilities** STV FTV WiFi ↺ ⅙ Gym Xmas New Year **Conf** Class 60 Board 40 Thtr 120 Del from £145* **Parking** 50 **Notes** LB Civ Wed 120

RYDE
Isle of Wight   Map 5 SZ59

Lakeside Park Hotel

★★★★ 75% HOTEL

tel: 01983 882266 **High St PO33 4LJ**
email: reception@lakesideparkhotel.com **web:** www.lakesideparkhotel.com
dir: A3054 towards Newport. Hotel on left after crossing Wotton Bridge

This hotel has picturesque views of the tidal lake and surrounding countryside. Bedrooms are well appointed with modern amenities and stylish design. Public areas feature a comfortable open-plan bar and lounge, and two restaurants that showcase the best of island produce. Sizable conference and banqueting facilities are available while the leisure area includes an indoor pool and spa therapy.

Rooms 44 (2 fmly) (16 GF) ₹ **Facilities** Spa FTV WiFi ☜ Sauna Steam room Relaxation room **Conf** Class 60 Board 40 Thtr 150 **Services** Lift Air con **Parking** 140 **Notes** ⊗ Civ Wed 120

Yelf's Hotel

★★★ 74% HOTEL

tel: 01983 564062 **Union St PO33 2LG**
email: manager@yelfshotel.com **web:** www.yelfshotel.com
dir: From Esplanade into Union St. Hotel on right

This former coaching inn has smart public areas including a busy bar, a separate lounge and an attractive dining room. Bedrooms are comfortably furnished and well equipped; some are located in an adjoining wing and some in an annexe. A conservatory lounge bar and stylish terrace are ideal for relaxing.

Rooms 40 (9 annexe) (5 fmly) (3 GF) (3 smoking) ₹ **Facilities** STV FTV WiFi Spa & treatments at sister hotel nearby **Conf** Class 30 Board 50 Thtr 100 **Services** Lift **Parking** 23 **Notes** ⊗ Civ Wed 100

Appley Manor Hotel

★★ 74% HOTEL

tel: 01983 564777 **Appley Rd PO33 1PH**
email: appleymanor@live.co.uk **web:** www.appley-manor.co.uk
dir: A3055 onto B3330. Hotel 0.25m on left

A Victorian manor house located only five minutes from the town and set in peaceful surroundings. The spacious bedrooms are well furnished and decorated. Dinner can be taken in the popular adjoining Manor Inn.

Rooms 12 (2 fmly) **S** £58-£60; **D** £68-£70 **Facilities** FTV WiFi **Conf** Class 40 Board 30 Thtr 40 **Parking** 60 **Notes** ⊗

RYE
East Sussex   Map 7 TQ92

The George in Rye

★★★★ 78%  HOTEL

tel: 01797 222114 **98 High St TN31 7JT**
email: stay@thegeorgeinrye.com **web:** www.thegeorgeinrye.com
dir: M20 junct 10, A2070 to Brenzett, A259 to Rye

This attractive 16th-century property, situated in the heart of historic Rye, has been sympathetically styled to retain many original features including a stunning Georgian ballroom complete with a minstrels' gallery. The bedrooms are stylishly appointed and filled with an abundance of thoughtful touches. Contemporary public areas include a bar, lounge and dining room plus an excellent alfresco area for summer dining.

Rooms 34 (3 GF) ₹ **D** £135-£145 (incl. bkfst)* **Facilities** FTV WiFi Xmas New Year **Conf** Class 65 Board 40 Thtr 100 **Notes** LB ⊗ Civ Wed 100

R

RYE *continued*

Mermaid Inn

★★★ 82% ◉◉ HOTEL

tel: 01797 223065 & 223788 **Mermaid St TN31 7EY**
email: info@mermaidinn.com web: www.mermaidinn.com
dir: A259, follow signs to town centre, then into Mermaid St

Situated near the top of a cobbled side street, this famous smugglers' inn is steeped in history, dating back to 1450 with 12th-century cellars. The charming interior has many architectural features such as attractive stone work. The bedrooms vary in size and style but all are tastefully furnished; there are no less than eight four-posters, and the Elizabethan and Dr Syn's Bedchambers are particularly noteworthy. Delightful public rooms include a choice of lounges, cosy bar and smart restaurant.

Rooms 31 (5 fmly) ⌂ **S** £90; **D** £150–£220 (incl. bkfst) **Facilities** FTV WiFi ☆ Xmas New Year **Conf** Class 40 Board 30 Thtr 50 Del £160 **Parking** 25 **Notes** LB ⊗

The Hope Anchor Hotel

★★★ 79% SMALL HOTEL

tel: 01797 222216 **Watchbell St TN31 7HA**
email: info@thehopeanchor.co.uk web: www.thehopeanchor.co.uk
dir: From A268, Quayside, right into Wish Ward, into Mermaid St, right into West St, right into Watchbell St, hotel at end

This historic inn sits high above the town with enviable views out over the harbour and Romney Marsh, and is accessible via delightful cobbled streets. There is a relaxed and friendly atmosphere within the cosy public rooms, while the attractively furnished bedrooms are well equipped and many enjoy good views over the marshes.

Rooms 16 (3 fmly) (1 GF) ⌂ **S** £75–£140; **D** £120–£170 (incl. bkfst)* **Facilities** FTV WiFi Xmas New Year **Conf** Class 30 Board 20 Thtr 40 Del from £160 to £220 **Parking** 12 **Notes** LB

Rye Lodge Hotel

★★★ 79% METRO HOTEL

tel: 01797 223838 & 226688 **Hilders Cliff TN31 7LD**
email: info@ryelodge.co.uk web: www.ryelodge.co.uk
dir: On one-way system follow town centre signs, through Landgate arch, hotel 100yds on right

Standing in an elevated position, Rye Lodge has panoramic views across Romney Marshes and the Rother Estuary. Traditionally styled bedrooms come in a variety of sizes; they are attractively decorated and thoughtfully equipped. Public rooms

feature indoor leisure facilities and the Terrace Room Restaurant where home-made dishes are offered. Lunch and afternoon tea are served on the flower-filled outdoor terrace in warmer months.

Rooms 19 (5 GF) ⌂ **Facilities** STV FTV WiFi ☆ HL ⊕ Aromatherapy Steam cabinet Sauna Exercise machines **Parking** 20

White Vine House

RESTAURANT WITH ROOMS

tel: 01797 224748 **24 High St TN31 7JF**
email: info@whitevinehouse.co.uk web: www.whitevinehouse.co.uk
dir: In town centre

Situated in the heart of the ancient Cinque Port town of Rye, this property's origins go back to the 13th century. The cellar is the oldest part, but the current building dates from 1560 and boasts an impressive Georgian frontage. The original timber framework is visible in many areas and certainly adds to the house's sense of history. The bedrooms have period furniture along with luxury bath or shower rooms; one bedroom has an antique four-poster.

Rooms 7 (1 fmly)

ST AGNES	Map 2 SW75
Cornwall	

Rose-in-Vale Country House Hotel

★★★★ 72% ◉ COUNTRY HOUSE HOTEL

tel: 01872 552202 **Mithian TR5 0QD**
email: reception@roseinvalehotel.co.uk web: www.roseinvalehotel.co.uk
dir: A30 S towards Redruth. At Chiverton Cross at rdbt take B3277 signed St Agnes. In 500mtrs follow tourist sign for Rose-in-Vale. Into Mithian, right at Miners Arms, down hill. Hotel on left

Peacefully located in a wooded valley, this Georgian manor house has a wonderfully relaxed atmosphere and abundant charm. Guests are assured of a warm welcome. Accommodation varies in size and style; several rooms are situated on the ground floor. An imaginative fixed-price menu featuring local produce is served in the spacious restaurant.

Rooms 23 (3 annexe) (1 fmly) (6 GF) ⌂ **S** £75–£180; **D** £90–£300 (incl. bkfst)* **Facilities** FTV WiFi ☆ ⌂ ☾ ♫ Xmas New Year **Conf** Class 50 Board 40 Thtr 75 Del from £100 to £250 **Services** Lift **Parking** 50 **Notes** LB No children 12yrs Closed 4 Jan–1 Feb Civ Wed 80

Beacon Country House Hotel

★★★ 75% SMALL HOTEL

tel: 01872 552318 **Goonvrea Rd TR5 0NW**
email: info@beaconhotel.co.uk web: www.beaconhotel.co.uk
dir: A30 onto B3277 to St Agnes. At rdbt left into Goonvrea Rd. Hotel 0.75m on right

Set in a quiet and attractive area away from the busy village, this family-run, relaxed hotel has splendid views over the countryside and along the coast to St Ives. Hospitality and customer care are great strengths, with guests assured of a very warm and friendly stay. Bedrooms are comfortable and well equipped, and many benefit from glorious views.

Rooms 11 (2 fmly) (2 GF) ⌂ **S** £70–£100; **D** £85–£140 (incl. bkfst)* **Facilities** FTV WiFi ☆ Xmas New Year **Conf** Class 20 Board 20 **Parking** 12 **Notes** LB No children 8yrs Closed 4–31 Jan

Rosemundy House Hotel

★★★ 71% HOTEL

tel: 01872 552101 **Rosemundy Hill TR5 0UF**
email: info@rosemundy.co.uk **web:** www.rosemundy.co.uk
dir: A30 to St Agnes, approx 3m. On entering village 1st right signed Rosemundy, hotel at foot of hill

This elegant Georgian house has been carefully restored and extended to provide comfortable bedrooms and spacious, inviting public areas. The hotel is set in well-maintained gardens complete with an outdoor pool which is available in warmer months. There is a choice of relaxing lounges and a cosy bar.

Rooms 46 (3 fmly) (9 GF) ↟ **Facilities** FTV WiFi ↻ Putt green 🦢 🎵 Xmas New Year **Conf** Board 80 **Parking** 50 **Notes** ⊗ No children 5yrs Closed 12-23 Dec & 2 Jan-12 Feb

---

ST ALBANS
Hertfordshire
Map 6 TL10

Sopwell House

★★★★ 79% 🏵 HOTEL

tel: 01727 864477 **Cottonmill Ln, Sopwell AL1 2HQ**
email: enquiries@sopwellhouse.co.uk **web:** www.sopwellhouse.co.uk
dir: M25 junct 21a, 1st exit rdbt to A405. A414 towards St Albans/Hatfield. Slip road Shenley, mini rdbt left

This fine country house hotel is situated in 12 acres of beautifully landscaped gardens and the house overlooks the hotel's golf course. Sopwell House Hotel was once the country home of Lord Mountbatten and has undergone major renovations in the last few years. The bedrooms are all very well appointed and leisure facilities are impressive. Afternoon teas are served in the comfortable lounges and there is a choice of restaurants for dinner.

Rooms 128 (16 annexe) (28 fmly) (7 GF) ↟ **S** £109-£159; **D** £134-£184 (incl. bkfst)* **Facilities** Spa STV FTV WiFi ↻ 🏊 Gym Sauna Steam room Dance studio Xmas New Year **Conf** Class 180 Board 110 Thtr 450 Del from £205 to £290* **Services** Lift Air con **Parking** 250 **Notes** LB ⊗ Civ Wed 380

Quality Hotel St Albans

★★★ 73% HOTEL

tel: 01727 857858 **232-236 London Rd AL1 1JQ**
email: st.albans@quality-hotels.net **web:** www.stalbans-hotels.co.uk
dir: M25 junct 22 follow A1081 to St Albans, after 2.5m hotel on left, before overhead bridge

This smartly presented property is conveniently situated close to the major road networks and the railway station. The contemporary style bedrooms have co-ordinated fabrics and a good range of useful facilities. Public rooms include an open-plan lounge bar and brasserie restaurant. The hotel has a leisure complex along with air-conditioned meeting rooms.

Rooms 81 (7 fmly) (14 GF) ↟ **S** £49-£90; **D** £69-£120 (incl. bkfst)* **Facilities** FTV WiFi ↻ 🏊 supervised Gym Saunarium Sunbed Beauty treatments **Conf** Class 40 Board 50 Thtr 200 Del from £95 to £150* **Services** Lift **Parking** 80 **Notes** ⊗

Ardmore House Hotel

★★★ 🅰 HOTEL

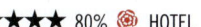
THE INDEPENDENTS
HOTEL ASSOCIATION

tel: 01727 859313 **54 Lemsford Rd AL1 3PR**
email: info@ardmorehousehotel.co.uk **web:** www.ardmorehousehotel.co.uk
dir: A1081 signed St Albans, through 3 sets of lights & 2 mini rdbts. Right at 3rd mini rdbt, through 2 sets of lights. Hotel on right in 800yds

Located in immaculate surroundings close to the town centre and cathedral, this extended Edwardian house and annexe provides a range of facilities much appreciated by a loyal commercial clientele. The practically furnished bedrooms offer a good range of facilities and the extensive public areas include a spacious conservatory dining room.

Rooms 40 (4 annexe) (5 fmly) (5 GF) ↟ **S** £67.50-£71.50; **D** £79.50-£145 (incl. bkfst) **Facilities** STV FTV WiFi ↻ **Conf** Class 50 Board 50 Thtr 130 Del from £140 to £150 **Parking** 40 **Notes** LB ⊗ Civ Wed 150

Premier Inn Luton South M1 Jct 9

Premier Inn

BUDGET HOTEL

tel: 0871 527 8334 **London Rd, Flamstead AL3 8HT**
web: www.premierinn.com
dir: M1 junct 9, A5 towards Dunstable

High quality, budget accommodation ideal for both families and business travellers. Spacious, en suite bedrooms feature tea and coffee making facilities, and Freeview TV in most hotels. Internet access and WiFi are available for a small fee. The adjacent family restaurant features a wide and varied menu. See also the Hotel Groups pages.

Rooms 75

ST ANNES

See Lytham St Annes

ST AUSTELL
Cornwall
Map 2 SX05

Carlyon Bay Hotel

★★★★ 80% 🏵 HOTEL

Brend Hotels

tel: 01726 812304 **Sea Rd, Carlyon Bay PL25 3RD**
email: reservations@carlyonbay.com **web:** www.carlyonbay.com
dir: From St Austell, follow signs for Charlestown. Carlyon Bay signed on left, hotel at end of Sea Rd

Built in the 1920s, this long-established hotel sits on the cliff top in 250 acres of grounds which include indoor and outdoor pools, a golf course and a spa. Bedrooms

S

continued

ST AUSTELL *continued*

are well maintained, and many have marvellous views across St Austell Bay. A good choice of comfortable lounges is available, while facilities for families include kids' clubs and entertainment.

Rooms 86 (14 fmly) ↟ S £75–£150; D £130–£410* **Facilities** Spa FTV WiFi ↘ ⊛ ⤳ ⚓ 18 ☺ Putt green Gym Hydrotherapy spa pool Hot stone beds ♫ Xmas New Year Child facilities **Conf** Thtr 150 **Services** Lift **Parking** 100 **Notes** LB ⊗ Civ Wed 100

See advert on page 383

The Cornwall Hotel, Spa & Estate

★★★★ 76% ⚘ COUNTRY HOUSE HOTEL

tel: 01726 874050 & 874051 **Pentewan Rd, Tregorrick PL26 7AB**
email: enquiries@thecornwall.com **web:** www.thecornwall.com
dir: A391 to St Austell then B3273 towards Mevagissey. Hotel approx 0.5m on right

Set in 43 acres of wooded parkland, this renovated manor house offers guests a real retreat. The restored White House has suites and traditionally styled bedrooms, and adjoining are the contemporary Woodland rooms ranging across standard, family, accessible, and also deluxe which have private balcony areas overlooking the Pentewan Valley. There are superb leisure facilities including the spa with luxury treatments, an infinity pool and state-of-the-art fitness centre. There is a choice of eating options - The Arboretum, the more informal Acorns, and the Drawing Room and Parkland Terrace for afternoon tea and cocktails respectively. This is an ideal base for visiting The Eden Project, The Lost Gardens of Heligan and south Cornwall fishing villages.

Rooms 65 (4 fmly) **S** £69–£285; **D** £79–£295 (incl. bkfst)* **Facilities** Spa STV FTV WiFi ↘ HL ⊛ ⤳ ⚓ Gym Xmas New Year **Conf** Class 30 Board 14 Thtr 50 Del from £97 to £260* **Services** Lift **Parking** 200 **Notes** LB Civ Wed 60

Boscundle Manor

★★★ 82% ⚘⚘ HOTEL

tel: 01726 813557 ▤ 01726 814997 **Boscundle PL25 3RL**
email: reservations@boscundlemanor.co.uk **web:** www.boscundlemanor.co.uk
dir: M5 to Exeter then A30 until Bodmin. A391 to St Austell. Turn Left onto A390 then left towards Tregrehan. Hotel drive is 300mtrs on left.

A charming and delightful family-run Manor House full of charm, located on the edge of Boscundle, set within five acres of its own private, well maintained and beautiful grounds and gardens. Friendly and attentive staff are eager to ensure guests have a relaxing and enjoyable stay. Accommodation is warm, comfortable and inviting, with a stylish and contemporary feel, yet still cosy. Food is of a high quality, with a good selection of wines and beers to match. Additional seating is offered in the relaxing lounge with open fireplaces; or maybe take a dip in the well-equipped indoor swimming pool, which is part of the excellent leisure facilities.

Rooms 14 (4 annexe) (4 fmly) **Facilities** WiFi ↘ ⊛ ⤳ Beauty treatments Xmas New Year **Notes** Civ Wed 150

Porth Avallen Hotel

★★★ 78% HOTEL

tel: 01726 812802 **Sea Rd, Carlyon Bay PL25 3SG**
email: info@porthavallen.co.uk **web:** www.porthavallen.co.uk
dir: A30 onto A391 to St Austell. Right onto A390. Left at lights, follow brown signs, left at rdbt, right into Sea Rd

This traditional hotel boasts panoramic views over the rugged Cornish coastline. It offers smartly appointed public areas and well-presented bedrooms, many with sea views. There is an oak-panelled lounge and conservatory; both are ideal for relaxation. Extensive dining options, including the stylish Reflections Restaurant, invite guests to choose from fixed-price, carte and all-day brasserie menus. The Olive Garden, inspired by the Mediterranean, is a lovely place to eat alfresco.

Rooms 28 (3 fmly) (3 GF) ↟ **Facilities** FTV WiFi Xmas New Year **Conf** Class 100 Board 80 Thtr 160 Del from £140 to £157* **Parking** 60 **Notes** ⊗ Civ Wed 160

BEST WESTERN Cliff Head Hotel

★★★ 75% HOTEL

tel: 01726 812345 **Sea Rd, Carlyon Bay PL25 3RB**
email: info@cliffheadhotel.com **web:** www.cliffheadhotel.com
dir: 2m E off A390

Set in extensive grounds and conveniently located for visiting the Eden Project, this hotel faces south and enjoys views over Carlyon Bay. A choice of lounges is provided, together with a seasonal swimming pool and sauna. Bay Restaurant offers a range of menus, which feature an interesting selection of dishes.

Rooms 57 (4 fmly) (11 GF) ♠ **Facilities** FTV WiFi ↘ Xmas **Conf** Class 90 Board 50 Thtr 150 **Parking** 60 **Notes** Civ Wed 70

The Pier House

★★★ 75% HOTEL

tel: 01726 67955 **Harbour Front, Charlestown PL25 3NJ**
email: pierhouse@btconnect.com **web:** www.pierhousehotel.com
dir: A390 to St Austell, at Mt Charles rdbt left into Charlestown Rd

This genuinely friendly hotel boasts a wonderful harbour location. The unspoilt working port has been the setting for many film and television productions. Most bedrooms have sea views, and the hotel's convivial Harbourside Inn is popular with locals and tourists alike. Locally caught fish features on the varied and interesting restaurant menu.

Rooms 28 (2 annexe) (3 fmly) (2 GF) ♠ **S** £60-£70; **D** £112-£146 (incl. bkfst)*
Facilities STV WiFi **Parking** 50 **Notes** ⊗ Closed 24-25 Dec

Premier Inn St Austell

BUDGET HOTEL

tel: 0871 527 9018 **St Austell Enterprise Park, Treverbyn Rd PL25 4EL**
web: www.premierinn.com
dir: A30 onto A391 signed St Austell. Through Bugle. Continue on A391 at rdbt. Continue to follow St Austell signs. 1st exit at Carclaze rdbt. Hotel at St Austell Enterprise Park

High quality, budget accommodation ideal for both families and business travellers. Spacious, en suite bedrooms feature tea and coffee making facilities, and Freeview TV in most hotels. Internet access and WiFi are available for a small fee. The adjacent family restaurant features a wide and varied menu. See also the Hotel Groups pages.

Rooms 61

ST HELENS
Merseyside

Map 15 SJ59

Premier Inn St Helens (A580/East Lancs)

BUDGET HOTEL

tel: 0871 527 9020 **Garswood Old Rd, East Lancs Rd WA11 7LX**
web: www.premierinn.com
dir: 3m from M6 junct 23, on A580 towards Liverpool

High quality, budget accommodation ideal for both families and business travellers. Spacious, en suite bedrooms feature tea and coffee making facilities, and Freeview TV in most hotels. Internet access and WiFi are available for a small fee. The adjacent family restaurant features a wide and varied menu. See also the Hotel Groups pages.

Rooms 44

Premier Inn St Helens South

BUDGET HOTEL

tel: 0871 527 9022 **Eurolink, Lea Green WA9 4TT**
web: www.premierinn.com
dir: M62 junct 7, A570 towards St Helens

Rooms 40

ST IVES
Cambridgeshire

Map 12 TL37

The Dolphin Hotel

★★★ 70% HOTEL

tel: 01480 466966 **London Rd PE27 5EP**
email: enquiries@dolphinhotelcambs.co.uk **web:** www.dolphinhotelcambs.co.uk
dir: A14 between Huntingdon & Cambridge onto A1096 towards St Ives. Left at 1st rdbt & immediately right. Hotel on left after 0.5m

This modern hotel sits by delightful water meadows on the banks of the River Ouse. Open-plan public rooms include a choice of bars and a pleasant restaurant offering fine river views. The bedrooms are modern and varied in style; some are in the hotel while others occupy an adjacent wing; all are comfortable and spacious. Conference and function suites are available.

Rooms 67 (37 annexe) (4 fmly) (22 GF) (2 smoking) ♠ **Facilities** FTV WiFi ↘ Fishing Gym **Conf** Class 50 Board 50 Thtr 150 **Parking** 400 **Notes** ⊗ RS 24 Dec-2 Jan Civ Wed 60

ST IVES
Cornwall

Map 2 SW54

Garrack Hotel & Restaurant

★★★ 79% ⚹ HOTEL

tel: 01736 796199 **Burthallan Ln, Higher Ayr TR26 3AA**
email: reception@garrack.com **web:** www.garrack.com
dir: Exit A30 for St Ives. From B3311 follow brown signs for Tate Gallery, then Garrack signs

Enjoying a peaceful, elevated position with splendid views across the harbour and Porthmeor Beach, the Garrack sits in its own delightful grounds and gardens. Bedrooms are comfortable and many have sea views. Public areas include a small leisure suite, a choice of lounges and an attractive restaurant, where locally sourced ingredients are used in the enjoyable dishes.

Rooms 18 (2 annexe) (2 fmly) (3 GF) **Facilities** FTV WiFi ❄ Gym Sauna Solarium New Year **Conf** Class 10 Board 10 Thtr 20 **Parking** 30

S

ST IVES continued

St Ives Harbour Hotel

★★★ 78% HOTEL

tel: 01736 795221 **The Terrace TR26 2BN**
email: stives@harbourhotels.co.uk **web:** www.stives-harbour-hotel.co.uk
dir: On A3074

This friendly hotel enjoys an enviable location with spectacular views of St Ives Bay. Extensive leisure facilities, a versatile function suite and a number of elegant and stylish lounges are available. The majority of bedrooms are appointed to a very high standard, and many rooms have spectacular sea views, as does the restaurant which looks out over the bay and golden sands below.

Rooms 46 (9 fmly) ⁂ **Facilities** Spa FTV WiFi ☺ Gym Steam room Sauna Xmas New Year **Conf** Class 20 Board 35 Thtr 130 **Services** Lift **Parking** 60 **Notes** Civ Wed 160

Primrose Valley

★★★ 75% METRO HOTEL

tel: 01736 794939 **Porthminster Beach TR26 2ED**
email: info@primroseonline.co.uk **web:** www.primroseonline.co.uk
dir: A3074 to St Ives, 25yds after town sign right into Primrose Valley, left under bridge, along beach front, left back under bridge, property on left

St Ives is just a short walk from this stylish, friendly, family-run establishment close to Porthminster Beach. The property is light and airy, and modernisation has resulted in good levels of comfort; some bedrooms have balconies with stunning views. There is a lounge and bar area, and breakfast features local produce and home-made items.

Rooms 10 ⁂ **S** £65-£160; **D** £75-£170 (incl. bkfst)* **Facilities** FTV WiFi ☺ **Parking** 11 **Notes** LB ⊗ No children 8yrs Closed 22-26 Dec

Tregenna Castle Hotel

★★★ 75% HOTEL

tel: 01736 795254 **TR26 2DE**
email: hotel@tregenna-castle.co.uk **web:** www.tregenna-castle.co.uk
dir: A30 from Exeter to Penzance, at Lelant take A3074 to St Ives, through Carbis Bay, main entrance signed on left

Sitting at the top of town in beautiful landscaped sub-tropical gardens with woodland walks, this popular hotel boasts spectacular views of St Ives. Many leisure facilities are available, including indoor and outdoor pools, a gym and a sauna. Families are particularly welcome. The individually designed bedrooms are generally spacious. There are two restaurants, the Trelawny Room and the Godrevy Room, while a brasserie provides lighter options in a less formal atmosphere.

Rooms 81 (37 fmly) (16 GF) ⁂ **Facilities** Spa STV FTV WiFi HL ☺ ↘ supervised ⚑ 18 ☺ Putt green ⚐ Gym Squash Steam room Badminton court ♫ Xmas New Year **Conf** Class 150 Board 30 Thtr 250 **Services** Lift **Parking** 200 **Notes** ⊗ Civ Wed 160

Chy-an-Albany Hotel

★★★ 74% HOTEL

tel: 01736 796759 **Albany Ter TR26 2BS**
email: info@chyanalbanyhotel.com **web:** www.chyanalbanyhotel.com
dir: A30 onto A3074 signed St Ives, hotel on left just before junct

Conveniently located, this pleasant hotel enjoys splendid sea views. The comfortable bedrooms come in a variety of sizes; some featuring balconies for enjoying those sea views. The friendly staff and the relaxing environment mean that some guests return on a regular basis. Freshly prepared and appetising cuisine is served in the dining room and a bar menu is also available.

Rooms 39 (9 fmly) ⁂ **Facilities** FTV WiFi **Conf** Class 30 Board 30 Thtr 50 **Services** Lift **Parking** 33 **Notes** ⊗ Civ Wed 70

Carbis Bay Hotel

★★★ 73% ☻ HOTEL

tel: 01736 795311 **Carbis Bay TR26 2NP**
email: info@carbisbayhotel.co.uk **web:** www.carbisbayhotel.co.uk
dir: A3074, through Lelant. 1m, at Carbis Bay 30yds before lights, right into Porthrepta Rd to hotel

In a peaceful location with access to its own white-sand beach, this hotel offers comfortable accommodation. The attractive public areas feature a smart bar and lounge, and a sun lounge overlooking the sea. Bedrooms, many with fine views, are well equipped. Interesting cuisine and particularly enjoyable breakfasts are offered. A small complex of luxury, self-catering apartments is available.

Rooms 47 (16 fmly) (3 GF) ⁂ **Facilities** Spa WiFi ↘ Fishing Private beach ♫ Xmas New Year **Conf** Class 80 Board 60 Thtr 120 **Parking** 200 **Notes** ⊗ Civ Wed 150

The Queens

★★ 85% ☻ HOTEL

tel: 01736 796468 📄 01736 799953 **High St TR26 1RR**
email: info@queenshotelstives.com **web:** www.queenshotelstives.com
dir: A3074 to town centre

Handily located in the centre of town, just a short stroll from the harbor, this is an ideal location for exploring the charms of St Ives. The bedrooms offer style and comfort with local Cornish artwork and lovely comfy beds. Bathrooms are also light, bright and modern. The relaxing bar and lounge is the venue for enjoyable award-winning cuisine with excellent local produce utilized in simple yet delicious dishes.

Rooms 10 (2 fmly) **S** £49-£109; **D** £59-£119* **Facilities** FTV WiFi

Cottage Hotel

★★ 74% HOTEL

tel: 01736 795252 **Boskerris Rd, Carbis Bay TR26 2PE**
email: cottage@leisureplex.co.uk **web:** www.leisureplex.co.uk
dir: From A30 take A3074 to Carbis Bay. Right into Porthreptor Rd. Just before rail bridge, left through railway car park into hotel car park

Set in quiet, lush gardens, this pleasant hotel offers friendly and attentive service. Smart bedrooms are pleasantly spacious and many rooms enjoy splendid views. Public areas are varied and include a snooker room, a comfortable lounge and a spacious dining room with sea views over the beach and Carbis Bay.

Rooms 80 (7 fmly) **Facilities** FTV WiFi ↘ Snooker ♫ Xmas New Year **Services** Lift **Parking** 20 **Notes** ⊗ Closed Dec-Feb (ex Xmas) RS Nov & Mar

ST LEONARDS-ON-SEA

See Hastings & St Leonards

ST MARY CHURCH

See Torquay

ST MARY'S Map 2 SV91
Cornwall (Isles of Scilly)

Tregarthen's Hotel

★★★ 80% HOTEL

tel: 01720 422540 **Hugh Town TR21 0PP**
email: reception@tregarthens-hotel.co.uk **web:** www.tregarthens-hotel.co.uk
dir: 100yds from town & quay

Opened in 1848 by Captain Tregarthen, this well-established hotel has impressive public areas that provide wonderful views overlooking St Mary's harbour and some of the many islands, including Tresco and Bryher. Bedrooms are well equipped and neatly furnished. Traditional cuisine is served in the restaurant.

Rooms 33 (1 annexe) (11 fmly) **Facilities** FTV WiFi Spa & beauty treatments available **Conf** Class 20 Board 30 Thtr 80 Del from £90 to £110* **Notes** Closed late Oct-mid Mar Civ Wed 100

ST MELLION Map 3 SX36
Cornwall

St Mellion International Resort

★★★★ 81% HOTEL

tel: 01579 351351 **PL12 6SD**
email: stmellion@crown-golf.co.uk **web:** www.st-mellion.co.uk
dir: From M5, A38 towards Plymouth & Saltash. St Mellion off A38 on A388 towards Callington & Launceston

Set in 450 acres of Cornish countryside, this impressive golfing and leisure complex has much to offer. A vast range of leisure facilities are provided, including three pools, spa facilities and a health club. In addition, the hotel also boasts a choice of championship golf courses. The Jack Nicklaus signature course has hosted many PGA tour events. The bedrooms provide contemporary comforts and many have views across the course. Public areas are equally stylish with a choice of dining options including An Boesti, a fine-dining restaurant overlooking the 18th green.

Rooms 80 (20 fmly) (18 GF) **Facilities** Spa FTV WiFi supervised 36 Putt green Gym Studio classes Lawn bowls Xmas New Year **Conf** Class 200 Board 80 Thtr 400 **Services** Lift Air con **Parking** 450 **Notes** Civ Wed 300

ST NEOTS Map 12 TL16
Cambridgeshire

The George Hotel & Brasserie

★★★ 88% HOTEL

tel: 01480 812300 **High St, Buckden PE19 5XA**
email: mail@thegeorgebuckden.com **web:** www.thegeorgebuckden.com
dir: 2m S of A1 & A14 junct at Buckden

The George Hotel is ideally situated in the heart of this historic town centre and is just a short drive from the A1. Public rooms feature a bustling ground-floor brasserie, which offers casual dining throughout the day and evening; there is also an informal lounge bar with an open fire and comfy seating. Bedrooms are stylish, tastefully appointed and thoughtfully equipped.

Rooms 12 (1 fmly) **D** £95-£150 (incl. bkfst)* **Facilities** STV WiFi **Conf** Class 30 Board 30 Thtr 50 Del £160* **Services** Lift **Parking** 25 **Notes** LB Civ Wed 60

Abbotsley Golf Hotel

★★★ 70% HOTEL

tel: 01480 474000 **Potton Rd, Eynesbury Hardwicke PE19 6XN**
email: membership@abbotsley.com **web:** www.abbotsley.com

Situated in a rural location on the outskirts of St Neots, this property is set in 250-acre grounds with two golf courses, a golf school and leisure complex. The well-equipped bedrooms are situated in a courtyard and another adjacent block; some rooms have views over the golf course. Public rooms include two bars, a conservatory dining room and a choice of lounges.

Rooms 42 (42 annexe) (2 fmly) (29 GF) **S** £59; **D** £95 (incl. bkfst) **Facilities** FTV WiFi 45 Putt green Gym New Year **Conf** Class 60 Board 60 Thtr 80 Del £95 **Parking** 200 **Notes** LB Civ Wed 90

ST NEOTS *continued*

Premier Inn St Neots (A1/Wyboston)

BUDGET HOTEL

tel: 0871 527 9024 **Great North Rd, Eaton Socon PE19 8EN**
web: www.premierinn.com
dir: Just off A1 at rdbt of A428 & B1428 before St Neots. 1m from St Neots rail station

High quality, budget accommodation ideal for both families and business travellers. Spacious, en suite bedrooms feature tea and coffee making facilities, and Freeview TV in most hotels. Internet access and WiFi are available for a small fee. The adjacent family restaurant features a wide and varied menu. See also the Hotel Groups pages.

Rooms 65

Premier Inn St Neots (Colmworth Park)

BUDGET HOTEL

tel: 0871 527 9026 **2 Marlborough Rd, Colmworth Business Park PE19 8YP**
web: www.premierinn.com
dir: From A1 N'bound: A428 towards Cambridge. 2nd exit at rdbt onto A4128 signed St Neots. Hotel on right. From A1 S'bound: follow A428 Cambridge signs. At rdbt 1st exit onto A4128 signed St Neots, hotel on right

Rooms 41

SALCOMBE	Map 3 SX73
Devon	

Soar Mill Cove Hotel

★★★★ 83% ◉◉ HOTEL

tel: 01548 561566 **Soar Mill Cove, Malborough TQ7 3DS**
email: info@soarmillcove.co.uk web: www.soarmillcove.co.uk
dir: 3m W of town off A381 at Malborough. Follow Soar signs

Situated amid spectacular scenery with dramatic sea views, this hotel is ideal for a relaxing stay. Family-run, with a committed team, keen standards of hospitality and service are upheld. Bedrooms are well equipped and many have private terraces. There are different seating areas where, if guests wish, impressive cream teas can be enjoyed, and for the more active, there's a choice of swimming pools. Local produce and seafood are used to good effect in the restaurant.

Rooms 22 (5 fmly) (21 GF) ♦ **S** £125-£204; **D** £149-£229 (incl. bkfst)* **Facilities** Spa FTV WiFi ♨ ♨ Putt green Gym Table tennis Games room Leisure complex ♫ Xmas **Conf** Class 50 Board 50 Thtr 100 **Parking** 30 **Notes** LB Closed 2 Jan-8 Feb Civ Wed 150

Thurlestone Hotel

★★★★ 83% ◉ HOTEL

tel: 01548 560382 **TQ7 3NN**
email: enquiries@thurlestone.co.uk web: www.thurlestone.co.uk

(For full entry see Thurlestone)

Salcombe Harbour Hotel

Ⓤ

tel: 01548 844444 **Cliff Rd TQ8 8JH**
email: salcombe@harbourhotels.co.uk web: www.salcombe-harbour-hotel.co.uk
dir: From A38 Exeter - Plymouth dual carriageway take A384 to Totnes then follow A381 (direct route to Kingsbridge & on to Salcombe). On entering Salcombe carry along Main Road, do not take town signs. Follow this road down hill into Bennett Road, after 0.25m hotel is on right.

Currently the rating for this establishment is not confirmed. This may be due to a change of ownership or because it has only recently joined the AA rating scheme. For further details please see the AA website: theAA.com

Rooms 50 (6 fmly) (6 GF) **S** £140-£585; **D** £150-£595 (incl. bkfst)* **Facilities** Spa FTV WiFi ♨ HL ♨ Gym Sauna Steam room Xmas New Year **Conf** Class 120 Board 40 Thtr 120 **Services** Lift **Parking** 50 **Notes** Civ Wed 120

SALE	Map 15 SJ79
Greater Manchester	

Premier Inn Manchester (Sale)

BUDGET HOTEL

tel: 0871 527 8716 **Carrington Ln, Ashton-upon-Mersey M33 5BL**
web: www.premierinn.com
dir: M60 junct 8, A6144(M) towards Carrington. Left at 1st lights, hotel on left

High quality, budget accommodation ideal for both families and business travellers. Spacious, en suite bedrooms feature tea and coffee making facilities, and Freeview TV in most hotels. Internet access and WiFi are available for a small fee. The adjacent family restaurant features a wide and varied menu. See also the Hotel Groups pages.

Rooms 43

SALISBURY	Map 5 SU12
Wiltshire	

Milford Hall Hotel

★★★★ 74% ◉ HOTEL

CLASSIC BRITISH HOTELS

tel: 01722 417411 & 424116 **206 Castle St SP1 3TE**
email: reception@milfordhallhotel.com web: www.milfordhallhotel.com
dir: Near junct of Castle St, A36 ring road & A345 Amesbury Road

This hotel offers high standards of accommodation and is within easy walking distance of the city centre. There are two categories of bedroom - traditional rooms in the original Georgian house, and spacious, modern rooms in a purpose-built extension; all are extremely well equipped. Meals are served in the smart brasserie where a varied choice of dishes is provided.

Rooms 45 (2 fmly) (22 GF) ♦ **S** £60-£140; **D** £60-£140 (incl. bkfst) **Facilities** STV FTV WiFi Xmas New Year **Conf** Class 90 Board 60 Thtr 200 Del from £150 to £180 **Parking** 60 **Notes** LB ⊗ Civ Wed 120

Mercure Salisbury White Hart Hotel

★★★★ 73% HOTEL

tel: 01722 327476 **St John St SP1 2SD**
email: H6616@accor.com **web:** www.mercure.com
dir: M3 juncts 7/8, A303 to A343 for Salisbury then A30. Follow city centre signs on ring road, into Exeter St, leading into St John St. Car park at rear on Brown St

There has been a hotel on this site since the 16th century. Bedrooms vary - some are contemporary and some are decorated in more traditional style, but all boast a comprehensive range of facilities. The bar and lounge areas are popular with guests and locals alike for morning coffees and afternoon teas.

Rooms 68 (6 fmly) **Facilities** STV WiFi Xmas New Year **Conf** Class 40 Board 40 Thtr 100 **Parking** 60 **Notes** Civ Wed 100

The Legacy Rose & Crown Hotel

★★★★ 71% HOTEL

tel: 08444 119046 & 0330 333 2846 **Harnham Rd SP2 8JQ**
email: res-roseandcrown@legacy-hotels.co.uk **web:** www.legacy-hotels.co.uk
dir: M3 junct 8, A303 & follow Salisbury Ring Road or M27 junct 2, A36 to Salisbury. A338 towards Harnham then Harnham Rd. Hotel on right

This 13th-century coaching inn, situated beside the river, enjoys picturesque views of Salisbury Cathedral, especially from the Pavilion Restaurant which provides a good range of dishes. Many original features are still retained in the heavy oak-beamed bars. All bedrooms and bathrooms are beautifully appointed. Excellent conference and banqueting facilities are available.

Rooms 32 (5 fmly) (5 GF) **Facilities** FTV WiFi Xmas New Year **Conf** Class 30 Board 26 Thtr 90 Del from £130 to £160* **Parking** 60 **Notes** ⊗ Civ Wed 100

Grasmere House Hotel

THE INDEPENDENTS
HOTEL ASSOCIATION

★★★ 71% HOTEL

tel: 01722 338388 **Harnham Rd SP2 8JN**
email: info@grasmerehotel.com **web:** www.grasmerehotel.com
dir: On A3094 on S side of Salisbury adjacent to Harnham church

This popular hotel, dating from 1896, has gardens that overlook the water meadows and the cathedral. The attractive bedrooms vary in size, some offer excellent quality and comfort, and some rooms are specially equipped for less mobile guests. In summer there is the option of dining on the pleasant outdoor terrace.

Rooms 38 (31 annexe) (16 fmly) (9 GF) **Facilities** STV FTV WiFi Fishing ⅂ Xmas New Year **Conf** Class 45 Board 45 Thtr 110 **Parking** 64 **Notes** Civ Wed 120

Premier Inn Salisbury

BUDGET HOTEL

tel: 0871 527 8956 **Pearce Way, Bishopsdown SP1 3YU**
web: www.premierinn.com
dir: From Salisbury take A30 towards Marlborough. 1m. Hotel off Hampton Park at rdbt

High quality, budget accommodation ideal for both families and business travellers. Spacious, en suite bedrooms feature tea and coffee making facilities, and Freeview TV in most hotels. Internet access and WiFi are available for a small fee. The adjacent family restaurant features a wide and varied menu. See also the Hotel Groups pages.

Rooms 62

SALTASH Map 3 SX45
Cornwall

China Fleet Country Club

★★★ 79% HOTEL

tel: 01752 848668 & 854661 **PL12 6LJ**
email: sales@china-fleet.co.uk **web:** www.china-fleet.co.uk
dir: A38 towards Plymouth/Saltash. Cross Tamar Bridge, take slip road before tunnel. Right at lights, 1st right follow signs, 0.5m

Set in 180 acres of stunning Cornish countryside overlooking the beautiful Tamar estuary, this hotel has easy access to Plymouth and the countryside. It offers an extensive range of leisure facilities including an impressive golf course. The one and two-bedroom apartments are located in annexe buildings; each has a kitchen, lounge and flexible sleeping arrangements. The dining options include a brasserie, a coffee shop and an award-winning Farm House Restaurant which offers interesting and imaginative choices.

Rooms 40 (39 fmly) (21 GF) **S** £74-£94; **D** £74-£94* **Facilities** Spa FTV WiFi ⊗ supervised ⅃ 18 Putt green Gym Squash Floodlit driving range Health & beauty suite Hairdresser Badminton Waterslide Xmas New Year **Conf** Class 100 Board 60 Thtr 300 Del from £136.95 to £142.95* **Services** Lift **Parking** 400 **Notes** ⊗ Civ Wed 300

SANDBANKS

See Poole

SANDIACRE Map 11 SK43
Derbyshire

Holiday Inn Derby/Nottingham

Holiday Inn

★★★ 74% HOTEL

tel: 0871 942 9062 **Bostocks Ln NG10 5NJ**
email: reservations-derby-nottingham@ihg.com **web:** www.hiderbyhotel.co.uk
dir: M1 junct 25 follow Sandiacre signs, hotel on right

This hotel is conveniently located by the M1, and is ideal for exploring Derby and Nottingham. The bedrooms are modern and smart. The restaurant offers a wide range of dishes for breakfast, lunch and dinner. The lounge/bar area is a popular meeting place, with food served all day.

Rooms 92 (31 fmly) (53 GF) **Facilities** STV FTV WiFi ⊗ HL Xmas New Year **Conf** Class 26 Board 30 Thtr 60 **Services** Air con **Parking** 200 **Notes** Civ Wed 50

S

SANDIWAY	Map 15 SJ67
Cheshire	

INSPECTORS' CHOICE

Nunsmere Hall Hotel

★★★★ ◉◉ COUNTRY HOUSE HOTEL

PRIMA

tel: 01606 889100 **Tarporley Rd CW8 2ES**
email: reception@nunsmere.co.uk **web:** www.nunsmere.co.uk
dir: M6 junct 18, A54 to Chester, at x-rds with A49 turn left towards Tarporley, hotel 2m on left

In an idyllic and peaceful setting of well-kept grounds, including a 60-acre lake, this delightful house dates back to 1900. Spacious bedrooms are individually styled, tastefully appointed to a very high standard and thoughtfully equipped. Guests can relax in the elegant lounges, the library or the oak-panelled bar. Dining in the Crystal Restaurant is a highlight and both a traditional carte and a gourmet menu are offered.

Rooms 36 (8 fmly) (2 GF) ⚐ **Facilities** FTV WiFi ⬇ 🏊 Xmas New Year **Conf** Class 24 Board 30 Thtr 50 Del from £149* **Services** Lift **Parking** 80 **Notes** Civ Wed 120

SANDOWN	Map 5 SZ58
Isle of Wight	

The Wight Montrene Hotel

★★ 80% HOTEL

tel: 01983 403722 **11 Avenue Rd PO36 8BN**
email: enquiries@wighthotel.co.uk **web:** www.wighthotel.co.uk
dir: 100yds after mini-rdbt between High St & Avenue Rd

A family hotel, set in secluded grounds, that is only a short walk from Sandown's beach and high street shops. Bedrooms are very welcoming and are either on the ground or first floor. Guests can relax in the heated swimming pool and enjoy the spa facility; there's also evening entertainment in the bar. The dinner menu changes nightly, and a plentiful breakfast is served in the colourful dining room.

Rooms 41 (18 fmly) (21 GF) ⚐ **S** £33-£50; **D** £66-£100 (incl. bkfst)* **Facilities** Spa FTV WiFi ☣ Gym Steam room Sauna Solarium Table tennis Full size snooker table ♫ Xmas New Year **Conf** Thtr 80 **Parking** 40 **Notes** LB

Sandringham Hotel

★★ 76% HOTEL

tel: 01983 406655 **Esplanade PO36 8AH**
email: info@sandringhamhotel.co.uk **web:** www.sandringhamhotel.co.uk

With a prime seafront location and splendid views, this is one of the largest hotels on the island. Comfortable public areas include a spacious lounge and a heated indoor swimming pool and jacuzzi. Bedrooms vary in size and many sea-facing rooms have a balcony. Regular entertainment is provided in the ballroom.

Rooms 110 (39 fmly) (6 GF) **Facilities** 🏊 ♫ Xmas **Services** Lift **Parking** 82 **Notes** ⊗

Bayshore Hotel

★★ 75% HOTEL

tel: 01983 403154 **12-16 Pier St PO36 8JX**
email: bayshore.sandown@alfatravel.co.uk **web:** www.leisureplex.co.uk
dir: From Broadway into Melville St, follow Tourist Information Office signs. Across High St, right opposite pier. Hotel on right

This large hotel is located on the seafront opposite the pier and offers extensive public rooms where live entertainment is provided in season. The bedrooms are well equipped and staff are very friendly and helpful.

Rooms 78 (18 fmly) ⚐ **Facilities** FTV WiFi ♫ Xmas New Year **Services** Lift **Notes** ⊗ Closed Dec-Feb (ex Xmas) RS Mar & Nov

Riviera Hotel

★★ 71% HOTEL

tel: 01983 402518 **2 Royal St PO36 8LP**
email: enquiries@rivierahotel.org.uk **web:** www.rivierahotel.org.uk
dir: At top of High St, beyond Post Office

Guests return year after year to this friendly and welcoming family-run hotel. It is located near to the High Street and just a short stroll from the beach, pier and shops. Bedrooms, including several at ground floor level, are very well furnished and comfortably equipped. Enjoyable home-cooked meals are served in the spacious dining room.

Rooms 43 (6 fmly) (11 GF) ⚐ **S** £40-£48; **D** £80-£96 (incl. bkfst)* **Facilities** FTV WiFi ♫ Xmas New Year **Parking** 30

SANDWICH	Map 7 TR35
Kent	

The Lodge at Prince's

★★★ 83% ◉◉ HOTEL

tel: 01304 611118 **Prince's Dr, Sandwich Bay CT13 9QB**
email: j.george@princesgolfclub.co.uk **web:** www.princesgolfclub.co.uk
dir: M2 onto A299 Thanet Way to Manston Airport, A256 to Sandwich, follow sign to golf course

A newly-built hotel in one of the most sought-after locations of the south east coast, The Lodge offers a choice of bedrooms within three adjoining Lodge Houses. Most rooms offer enviable views of the golf course or the Bay of Sandwich. All rooms have been carefully designed and offer a range of practical amenities including club storage. Award-winning cuisine is served in The Brasserie on the Bay.

Rooms 38 (24 annexe) (1 fmly) (12 GF) ⚐ **Facilities** FTV WiFi ⬇ HL ⚘ 27 Putt green Gym Xmas New Year **Conf** Class 60 Board 50 Thtr 120 Del from £110 to £190* **Services** Lift **Parking** 50 **Notes** ⊗

S

SAUNTON
Devon

Map 3 SS43

Saunton Sands Hotel

★★★★ 80% ⊛ HOTEL

tel: 01271 890212 **EX33 1LQ**
email: reservations@sauntonsands.com **web:** www.sauntonsands.com
dir: Exit A361 at Braunton, signed Croyde B3231, hotel 2m on left

Stunning sea views and direct access to five miles of sandy beach are just two of the highlights at this popular hotel. The majority of sea-facing rooms have balconies, and splendid views can be enjoyed from all of the public areas, which include comfortable lounges. In addition to the dining room, in summer an outside grill has tables on the terrace overlooking the sea. Alternatively, The Sands café/bar, an informal eating option, is a successful innovation located on the beach.

Rooms 92 (39 fmly) ☞ **S** £75-£270; **D** £150-£540 (incl. bkfst)* **Facilities** Spa STV FTV WiFi ⊳ ⓧ ⤳ ⌣ Putt green Gym Squash Sauna Sun shower Snooker room ♫ Xmas New Year Child facilities **Conf** Class 180 Board 50 Thtr 200 **Services** Lift **Parking** 140 **Notes** LB ⊗ Civ Wed 200

See advert on below

SAWBRIDGEWORTH
Hertfordshire

Map 6 TL41

Manor of Groves Hotel, Golf & Country Club

★★★ 79% HOTEL

tel: 01279 600777 **High Wych CM21 0JU**
email: info@manorofgroves.co.uk **web:** www.manorofgroves.com
dir: A1184 to Sawbridgeworth, left to High Wych, right at village green & hotel 200yds left

Manor of Groves Hotel is a delightful Georgian manor house set in 150 acres of secluded grounds and gardens, with its own 18-hole championship golf course and superb leisure facilities. Public rooms include an imposing open-plan glass atrium that features a bar, lounge area and modern restaurant. The spacious bedrooms are smartly decorated and equipped with modern facilities.

Rooms 80 (2 fmly) (17 GF) ☞ **S** £68-£133; **D** £78-£163 (incl. bkfst) **Facilities** Spa FTV WiFi ⊳ ⓧ supervised ⌁ 18 Putt green Gym Dance studio Beauty salon Sauna Steam rooms Xmas New Year **Conf** Class 250 Board 50 Thtr 500 Del from £130 to £165 **Services** Lift **Parking** 350 **Notes** LB ⊗ RS 24-26 Dec Civ Wed 300

S

SCARBOROUGH
North Yorkshire   Map 17 TA08

Crown Spa Hotel

★★★★ 79% HOTEL

tel: 01723 357400 **Esplanade YO11 2AG**
email: info@crownspahotel.com **web:** www.crownspahotel.com
dir: On A64 follow town centre signs to lights opposite railway station, turn right over Valley Bridge, 1st left, right into Belmont Rd to cliff top

This well-known hotel has an enviable position overlooking the harbour and South Bay, and most of the front-facing bedrooms have excellent views. All the bedrooms, including suites, are contemporary and have the latest amenities including feature bathrooms. An extensive range of treatments are available in the outstanding spa.

Rooms 115 (42 fmly) 🛏 **Facilities** Spa FTV WiFi ↘ HL 🏊 Gym Fitness classes Massage Sauna Steam room Xmas New Year **Conf** Class 100 Board 80 Thtr 260 **Services** Lift **Parking** 17 **Notes** ⊗ Civ Wed 260

Palm Court Hotel

★★★ 82% ❀ HOTEL

tel: 01723 368161 **St Nicholas Cliff YO11 2ES**
email: info@palmcourt-scarborough.co.uk **web:** www.palmcourtscarborough.co.uk
dir: Follow signs for town centre & town hall, hotel before town hall on right

The public rooms are spacious and comfortable at this modern, town centre hotel. Traditional cooking is provided in the attractive restaurant and staff are friendly and helpful. Bedrooms are quite delightfully furnished and well equipped. Extra facilities include a swimming pool and free, covered parking.

Rooms 40 (11 fmly) 🛏 **Facilities** FTV WiFi 🏊 Xmas New Year **Conf** Class 70 Board 60 Thtr 80 Del from £99.50 to £129.50 **Services** Lift **Parking** 40 **Notes** ⊗ Civ Wed 80

Ambassador Spa Hotel

★★★ 80% HOTEL

tel: 01723 362841 **Centre of the Esplanade YO11 2AY**
email: ask@ambassadorspahotel.co.uk **web:** www.ambassadorspahotel.co.uk
dir: A64, right at mini rdbt opposite B&Q, right at next mini rdbt, immediately left into Avenue Victoria to cliff top

Standing on the South Cliff with excellent views over the bay, this friendly hotel offers well-equipped bedrooms; some are executive rooms, some have sea views. A spa with pool and many rejuvenating and pampering facilities is available. Entertainment is provided during the summer season.

Rooms 56 (10 fmly) (1 GF) 🛏 **S** £39-£89; **D** £79-£129 (incl. bkfst) **Facilities** Spa FTV WiFi ↘ 🏊 Sauna Spa bath Xmas New Year **Conf** Class 60 Board 40 Thtr 120 Del from £99 to £149 **Services** Lift Air con **Notes** LB ⊗ Civ Wed 120

Esplanade Hotel

★★★ 70% HOTEL

tel: 01723 360382 **Belmont Rd YO11 2AA**
email: enquiries@theesplanade.co.uk **web:** www.theesplanade.co.uk
dir: From town centre over Valley Bridge, left then immediately right into Belmont Rd, hotel 100mtrs on right

This large hotel enjoys a superb position overlooking South Bay and the harbour. Both the terrace, leading from the lounge bar, and the restaurant, with its striking oriel window, benefit from magnificent views. Bedrooms are comfortably furnished and are well equipped. Touring groups are also well catered for.

Rooms 70 (7 fmly) 🛏 **S** £39-£67; **D** £78-£134 (incl. bkfst)* **Facilities** FTV WiFi Xmas New Year **Conf** Class 100 Board 30 Thtr 120 Del from £40 to £80* **Services** Lift **Parking** 15 **Notes** LB RS 2 Jan-9 Feb

Red Lea Hotel

★★★ 70% HOTEL

tel: 01723 362431 **Prince of Wales Ter YO11 2AJ**
email: info@redleahotel.co.uk **web:** www.redleahotel.co.uk
dir: Follow South Cliff signs. Prince of Wales Terrace is off Esplanade opposite cliff lift

This friendly, family-run hotel is situated close to the cliff lift. Bedrooms are well equipped and comfortably furnished, and many at the front have picturesque views of the coast. There are two large lounges and a spacious dining room where good-value, traditional food is served.

Rooms 66 (7 fmly) 🛏 **Facilities** FTV WiFi 🏊 Xmas New Year **Conf** Class 25 Board 25 Thtr 40 **Services** Lift **Notes** ⊗

The Cumberland

★★ 76% HOTEL

tel: 01723 361826 **Belmont Rd YO11 2AB**
email: cumberland@alfatravel.co.uk **web:** www.leisureplex.co.uk
dir: A64 onto B1437, left at A165 towards town centre. Right into Ramshill Rd, right into Belmont Rd

On the South Cliff, convenient for the spa complex, beach and town centre shops, this hotel offers comfortably appointed bedrooms; each floor can be accessed by lift. Entertainment is provided most evenings and the meals are carefully prepared.

Rooms 86 (6 fmly) 🛏 **S** £39-£50; **D** £62-£84 (incl. bkfst)* **Facilities** FTV WiFi 🎵 Xmas New Year **Services** Lift **Notes** LB ⊗ Closed Jan RS Nov-Dec & Feb

The Mount Hotel

★★ 76% HOTEL

tel: 01723 360961 **Cliff Bridge Ter, Saint Nicholas Cliff YO11 2HA**
email: info@mounthotel.com **web:** www.mounthoteluk.co.uk
dir: On one-way system. From A165 (Valley Bridge Rd) left into Somerset Terrace, straight on at lights, straight on at rdbt (Palm Court Hotel on right). Next right into St Nicholas Cliff. Hotel at end on right

Standing in a superb, elevated position and enjoying magnificent views of the South Bay, this elegant Regency hotel is operated to high standards. The richly furnished and comfortable public rooms are inviting, and the well-equipped bedrooms have been attractively decorated. The spacious deluxe rooms are mini-suites.

Rooms 50 (3 fmly) 🛏 **Facilities** FTV WiFi ↘ New Year **Conf** Class 24 Board 18 Thtr 26 **Services** Lift

Park Manor Hotel

★★ 75% HOTEL

tel: 01723 372090 **Northstead Manor Dr YO12 6BB**
email: info@parkmanor.co.uk **web:** www.parkmanor.co.uk
dir: Off A165, adjacent to Peasholm Park

Enjoying a peaceful residential setting with sea views, this smartly presented, friendly hotel provides the seaside tourist with a wide range of facilities. Bedrooms vary in size and style but all are smartly furnished and well equipped. There is a spacious lounge, smart restaurant, games room and indoor pool plus a steam room for relaxation.

Rooms 41 (6 fmly) (1 GF) ❦ S £45-£56; D £90-£123 (incl. bkfst)* **Facilities** FTV WiFi ⓢ Pool table Spa bath Steam room Table tennis New Year **Conf** Class 20 Board 20 Thtr 30 Del from £75 to £89* **Services** Lift **Parking** 20 **Notes** LB ⊗ Closed 26 Dec RS 25 Dec

Premier Inn Scarborough

BUDGET HOTEL

tel: 0871 527 9292 **Falconer Rd YO11 2EN**
web: www.premierinn.com
dir: From A64 into Seamer Rd, follow rail station signs. Right into Valley Bridge Rd. At 1st lights follow Town Hall signs into Somerset St (towards Brunswick shopping centre). At lights follow Town Hall signs into Falconers Rd

High quality, budget accommodation ideal for both families and business travellers. Spacious, en suite bedrooms feature tea and coffee making facilities, and Freeview TV in most hotels. Internet access and WiFi are available for a small fee. The adjacent family restaurant features a wide and varied menu. See also the Hotel Groups pages.

Rooms 74

SCOTTER	Map 17 SE80
Lincolnshire	

The White Swan

RESTAURANT WITH ROOMS

tel: 01724 763061 📠 01652 651493 **9 The Green DN21 3UD**
email: info@whiteswanscotter.com **web:** www.whiteswanscotter.com

This smartly presented property has been fully refurbished to provide stylish, contemporary accommodation in a peaceful village location. The restaurant is modern with vaulted ceilings and is split over three levels, whilst there is also a traditional pub called The Mucky Duck. A lounge bar and impressive garden add to the range of areas for guests to relax. Weddings and other special events are also well catered for. Accommodation rates include a continental breakfast but a choice of breakfast options are also available.

Rooms 11 (1 fmly)

SCUNTHORPE	Map 17 SE81
Lincolnshire	

Forest Pines Hotel & Golf Resort

★★★★ 80% ⓗ HOTEL

QHOTELS
INSPIRED BY YOU

tel: 01652 650770 **Ermine St, Broughton DN20 0AQ**
email: forestpines@qhotels.co.uk **web:** www.qhotels.co.uk
dir: 200yds from M180 junct 4, on Brigg-Scunthorpe rdbt

This smart hotel provides a comprehensive range of leisure facilities. Extensive conference rooms, a modern health and beauty spa, and a championship golf course ensure that it is a popular choice with both corporate and leisure guests. The well-equipped bedrooms are modern, spacious, and appointed to a good standard. Extensive public areas include a choice of dining options, with fine dining available in The Eighteen57 fish restaurant, and more informal eating in the Grill Bar. QHotels is the AA Hotel Group of the Year 2014-15.

Rooms 188 (66 fmly) (67 GF) ❦ **Facilities** Spa STV FTV WiFi ⓢ ⌁ 27 Putt green Gym Mountain bikes Jogging track Xmas New Year **Conf** Class 170 Board 96 Thtr 370 **Services** Lift **Parking** 400 **Notes** Civ Wed 250

Premier Inn Scunthorpe

BUDGET HOTEL

tel: 0871 527 8960 **Lakeside Retail Park, Lakeside Parkway DN16 3UA**
web: www.premierinn.com
dir: M180 junct 4, A18 towards Scunthorpe. At Morrisons rdbt left onto Lakeside Retail Park, hotel behind Morrisons petrol station

High quality, budget accommodation ideal for both families and business travellers. Spacious, en suite bedrooms feature tea and coffee making facilities, and Freeview TV in most hotels. Internet access and WiFi are available for a small fee. The adjacent family restaurant features a wide and varied menu. See also the Hotel Groups pages.

Rooms 60

SEAHAM	Map 19 NZ44
County Durham	

Seaham Hall

★★★★★ 86% ⓖⓖ HOTEL

tel: 0191 516 1400 **Lord Byron's Walk SR7 7AG**
email: hotel@seaham-hall.com **web:** www.seaham-hall.co.uk
dir: From A19 take B1404 to Seaham. At lights straight over level crossing. Hotel approx 0.25m on right

This unique hotel benefits from a wonderful coastal location. The interior is sumptuously furnished with all rooms boasting the highest quality fixtures, fittings and furniture. Many have feature bathrooms and the garden rooms have their own patio and garden areas. Public areas boast quality and luxury throughout, while the Spa is just an amazing place with many treatment rooms, outside hot tubs and a full compliment of saunas, steam rooms, a pool and fully equipped gym. The two dining options are the fine-dining Blunos sea grill restaurant, and the authentic Ozone Pan-Asian restaurant.

Rooms 20 (4 GF) ❦ D £285-£785 (incl. bkfst)* **Facilities** Spa STV FTV WiFi ⓗ HL ⓢ Putt green ⌁ Gym Games Room Xmas New Year **Conf** Class 48 Board 40 Thtr 100 **Services** Lift Air con **Parking** 120 **Notes** ⊗ Civ Wed 100

SEAHOUSES	Map 21 NU23
Northumberland	

The Links Hotel

★★ 79% SMALL HOTEL

tel: 01665 720062 **8 King St NE68 7XP**
email: linkshotel@hotmail.com **web:** www.linkshotel-seahouses.co.uk
dir: Off A1 at Browleside & follow signs along country road

This family-owned small hotel is in the heart of Seahouses. The restaurant is popular with residents and locals alike, offering relaxed and informal dining with quality home cooking and generous portions. Bedrooms are well presented and equipped and some off-road parking is available.

Rooms 14 (4 annexe) (2 fmly) (2 GF) ❦ S £43-£51; D £66-£82 (incl. bkfst)* **Facilities** STV FTV WiFi ⓗ Xmas New Year **Parking** 14

S

SEASCALE
Cumbria   Map 18 NY00

Sella Park House Hotel

★★★★ 77%  COUNTRY HOUSE HOTEL

tel: 0845 450 6445 & 01946 841601 **Calderbridge CA20 1DW**
email: info@penningtonhotels.com **web:** www.penningtonhotels.com
dir: From A595 at Calderbridge, follow sign for North Gate. Hotel 0.5m on left

This property, which some believe dates back to the 13th century, is set in six acres of mature grounds which lead down to the River Calder. The individually designed bedrooms are very well appointed and have many extras; public areas are comfortable and welcoming. Food in the Priory Restaurant is a highlight with local produce at the heart of each menu selection.

Rooms 16 (5 annexe) (2 GF) ⌁ **S** £80-£120; **D** £100-£140 (incl. bkfst)* **Facilities** FTV WiFi ⌁ HL Fishing Xmas New Year **Conf** Class 80 Board 80 Thtr 300 Del from £100 to £137.50* **Parking** 30 **Notes** LB Civ Wed 150

SEAVIEW
Isle of Wight   Map 5 SZ69

The Seaview Hotel & Restaurant

★★★ 82% HOTEL

tel: 01983 612711 **High St PO34 5EX**
email: reception@seaviewhotel.co.uk **web:** www.seaviewhotel.co.uk
dir: From B3330 (Ryde-Seaview road), turn left via Puckpool along seafront

Located in the quiet and tranquil area of Seaview, the hotel is just a short walk from the seafront, and there are views from the front terrace, especially enjoyable in the summer months. Bedrooms are split between three main areas yet all offer modern and stylish accommodation; all have free broadband, DVD TVs plus slippers and robes. There is a modern restaurant where guests can enjoy meals, and there is also The Pump Bar with very traditional decor which is popular with both residents and locals alike.

Rooms 29 (4 fmly) (5 GF) ⌁ **Facilities** FTV WiFi ⌁ Use of nearby sports club New Year **Conf** Class 20 Board 20 Thtr 20 **Parking** 10 **Notes** Closed 22-26 Dec

Priory Bay Hotel

★★★ 80%  HOTEL

tel: 01983 613146 **Priory Dr PO34 5BU**
email: enquiries@priorybay.co.uk **web:** www.priorybay.co.uk
dir: B3330 towards Seaview, through Nettlestone. NB do not follow Seaview turn, but continue 0.5m to hotel sign

This peacefully located hotel has much to offer and comes complete with its own stretch of private beach and 6-hole golf course. Bedrooms are a wonderful mix of styles, all of which provide much comfort and character. Public areas are equally impressive with a choice of enticing lounges to relax and unwind in. The kitchen creates interesting and imaginative dishes, using the excellent island produce as much as possible.

Rooms 22 (4 annexe) (6 fmly) (2 GF) ⌁ **S** £90-£225; **D** £160-£300 (incl. bkfst)* **Facilities** FTV WiFi ⌁ ⌁ 6 ⌁ ⌁ Private beach Xmas New Year **Conf** Class 60 Board 40 Thtr 80 Del from £140 to £205* **Parking** 100 **Notes** LB ⌁ Civ Wed 300

SEDGEFIELD
County Durham   Map 19 NZ32

BEST WESTERN PLUS Hardwick Hall Hotel

★★★★ 79% HOTEL   **Best Western PLUS**

tel: 01740 620253 **TS21 2EH**
email: info@hardwickhallhotel.co.uk **web:** www.hardwickhallhotel.co.uk
dir: Exit A1(M) junct 60 towards Sedgefield, left at 1st rdbt, hotel 400mtrs on left

Set in extensive parkland, this 18th-century house suits both leisure and corporate guests. It is a top conference and function venue offering an impressive meeting and banqueting complex. Luxurious accommodation includes contemporary rooms, and some with antique furnishings. All are appointed to the same high standard, many have feature bathrooms, and some have stunning views over the lake. Both the modern lounge bar and cellar bistro have a relaxed atmosphere.

Rooms 51 (6 fmly) (12 GF) ⌁ **Facilities** STV FTV WiFi ⌁ Xmas New Year **Conf** Class 100 Board 80 Thtr 700 **Services** Lift **Parking** 300 **Notes** ⌁ Civ Wed 450

SEDGEMOOR MOTORWAY SERVICE AREA (M5)
Somerset   Map 4 ST35

Days Inn Sedgemoor - M5

BUDGET HOTEL

tel: 01934 750831 **Sedgemoor BS24 0JL**
email: sedgemoor.hotel@welcomebreak.co.uk **web:** www.welcomebreak.co.uk
dir: M5 northbound junct 21/22

This modern building offers accommodation in smart, spacious and well-equipped bedrooms, suitable for families and business travellers, and all with en suite bathrooms. Continental breakfast is available and other refreshments may be taken at the nearby family restaurant. See also the Hotel Groups pages.

Rooms 40 (22 fmly) (19 GF) (8 smoking)

SHAFTESBURY
Dorset   Map 4 ST82

BEST WESTERN The Royal Chase Hotel

★★★ 71% HOTEL   **Best Western**

tel: 01747 853355 **Royal Chase Roundabout SP7 8DB**
email: reception@theroyalchasehotel.co.uk **web:** www.theroyalchasehotel.co.uk
dir: A303 to A350 signed Blandford Forum. Avoid town centre, follow road to 3rd rdbt

Equally suitable for both leisure and business guests, this well-known local landmark is situated close to the famous Gold Hill. Both Standard and Crown bedrooms offer good levels of comfort and quality. In addition to the fixed-price menu in the Byzant Restaurant, guests have the option of eating more informally in the convivial bar.

Rooms 33 (13 fmly) (6 GF) ⌁ **S** £65-£95; **D** £90-£130 (incl. bkfst) **Facilities** FTV WiFi ⌁ ⌁ Turkish steam room Spa pool Xmas New Year **Conf** Class 90 Board 50 Thtr 180 Del £139 **Parking** 100 **Notes** LB Civ Wed 76

La Fleur de Lys Restaurant with Rooms

 RESTAURANT WITH ROOMS

tel: 01747 853717 📄 01747 853130 **Bleke St SP7 8AW**
email: info@lafleurdelys.co.uk **web:** www.lafleurdelys.co.uk
dir: From junct of A30 & A350, 0.25m towards town centre

Located just a few minutes' walk from the famous Gold Hill, this light and airy restaurant with rooms combines efficient service in a relaxed and friendly atmosphere. Bedrooms, which are suitable for both business and leisure guests, vary in size but all are well equipped, comfortable and tastefully furnished. A relaxing guest lounge and courtyard are available for afternoon tea or pre-dinner drinks.

Rooms 8 (2 fmly)

SHANKLIN   Map 5 SZ58
Isle of Wight

Channel View Hotel

★★★ 79% HOTEL

tel: 01983 862309 **Hope Rd PO37 6EH**
email: enquiries@channelviewhotel.co.uk **web:** www.channelviewhotel.co.uk
dir: Exit A3055 at Esplanade & Beach sign. Hotel 250mtrs on left

With an elevated cliff-top location overlooking Shanklin Bay, several rooms at this hotel enjoy pleasant views and all are very well decorated and furnished. The hotel is family run, and guests can enjoy efficient service, regular evening entertainment, a heated indoor swimming pool and holistic therapy.

Rooms 56 (15 fmly) 🐾 **S** £44-£64; **D** £88-£128 (incl. bkfst) **Facilities** FTV WiFi ⏱ ❄ Holistic therapies Aromatherapy 🎵 **Services** Lift **Parking** 32 **Notes** LB Closed Jan-Feb

Melbourne Ardenlea Hotel

★★ 78% HOTEL

tel: 01983 862596 **4-6 Queens Rd PO37 6AN**
email: reservations@mahotel.co.uk **web:** www.mahotel.co.uk
dir: A3055 to Shanklin. Then follow signs to Ventnor via A3055 (Queens Rd). Hotel just before end of road on right

This quietly located hotel is within easy walking distance of the town centre and the lift down to the promenade. Bedrooms are traditionally furnished and guests can enjoy the various spacious public areas including a welcoming bar and a large heated indoor swimming pool.

Rooms 54 (5 fmly) (6 GF) 🐾 **Facilities** FTV WiFi ❄ Sauna 🎵 Xmas New Year **Conf** Class 24 Board 20 Thtr 80 **Services** Lift **Parking** 26 **Notes** Closed 1-15 Jan

Auckland Hotel

★★ 72% HOTEL

tel: 01983 862960 **1O Queens Rd PO37 6AN**
email: aucklandhotel@tiscali.co.uk

This family-run hotel is located in the heart of Shanklin. Bedrooms are traditional in style yet spacious and all front rooms benefit from balconies with views of Sandown Beach. There is a spacious bar often providing evening entertainment and a restaurant where both dinner and breakfast are served daily. This hotel has ample off-road parking and is within just a short walk of the Cliff Lift providing easy access to the seafront.

Rooms 30 **S** £35-£45; **D** £70-£90 (incl. bkfst)* **Facilities** FTV WiFi 🎵 **Parking** 16 **Notes** ⊗ Closed Dec-Feb

Malton House Hotel

★★ 69% HOTEL

tel: 01983 865007 **8 Park Rd PO37 6AY**
email: couvoussis@maltonhouse.freeserve.co.uk **web:** www.maltonhouse.co.uk
dir: Up hill from Hope Rd lights then 3rd left

A well-kept Victorian hotel set in its own gardens in a quiet area, conveniently located for cliff-top walks and the public lift down to the promenade. The bedrooms are comfortable and public rooms include a small lounge, a separate bar and a dining room where traditional homemade meals are served.

Rooms 12 (3 fmly) (2 GF) **S** £34-£38; **D** £60-£70 (incl. bkfst)* **Facilities** WiFi **Parking** 12 **Notes** LB ⊗ No children 3yrs Closed Oct-Apr

SHAP   Map 18 NY51
Cumbria

BEST WESTERN Shap Wells Hotel

★★★ 77% HOTEL

tel: 01931 716628 **CA1O 3QU**
email: reservations@shapwellshotel.com **web:** www.bw-shapwellshotel.co.uk
dir: Between A6 & B6261, 4m S of Shap

This hotel occupies a wonderful secluded position amid trees and waterfalls. Extensive public areas include function and meeting rooms, a well-stocked bar, a choice of lounges and a spacious restaurant. Bedrooms vary in size and style but all are equipped with the expected facilities.

Rooms 100 (9 annexe) (10 fmly) (10 GF) 🐾 **Facilities** FTV WiFi ⏱ Games room Cardiovascular gym 🎵 Xmas New Year **Conf** Class 80 Board 40 Thtr 170 **Services** Lift **Parking** 200 **Notes** Closed 2-24 Jan Civ Wed 150

SHEFFIELD   Map 16 SK49
South Yorkshire

Copthorne Hotel Sheffield

★★★★ 79%  HOTEL

tel: 0114 252 5480 **Sheffield United Football Club, Bramhall Ln S2 4SU**
email: reservations.sheffield@millenniumhotels.co.uk
web: www.millenniumhotels.co.uk/copthornesheffield
dir: M1 junct 33/A57. At Park Square rdbt follow A61 (Chesterfield Rd). Follow brown signs for Bramall Lane

This modern and stylish hotel is situated in the centre of Sheffield. Located next to the home of Sheffield United FC, it offers contemporary public areas and an award-winning restaurant on the ground floor. A well-equipped gym is situated on the first floor. Bedrooms are spacious and comfortable. Ample parking is a plus in this central location.

Rooms 158 (23 fmly) 🐾 **Facilities** STV FTV WiFi ⏱ Fitness room **Conf** Class 150 Board 40 Thtr 400 **Services** Lift Air con **Parking** 250 **Notes** ⊗

S

SHEFFIELD *continued*

Whitley Hall Hotel

★★★★ 78%  HOTEL

tel: 0114 245 4444 & 246 0456 **Elliott Ln, Grenoside S35 8NR**
email: reservations@whitleyhall.com **web:** www.whitleyhall.com
dir: A61 past football ground, 2m, right just before Norfolk Arms, left at bottom of hill.
Hotel on left

This 16th-century house stands in 20 acres of landscaped grounds and gardens.
Public rooms are full of character and interesting architectural features, and
command the best views of the gardens. The individually styled bedrooms are
furnished in keeping with the country house setting, as are the oak-panelled
restaurant and bar.

Rooms 32 (3 annexe) (2 fmly) (8 GF) S £85-£125; **D** £85-£125* **Facilities** STV FTV
WiFi ⚓ **Conf** Class 50 Board 34 Thtr 70 Del from £140 to £180* **Services** Lift
Parking 100 **Notes** LB ⊗ Civ Wed 100

Mercure Sheffield St Paul's Hotel & Spa

★★★★ 77% HOTEL

tel: 0114 278 2000 **119 Norfolk St S1 2JE**
email: h6628@accor.com **web:** www.mercure.com
dir: M1 junct 33, 4th exit at rdbt, left at 1st lights, right at 2nd in front of Crucible
Theatre

This modern, luxury hotel enjoys a central location close to key attractions in the
city. Open-plan public areas are situated in a steel and glass atrium and include a
popular Champagne bar, the Yard Restaurant and Zucca, an Italian Bistro.
Bedrooms are superbly presented and richly furnished. The Vital health and beauty
treatment centre provides a fabulous thermal suite.

Rooms 163 (40 fmly) **Facilities** Spa WiFi ⚓ Sauna Steam room Snail shower Ice
fountain Fitness classes Xmas New Year **Conf** Class 400 Board 30 Thtr 600
Services Lift Air con **Notes** ⊗ Civ Wed 350

Kenwood Hall

★★★★ 73% HOTEL

tel: 0114 258 3811 **Kenwood Rd S7 1NQ**
web: www.principal-hayley.com
dir: A61 (Barnsley ring road) into St Mary's Rd. Straight over rdbt, left into London Rd,
right at lights. 2nd exit at 2nd rdbt, hotel ahead

A smart, modern hotel peacefully located in a residential suburb a few miles from
the city centre. The stylishly decorated bedrooms are spacious, quiet and well

equipped. The hotel also has an extensive range of leisure and meeting facilities,
and secure parking is located in extensive landscaped gardens.

Rooms 114 (8 fmly) **Facilities** STV WiFi ⚓ Fishing Gym Steam room Sauna Solarium
Beauty treatment rooms New Year **Conf** Class 100 Board 60 Thtr 250 **Services** Lift
Parking 150 **Notes** Civ Wed 260

Novotel Sheffield Centre

★★★★ 72% HOTEL

tel: 0114 278 1781 **50 Arundel Gate S1 2PR**
email: h1348@accor.com **web:** www.novotel.com
dir: Between Registry Office & Crucible/Lyceum Theatres, follow signs to Town Hall/
Theatres & Hallam University

In the heart of the city centre, this hotel has stylish public areas including a very
modern restaurant, indoor swimming pool and a range of meeting rooms. Spacious
bedrooms are suitable for family occupation, and the Novation rooms are ideal for
business users.

Rooms 144 (136 fmly) ⚓ **Facilities** STV FTV WiFi ⚓ Gym Steam room Xmas New
Year **Conf** Class 180 Board 100 Thtr 220 **Services** Lift Air con **Parking** 60
Notes Civ Wed 180

BEST WESTERN PLUS Aston Hall Hotel

★★★ 82% HOTEL

tel: 0114 287 2309 **Worksop Rd, Aston S26 2EE**
email: reservations@astonhallhotel.co.uk **web:** www.astonhallhotel.co.uk
dir: M1 junct 31, follow A57 to Sheffield & follow signs to hotel

Originally built as a manor house and set in spacious grounds with open views
across the countryside to the south of the city, this hotel is well located for the M1,
Meadowhall, the city or touring. Extensive conference, banqueting facilities and
picturesque grounds make it an ideal wedding venue. Bedrooms are comfortable
and well equipped.

Rooms 52 (6 annexe) (13 GF) ⚓ **Facilities** FTV WiFi ⚓ Gym Xmas New Year
Conf Class 200 Board 60 Thtr 300 **Services** Lift **Parking** 90 **Notes** ⊗ Civ Wed 300

BEST WESTERN PLUS Mosborough Hall Hotel

★★★ 82% HOTEL

tel: 0114 248 4353 **High St, Mosborough S20 5EA**
email: hotel@mosboroughhall.co.uk **web:** www.mosboroughhall.co.uk
dir: M1 junct 30, A6135 towards Sheffield. Follow Eckington/Mosborough signs 2m. Sharp
bend at top of hill, hotel on right

This 16th-century, Grade II listed manor house is set in gardens not far from the M1
and is convenient for the city centre. The bedrooms offer very high quality and good

amenities; some are very spacious. There is a galleried lounge and conservatory bar, and freshly prepared dishes are served in the traditional style dining room.

Rooms 44 (17 GF)  **Facilities** FTV WiFi ⌕ Spa & beauty treatments Xmas New Year **Conf** Class 125 Board 70 Thtr 220 **Parking** 100 **Notes** Civ Wed 250

BEST WESTERN Cutlers Hotel

★★★ 72% HOTEL

tel: 0114 273 9939 **Theatreland George St S1 2PF**
email: enquiries@cutlershotel.co.uk **web:** www.cutlershotel.co.uk
dir: M1 junct 33. At Park Sq follow signs to City Centre & Theatres. At top of Commercial St, left into Arundel Gate. Into right lane, at lights right into Norfolk St, 2nd right into George St. Hotel 50mtrs on left

Situated in the heart of the city, near the theatres and only minutes from the bus and railway stations. Each of the bedrooms has a flat-screen TV, iPod docking station, free WiFi and broadband access. Mariano's Restaurant & Bar on the upper mezzanine level offers a relaxed atmosphere. A function room is also available. Discounted overnight parking is provided in the nearby public car park.

Rooms 45 (2 fmly) **Facilities** STV FTV WiFi Beauty treatment rooms Xmas New Year **Conf** Class 20 Board 25 Thtr 80 **Services** Lift **Notes** ⊗ Civ Wed 60

Ibis Sheffield City Centre

BUDGET HOTEL

tel: 0114 241 9600 **Shude Hill S1 2AR**
email: H2891@accor.com **web:** www.ibishotel.com
dir: M1 junct 33, follow signs to Sheffield City Centre (A630/A57), at rdbt take 5th exit, signed Ponds Forge, for hotel

Modern, budget hotel offering comfortable accommodation in bright and practical bedrooms. Breakfast is self-service and dinner is available in the restaurant. See also the Hotel Groups pages.

Rooms 95 (15 fmly) (3 GF)  **S** £39-£79; **D** £39-£79*

Premier Inn Sheffield (Arena)

BUDGET HOTEL

tel: 0871 527 8964 **Attercliffe Common Rd S9 2LU**
web: www.premierinn.com
dir: M1 junct 34, follow signs to city centre. Hotel opposite Arena

High quality, budget accommodation ideal for both families and business travellers. Spacious, en suite bedrooms feature tea and coffee making facilities, and Freeview TV in most hotels. Internet access and WiFi are available for a small fee. The adjacent family restaurant features a wide and varied menu. See also the Hotel Groups pages.

Rooms 61

Premier Inn Sheffield City Centre

BUDGET HOTEL

tel: 0871 527 8972 **Young St, St Marys Gate S1 4LA**
web: www.premierinn.com
dir: M1 junct 33, A630, A57 follow Sheffield City Centre signs. At Park Square rdbt 3rd exit signed A61/Chesterfield. At Granville Square right onto A61 signed Ring Rd. Keep in left lane. At rdbt 3rd exit signed A621. Left into Cumberland St. Left into South Lane. Right into Young St

Rooms 122

Premier Inn Sheffield City Centre Angel St

BUDGET HOTEL

tel: 0871 527 8970 **Angel St, (Corner of Bank Street) S3 8LN**
web: www.premierinn.com
dir: M1 junct 33, follow city centre, A630, A57 signs. At Park Square rdbt 4th exit (A61 Barnsley). Left at 4th lights into Snig Hill, right at lights into Bank St

Rooms 160

Premier Inn Sheffield (Meadowhall)

BUDGET HOTEL

tel: 0871 527 8966 **Sheffield Rd, Meadowhall S9 2YL**
web: www.premierinn.com
dir: On A6178 approx 6m from city centre

Rooms 103

| **SHEPTON MALLET** | **Map 4 ST64** |
| Somerset | |

Charlton House Spa Hotel

★★★★ 76% ⊛⊛ HOTEL

tel: 01749 342008 **Charlton Rd BA4 4PR**
email: gm.charltonhousehotel@bannatyne.co.uk **web:** www.bannatyne.co.uk
dir: On A361 towards Frome, 1m from town centre

A peaceful location with grounds and relaxing spa facilities are just part of the charm of this interesting hotel. Individually designed bedrooms include larger suites and a luxurious lodge in the garden. Guests can relax in the 'shabby chic' lounges or bar area, or in the warmer months there's plenty of outdoor seating. Dinner in the stylish restaurant offers a selection of carefully prepared, high quality dishes. The spa offers a wide range of facilities including treatment rooms, hydrotherapy pool, crystal room, sauna and a fitness studio to name but a few. The hotel is a popular wedding venue.

Rooms 28 (6 annexe) (3 fmly) (12 GF)  **D** £100-£400 (incl. bkfst) **Facilities** Spa FTV WiFi ⓢ ♨ Gym Sauna Steam room Laconium Experience showers Xmas New Year **Conf** Class 50 Board 30 Thtr 90 Del from £170 to £219* **Parking** 70 **Notes** LB ⊗ Civ Wed 120

| **SHERBORNE** | **Map 4 ST61** |
| Dorset | |

Eastbury Hotel

★★★ 79% ⊛⊛ HOTEL

tel: 01935 813131 **Long St DT9 3BY**
email: enquiries@theeastburyhotel.co.uk **web:** www.theeastburyhotel.co.uk
dir: From A30 W'bound, left into North Rd, then St Swithin's, left at bottom, hotel 800yds on right

Much of the original Georgian charm and elegance is maintained at this smart, comfortable hotel. Just five minutes' stroll from the abbey and close to the town centre, the Eastbury's friendly and attentive staff ensure a relaxed and enjoyable stay. Award-winning cuisine is served in the attractive dining room, overlooking the walled garden, with an alfresco bistro option also available.

Rooms 23 (1 fmly) (3 GF)  **Facilities** FTV WiFi ⌕ ☘ New Year **Conf** Class 40 Board 28 Thtr 80 **Parking** 30 **Notes** Civ Wed 80

S

SHERBORNE *continued*

BEST WESTERN The Grange at Oborne

★★★ 79% HOTEL

tel: 01935 813463 **Oborne DT9 4LA**
email: reception@thegrange.co.uk **web:** www.thegrangeatoborne.co.uk
dir: Exit A30, follow signs through village

Set in beautiful gardens in a quiet hamlet, this 200-year-old, family-run hotel has a wealth of charm and character. It offers friendly hospitality together with attentive service. Bedrooms are comfortable and tastefully appointed, public areas are elegantly furnished and the popular restaurant offers a good selection of dishes.

Rooms 18 (3 fmly) (2 GF) ☎ **S** £88-£139; **D** £99-£169 (incl. bkfst)* **Facilities** STV WiFi ☽ Xmas New Year **Conf** Class 40 Board 30 Thtr 80 Del from £148.95* **Parking** 45 **Notes** LB ⊗ Civ Wed 120

The Sherborne Hotel

★★★ 66% HOTEL

tel: 01935 813191 **Horsecastles Ln DT9 6BB**
email: info@sherbornehotel.co.uk **web:** www.sherbornehotel.co.uk
dir: At junct of A30 & A352

This hotel is in a quiet location with attractive grounds, yet is only just off a main road. The bedrooms are spacious and well equipped, the open-plan lounge and bar area are comfortable, and satellite TV is provided. There is a good range of dishes to choose from and the dining room looks out to the garden.

Rooms 60 (24 GF) ☎ **S** £69; **D** £89 (incl. bkfst)* **Facilities** FTV WiFi HL ⊌ Concessionary swimming rates at leisure centre opposite ♫ Xmas New Year **Conf** Class 35 Board 30 Thtr 80 **Parking** 90 **Notes** LB ⊗

SHERINGHAM	Map 13 TG14
Norfolk	

Dales Country House Hotel

★★★★ 83% ◉◉ HOTEL

tel: 01263 824555 **Lodge Hill, Upper Sheringham NR26 8TJ**
email: dales@mackenziehotels.com **web:** www.mackenziehotels.com
dir: From Sheringham take B1157 to Upper Sheringham. Through village, hotel on left

Superb Grade II listed building situated in extensive landscaped grounds on the edge of Sheringham Park. The attractive public rooms are full of original character; they include a choice of lounges as well as an intimate restaurant and a cosy lounge bar. The spacious bedrooms are individually decorated with co-ordinated soft furnishings and many thoughtful touches.

Rooms 21 (5 GF) ☎ **S** fr £103; **D** fr £166 (incl. bkfst)* **Facilities** WiFi ⊌ ⊌ Giant garden chess & jenga Xmas New Year **Conf** Class 20 Board 27 Thtr 40 Del from £140* **Services** Lift **Parking** 50 **Notes** LB No children 14yrs

Beaumaris Hotel

★★ 79% HOTEL

tel: 01263 822370 **South St NR26 8LL**
email: beauhotel@aol.com **web:** www.thebeaumarishotel.co.uk
dir: Exit A148, left at rdbt, 1st right over rail bridge, 1st left by church, 1st left into South St

The Beaumaris Hotel is situated in a peaceful side road just a short walk from the beach, town centre and golf course. This friendly hotel has been owned and run by the same family for over 60 years and continues to provide comfortable, thoughtfully equipped accommodation throughout. Public rooms feature a smart dining room, a cosy bar and two quiet lounges.

Rooms 21 (5 fmly) (2 GF) ☎ **Facilities** FTV WiFi **Parking** 25 **Notes** ⊗ Closed mid Dec-1 Mar

SHIFNAL	Map 10 SJ70
Shropshire	

Park House Hotel

★★★★ 76% ◉ HOTEL

tel: 01952 460128 **Park St TF11 9BA**
email: reception@parkhousehotel.net **web:** www.parkhousehotel.net
dir: M54 junct 4, A464 (Wolverhampton road) for approx 2m, under railway bridge, hotel 100yds on left

Park House Hotel was created from what were originally two country houses of very different architectural styles. Located on the edge of this historic market town, it offers guests easy access to motorway networks, a choice of banqueting and meeting rooms, plus leisure facilities. Butlers Bar and Restaurant is the setting for imaginative food. Service is friendly and attentive.

Rooms 54 (16 annexe) (4 fmly) (8 GF) (4 smoking) ☎ **S** £75-£120; **D** £90-£150 (incl. bkfst)* **Facilities** STV FTV WiFi ☽ ⊛ Gym Steam room Sauna Xmas New Year **Conf** Class 80 Board 40 Thtr 160 Del from £125 to £137.50* **Services** Lift **Parking** 90 **Notes** LB Civ Wed 200

SHIPLEY	Map 19 SE13
West Yorkshire	

Ibis Bradford Shipley

BUDGET HOTEL

tel: 01274 589333 **Quayside, Salts Mill Rd BD18 3ST**
email: H3158@accor.com **web:** www.ibis.com
dir: Follow tourist signs for Salts Mill. Follow A650 signs through Bradford for approx 5m to Shipley

Modern, budget hotel offering comfortable accommodation in bright and practical bedrooms. Breakfast is self-service and dinner is available in the restaurant. See also the Hotel Groups pages.

Rooms 78 (20 fmly) (22 GF) **Conf** Class 16 Board 18 Thtr 20

SHREWSBURY
Shropshire

Map 15 SJ41

Albright Hussey Manor Hotel & Restaurant

★★★★ 77% ◉◉ HOTEL

tel: 01939 290571 & 290523 **Ellesmere Rd SY4 3AF**
email: info@albrighthussey.co.uk **web:** www.albrighthussey.co.uk
dir: 2.5m N of Shrewsbury on A528, follow signs for Ellesmere

The estate was mentioned in the Domesday Book, but the current manor house is Tudor, dating from around 1524, and is approached over a moat. This Grade II listed, partly black-and-white timbered building maintains an abundance of original features including huge open fireplaces, oak-panelling and beams. The bedrooms, including four-poster rooms, are situated in either the sumptuously appointed main house or in the more modern wing. There's an intimate, award-winning restaurant and a comfortable cocktail bar and lounge.

Rooms 26 (4 fmly) (8 GF) ☜ **Facilities** FTV WiFi ⤵ Xmas New Year **Conf** Class 180 Board 80 Thtr 250 Del from £120 to £145* **Parking** 100 **Notes** Civ Wed 180

Mercure Shrewsbury Albrighton Hall Hotel & Spa

★★★★ 75% COUNTRY HOUSE HOTEL

tel: 01939 291000 **Albrighton SY4 3AG**
email: H6629@accor.com **web:** www.mercure.com
dir: From S: M6 junct 10a to M54 to end. From N: M6 junct 12 to M5 then M54. Follow signs Harlescott & Ellesmere to A528

Dating back to 1630, this former ancestral home is set in 15 acres of attractive gardens. The bedrooms are generally spacious and the stable rooms are particularly popular. Elegant public rooms have rich oak panelling and there is a modern, well-equipped health and fitness centre.

Rooms 87 (16 annexe) (6 fmly) (21 GF) ☜ **Facilities** Spa STV WiFi HL ⊗ ⤵ Gym Squash Thermal suite Relax room Spray tan Aerobics Xmas New Year **Conf** Class 150 Board 80 Thtr 300 Del from £99 to £149* **Services** Lift **Parking** 200 **Notes** ⊗ Civ Wed 250

Prince Rupert Hotel

CLASSIC
BRITISH HOTELS

★★★★ 75% HOTEL

tel: 01743 499955 **Butcher Row SY1 1UQ**
email: reservations@prince-rupert-hotel.co.uk **web:** www.prince-rupert-hotel.co.uk
dir: Follow town centre signs, over English Bridge & Wyle Cop Hill. Right into Fish St, hotel 200yds

Parts of this popular town centre hotel date back to medieval times and many bedrooms have exposed beams and other original features. Luxury suites, family rooms and rooms with four-poster beds are all available. As an alternative to the main Royalist Restaurant, diners have a less formal option in Chambers, a popular brasserie. The Camellias Tea Rooms are adjacent, providing snacks and afternoon teas. The hotel's valet parking service is also commendable.

Rooms 70 (2 fmly) ☜ **S** £75-£95; **D** £105-£185 (incl. bkfst) **Facilities** FTV WiFi ⤵ Gym Weight training Steam shower Sauna Snooker room Hair salon Xmas New Year **Conf** Class 80 Board 40 Thtr 120 Del from £140 to £160 **Services** Lift **Parking** 70 **Notes** LB ⊗

Rowton Castle Hotel

★★★ 88% HOTEL

tel: 01743 884044 **Halfway House SY5 9EP**
email: post@rowtoncastle.com **web:** www.rowtoncastle.com
dir: From A5 near Shrewsbury take A458 to Welshpool. Hotel 4m on right

Standing in 17 acres of grounds where a castle has stood for nearly 800 years, this Grade II listed building dates in parts back to 1696. Many original features remain, including the oak panelling in the restaurant and a magnificent carved oak fireplace. Most bedrooms are spacious and all have modern facilities; some have four-poster beds. The hotel has a well deserved reputation for its food and is a popular venue for weddings.

Rooms 19 (3 fmly) **S** £79-£99; **D** £124-£229 (incl. bkfst) **Facilities** WiFi **Conf** Class 30 Board 30 Thtr 80 Del from £115 to £120 **Parking** 100 **Notes** LB ⊗ Civ Wed 110

Lion & Pheasant Hotel

★★★ 80% ◉◉ TOWN HOUSE HOTEL

tel: 01743 770345 **49-50 Wyle Cop SY1 1XJ**
email: info@lionandpheasant.co.uk **web:** www.lionandpheasant.co.uk
dir: From S & E: pass abbey, cross river on English Bridge to Wyle Cop, hotel on left. From N & W: follow Town Centre signs on one-way system to Wyle Cop. Hotel at bottom of hill on right

This 16th-century property stands on Wyle Cop, part of the historic centre of Shrewsbury. The interior décor is minimalist and uses natural materials such as limed oak, linens and silks. The bedrooms are of a high standard and include twin, double and family rooms. Award-winning food is offered in the first-floor restaurant and also in the ground-floor bar area.

Rooms 22 (2 fmly) ☜ **Facilities** FTV WiFi ⤵ **Conf** Class 30 Board 30 Thtr 30 **Parking** 15 **Notes** ⊗ Closed 25-26 Dec

S

SHREWSBURY *continued*

Lord Hill Hotel

★★★ 77% HOTEL

tel: 01743 232601 **Abbey Foregate SY2 6AX**
email: reception@thelordhill.co.uk **web:** www.thelordhill.co.uk
dir: From M54 take A5, left at 1st rdbt , at 2nd rdbt 4th exit into London Rd. At next rdbt (Lord Hill Column) take 3rd exit, hotel 300yds on left

This pleasant, attractively appointed hotel is located close to the town centre. Most of the modern bedrooms are set in a separate purpose-built property, but those in the main building include one with a four-poster, as well as full suites. Public areas include a conservatory restaurant and spacious function suites.

Rooms 35 (24 annexe) (2 fmly) (8 GF) ⚲ **Facilities** FTV WiFi ⟿ Xmas New Year **Conf** Class 180 Board 180 Thtr 250 **Parking** 110 **Notes** Civ Wed 250

Abbots Mead Hotel

★★ 75% METRO HOTEL

tel: 01743 235281 **9 St Julian's Friars SY1 1XL**
email: res@abbotsmeadhotel.co.uk **web:** www.abbotsmeadhotel.co.uk
dir: From S into town, 2nd left after English Bridge

This well maintained Georgian town house is located in a quiet cul-de-sac, near the English Bridge and close to both the River Severn and town centre with its many restaurants. Bedrooms are compact, neatly decorated and well equipped. Two lounges are available in addition to an attractive dining room, the setting for breakfasts, and dinner parties by prior arrangement.

Rooms 16 (2 fmly) **Facilities** WiFi **Parking** 10 **Notes** Closed certain days at Xmas

Premier Inn Shrewsbury (Harmers Hill)

BUDGET HOTEL

tel: 0871 527 8974 **Wem Rd, Harmer Hill SY4 3DS**
web: www.premierinn.com
dir: M54 junct 7, A5 signed Telford for approx 7m, at rdbt take A49, approx 3m. At next 2 rdbts 2nd exit, at next rdbt 4th exit signed Ellesmere & A528. In approx 3m hotel on left

High quality, budget accommodation ideal for both families and business travellers. Spacious, en suite bedrooms feature tea and coffee making facilities, and Freeview TV in most hotels. Internet access and WiFi are available for a small fee. The adjacent family restaurant features a wide and varied menu. See also the Hotel Groups pages.

Rooms 20

Premier Inn Shrewsbury Town Centre

BUDGET HOTEL

tel: 0871 527 9402 **Smithfield Rd SY1 1QB**
web: www.premierinn.com
dir: Please phone for directions

Rooms 136

Drapers Hall

 RESTAURANT WITH ROOMS

tel: 01743 344679 **10 Saint Mary's Place SY1 1DZ**
email: goodfood@drapershallrestaurant.co.uk **web:** www.drapershallrestaurant.co.uk
dir: From A5191 (Saint Mary's St) on one-way system into St Mary's Place

This 16th-century, timber-framed property is situated in the heart of the market town of Shrewsbury. It provides high quality accommodation, including two suites, with modern facilities. Careful preservation of the original beams and wood panels, together with beautiful wooden furniture, has created a harmony between the past and present. Accomplished dining, headed up by Nigel Huxley, can be enjoyed in the main restaurant.

Rooms 6 (2 fmly)

Porter House SY1

 RESTAURANT WITH ROOMS

tel: 01743 358870 & 761220 ▤ 01743 344422 **15 Saint Mary's St SY1 1EQ**
email: hello@porterhousesy1.co.uk **web:** www.porterhousesy1.co.uk
dir: Follow one-way system around town, opposite St Mary's church

This fine property is located in the heart of the town. Its name comes from a eccentric squire in the 18th century who squandered a fortune and then landed in jail for his drunken and riotous behaviour. The four individually designed bedrooms, including a suite, are very comfortable and have spacious and contemporary bathrooms. Downstairs the award-winning, vibrant bar and restaurant specialises in British food with a classic twist. Breakfast offers a quality range of dishes. Secure parking is available in a nearby public car park.

Rooms 4 (1 fmly)

SIDLESHAM	Map 5 SZ89
West Sussex	

The Crab & Lobster

 RESTAURANT WITH ROOMS

tel: 01243 641233 **Mill Ln PO20 7NB**
email: enquiries@crab-lobster.co.uk **web:** www.crab-lobster.co.uk
dir: A27 onto B2145 signed Selsey. 1st left after garage at Sidlesham into Rookery Ln to Crab & Lobster

Hidden away on the south coast near Pagham Harbour and only a short drive from Chichester is the stylish Crab & Lobster. Bedrooms are superbly appointed, and bathrooms are a feature with luxury toiletries and powerful 'raindrop' showers. Guests can enjoy lunch or dinner in the smart restaurant where the menu offers a range of locally caught fresh fish together with other regionally-sourced, seasonal produce.

Rooms 4

THE MOST LUXURIOUS CHOICE IN EAST DEVON

Victoria
AA ★★★★ HOTEL

Perfectly positioned on Sidmouth's famous esplanade, the Victoria is one of the resort's finest and most picturesque hotels. It's extensive leisure facilities include indoor & outdoor pools, putting green, tennis court, snooker room and a luxurious spa area with sauna, spa bath, hot beds and treatment room. The hotel's restaurant has been awarded an AA Rosette for fine cuisine.

To make a booking please
call 01395 512651
or visit **www.victoriahotel.co.uk**

The Belmont Hotel
AA ★★★★

The Belmont too commands spectacular views from the famous esplanade. As inviting in January as July, the hotel offers fine cuisine and superb service that brings guests back year after year. With the indoor and outdoor leisure facilities of the adjacent Victoria Hotel at your disposal, the Belmont provides the perfect location for your holiday.

To make a booking please
call 01395 512555
or visit **www.belmont-hotel.co.uk**

Brend Hotels

SIDMOUTH
Devon

Map 3 SY18

The Victoria Hotel

★★★★ 83% 🌹 HOTEL

tel: 01395 512651 **The Esplanade EX10 8RY**
email: reservations@victoriahotel.co.uk **web:** www. victoriahotel.co.uk
dir: On seafront

This imposing building, with manicured gardens, is situated overlooking the town. Wonderful sea views can be enjoyed from many of the comfortable bedrooms and elegant lounges. With indoor and outdoor leisure facilities, the hotel caters to a year-round clientele. Carefully prepared meals are served in the refined atmosphere of the restaurant. The staff provide a professional and friendly service.

Rooms 62 (6 fmly) 🏷 **S** £140-£370; **D** £185-£370* **Facilities** FTV WiFi ⌨ 🏊 🏌 ⚲ Putt green Hot stone relaxation beds Spa bath Sauna Beauty treatment room Games room ♫ Xmas New Year Child facilities **Conf** Thtr 60 **Services** Lift **Parking** 100 **Notes** LB ⊗

See advert on page 401

Hotel Riviera

★★★★ 82% 🌹🌹 HOTEL

tel: 01395 515201 **The Esplanade EX10 8AY**
email: enquiries@hotelriviera.co.uk **web:** www.hotelriviera.co.uk
dir: M5 junct 30 & follow A3052

Overlooking the sea and close to the town centre, the Riviera is a fine example of Regency architecture. The large number of guests that become regular visitors here are testament to the high standards of service and hospitality offered. The front-facing bedrooms benefit from wonderful sea views, and the daily-changing menu places an emphasis on fresh, local produce.

Rooms 26 (6 fmly) 🏷 **S** £114-£209; **D** £208-£398 (incl. bkfst & dinner)* **Facilities** FTV WiFi ⌨ ♫ Xmas New Year **Conf** Class 60 Board 30 Thtr 85 **Services** Lift **Parking** 26 **Notes** LB

See advert on opposite page

The Belmont Hotel

★★★★ 77% HOTEL

tel: 01395 512555 **The Esplanade EX10 8RX**
email: reservations@belmont-hotel.co.uk **web:** www.belmont-hotel.co.uk
dir: On seafront

Prominently positioned on the seafront just a few minutes' walk from the town centre, this traditional hotel has many returning guests. A choice of comfortable lounges provides ample space for relaxation, and the air-conditioned restaurant has a pianist playing most evenings. Bedrooms are attractively furnished and many have fine views over the esplanade. Leisure facilities are available at the adjacent sister hotel, The Victoria.

Rooms 50 (1 fmly) (2 GF) 🐾 **S** £130-£245; **D** £160-£245* **Facilities** STV WiFi ⚓ Putt green Leisure facilities available at sister hotel 🎵 Xmas New Year Child facilities **Conf** Thtr 50 **Services** Lift **Parking** 45 **Notes** LB ⊗ Civ Wed 110

See advert on page 401

Westcliff Hotel

★★★ 81% HOTEL

tel: 01395 513252 **Manor Rd EX10 8RU**
email: stay@westcliffhotel.co.uk **web:** www.westcliffhotel.co.uk
dir: Exit A3052 to Sidmouth then to seafront & esplanade, turn right, hotel directly ahead

This charming hotel is ideally located within walking distance of Sidmouth's elegant promenade and beaches. The spacious lounges and the cocktail bar open onto a terrace which leads to the pool and croquet lawn. Bedrooms, several with balconies and glorious sea views, are spacious and comfortable, whilst the restaurant offers a choice of well-prepared dishes.

Rooms 40 (1 fmly) (5 GF) 🐾 **Facilities** FTV WiFi ⚓ Putt green Xmas New Year **Conf** Class 20 Board 15 Thtr 30 **Services** Lift **Parking** 40 **Notes** Civ Wed 80

S

SIDMOUTH *continued*

Bedford Hotel

★★★ 79% HOTEL

tel: 01395 513047 **Esplanade EX10 8NR**
email: info@bedfordhotelsidmouth.co.uk **web:** www.bedfordhotelsidmouth.co.uk
dir: M5 junct 30, A3052 & to Sidmouth. Hotel at centre of Esplanade

Situated on the seafront, this long established, family-run hotel provides a warm welcome and relaxing atmosphere. Bedrooms are well appointed and many have the added bonus of wonderful sea views. Public areas combine character and comfort with a choice of lounges in which to relax. In addition to the hotel dining room, Pyne's bar and restaurant offers an interesting range of dishes in a convivial environment.

Rooms 40 (1 GF) **Facilities** FTV Xmas **Services** Lift **Parking** 6

Kingswood & Devoran Hotel

★★★ 77% HOTEL

tel: 01395 516367 & 08000 481731 **The Esplanade EX10 8AX**
email: kingswoodanddevoran@hotels-sidmouth.co.uk **web:** www.hotels-sidmouth.co.uk
dir: M5 junct 30, A3052 signed Sidmouth on right, follow Station Rd down to Esplanade

This seafront hotel continues to offer friendly hospitality and service. Many bedrooms enjoy the sea views; all are well appointed and have smart bathrooms. Cuisine is pleasant and offers enjoyable dining featuring freshly prepared dishes.

Rooms 49 (8 fmly) (1 GF) ❦ **S** £55-£75; **D** £130-£180 (incl. bkfst)* **Facilities** FTV WiFi Xmas New Year **Conf** Class 30 Board 40 Thtr 60 **Services** Lift **Parking** 23 **Notes** Closed 27 Dec-10 Feb

Royal Glen Hotel

★★★ 77% HOTEL

tel: 01395 513221 & 513456 **Glen Rd EX10 8RW**
email: info@royalglenhotel.co.uk **web:** www.royalglenhotel.co.uk
dir: A303 to Honiton, A375 to Sidford, follow seafront signs, right onto esplanade, right at end into Glen Rd

This historic 17th-century, Grade I listed hotel has been owned by the same family for several generations. The comfortable bedrooms are furnished in period style. Guests may use the well-maintained gardens and a heated indoor pool, and can enjoy well-prepared food in the elegant dining room.

Rooms 32 (3 fmly) (3 GF) ❦ **S** £48-£74; **D** £96-£148 (incl. bkfst)* **Facilities** FTV WiFi ☂ Gym Therapy room (Massage & Aromatherapy) **Services** Lift **Parking** 22 **Notes** LB Closed Dec-21 Feb

Hotel Elizabeth

★★★ 75% HOTEL

tel: 01395 513503 & 08000 481731 **The Esplanade EX10 8AT**
email: elizabeth@hotels-sidmouth.co.uk **web:** www.hotels-sidmouth.co.uk
dir: M5 junct 30, A3052 to Sidmouth. 1st exit on right to Sidmouth, left onto esplanade

Occupying a prime location on the Esplanade, this elegant hotel attracts many loyal guests who return to enjoy the relaxed atmosphere and attentive service. Bedrooms are both comfortable and smartly appointed; all have sea views and some have balconies. The spacious lounge and sunny patio, with wonderful views across the bay, are perfect places to sit and just watch the world go by.

Rooms 28 (3 fmly) (1 GF) ❦ **S** £57-£65; **D** £114-£130 (incl. bkfst)* **Facilities** FTV WiFi Xmas **Services** Lift **Parking** 16 **Notes** ⊗ Closed 28 Dec-10 Feb

The Royal York & Faulkner Hotel

★★★ 75% HOTEL

tel: 01395 513043 & 0800 220714 **The Esplanade EX10 8AZ**
email: stay@royalyorkhotel.co.uk **web:** www.royalyorkhotel.co.uk
dir: M5 junct 30 take A3052, 10m to Sidmouth, hotel in centre of Esplanade

This seafront hotel, owned and run by the same family for over 60 years, maintains its Regency charm and grandeur. The attractive bedrooms vary in size, and many have balconies and sea views. Public rooms are spacious, and traditional dining is offered, alongside Blinis Café-Bar, which is more contemporary in style and offers coffees, lunch and afternoon tea. The spa facilities include a hydrotherapy pool, steam room, sauna and a variety of treatments.

Rooms 70 (2 annexe) (8 fmly) (5 GF) ❦ **S** £56.50-£97.50; **D** £113-£216 (incl. bkfst & dinner)* **Facilities** Spa FTV WiFi ☂ HL Hydrotherapy pool Steam Room Sauna Complimentary use of pool (200yds from hotel) ♫ Xmas New Year **Services** Lift **Parking** 20 **Notes** LB Closed Jan

Hunters Moon Hotel

★★ 83% HOTEL

tel: 01395 513380 **Sid Rd EX10 9AA**
email: huntersmoon.hotel@virgin.net **web:** www.huntersmoonhotel.com
dir: From Exeter on A3052 to Sidford, right at lights into Sidmouth, 1.5m, at cinema turn left. Hotel in 0.25m

Set in three acres of attractive and well-tended grounds, Hunters Moon Hotel is a friendly, family-run establishment located in a quiet area within walking distance of the town and esplanade. The light and airy bedrooms, some at ground floor level, are comfortable and well equipped. There is a lounge and a cosy bar. The restaurant provides a choice of imaginative dishes, and weather permitting, tea may be taken on the lawn.

Rooms 33 (4 fmly) (11 GF) ❦ **S** £62-£65; **D** £118-£124 (incl. bkfst)* **Facilities** FTV WiFi ☂ Putt green Xmas **Parking** 33 **Notes** LB No children 3yrs Closed Jan-Feb RS Dec

Mount Pleasant Hotel

★★ 82% HOTEL

tel: 01395 514694 **Salcombe Rd EX10 8JA**
web: www.mountpleasant-hotel.co.uk
dir: Exit A3052 at Sidford x-rds, in 1.25m turn left into Salcombe Rd, opposite Radway Cinema. Hotel on right after bridge

Quietly located within almost an acre of gardens, this modernised Georgian hotel is minutes from the town centre and seafront. Bedrooms and public areas provide good levels of comfort and high quality furnishings. Guests return on a regular basis, especially to experience the friendly, relaxed atmosphere. The light and airy restaurant overlooks the pleasant garden and offers a daily-changing menu of imaginative, yet traditional home-cooked dishes.

Rooms 17 (1 fmly) (3 GF) **S** £67-£83; **D** £134-£166 (incl. bkfst & dinner)* **Facilities** Putt green **Parking** 20 **Notes** ⊗ No children 8yrs Closed Dec-Feb

The Salty Monk

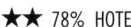 RESTAURANT WITH ROOMS

tel: 01395 513174 **Church St, Sidford EX10 9QP**
email: saltymonk@btconnect.com **web:** www.saltymonk.co.uk
dir: On A3052 opposite church in Sidford

Set in the village of Sidford, this attractive property dates from the 16th century. There's oodles of style and appeal here and each bedroom has a unique identity. Bathrooms are equally special with multi-jet showers, spa baths and cosseting robes and towels. The output from the kitchen is impressive with excellent local produce very much in evidence, served in the elegant surroundings of the restaurant. A mini spa facility is available.

Rooms 6 (1 annexe)

SILLOTH
Cumbria   Map 18 NY15

The Golf Hotel

★★ 78% HOTEL

tel: 016973 31438 **Criffel St CA7 4AB**
email: info@golfhotelsilloth.co.uk **web:** www.golfhotelsilloth.co.uk

A friendly welcome waits at this hotel which occupies a prime position in the centre of the historic market town, and is a popular meeting place for the local community. Bedrooms are mostly well proportioned and are comfortably equipped. The lounge bar is a popular venue for dining, with a wide range of dishes on offer.

Rooms 22 (2 fmly) ✆ **S** £50-£70; **D** £90-£150 (incl. bkfst)* **Facilities** FTV WiFi ⌨ Xmas New Year **Conf** Class 50 Board 30 Thtr 100 Del from £110 to £130* **Notes** LB Civ Wed 100

SILVERSTONE
Northamptonshire   Map 11 SP64

Premier Inn Silverstone

BUDGET HOTEL

tel: 0871 527 8976 **Brackley Hatch, Syresham NN13 5TX**
web: www.premierinn.com
dir: On A43 near Silverstone

High quality, budget accommodation ideal for both families and business travellers. Spacious, en suite bedrooms feature tea and coffee making facilities, and Freeview TV in most hotels. Internet access and WiFi are available for a small fee. The adjacent family restaurant features a wide and varied menu. See also the Hotel Groups pages.

Rooms 41

SITTINGBOURNE
Kent   Map 7 TQ96

Hempstead House Country Hotel

★★★ 86% ◉ HOTEL

tel: 01795 428020 **London Rd, Bapchild ME9 9PP**
email: info@hempsteadhouse.co.uk **web:** www.hempsteadhouse.co.uk
dir: 1.5m from town centre on A2 towards Canterbury

Expect a warm welcome at this charming detached Victorian property, situated amidst four acres of mature landscaped gardens. Bedrooms are attractively decorated with lovely co-ordinated fabrics, and are tastefully furnished and equipped with many thoughtful touches. Public rooms feature a choice of elegant lounges as well as a superb conservatory dining room. In summer guests can eat on the terraces. There is a spa and fitness studio.

Rooms 34 (7 fmly) (1 GF) ✆ **S** £85-£115; **D** £110-£160 (incl. bkfst)* **Facilities** Spa STV FTV WiFi ☒ ⌣ Gym Fitness studio Steam room Sauna Hydrotherapy pool Xmas New Year **Conf** Class 150 Board 100 Thtr 150 Del £152.50* **Services** Lift **Parking** 200 **Notes** LB Civ Wed 150

Premier Inn Sittingbourne

BUDGET HOTEL

tel: 9871 527 8978 **Bobbing Corner, Sheppy Way, Bobbing ME9 8RZ**
web: www.premierinn.com
dir: M2 junct 5, A249 towards Sheerness, approx 2m. Take 1st slip road after A2 underpass. At rdbt take 1st exit, hotel on left

High quality, budget accommodation ideal for both families and business travellers. Spacious, en suite bedrooms feature tea and coffee making facilities, and Freeview TV in most hotels. Internet access and WiFi are available for a small fee. The adjacent family restaurant features a wide and varied menu. See also the Hotel Groups pages.

Rooms 40

S

SKEGNESS
Lincolnshire

Map 17 TF56

BEST WESTERN The Vine Hotel

★★★ 77% HOTEL

tel: 01754 763018 & 610611 **Vine Rd, Seacroft PE25 3DB**
email: info@thevinehotel.com **web:** www.bw-vinehotel.co.uk
dir: A52 to Skegness, S towards Gibraltar Point, right into Drummond Rd, 0.5m, right into Vine Rd

With its long history this traditional hotel is something of a local landmark. The smartly decorated bedrooms are well equipped and comfortably appointed. Public areas include two character bars that serve excellent local beers. Freshly prepared dishes are offered in the bar and the restaurant; service is both friendly and helpful.

Rooms 25 (3 fmly) **Facilities** FTV WiFi Xmas New Year **Conf** Class 25 Board 30 Thtr 100 **Parking** 50 **Notes** ⊗ Civ Wed 100

BEST WESTERN North Shore Hotel & Golf Course

★★★ 72% HOTEL

tel: 01754 763298 **North Shore Rd PE25 1DN**
email: info@northshorehotel.co.uk **web:** www.northshorehotel.co.uk
dir: 1m N of town centre on A52, turn right into North Shore Rd, opposite Fenland laundry

This hotel enjoys an enviable position on the beachfront, adjacent to its own championship golf course and only ten minutes from the town centre. Spacious public areas include a terrace bar serving informal meals and real ales, a formal restaurant and impressive function rooms. Bedrooms are smartly decorated and thoughtfully equipped.

Rooms 34 (3 annexe) (4 fmly) (3 GF) ⌕ **Facilities** FTV WiFi ⌕ 18 Putt green Xmas New Year **Conf** Class 60 Board 60 Thtr 220 **Parking** 100 **Notes** ⊗ Civ Wed 180

See advert on opposite page

SKIPTON
North Yorkshire

Map 18 SD95

The Coniston Hotel & Country Estate

★★★★ 77% HOTEL

tel: 01756 748080 **Coniston Cold BD23 4EA**
email: info@theconistonhotel.com **web:** www.theconistonhotel.com
dir: On A65, 6m NW of Skipton

This privately owned hotel set in 1,400 acres of prime country estate is a haven for both leisure and corporate guests. All bedrooms and bathrooms are appointed to a very high standard; the bedroom wing offers large rooms with balconies. The reception, bar and restaurant have style and elegance, and the stunning spa adds to the impressive list of activities for guests.

Rooms 71 (13 fmly) (35 GF) ⌕ **S** £99-£131; **D** £116-£150 (incl. bkfst) **Facilities** STV FTV WiFi Fishing Clay pigeon shooting Falconry centre The Land Rover Experience Fly fishing Xmas New Year **Conf** Class 80 Board 50 Thtr 200 Del from £135 **Services** Lift **Parking** 170 **Notes** LB Civ Wed 120

Herriots Hotel

★★★ 80% HOTEL

tel: 01756 792781 **Broughton Rd BD23 1RT**
email: info@herriotsforleisure.co.uk **web:** www.herriotsforleisure.co.uk
dir: 2m from A59 at entrance to town; 50yds from railway station

This friendly hotel is situated in the centre of the delightful market town of Skipton and is just a short walk from the canal; the nearby railway has links to Leeds and the Settle to Carlisle route with its breathtaking scenery. The well-equipped bedrooms are contemporary in style yet maintain the character of this Victorian listed building; some rooms have French doors that overlook the canal; the largest rooms have four-posters and spas, and can be converted to accommodate families. Rhubarb restaurant offers British cuisine with a Yorkshire 'twist' that is based on local, seasonal produce.

Rooms 23 (3 fmly) ⌕ **S** £60-£75; **D** £85-£110 (incl. bkfst)* **Facilities** FTV WiFi ⌕ Private access onto Leeds Liverpool Canal Xmas New Year **Conf** Class 50 Board 52 Thtr 100 Del from £125 to £145* **Services** Lift **Parking** 26 **Notes** LB ⊗ Civ Wed 80

Rendezvous Hotel

★★★ 78% HOTEL

tel: 01756 700100 **Keighley Rd BD23 2TA**
email: reservations@rendezvous-skipton.com **web:** www.rendezvous-skipton.co.uk
dir: On A6131 (Keighley road) S from town centre

Located beside the canal just outside the town, the hotel has the advantage of plenty of parking and a leisure club with pool and gym. Bedrooms are well equipped and spacious, and have delightful views over the rolling countryside. There are extensive conference facilities. This hotel makes an ideal base for touring The Dales.

Rooms 80 (10 fmly) (13 GF) 🐾 **S** £65-£105; **D** £65-£105* **Facilities** FTV WiFi 🏊 supervised Gym Xmas New Year **Conf** Class 250 Board 120 Thtr 500 Del from £99 to £145* **Services** Lift **Parking** 80 **Notes** LB 🚫 Civ Wed 120

Premier Inn Skipton North (Gargrave)

BUDGET HOTEL

tel: 0871 527 8980 **Hellifield Rd, Gargrave BD23 3NB**
web: www.premierinn.com
dir: NW of Skipton at rdbt junct of A59 & A65, take A65 signed Kendal, Settle & Gargrave. 3.5m. Through Gargrave. Hotel on left

High quality, budget accommodation ideal for both families and business travellers. Spacious, en suite bedrooms feature tea and coffee making facilities, and Freeview TV in most hotels. Internet access and WiFi are available for a small fee. The adjacent family restaurant features a wide and varied menu. See also the Hotel Groups pages.

Rooms 21

SLOUGH	
Berkshire	Map 6 SU97

Hilton London Heathrow Airport Terminal 5

★★★★ 82% 🌸 HOTEL

tel: 01753 686860 **Poyle Rd, Colnbrook SL3 0FF**
email: heathrowairportterminal5.info@hilton.com **web:** www.hilton.com/heathrowt5

Hilton London Heathrow Airport Terminal 5, is located just one mile from Terminal 5 with easy access to the M25. Bedrooms offer practical and modern amenities such as soundproof windows and high quality comfortable beds, so that guests will enjoy a peaceful night sleep. A complimentary shuttle service is available to businesses in Stockley Park and Bedfront Lakes. It is an ideal venue for conferences, meetings and banqueting events for up to 1,000 guests. There are two restaurants for guests

to dine in, including The Gallery offering traditional British dishes, or enjoy pan-Indian cuisine at Mr Todiwala's. Guests can relax in the luxury onsite Spa and 24 Fitness Centre.

Rooms 350 (4 fmly) 🐾 **S** £89.25-£619; **D** £89.25-£619 **Facilities** Spa STV FTV WiFi 🏊 Gym **Conf** Class 430 Board 78 Thtr 1400 Del from £169 to £329 **Services** Lift Air con **Parking** 486 **Notes** 🚫 Civ Wed 1170

Copthorne Hotel Slough-Windsor

★★★★ 75% HOTEL

tel: 01753 516222 **400 Cippenham Ln SL1 2YE**
email: sales.slough@millenniumhotels.co.uk **web:** www.millenniumhotels.co.uk
dir: M4 junct 6, A355 towards Slough. At next rdbt left & left again for hotel entrance

Conveniently located for the motorway and for Heathrow Airport, this modern hotel of striking design offers visitors a wide range of indoor leisure facilities; Bugis Street Brasserie offers menus of Chinese, Malaysian and Singaporean dishes. Bedrooms provide a useful range of extras including climate control and satellite TV. The hotel offers a discounted entrance fee to some of the attractions in the area.

Rooms 219 (53 fmly) (6 smoking) 🐾 **S** £48-£286.80; **D** £48-£286.80* **Facilities** STV FTV WiFi 🏊 🐾 Gym Steam room Sauna Beauty treatment room **Conf** Class 160 Board 60 Thtr 280 **Services** Lift **Parking** 303 **Notes** LB Civ Wed 280

Premier Inn Slough

BUDGET HOTEL

tel: 0871 527 8982 **76 Uxbridge Rd SL1 1SU**
web: www.premierinn.com
dir: 2m from M4 junct 5, 3m from junct 6. Just off A4

High quality, budget accommodation ideal for both families and business travellers. Spacious, en suite bedrooms feature tea and coffee making facilities, and Freeview TV in most hotels. Internet access and WiFi are available for a small fee. The adjacent family restaurant features a wide and varied menu. See also the Hotel Groups pages.

Rooms 84

S

SOLIHULL
West Midlands

Map 10 SP17

See also **Dorridge**

The St Johns Hotel

★★★★ 75% HOTEL

tel: 0121 711 3000 & 712 7601 **651 Warwick Rd B91 1AT**
email: enquiries.stjohns@principal-hayley.com **web:** www.principal-hayley.com
dir: M42 junct 5, A41 (Solihull Bypass) signed Solihull. At lights left into Load Ln (signed Solihull Town Centre). At next rdbt 3rd exit onto B425 (Warwick Rd). Hotel on right

With its town centre location, this modern hotel is conveniently situated for the NEC, Birmingham and many local attractions. Bedrooms are air conditioned, attractively decorated and equipped with a comprehensive range of extras. The hotel provides extensive conference facilities, an indoor leisure facility and extensive parking.

Rooms 180 (1 fmly) (9 GF) ✦ **Facilities** STV FTV WiFi HL ⓢ Gym Sauna Steam room Nail treatment room Massage parlour Xmas New Year **Conf** Class 350 Board 40 Thtr 700 Del from £129 to £199 **Services** Lift Air con **Parking** 300 **Notes** Civ Wed 350

Premier Inn Solihull (Hockley Heath)

BUDGET HOTEL

tel: 0871 527 8984 **Stratford Rd, Hockley Heath B94 6NX**
web: www.premierinn.com
dir: On A3400, 2m S of M42 junct 4

High quality, budget accommodation ideal for both families and business travellers. Spacious, en suite bedrooms feature tea and coffee making facilities, and Freeview TV in most hotels. Internet access and WiFi are available for a small fee. The adjacent family restaurant features a wide and varied menu. See also the Hotel Groups pages.

Rooms 55

Premier Inn Solihull North

BUDGET HOTEL

tel: 0871 527 8988 **Stratford Rd, Shirley B90 3AG**
web: www.premierinn.com
dir: M42 junct 4 follow signs for Birmingham. Hotel in Shirley town centre on A34

Rooms 43

Premier Inn Solihull (Shirley)

BUDGET HOTEL

tel: 0871 527 8986 **Stratford Rd, Shirley B90 4EP**
web: www.premierinn.com
dir: M42 junct 4, A34N. Hotel in 1m

Rooms 51

Premier Inn Solihull Town Centre

BUDGET HOTEL

tel: 0871 527 9366 **Station Rd B91 3RX**
web: www.premierinn.com
dir: M42 junct 5. At rdbt, take 3rd exit onto A41. At lights, turn left onto Lode Lane. At rdbt, take 2nd exit & continue down Lode Lane. At rdbt take 1st exit onto Station Road

Rooms 115

Hampton Manor

◉◉ RESTAURANT WITH ROOMS

tel: 01675 446080 🖷 01675 443838 **Swadowbrook Ln, Hampton-in-Arden B92 0EN**
email: info@hamptonmanor.eu **web:** www.hamptonmanor.eu
dir: M42 junct 6 follow signs for A45 (Birmingham). At 1st rdbt, 1st exit onto B4438 (Catherine de Barnes Ln). Left into Shadowbrook Ln

Hampton Manor is set within 45 acres of mature woodland, only minutes from Birmingham's major air, rail and road links and the National Exhibition Centre (NEC). The manor has received major renovation and now offers luxurious accommodation with a contemporary and sophisticated style whilst maintaining many of its original features and heritage. The bedrooms are all beautifully and uniquely designed and boast sumptuous beds. Fine dining can be enjoyed at Peel's restaurant, which is a fabulous venue for innovative cooking, and will prove the highlight of any stay.

Rooms 15 (3 fmly)

SOURTON
Devon

Map 3 SX59

Collaven Manor Hotel

★★ 80% COUNTRY HOUSE HOTEL

tel: 01837 861522 **EX20 4HH**
email: collavenmanor@supanet.com **web:** www.collavenmanor.co.uk
dir: A30 onto A386 to Tavistock, hotel 2m on right

This delightful 15th-century manor house is quietly located in five acres of well-tended grounds. The friendly proprietors provide attentive service and ensure a relaxing environment. Charming public rooms have old oak beams and granite fireplaces, provide a range of comfortable lounges, and include a well stocked bar. In the restaurant, a daily-changing menu offers interesting dishes.

Rooms 8 (1 fmly) ✦ **S** £77-£89; **D** £98-£150 (incl. bkfst)* **Facilities** FTV WiFi ⓢ ⚐ Bowls **Conf** Class 20 Board 16 Thtr 30 **Parking** 50 **Notes** LB Closed Dec-Jan Civ Wed 50

SOUTHAMPTON
Hampshire

Map 5 SU41

See also **Botley**

Botleigh Grange Hotel

★★★★ 75% ◉ HOTEL

tel: 01489 787700 & 776969 **Grange Rd, Hedge End SO30 2GA**
email: info@botleighgrangehotel.net **web:** www.botleighgrangehotel.net
dir: M27 junct 7, A334 to Botley, hotel 1m on left

This impressive mansion, situated close to the M27, displays good quality throughout. The bedrooms are spacious with a good range of facilities. Public areas include a large conference room and a pleasant terrace with views overlooking the gardens and lake. The restaurant offers interesting menus using fresh, local produce.

Rooms 56 (10 fmly) (9 GF) **S** £65-£145; **D** £85-£165 (incl. bkfst)* **Facilities** Spa STV FTV WiFi ⓢ ⓢ supervised Putt green Fishing Sauna Steam room Relaxation room Monsoon showers Xmas New Year **Conf** Class 120 Board 40 Thtr 500 Del from £130 to £180 **Services** Lift **Parking** 300 **Notes** LB Civ Wed 180

Novotel Southampton

★★★★ 74% HOTEL

tel: 023 8033 0550 **1 West Quay Rd SO15 1RA**
email: H1073@accor.com **web:** www.novotel.com
dir: M27 junct 3, follow city centre/A33 signs. In 1m take right lane for West Quay & Dock Gates 4-10. Hotel entrance on left. Turn at lights by McDonalds, left at rdbt, hotel straight ahead

A modern, purpose-built hotel situated close to the city centre, railway station, ferry terminal and major road networks. The brightly decorated bedrooms are ideal for families and business guests; four rooms have facilities for the less mobile. The open-plan public areas include the Garden Brasserie, a bar and a leisure complex.

Rooms 121 (50 fmly) **Facilities** STV FTV WiFi Gym Sauna **Conf** Class 250 Board 150 Thtr 450 **Services** Lift **Parking** 300 **Notes** Civ Wed 300

Mercure Southampton Centre Dolphin Hotel

★★★★ 71% HOTEL

tel: 023 8038 6460 **34-35 High St SO14 2HN**
email: H7876@accor.com **web:** www.mercure.com
dir: From A33 follow signs for Docks, Old Town & Isle of Wight ferry. At ferry terminal right into High Street, hotel 400yds on left

Originally a coaching inn, this hotel enjoys a central location set almost in the heart of the town, yet close to the ferry terminals. The bedrooms are appointed to a high standard, and public areas include a traditional bar, popular restaurant and two meeting rooms. Parking at the rear of the hotel is an added bonus.

Rooms 99 (9 annexe) (6 fmly) (27 GF) **Facilities** FTV WiFi Xmas New Year **Conf** Class 50 Board 40 Thtr 120 **Services** Lift **Parking** 80 **Notes** Civ Wed 120

BEST WESTERN Chilworth Manor

★★★ 78% HOTEL

tel: 023 8076 7333 **Chilworth SO16 7PT**
email: sales@chilworth-manor.co.uk **web:** www.bw-chilworthmanor.co.uk
dir: 1m from M3/M27 junct on A27 Romsey Rd N from Southampton. Pass Chilworth Arms on left, in 200mtrs turn left at Southampton Science Park sign. Hotel immediately right

Set in 12 acres of delightful grounds, this attractive Edwardian manor house is conveniently located for Southampton and also the New Forest National Park. Bedrooms are located in both the main house and an adjoining wing. The hotel is particularly popular as both a conference and a wedding venue.

Rooms 95 (6 fmly) (23 GF) **S** £69-£109; **D** £79-£149 **Facilities** Spa FTV WiFi Gym Trail walking Giant chess Petanque New Year **Conf** Class 50 Board 50 Thtr 130 Del from £135 to £155 **Services** Lift **Parking** 200 **Notes** LB Civ Wed 105

Holiday Inn Southampton

★★★ 77% HOTEL

tel: 0871 942 9073 **Herbert Walker Av SO15 1HJ**
email: southamptonhi@ihg.com **web:** www.holidayinn.co.uk
dir: M27 junct 3 follow 'Dockgate 1-10 & Southampton Waterfront' signs. Hotel adjacent to Dock Gate 8

Convenient for both the port and town centre, this modern hotel is popular with both business and leisure guests. The well-equipped bedrooms are comfortably furnished. Public areas include an informal lounge bar and a contemporary restaurant offering an extensive range of popular dishes. Conference and leisure facilities are also available.

Rooms 130 (6 fmly) (2 smoking) **Facilities** STV WiFi supervised Gym New Year **Conf** Class 120 Board 80 Thtr 200 **Services** Lift Air con **Parking** 180 **Notes** Civ Wed

The Elizabeth House Hotel

★★ 81% HOTEL

tel: 023 8022 4327 **42-44 The Avenue SO17 1XP**
email: mail@elizabethhousehotel.com **web:** www.elizabethhousehotel.com
dir: On A33, hotel on left after Southampton Common, before main lights

This hotel is conveniently situated close to the city centre, so provides an ideal base for both business and leisure guests. The bedrooms are well equipped and are attractively furnished with comfort in mind. There is also a cosy and atmospheric bistro in the cellar where evening meals are served.

Rooms 27 (7 annexe) (9 fmly) (8 GF) **S** £65-£75.50; **D** £75-£87.50 (incl. bkfst)* **Facilities** FTV WiFi **Conf** Class 24 Board 24 Thtr 40 Del £112.50* **Parking** 31

Holiday Inn Express Southampton M27 Jct 7

BUDGET HOTEL

tel: 023 8060 6060 **Botley Rd, West End SO30 3XA**
email: reservations@expressbyholidayinn.uk.net **web:** www.hiesouthamptonhotel.com
dir: M27 junct 7, follow brown Ageas Bowl signs. Hotel 1m from junct 7 at entrance to The Ageas Bowl on corner Marshall Drive & Botley Rd

Set in landscaped gardens this hotel, adjacent to the Ageas Bowl, is conveniently located for Southampton Airport, Cruise Terminal and Docks and has ample free parking. There is an air-conditioned conservatory restaurant serving freshly prepared evening meals and complimentary hot breakfast and a fully licensed bar and lounge area with a 42" plasma TV. The hotel offers high speed WiFi throughout. Leisure facilities are available at the adjacent Virgin Active Leisure Centre for an additional fee. See also the Hotel Groups pages.

Rooms 176 (129 fmly) (38 GF) (9 smoking) **S** £48-£109; **D** £48-£109 (incl. bkfst)* **Conf** Class 26 Board 20 Thtr 52 Del from £99 to £109*

Ibis Southampton Centre

BUDGET HOTEL

tel: 023 8063 4463 **West Quay Rd, Western Esplanade SO15 1RA**
email: H1039@accor.com **web:** www.ibishotel.com
dir: M27 junct 3, M271, left to city centre (A35), follow Old Town Waterfront to 4th lights, left, left again, hotel opposite station

Modern, budget hotel offering comfortable accommodation in bright and practical bedrooms. Breakfast is self-service and dinner is available in the restaurant. See also the Hotel Groups pages.

Rooms 93 **Conf** Class 50 Board 40 Thtr 80

Premier Inn Southampton Airport

BUDGET HOTEL

tel: 0871 527 8998 **Mitchell Way SO18 2XU**
web: www.premierinn.com
dir: M27 junct 5, A335 towards Eastleigh. Right at rdbt into Wide Lane. 1st exit at next rdbt into Mitchell Way

High quality, budget accommodation ideal for both families and business travellers. Spacious, en suite bedrooms feature tea and coffee making facilities, and Freeview TV in most hotels. Internet access and WiFi are available for a small fee. The adjacent family restaurant features a wide and varied menu. See also the Hotel Groups pages.

Rooms 121

S

SOUTHAMPTON *continued*

Premier Inn Southampton City Centre

BUDGET HOTEL

tel: 0871 527 9266 **6 Dials, New Rd SO14 0YN**
web: www.premierinn.com
dir: M27 junct 5, A335 signed City Centre. At Charlotte Place rdbt take 3rd exit into East Park Terrace, 1st left into New Rd. Hotel on right

Rooms 172

Premier Inn Southampton North

BUDGET HOTEL

tel: 0871 527 9002 **Romsey Rd, Nursling SO16 0XJ**
web: www.premierinn.com
dir: M27 junct 3, M271 towards Romsey. At next rdbt take 3rd exit towards Southampton (A3057). Hotel 1.5m on right

Rooms 32

Premier Inn Southampton West Quay

BUDGET HOTEL

tel: 0871 527 9298 **Harbour Pde SO15 1ST**
web: www.premierinn.com
dir: M27 junct 3, follow M271(S)/Southampton/The Docks signs, onto M271, at Redbridge rdbt onto A35 follow Southampton/The Docks/A3024 signs. Merge onto A35 (Redbridge Rd), continue onto Millbrook Flyover/A3024, right at West Quay Rd/A3057, left after Ikea into Harbour Parade

Rooms 155

Ennio's Restaurant & Boutique Rooms

RESTAURANT WITH ROOMS

tel: 023 8022 1159 & 07748 966113 023 8039 9849 **Town Quay Rd SO14 3AS**
email: info@ennios.co.uk **web:** www.ennios.co.uk
dir: Opposite Red Funnel Ferry terminal

This fine property offers luxurious accommodation on Southampton's Waterfront. All rooms are en suite and are furnished to a very high standard including mini-bars and over-sized showers. Downstairs there is the popular Ennio's Restaurant and bar, which is the ideal setting in which to dine. There is also limited parking available at the rear.

Rooms 10

SOUTH CAVE	Map 17 SE93
East Riding of Yorkshire	

Cave Castle Hotel & Country Club

★★★ 78% HOTEL

tel: 01430 422245 **Church Hill HU15 2EU**
email: info@cavecastlehotel.com **web:** www.cavecastlehotel.com
dir: In village, opposite school

This beautiful Victorian manor retains original turrets, stone features and much charm, together with modern comforts and style. It stands in 150 acres of meadow and parkland that provide a peaceful setting. Bedrooms are a careful mix of

traditional and contemporary styles. Public areas include a well-equipped leisure complex and pool.

Rooms 70 (14 GF) **Facilities** Spa WiFi supervised 18 Putt green Fishing Gym New Year **Conf** Class 150 Board 100 Thtr 250 **Services** Lift **Parking** 100 **Notes** Civ Wed 150

SOUTH CERNEY	Map 5 SU09
Gloucestershire	

Cotswold Water Park Four Pillars Hotel

★★★★ 80% HOTEL

tel: 0800 374692 & 01285 864000 **Lake 6 Spine Road East GL7 5FP**
email: waterpark@four-pillars.co.uk **web:** www.cotswoldwaterparkhotel.co.uk
dir: Off A419, 3m from Cirencester (NB for Sav Nav use GL7 5TL)

This impressive hotel has well-appointed bedrooms and suites, conference facilities for up to 800 delegates, a spa with an 11-metre pool, a gym, a hydro pool and treatment rooms. An excellent range of dining options is available, and a large car park is provided.

Rooms 328 (58 fmly) (126 GF) **S** £79-£129; **D** £99-£149 (incl. bkfst)
Facilities Spa FTV WiFi Fishing Gym Beauty treatment rooms & therapies Steam room Sauna Xmas New Year **Conf** Class 350 Board 68 Thtr 500 Del from £130 to £175 **Services** Lift **Parking** 500 **Notes** LB Civ Wed 370

SOUTHEND-ON-SEA	Map 7 TQ88
Essex	

The Roslin Beach Hotel

★★★★ 82% HOTEL

tel: 01702 586375 **Thorpe Esplanade, Thorpe Bay SS1 3BG**
email: info@roslinhotel.com **web:** www.roslinhotel.com
dir: A127, follow Southend-on-Sea signs. Hotel between Walton Rd & Clieveden Rd on seafront

This friendly hotel is situated at the quiet end of the esplanade, overlooking the beach and sea. The spacious bedrooms are pleasantly decorated and thoughtfully equipped; some rooms have superb sea views. Public rooms include a large lounge bar, the Mulberry Restaurant and a smart conservatory which overlooks the sea.

Rooms 62 (5 fmly) (11 GF) **S** £65-£95; **D** £80-£145 (incl. bkfst)* **Facilities** Spa FTV WiFi Gym Xmas New Year **Conf** Class 65 Board 45 Thtr 90 Del from £136* **Parking** 48 **Notes** LB Civ Wed 100

Holiday Inn Southend

★★★ 81% @ HOTEL

 Holiday Inn

tel: 01702 543001 **77 Eastwoodbury Crescent SS2 6XG**
email: reservations@hisouthend.com **web:** www.hisouthend.com
dir: M25 junct 29, A127 follow signs to London Southend Airport. Hotel 2mins away

Built in 2012, Holiday Inn Southend offers a range of modern, well-appointed, stylish bedrooms. The public areas look very smart and have an open-plan contemporary image, and lounges are fitted out with designer furniture and seating. The award-winning 1935 Restaurant is situated on the fifth floor and overlooks the main runway of Southend airport. There are a range of conference facilities and business suites available along with secure parking for guests.

Rooms 129 (17 fmly) **Facilities** STV FTV WiFi Gym Xmas New Year **Conf** Class 50 Board 40 Thtr 140 **Services** Lift Air con **Parking** 250 **Notes** Civ Wed 140

Westcliff Hotel

★★★ 78% HOTEL

tel: 01702 345247 **Westcliff Pde, Westcliff-on-Sea SSO 7QW**
email: westcliff@zolahotels.com **web:** www.westcliff-hotel.co.uk
dir: M25 junct 29, A127 towards Southend, follow signs for Cliffs Pavillion when approaching town centre

This impressive Grade II listed Victorian building is situated in an elevated position overlooking gardens and cliffs with views to the sea beyond. The spacious bedrooms are tastefully decorated and thoughtfully equipped; many have lovely sea views. Public rooms include a smart conservatory-style restaurant, a spacious lounge and a range of function rooms.

Rooms 55 (2 fmly) ⌁ **S** £55-£69; **D** £80-£109 (incl. bkfst) **Facilities** FTV WiFi ♬ Xmas New Year **Conf** Class 90 Board 64 Thtr 225 **Services** Lift **Notes** ⊛ Civ Wed 120

Camelia Hotel

★★★ Ⓐ HOTEL

tel: 01702 587917 **176-178 Eastern Esplanade, Thorpe Bay SS1 3AA**
email: bookings@cameliahotel.com **web:** www.cameliahotel.com
dir: From A13 or A127 follow signs to Southend seafront; on seafront left, hotel 1m E of pier

Situated on the seafront with views of the Thames Estuary, this hotel has individually designed bedrooms including four-poster rooms and a honeymoon suite. There is a smart, air-conditioned restaurant offering both set and carte menus, and in summer a patio overlooking the sea for enjoying a relaxing drink.

Rooms 28 (8 annexe) (3 fmly) (8 GF) ⌁ **S** £60-£78; **D** £84-£130* **Facilities** FTV WiFi ⌁ **Parking** 100 **Notes** ⊛

Premier Inn Southend Airport

BUDGET HOTEL

 Premier Inn

tel: 0871 527 9008 **Thanet Grange SS2 6GB**
web: www.premierinn.com
dir: At A127 & B1013 junct

High quality, budget accommodation ideal for both families and business travellers. Spacious, en suite bedrooms feature tea and coffee making facilities, and Freeview TV in most hotels. Internet access and WiFi are available for a small fee. The adjacent family restaurant features a wide and varied menu. See also the Hotel Groups pages.

Rooms 80

Premier Inn Southend-on-Sea (Thorpe Bay)

BUDGET HOTEL

tel: 0871 527 9006 **213 Eastern Esplanade SS1 3AD**
web: www.premierinn.com
dir: Follow signs for A1159 (A13) Shoebury onto dual carriageway. At rdbt, follow signs for Thorpe Bay & seafront, at seafront turn right. Hotel on right

Rooms 43

SOUTH MIMMS SERVICE AREA (M25)	Map 6 TL20
Hertfordshire	

Days Inn South Mimms - M25

BUDGET HOTEL

 Welcome Break

tel: 01707 665440 **Bignells Corner, Potters Bar EN6 3QQ**
email: south.mimms@welcomebreak.co.uk **web:** www.welcomebreak.co.uk
dir: M25 junct 23, at rdbt follow signs

This modern building offers accommodation in smart, spacious and well-equipped bedrooms, suitable for families and business travellers, and all with en suite bathrooms. Continental breakfast is available and other refreshments may be taken at the nearby family restaurant. See also the Hotel Groups pages.

Rooms 75 (19 fmly) (23 GF) (10 smoking)

Premier Inn South Mimms/Potters Bar

BUDGET HOTEL

Premier Inn

tel: 0871 527 8990 **Swanland Rd EN6 3NH**
web: www.premierinn.com
dir: M25 junct 23 & A1 take services exit off main rdbt then 1st left & follow hotel signs

High quality, budget accommodation ideal for both families and business travellers. Spacious, en suite bedrooms feature tea and coffee making facilities, and Freeview TV in most hotels. Internet access and WiFi are available for a small fee. The adjacent family restaurant features a wide and varied menu. See also the Hotel Groups pages.

Rooms 142

SOUTH MOLTON	Map 3 SS72
Devon	

The George Hotel

★★ 78% HOTEL

tel: 01769 572514 **1 Broad St EX36 3AB**
email: info@georgehotelsouthmolton.co.uk **web:** www.georgehotelsouthmolton.co.uk
dir: Exit A361 at rdbt signed South Molton, 1.5m to centre

Retaining many of its original features, this charming 17th-century hotel is situated in the centre of town. Providing comfortable accommodation, complemented by informal and friendly service, this hotel is an ideal base for touring the area. Regularly changing menus, featuring local produce, are offered in both the restaurant and the bar, which also serves real ales.

Rooms 10 (1 fmly) ⌁ **Facilities** FTV WiFi ♬ **Conf** Class 30 Board 30 Thtr 100 **Parking** 12 **Notes** ⊛ RS 1st wk Jan

S

SOUTH NORMANTON	Map 16 SK45
Derbyshire	

The Derbyshire Hotel

★★★★ 74% HOTEL

tel: 01773 812000 **Carter Lane East DE55 2EH**
email: reservations.derbyshire@principal-hayley.com **web:** www.principal-hayley.com
dir: M1 junct 28, E on A38 to Mansfield

Conveniently located by the motorway, this hotel offers comfortable accommodation and a relaxed informal atmosphere through the lounge bar and restaurant. The conference and meeting rooms are appointed to a smart modern standard; delegates also have use of on-site sauna, jacuzzi and steam room in the spa.

Rooms 157 (10 fmly) (61 GF) **S** £69-£149; **D** £69-£149* **Facilities** Spa STV WiFi ⌘ 🕹 Gym Steam room Sauna New Year **Conf** Class 120 Board 25 Thtr 250 Del from £118.80 to £169* **Parking** 220 **Notes** LB ⊗ Civ Wed 150

Premier Inn Mansfield

BUDGET HOTEL

tel: 0871 527 8758 **Carter Lane East DE55 2EH**
web: www.premierinn.com
dir: M1 junct 28, A38 signed Mansfield. Entrance 200yds on left

High quality, budget accommodation ideal for both families and business travellers. Spacious, en suite bedrooms feature tea and coffee making facilities, and Freeview TV in most hotels. Internet access and WiFi are available for a small fee. The adjacent family restaurant features a wide and varied menu. See also the Hotel Groups pages.

Rooms 82

SOUTHPORT	Map 15 SD31
Merseyside	

Vincent Hotel

★★★★ 80% 🏵🏵 TOWN HOUSE HOTEL

tel: 01704 883800 **98 Lord St PR8 1JR**
email: manager@thevincenthotel.com **web:** www.thevincenthotel.com
dir: M58 junct 3, follow signs to Ormskirk & Southport

This stylish, boutique property occupies a prime location on Southport's famous boulevard. Bedrooms, some with views of the beach, are appointed to a high standard with oversized beds, extremely well stocked mini-bars and stylish en suites with deep tubs. Public areas include a trendy cocktail bar, and an all-day dining concept. The friendly staff offer a professional and personalised service.

Rooms 59 (2 fmly) 🐾 **D** £93-£695* **Facilities** Spa STV FTV WiFi ⌘ Gym **Conf** Class 96 Board 50 Thtr 196 Del from £130* **Services** Lift Air con **Parking** 50 **Notes** ⊗ Civ Wed 150

BEST WESTERN Royal Clifton Hotel & Spa

★★★ 75% HOTEL

tel: 01704 533771 **Promenade PR8 1RB**
email: sales@royalclifton.co.uk **web:** www.royalclifton.co.uk
dir: Adjacent to Marine Lake

This grand, traditional hotel benefits from a prime location on the promenade. Bedrooms range in size and style, but all are comfortable and thoughtfully equipped. Public areas include the lively Bar C, the elegant Pavilion Restaurant and

a modern, well-equipped leisure club. Extensive conference and banqueting facilities make this hotel a popular function venue.

Rooms 120 (23 fmly) (6 GF) **Facilities** Spa STV WiFi ⌘ 🕹 supervised Gym Hair & beauty Sauna Steam room Aromatherapy 🎵 Xmas New Year **Conf** Class 100 Board 65 Thtr 250 **Services** Lift **Parking** 60 **Notes** ⊗ Civ Wed 150

Balmoral Lodge Hotel

★★ 74% SMALL HOTEL

tel: 01704 544298 **41 Queens Rd PR9 9EX**
email: balmorallg@aol.com **web:** www.balmorallodge.co.uk
dir: On edge of town on A565 (Preston road). E at rdbt at North Lord St, left at lights, hotel 200yds on left

Situated in a quiet residential area, this popular friendly hotel is ideally situated just 50 yards from Lord Street. Bedrooms are comfortably appointed and family rooms are available. In addition to the restaurant which offers freshly prepared dishes, there is a choice of lounges including a comfortable lounge bar.

Rooms 15 (4 annexe) (3 fmly) (4 GF) **S** £25-£39; **D** £38-£90 (incl. bkfst)*
Facilities STV FTV WiFi ⌘ **Conf** Class 30 Board 30 Thtr 30 Del from £50 to £90*
Parking 12 **Notes** LB

Premier Inn Southport Central

BUDGET HOTEL

tel: 0871 527 9012 **Marine Dr PR8 1RY**
web: www.premierinn.com
dir: From Southport follow Promenade & Marine Drive signs. Hotel at junct of Marine Parade & Marine Drive

High quality, budget accommodation ideal for both families and business travellers. Spacious, en suite bedrooms feature tea and coffee making facilities, and Freeview TV in most hotels. Internet access and WiFi are available for a small fee. The adjacent family restaurant features a wide and varied menu. See also the Hotel Groups pages.

Rooms 59

SOUTHSEA

See Portsmouth & Southsea

SOUTH SHIELDS	Map 21 NZ36
Tyne & Wear	

BEST WESTERN The Sea Hotel

★★★ 75% HOTEL

tel: 0191 427 0999 **Sea Rd NE33 2LD**
email: info@seahotel.co.uk **web:** www.seahotel.co.uk
dir: A1(M), past Washington Services onto A194. Then A183 through town centre along Ocean Rd. Hotel on seafront

Dating from the 1930s, this long-established business hotel overlooks the boating lake and the Tyne estuary. Bedrooms are generally spacious and well equipped and include five annexe rooms with wheelchair access. A range of generously portioned meals is served in both the bar and restaurant.

Rooms 37 (5 annexe) (5 fmly) (5 GF) 🐾 **Facilities** FTV WiFi ⌘ New Year
Conf Class 100 Board 50 Thtr 200 Del from £89 to £109* **Parking** 70 **Notes** RS 26 Dec

Premier Inn South Shields (Port of Tyne)

BUDGET HOTEL

tel: 0871 527 8992 **Hobson Av, Newcastle Rd NE34 9PQ**
web: www.premierinn.com
dir: A1(M) onto A194(M). 2nd exit at rdbt into Leam Lane (A194). At next rdbt 2nd exit, next rdbt 3rd exit, next rdbt 2nd exit (A194), next rdbt 2nd exit. Hotel on left adjacent to Taybarns

High quality, budget accommodation ideal for both families and business travellers. Spacious, en suite bedrooms feature tea and coffee making facilities, and Freeview TV in most hotels. Internet access and WiFi are available for a small fee. The adjacent family restaurant features a wide and varied menu. See also the Hotel Groups pages.

Rooms 66

SOUTHWOLD	Map 13 TM57
Suffolk	

Swan Hotel

★★★★ 78% 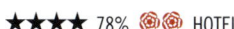 HOTEL

tel: 01502 722186 **Market Place IP18 6EG**
email: swan.hotel@adnams.co.uk **web:** www.adnams.co.uk
dir: A1095 to Southwold. Hotel in town centre. Parking via archway to left of building

The Swan Hotel is a charming 17th-century coaching inn situated in the heart of this bustling town centre overlooking the market place. Public rooms feature an elegant restaurant, a comfortable drawing room, a cosy bar and a lounge where guests can enjoy afternoon tea. The spacious bedrooms are attractively decorated, tastefully furnished and thoughtfully equipped.

Rooms 42 (17 annexe) (11 fmly) (17 GF) ☞ **Facilities** FTV WiFi HL Beauty treatment room Xmas New Year **Conf** Class 40 Board 30 Thtr 80 **Services** Lift **Parking** 42 **Notes** Civ Wed 60

The Blyth Hotel

★★ 85%  SMALL HOTEL

tel: 01502 722632 **Station Rd IP18 6AY**
email: reception@blythhotel.com **web:** www.blythhotel.com
dir: A12 onto A1095 signed Southwold

Expect a warm welcome at this delightful family run hotel which is situated just a short walk from the town centre. The spacious public rooms include a smart residents' lounge, an open-plan bar and a large restaurant. Bedrooms are tastefully appointed with co-ordinated fabrics and have many thoughtful touches.

Rooms 13 ☞ **Facilities** FTV WiFi Xmas New Year **Conf** Class 20 Board 12 Thtr 20 **Parking** 8

Sutherland House

 RESTAURANT WITH ROOMS

tel: 01502 724544 **56 High St IP18 6DN**
email: enquiries@sutherlandhouse.co.uk **web:** www.sutherlandhouse.co.uk
dir: A1095 into Southwold, on High St on left after Victoria St

Situated in the heart of the bustling town centre, this delightful 16th-century house has a wealth of character - oak beams, exposed brickwork, open fireplaces and two superb ornate plasterwork ceilings. The stylish bedrooms are tastefully decorated using co-ordinated fabrics and include many thoughtful touches. Public rooms feature a large open-plan contemporary restaurant with plush furniture. There's a modern British menu created with care, and the food miles are listed alongside each dish.

Rooms 4 (1 fmly)

SPALDING	Map 12 TF22
Lincolnshire	

Woodlands Hotel

★★★ 73% SMALL HOTEL

tel: 01775 769933 **80 Pinchbeck Rd PE11 1QF**
email: reservations@woodlandshotelspalding.com
web: www.woodlandshotelspalding.com
dir: 10mins walk from City Centre

A delightful Victorian house ideally situated just a short walk from the town centre. The public areas have many original features; they include the Oakleaf dining room, the Silver Birch meeting room and the Willows bar. The smartly decorated bedrooms have lovely co-ordinated soft furnishings and many thoughtful touches.

Rooms 17 (5 GF) **S** £65-£75; **D** £75-£95 (incl. bkfst)* **Facilities** FTV WiFi ⌁ HL **Conf** Class 30 Board 30 Thtr 60 **Parking** 30 **Notes** ⊗ Civ Wed 65

SPENNYMOOR	Map 19 NZ23
County Durham	

BEST WESTERN Whitworth Hall Hotel

★★★ 79% HOTEL

tel: 01388 811772 **Whitworth Hall Country Park DL16 7QX**
email: enquiries@whitworthhall.co.uk **web:** www.whitworthhall.co.uk
dir: A688 to Spennymoor, then Bishop Auckland. At rdbt right to Middlestone Moor. Left at lights, hotel on right

This hotel, peacefully situated in its own grounds in the centre of the deer park, offers comfortable accommodation. Spacious bedrooms, some with excellent views, offer stylish and elegant decor. Public areas include a choice of restaurants and bars, a bright conservatory and well-equipped function and conference rooms.

Rooms 29 (17 GF) **S** £65-£105; **D** £65-£105* **Facilities** FTV WiFi ⌁ Fishing **Conf** Class 40 Board 30 Thtr 100 Del from £120 to £140* **Parking** 100 **Notes** LB ⊗ Civ Wed 120

S

STAFFORD
Staffordshire
Map 10 SJ92

The Moat House

★★★★ 82% HOTEL

tel: 01785 712217 **Lower Penkridge Rd, Acton Trussell ST17 ORJ**
email: info@moathouse.co.uk **web:** www.moathouse.co.uk
dir: M6 junct 13 onto A449 through Acton Trussell. Hotel on right on exiting village

This 17th-century timbered building, with an idyllic canal-side setting, has been skilfully extended. Bedrooms are stylishly furnished, well equipped and comfortable. The bar offers a range of snacks and the restaurant boasts a popular fine dining option where the head chef displays his skills using top quality produce.

Rooms 41 (4 fmly) (15 GF) **Facilities** WiFi New Year **Conf** Class 60 Board 50 Thtr 200 **Services** Lift **Parking** 200 **Notes** ⊗ Closed 25 Dec Civ Wed 150

Tillington Hall Hotel

★★★ 75% HOTEL

tel: 01785 253531 **Eccleshall Rd ST16 1JJ**
email: reservations@tillingtonhall.co.uk **web:** www.tillingtonhall.co.uk
dir: M6 junct 14, A5013 towards Stafford. Hotel 0.5m on left

Located close to the M6, this modern hotel is ideal for both business and leisure guests. There is a spacious restaurant, relaxing coffee lounge and smart bar, alongside a range of function rooms for meetings and events, including the new Garden Suite. Complimentary WiFi access is available.

Rooms 91 (4 fmly) (25 GF) ⌁ **Facilities** FTV WiFi HL Xmas New Year **Conf** Class 150 Board 75 Thtr 300 **Services** Lift **Parking** 200 **Notes** ⊗ Civ Wed 300

Premier Inn Stafford North (Hurricane)

BUDGET HOTEL

tel: 0871 527 9030 **1 Hurrican Close ST16 1GZ**
web: www.premierinn.com
dir: M6 junct 14, A34 towards Stafford. Hotel approx 2m NW of town centre

High quality, budget accommodation ideal for both families and business travellers. Spacious, en suite bedrooms feature tea and coffee making facilities, and Freeview TV in most hotels. Internet access and WiFi are available for a small fee. The adjacent family restaurant features a wide and varied menu. See also the Hotel Groups pages.

Rooms 96

Premier Inn Stafford North (Spitfire)

BUDGET HOTEL

tel: 0871 527 9032 **1 Spitfire Close ST16 1GX**
web: www.premierinn.com
dir: M6 junct 14, A34 N. Hotel approx 1m on left

Rooms 60

STAINES-UPON-THAMES
Surrey
Map 6 TQ07

Mercure London Staines Thames Lodge

★★★ 78% HOTEL

tel: 01784 464433 **Thames St TW18 4SJ**
email: h6620@accor.com **web:** www.mercure.com
dir: M25 junct 13. Follow A30/town centre signs (bus station on right). Hotel straight ahead

Located on the banks of the River Thames in a bustling town, this hotel is well positioned for both business and leisure travellers. Meals are served in the Riverside Restaurant, and snacks are available in the spacious lounge/bar; weather permitting the terrace provides a good place for a drink on a summer evening. On-site parking is an additional bonus.

Rooms 88 (17 fmly) (31 GF) **Facilities** STV FTV WiFi Moorings Xmas New Year **Conf** Class 40 Board 20 Thtr 40 **Parking** 40

STAMFORD
Lincolnshire
Map 11 TF00

The William Cecil

★★★★ 81% HOTEL

tel: 01780 750070 **High St, St Martins PE9 2LJ**
email: enquiries@thewilliamcecil.co.uk **web:** www.thewilliamcecil.co.uk
dir: Exit A1 signed Stamford & Burghley Park. Hotel 1st building on right on entering town

This lovely refurbished property is situated on the edge of town within the Burghley Estate. The stylish bedrooms are spacious, individually decorated and have lots of extra little touches. The public rooms include a lounge bar with plush seating and a panelled restaurant. A smart terrace is available for alfresco dining when the weather permits.

Rooms 27 (2 fmly) (5 GF) ⌁ **S** £75-£180; **D** £85-£190 (incl. bkfst) **Facilities** FTV WiFi ⌁ Xmas New Year **Conf** Class 60 Board 40 Thtr 120 Del from £150 to £190* **Parking** 60 **Notes** Civ Wed 120

The George of Stamford

★★★★ 79% HOTEL

tel: 01780 750750 & 750700 (res) **71 St Martins PE9 2LB**
email: reservations@georgehotelofstamford.com **web:** www.georgehotelofstamford.com
dir: A1, 15m N of Peterborough onto B1081, hotel 1m on left

Steeped in hundreds of years of history, this delightful coaching inn provides spacious public areas that include a choice of dining options, inviting lounges, a business centre and a range of quality shops. A highlight is afternoon tea, taken in the colourful courtyard when the weather permits. Bedrooms are stylishly appointed and range from traditional to contemporary in design.

Rooms 47 **S** £95–£115; **D** £165–£290 (incl. bkfst)* **Facilities** STV WiFi ↻ ⟊ Complimentary membership to local gym Xmas New Year **Conf** Class 25 Board 25 Thtr 50 Del from £150 to £180* **Parking** 110 **Notes** LB Civ Wed 50

Crown Hotel

★★★ 82% HOTEL

tel: 01780 763136 **All Saints Place PE9 2AG**
email: reservations@thecrownhotelstamford.co.uk
web: www.thecrownhotelstamford.co.uk
dir: A1 onto A43, through town to Red Lion Sq, hotel behind All Saints Church

This small, privately owned hotel where hospitality is spontaneous and sincere, is ideally situated in the town centre. Unpretentious British food is served in the modern dining areas and the spacious bar is popular with locals. Bedrooms are appointed to a very high standard being quite contemporary in style and very well equipped; some have four-poster beds. Additional 'superior' rooms are located in a renovated Georgian town house just a short walk up the street.

Rooms 28 (10 annexe) (1 fmly) (1 GF) ↻ **S** £80–£115; **D** £80–£165 (incl. bkfst)* **Facilities** FTV WiFi ↻ Use of local health/gym club Xmas New Year **Conf** Class 12 Board 12 Thtr 20 Del from £140 to £160* **Parking** 21 **Notes** LB ⊗

Candlesticks

RESTAURANT WITH ROOMS

tel: 01780 764033 📄 01780 756071 **1 Church Ln PE9 2JU**
email: info@candlestickshotel.co.uk **web:** www.candlestickshotel.co.uk
dir: B1081 into Stamford. Left onto A43. Right into Worthorpe Rd, right into Church Ln

Candlesticks is a 17th-century property situated in a quiet lane in the oldest part of Stamford just a short walk from the centre of town. The bedrooms are pleasantly decorated and equipped with a good range of useful extras. Public rooms feature Candlesticks restaurant and a cosy bar.

Rooms 8

STANDISH	Map 15 SD51
Greater Manchester	

Premier Inn Wigan North

BUDGET HOTEL

tel: 0871 527 9166 **Almond Brook Rd WN6 0SS**
web: www.premierinn.com
dir: M6 junct 27 follow signs for Standish. Left at T-junct, then 1st right

High quality, budget accommodation ideal for both families and business travellers. Spacious, en suite bedrooms feature tea and coffee making facilities, and Freeview TV in most hotels. Internet access and WiFi are available for a small fee. The adjacent family restaurant features a wide and varied menu. See also the Hotel Groups pages.

Rooms 36

STANLEY	Map 19 NZ15
County Durham	

BEST WESTERN Beamish Hall Hotel

★★★★ 72% COUNTRY HOUSE HOTEL

tel: 01207 233733 **Beamish DH9 0YB**
email: info@beamish-hall.co.uk **web:** www.beamish-hall.co.uk
dir: A693 to Stanley. Follow signs for hotel & Beamish Museum. Left at museum entrance. Hotel on left 0.2m after golf club

This hotel is set in 24 acres of impeccably maintained grounds and can trace its history back many centuries. The public areas are elegant, with leather suites and wooden floors, and the beautifully decorated dining room has a real feeling of grandeur, with high ceilings and wonderful views of the gardens. All the bedrooms are stylishly designed and well equipped, and include larger rooms that have jacuzzi baths and separate showers; some of the premier rooms are interconnecting, and there is also a two bedroom apartment with its own kitchen and family room.

Rooms 42 (18 fmly) (4 GF) **Facilities** STV FTV WiFi ↻ Xmas New Year **Conf** Class 160 Board 160 Thtr 300 Del from £110 to £165* **Services** Lift **Parking** 300 **Notes** ⊗ Civ Wed 200

STANSTED AIRPORT	Map 6 TL52
Essex	

See also **Birchanger Green Motorway Service Area (M11)**

Premier Inn Stansted Airport

BUDGET HOTEL

tel: 0871 527 9352 **Thremhall Av, Stansted Airport CM24 1PY**
web: www.premierinn.com
dir: M11 junct 8/8a, follow signs Stanstead Airport Terminal. Main rdbt 3rd exit follow signs mid-stay car park. Adjacent BP Petrol Station

High quality, budget accommodation ideal for both families and business travellers. Spacious, en suite bedrooms feature tea and coffee making facilities, and Freeview TV in most hotels. Internet access and WiFi are available for a small fee. The adjacent family restaurant features a wide and varied menu. See also the Hotel Groups pages.

Rooms 303 (22 fmly)

STANSTED MOUNTFITCHET	Map 12 TL52
Essex	

Linden House

 RESTAURANT WITH ROOMS

tel: 01279 813003 **1-3 Silver St CM24 8HA**
email: stay@lindenhousestansted.co.uk **web:** www.lindenhousestansted.co.uk
dir: M11 junct 8 towards Newport on A120, on right after windmill

Linden House enjoys a prominent position in the heart of Stansted and is a short drive from the airport. This fine property has individually designed bedrooms, which are all beautifully presented and very luxurious. The cosy bar is ideal for pre-dinner drinks with a good choice of local ales and an extensive wine list. The award-winning restaurant serves great food, service is attentive and there is a lovely atmosphere in the evenings. Visitors arriving late should note that on Sunday the restaurant takes its last order at 6pm. Freshly cooked breakfasts are not to be missed. Free WiFi is available throughout the property and parking is available nearby.

Rooms 9

S

STEEPLE ASTON
Oxfordshire

Map 11 SP42

The Holt Hotel

★★★ 75% HOTEL

tel: 01869 340259 **Oxford Rd OX25 5QQ**
email: info@holthotel.co.uk **web:** www.holthotel.co.uk
dir: At junct of B4030 & A4260

This attractive former coaching inn has given hospitality to many over the centuries, not least to Claude Duval, a notorious 17th-century highwayman. Today guests are offered well-equipped, modern bedrooms and attractive public areas, which include a relaxing bar, restaurant and a well-appointed lounge. A selection of meeting rooms is available.

Rooms 86 (19 fmly) (20 GF) (8 smoking) **S** £59-£84; **D** £74-£109 (incl. bkfst)* **Facilities** FTV WiFi Xmas New Year **Conf** Class 57 Board 32 Thtr 140 Del from £120 to £140* **Parking** 200 **Notes** Civ Wed 120

STEVENAGE
Hertfordshire

Map 12 TL22

Holiday Inn Stevenage

★★★★ 75% HOTEL

tel: 01438 722727 & 346060 **St George's Way SG1 1HS**
email: reservations@histevenage.com **web:** www.histevenage.com
dir: A1(M) junct 7 take A602 to Stevenage, across 1st rdbt, 1st exit at 2nd rdbt, 2nd exit at next rdbt along St George's Way. Hotel 100yds on right

Situated in the heart of the town centre and just 25 minutes from central London by train. Bedrooms are air conditioned and well equipped; ideal for business and leisure travellers. Public areas are smart, capacious and stylish, and as well as a comfortable bar and restaurant, there is a mini gym. Parking is limited.

Rooms 140 (12 fmly) **S** fr £39; **D** fr £39* **Facilities** STV FTV WiFi HL Gym Xmas New Year **Conf** Class 200 Board 200 Thtr 400 Del from £115 to £175 **Services** Lift Air con **Parking** 23 **Notes** Civ Wed 400

Novotel Stevenage

★★★ 79% HOTEL

tel: 01438 346100 **Knebworth Park SG1 2AX**
email: H0992@accor.com **web:** www.novotel.com
dir: A1(M) junct 7, at entrance to Knebworth Park

Ideally situated just off the A1(M) is this purpose built hotel, which is a popular business and conference venue. Bedrooms are pleasantly decorated and equipped with a good range of useful extras. Public rooms include a large open plan lounge bar serving a range of snacks, and a smartly appointed restaurant.

Rooms 101 (20 fmly) (30 GF) **Facilities** STV WiFi Use of local health club New Year **Conf** Class 80 Board 70 Thtr 150 **Services** Lift **Parking** 120 **Notes** Civ Wed 120

BEST WESTERN Roebuck Inn

★★★ 73% HOTEL

tel: 01438 365445 & 365653 **London Rd, Broadwater SG2 8DS**
email: book@roebuckinn.com **web:** www.roebuckinn.com
dir: A1(M) junct 7, right towards Stevenage. At 2nd rdbt take 2nd exit signed Roebuck-London/Knebworth/B197. Hotel in 1.5m

Suitable for both the business and leisure traveller, this hotel provides spacious contemporary accommodation in well-equipped bedrooms. The older part of the building, where there is a restaurant and a cosy public bar with log fire and real ales, dates back to the 15th century.

Rooms 26 (8 fmly) (13 GF) **Facilities** STV FTV WiFi Xmas New Year **Conf** Class 20 Board 30 Thtr 50 Del from £125 to £145* **Parking** 50 **Notes** ⊗

Ibis Stevenage Centre

BUDGET HOTEL

tel: 01438 779955 **Danestrete SG1 1EJ**
email: H2794@accor.com **web:** www.ibishotel.com
dir: In town centre adjacent to Tesco & Westgate multi storey car park

Modern, budget hotel offering comfortable accommodation in bright and practical bedrooms. Breakfast is self-service and dinner is available in the restaurant. See also the Hotel Groups pages.

Rooms 98

Premier Inn Stevenage Central

BUDGET HOTEL

tel: 0871 527 9034 **Six Hills Way, Horizon Technology Park SG1 2DD**
web: www.premierinn.com
dir: A1(M) junct 7, follow Stevenage signs. Left into Gunnels Wood Rd. (NB do not use underpass). Left at next rdbt. Hotel in Horizon Technology Park on left

High quality, budget accommodation ideal for both families and business travellers. Spacious, en suite bedrooms feature tea and coffee making facilities, and Freeview TV in most hotels. Internet access and WiFi are available for a small fee. The adjacent family restaurant features a wide and varied menu. See also the Hotel Groups pages.

Rooms 115

Premier Inn Stevenage North

BUDGET HOTEL

tel: 0871 527 9036 **Corey's Mill Ln SG1 4AA**
web: www.premierinn.com
dir: A1(M) junct 8, at intersection with A602 - Hitchin Rd & Corey's Mill Lane

Rooms 41

STEYNING
West Sussex

Map 6 TQ11

BEST WESTERN Old Tollgate Hotel & Restaurant

★★★ 78% HOTEL

tel: 01903 879494 **The Street, Bramber BN44 3WE**
email: info@oldtollgatehotel.com web: www.oldtollgatehotel.com
dir: From A283 at Steyning rdbt to Bramber. Hotel 200yds on right

As its name suggests, this well-presented hotel is built on the site of the old toll house. The spacious bedrooms are smartly designed and are furnished to a high standard; eight rooms are air conditioned and have smart power showers. Open for both lunch and dinner, the popular carvery-style restaurant offers an extensive choice of dishes.

Rooms 38 (28 annexe) (5 fmly) (14 GF) ↟ **S** £64-£168; **D** £64-£168 (incl. bkfst)*
Facilities STV WiFi ⇗ HL New Year **Conf** Class 32 Board 24 Thtr 50 Del £144*
Services Lift **Parking** 60 **Notes** LB ⊗ Civ Wed 70

STILTON
Cambridgeshire

Map 12 TL18

Bell Inn Hotel

★★★ 81% ❀ HOTEL

tel: 01733 241066 **Great North Rd PE7 3RA**
email: reception@thebellstilton.co.uk web: www.thebellstilton.co.uk
dir: A1(M) junct 16, follow Stilton signs. Hotel in village centre

This delightful inn is steeped in history and retains many original features, with imaginative food served in both the character village bar/brasserie and the elegant beamed first floor restaurant; refreshments can be enjoyed in the attractive courtyard and rear gardens when weather permits. Individually designed bedrooms are stylish and equipped to a high standard.

Rooms 22 (3 annexe) (1 fmly) (3 GF) ↟ **S** £80-£120; **D** £108-£140 (incl. bkfst)*
Facilities STV FTV WiFi **Conf** Class 46 Board 50 Thtr 130 Del from £125 to £143*
Parking 30 **Notes** LB ⊗ Closed 25 Dec (pm) RS 26 Dec (pm) & 1 Jan (pm) Civ Wed 130

STOCK
Essex

Map 6 TQ69

Greenwoods Hotel & Spa

★★★★ 78% HOTEL

tel: 01277 829990 & 829205 **Stock Rd CM4 9BE**
email: info@greenwoodshotel.co.uk web: www.greenwoodshotel.co.uk
dir: A12 junct 16 take B1007 signed Billericay. Hotel on right on entering village

Greenwoods is a beautiful 17th-century, Grade II listed manor house set in extensive landscaped gardens. All bedrooms are tastefully appointed, with marble bathrooms and a wide range of extras; the premier rooms have spa baths and antique beds. The spa facilities are impressive offering the latest beauty treatments, together with saunas, a jacuzzi, steam rooms, a monsoon shower and a 20-metre pool.

Rooms 39 (6 GF) ↟ **Facilities** Spa STV FTV WiFi ⇗ 🏊 Gym Steam room Sauna Monsoon shower New Year **Conf** Class 70 Board 52 Thtr 110 **Services** Lift **Parking** 100 **Notes** ⊗ No children 16yrs Closed 26 Dec & 1 Jan Civ Wed 110

STOCKBRIDGE
Hampshire

Map 5 SU33

The Greyhound on the Test

◉◉ ❀ RESTAURANT WITH ROOMS

tel: 01264 810833 **31 High St SO20 6EY**
email: info@thegreyhoundonthetest.co.uk web: www.thegreyhoundonthetest.co.uk
dir: 9m NW of Winchester, 8m S of Andover. Off A303

This charming restaurant with rooms has the River Test at its rear and serves great food. In addition, the luxury bedrooms are generally spacious, beautifully styled and come with a host of extras. Bathrooms are modern and come with high quality towels and toiletries. There is also ample parking and well kept grounds.

Rooms 7

S

STOCKPORT
Greater Manchester

Map 16 SJ89

See also **Manchester Airport**

Bredbury Hall Hotel & Country Club

★★★ 78% HOTEL

tel: 0161 430 7421 **Goyt Valley, Bredbury SK6 2DH**
email: reservations@bredburyhallhotel.com web: www.bredburyhallhotel.com
dir: M60 junct 25 signed Bredbury, right at lights, left onto Osbourne St, hotel 500mtrs on right

With views over open countryside, this large, modern hotel is conveniently located for the M60. The well-equipped bedrooms are spacious and comfortable, and the restaurant serves a very wide range of freshly prepared dishes. Additional facilities include a fitness suite, complimentary WiFi and conference rooms accommodating up to 200 delegates.

Rooms 148 (2 fmly) (50 GF) ⚲ **S** £69-£199; **D** £69-£199* **Facilities** STV FTV WiFi ⊳ Fishing Gym Night club (Fri & Sat eve) ♫ Xmas New Year **Conf** Class 120 Board 60 Thtr 200 Del from £120 to £125* **Services** Lift **Parking** 450 **Notes** ⊗ Civ Wed 80

Alma Lodge Hotel

★★★ 74% HOTEL

tel: 0161 483 4431 **149 Buxton Rd SK2 6EL**
email: reception@almalodgehotel.com web: www.almalodgehotel.com
dir: M60 junct 1 at rdbt take 2nd exit under rail viaduct at lights opposite. At Debenhams turn right onto A6. Hotel approx 1.5m on left

A large hotel located on the main road close to the town, offering modern and well-equipped bedrooms. It is family-owned and run and serves a good range of quality Italian cooking in Luigi's restaurant. Good function rooms and free internet access are also available.

Rooms 52 (32 annexe) (2 fmly) **S** £45-£55; **D** £62-£69 (incl. bkfst)* **Facilities** FTV WiFi **Conf** Class 100 Board 60 Thtr 250 **Parking** 120 **Notes** ⊗ RS BHs Civ Wed 200

The Wycliffe Hotel

★★★ 74% HOTEL

tel: 0161 477 5395 **74 Edgeley Rd, Edgeley SK3 9NQ**
email: reception@wycliffe-hotel.com web: www.wycliffe-hotel.com
dir: M60 junct 2, follow A560 Stockport signs, right at 1st lights, hotel 0.5m on left

The Wycliffe is a family-run hotel close to the town centre and convenient for Manchester airport. The contemporary bedrooms are very well maintained and well-equipped, with LCD TVs and data ports provided. There is a well-stocked bar and a popular restaurant where the menu has an Italian bias. There is also a large car park.

Rooms 14 (3 fmly) (2 GF) **S** £65.50-£67.50; **D** £77.95 (incl. bkfst)* **Facilities** FTV WiFi **Conf** Class 20 Board 20 Thtr 30 Del £99* **Parking** 46 **Notes** ⊗ Closed 25-27 Dec RS BHs

Premier Inn Manchester Airport Heald Green

BUDGET HOTEL

tel: 0871 527 8734 **Finney Ln, Heald Green SK8 3QH**
web: www.premierinn.com
dir: M56 junct 5 follow signs to Terminal 1, at rdbt take 2nd exit, at next rdbt follow Cheadle signs. Left at lights, right at next lights

High quality, budget accommodation ideal for both families and business travellers. Spacious, en suite bedrooms feature tea and coffee making facilities, and Freeview TV in most hotels. Internet access and WiFi are available for a small fee. The adjacent family restaurant features a wide and varied menu. See also the Hotel Groups pages.

Rooms 66

Premier Inn Stockport Central

BUDGET HOTEL

tel: 0871 527 9040 **Churchgate SK1 1YG**
web: www.premierinn.com
dir: M60 junct 27, A626 towards Marple. Right at Spring Gardens

Rooms 46

Premier Inn Stockport South

BUDGET HOTEL

tel: 0871 527 9042 **Buxton Rd, Heaviley SK2 6NB**
web: www.premierinn.com
dir: On A6, 1.5m from town centre

Rooms 40

STOCKTON-ON-TEES
County Durham

Map 19 NZ41

BEST WESTERN Parkmore Hotel & Leisure Club

★★★ 80% HOTEL

tel: 01642 786815 **636 Yarm Rd, Eaglescliffe TS16 0DH**
email: enquiries@parkmorehotel.co.uk web: www.parkmorehotel.co.uk
dir: Exit A19 at Crathorne, A67 to Yarm. Through Yarm right onto A135 to Stockton. Hotel 1m on left

Set in its own gardens, this smart hotel has grown from its Victorian house origins to provide stylish public areas, as well as extensive leisure and beauty facilities including a hydrotherapy pool. There are also conference facilities. The well-equipped bedrooms include junior suites. The restaurant known as J's@636 has a reputation for creative meals, and service is friendly and obliging.

Rooms 55 (8 fmly) (9 GF) **Facilities** Spa FTV WiFi ⊳ ⊗ supervised Gym Dance studio Hydrotherapy Sauna Steam room Xmas New Year **Conf** Class 40 Board 40 Thtr 100 **Parking** 90 **Notes** Civ Wed 90

S

Premier Inn Stockton-on-Tees/Hartlepool

BUDGET HOTEL

tel: 0871 527 9044 **Coal Ln, Wolviston TS22 5PZ**
web: www.premierinn.com
dir: A1(M) junct 60, A689, follow Teeside then Hartlepool signs. Hotel on left at A89 & A19 junct

High quality, budget accommodation ideal for both families and business travellers. Spacious, en suite bedrooms feature tea and coffee making facilities, and Freeview TV in most hotels. Internet access and WiFi are available for a small fee. The adjacent family restaurant features a wide and varied menu. See also the Hotel Groups pages.

Rooms 49

Premier Inn Stockton-on-Tees/Middlesbrough

BUDGET HOTEL

tel: 0871 527 9048 **Whitewater Way, Thornaby TS17 6QB**
web: www.premierinn.com
dir: A19, A66 towards Stockton & Darlington. Take 1st exit signed Teeside Park/Teesdale. Right at lights over viaduct bridge rdbt & Tees Barrage

Rooms 62

Premier Inn Stockton-on-Tees West

BUDGET HOTEL

tel: 0871 527 9046 **Yarm Rd TS18 3RT**
web: www.premierinn.com
dir: A1(M) junct 60, A689 towards Teeside. Follow Hartlepool signs. Hotel on left at A689 & A19 interchange

Rooms 40

STOKE-BY-NAYLAND
Suffolk
Map 13 TL93

The Crown

★★★ 87% SMALL HOTEL

tel: 01206 262001 & 262346 **CO6 4SE**
email: reservations@crowninn.net **web:** www.crowninn.net
dir: Follow Stoke-by-Nayland signs from A12 & A134. Hotel in village off B1068 towards Higham

Situated in a picturesque village, The Crown, with an award-winning restaurant, has a reputation for making everyone feel welcome. It offers quiet, individually decorated rooms that look out over the countryside. Ground floor rooms, including three with a terrace, are of a contemporary design while upstairs rooms are in a country-house style; each room has WiFi, DVDs and luxury toiletries.

Rooms 11 (1 fmly) (8 GF) ♨ **S** £95–£150; **D** £130–£245 (incl. bkfst)* **Facilities** FTV WiFi ♨ New Year **Conf** Board 10 Del from £162 to £174* **Parking** 49 **Notes** LB ⊗

STOKE D'ABERNON
Surrey
Map 6 TQ15

Woodlands Park Hotel

★★★★ 81% HOTEL

tel: 01372 843933 & 0845 072 7581 **Woodlands Ln KT11 3QB**
email: woodlandspark@handpicked.co.uk
web: www.handpickedhotels.co.uk/woodlandspark
dir: A3 exit at Cobham. Through town centre & Stoke D'Abernon, left at garden centre into Woodlands Lane, hotel 0.5m on right

Originally built for the Bryant family, of the matchmaking firm Bryant & May, this lovely Victorian mansion enjoys an attractive parkland setting in ten and a half acres of Surrey countryside. Bedrooms in the wing are contemporary in style while those in the main house are more traditionally decorated. The hotel boasts two dining options, Benson's Brasserie and the Oak Room Restaurant.

Rooms 57 (4 fmly) ♨ **D** £135–£329 (incl. bkfst)* **Facilities** FTV WiFi ♨ HL ⛳ Xmas New Year **Conf** Class 20 Board 50 Thtr 150 **Services** Lift Air con **Parking** 150 **Notes** LB ⊗ Civ Wed 200

STOKE-ON-TRENT
Staffordshire
Map 10 SJ84

BEST WESTERN PLUS Stoke-on-Trent Moat House

★★★★ 73% HOTEL

tel: 01782 609988 **Etruria Hall, Festival Way, Festival Park ST1 5BQ**
email: reservations.stoke@qmh-hotels.com **web:** www.bw-stokeontrentmoathouse.co.uk
dir: M6 junct 15 (or junct 16), A500, follow A53 & Festival Park signs. Keep in left lane, take 1st slip road on left. Left at island, hotel opposite at next island

This large, modern hotel is located in Stoke's Festival Park, which adjoins Etruria Hall, the former home of Josiah Wedgwood. Bedrooms are spacious and well equipped, and include family rooms, suites and executive rooms. Public areas include a spacious lounge bar and restaurant as well as a business centre, extensive conference facilities and a leisure club.

Rooms 147 **S** £45–£169; **D** £45–£169 (incl. bkfst)* **Facilities** Spa FTV WiFi ♨ supervised Gym **Conf** Class 400 Board 40 Thtr 650 Del from £89 to £169* **Services** Lift Air con **Parking** 250 **Notes** LB ⊗ Civ Wed 400

Premier Inn Stoke-on-Trent (Hanley)

BUDGET HOTEL

tel: 0871 527 9476 **Etruria Rd, Hanley ST1 5NH**
web: www.premierinn.com
dir: M6 junct 15, A500. 4.3m, take 5th slip road for A53 (City Centre, Hanley). At rdbt take 4th exit signed Etruria & A53. Keep in left lane until passing flyover entrance. At rdbt take 3rd exit, hotel on right

High quality, budget accommodation ideal for both families and business travellers. Spacious, en suite bedrooms feature tea and coffee making facilities, and Freeview TV in most hotels. Internet access and WiFi are available for a small fee. The adjacent family restaurant features a wide and varied menu. See also the Hotel Groups pages.

Rooms 96

S

STOKE-ON-TRENT *continued*

Premier Inn Stoke (Trentham Gardens)

BUDGET HOTEL

tel: 9871 527 9050 **Stone Rd, Trentham ST4 8JG**
web: www.premierinn.com
dir: M6 junct 15, A500, follow Trentham signs. At rdbt 3rd exit onto A34, 2m to hotel on right in Trentham Gardens

Rooms 119

Weathervane

BUDGET HOTEL

tel: 01782 388799 **Lysander Rd ST3 7WA**
email: 5305@greenking.co.uk **web:** www.oldenglish.co.uk

A few minutes from the A50 and convenient for both the city and industrial areas, this popular, modern pub and restaurant, under the 'Hungry Horse' brand, provides hearty, well-cooked food at reasonable prices. Adjacent bedrooms are furnished for both commercial and leisure customers. See also the Hotel Groups pages.

Rooms 39 (8 fmly) (18 GF) **Conf** Class 20 Board 20 Thtr 20

STOKE POGES	**Map 6 SU98**
Buckinghamshire	

INSPECTORS' CHOICE

Stoke Park

★★★★★ ◉◉◉ HOTEL

tel: 01753 717171 **Park Rd SL2 4PG**
email: info@stokepark.com **web:** www.stokepark.com
dir: M4 junct 6, A355 towards Slough, B416 (Park Rd). Hotel 1.25m on right

Located within 300 acres of beautiful parkland created by 'Capability' Brown and Humphry Repton, this hotel offers outstanding leisure and sporting facilities. Inside the stunning mansion house, designed by George III's architect, the public areas display lavish opulence throughout and the bedrooms have a luxurious and classic feel. In contrast, the Pavilion features more contemporary bedrooms and public areas; as well as extensive state-of-the-art health and beauty facilities. The hotel has a championship golf course, tennis courts, and three restaurants, including the award-winning Humphry's and the more informal Italian brasserie, San Marco. There are bars, lounges and meeting rooms as well.

Rooms 49 (28 annexe) (6 fmly) **D** £290-£1500* **Facilities** Spa STV FTV WiFi ⓘ ⓘ ⓘ 27 ⓘ Putt green Fishing ⓘ Gym Indoor golf swing studio Creche Games room Playground Hot yoga studio New Year Child facilities **Conf** Class 30 Board 34 Thtr 80 Del from £299* **Services** Lift **Parking** 460 **Notes** ⓧ Closed 24-26 Dec Civ Wed 120

Stoke Place

★★★★ 76% ◉◉◉ HOTEL

tel: 01753 534790 **Stoke Green SL2 4HT**
email: enquiries@stokeplace.co.uk **web:** www.stokeplace.co.uk
dir: A355, right at 1st lights to A4 Bath Rd. At 1st rdbt take 2nd exit onto Stoke Rd. B416 to Stoke Green. Hotel 200mtrs on right

Originally built in 1690 and set in 26 acres of 'Capability' Brown designed gardens, this is a delightful William and Mary style manor house. It offers a range of stylish modern bedrooms that are equipped to a very high standard; rear-facing rooms have fantastic view of the garden. Guests can relax in the peaceful lounge and enjoy afternoon tea if they wish. The award-winning Garden Restaurant serves imaginative dishes and the tranquil bar area is ideal for post-dinner drinks.

Rooms 39 (15 annexe) (14 GF) ⓘ **S** £120-£200; **D** £130-£210 (incl. bkfst)*
Facilities STV FTV WiFi ⓘ Fishing ⓘ Gym Outdoor jogging track Bicycles Boule pitch Giant kids games Xmas New Year **Conf** Class 100 Board 60 Thtr 200 Del from £220 to £280* **Parking** 120 **Notes** LB Civ Wed 150

STON EASTON	**Map 4 ST65**
Somerset	

INSPECTORS' CHOICE

Ston Easton Park Hotel

★★★★ ◉◉ COUNTRY HOUSE HOTEL

tel: 01761 241631 **BA3 4DF**
email: reception@stoneaston.co.uk **web:** www.stoneaston.co.uk
dir: On A37

Surrounded by The Mendips, this outstanding Palladian mansion lies in extensive parklands that were landscaped by Humphrey Repton. The architecture and decorative features are stunning. The state rooms include one of England's earliest surviving Print Rooms, and the Palladian Saloon is considered one of Somerset's finest rooms. There is even an Edwardian kitchen that guests might like to take a look at. The helpful and attentive team provide a very efficient service, and the award-winning cuisine uses organic produce from the hotel's own kitchen garden. The bedrooms and bathrooms are all appointed to an excellent standard.

Rooms 22 (3 annexe) (2 fmly) ⓘ **S** £130-£300; **D** £226-£406 (incl. bkfst)*
Facilities FTV WiFi ⓘ ⓘ Fishing ⓘ Archery Clay pigeon shooting Quad bikes Hot air ballooning Xmas New Year **Conf** Class 60 Board 30 Thtr 100 Del from £180 to £250* **Parking** 120 **Notes** LB Civ Wed 120

STOURPORT-ON-SEVERN
Worcestershire

Map 10 SO87

Menzies Hotels Birmingham / Stourport Manor

MenziesHotels

★★★★ 77% HOTEL

tel: 01299 289955 **35 Hartlebury Rd DY13 9JA**
email: stourport@menzieshotels.co.uk **web:** www.menzieshotels.co.uk
dir: M5 junct 6, A449 towards Kidderminster, B4193 towards Stourport. Hotel on right

Once the home of Prime Minister Sir Stanley Baldwin, this much extended country house is set in attractive grounds. A number of bedrooms and suites are located in the original building, although the majority are in a more modern, purpose-built section. Spacious public areas include a range of lounges, a popular restaurant, a leisure club and conference facilities.

Rooms 68 (17 fmly) (31 GF) ☏ **S** £49-£119; **D** £49-£119 **Facilities** FTV WiFi ⇄ 🎾 ♨ Putt green Gym Squash Xmas New Year **Conf** Class 110 Board 100 Thtr 400 Del from £99 to £155 **Parking** 300 **Notes** LB Civ Wed 300

STOWMARKET
Suffolk

Map 13 TM05

Cedars Hotel

THE INDEPENDENTS
HOTEL ASSOCIATION

★★★ 75% HOTEL

tel: 01449 612668 **Needham Rd IP14 2AJ**
email: info@cedarshotel.co.uk **web:** www.cedarshotel.co.uk
dir: A14 junct 50, A1120 towards Stowmarket. At junct with A1113 turn right. Hotel on right

Expect a friendly welcome at this privately owned hotel, which is situated just off the A14 within easy reach of the town centre. Public rooms are full of charm and character with features such as exposed beams and open fireplaces. Bedrooms are pleasantly decorated and thoughtfully equipped with modern facilities.

Rooms 25 (3 fmly) (9 GF) ☏ **Facilities** WiFi **Conf** Class 60 Board 40 Thtr 150 **Parking** 75 **Notes** Closed 25 Dec-1 Jan

STOW-ON-THE-WOLD
Gloucestershire

Map 10 SP12

Number Four at Stow Hotel & Restaurant

★★★★ 77% ⊛⊛ SMALL HOTEL

tel: 01451 830297 **Fosseway GL54 1JX**
email: reservations@hotelnumberfour.co.uk **web:** www.hotelnumberfour.co.uk
dir: A424 - Burford to Stow Road

This hotel is situated in one of the most picturesque areas of the Cotswolds. Service is relaxed and friendly, and the bedrooms are very stylish and beautifully presented. The award-winning Cutler's Restaurant serves imaginative dishes using the finest in local produce. Public areas include a contemporary lounge area and a well-equipped business suite.

Rooms 18 (5 fmly) (12 GF) **S** £100-£140; **D** £120-£160 (incl. bkfst)* **Facilities** FTV WiFi **Conf** Class 15 Board 28 Thtr 50 Del from £180 to £220* **Services** Air con **Parking** 50 **Notes** ⊗ Closed 23-29 Dec

Wyck Hill House Hotel & Spa

"bespoke"

★★★★ 76% ⊛⊛ HOTEL

tel: 01451 831936 **Burford Rd GL54 1HY**
email: info@wyckhillhousehotel.co.uk **web:** www.wyckhillhousehotel.co.uk
dir: Exit A429. Hotel 1m on right

This charming 18th-century house enjoys superb views across the Windrush Valley and is ideally positioned for a relaxing weekend exploring the Cotswolds. The spacious and thoughtfully equipped bedrooms provide high standards of comfort and quality, located both in the main house and also the original coach house. Elegant public rooms include a cosy bar, library and the magnificent front hall with crackling log fire. The imaginative cuisine makes extensive use of local produce.

Rooms 60 (22 annexe) (4 GF) ☏ **Facilities** Spa FTV WiFi Sauna Steam room Xmas New Year **Conf** Class 50 Board 50 Thtr 150 **Services** Lift **Parking** 100 **Notes** ⊗ Civ Wed 120

Stow Lodge Hotel

★★★ 77% SMALL HOTEL

tel: 01451 830485 **The Square GL54 1AB**
email: enquiries@stowlodge.co.uk **web:** www.stowlodge.co.uk
dir: In town centre

Situated in smart grounds, this family-run hotel has direct access to the market square and provides high standards of customer care. Bedrooms are offered both within the main building and in the converted coach house, all of which provide similar standards of homely comfort. Extensive menus and an interesting wine list make for an enjoyable dining experience.

Rooms 21 (10 annexe) (1 fmly) ☏ **S** £70-£140; **D** £91-£160 (incl. bkfst) **Facilities** WiFi **Parking** 30 **Notes** LB ⊗ No children 5yrs Closed Xmas-end Jan

STRATFORD-UPON-AVON
Warwickshire

Map 10 SP25

INSPECTORS' CHOICE

Ettington Park Hotel

HandPICKED
HOTELS
BUILT FOR PLEASURE

★★★★ ⊛⊛ COUNTRY HOUSE HOTEL

tel: 01789 450123 & 0845 072 7454 **CV37 8BU**
email: ettingtonpark@handpicked.co.uk
web: www.handpickedhotels.co.uk/ettingtonpark

(For full entry see Alderminster)

Symbols and abbreviations are explained on page 7

S

STRATFORD-UPON-AVON *continued*

Menzies Welcombe Hotel Spa & Golf Club

★★★★ 85% HOTEL

tel: 01789 295252 **Warwick Rd CV37 0NR**
email: welcombe@menzieshotels.co.uk **web:** www.menzieshotels.co.uk
dir: M40 junct 15, A46 towards Stratford-upon-Avon, at rdbt follow signs for A439. Hotel 3m on right

This Jacobean manor house is set in 157 acres of landscaped parkland. Public rooms are impressive, especially the lounge with its wood panelling and ornate marble fireplace, and the gentleman's club-style bar. Bedrooms in the original building are stylish and gracefully proportioned; those in the garden wing are comfortable and thoughtfully equipped. The spa development incorporates advanced, luxurious facilities and treatments.

Rooms 85 (12 fmly) (11 GF) **S** £103-£215; **D** £103-£215* **Facilities** Spa STV FTV WiFi 18 Putt green Gym Xmas New Year **Conf** Class 65 Board 40 Thtr 200 Del from £149 to £230* **Parking** 200 **Notes** LB Civ Wed 120

Macdonald Alveston Manor

MACDONALD HOTELS & RESORTS

★★★★ 81% HOTEL

tel: 0844 879 9138 **Clopton Bridge CV37 7HP**
email: sales.alvestonmanor@macdonald-hotels.co.uk **web:** www.macdonaldhotels.co.uk
dir: On rdbt, S of Clopton Bridge

A striking red-brick and timbered façade, well-tended grounds, and a giant cedar tree all contribute to the charm of this well-established hotel, just five minutes from Stratford. The bedrooms vary in size and character, and the coach house conversion offers an impressive mix of full and junior suites. The superb leisure complex offers a 20-metre swimming pool, steam room, sauna, a high-tech gym and a host of beauty treatments.

Rooms 113 (8 fmly) (45 GF) **Facilities** Spa FTV WiFi supervised Gym Technogym Beauty treatments Sauna Steam room Xmas New Year **Conf** Class 80 Board 40 Thtr 140 **Services** Air con **Parking** 150 **Notes** Civ Wed 110

The Arden Hotel

EDEN HOTEL COLLECTION

★★★★ 80% HOTEL

tel: 01789 298682 **Waterside CV37 6BA**
email: enquiries@theardenhotelstratford.com **web:** www.theardenhotelstratford.com
dir: M40 junct 15 follow signs to town centre. At Barclays Bank rdbt left onto High St, 2nd left onto Chapel Lane (Nash's House on left). Hotel car park on right in 40yds

This property is on the same road as the world famous Royal Shakespeare and Swan theatres, and just a short walk from the town centre. The bedrooms and bathrooms have been tastefully designed and have quality fixtures and fittings. The dedicated team provide polite and professional service. Award-winning cuisine is served in the popular restaurant. Ample secure parking is available. Eden Hotel Collection is the AA Small Hotel Group of the Year 2014-15.

Rooms 45 (6 fmly) (17 GF) **S** £122.50-£252.50; **D** £145-£405 (incl. bkfst)* **Facilities** FTV WiFi Xmas New Year **Conf** Class 18 Board 28 Thtr 50 Del from £165 to £195* **Services** Air con **Parking** 50 **Notes** LB Civ Wed 90

The Stratford

★★★★ 80% HOTEL

tel: 01789 271000 & 271007 **Arden St CV37 6QQ**
email: thestratfordreservations@qhotels.co.uk **web:** www.qhotels.co.uk
dir: A439 into Stratford. In town follow A3400/Birmingham, at lights left into Arden St, hotel 150yds on right

Situated adjacent to the hospital, this eye-catching modern hotel with its red-brick façade is within walking distance of the town centre. The hotel offers modern, well-equipped and spacious bedrooms. The open-plan public areas include a comfortable lounge, a small, atmospheric bar and a spacious restaurant with exposed beams. QHotels is the AA Hotel Group of the Year 2014-15.

Rooms 102 (7 fmly) (14 GF) **Facilities** STV WiFi Gym Free use of Stratford Manor's leisure facilities Xmas New Year **Conf** Class 66 Board 54 Thtr 132 **Services** Lift Air con **Parking** 92 **Notes** Civ Wed 132

Billesley Manor Hotel

★★★★ 79% HOTEL

tel: 01789 279955 **Billesley, Alcester B49 6NF**
email: billesleymanor@pumahotels.co.uk **web:** www.pumahotels.co.uk
dir: A46 towards Evesham. Over 3 rdbts, right for Billesley after 2m

This 16th-century manor is set in peaceful grounds and parkland with a delightful yew topiary garden and fountain. The spacious bedrooms and suites, most in traditional country-house style, are thoughtfully designed and well equipped. Conference facilities and some of the bedrooms are found in the cedar barns. Public areas retain many original features, such as oak panelling, fireplaces and exposed stone.

Rooms 72 (29 annexe) (5 GF) **Facilities** Spa WiFi supervised Gym Steam room Beauty treatments Yoga studio Xmas New Year **Conf** Class 60 Board 50 Thtr 100 Del from £135 to £189* **Parking** 100 **Notes** Civ Wed 75

Holiday Inn Stratford-upon-Avon

★★★★ 77% HOTEL

tel: 0871 942 9270 & 01789 279988 **Bridgefoot CV37 6YR**
email: histratford@qmh-hotels.com **web:** www.holidayinn.co.uk
dir: A439 to Stratford-upon-Avon. On entering town bear left, hotel 200mtrs on left

This large modern hotel sits beside the River Avon in landscaped grounds and has ample parking. Bedrooms have a light contemporary feel and are equipped with a good range of facilities that include air conditioning and WiFi. Day rooms include a terrace lounge and bar, a carvery restaurant and the Club Moativation health and fitness facility that is popular with both corporate and leisure guests.

Rooms 259 (8 fmly) **Facilities** STV WiFi supervised Gym Sauna Steam room Solarium Beauty Salon Xmas New Year **Conf** Class 340 Board 42 Thtr 550 **Services** Lift Air con **Parking** 350 **Notes**

Macdonald Swan's Nest Hotel

★★★★ 77% HOTEL

tel: 0844 879 9140 **Bridgefoot CV37 7LT**
email: sales.swansnest@macdonald-hotels.co.uk
web: www.macdonald-hotels.co.uk/swansnest
dir: A439 towards Stratford, follow one-way system, left over bridge (A3400), hotel on right

Dating back to the 17th century, this hotel is said to be one of the earliest brick-built houses in Stratford. It occupies a prime position on the banks of the River

Avon and is ideally situated for exploring the town. Bedrooms and bathrooms are appointed to a high standard with some thoughtful guest extras provided.

Rooms 68 (2 fmly) (25 GF) 🐾 **Facilities** FTV WiFi ⬡ Use of facilities at Macdonald Alveston Manor New Year **Conf** Class 70 Board 56 Thtr 150 **Parking** 80 **Notes** Civ Wed 150

Stratford Manor

★★★★ 77% HOTEL

tel: 01789 731173 **Warwick Rd CV37 OPY**
email: stratfordmanor@qhotels.co.uk **web:** www.qhotels.co.uk
dir: M40 junct 15, A46 signed Stratford. At 2nd rdbt take A439 signed Stratford Town Centre. Hotel 1m on left. Or from Stratford centre take A439 signed Warwick & M40. Hotel 3m on right

Just outside Stratford, this hotel is set against a rural backdrop with lovely gardens and ample parking. Public areas include a stylish lounge bar and a contemporary restaurant. Service is both professional and helpful. Bedrooms are smartly appointed, spacious and have generously sized beds and a range of useful facilities. The leisure centre boasts a large indoor pool. QHotels is the AA Hotel Group of the Year 2014-15.

Rooms 104 (8 fmly) (24 GF) 🐾 **Facilities** Spa WiFi ⬡ HL 🐾 ♨ Gym Sauna Steam room Xmas New Year **Conf** Class 120 Board 100 Thtr 350 **Services** Lift **Parking** 220 **Notes** Civ Wed 150

The Legacy Falcon Hotel

★★★★ 74% 🏵 HOTEL

tel: 08444 119005 & 0330 333 2805 **Chapel St CV37 6HA**
email: res-falcon@legacy-hotels.co.uk **web:** www.legacy-hotels.co.uk
dir: M40 junct 15, A46, A349, A3400 towards Stratford. Into one-way system into right lane marked Town Centre. At rdbt (Barclays Bank facing) left into High St. 2nd right into Scholars Lane

Situated in the heart of the town just a short walk from all the Shakespeare properties, this hotel dates back to 1500. In the 17th century an extra storey was added. Bedrooms provide contemporary accommodation and the public areas are cosy. Service is provided by a friendly team. The restaurant provides good quality cuisine using fresh, local ingredients.

Rooms 83 (11 annexe) (6 fmly) (3 GF) 🐾 **S** £79-£155; **D** £79-£155* **Facilities** STV WiFi ⬡ Xmas New Year **Conf** Class 80 Board 50 Thtr 150 Del from £139 to £185* **Services** Lift **Parking** 120 **Notes** LB Civ Wed 150

Mercure Stratford-upon-Avon Shakespeare Hotel

★★★★ 73% 🏵 HOTEL

tel: 01789 294997 **Chapel St CV37 6ER**
email: h6630@accor.com **web:** www.mercure.com
dir: M40 junct 15. Follow signs for Stratford town centre on A439. Follow one-way system into Bridge St. Left at rdbt, hotel 200yds on left opposite HSBC bank

Dating back to the early 17th century, The Shakespeare is one of the oldest hotels in this historic town. The hotel name represents one of the earliest exploitations of Stratford as the birthplace of one of the world's leading playwrights. With exposed beams and open fires, the public rooms retain an ambience reminiscent of this era. Bedrooms are appointed to a good standard and remain in keeping with the style of the property.

Rooms 78 (11 annexe) (3 GF) 🐾 **Facilities** WiFi Xmas New Year **Conf** Class 45 Board 40 Thtr 90 **Services** Lift **Parking** 31 **Notes** Civ Wed 100

BEST WESTERN Grosvenor Hotel

★★★ 77% HOTEL

tel: 01789 269213 & 414030 **Warwick Rd CV37 6YT**
email: res@bwgh.co.uk **web:** www.bwgh.co.uk
dir: M40 junct 15, follow Stratford signs to A439 (Warwick Rd). Hotel 7m, on one-way system

This hotel is a short distance from the town centre and many historic attractions. Bedroom styles and sizes vary, and the friendly staff offer an efficient service. Refreshments are served in the lounge all day, and room service is available. The Garden Room restaurant offers a choice of dishes from set price and carte menus.

Rooms 73 (16 fmly) (25 GF) **S** £65-£145; **D** £65-£145* **Facilities** STV FTV WiFi ⬡ Xmas New Year **Conf** Class 45 Board 50 Thtr 100 Del from £125 to £145* **Parking** 46 **Notes** LB ⊗ Civ Wed 100

Premier Inn Stratford-upon-Avon Central

BUDGET HOTEL

tel: 0871 527 9282 **Payton Rd CV37 6UQ**
web: www.premierinn.com
dir: A439, A4300 signed Stratford-upon-Avon. Hotel on left

High quality, budget accommodation ideal for both families and business travellers. Spacious, en suite bedrooms feature tea and coffee making facilities, and Freeview TV in most hotels. Internet access and WiFi are available for a small fee. The adjacent family restaurant features a wide and varied menu. See also the Hotel Groups pages.

Rooms 87

Premier Inn Stratford-upon-Avon Waterways

BUDGET HOTEL

tel: 0871 527 9316 **The Waterways, Birmingham Rd CV37 0AZ**
web: www.premierinn.com
dir: A3400 (Birmingham Rd) towards town centre, pass large retail park on left. Straight over mini rdbt, approx 150yds. Hotel on right

Rooms 130

STREET
Somerset   Map 4 ST43

Wessex Hotel

★★★ 67% HOTEL

tel: 01458 443383 **High St BA16 0EF**
email: info@wessexhotel.com **web:** www.wessexhotel.com
dir: From A303, onto B3151 to Somerton. Then 7m, pass lights by Millfield School. Left at mini-rdbt

The Wessex Hotel is centrally located in this popular town, with easy access to all the shops and attractions. The bedrooms and bathrooms vary slightly in size but most rooms provide good levels of quality and comfort. A wide range of snacks and refreshments is available throughout the day, including a regular carvery at dinner. Entertainment is often offered in the main season.

Rooms 51 (9 fmly) **Facilities** FTV WiFi 🎵 Xmas New Year **Conf** Class 120 Board 80 Thtr 400 **Services** Lift **Parking** 70 **Notes** ⊗

S

The Bear of Rodborough

★★★ 82% HOTEL

tel: 01453 878522 **Rodborough Common GL5 5DE**
email: info@bearofrodborough.info **web:** www.cotswold-inns-hotels.co.uk/bear
dir: M5 junct 13, A419 to Stroud. Follow signs to Rodborough. Up hill, left at top at
T-junct. Hotel on right

This popular 17th-century coaching inn is situated high above Stroud in acres of
National Trust parkland. Character abounds in the lounges and cocktail bar, and in
the Box Tree Restaurant where the cuisine utilises fresh local produce. Bedrooms
offer equal measures of comfort and style with plenty of extra touches. There is also
a traditional and well-patronised public bar.

Rooms 46 (2 fmly) **S** £85-£95; **D** £140-£150 (incl. bkfst)* **Facilities** FTV WiFi Xmas
New Year **Conf** Class 35 Board 30 Thtr 60 **Parking** 70 **Notes** LB Civ Wed 70

Burleigh Court Hotel

★★★ 81% 🌸 HOTEL

tel: 01453 883804 **Burleigh, Minchinhampton GL5 2PF**
email: burleighcourt@aol.com **web:** www.burleighcourthotel.co.uk
dir: From Stroud A419 towards Cirencester. Right after 2.5m signed Burleigh &
Minchinhampton. Left after 500yds signed Burleigh Court. Hotel 300yds on right

Dating back to the 18th century, this former gentleman's manor house is in a
secluded and elevated, though accessible, position with some wonderful
countryside views. Public rooms are elegantly styled and include an oak-panelled
bar for pre-dinner drinks beside a crackling fire. Combining comfort and quality, no
two bedrooms are alike; some are in an adjoining coach house.

Rooms 18 (7 annexe) (2 fmly) (3 GF) 🐾 **S** £100-£120; **D** £160-£220 (incl. bkfst)*
Facilities WiFi 🐾 🦢 New Year **Conf** Class 30 Board 30 Thtr 50 Del £180*
Parking 40 **Notes** LB Closed 24-26 Dec Civ Wed 50

Premier Inn Stroud

BUDGET HOTEL

tel: 0871 527 9052 **Stratford Lodge, Stratford Rd GL5 4AF**
web: www.premierinn.com
dir: M5 junct 13, A419 to town centre, follow Leisure Centre signs. Hotel adjacent to Tesco
superstore

High quality, budget accommodation ideal for both families and business
travellers. Spacious, en suite bedrooms feature tea and coffee making facilities,

and Freeview TV in most hotels. Internet access and WiFi are available for a small
fee. The adjacent family restaurant features a wide and varied menu. See also the
Hotel Groups pages.

Rooms 32

The Boars Head Hotel

★★★ 75% HOTEL

tel: 01283 820344 **Lichfield Rd DE6 5GX**
email: enquiries@boars-head-hotel.co.uk **web:** www.boars-head-hotel.co.uk
dir: A50 onto A515 towards Lichfield, hotel 1m on right

This popular hotel offers comfortable accommodation in well-equipped bedrooms.
There is a relaxed atmosphere in the public rooms, which consist of several bars
and dining options. The beamed lounge bar provides informal dining thanks to a
popular carvery, while the restaurant and cocktail bar offer a more formal
environment.

Rooms 23 (1 annexe) (14 GF) **S** £59.95-£69.95; **D** £69.95-£79.95 (incl. bkfst)*
Facilities STV WiFi Xmas New Year **Parking** 85 **Notes** LB

The Legacy Mill Hotel

U

tel: 0844 411 9496 & 0330 333 2996 **Walnut Tree Ln CO10 1BD**
email: info@themillhotelsudbury.co.uk **web:** www.legacy-hotels.co.uk
dir: A12 direction Harwich (from London) exit junct 27 onto A134, 2nd exit into A133, rdbt
1st exit onto A134, straight over 7 rdbts, 2nd exit onto Newton Road, A131, turn right

Currently the rating for this establishment is not confirmed. This may be due to a
change of ownership or because it has only recently joined the AA rating scheme.
For further details please see the AA website: theAA.com

Rooms 62 (10 annexe) (8 fmly) (12 GF) 🐾 **Facilities** FTV WiFi 🐾 Xmas New Year
Conf Class 56 Board 40 Thtr 80 Del from £115 to £150* **Parking** 45
Notes Civ Wed 80

The Case Restaurant with Rooms

🌸 RESTAURANT WITH ROOMS

tel: 01787 210483 📠 01787 211725 **Further St, Assington CO10 5LD**
email: restaurant@thecaserestaurantwithrooms.co.uk
web: www.thecaserestaurantwithrooms.co.uk
dir: Exit A12 at Colchester onto A134 to Sudbury. 7m, establishment on left

The Case Restaurant with Rooms offers dining in comfortable surroundings, along
with luxurious accommodation in bedrooms that all enjoy independent access.
Some bathrooms come complete with corner jacuzzi, while internet access comes as
standard. In the restaurant, local produce is used in all dishes, and bread and
delicious desserts are made fresh every day.

Rooms 7 (2 fmly)

Premier Inn Sunbury (Kempton Park)

BUDGET HOTEL PLAN 1 A1

tel: 0871 527 9054 **Staines Road West, Sunbury Cross TW16 7AT**
web: www.premierinn.com
dir: M25 junct 12, onto M3 signed London & Richmond. Exit at junct 1, take 1st exit at rdbt into Staines Road West (A308). 1st left into Crossways. Hotel on right

High quality, budget accommodation ideal for both families and business travellers. Spacious, en suite bedrooms feature tea and coffee making facilities, and Freeview TV in most hotels. Internet access and WiFi are available for a small fee. The adjacent family restaurant features a wide and varied menu. See also the Hotel Groups pages.

Rooms 109

Sunderland Marriott Hotel

★★★★ 75% HOTEL

tel: 0191 529 2041 **Queen's Pde, Seaburn SR6 8DB**
email: mhrs.nclsl.frontoffice@marriotthotels.com **web:** www.sunderlandmarriott.co.uk
dir: A19, A184 (Boldon/Sunderland North), 3m. At rdbt left, then right. At rdbt left, follow to coast. Turn right, hotel on right

Comfortable and spacious bedrooms, some with fabulous views of the North Sea and vast expanses of sandy beach, are provided at this seafront hotel. Public rooms are bright and modern and a number of meeting rooms are available. The hotel is conveniently located for access to the local visitor attractions.

Rooms 82 (6 fmly) ✆ **Facilities** STV WiFi ➷ HL 🏊 Gym Xmas New Year
Conf Class 120 Board 70 Thtr 300 Del from £134 to £160 **Services** Lift **Parking** 110
Notes ⊗ Civ Wed 160

BEST WESTERN Roker Hotel

★★★ 79% HOTEL

tel: 0191 567 1786 **Roker Ter, Roker SR6 9ND**
email: info@rokerhotel.co.uk **web:** www.tavistockleisure.com

This modern hotel offers stunning views of the coastline. Well-equipped bedrooms come in a variety of sizes, and several have feature bathrooms. Functions, conferences and weddings are all well catered for with a variety of rooms and spaces available including The Harbour Suite. The late-opening R Bar serves food all day and the hotel's restaurant, the Tavistock Retro Italia, offers a vibrant atmosphere.

Rooms 43 (8 fmly) (3 GF) ✆ **Facilities** STV FTV WiFi ➷ 🎵 Xmas New Year
Conf Class 150 Board 100 Thtr 300 **Services** Lift Air con **Parking** 150 **Notes** ⊗
Civ Wed 350

Premier Inn Sunderland A19/A1231

BUDGET HOTEL

tel: 0871 527 9058 **Wessington Way, Castletown SR5 3HR**
web: www.premierinn.com
dir: From A19 take A1231 towards Sunderland. Hotel 100yds

High quality, budget accommodation ideal for both families and business travellers. Spacious, en suite bedrooms feature tea and coffee making facilities, and Freeview TV in most hotels. Internet access and WiFi are available for a small fee. The adjacent family restaurant features a wide and varied menu. See also the Hotel Groups pages.

Rooms 61

Premier Inn Sunderland North West

BUDGET HOTEL

tel: 0871 527 9056 **Timber Beach Rd, off Wessington Way, Castletown
SR5 3XG**
web: www.premierinn.com
dir: A1(M) junct 65, A1231 towards Sunderland, cross over A19

Rooms 63

Holiday Inn London - Kingston South

★★★★ 76% HOTEL PLAN 1 C1

tel: 020 8786 6565 & 8786 6500 **Kingston Tower, Portsmouth Rd KT6 5QQ**
email: enquiries@hikingston.co.uk **web:** www.hikingston.co.uk
dir: M25 junct 10, A3, left onto A243, 3rd exit at rdbt. At lights left onto A307

This hotel occupies a convenient location overlooking the River Thames just outside Kingston-upon-Thames and close to Surbiton. Many front-facing bedrooms have beautiful river views; all are comfortable and stylish. The public areas include a small yet well-equipped fitness room. Complimentary parking and WiFi are also available.

Rooms 116 (2 fmly) ✆ **Facilities** STV FTV WiFi ➷ HL Gym **Conf** Class 125 Board 60
Thtr 250 **Services** Lift Air con **Parking** 120 **Notes** Civ Wed 300

S

Holiday Inn London - Sutton

★★★ 78% HOTEL

tel: 020 8234 1100 & 020 8234 1104 **Gibson Rd SM1 2RF**
email: sales-sutton@ihg.com **web:** www.hilondonsuttonhotel.co.uk
dir: M25 junct 8, A217, B2230. Pass rail station, follow one-way system in right lane. At lights, right then immediately left, left into Gibson Rd

Well located for many famous attractions such as Chessington World of Adventure, the All-England Tennis Club at Wimbledon and Epsom Racecourse, this hotel offers air-conditioned bedrooms ranging from standard to executive, a variety of conference rooms, and leisure facilities with a swimming pool.

Rooms 119 (4 fmly) **Facilities** Spa STV FTV WiFi ➷ HL 🏊 supervised Gym Xmas New
Year **Conf** Class 100 Board 70 Thtr 180 **Services** Lift Air con **Parking** 115 **Notes** ⊗
Civ Wed 160

SUTTON COLDFIELD West Midlands	Map 10 SP19

New Hall Hotel & Spa

★★★★ 82%  HOTEL

tel: 0845 072 7577 & 0121 378 2442 **Walmley Rd B76 1QX**
email: newhall@handpicked.co.uk **web:** www.handpickedhotels.co.uk/newhall
dir: M42 junct 9, A4097, 2m to rdbt, take 2nd exit signed Walmley. Take 2nd exit from next 5 rdbts follow Sutton Coldfield signs. At 6th rdbt take 3rd exit follow Sutton Coldfield signs. Hotel on left

Situated in 26 acres of beautiful grounds this hotel is reputed to be the oldest inhabited, moated house in the country. The house's medieval charm and character combine well with 21st-century guest facilities. Executive and luxury suites are available. Public areas, with their fine panelling and mullioned stained-glass windows include the magnificent Great Chamber.

Rooms 60 (14 fmly) (25 GF) ⚓ **S** £151; **D** £161 (incl. bkfst)* **Facilities** Spa STV FTV WiFi ⟳ supervised ⚃ 9 ⚑ Fishing ⚑ Gym Steam room Pitch & putt Xmas New Year **Conf** Class 75 Board 35 Thtr 150 Del £188* **Parking** 80 **Notes** LB ⊗ Civ Wed 75

BEST WESTERN PREMIER Moor Hall Hotel & Spa

★★★★ 80% ⚘ HOTEL

tel: 0121 308 3751 **Moor Hall Dr, Four Oaks B75 6LN**
email: mail@moorhallhotel.co.uk **web:** www.moorhallhotel.co.uk
dir: A38 onto A453 towards Sutton Coldfield, right at lights into Weeford Rd. Hotel 150yds on left

Although only a short distance from the city centre this hotel enjoys a peaceful setting, overlooking extensive grounds and an adjacent golf course. Bedrooms are well equipped and executive rooms are particularly spacious. Public rooms include the formal Oak Room Restaurant, and the informal Country Kitchen which offers a carvery and blackboard specials. The hotel also has a well-equipped spa with pool, sauna, steam room, jacuzzi and treatment rooms.

Rooms 82 (5 fmly) (33 GF) ⚓ **S** £45-£149; **D** £75-£169 (incl. bkfst) **Facilities** Spa FTV WiFi ⚑ HL ⟳ Gym Aerobics studio Sauna Steam room **Conf** Class 120 Board 45 Thtr 250 Del from £140 to £160 **Services** Lift **Parking** 170 **Notes** LB ⊗ Civ Wed 180

Ramada Birmingham, Sutton Coldfield

★★★ 73% HOTEL

tel: 0121 351 3111 **Penns Ln, Walmley B76 1LH**
email: enquiries@ramadasuttonhotel.co.uk **web:** www.ramadasuttonhotel.co.uk
dir: From S: M6 junct 5 A452, 3rd rdbt right into Eachelhurst Rd, left at lights into Penns Lane. From N/W: M6 junct 6, Sutton Coldfield A5127, follow signs, 2m on at lights (Macdonalds) 4th right into Penns Lane

This hotel offers comfortable bedrooms which are fully equipped with a range of thoughtful accessories. The public areas provide a leisure facility with a well-equipped gym, alongside a smart lounge bar and function rooms.

Rooms 170 (23 annexe) (26 fmly) (48 GF) ⚓ **Facilities** Spa STV FTV WiFi ⟳ Fishing Gym Squash Sauna Steam room Studio Hair salon New Year **Conf** Class 200 Board 80 Thtr 600 **Services** Lift **Parking** 500 **Notes** Civ Wed 200

Premier Inn Birmingham North (Sutton Coldfield)

BUDGET HOTEL

tel: 0871 527 8088 **Whitehouse Common Rd B75 6HD**
web: www.premierinn.com
dir: M42 junct 9, A446 towards Lichfield, then A453 to Sutton Coldfield. Left into Whitehouse Common Rd, hotel on left

High quality, budget accommodation ideal for both families and business travellers. Spacious, en suite bedrooms feature tea and coffee making facilities, and Freeview TV in most hotels. Internet access and WiFi are available for a small fee. The adjacent family restaurant features a wide and varied menu. See also the Hotel Groups pages.

Rooms 42

SUTTON SCOTNEY Hampshire	Map 5 SU43

Norton Park

★★★★ 79% HOTEL

tel: 0845 074 0055 & 01962 763000 **SO21 3NB**
email: nortonpark@qhotels.co.uk **web:** www.qhotels.co.uk
dir: From A303 & A34 junct follow signs to Sutton Scotney. Hotel on Micheldever Station Rd (old A30), 1m from Sutton Scotney

Set in 54 acres of beautiful parkland in the heart of Hampshire, Norton Park offers both business and leisure guests a great range of amenities. Dating from the 16th century, the hotel is complemented by extensive buildings housing the bedrooms, and public areas which include a superb leisure club and numerous conference facilities. Ample parking is available. QHotels is the AA Hotel Group of the Year 2014-15.

Rooms 175 (11 fmly) (80 GF) ⚓ **Facilities** Spa WiFi ⟳ supervised ⚑ Gym Steam room Sauna Experience shower Ice fountain Xmas New Year **Conf** Class 250 Board 80 Thtr 340 **Services** Lift **Parking** 220 **Notes** Civ Wed 340

SWAFFHAM Norfolk	Map 13 TF80

BEST WESTERN George Hotel

★★★ 73% HOTEL

tel: 01760 721238 **Station St PE37 7LJ**
email: georgehotel@bestwestern.co.uk **web:** www.georgehotelswaffham.co.uk
dir: From the S: M11 junct 9, merge onto A11, continue on A14 exit 38, join A11, at rdbt 2nd exit A1065. From the N: A1, A17, A47

Located in the centre of historic Swaffham and originally a 16th-century coaching inn, the hotel now offers a range of bedroom styles and sizes. Meals are served everyday in The Green Room restaurant or in the bar for a more informal dining experience. A suitable base for those exploring the North Norfolk Coast.

Rooms 28 (2 fmly) (8 GF) ⚓ **S** £50-£85; **D** £55-£95 (incl. bkfst)* **Facilities** FTV WiFi ⚑ **Conf** Class 60 Board 50 Thtr 160 Del from £85 to £135* **Parking** 60 **Notes** LB RS 24-26 Dec

S

SWANAGE Map 5 SZ07
Dorset

The Pines Hotel

★★★ 80% HOTEL

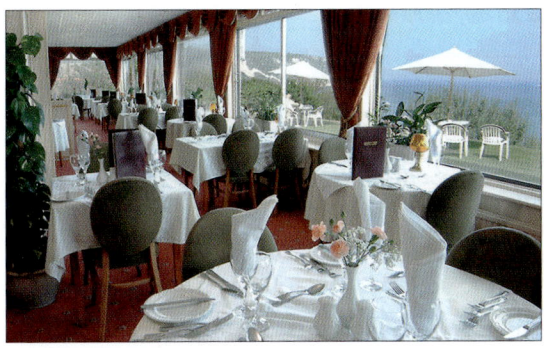

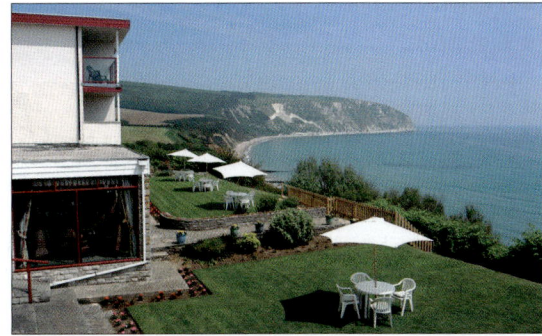

tel: 01929 425211 **Burlington Rd BH19 1LT**
email: reservations@pineshotel.co.uk **web:** www.pineshotel.co.uk
dir: A351 to seafront, left then 2nd right. Hotel at end of road

Enjoying a peaceful location with spectacular views over the cliffs and sea, The Pines is a pleasant place to stay. Many of the comfortable bedrooms have sea views. Guests can take tea in the lounge, enjoy appetising bar snacks in the attractive bar, and dine on interesting cuisine in the restaurant.

Rooms 41 (26 fmly) (6 GF) **S** £72; **D** £144-£194 (incl. bkfst)* **Facilities** FTV WiFi Xmas New Year **Conf** Class 80 Board 80 Thtr 80 Del from £87.80 to £112.80* **Services** Lift **Parking** 60 **Notes** LB

See advert below

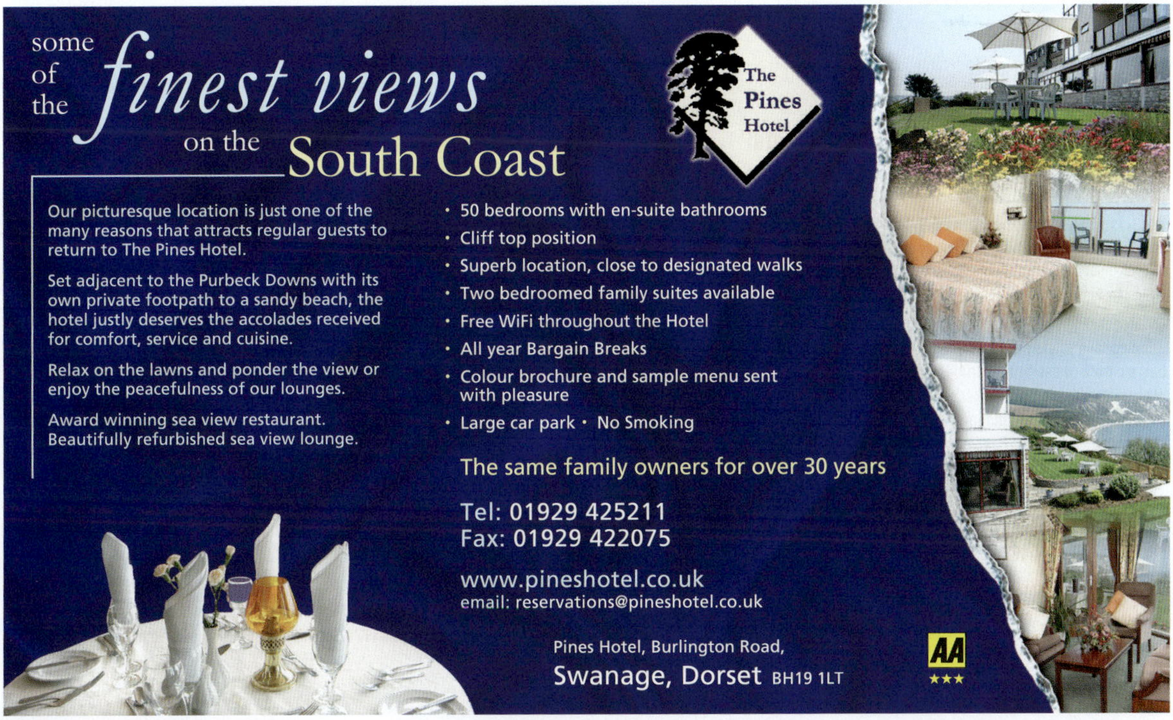

SWANAGE *continued*

Grand Hotel

★★★ 72% HOTEL

tel: 01929 423353 **Burlington Rd BH19 1LU**
email: reservations@grandhotelswanage.co.uk **web:** www.grandhotelswanage.co.uk

Dating back to 1898, this hotel is located on the Isle of Purbeck and has spectacular views across Swanage Bay and Peveril Point. Bedrooms are individually decorated and well equipped; public rooms offer a number of choices from relaxing lounges to extensive leisure facilities. The hotel also has its own private beach.

Rooms 30 (2 fmly) **S** fr £55; **D** fr £110 (incl. bkfst)* **Facilities** FTV WiFi supervised Gym Table tennis Beauty treatment room Sauna Solarium Xmas New Year **Conf** Class 40 Board 40 Thtr 120 Del from £79* **Services** Lift **Parking** 15 **Notes** LB ⊗

SWANLEY	Map 6 TQ56
Kent	

Premier Inn Swanley

BUDGET HOTEL

tel: 0871 527 9288 **London Rd BR8 7QD**
web: www.premierinn.com
dir: M25 junct 3, B2173 towards Swanley. At rdbt 2nd exit onto B258 (High St). At next rdbt 4th exit into Swanley Ln, 1st exit into Bartholomew Way, at next rdbt 3rd exit into London Rd

High quality, budget accommodation ideal for both families and business travellers. Spacious, en suite bedrooms feature tea and coffee making facilities, and Freeview TV in most hotels. Internet access and WiFi are available for a small fee. The adjacent family restaurant features a wide and varied menu. See also the Hotel Groups pages.

Rooms 61

SWINDON	Map 5 SU18
Wiltshire	

BEST WESTERN PLUS Blunsdon House Hotel

★★★★ 74% HOTEL

tel: 01793 721701 **Blunsdon SN26 7AS**
email: reservations@blunsdonhouse.co.uk **web:** www.blunsdonhouse.co.uk
dir: M4 junct 15, A419 towards Cirencester. Exit at Turnpike junct, right, follow brown hotel signs

Located just to the north of Swindon, Blunsdon House is set in 30 acres of well-kept grounds, and offers extensive leisure facilities and spacious day rooms. The hotel has a choice of eating and drinking options in three bars and two restaurants; the lively and informal Christopher's, and Nichols for fine dining. Bedrooms are comfortably furnished, and include family rooms with bunk beds and the contemporary spacious Pavilion rooms.

Rooms 108 (17 fmly) (27 GF) ⟑ **S** £71-£149; **D** £71-£149* **Facilities** Spa STV FTV WiFi ⟑ HL ⊗ ♪ 9 ⚲ Putt green Gym Squash Beauty therapy Woodland walk Xmas New Year Child facilities **Conf** Class 200 Board 55 Thtr 300 **Services** Lift **Parking** 300 **Notes** LB ⊗ Civ Wed 200

The Pear Tree at Purton

★★★ 81% ⚛⚛ HOTEL

tel: 01793 772100 **Church End SN5 4ED**
email: stay@peartreepurton.co.uk **web:** www.peartreepurton.co.uk

(For full entry see Purton)

Chiseldon House Hotel

★★★ 78% ⚛ HOTEL

tel: 01793 741010 **New Rd, Chiseldon SN4 ONE**
email: welcome@chiseldonhouse.com **web:** www.chiseldonhouse.com
dir: M4 junct 15, A346 signed Marlborough. In 0.5m right onto B4500, 0.25m, hotel on right

Conveniently located for access to the M4, Chiseldon House is in a quiet location and has a relaxed ambience. Bedrooms include a number of larger rooms but all are comfortably furnished. The award-winning restaurant offers a selection of carefully prepared dishes utilising high quality produce. Guests are welcome to enjoy the pleasant garden with outdoor seating.

Rooms 21 (4 fmly) ⟑ **Facilities** FTV WiFi ⟑ **Conf** Class 20 Board 32 Thtr 65 **Parking** 50 **Notes** ⊗ Civ Wed 85

Holiday Inn Swindon

★★★ 78% HOTEL

tel: 01793 817000 & 0871 942 9079 **Marlborough Rd SN3 6AQ**
email: swindon@ihg.com **web:** www.holidayinn.co.uk
dir: M4 junct 15, A419 towards Swindon. Take A4259 for 1m. Hotel on right opposite Sun Inn

With convenient access to both the M4 and Swindon's centre, this hotel provides an ideal base for business or leisure guests. Bedrooms are well decorated and have a good range of useful extras. Guests can enjoy the facilities of The Spirit Health and Fitness Club and then relax in the comfortable bar. A good selection of dishes is available whether by way of room service, lounge snacks or the welcoming, informal restaurant.

Rooms 99 (25 fmly) (48 GF) (4 smoking) **Facilities** STV FTV WiFi ⟑ HL ⊗ supervised Gym **Conf** Class 30 Board 30 Thtr 60 Del from £99 to £155* **Services** Air con **Parking** 120 **Notes** ⊗ Civ Wed 80

Stanton House Hotel

★★★ 78% HOTEL

tel: 0843 507 1388 **The Avenue, Stanton Fitzwarren SN6 7SD**
email: reception@stantonhouse.co.uk **web:** www.stantonhouse.co.uk
dir: A419 onto A361 towards Highworth, left towards Stanton Fitzwarren about 600yds, hotel on left

Extensive grounds and superb gardens surround this Cotswold-stone manor house: the park and Stanton Lake are accessible to guests and provide great walks. Smart, well-maintained bedrooms have been equipped with modern comforts. Public areas include a conservatory, a bar and two eating options - The Rosemary Restaurant offering a wide choice of Japanese and European dishes, and the Mt Fuji Restaurant specialising in authentic Japanese food in traditional surroundings. The friendly, multi-lingual staff create a relaxing atmosphere for their guests.

Rooms 78 (27 GF) ⟑ **Facilities** STV WiFi Xmas New Year **Conf** Class 70 Board 40 Thtr 110 Del from £104 to £112* **Services** Lift **Parking** 110 **Notes** ⊗ Civ Wed 110

S

Mercure Swindon South Marston Hotel & Spa

★★★ 74% HOTEL

tel: 01793 833700 **Old Vicarage Ln, South Marston SN3 4SH**
email: info@southmarstonhotel.com **web:** www.mercure.com
dir: M4 junct 15, A419 N to Cirencester. Exit 2nd junct signed A420 Oxford, left to South Marston. Hotel past pub on left

Located just outside Swindon, this hotel offers smart, modern, well-appointed bedrooms and spacious public areas. Leisure facilities include a spa with health and beauty treatments, a well-equipped gym and a 23-metre pool. The light and airy restaurant serves modern British cuisine. Free WiFi is available throughout.

Rooms 60 (7 fmly) (30 GF) **Facilities** Spa FTV WiFi ⓑ ⓢ Gym Squash Sauna Steam room Fitness studio Spinning room **Conf** Class 75 Board 60 Thtr 150 Del from £105 to £145* **Parking** 200 **Notes** ⊗ Civ Wed 120

Marsh Farm Hotel

★★★ 71% HOTEL

tel: 01793 842800 & 848044 **Coped Hall, Royal Wootton Bassett SN4 8ER**
email: info@marshfarmhotel.co.uk **web:** www.marshfarmhotel.co.uk
dir: M4 junct 16 onto A3102, straight on at 1st rdbt, right at 2nd rdbt. Hotel 200yds on left

The well decorated and comfortably furnished bedrooms at this hotel are situated in converted barns and extensions around the original farmhouse, which is set in its own grounds less than a mile from the M4. A relaxed and welcoming atmosphere prevails especially at dinner, when an extensive range of dishes to suit all tastes, is offered in the conservatory restaurant.

Rooms 50 (39 annexe) (1 fmly) (16 GF) ⓡ **S** £53–£73; **D** £63–£135 (incl. bkfst)*
Facilities FTV WiFi Beauty salon Use of nearby leisure centre New Year **Conf** Class 60 Board 50 Thtr 120 **Parking** 100 **Notes** ⊗ Closed 26-30 Dec RS 25 Dec Civ Wed 100

Campanile Swindon

BUDGET HOTEL

tel: 01793 514777 **Delta Business Park, Great Western Way SN5 7XG**
email: swindon@campanile.com **web:** www.campanile.com
dir: M4 junct 16, A3102 towards Swindon. After 2nd rdbt, 2nd exit onto Welton Rd (Delta Business Park), 1st left

This modern building offers accommodation in smart, well-equipped bedrooms, all with en suite bathrooms. Refreshments may be taken at the informal bistro. See also the Hotel Groups pages.

Rooms 120 (6 fmly) (22 GF) ⓡ **Conf** Class 40 Board 40 Thtr 70

Premier Inn Swindon Central

BUDGET HOTEL

tel: 0871 527 9064 **Kembrey Business Park, Kembrey St SN2 8YS**
web: www.premierinn.com
dir: M4 junct 15, A419 (Swindon bypass) towards Cirencester. In 6m at Turnpike Rdbt 1st left. Hotel on left in 2m

High quality, budget accommodation ideal for both families and business travellers. Spacious, en suite bedrooms feature tea and coffee making facilities, and Freeview TV in most hotels. Internet access and WiFi are available for a small fee. The adjacent family restaurant features a wide and varied menu. See also Hotel Groups pages.

Rooms 50

Premier Inn Swindon North

BUDGET HOTEL

tel: 0871 527 9066 **Broad Bush, Blunsdon SN26 8DJ**
web: www.premierinn.com
dir: N of Swindon. 5m from M4 junct 15. At junct of A419 & B4019

Rooms 62

Premier Inn Swindon West

BUDGET HOTEL

tel: 0871 527 9068 **Great Western Way SN5 8UY**
web: www.premierinn.com
dir: M4 junct 16, A3102 to Lydiard Fields. Past Hilton, entrance on left. (NB for Sat Nav use SN5 8UB)

Rooms 63

| TADWORTH | Map 6 TQ25 |
| Surrey | |

Premier Inn Epsom South

BUDGET HOTEL

tel: 0871 527 8382 **Brighton Rd, Burgh Heath KT20 6BW**
web: www.premierinn.com
dir: Just off M25 junct 8 on A217 towards Sutton

High quality, budget accommodation ideal for both families and business travellers. Spacious, en suite bedrooms feature tea and coffee making facilities, and Freeview TV in most hotels. Internet access and WiFi are available for a small fee. The adjacent family restaurant features a wide and varied menu. See also the Hotel Groups pages.

Rooms 76

| TAMWORTH | Map 10 SK20 |
| Staffordshire | |

Drayton Court Hotel

★★ 85% HOTEL

tel: 01827 285805 **65 Coleshill St, Fazeley B78 3RG**
email: draytoncthotel@yahoo.co.uk **web:** www.draytoncourthotel.co.uk
dir: M42 junct 9, A446 to Lichfield, at next rdbt right onto A4091. 2m, Drayton Manor Theme Park on left. Hotel on right

Conveniently located close to the M42, this lovingly restored hotel offers bedrooms that are elegant and have been thoughtfully equipped to suit both business and leisure guests. Beds are particularly comfortable, and one room has a four-poster. Public areas include a panelled bar, a relaxing lounge and an attractive restaurant.

Rooms 19 (3 fmly) **Facilities** WiFi ⓑ **Conf** Board 12 **Parking** 23 **Notes** ⊗ Closed 22 Dec-1 Jan

T

TAMWORTH *continued*

Premier Inn Tamworth Central

BUDGET HOTEL

tel: 0871 527 9070 **Bonehill Rd, Bitterscote B78 3HQ**
web: www.premierinn.com
dir: M42 junct 10, A5 towards Tamworth. Left in 3m onto A51 signed Tamworth. Straight on at 1st rdbt. At next rdbt 3rd exit. Hotel adjacent to Ladybridge Beefeater

High quality, budget accommodation ideal for both families and business travellers. Spacious, en suite bedrooms feature tea and coffee making facilities, and Freeview TV in most hotels. Internet access and WiFi are available for a small fee. The adjacent family restaurant features a wide and varied menu. See also the Hotel Groups pages.

Rooms 58

Premier Inn Tamworth South

BUDGET HOTEL

tel: 0871 527 9072 **Watling St, Wilnecote B77 5PN**
web: www.premierinn.com
dir: M42 junct 10, A5 towards Tamworth. Left in 200yds signed Wilnecote/B5404. Left at next rdbt, hotel on left

Rooms 58

| TANKERSLEY | Map 16 SK39 |
South Yorkshire

Tankersley Manor

★★★★ 77% HOTEL

tel: 01226 744700 **Church Ln S75 3DQ**
email: tankersleymanor@qhotels.co.uk **web:** www.qhotels.co.uk
dir: M1 junct 36, A61 (Sheffield Rd)

High on the moors with views over the countryside, this 17th-century residence is well located for major cities, tourist attractions and motorway links. Where appropriate, bedrooms retain original features such as exposed beams or Yorkshire-stone window sills. The hotel has a newly refurbished bar and brasserie which has old beams and open fires. A well-equipped leisure centre is also available. QHotels is the AA Hotel Group of the Year 2014-15.

Rooms 98 (10 fmly) (16 GF) ⚡ **S** £69-£109; **D** £85-£125 (incl. bkfst)* **Facilities** Spa STV FTV WiFi ↳ 🎣 Gym Swimming lessons Beauty treatments Xmas New Year **Conf** Class 200 Board 100 Thtr 400 Del from £119 to £149* **Services** Lift **Parking** 350 **Notes** Civ Wed 250

Premier Inn Sheffield/Barnsley M1 Jct 36

BUDGET HOTEL

tel: 0871 527 8968 **Maple Rd S75 3DL**
web: www.premierinn.com
dir: M1 junct 35A (N'bound exit only), A616 for 2m. From M1 junct 36, A61 towards Sheffield

High quality, budget accommodation ideal for both families and business travellers. Spacious, en suite bedrooms feature tea and coffee making facilities, and Freeview TV in most hotels. Internet access and WiFi are available for a small fee. The adjacent family restaurant features a wide and varied menu. See also the Hotel Groups pages.

Rooms 62

| TAPLOW | Map 6 SU98 |
Buckinghamshire

Cliveden

★★★★★ ◉◉◉ COUNTRY HOUSE HOTEL

tel: 01628 668561 **SL6 0JF**
email: info@clivedenhouse.co.uk **web:** www.clivedenhouse.co.uk
dir: M4 junct 7, A4 towards Maidenhead, 1.5m, onto B476 towards Taplow, 2.5m, hotel on left

This wonderful stately home stands at the top of a gravelled boulevard. Visitors are treated as house-guests and staff recapture the tradition of fine hospitality. Bedrooms have individual quality and style, and reception rooms retain a timeless elegance. Exceptional leisure facilities include cruises along Cliveden Reach and massages in the Pavilion. The Terrace Restaurant with its delightful views has been awarded two AA Rosettes.

Rooms 39 (1 annexe) (16 fmly) (10 GF) 🐾 **Facilities** Spa STV FTV WiFi 🕐 🏹 ⛵ 🦢 Gym Squash Full range of beauty treatments 3 vintage boats 🎵 Xmas New Year **Conf** Class 48 Board 40 Thtr 120 Del from £315 to £355* **Services** Lift **Parking** 60 **Notes** Civ Wed 150

Taplow House Hotel

★★★★ 74% HOTEL

tel: 01628 670056 **Berry Hill SL6 0DA**
email: reception@taplowhouse.com **web:** www.taplowhouse.com
dir: Exit A4 onto Berry Hill, hotel 0.5m on right

This elegant Georgian manor is set amid beautiful gardens and has been skilfully restored. Character public rooms are pleasing and include a number of air-conditioned conference rooms and an elegant restaurant. Comfortable bedrooms are individually decorated and furnished to a high standard.

Rooms 32 (4 fmly) (2 GF) 🐾 **S** £89-£209; **D** £109-£229 **Facilities** STV FTV WiFi 🦢 Complimentary use of private leisure facilities 1m from hotel Xmas New Year **Conf** Class 50 Board 50 Thtr 120 **Services** Air con **Parking** 100 **Notes** LB ⊗ Civ Wed 100

TARPORLEY	Map 15 SJ56
Cheshire	

Macdonald Portal Hotel Golf & Spa

★★★★ 79% ✿ HOTEL

MACDONALD
HOTELS & RESORTS

tel: 0844 879 9082 **Cobblers Cross Ln CW6 ODJ**
email: general.portal@macdonaldhotels.co.uk
web: www.macdonaldhotels.co.uk/theportal
dir: M6 junct 18, A54 towards Middlewich/Winsford. Left onto A49, through Cotebrook. In approx 1m follow signs for hotel

This hotel is located in beautiful rolling countryside and provides a luxury base for both the leisure and business guest. The spacious and well-equipped bedrooms have bathrooms with baths and power showers. Extensive leisure facilities include a superb spa, state-of-the-art fitness equipment, three golf courses and a golf academy. The Ranulf Restaurant delivers skilfully prepared, innovative cooking, as well as an excellent breakfast. Staff throughout are very friendly and nothing is too much trouble.

Rooms 85 (29 GF) ✿ **Facilities** Spa STV FTV WiFi ↘ HL ✪ ♨ 45 Putt green Gym Golf academy Outdoor pursuits New Year **Conf** Class 180 Board 60 Thtr 250 **Services** Lift **Parking** 250 **Notes** Civ Wed 250

TAUNTON	Map 4 ST22
Somerset	

Castle Hotel

★★★★ 77% ✿✿ HOTEL

tel: 01823 272671 **Castle Green TA1 1NF**
email: reception@the-castle-hotel.com **web:** www.the-castle-hotel.com
dir: M5 junct 25/26 follow signs to town centre then brown tourist signs to hotel

The Castle Hotel has enjoyed a strong reputation for many years, today it keeps those same standards that achieved its recognition and fame and offers spacious and comfortable rooms and interesting features throughout. Hospitality is a clear strength and guests are very positively welcomed here. Cuisine remains a highlight at the Castle; there are two dining options, the contemporary Brazz offers relaxed dining, while the Grill has a fine dining concept.

Rooms 44 (5 fmly) ✿ **S** £89-£109; **D** £155-£225* **Facilities** FTV WiFi Xmas New Year **Conf** Class 35 Board 35 Thtr 100 **Del** from £185 to £199* **Services** Lift **Parking** 50 **Notes** LB Civ Wed 90

The Mount Somerset Hotel & Spa

★★★★ 77% ✿✿ COUNTRY HOUSE HOTEL

EDEN HOTEL COLLECTION

tel: 01823 442500 **Lower Henlade TA3 5NB**
email: info@mountsomersethotel.co.uk **web:** www.mountsomersethotel.co.uk
dir: M5 junct 25, A358 towards Chard/Ilminster, at Henlade right into Stoke Rd, left at T-junct at end, then right into drive

From its elevated and rural position, this impressive Regency house has wonderful views over Taunton Vale. There are impressive quality and comfort levels throughout in the stylish bedrooms and bathrooms. The elegant public rooms combine style and flair with an engaging and intimate atmosphere. In addition to the daily-changing, fixed-price menu, a carefully selected seasonal carte is available in the restaurant. Eden Hotel Collection is the AA Small Hotel Group of the Year 2014-15.

Rooms 19 (1 fmly) ✿ **S** £99-£190; **D** £125-£270 (incl. bkfst)* **Facilities** Spa FTV WiFi ♨ Gym Hydrotherapy pool Sauna Steam room Experience showers Xmas New Year **Conf** Class 60 Board 35 Thtr 70 **Del** from £159 to £199* **Services** Lift **Parking** 100 **Notes** LB Civ Wed 80

Salisbury House Hotel

★★★ 73% METRO HOTEL

tel: 01823 272083 **14 Billetfield TA1 3NN**
email: res@salisburyhousehotel.co.uk **web:** www.salisburyhousehotel.co.uk

Centrally and conveniently located, this elegant establishment dates back to the 1850s and retains many original features such as stained-glass windows and a wonderful oak staircase. Bedrooms provide impressive levels of comfort and quality with well-equipped, modern bathrooms. Public areas reflect the same high standards that are a hallmark throughout this hotel.

Rooms 17 (4 fmly) (6 GF) (2 smoking) ✿ **Facilities** FTV WiFi ↘ **Parking** 17 **Notes** ⊗

Corner House Hotel

★★★ 71% HOTEL

tel: 01823 284683 **Park St TA1 4DQ**
email: res@corner-house.co.uk **web:** www.corner-house.co.uk
dir: 0.3m from town centre. Hotel on junct of Park St & A38 - Wellington Rd

The unusual Victorian façade of the Corner House, with its turrets and stained-glass windows, belies the wealth of innovation, quality and style to be found inside. The contemporary bedrooms have state-of-the-art facilities including flat-screen TVs, ample working space, and fridges with complimentary water and fresh milk. The smart public areas include the convivial bar and the relaxed and enjoyable 'Wine & Sausage' eating rooms. Free WiFi is available throughout the hotel.

Rooms 44 (9 annexe) (4 fmly) (5 GF) **Facilities** FTV WiFi ↘ **Conf** Class 32 Board 26 Thtr 45 **Parking** 30 **Notes** ⊗

Premier Inn Taunton Central (North)

BUDGET HOTEL

Premier Inn

tel: 0871 527 9076 **Massingham Park, Priorswood Rd TA2 7RX**
web: www.premierinn.com
dir: M5 junct 25, A358 into Taunton, at 2nd rdbt right onto Obridge Viaduct. Hotel at next rdbt

High quality, budget accommodation ideal for both families and business travellers. Spacious, en suite bedrooms feature tea and coffee making facilities, and Freeview TV in most hotels. Internet access and WiFi are available for a small fee. The adjacent family restaurant features a wide and varied menu. See also the Hotel Groups pages.

Rooms 40

Premier Inn Taunton East

BUDGET HOTEL

tel: 0871 527 9080 **81 Bridgwater Rd TA1 2DU**
web: www.premierinn.com
dir: M5 junct 25 follow signs to Taunton. Straight on at 1st rdbt, keep left at Creech Castle lights, hotel 200yds on right

Rooms 40

T

TAUNTON *continued*

Premier Inn Taunton (Ruishton)

BUDGET HOTEL

tel: 0871 527 9074 **Ruishton Ln, Ruishton TA3 5LU**
web: www.premierinn.com
dir: Just off M5 junct 25 on A38

Rooms 38

| TAVISTOCK | Map 3 SX47 |
| Devon | |

The Horn of Plenty

★★★ 85% ◉◉ HOTEL

tel: 01822 832528 **Gulworthy PL19 8JD**
email: enquiries@thehornofplenty.co.uk **web:** www.thehornofplenty.co.uk
dir: From Tavistock take A390 W for 3m. Right at Gulworthy Cross. In 400yds turn left, hotel in 400yds on right

With stunning views over the Tamar Valley, The Horn of Plenty maintains its reputation as one of Britain's best country-house hotels. Bedrooms are well equipped and have many thoughtful extras. The garden rooms offer impressive levels of both quality and comfort, while award-winning cuisine is served with accomplished skill and a passion for local produce.

Rooms 10 (6 annexe) (3 fmly) (4 GF) ✆ **S** £85-£215; **D** £95-£225 (incl. bkfst)* **Facilities** FTV WiFi ⬩ HL Falconry Xmas New Year **Conf** Class 22 Board 14 Thtr 22 Del from £140 to £270* **Parking** 25 **Notes** Civ Wed 80

Bedford Hotel

★★★ 78% ◉ HOTEL

tel: 01822 613221 **1 Plymouth Rd PL19 8BB**
email: enquiries@bedford-hotel.co.uk **web:** www.bedford-hotel.co.uk
dir: M5 junct 31, A30 (Launceston/Okehampton). Then A386 to Tavistock, follow town centre signs. Hotel opposite church

Built on the site of a Benedictine abbey, this impressive castellated building has been welcoming visitors for over 200 years. Very much a local landmark, the hotel offers comfortable and relaxing public areas, all reflecting charm and character throughout. Bedrooms are traditionally styled with contemporary comforts, whilst the Woburn Restaurant provides a refined setting for enjoyable cuisine.

Rooms 31 (2 fmly) (5 GF) **S** £70-£95; **D** £140-£180 (incl. bkfst) **Facilities** FTV WiFi ⬩ Xmas New Year **Conf** Class 100 Board 60 Thtr 160 Del £145 **Parking** 45 **Notes** LB Civ Wed 120

| TEBAY | Map 18 NY60 |
| Cumbria | |

Westmorland Hotel

★★★ 82% HOTEL

tel: 015396 24351 **Westmorland Place, Orton CA10 3SB**
email: reservations@westmorlandhotel.com **web:** www.westmorlandhotel.com
dir: Signed from Tebay Services M6 between junct 38 & 39 N'bound & S'bound

With fine views over rugged moorland, this modern and friendly hotel is ideal for conferences and meetings. Bedrooms are spacious and comfortable, with executive

rooms being particularly well equipped. Open-plan public areas provide a Tyrolean touch and include a split-level restaurant.

Rooms 51 (5 fmly) (12 GF) ✆ **Facilities** FTV WiFi HL Xmas New Year **Conf** Class 24 Board 30 Thtr 120 **Services** Lift **Parking** 60 **Notes** Civ Wed 120

| TEIGNMOUTH | Map 3 SX97 |
| Devon | |

Cliffden Hotel

★★★ 74% HOTEL

tel: 01626 770052 **Dawlish Rd TQ14 8TE**
email: cliffden.hotel@visionhotels.co.uk **web:** www.visionhotels.co.uk
dir: M5 junct 31, A380, B3192 to Teignmouth. Down hill on Exeter Rd to lights, left to rdbt (station on left). Left, follow Dawlish signs. Up hill. Hotel next right

While this hotel mainly caters for visually impaired guests, their families, friends and guide dogs, it offers a warm welcome to all. This establishment is a listed Victorian building set in six acres of delightful gardens overlooking a small valley. Bedrooms are comfortable, very spacious and thoughtfully equipped. There are also leisure facilities and, of course, special provision for guide dogs.

Rooms 47 (8 fmly) (10 GF) ✆ **S** £55-£70; **D** £99-£139 (incl. bkfst)* **Facilities** FTV WiFi ⬩ supervised ♫ Xmas New Year **Conf** Class 30 Board 30 Thtr 50 Del from £70 to £100* **Services** Lift **Parking** 25 **Notes** Civ Wed 60

| TELFORD | Map 10 SJ60 |
| Shropshire | |

Telford Hotel & Golf Resort

★★★★ 79% HOTEL

tel: 01952 429977 **Great Hay Dr, Sutton Heights TF7 4DT**
email: telford@qhotels.co.uk **web:** www.qhotels.co.uk
dir: M54 junct 4, A442. Follow signs for Telford Golf Club

Set on the edge of Telford with panoramic views of the famous Ironbridge Gorge, this hotel offers excellent standards. Smart bedrooms are complemented by spacious public areas, large conference facilities, a spa with treatment rooms, a golf course and a driving range. Ample parking is available. QHotels is the AA Hotel Group of the Year 2014-15.

Rooms 114 (8 fmly) (50 GF) ✆ **Facilities** Spa STV WiFi ⬩ ⛷ 18 Putt green Gym Xmas New Year **Conf** Class 220 Board 100 Thtr 350 **Services** Lift **Parking** 200 **Notes** Civ Wed 250

BEST WESTERN Valley Hotel

★★★ 82% ◉◉ HOTEL

tel: 01952 432247 **Ironbridge TF8 7DW**
email: info@thevalleyhotel.co.uk **web:** www.thevalleyhotel.co.uk
dir: M6, M54 junct 6 onto A5223 to Ironbridge

This privately owned hotel is situated in attractive gardens, close to the famous Iron Bridge. It was once the home of the Maws family who manufactured ceramic tiles, and fine examples of their craft are found throughout the house. Bedrooms vary in size and are split between the main house and a mews development; imaginative meals are served in the attractive Chez Maws restaurant.

Rooms 44 (3 fmly) (6 GF) ✆ **Facilities** FTV WiFi ⬩ **Conf** Class 80 Board 60 Thtr 150 Del from £125 to £160* **Services** Lift **Parking** 70 **Notes** ⊗ Closed 24 Dec-2 Jan RS 25 Dec Civ Wed 150

Hadley Park House

★★★ 80%  HOTEL

tel: 01952 677269 **Hadley Park TF1 6QJ**
email: info@hadleypark.co.uk **web:** www.hadleypark.co.uk
dir: Off Hadley Park Island exit A442 to Whitchurch

Located in Telford, but close to Ironbridge, this elegant Georgian mansion is situated in three acres of its own grounds. Bedrooms are spacious and well equipped. There is a comfortable bar and lounge, and meals are served in the attractive conservatory-style restaurant.

Rooms 22 (6 fmly) (5 GF) **Facilities** STV FTV WiFi ᐅ Xmas New Year **Conf** Class 60 Board 40 Thtr 200 **Parking** 60 **Notes** ⊗ Civ Wed 200

Mercure Telford Madeley Court Hotel

★★★ 77% HOTEL

tel: 01952 680068 **Castlefields Way, Madeley TF7 5DW**
email: enquiries@hotels-telford.com **web:** www.hotels-telford.com
dir: A464 to Telford then A442, A4169 to Castlefields rdbt, 1st exit onto B4373. Hotel 200yds on left

This beautifully restored 16th-century manor house is set in extensive grounds and gardens. Bedrooms vary between character rooms and the newer annexe rooms. Public areas consist of two wood-panelled lounges, a lakeside bar and at the centre of the original manor house, The Priory restaurant. The 16th-century Grade I listed mill house makes a lovely location for wedding receptions.

Rooms 49 (49 annexe) (4 fmly) (21 GF) **Facilities** FTV WiFi Xmas New Year **Conf** Class 150 Board 50 Thtr 175 **Parking** 150 **Notes** Civ Wed 175

Premier Inn Telford Central

BUDGET HOTEL

tel: 0871 527 9082 **Euston Way TF3 4LY**
web: www.premierinn.com
dir: M54 junct 5 follow Central Railway Station signs. Hotel at 2nd exit off rdbt signed railway station

High quality, budget accommodation ideal for both families and business travellers. Spacious, en suite bedrooms feature tea and coffee making facilities, and Freeview TV in most hotels. Internet access and WiFi are available for a small fee. The adjacent family restaurant features a wide and varied menu. See also the Hotel Groups pages.

Rooms 62

Premier Inn Telford North (Donnington)

BUDGET HOTEL

tel: 0871 527 9084 **Donnington Wood Way, Donnington TF2 8LE**
web: www.premierinn.com
dir: From Telford M54 junct 4, B5060 (Redhill Way) signed Donnington. At rdbt straight on (becomes Donnington Wood Way then School Rd). At mini rdbt take 1st left into Wellington Rd (hotel adjacent to McDonalds & Shell garage)

Rooms 20

TELFORD SERVICE AREA (M54)   Map 10 SJ70
Shropshire

Days Inn Telford - M54

BUDGET HOTEL

tel: 01952 238400 **Telford Services, Priorslee Rd TF11 8TG**
email: telford.hotel@welcomebreak.co.uk **web:** www.welcomebreak.co.uk
dir: At M54 junct 4

This modern building offers accommodation in smart, spacious and well-equipped bedrooms, suitable for families and business travellers, and all with en suite bathrooms. Continental breakfast is available, and other refreshments may be taken at the nearby family restaurant. See also the Hotel Groups pages.

Rooms 48 (45 fmly) (21 GF) (9 smoking) **Conf** Board 8

TEMPLE SOWERBY   Map 18 NY62
Cumbria

Temple Sowerby House Hotel & Restaurant

★★★ 88%  COUNTRY HOUSE HOTEL

tel: 017683 61578 **CA10 1RZ**
email: stay@templesowerby.com **web:** www.templesowerby.com
dir: 7m from M6 junct 40, midway between Penrith & Appleby, in village centre

The hotel is set in the heart of the Eden Valley, ideal for exploring the northern Lake District and Pennine Fells. Bedrooms are comfortable and stylish, most feature ultra-modern bathrooms, and there is a choice of pleasant lounges. The restaurant, with picture windows overlooking the beautiful walled garden, is a splendid place to enjoy the award-winning cuisine. Staff throughout are friendly and keen to please.

Rooms 12 (4 annexe) (2 GF) ⟨ **S** £99-£110; **D** £140-£170 (incl. bkfst) **Facilities** FTV WiFi ᐅ 🍴 New Year **Conf** Class 20 Board 20 Thtr 30 Del from £170 to £190 **Parking** 15 **Notes** LB ⊗ No children 12yrs Closed 20-29 Dec Civ Wed 40

TENTERDEN   Map 7 TQ83
Kent

Little Silver Country Hotel

★★★ 80% HOTEL

tel: 01233 850321 & 0845 166 2516 **Ashford Rd, St Michael's TN30 6SP**
email: enquiries@little-silver.co.uk **web:** www.little-silver.co.uk
dir: M20 junct 8, A274 signed Tenterden

Located just outside the charming town of Tenterden and within easy reach of many local Kent attractions, this charming hotel is ideal for leisure and business guests as well as being a popular wedding venue. Bedrooms are spaciously appointed and well equipped; many boast spa baths. There are a spacious lounge, small bar and a modern restaurant that overlooks beautifully tended gardens.

Rooms 16 (1 fmly) (6 GF) ⟨ **S** £65-£100; **D** £99-£160 (incl. bkfst)* **Facilities** FTV WiFi ᐅ Xmas **Conf** Class 50 Board 25 Thtr 75 Del £123.50* **Parking** 70 **Notes** LB ⊗ Civ Wed 120

T

TENTERDEN *continued*

London Beach Country Hotel, Spa & Golf Club

★★★ 70% HOTEL

tel: 01580 766279 **Ashford Rd TN30 6HX**
email: enquiries@londonbeach.com **web:** www.londonbeach.com
dir: M20 junct 9, A28 follow signs to Tenterden (10m). Hotel on right 1m before Tenterden

A modern purpose-built hotel situated in mature grounds on the outskirts of Tenterden. The spacious bedrooms are smartly decorated with co-ordinated soft furnishings, and most rooms have balconies with superb views over the golf course. The open-plan public rooms feature a brasserie-style restaurant, where a good choice of dishes is served.

Rooms 26 (2 fmly) (3 smoking) ❦ **S** £75-£110; **D** £110-£150 (incl. bkfst)*
Facilities Spa FTV WiFi ⬥ ⊛ ⌇ 9 Putt green Fishing Gym Driving range Health club Xmas New Year **Conf** Class 75 Board 40 Thtr 100 Del from £135* **Services** Lift **Parking** 100 **Notes** LB ⊗ Civ Wed 100

TETBURY	
Gloucestershire	Map 4 ST89

Calcot Manor

★★★★ ◎◎ HOTEL

tel: 01666 890391 **Calcot GL8 8YJ**
email: reception@calcotmanor.co.uk **web:** www.calcotmanor.co.uk
dir: 3m W of Tetbury at A4135 & A46 junct

Cistercian monks built the ancient barns and stables around which this lovely English farmhouse is set. No two rooms are identical, and each is beautifully decorated and equipped with modern comforts. Sumptuous sitting rooms, with crackling log fires in the winter, look out over immaculate gardens. There are two dining options: the elegant conservatory restaurant and the informal Gumstool Inn. There are also ample function rooms. The health and leisure spa includes an indoor pool, high-tech gym, massage tables, complementary therapies and much more. For children, a supervised crèche and 'playzone' are a great attraction.

Rooms 35 (23 annexe) (13 fmly) (17 GF) ❦ **S** £252-£441; **D** £280-£490 (incl. bkfst)*
Facilities Spa STV WiFi ⬥ ⬦ ⬥ ⊛ ⌇ Gym Clay pigeon shooting Archery Cycling Running track Xmas New Year Child facilities **Conf** Class 70 Board 35 Thtr 120 Del from £300* **Parking** 150 **Notes** LB ⊗ Civ Wed 100

Hare & Hounds Hotel

★★★★ 78% ◎◎ HOTEL

tel: 01666 881000 **Westonbirt GL8 8QL**
email: reception@hareandhoundshotel.com **web:** www.hareandhoundshotel.com
dir: 2.5m SW of Tetbury on A433

This popular hotel, set in extensive grounds, is situated close to Westonbirt Arboretum and has remained under the same ownership for over 50 years. The stylish bedrooms are individually designed; those in the main house are more traditional and the cottage rooms are contemporary. The public rooms include an informal bar and light, airy lounges - one with a log fire lit in colder months. Guests can eat either in the bar or the attractive Beaufort Restaurant.

Rooms 42 (21 annexe) (8 fmly) (13 GF) ❦ **S** £88-£109; **D** £158-£198 (incl. bkfst)*
Facilities FTV WiFi ⬥ ⌇ Beauty treatment room Xmas New Year **Conf** Class 80 Board 40 Thtr 120 **Parking** 85 **Notes** LB Civ Wed 200

The Close Hotel

★★★ 88% ◎◎ HOTEL

tel: 01666 502272 ▤ 01666 504401 **Long St GL8 8AQ**
email: info@theclose-hotel.com **web:** www.theclose-hotel.com
dir: M4 junct 17 onto A429 or M5 junct 14 onto B4509, follow Tetbury signs

Even with its town centre location, the Close Hotel retains a country-house feel that has made this a favourite with many for years. Bedrooms are striking and well equipped, with thoughtful touches such as homemade biscuits and bottled water. The public rooms provide a choice of relaxing areas with log fires lit in the winter. In the summer, guests can enjoy the terrace in the attractive walled garden.

Rooms 18 **S** £130-£170; **D** £140-£230 (incl. bkfst)* **Facilities** FTV WiFi Xmas New Year **Conf** Board 22 Thtr 50 **Parking** 10 **Notes** LB

The Priory Inn

★★★ 77% SMALL HOTEL

tel: 01666 502251 **London Rd GL8 8JJ**
email: info@theprioryinn.co.uk **web:** www.theprioryinn.co.uk
dir: On A433 (Cirencester to Tetbury road). Hotel 200yds from Market Square

A warm welcome is assured at this attractive inn where friendly service is a high priority. Public areas and bedrooms have a contemporary style that mixes well with more traditional features, such as an open fireplace in the cosy bar dining room. Cuisine, using locally sourced produce, is offered on a menu that should suit all tastes.

Rooms 14 (1 fmly) (4 GF) **S** £85-£135; **D** £99-£135 (incl. bkfst)* **Facilities** FTV WiFi ⌇ **Conf** Class 28 Board 28 Thtr 30 Del £125* **Parking** 35 **Notes** LB ⊗

Snooty Fox

★★★ 77% SMALL HOTEL

tel: 01666 502436 **Market Place GL8 8DD**
email: res@snooty-fox.co.uk **web:** www.snooty-fox.co.uk
dir: In town centre

Centrally situated, this 16th-century coaching inn retains original features and is a popular venue for weekend breaks. The relaxed and friendly atmosphere, the high standard of accommodation, and the food offered in the bar and restaurant, are all very good reasons why many guests return here time and again.

Rooms 12 **S** £65-£130; **D** £75-£210 (incl. bkfst)* **Facilities** FTV WiFi ⬥ Xmas New Year **Conf** Class 12 Board 16 Thtr 24 Del £118* **Notes** LB

TEWKESBURY	Map 10 SO83
Gloucestershire	

Premier Inn Tewkesbury Central

BUDGET HOTEL

tel: 0871 527 9088 **Shannon Way, Ashchurch GL20 8ND**
web: www.premierinn.com
dir: M5 junct 9, A438 towards Tewkesbury, hotel 400yds on right

High quality, budget accommodation ideal for both families and business travellers. Spacious, en suite bedrooms feature tea and coffee making facilities, and Freeview TV in most hotels. Internet access and WiFi are available for a small fee. The adjacent family restaurant features a wide and varied menu. See also the Hotel Groups pages.

Rooms 40

THETFORD	Map 13 TL88
Norfolk	

Premier Inn Thetford

BUDGET HOTEL

tel: 0871 527 9090 **Lynn Wood, Maine St IP24 3PG**
web: www.premierinn.com
dir: From A11 N follow Thetford signs. At 3rd rdbt 1st exit for town centre into Brandon Rd. 1st exit into Maine St

High quality, budget accommodation ideal for both families and business travellers. Spacious, en suite bedrooms feature tea and coffee making facilities, and Freeview TV in most hotels. Internet access and WiFi are available for a small fee. The adjacent family restaurant features a wide and varied menu. See also the Hotel Groups pages.

Rooms 40

THIRSK	Map 19 SE48
North Yorkshire	

White Horse Lodge Hotel

★★★ 72% HOTEL

tel: 01845 522293 **Sutton Rd YO7 2ER**
email: enquiries@whitehorselodgehotel.co.uk **web:** www.whitehorselodgehotel.co.uk
dir: A1 or A19 to Thirsk, A170 signed Helmsley/Scarborough. Hotel approx 1.3m on left

This hotel is located just a short drive from Thirsk's centre and the racecourse, as well as being only 20 minutes from York. The hotel is smart with well-appointed bedrooms; all have the modern facilities including free WiFi. Real ales are served in the large, modern bar and the restaurant serves home-cooked food, based on produce from local suppliers. The lodge has attractive gardens, and ample parking is provided.

Rooms 14 (1 fmly) (4 GF) **Facilities** FTV WiFi **Conf** Class 40 Board 30 Thtr 60 **Parking** 30 **Notes** Closed mid Dec-early Jan

THORNBURY	Map 4 ST69
Gloucestershire	

Thornbury Castle

★★★ COUNTRY HOUSE HOTEL

tel: 01454 281182 **Castle St BS35 1HH**
email: info@thornburycastle.co.uk **web:** www.thornburycastle.co.uk
dir: On A38 N'bound from Bristol take 1st turn to Thornbury. At end of High St left into Castle St, follow brown sign, entrance to Castle on left behind St Mary's Church

History fans may be interested to learn that Henry VIII ordered the first owner of this castle to be beheaded! Guests today have the opportunity of sleeping in historical surroundings fitted out with all the modern amenities. Most rooms have four-poster or coronet beds and real fires, and guests can even choose to sleep in the Duke's Bedchamber where King Henry and Anne Boleyn once slept, or in the Tower Suite that has reputedly the widest four-poster bed in England. Tranquil lounges enjoy views over the wonderful gardens, while elegant, wood-panelled dining rooms make memorable settings for a leisurely award-winning meal. Activities include falconry and archery and the castle has its own vineyard. Thornbury is, of course, a popular wedding venue.

Rooms 27 (3 fmly) (4 GF) **Facilities** STV FTV WiFi Archery Helicopter rides Clay pigeon shooting Massage treatment Xmas New Year **Conf** Class 40 Board 30 Thtr 70 **Parking** 50 **Notes** Civ Wed 70

THORNTON HOUGH	Map 15 SJ38
Merseyside	

Thornton Hall Hotel and Spa

★★★★ 79% HOTEL

tel: 0151 336 3938 & 353 3717 **Neston Rd CH63 1JF**
email: reservations@thorntonhallhotel.com **web:** www.thorntonhallhotel.com
dir: M53 junct 4, B5151/Neston onto B5136 to Thornton Hough (signed)

Dating back to the mid 1800s, this country-house hotel has been carefully extended and restored. Public areas include an impressive leisure spa boasting excellent facilities, a choice of restaurants and a spacious bar. Bedrooms vary in style and include feature rooms in the main house and more contemporary rooms in the garden wing. Delightful grounds and gardens, and impressive function facilities make this a popular wedding venue.

Rooms 62 (6 fmly) (28 GF) **Facilities** Spa STV FTV WiFi Gym Outdoor spa pools **Conf** Class 225 Board 80 Thtr 650 **Parking** 250 **Notes** Civ Wed 500

THORPENESS
Suffolk   Map 13 TM45

Thorpeness Hotel
    T|A|HOTEL COLLECTION

★★★ 83% ⚫ HOTEL

tel: 01728 452176 **Lakeside Av IP16 4NH**
email: info@thorpeness.co.uk **web:** www.thorpeness.co.uk
dir: A1094 towards Aldeburgh, take coast road N for 2m

Ideally situated in an unspoilt, tranquil setting close to Aldeburgh and Snape Maltings. The extensive public rooms include a choice of lounges, a restaurant, a smart bar, a snooker room and clubhouse. The spacious bedrooms are pleasantly decorated, tastefully furnished and equipped with modern facilities. An 18-hole golf course and tennis courts are also available.

Rooms 36 (36 annexe) (10 fmly) (10 GF) ☞ **Facilities** WiFi HL ⚓ 18 ⛳ Putt green Fishing Cycle hire Rowing boat hire Birdwatching Xmas New Year **Conf** Class 30 Board 24 Thtr 130 Del £150* **Parking** 80 **Notes** Civ Wed 130

THURLASTON
Warwickshire   Map 11 SP47

Draycote Hotel

★★★ 75% HOTEL

tel: 01788 521800 **London Rd CV23 9LF**
email: mail@draycotehotel.co.uk **web:** www.draycotehotel.co.uk
dir: M1 junct 17 onto M45, A45. Hotel 500mtrs on left

Located in the picturesque Warwickshire countryside and within easy reach of motorway networks, this hotel offers modern, comfortable and well-equipped accommodation with a relaxed and friendly welcome. The hotel has a challenging golf course.

Rooms 49 (24 fmly) (24 GF) ☞ **S** £55.50-£78.50; **D** £62-£92 (incl. bkfst)* **Facilities** FTV WiFi ⚓ ⚓ 18 Putt green Golf driving range Chipping green New Year **Conf** Class 78 Board 30 Thtr 250 Del from £99 to £160* **Parking** 150 **Notes** LB ⊗ Civ Wed 170

THURLESTONE
Devon   Map 3 SX64

Thurlestone Hotel

★★★★ 83% ⚫ HOTEL

tel: 01548 560382 **TQ7 3NN**
email: enquiries@thurlestone.co.uk **web:** www.thurlestone.co.uk
dir: A38, A384 into Totnes, A381 towards Kingsbridge, A379 towards Churchstow, onto B3197. Into lane signed to Thurlestone

This perennially popular hotel has been in the same family-ownership since 1896 and continues to go from strength to strength. A vast range of facilities is available for all the family including indoor and outdoor pools, a golf course and a beauty salon. Bedrooms are equipped to ensure a comfortable stay with many having wonderful views of the south Devon coast. The range of eating options includes the elegant and stylish restaurant with its stunning views.

Rooms 65 (23 fmly) ☞ **S** £75-£130; **D** £150-£450 (incl. bkfst)* **Facilities** Spa STV FTV WiFi ⚓ ⚓ ⚓ supervised ⚓ 9 ⛳ Putt green ⚓ Gym Squash Badminton Table tennis Games & Snooker room Toddler room Beauty treatment room ♫ Xmas New Year Child facilities **Conf** Class 100 Board 40 Thtr 150 Del from £140 to £300* **Services** Lift **Parking** 121 **Notes** LB Closed 1-2 wks Jan Civ Wed 160

THURSFORD
Norfolk   Map 13 TF93

The Old Forge Seafood Restaurant

⚫ RESTAURANT WITH ROOMS

tel: 01328 878345 **Fakenham Rd NR21 0BD**
email: sarah.goldspink@btconnect.com **web:** www.seafoodnorthnorfolk.co.uk
dir: On A148 (Fakenham to Holt road)

Expect a warm welcome at this delightfully relaxed restaurant with rooms. The open-plan public areas include a lounge bar with comfy sofas, and an intimate restaurant with pine tables. Bedrooms are pleasantly decorated and equipped with a good range of useful facilities.

Rooms 3

TICEHURST
East Sussex   Map 6 TQ63

Dale Hill Hotel & Golf Club

★★★★ 80% ⚫ HOTEL

tel: 01580 200112 **TN5 7DQ**
email: info@dalehill.co.uk **web:** www.dalehill.co.uk
dir: M25 junct 5, A21. 5m after Lamberhurst right at lights onto B2087 to Flimwell. Hotel 1m on left

This modern hotel is situated just a short drive from the village. Extensive public rooms include a lounge bar, a conservatory brasserie, a formal restaurant and the Spike Bar, which is mainly frequented by golf club members and has a lively atmosphere. The hotel also has two superb 18-hole golf courses, a swimming pool and gym.

Rooms 35 (8 fmly) (23 GF) **S** £65-£170; **D** £75-£180 (incl. bkfst)* **Facilities** FTV WiFi ⚓ ⚓ 36 Putt green Gym Covered driving range Pool table Xmas New Year **Conf** Class 50 Board 50 Thtr 120 Del from £129* **Services** Lift **Parking** 220 **Notes** LB ⊗ Civ Wed 150

T

TINTAGEL
Cornwall
Map 2 SX08

Atlantic View Hotel

★★ 78% SMALL HOTEL

tel: 01840 770221 **Treknow PL34 OEJ**
email: atlantic-view@eclipse.co.uk **web:** www.atlanticviewhoteltintagel.co.uk
dir: B3263 to Tregatta, turn left into Treknow, hotel on road to Trebarwith Strand Beach

Conveniently located for all the attractions of Tintagel, this family-run hotel has a wonderfully relaxed and welcoming atmosphere. Public areas include a bar, comfortable lounge, TV/games room and heated swimming pool. Bedrooms are generally spacious and some have the added advantage of distant sea views.

Rooms 9 (1 fmly) S £68-£74; **D** £136-£148 (incl. bkfst & dinner)* **Facilities** FTV WiFi Pool table **Parking** 10 **Notes** Closed Nov-Feb RS Mar

TITCHWELL
Norfolk
Map 13 TF74

Titchwell Manor Hotel

★★★ 87% ◎◎◎ HOTEL

tel: 01485 210221 **PE31 8BB**
email: margaret@titchwellmanor.com **web:** www.titchwellmanor.com
dir: On A149 (coast road) between Brancaster & Thornham

Friendly family-run hotel ideally placed for touring the north Norfolk coastline. The tastefully appointed bedrooms are very comfortable; some in the adjacent annexe offer ground floor access. Smart public rooms include a lounge area, relaxed informal bar and the delightful Conservatory Restaurant, overlooking the walled garden. Head Chef Eric Snaith produces imaginative menus that feature quality local produce and fresh fish.

Rooms 27 (19 annexe) (4 fmly) (16 GF) **Facilities** FTV WiFi Xmas New Year **Conf** Class 50 Board 30 Thtr 30 **Parking** 50 **Notes** Civ Wed 80

TOLLESHUNT KNIGHTS
Essex
Map 7 TL91

Crowne Plaza Resort Colchester - Five Lakes

★★★★ 78% ◎ HOTEL

tel: 01621 868888 **Colchester Rd CM9 8HX**
email: enquiries@cpcolchester.co.uk **web:** www.cpcolchester.co.uk
dir: Exit A12 at Kelvedon, follow brown signs through Tiptree to hotel

This hotel is set amidst 320 acres of open countryside, featuring two golf courses. The spacious bedrooms are furnished to a high standard and have excellent

facilities. The public rooms offer a high degree of comfort and include five bars, two restaurants and a large lounge. The property also boasts extensive leisure facilities.

Rooms 194 (80 annexe) (4 fmly) (40 GF) S £85-£150; **D** £95-£160 (incl. bkfst) **Facilities** Spa STV FTV WiFi 36 Putt green Gym Squash Sauna Steam room Badminton Aerobics Studio Nail lounge Relaxation room Xmas New Year **Conf** Class 700 Board 60 Thtr 2000 Del from £130 to £165 **Services** Lift **Parking** 550 **Notes** LB Civ Wed 250

TONBRIDGE
Kent
Map 6 TQ54

BEST WESTERN Rose & Crown Hotel

★★★ 78% HOTEL

tel: 01732 357966 **125 High St TN9 1DD**
email: rose.crown@bestwestern.co.uk **web:** www.roseandcrowntonbridge.co.uk

A 15th-century coaching inn situated in the heart of this bustling town centre. The public areas are light and airy yet still retain much original character such as oak beams and Jacobean panelling. Food is served throughout the day in the Oak Room Bar & Grill. Bedrooms are stylishly decorated, spacious and well presented; amenities include free WiFi.

Rooms 56 (3 fmly) (10 GF) S £65-£85; **D** £85-£145* **Facilities** FTV WiFi **Conf** Class 60 Board 60 Thtr 80 Del from £125 to £185 **Parking** 43 **Notes** Closed 27 Dec-5 Jan RS 24-26 Dec

Premier Inn Tonbridge

BUDGET HOTEL

tel: 0871 527 9096 **Pembury Rd TN11 0NA**
web: www.premierinn.com
dir: 11m from M25 junct 5. Follow A21 towards Hastings, pass A26 (Tunbridge Wells) junct. Exit at next junct, 1st exit at rdbt

High quality, budget accommodation ideal for both families and business travellers. Spacious, en suite bedrooms feature tea and coffee making facilities, and Freeview TV in most hotels. Internet access and WiFi are available for a small fee. The adjacent family restaurant features a wide and varied menu. See also the Hotel Groups pages.

Rooms 40

Premier Inn Tonbridge North

BUDGET HOTEL

tel: 0871 527 9098 **Hilden Manor, London Rd TN10 3AN**
web: www.premierinn.com
dir: From A21 follow Seven Oaks & Hildenborough signs. At rdbt take 2nd exit onto B245 signed Hildenborough. In 2m hotel on right

Rooms 41

TORBAY

See Brixham, Paignton & Torquay

T

TORQUAY
Devon

Map 3 SX96

The Imperial Hotel

★★★★ 81%  HOTEL

PUMA HOTELS COLLECTION

tel: 01803 294301 **Park Hill Rd TQ1 2DG**
email: imperialtorquay@pumahotels.co.uk **web:** www.pumahotels.co.uk
dir: A380 towards seafront. Turn left to harbour, right at clocktower. Hotel 300yds on right

This hotel has an enviable location with extensive views of the coastline. Traditional in style, the public areas are elegant and offer a choice of dining options including the Regatta Restaurant, with its stunning views over the bay. Bedrooms are spacious, most with private balconies, and the hotel has an extensive range of indoor and outdoor leisure facilities.

Rooms 152 (14 fmly) **Facilities** Spa STV WiFi ⏧ ⮜ supervised ⌇ Gym Squash Beauty salon Hairdresser Steam room ♫ Xmas New Year **Conf** Class 200 Board 30 Thtr 350 **Services** Lift **Parking** 140 **Notes** Civ Wed 250

Grand Hotel

★★★★ 77%  HOTEL

R RICHARDSON HOTELS *Where Memories are Made*

tel: 01803 296677 **Sea Front TQ2 6NT**
email: reservations@grandtorquay.co.uk **web:** www.grandtorquay.co.uk
dir: A380 to Torquay. At seafront turn right, then 1st right. Hotel on corner, entrance 1st on left

Within level walking distance of the town, this large Edwardian hotel overlooks the bay and offers modern facilities. Many of the bedrooms, some with balconies, enjoy the best of the views, but all are very well equipped. The Compass Bar also benefits from the stunning views, and offers an informal alternative to the Gainsborough Restaurant.

Rooms 132 (32 fmly) (3 GF) ⏧ **Facilities** FTV WiFi ⏧ ⏧ ⮜ supervised ⌇ Gym Beauty clinic Car valeting Xmas New Year **Conf** Class 150 Board 60 Thtr 250 **Services** Lift **Parking** 57 **Notes** Civ Wed 250

Palace Hotel

★★★★ 72% HOTEL

tel: 01803 200200 **Babbacombe Rd TQ1 3TG**
email: info@palacetorquay.co.uk **web:** www.palacetorquay.co.uk
dir: Towards harbour, left by clocktower into Babbacombe Rd, hotel on right after 1m

Set in 25 acres of stunning, beautifully tended wooded grounds, the Palace offers a tranquil environment. Suitable for business and leisure, the hotel boasts a huge range of well-presented indoor and outdoor facilities. Much of the original charm and grandeur is still in evidence, particularly in the dining room. Many of the bedrooms enjoy views of the magnificent gardens.

Rooms 141 (7 fmly) **Facilities** WiFi ⏧ ⮜ ⌇ 9 ⌇ Putt green ⌇ Gym Squash Table tennis Snooker Childrens' play area Xmas New Year **Conf** Class 800 Board 40 Thtr 1000 **Services** Lift **Parking** 140 **Notes** ⊗ Civ Wed

The Headland Hotel

★★★ 83%  HOTEL

tel: 01803 295666 **Daddyhole Rd TQ1 2EF**
email: info@headlandtorquay.com **web:** www.headlandtorquay.com
dir: A380 to Torquay sea front, left then far side of harbour, up hill, 500mtrs & turn right

This hotel has a delightful location set apart from the bustle of town, but within easy walking distance of the numerous attractions. Having some splendid grounds and an elevated view of the bay, the hotel has an enviable position. Bedrooms are very comfortably appointed, many with sea views. Cuisine is a highlight, and the friendly team offer attentive service.

Rooms 78 (16 fmly) (7 GF) ⏧ **Facilities** FTV WiFi ⮜ ⌇ Gym ♫ Xmas New Year **Conf** Class 50 Board 40 Thtr 150 **Services** Lift **Parking** 42 **Notes** ⊗ Civ Wed 150

BEST WESTERN Hotel Gleneagles

★★★ 80% HOTEL

Best Western

tel: 01803 293637 **Asheldon Rd, Wellswood TQ1 2QS**
email: enquiries@hotel-gleneagles.com **web:** www.hotel-gleneagles.com
dir: A380 onto A3022 to A379, follow to St Mathias Church, turn right into Asheldon Rd

From its hillside location, looking out over Anstey's Cove towards Lyme Bay, this peacefully located hotel is appointed to an impressive standard. Stylish public areas combine comfort, flair and quality with ample space in which to find a quiet spot and unwind. Bedrooms also have a contemporary feel; many have balconies or patios. The pool area has a real Riviera feel, with elegant Lloyd Loom sun loungers and palm trees.

Rooms 41 (2 fmly) (5 GF) ⏧ **Facilities** FTV WiFi ⏧ ⮜ Xmas New Year **Conf** Class 20 Board 25 Thtr 40 **Services** Lift **Parking** 21 **Notes** Civ Wed

Corbyn Head Hotel

★★★ 79%  HOTEL

tel: 01803 213611 **Torbay Rd, Sea Front TQ2 6RH**
email: info@corbynhead.com **web:** www.corbynhead.com
dir: Follow signs to Torquay seafront, turn right on seafront. Hotel on right with green canopies

This hotel occupies a prime position overlooking Torbay, and offers well-equipped bedrooms, many with sea views and some with balconies. The staff are friendly and welcoming, and a well-stocked bar and comfortable lounge are available. Guests can enjoy fine dining in the Harbour View Restaurant, with attentive service assured.

Rooms 45 (4 fmly) (9 GF) **Facilities** FTV WiFi ⮜ Squash Use of leisure facilities at sister hotel ♫ Xmas New Year **Conf** Class 30 Board 30 Thtr 80 **Parking** 50 **Notes** Civ Wed 85

Livermead House Hotel

★★★ 75% HOTEL

tel: 01803 294361 & 294363 **Torbay Rd TQ2 6QJ**
email: info@livermead.com **web:** www.livermead.com
dir: From seafront turn right, follow A379 towards Paignton & Livermead, hotel opposite Institute Beach

Having a splendid waterfront location, this hotel dates back to the 1820s, and is where Charles Kingsley is said to have written *The Water Babies*. Bedrooms vary in size and style; excellent public rooms are popular for private parties and meetings, and a range of leisure facilities is provided. Enjoyable cuisine is served in the impressive restaurant.

Rooms 67 (6 fmly) (2 GF) **Facilities** WiFi ↘ Gym Squash Sauna Games room ♫
Xmas **Conf** Class 175 Board 80 Thtr 250 **Services** Lift **Parking** 131
Notes Civ Wed 250

BEST WESTERN Livermead Cliff Hotel

★★★ 72% HOTEL

tel: 01803 299666 **Torbay Rd TQ2 6RQ**
email: info@livermeadcliff.co.uk **web:** www.livermeadcliff.co.uk
dir: A379, A3022 to Torquay, towards seafront, turn right towards Paignton. Hotel 600yds on seaward side

Situated at the water's edge, this long-established hotel offers friendly service and traditional hospitality. The splendid views can be enjoyed from the lounge, bar and dining room. Alternatively, guests can take advantage of refreshment on the wonderful terrace and enjoy one of the best outlooks in the bay. Bedrooms, many with sea views and some with balconies, are comfortable and well equipped; a range of room sizes is available.

Rooms 65 (17 fmly) ♠ **Facilities** FTV WiFi Fishing Use of facilities at sister hotel Xmas New Year **Conf** Class 60 Board 40 Thtr 120 **Services** Lift **Parking** 80
Notes Civ Wed 200

Abbey Lawn Hotel

★★★ 67% HOTEL

tel: 01803 299199 & 203181 **Scarborough Rd TQ2 5UQ**
email: nburfitt@holdsworthhotels.co.uk

Conveniently located for both the seafront and town centre, this is an ideal base for visiting the attractions of the 'English Riviera'. Many of the bedrooms, including the four-poster suite, benefit from lovely sea views. Facilities include a health club with extensive leisure activities, plus indoor and outdoor pools. Traditional cuisine is served in the elegant restaurant, and evening entertainment is a regular feature in the ballroom.

Rooms 57 (3 fmly) **Facilities** ↘ Gym ♫ Xmas New Year **Services** Lift **Parking** 20
Notes ⊗ Closed Jan

The Heritage Hotel

★★ 75% HOTEL

tel: 01803 299332 **Seafront, Shedden Hill TQ2 5TY**
email: enquiries@heritagehoteltorquay.co.uk **web:** www.heritagehoteltorquay.co.uk
dir: A380 to Torquay follow signs to seafront. Hotel on left

In an elevated position overlooking Tor Abbey Sands, this hotel is a short walk from both the harbour and the shops. The bedrooms are traditionally furnished and come in various sizes; all have sea views except one. There is a variety of eating options based on American food themes, and a large sun deck for relaxation in summer.

Rooms 24 (24 fmly) (4 GF) ♠ **S** £40-£50; **D** £70-£90 (incl. bkfst) **Facilities** STV FTV WiFi ⊕ Gym **Services** Lift **Parking** 40 **Notes** LB ⊗

Regina Hotel

★★ 71% HOTEL

tel: 01803 292904 **Victoria Pde TQ1 2BE**
email: regina@leisureplex.co.uk **web:** www.leisureplex.co.uk
dir: Into Torquay, follow harbour signs, hotel on outer corner of harbour

This hotel enjoys a pleasant and convenient location right on the harbourside, a short stroll from the town's attractions. Bedrooms, some with harbour views, vary in size. Entertainment is provided on most nights and there is a choice of bars.

Rooms 68 (5 fmly) **Facilities** FTV ♫ Xmas New Year **Services** Lift **Parking** 6 **Notes** ⊗ Closed Jan & part Feb RS Nov-Dec (ex Xmas) & Feb-Mar

Anchorage Hotel

★★ 67% HOTEL

tel: 01803 326175 **Cary Park, Aveland Rd, Babbacombe TQ1 3PT**
email: enquiries@anchoragehotel.co.uk **web:** www.anchoragehotel.co.uk

Quietly located in a residential area and providing a friendly welcome, this family-run establishment enjoys a great deal of repeat business. Bedrooms come in a range of sizes but all rooms are neatly presented. Evening entertainment is provided regularly in the large and comfortable lounge.

Rooms 56 (5 fmly) (17 GF) **S** £32.50-£54; **D** £63-£108 (incl. bkfst & dinner)*
Facilities FTV WiFi ↘ ♫ Xmas New Year **Services** Lift **Parking** 26 **Notes** LB

T

TORQUAY *continued*

Ashley Court Hotel

★★ 64% HOTEL

tel: 01803 292417 **107 Abbey Rd TQ2 5NP**
email: reception@ashleycourt.co.uk web: www.ashleycourt.co.uk
dir: A380 to seafront, left to Shedden Hill to lights, hotel opposite

Located close to the town centre and within easy strolling distance of the seafront, this hotel offers a warm welcome to guests. Bedrooms are pleasantly appointed and some have sea views. The outdoor pool and patio are popular with guests wishing to soak up some sunshine. Live entertainment is provided every night throughout the season.

Rooms 83 (12 fmly) (8 GF) (14 smoking) **Facilities** Games room Xmas New Year **Services** Lift **Parking** 42 **Notes** Closed 3 Jan-1 Feb

Premier Inn Torquay

BUDGET HOTEL

tel: 0871 527 9102 **Seafront, Belgrave Rd TQ2 5HE**
web: www.premierinn.com
dir: On A380 into Torquay, continue to lights (Torre Station on right). Right into Avenue Road to Kings Drive. Left at seafront, hotel at lights

High quality, budget accommodation ideal for both families and business travellers. Spacious, en suite bedrooms feature tea and coffee making facilities, and Freeview TV in most hotels. Internet access and WiFi are available for a small fee. The adjacent family restaurant features a wide and varied menu. See also the Hotel Groups pages.

Rooms 83

Orestone Manor

RESTAURANT WITH ROOMS

tel: 01803 328098 **Rockhouse Ln, Maidencombe TQ1 4SX**
email: info@orestonemanor.com web: www.orestonemanor.com
dir: N of Torquay on A379, on sharp bend in village of Maidencombe

Set in an fabulous location overlooking the bay, Orestone Manor has a long history of providing fine food and very comfortable accommodation, coupled with friendly, attentive service. Log fires burn in cooler months, and there is a conservatory, a bar and a sitting room for guests to enjoy. AA Rosettes have been awarded for the uncomplicated modern cuisine which is based on quality local produce.

Rooms 10 (1 annexe) (6 fmly)

TRING	Map 6 SP91
Hertfordshire	

Pendley Manor Hotel

★★★★ 75% HOTEL

tel: 01442 891891 **Cow Ln HP23 5QY**
email: info@pendley-manor.co.uk web: www.pendley-manor.co.uk
dir: M25 junct 20, A41 (Tring exit). At rdbt follow Berkhamsted/London signs. 1st left signed Tring Station & Pendley Manor

Pendley Manor Hotel is an impressive Victorian mansion set in extensive and mature landscaped grounds where peacocks roam. The spacious bedrooms are situated in both the manor house and the wing, and offer a useful range of facilities. Public areas include a cosy bar, a conservatory lounge and an intimate restaurant as well as a leisure centre.

Rooms 72 (17 fmly) (17 GF) **Facilities** Spa FTV WiFi Gym Steam room Dance Studio Sauna Snooker room **Conf** Class 80 Board 80 Thtr 250 **Services** Lift **Parking** 150 **Notes** Civ Wed 160

Premier Inn Tring

BUDGET HOTEL

tel: 0871 527 9104 **Tring Hill HP23 4LD**
web: www.premierinn.com
dir: M25 junct 20, A41 towards Aylesbury, at end of Hemel Hempstead/Tring bypass straight on at rdbt, hotel approx 100yds on right

High quality, budget accommodation ideal for both families and business travellers. Spacious, en suite bedrooms feature tea and coffee making facilities, and Freeview TV in most hotels. Internet access and WiFi are available for a small fee. The adjacent family restaurant features a wide and varied menu. See also the Hotel Groups pages.

Rooms 30

TROWBRIDGE	Map 4 ST85
Wiltshire	

Fieldways Hotel & Health Club

★★ 69% SMALL HOTEL

tel: 01225 768336 **Hilperton Rd BA14 7JP**
email: fieldwayshotel@yahoo.co.uk web: www.fieldwayshealthhotel.co.uk
dir: A361 from Trowbridge towards Melksham, Chippenham, Devizes. Hotel last property on left

Originally part of a Victorian mansion this hotel is quietly set in well-kept grounds and provides a pleasant combination of spacious, comfortably furnished bedrooms. There are two splendid wood-panelled dining rooms, one of which is impressively finished in oak, pine, rosewood and mahogany. The indoor leisure facilities include a gym, a pool and treatment rooms; 'Top to Toe' days are especially popular.

Rooms 13 (5 annexe) (2 fmly) (2 GF) **S** £60; **D** £80-£90 (incl. bkfst) **Facilities** Spa FTV WiFi Gym Range of beauty treatments/massage Pampering days **Conf** Class 40 Board 20 Thtr 40 **Parking** 70 **Notes** LB

Premier Inn Trowbridge

BUDGET HOTEL

tel: 0871 527 9444 **St Stephens Place BA14 8AH**
web: www.premierinn.com
dir: M4 junct 17, A429 (Chippenham). A350 (Warminster & Poole). 12m. After Seminton rdbt, at 2nd lights right into West Ashton Rd (Trowbridge). At 1st mini rdbt 2nd exit, at 2nd mini rdbt into County Way. At major rdbt 5th exit into Castle St. At mini rdbt 3rd exit, hotel on right

High quality, budget accommodation ideal for both families and business travellers. Spacious, en suite bedrooms feature tea and coffee making facilities, and Freeview TV in most hotels. Internet access and WiFi are available for a small fee. The adjacent family restaurant features a wide and varied menu. See also the Hotel Groups pages.

Rooms 80

| **TRURO** | Map 2 SW84 |
| Cornwall | |

The Alverton Hotel

★★★★ 76% ⦿ HOTEL

tel: 01872 276633 **Tregolls Rd TR1 1ZQ**
email: stay@thealverton.co.uk **web:** www.thealverton.co.uk
dir: From A30 at Carland Cross take A39 to Truro. At lights right onto A39 (Tregolls Rd) signed Truro/Falmouth

The Alverton Hotel is a beautiful Grade II listed building which was previously a convent. The bedrooms are smartly decorated, and there is a comfortable lounge/cocktail bar, as well as an attractive restaurant that serves popular meals using locally-sourced produce. Parking is available.

Rooms 33 (4 fmly) (3 GF) **Facilities** FTV WiFi ⌁ Xmas New Year **Conf** Class 50 Board 30 Thtr 140 **Parking** 71 **Notes** Civ Wed 90

Mannings Hotel

★★★ 86% HOTEL

tel: 01872 270345 **Lemon St TR1 2QB**
email: reception@manningshotels.co.uk **web:** www.manningshotels.co.uk
dir: A30 to Carland Cross then Truro. Follow brown signs to hotel in city centre

This popular hotel is located in the heart of Truro and offers an engaging blend of traditional and contemporary. Public areas have a stylish atmosphere with the bar and restaurant proving popular with locals and residents alike. A wide choice of appetising dishes is available, including ethnic, classic and vegetarian as well as daily specials. Bedrooms are pleasantly appointed.

Rooms 43 (9 annexe) (4 fmly) (3 GF) ⌁ **S** £65-£79; **D** £85-£109 (incl. bkfst)*
Facilities FTV WiFi **Parking** 43 **Notes** LB ⊗ Closed 25-26 Dec

Follow us on Facebook
www.facebook.com/TheAAUK

Premier Inn Truro

BUDGET HOTEL

tel: 0871 527 9106 **Old Carnon Hill, Carnon Downs TR3 6JT**
web: www.premierinn.com
dir: On A39 (Truro to Falmouth road), 3m SW of Truro

High quality, budget accommodation ideal for both families and business travellers. Spacious, en suite bedrooms feature tea and coffee making facilities, and Freeview TV in most hotels. Internet access and WiFi are available for a small fee. The adjacent family restaurant features a wide and varied menu. See also the Hotel Groups pages.

Rooms 62

| **TUNBRIDGE WELLS (ROYAL)** | Map 6 TQ53 |
| Kent | |

The Spa Hotel

★★★★ 81% ⦿ HOTEL

tel: 01892 520331 **Mount Ephraim TN4 8XJ**
email: reservations@spahotel.co.uk **web:** www.spahotel.co.uk
dir: A21 to A26, follow A264 East Grinstead signs, hotel on right

Set in 14 acres of beautifully tended grounds, this imposing 18th-century mansion offers spacious, modern bedrooms that are stylishly decorated and thoughtfully equipped. The public rooms include the Chandelier Restaurant, a champagne bar and the Orangery which complements the traditional lounge. There are extensive meeting and health club facilities, and a spa offering treatment rooms. It is also licensed for civil wedding ceremonies.

Rooms 70 (4 fmly) (1 GF) ⌁ **S** £110-£120; **D** £160-£230* **Facilities** Spa STV FTV WiFi ⌀ ⌀ ⌀ Gym Xmas New Year **Conf** Class 90 Board 90 Thtr 300 Del from £135 to £160* **Services** Lift **Parking** 150 **Notes** LB ⊗ Civ Wed 150

Hotel du Vin Tunbridge Wells

★★★★ 74% ⦿ TOWN HOUSE HOTEL

tel: 01892 526455 **Crescent Rd TN1 2LY**
email: reception.tunbridgewells@hotelduvin.com **web:** www.hotelduvin.com
dir: Follow town centre, to main junct of Mount Pleasant Rd & Crescent Rd/Church Rd. Hotel 150yds on right just past Phillips House

This impressive Grade II listed building dates from 1762, and as a princess, Queen Victoria often stayed here. The spacious bedrooms are available in a range of sizes, beautifully and individually appointed, and equipped with a host of thoughtful extras. Public rooms include a bistro-style restaurant, two elegant lounges and a small bar.

Rooms 34 ⌁ **Facilities** STV WiFi Boules court in garden **Conf** Class 40 Board 25 Thtr 60 **Services** Lift **Parking** 30 **Notes** Civ Wed 84

T

TUNBRIDGE WELLS (ROYAL) *continued*

Mercure Tunbridge Wells

★★★★ 73% HOTEL

tel: 0844 815 9074 **8 Tonbridge Rd, Pembury TN2 4QL**
email: sales.mercuretunbridgewells@jupiterhotels.co.uk **web:** www.jupiterhotels.co.uk
dir: M25 junct 5, A21 S. Left at 1st rdbt signed Pembury Hospital. Hotel on left, 400yds past hospital

Built in the style of a traditional Kentish oast house, this well presented hotel is conveniently located just off the A21 with easy access to the M25. Bedrooms are comfortably appointed for both business and leisure guests. Public areas include a leisure club and a range of meeting rooms.

Rooms 84 (8 fmly) (40 GF) ⚓ **Facilities** STV FTV WiFi ↘ HL ⚡ Steam room Sauna Xmas New Year **Conf** Class 80 Board 50 Thtr 150 **Parking** 200 **Notes** Civ Wed 150

Russell Hotel

★★ 65% METRO HOTEL

tel: 01892 544833 **80 London Rd TN1 1DZ**
email: sales@russell-hotel.com **web:** www.russell-hotel.com
dir: From Tunbridge Wells A26 junct with Lime Hill Road turn (no through road)

This detached Victorian property is situated just a short walk from the centre of town. The generously proportioned bedrooms in the main house are pleasantly decorated and well equipped. In addition, there are several smartly appointed self-contained suites in an adjacent building. The public rooms include a lounge and cosy bar.

Rooms 26 (5 annexe) (5 fmly) (1 GF) **Facilities** FTV WiFi **Conf** Class 10 Board 10 Thtr 10 **Parking** 14 **Notes** ⊗

TURNERS HILL
West Sussex   Map 6 TQ33

Alexander House Hotel & Utopia Spa

★★★★★ 86% ◉◉◉ HOTEL

tel: 01342 714914 **East St RH10 4QD**
email: admin@alexanderhouse.co.uk **web:** www.alexanderhouse.co.uk
dir: 6m from M23 junct 10, on B2110 between Turners Hill & East Grinstead

Set in 175 acres of parkland and landscaped gardens, this delightful country house hotel dates back to the 17th century. Most of the bedrooms are very spacious and all have luxurious bathrooms; the rooms in the most recent wing are particularly stunning. There are two options for dining - the AG's Grill which has been awarded AA Rosettes, or the lively Reflections which is set around an open courtyard, ideal for eating alfresco. The Utopia Spa has a state-of-the-art pool and gym, as well as specialised treatments.

Rooms 38 (13 fmly) (1 GF) ⚓ **S** £155-£695; **D** £155-£695 **Facilities** Spa STV FTV WiFi ⚡ 🏊 ⛳ Gym Clay shooting Archery Mountain bikes Pony trekking Xmas New Year **Conf** Class 70 Board 40 Thtr 150 **Del** from £275 **Services** Lift **Parking** 100 **Notes** ⊗ Civ Wed 100

TWICKENHAM
Greater London

Premier Inn Twickenham East

BUDGET HOTEL PLAN 1 B2

tel: 0871 527 9108 **Corner Sixth Cross, Staines Rd TW2 5PE**
web: www.premierinn.com
dir: M25 junct 12 onto M3, follow Central London signs, at end of M3 becomes A316. Straight on at 1st rdbt. Hotel 500yds on left

High quality, budget accommodation ideal for both families and business travellers. Spacious, en suite bedrooms feature tea and coffee making facilities, and Freeview TV in most hotels. Internet access and WiFi are available for a small fee. The adjacent family restaurant features a wide and varied menu. See also the Hotel Groups pages.

Rooms 17

Premier Inn Twickenham Stadium

BUDGET HOTEL PLAN 1 B2

tel: 0871 527 9110 **Chertsey Rd, Whitton TW2 6LS**
web: www.premierinn.com
dir: From M3 onto A316, then A305 signed Twickenham. At Hospital Bridge Rdbt 3rd exit into Hospital Bridge Rd. Take B358 signed Teddington. Becomes Sixth Cross Rd. Hotel on left

Rooms 31

TWO BRIDGES
Devon   Map 3 SX67

Two Bridges Hotel

★★★ 78% ◉ HOTEL

tel: 01822 892300 **PL20 6SW**
email: enquiries@twobridges.co.uk **web:** www.twobridges.co.uk
dir: At junct of B3212 & B3357

This wonderfully relaxing hotel is set in the heart of the Dartmoor National Park, in a beautiful riverside location. Three standards of comfortable rooms provide every modern convenience, and include four-poster rooms. There is a choice of lounges, and fine dining is available in the restaurant, where menus feature local game and other seasonal produce.

Rooms 33 (2 fmly) (10 GF) **S** £70-£105; **D** £140-£210 (incl. bkfst) **Facilities** STV WiFi Fishing Xmas New Year **Conf** Class 60 Board 40 Thtr 130 **Del** from £135 to £145 **Parking** 100 **Notes** LB Closed 7-14 Sep Civ Wed 130

TYNEMOUTH
Tyne & Wear   Map 21 NZ36

Grand Hotel

★★★ 82% HOTEL

tel: 0191 293 6666 **Grand Pde NE30 4ER**
email: reservations@grandhotel-uk.com **web:** www.grandhotel-uk.com
dir: A1058 for Tynemouth. At coast rdbt turn right. Hotel on right approx 0.5m

This grand Victorian building offers stunning views of the coast. Bedrooms come in a variety of styles and are well equipped, tastefully decorated and have impressive bathrooms. In addition to the restaurant there are two bars. The elegant and imposing staircase is a focal point, and is a favourite spot for the bride and groom to have their photograph taken after their wedding here.

Rooms 46 (6 annexe) (14 fmly) S £85-£170; **D** £88-£183 (incl. bkfst)*
Facilities STV FTV WiFi Xmas New Year **Conf** Class 40 Board 40 Thtr 130
Services Lift **Parking** 16 **Notes** LB ⊗ RS Sun evening Civ Wed 120

UCKFIELD
East Sussex Map 6 TQ42

Buxted Park Hotel
★★★★ ◎◎ HOTEL

tel: 01825 733333 & 0845 458 0901 **Buxted TN22 4AY**
email: buxtedpark@handpicked.co.uk **web:** www.handpickedhotels.co.uk/buxtedpark
dir: From A26 (Uckfield bypass) take A272 signed Buxted. Through lights, hotel 1m on right

An attractive Grade II listed Georgian mansion dating back to the 17th century. The property is set amidst 300 acres of beautiful countryside and landscaped gardens. The stylish, thoughtfully equipped bedrooms are split between the main house and the modern Garden Wing. An interesting choice of dishes is served in the restaurant.

Rooms 44 (7 fmly) (16 GF) S £103-£388; **D** £103-£398 (incl. bkfst)* **Facilities** STV WiFi HL Fishing Gym Orienteering Walking trail Snooker room Xmas New Year **Conf** Class 80 Board 42 Thtr 180 Del from £125 to £190* **Services** Lift **Parking** 100 **Notes** LB ⊗ Civ Wed 120

East Sussex National Golf Resort & Spa
★★★★ 79% ◎ HOTEL

tel: 01825 880088 **Little Horsted TN22 5ES**
email: reception@eastsussexnational.co.uk **web:** www.eastsussexnational.co.uk
dir: M25 junct 6, A22 signed East Grinstead & Eastbourne. Straight on at rdbt junct of A22 & A26 (Little Horsted). At next rdbt right to hotel

This modern hotel is located in a lovely country location and offers a super range of facilities with two golf courses and an impressive leisure suite. In addition there are also conference and meeting facilities. The bedrooms are spacious and have good facilities; all have delightful views across the golf course to the countryside beyond. The cuisine is enjoyable; particularly at breakfast, which is served in the restaurant that overlooks the course.

Rooms 104 (3 fmly) (36 GF) **Facilities** Spa STV FTV WiFi 36 Putt green Gym Academy of Golf Xmas New Year **Conf** Class 200 Board 50 Thtr 450 **Services** Lift Air con **Parking** 500 **Notes** ⊗ Civ Wed 250

Horsted Place
★★★ ◎◎ HOTEL

tel: 01825 750581 **Little Horsted TN22 5TS**
email: hotel@horstedplace.co.uk **web:** www.horstedplace.co.uk
dir: From Uckfield 2m S on A26 towards Lewes

This property is one of Britain's finest examples of Gothic revivalist architecture, and much of the 1850s building was designed by Augustus Pugin. The hotel is situated in extensive landscaped grounds, with a tennis court and croquet lawn, and is adjacent to the East Sussex National Golf Club. The spacious bedrooms, in a range of both sizes and designs, are attractively decorated, tastefully furnished, and equipped with many thoughtful touches such as flowers and books. Most bedrooms also have a separate sitting area. Formal dining can be enjoyed in the elegant dining room (no children after 7pm) where the menus are based on quality seasonal produce. Pre-dinner drinks and after-dinner coffees can be enjoyed either in the Drawing Room or on the terrace overlooking the garden.

Rooms 20 (3 annexe) (5 fmly) (2 GF) S £145-£360; **D** £145-£360 (incl. bkfst)* **Facilities** STV FTV WiFi 36 Free use of gym & indoor pool at nearby hotel Xmas New Year **Conf** Class 50 Board 40 Thtr 80 Del from £170* **Services** Lift **Parking** 32 **Notes** LB ⊗ No children 7yrs Civ Wed 100

ULLESTHORPE
Leicestershire Map 11 SP58

BEST WESTERN PLUS Ullesthorpe Court Hotel & Golf Club

★★★★ 75% HOTEL

tel: 01455 209023 **Frolesworth Rd LE17 5BZ**
email: bookings@ullesthorpecourt.co.uk **web:** www.bw-ullesthorpecourt.co.uk
dir: M1 junct 20 towards Lutterworth. Follow brown tourist signs

Complete with its own golf club, this impressively equipped hotel is within easy reach of the motorway network, NEC and Birmingham airport. Public areas include both formal and informal eating options and extensive conference and leisure facilities. Spacious bedrooms are thoughtfully equipped for both the business and leisure guest, and a four-poster room is available.

Rooms 72 (3 fmly) (16 GF) **Facilities** Spa STV WiFi supervised 18 Putt green Gym Beauty room Steam room Sauna Snooker room New Year **Conf** Class 48 Board 30 Thtr 80 Del from £110 to £150* **Services** Lift **Parking** 280 **Notes** ⊗ RS 25-26 Dec Civ Wed 120

ULLSWATER

See Glenridding & Patterdale

UPPER SLAUGHTER
Gloucestershire   Map 10 SP12

INSPECTORS' CHOICE

Lords of the Manor

★★★★ ⚜⚜⚜ COUNTRY HOUSE HOTEL

tel: 01451 820243 **GL54 2JD**
email: reservations@lordsofthemanor.com **web:** www.lordsofthemanor.com
dir: 2m W of A429. Exit A40 onto A429, take 'The Slaughters' turn. Through Lower Slaughter for 1m to Upper Slaughter. Hotel on right

This wonderfully welcoming 17th-century manor house hotel sits in eight acres of gardens and parkland surrounded by Cotswold countryside. A relaxed atmosphere, underpinned by professional and attentive service is the hallmark here, so that guests are often reluctant to leave. The hotel has elegant public rooms that overlook the immaculate lawns, and the restaurant is the venue for consistently impressive cuisine. Bedrooms have much character and charm, combined with the extra touches expected of a hotel of this stature.

Rooms 26 (4 fmly) (9 GF) 🐾 **S** £180-£500; **D** £225-£600 (incl. bkfst)* **Facilities** FTV WiFi Fishing 🌳 Xmas New Year **Conf** Class 20 Board 20 Thtr 30 Del from £225* **Parking** 40 **Notes** Civ Wed 80

Find out more about the AA Hotel Groups of the Year see pages 15 & 16

UPPINGHAM
Rutland   Map 11 SP89

The Lake Isle

⚜⚜ RESTAURANT WITH ROOMS

tel: 01572 822951 📠 01572 824400 **16 High Street East LE15 9PZ**
email: info@lakeisle.co.uk **web:** www.lakeisle.co.uk
dir: From A47, turn left at 2nd lights, 100yds on right

This attractive town house centres around a delightful restaurant and small elegant bar. There is also an inviting first-floor guest lounge, and the bedrooms are extremely well appointed and thoughtfully equipped; spacious split-level cottage suites situated in a quiet courtyard are also available. The imaginative cooking and an extremely impressive wine list are highlights here.

Rooms 12 (3 annexe) (1 fmly)

UPTON UPON SEVERN
Worcestershire   Map 10 SO84

White Lion Hotel

★★★ 74% ⚜ HOTEL

tel: 01684 592551 **21 High St WR8 OHJ**
email: reservations@whitelionhotel.biz **web:** www.whitelionhotel.biz
dir: A422, A38 towards Tewkesbury. In 8m take B4104, after 1m cross bridge, turn left to hotel, past bend on left

Famed for being the inn depicted in Henry Fielding's novel *Tom Jones*, this 16th-century hotel is a reminder of 'Old England' with features such as exposed beams and wall timbers still remaining. The quality furnishing and the decor throughout enhance its character; the bedrooms are smart and include one four-poster room.

Rooms 13 (2 annexe) (2 fmly) (2 GF) 🐾 **S** £65-£90; **D** £90-£99 (incl. bkfst)* **Facilities** FTV WiFi **Parking** 14 **Notes** LB Closed 1 Jan RS 25 Dec

UTTOXETER
Staffordshire   Map 10 SK03

Premier Inn Uttoxeter

BUDGET HOTEL

tel: 0871 527 9112 **Derby Rd ST14 5AA**
web: www.premierinn.com
dir: At junct of A50 & B5030 on outskirts of Uttoxeter, 7m S of Alton Towers Theme Park

High quality, budget accommodation ideal for both families and business travellers. Spacious, en suite bedrooms feature tea and coffee making facilities, and Freeview TV in most hotels. Internet access and WiFi are available for a small fee. The adjacent family restaurant features a wide and varied menu. See also the Hotel Groups pages.

Rooms 41

VENTNOR   Map 5 SZ57
Isle of Wight

The Royal Hotel

★★★★ 80% ⊛⊛ HOTEL

tel: 01983 852186 **Belgrave Rd PO38 1JJ**
email: enquiries@royalhoteliow.co.uk **web:** www.royalhoteliow.co.uk
dir: A3055 into Ventnor follow one-way system, after lights left into Belgrave Rd. Hotel on right

This smart hotel enjoys a central yet peaceful location in its own gardens, complete with an outdoor pool. Spacious, elegant public areas include a bright conservatory, bar and lounge. Bedrooms, appointed to a high standard, vary in size and style. Staff are friendly and efficient, particularly in the smart restaurant, where modern British cuisine is offered.

Rooms 53 (9 fmly) ✆ **S** £110-£145; **D** £185-£285 (incl. bkfst)* **Facilities** FTV WiFi ✴
Xmas New Year **Conf** Class 40 Board 24 Thtr 100 Del from £160 to £270*
Services Lift **Parking** 50 **Notes** LB ⊗ Closed 1st 2 wks Jan Civ Wed 120

Eversley Hotel

★★★ 75% HOTEL

tel: 01983 852244 & 852462 **Park Av PO38 1LB**
email: eversleyhotel@yahoo.co.uk **web:** www.eversleyhotel.uk.com
dir: On A3055 W of Ventnor, next to Ventnor Park

Located west of Ventnor, this hotel enjoys a quiet location and has some rooms with garden and pool views. The spacious restaurant is sometimes used for local functions, and there are a bar, television room, lounge area, and card room as well as a jacuzzi and gym. Bedrooms are generally a good size.

Rooms 28 (6 fmly) (2 GF) ✆ **S** £35-£85; **D** £69-£120 (incl. bkfst)* **Facilities** STV FTV
WiFi ✴ Gym Xmas New Year **Conf** Class 60 Board 20 **Parking** 23 **Notes** Closed 30 Nov-22 Dec & 2 Jan-8 Feb

Ventnor Towers Hotel

★★★ 70% HOTEL

tel: 01983 852277 **54 Madeira Rd PO38 1QT**
email: reservations@ventnortowers.com **web:** www.ventnortowers.com
dir: From E, 1st left off A3055 just before pelican crossing

This mid-Victorian hotel, set in spacious grounds with a path that leads down to the shore, is high above the bay and enjoys splendid sea views. Many potted plants and fresh flowers grace the day rooms, which include two lounges and a spacious bar. Bedrooms include two four-poster rooms and some that have their own balconies.

Rooms 25 (4 fmly) (6 GF) **Facilities** WiFi ✴ ♨ 9 ⛳ Putt green Xmas New Year
Conf Class 60 Board 44 Thtr 100 **Parking** 20 **Notes** Civ Wed 150

The Wellington Hotel

★★★ ⒶHOTEL

tel: 01983 856600 **Belgrave Rd PO38 1JH**
email: enquiries@thewellingtonhotel.net **web:** www.thewellingtonhotel.net

This hotel, a commanding white building with ornate balconies, has amazing sea views. Double, twin and deluxe bedrooms are on offer and very nearly all have uninterrupted views of the sea. Each has an understated decor in calming colour schemes.

Rooms 28 (5 fmly) (7 GF) **S** £82-£92; **D** £112-£122 (incl. bkfst)* **Facilities** FTV WiFi
⇗ **Parking** 10 **Notes** LB ⊗

INSPECTORS' CHOICE

The Hambrough

RESTAURANT WITH ROOMS ⊛⊛⊛

tel: 01983 856333 ⎙ 01983 857260 **Hambrough Rd PO38 1SQ**
email: info@thehambrough.com **web:** www.thehambrough.com
dir: Phone for directions

A former Victorian villa set on the hillside above Ventnor and with memorable views out to sea, The Hambrough has a modern, stylish interior with well-equipped and boutique-style accommodation. The kitchen team's passion for food is clearly evident in the superb cuisine served in the minimalistic styled restaurant.

Rooms 7 (3 fmly)

V

VERYAN
Cornwall

Map 2 SW93

INSPECTORS' CHOICE

The Nare

★★★★ ◉◉ COUNTRY HOUSE HOTEL

tel: 01872 501111 **Carne Beach TR2 5PF**
email: stay@narehotel.co.uk **web:** www.narehotel.co.uk
dir: A3078 from Tregony, approx 1.5m. Left at Veryan sign, through village towards sea & hotel

The Nare offers a relaxed, country-house atmosphere in a spectacular coastal setting. The elegantly designed bedrooms, many with balconies, have fresh flowers, carefully chosen artwork and antiques that contribute to their engaging individuality. A choice of dining options is available, from light snacks to superb local seafood.

Rooms 37 (7 fmly) (7 GF) ⟨S £143-£276; **D** £276-£791 (incl. bkfst)* **Facilities** Spa FTV WiFi ⟨⟩ ⟨ Gym Health & beauty clinic Sauna Steam room Hotel sailing boat Shooting Xmas New Year **Services** Lift **Parking** 80 **Notes** LB

WADDESDON
Buckinghamshire

Map 11 SP71

The Five Arrows

◉◉ RESTAURANT WITH ROOMS

tel: 01296 651727 ▤ 01296 655716 **High St HP18 0JE**
email: five.arrows@nationaltrust.org.uk **web:** www.thefivearrows.com
dir: On A41 in Waddesdon. Into Baker St for car park

This Grade II listed building with its elaborate Elizabethan-style chimney stacks stands at the gates of Waddesdon Manor and was named after the Rothschild family emblem. Individually styled en suite bedrooms are comfortable and well appointed. Friendly staff are on hand to offer a warm welcome. Alfresco dining is possible in the warmer months.

Rooms 11

WAKEFIELD
West Yorkshire

Map 16 SE32

See also **Liversedge**

Waterton Park Hotel

★★★★ 80% ◉ HOTEL

tel: 01924 257911 & 249800 **Walton Hall, The Balk, Walton WF2 6PW**
email: info@watertonparkhotel.co.uk **web:** www.watertonparkhotel.co.uk
dir: 3m SE off B6378. Exit M1 junct 39 towards Wakefield. At 3rd rdbt right for Crofton. At 2nd lights right & follow signs

This Georgian mansion, built on an island in the centre of a 26-acre lake is in a truly idyllic setting. The main house contains many feature bedrooms, and the annexe houses more spacious rooms, all equally well equipped with modern facilities; most of the bedrooms have views over the lake or the 18-hole golf course. The delightful beamed restaurant, two bars and leisure club are located in the old hall, and there is a licence for civil weddings.

Rooms 65 (43 annexe) (5 fmly) (23 GF) ⟨S £70-£120; **D** £99-£185 (incl. bkfst)* **Facilities** STV FTV WiFi ⟨⟩ ⟨ supervised Fishing Gym Steam room Sauna New Year **Conf** Class 80 Board 80 Thtr 150 Del from £130 to £175* **Services** Lift **Parking** 200 **Notes** LB ⊗ Civ Wed 130

Cedar Court Hotel Wakefield

THE INDEPENDENTS
HOTEL ASSOCIATION

★★★★ 73% HOTEL

tel: 01924 276310 **Denby Dale Rd WF4 3QZ**
email: sales@cedarcourthotels.co.uk **web:** www.cedarcourthotels.co.uk
dir: Adjacent to M1 junct 39

This hotel enjoys a convenient location just off the M1. Traditionally styled bedrooms offer a good range of facilities while open-plan public areas include a busy bar and restaurant operation. Conferences and functions are extremely well catered for and a modern leisure club completes the picture.

Rooms 149 (2 fmly) (74 GF) ⟨S £49-£99; **D** £49-£99* **Facilities** FTV WiFi ⟨⟩ ⟨ supervised Gym Sauna Steam room Beauty treatment room Xmas New Year **Conf** Class 140 Board 80 Thtr 400 Del from £119.95 to £124.95 **Services** Lift **Parking** 350 **Notes** LB Civ Wed 250

Campanile Wakefield

Campanile

BUDGET HOTEL

tel: 01924 201054 **Monckton Rd WF2 7AL**
email: wakefield@campanile.com **web:** www.campanile.com
dir: M1 junct 39, A636, 1m towards Wakefield, left into Monckton Rd, hotel on left

This modern building offers accommodation in smart, well-equipped bedrooms, all with en suite bathrooms. Refreshments may be taken at the informal bistro. See also the Hotel Groups pages.

Rooms 72 (72 annexe) (21 GF) **S** £35-£44; **D** £35-£48* **Conf** Class 15 Board 15 Thtr 25 Del from £52 to £70*

Premier Inn Wakefield Central

BUDGET HOTEL

tel: 0871 527 9114 **Thornes Park, Denby Dale Rd WF2 8DY**
web: www.premierinn.com
dir: M1 junct 41, A650 towards Wakefield. Approx 1.5m. Hotel on right

High quality, budget accommodation ideal for both families and business travellers. Spacious, en suite bedrooms feature tea and coffee making facilities, and Freeview TV in most hotels. Internet access and WiFi are available for a small fee. The adjacent family restaurant features a wide and varied menu. See also the Hotel Groups pages.

Rooms 42

Premier Inn Wakefield City North

BUDGET HOTEL

tel: 0871 527 9116 **Paragon Business Park, Herriot Way WF1 2UJ**
web: www.premierinn.com
dir: M1 junct 41, A650 (Bradford Rd) for approx 1.5m towards Wakefield centre. Hotel on right adjacent to Bannatynes Health Club

Rooms 47

Premier Inn Wakefield South M1 Jct 39

BUDGET HOTEL

tel: 0871 527 9118 **Calder Park, Denby Dale Rd WF4 3BB**
web: www.premierinn.com
dir: M1 junct 39, A636 towards Wakefield. At 1st rdbt 1st exit into Calder Park. Hotel on right

Rooms 74

WALLASEY
Merseyside   Map 15 SJ29

Grove House Hotel

★★★ 82% HOTEL

tel: 0151 639 3947 & 630 4558 **Grove Rd CH45 3HF**
email: reception@thegrovehouse.co.uk **web:** www.thegrovehouse.co.uk
dir: M53 junct 1, A554 (Wallasey New Brighton), right after church into Harrison Drive, left after Windsors Garage into Grove Rd

Ideally situated for Liverpool and the M53, this friendly hotel offers attractive and comfortable bedrooms, which come with a wealth of extras. Well-cooked meals are served in the elegant panelled dining room. Weddings and conferences also catered for.

Rooms 14 (7 fmly) ♠ **S** £59; **D** £79-£99* **Facilities** FTV WiFi **Conf** Class 30 Board 50 Thtr 50 Del from £89 to £99* **Parking** 28 **Notes** ⊗ RS BHs Civ Wed 50

WALLINGFORD
Oxfordshire   Map 5 SU68

The George

★★★ 73% HOTEL

tel: 01491 836665 **High St OX10 0BS**
email: info@george-hotel-wallingford.com **web:** www.peelhotels.co.uk
dir: E side of A329, N end of Wallingford

Old world charm and modern facilities merge seamlessly in this former coaching inn. Bedrooms in the main house have character in abundance. Those in the wing have a more contemporary style, but all are well equipped and attractively decorated. Diners can choose between the restaurant and bistro, or relax in the cosy bar.

Rooms 39 (1 fmly) (9 GF) ♠ **S** £100-£125; **D** £110-£135 (incl. bkfst)* **Facilities** STV WiFi Xmas New Year **Conf** Class 60 Board 50 Thtr 150 Del from £125 to £145* **Parking** 40 **Notes** LB ⊗ Civ Wed 100

WALSALL
West Midlands   Map 10 SP09

Fairlawns Hotel & Spa

★★★★ 77% ⑧⑧ HOTEL

tel: 01922 455122 **178 Little Aston Rd WS9 0NU**
email: reception@fairlawns.co.uk **web:** www.fairlawns.co.uk
dir: Exit A452 towards Aldridge at x-roads with A454. Hotel 600yds on right

In a rural location with immaculate landscaped grounds, this constantly improving hotel offers a wide range of facilities and modern, comfortable bedrooms. Family rooms, one with a four-poster bed, and suites are also available. The Fairlawns Restaurant serves a wide range of award-winning seasonal dishes. The extensive, comprehensively equipped leisure complex is mainly for adult use as there is restricted availability to young people.

Rooms 58 (8 fmly) (1 GF) (3 smoking) ♠ **Facilities** Spa STV FTV WiFi ▷ ⊗ supervised ⊰ ⊱ Gym Dance studio Beauty salon Bathing suite Floatation suite Sauna Aromatherapy room New Year **Conf** Class 40 Board 30 Thtr 80 Del from £125 to £159.50* **Services** Lift **Parking** 150 **Notes** RS 24 Dec-2 Jan Civ Wed 100

BEST WESTERN Baron's Court Hotel

★★★ 74% HOTEL

tel: 01543 452020 **Walsall Rd, Walsall Wood WS9 9AH**
email: yvonne.hyde@bwbaronscourthotel.com **web:** www.bwbaronscourthotel.com
dir: 3.5m out of Walsall town centre, just N of Birmingham, close to M6 Toll

This hotel prides itself on warm hospitality and is conveniently situated for business guests visiting this area. The lounge, bar and restaurant are modern and thoughtfully designed. Conference facilities are available, along with ample car parking.

Rooms 94 (10 fmly) ♠ **S** £35-£100; **D** £39-£115* **Facilities** WiFi ▷ Xmas New Year **Conf** Class 42 Board 40 Thtr 180 Del from £79 to £89* **Services** Lift **Parking** 123 **Notes** LB Civ Wed 120

W

WALLSALL *continued*

Holiday Inn Express Walsall M6 Jct 10

BUDGET HOTEL

tel: 01922 705250 **Tempus Ten, Tempus Dr WS2 8TJ**
email: admin@hiexwalsall.com **web:** www.hiexpress.co.uk
dir: M6 junct 10/A454 to Walsall. Right at 1st lights, hotel 200mtrs on right

A modern hotel ideal for families and business travellers. Fresh and uncomplicated, the spacious rooms include Sky TV, power shower and tea and coffee-making facilities. Continental buffet breakfast is included in the room rate; other meals may be taken at the nearby family pub or restaurant. See also the Hotel Groups pages.

Rooms 120 (77 fmly) (30 GF) ✆ **S** £30-£150; **D** £30-£150 (incl. bkfst) **Conf** Class 45 Board 36 Thtr 60 Del from £70 to £130

Premier Inn Walsall M6 Jct 10

BUDGET HOTEL

tel: 0871 527 9120 **Bentley Green, Bentley Road North WS2 0WB**
web: www.premierinn.com
dir: M6 junct 10, A454 signed Wolverhampton. 2nd exit (Ansons junct). Left at rdbt, 1st left at next rdbt, hotel on right

High quality, budget accommodation ideal for both families and business travellers. Spacious, en suite bedrooms feature tea and coffee making facilities, and Freeview TV in most hotels. Internet access and WiFi are available for a small fee. The adjacent family restaurant features a wide and varied menu. See also the Hotel Groups pages.

Rooms 40

Premier Inn Walsall Town Centre

BUDGET HOTEL

tel: 0871 527 9374 **Waterfront, Wolverhampton St WS2 8LR**
web: www.premierinn.com
dir: M6 junct 10/A454 Wolverhampton Road to Walsall. Continue on A454. Follow signs for Crown Wharf Shopping Centre. Premier Inn situated on right on Wolverhampton Street

Rooms 100 (75 fmly)

WALTHAM ABBEY
Essex

Map 6 TL30

Premier Inn Waltham Abbey

BUDGET HOTEL

tel: 0871 527 9122 **Sewardstone Rd EN9 3QF**
web: www.premierinn.com
dir: M25 junct 26, A121 towards Waltham Abbey. Left onto A112, hotel 0.5m on left

High quality, budget accommodation ideal for both families and business travellers. Spacious, en suite bedrooms feature tea and coffee making facilities, and Freeview TV in most hotels. Internet access and WiFi are available for a small fee. The adjacent family restaurant features a wide and varied menu. See also the Hotel Groups pages.

Rooms 93

WANSFORD
Cambridgeshire

Map 12 TL09

The Haycock Hotel

★★★ 87% ◉ HOTEL

tel: 01780 782223 & 781124 **PE8 6JA**
email: sales@thehaycock.co.uk **web:** www.macdonaldhotels.co.uk/haycock
dir: A1 junct to A47 Leicester

A charming 17th-century coaching inn set in attractive landscaped grounds in a peaceful village location. The smartly decorated bedrooms are tastefully furnished and thoughtfully equipped. Public rooms include a choice of restaurants, a lounge bar, a cocktail bar and a stylish lounge. The hotel has a staffed business centre, and banqueting facilities are also available.

Rooms 48 (1 fmly) (14 GF) ✆ **S** £77-£127; **D** £87-£137 (incl. bkfst)* **Facilities** FTV WiFi ⊹ Beauty treatment room New Year **Conf** Class 100 Board 45 Thtr 300 Del from £125 to £135* **Parking** 300 **Notes** Civ Wed 200

WANTAGE
Oxfordshire

Map 5 SU38

La Fontana Restaurant with Accommodation

RESTAURANT WITH ROOMS

tel: 01235 868287 📠 01235 868019 **Oxford Rd, East Hanney OX12 0HP**
email: anna@la-fontana.co.uk **web:** www.la-fontana.co.uk
dir: A338 from Wantage towards Oxford. Restaurant on right in East Hanney

Guests are guaranteed a warm welcome at this family-run Italian restaurant located on the outskirts of the busy town of Wantage. The stylish bedrooms are individually designed, well equipped and very comfortable. Dinner should not be missed - the menu features a wide range of regional Italian specialities.

Rooms 15 (7 annexe) (2 fmly)

WARMINSTER
Wiltshire

Map 4 ST84

The Bishopstrow Hotel & Spa

★★★★ 79% ◉ HOTEL

tel: 01985 212312 **Borenam Rd BA12 9HH**
web: www.bishopstrow.co.uk
dir: From rdbt on A36 take B3414 towards Warminster. Follow brown hotel signs

The Bishopstrow Hotel is set in 27 acres of delightful grounds which include modern spa facilities, tennis courts and country walks. Bedrooms are comfortable and stylish, and all are well appointed. Public areas offer several day rooms, and retain the style of the original house. Cuisine is a feature here, and menus offer fresh and local produce.

Rooms 32 (2 annexe) (26 fmly) (9 GF) ✆ **S** £120-£475; **D** £150-£505 (incl. bkfst)* **Facilities** Spa STV FTV WiFi ⊛ ⊰ ⊱ Fishing Gym Thermal rooms Relaxation room Dual treatment room Xmas New Year **Conf** Class 40 Board 36 Thtr 60 Del from £180 to £220* **Parking** 70 **Notes** Civ Wed 82

WARRINGTON
Cheshire

Map 15 SJ68

The Park Royal

★★★★ 80% HOTEL

QHOTELS
INSPIRED BY YOU

tel: 01925 730706 **Stretton Rd, Stretton WA4 4NS**
email: parkroyalreservations@qhotels.co.uk **web:** www.qhotels.co.uk
dir: M56 junct 10, A49 to Warrington, at lights turn right to Appleton Thorn, 1st right into Spark Hall Close, hotel on left

This modern hotel enjoys a peaceful setting, yet is conveniently located just minutes from the M56. The bedrooms are contemporary, well furnished and attractively co-ordinated. Spacious, stylish public areas include extensive conference and function facilities and a comprehensive leisure centre complete with outdoor tennis courts and a spa. Complimentary WiFi is also provided. QHotels is the AA Hotel Group of the Year 2014-15.

Rooms 146 (31 fmly) (31 GF) 🐾 **Facilities** Spa FTV WiFi 🌀 🏊 Gym Dance studio Sauna Xmas New Year **Conf** Class 180 Board 90 Thtr 400 **Services** Lift **Parking** 400 **Notes** Civ Wed 300

BEST WESTERN Fir Grove Hotel

★★★ 78% HOTEL

Best Western

tel: 01925 267471 **Knutsford Old Rd WA4 2LD**
email: firgrove@bestwestern.co.uk **web:** www.bw-firgrovehotel.co.uk
dir: M6 junct 20, follow signs for A50 to Warrington for 2.4m, before swing bridge over canal, turn right & right again

Situated in a quiet residential area, this hotel is convenient for both the town centre and the motorway network. Comfortable, smart bedrooms, including spacious executive rooms, offer some excellent extra facilities such as iPod docking stations. Public areas include a smart lounge/bar, a neatly appointed restaurant, and excellent function and meeting facilities.

Rooms 52 (3 fmly) (20 GF) **Facilities** STV FTV WiFi 🐾 Xmas New Year **Conf** Class 150 Board 50 Thtr 300 **Parking** 100 **Notes** Civ Wed 180

Holiday Inn Warrington

★★★ 76% HOTEL

Holiday Inn

tel: 0871 942 9087 **Woolston Grange Av, Woolston WA1 4PX**
web: www.hiwarringtonhotel.co.uk
dir: M6 junct 21, follow signs for Birchwood

Ideally located within the M62 and M56 interchange, this hotel provides the ideal base for all areas of the north-west region for both corporate and leisure guests. Rooms are spacious and well equipped, and a wide choice of meals is available in the comfortable restaurant and cosy bar. Meeting and conference facilities are also available.

Rooms 96 (40 fmly) (9 GF) **Facilities** STV FTV WiFi 🐾 HL Xmas New Year **Conf** Board 20 Thtr 30 **Services** Lift Air con **Parking** 101

Premier Inn Warrington A49/M62 Jct 9

BUDGET HOTEL

tel: 0871 527 9128 **Winwick Rd WA2 8RN**
web: www.premierinn.com
dir: M62 junct 9 towards Warrington, hotel 100yds

High quality, budget accommodation ideal for both families and business travellers. Spacious, en suite bedrooms feature tea and coffee making facilities, and Freeview TV in most hotels. Internet access and WiFi are available for a small fee. The adjacent family restaurant features a wide and varied menu. See also the Hotel Groups pages.

Rooms 74

Premier Inn Warrington Centre

BUDGET HOTEL

tel: 0871 527 9126 **1430 Centre Park, Park Boulevard WA1 1PR**
web: www.premierinn.com
dir: Take A49 to Brian Beven Island Rdbt, into Park Boulevard (Centre Park). Over bridge. Hotel on right

Rooms 42

Premier Inn Warrington (M6 Jct 21)

BUDGET HOTEL

tel: 0871 527 9124 **Manchester Rd, Woolston WA1 4GB**
web: www.premierinn.com
dir: Just off M6 junct 21 on A57 to Warrington

Rooms 105

Premier Inn Warrington North

BUDGET HOTEL

tel: 0871 527 9128 **Winwick Rd WA2 8RN**
web: www.premierinn.com
dir: M62 junct 9, A49 signed Warrington. At next rdbt follow Town Centre signs. Straight on at next rdbt, left into Warrington Collegiate Camp

Rooms 74

Premier Inn Warrington North East

BUDGET HOTEL

tel: 0871 527 9130 **Golborne Rd, Winwick WA2 8LF**
web: www.premierinn.com
dir: M6 junct 22, A573 towards Newton-le-Willows. Dual carriageway to end, take 3rd exit at rdbt. Hotel adjacent to church

Rooms 42

Premier Inn Warrington South

BUDGET HOTEL

tel: 0871 527 9134 **Tarporley Rd, Stretton WA4 4NB**
web: www.premierinn.com
dir: Just off M56 junct 10. Follow A49 to Warrington, left at 1st lights

Rooms 29

W

WARWICK
Warwickshire

Map 10 SP26

See also **Leamington Spa (Royal) & Wroxall**

Ardencote Manor Hotel & Spa

★★★★ 80% 🏵🏵 HOTEL

tel: 01926 843111 **The Cumsey, Lye Green Rd, Claverdon CV35 8LT**
email: hotel@ardencote.com **web:** www.ardencote.com

(For full entry see Claverdon)

Chesford Grange

★★★★ 77% HOTEL

tel: 01926 859331 **Chesford Bridge CV8 2LD**
email: chesfordreservations@qhotels.co.uk **web:** www.qhotels.co.uk

(For full entry see Kenilworth)

Premier Inn Warwick

BUDGET HOTEL

tel: 0871 527 9320 **Opus 40, Birmingham Rd CV34 5JL**
web: www.premierinn.com
dir: M40 junct 15, A46 (Warick bypass) towards Warwick. Follow A425 signs. From A425 1st left into industrial estate (Opus 40). Hotel 200yds, opposite IBM office

High quality, budget accommodation ideal for both families and business travellers. Spacious, en suite bedrooms feature tea and coffee making facilities, and Freeview TV in most hotels. Internet access and WiFi are available for a small fee. The adjacent family restaurant features a wide and varied menu. See also the Hotel Groups pages.

Rooms 124

WARWICK MOTORWAY SERVICE AREA (M40)
Warwickshire

Map 10 SP35

Days Inn Warwick North - M40

BUDGET HOTEL

tel: 01926 651681 **Warwick Services, M40 Northbound Junction 12-13, Banbury Rd CV35 OAA**
email: warwick.north.hotel@welcomebreak.co.uk **web:** www.welcomebreak.co.uk
dir: M40 northbound between junct 12 & 13

This modern building offers accommodation in smart, spacious and well-equipped bedrooms, suitable for families and business travellers, and all with en suite bathrooms. Continental breakfast is available and other refreshments may be taken at the nearby family restaurant. See also the Hotel Groups pages.

Rooms 54 (45 fmly) (8 smoking) **S** £25-£70; **D** £25-£70* **Conf** Board 30 Del £120*

Days Inn Warwick South - M40

BUDGET HOTEL

tel: 01926 652081 **Warwick Services, M40 Southbound, Banbury Rd CV35 OAA**
email: warwick.south.hotel@welcomebreak.co.uk **web:** www.welcomebreak.co.uk
dir: M40 southbound between junct 14 & 12

Rooms 40 (30 fmly) (19 GF) (4 smoking)

WASHINGTON
Tyne & Wear

Map 19 NZ35

Holiday Inn Washington

★★★ 79% HOTEL

tel: 0871 942 9084 **Emerson District 5 NE37 1LB**
email: washingtonhi@ihg.com **web:** www.hiwashingtonhotel.co.uk
dir: Just off A1(M) junct 64. Left at rdbt, hotel on left

This is an ideally located hotel, just off the A1(M), and near to historic Durham, Sunderland and Newcastle's city centre. It is well established and noted for its friendly staff. Bedrooms are air conditioned, and executive rooms are available. The eating options are Traders Restaurant and the lounge bar area.

Rooms 136 (6 GF) (4 smoking) **Facilities** STV FTV WiFi 🏊 Xmas New Year **Conf** Class 60 Board 50 Thtr 100 **Services** Lift Air con **Parking** 200 **Notes** Civ Wed 150

Campanile Washington

BUDGET HOTEL

tel: 0191 416 5010 **Emerson Rd, District 5 NE37 1LE**
email: washington@campanile.com **web:** www.campanile.com
dir: A1(M) junct 64, A195 to Washington, 1st left at rdbt into Emerson Rd. Hotel 800yds on left

This modern building offers accommodation in smart, well-equipped bedrooms, all with en suite bathrooms. Refreshments may be taken at the informal bistro. See also the Hotel Groups pages.

Rooms 79 (79 annexe) (1 fmly) (28 GF) **S** £39-£150; **D** £39-£150* **Conf** Class 15 Board 25 Thtr 40 Del from £80 to £95*

Premier Inn Newcastle (Washington)

BUDGET HOTEL

tel: 0871 527 9136 **Emerson Rd NE37 1LB**
web: www.premierinn.com
dir: A1(M) junct 64, A195, follow Emerson signs. Left at rdbt, hotel 250yds left

High quality, budget accommodation ideal for both families and business travellers. Spacious, en suite bedrooms feature tea and coffee making facilities, and Freeview TV in most hotels. Internet access and WiFi are available for a small fee. The adjacent family restaurant features a wide and varied menu. See also the Hotel Groups pages.

Rooms 74

WATERMILLOCK
Cumbria

Map 18 NY42

Rampsbeck Country House Hotel

★★★★ ◎◎ HOTEL

tel: 017684 86442 **CA11 0LP**
email: enquiries@rampsbeck.co.uk **web:** www.rampsbeck.co.uk
dir: M6 junct 40, A592 to Ullswater, at T-junct (with lake opposite) turn right, hotel 1.5m

This fine country house lies in 18 acres of parkland on the shores of Lake Ullswater, and is furnished with many period and antique pieces. There are three delightful lounges, an elegant restaurant and a traditional bar. Bedrooms come in three grades; the most spacious of which are spectacular and overlook the lake. Service is attentive and the award-winning cuisine a real highlight.

Rooms 19 (1 fmly) (1 GF) ⌁ **S** £154.75-£265; **D** £259.50-£430 (incl. bkfst & dinner)*
Facilities STV FTV WiFi Putt green ⛵ Private boat trips on Lake Ullswater Xmas New Year **Conf** Class 10 Board 15 Thtr 15 **Parking** 25 **Notes** Civ Wed 60

Macdonald Leeming House

★★★★ 76% ◎ HOTEL

tel: 0844 879 9142 **CA11 0JJ**
email: leeminghouse@macdonald-hotels.co.uk **web:** www.macdonaldhotels.co.uk
dir: M6 junct 40, A66 to Keswick. At rdbt take A592 (Ullswater). 5m to T-junct, right - A592. Hotel on left

This hotel enjoys a superb location, being set in 20 acres of mature wooded gardens in the Lake District National Park, and overlooking Ullswater and the towering fells. Many rooms offer views of the lake and the rugged mountains beyond, with more than half having their own balcony. Public rooms include three sumptuous lounges, a cosy bar and library.

Rooms 41 (1 fmly) (10 GF) **Facilities** WiFi Fishing ⛵ Xmas New Year **Conf** Class 40 Board 30 Thtr 80 **Parking** 50 **Notes** Civ Wed 80

WATFORD
Hertfordshire

Map 6 TQ19

Mercure London Watford Hotel

★★★★ 71% HOTEL

tel: 0844 815 9056 **A41, Watford Bypass WD25 8JH**
email: info@mercurewatford.co.uk **web:** www.jupiterhotels.co.uk
dir: M1 junct 5, A41 S to London. Straight on at island, hotel 1m on left

The Hotel is situated on the outskirts of London close to the M1, M25, A1(M) motorways, and Luton and London Heathrow airports. The bedrooms are smartly appointed and equipped with modern facilities including WiFi and satellite TV. Public rooms include The Brasserie restaurant and bar; guests also have the use of the leisure facilities with a heated pool.

Rooms 218 **Facilities** WiFi ↓ ❄ Gym Sauna Steam room Beauty treatments **Conf** Class 120 Board 58 Thtr 200 **Parking** 250 **Notes** Civ Wed 200

BEST WESTERN White House

★★★ 74% HOTEL

tel: 01923 237316 **Upton Rd WD18 0JF**
email: info@whitehousehotel.co.uk **web:** www.bw-whitehousehotel.co.uk
dir: From centre ring road, exit left into Upton Rd, hotel on left

This popular commercial hotel is situated within easy walking distance to the town centre. Bedrooms are pleasantly decorated and offer a good range of facilities that include interactive TV with internet. The public areas are open plan; they include a comfortable lounge/bar, cosy snug and an attractive conservatory restaurant with a sunny open terrace for summer dining. Functions suites are also available.

Rooms 57 (3 fmly) (8 GF) **S** £59-£99; **D** £69-£109 (incl. bkfst)* **Facilities** FTV WiFi HL **Conf** Class 80 Board 50 Thtr 150 Del from £125 to £155* **Services** Lift **Parking** 50 **Notes** ⊗ RS 25 Dec-2 Jan Civ Wed 120

Premier Inn Watford Centre

BUDGET HOTEL

tel: 0871 527 9140 **Timms Meadow, Water Ln WD17 2NJ**
web: www.premierinn.com
dir: M1 junct 5, A41 into town centre. At rdbt take 3rd exit, stay in left lane through lights. Take 1st left into Water Ln. Hotel on left

High quality, budget accommodation ideal for both families and business travellers. Spacious, en suite bedrooms feature tea and coffee making facilities, and Freeview TV in most hotels. Internet access and WiFi are available for a small fee. The adjacent family restaurant features a wide and varied menu. See also the Hotel Groups pages.

Rooms 105

Premier Inn Watford (Croxley Green)

BUDGET HOTEL

tel: 0871 527 9138 **2 Ascot Rd WD18 8AD**
web: www.premierinn.com
dir: M25 junct 18, A404 signed Watford/Rickmansworth, left at 1st rdbt signed A412 Watford. Follow Croxley Green Business Park/Watford signs, at 4th rdbt, 3rd exit. M1 junct 5, A41 towards Watford, follow Watford West & Rickmansworth A412 signs. Then Croxley Green Business Park signs

Rooms 121

W

WATFORD *continued*

Premier Inn Watford North

BUDGET HOTEL

tel: 0871 527 9142 **859 St Albans Rd, Garston WD25 0LH**
web: www.premierinn.com
dir: M1 junct 6, A405 towards Watford. At 2nd lights onto A412 (St Albans Rd). Into TGI Friday's car park. Hotel directly behind

Rooms 45

WATTON	Map 13 TF90
Norfolk	

Broom Hall Country Hotel

★★★ 77% COUNTRY HOUSE HOTEL

tel: 01953 882125 **Richmond Rd, Saham Toney IP25 7EX**
email: enquiries@broomhallhotel.co.uk **web:** www.broomhallhotel.co.uk
dir: From A11 at Thetford onto A1075 to Watton (12m), B1108 towards Swaffham, in 0.5m at rdbt turn right to Saham Toney, hotel 0.5m on left. From A47 take A1075, left onto B1108

A delightful Victorian country house situated down a private drive and set in mature landscaped gardens surrounded by parkland. The well-equipped bedrooms are split between the main house and an adjacent building. Public rooms include a relaxing lounge, a brasserie restaurant, a lounge bar, a conservatory and a smart restaurant. There is an indoor swimming pool.

Rooms 15 (5 annexe) (3 fmly) (5 GF) ✆ **S** £75-£125; **D** £85-£175 (incl. bkfst) **Facilities** FTV WiFi ☒ Massage Beauty treatments **Conf** Class 30 Board 22 Thtr 80 Del from £115 to £165 **Parking** 30 **Notes** LB Closed 24 Dec-4 Jan Civ Wed 70

WELLESBOURNE	Map 10 SP25
Warwickshire	

Walton Hall

★★★★ 82% ⑳⑳ COUNTRY HOUSE HOTEL

tel: 01789 842424 **Walton CV35 9HU**
email: waltonhall.mande@pumahotels.co.uk **web:** www.pumahotels.co.uk
dir: A429 through Barford towards Wellesbourne, right after watermill, follow signs to hotel

Sitting in 65 acres of beautiful countryside, this hotel is just 10 minutes from the M40. It has a fascinating history, with parts dating back to the 1500s. The property has been appointed in a style that combines both the traditional and the modern. The individually designed bedrooms, many with stunning views over the lake and garden, have plasma screen TVs, DVD players and safes big enough for a laptop. Premium rooms and suites are available. The award-winning Moncreiffe Restaurant is situated in the hall and has views over the lovely gardens.

Rooms 37 **Facilities** Spa STV FTV WiFi ☒ supervised Gym Dance studio Beauty salon Xmas New Year **Conf** Class 60 Board 30 Thtr 200 Del from £145 to £255* **Services** Air con **Parking** 240 **Notes** ⊗ Civ Wed 200

Walton Hotel

★★★★ 76% HOTEL

tel: 01789 842424 **Walton CV35 9HU**
email: waltonhotel@pumahotels.co.uk **web:** www.pumahotels.co.uk

Set in 65 acres of open countryside within easy striking distance of Stratford-upon-Avon and Warwick. The modern bedrooms are spacious and very well equipped;

many of the rooms have their own terrace. The hotel has a range of facilities including a spa, a choice of restaurants and a Victorian garden.

Rooms 149 (19 annexe) (40 GF) ✆ **S** £70-£160; **D** £90-£180 (incl. bkfst)* **Facilities** Spa WiFi HL ☒ ♨ Gym ♫ Xmas New Year **Conf** Class 27 Board 28 Thtr 70 Del from £130 to £160* **Services** Lift **Parking** 300 **Notes** LB Civ Wed 100

WELLINGBOROUGH	Map 11 SP86
Northamptonshire	

Ibis Wellingborough

BUDGET HOTEL

tel: 01933 228333 **Enstone Court NN8 2DR**
email: H3164@accor.com **web:** www.ibishotel.com
dir: At junct of A45 & A509 towards Kettering, SW outskirts of Wellingborough

Modern, budget hotel offering comfortable accommodation in bright and practical bedrooms. Breakfast is self-service and dinner is available in the restaurant. See also the Hotel Groups pages.

Rooms 78 (19 fmly) (22 GF) ✆ **Conf** Thtr 20

Premier Inn Wellingborough

BUDGET HOTEL

tel: 0871 527 9144 **London Rd NN8 2DP**
web: www.premierinn.com
dir: 0.5m from town centre on A5193, near Dennington Industrial Estate

High quality, budget accommodation ideal for both families and business travellers. Spacious, en suite bedrooms feature tea and coffee making facilities, and Freeview TV in most hotels. Internet access and WiFi are available for a small fee. The adjacent family restaurant features a wide and varied menu. See also the Hotel Groups pages.

Rooms 40

WELLS	Map 4 ST54
Somerset	

BEST WESTERN PLUS Swan Hotel

★★★ 86% ⑳⑳ HOTEL

tel: 01749 836300 **Sadler St BA5 2RX**
email: info@swanhotelwells.co.uk **web:** www.swanhotelwells.co.uk
dir: A39, A371, on entering Wells follow signs for Hotels & Deliveries. Hotel on right opposite cathedral

Situated in the shadow of Wells Cathedral, this privately owned hotel enjoys a truly stunning location and extends a genuinely friendly welcome. Full of character and with a rich history, the hotel has been restored and extended to provide high levels of quality and comfort. Guests can choose between the larger, period bedrooms in the main building or the more contemporary coach house rooms. Dinner in the oak-panelled restaurant should not be missed.

Rooms 51 (3 fmly) (4 GF) ✆ **S** £100-£122; **D** £124-£197 (incl. bkfst)* **Facilities** FTV WiFi Gym Xmas New Year **Conf** Class 45 Board 40 Thtr 120 Del £140* **Parking** 30 **Notes** LB ⊗ Civ Wed 90

White Hart Hotel

★★ 78% HOTEL

tel: 01749 672056 **Sadler St BA5 2RR**
email: info@whitehart-wells.co.uk **web:** www.whitehart-wells.co.uk
dir: Sadler St at start of one-way system. Hotel opposite cathedral

A former coaching inn dating back to the 15th century, this hotel offers comfortable, modern accommodation. Some bedrooms are in an adjoining former stable block and some are at ground-floor level. Public areas include a guest lounge, a bar and the popular restaurant, Brufani's, where delicious steaks and gourmet burgers are in high demand.

Rooms 15 (3 fmly) (2 GF) **S** £80-£90; **D** £85-£115 (incl. bkfst) **Facilities** WiFi Xmas New Year **Conf** Class 50 Board 35 Thtr 150 **Parking** 17 **Notes** LB Civ Wed 100

Ancient Gate House Hotel

★★ 74% ❀ HOTEL

tel: 01749 672029 **20 Sadler St BA5 2SE**
email: info@ancientgatehouse.co.uk **web:** www.ancientgatehouse.co.uk
dir: 1st hotel on left on cathedral green

Guests are treated to good old-fashioned hospitality and a friendly informal atmosphere at this charming hotel which is full of character. Bedrooms, many with unrivalled cathedral views and four-poster beds, are smartly appointed and stylishly co-ordinated. The Rugantino Restaurant remains popular, offering a mix of traditional and contemporary Italian dishes.

Rooms 9 ✆ **S** £80-£95; **D** £85-£130 (incl. bkfst) **Facilities** FTV WiFi Xmas New Year **Notes** LB Closed 27-29 Dec

---

Tewin Bury Farm Hotel

★★★★ 80% ❀❀ HOTEL

tel: 01438 717793 **Hertford Road (B1000) AL6 0JB**
email: reservations@tewinbury.co.uk **web:** www.tewinbury.co.uk
dir: From N: A1(M) junct 6, 1st exit signed A1000, at next rdbt 1st exit towards Digswell. 0.1m straight on at rdbt. 1m on B100. Hotel on left

Situated not far from the A1(M) and within easy reach of Stevenage and Knebworth House, this delightful country-house hotel is part of a thriving farm. Stylish, well-equipped bedrooms of varying sizes are perfectly suited for both leisure and business guests. An award-winning restaurant and meeting rooms are all part of this family-run establishment.

Rooms 29 (20 annexe) (6 fmly) (21 GF) ✆ **Facilities** FTV WiFi ⟴ Fishing Cycling Xmas New Year **Conf** Class 300 Board 40 Thtr 500 **Services** Lift **Parking** 400 **Notes** ⊗ Civ Wed 300

BEST WESTERN Homestead Court Hotel

★★★ 77% HOTEL

tel: 01707 324336 **Homestead Ln AL7 4LX**
email: enquiries@homesteadcourt.co.uk **web:** www.bwhomesteadcourt.co.uk
dir: Exit A1000, left at lights at Bushall Hotel. Right at rdbt into Howlands, 2nd left at Hollybush public house into Hollybush Lane. 2nd right at War Memorial into Homestead Lane

This family run hotel enjoys a quiet location and is a short drive from the centre of Welwyn Garden City and the major road network. Bedrooms are all attractively presented and very well equipped. Free WiFi is available throughout the hotel and there is an extensive choice on the restaurant menu. Ample secure parking is provided and the cosy lounge is a popular casual dining venue.

Rooms 74 (8 annexe) (6 fmly) (2 GF) (2 smoking) **Facilities** STV WiFi ⟴ **Conf** Class 200 Board 60 Thtr 300 **Services** Lift **Parking** 70 **Notes** ⊗ Civ Wed 110

Premier Inn Welwyn Garden City

BUDGET HOTEL

tel: 0871 527 9146 **Stanborough Rd AL8 6DQ**
web: www.premierinn.com
dir: A1(M) junct 4, A6129

High quality, budget accommodation ideal for both families and business travellers. Spacious, en suite bedrooms feature tea and coffee making facilities, and Freeview TV in most hotels. Internet access and WiFi are available for a small fee. The adjacent family restaurant features a wide and varied menu. See also the Hotel Groups pages.

Rooms 90

W

WEMBLEY
Greater London

Quality Hotel London - Wembley & Conference Centre

★★★ 70% HOTEL PLAN 1 C5

tel: 020 8733 9000 **Empire Way HA9 0NH**
email: sales@hotels-wembley.com **web:** www.qualityhotelwembley.co.uk
dir: M1 junct 6, A406, right onto A404. Right onto Empire Way, after rdbt at lights. Hotel on right

Conveniently situated within walking distance of both the Arena and conference centres this modern hotel offers smart, comfortable, spacious bedrooms; many are air conditioned. All rooms offer an excellent range of amenities. Air-conditioned public areas include a large restaurant serving a wide range of contemporary dishes.

Rooms 165 (70 fmly) (3 GF) (48 smoking) **S** £39-£500; **D** £39-£500* **Facilities** STV FTV WiFi ↘ **Conf** Class 90 Board 90 Thtr 150 Del from £85 to £250* **Services** Lift Air con **Parking** 65 **Notes** LB ⊛

Ibis London Wembley

ibis

BUDGET HOTEL PLAN 1 C4

tel: 020 8453 5100 **Southway HA9 6BA**
email: H3141@accor.com **web:** www.ibishotel.com
dir: From Hanger Lane on A40, take A406 N, exit at Wembley. A404 to lights junct with Wembley Hill Rd, right, 1st right into Southway. Hotel 75mtrs on left

Modern, budget hotel offering comfortable accommodation in bright and practical bedrooms. Breakfast is self-service and dinner is available in the restaurant. See also the Hotel Groups pages.

Rooms 210 (44 fmly) ↗ **S** fr £40; **D** fr £40

Premier Inn London Wembley Stadium

BUDGET HOTEL PLAN 1 C5

tel: 0871 527 8682 **151 Wembley Park Dr HA9 8HQ**
web: www.premierinn.com
dir: A406 (North Circular) take A404 towards Wembley. 2m right into Wembley Hill Rd, keep right into Empire Way (B4565), pass Wembley Arena on right, keep right around petrol station. Hotel 200yds on left

High quality, budget accommodation ideal for both families and business travellers. Spacious, en suite bedrooms feature tea and coffee making facilities, and Freeview TV in most hotels. Internet access and WiFi are available for a small fee. The adjacent family restaurant features a wide and varied menu. See also the Hotel Groups pages.

Rooms 154

WEST AUCKLAND
County Durham — Map 19 NZ12

The Manor House Hotel

★★★ 78% HOTEL

tel: 01388 834834 **The Green DL14 9HW**
email: enquiries@manorhousehotelcountydurham.co.uk
web: www.manorhousehotelcountydurham.co.uk
dir: A1(M) junct 58, A68 to West Auckland. At T-junct left, hotel 150yds on right

This historic manor house, dating back to the 14th century, is full of character. Welcoming log fires await guests on cooler evenings. Comfortable bedrooms are individual in style, tastefully furnished and well equipped. The brasserie and Juniper's restaurant both offer an interesting selection of freshly prepared dishes. Well-equipped leisure facilities are available and the Beauty Rooms offer a range of beauty and holistic treatments, with spa packages also available.

Rooms 35 (11 annexe) (6 fmly) (3 GF) ↗ **Facilities** Spa FTV WiFi ⊛ Gym Steam room Sauna Xmas New Year **Conf** Class 80 Board 50 Thtr 100 **Parking** 150 **Notes** Civ Wed 120

WEST BAY

See Bridport

WEST BROMWICH
West Midlands — Map 10 SP09

Premier Inn West Bromwich

BUDGET HOTEL

tel: 0871 527 9148 **New Gas St B70 0NP**
web: www.premierinn.com
dir: M5 junct 1, A41 (Expressway) towards Wolverhampton. At 3rd rdbt, hotel on right

High quality, budget accommodation ideal for both families and business travellers. Spacious, en suite bedrooms feature tea and coffee making facilities, and Freeview TV in most hotels. Internet access and WiFi are available for a small fee. The adjacent family restaurant features a wide and varied menu. See also the Hotel Groups pages.

Rooms 40

Premier Inn West Bromwich Central

BUDGET HOTEL

tel: 0871 527 9150 **144 High St B70 6JJ**
web: www.premierinn.com
dir: M5 junct 1 towards town centre, hotel 2m

Rooms 85

WEST DRAYTON

Hotels are listed under Heathrow Airport

WEST THURROCK
Essex

Map 6 TQ57

Ibis London Thurrock

BUDGET HOTEL

tel: 01708 686000 **Weston Av RM20 3JQ**
email: H2176@accor.com **web:** www.ibishotel.com
dir: M25 junct 31 to West Thurrock Services, right at 1st & 2nd rdbts, left at 3rd rdbt. Hotel on right in 500yds

Modern, budget hotel offering comfortable accommodation in bright and practical bedrooms. Breakfast is self-service and dinner is available in the restaurant. See also the Hotel Groups pages.

Rooms 102 (18 GF)

Premier Inn Thurrock East

BUDGET HOTEL

tel: 0871 527 9092 **Fleming Rd, Unicorn Estate, Chafford Hundred RM16 6YJ**
web: www.premierinn.com
dir: From A13 follow Lakeside Shopping Centre signs. Right at 1st rdbt, straight on at next rdbt, then 1st slip road. Left at next rdbt

High quality, budget accommodation ideal for both families and business travellers. Spacious, en suite bedrooms feature tea and coffee making facilities, and Freeview TV in most hotels. Internet access and WiFi are available for a small fee. The adjacent family restaurant features a wide and varied menu. See also the Hotel Groups pages.

Rooms 62

Premier Inn Thurrock West

BUDGET HOTEL

tel: 0871 527 9094 **Stonehouse Ln RM19 1NS**
web: www.premierinn.com
dir: From N: M25 junct 31, A1090 to Purfleet. (NB do not cross Dartford Bridge or follow signs for Lakeside). From S: M25 junct 31. On approach to Dartford Tunnel, bear far left signed Dagenham. After tunnel, hotel at top of slip road

Rooms 161

WEST WITTON
North Yorkshire

Map 19 SE08

The Wensleydale Heifer

RESTAURANT WITH ROOMS

tel: 01969 622322 **Main St DL8 4LS**
email: info@wensleydaleheifer.co.uk **web:** www.wensleydaleheifer.co.uk
dir: A1 to Leeming Bar junct, A684 towards Bedale for approx 10m to Leyburn, then towards Hawes 3.5m to West Witton

Describing itself as 'boutique style', this 17th-century former coaching inn is very much of the 21st century. The bedrooms, with Egyptian cotton linen and Molton Brown toiletries as standard, are each designed with an interesting theme - for example, Black Sheep, Night at the Movies, True Romantics and Shooters, and for chocolate lovers there's a bedroom where they can eat as much chocolate as they like! The food is very much the focus here in both the informal fish bar and the contemporary style restaurant. The kitchen prides itself on sourcing the freshest fish and locally reared meats.

Rooms 13 (4 annexe) (2 fmly)

WESTLETON
Suffolk

Map 13 TM46

The Westleton Crown

★★★ 79% HOTEL

tel: 01728 648777 **The Street IP17 3AD**
email: info@westletoncrown.co.uk **web:** www.westletoncrown.co.uk
dir: A12 N, turn right for Westleton just after Yoxford. Hotel opposite on entering Westleton

The Westleton Crown is a charming coaching inn situated in a peaceful village location just a few minutes from the A12. Public rooms include a smart, award-winning restaurant, comfortable lounge, and busy bar with exposed beams and open fireplaces. The stylish bedrooms are tastefully decorated and equipped with many thoughtful little extras.

Rooms 34 (22 annexe) (5 fmly) (13 GF) **S** £80-£100; **D** £95-£215 (incl. bkfst)*
Facilities FTV WiFi ᐅ Xmas New Year **Conf** Class 40 Board 30 Thtr 60 **Parking** 34 **Notes** LB Civ Wed 90

WESTON-ON-THE-GREEN
Oxfordshire

Map 11 SP51

The Manor At Weston-On-The-Green

★★★★ 83% COUNTRY HOUSE HOTEL

tel: 01869 350621 **Northampton Rd OX25 3QL**
email: house@themanorweston.co.uk **web:** www.themanorweston.com

The Manor is an outstanding country house hotel, offering traditional values and outstanding quality. The gardens are a real delight and taking afternoon tea here is a must. The hotel has been carefully restored and refurbished to a very high standard. Bedrooms are classic in design, but still enjoy all modern day accessories. Dinner in the feature restaurant with its wood panelled walls and gallery area is a highlight of any stay. Professional staff guarantee a seamless experience.

Rooms 25 **Facilities** ᐟ supervised ᐟ ᐟ **Conf** Board 20 Thtr 100 **Notes** Civ Wed 120

W

WESTON-SUPER-MARE
Somerset

Map 4 ST36

The Royal Hotel

★★★ 77% HOTEL

tel: 01934 423100 **1 South Pde BS23 1JP**
email: reservations@royalhotelweston.com web: www.royalhotelweston.com
dir: M5 junct 21, follow signs to seafront. Hotel next to Winter Gardens Pavillion

The Royal, which opened in 1810, was the first hotel in Weston and occupies a prime seafront position. It is a grand building and many of the bedrooms, including some with sea views, are spacious and comfortable; family apartments are also available. Public areas include a choice of bars and a restaurant which offers a range of dishes to meet all tastes. Entertainment is provided during the season.

Rooms 44 (3 annexe) (8 fmly) ♠ S £73-£83; (incl. bkfst)* Facilities FTV WiFi HL Beauty treatment room Hair salon ♬ Conf Class 100 Board 60 Thtr 200 Del from £105 to £150* Services Lift Parking 152 Notes LB ⊗ Civ Wed 200

See advert on opposite page

Beachlands Hotel

★★★ 75% HOTEL

tel: 01934 621401 **17 Uphill Road North BS23 4NG**
email: info@beachlandshotel.com web: www.beachlandshotel.com
dir: M5 junct 21, follow signs for hospital. At hospital rdbt follow signs for beach, hotel 300yds before beach

This popular hotel is very close to the 18-hole links course and a short walk from the seafront. Elegant public areas include a bar, a choice of lounges and a bright dining room. Bedrooms vary slightly in size, but all are well equipped for both the business and leisure guest. There is the added bonus of a 10-metre indoor pool and a sauna.

Rooms 21 (6 fmly) (11 GF) ♠ S £65-£105; D £102-£139.75 (incl. bkfst)* Facilities FTV WiFi ⊛ Sauna Beauty treatment room New Year Conf Class 20 Board 30 Thtr 60 Del from £102 to £117.75* Parking 28 Notes LB ⊗ Closed 23-29 Dec Civ Wed 110

Lauriston Hotel

★★★ 68% HOTEL

tel: 01934 620758 **6-12 Knightstone Rd BS23 2AN**
email: lauriston.hotel@actionforblindpeople.org.uk web: www.visionhotels.co.uk
dir: 1st right after Winter Gardens, hotel entrance adjacent to Grand Pier

A friendly welcome is assured at the Lauriston, a pleasant hotel located right on the seafront, just a few minutes' stroll from the pier. The hotel welcomes everyone but caters especially for the visually impaired, their families, friends and guide dogs. There are comfortable and well-appointed bedrooms; and special facilities for guide dogs are, of course, available.

Rooms 37 (2 fmly) (8 GF) ♠ Facilities FTV WiFi ♭ HL ♬ Xmas New Year Child facilities Conf Class 12 Board 10 Thtr 18 Services Lift Parking 16 Notes Civ Wed 60

Anchor Head Hotel

★★ 69% HOTEL

Leisureplex

tel: 01934 620880 **19 Claremont Crescent, Birnbeck Rd BS23 2EE**
email: anchor.weston@alfatravel.co.uk web: www.leisureplex.co.uk
dir: M5 junct 21, A370 to seafront, right, past Grand Pier towards Brimbeck Pier. Hotel at end of terrace on left

Enjoying a very pleasant location with views across the bay, the Anchor Head offers a varied choice of comfortable lounges and a relaxing outdoor patio area. Bedrooms and bathrooms are traditionally furnished and include several ground-floor rooms. Dinner and breakfast are served in the spacious dining room that also benefits from sea views.

Rooms 52 (1 fmly) (5 GF) ♠ S £36-£48; D £56-£80 (incl. bkfst)* Facilities FTV ♬ Xmas New Year Services Lift Notes ⊗ Closed Dec-Feb (ex Xmas) RS Mar & Nov

Premier Inn Weston-Super-Mare East

BUDGET HOTEL

Premier Inn

tel: 0871 527 9156 **Hutton Moor Rd BS22 8LY**
web: www.premierinn.com
dir: M5 junct 21, A370 towards Weston-Super-Mare. After 3rd rbt right at lights into Hutton Moor Leisure Centre. Left, into car park

High quality, budget accommodation ideal for both families and business travellers. Spacious, en suite bedrooms feature tea and coffee making facilities, and Freeview TV in most hotels. Internet access and WiFi are available for a small fee. The adjacent family restaurant features a wide and varied menu. See also the Hotel Groups pages.

Rooms 88

Premier Inn Weston-Super-Mare (Seafront)

BUDGET HOTEL

tel: 0871 527 9378 **Dolphin Square, Beach Rd BS23 1TT**
web: www.premierinn.com
dir: M5 junction 21, A370 towards Weston-Super-Mare town centre. At double mini rdbt 2nd exit, 1st exit into Oxford St. At end, left into Beach Rd. Left into Carlton St. Hotel on left

Rooms 112

The Royal Hotel

Weston-super-Mare

Telephone: 01934 423100

This charismatic historic & luxuriously appointed Georgian Hotel is centrally located in a unique location enjoying both a wonderful sea view and close proximity to the promenade, Grand Pier, Shopping Centre & high Street.

- **3 Star Seafront Hotel**
- **Shopping Centre 200 Metres**
- **Themed Luxury Rooms**
- **Ala Carte Restaurant**
- **Late Licence Bar & Bar Menu**
- **Entertainment Friday Nights**
- **Sunday and Midweek Carvery**
- **Special Offers & Breaks**
- **Beauty Room & Hair Salon**
- **Electric Car Charging Station**

www.royalhotelweston.com

Download our Free App!

W

WESTON-UNDER-REDCASTLE
Shropshire   Map 15 SJ52

Hawkstone Park Hotel

★★★ 77% HOTEL

tel: 01948 841700 **SY4 5UY**
email: enquiries@hawkstone.co.uk **web:** www.princial-hayley.com
dir: 1m E of A49 between Shrewsbury & Whitchurch

Built in the 1700s, this splendid former coaching inn is set in 400 acres of lovely scenery which includes two championship golf courses and the much remarked upon 18th-century follies. The bedrooms are comfortably appointed and well equipped for both leisure and business guests, and the public areas include conference facilities and a pleasant dining room.

Rooms 67 (19 annexe) (2 fmly) (26 GF) ⌁ **Facilities** STV WiFi ⌁ HL ⌁ 42 Putt green ⌁ Xmas New Year **Conf** Class 90 Board 50 Thtr 200 **Parking** 200 **Notes** Civ Wed 200

WETHERBY
West Yorkshire   Map 16 SE44

INSPECTORS' CHOICE

Wood Hall Hotel & Spa

★★★★ ◉◉ HOTEL

tel: 01937 587271 **Trip Ln, Linton LS22 4JA**
email: woodhall@handpicked.co.uk **web:** www.handpickedhotels.co.uk/woodhall
dir: From Wetherby take Harrogate road N (A661) for 0.5m, left to Sicklinghall & Linton. Cross bridge, left to Linton & Wood Hall. Turn right opposite Windmill Inn, 1.25m to hotel

A long sweeping drive leads to this delightful Georgian house situated in 100 acres of parkland. Spacious bedrooms are appointed to an impressive standard and feature comprehensive facilities, including large plasma-screen TVs. Public rooms reflect the same elegance and include a smart drawing room and dining room, both with fantastic views.

Rooms 44 (30 annexe) (5 fmly) ⌁ **Facilities** Spa STV FTV WiFi ⌁ HL ⌁ Fishing Gym Beauty spa Xmas New Year **Conf** Class 70 Board 40 Thtr 100 **Services** Lift **Parking** 200 **Notes** ⌁ Civ Wed 100

The Bridge Hotel & Spa

★★★★ 77% HOTEL

tel: 01937 580115 **Walshford LS22 5HS**
email: info@bridgewetherby.co.uk **web:** www.bridgewetherby.co.uk
dir: From N exit A1(M) at junct 47 (York) or S junct 46 (Wetherby Race Centre), 1st left Walshford, follow brown tourist signs

The Bridge Hotel is located close to the A1, with spacious public areas and a good range of services, making this an ideal venue for business or leisure. The stylish bedrooms are comfortable and well equipped. There is a choice of bars and a large open-plan restaurant. Conference and banqueting suites are also available.

Rooms 30 (2 fmly) (10 GF) **S** £65-£135; **D** £75-£150 (incl. bkfst) **Facilities** Spa FTV WiFi ⌁ Gym Xmas New Year **Conf** Class 50 Board 50 Thtr 200 Del from £120 to £150 **Parking** 150 **Notes** LB Civ Wed 150

Mercure Wetherby Hotel

★★★ 73% HOTEL

tel: 0844 815 9067 **Leeds Rd LS22 5HE**
email: info@mercurewetherby.co.uk **web:** www.jupiterhotels.co.uk
dir: A1/A659, then follow A168. Hotel on rdbt

This modern hotel is well located for motorway access and as well as being close to the historic market town of Wetherby, it is also convenient for Leeds, Harrogate and York. Leeds Bradford Airport is just eight miles away. There is a spacious restaurant and adjacent bar. The Brasserie menu features bistro dishes and daily Chef's specials. Extensive conference facilities are provided with 13 naturally lit meeting rooms available. Complimentary WiFi access is another highlight.

Rooms 103 **Facilities** WiFi ⌁ **Conf** Class 60 Board 50 Thtr 140 **Parking** 167 **Notes** Civ Wed 100

Days Inn Wetherby

BUDGET HOTEL

tel: 01937 547557 **Junction 46 A1(M), Kirk Deighton LS22 5GT**
email: reservations@daysinnwetherby.co.uk **web:** www.daysinnwetherby.co.uk
dir: A1(M) junct 46 at Moto Service Area

This modern building offers accommodation in smart, spacious and well-equipped bedrooms, suitable for families and business travellers, and all with en suite bathrooms. Continental breakfast is available and other refreshments may be taken at the nearby family restaurant. See also the Hotel Groups pages.

Rooms 129 (33 fmly) (35 GF) ⌁ **S** £49-£120; **D** £49-£120* **Conf** Class 20 Board 20 Thtr 30

WEYBRIDGE
Surrey   Map 6 TQ06

Brooklands Hotel

★★★★ 82% ◉◉ HOTEL

tel: 01932 335700 **Brooklands Dr KT13 0SL**
email: info@brooklandshotelsurrey.com **web:** www.brooklandshotelsurrey.com
dir: Telephone for detailed directions

Overlooking the historic motoring racing circuit, this hotel has stunning design that reflects the art deco style and that of the Mercedes Benz racetrack's heyday in the 1920 and 30s. The bedrooms are notably spacious and very comfortable with many contemporary facilities; all have floor-to-ceiling windows, and many come with balconies overlooking the racetrack. There is a wealth of public areas including

W

leisure and meeting rooms as well as a spa. The contemporary 1907 Restaurant, Bar and Grill offers imaginative menus.

Rooms 120 (16 fmly) Facilities **Spa** STV FTV WiFi Gym New Year **Conf** Class 86 Board 90 Thtr 174 **Services** Lift Air con **Parking** 120 **Notes** Civ Wed 174

Oatlands Park Hotel

★★★★ 77% HOTEL

tel: 01932 847242 **146 Oatlands Dr KT13 9HB**
email: info@oatlandsparkhotel.com **web:** www.oatlandsparkhotel.com
dir: Through High Street to Monument Hill mini rdbt. Left into Oatlands Drive. Hotel 500yds on left

Once a palace for Henry VIII, this impressive building sits in extensive grounds encompassing tennis courts, a gym and a 9-hole golf course. The spacious lounge and bar create a wonderful first impression with tall marble pillars and plush comfortable seating. Most of the bedrooms are very spacious, and all are well equipped.

Rooms 144 (24 fmly) (30 GF) Facilities STV WiFi HL 9 Putt green Gym Jogging course Fitness suite Xmas New Year **Conf** Class 150 Board 80 Thtr 300 Del from £170 to £240* **Services** Lift Air con **Parking** 180 **Notes** Civ Wed 220

BEST WESTERN Ship Hotel

★★★ 78% HOTEL

tel: 01932 848364 **Monument Green KT13 8BQ**
email: reservations@desboroughhotels.com **web:** www.shiphotel.co.uk
dir: M25 junct 11, at 3rd rdbt left into High St. Hotel 300yds on left

This former coaching inn has retained much of its period charm and is now a spacious and comfortable hotel. Bedrooms, some overlooking a delightful courtyard, are spacious and cheerfully decorated. Public areas include a lounge and cocktail bar, restaurant and a popular pub. The high street location and private parking are a bonus.

Rooms 76 (2 fmly) Facilities FTV WiFi Xmas New Year **Conf** Class 70 Board 60 Thtr 180 Del from £110 to £145* **Services** Lift **Parking** 65 **Notes** Civ Wed 120

WEYMOUTH	Map 4 SY67
Dorset	

BEST WESTERN Hotel Rembrandt

★★★ 74% HOTEL

tel: 01305 764000 **12-18 Dorchester Rd DT4 7JU**
email: reception@hotelrembrandt.co.uk **web:** www.hotelrembrandt.co.uk
dir: On A354 from Dorchester, turn left at Manor rdbt & proceed for 0.75m

Only a short distance from the seafront and the town centre, this hotel is ideal for visiting local attractions. Facilities include a spa, gym and heated pool; a bar and extensive meeting rooms. The restaurant offers an impressive carvery and carte menu, which proves popular with locals and residents alike.

Rooms 78 (27 fmly) (5 GF) S £80-£100; D £80-£137.50 (incl. bkfst)* **Facilities** STV FTV WiFi Gym Steam room Sauna Beautician Beauty treatment room **Conf** Class 100 Board 60 Thtr 200 Del from £115 to £125* **Services** Lift **Parking** 80 **Notes** LB Civ Wed 100

Hotel Rex

★★★ 71% HOTEL

tel: 01305 760400 **29 The Esplanade DT4 8DN**
email: rex@kingshotels.co.uk **web:** www.kingshotels.co.uk
dir: On seafront opposite Alexandra Gardens

Originally built as the summer residence for the Duke of Clarence, this hotel benefits from a seafront location with stunning views across Weymouth Bay. Bedrooms, including several sea-facing rooms, are well equipped. A wide range of imaginative dishes is served in the popular and attractive restaurant.

Rooms 31 (2 fmly) S £50-£70; D £80-£125 (incl. bkfst)* **Facilities** FTV WiFi New Year **Conf** Class 30 Board 25 Thtr 40 Del from £65 to £95* **Services** Lift **Parking** 10 **Notes** LB Closed Xmas

Crown Hotel

★★ 75% HOTEL

tel: 01305 760800 **51-53 St Thomas St DT4 8EQ**
email: crown@kingshotels.co.uk **web:** www.kingshotels.co.uk
dir: From Dorchester, A354 to Weymouth. Follow Back Water on left & cross 2nd bridge

This popular hotel is conveniently located adjacent to the old harbour and is ideal for shopping, local attractions and transportation links, including the ferry. Public areas include an extensive bar, ballroom and comfortable residents' lounge on the first floor. Themed events, such as mock cruises, are a speciality.

Rooms 86 (15 fmly) Facilities WiFi New Year **Services** Lift **Parking** 14 **Notes** Closed Xmas

Fairhaven Hotel

★★ 71% HOTEL

tel: 01305 760200 **37 The Esplanade DT4 8DH**
email: fairhaven@kingshotels.co.uk **web:** www.kingshotels.co.uk
dir: On right just before Alexandra Gardens

A popular sea-facing, family-run hotel which has a friendly young team of staff. Bedrooms are comfortable and well maintained, and the hotel boasts two bars, one with panoramic views of the bay. Entertainment is provided most nights during the season.

Rooms 82 (21 fmly) (1 GF) Facilities WiFi **Services** Lift **Parking** 16 **Notes** Closed Nov-1 Mar

Hotel Central

★★ 71% HOTEL

tel: 01305 760700 **17-19 Maiden St DT4 8BB**
email: central@kingshotels.co.uk **web:** www.kingshotels.co.uk
dir: In town centre

Well located for the town, the beach and the ferries to the Channel Islands, and with off-road parking, this privately owned hotel has friendly staff and comfortable bedrooms. Three rooms are designed for guests with limited mobility. The pleasant dining room offers a varied menu and live entertainment is provided during the season.

Rooms 28 (5 fmly) (4 GF) Facilities **Services** Lift **Parking** 16 **Notes** Closed mid Dec-1 Mar

W

WEYMOUTH *continued*

Premier Inn Weymouth

BUDGET HOTEL

tel: 0871 527 9384 **Gateway Business Park, Mercury Rd DT3 5HJ**
web: www.premierinn.com
dir: M27 junct 1, A31 towards Bournemouth, A35 towards Dorchester. 1st exit at rdbt onto A354 (Weymouth road). At 3rd rdbt take 1st exit into Dorchester Rd. Left into Mercery Rd

High quality, budget accommodation ideal for both families and business travellers. Spacious, en suite bedrooms feature tea and coffee making facilities, and Freeview TV in most hotels. Internet access and WiFi are available for a small fee. The adjacent family restaurant features a wide and varied menu. See also the Hotel Groups pages.

Rooms 60

Premier Inn Weymouth Seafront

BUDGET HOTEL

tel: 0871 527 9158 **Lodmoor Country Park, Preston Beach Rd, Green Hill DT4 7SX**
web: www.premierinn.com
dir: Follow signs to Weymouth then brown route signs to Lodmoor Country Park (height restriction 9' 4" at barrier). Hotel adjacent to Lodmoor Brewers Fayre. NB for Sat Nav use DT4 7SL

Rooms 64

WHITBY	Map 19 NZ81
North Yorkshire	

The Cliffemount Hotel

★★★ 82% @@ SMALL HOTEL

tel: 01947 840103 **Bank Top Ln, Runswick Bay TS13 5HU**
email: info@cliffemounthotel.co.uk **web:** www.cliffemounthotel.co.uk
dir: Exit A174, 8m N of Whitby, 1m to end

Overlooking Runswick Bay this property offers a relaxed and romantic atmosphere with open fires and individual, carefully designed bedrooms; some have a private balcony overlooking the bay. Dining is recommended; the food is modern British in style, using locally sourced fresh seafood and game from nearby estates.

Rooms 20 (4 fmly) (5 GF) **S** £65-£195; **D** £85-£195 (incl. bkfst)* **Facilities** FTV WiFi Xmas New Year **Conf** Class 25 Board 16 Thtr 25 Del from £95 to £150* **Parking** 25 **Notes** LB

Saxonville Hotel

★★★ 78% HOTEL

tel: 01947 602631 **Ladysmith Av, Argyle Rd YO21 3HX**
email: newtons@saxonville.co.uk **web:** www.saxonville.co.uk
dir: A174 to North Promenade. Turn inland at large four-towered building visible on West Cliff, into Argyle Rd, then 1st right

The friendly service is noteworthy at this long-established holiday hotel. Well maintained throughout, it offers comfortable bedrooms and inviting public areas that include a well-proportioned restaurant where quality dinners are served.

Rooms 23 (2 fmly) (1 GF) **S** £48-£68; **D** £96-£156 (incl. bkfst)* **Facilities** WiFi **Conf** Class 40 Board 40 Thtr 100 Del from £75 to £120* **Parking** 20 **Notes** ⊗ Closed Dec-Jan RS Feb-Mar

Estbek House

@@ RESTAURANT WITH ROOMS

tel: 01947 893424 ▤ 01947 893625 **East Row, Sandsend YO21 3SU**
email: info@estbekhouse.co.uk **web:** www.estbekhouse.co.uk
dir: From Whitby take A174. In Sandsend, left into East Row

The speciality seafood restaurant on the first floor is the focus of this listed building in a small coastal village north west of Whitby. The seasonal menu is based on local fresh local ingredients, and is overseen by Tim the chef, who has guided his team to 2 AA Rosette standard. The unique Australian/New Zealand Wine list is managed by David. There is also a small bar and breakfast room, and five individually appointed bedrooms offering high levels of comfort.

Rooms 4

WHITCHURCH	Map 15 SJ54
Shropshire	

Macdonald Hill Valley Spa, Hotel & Golf

★★★★ 78% HOTEL

tel: 0844 879 9049 **Tarporley Rd SY13 4JH**
email: general.hillvalley@macdonald-hotels.co.uk
web: www.macdonald-hotels.co.uk/hillvalley
dir: 2nd exit off A41 towards Whitchurch

Located in rural surroundings on the town's outskirts, this modern hotel is surrounded by two golf courses, and a very well equipped leisure spa is also available. Spacious bedrooms, with country views, are furnished in minimalist style and public areas include a choice of bar lounges and extensive conference facilities.

Rooms 80 (15 fmly) (27 GF) ☞ **Facilities** Spa STV FTV WiFi ⌕ ⊛ ↲ 36 Putt green Gym Mud Rasul Xmas New Year **Conf** Class 150 Board 150 Thtr 300 **Services** Lift **Parking** 300 **Notes** Civ Wed 300

WHITEHAVEN	Map 18 NX91
Cumbria	

Premier Inn Whitehaven

BUDGET HOTEL

tel: 0871 527 9160 **Howgate CA28 6PL**
web: www.premierinn.com
dir: On A595 just outside Whitehaven

High quality, budget accommodation ideal for both families and business travellers. Spacious, en suite bedrooms feature tea and coffee making facilities, and Freeview TV in most hotels. Internet access and WiFi are available for a small fee. The adjacent family restaurant features a wide and varied menu. See also the Hotel Groups pages.

Rooms 47

WHITLEY BAY
Tyne & Wear — Map 21 NZ37

The Royal Hotel

★★★ 75% HOTEL

tel: 0191 252 4777 **13-17 East Pde NE26 1AP**
email: info@royalhotelwhitleybay.co.uk **web:** www.royalhotelwhitleybay.co.uk
dir: From Whitley Bay Metro station left onto Station Square, bear right onto Victoria Terrace, right onto North Parade then right & right again, then left

Overlooking the sea front, this refurbished hotel offers warm hospitality from a friendly team. Bedrooms are well appointed, and the recently opened Noir Drinks Lounge adds a new dimension to the operation. Tapas are served in this area with the option to take dinner in the Italian restaurant next door. Limited off-road car parking is available to the front of the hotel.

Rooms 37 📞 **Facilities** FTV WiFi ⅃ **Parking** 10 **Notes** ⊗ Closed 23 Dec-2 Jan

WHITSTABLE
Kent — Map 7 TR16

Premier Inn Whitstable

BUDGET HOTEL

tel: 0871 527 9162 **Thanet Way CT5 3DB**
web: www.premierinn.com
dir: 2m W of town centre on B2205

High quality, budget accommodation ideal for both families and business travellers. Spacious, en suite bedrooms feature tea and coffee making facilities, and Freeview TV in most hotels. Internet access and WiFi are available for a small fee. The adjacent family restaurant features a wide and varied menu. See also the Hotel Groups pages.

Rooms 41

WHITTLEBURY
Northamptonshire — Map 11 SP64

Whittlebury Hall

★★★★ 80% ⊛⊛ HOTEL

tel: 01327 857857 **NN12 8QH**
email: reservations@whittleburyhall.co.uk **web:** www.whittleburyhall.co.uk
dir: A43, A413 towards Buckingham, through Whittlebury, turn for hotel on right, signed

A purpose-built, Georgian-style country house hotel with excellent spa and leisure facilities and pedestrian access to the Silverstone circuit. Grand public areas include F1 car racing memorabilia and the accommodation includes some lavishly appointed suites. Food is a strength, with a choice of various dining options. Particularly noteworthy are the afternoon teas in the spacious, comfortable lounge and the fine dining in Murray's Restaurant.

Rooms 212 (4 fmly) (13 smoking) **Facilities** Spa FTV WiFi ⅃ Gym Beauty treatments Relaxation room Hair studio Heat & Ice experience Leisure club ⅃ Xmas New Year **Conf** Class 175 Board 40 Thtr 500 **Services** Lift **Parking** 450 **Notes** ⊗

WIDNES
Cheshire — Map 15 SJ58

Premier Inn Widnes

BUDGET HOTEL

tel: 0871 527 9306 **Venture Fields WA8 0GY**
web: www.premierinn.com
dir: M62 junct 7. At Rainhill Stoops rdbt 2nd exit onto A557 (Widnes). Left into Earle Rd (Widnes Waterfront), into Venture Field Leisure Entertainment complex. Hotel on left

High quality, budget accommodation ideal for both families and business travellers. Spacious, en suite bedrooms feature tea and coffee making facilities, and Freeview TV in most hotels. Internet access and WiFi are available for a small fee. The adjacent family restaurant features a wide and varied menu. See also the Hotel Groups pages.

Rooms 60

WIGAN
Greater Manchester — Map 15 SD50

Wrightington Hotel & Country Club

★★★★ 75% ⊛ HOTEL

tel: 01257 425803 **Moss Ln, Wrightington WN6 9PB**
email: info@wrightingtonhotel.co.uk **web:** www.wrightingtonhotel.co.uk
dir: M6 junct 27, 0.25m W, hotel on right after church

Situated in open countryside close to the M6, this privately owned hotel offers friendly hospitality. Accommodation is well equipped and spacious, and public areas include an extensive leisure complex complete with hair salon, boutique and sports injury lab. Blazers Restaurant, two bars and air-conditioned banqueting facilities appeal to a broad market.

Rooms 73 (6 fmly) (36 GF) **Facilities** Spa STV FTV WiFi ⅃ Gym Squash Hairdressing salon Sports injury clinic New Year **Conf** Class 120 Board 40 Thtr 200 **Services** Lift **Parking** 240 **Notes** Civ Wed 100

Macdonald Kilhey Court Hotel

★★★★ 73% ⊛ HOTEL

tel: 0844 879 9045 & 01257 472100 **Chorley Rd, Standish WN1 2XN**
email: general.kilheycourt@macdonald-hotels.co.uk
web: www.macdonaldhotels.co.uk/kilheycourt
dir: M6 junct 27, A5209 Standish, over at lights, past church on right, left at rdbt (1st exit), hotel on right 350yds. M61 junct 6, signed Wigan & Haigh Hall. 3m & right at rdbt (2nd exit). Hotel 0.5m on right

Macdonald Kilhey Court Hotel is peacefully located in its own grounds yet is convenient for the motorway network. Bedrooms are divided between the Victorian house and the modern extension, while public areas have original features, and the split-level restaurant has views over the Worthington Lakes. There are eleven meeting rooms, ideal for exhibitions, and extensive landscaped grounds available for weddings. Facilities also include an indoor pool and spa.

Rooms 62 (18 fmly) (8 GF) **Facilities** Spa STV FTV WiFi ⅃ HL Gym Aerobics classes Beauty treatments Xmas New Year **Conf** Class 180 Board 60 Thtr 400 **Services** Lift **Parking** 200 **Notes** Civ Wed 300

W

WIGAN *continued*

Mercure Wigan Oak Hotel

★★★ 77% HOTEL

tel: 01942 826888 **Orchard St WN1 3SS**
email: enquiries@hotels-wigan.com **web:** www.hotels-wigan.com
dir: From S: M6 junct 25, A49 signed Wigan then B5238, right after Grand Arcade Shopping. From N: M6 junct 27, A5209, right onto A49, left at lights, hotel opposite Tesco

This modern and stylish hotel is situated in the centre of Wigan; easily accessed from the M6 and M61 and well positioned for public transport. The bedrooms are both comfortable and well equipped and public rooms include the restaurant, conservatory and popular bar. There is free WiFi throughout, and conference and events facilities are available. Ample parking is a plus in this central location.

Rooms 88 (7 fmly) (16 GF) ✿❀ **S** £55-£105; **D** £55-£105* **Facilities** FTV WiFi ⊾ New Year **Conf** Class 80 Board 40 Thtr 160 Del from £85 to £125* **Services** Lift **Parking** 100 **Notes** LB Civ Wed 50

Premier Inn Haydock Park (Wigan South)

BUDGET HOTEL

tel: 0871 527 8502 **53 Warrington Rd, Ashton-in-Makerfield WN4 9PJ**
web: www.premierinn.com
dir: Just off M6 junct 23, A49 towards Wigan

High quality, budget accommodation ideal for both families and business travellers. Spacious, en suite bedrooms feature tea and coffee making facilities, and Freeview TV in most hotels. Internet access and WiFi are available for a small fee. The adjacent family restaurant features a wide and varied menu. See also the Hotel Groups pages.

Rooms 30

Premier Inn Wigan M6 Jct 25

BUDGET HOTEL

tel: 0871 527 9164 **Warrington Rd, Marus Bridge WN3 6XB**
web: www.premierinn.com
dir: M6 junct 25 (N'bound). At rdbt left, hotel on left

Rooms 40

Premier Inn Wigan West

BUDGET HOTEL

tel: 0871 527 9168 **Orrell Rd, Orrell WN5 8HQ**
web: www.premierinn.com
dir: M6 junct 26 follow signs for Upholland & Orrell. At 1st lights turn left. Hotel on right behind Priory Wood Beefeater

Rooms 40

The Beeches

RESTAURANT WITH ROOMS

tel: 01257 426432 & 421316 📠 01257 427503 **School Ln, Standish WN6 OTD**
email: mail@beecheshotel.co.uk **web:** www.beecheshotel.co.uk
dir: M6 junct 27, A5209 into Standish & into School Ln

Just a mile away from junction 27 of the M6, this privately owned, spacious Victorian property is set in pleasant gardens. Bedrooms are well equipped and offer

modern facilities. A wide choice of food is offered in the brasserie. The beautifully presented Piano Lounge also offers live entertainment on Friday and Saturday evenings.

Rooms 10 (4 fmly)

BEST WESTERN Willerby Manor Hotel

★★★ 83% ❀ HOTEL

tel: 01482 652616 **Well Ln HU10 6ER**
email: willerbymanor@bestwestern.co.uk **web:** www.willerbymanor.co.uk
dir: Exit A63, signed Humber Bridge. Right at rdbt by Waitrose. At next rdbt hotel signed

Set in a quiet residential area, amid well-tended gardens, this hotel was originally a private mansion; it has now been thoughtfully extended to provide very comfortable bedrooms, equipped with many useful extras. There are extensive leisure facilities and a wide choice of meals offered in the contemporary Figs Brasserie which has an impressive heated outdoor area.

Rooms 63 (6 fmly) (20 GF) (1 smoking) ✿❀ **S** £67-£100; **D** £108-£128 (incl. bkfst)* **Facilities** STV FTV WiFi HL ⊛ supervised ⛳ Gym Steam room Beauty treatment room Aerobic classes New Year **Conf** Class 200 Board 100 Thtr 500 Del £170* **Parking** 300 **Notes** LB Closed 24-26 Dec Civ Wed 150

Mercure Hull Grange Park Hotel

★★★ 75% HOTEL

tel: 0844 815 9037 **Grange Park Ln HU10 6EA**
email: info@mercurehull.co.uk **web:** www. jupiterhotels.co.uk
dir: A164 to Beverley signed Willerby Shopping Park. Left at rdbt into Grange Park Lane, hotel at end

Originally a 19th-century manor house, this modern hotel provides comfortable accommodation tucked away in 12 acres of landscaped gardens. The location is peaceful yet convenient for the historic market town of Beverley. Hull city centre is only five miles away. Extensive meeting rooms are in a self contained conference centre with complimentary WiFi throughout. The hotel also boasts a health club with indoor swimming pool.

Rooms 100 **Facilities** WiFi ⊾ ⊛ Gym Sauna Steam room **Conf** Class 250 Board 80 Thtr 550 **Parking** 600 **Notes** Civ Wed 550

Crossways

❀❀ RESTAURANT WITH ROOMS

tel: 01323 482455 📠 01323 487811 **Lewes Rd BN26 5SG**
email: stay@crosswayshotel.co.uk **web:** www.crosswayshotel.co.uk
dir: On A27 between Lewes & Polegate, 2m E of Alfriston rdbt

Proprietors Davis Stott and Clive James have been welcoming guests to this elegant restaurant with rooms for over 25 years. Crossways sits amid stunning gardens and attractively tended grounds. The well-presented bedrooms are tastefully decorated and provide an abundance of thoughtful amenities including free WiFi. Guest comfort is paramount and the naturally warm hospitality ensures guests often return.

Rooms 7

W

WILMSLOW
See **Manchester Airport**

WIMBORNE MINSTER
Dorset   Map 5 SZ06

Les Bouviers Restaurant with Rooms

 RESTAURANT WITH ROOMS

tel: 01202 889555 📠 01202 639428 **Arrowsmith Rd, Canford Magna BH21 3BD**
email: info@lesbouviers.co.uk **web:** www.lesbouviers.co.uk
dir: A31 onto A349. Left in 0.6m. In approx 1m right into Arrowsmith Rd. Establishment approx 100yds on right

Les Bouviers is an excellent restaurant with rooms in a great location, set in five and a half acres of grounds. Food is a highlight of any stay here as is the friendly, attentive service. Chef patron James Coward's team turn out impressive cooking, which has been recognised with two AA Rosettes. The bedrooms are extremely well equipped and the beds are supremely comfortable. Cream teas can be taken on the terrace.

Rooms 6 (4 fmly)

WINCANTON
Somerset   Map 4 ST72

Holbrook House

★★★ 85% COUNTRY HOUSE HOTEL

tel: 01963 824466 & 828844 **Holbrook BA9 8BS**
email: enquiries@holbrookhouse.co.uk **web:** www.holbrookhouse.co.uk
dir: From A303 at Wincanton left onto A371 towards Castle Cary & Shepton Mallet

This handsome country house offers a unique blend of quality and comfort combined with a friendly atmosphere. Set in 17 acres of peaceful gardens and wooded grounds, Holbrook House makes a perfect retreat. The restaurant provides a selection of innovative dishes prepared with enthusiasm and served by a team of caring staff.

Rooms 21 (5 annexe) (2 fmly) (5 GF) ⚄ **Facilities** Spa FTV WiFi ⚄ ⚄ ⚄ Gym Exercise classes Sauna Steam room Fitness suite ♫ Xmas New Year **Conf** Class 100 Board 55 Thtr 200 **Parking** 100 **Notes** LB Civ Wed 250

WINCHCOMBE
Gloucestershire   Map 10 SP02

Wesley House

 RESTAURANT WITH ROOMS

tel: 01242 602366 📠 01242 609046 **High St GL54 5LJ**
email: enquiries@wesleyhouse.co.uk **web:** www.wesleyhouse.co.uk
dir: In town centre

This 15th-century, half-timbered property is named after John Wesley, founder of the Methodist Church, who stayed here while preaching in the town. Bedrooms are small but full of character. In the rear dining room, a unique lighting system changes colour to suit the mood required, and also highlights the various floral displays created by a world-renowned flower arranger. A glass atrium covers the outside terrace.

Rooms 5

WINCHESTER
Hampshire   Map 5 SU42

Lainston House, an Exclusive Hotel

★★★★★  86% HOTEL

tel: 01962 776088 **Sparsholt SO21 2LT**
email: enquiries@lainstonhouse.com **web:** www.lainstonhouse.com
dir: 2m NW off B3049 towards Stockbridge

This graceful example of a William and Mary House enjoys a countryside location amidst mature grounds and gardens. Staff provide good levels of courtesy and care with a polished, professional service. Bedrooms are tastefully appointed and include some spectacular, spacious rooms with stylish handmade beds and stunning bathrooms. Public rooms include a cocktail bar built entirely from a single cedar and stocked with an impressive range of rare drinks and cigars.

Rooms 49 (6 fmly) (18 GF) ⚄ S £165-£745; D £165-£745* **Facilities** STV FTV WiFi ⚄ ⚄ Fishing ⚄ Gym Archery Clay pigeon shooting Cycling Hot air ballooning On-site falconer ♫ Xmas New Year **Conf** Class 80 Board 40 Thtr 166 Del from £250* **Parking** 200 **Notes** LB Civ Wed 200

Holiday Inn Winchester

★★★★ 78%  HOTEL

tel: 01962 670700 & 0871 942 9188 **Telegraph Way, Morn Hill SO21 1HZ**
email: info@hiwinchester.co.uk **web:** www.hiwinchester.co.uk
dir: M3 junct 9, A31 signed Alton, A272 & Petersfield. 1st exit at rdbt onto A31, 1.6m, take 1st exit into Alresford Rd, left into Telegraph Way

Located a few miles from the historic city of Winchester and within easy reach of the south's transport links, this modern, purpose-built property is presented to a high standard. Bedrooms are spacious and well-equipped for both the business and leisure guest. Enjoyable cuisine is served in the restaurant and there is a very good range of freshly prepared dishes to choose from. Conference facilities and ample parking are available.

Rooms 141 (7 fmly) (60 GF) ⚄ **Facilities** STV FTV WiFi ⚄ HL Gym Xmas New Year **Conf** Class 110 Board 120 Thtr 250 **Services** Lift Air con **Parking** 167 **Notes** ⊗ Civ Wed 200

W

WINCHESTER *continued*

The Winchester Hotel & Spa

★★★★ 76% HOTEL

tel: 01962 709988 **Worthy Ln SO23 7AB**
email: info@thewinchesterhotel.co.uk **web:** www.thewinchesterhotel.co.uk
dir: A33 then A3047, hotel 1m on right

This hotel is just a few minutes' walk from the city centre, is very smartly appointed throughout, and includes a great leisure centre. The staff are extremely friendly and helpful, and praiseworthy food is served in the contemporary Hutton's Brasserie.

Rooms 96 (6 GF) **S** £80–£170; **D** £80–£180 (incl. bkfst)* **Facilities** Spa FTV WiFi
Gym Sauna Steam room Xmas New Year **Conf** Class 100 Board 40 Thtr 200
Del from £120 to £180* **Services** Lift Air con **Parking** 47 **Notes** LB Civ Wed 180

Hotel du Vin Winchester

★★★★ 74% ❀❀ TOWN HOUSE HOTEL

tel: 01962 841414 **Southgate St SO23 9EF**
email: info@winchester.hotelduvin.com **web:** www.hotelduvin.com
dir: M3 junct 11 towards Winchester, follow signs. Hotel in approx 2m on left just past cinema

Continuing to set high standards, this inviting hotel is best known for its high profile bistro. The individually designed bedrooms have all the Hotel du Vin signature touches including fine Egyptian cotton linen, power showers and WiFi. The bistro serves imaginative yet simply cooked dishes from a seasonal, daily-changing menu.

Rooms 24 (4 annexe) (4 GF) **S** £145–£195; **D** £145–£195* **Facilities** STV WiFi
Xmas New Year **Conf** Class 30 Board 20 Thtr 40 **Services** Air con **Parking** 35
Notes LB Civ Wed 60

Mercure Winchester Wessex Hotel

★★★★ 73% HOTEL

tel: 01962 861611 **Paternoster Row SO23 9LQ**
email: H6619@accor.com **web:** www.mercure.com
dir: M3 junct 10, 2nd exit at rdbt signed Winchester/B3330. Right at lights, left at 2nd rdbt. Over small bridge, straight on at next rdbt into Broadway. Past Guildhall, 1st left into Colebrook St. Hotel 50yds on right

Occupying an enviable location in the centre of this historic city and adjacent to the spectacular cathedral, Mercure Winchester Wessex Hotel is quietly situated on a side street. Inside, the atmosphere is restful and welcoming, with public areas and some bedrooms enjoying unrivalled views of the hotel's centuries-old neighbour.

Rooms 94 (6 fmly) **S** £75–£160; **D** £75–£160* **Facilities** STV WiFi Xmas New Year
Conf Class 25 Board 40 Thtr 100 Del from £120 to £160* **Services** Lift **Parking** 30
Notes LB Civ Wed 120

Marwell Hotel

★★★ 81% ❀❀ HOTEL

tel: 01962 777681 **Thompsons Ln, Colden Common, Marwell SO21 1JY**
email: info@marwellhotel.co.uk **web:** www.marwellhotel.co.uk
dir: B3354 through Twyford. 1st exit at rdbt (B3354), left onto B2177 signed Bishop Waltham. Left into Thompsons Ln after 1m, hotel on left

Taking its theme from the adjacent zoo, this unusual hotel is based on the famous TreeTops safari lodge in Kenya. The well-equipped bedrooms, split between four lodges, convey a safari style, while the smart public areas include an airy lobby bar and an 'Out of Africa' themed restaurant. There is also a selection of meeting and leisure facilities.

Rooms 68 (10 fmly) (38 GF) **S** £49–£110; **D** £49–£125* **Facilities** FTV WiFi 36
Putt green Gym Sauna New Year Child facilities **Conf** Class 60 Board 60 Thtr 175
Parking 120 **Notes** LB Civ Wed 150

WINDERMERE	Map 18 SD49
Cumbria	

INSPECTORS' CHOICE

Holbeck Ghyll Country House Hotel

★★★★ ❀❀❀ COUNTRY HOUSE HOTEL

tel: 015394 32375 **Holbeck Ln LA23 1LU**
email: stay@holbeckghyll.com **web:** www.holbeckghyll.com
dir: 3m N of Windermere on A591, right into Holbeck Lane (signed Troutbeck), hotel 0.5m on left

Holbeck Ghyll sits high up overlooking the majestic Lake Windermere surrounded by well maintained grounds. The original house was bought in 1888 by Lord Lonsdale, the first president of the AA, who used it as a hunting lodge. Guests today will find that this is a delightful place where the service is professional and attentive. There are beautifully designed, spacious bedrooms situated in the main house and also in lodges in the grounds; each has lake views and some have patios. There are also The Shieling and Miss Potter suites. Each bedroom has Egyptian cotton linens, fresh flowers, LCD satellite TV, CD/DVD players, bathrobes and a decanter of damson gin. The restaurant impresses with its award-winning cuisine. The hotel also has a health spa, gym and boutique store.

Rooms 26 (13 annexe) (5 fmly) (11 GF) **S** £130–£307; **D** £160–£515 (incl. bkfst)
Facilities Spa FTV WiFi Sauna Steam room Beauty massage Xmas New Year
Conf Class 40 Board 30 Thtr 60 Del £250 **Parking** 34 **Notes** LB Civ Wed 60

Linthwaite House Hotel & Restaurant

★★★★ ◉◉◉ COUNTRY HOUSE HOTEL

tel: 015394 88600 **Crook Rd LA23 3JA**
email: stay@linthwaite.com **web:** www.linthwaite.com
dir: A591 towards The Lakes for 8m to large rdbt, take 1st exit (B5284), 6m, hotel on left. 1m past Windermere golf club

Linthwaite House is set in 14 acres of hilltop grounds and enjoys stunning views over Lake Windermere. Inviting public rooms include an attractive conservatory and adjoining lounge, and an elegant restaurant which occupies three rooms and offers menus based on the finest local ingredients. Bedrooms, which are individually decorated, combine contemporary furnishings with classical styles; all are thoughtfully equipped and include CD players, radios and free WiFi. There is also a Garden Suite and the luxurious Loft Suite which even has a retractable roof and telescope for star gazing. Service and hospitality are attentive and friendly.

Rooms 30 (1 fmly) (7 GF) ✎ **S** £136-£195; **D** £202-£650 (incl. bkfst & dinner)*
Facilities STV FTV WiFi ♇ Putt green Fishing ⚓ Beauty treatments Massage Access to nearby spa with pool & gym Xmas New Year **Conf** Class 22 Board 25 Thtr 54
Parking 40 **Notes** LB Civ Wed 64

Gilpin Hotel & Lake House

★★★★ ◉◉◉ HOTEL

tel: 015394 88818 **Crook Rd LA23 3NE**
email: hotel@the gilpin.co.uk **web:** www.thegilpin.co.uk
dir: M6 junct 36, A590, A591 to rdbt N of Kendal, onto B5284, hotel 5m on right

This smart Victorian residence is set amidst delightful gardens leading to the fells, and is just a short drive from the lake. The individually designed bedrooms are stylish and a number benefit from private terraces; all are spacious and thoughtfully equipped, and each has a private sitting room. In addition there are luxury Garden Suites that lead onto private gardens with cedar wood hot tubs. The welcoming atmosphere is notable and the attractive day rooms are perfect for relaxing, perhaps beside a real fire. Eating in any of the quartet of dining rooms is a must. The Lake House situated a mile from the main hotel offers an additional six suites, spa and stunning lakeside views.

Rooms 26 (12 annexe) (1 fmly) (12 GF) ✎ **S** £225-£565; **D** £335-£605 (incl. bkfst & dinner)* **Facilities** WiFi ♇ ⚓ Free membership at local leisure club Xmas New Year **Parking** 40 **Notes** LB ⊗ No children 7yrs Civ Wed 25

Macdonald Old England Hotel & Spa

★★★★ 84% ◉◉ HOTEL

tel: 0844 879 9144 **Church St, Bowness LA23 3DF**
email: sales.oldengland@macdonald-hotels.co.uk **web:** www.macdonaldhotels.co.uk
dir: Through Windermere to Bowness, straight across at mini-rdbt. Hotel behind church on right

This hotel stands right on the shore of England's largest lake and boasts superb views, especially through the floor-to-ceiling windows in the Vinand Restaurant. There are several bedroom types; standard, executive and suites; some rooms have been designed for wheelchairs users. The spa has a 20-metre pool, a gym, sauna and steam room.

Rooms 106 (6 fmly) (14 GF) ✎ **Facilities** Spa STV WiFi ⊙ supervised Gym Private jetties Rock sauna Aromatherapy shower Steam room Ice room Xmas New Year **Conf** Class 60 Board 25 Thtr 150 **Services** Lift **Parking** 90 **Notes** ⊗ Civ Wed 100

W

WINDERMERE *continued*

Low Wood Bay

English Lakes
Hotels Resorts & Venues

★★★★ 80% HOTEL

tel: 015394 33338 & 0845 850 3502 **LA23 1LP**
email: lowwoodbay@englishlakes.co.uk web: www.englishlakes.co.uk
dir: M6 junct 36, A590, A591 to Windermere, then 3m towards Ambleside, hotel on right

Benefiting from a lakeside location, this hotel offers an excellent range of leisure and conference facilities. Bedrooms, many with panoramic lake views, are attractively furnished, and include a number of larger executive rooms and suites. There is a choice of bars, a spacious restaurant and the more informal Café del Lago. The poolside bar offers internet access.

Rooms 111 (13 fmly) (21 GF) ➧ **S** £110-£150; **D** £110-£150 (incl. bkfst)*
Facilities Spa FTV WiFi ➔ ➔ supervised Fishing ➤ Gym Squash Watersports centre offering water skiing & canoeing Beauty salon Marina Xmas New Year
Conf Class 180 Board 150 Thtr 340 Del from £108* **Services** Lift **Parking** 200
Notes LB Civ Wed 280

Lindeth Howe Country House Hotel & Restaurant

CLASSIC
BRITISH HOTELS

★★★★ 79% ◉◉ COUNTRY HOUSE HOTEL

tel: 015394 45759 **Lindeth Dr, Longtail Hill LA23 3JF**
email: hotel@lindeth-howe.co.uk web: www.lindeth-howe.co.uk
dir: Exit A592, 1m S of Bowness onto B5284 (Longtail Hill) signed Kendal & Lancaster, hotel last driveway on right

Historic photographs commemorate the fact that this delightful house was once the family home of Beatrix Potter. Secluded in landscaped grounds, it enjoys views across the valley and Lake Windermere. Public rooms are plentiful and inviting, with the restaurant being the perfect setting for modern country-house cooking. Deluxe and superior bedrooms are spacious and smartly appointed.

Rooms 34 (3 fmly) (2 GF) ➧ **Facilities** FTV WiFi ➔ Gym Sauna Fitness room Xmas New Year **Conf** Class 20 Board 18 Thtr 30 Del £180* **Parking** 50 **Notes** ⊗ Closed 4-16 Jan Civ Wed 100

Storrs Hall Hotel

★★★★ 76% ◉◉ HOTEL

tel: 015394 47111 **Storrs Park LA23 3LG**
email: enquiries@storrshall.com web: www.storrshall.com
dir: On A592, 2m S of Bowness, on Newby Bridge road

Set in 17 acres of landscaped grounds by the lakeside, this imposing Georgian mansion is delightful. There are numerous lounges to relax in, furnished with fine art and antiques. Individually styled bedrooms are generally spacious and boast

impressive bathrooms. Imaginative cuisine is served in the elegant restaurant, which offers fine views across the lawn to the lake and fells beyond.

Rooms 30 **S** £90-£152.50; **D** £120-£245 (incl. bkfst)* **Facilities** FTV WiFi Fishing ➤ In-room beauty treatments Xmas New Year **Conf** Class 35 Board 24 Thtr 50 Del from £150 to £250* **Parking** 50 **Notes** LB Civ Wed 94

Beech Hill Hotel

★★★★ 75% ◉ HOTEL

tel: 015394 42137 **Newby Bridge Rd LA23 3LR**
email: reservations@beechhillhotel.co.uk web: www.beechhillhotel.co.uk
dir: M6 junct 36, A591 to Windermere. Left onto A592 towards Newby Bridge. Hotel 4m from Bowness-on-Windermere

Located on the edge of Lake Windermere, the panoramic views across the lake to the Cumbrian fells beyond are impressive. The bedrooms are well appointed and some have balconies overlooking the lake. The open areas, for enjoying coffee or drinks, prove very popular in the summer, and there are cosy lounges with log fires, a fine restaurant, leisure facilities and landscaped gardens. High standards of service can be expected from the attentive, informative and very friendly staff.

Rooms 57 (5 fmly) (4 GF) ➧ **S** £69-£99; **D** £89-£395 (incl. bkfst)* **Facilities** FTV WiFi ➔ Fishing Solarium ♬ Xmas New Year **Parking** 70 **Notes** ⊗ Civ Wed 130

The Samling

★★★ ◉◉◉ HOTEL

tel: 015394 31922 **Ambleside Rd LA23 1LR**
email: info@thesamlinghotel.co.uk web: www.thesamlinghotel.co.uk
dir: M6 junct 36, A591 through Windermere towards Ambleside. 2m. 300yds past Low Wood Water Sports Centre just after sharp bend turn right into hotel entrance

This stylish house, built in the late 1700s, is situated in 67 acres of grounds and enjoys an elevated position overlooking Lake Windermere. The spacious, beautifully furnished bedrooms and suites, some in adjacent buildings, are thoughtfully equipped and all have superb bathrooms. Public rooms include a sumptuous drawing room, a small library and an elegant dining room where imaginative, skilfully prepared food is served.

Rooms 11 (6 annexe) (6 fmly) (6 GF) ➧ **D** £220-£360 (incl. bkfst)* **Facilities** STV FTV WiFi ➔ ➤ Xmas New Year **Conf** Board 14 Thtr 30 Del £340 **Parking** 20 **Notes** LB Civ Wed 50

W

Lindeth Fell Country House Hotel

★★★ 87% ◎ COUNTRY HOUSE HOTEL

tel: 015394 43286 & 44287 **Lyth Valley Rd, Bowness-on-Windermere LA23 3JP**
email: kennedy@lindethfell.co.uk **web:** www.lindethfell.co.uk
dir: 1m S of Bowness on A5074

Enjoying delightful views, this smart Edwardian residence stands in seven acres of glorious, landscaped gardens. Bedrooms, which vary in size and style, are comfortably equipped. Skilfully prepared dinners are served in the spacious dining room that commands fine views. The resident owners and their attentive, friendly staff provide high levels of hospitality and service.

Rooms 14 (2 fmly) (1 GF) ♠ **S** £63.50-£90; **D** £127-£220 (incl. bkfst)* **Facilities** FTV WiFi Putt green Fishing ♨ Bowling Xmas New Year **Conf** Class 12 Board 12 **Parking** 20 **Notes** LB ⊗ Closed 2-31 Jan

Cedar Manor Hotel & Restaurant

★★★ 86% ◎◎ SMALL HOTEL

tel: 015394 43192 & 45970 **Ambleside Rd LA23 1AX**
email: info@cedarmanor.co.uk **web:** www.cedarmanor.co.uk
dir: From A591 follow signs to Windermere. Hotel on left just beyond St Mary's Church

Built in 1854 as a country retreat, this lovely old house enjoys a peaceful location that is within easy walking distance of the town centre. Bedrooms, some on the ground floor, are attractive and well equipped, with a luxurious annexe suite available for longer stays or romantic getaways. There is a comfortable lounge bar where guests can relax before enjoying dinner in the well-appointed dining room.

Rooms 10 (1 annexe) (1 fmly) (3 GF) ♠ **S** £100-£365; **D** £105-£385 (incl. bkfst)* **Facilities** FTV WiFi New Year **Conf** Board 10 Del from £149 to £199* **Parking** 11 **Notes** LB ⊗ Closed 3-21 Jan

Miller Howe Hotel

★★★ 86% ◎◎ COUNTRY HOUSE HOTEL

tel: 015394 42536 **Rayrigg Rd LA23 1EY**
email: info@millerhowe.com **web:** www.millerhowe.com
dir: M6 junct 36, A591 past Windermere, left at rdbt towards Bowness

This long established hotel enjoys a lakeside setting amidst delightful landscaped gardens. The bright and welcoming day rooms include sumptuous lounges, a conservatory and an opulently decorated restaurant. Imaginative dinners make use of fresh, local produce where possible and there is an extensive, well-balanced wine list. Stylish bedrooms, many with fabulous lake views, include well-equipped cottage rooms and a number with whirlpool baths.

Rooms 15 (3 annexe) (1 GF) ♠ **Facilities** FTV WiFi ♨ HL Xmas New Year **Parking** 35 **Notes** Civ Wed 75

Hillthwaite

★★★ 79% HOTEL

tel: 015394 43636 & 46691 **Thornbarrow Rd LA23 2DF**
email: reception@hillthwaite.com **web:** www.hillthwaite.com
dir: M6 junct 36, A591 Windermere, follow lane road through village (A5074), left opposite Goodley Dale School, approx 0.5m from A591

The family-owned Hillthwaite hotel, set in three acres of landscaped gardens between Windermere and Bowness, is one of the area's highest hotels, overlooking Lake Windermere with magnificent panoramic views over to Langdale Pikes, Crinkle Crags and Coniston Old Man. Individually designed rooms are maintained to a high standard, some with splendid four-poster beds and jacuzzi baths, and most with lake or fell views. Public rooms on the ground floor include a comfortable lounge with well-stocked bar, a feature conservatory and impressive restaurant with stunning views of the South Lakes skyline. Leisure facilities include a heated swimming pool, steam room and sauna.

Rooms 33 (4 fmly) (2 GF) **Facilities** FTV WiFi ⊗ Sauna Steam room New Year **Parking** 30

Windermere Manor Hotel

★★★ 78% HOTEL

tel: 01539 445801 **Rayrigg Rd LA23 1ES**
email: windermere@actionforblindpeople.org.uk **web:** www.visionhotels.co.uk
dir: A591 towards Ambleside. At mini-rdbt turn left, hotel 1st on left

Set above the shores of Lake Windermere in wooded landscaped gardens, this former manor house has been restored to its original splendour. The bedrooms and suites are smart and well appointed. The attractive dining room has an unusual barrel-vaulted wooden roof and serves delicious home cooking. The hotel extends a warm welcome to everyone but caters especially for the visually impaired, their families, friends and guide dogs. Special facilities for guide dogs are provided.

Rooms 35 (7 annexe) (2 fmly) (10 GF) ♠ **Facilities** FTV WiFi HL ⊗ supervised Gym Xmas New Year **Conf** Class 30 Board 15 Thtr 40 **Services** Lift **Parking** 28 **Notes** Civ Wed 40

Craig Manor

★★★ 74% HOTEL

tel: 015394 88877 **Lake Rd LA23 2JF**
email: info@craigmanor.co.uk **web:** www.craigmanor.co.uk
dir: A590, then A591 into Windermere, left at Windermere Hotel, through village, pass Magistrates' Court, hotel on left

Situated in the heart of the Lake District, Craig Manor has a relaxed and friendly atmosphere with professional staff providing attentive service. Bedrooms are comfortable and well equipped, and some rooms offer stunning views across the lake. The attractive and elegant lake-facing restaurant serves an excellent choice of quality dishes. The large car park is a further benefit in this popular tourist resort.

Rooms 16 ♠ **S** £75-£131; **D** £80-£150 (incl. bkfst)* **Parking** 39 **Notes** LB

W

WINDSOR
Berkshire

Map 6 SU97

INSPECTORS' CHOICE

Macdonald Windsor Hotel

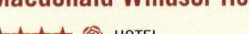

★★★★ @ HOTEL

tel: 0844 879 9101 **23 High St SL4 1LH**
email: gm.windsor@macdonaldwindsor.co.uk **web:** www.macdonaldhotels.co.uk
dir: M4 junct 6 A355, take A332, rdbt 1st exit signed towncentre. In 0.7m turn left into Bachelors Acre

Just across the street from Windsor Castle, this hotel is an ideal base for visiting the castle, and all the other famous attractions of the town. It has well-appointed contemporary, designer-led bedrooms, some overlooking the castle, that are decorated in soft shades to create a calm atmosphere, and include flat-screen TVs and Bose iPod docks. The Scottish Steak Club@ Caleys restaurant offers a relaxed and informal dining venue, and 24-hour room service is also available. There is complimentary WiFi in the bedrooms and the conference rooms. The hotel has excellent wedding facilities.

Rooms 120 (4 fmly) ☂ **Facilities** FTV WiFi ⌕ HL ♫ **Conf** Class 80 Board 35 Thtr 100 **Services** Lift Air con **Parking** 42 **Notes** Civ Wed 100

Oakley Court Hotel

principal hayley

★★★★ 81% @@ HOTEL

tel: 01753 609988 & 609900 **Windsor Rd, Water Oakley SL4 5UR**
email: reservations@theoakleycourthotel.com **web:** www.principal-hayley.com
dir: M4 junct 6, A355, then A332 towards Windsor, right onto A308 towards Maidenhead. Pass racecourse, hotel 2.5m on right

Built in 1859 this splendid Victorian Gothic mansion is enviably situated in extensive grounds that lead down to the Thames. All bedrooms are spacious, beautifully furnished and many enjoy river views. Extensive public areas include a range of comfortable lounges and the Oakleaf Restaurant. The comprehensive leisure facilities include a 9-hole golf course.

Rooms 118 (108 annexe) (6 fmly) (42 GF) **Facilities** WiFi HL ⓢ ♨ 9 ♨ Putt green ♨ Gym Boating Sauna Steam room Snooker Xmas New Year **Conf** Class 90 Board 50 Thtr 170 **Services** Air con **Parking** 200 **Notes** ⊗ Civ Wed 170

Mercure Windsor Castle Hotel

★★★★ 77% @@ HOTEL

tel: 01753 851577 **18 High St SL4 1LJ**
email: h6618@accor.com **web:** www.mercure.com
dir: M4 junct 6/M25 junct 15, follow signs to Windsor town centre & castle. Hotel at top of hill opposite Guildhall

This is one of the oldest hotels in Windsor, beginning life as a coaching inn in the 16th century. Located opposite Windsor Castle, it is an ideal base from which to explore the town and its royal connections. Stylish bedrooms are thoughtfully equipped and include four-poster and executive rooms. Public areas are spacious and tastefully decorated.

Rooms 108 (70 annexe) (18 fmly) (3 GF) ☂ **Facilities** STV FTV WiFi Xmas New Year **Conf** Class 150 Board 50 Thtr 400 **Services** Lift Air con **Parking** 135 **Notes** ⊗ Civ Wed 300

Sir Christopher Wren Hotel and Spa

SAROVA HOTELS

★★★★ 76% @ HOTEL

tel: 01753 442400 **Thames St SL4 1PX**
email: wrens@sarova.co.uk **web:** www.sarova.com
dir: M4 junct 6, at 1st exit follow signs to Windsor, 1st major exit on left, left at lights

Located by the side of the Thames and close to the Eton Bridge stands this well presented hotel. Bedrooms vary - with both traditional and contemporary tastes catered for. There are comfortable lounges, a popular restaurant with great views of the river, and also a well-equipped leisure club. Limited parking is available.

Rooms 99 (42 annexe) (5 fmly) (10 GF) ☂ **S** £110-£180; **D** £130-£395* **Facilities** Spa STV WiFi ⌕ Gym Sauna ♫ Xmas New Year **Conf** Class 50 Board 45 Thtr 100 Del from £200 to £300* **Parking** 14 **Notes** ⊗ Civ Wed 100

Christopher Hotel

★★★ 80% HOTEL

tel: 01753 852359 **110 High St, Eton SL4 6AN**
email: reservations@thechristopher.co.uk **web:** www.thechristopher.co.uk
dir: M4 junct 5 (Slough E), Colnbrook Datchet Eton (B470). At rdbt 2nd exit for Datchet. Right at mini rdbt (Eton), left into Eton Rd (3rd rdbt). Left, hotel on right

This hotel benefits from an ideal location in Eton, being only a short stroll across the pedestrian bridge from historic Windsor Castle and the many other attractions the town has to offer. The hotel has comfortable and smartly decorated accommodation, and a wide range of dishes is available in the informal bar and grill. A stylish room is available for private dining or for meetings.

Rooms 34 (23 annexe) (10 fmly) (22 GF) ☂ **S** £100-£144; **D** £152-£205* **Facilities** FTV WiFi ⌕ Xmas New Year **Conf** Board 10 Thtr 30 Del from £178 to £200* **Parking** 19 **Notes** LB

WINTERINGHAM
Lincolnshire
Map 17 SE92

Winteringham Fields

 RESTAURANT WITH ROOMS

tel: 01724 733096 01724 733898 **DN15 9ND**
email: reception@winteringhamfields.co.uk **web:** www.winteringhamfields.co.uk
dir: In village centre at x-rds

This highly regarded restaurant with rooms, located deep in the countryside at Winteringham village, is six miles west of the Humber Bridge. Public rooms and bedrooms, some of which are housed in renovated barns and cottages, are delightfully luxurious. There is an abundance of charm, and period features are combined with rich furnishings and fabrics. The award-winning food is a highlight of any stay and guests can expect highly skilled dishes, excellent quality and stunning presentation.

Rooms 11 (7 annexe) (2 fmly)

WISBECH
Cambridgeshire
Map 12 TF40

Crown Lodge Hotel

THE INDEPENDENTS
HOTEL ASSOCIATION

★★★ 85% HOTEL

tel: 01945 773391 & 772206 **Downham Rd, Outwell PE14 8SE**
email: office@thecrownlodgehotel.co.uk **web:** www.thecrownlodgehotel.co.uk
dir: On A1122, approx 5m from Wisbech

A friendly, privately owned hotel situated in a peaceful location on the banks of Well Creek, a short drive from Wisbech. The bedrooms are pleasantly decorated, with co-ordinated fabrics and modern facilities. The public areas are very stylish; they include a lounge bar, brasserie restaurant and a large seating area with plush leather sofas.

Rooms 10 (1 fmly) (10 GF) **Facilities** FTV WiFi Squash **Conf** Class 60 Board 40 Thtr 80 **Services** Air con **Parking** 55 **Notes** Closed 25-26 Dec & 1 Jan

WITNEY
Oxfordshire
Map 5 SP31

Oxford Witney Four Pillars Hotel

★★★★ 75% HOTEL

tel: 0800 374692 & 01993 779777 **Ducklington Ln OX28 4TJ**
email: witney@four-pillars.co.uk **web:** www.four-pillars.co.uk/witney
dir: M40 junct 9, A34 to A40, exit A415 Witney/Abingdon. Hotel on left, 2nd exit for Witney

This attractive modern hotel is close to Oxford and Burford and offers spacious, well-equipped bedrooms. The cosy Spinners Bar has comfortable seating areas and the popular Weavers Restaurant offers a good range of dishes. Other amenities include extensive function and leisure facilities, complete with indoor swimming pool.

Rooms 87 (14 fmly) (21 GF) **S** £80-£150; **D** £80-£150 **Facilities** FTV WiFi Gym Steam room Sauna Xmas New Year **Conf** Class 76 Board 44 Thtr 150 Del from £99 to £186 **Parking** 120 **Notes** LB Civ Wed 150

Premier Inn Witney

Premier Inn

BUDGET HOTEL

tel: 0871 527 9488 **Beech House, Ducklington Ln OX28 4JF**
web: www.premierinn.com
dir: M40 junct 8 or junct 9 follow Oxford signs, A40 towards Cheltenham. Take A415 (Witney & Abingdon). At bottom of slip road follow Witney signs. Straight on at lights, hotel on right

High quality, budget accommodation ideal for both families and business travellers. Spacious, en suite bedrooms feature tea and coffee making facilities, and Freeview TV in most hotels. Internet access and WiFi are available for a small fee. The adjacent family restaurant features a wide and varied menu. See also the Hotel Groups pages.

Rooms 57

W

WOBURN
Bedfordshire

Map 11 SP93

Woburn Hotel

★★★ 86% ◉◉ HOTEL

tel: 01525 290441 **George St MK17 9PX**
email: inn@woburn.co.uk **web:** www.woburn.co.uk/inn
dir: M1 junct 13, towards Woburn. In Woburn left at T-junct, hotel in village

This inn provides a high standard of accommodation. Bedrooms are divided between the original house, a modern extension and some stunning cottage suites. Public areas include the beamed, club-style Tavistock Bar, a range of meeting rooms and an attractive restaurant with interesting dishes on offer.

Rooms 55 (7 annexe) (4 fmly) (25 GF) ⬤ **S** £130-£140; **D** £150-£280* **Facilities** FTV WiFi ⬤ 54 Putt green Concessionary rate to access Woburn Safari Park & Woburn Abbey Xmas New Year **Conf** Class 30 Board 35 Thtr 60 Del from £150 to £180* **Parking** 80 **Notes** LB ⊗ Civ Wed 60

WOKING
Surrey

Map 6 TQ05

Premier Inn Woking

BUDGET HOTEL

tel: 0871 527 9182 **Bridge Barn Ln, Horsell GU21 6NL**
web: www.premierinn.com
dir: From A324 at rdbt into Parley Drive. Left at next rdbt into Goldsworth Rd

High quality, budget accommodation ideal for both families and business travellers. Spacious, en suite bedrooms feature tea and coffee making facilities, and Freeview TV in most hotels. Internet access and WiFi are available for a small fee. The adjacent family restaurant features a wide and varied menu. See also the Hotel Groups pages.

Rooms 34

Premier Inn Woking Town Centre

BUDGET HOTEL

tel: 0871 527 9462 **Eurobet House, Church Street West GU21 6HT**
web: www.premierinn.com
dir: See website for detailed directions

Rooms 105

WOLVERHAMPTON
West Midlands

Map 10 SO99

Novotel Wolverhampton

★★★ 81% HOTEL

tel: 01902 871100 **Union St WV1 3JN**
email: H1188@accor.com **web:** www.novotel.com
dir: 6m from M6 junct 10. A454 to Wolverhampton. Hotel on main ring road

This large, modern, purpose-built hotel stands close to the town centre. It provides spacious, smartly presented and well-equipped bedrooms, all of which contain convertible bed settees for family occupancy. In addition to the open-plan lounge and bar area, there is an attractive brasserie-style restaurant, which overlooks an attractive patio garden.

Rooms 132 (9 fmly) ⬤ **S** £65-£149; **D** £65-£149* **Facilities** FTV WiFi ⬤ **Conf** Class 100 Board 80 Thtr 200 Del from £99 to £149* **Services** Lift **Parking** 120 **Notes** RS 23 Dec-4 Jan Civ Wed 170

Mercure Wolverhampton Goldthorn Hotel

★★★ 74% HOTEL

tel: 01902 429216 **126 Penn Rd WV3 OER**
email: enquiries@hotels-wolverhampton.com **web:** www.hotels-wolverhampton.com
dir: A454 then A449 signed Kidderminster. Hotel 1m on right

This hotel is situated just on the outskirts of the old town and offers easy access to major motorway networks. The bedrooms are comfortable and well equipped; free WiFi is available throughout the hotel. The leisure facilities include a health club with a swimming pool, gym, steam room and sauna. There is also free on-site parking.

Rooms 74 (16 annexe) (12 fmly) (4 GF) **S** £35-£45; **D** £58-£90* **Facilities** FTV WiFi ⬤ Gym Sauna Steam room **Conf** Class 70 Board 40 Thtr 140 Del from £85 to £125* **Parking** 100 **Notes** LB Civ Wed 100

Quality Hotel Wolverhampton

★★★ 70% HOTEL

tel: 01902 424433 **Tettenhall Rd WV1 4SW**
email: reception@qualityhotelwolverhampton.com
web: www.qualityhotelwolverhampton.com
dir: A41 junct 3, 1st exit at rdbt. Follow signs for Tettenhall. In Tettenhall Rd, hotel on left

This hotel is located a short walk from the city centre and the railway station, with convenient access to the motorway networks. Bedrooms provide modern comfort with contemporary decor. Complimentary WiFi is available throughout the hotel. The Americano steakhouse and bar offers American-style dishes, with exotic meats a speciality. There are seven air-conditioned conference and banqueting suites.

Rooms 60 (3 fmly) **Facilities** STV FTV WiFi ⬤ Xmas New Year **Conf** Class 300 Board 60 Thtr 500 **Services** Lift **Parking** 120 **Notes** ⊗ Civ Wed 500

Premier Inn Wolverhampton City Centre

BUDGET HOTEL

tel: 0871 527 9186 **Broad Gauge Way WV10 OBA**
web: www.premierinn.com
dir: M6 junct 10, A454 signed Wolverhampton for approx 2m. Right into Neachalls Ln (signed Wednesfield). 0.75m. At rdbt 1st exit onto A4124 (Wednesfield Way). 1st exit at next rdbt. 2nd exit at 3rd rdbt. At 2nd lights left into Sun St. 1st right, hotel at end of road

High quality, budget accommodation ideal for both families and business travellers. Spacious, en suite bedrooms feature tea and coffee making facilities, and Freeview TV in most hotels. Internet access and WiFi are available for a small fee. The adjacent family restaurant features a wide and varied menu. See also the Hotel Groups pages.

Rooms 88

Premier Inn Wolverhampton North

BUDGET HOTEL

tel: 0871 527 9184 **Greenfield Ln, Stafford Rd WV10 6TA**
web: www.premierinn.com
dir: M54 junct 2. Hotel at lights in approx 100yds

Rooms 77

W

WOMBWELL
South Yorkshire   Map 16 SE40

Premier Inn Barnsley (Dearne Valley)

BUDGET HOTEL

tel: 0871 527 8050 **Meadow Gate, Dearne Valley S73 0UN**
web: www.premierinn.com
dir: M1 junct 36 E'bound, A6195 towards Doncaster (5m). Hotel at rdbt adjacent to Meadows Brewers Fayre

High quality, budget accommodation ideal for both families and business travellers. Spacious, en suite bedrooms feature tea and coffee making facilities, and Freeview TV in most hotels. Internet access and WiFi are available for a small fee. The adjacent family restaurant features a wide and varied menu. See also the Hotel Groups pages.

Rooms 41

WOOBURN COMMON
Buckinghamshire   Map 6 SU98

Chequers Inn
★★★ 79%  HOTEL

tel: 01628 529575 **Kiln Ln, Wooburn HP10 0JQ**
email: info@chequers-inn.com **web:** www.chequers-inn.com
dir: M40 junct 2, A40 through Beaconsfield Old Town towards High Wycombe. 2m from town left into Broad Ln. Inn 2.5m

This 17th-century inn enjoys a peaceful, rural location beside the common. Bedrooms feature stripped-pine furniture, co-ordinated fabrics and an excellent range of extra facilities. The bar, with its massive oak post, beams and flagstone floor; and the restaurant, which overlooks a pretty patio, are very much focal points here.

Rooms 17 (8 GF) **S** £85-£99.50; **D** £90-£140* **Facilities** FTV WiFi **Conf** Class 30 Board 20 Thtr 50 Del from £155* **Parking** 60 **Notes** ⊗

WOODALL MOTORWAY SERVICE AREA (M1)
South Yorkshire   Map 16 SK48

Days Inn Sheffield - M1

BUDGET HOTEL

tel: 0114 248 7992 **Woodall Service Area S26 7XR**
email: woodall.hotel@welcomebreak.co.uk **web:** www.welcomebreak.co.uk
dir: M1, between juncts 30 & 31 S'bound, at Woodall Services

This modern building offers accommodation in smart, spacious and well-equipped bedrooms, suitable for families and business travellers, and all with en suite bathrooms. Continental breakfast is available and other refreshments may be taken at the nearby family restaurant. See also the Hotel Groups pages.

Rooms 38 (32 fmly) (16 GF) (6 smoking) **Conf** Board 10

WOODBRIDGE
Suffolk   Map 13 TM24

Seckford Hall Hotel
★★★★ 80%  HOTEL   

tel: 01394 385678 **IP13 6NU**
email: reception@seckford.co.uk **web:** www.seckford.co.uk
dir: Signed on A12 - NB do not follow signs for town centre

Seckford Hall is an elegant Tudor manor house set amid landscaped grounds just off the A12. It is reputed that Queen Elizabeth I visited this property, and it retains much of its original character. Public rooms include a superb panelled lounge, a cosy bar and an intimate restaurant. The spacious bedrooms are attractively decorated, tastefully furnished and thoughtfully equipped.

Rooms 32 (10 annexe) (4 fmly) (7 GF) **Facilities** WiFi ⊙ Putt green Fishing Gym Beauty salon & treatment room Xmas New Year **Conf** Class 46 Board 40 Thtr 100 **Parking** 100 **Notes** Civ Wed 120

The Crown at Woodbridge
★★★ 87% HOTEL   T|A|HOTEL COLLECTION

tel: 01394 384242 **2 Thoro'fare IP12 1AD**
email: info@thecrownatwoodbridge.co.uk **web:** www.thecrownatwoodbridge.co.uk
dir: A12 follow signs for Woodbridge onto B1438. 1.25m from rdbt left into Quay St. Hotel on right approx 100yds

This 17th-century property offers contemporary-style accommodation throughout. The open-plan public areas are tastefully appointed and include a large lounge bar, a restaurant and a private dining room. The stylish bedrooms are tastefully appointed and equipped with modern facilities.

Rooms 10 (2 fmly) **S** £90-£170; **D** £90-£170 (incl. bkfst)* **Facilities** STV WiFi **Parking** 40 **Notes** LB ⊗

WOODBURY
Devon   Map 3 SY08

Woodbury Park Hotel and Golf Club
★★★★ 76% HOTEL

tel: 01395 233382 **Woodbury Castle EX5 1JJ**
email: enquiries@woodburypark.co.uk **web:** www.woodburypark.co.uk
dir: M5 junct 30, A376 then A3052 towards Sidmouth, onto B3180, hotel signed

Situated in 500 acres of beautiful and unspoilt countryside, yet within easy reach of Exeter and the M5, this hotel offers smart, well-equipped and immaculately presented accommodation together with a host of sporting and banqueting facilities. There is a choice of golf courses, a Bodyzone beauty centre and enjoyable dining in the Atrium Restaurant.

Rooms 60 (4 annexe) (4 fmly) (28 GF) ⌒ **S** £79-£95; **D** £89-£110 (incl. bkfst) **Facilities** Spa STV FTV WiFi ⋎ ⊙ ⌕ 27 ⚑ Putt green Fishing Gym Squash Beauty salon Football pitch Driving range Fitness studio Cinema suite Xmas New Year **Conf** Class 100 Board 40 Thtr 250 Del from £130.50 to £145 **Services** Lift **Parking** 400 **Notes** LB ⊗ Civ Wed 150

W

WOODFORD BRIDGE
Greater London   Map 6 TQ49

Menzies Hotels London Chigwell Prince Regent

MenziesHotels

★★★★ 74% HOTEL

tel: 020 8505 9966 **Manor Rd IG8 8AE**
email: princeregent@menzieshotels.co.uk **web:** www.menzieshotels.co.uk
dir: From A113 (Chigwell Rd) S of Chigwell into B173 (Manor Rd

Situated on the edge of Woodford Bridge and Chigwell, this hotel with delightful rear gardens, offers easy access into London as well as to the M11 and M25. There is a good range of spacious, well-equipped bedrooms. Extensive conference and banqueting facilities are particularly well appointed, and are very suitable for weddings or business events.

Rooms 61 (4 fmly) (15 GF) (6 smoking) ✆ **S** £70-£150; **D** £70-£150 **Facilities** STV FTV WiFi ↘ Xmas New Year **Conf** Class 180 Board 80 Thtr 400 Del from £125 to £140 **Services** Lift **Parking** 225 **Notes** LB Civ Wed 350

WOODHALL SPA
Lincolnshire   Map 17 TF16

Petwood

★★★ 73% HOTEL

tel: 01526 352411 **Stixwould Rd LN10 6QG**
email: reception@petwood.co.uk **web:** www.petwood.co.uk
dir: From Sleaford take A153 (signed Skegness). At Tattershall turn left on B1192. Hotel is signed from village

This lovely Edwardian house, set in 30 acres of gardens and woodlands, is adjacent to Woodhall Golf Course. Built in 1905, the house was used by 617 Squadron, the famous Dambusters, as an officers' mess during World War II. Bedrooms and public

areas are spacious and comfortable, and retain many original features. Weddings and conferences are well catered for in modern facilities.

Rooms 53 (3 GF) ✆ **Facilities** FTV WiFi HL Putt green ↘ ♫ Xmas New Year **Conf** Class 100 Board 50 Thtr 250 Del from £130* **Services** Lift **Parking** 140 **Notes** Civ Wed 200

Golf Hotel

★★★ 70% HOTEL

tel: 01526 353535 **The Broadway LN10 6SG**
email: reception@thegolf-hotel.com **web:** www.thegolf-hotel.com
dir: From Lincoln take B1189 to Metheringham onto B1191 towards Woodhall Spa. Hotel on left in approx 500yds from rdbt

Located near the centre of the village, this traditional hotel is ideally situated to explore the Lincolnshire countryside and coast. The adjacent golf course makes this a popular venue for golfers, and the hotel's hydrotherapy suite uses the original spa water supplies. Bedrooms vary in size.

Rooms 50 (2 fmly) (8 GF) (3 smoking) **Facilities** Spa STV WiFi Xmas New Year **Conf** Class 50 Board 50 Thtr 120 **Services** Lift **Parking** 100 **Notes** Civ Wed 150

WOODLANDS
Hampshire   Map 5 SU31

Woodlands Lodge Hotel

★★★ 79% ❀ HOTEL

tel: 023 8029 2257 **Bartley Rd, Woodlands SO40 7GN**
email: reception@woodlands-lodge.co.uk **web:** www.woodlands-lodge.co.uk
dir: M27 junct 2, left at rdbt towards Fawley. 2nd rdbt right towards Cadnam. 1st left at White Horse pub onto Woodlands Rd, over cattle grid

An 18th-century former hunting lodge, this hotel is set in four acres of impressive and well-tended grounds on the edge of the New Forest. Well-equipped bedrooms come in varying sizes and styles and a number of bathrooms have a jacuzzi bath. Public areas include a pleasant lounge and intimate cocktail bar.

Rooms 17 (3 fmly) (3 GF) ✆ **S** £49-£149; **D** £54-£229 (incl. bkfst)* **Facilities** FTV WiFi Xmas New Year **Conf** Class 20 Board 20 Thtr 65 Del from £100 to £200* **Parking** 60 **Notes** LB Civ Wed 100

WOODSTOCK
Oxfordshire   Map 11 SP41

The Feathers Hotel

★★★★ 78% ❀❀ TOWN HOUSE HOTEL

tel: 01993 812291 **Market St OX20 1SX**
email: reception@feathers.co.uk **web:** www.feathers.co.uk
dir: From A44 Oxford to Woodstock, 1st left after lights. Hotel on left

This intimate and unique hotel enjoys a town centre location with easy access to nearby Blenheim Palace. Public areas are elegant and full of traditional character from the cosy drawing room to the atmospheric restaurant. Individually styled bedrooms are appointed to a high standard and are furnished with attractive period and reproduction furniture.

Rooms 21 (5 annexe) (4 fmly) (2 GF) ✆ **Facilities** FTV WiFi ↘ Xmas New Year **Conf** Class 18 Board 20 Thtr 40 Del from £180 to £300*

W

Macdonald Bear Hotel

★★★★ 77% ◎◎ HOTEL

tel: 0844 879 9143 **Park St OX20 1SZ**
email: general.bear@macdonaldhotels.co.uk **web:** www.macdonaldhotels.co.uk
dir: M40 junct 9 follow signs for Oxford & Blenheim Palace. A44 to town centre, hotel on left

With its ivy-clad façade, oak beams and open fireplaces, this 13th-century coaching inn exudes charm and cosiness. The bedrooms are decorated in a modern style that remains in keeping with the historic character of the building. Public rooms include a variety of function rooms, an intimate bar area and an attractive restaurant where attentive service and good food are offered.

Rooms 54 (18 annexe) (1 fmly) (8 GF) ➚⊗ **D** £119-£425 **Facilities** FTV WiFi Xmas New Year **Conf** Class 12 Board 24 Thtr 40 Del from £150 to £280 **Parking** 40 **Notes** LB

Kings Arms Hotel

★★★ 79% ◎ HOTEL

tel: 01993 813636 **19 Market St OX20 1SU**
email: stay@kingshotelwoodstock.co.uk **web:** www.kings-hotel-woodstock.co.uk
dir: In town centre, on corner of Market St & A44

This appealing and contemporary hotel is situated in the centre of town just a short walk from Blenheim Palace. Public areas include an attractive bistro-style restaurant and a smart bar. Bedrooms and bathrooms are comfortably furnished and well equipped, and appointed to a high standard.

Rooms 15 ➚ **Facilities** FTV WiFi Xmas New Year **Notes** ⊗ No children 12yrs

Hope House Woodstock

AA Advertised

tel: 01993 815990 & 07587 775040 **14 Oxford St OX20 1TS**
email: stay@hopehousewoodstock.co.uk **web:** www.hopehousewoodstock.co.uk
dir: M40 junct 8, A40 towards Oxford, A44 towards Woodstock. Left into Hewsington Rd on right after Punch Bowl pub

Built in the early 18th century for a local councillor and mayor, Hope House is one of a few grand houses in Woodstock built at the same time as Blenheim Palace, in the same architectural style, and to which it is seen as a sister property. The Money family owned and operated glove-making factories in Woodstock, and held a Royal Warrant to supply Queen Victoria with leather boots, saddles and gloves. The Moneys have lived here for centuries and it is still owned and operated by a descendant of the family. There are three suites and an apartment, all of which are sumptuously decorated and equipped. Breakfast is very special, using locally sourced produce and home-made sausages.

Rooms 6 (1 annexe) (2 fmly) (1 GF) ➚⊗ **S** £295-£495; **D** £350-£495 (incl. bkfst) **Facilities** STV FTV WiFi ⅃ Fishing Beauty treatments **Services** Air con **Parking** 5 **Notes** ⊗ No children 12yrs

WOODY BAY
Devon
Map 3 SS64

Woody Bay Hotel

★★ 78% HOTEL

tel: 01598 763264 & 763563 **EX31 4QX**
email: info@woodybayhotel.co.uk **web:** www.woodybayhotel.co.uk
dir: Signed from A39 between Blackmoor Gate & Lynton

Popular with walkers, this Victorian country style hotel is perfectly situated to enjoy sweeping views over Woody Bay. Bedrooms vary in style and size, but all boast truly

magnificent views across dense woodland to the sea beyond. The same views can be enjoyed from the restaurant where local fish features prominently on the imaginative menus.

Rooms 5 (1 fmly) **Facilities** WiFi ⅃ **Parking** 7 **Notes** ⊗ No children 10 yrs Closed Dec-Jan RS Nov & Feb

WOOKEY HOLE
Somerset
Map 4 ST54

Wookey Hole Hotel

★★ 74% HOTEL

tel: 01749 672243 **BA5 1BB**
email: witch@wookey.co.uk **web:** www.wookey.co.uk

This impressive, newly-built hotel is located in the heart of the pretty village, famous for its magnificent cave system and just a couple of miles from the historic cathedral city of Wells. The bedrooms are modern, spacious and comfortable, with both family and connecting rooms available. Additional facilities include a bar and restaurant. There is ample parking provision.

Rooms 58 (37 fmly) (27 GF) **Facilities** FTV WiFi ⅃ 9 hole adventure golf course Xmas New Year **Conf** Class 200 Board 200 Thtr 450 Del from £50 to £150* **Services** Lift **Parking** 800 **Notes** ⊗ Civ Wed 250

WOOLACOMBE
Devon
Map 3 SS44

Watersmeet Hotel

★★★★ 76% ◎◎ HOTEL

tel: 01271 870333 **EX34 7EB**
email: info@watersmeethotel.co.uk **web:** www.watersmeethotel.co.uk
dir: B3343 into Woolacombe, right onto esplanade, hotel 0.75m on left

With magnificent views, and steps leading directly to the beach, this popular hotel offers guests attentive service and a relaxing atmosphere. Bedrooms benefit from the wonderful sea views and some have private balconies. Diners in the attractive tiered restaurant can admire the beautiful sunsets while enjoying an innovative range of dishes offered on the fixed-price menu. Both indoor and outdoor pools are available.

Rooms 25 (4 fmly) (3 GF) ➚ **Facilities** FTV WiFi ⅃ ⊛ ⇲ ⅃ Steam room ♫ Xmas New Year **Conf** Board 20 Thtr 20 **Services** Lift **Parking** 38 **Notes** ⊗ Civ Wed 60

W

WOOLACOMBE continued

The Woolacombe Bay Hotel

★★★★ 74% HOTEL

tel: 01271 870388 **South St EX34 7BN**
email: enquiries@woolacombebayhotel.co.uk **web:** www.woolacombebayhotel.com
dir: A361 onto B3343 to Woolacombe. Hotel in centre

Overlooking one of the finest beaches in England, this privately owned hotel offers a warm welcome. Public areas are spacious and comfortable, and many of the stylishly furnished and well-equipped bedrooms have balconies with splendid views over the bay. New bathroom suites certainly add to the feeling of luxury. In addition to the elegant surroundings of Doyle's Restaurant, The Bay Brasserie is available as an informal alternative. Extensive leisure facilities are also provided, including a health club, a spa and a very stylish lido.

Rooms 68 (26 fmly) (2 GF) ♠ **S** £55-£128; **D** £110-£296 (incl. bkfst)* **Facilities** Spa FTV WiFi ⊗ ⤳ ♨ 9 ☺ Gym Squash Paddling pool Table tennis Snooker Steam room Sauna Outdoor short mat bowls Xmas New Year **Conf** Class 150 Board 150 Thtr 200 Del from £105 to £135* **Services** Lift **Parking** 150 **Notes** LB ⊗ Closed 2 Jan-14 Feb Civ Wed 150

Trimstone Manor Country House Hotel

★★★ Ⓐ

tel: 01271 862841 & 868050 **Trimstone EX34 8NR**
email: info@trimstone.co.uk **web:** www.trimstone.co.uk
dir: M5 junct 27 towards Barnstaple, A361, through Braunton & Knowle. Left into Trimstone Lane after 1m, hotel 300yds on left.

With a history that goes back to the Domesday Book and parts of the building dating back 400 years, this manor house, in 44-acre landscaped grounds, is situated near the sandy beaches at Saunton Sands, Woolacombe and Croyde. The public areas include a lounge bar, Tyme Restaurant, a swimming pool, sauna, gym and games room; outside there is a terrace - perfect for enjoying a drink while enjoying the views.

Rooms 15 (2 fmly) (3 GF) ♠ **Facilities** FTV WiFi ⊗ ☺ Gym Sauna Games room **Conf** Class 45 Board 40 Thtr 100 **Parking** 20 **Notes** Civ Wed 179

WORCESTER
Worcestershire   Map 10 SO85

Premier Inn Worcester

BUDGET HOTEL

tel: 0871 527 9188 **Wainwright Way, Warndon WR4 9FA**
web: www.premierinn.com
dir: M5 junct 6. At entrance of Warndon commercial development area

High quality, budget accommodation ideal for both families and business travellers. Spacious, en suite bedrooms feature tea and coffee making facilities, and Freeview TV in most hotels. Internet access and WiFi are available for a small fee. The adjacent family restaurant features a wide and varied menu. See also the Hotel Groups pages.

Rooms 60

Premier Inn Worcester City Centre

BUDGET HOTEL

tel: 0871 527 9456 **Cricket Ground, New Rd WR2 4QQ**
web: www.premierinn.com
dir: M5 junct 7 (Worcester South), A44 signed Worcester City Centre. At next rdbt 2nd exit (A44 & Worcester City Centre) keep in left lane. At Worcester Cathedral continue on A44, straight on at 3 sets of lights

Rooms 120

WORKINGTON
Cumbria   Map 18 NY02

Washington Central Hotel

★★★★ 76% HOTEL

tel: 01900 65772 **Washington St CA14 3AY**
email: kawildwchotel@aol.com **web:** www.washingtoncentralhotelworkington.com
dir: M6 junct 40, A66 to Workington. Left at lights, hotel on right

Enjoying a prominent town centre location, this modern hotel boasts memorably hospitable staff. The well-maintained and comfortable bedrooms are equipped with a range of thoughtful extras. Public areas include numerous lounges, a spacious bar, Caesars leisure club, a smart restaurant and a popular coffee shop. The comprehensive conference facilities are ideal for meetings and weddings.

Rooms 57 (12 fmly) ♠ **S** £95-£120; **D** £140-£200 (incl. bkfst)* **Facilities** FTV WiFi ↳ ⊗ supervised Gym Sauna Steam room New Year **Conf** Class 200 Board 100 Thtr 300 Del £145* **Services** Lift **Parking** 25 **Notes** LB ⊗ Civ Wed 300

WORKSOP
Nottinghamshire   Map 16 SK57

BEST WESTERN Lion Hotel

★★★ 80% HOTEL

tel: 01909 477925 **112 Bridge St S80 1HT**
email: reception@thelionworksop.co.uk **web:** www.bw-lionhotel.co.uk
dir: A57 to town centre, turn right at Sainsburys, follow to Norfolk Arms, turn left

This former coaching inn lies on the edge of the main shopping precinct, with a car park to the rear. It has been extended to offer modern accommodation that includes excellent executive rooms. A wide range of interesting dishes is offered in both the restaurant and bar.

Rooms 46 (3 fmly) (7 GF) 🎿 **S** £71-£91; **D** £75-£95 (incl. bkfst) **Facilities** STV FTV WiFi 🏌 Xmas New Year **Conf** Class 80 Board 70 Thtr 160 Del from £120 to £145 **Services** Lift **Parking** 50 **Notes** LB Civ Wed 150

WORSLEY
Greater Manchester   Map 15 SD70

Novotel Manchester West

★★★ 74% HOTEL

tel: 0161 799 3535 **Worsley Brow M28 2YA**
email: H0907@accor.com **web:** www.novotel.com
dir: Adjacent to M60 junct 13

Well placed for access to the Peak District and the Lake District, as well as Manchester, this modern hotel successfully caters for both families and business guests. The spacious bedrooms have sofa beds and a large work area; the hotel has an outdoor swimming pool, children's play area and secure parking.

Rooms 119 (10 fmly) (41 GF) 🎿 **Facilities** STV WiFi 🏌 HL Gym Xmas New Year **Conf** Class 130 Board 60 Thtr 220 **Services** Lift **Parking** 95 **Notes** Civ Wed 140

WORTHING
West Sussex   Map 6 TQ10

Ardington Hotel

★★★ 80% HOTEL

tel: 01903 230451 **Steyne Gardens BN11 3DZ**
email: reservations@ardingtonhotel.co.uk **web:** www.ardingtonhotel.co.uk
dir: A27 to Lancing, to seafront. Follow signs for Worthing. Left at church into Steyne Gardens

Overlooking Steyne Gardens adjacent to the seafront, this popular hotel offers well-appointed bedrooms with a good range of facilities. There's a stylishly modern lounge/bar with ample seating, where a light menu is available throughout the day. The popular restaurant offers local seafood and a choice of modern dishes. WiFi is available in the lounge/bar.

Rooms 45 (4 fmly) (12 GF) **Facilities** STV FTV WiFi **Conf** Class 60 Board 35 Thtr 140 **Notes** Closed 25 Dec-4 Jan

WOTTON-UNDER-EDGE
Gloucestershire   Map 4 ST79

Tortworth Court Four Pillars Hotel

★★★★ 78% 🌸 HOTEL

tel: 0800 374 692 & 01454 263000 **Tortworth GL12 8HH**
email: tortworth@four-pillars.co.uk **web:** www.four-pillars.co.uk/tortworth
dir: M5 junct 14, B4509 towards Wotton. 1st right into Tortworth Rd next right, hotel 0.5m on right

Set in 30 acres of parkland, this Gothic mansion displays original features cleverly combined with contemporary additions. Elegant public rooms include a choice of dining options, one housed within the library, with another in the atrium. Bedrooms are well equipped, and additional facilities include a host of conference rooms and a leisure centre.

Rooms 190 (25 fmly) (74 GF) **S** £59-£139; **D** £79-£159 (incl. bkfst) **Facilities** Spa FTV WiFi 🏊 ⛵ Gym Steam room Sauna Xmas New Year **Conf** Class 200 Board 80 Thtr 400 Del from £125 to £185 **Services** Lift **Parking** 200 **Notes** LB ⊗ Civ Wed 400

WREA GREEN
Lancashire   Map 18 SD33

The Spa Hotel at Ribby Hall Village

★★★★ 80% 🌸🌸 HOTEL

tel: 01772 671111 & 0800 085 1717 **Ribby Hall Village, Ribby Rd PR4 2PR**
email: enquiries@ribbyhall.co.uk **web:** www.ribbyhall.co.uk/spa-hotel
dir: M55 junct 33 follow A585 towards Kirkham & brown tourist signs for Ribby Hall Village. Straight across 3 rdbts. Ribby Hall Village 200yds on left

Set in one hundred acres of rolling countryside, Ribby Hall is a tranquil and relaxing place to stay. The well appointed bedrooms are comfortable. The spa has a range of facilities including an outdoor pool and sauna, and hotel also has a gym and treatment rooms.

Rooms 42 (14 GF) 🎿 **Facilities** Spa STV FTV WiFi 🏌 ⛱ Fishing Gym Squash Aqua thermal journey Champagne bar Xmas New Year **Services** Lift Air con **Parking** 124 **Notes** ⊗ No children 18yrs

W

WROTHAM
Kent

Map 6 TQ65

Holiday Inn Maidstone Sevenoaks

★★★ 77% HOTEL

tel: 0871 942 9054 & 01732 781510 **London Rd, Wrotham Heath TN15 7RS**
email: reservations-maidstone@ihg.com **web:** www.holidayinn.co.uk
dir: M26 junct 2A onto A20. Hotel on left

This purpose-built hotel is located within easy reach of the world-famous Brands Hatch racing circuit as well as historic Leeds and Hever Castles. Bedrooms are very spacious, and comfortably furnished with many accessories. A bar, restaurant and lounges are also available as well as a range of modern meeting rooms and a fully equipped leisure centre.

Rooms 105 (16 fmly) (6 GF) (2 smoking) **Facilities** STV WiFi 🕲 supervised Gym Steam room Sauna Beaty treatment room New Year **Conf** Class 35 Board 30 Thtr 100 **Services** Air con **Parking** 120 **Notes** ⊗ Civ Wed 100

Premier Inn Sevenoaks/Maidstone

BUDGET HOTEL

tel: 0871 527 8962 **London Rd, Wrotham Heath TN15 7RX**
web: www.premierinn.com
dir: M26 junct 2a, A20 S. At lights left onto A20 towards West Malling. Hotel on right.

High quality, budget accommodation ideal for both families and business travellers. Spacious, en suite bedrooms feature tea and coffee making facilities, and Freeview TV in most hotels. Internet access and WiFi are available for a small fee. The adjacent family restaurant features a wide and varied menu. See also the Hotel Groups pages.

Rooms 40

WROXALL
Warwickshire

Map 10 SP27

Wroxall Abbey Estate

★★★★ 74% HOTEL

tel: 01926 484470 & 486730 **Birmingham Rd CV35 7NB**
email: info@wroxall.com **web:** www.wroxall.com
dir: Between Solihull & Warwick on A4141

Situated in 27 acres of open parkland, yet only 10 miles from the NEC and Birmingham International Airport, this hotel is a magnificent Victorian mansion. Some of the individually designed bedrooms have traditional decor but there are some modern loft rooms as well; some rooms have four-posters. Sonnets Restaurant, with its impressive fireplace and oak panelling, makes the ideal setting for fine dining.

Rooms 70 (22 annexe) (10 GF) 🕲 **S** £69-£199; **D** £79-£299* **Facilities** Spa STV WiFi 🕲 ☁ Fishing ⚘ Gym Ten-pin bowling Walking & jogging trail Table tennis 🎵 Xmas New Year **Conf** Class 80 Board 60 Thtr 160 Del from £139 to £169 **Services** Lift **Parking** 200 **Notes** ⊗ No children 12yrs Civ Wed 200

YARM
North Yorkshire

Map 19 NZ41

Judges Country House Hotel

★★★★ ◉◉◉ COUNTRY HOUSE HOTEL

tel: 01642 789000 **Kirklevington Hall TS15 9LW**
email: enquiries@judgeshotel.co.uk **web:** www.judgeshotel.co.uk
dir: 1.5m from A19. At A67 junct, follow Yarm road, hotel on left

Formerly a lodging for local circuit judges, this gracious mansion lies in landscaped grounds through which a stream runs. Stylish bedrooms are individually decorated and come with plenty of extras; four-poster bedrooms and suites are available. The Conservatory restaurant serves award-winning cuisine, and private dining for a small number of guests is available in the wine cellar. Judges is a popular wedding venue. The genuinely caring and attentive service from the staff is truly memorable.

Rooms 21 (3 fmly) (5 GF) 🕲 **S** £99-£105; **D** £120-£220* **Facilities** FTV WiFi ⚘ ⚘ Gym Mountain bikes Nature trails Beauty treatment room Xmas New Year **Conf** Class 50 Board 38 Thtr 80 Del from £220 to £260* **Parking** 102 **Notes** LB ⊗ Civ Wed 200

W

Crathorne Hall Hotel

★★★★  HOTEL

tel: 01642 700398 **Crathorne TS15 0AR**
email: crathornehall@handpicked.co.uk
web: www.handpickedhotels.co.uk/crathorne-hall
dir: From A19 take slip road signed Teesside Airport & Kirklevington, right signed Crathorne to hotel

This splendid Edwardian hall sits in its own landscaped grounds and enjoys fine views of the Leven Valley and rolling Cleveland Hills. The impressively equipped bedrooms and delightful public areas offer sumptuous levels of comfort, with elegant antique furnishings that complement the hotel's architectural style. All bedrooms and suites offer large flat-screen TVs and free broadband among their many facilities. The elegant Leven Restaurant is a traditional setting for fine dining; there's also the Drawing Room for lighter food options. Weather permitting, alfresco eating is available on the terrace, and afternoon tea is always popular. Conference and banqueting facilities are available.

Rooms 37 (10 fmly) **Facilities** STV FTV WiFi HL Jogging track Clay pigeon shooting Xmas **Conf** Class 75 Board 60 Thtr 120 **Services** Lift **Parking** 88 **Notes** Civ Wed 90

Follow us on twitter
@TheAA_Lifestyle

YARMOUTH
Isle of Wight

Map 5 SZ38

The George Hotel

★★★ HOTEL

tel: 01983 760331 **Quay St P041 0PE**
email: res@thegeorge.co.uk **web:** www.thegeorge.co.uk
dir: Between castle & pier

This delightful 17th-century hotel enjoys a wonderful location at the water's edge, adjacent to the castle and the quay. Public areas include a bright brasserie where organic and local produce are utilised, a cosy bar and an inviting lounge. Individually styled bedrooms, with many thoughtful extras, are beautifully appointed; some benefit from spacious balconies. The hotel's motor yacht is available for guests to hire.

Rooms 19 (1 GF) **S** £99-£137.50; **D** £190-£287 (incl. bkfst)* **Facilities** STV WiFi Sailing from Yarmouth Mountain biking Xmas New Year **Conf** Class 20 Board 20 Thtr 40 Del from £185* **Notes** LB No children 10yrs

---

Norton Grange Coastal Village

Warner Leisure Hotels
Life begins at Warner

AA Advertised

tel: 01983 760 323 **P041 0SD**
web: www.warnerleisurehotels.co.uk
dir: From Yarmouth Ferry Terminal leaving Yarmouth harbour, turn right at rdbt, follow road across Yarmouth bridge (A3054). After approx 0.5m hotel on right after bend

Sitting pretty in one of the UK's sunniest spots just five minutes from Yarmouth ferry port, with access to scenic coastal walks, this friendly chalet village is a favourite for sunseekers. A wide range of leisure activities is on offer, and there is nightly entertainment on the popular half-board breaks. This is an adults only (over 21 years) hotel.

Rooms 208 **Facilities** FTV WiFi supervised Putt green Gym Xmas New Year **Parking** 208 **Notes** No children 21yrs Closed Jan-Feb

Y

YATELEY
Hampshire

Map 5 SU86

Casa Hotel & Marco Pierre White Restaurant

★★★ 78%  HOTEL

tel: 01252 873275 **Handford Ln GU46 6BT**
email: reservations@casadeicesari.co.uk **web:** www.thecasahoteluk.com
dir: M3 junct 4a, follow signs for town centre. Hotel signed

This delightful hotel where a warm welcome is guaranteed is ideally located for transport networks. It boasts rooms with quality and comfort, and the Marco Pierre White, Wheeler's of St James's Restaurant, which is very popular locally, serves an extensive traditional menu.

Rooms 63 (2 fmly) (15 GF) (33 smoking) **Facilities** FTV WiFi ⓦ Xmas New Year **Conf** Class 60 Board 60 Thtr 180 **Services** Lift **Parking** 80 **Notes** ⊗ Civ Wed 120

YATTON
Somerset

Map 4 ST46

Bridge Inn

BUDGET HOTEL

tel: 01934 839100 & 839101 **North End Rd BS49 4AU**
email: bridge.yatton@newbridgeinns.co.uk **web:** www.oldenglish.co.uk
dir: M5 junct 20, B3133 to Yatton. 1st left at rdbt, 1st left at 2nd rdbt. Hotel 2.5m on right

This establishment offers spacious, well-equipped bedrooms, and the bar/restaurant serves a variety of dishes throughout the day in a relaxed and informal environment. Breakfast is a self-service buffet plus a full English breakfast served at the table. There is also a play zone area for children. See also the Hotel Groups pages.

Rooms 41 (4 fmly) (20 GF) ⬆ **Conf** Class 30 Board 50 Thtr 100

YAXLEY
Suffolk

Map 13 TM17

The Auberge

◉◉ RESTAURANT WITH ROOMS

tel: 01379 783604 📠 01379 788486 **Ipswich Rd IP23 8BZ**
email: aubmail@the-auberge.co.uk **web:** www.the-auberge.co.uk
dir: On A140 between Norwich & Ipswich at x-rds with B1117

A warm welcome awaits at The Auberge, a charming 15th-century property, which was once a rural pub but is now a smart restaurant with rooms. The restaurant has gained two AA Rosettes for the good use of fresh, quality produce in well-crafted dishes. The public areas have a wealth of character, such as exposed brickwork and beams, and the grounds are particularly well kept and attractive. The spacious bedrooms are tastefully appointed and have many thoughtful touches; one bedroom has a four-poster.

Rooms 11 (11 annexe) (2 fmly)

YELVERTON
Devon

Map 3 SX56

Moorland Garden Hotel

★★★ 82% HOTEL

tel: 01822 852245 **Yelverton PL20 6DA**
email: stay@moorlandgardenhotel.co.uk **web:** www.moorlandgardenhotel.co.uk
dir: A38 from Exeter to Plymouth, then A386 towards Tavistock. 5m onto open moorland, hotel 1m on left

This hotel has a great location for either the city or Dartmoor, and sits in delightful gardens. Bedrooms are spacious, all with garden views and some with impressive balconies. There is a choice of dining as well as a range of meeting and function rooms. Pleasant Devon cream teas are served in the garden in warmer months.

Rooms 44 (5 fmly) (17 GF) ⬆⬆ **S** £85-£150; **D** £100-£155 (incl. bkfst)* **Facilities** FTV WiFi ⓦ HL Xmas New Year **Conf** Class 60 Board 50 Thtr 170 Del from £125 to £145* **Parking** 75 **Notes** LB Civ Wed 160

YEOVIL
Somerset

Map 4 ST51

The Yeovil Court Hotel & Restaurant

★★★ 79% ◉◉ HOTEL

tel: 01935 863746 **West Coker Rd BA20 2HE**
email: unwind@yeovilhotel.com **web:** www.yeovilcourthotel.com
dir: 2.5m W of town centre on A30

This comfortable, family-run hotel offers a very relaxed and caring atmosphere. Bedrooms are well equipped and neatly presented; some are located in an adjacent building. Public areas consist of a smart lounge, a popular bar and an attractive restaurant. Menus combine an interesting selection that includes lighter options and dishes suited to special occasion dining.

Rooms 30 (12 annexe) (3 fmly) (11 GF) **Facilities** FTV WiFi ⓦ **Conf** Class 18 Board 30 Thtr 50 **Parking** 65 **Notes** RS Sat lunch, 25 Dec eve & 26 Dec Civ Wed 70

Premier Inn Yeovil

BUDGET HOTEL

tel: 0871 527 9192 **Alvington Ln, Brympton BA22 8UX**
web: www.premierinn.com
dir: M5 junct 25, A358, A303 follow Yeovil signs. At rdbt onto A3088. At next rdbt 1st left, at next rdbt turn left. Hotel on left

High quality, budget accommodation ideal for both families and business travellers. Spacious, en suite bedrooms feature tea and coffee making facilities, and Freeview TV in most hotels. Internet access and WiFi are available for a small fee. The adjacent family restaurant features a wide and varied menu. See also the Hotel Groups pages.

Rooms 20

Little Barwick House

 RESTAURANT WITH ROOMS

tel: 01935 423902 📠 01935 420908 **Barwick Village BA22 9TD**
email: littlebarwick@hotmail.com **web:** www.littlebarwickhouse.co.uk
dir: From Yeovil A37 towards Dorchester, left at 1st rdbt, 1st left, 0.25m on left

Situated in a quiet hamlet in three and half acres of gardens and grounds, this listed Georgian dower house is an ideal retreat for those seeking peaceful surroundings and good food. Just one of the highlights of a stay here is a meal in the restaurant, where good use is made of local ingredients. Each of the bedrooms has its own character, and a range of thoughtful extras such as fresh flowers, bottled water and magazines is provided.

Rooms 6

YORK
North Yorkshire   **Map 16 SE65**

See also **Aldwark & Escrick**

Cedar Court Grand Hotel & Spa

★★★★★ 86% HOTEL

tel: 01904 380038 **Station Rise YO1 6HT**
email: info@cedarcourtgrand.co.uk **web:** www.cedarcourtgrand.co.uk
dir: In city centre, near station

Located in the heart of the city, this majestic Edwardian building, originally built in 1908, has been transformed into a luxury hotel. Spacious, air-conditioned accommodation offers deeply comfortable rooms with luxurious bathrooms. Public areas are equally impressive with a range of delightful lounges, a modern spa in the former vaults, and excellent meeting rooms. The Grill offers a high standard of cooking with modern, classic dishes on the menus, plus afternoon tea. Valet parking is a great asset given the hotel's central location.

Rooms 107 (14 GF) 🐾 **S** £130-£300; **D** £130-£300* **Facilities** Spa FTV WiFi 🏊 supervised Gym Sauna Steam room Xmas New Year **Conf** Class 60 Board 50 Thtr 120 Del from £180 to £250* **Services** Lift Air con **Notes** ⊗ Civ Wed 120

Middlethorpe Hall & Spa

★★★★ HOTEL

tel: 01904 641241 **Bishopthorpe Rd, Middlethorpe YO23 2GB**
email: info@middlethorpe.com **web:** www.middlethorpe.com
dir: A1/A64 follow York West (A1036) signs, then Bishopthorpe, Middlethorpe racecourse signs

This fine house, dating from the reign of William and Mary, sits in acres of beautifully landscaped gardens. The bedrooms vary in size but all are comfortably furnished; some are located in the main house, and others are in a cottage and converted courtyard stables. Public areas include a small spa and a stately drawing room where afternoon tea is quite an event. The delightful panelled restaurant is a perfect setting for enjoying the imaginative cuisine.

Rooms 29 (19 annexe) (2 fmly) (10 GF) 🐾 **S** £129-£159; **D** £199-£279 (incl. bkfst)* **Facilities** Spa FTV WiFi 🏊 🎾 ⛳ Gym Xmas New Year **Conf** Class 30 Board 25 Thtr 56 Del from £175 to £190* **Services** Lift **Parking** 71 **Notes** LB No children 6yrs RS 25 & 31 Dec Civ Wed 56

Hotel du Vin York

★★★★ 81% HOTEL

tel: 01904 557350 **89 The Mount YO24 1AX**
email: info.york@hotelduvin.com **web:** www.hotelduvin.com
dir: A1036 towards city centre, 6m. Hotel on right through lights.

This Hotel du Vin offers luxury and quality that will cosset even the most discerning guest. Bedrooms are decadent in design and the bathrooms have huge monsoon showers and feature baths. Dinner in the bistro provides a memorable highlight thanks to exciting menus and a superb wine list. Staff throughout are naturally friendly, nothing is too much trouble.

Rooms 44 (3 fmly) (14 GF) 🐾 **S** £99-£450; **D** £99-£450* **Facilities** STV FTV WiFi 🏊 **Conf** Class 8 Board 22 Thtr 22 **Services** Lift Air con **Parking** 18 **Notes** LB Civ Wed 50

Y

YORK *continued*

The Grange Hotel

★★★★ 78%  HOTEL

tel: 01904 644744 **1 Clifton YO30 6AA**
email: info@grangehotel.co.uk **web:** www.grangehotel.co.uk
dir: On A19 York/Thirsk road, approx 500yds from city centre

This bustling Regency town house is just a few minutes' walk from the centre of York. A professional service is efficiently delivered by caring staff in a very friendly and helpful manner. Public rooms are comfortable and have been stylishly furnished; these include two dining options, the popular and informal Cellar Bar, and main hotel restaurant The Ivy Brasserie, which offers fine dining in a lavishly decorated environment. The individually designed bedrooms are comfortably appointed and have been thoughtfully equipped.

Rooms 36 (6 GF) **S** £99-£147; **D** £119-£178* **Facilities** STV FTV WiFi Use of nearby health club (chargeable) Xmas New Year **Conf** Class 24 Board 24 Thtr 50 Del from £145 to £173.95 **Parking** 26 **Notes** Civ Wed 90

York Marriott Hotel

★★★★ 78% HOTEL

tel: 01904 701000 **Tadcaster Rd YO24 1QQ**
email: mhrs.qqyyk.dos@marriott.com **web:** www.yorkmarriott.co.uk
dir: From A64 at York 'West' onto A1036, follow signs to city centre. Approx 1.5m, hotel on right after church and lights

Overlooking the racecourse and Knavesmire Parkland, this hotel offers modern accommodation, including family rooms, all with comfort cooling. Within the hotel, guests enjoy the use of extensive leisure facilities including indoor pool, putting green and tennis court. For those wishing to explore the historic and cultural attractions, the city is less than a mile away.

Rooms 151 (45 fmly) (27 GF) **Facilities** Spa STV FTV WiFi HL Gym Beauty treatments Xmas New Year **Conf** Class 90 Board 40 Thtr 190 **Services** Lift Air con **Parking** 140 **Notes** Civ Wed 140

The Royal York Hotel & Events Centre

★★★★ 77% HOTEL

tel: 01904 653681 **Station Rd YO24 1AA**
email: royalyork.reservations@principal-hayley.com **web:** www.principal-hayley.com
dir: Adjacent to railway station

Situated in three acres of landscaped grounds in the very heart of the city, this Victorian railway hotel has views over the city and York Minster. Contemporary bedrooms are divided between those in the main hotel and the air-conditioned garden mews. There is also a leisure complex and state-of-the-art conference centre.

Rooms 167 (8 fmly) **Facilities** FTV WiFi Gym Steam room Weights room Xmas New Year **Conf** Class 250 Board 80 Thtr 410 **Services** Lift **Parking** 80 **Notes** Civ Wed 160

BEST WESTERN PLUS Dean Court Hotel

★★★★ 76% HOTEL

tel: 01904 625082 **Duncombe Place YO1 7EF**
email: sales@deancourt-york.co.uk **web:** www.deancourt-york.co.uk
dir: In city centre opposite York Minster

This smart hotel enjoys a central location overlooking The Minster, and guests will find the service is particularly friendly and efficient. Bedrooms are stylishly appointed and vary in size. Public areas are elegant in a contemporary style and include the popular D.C.H. restaurant which enjoys wonderful views of the cathedral, and The Court café-bistro and bar where a more informal, all-day menu is offered. Valet parking is available.

Rooms 37 (4 fmly) **S** £100-£150; **D** £120-£275 (incl. bkfst)* **Facilities** FTV WiFi Xmas New Year **Conf** Class 12 Board 32 Thtr 50 Del from £160 to £190* **Services** Lift **Parking** 30 **Notes** LB Civ Wed 50

Novotel York Centre

★★★★ 76% HOTEL

tel: 01904 611660 **Fishergate YO10 4FD**
email: H0949@accor.com **web:** www.novotel.com
dir: A19 north to city centre, hotel set back on left

Set just outside the ancient city walls, this modern, family-friendly hotel is conveniently located for visitors to the city. Bedrooms feature bathrooms with a separate toilet room, plus excellent desk space and sofa beds. Four rooms are equipped for less able guests. The hotel's facilities include indoor and outdoor children's play areas and an indoor pool.

Rooms 124 (124 fmly) **Facilities** STV FTV WiFi HL Xmas New Year **Conf** Class 100 Board 120 Thtr 210 Del from £120 to £185* **Services** Lift **Parking** 140

Marmadukes Hotel

★★★★ 75% TOWN HOUSE HOTEL

tel: 01904 640101 **4-5 St Peters Grove, Bootham YO30 6AQ**
email: reservations@marmadukesyork.com **web:** www.marmadukesyork.com
dir: A1036 signed York for approx 6m past train station then signed Inner Ring Rd. Over Lendal bridge, at lights left onto A19 (Bootham Bar) for 0.4m, right into St Peters Grove

Quietly situated just a short walk from the Minster, Marmadukes is a classically furnished, period property with all the expected modern amenities. Steeped in history and with a Roman burial ground underneath the lawn, it also has a sauna and a spa bath in the grounds. The bedrooms have antique furniture and many of the bathrooms have roll-top baths. The public areas, including the conservatory-style breakfast room, are equally impressive with an air of spaciousness.

Rooms 21 (2 fmly) (2 GF) ℕ **Facilities** FTV WiFi ♨ Sauna **Conf** Class 20 Board 16 Thtr 20 **Parking** 14 **Notes** ⊗ Civ Wed 50

Mercure York Fairfield Hotel

★★★★ 73% COUNTRY HOUSE HOTEL

tel: 0844 815 9038 **Shipton Rd, Skelton YO30 1XW**
email: gm.mercureyorkfairfieldmanor@jupiterhotels.co.uk **web:** www.jupiterhotels.co.uk
dir: Exit A1237 onto A19, hotel 0.5m on left

This stylish Georgian mansion stands in six acres of private grounds on the outskirts of the city. The contemporary bedrooms, styled in reds or blues, have broadband access and flat-screen TVs; some rooms have garden and courtyard views. The suites have either four-poster or king-size beds and a separate seating area. Kilby's Restaurant serves bistro food, and 24-hour room service is available. There are good conference facilities.

Rooms 89 (20 fmly) (24 GF) ℕ **Facilities** WiFi ♨ HL Xmas New Year **Conf** Class 72 Board 60 Thtr 180 **Services** Lift **Parking** 130 **Notes** ⊗ Civ Wed 150

The Churchill Hotel

★★★ 83% ⚜⚜ HOTEL

tel: 01904 644456 **65 Bootham YO30 7DQ**
email: info@churchillhotel.com **web:** www.churchillhotel.com
dir: On A19 (Bootham), W from York Minster, hotel 250yds on right

A late Georgian manor house set in its own grounds, just a short walk from the Minster and other attractions. Period features and interesting artefacts relating to Winston Churchill are incorporated into smart contemporary design and up-to-date technology. Public areas include the Piano Bar & Restaurant, where innovative menus feature high quality, local produce.

Rooms 32 (4 fmly) (5 GF) **Facilities** WiFi 🎵 Xmas New Year **Conf** Class 50 Board 30 Thtr 100 **Services** Lift **Parking** 40 **Notes** Civ Wed 70

Mount Royale

★★★ 80% ⚜⚜ HOTEL

tel: 01904 628856 **The Mount YO24 1GU**
email: reservations@mountroyale.co.uk **web:** www.mountroyale.co.uk
dir: W on A1036, 0.5m after racecourse. Hotel on right after lights

This friendly hotel, a listed building from the 1830s, offers comfortable bedrooms in a variety of styles, several leading onto the delightful gardens. Public rooms include a lounge, a meeting room and a cosy bar; the hotel has an outdoor pool, a sauna and a hot tub plus a beauty therapist. There is a separate restaurant called Oxo's on The Mount, and a cocktail lounge overlooking the gardens. Limited car parking is also available.

Rooms 24 (3 fmly) (6 GF) ℕ S £95-£185; D £125-£265 (incl. bkfst)* **Facilities** Spa FTV WiFi 🏃 supervised Beauty treatment centre Sauna Steam room Xmas New Year **Conf** Board 25 Thtr 35 Del £145 **Parking** 27 **Notes** LB

BEST WESTERN Kilima Hotel

★★★ 79% HOTEL

tel: 01904 625787 **129 Holgate Rd YO24 4AZ**
email: sales@kilima.co.uk **web:** www.kilima.co.uk
dir: On A59, 1m from York city ctr

This establishment, a former rectory, is conveniently situated within easy walking distance of the city centre. There is a relaxed and friendly atmosphere with professional, friendly staff providing attentive service. Bedrooms are comfortable and well equipped. There is an indoor pool, a fitness centre and a Turkish steam room.

Rooms 26 (4 fmly) (10 GF) S £50-£110; D £75-£220 (incl. bkfst) **Facilities** FTV WiFi ♨ 🏊 Gym Leisure complex Steam room Fitness suite Xmas **Conf** Board 14 Del from £75 to £140 **Parking** 26 **Notes** LB ⊗

BEST WESTERN York Pavilion Hotel

★★★ 79% HOTEL

tel: 01904 622099 & 239900 **45 Main St, Fulford YO10 4PJ**
email: reservations@yorkpavilionhotel.com **web:** www.yorkpavilionhotel.com
dir: Exit A64 (York ring road) at A19 junct towards York. Hotel 0.5m on right opposite Pavilion Court

An attractive Georgian hotel situated in its own grounds. All the bedrooms are individually designed to a high specification; some are in the old house and some in the converted stables set around a garden terrace. There is a comfortable lounge, a conference centre and an inviting brasserie-style restaurant with a regularly changing menu.

Rooms 57 (4 fmly) (11 GF) ℕ S £80-£125; D £110-£160 (incl. bkfst) **Facilities** FTV WiFi ♨ Xmas New Year **Conf** Class 80 Board 50 Thtr 150 Del from £110 to £150 **Parking** 55 **Notes** LB Civ Wed 150

The Parsonage Country House Hotel

★★★ 79% COUNTRY HOUSE HOTEL

tel: 01904 728111 **York Rd YO19 6LF**
email: reservations@parsonagehotel.co.uk **web:** www.parsonagehotel.co.uk

(For full entry see Escrick)

YORK *continued*

BEST WESTERN Monkbar Hotel

★★★ 77% HOTEL

tel: 01904 638086 **Monkbar YO31 7JA**
email: sales@monkbarhotel.co.uk **web:** www.monkbarhotel.co.uk
dir: A64 onto A1079 to city, turn right at city walls, take middle lane at lights. Hotel on right

This smart hotel enjoys a prominent position adjacent to the city walls, and is just a few minutes' walk from York Minster. Individually styled bedrooms are well equipped for both business and leisure guests. Spacious public areas include comfortable lounges, a traditional Yorkshire bar, an airy restaurant and impressive meeting and training facilities.

Rooms 99 (8 fmly) (2 GF) ☝ **Facilities** FTV WiFi ☝ HL Xmas New Year **Conf** Class 80 Board 50 Thtr 140 **Services** Lift **Parking** 66 **Notes** Civ Wed 80

Lady Anne Middleton's Hotel

★★ 72% HOTEL

tel: 01904 611570 **Skeldergate YO1 6DS**
email: bookings@ladyannes.co.uk **web:** www.ladyannes.co.uk
dir: From A64 (Leeds) A1036 towards city centre. Right at City Walls lights, keep left, 1st left before bridge, then 1st left into Cromwell Rd. Hotel on right

This hotel has been created from several listed buildings and is very well located in the centre of York. Bedrooms are comfortably equipped. Among its amenities is a

bar-lounge and a dining room where a satisfying range of food is served. An extensive fitness club is also available along with private parking.

Rooms 56 (19 annexe) (15 fmly) (17 GF) ☝ **S** fr £75.50; **D** fr £80 **Facilities** FTV WiFi ☝ ☝ Gym Fitness centre Beauty treatments Massage ♫ **Conf** Class 36 Board 36 Thtr 60 Del from £165 to £210 **Parking** 40 **Notes** LB ⊗ Closed 24-26 Dec Civ Wed 60

Jorvik Hotel

Ⓤ

tel: 01904 653511 **50-52 Marygate YO30 7BH**
email: info@jorvikhotel.co.uk **web:** www.jorvikhotel.co.uk

Currently the rating for this establishment is not confirmed. This may be due to a change of ownership or because it has only recently joined the AA rating scheme. For further details please see the AA website: theAA.com

Rooms 22 (3 fmly) (8 GF) ☝ **Facilities** FTV WiFi **Conf** Class 20 Board 20 Thtr 20 **Services** Air con **Notes** ⊗ Closed 25-26 Dec

Ibis York Centre

BUDGET HOTEL

tel: 01904 658301 **77 The Mount YO24 1BN**
email: H6390@accor.com **web:** www.ibishotel.com
dir: A64/A1036 follow signs to city centre, hotel on right

Modern, budget hotel offering comfortable accommodation in bright and practical bedrooms. Breakfast is self-service and dinner is available in the restaurant. See also the Hotel Groups pages.

Rooms 91 (11 fmly) (3 GF) ☝ **Conf** Class 16 Board 16 Thtr 24

Premier Inn York City (Blossom St North)

BUDGET HOTEL

tel: 0871 527 9196 **20 Blossom St YO24 1AJ**
web: www.premierinn.com
dir: 12m from A1 junct 47, off A59

High quality, budget accommodation ideal for both families and business travellers. Spacious, en suite bedrooms feature tea and coffee making facilities, and Freeview TV in most hotels. Internet access and WiFi are available for a small fee. The adjacent family restaurant features a wide and varied menu. See also the Hotel Groups pages.

Rooms 86

ISLE OF MAN

Premier Inn York City (Blossom St South)

BUDGET HOTEL

tel: 0871 527 9194 **28-40 Blossom St YO24 1AJ**
web: www.premierinn.com
dir: From S, E & W: A64, A1036 (signed York West). From N: A1 (or A19), A59, follow city centre signs. At lights left onto A1036. Hotel on left just after cinema. (NB no drop-off point, parking at NCP, Queens St)

Rooms 91

Premier Inn York North

BUDGET HOTEL

tel: 0871 527 9198 **Shipton Rd YO30 5PA**
web: www.premierinn.com
dir: From A1237 (ring road), A19 (Shipton Road South) signed York Centre. Hotel on right in Clifton Park

Rooms 49

Premier Inn York North West

BUDGET HOTEL

tel: 0871 527 9200 **White Rose Close, York Business Park, Nether Poppleton YO26 6RL**
web: www.premierinn.com
dir: On A1237 between A19 (Thirsk road) & A59 (Harrogate road)

Rooms 64

Premier Inn York South West

BUDGET HOTEL

tel: 0871 527 9202 **Bilbrough Top, Colton YO23 3PP**
web: www.premierinn.com
dir: On A64 between Tadcaster & York

Rooms 61

YOXFORD   Map 13 TM36
Suffolk

Satis House Hotel

★★★ 88% ◎◎ COUNTRY HOUSE HOTEL

tel: 01728 668418 **IP17 3EX**
email: enquiries@satishouse.co.uk **web:** www.satishouse.co.uk
dir: Off A12 between Ipswich & Lowestoft. 9m E Aldeburgh & Snape

Expect a warm welcome from the caring hosts at this delightful 18th-century, Grade II listed property set in three acres of parkland. The stylish public areas have a really relaxed atmosphere; they include a choice of dining rooms, a smart bar and a cosy lounge. The individually decorated bedrooms are tastefully appointed and thoughtfully equipped.

Rooms 12 (4 annexe) (1 fmly) (4 GF) ♠ **Facilities** STV FTV WiFi ♭ Xmas New Year **Conf** Class 40 Board 20 Thtr 40 **Parking** 30 **Notes** Closed 23-27 Dec Civ Wed 50

DOUGLAS   Map 24 SC37

Mount Murray Hotel and Country Club

★★★★ 70% HOTEL

tel: 01624 661111 **Santon IM4 2HT**
email: hotel@mountmurray.com **web:** www.mountmurray.com
dir: 4m from Douglas towards airport. Hotel signed at Santon

This large, modern hotel and country club offers a wide range of sporting and leisure facilities, and a superb health and beauty salon. The attractively appointed public areas provide a choice of bars and eating options, including the Mallards Restaurant. The spacious bedrooms are well equipped and many enjoy fine views over the 200-acre grounds and golf course. There is a very large conference suite.

Rooms 10 (2 fmly) (4 GF) ♠ **S** £65-£189; **D** £85-£249 (incl. bkfst)* **Facilities** FTV WiFi ♭ ❄ ↻ 18 Putt green Gym Squash Driving range New Year **Conf** Class 200 Board 100 Thtr 300 **Services** Lift **Parking** 400 **Notes** LB ❀ Civ Wed 120

Admiral House Hotel

★★★ 78% ◎◎ HOTEL

tel: 01624 629551 **12 Loch Promenade IM1 2LX**
email: enquiries@admiralhouse.com **web:** www.admiralhouse.com
dir: Located 2 mins from Douglas Ferry Terminal. 20 mins from airport

Admiral House Hotel is a grand Victorian building with stunning views over Douglas Bay. Spacious bedrooms and public areas combine period features with contemporary style. The JAR restaurant is a highlight, offering excellent food, a stylish setting and professional service. There is also a modern champagne and cocktail bar, and IGI's Café serves snacks and light meals throughout the day. Complimentary WiFi is provided throughout.

Rooms 23 (3 fmly) ♠ **Facilities** FTV WiFi ♭ ♫ Xmas New Year **Services** Lift **Notes** ❀

Channel Islands

GUERNSEY

CASTEL   Map 24

Cobo Bay Hotel

★★★ 87%  HOTEL

tel: 01481 257102 **Coast Rd, Cobo GY5 7HB**
email: reservations@cobobayhotel.com **web:** www.cobobayhotel.com
dir: From airport turn right, follow road to W coast at L'Eree. Turn right onto coast road for 3m to Cobo Bay. Hotel on right

As the name implies, this popular hotel is situated on the seafront overlooking Cobo Bay. The well-equipped bedrooms are pleasantly decorated; many of the front rooms have balconies and there is a secluded sun terrace to the rear. Public rooms include the Chesterfield Bar with its leather sofas and armchairs and a welcoming award-winning restaurant and terrace with stunning views of the bay.

Rooms 34 (4 fmly) 🐾 **S** £59-£99; **D** £99-£215 (incl. bkfst)* **Facilities** STV FTV WiFi ꜟ Sauna Steam room **Conf** Class 30 Board 30 Thtr 100 Del from £99 to £250*
Services Lift **Parking** 20 **Notes** LB ⊗

FOREST   Map 24

Le Chene Hotel

★★ 69% HOTEL

tel: 01481 235566 **Forest Rd GY8 0AH**
email: info@lechene.co.uk **web:** www.lechene.co.uk
dir: Between airport & St Peter Port. From airport left to St Peter Port. Hotel on right after 1st lights

This Victorian manor house is well located for guests wishing to explore Guernsey's spectacular south coast. The building has been skilfully extended to house a range of well-equipped, modern bedrooms. There is a swimming pool, a cosy cellar bar and a varied range of enjoyable freshly cooked dishes at dinner.

Rooms 26 (2 fmly) (1 GF) (1 smoking) **S** £35-£60; **D** £60-£130 (incl. bkfst)*
Facilities WiFi ꜟ Library Outdoor sauna **Parking** 20 **Notes** LB ⊗ Closed Oct-Mar

ST MARTIN   Map 24

INSPECTORS' CHOICE

Bella Luce Hotel, Restaurant & Spa

★★★★ ◉◉ SMALL HOTEL

tel: 01481 238764 **La Fosse GY4 6EB**
email: wakeup@bellalucehotel.com **web:** www.bellalucehotel.com
dir: From airport, turn left to St Martin. At 3rd set of lights continue 30yds, turn right, straight on to hotel

This delightful hotel has taken a dramatic jump in to the contemporary and luxurious; a recent refurbishment has brought stylish bedrooms with comfortable beds and designer furnishings, superb bathrooms and up-to-the-minute technology. Public rooms have many interesting features and lots of soft settees and nooks and crannies where guests can relax. The restaurant offers the best produce Guernsey can provide, and chef has a keen sense of adventure. Staff are friendly and attentive, and make sure guests feel welcome.

Rooms 23 (4 fmly) (2 GF) **Facilities** STV FTV WiFi ꜞ ♨ 18 Fishing Gym Sauna
Conf Class 18 Board 25 Thtr 40 **Parking** 33 **Notes** ⊗ Closed 1st 2 wks Jan

La Barbarie Hotel

★★★ 82% ◉ HOTEL

tel: 01481 235217 **Saints Rd, Saints Bay GY4 6ES**
email: reservations@labarbariehotel.com **web:** www.labarbariehotel.com
dir: At lights in St Martin take road to Saints Bay. Hotel on right at end of Saints Rd

This former priory dates back to the 17th century and retains much charm and style. Staff help to create a very friendly and attentive atmosphere, and the modern

continued

CHANNEL ISLANDS

ST MARTIN *continued*

facilities offer guests a relaxing stay. Excellent choices and fresh local ingredients form the basis of the interesting menus in the attractive restaurant and bar.

Rooms 30 (8 GF) **Facilities** STV WiFi ⚡ **Parking** 50 **Notes** ⊗ Closed Nov-11 Mar

Hotel Jerbourg

★★★ 79% 🌸 HOTEL

tel: 01481 238826 **Jerbourg Point GY4 6BJ**
email: stay@hoteljerbourg.com **web:** www.hoteljerbourg.com
dir: From airport turn left to St Martin, right at filter, straight on at lights, hotel at end of road on right

This hotel boasts excellent sea views from its cliff-top location. Public areas are smartly appointed and include an extensive bar/lounge and bright conservatory-style restaurant. In addition to the fairly extensive carte, a daily-changing menu is available. Bedrooms are well presented and comfortable, and the luxury bay rooms are generally more spacious.

Rooms 32 (4 fmly) (5 GF) **S** £79-£169; **D** £94-£179 (incl. bkfst)* **Facilities** FTV WiFi ⚡ Petanque Xmas New Year **Parking** 50 **Notes** LB ⊗ Closed 5 Jan-1 Mar

La Villette Hotel & Leisure Suite

★★★ 79% HOTEL

tel: 01481 235292 **GY4 6QG**
email: reservations@lavillettehotel.co.uk **web:** www.lavillettehotel.co.uk
dir: Turn left from airport. Follow road past La Trelade Hotel. Take next right, hotel on left

Set in spacious grounds, this peacefully located, family-run hotel has a friendly atmosphere. The well-equipped bedrooms are spacious and comfortable. Live music is a regular feature in the large bar, while in the separate restaurant a fixed-price menu is provided. Residents have use of the excellent indoor leisure facilities, and there are also beauty treatments and a hairdressing salon.

Rooms 35 (3 fmly) (14 GF) 📞 **S** £53-£60; **D** £90-£103 (incl. bkfst)* **Facilities** FTV WiFi ⓧ supervised ⚡ Gym Steam room Leisure suite Beauty salon Hairdresser Petanque Xmas New Year **Conf** Board 40 Thtr 80 **Services** Lift **Parking** 50 **Notes** ⊗

Saints Bay Hotel

★★★ 77% HOTEL

tel: 01481 238888 **Icart Rd GY4 6JG**
email: info@saintsbayhotel.com **web:** www.saintsbayhotel.com
dir: From St Martin take Saints Rd into Icart Rd

Ideally situated in an elevated position near Icart Point headland and above the fishing harbour at Saints Bay, this hotel has superb views. The spacious public rooms include a smart lounge bar, a first-floor lounge and a smart conservatory restaurant that overlooks the swimming pool. Bedrooms are pleasantly decorated and thoughtfully equipped.

Rooms 35 (1 fmly) (13 GF) **Facilities** FTV WiFi ⚡ Xmas New Year **Parking** 15 **Notes** ⊗

ST PETER PORT   **Map 24**

The Old Government House Hotel & Spa

★★★★★ 81% 🌸 HOTEL   THE **RED CARNATION** HOTEL COLLECTION

tel: 01481 724921 **St Ann's Place GY1 2NU**
email: ogh@theoghhotel.com **web:** www.theoghhotel.com
dir: At junct of St Julian's Ave & St Anns Place

The affectionately known OGH is one of the island's leading hotels. Located in the heart of St Peter Port, it is the perfect base from which to explore Guernsey and the other islands of the Bailiwick. Bedrooms vary in size but all are comfortable, and offer high quality accommodation. There is an indulgent health club and spa, and the eating options are the OGH Brasserie, and award-winning Governor's that offers local produce with a French twist.

Rooms 62 (3 annexe) (6 fmly) 📞 **S** £183-£208; **D** £183-£500 (incl. bkfst)* **Facilities** Spa STV WiFi ⓦ HL ⚡ Gym Steam room Sauna Spa pools Relaxation room ♫ Xmas New Year **Conf** Class 69 Board 66 Thtr 200 Del from £280.50 to £597.50* **Services** Lift Air con **Parking** 20 **Notes** LB

Fermain Valley Hotel

★★★★ 79% 🌸🌸 HOTEL

tel: 0800 316 0314 & 01481 235666 **Fermain Ln GY1 1ZZ**
email: info@fermainvalley.com **web:** www.fermainvalley.com
dir: Turn left from airport, follow Forest Rd, right into Le Route de Sausmarez, right into Fermain Lane at Fermain Tavern. Hotel 100mtrs on left

This hotel occupies an amazing location high above Fermain Bay with far reaching views out to sea; there are lovely walks along the cliff or down the lanes from the hotel. The delightfully furnished bedrooms, some with balconies, have either views of the sea, the valley or the well tended gardens. Informal eating is available in the stylish Rock Garden bar, and in summer on the terrace; the Valley Restaurant is the fine dining option. The leisure facilities include a pool, a sauna and a private cinema. The well-trained staff provide warm and friendly service.

Rooms 45 (13 annexe) (2 fmly) 📞 **S** £70-£115; **D** £105-£230 (incl. bkfst) **Facilities** STV FTV WiFi ⓦ ⓧ 3D Cinema Sauna ♫ Xmas New Year **Conf** Class 70 Board 45 Thtr 100 Del £116.50 **Services** Lift **Parking** 50 **Notes** ⊗

The Duke of Richmond Hotel

THE RED CARNATION HOTEL COLLECTION

★★★★ 79% HOTEL

tel: 01481 726221 **Cambridge Park GY1 1UY**
email: manager@dukeofrichmond.com **web:** www.dukeofrichmond.com
dir: On corner of Cambridge Park & L'Hyvreuse Ave, opposite leisure centre

Peacefully located in a mainly residential area overlooking Cambridge Park, this hotel has comfortable, well-appointed bedrooms that vary in size. Public areas include a spacious lounge, a terrace and the unique Sausmarez Bar, with its nautical theme. The smartly uniformed team of staff provide professional standards of service.

Rooms 73 (11 fmly) S £145-£175; **D** £145-£400 (incl. bkfst)* **Facilities** STV WiFi HL Xmas New Year **Conf** Class 80 Board 40 Thtr 300 Del from £222.50 to £477.50* **Services** Lift Air con **Parking** 5 **Notes** LB

St Pierre Park Hotel

★★★★ 74% HOTEL

tel: 01481 728282 **Rohais GY1 1FD**
email: reservations@stpierrepark.co.uk **web:** www.stpierrepark.co.uk
dir: From harbour straight over rdbt, up hill through 3 sets of lights. Right at filter, to lights. Straight ahead, hotel 100mtrs on left

Peacefully located on the outskirts of town amidst 45 acres of grounds, this well established hotel also features a 9-hole golf course. Most of the bedrooms overlook the pleasant gardens and have either a balcony or a terrace. Public areas include a choice of restaurants and a stylish bar which opens onto a spacious terrace, overlooking an elegant water feature.

Rooms 131 (5 fmly) (20 GF) **Facilities** Spa STV WiFi 9 Putt green Gym Bird watching Children's playground Crazy golf Xmas **Conf** Class 120 Board 70 Thtr 200 Del from £174 to £234 **Services** Lift **Parking** 150 **Notes**

BEST WESTERN Hotel de Havelet

★★★ 82% HOTEL

tel: 01481 722199 **Havelet GY1 1BA**
email: stay@dehaveletguernsey.com **web:** www.dehaveletguernsey.com
dir: From airport follow signs for St Peter Port through St. Martins. At bottom of 'Val de Terres' hill turn left at top of hill, hotel on right

This extended Georgian hotel looks over the harbour to Castle Cornet. Many of the well-equipped bedrooms are set around a pretty colonial-style courtyard. Day rooms in the original building have period elegance; the restaurant and bar are on the other side of the car park in converted stables.

Rooms 34 (4 fmly) (9 GF) S £90-£130; **D** £106-£170 (incl. bkfst)* **Facilities** FTV WiFi Sauna Steam room Xmas New Year **Conf** Class 20 Board 18 Thtr 30 Del from £125 to £175* **Parking** 40 **Notes** LB

Duke of Normandie Hotel

★★★ 80% HOTEL

tel: 01481 721431 **Lefebvre St GY1 2JP**
email: enquiries@dukeofnormandie.com **web:** www. dukeofnormandie.com
dir: From harbour rdbt St Julians Ave, 3rd left into Anns Place, continue to right, up hill, then left into Lefebvre St, archway entrance on right

An 18th-century hotel situated close to the high street and just a short stroll from the harbour. Bedrooms vary in style and include some that have their own access from the courtyard. Public areas feature a smart brasserie, a contemporary lounge/lobby area and a busy bar with beams and an open fireplace.

Rooms 37 (17 annexe) (8 GF) S £49-£70; **D** £120-£150 (incl. bkfst) **Facilities** STV WiFi **Parking** 10 **Notes** LB

Les Rocquettes Hotel

★★★ 80% HOTEL

tel: 01481 722146 **Les Gravees GY1 1RN**
email: stay@lesrocquettesguernsey.com **web:** www.lesrocquettesguernsey.com
dir: From ferry terminal take 2nd exit at rdbt, through 5 sets of lights. After 5th lights into Les Gravees. Hotel on right opposite church

This late 18th-century country mansion is in a good location close to St Peter Port and Beau Sejour. Bedrooms come in three grades - Deluxe, Superior and Standard, but all have plenty of useful facilities. Guests can eat in Oaks restaurant and bar. The hotel has attractive lounge areas on three levels; there is a health suite with a gym and swimming pool with an integrated children's pool.

Rooms 51 (5 fmly) S £58-£125; **D** £88-£144 (incl. bkfst)* **Facilities** FTV WiFi supervised Gym Beauty treatment room Sauna Steam room Whirlpool New Year **Conf** Class 60 Board 60 Thtr 100 Del from £120 to £160* **Services** Lift **Parking** 60 **Notes** LB

ST PETER PORT *continued*

BEST WESTERN Moores Hotel

★★★ 79% HOTEL

tel: 01481 724452 **Pollet GY1 1WH**
email: stay@mooresguernsey.com **web:** www.mooresguernsey.com
dir: Left at airport, follow signs to St Peter Port. Fort Road to seafront, straight on, turn left before rdbt, to hotel

This elegant granite town house is situated in the heart of St Peter Port among the shops and amenities. Public rooms feature a smart conservatory restaurant which leads out onto a first-floor terrace for alfresco dining; there is also a choice of lounges and bars as well as a patisserie. Bedrooms are pleasantly decorated and thoughtfully equipped.

Rooms 49 (3 annexe) (8 fmly) ➽ **S** £90-£135; **D** £110-£250 (incl. bkfst)*
Facilities FTV WiFi ➷ Gym Sauna Xmas New Year **Conf** Class 20 Board 18 Thtr 40 Del from £120 to £170* **Services** Lift **Notes** LB ⊗

ST SAVIOUR — Map 24

The Farmhouse Hotel

★★★★ 84% ❀ SMALL HOTEL

tel: 01481 264181 **Route Des Bas Courtils GY7 9YF**
email: enquiries@thefarmhouse.gg **web:** www.thefarmhouse.gg
dir: From airport turn left. Approx 1m left at lights. 100mtrs, left, around airport runway perimeter. 1m, left at staggered junct. Hotel in 100mtrs on right. For directions from harbour please see hotel website or contact hotel

This hotel provides spacious accommodation with amazingly comfortable beds and state-of-the-art bathrooms with under-floor heating. Guests can choose from various stylish dining options including alfresco eating in the warmer months. The outdoor swimming pool is available to guests in the summer and there are lots of countryside walks to enjoy.

Rooms 14 (7 fmly) ➽ **S** £139-£279; **D** £139-£279 (incl. bkfst)* **Facilities** STV WiFi ➷ ⤸ **Conf** Class 130 Board 30 Thtr 150 Del from £195 to £295* **Services** Air con **Parking** 80 **Notes** LB ⊗

VALE — Map 24

Peninsula Hotel

★★★ 80% HOTEL

tel: 01481 248400 **Les Dicqs GY6 8JP**
email: peninsula@guernsey.net **web:** www.peninsulahotelguernsey.com
dir: On coast road at Grand Havre Bay

Adjacent to the sandy beach and set in five acres of grounds, this modern hotel provides comfortable accommodation. Bedrooms have an additional sofa bed to suit families and good workspace for the business traveller. Both fixed-price and carte menus are served in the restaurant, or guests can eat informally in the bar.

Rooms 99 (99 fmly) (27 GF) (2 smoking) ➽ **Facilities** STV WiFi ➷ Putt green Petanque Children's playground Xmas New Year **Conf** Class 100 Board 105 Thtr 250 **Services** Lift **Parking** 120 **Notes** ⊗ Closed Jan

HERM

HERM — Map 24

White House Hotel

★★★ 83% ◉◉ HOTEL

tel: 01481 750075 **GY1 3HR**
email: hotel@herm.com **web:** www.herm.com
dir: Transport to island by catamaran ferry from St Peter Port, Guernsey

Enjoying a unique island setting, this attractive hotel is just 20 minutes from Guernsey by sea. Set in well-tended gardens, the hotel offers neatly decorated bedrooms, located in either the main house or adjacent cottages; the majority of rooms have sea views. Guests can relax in one of several lounges, enjoy a drink in one of two bars and choose from two dining options.

Rooms 40 (23 annexe) (23 fmly) (7 GF) **Facilities** WiFi ➷ ⏆ ⤸ Fishing trips Yacht & motor boat charters **Conf** Board 10 Thtr 50 **Notes** ⊗ Closed Nov-Mar

JERSEY

GOREY
Map 24

The Moorings Hotel & Restaurant

★★★ 83% ◉◉ HOTEL

tel: 01534 853633 **Gorey Pier JE3 6EW**
email: reservations@themooringshotel.com **web:** www.themooringshotel.com
dir: At foot of Mont Orgueil Castle

Enjoying an enviable position by the harbour, the heart of this hotel is the restaurant where a selection of menus offers an extensive choice of dishes. Other public areas include a bar, coffee shop and a comfortable first-floor residents' lounge. Bedrooms at the front have a fine view of the harbour; three have access to a balcony. A small sun terrace at the back of the hotel is available to guests.

Rooms 15 ↟ **S** £69.50-£92; **D** £139-£184 (incl. bkfst)* **Facilities** FTV WiFi ↳ Xmas New Year **Conf** Class 20 Board 20 Thtr 20 Del from £130 to £240* **Notes** LB ⊗

Old Court House Hotel

★★★ 72% HOTEL

tel: 01534 854444 **JE3 9FS**
email: info@ochhoteljersey.com **web:** www.ochhoteljersey.com

Situated on the east of the island, a short walk from the beach, this long established hotel continues to have a loyal following for its relaxed atmosphere and friendly staff. Bedrooms are of a similar standard throughout and some have balconies overlooking the gardens. Spacious public areas include a comfortable, quiet lounge, a restaurant, and a large bar with a dance floor.

Rooms 58 (4 fmly) (9 GF) **S** £53-£80; **D** £106-£160 (incl. bkfst)* **Facilities** FTV WiFi ↟ **Services** Lift **Parking** 40 **Notes** LB Closed Oct-Apr

The Dolphin Hotel and Restaurant

★★ 75% HOTEL

tel: 01534 853370 **Gorey Pier JE3 6EW**
email: dolphinhotel@jerseymail.co.uk **web:** www.dolphinhoteljersey.com
dir: At foot of Mont Orgueil Castle

Located on the main harbour at Gorey, many bedrooms at this popular hotel enjoy views over the sea and beaches. The relaxed and friendly style is apparent from the moment of arrival, and the busy restaurant and bar are popular with locals and tourists alike. Outdoor seating is available in season, and fresh fish and seafood are included on the menu.

Rooms 16 **S** £45-£58.50; **D** £90-£117 (incl. bkfst)* **Facilities** STV WiFi ↳ ♫ Xmas New Year **Conf** Class 20 Board 20 Thtr 20 **Notes** LB ⊗

ROZEL
Map 24

Château la Chaire

★★★★ 80% ◉◉ HOTEL

tel: 01534 863354 **Rozel Bay JE3 6AJ**
email: res@chateau-la-chaire.co.uk **web:** www.chateau-la-chaire.co.uk
dir: From St Helier on B38 turn left in village by Rozel Bay Inn, hotel 100yds on right

Built as a gentleman's residence in 1843, Château la Chaire is a haven of peace and tranquillity, set in a secluded wooded valley. Picturesque Rozel Harbour is within easy walking distance, and the house is surrounded by terraced gardens and woods. The helpful staff deliver high standards of guest care, and imaginative menus, making the best use of local produce, are served in the oak-panelled dining room, the conservatory, or on the terrace when the weather permits. Bedroom and suite styles and sizes vary, but all are beautifully appointed and include many nice touches such as towelling robes, slippers, flowers and DVD players. Free WiFi is available throughout the hotel.

Rooms 14 (2 fmly) (1 GF) ↟ **S** £85-£130; **D** £125-£325 (incl. bkfst)* **Facilities** FTV WiFi ↳ Xmas New Year **Conf** Class 20 Board 20 Thtr 20 Del from £125 to £185* **Parking** 30 **Notes** LB ⊗ No children 7yrs Civ Wed 60

ST BRELADE
Map 24

The Atlantic Hotel

★★★★ ◉◉◉◉ HOTEL

tel: 01534 744101 **Le Mont de la Pulente JE3 8HE**
email: info@theatlantichotel.com **web:** www.theatlantichotel.com
dir: From Petit Port turn right into Rue de la Sergente, right again, hotel signed

Adjoining the manicured fairways of La Moye championship golf course, this hotel enjoys a peaceful setting with breathtaking views over St Ouen's Bay. Stylish bedrooms look onto the course or the sea, and offer a blend of high quality and reassuring comfort. An air of understated luxury is apparent throughout, and the attentive service achieves the perfect balance of friendliness and professionalism. The Ocean restaurant's very talented chef, Mark Jordan, uses the best island produce to create outstanding and impeccably modern cuisine.

Rooms 50 (8 GF) ↟ **S** £100-£200; **D** £150-£550 (incl. bkfst)* **Facilities** STV WiFi ↳ 🏊 ↟ 🏋 Gym Saunas Xmas New Year **Conf** Class 40 Board 20 Thtr 60 Del from £200 to £250* **Services** Lift **Parking** 60 **Notes** LB ⊗ Closed 2 Jan-6 Feb Civ Wed 80

ST BRELADE *continued*

L'Horizon Beach Hotel and Spa

★★★★ 85% ❀❀ HOTEL

tel: 01534 743101 **St Brelade's Bay JE3 8EF**
email: lhorizon@handpicked.co.uk **web:** www.handpickedhotels.co.uk/lhorizon
dir: From airport right at rdbt towards St Brelades & Red Houses. Through Red Houses, hotel 300mtrs on right in centre of bay

The combination of a truly wonderful setting on the golden sands of St Brelade's Bay, a relaxed atmosphere and excellent facilities prove a winning formula here. Bedrooms are stylish and have a real contemporary feel, all with plasma TVs and a host of extras; many have balconies or terraces and superb sea views. Spacious public areas include a spa and leisure club, a choice of dining options and relaxing lounges.

Rooms 105 (1 fmly) (15 GF) ➧ **S** £75-£180; **D** £122-£305 (incl. bkfst)*
Facilities Spa STV FTV WiFi ⓑ ⓡ ⓢ Gym Windsurfing Water skiing Sailing Sauna Steam room ♫ Xmas New Year **Conf** Class 100 Board 50 Thtr 250 Del from £145 to £380* **Services** Lift **Parking** 125 **Notes** LB ⊗ Civ Wed 240

St Brelade's Bay Hotel

★★★★ 81% HOTEL

tel: 01534 746141 **JE3 8EF**
web: www.stbreladesbayhotel.com
dir: SW corner of island

The hotel, set in five-acres of gardens, enjoys a fabulous location with unobstructed views overlooking St Brelade's Bay, and a sandy beach right on the doorstep. Bedrooms are beautifully presented and equipped to a very high standard. They include two-bedroom suites, family rooms and superb penthouse suites that have large balconies, and even telescopes. The relaxing public areas include a stylish, comfortable lounge along with a spacious bar. The gardens feature a pool area, terraces for relaxing and eating, and a tennis court. A superb leisure and fitness centre with state-of-the-art equipment is another attraction. Attentive friendly service is guaranteed in the elegant restaurant with its sea views.

Rooms 77 (8 fmly) ➧ **Facilities** Spa FTV WiFi ⓡ ⓣ ⓢ Gym Beauty treatment rooms ♫ Xmas New Year **Conf** Class 30 Board 12 Thtr 60 **Services** Lift **Parking** 90 **Notes** ⊗ Civ Wed 70

Hotel La Place

★★★★ 75% ❀ HOTEL

tel: 01534 744261 **Route du Coin, La Haule JE3 8BT**
email: reservations@hotellaplacejersey.com **web:** www.hotellaplacejersey.com
dir: Off main St Helier/St Aubin coast road at La Haule Manor (B25). Up hill, 2nd left (to Red Houses), 1st right. Hotel 100mtrs on right

Developed around a 17th-century farmhouse, this hotel is well placed for exploration of the island. Attentive, friendly service is very much part of the ethos here. Many of the bedrooms have benefited from an impressive refurbishment program and offer high levels of quality and comfort; some have private patios and direct access to the pool area. The cocktail bar is popular for pre-dinner drinks, and the stylish lounge is a perfect place to sit back and enjoy the tranquil delights of this peaceful setting. Cuisine is also an important feature here with the menu offering a good range of local, seasonal produce, served within the elegant restaurant.

Rooms 42 (1 fmly) (10 GF) **Facilities** STV WiFi ⓣ Discount at Les Ormes Country Club Xmas **Conf** Class 40 Board 40 Thtr 100 **Parking** 100 **Notes** Civ Wed 100

Beau Rivage Hotel

★★★ 77% HOTEL

tel: 01534 745983 **St Brelade's Bay JE3 8EF**
email: beau@jerseyweb.demon.co.uk **web:** www.jersey.co.uk/hotels/beau
dir: Sea side of coast road in centre of St Brelade's Bay, 1.5m S of airport

With direct access to one of Jersey's most popular beaches, residents and non-residents alike are welcome to this hotel's bar and terrace. All of the well-equipped bedrooms are now suites, most have wonderful sea views, and some have the bonus of balconies. Residents have a choice of lounges, plus a sun deck exclusively for their use. A range of dishes, featuring English and Continental cuisine, is available from a selection of menus in either the bar or the main bistro restaurant.

Rooms 12 (12 fmly) (12 smoking) ➧ **D** £57-£177* **Facilities** STV FTV WiFi Games room **Services** Lift **Parking** 16 **Notes** ⊗ RS Nov-Mar Civ Wed 80

Highlands Hotel

★★★ 72% HOTEL

tel: 01534 744288 **Corbiere JE3 8HN**
email: enquiries@highlandshotel.com **web:** www.highlandshotel.com
dir: 3m from Jersey airport. Very close to Corbiere Lighthouse

This hotel has an enviable location, ideally suited to touring and walking the island and is close to the coast and beaches of St Brelades Bay. There are several leisure facilities, including a swimming pool, and games room. The restaurant and many of the bedrooms have delightful views. Bedrooms and bathrooms are very pleasantly appointed in a bright and attractive style.

Rooms 49 (5 fmly) ➧ **S** £50-£60; **D** £90-£140 (incl. bkfst)* **Facilities** FTV WiFi ⓑ ⓣ Gym **Services** Lift **Parking** 60 **Notes** LB Closed Oct-May

ST CLEMENT — Map 24

Pontac House Hotel

★★★ 74% HOTEL

tel: 01534 857771 **St Clements Bay JE2 6SE**
email: info@pontachouse.com **web:** www.pontachouse.com
dir: 10 mins from St Helier

Overlooking the sandy beach of St Clement's Bay, this hotel is located on the south eastern corner of Jersey. Many guests return on a regular basis to experience the friendly, relaxed style of service. The bedrooms, most with splendid views, are comfortable and well equipped. Varied menus, featuring local seafood, are on offer each evening.

Rooms 27 (1 fmly) (5 GF) ➦ **S** £40-£52; **D** £80-£130 (incl. bkfst)* **Facilities** FTV WiFi ⚡ **Parking** 35 **Notes** Closed 1 Dec-1 Apr

The Samares Coast Hotel

★★★ 74% HOTEL

tel: 01534 723411 & 873006 **St Clement's Coast Rd JE2 6SB**
email: admin@morvanhotels.com **web:** www.morvanhotels.com
dir: On main esplanade

This hotel is situated on the south coast in a prime seafront location with delightful views from the restaurant and many of the bedrooms. All rooms are well appointed and the sea-facing balcony rooms prove especially popular. Facilities include a leisure complex with swimming pool and gym, and there are pleasant gardens. Carefully prepared dishes are offered in the comfortable restaurant.

Rooms 52 (4 annexe) (5 fmly) (14 GF) **Facilities** STV FTV WiFi ⚡ ⚡ Gym Steam room **Services** Lift **Parking** 35 **Notes** ⊗ Closed Nov-Mar

ST HELIER — Map 24

Grand Jersey

★★★★★ 80% ◉◉◉ HOTEL

PRIDE OF BRITAIN HOTELS

tel: 01534 722301 **The Esplanade JE2 3QA**
email: reservations@grandjersey.com **web:** www.grandjersey.com
dir: Located on St Helier seafront

A local landmark, the Grand Hotel has pleasant views across St Aubin's Bay to the front, and the bustling streets of St Helier to the rear. The hotel is elegant and contemporary in design with a real touch of grandeur throughout. The air-conditioned bedrooms, including six suites, come in a variety of designs, but all have luxurious beds, ottomans and LCD TVs. The spacious public areas, many looking out onto the bay, include the very popular Champagne Lounge, Victorias brasserie, and the impressive and intimate Tassili fine-dining restaurant. There is a large terrace for alfresco eating in the summer months, and the spa offers an indoor pool, gym and treatment rooms.

Rooms 123 (18 fmly) (6 GF) ➦ **Facilities** Spa STV FTV WiFi ⬧ ⚡ Gym ♬ Xmas New Year **Conf** Class 100 Board 50 Thtr 180 **Services** Lift Air con **Parking** 27 **Notes** ⊗ Civ Wed 180

The Club Hotel & Spa

★★★★ ◉◉◉◉ TOWN HOUSE HOTEL

tel: 01534 876500 **Green St JE2 4UH**
email: reservations@theclubjersey.com **web:** www.theclubjersey.com
dir: 5 mins walk from main shopping centre

This swish, town house hotel is conveniently located close to the centre of town and features stylish, contemporary decor throughout. All the guest rooms and suites have power showers and state-of-the-art technology including wide-screen LCD TV, DVD and CD systems. The choice of restaurants includes Bohemia, a sophisticated eating option that continues to offer outstanding cuisine. For relaxation there is an elegant spa with a luxurious range of treatments.

Rooms 46 (4 fmly) (4 GF) **S** £99-£445; **D** £99-£445 (incl. bkfst)* **Facilities** Spa STV FTV WiFi ⬧ ⚡ Sauna Steam room Salt cabin Hydrothermal bench Rasul room New Year **Conf** Class 60 Board 34 Thtr 80 Del from £145 to £215* **Services** Lift Air con **Parking** 32 **Notes** LB ⊗ Closed 24-30 Dec Civ Wed 84

The Royal Yacht

★★★★ 84% ◉◉ HOTEL

tel: 01534 720511 **The Weighbridge JE2 3NF**
email: reception@theroyalyacht.com **web:** www.theroyalyacht.com
dir: In town centre, opposite marina & harbour

Overlooking the marina and steam clock, the Royal Yacht is thought to be the oldest established hotel on the island. Although it has a long history, it is very much a

continued

ST HELIER *continued*

21st-century hotel, with state-of-the-art technology in all the bedrooms and the two penthouse suites. There is a range of impressive dining options to suit all tastes, with Sirocco's Restaurant offering high quality local produce. In addition to a choice of bars and conference facilities guests can enjoy the luxury spa with an indoor pool and gym.

Rooms 110 🐾 **S** £99-£145; **D** £99-£240 (incl. bkfst)* **Facilities** Spa STV WiFi ↘ 🐾 Gym 🎵 Xmas New Year **Conf** Class 150 Board 40 Thtr 280 Del from £139* **Services** Lift Air con **Notes** LB ⊗ Civ Wed 250

See advert on opposite page

Pomme d'Or Hotel

★★★★ 80% HOTEL

tel: 01534 880110 **Liberation Square JE1 3UF**
email: enquiries@pommedorhotel.com **web:** www.pommedorhotel.com
dir: Opposite harbour

This historic hotel overlooks Liberation Square and the marina and offers comfortably furnished, well-equipped bedrooms. Popular with the business fraternity, a range of conference facilities and meeting rooms are available. Dining options include The Harbour Room Carvery and the café bar.

Rooms 143 (3 fmly) 🐾 **Facilities** STV FTV WiFi ↘ Free use of The Aquadome at The Merton Hotel Xmas New Year **Conf** Class 100 Board 50 Thtr 220 Del from £155 to £200* **Services** Lift Air con **Notes** ⊗ Civ Wed 100

Radisson Blu Waterfront Hotel, Jersey

★★★★ 78% HOTEL

tel: 01534 671100 & 671173 **The Waterfront, La Rue de L'Etau JE2 3WF**
email: info.jersey@radissonblu.com **web:** www.radissonblu.com/hotel-jersey
dir: Follow signs to St Helier. From A2 follow signs to harbour. At rdbt just before harbour take 2nd exit, continue to hotel

Most of the bedrooms at this purpose-built hotel have fabulous views of the coastline. Facilities include a popular brasserie, cocktail bar, lounges, indoor heated pool, gym, sauna and steam room. A wide range of meeting rooms provides conference facilities for delegates; parking is extensive.

Rooms 195 🐾 **D** £85-£145* **Facilities** Spa STV WiFi ↘ HL 🐾 Gym Sauna Steam room 🎵 Xmas New Year **Conf** Class 184 Board 30 Thtr 400 **Services** Lift Air con **Parking** 70 **Notes** LB ⊗ Civ Wed 400

Hotel Savoy

★★★★ 74% HOTEL

tel: 01534 727521 **37 Rouge Bouillon JE2 3ZA**
email: info@thesavoy.biz **web:** www.hotelsavoyjersey.com
dir: From airport 1st exit at rdbt. At next rdbt 2nd exit right, down Beaumont Hill. At bottom left, along coast onto dual carriageway. At 3rd lights 1st left. Right at end. Remain in right lane, into left lane before hospital. Hotel on left opposite police station

This family-run hotel, a manor house dating from the 19th century, sits peacefully in its own grounds, just a short walk from the main shopping area in St Helier. It offers spacious, comfortable accommodation and smart public rooms. The Montana Restaurant serves carefully prepared, imaginative cuisine. A car park and leisure facilities are also available.

Rooms 56 (2 fmly) (10 GF) 🐾 **Facilities** STV FTV WiFi ↘ 🐾 Gym 🎵 Xmas New Year **Conf** Class 70 Board 12 Thtr 120 **Services** Lift **Parking** 46 **Notes** ⊗ Closed Jan-Feb Civ Wed 80

BEST WESTERN Royal Hotel

★★★ 79% ⊛ HOTEL

tel: 01534 726521 & 873006 **David Place JE2 4TD**
email: enquiries@royalhoteljersey.com **web:** www.royalhoteljersey.com
dir: From Airport: In St Helier on Victoria Ave, left by Grand Hotel into Peirson Rd. Follow one-way system into Cheapside. Left at filter, follow Ring Rd signs into Rouge Boullion (A14). At rdbt right, stay in right lane, right at lights into Midvale Rd. Through 2 lights, hotel on left

This long established hotel is located in the centre of town and is within walking distance of the business district and shops. Seasons Restaurant offers a modern approach to dining, and the adjoining bar provides a relaxed venue for residents and locals alike. The bedrooms are individually styled. Extensive conference facilities are available.

Rooms 89 (4 fmly) 🐾 **S** £58-£81; **D** £76-£125* **Facilities** FTV WiFi ↘ Gym Xmas New Year **Conf** Class 120 Board 80 Thtr 300 Del £141* **Services** Lift **Parking** 15 **Notes** LB ⊗ Civ Wed 30

The Norfolk Lodge Hotel

★★★ 75% HOTEL

tel: 01534 722950 & 873006 **Rouge Bouillon JE2 3ZB**
email: admin@morvanhotels.com **web:** www.morvanhotels.com

Centrally located and just a short walk to the main town, this popular hotel has a large number of regularly returning guests. Bedrooms are well decorated and equipped, and include some on the ground floor. In addition to an indoor swimming pool, the hotel offers regular evening entertainment during the main season. A range of well-prepared dishes is offered at dinner in the spacious restaurant.

Rooms 101 (11 annexe) (8 fmly) (15 GF) 🐾 **Facilities** FTV WiFi 🐾 Children's pool 🎵 **Services** Lift **Parking** 40 **Notes** ⊗ Closed Nov-Mar

CHANNEL ISLANDS

ST HELIER *continued*

Hampshire Hotel

★★★ 74% HOTEL

tel: 01534 724115 **53 Val Plaisant JE2 4TB**
email: info@hampshirehotel.je **web:** www.hampshirehotel.je

Located a short walk from the town centre, this hotel features spacious public areas and comfortable bedrooms. There are premier, standard and family rooms, each with a flat-screen TV. The spacious restaurant features seasonal changing dinner menus of popular dishes; at breakfast a wide choice is offered. The outdoor swimming pool and sun terrace are popular in the summer months.

Rooms 42 (2 fmly) (5 GF) **S** £42-£67; **D** £71-£101 (incl. bkfst)* **Facilities** STV WiFi ↳ ⌇ Xmas New Year **Services** Lift **Parking** 30 **Notes** ⊗

The Monterey Hotel

★★★ 74% HOTEL

tel: 01534 724762 & 873006 **St Saviour's Rd JE2 7LA**
email: monterey@morvanhotels.com **web:** www.morvanhotels.com

Conveniently located for the town, this comfortable hotel has the added benefit of ample parking and a range of leisure facilities including an indoor pool. Bedrooms are well decorated and furnished, and include a number of superior rooms. The relaxing bar area is open all day, and a good range of freshly prepared dishes is offered each evening.

Rooms 73 (6 fmly) (9 GF) **Facilities** FTV WiFi ↳ ⌇ Gym Steam room Xmas New Year **Conf** Class 12 Board 22 Thtr 40 **Services** Lift **Parking** 40 **Notes** ⊗

The Hotel Revere

★★★ 72% HOTEL

tel: 01534 611111 **Kensington Place JE2 3PA**
email: reservations@revere.co.uk **web:** www.revere.co.uk
dir: From Esplanade left after Grand Hotel

Situated on the west side of the town and convenient for the centre and harbour side, this hotel dates back to the 17th century and retains many period features. The style here is engagingly different, and bedrooms are individually decorated. There are three dining options and a small sun terrace.

Rooms 56 (2 fmly) (4 GF) ⌇ **S** £70-£90; **D** £100-£140 (incl. bkfst)* **Facilities** FTV WiFi ⌇ ♫ Xmas New Year **Notes** LB ⊗ Civ Wed 50

Apollo Hotel

★★★ 66% HOTEL

tel: 01534 725441 **St Saviours Rd JE2 4GJ**
email: reservations@huggler.com **web:** www.huggler.com
dir: On St Saviours Rd at junct with La Motte St

Centrally located, this popular hotel has a relaxed, informal atmosphere. Bedrooms are comfortably furnished and include useful extras. Many guests return regularly to enjoy the variety of leisure facilities including an outdoor pool with water slide and indoor pool with separate jacuzzi. The cocktail bar is an ideal place for a pre-dinner drink.

Rooms 85 (5 fmly) **S** £42-£120; **D** £49-£150 (incl. bkfst)* **Facilities** FTV WiFi ⊛ supervised ⌇ supervised Gym Xmas New Year **Conf** Class 100 Board 80 Thtr 150 **Services** Lift **Parking** 40 **Notes** ⊗

Millbrook House Hotel

★★ 76% HOTEL

tel: 01534 733036 **Rue De Trachy, Millbrook JE2 3JN**
email: millbrook.house@jerseymail.co.uk **web:** www.millbrookhousehotel.com
dir: 1.5m W of town off A1

Peacefully located within its own grounds, this small, personally run hotel offers a friendly welcome and relaxing ambience. Bedrooms and bathrooms vary in size; many have pleasant, countryside views. In addition to outdoor seating in the warmer months, guests can relax in the library, maybe with a drink before dinner.

Rooms 24 (2 fmly) (6 GF) **S** £30-£45; **D** £55-£80* **Facilities** WiFi Putt green **Services** Lift **Parking** 20 **Notes** Closed Oct-13 May

Westhill Country Hotel

★★ 74% COUNTRY HOUSE HOTEL

tel: 01534 723260 **Mont-a-l'abbe JE2 3HB**
email: info@westhillhoteljersey.com **web:** www.westhillhoteljersey.com
dir: Telephone for detailed directions

Set in its own beautifully landscaped gardens this hotel enjoys a prominent position just on the outskirts of St Helier. Service is attentive and guests are guaranteed a warm welcome and genuine hospitality throughout the hotel. The bedrooms are spacious and well equipped; several rooms have commanding views over the gardens to the countryside beyond. Public areas include a stylish lounge bar and popular restaurant. Free WiFi is available in the public areas and the swimming pool proves very popular with guests.

Rooms 90 (20 fmly) (16 GF) ⌇ **S** £47-£61; **D** £94-£102 (incl. bkfst)* **Facilities** FTV WiFi ⌇ ♫ **Conf** Class 80 Board 40 Thtr 60 **Parking** 75 **Notes** ⊗ Closed early Oct-early Apr Civ Wed 75

Sarum Hotel

★★ 63% METRO HOTEL

tel: 01534 758163 **19/21 New St Johns Rd JE2 3LD**
email: sarum@welcome.je **web:** www.jersey.co.uk/hotels/sarum
dir: On NW edge of St Helier, 0.5m from town centre

This hotel, just 600yds from the beach, offers self-catering bedrooms and a number of suites. The friendly staff provide a warm welcome, and there is a spacious recreational lounge with pool tables, plasma-screen TV and internet access. A garden and outdoor pool are also available. Local restaurants are just a short walk away, and bar snacks are available throughout the day.

Rooms 52 (5 annexe) (6 fmly) (2 GF) (52 smoking) **Facilities** FTV WiFi ⌇ Games room **Services** Lift **Parking** 10 **Notes** ⊗

Fort D'Auvergne Hotel

Ⓤ

tel: 01534 879960 & 731684 🖹 01534 876306 **Harve des Pas JE2 4UQ**
email: fort@morvanhotels.com **web:** www.morvanhotels.com

Currently the rating for this establishment is not confirmed. This may be due to a change of ownership or because it has only recently joined the AA rating scheme. For further details please see the AA website: theAA.com

Rooms 65 (4 fmly) (9 GF) ⌇ **Facilities** FTV WiFi ⊛ ♫ Child facilities **Services** Lift **Notes** ⊗ Closed 19 Oct-1 Apr

ST MARY　Map 24

West View Hotel

★★ 72% HOTEL

tel: 01534 481643 **La Grande Rue JE3 3BD**
email: westview@jerseymail.co.uk web: www.westviewhoteljersey.com
dir: At junct of B33 & C103

Located in the quiet parish of St Mary, this welcoming hotel is close to the delightful walks and cycle routes of the north coast. Bedrooms here are well equipped especially the larger, superior rooms. Entertainment is provided in the lounge bar during the summer months, when guests can also enjoy a swim in the heated outdoor pool.

Rooms 42 (3 fmly) (18 GF) **S** £39-£49; **D** £68-£96 (incl. bkfst)* **Facilities** FTV WiFi ⚡ **Parking** 38 **Notes** ⊗ Closed Nov-Mar

ST PETER　Map 24

Greenhills Country Hotel

★★★★ 76% ◉ COUNTRY HOUSE HOTEL

tel: 01534 481042 **Mont de L'Ecole JE3 7EL**
email: reserve@greenhillshotel.com web: www.greenhillshotel.com
dir: Follow signs to St Peter's Village, the A11, turn into Le Mont de l'ecole, Hotel on left

Located in the rural centre of Jersey, this relaxing country-house hotel, with delightful gardens, has a lovely atmosphere. Bedrooms extend from the main building around the courtyard; all are modern and well equipped with satellite LED TVs, luxurious bathrobes, white duck down duvets and linen. A varied menu, based on fresh local produce, is served in the restaurant, and guests also have use of the Aquadome at the Merton Hotel.

Rooms 31 (2 fmly) (9 GF) **S** £60-£80; **D** £81-£162 (incl. bkfst)* **Facilities** STV FTV WiFi ⚡ Free use of Merton Hotel's Aquadome & Leisure Centre **Conf** Class 12 Board 16 Thtr 20 Del from £100 to £130* **Parking** 40 **Notes** LB ⊗ Closed mid Dec-early Feb Civ Wed 40

ST SAVIOUR　Map 24

INSPECTORS' CHOICE

Longueville Manor Hotel

★★★★★ ◉◉◉ HOTEL

tel: 01534 725501 **JE2 7WF**
email: info@longuevillemanor.com web: www.longuevillemanor.com
dir: A3 E from St Helier towards Gorey. Hotel 1m on left

Dating back to the 13th century, there is something very special about Longueville Manor, which is why so many guests return time and again. It is set in 16 acres of grounds including woodland walks, a spectacular rose garden, Victorian kitchen garden and a lake. Bedrooms have great style and individuality boasting fresh flowers, fine embroidered bed linen and a host of extras. The very accomplished cuisine is also a highlight of any stay. In summer the pool and terrace are popular spots, plus there are also croquet and tennis courts. Families are particularly welcome, and there are extra activities arranged for children, including an adventure zone to explore. They also have their own menus and DVD library. The committed team of staff create a welcoming atmosphere and every effort is made to ensure a memorable stay.

Rooms 30 (1 annexe) (7 GF) ⚡ **S** £100-£387.50; **D** £175-£575 (incl. bkfst)* **Facilities** STV WiFi ◊ ⚡ 🏊 ⛳ Mini-gym, Treatment room Xmas New Year **Conf** Class 30 Board 30 Thtr 45 **Services** Lift **Parking** 40 **Notes** LB Civ Wed 40

TRINITY　Map 24

Water's Edge Hotel

★★★ 75% ◉ HOTEL

tel: 01534 862777 **Bouley Bay JE3 5AS**
email: admin@watersedgejersey.com web: www.watersedgejersey.com
dir: On NE coast. 4m from St Helier & 7.4m from Jersey Airport

Set in the tranquil surroundings of Bouley Bay on the north coast, this hotel is situated exactly as its name conveys. The well-furnished bedrooms offer high standards of quality and comfort, and the vast majority enjoy delightful views of either the garden or over the bay towards France. A range of modern British dishes, including fresh seafood, is offered in the comfortable dining room which also benefits from the splendid views. Free WiFi is available.

Rooms 50 (6 fmly) **S** £49.95-£69.95; **D** £70-£134 (incl. bkfst)* **Facilities** FTV WiFi ⚡ **Services** Lift **Parking** 20 **Notes** LB ⊗ Closed mid Oct-mid Apr

SARK

SARK　Map 24

Stocks Hotel

★★★★ 79% ◉◉ SMALL HOTEL

tel: 01481 832001 & 832444 **GY10 1SD**
email: reception@stockshotel.com web: www.stockshotel.com
dir: Ferry to Guernsey then to Sark. Trocador bus from harbour to top of island. Horse & carriage available for transfer to hotel (chargeable) or walk approx 20 mins

Sark is a delight; with no cars, transport is horse and cart, tractor or bicycle, and therefore the island is a very tranquil place. The hotel has spacious, comfortable rooms, which are attractively appointed. There are several lounges, and a cosy bar, as well as two dining options; the Brasserie is at the poolside and offers al fresco dining, while the main restaurant is more formal. The gardens provide much for the kitchen, and the stables house the hotel's own team of cart pullers.

Rooms 23 (2 fmly) (3 GF) ⚡ **S** £239-£259; **D** £245-£266 (incl. bkfst) **Facilities** STV FTV WiFi ◊ ⚡ Gym Treatment room Xmas New Year **Conf** Class 70 Board 12 Thtr 70 Del from £299 to £399 **Notes** LB Closed 3 Jan-1 Mar RS Mar & Nov-Dec

Scotland

ABERDEEN
City of Aberdeen   Map 23 NJ90

See also **Aberdeen Airport**

Norwood Hall Hotel

★★★★ 81% 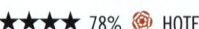 HOTEL

tel: 01224 868951 **Garthdee Rd, Cults AB15 9FX**
email: info@norwood-hall.co.uk **web:** www.norwood-hall.co.uk
dir: Off A90, at 1st rdbt cross Bridge of Dee, left at rdbt onto Garthdee Rd (B&Q & Sainsburys on left) continue to hotel sign

This imposing Victorian mansion has retained many of its original features, most notably the fine oak staircase, stained glass and ornately decorated walls and ceilings. Accommodation varies in style from individually designed bedrooms in the main house to the newest contemporary bedrooms. The extensive grounds ensure the hotel is popular as a wedding venue.

Rooms 73 (14 GF) **Facilities** STV FTV WiFi ↕ Xmas New Year **Conf** Class 100 Board 70 Thtr 200 **Services** Lift **Parking** 140 **Notes** ⊗ Civ Wed 150

Mercure Aberdeen Ardoe House Hotel & Spa

★★★★ 78% 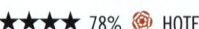 HOTEL

tel: 01224 860600 **South Deeside Rd, Blairs AB12 5YP**
email: h6626@accor.com **web:** www.mercure.com/AberdeenHotels
dir: 4m W of city off B9077, follow for 3m, hotel on left

From its elevated position on the banks of the River Dee, this 19th-century baronial-style mansion commands excellent countryside views. Beautifully decorated, thoughtfully equipped bedrooms are located in the main house, and in the more modern extension. Public rooms include a spa and leisure club, a cosy lounge and whisky bar and impressive function facilities.

Rooms 120 (7 fmly) **Facilities** Spa FTV WiFi ↕ HL ⊛ supervised ⌣ Gym Sauna Steam room Dance studio Xmas New Year **Conf** Class 200 Board 150 Thtr 600 **Services** Lift Air con **Parking** 200 **Notes** Civ Wed

Malmaison Aberdeen

★★★★ 74% 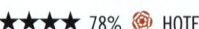 HOTEL

Malmaison
hotels that dare to be different

tel: 0844 693 0649 & 01224 327370 **49-53 Queens Rd AB15 4YP**
email: info.aberdeen@malmaison.com **web:** www.malmaison.com
dir: A90, 3rd exit into Queens Rd at 3rd rdbt, hotel on right

Popular with business travellers and as a function venue, this well-established hotel lies east of the city centre. Public areas include an attractive reception lounge and an intimate restaurant featuring a Josper Grill, plus the modern bar which remains a popular choice for many regulars whether it be for a bar meal or bottle of wine from the extensive cellar. There are two styles of accommodation, with the superior rooms being particularly comfortable and well equipped.

Rooms 79 (10 GF) **S** £129-£350; **D** £149-£450* **Facilities** Spa STV FTV WiFi ↕ Gym Steam room Xmas New Year **Conf** Class 12 Board 25 Thtr 30 **Services** Lift **Parking** 30 **Notes** LB Civ Wed 30

Copthorne Hotel Aberdeen

★★★★ 74% HOTEL

MILLENNIUM
HOTELS AND RESORTS
MILLENNIUM • COPTHORNE

tel: 01224 630404 **122 Huntly St AB10 1SU**
email: reservations.aberdeen@millenniumhotels.co.uk
web: www.millenniumhotels.co.uk/aberdeen
dir: West end of city centre, off Union St, up Rose St, hotel 0.25m on right on corner with Huntly St

Situated just outside of the city centre, this hotel offers friendly, attentive service. The smart bedrooms are well proportioned and guests will appreciate the added quality of the Connoisseur rooms. The West End Bistro and Bar provides a relaxed atmosphere in which to enjoy a drink or a meal; a great traditional steak and grill selection is on offer.

Rooms 87 (15 fmly) **Facilities** STV FTV WiFi HL New Year **Conf** Class 100 Board 70 Thtr 200 **Services** Lift **Notes** RS 24-26 Dec Civ Wed 180

Maryculter House Hotel

★★★★ 71% 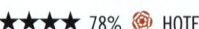 HOTEL

tel: 01224 732124 **South Deeside Rd, Maryculter AB12 5GB**
email: info@maryculterhousehotel.com **web:** www.maryculterhousehotel.com
dir: Exit A90 S of Aberdeen onto B9077. Hotel 8m on right, 0.5m beyond Deeside Holiday Park

Set in grounds on the banks of the River Dee, this charming Scottish mansion dates back to medieval times and is now a popular wedding and conference venue. Exposed stonework and open fires feature in the oldest parts, which house the cocktail bar and Priory Restaurant. Lunch and breakfast are taken overlooking the river; bedrooms are equipped especially with business travellers in mind.

Rooms 39 (1 fmly) (16 GF) **Facilities** FTV WiFi ↕ Fishing Xmas New Year **Conf** Class 100 Board 50 Thtr 180 Del £190* **Parking** 65 **Notes** Civ Wed 200

The Craighaar Hotel

★★★ 78% HOTEL

tel: 01224 712275 **Waterton Rd, Bucksburn AB21 9HS**
email: info@craighaar.co.uk **web:** www.craighaarhotel.com
dir: From A96 (Airport/Inverness) onto A947, hotel signed

Conveniently located for the airport, this welcoming hotel is a popular base for business people and tourists alike. Guests can make use of a quiet library lounge, and enjoy meals in the bar or restaurant. All bedrooms are well equipped, plus there is a wing of duplex suites that provide additional comfort.

Rooms 53 (6 fmly) (16 GF) **S** £119; **D** £135 (incl. bkfst)* **Facilities** STV FTV WiFi ↕ Library **Conf** Class 33 Board 30 Thtr 90 Del £129.50* **Parking** 80 **Notes** LB ⊗ Closed 25-26 Dec Civ Wed 40

The Mariner Hotel

★★★ 78% HOTEL

tel: 01224 588901 **349 Great Western Rd AB10 6NW**
email: info@themarinerhotel.co.uk **web:** www.themarinerhotel.co.uk
dir: E off Anderson Drive (A90) at Great Western Rd. Hotel on right on corner of Gray St

This well maintained, family-operated hotel is located west of the city centre. The smart, spacious bedrooms are well equipped and particularly comfortable, with executive suites available. The public rooms are restricted to the lounge bar, which is food driven, and the Atlantis Restaurant that showcases the region's wide choice of excellent seafood and meats.

Rooms 25 (8 annexe) (1 fmly) (4 GF) ↖ **S** £60–£100; **D** £75–£160 (incl. bkfst)*
Facilities FTV WiFi New Year **Parking** 51 **Notes** ⊗

bauhaus hotel

⋃ HOTEL

tel: 01224 212122 **52-60 Langstane Place AB11 6EN**
web: www.thebauhaus.co.uk
dir: Centre of Aberdeen

Designed around the principles of the German Bauhaus movement of the 1920s with its simplified, modern and minimal industrial design, this modern hotel provides a level of design rarely seen in UK hotels. Deeply comfortable in all areas with striking artwork, vibrant colours and a nod to the industrial past with exposed brick walls and metal work. Bedrooms are designed with luxury and comfort in mind and feature smartTVs. Public areas include two feature bars and grants@bauhaus serving modern food from an open kitchen. For further details please see the AA website: theAA.com

Rooms 39 ↖ **S** £65–£121; **D** £85–£210 (incl. bkfst)* **Facilities** FTV WiFi ↘
Conf Class 22 Board 22 Thtr 40 Del from £185 to £195* **Services** Lift **Notes** LB ⊗

Holiday Inn Express Aberdeen

BUDGET HOTEL

tel: 01224 227250 **Exhibition & Conference Centre, Parkway East, Bridge of Don AB23 8AJ**
email: info@hieaberdeenexhibitioncentre.co.uk **web:** www.hiexpress.co.uk
dir: Follow A90 northbound for Aberdeen Exhibition Conference Centre, located 2m from City Centre

A modern hotel ideal for families and business travellers. Fresh and uncomplicated, the spacious rooms include Sky TV, power shower and tea and coffee-making facilities. Continental buffet breakfast is included in the room rate; other meals may be taken at the nearby family pub or restaurant. See also the Hotel Groups pages.

Rooms 135 (100 fmly) ↖ **Conf** Class 16 Board 30 Thtr 48

Ibis Aberdeen Centre Hotel

BUDGET HOTEL

tel: 01224 285820 **15 Shiprow AB11 5BY**
email: H5170@accor.com **web:** www.ibis.com

Situated in a convenient location in the heart of Aberdeen, the newly constructed hotel provides a comfortable place to stay in a modern environment. Attractive and spacious bedrooms are equipped with a host of features including flat-screen TVs and WiFi access. Snacks are available 24 hours of the day and breakfast is offered in the stylish restaurant. Parking is available adjacent to the hotel. See also the Hotel Groups pages.

Rooms 107 ↖ **S** £45–£165; **D** £45–£165*

A

ABERDEEN *continued*

Premier Inn Aberdeen Central West

BUDGET HOTEL

tel: 0871 527 8006 **North Anderson Dr AB15 6DW**
web: www.premierinn.com
dir: Into Aberdeen from S on A90 follow airport signs. Hotel 1st left after fire station. (NB for Sat Nav use AB15 6TP)

High quality, budget accommodation ideal for both families and business travellers. Spacious, en suite bedrooms feature tea and coffee making facilities, and Freeview TV in most hotels. Internet access and WiFi are available for a small fee. The adjacent family restaurant features a wide and varied menu. See also the Hotel Groups pages.

Rooms 62

Premier Inn Aberdeen City Centre

BUDGET HOTEL

tel: 0871 527 8008 **Inverlair House, West North St AB24 5AS**
web: www.premierinn.com
dir: A90 onto A9013 into city centre. Take A956 towards King St, 1st left into Meal Market St

Rooms 162

Premier Inn Aberdeen North (Murcar)

BUDGET HOTEL

tel: 0871 527 8010 **Ellon Rd, Murcar, Bridge of Don AB23 8BP**
web: www.premierinn.com
dir: From city centre take A90 N follow Peterhead signs. At rdbt 2m after Aberdeen Exhibition & Conference Centre, left onto B999. Hotel on right

Rooms 40

Premier Inn Aberdeen South

BUDGET HOTEL

tel: 0871 527 8012 **Mains of Balquharn, Portlethen AB12 4QS**
web: www.premierinn.com
dir: From A90 follow Portlethen & Badentoy Park signs. Hotel on right

Rooms 40

Premier Inn Aberdeen (Westhill)

BUDGET HOTEL

tel: 0871 527 8004 **Straik Rd, Westhill AB32 6HF**
web: www.premierinn.com
dir: On A944 towards Alford, hotel adjacent to Tesco

Rooms 61

ABERDEEN AIRPORT	Map 23 NJ81
City of Aberdeen	

Aberdeen Marriott Hotel

★★★★ 76% HOTEL

tel: 01224 770011 **Overton Circle, Dyce AB21 7AZ**
email: reservations.scotland@marriotthotels.com **web:** www.aberdeenmarriott.co.uk
dir: Follow A96 to Bucksburn, right at rdbt onto A947. Hotel in 2m at 2nd rdbt

Close to the airport and conveniently located for the business district, this purpose-built hotel is a popular conference venue. The well-proportioned bedrooms come with many thoughtful extras. Public areas include an informal bar and lounge, a split-level restaurant and a leisure centre that can be accessed directly from a number of bedrooms.

Rooms 155 (81 fmly) (61 GF) **Facilities** STV WiFi HL ⓑ supervised Gym Saunas (male & female) Solarium Xmas New Year **Conf** Class 200 Board 60 Thtr 400 **Services** Air con **Parking** 220 **Notes** ⊗ Civ Wed 90

Menzies Hotels Aberdeen Airport Dyce

★★★ 77% HOTEL

tel: 01224 723101 **Farburn Ter, Dyce AB21 7DW**
email: dyce@menzieshotels.co.uk **web:** www.menzieshotels.co.uk
dir: A96/A947 airport E after 1m turn left at lights. Hotel in 250yds

This hotel is very convenient for air travellers and for those wishing to explore this lovely Highland area. The spacious, well-equipped bedrooms have all the expected up-to-date amenities. The public areas are welcoming and include a contemporary brasserie. Secure parking and WiFi are also provided.

Rooms 212 (212 annexe) (3 fmly) (107 GF) (54 smoking) **S** £48-£209; **D** £53-£209* **Facilities** STV FTV WiFi Xmas New Year **Conf** Class 160 Board 120 Thtr 400 Del from £180 to £240* **Parking** 150 **Notes** LB Civ Wed 220

Premier Inn Aberdeen Airport (Dyce)

BUDGET HOTEL

tel: 0871 527 9460 **Aberdeen Airport Main Terminal, Argyll Way, Dyce AB21 0BN**
web: www.premierinn.com
dir: From N on A96 follow Aberdeen signs. At rdbt 1st exit into Dyce Dr signed Airport. At 2nd lights right into Argyll Rd. Hotel on right. From S on A90 follow Airport & A96 signs. Take A96 (Inverurie road) at 2nd rdbt 3rd exit into Dyce Drive (proceed as above)

High quality, budget accommodation ideal for both families and business travellers. Spacious, en suite bedrooms feature tea and coffee making facilities, and Freeview TV in most hotels. Internet access and WiFi are available for a small fee. The adjacent family restaurant features a wide and varied menu. See also the Hotel Groups pages.

Rooms 100

ABERDOUR
Fife
Map 21 NT18

The Woodside Hotel

★★★ △ HOTEL

tel: 01383 860328 **High St KY3 0SW**
email: reception@thewoodsidehotel.co.uk **web:** www.thewoodsidehotel.co.uk
dir: M90 junct 1, E on A291 for 5m, hotel on left on entering village

The Woodside Hotel is a 19th-century mansion in the Fife Hills that looks out over the Earl of Moray's estate to the lovely Firth of Fife beyond. Each of the bedrooms is named after a Scottish clan, and include a spacious family room and the Rennie Suite with a four-poster bed. The hotel has facilities for conferences, weddings and banquets.

Rooms 20 (1 fmly) ➤ **Facilities** FTV WiFi **Conf** Class 80 Board 30 Thtr 60 **Parking** 22 **Notes** ⊗ Closed 25 Dec & 1 Jan

ABERFOYLE
Stirling
Map 20 NN50

Macdonald Forest Hills Hotel & Resort

★★★★ 80% ◉ HOTEL

tel: 0844 879 9057 & 01877 389500 **Kinlochard FK8 3TL**
email: general.foresthills@macdonald-hotels.co.uk
web: www.macdonald-hotels.co.uk/foresthills
dir: A84, A873, A81 to Aberfoyle onto B829

Situated in the heart of The Trossachs with wonderful views of Loch Ard, this popular hotel forms part of a resort complex offering a range of indoor and outdoor facilities. The main hotel has relaxing lounges and a restaurant that all overlook the landscaped gardens. A separate building houses the leisure centre, lounge bar and bistro.

Rooms 55 (16 fmly) (12 GF) ➤ **Facilities** Spa STV FTV WiFi ⊗ ⌇ Gym Children's club Snooker Watersports Quad biking Archery Clay pigeon shooting ♫ Xmas New Year **Conf** Class 60 Board 20 Thtr 120 Del from £135 to £155* **Services** Lift **Parking** 100 **Notes** Civ Wed 100

ABERLADY
East Lothian
Map 21 NT47

Ducks at Kilspindie

◉◉ RESTAURANT WITH ROOMS

tel: 01875 870682 ▤ 01875 870504 **Main St EH32 0RE**
email: kilspindie@ducks.co.uk **web:** www.ducks.co.uk
dir: A1 (Bankton junct) take 1st exit to North Berwick. At next rdbt 3rd exit onto A198 signed Longniddry, left towards Aberlady. At T-junct, facing river, right to Aberlady

The name of this restaurant with rooms is referenced around the building - Ducks Restaurant for award-winning cuisine; Donald's Bistro and the Ducklings informal coffee shop. The warm and welcoming public areas include a great bar offering real ales and various objets d'art. The bedrooms are comfortable and well-appointed with stylish en suites. The team are informal and friendly, taking the time to chat to their guests.

Rooms 23 (1 fmly)

ABINGTON MOTORWAY SERVICE AREA (M74)
South Lanarkshire
Map 21 NS92

Days Inn Abington - M74

BUDGET HOTEL

tel: 01864 502782 **ML12 6RG**
email: abington.hotel@welcomebreak.co.uk **web:** www.welcomebreak.co.uk
dir: M74 junct 13, accessible from N'bound and S'bound carriageways

This modern building offers accommodation in smart, spacious and well-equipped bedrooms, suitable for families and business travellers, and all with en suite bathrooms. Continental breakfast is available and other refreshments may be taken at the nearby family restaurant. See also the Hotel Groups pages.

Rooms 54 (50 fmly) (4 smoking) **S** £60; **D** £66* **Conf** Board 10

ARDUAINE
Argyll & Bute
Map 20 NM71

Loch Melfort Hotel

★★★ 83% ◉◉ HOTEL

tel: 01852 200233 **PA34 4XG**
email: reception@lochmelfort.co.uk **web:** www.lochmelfort.co.uk
dir: On A816, midway between Oban & Lochgilphead

Enjoying one of the finest locations on the West Coast, this popular, family-run hotel has outstanding views across Asknish Bay towards the Islands of Jura, Scarba and Shuna. Accommodation is provided in either the balconied rooms of the Cedar wing or the more traditional rooms in the main hotel. Dining options include the main restaurant with stunning views or the more informal bistro.

Rooms 25 (20 annexe) (2 fmly) (10 GF) ➤ **S** £104-£174; **D** £148-£268 (incl. bkfst)* **Facilities** WiFi 4 moorings Childrens' play park Xmas New Year **Conf** Class 40 Board 20 Thtr 50 **Parking** 50 **Notes** LB Closed 3 wks beginning Dec & 3 wks mid Jan RS Winter Civ Wed 100

AUCHENCAIRN
Dumfries & Galloway
Map 21 NX75

Balcary Bay Hotel

★★★ 88% ◉◉ HOTEL

tel: 01556 640217 & 640311 **DG7 1QZ**
email: reservations@balcary-bay-hotel.co.uk **web:** www.balcary-bay-hotel.co.uk
dir: On A711 between Dalbeattie & Kirkcudbright, hotel 2m from Auchencairn

Taking its name from the bay on which it lies, this hotel has lawns running down to the shore. The larger bedrooms enjoy stunning views over the bay, while others overlook the gardens. The comfortable public areas are very relaxing. Imaginative dishes feature at dinner, accompanied by a good wine list.

Rooms 20 (1 fmly) (3 GF) ➤ **S** £84; **D** £156-£186 (incl. bkfst) **Facilities** FTV WiFi **Parking** 50 **Notes** Closed 1st Sun Dec-1st Fri Feb

A

AUCHTERARDER
Perth & Kinross

Map 21 NN91

INSPECTORS' CHOICE

The Gleneagles Hotel

★★★★★ ◉◉◉◉ HOTEL

tel: 01764 662231 & 0800 169 2984 **PH3 1NF**
email: resort.sales@gleneagles.com **web:** www.gleneagles.com
dir: Off A9 at exit for A823 follow signs for Gleneagles Hotel

With its international reputation for high standards, this grand hotel provides something for everyone. Set in 850 acres of glorious countryside, Gleneagles offers a peaceful retreat, as well as many sporting activities, including the famous championship golf courses. All bedrooms are appointed to a high standard and offer both traditional and contemporary styles. Stylish public areas include various dining options: the Deseo 'Mediterranean Food Market' eaterie; The Strathearn, with two AA Rosettes; as well as inspired cooking at Andrew Fairlie at Gleneagles, a restaurant with four AA Rosettes. There's also the Clubhouse and many bars. The award-winning EPSA spa offers the very latest treatments to restore both body and soul. Service is always professional - the staff are friendly and nothing is too much trouble.

Rooms 232 (115 fmly) (11 GF) **Facilities** Spa STV FTV WiFi ⓑ supervised ⅂
supervised ⅃ 54 ⏚ Putt green Fishing ⏚ Gym Falconry Off-road driving Golf Archery Clay shooting Gundog School Horse riding Xmas New Year Child facilities **Conf** Class 240 Board 60 Thtr 360 **Services** Lift **Parking** 300 **Notes** Civ Wed 360

AVIEMORE
Highland

Map 23 NH81

Macdonald Aviemore Resort

MACDONALD HOTELS & RESORTS

★★★★ 74% HOTEL

tel: 01479 815100 **PH22 1PN**
email: general@aviemorehighlandresort.com **web:** www.macdonald-hotels.co.uk
dir: From N: Exit A9 to Aviemore (B970). Right at T-junct, through village. Right (2nd exit) at 1st rdbt into Macdonald Aviemore Highland Resort, follow reception signs. From S: Exit A9 to Aviemore, left at T-junct. Immediately after Esso garage, turn left into Resort

This hotel is part of the Aviemore Highland Resort which boasts a wide range of activities including a championship golf course. The modern, well-equipped bedrooms suit business, leisure guests and families, and Aspects Restaurant is the fine dining option. In addition there is a state-of-the-art gym, spa treatments and a 25-metre pool with a wave machine and flume.

Rooms 151 (10 fmly) (44 GF) **Facilities** Spa STV FTV WiFi ⓑ supervised ⅃ 18 Putt green Fishing Gym Steam room Sauna Children's indoor & outdoor playgrounds Xmas New Year **Conf** Class 610 Board 38 Thtr 1000 **Services** Lift **Parking** 500 **Notes** Civ Wed 300

AYR
South Ayrshire

Map 20 NS32

Fairfield House Hotel

★★★★ 76% ◉◉ HOTEL

tel: 01292 267461 **12 Fairfield Rd KA7 2AR**
email: reservations@fairfieldhotel.co.uk **web:** www.fairfieldhotel.co.uk
dir: From A77 towards Ayr South (A30). Follow town centre signs, down Miller Rd, left, then right into Fairfield Rd

Situated in a leafy cul-de-sac close to the esplanade, this hotel enjoys stunning seascapes towards the Isle of Arran. Bedrooms are in either modern or classical styles, the latter featuring impressive bathrooms. Public areas provide stylish, modern rooms in which to relax. Skilfully prepared meals are served in the casual brasserie or elegant restaurant.

Rooms 44 (4 annexe) (3 fmly) (9 GF) **Facilities** FTV WiFi ⓑ supervised Gym Fitness room Sauna Steam room Xmas New Year **Conf** Class 80 Board 40 Thtr 120 **Services** Lift **Parking** 50 **Notes** ⊗ Civ Wed 150

Enterkine Country House

★★★★ 75% ◉◉ COUNTRY HOUSE HOTEL

tel: 01292 520580 **Annbank KA6 5AL**
email: mail@enterkine.com **web:** www.enterkine.com
dir: 5m E of Ayr on B743

This luxurious art deco country mansion dates from the 1930s and retains many original features, notably some splendid bathroom suites. The focus is very much on dining, and in country house tradition there is no bar, drinks being served in the elegant lounge and library. The well-proportioned bedrooms are furnished and equipped to high standards, many with lovely countryside views.

Rooms 14 (8 annexe) (2 fmly) (3 GF) ⓑ **S** £60-£85; **D** £70-£195 (incl. bkfst) **Facilities** FTV WiFi Xmas New Year **Conf** Class 140 Board 140 Thtr 200 Del from £120 to £140 **Parking** 40 **Notes** LB Civ Wed 250

Mercure Ayr Hotel

★★★ 74% HOTEL

Mercure
HOTELS

tel: 0844 815 9005 **Dalblair Rd KA7 1UG**
email: info@mercureayr.co.uk **web:** www.jupiterhotels.co.uk
dir: M77 towards Prestwick Airport, then A77 Ayr, 1st rdbt 3rd exit, 2nd rdbt straight over, left at lights, then 2nd lights turn left, bottom of road turn right, hotel on left

This hotel is situated in a central location in Ayr, and many bedrooms benefit from sea views. The property is ideally located for both business and leisure travellers and the area boasts many golf courses within easy reach; indeed the hotel even has its own golf simulator. Bedrooms and bathrooms are presented to a modern standard with a range of extras including free WiFi. A leisure club and Brasserie restaurant are also provided for guests.

Rooms 118 (4 fmly) ⓑ **Facilities** FTV WiFi ⓑ supervised Gym Beauty treatment room **Services** Lift **Parking** 45 **Notes** ⊗ Civ Wed 70

B

Premier Inn Ayr A77/Racecourse

BUDGET HOTEL

tel: 0871 527 9416 **Wheatpark Place KA8 9RT**
web: www.premierinn.com
dir: Please phone for directions

High quality, budget accommodation ideal for both families and business travellers. Spacious, en suite bedrooms feature tea and coffee making facilities, and Freeview TV in most hotels. Internet access and WiFi are available for a small fee. The adjacent family restaurant features a wide and varied menu. See also the Hotel Groups pages.

Rooms 84

Premier Inn Ayr/Prestwick Airport

BUDGET HOTEL

tel: 0871 527 8038 **Kilmarnock Rd, Monkton KA9 2RJ**
web: www.premierinn.com
dir: At Dutch House Rdbt (at junct of A77 & A78) at Monkton

Rooms 64

BALLANTRAE
South Ayrshire   Map 20 NX08

INSPECTORS' CHOICE

Glenapp Castle

★★★★★  HOTEL

tel: 01465 831212 **KA26 0NZ**
email: enquiries@glenappcastle.com **web:** www.glenappcastle.com
dir: S through Ballantrae, cross bridge over River Stinchar, 1st right, hotel gates 1m

Friendly hospitality and attentive service prevail at this stunning Victorian castle, set in extensive private grounds to the south of the village. Impeccably furnished bedrooms are graced with antiques and period pieces, and include two master rooms and a ground-floor family suite. Breathtaking views of Arran and Ailsa Craig can be enjoyed from the delightful, sumptuous day rooms and from many of the bedrooms. Guests should make a point of walking round the wonderful 36-acre grounds, and take a look at the azalea pond, walled vegetable gardens and restored Victorian greenhouses.

Rooms 17 (2 fmly) (7 GF) ✆ **S** £280-£490; **D** £450-£670 (incl. bkfst & dinner) **Facilities** FTV WiFi ⊁ ⬆ ⬇ Woodland walks New Year **Conf** Class 12 Board 25 Thtr 25 Del from £240 to £265 **Services** Lift **Parking** 20 **Notes** LB Closed Jan-mid Mar & Xmas week Civ Wed 40

BALLATER
Aberdeenshire   Map 23 NO39

INSPECTORS' CHOICE

Darroch Learg Hotel

★★★  SMALL HOTEL

tel: 013397 55443 **Braemar Rd AB35 5UX**
email: enquiries@darrochlearg.co.uk **web:** www.darrochlearg.co.uk
dir: On A93, W of Ballater

Set high above the road in extensive wooded grounds, this long-established hotel offers superb views over the hills and countryside of Royal Deeside. Nigel and Fiona Franks are caring and attentive hosts who improve their hotel every year. Bedrooms, some with four-poster beds, are individually styled, bright and spacious. Food is a highlight of any visit, whether it is a freshly prepared breakfast or the fine cuisine served in the delightful conservatory restaurant.

Rooms 12 (1 GF) **S** £95-£160; **D** £140-£250 (incl. bkfst)* **Facilities** New Year **Conf** Board 12 Thtr 25 Del from £155 to £220* **Parking** 15 **Notes** Closed Xmas & Jan (ex New Year)

B

BALLATER *continued*

Loch Kinord Hotel

★★★ 79% HOTEL

tel: 013398 85229 **Ballater Rd, Dinnet AB34 5JY**
email: stay@lochkinord.com **web:** www.lochkinord.com
dir: Between Aboyne & Ballater, on A93, in Dinnet

Family-run, this roadside hotel is well located for leisure and sporting pursuits. It has lots of character and a friendly atmosphere. There are two bars, one outside and a cosy one inside, plus a dining room with a bold colour scheme. Bedrooms are stylish and have smart bathrooms.

Rooms 20 (3 fmly) (4 GF) ⋒ **Facilities** FTV WiFi ⅃ Xmas **Conf** Class 30 Board 30 Thtr 40 **Parking** 20 **Notes** Civ Wed 50

BALLOCH
West Dumbartonshire

Map 20 NS38

Cameron House on Loch Lomond

★★★★★ 85% ◉◉ HOTEL

tel: 01389 755565 **G83 8QZ**
email: reservations@cameronhouse.co.uk **web:** www.devere.co.uk
dir: M8 (W) junct 30 for Erskine Bridge. A82 for Crainlarich. 14m, at rdbt signed Luss, hotel on right

Enjoying an idyllic location on the banks of Loch Lomond in over 100 acres of wooded parkland, this stylish hotel offers an excellent range of leisure facilities. These include two golf courses, a world-class spa and a host of indoor and outdoor sporting activities. A choice of restaurants and bars cater for all tastes and include the Scottish-themed Cameron Grill and a fine dining operation, Martin Wishart at Loch Lomond. Bedrooms are stylish, well equipped and many boast wonderful loch views.

Rooms 132 (9 fmly) (18 GF) ⋒ **D** £159-£310 (incl. bkfst)* **Facilities** Spa STV WiFi ⅃ HL 🏊 supervised ⚓ 27 ⛳ Fishing ⅃ Gym Squash Motor boat on Loch Lomond Hairdresser Sea plane Falconry Archery Segways Xmas New Year **Conf** Class 180 Board 80 Thtr 300 Del from £195 to £300* **Services** Lift Air con **Parking** 200 **Notes** LB ⊗ Civ Wed 200

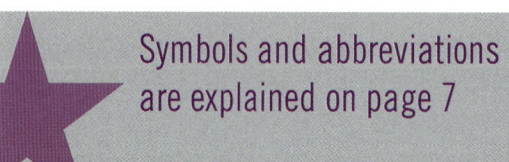

Symbols and abbreviations are explained on page 7

BANCHORY
Aberdeenshire

Map 23 NO69

Raemoir House Hotel

★★★ 85% ◉◉ COUNTRY HOUSE HOTEL

tel: 01330 824884 **Raemoir AB31 4ED**
email: hotel@raemoir.com **web:** www.raemoir.com
dir: A93 to Banchory then A980, hotel at x-rds after 2.5m

Raemoir House is a beautiful Georgian country house set in eleven acres of secluded, peaceful grounds, close to Aberdeen and perfectly situated for the Whisky, Castle and Golf trails. The individually styled bedrooms feature all modern comforts including WiFi access. Cooking is a highlight with delicious meals served in the Oval Dining Room. The hotel has a helicopter pad.

Rooms 20 (6 annexe) (1 fmly) (3 GF) ⋒ **S** £105-£150; **D** £165-£310 (incl. bkfst)* **Facilities** FTV WiFi ⅃ 🍴 Xmas New Year **Conf** Class 50 Board 40 Thtr 80 Del £180* **Parking** 30 **Notes** LB No children 12yrs Civ Wed 70

BEST WESTERN Burnett Arms Hotel

★★★ 71% SMALL HOTEL

tel: 01330 824944 **25 High St AB31 5TD**
email: theburnett@btconnect.com **web:** www.bw-burnettarms.co.uk
dir: Town centre on N side of A93

This popular hotel is located in the heart of the town centre and gives easy access to the many attractions of Royal Deeside. Public areas include a choice of eating and drinking options, with food served in the restaurant, bar and foyer lounge. Bedrooms are thoughtfully equipped and comfortably modern.

Rooms 18 (1 fmly) ⋒ **S** £73-£85; **D** £94-£105 (incl. bkfst) **Facilities** STV FTV WiFi Xmas New Year **Conf** Class 50 Board 50 Thtr 100 Del from £113 to £125 **Parking** 22

C

BATHGATE
West Lothian

Map 21 NS96

Premier Inn Livingston (Bathgate)

BUDGET HOTEL

tel: 0871 527 8630 **Starlaw Rd EH48 1LQ**
web: www.premierinn.com
dir: M8 junct 3A. At 1st rdbt 1st exit (Bathgate). Over bridge, at 2nd rdbt take 1st exit. Hotel 200yds on left

High quality, budget accommodation ideal for both families and business travellers. Spacious, en suite bedrooms feature tea and coffee making facilities, and Freeview TV in most hotels. Internet access and WiFi are available for a small fee. The adjacent family restaurant features a wide and varied menu. See also the Hotel Groups pages.

Rooms 74

BEAULY
Highland

Map 23 NH54

Priory Hotel

★★★ 75% HOTEL

tel: 01463 782309 & 784920 **The Square IV4 7BX**
email: reservations@priory-hotel.com **web:** www.priory-hotel.com
dir: Signed from A832, into Beauly, hotel in square on left

This popular hotel occupies a central location in the town square. Standard and executive rooms are on offer, both providing a good level of comfort and range of facilities. Food is served throughout the day in the open-plan public areas, with menus offering a first rate choice.

Rooms 38 (3 fmly) (1 GF) ↖ **S** £57.50-£67.50; **D** £79.50-£110 (incl. bkfst)* **Facilities** STV FTV WiFi Xmas New Year **Conf** Class 40 Board 30 Thtr 40 Del from £75 to £95* **Services** Lift **Parking** 20 **Notes** LB ⊗

BOTHWELL
South Lanarkshire

Map 20 NS75

Bothwell Bridge Hotel

★★★ 78% HOTEL

tel: 01698 852246 **89 Main St G71 8EU**
email: reception@bothwellbridge-hotel.com **web:** www.bothwellbridge-hotel.com
dir: M74 junct 5 & follow signs to Uddingston, right at mini-rdbt. Hotel just past shops on left

This red-sandstone mansion house is a popular business, function and conference hotel and is conveniently placed for the motorway. Most bedrooms are spacious and all are well equipped. The conservatory is a bright and comfortable restaurant serving an interesting variety of Italian influenced dishes. The lounge bar offers a comfortable seating area that proves popular as a stop for coffee.

Rooms 90 (14 fmly) (13 GF) **S** £64-£69.50; **D** £75-£82.50 (incl. bkfst)* **Facilities** STV FTV WiFi ↕ HL ♫ Xmas New Year **Conf** Class 80 Board 50 Thtr 200 Del from £86.50 to £103* **Services** Lift **Parking** 125 **Notes** LB ⊗ Civ Wed 200

Find out more about Hotel Bathrooms in our feature on page 26

CALLANDER
Stirling

Map 20 NN60

Roman Camp Country House Hotel

★★★ ❀❀❀ COUNTRY HOUSE HOTEL

tel: 01877 330003 **FK17 8BG**
email: mail@romancamphotel.co.uk **web:** www.romancamphotel.co.uk
dir: N on A84, left at east end of High Street. 300yds to hotel

Built in the 17th century and originally used as a shooting lodge, this charming country house has a rich history, and has been in the same ownership for over twenty years. Twenty acres of gardens and grounds lead down to the River Teith, and the town centre and its attractions are only a short walk away. Each bedroom is individually and elegantly designed, and offers much pampering comfort. Food is a highlight of any stay and menus are dominated by high-quality Scottish produce that is sensitively treated by the talented kitchen team. Real fires warm the atmospheric public areas and service is friendly yet professional.

Rooms 15 (4 fmly) (7 GF) ↖ **S** £110-£185; **D** £160-£225 (incl. bkfst) **Facilities** STV FTV WiFi ↕ Fishing Xmas New Year **Conf** Class 60 Board 30 Thtr 120 Del from £185 to £225 **Parking** 80 **Notes** LB Civ Wed 150

CLYDEBANK
West Dumbartonshire

Map 20 NS47

Beardmore Hotel

★★★★ 75% ❀ HOTEL

tel: 0141 951 6000 **Beardmore St G81 4SA**
email: info@beardmore.scot.nhs.uk **web:** www.thebeardmore.com
dir: M8 junct 19, follow signs for Clydeside Expressway to Glasgow road, then A814 (Dumbarton road), then follow Clydebank Business Park signs. Hotel on left

Attracting plenty of business and conference custom, this stylish modern hotel lies beside the River Clyde and shares an impressive site with a hospital (although the latter does not intrude). Spacious and imposing public areas include the stylish restaurant providing innovative contemporary Scottish cooking, the recently added Central Plaza café, and The BBar lounge which offers a more extensive choice of lighter dishes. The leisure facilities include a 15-metre swimming pool, sauna and steam room. All bedrooms come with iMac entertainment systems.

Rooms 168 **Facilities** STV FTV WiFi ↕ ⊛ supervised Gym Sauna Steam room Xmas New Year **Conf** Class 84 Board 27 Thtr 240 **Services** Lift Air con **Parking** 300 **Notes** ⊗ Civ Wed 170

C

COMRIE
Perth & Kinross

Map 21 NN72

Royal Hotel

★★★ 79% 🌸 SMALL HOTEL

tel: 01764 679200 **Melville Square PH6 2DN**
email: reception@royalhotel.co.uk **web:** www.royalhotel.co.uk
dir: A9 on A822 to Crieff, then B827 to Comrie. Hotel in main square on A85

The traditional façade gives little indication of the style and elegance to be found inside this long-established hotel located in the village centre. Public areas include a bar and library, a bright modern restaurant and a conservatory-style brasserie. The bedrooms are tastefully appointed and furnished with smart reproduction antiques.

Rooms 13 (2 annexe) **Facilities** STV WiFi Fishing Shooting arranged New Year **Conf** Class 10 Board 20 Thtr 20 **Parking** 22 **Notes** Closed 25-26 Dec

---

CONNEL
Argyll & Bute

Map 20 NM93

Falls of Lora Hotel

THE INDEPENDENTS
HOTEL ASSOCIATION

★★★ 73% HOTEL

tel: 01631 710483 **PA37 1PB**
email: enquiries@fallsoflora.com **web:** www.fallsoflora.com
dir: From Glasgow take A82, A85. Hotel 0.5m past Connel sign (5m before Oban)

Personally run and welcoming, this long-established and thriving holiday hotel enjoys inspiring views over Loch Etive. The spacious ground floor takes in a comfortable, traditional lounge and a cocktail bar with over a hundred whiskies and an open log fire. Guests can eat in the popular, informal bistro, which is open all

day. Bedrooms come in a variety of styles, ranging from the cosy standard rooms to high quality luxury rooms.

Rooms 30 (4 fmly) (4 GF) 🐾 **S** £55.50-£83.50; **D** £59-£159 (incl. bkfst)*
Facilities FTV WiFi Child facilities **Conf** Class 20 Board 15 Thtr 45 **Parking** 40
Notes LB Closed mid Dec & Jan

See advert on page 535

CUMBERNAULD
North Lanarkshire

Map 21 NS77

The Westerwood Hotel & Golf Resort

QHOTELS
INSPIRED
BY YOU

★★★★ 79% 🌸 HOTEL

tel: 01236 457171 **1 St Andrews Dr, Westerwood G68 0EW**
email: westerwood@qhotels.co.uk **web:** www.qhotels.co.uk
dir: M80 junct 6, follow signs for hotel

This stylish, contemporary hotel enjoys an elevated position within 400 acres at the foot of the Campsie Hills. Accommodation is provided in spacious, bright bedrooms, many with super bathrooms, and day rooms include sumptuous lounges and an airy restaurant; extensive golf, fitness and conference facilities are available. QHotels is the AA Hotel Group of the Year 2014-15.

Rooms 148 (16 fmly) (49 GF) **Facilities** Spa STV WiFi 🐾 🏌 ♨ 18 ⛳ Putt green Gym Beauty salon Relaxation room Sauna Steam room Xmas New Year **Conf** Class 120 Board 60 Thtr 400 **Services** Lift **Parking** 250 **Notes** Civ Wed 350

D

Premier Inn Glasgow (Cumbernauld)

BUDGET HOTEL

tel: 0871 527 8424 **4 South Muirhead Rd G67 1AX**
web: www.premierinn.com
dir: From A80, A8011 follow Cumbernauld & town centre signs. Hotel opposite Asda & McDonalds

High quality, budget accommodation ideal for both families and business travellers. Spacious, en suite bedrooms feature tea and coffee making facilities, and Freeview TV in most hotels. Internet access and WiFi are available for a small fee. The adjacent family restaurant features a wide and varied menu. See also the Hotel Groups pages.

Rooms 37

DALKEITH
Midlothian   Map 21 NT36

Premier Inn Edinburgh (Dalkeith)

BUDGET HOTEL

tel: 0871 527 9290 **Melville Dykes Rd EH18 1AN**
web: www.premierinn.com
dir: Exit A720 at Sheriffhall rdbt onto A7 signed Galashiels/Harwick/Carlisle. At 2nd rdbt take 3rd exit into Melville Dykes Rd (A768). Hotel on left

High quality, budget accommodation ideal for both families and business travellers. Spacious, en suite bedrooms feature tea and coffee making facilities, and Freeview TV in most hotels. Internet access and WiFi are available for a small fee. The adjacent family restaurant features a wide and varied menu. See also the Hotel Groups pages.

Rooms 40

DORNOCH
Highland   Map 23 NH78

Dornoch Castle Hotel

 ★★★ 75% 🏵 HOTEL

tel: 01862 810216 **Castle St IV25 3SD**
email: enquiries@dornochcastlehotel.com **web:** www.dornochcastlehotel.com
dir: 2m N of Dornoch Bridge on A9, turn right to Dornoch. Hotel in village centre

Situated opposite the cathedral, this fully restored ancient castle has become a popular wedding venue. Within the original castle are some splendid themed bedrooms, and elsewhere the more modern bedrooms have all of the expected facilities. There is a character bar and a delightful conservatory restaurant overlooking the garden.

Rooms 23 (3 fmly) (4 GF) � **S** £63-£73; **D** £99-£250 (incl. bkfst)* **Facilities** FTV WiFi New Year **Conf** Class 40 Board 30 Thtr 60 **Parking** 16 **Notes** LB ⊗ Closed 24-26 Dec & 2nd wk Jan

DRYMEN
Stirling   Map 20 NS48

Winnock Hotel

★★★ 74% HOTEL

tel: 01360 660245 **The Square G63 0BL**
email: info@winnockhotel.com **web:** www.winnockhotel.com
dir: From S: M74 onto M8 junct 16b through Glasgow. Follow A809 to Aberfoyle

Occupying a prominent position overlooking the village green, this popular hotel offers well-equipped bedrooms of various sizes and styles. The public rooms include a bar, a lounge and an attractive formal dining room that serves dishes of good, locally sourced food.

Rooms 73 (18 fmly) (19 GF) 🌙 **Facilities** FTV WiFi 🐾 Xmas New Year **Conf** Class 60 Board 70 Thtr 140 **Parking** 60 **Notes** ⊗ Civ Wed 150

DUMBARTON
East Dunbartonshire   Map 20 NS37

Premier Inn Dumbarton

BUDGET HOTEL

tel: 0871 527 9274 **Lomondgate Dr G82 2QU**
web: www.premierinn.com
dir: From Glasgow follow A82 towards Crainlarich, right at Lomondgate rdbt onto A813, hotel on right. From N: A82 towards Glasgow, left at Lomondgate rdbt onto A813, hotel on right

High quality, budget accommodation ideal for both families and business travellers. Spacious, en suite bedrooms feature tea and coffee making facilities, and Freeview TV in most hotels. Internet access and WiFi are available for a small fee. The adjacent family restaurant features a wide and varied menu. See also the Hotel Groups pages.

Rooms 60

DUMFRIES
Dumfries & Galloway   Map 21 NX97

Cairndale Hotel & Leisure Club

★★★ 81% HOTEL

tel: 01387 254111 **English St DG1 2DF**
email: sales@cairndalehotel.co.uk **web:** www.cairndalehotel.co.uk
dir: From S on M6 take A75 to Dumfries, left at 1st rdbt, cross rail bridge to lights, hotel 1st building on left

Within walking distance of the town centre, this hotel provides a wide range of amenities, including leisure facilities and an impressive conference and entertainment centre. Bedrooms range from stylish suites to cosy singles. There's a choice of eating options in the evening. The Reivers Restaurant is smartly modern with food to match.

Rooms 91 (22 fmly) (5 GF) 🌙 **Facilities** WiFi 🛝 supervised Gym Steam room Sauna Beauty treatment room ♬ Xmas New Year **Conf** Class 150 Board 50 Thtr 300 **Services** Lift **Parking** 100 **Notes** Civ Wed 300

DUMFRIES *continued*

BEST WESTERN Station Hotel

★★★ 80% HOTEL

tel: 01387 254316 **49 Lovers Walk DG1 1LT**
email: info@stationhotel.co.uk **web:** www.stationhoteldumfries.co.uk
dir: A75, follow signs to town centre, hotel opposite railway station

This friendly Victorian hotel offers stylish, well-equipped bedrooms that feature satellite TVs and free WiFi; three rooms have four-poster beds and spa baths. The Courtyard restaurant creates an informal atmosphere where guests can enjoy a popular range of dishes at dinner; in addition, good-value meals are served at lunchtime in either the lounge bar or on the patio in warmer weather. There is a delightful small garden to relax in.

Rooms 32 ✆ **S** £60-£70; **D** £80-£103 (incl. bkfst) **Facilities** FTV WiFi ⮧ Use of local gym **Conf** Class 35 Board 30 Thtr 80 Del from £103 to £135 **Services** Lift **Parking** 34 **Notes** LB ⊗ Closed 26 Dec & 2 Jan RS 25 Dec & 1 Jan Civ Wed 50

Premier Inn Dumfries

BUDGET HOTEL

tel: 0871 527 8316 **Annan Rd, Collin DG1 3JX**
web: www.premierinn.com
dir: At rdbt junct of Euroroute bypass (A75) & A780

High quality, budget accommodation ideal for both families and business travellers. Spacious, en suite bedrooms feature tea and coffee making facilities, and Freeview TV in most hotels. Internet access and WiFi are available for a small fee. The adjacent family restaurant features a wide and varied menu. See also the Hotel Groups pages.

Rooms 40

DUNDEE	Map 21 NO43
City of Dundee	

Malmaison Dundee

★★★★ 79% ◉ HOTEL

tel: 0844 693 0661 ◳ 01382 221422 **44 Whitehall Crescent DD1 4AY**
web: www.malmaison.com

This iconic building has been delightfully restored, and with its gold top, it shines as a beacon of style and quality. Lovingly restored, the public areas are stylish and plush, the staircase is very notable for its ironwork, and the restaurant for its views. Bedrooms are very well appointed and the hotel has a number of meeting rooms available. Cuisine is a feature and a range of menu options are available.

Rooms 91 **S** £79-£139; **D** £89-£149 (incl. bkfst)* **Facilities** FTV WiFi **Conf** Thtr 278

DoubleTree by Hilton Dundee

★★★★ 76% ◉ HOTEL

tel: 01382 641122 **Kingsway West DD2 5JT**
email: reception@doubletreedundee.co.uk **web:** www.doubletree.com
dir: From A90 (Kingsway) at rdbt junct with A85, follow hotel signs

Well located off Kingsway West with ample parking, this hotel offers contemporary bedrooms that are equipped with many thoughtful extras. The restaurant overlooks the gardens which are a feature at this hotel. A good leisure club includes a gym, steam room and sauna. The hotel is a popular wedding venue.

Rooms 95 (11 fmly) (45 GF) ✆ **Facilities** STV FTV WiFi ⓢ supervised Gym Sauna Steam room Xmas New Year **Conf** Class 50 Board 45 Thtr 100 **Parking** 140 **Notes** ⊗ Civ Wed 100

Apex City Quay Hotel & Spa

★★★★ 76% HOTEL

tel: 0845 365 0000 & 01382 202404 **1 West Victoria Dock Rd DD1 3JP**
email: dundee.reservations@apexhotels.co.uk **web:** www.apexhotels.co.uk
dir: A85/Riverside Drive to Discovery Quay. Exit rdbt for City Quay

This stylish, purpose-built hotel occupies an enviable position at the heart of Dundee's regenerated quayside. Bedrooms, including a number of smart suites, feature the very latest in design. Warm hospitality and professional service are an integral part of the hotel's appeal. Public areas are open-plan with panoramic windows and contemporary dining options. The luxurious Yu Spa completes the package.

Rooms 151 (17 fmly) ✆ **S** £90-£280; **Facilities** Spa FTV WiFi ⮧ HL ⓢ Gym Steam room Sauna Xmas New Year **Conf** Class 180 Board 120 Thtr 375 Del from £135 to £305 **Services** Lift **Parking** 150 **Notes** LB ⊗ RS 11 Jul-2 Aug Civ Wed 300

Premier Inn Dundee Centre

BUDGET HOTEL

tel: 0871 527 8320 **Discovery Quay, Riverside Dr DD1 4XA**
web: www.premierinn.com
dir: Follow signs for Discovery Quay, hotel on waterfront

High quality, budget accommodation ideal for both families and business travellers. Spacious, en suite bedrooms feature tea and coffee making facilities, and Freeview TV in most hotels. Internet access and WiFi are available for a small fee. The adjacent family restaurant features a wide and varied menu. See also the Hotel Groups pages.

Rooms 40

Premier Inn Dundee East

BUDGET HOTEL

tel: 0871 527 8322 **115-117 Lawers Dr, Panmurefield Village, Broughty Ferry DD5 3UP**
web: www.premierinn.com
dir: From N: A92 (Dundee & Arbroath). Hotel 1.5m after Sainsbury's. From S: A90. At end of dual carriageway follow Dundee to Arbroath signs

Rooms 60

Premier Inn Dundee (Monifieth)

BUDGET HOTEL

tel: 0871 527 8318 **Ethiebeaton Park, Arbroath Rd, Monifieth DD5 4HB**
web: www.premierinn.com
dir: From A90 (Kingsway Rd) follow Carnoustie/Arbroath (A92) signs

Rooms 40

Premier Inn Dundee North

BUDGET HOTEL

tel: 0871 527 8324 **Camperdown Leisure Park, Dayton Dr, Kingsway DD2 3SQ**
web: www.premierinn.com
dir: 2m N of city centre on A90 at junct with A923, adjacent to cinema. At entrance to Camperdown Country Park

Rooms 78

E

Premier Inn Dundee West

BUDGET HOTEL

tel: 0871 527 8326 **Kingsway West DD2 5JU**
web: www.premierinn.com
dir: On A90 towards Aberdeen adjacent to Technology Park rdbt

Rooms 64

DUNFERMLINE
Fife
Map 21 NT08

King Malcolm Hotel

★★★ 73% HOTEL

tel: 01383 722611 **Queensferry Rd KY11 8DS**
email: info@kingmalcolm-hotel-dunfermline.com **web:** www.peelhotels.co.uk
dir: On A823, S of town

Located to the south of the city, this purpose-built hotel remains popular with business clientele and is convenient for access to both Edinburgh and Fife. Public rooms include a smart foyer lounge and a conservatory bar, as well as a restaurant. Bedrooms, although not large, are well laid out and well equipped.

Rooms 48 (2 fmly) (24 GF) **Facilities** STV WiFi 🎵 Xmas New Year **Conf** Class 60 Board 50 Thtr 150 **Parking** 60 **Notes** Civ Wed 120

Premier Inn Dunfermline

BUDGET HOTEL

tel: 0871 527 8328 **4-12 Whimbrel Place, Fife Leisure Park KY11 8EX**
web: www.premierinn.com
dir: M90 junct 3 (Forth Road Bridge exit) 1st left at lights signed Duloch Park. 1st left into Fife Leisure Park

High quality, budget accommodation ideal for both families and business travellers. Spacious, en suite bedrooms feature tea and coffee making facilities, and Freeview TV in most hotels. Internet access and WiFi are available for a small fee. The adjacent family restaurant features a wide and varied menu. See also the Hotel Groups pages.

Rooms 40

DUNOON
Argyll & Bute
Map 20 NS17

Selborne Hotel

★★ 76% HOTEL

tel: 01369 702761 **Clyde St, West Bay PA23 7HU**
email: selborne.dunoon@alfatravel.co.uk **web:** www.leisureplex.co.uk
dir: From Caledonian MacBrayne pier. Past castle, left into Jane St, right into Clyde St. Ferry crossing to Dunoon via Greenock

This holiday hotel is situated overlooking the West Bay and provides unrestricted views of the Clyde Estuary towards the Isles of Cumbrae. Tour groups are especially well catered for in this good-value establishment, which offers entertainment most nights. Bedrooms are comfortable and many have sea views.

Rooms 98 (6 fmly) (14 GF) 📶 🛎 **S** £36-£52; **D** £56-£88 (incl. bkfst)* **Facilities** FTV WiFi HL Pool table Table tennis 🎵 Xmas New Year **Services** Lift **Parking** 30 **Notes** LB ⊗ Closed Dec-Feb (ex Xmas) RS Nov & Mar

---

EAST KILBRIDE
South Lanarkshire
Map 20 NS65

Macdonald Crutherland House

★★★★ 75% ⬤⬤ HOTEL

tel: 0844 879 9039 **Strathaven Rd G75 0QZ**
email: crutherland@macdonald-hotels.co.uk
web: www.macdonaldhotels.co.uk/crutherland
dir: Follow A726 signed Strathaven, straight over Torrance rdbt, hotel on left after 250yds

This mansion is set in 37 acres of landscaped grounds two miles from the town centre. Behind its Georgian façade is a very relaxing hotel with elegant public areas plus extensive banqueting and leisure facilities. The bedrooms are spacious and comfortable. Staff provide good levels of attention and enjoyable meals are served in the restaurant.

Rooms 75 (16 fmly) (16 GF) **Facilities** Spa STV WiFi 🕹 Gym Sauna Steam room Xmas New Year **Conf** Class 100 Board 50 Thtr 500 **Services** Lift **Parking** 200 **Notes** ⊗ Civ Wed 300

Premier Inn Glasgow East Kilbride

BUDGET HOTEL

tel: 0871 527 8446 **5 Lee's Burn Court, Nerston G74 3XB**
web: www.premierinn.com
dir: M74 junct 5, follow East Kilbride/A725 signs. Into right lane, follow Glasgow/A749 signs. At lights left onto A749 signed East Kilbride Town Centre (A725). Take slip road to Lee's Burn Court

High quality, budget accommodation ideal for both families and business travellers. Spacious, en suite bedrooms feature tea and coffee making facilities, and Freeview TV in most hotels. Internet access and WiFi are available for a small fee. The adjacent family restaurant features a wide and varied menu. See also the Hotel Groups pages.

Rooms 44

Premier Inn Glasgow East Kilbride Central

BUDGET HOTEL

tel: 0871 527 8450 **Brunel Way, The Murray G75 0LD**
web: www.premierinn.com
dir: M74 junct 5, follow East Kilbride A725 signs, then Paisley A726 signs, left at Murray Rdbt, left into Brunel Way

Rooms 40

Premier Inn Glasgow East Kilbride (Peel Park)

BUDGET HOTEL

tel: 0871 527 8448 **Eaglesham Rd G75 8LW**
web: www.premierinn.com
dir: 8m from M74 junct 5 on A726 at rdbt of B764

Rooms 42

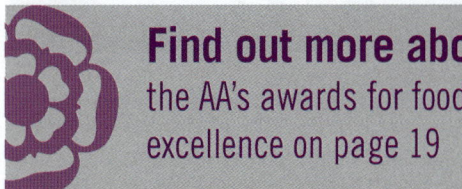

Find out more about the AA's awards for food excellence on page 19

EAST LINTON
East Lothian — Map 21 NT67

The Linton

 RESTAURANT WITH ROOMS

tel: 01620 860202 **3 Bridgend EH40 3AF**
email: infolinton@aol.com **web:** www.thelintonhotel.co.uk
dir: From A1, follow signs for East Linton, 3m

The Linton is located in a quiet conservation village within easy distance of Edinburgh, the East Lothian coast and numerous golf courses. Award-winning food promotes local suppliers with a menu that has something for everybody. The pub serves real ales and is warm and welcoming. Bedrooms are individually appointed with many modern useful extras provided as standard. The garden to the rear is a real suntrap with just the chime of the church clock to disturb the peace.

Rooms 7 (2 fmly)

EDDLESTON
Scottish Borders — Map 21 NT24

The Horseshoe Restaurant with Rooms

 RESTAURANT WITH ROOMS

tel: 01721 730225 📠 01721 730268 **EH45 8QP**
email: reservations@horseshoeinn.co.uk **web:** www.horseshoeinn.co.uk
dir: A703, 5m N of Peebles

The Horseshoe is five miles north of Peebles and only 18 miles south of Edinburgh. Originally a blacksmith's shop, it has a very good reputation for its delightful atmosphere and excellent cuisine. There are eight luxuriously appointed and individually designed bedrooms. Please note children are welcome but dinner is not served to under fives except in private dining room.

Rooms 8 (1 fmly)

EDINBURGH
City of Edinburgh — Map 21 NT27

The Balmoral

★★★★★  HOTEL

tel: 0131 556 2414 **1 Princes St EH2 2EQ**
email: reservations.balmoral@roccofortehotels.com **web:** www.roccofortehotels.com
dir: Follow city centre signs. Hotel at E end of Princes St, adjacent to Waverley Station

This elegant hotel enjoys a prestigious address at the top of Princes Street, with fine views over the city and the castle. Bedrooms and suites are stylishly furnished and decorated, all boasting a thoughtful range of extras and impressive marble bathrooms. Hotel amenities include a Roman-style health spa, extensive function facilities, a choice of bars and two very different dining options - Number One offers inspired fine dining whilst Hadrians is a bustling, informal brasserie.

Rooms 188 (22 fmly) (15 smoking) **Facilities** Spa STV WiFi ▷ ⓧ Gym ♫ Xmas New Year **Conf** Class 180 Board 60 Thtr 350 **Services** Lift Air con **Parking** 100 **Notes** ⊗ Civ Wed 120

Prestonfield

★★★★★ ◉◉ TOWN HOUSE HOTEL

tel: 0131 225 7800 **Priestfield Rd EH16 5UT**
email: reservations@prestonfield.com **web:** www.prestonfield.com
dir: A7 towards Cameron Toll. 200mtrs beyond Royal Commonwealth Pool, into Priestfield Rd

This centuries-old landmark has been lovingly restored and enhanced to provide deeply comfortable and dramatically furnished bedrooms. The building demands to be explored: from the tapestry lounge and the whisky room to the restaurant, where the walls are adorned with pictures of former owners. Facilities and services are up-to-the-minute, and carefully prepared meals are served in the award-winning Rhubarb restaurant.

Rooms 23 (6 GF) 🐾 **D** £295-£475 (incl. bkfst)* **Facilities** STV FTV WiFi ▷ ⚘ 18 Putt green ⚑ Xmas New Year **Conf** Class 500 Board 40 Thtr 700 **Services** Lift **Parking** 250 **Notes** Civ Wed 350

Waldorf Astoria Edinburgh - The Caledonian

★★★★★ 87% ◉◉◉ HOTEL

tel: 0131 222 8888 **Princes St EH1 2AB**
web: www.thecaledonianedinburgh.com
dir: Situated on east end of Princess St, on Rutland St & Lothian Rd

Known locally as "the Caley", the Caledonian was built in the age of steam and has recently benefitted from a £24 million transformation without losing any of the charm and character that has made it famous. Spacious bedrooms and en suites offer comfort and luxury, and there is a choice of award-wining restaurants and wonderful public areas.

Rooms 241 (10 fmly) 🐾 **S** £175-£399; **D** £175-£399* **Facilities** Spa STV WiFi ▷ HL ⓧ Gym Sauna Steam room Xmas New Year **Conf** Class 120 Board 80 Thtr 300 Del from £200 to £350* **Services** Lift Air con **Parking** 39 **Notes** LB ⊗ Civ Wed 300

E

Hotel Missoni Edinburgh

★★★★★ 85%  HOTEL

tel: 0131 220 6666 **1 George IV Bridge EH1 1AD**
email: info.edinburgh@hotelmissoni.com **web:** www.hotelmissoni.com
dir: At corner of Royal Mile & George IV Bridge

As we go to print we have been advised that this establishment is now called Q & V Royal Mile Hotel. Located on the corner of the George IV Bridge and the Royal Mile in the heart of the old town, this hotel's design is strikingly different. Bold use of black and white and vivid colours together with strong patterns creates a stunning impression. Stylish bedrooms, some with great city views, have iPod/AV hook-up, WiFi, coffee machines, and bathrooms with walk-in showers as standard. The buzzing cocktail bar and Cucina Missoni, for modern Italian cuisine, attract locals and residents alike.

Rooms 136 **Facilities** Spa STV FTV WiFi ⬠ Gym Xmas New Year **Conf** Class 24 Board 24 Thtr 63 **Services** Lift Air con **Parking** 13

Sheraton Grand Hotel & Spa

★★★★★ 84% HOTEL

tel: 0131 229 9131 **1 Festival Square EH3 9SR**
email: grandedinburgh@sheraton.com **web:** www.sheraton.com/grandedinburgh
dir: Follow City Centre signs (A8). Through Shandwick Place, right at lights into Lothian Rd. Right at next lights. Hotel on left at next lights

This modern hotel boasts one of the best spas in Scotland - the external top floor hydro pool is definitely worth a look, while the thermal suite provides a unique venue for serious relaxation. The spacious bedrooms are available in a variety of styles, and the suites prove very popular. There is a wide range of dishes available in the One Square Bar and Restaurant.

Rooms 269 ⬠ **D** £155-£595* **Facilities** Spa STV FTV WiFi ⬠ ⬠ ⬠ Gym Indoor/outdoor hydropool Kinesis studio Thermal suite Fitness studio ⬠ Xmas New Year **Conf** Class 350 Board 120 Thtr 500 Del from £250 to £350* **Services** Lift Air con **Parking** 122 **Notes** ⬠ Civ Wed 485

The Howard

★★★★★ 83%  TOWN HOUSE HOTEL

tel: 0131 537 3500 **34 Great King St EH3 6QH**
email: reserve@thehoward.com **web:** www.thehoward.com
dir: E on Queen St, 2nd left, Dundas St. Through 3 lights, right, hotel on left

Quietly elegant and splendidly luxurious, The Howard provides an intimate and high quality experience for the discerning traveller. It comprises three linked Georgian houses and is situated just a short walk from Princes Street. The sumptuous bedrooms and suites, in a variety of styles, have well-equipped bathrooms and a host of thoughtful touches. Ornate chandeliers and lavish drapes adorn the drawing room, while the Atholl Dining Room contains unique hand-painted murals dating from the 19th century.

Rooms 18 (3 fmly) (2 GF) ⬠ **Facilities** STV FTV WiFi ⬠ HL Xmas New Year **Conf** Class 28 Board 28 Thtr 28 **Services** Lift **Parking** 12 **Notes** ⬠ Civ Wed 28

Norton House Hotel & Spa

HANDPICKED HOTELS
BUILT FOR PLEASURE

★★★★ ⬠⬠⬠ HOTEL

tel: 0131 333 1275 **Ingliston EH28 8LX**
email: nortonhouse@handpicked.co.uk **web:** www.handpickedhotels.co.uk/nortonhouse
dir: Off A8, 5m W of city centre

This extended Victorian mansion, set in 55 acres of parkland, is peacefully situated just outside the city and is convenient for the airport. The original building dates from 1840, and was bought nearly 40 years later by John Usher of the Scottish brewing family. Today both the contemporary bedrooms and the very spacious, traditional ones have an impressive range of accessories including large flat-screen satellite TVs, DVD/CD players and free high speed internet access. Executive rooms have more facilities, of course, including MP3 connection and 'tlevision' TVs at the end of the baths. Public areas take in a choice of lounges as well as dining options, with a popular brasserie and the intimate Ushers Restaurant. There is a health club, and a spa which offers a long list of treatments.

Rooms 83 (10 fmly) (20 GF) ⬠ **S** £106-£219; **D** £116-£229 (incl. bkfst)*
Facilities Spa STV WiFi ⬠ HL ⬠ Gym Archery Laser Clay shooting Quad biking Xmas New Year **Conf** Class 100 Board 60 Thtr 300 Del from £134 to £229* **Services** Lift **Parking** 200 **Notes** LB ⬠ Civ Wed 140

Dalmahoy, A Marriott Hotel & Country Club

★★★★ 81% ⬠ HOTEL

tel: 0131 333 1845 **Kirknewton EH27 8EB**
email: mhrs.edigs.frontdesk@marriotthotels.com **web:** www.marriottdalmahoy.co.uk
dir: A720 (Edinburgh City Bypass) onto A71 towards Livingston, hotel on left in 2m

The rolling Pentland Hills and beautifully kept parkland provide a stunning setting for this imposing Georgian mansion. With two championship golf courses and a health and beauty club, there is plenty here to occupy guests. Bedrooms are spacious and most have fine views, while public rooms offer a choice of formal and informal drinking and dining options.

Rooms 215 (172 annexe) (59 fmly) (6 smoking) ⬠ **Facilities** Spa STV WiFi ⬠ HL ⬠ ⬠ 36 ⬠ Putt green Gym Health & beauty treatments Steam room Dance studio Driving range Golf lessons Xmas New Year **Conf** Class 200 Board 120 Thtr 300 **Services** Lift Air con **Parking** 350 **Notes** ⬠ Civ Wed 250

EDINBURGH *continued*

Hotel du Vin Edinburgh

★★★★ 80% TOWN HOUSE HOTEL

tel: 0131 247 4900 **11 Bristo Place EH1 1EZ**
web: www.hotelduvin.com
dir: M8 junct 1, A720 (signed Kilmarnock/W Calder/Edinburgh W). Right at fork, follow A720 signs, merge onto A720. Take exit signed A703. At rdbt take A702/Biggar Rd. 3.5m. Right into Lauriston Pl which becomes Forrest Rd. Right at Bedlam Theatre. Hotel on right

This hotel offers very stylish and comfortable accommodation; all bedrooms display the Hotel du Vin trademark facilities - air conditioning, free WiFi, plasma TVs, monsoon showers and Egyptian cotton linen to name but a few. Public areas include a whisky snug, and a mezzanine bar that overlooks the brasserie where modern Scottish cuisine is served. For the wine connoisseur there's La Roche tasting room where wines from around the world can be appreciated.

Rooms 47  **S** £99-£750; **D** £99-£750* **Facilities** STV FTV WiFi ⌕ **Conf** Class 10 Board 26 Thtr 30 Del from £165 to £350* **Services** Lift Air con **Notes** Civ Wed 28

Apex International Hotel

★★★★ 79% HOTEL

tel: 0845 365 0000 & 0131 300 3456 **31/35 Grassmarket EH1 2HS**
email: edinburgh.reservations@apexhotels.co.uk **web:** www.apexhotels.co.uk
dir: Into Lothian Rd at west end of Princes St, 1st left into King Stables Rd, leads into Grassmarket

A sister to the Apex City Hotel close by, the International lies in a historic yet trendy square in the shadow of Edinburgh Castle. It has a versatile business and conference centre, and also Yu Time leisure and fitness facility with a stainless steel ozone pool. Bedrooms are contemporary in style and very well equipped. The fifth-floor restaurant boasts stunning views of the castle.

Rooms 169 (99 fmly)  **Facilities** FTV WiFi⎙ ⊛ Gym Tropicarium Xmas New Year **Conf** Class 80 Board 40 Thtr 200 **Services** Lift **Parking** 60 **Notes** ⊗ Civ Wed 200

George Hotel Edinburgh

★★★★ 79% HOTEL

tel: 0131 225 1251 **19-21 George St EH2 2PB**
email: enquiries.thegeorge@principal-hayley.com **web:** www.principal-hayley.com
dir: In city centre

A long-established hotel, the George enjoys a city centre location. The splendid public areas have many original features such as intricate plasterwork, a marble-floored foyer and chandeliers. The Tempus Bar offers menus that feature a wide range of dishes to suit most tastes. The elegant, modern bedrooms come in a mix of sizes and styles; the upper ones having fine city views.

Rooms 249 (20 fmly) (4 GF) **S** £109-£399; **D** £109-£399 **Facilities** STV WiFi⎙ HL Xmas New Year **Conf** Class 120 Board 50 Thtr 300 **Services** Lift **Notes** LB ⊗ Civ Wed 300

Apex City Hotel

★★★★ 78%  HOTEL

tel: 0845 365 0000 & 0131 243 3456 **61 Grassmarket EH1 2HJ**
email: edinburgh.reservations@apexhotels.co.uk **web:** www.apexhotels.co.uk
dir: Into Lothian Rd at west end of Princes St, 1st left into King Stables Rd. Leads into Grassmarket

This modern, stylish hotel lies in a historic yet trendy square dominated by Edinburgh Castle above. The design-led bedrooms are fresh and contemporary and each has artwork by Richard Demarco. Agua Bar and Restaurant is a smart open-plan area in dark wood and chrome that serves a range of meals and cocktails. Residents can use the spa at a sister hotel, Apex International, which is nearby.

Rooms 119 (6 fmly) **Facilities** FTV WiFi ⌕ Complimentary use of leisure facilities at Apex International Hotel Xmas **Conf** Class 30 Board 34 Thtr 70 **Services** Lift **Notes** ⊗ Civ Wed 60

Apex Waterloo Place Hotel

★★★★ 78%  HOTEL

tel: 0845 365 0000 & 0131 523 1819 **23-27 Waterloo Place EH1 3BH**
email: edinburgh.reservations@apexhotels.co.uk **web:** www.apexhotels.co.uk
dir: At E end of Princes St. Telephone for detailed directions

This stunning hotel provides a state-of-the-art experience with slick interior design. Bedrooms, many with city views, are well appointed for both the business and leisure guest; stunning duplex suites provide extra space, surround-sound TV systems and luxurious feature bathrooms. The restaurant provides an appealing menu both at dinner and breakfast. There is also a well-equipped fitness centre, indoor pool and treatment rooms. The hotel has direct, pedestrian access to Edinburgh's Waverley Station.

Rooms 186 (5 fmly) (15 GF) **Facilities** FTV WiFi ⌕ ⊛ Gym Sauna Steam rooms Xmas New Year **Conf** Class 70 Board 40 Thtr 150 **Services** Lift Air con **Notes** ⊗ Civ Wed 80

Crowne Plaza Edinbugh - The Roxburghe Hotel

★★★★ 78% HOTEL

tel: 0871 423 4942 **38 Charlotte Square EH2 4HQ**
email: info@theroxburghe.co.uk **web:** www.theroxburghe.com
dir: On corner of Charlotte Sq & George St

This long-established hotel lies in the heart of the city overlooking Charlotte Square Gardens. Public areas are inviting and include relaxing lounges, a choice of bars (in the evening) and an inner concourse that looks onto a small lawned area. Smart bedrooms come in both classic and contemporary styles. There is a secure underground car park.

Rooms 199 (3 fmly) **Facilities** Spa STV FTV WiFi ⊛ Gym Dance studio Sauna Steam room Xmas New Year **Conf** Class 160 Board 50 Thtr 300 **Services** Lift Air con **Parking** 20 **Notes** ⊗ Civ Wed 280

Novotel Edinburgh Park

★★★★ 78% HOTEL

tel: 0131 446 5600 **15 Lochside Av EH12 9DJ**
email: h6515@accor.com **web:** www.novotel.com
dir: Near Hermiston Gate shopping area

Located just off the city by-pass and within minutes of the airport, this modern hotel offers bedrooms that are spacious and comfortable. The public areas include the open-plan lobby, a bar and a restaurant offering diverse and informal dishes. A swimming pool and small gym are also available to guests.

Rooms 170 (130 fmly)  **Facilities** WiFi HL ⊛ **Conf** Class 60 Board 40 Thtr 150 **Services** Lift **Parking** 96 **Notes** Civ Wed 90

E

DoubleTree by Hilton Edinburgh City Centre

★★★★ 77% HOTEL

tel: 0131 221 5555 **34 Bread St EH3 9AF**
web: www.doubletree.com
dir: A71 to Haymarket Station. Straight on at junct & right on Torphichen St, left onto Morrison St, straight on to Bread St, hotel on right

Recently rebranded to DoubleTree by Hilton with a £4.2 million renovation, this hotel was originally built in 1892 as a Co-op, which once employed Sean Connery as a milkman. Bedrooms are spacious and cater well for the needs of the modern guest. Public areas are warm and welcoming, and are enhanced with black and white photographs. The SKYbar, Monboddo Bar and the Bread Street Brasserie offer comfortable and relaxed surroundings for drinks and meals. A number of bedrooms offer views onto Edinburgh Castle.

Rooms 138 (4 fmly) ⬥ **S** £59–£450; **D** £59–£450* **Facilities** FTV WiFi ⬥ Gym **Conf** Class 80 Board 30 Thtr 200 Del from £129 to £279* **Services** Lift Air con **Notes** LB ⊗ Civ Wed 200

Edinburgh Marriott Hotel

★★★★ 77% HOTEL

tel: 0131 334 9191 **111 Glasgow Rd EH12 8NF**
email: edinburgh@marriotthotels.com **web:** www.edinburghmarriott.co.uk
dir: M8 junct 1 for Gogar, at rdbt turn right for city centre, hotel on right

This smart, modern hotel is located on the city's western edge which is convenient for the bypass, airport, showground and business park. Public areas include an attractive marbled foyer, extensive conference facilities and a restaurant serving a range of international dishes. The air-conditioned bedrooms are spacious and equipped with a range of extras.

Rooms 245 (76 fmly) (64 GF) ⬥ **D** £85–£200 **Facilities** FTV WiFi ⬥ HL ⬥ Gym Steam room Sauna Beauty treatment room Xmas New Year **Conf** Class 120 Board 50 Thtr 250 Del from £130 to £200 **Services** Lift Air con **Parking** 300 **Notes** LB Civ Wed 80

Malmaison Edinburgh

★★★★ 76% ⊛ HOTEL

tel: 0844 693 0652 **One Tower Place EH6 7BZ**
email: edinburgh@malmaison.com **web:** www.malmaison.com
dir: A900 from city centre towards Leith, at end of Leith Walk, through 3 sets of lights, left into Tower St. Hotel on right at end of road

The trendy Port of Leith is home to this stylish Malmaison. Inside, bold contemporary designs create a striking effect. Bedrooms are comprehensively equipped with CD players, mini-bars and loads of individual touches. Ask for one of the stunning superior rooms for a really memorable stay. The smart brasserie and a café bar are popular with the local clientele.

Rooms 100 (18 fmly) ⬥ **D** £85–£199 (incl. bkfst)* **Facilities** STV FTV WiFi ⬥ Gym Xmas New Year **Conf** Class 32 Board 32 Thtr 80 Del from £140 to £185* **Services** Lift **Parking** 50 **Notes** LB Civ Wed 70

Crowne Plaza Edinburgh - Royal Terrace

★★★★ 76% HOTEL

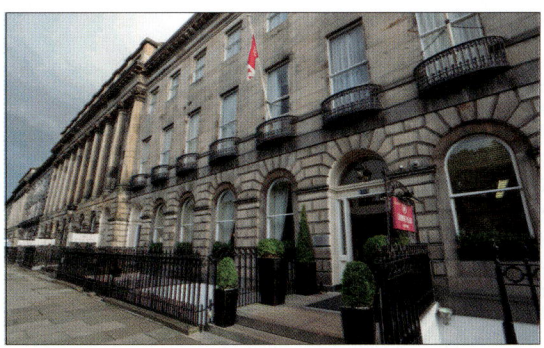

tel: 0131 557 3222 **18 Royal Ter EH7 5AQ**
email: sales@royalterracehotel.co.uk **web:** www.royalterracehotel.co.uk
dir: A8 to city centre, follow one-way system, left into Charlotte Sq. At end right into Queens St. Left at rdbt. At next island right into London Rd, right into Blenheim Place leading to Royal Terrace

Forming part of a quiet Georgian terrace in the heart of the city, this hotel offers bedrooms that successfully blend the historic architecture of the building with state-of-the-art facilities. Although most rooms afford lovely views, the top floor rooms provide excellent panoramas over the city to the Firth of Forth. The Club Lounge provides an exclusive space for Club Room guests. The hotel's leisure club has a swimming pool and steam room. Dinners are served in the Terrace Brasserie

Rooms 97 (13 fmly) (7 GF) **Facilities** WiFi ⬥ Gym Steam room Sauna Aromatherapy shower Xmas New Year **Conf** Class 40 Board 40 Thtr 100 **Services** Lift **Notes** ⊗ Civ Wed 80

Holiday Inn Edinburgh

★★★★ 76% HOTEL

tel: 0871 942 9026 **Corstorphine Rd EH12 6UA**
email: edinburghhi@ihg.com **web:** www.hiedinburghhotel.co.uk
dir: On A8, adjacent to Edinburgh Zoo

A modern hotel situated three miles west of Edinburgh and near Edinburgh Business Park. The hotel enjoys panoramic views of the Pentland Hills and makes a good base for visiting the attractions of the city. Bedrooms include family and executive rooms. The eating options are Traders Restaurant or Sampans Oriental Restaurant, as well as a café and bar. The Spirit Health and Fitness Club has a gym, swimming pool, sauna, spa and beauty treatments. There is also a conference centre.

Rooms 303 (76 fmly) **Facilities** Spa STV FTV WiFi ⬥ HL ⬥ supervised Gym New Year **Conf** Class 60 Board 45 Thtr 120 Del from £125 to £185* **Services** Lift Air con **Parking** 60 **Notes** ⊗ Civ Wed 80

EDINBURGH *continued*

Macdonald Holyrood Hotel

★★★★ 76% HOTEL

tel: 0870 1942106 **Holyrood Rd EH8 8AU**
email: general.holyrood@macdonald-hotels.co.uk
web: www.macdonaldhotels.co.uk/holyrood
dir: Parallel to Royal Mile, near Holyrood Palace & Dynamic Earth

Situated just a short walk from Holyrood Palace, this impressive hotel lies next to the Scottish Parliament building. Air-conditioned bedrooms are comfortably furnished, whilst the Club floor boasts a private lounge. Full business services complement the extensive conference suites.

Rooms 156 (16 fmly) (13 GF) **Facilities** Spa STV FTV WiFi ♦ ☜ Gym Sauna Steam room Library ♫ Xmas New Year **Conf** Class 100 Board 80 Thtr 200 **Services** Lift Air con **Parking** 38 **Notes** Civ Wed 100

Novotel Edinburgh Centre

★★★★ 75% HOTEL

tel: 0131 656 3500 **Lauriston Place, Lady Lawson St EH3 9DE**
email: H3271@accor.com **web:** www.novotel.com
dir: From Edinburgh Castle right onto George IV Bridge from Royal Mile. Follow to junct, then right into Lauriston Place. Hotel 700mtrs on right

This modern hotel is located in the centre of the city, close to Edinburgh Castle. Smart and stylish public areas include a cosmopolitan bar, brasserie-style restaurant and indoor leisure facilities. The air-conditioned bedrooms feature a comprehensive range of extras and bathrooms with baths and separate shower cabinets.

Rooms 180 (146 fmly) ☜ **Facilities** STV WiFi ♦ HL ☜ Gym Sauna Steam room Xmas New Year **Conf** Class 50 Board 32 Thtr 80 **Services** Lift Air con **Parking** 15

The Carlton Hotel

★★★★ 73% HOTEL

tel: 0131 472 3000 **North Bridge EH1 1SD**
email: carlton@pumahotels.co.uk **web:** www.pumahotels.co.uk
dir: On North Bridge which links Princes St to The Royal Mile

The Carlton occupies a city centre location just off the Royal Mile. Inside, it is modern and stylish in design, with an impressive open-plan reception/lobby, spacious first-floor lounge, bar and restaurant, plus a basement leisure club. Bedrooms, many air-conditioned, are generally spacious, with an excellent range of accessories.

Rooms 189 (20 fmly) **Facilities** Spa STV WiFi HL ☜ supervised Gym Squash Dance studio Exercise classes Xmas New Year **Conf** Class 110 Board 60 Thtr 220 **Services** Lift **Notes** Civ Wed 160

Apex European Hotel

★★★ 85% HOTEL

tel: 0845 365 0000 & 0131 474 3456 **90 Haymarket Ter EH12 5LQ**
email: edinburgh.reservations@apexhotels.co.uk **web:** www.apexhotels.co.uk
dir: A8 to city centre, 100mtrs from Haymarket Railway Station

Lying just west of the city centre, close to Haymarket Station and handy for the Conference Centre, this modern hotel is popular with business travellers. Smart, stylish bedrooms offer an excellent range of facilities and have been designed with work requirements in mind. Public areas include Metro, an informal bistro. Service is friendly and pro-active.

Rooms 66 (3 GF) ☜ **Facilities** FTV WiFi ♦ New Year **Conf** Class 30 Board 36 Thtr 80 **Services** Lift **Parking** 10 **Notes** ⊗ Closed 24-27 Dec & 3-10 Jan

Dalhousie Castle and Aqueous Spa

★★★ 82% ◉◉ HOTEL

tel: 01875 820153 **Bonnyrigg EH19 3JB**
email: info@dalhousiecastle.co.uk **web:** www.dalhousiecastle.co.uk
dir: A7 S from Edinburgh through Lasswade/Newtongrange, right at Shell Garage (B704), hotel 0.5m from junct

A popular wedding venue, this imposing medieval castle sits amid lawns and parkland and even has a falconry. Bedrooms offer a mix of styles and sizes, including richly decorated themed rooms named after various historical figures. The Dungeon restaurant provides an atmospheric setting for dinner, and the less formal Orangery serves food all day. The spa offers many relaxing and therapeutic treatments and hydro facilities.

Rooms 35 (6 annexe) (3 fmly) ☜ **S** £83-£285; **D** £98-£300 (incl. bkfst)*
Facilities Spa FTV WiFi Fishing Falconry Clay pigeon shooting Archery Xmas New Year **Conf** Class 60 Board 45 Thtr 120 Del from £180 to £360* **Parking** 110 **Notes** Civ Wed 100

BEST WESTERN Kings Manor

★★★ 82% HOTEL

tel: 0131 669 0444 & 468 8003 **100 Milton Road East EH15 2NP**
email: reservations@kingsmanor.com **web:** www.kingsmanor.com
dir: A720 E to Old Craighall junct, left into city, right at A1/A199 junct, hotel 400mtrs on right

Lying on the eastern side of the city and convenient for the by-pass, this hotel is popular with business guests, tour groups and for conferences. It boasts a fine leisure complex and a bright modern bistro, which complements the quality, creative cooking in the main restaurant.

Rooms 95 (8 fmly) (13 GF) ☜ **Facilities** Spa STV FTV WiFi ♦ ☜ ⌣ Gym Health & beauty salon Steam room Sauna **Conf** Class 80 Board 60 Thtr 160 **Services** Lift **Parking** 130 **Notes** Civ Wed 100

Holiday Inn Edinburgh West

★★★ 80% HOTEL

tel: 0871 942 9025 **107 Queensferry Rd EH4 3HL**
email: reservations-edinburghcitywest@ihg.com **web:** www.holidayinn.co.uk
dir: On A90 approx 1m from city centre

Situated on the north-west side of the city, close to Murrayfield Stadium and just five miles from the airport, this purpose-built hotel has a bright contemporary look. The colourful, modern bedrooms are well equipped and three specifications are available - with two double beds; with a double bed and sofa; or with a double bed and separate lounge. Some have great views of the city too. There is limited free parking.

Rooms 101 (65 fmly) **D** £50-£260* **Facilities** STV FTV WiFi ♦ HL New Year **Conf** Class 60 Board 50 Thtr 140 Del from £80 to £180* **Services** Lift Air con **Parking** 80 **Notes** LB ⊗ Civ Wed 120

E

Mercure Edinburgh City - Princes Street Hotel

★★★ 78% HOTEL

tel: 0844 815 9017 **Princes St EH2 2DG**
email: info@mercureedinburgh.co.uk **web:** www.mercureedinburgh.co.uk
dir: Opposite Scott Monument & Waverley Station. At east end of Princes St

With an enviable location in the heart of Princes Street, offering excellent views of the castle you really cannot be any more central. The front-facing bedrooms are more spacious; some benefit from a balcony but all are well appointed. The large popular restaurant benefits from the wonderful views.

Rooms 158 **Facilities** WiFi **Conf** Class 40 Board 27 Thtr 70

Old Waverley Hotel

★★★ 78% HOTEL

tel: 0131 556 4648 **43 Princes St EH2 2BY**
email: reservations@oldwaverley.co.uk **web:** www.oldwaverley.co.uk
dir: In city centre, opposite Scott Monument, Waverley Station & Jenners

Occupying a commanding position opposite Sir Walter Scott's famous monument on Princes Street, this hotel lies right in the heart of the city close to the station. The comfortable public rooms are all on first-floor level and along with front-facing bedrooms enjoy the fine views.

Rooms 85 (5 fmly) **Facilities** WiFi ▷ Leisure facilities at sister hotel **Services** Lift **Notes** ⊛

Ibis Edinburgh Centre Royal Mile

BUDGET HOTEL

tel: 0131 240 7000 **6 Hunter Square, off The Royal Mile EH1 1QW**
email: H2039@accor.com **web:** www.ibishotel.com
dir: M8/M9/A1 over North Bridge (A7) & High St, take 1st right off South Bridge, into Hunter Sq

Modern, budget hotel offering comfortable accommodation in bright and practical bedrooms. Breakfast is self-service and dinner is available in the restaurant. See also the Hotel Groups pages.

Rooms 99 (2 GF) ↻ **S** £45-£239; **D** £45-£239

Premier Inn Edinburgh Airport (Newbridge)

BUDGET HOTEL

tel: 0871 527 9284 **2A Kirkliston Rd, Newbridge EH28 8SL**
web: www.premierinn.com
dir: M9 junct 1, A89 signed Broxburn. At lights turn right, then 2nd right

High quality, budget accommodation ideal for both families and business travellers. Spacious, en suite bedrooms feature tea and coffee making facilities, and Freeview TV in most hotels. Internet access and WiFi are available for a small fee. The adjacent family restaurant features a wide and varied menu. See also the Hotel Groups pages.

Rooms 119

Premier Inn Edinburgh City Centre (Haymarket)

BUDGET HOTEL

tel: 0871 527 8368 **1 Morrison Link EH3 8DN**
web: www.premierinn.com
dir: Adjcent to Edinburgh International Conference Centre

Rooms 281

Premier Inn Edinburgh City Centre (Princess St)

BUDGET HOTEL

tel: 0871 527 9358 **122-123 Princess St EH2 4AD**
web: www.premierinn.com
dir: From Edinburgh bypass (A720) onto A702, take A700. NB Princes St is not accessible by car - it is advisable to park in Castle Terrace Car Park (EH1 2EW)

Rooms 97

Premier Inn Edinburgh City Lauriston Place

BUDGET HOTEL

tel: 0871 527 8366 **82 Lauriston Place, Lady Lawson St EH3 9DG**
web: www.premierinn.com
dir: A8 onto A702 (Lothian Rd). Left into Lauriston Place. Hotel on left

Rooms 112

Premier Inn Edinburgh East

BUDGET HOTEL

tel: 0871 527 8370 **228 Willowbrae Rd EH8 7NG**
web: www.premierinn.com
dir: M8 junct 1, A720 S for 12m, then A1. At Asda rdbt turn left. In 2m, hotel on left before Esso garage

Rooms 39

Premier Inn Edinburgh (Inveresk)

BUDGET HOTEL

tel: 0871 527 8358 **Carberry Rd, Inveresk, Musselburgh EH21 8PT**
web: www.premierinn.com
dir: From A1 follow Dalkeith (A6094) signs. At rdbt turn right, hotel 300yds on right

Rooms 40

Premier Inn Edinburgh (Leith)

BUDGET HOTEL

tel: 0871 527 8360 **51-53 Newhaven Place, Leith EH6 4TX**
web: www.premierinn.com
dir: From A1 follow coast road through Leith. Pass Ocean Terminal, straight ahead at mini-rdbt, 2nd exit signed Harry Ramsden's car park

Rooms 60

E

EDINBURGH *continued*

Premier Inn Edinburgh Park (The Gyle)

BUDGET HOTEL

tel: 0871 527 9336 **Edinburgh Park (Airport), 1 Lochside Court EH12 9FX**
web: www.premierinn.com
dir: M8 junct 1, A720 (city bypass). At Gogar rdbt 3rd exit follow South Gyle/station signs. Into right lane approaching Gyle rdbt, 3rd exit, follow Edinburgh Park train station signs into Lochside Cres. Straight on at 2 rdbts, 400yds. Hotel on left

Rooms 120

INSPECTORS' CHOICE

21212

 RESTAURANT WITH ROOMS

tel: 0131 523 1030 & 0845 222 1212 **3 Royal Ter EH7 5AB**
email: reservations@21212restaurant.co.uk **web:** www.21212restaurant.co.uk
dir: Calton Hill, city centre

A real jewel in Edinburgh's crown, this establishment takes its name from the number of choices at each course on the five-course dinner menu. Located on the prestigious Royal Terrace this is a light and airy, renovated Georgian town house stretching over four floors. The four individually designed bedrooms epitomise luxury living and the bathrooms certainly have the wow factor. At the heart of this restaurant with rooms is the creative, award-winning cooking of Paul Kitching. Service throughout is friendly and very attentive.

Rooms 4

INSPECTORS' CHOICE

The Witchery by the Castle

 RESTAURANT WITH ROOMS

tel: 0131 225 5613 📠 0131 220 4392 **Castlehill, The Royal Mile EH1 2NF**
email: mail@thewitchery.com **web:** www.thewitchery.com
dir: Top of Royal Mile at gates of Edinburgh Castle

Originally built in 1595, The Witchery by the Castle is situated in a historic building at the gates of Edinburgh Castle. The two luxurious and theatrically decorated suites, known as the Inner Sanctum and the Old Rectory are located above the restaurant and are reached via a winding stone staircase. Filled with antiques, opulently draped beds, large roll-top baths and a plethora of memorabilia, this ancient and exciting establishment is often described as one of the country's most romantic destinations.

Rooms 9 (5 annexe)

ELGIN
Moray

Map 23 NJ26

Mansion House Hotel

★★★ 81% HOTEL

tel: 01343 548811 **The Haugh IV30 1AW**
email: reception@mhelgin.co.uk **web:** www.mansionhousehotel.co.uk
dir: Exit A96 into Haugh Rd, then 1st left

Set in grounds by the River Lossie, this baronial mansion is popular with leisure and business guests as well as being a lovely wedding venue. Bedrooms are spacious and many have views of the river. Extensive public areas include a choice of restaurants, with a bistro that contrasts nicely with the classical main restaurant. There is an indoor pool and a beauty and hair salon.

Rooms 23 (6 fmly) (5 GF) 🐾 **S** £95-£124; **D** £135-£202 (incl. bkfst)* **Facilities** STV FTV WiFi ♨ 🏃 supervised Gym Hair studio Beauty treatment room New Year **Conf** Class 100 Board 20 Thtr 180 **Parking** 50 **Notes** LB ⊗ Civ Wed 160

Premier Inn Elgin

BUDGET HOTEL

tel: 0871 527 8372 **15 Linkwood Way IV30 1HY**
web: www.premierinn.com
dir: On A96, 1.5m E of city centre

High quality, budget accommodation ideal for both families and business travellers. Spacious, en suite bedrooms feature tea and coffee making facilities, and Freeview TV in most hotels. Internet access and WiFi are available for a small fee. The adjacent family restaurant features a wide and varied menu. See also the Hotel Groups pages.

Rooms 40

F

ERISKA
Argyll & Bute

Map 20 NM94

Isle of Eriska Hotel, Spa & Golf

★★★★★ ⚜⚜⚜ COUNTRY HOUSE HOTEL

tel: 01631 720371 **PA37 1SD**
email: office@eriska-hotel.co.uk **web:** www.eriska-hotel.co.uk
dir: Exit A85 at Connel, onto A828, 4m, follow hotel signs from N of Benderloch

Situated on its own private island with delightful beaches and walking trails, this hotel is in a tranquil setting, perfect for total relaxation. The spacious bedrooms are very comfortable and boast some fine antique pieces. Local seafood, meats and game feature prominently on the award-winning menu, as do vegetables and herbs grown in the hotel's kitchen garden. Leisure facilities include an indoor pool, gym and spa treatment rooms.

Rooms 23 (6 fmly) (2 GF) ✿ **S** £250-£350; **D** £360-£480 (incl. bkfst)* **Facilities** Spa FTV WiFi ↝ ⚑ supervised ⚓ 9 ⛳ Putt green Fishing 🏌 Gym Squash Sauna Steam room Skeet shooting Nature trails Indoor tennis Badminton Xmas New Year **Conf** Class 30 Board 30 Thtr 30 Del from £300 to £400* **Parking** 40 **Notes** LB Closed Jan Civ Wed 50

FALKIRK
Falkirk

Map 21 NS88

Premier Inn Falkirk Central

BUDGET HOTEL

tel: 0871 527 8388 **Main St, Camelon FK1 4DS**
web: www.premierinn.com
dir: From Falkirk A803 signed Glasgow. At mini-rdbt right, continue on A803. At Rosebank rdbt 2nd exit signed Glasgow & Stirling

High quality, budget accommodation ideal for both families and business travellers. Spacious, en suite bedrooms feature tea and coffee making facilities, and Freeview TV in most hotels. Internet access and WiFi are available for a small fee. The adjacent family restaurant features a wide and varied menu. See also the Hotel Groups pages.

Rooms 31

Premier Inn Falkirk (Larbert)

BUDGET HOTEL

tel: 0871 527 8390 **Glenbervie Business Park, Bellsdyke Rd, Larbert FK5 4EG**
web: www.premierinn.com
dir: Just off A88. Approx 1m from M876 junct 2

Rooms 60

FINTRY
Stirling

Map 20 NS68

Culcreuch Castle Hotel & Estate

★★★ 80% HOTEL

tel: 01360 860555 **Kippen Rd G63 0LW**
email: info@culcreuch.com **web:** www.culcreuch.com
dir: On B822, 17m W of Stirling

Peacefully located in 1,600 acres of parkland, this ancient castle dates back to 1296. Tastefully restored accommodation is in a mixture of individually themed castle rooms, some with four-poster beds, and more modern courtyard rooms which are suitable for families. Period style public rooms include a bar, serving light meals, an elegant lounge and a wood-panelled dining room.

Rooms 14 (4 annexe) (4 fmly) (4 GF) ✿ **S** £76-£110; **D** £102-£190 (incl. bkfst)* **Facilities** STV FTV WiFi ↝ New Year **Conf** Class 70 Board 30 Thtr 140 Del £99* **Parking** 80 **Notes** LB ⊗ Closed 4-18 Jan & 25-26 Dec RS 19 Jan-mid Mar Civ Wed 110

FORRES
Moray

Map 23 NJ05

Cluny Bank

⊚ RESTAURANT WITH ROOMS

tel: 01309 674304 ▤ 01309 638206 **69 St Leonards Rd IV36 1DW**
email: info@clunybankhotel.co.uk **web:** www.clunybankhotel.co.uk

Historic, listed Cluny Bank occupies a quiet location within walking distance of the centre of Forres, and is an ideal base for exploring the North East of Scotland. Family-run, the building retains many original architectural features. Public areas include the 'Altyre Bar' with a wide range of whiskies, and 'Franklin's Restaurant' where a real taste of Moray can be experienced. Room service, complimentary WiFi and memorable breakfasts are also provided for guests.

Rooms 7 (1 annexe)

F

FORT AUGUSTUS
Highland   Map 23 NH30

The Lovat, Loch Ness

★★★ 88% ◉◉◉ HOTEL

tel: 01456 459250 & 0845 450 1100 **Loch Ness Side PH32 4DU**
email: info@thelovat.com **web:** www.thelovat.com
dir: A82 between Fort William & Inverness

This charming hotel enjoys an elevated position in the pretty town of Fort Augustus with views over Loch Ness. It has impressively styled bedrooms with a host of thoughtful extras. Inviting public areas include a comfortable lounge with a log fire, a stylish bar, and contemporary restaurant where food is cooked with skill and care. The hotel has an admirable green policy, and the hospitality and commitment to guest care will leave a lasting impression.

Rooms 28 (1 fmly) (7 GF) ⚓ **S** £75-£280; **D** £85-£295 (incl. bkfst)* **Facilities** FTV WiFi ▷ Beauty treatment room Xmas New Year **Conf** Class 32 Board 24 Thtr 70 Del from £145 to £175* **Services** Lift **Parking** 30 **Notes** LB Civ Wed 150

Inchnacardoch Lodge Hotel

★★★ 71% ◉ SMALL HOTEL

tel: 01456 450900 **Inchnacardoch Bay PH32 4BL**
email: happy@inchhotel.com **web:** www.inchhotel.com
dir: On A82. Turn right before entering Fort Augustus from Inverness

This 150-year-old former hunting lodge is set on the hillside looking over the south end of Loch Ness, making it a perfect base for exploring the Highlands. Guests can expect the finest hospitality here from staff that are always eager to please. The bedrooms are very individual in style; the Bridal Suite is a very well appointed room with stunning views. The award-winning Yard Restaurant serves dishes based on the plentiful supply of local game and seafood.

Rooms 18 (2 fmly) **S** £50-£100; **D** £75-£155 (incl. bkfst) **Facilities** FTV WiFi Fishing Xmas New Year **Conf** Class 30 Board 26 Thtr 45 Del £239* **Parking** 30 **Notes** Civ Wed 35

FORTINGALL
Perth & Kinross   Map 20 NN74

Fortingall Hotel

★★★★ 81% ◉◉ SMALL HOTEL

tel: 01887 830367 & 830368 **PH15 2NQ**
email: hotel@fortingallhotel.com **web:** www.fortingallhotel.com
dir: B846 from Aberfeldy for 6m, left signed Fortingall for 3m. Hotel in village centre

Appointed to a very high standard, this hotel has plenty of charm. It lies at the foot of wooded hills in the heart of Glen Lyon. All the bedrooms are very well equipped and have an extensive range of thoughtful extras. The comfortable lounge, with its log fire, is ideal for pre-dinner drinks, and the small bar is full of character.

Rooms 10 (1 fmly) **S** £150; **D** £275 (incl. bkfst & dinner)* **Facilities** STV WiFi ▷ Fishing Deer stalking Grouse shoots Munro bagging Clay pigeon Guided walks ♫ Xmas New Year **Conf** Board 20 Thtr 40 **Parking** 20 **Notes** Civ Wed 30

FORT WILLIAM
Highland   Map 22 NN17

Inverlochy Castle Hotel

★★★★★ ◉◉◉ COUNTRY HOUSE HOTEL

tel: 01397 702177 **Torlundy PH33 6SN**
email: info@inverlochy.co.uk **web:** www.inverlochycastlehotel.com
dir: Accessible from either A82 (Glasgow-Fort William) or A9 (Edinburgh-Dalwhinnie). Hotel 3m N of Fort William on A82, in Torlundy

With Ben Nevis as its backdrop, this imposing and gracious castle sits amidst extensive gardens and grounds overlooking the hotel's own loch. Lavishly appointed in classic country-house style, spacious bedrooms are extremely comfortable and boast flat-screen TVs and laptops with internet access. The sumptuous main hall and lounge provide the perfect setting for afternoon tea or a pre-dinner cocktail, while imaginative modern British cuisine is served in one of three dining rooms. A snooker room and DVD library are also available.

Rooms 17 (6 fmly) ⚓ **S** £280-£395; **D** £450-£550 (incl. bkfst)* **Facilities** STV FTV WiFi ◔ ⚓ Fishing on loch Massage Riding Hunting Stalking Clay pigeon shooting Archery ♫ Xmas New Year **Conf** Class 20 Board 20 Thtr 50 **Parking** 17 **Notes** Civ Wed 80

Moorings Hotel

★★★★ 75% HOTEL

tel: 01397 772797 **Banavie PH33 7LY**
email: reservations@moorings-fortwilliam.co.uk **web:** www.moorings-fortwilliam.co.uk
dir: Take A830 (N from Fort William), cross Caledonian Canal, 1st right

Located on the Caledonian Canal next to a series of locks known as Neptune's Staircase and close to Thomas Telford's house, this hotel has a dedicated team

F

offering friendly service. Accommodation comes in two distinct styles and the newer rooms are particularly appealing. Meals can be taken in the bars or the spacious dining room.

Rooms 27 (2 fmly) (1 GF) 🐾 **S** £85-£145; **D** £105-£155 (incl. bkfst)* **Facilities** STV WiFi Gym New Year **Conf** Class 60 Board 40 Thtr 140 **Parking** 60 **Notes** Closed 24-26 Dec Civ Wed 120

Alexandra Hotel

★★★ 73% HOTEL

tel: 01397 702241 **The Parade PH33 6AZ**
email: salesalexandra@strathmorehotels.com **web:** www.strathmorehotels.com
dir: Off A82. Hotel opposite railway station

This charming old hotel enjoys a prominent position in the town centre and is just a short walk from all the major attractions. Front-facing bedrooms have views over the town and the spectacular Nevis mountain range. There is a choice of restaurants, including a bistro serving meals until late, along with several stylish and very comfortable lounges.

Rooms 93 (2 fmly) **Facilities** WiFi Free use of nearby leisure club 🎵 Xmas New Year **Conf** Class 100 Board 40 Thtr 120 **Services** Lift **Parking** 50

See advert on page 499

Ben Nevis Hotel & Leisure Club

★★ 75% HOTEL

tel: 01397 702331 **North Rd PH33 6TG**
email: bennevismanager@strathmorehotels.com **web:** www.strathmorehotels.com
dir: Off A82

This popular hotel is ideally situated on the outskirts of Fort William. It provides comfortable, well equipped bedrooms; many with views of the impressive Nevis mountains. The hotel's leisure centre is a firm favourite with guests at the hotel.

Rooms 119 (3 fmly) (30 GF) **Facilities** WiFi 🏊 supervised Gym Beauty salon 🎵 Xmas New Year **Conf** Class 60 Board 40 Thtr 150 **Parking** 100 **Notes** Civ Wed 60

See advert on page 499

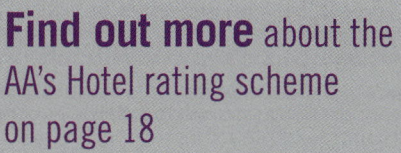

Find out more about the AA's Hotel rating scheme on page 18

Follow us on twitter @TheAA_Lifestyle

FORT WILLIAM *continued*

Croit Anna Hotel

★★ 74% HOTEL

tel: 01397 702268 **Achintore Rd, Drimarben PH33 6RR**
email: croitanna@leisureplex.co.uk **web:** www.leisureplex.co.uk
dir: From Glencoe on A82 into Fort William, hotel 1st on right

Located on the edge of Loch Linnhe, just two miles out of town, this hotel offers some spacious bedrooms, many with fine views over the loch. There is a choice of two comfortable lounges and a large airy restaurant. The hotel appeals to coach parties and independent travellers alike.

Rooms 90 (5 fmly) (13 GF) **Facilities** FTV WiFi Pool table ♫ Xmas New Year **Parking** 25 **Notes** ⊗ Closed Dec-Jan (ex Xmas) RS Nov, Feb, Mar

Premier Inn Fort William

BUDGET HOTEL

tel: 0871 527 8402 **Loch Iall, An Aird PH33 6AN**
web: www.premierinn.com
dir: N end of Fort William Shopping Centre, just off A82 (ring road)

High quality, budget accommodation ideal for both families and business travellers. Spacious, en suite bedrooms feature tea and coffee making facilities, and Freeview TV in most hotels. Internet access and WiFi are available for a small fee. The adjacent family restaurant features a wide and varied menu. See also the Hotel Groups pages.

Rooms 40

GALASHIELS	Map 21 NT43
Scottish Borders	

Kingsknowes Hotel

★★★ 79% HOTEL

tel: 01896 758375 **Selkirk Rd TD1 3HY**
email: enq@kingsknowes.co.uk **web:** www.kingsknowes.co.uk
dir: Exit A7 at Galashiels/Selkirk rdbt

An imposing turreted mansion, this hotel lies in attractive gardens on the outskirts of town close to the River Tweed. It boasts elegant public areas and many spacious bedrooms, some with excellent views. There is a choice of bars, one with a popular menu to supplement the restaurant.

Rooms 12 (2 fmly) ✆ **Facilities** FTV WiFi HL **Conf** Class 40 Board 30 Thtr 80 **Parking** 65 **Notes** Civ Wed 75

GATEHOUSE OF FLEET	Map 20 NX55
Dumfries & Galloway	

Cally Palace Hotel

★★★★ 77% COUNTRY HOUSE HOTEL

tel: 01557 814341 **DG7 2DL**
email: info@callypalace.co.uk **web:** www.callypalace.co.uk
dir: From M6 & A74, signed A75 Dumfries then Stranraer. At Gatehouse-of-Fleet right onto B727, left at Cally

A resort hotel with extensive leisure facilities, this grand 18th-century building is set in 500 acres of forest and parkland that incorporates its own golf course. Bedrooms are spacious and well equipped, while public rooms retain a quiet

elegance. The short dinner menu focuses on freshly prepared dishes; a pianist plays most nights and the wearing of jacket and tie is obligatory (for gentlemen).

Rooms 55 (7 fmly) (4 GF) ✆ **S** fr £75; **D** fr £150* **Facilities** STV FTV WiFi ⊛ ⌇ 18 ⌣ Putt green Fishing ⌇ Gym Table tennis Practice fairway Xmas New Year **Conf** Class 40 Board 25 Thtr 40 **Services** Lift **Parking** 100 **Notes** ⊗ Closed Jan-early Feb Civ Wed 130

GLASGOW	Map 20 NS56
City of Glasgow	

See also **Clydebank & Uplawmoor**

Blythswood Square

★★★★★ 86% ◉◉ HOTEL

tel: 0141 248 8888 **11 Blythswood Square G2 4AD**
email: reserve@blythswoodsquare.com **web:** www.blythswoodsquare.com

Built in 1821, and restored to its former glory, this was the headquarters of the Royal Scottish Automobile Club which was the official start point for the 1955 Monte Carlo Rally. The bedrooms and bathrooms are sumptuous, and include suites and a penthouse. Afternoon tea and cocktails are served in the 35-metre, first-floor Salon Lounge, and the award-winning restaurant occupies the old RSAC's ballroom. The Spa includes a fantastic thermal suite.

Rooms 100 (5 GF) ✆ **S** £100-£280; **D** £110-£280 (incl. bkfst)* **Facilities** Spa STV WiFi ⌇ ⊛ Gym Thermal experience Xmas New Year **Conf** Board 80 Thtr 130 **Services** Lift Air con **Notes** Civ Wed 80

Hotel du Vin at One Devonshire Gardens

★★★★ ◉◉◉ TOWN HOUSE HOTEL

tel: 0844 736 4256 **1 Devonshire Gardens G12 0UX**
email: info.odg@hotelduvin.com **web:** www.hotelduvin.com
dir: M8 junct 17, follow signs for A82, in 1.5m left into Hyndland Rd, 1st right, right at mini rdbt, right at end

Situated in a tree-lined Victorian terrace this luxury 'boutique' hotel has stunning, individually designed bedrooms and suites that have the trademark Egyptian linens and seriously good showers. The oak-panelled Bistro offers a daily-changing menu of both classic and modern dishes with a Scottish influence. Naturally, wine is an important part of the equation here, and knowledgeable staff can guide guests around the impressive wine list.

Rooms 49 (7 GF) ✆ **S** £109-£975; **D** £109-£975 **Facilities** STV WiFi Gym Beauty treatment room Tennis & Squash facilities at nearby club Xmas New Year **Conf** Class 30 Board 30 Thtr 50 Del from £165 to £275 **Notes** LB Civ Wed 70

Menzies Hotels - Glasgow

★★★★ 78% HOTEL

tel: 0141 222 2929 & 270 2323 **27 Washington St G3 8AZ**
email: glasgow@menzieshotels.co.uk **web:** www.menzieshotels.co.uk
dir: M8 junct 19, follow signs for SECC & Broomielaw. Left at lights

Centrally located, this modern hotel is a short drive from the airport and a short walk from the centre of the city. Bedrooms are generally spacious and boast a range of facilities, including high-speed internet access. Facilities include a brasserie restaurant and an impressive indoor leisure facility.

Rooms 141 (16 fmly) (2 smoking) **D** £70-£152* **Facilities** Spa STV FTV WiFi 🏊 supervised Gym Xmas New Year **Conf** Class 80 Board 70 Thtr 160 Del from £115 to £165* **Services** Lift Air con **Parking** 50 **Notes** LB Civ Wed 150

Malmaison Glasgow

★★★★ 76% ◉ HOTEL

tel: 0844 693 0653 **278 West George St G2 4LL**
email: reception.glasgow@malmaison.com **web:** www.malmaison.com
dir: From S & E: M8 junct 18 (Charing Cross). From W & N: M8 city centre

Built around a former church in the historic Charing Cross area, this hotel is a smart, contemporary establishment offering impressive levels of service and hospitality. Bedrooms are spacious and feature a host of modern facilities, such as CD players and mini bars. Dining is a treat here, with French brasserie-style cuisine, backed up by an excellent wine list, served in the original crypt.

Rooms 72 (4 fmly) (19 GF) ⟟ **S** £89-£175; **D** £89-£175* **Facilities** STV WiFi ⤵ Gym Cardiovascular equipment New Year **Conf** Class 16 Board 22 Thtr 40 Del from £150 to £230* **Services** Lift **Notes** LB Civ Wed 60

Beardmore Hotel

★★★★ 75% ◉ HOTEL

tel: 0141 951 6000 **Beardmore St G81 4SA**
email: info@beardmore.scot.nhs.uk **web:** www.thebeardmore.com

(For full entry see Clydebank)

Grand Central Hotel

★★★★ 75% HOTEL

tel: 0141 240 3700 **99 Gordon St G1 3SF**
email: grandcentralhotel@principal-hayley.com **web:** www.principal-hayley.com
dir: M8 junct 19 towards city centre turn left at Hope St. Hotel 200mtrs on right

This is the place where John Logie Baird transmitted the world's first long-distance television pictures in 1927, and this 'grand old lady' of the Glasgow hotel scene is appointed to a very good standard. The decor is a blend of contemporary, art deco and original Victorian styles. Bedrooms are well equipped and suit business travellers especially. There is Champagne Central, a glamorous bar, the Tempus Bar and Restaurant, and Deli Central (with direct access to the Central Station) which is an eat-in deli and a take-away. Ample meeting facilities are available, and NCP car parks are nearby.

Rooms 186 (13 fmly) ⟟ **Facilities** FTV WiFi New Year **Conf** Class 350 Board 60 Thtr 500 **Services** Lift **Notes** ⊗ Civ Wed 500

Millennium Hotel Glasgow

★★★★ 74% HOTEL

tel: 0141 332 6711 **George Square G2 1DS**
email: glasgow.reservations@millenniumhotels.co.uk **web:** www.millenniumhotels.co.uk
dir: M8 junct 15 through 4 sets of lights, at 5th left into Hanover St. George Sq directly ahead, hotel on right

Right in the heart of the city, this hotel has pride of place overlooking George Square. Inside, the property has a contemporary air, with a spacious reception concourse and a glass veranda overlooking the square. There is a stylish brasserie and separate lounge bar, and bedrooms come in a variety of sizes.

Rooms 116 (17 fmly) ⟟ **Facilities** STV WiFi New Year **Conf** Class 24 Board 32 Thtr 40 **Services** Lift **Notes** ⊗ Closed 25 Dec Civ Wed 120

Novotel Glasgow Centre

★★★★ 71% HOTEL

tel: 0141 222 2775 **181 Pitt St G2 4DT**
email: H3136@accor.com **web:** www.novotel.com
dir: M8 junct 18 for Charing Cross. Follow to Sauchiehall St. 3rd right

Enjoying a convenient city centre location and with limited parking spaces, this hotel is ideal for both business and leisure travellers. Well-equipped bedrooms are brightly decorated and offer functional design. Modern public areas include a small fitness club and a brasserie serving a range of meals all day.

Rooms 139 (139 fmly) **Facilities** WiFi ⤵ Gym Sauna Steam room Xmas **Conf** Class 20 Board 20 Thtr 40 **Services** Lift Air con **Parking** 19

Holiday Inn Glasgow City Centre - Theatreland

★★★ 83% ◉ HOTEL

tel: 0141 352 8300 **161 West Nile St G1 2RL**
email: reservations@higlasgow.com **web:** www.holidayinn.co.uk
dir: M8 junct 16, follow signs for Royal Concert Hall, hotel opposite

Built on a corner site close to the Theatre Royal Concert Hall and the main shopping areas, this contemporary hotel features the popular La Bonne Auberge French restaurant, a bar area and conservatory. Bedrooms are well equipped and comfortable; suites are available. Staff are friendly and attentive.

Rooms 113 (20 fmly) (10 smoking) ⟟ **Facilities** STV FTV WiFi **Conf** Class 60 Board 60 Thtr 100 **Services** Lift Air con **Notes** ⊗

Uplawmoor Hotel

★★★ 77% ◉ SMALL HOTEL

tel: 01505 850565 **Neilston Rd G78 4AF**
email: info@uplawmoor.co.uk **web:** www.uplawmoor.co.uk

(For full entry see Uplawmoor)

G

GLASGOW *continued*

Mercure Glasgow City Hotel

★★★ 74% HOTEL

tel: 0844 815 9017 **201 Ingram St G1 1DQ**
email: info@mercureedinburgh.co.uk **web:** www.jupiterhotels.co.uk
dir: M8 junct 15, straight through 4 lights, left at 5th into Hanover St, left into George Sq, right into Frederick St. Right at 2nd lights into Ingram St

This hotel enjoys a fantastic location in the heart of Glasgow with great access to shops, bars and restaurants. Bedrooms provide modern accommodation and a host of accessories including flat screen televisions and complimentary WiFi. Extensive conference facilities and the popular Bagio Café Bar mean you may not need to leave the hotel.

Rooms 91 **Facilities** New Year **Conf** Class 40 Board 40 Thtr 80 Del from £115 to £300* **Services** Lift **Parking** 30 **Notes** Civ Wed 80

Campanile Glasgow

Campanile

BUDGET HOTEL

tel: 0141 287 7700 **10 Tunnel St G3 8HL**
email: glasgow@campanile.com **web:** www.campanile.com
dir: M8 junct 19, follow signs to SECC. Hotel adjacent to SECC

This modern building offers accommodation in smart, well-equipped bedrooms, all with en suite bathrooms. Refreshments may be taken at the informal bistro. See also the Hotel Groups pages.

Rooms 104 (2 fmly) (21 GF) ⌾ **Conf** Class 60 Board 90 Thtr 150

Ibis Glasgow

BUDGET HOTEL

tel: 0141 225 6000 & 619 9000 **220 West Regent St G2 4DQ**
email: H3139@accor.com **web:** www.ibis.com

Modern, budget hotel offering comfortable accommodation in bright and practical bedrooms. Breakfast is self-service and meals are also available in the café-bar 24 hours. See also the Hotel Groups pages.

Rooms 141 ⌾ **S** £47-£249; **D** £47-£249

Premier Inn Glasgow (Bearsden)

BUDGET HOTEL

tel: 0871 527 8418 **279 Milngavie Rd G61 3DQ**
web: www.premierinn.com
dir: M8 junct 16, A81. Pass Asda on right. Hotel on left, behind The Burnbrae

High quality, budget accommodation ideal for both families and business travellers. Spacious, en suite bedrooms feature tea and coffee making facilities, and Freeview TV in most hotels. Internet access and WiFi are available for a small fee. The adjacent family restaurant features a wide and varied menu. See also the Hotel Groups pages.

Rooms 61

Premier Inn Glasgow (Bellshill)

BUDGET HOTEL

tel: 0871 527 8421 **New Edinburgh Rd, Bellshill ML4 3PD**
web: www.premierinn.com
dir: M74 junct 5, A725. Follow Bellshill A721 signs, bear left. At rdbt left, follow Tannochside sign. At next rdbt left into Bellziehill Rd. Hotel on right

Rooms 40

Premier Inn Glasgow (Cambuslang/M74 Jct 1)

BUDGET HOTEL

tel: 0871 527 8422 **Cambuslang Investment Park, Off London Rd G32 8YX**
web: www.premierinn.com
dir: At end of M74, turn right at rdbt. At 1st lights turn right, at 2nd lights straight ahead. Hotel on right

Rooms 40

Premier Inn Glasgow City Centre

BUDGET HOTEL

tel: 0871 527 9360 **St Andrew House, 141 West Nile St G1 2RN**
web: www.premierinn.com
dir: Please telephone for detailed directions

Rooms 210

Premier Inn Glasgow City Centre Argyle St

BUDGET HOTEL

tel: 0871 527 8436 **377 Argyle St G2 8LL**
web: www.premierinn.com
dir: From S: M8 junct 19, at pedestrian lights left into Argyle St. Hotel 200yds on right

Rooms 121

Premier Inn Glasgow City Centre (Charing Cross)

BUDGET HOTEL

tel: 0871 527 8438 **10 Elmbank Gardens G2 4PP**
web: www.premierinn.com
dir: Telephone for directions

Rooms 278

Premier Inn Glasgow City Centre (George Square)

BUDGET HOTEL

tel: 0871 527 8440 **187 George St G1 1YU**
web: www.premierinn.com
dir: M8 junct 15, into Stirling Rd. Right into Cathedral St. At 1st lights left into Montrose St. Hotel after 1st lights

Rooms 239

Premier Inn Glasgow City Centre South

BUDGET HOTEL

tel: 0871 527 8442 **80 Ballater St G5 0TW**
web: www.premierinn.com
dir: M8 junct 21 follow East Kilbride signs, right onto A8 into Kingston St. Right into South Portland St, left into Norfolk St, through Gorbals St into Ballater St

Rooms 114

Premier Inn Glasgow East

BUDGET HOTEL

tel: 0871 527 8444 **601 Hamilton Rd, Uddington G71 7SA**
web: www.premierinn.com
dir: At entrance to Glasgow Zoo, adjacent to junct 4 of M73 & M74

Rooms 66

GLASGOW AIRPORT   Map 20 NS46
Renfrewshire

Holiday Inn Glasgow Airport

★★★ 77% HOTEL

tel: 0871 942 9031 & 0141 887 1266 **Abbotsinch PA3 2TE**
email: operations-glasgow@ihg.com **web:** www.higlasgowairporthotel.co.uk
dir: From E: M8 junct 28, follow hotel signs. From W: M8 junct 29, airport slip road to hotel

Holiday Inn Glasgow Airport is located within the airport grounds and is within walking distance of the terminal. Bedrooms are well appointed and cater for the needs of the modern traveller; all have mini bars. The open-plan public areas are relaxing as is the restaurant which offers a wide ranging a la carte menu. WiFi is available in all areas of the hotel.

Rooms 300 (6 fmly) **Facilities** STV FTV WiFi ↹ HL **Conf** Class 150 Board 75 Thtr 300
Services Lift Air con **Parking** 56 **Notes** Civ Wed 250

Premier Inn Glasgow Airport

BUDGET HOTEL

tel: 0871 527 8434 **Whitecart Rd, Glasgow Airport PA3 2TH**
web: www.premierinn.com
dir: M8 junct 28, follow airport signs for Long Stay & Car Park 3 (Premier Inn signed). At 1st rdbt right into St Andrews Drive. At next rdbt right into Whitecart Rd. Under motorway. Left at garage. Hotel on right

High quality, budget accommodation ideal for both families and business travellers. Spacious, en suite bedrooms feature tea and coffee making facilities, and Freeview TV in most hotels. Internet access and WiFi are available for a small fee. The adjacent family restaurant features a wide and varied menu. See also the Hotel Groups pages.

Rooms 104

Premier Inn Glasgow (Paisley)

BUDGET HOTEL

tel: 0871 527 8432 **Phoenix Retail Park PA1 2BH**
web: www.premierinn.com
dir: M8 junct 28a, A737 signed Irvine, take 1st exit signed Linwood, left at 1st rdbt to Phoenix Park

Rooms 40

GLENEAGLES
See Auchterarder

GLENFINNAN   Map 22 NM98
Highland

G

The Prince's House

★★★ 77% ◉◉ SMALL HOTEL

tel: 01397 722246 **PH37 4LT**
email: princeshouse@glenfinnan.co.uk **web:** www.glenfinnan.co.uk
dir: On A830, 0.5m on right past Glenfinnan Monument. 200mtrs from railway station

This delightful hotel enjoys a well deserved reputation for fine food and excellent hospitality. The hotel has inspiring views and sits close to where 'Bonnie' Prince Charlie raised the Jacobite standard. Comfortably appointed bedrooms offer pleasing decor. Excellent local game and seafood can be enjoyed in the restaurant and the bar.

Rooms 9 ➘ **S** £70-£80; **D** £110-£160 (incl. bkfst)* **Facilities** STV FTV WiFi Fishing New Year **Conf** Class 20 Thtr 40 **Parking** 18 **Notes** LB ✖ Closed Nov, Xmas, Jan-Feb RS Oct, Dec & Mar

GLENROTHES   Map 21 NO20
Fife

Premier Inn Glenrothes

BUDGET HOTEL

tel: 0871 527 8454 **Beaufort Dr, Bankhead Roundabout KY7 4UJ**
web: www.premierinn.com
dir: M90 junct 2a N'bound, A92 to Glenrothes. At 2nd rbt (Bankhead) take 3rd exit. Hotel on left

High quality, budget accommodation ideal for both families and business travellers. Spacious, en suite bedrooms feature tea and coffee making facilities, and Freeview TV in most hotels. Internet access and WiFi are available for a small fee. The adjacent family restaurant features a wide and varied menu. See also the Hotel Groups pages.

Rooms 41

GRANGEMOUTH
Falkirk

Map 21 NS98

The Grange Manor

★★★★ 76% HOTEL

tel: 01324 474836 **Glensburgh FK3 8XJ**
email: info@grangemanor.co.uk **web:** www.grangemanor.co.uk
dir: E: M9 junct 6, hotel 200mtrs to right. W: M9 junct 5, A905 for 2m

Located south of town and close to the M9, this stylish hotel, popular with business and corporate clientele, benefits from hands-on family ownership. It offers spacious, high quality accommodation with superb bathrooms. Public areas include a comfortable foyer area, a lounge bar and a smart restaurant. Cook's bar and restaurant is adjacent to the main house in the converted stables. Staff throughout are very friendly.

Rooms 36 (30 annexe) (6 fmly) (15 GF) **Facilities** FTV WiFi Xmas New Year
Conf Class 68 Board 40 Thtr 120 **Services** Lift **Parking** 154 **Notes** ✆ Civ Wed 120

GRANTOWN-ON-SPEY
Highland

Map 23 NJ02

Grant Arms Hotel

★★★ 81% HOTEL

tel: 01479 872526 **25-27 The Square PH26 3HF**
email: info@grantarmshotel.com **web:** www.grantarmshotel.com
dir: Exit A9 N of Aviemore onto A95

Conveniently located in the centre of the town, this fine hotel is appointed to a high standard yet still retains the building's traditional character. The spacious bedrooms are stylishly presented and very well equipped. The Garden Restaurant is a popular venue for dinner, and lighter snacks can be enjoyed in the comfortable bar. Modern conference facilities are available and the hotel is very popular with birdwatchers and wildlife enthusiasts.

Rooms 50 (7 fmly) ⋏ **S** £85-£105; **D** £170-£210 (incl. bkfst & dinner)* **Facilities** FTV WiFi ⮴ Birdwatching & Wildlife Club ♫ Xmas New Year **Conf** Class 30 Board 16 Thtr 70 Del £95* **Services** Lift **Notes** LB

GREENOCK
Inverclyde

Map 20 NS27

Premier Inn Greenock

BUDGET HOTEL

tel: 0871 527 8476 **The Point, 1-3 James Watt Way PA15 2AD**
web: www.premierinn.com
dir: A8 to Greenock. At rdbt junct of East Hamilton St & Main St (McDonalds visable on right) take 3rd exit. Hotel on left

High quality, budget accommodation ideal for both families and business travellers. Spacious, en suite bedrooms feature tea and coffee making facilities, and Freeview TV in most hotels. Internet access and WiFi are available for a small fee. The adjacent family restaurant features a wide and varied menu. See also the Hotel Groups pages.

Rooms 17

GRETNA SERVICE AREA (A74(M))
Dumfries & Galloway

Map 21 NY36

Days Inn Gretna Green - M74

BUDGET HOTEL

tel: 01461 337566 **Welcome Break Service Area DG16 5HQ**
email: gretna.hotel@welcomebreak.co.uk **web:** www.welcomebreak.co.uk
dir: Between junct 21 & 22 of A74(M) - accessible from both N'bound & S'bound carriageways

This modern building offers accommodation in smart, spacious and well-equipped bedrooms suitable for families and business travellers, and all with en suite bathrooms. Continental breakfast is available and other refreshments may be taken at the nearby family restaurant. See also the Hotel Groups pages.

Rooms 64 (54 fmly) (64 GF)

GRETNA (WITH GRETNA GREEN)
Dumfries & Galloway

Map 21 NY36

Smiths at Gretna Green

★★★★ 80% ⧉⧉ HOTEL

CLASSIC
BRITISH HOTELS

tel: 01461 337007 **Gretna Green DG16 5EA**
email: info@smithsgretnagreen.com **web:** www.smithsgretnagreen.com
dir: From M74 junct 22 follow signs to Old Blacksmith's Shop. Hotel opposite

Located next to the World Famous Old Blacksmith's Shop Centre just off the motorway linking Scotland and England. The bedrooms offer a spacious environment, complete with flat-screen TVs, DVD players and broadband. Family rooms feature a separate children's area with bunk beds, each with its own TV. Three suites and a penthouse apartment are also available. Open-plan contemporary day rooms lead to the brasserie restaurant; impressive conference and banqueting facilities are provided.

Rooms 50 (8 fmly) ⋏ **S** £65-£135; **D** £75-£145 (incl. bkfst) **Facilities** STV FTV WiFi ⮴ HL Beauty treatment room New Year **Conf** Class 100 Board 40 Thtr 250 Del from £105 to £135 **Services** Lift Air con **Parking** 115 **Notes** Civ Wed 150

The Gables Hotel

★★★ 80% HOTEL

tel: 01461 338300 **1 Annan Rd DG16 5DQ**
email: reservations@gables-hotel-gretna.co.uk **web:** www.gables-hotel-gretna.co.uk
dir: M74 S or M6/M74 N follow signs for Gretna. At rdbt at Gretna Gateway take exit onto Annan Rd, hotel 200yds on right

This Grade II listed hotel is located close to the Gretna Gateway and is ideally located to explore both Galloway and the Border City of Carlisle. Bedrooms offer comfortable and well-appointed accommodation. The main restaurant offers a carte menu with a range of freshly prepared dishes, whilst Saddlers bar provides light snacks and meals.

Rooms 31 (5 fmly) (10 GF) ⋏ **Facilities** FTV WiFi Xmas New Year **Conf** Class 60 Board 48 Thtr 100 **Parking** 60 **Notes** ✆ Civ Wed 100

HAWICK
Scottish Borders   Map 21 NT51

Mansfield House Hotel

★★★ 80% HOTEL

tel: 01450 360400 **Weensland Rd TD9 8LB**
email: reception@themansfieldhousehotel.co.uk **web:** www.themansfieldhousehotel.com
dir: A7 to Hawick onto A698 (Weensland Rd). Hotel 0.75m on right

This hotel is set in its own mature grounds at the top of a hill with spectacular views over Hawick. The bedrooms, located on the basement level and the first floor, differ in size and include the fantastic Tower Room accessed via a steep, narrow staircase - but the climb is well worth the effort! Public areas are welcoming and the style is in keeping with the age of the building. The restaurant proudly uses local, quality ingredients for the menus.

Rooms 16 (2 fmly) 🐾 **S** £85; **D** £110-£175 (incl. bkfst)* **Facilities** FTV WiFi ☼ Xmas New Year **Conf** Class 160 Board 60 Thtr 160 **Parking** 25 **Notes** LB ⊗ Civ Wed 120

INVERGARRY
Highland   Map 22 NH30

Glengarry Castle Hotel

★★★ 81% ◉ COUNTRY HOUSE HOTEL

tel: 01809 501254 **PH35 4HW**
email: castle@glengarry.net **web:** www.glengarry.net
dir: On A82, 0.5m from A82/A87 junct

This charming country-house hotel is set in 50 acres of grounds on the shores of Loch Oich. The spacious day rooms include comfortable sitting rooms with lots to read and board games to play. The classical dining room boasts an innovative menu that showcases local Scottish produce. The smart bedrooms vary in size and style but all boast magnificent loch or woodland views.

Rooms 26 (2 fmly) 🐾 **S** £78-£88; **D** £115-£180 (incl. bkfst) **Facilities** FTV WiFi ⌂ Fishing **Parking** 30 **Notes** Closed mid Nov-mid Mar

INVERGORDON
Highland   Map 23 NH76

Kincraig Castle Hotel

★★★★ 77% ◉◉ COUNTRY HOUSE HOTEL

tel: 01349 852587 **IV18 0LF**
email: info@kincraig-house-hotel.co.uk **web:** www.kincraig-house-hotel.co.uk
dir: Off A9 past Alness towards Tain. Hotel on left 0.25m past Rosskeen Church

This imposing castle is set in well-tended grounds in an elevated position with views over the Cromarty Firth. It offers smart, individually designed, well-equipped bedrooms with satellite TVs, and inviting public areas that retain the original features. However, it is the friendly service and commitment to guest care that will leave a lasting impression.

Rooms 15 (1 fmly) (1 GF) 🐾 **Facilities** STV WiFi ☼ Xmas New Year **Conf** Class 30 Board 24 Thtr 50 **Parking** 30 **Notes** Civ Wed 70

INVERKEILOR
Angus   Map 23 NO64

Gordon's

◉◉◉ RESTAURANT WITH ROOMS

tel: 01241 830364 **Main St DD11 5RN**
email: gordonsrest@aol.com **web:** www.gordonsrestaurant.co.uk
dir: Exit A92 between Arbroath & Montrose into Inverkeilor

It's worth a detour off the main road to this family-run restaurant with rooms set in the centre of the village. The award-winning evening meals and the excellent breakfasts are equally memorable. A huge fire dominates the restaurant on cooler evenings. The attractive bedrooms are tastefully decorated and thoughtfully equipped; the larger two are furnished in pine.

Rooms 5 (1 annexe)

INVERNESS
Highland   Map 23 NH64

The New Drumossie Hotel

★★★★ 77% ◉◉ HOTEL

tel: 01463 236451 & 0870 194 2110 **Old Perth Rd IV2 5BE**
email: stay@drumossiehotel.co.uk **web:** www.drumossiehotel.co.uk
dir: From A9 follow signs for Culloden Battlefield, hotel on left after 1m

Set in nine acres of landscaped hillside grounds south of Inverness, this hotel has fine views of the Moray Firth towards Ben Wyvis. Art deco style decoration together with a country-house atmosphere are found throughout. Service is friendly and attentive, the food imaginative and enjoyable and the bedrooms spacious and well presented. The main function room is probably the largest in this area.

Rooms 44 (10 fmly) (6 GF) 🐾 **Facilities** STV FTV WiFi HL Fishing New Year **Conf** Class 200 Board 40 Thtr 500 **Services** Lift **Parking** 200 **Notes** ⊗ Civ Wed 400

Loch Ness Country House Hotel

★★★★ 76% ◉◉ SMALL HOTEL

tel: 01463 230512 **Loch Ness Rd IV3 8JN**
email: info@lochnesscountryhousehotel.co.uk **web:** www.lochnesscountryhousehotel.co.uk
dir: On A82, 1m from Inverness town boundary

Built in the Georgian era, this fine house is perfectly situated in its own six acre private Highland estate. The hotel has luxurious bedrooms, four of which are in the garden suite cottages. The stylish restaurant serves the best of local produce and guests have a choice of cosy well-appointed lounges for after dinner drinks. The terrace is ideal for relaxing and has splendid views over the landscaped gardens towards Inverness.

Rooms 13 (2 annexe) (8 fmly) (3 GF) **S** £80-£185; **D** £90-£265 (incl. bkfst)* **Facilities** FTV WiFi Xmas New Year **Conf** Class 40 Board 40 Thtr 100 Del from £120 to £240* **Parking** 50 **Notes** LB Civ Wed 150

I

INVERNESS *continued*

Bunchrew House Hotel

★★★★ 75% ◉◉ COUNTRY HOUSE HOTEL

tel: 01463 234917 **Bunchrew IV3 8TA**
email: welcome@bunchrewhousehotel.com **web:** www.bunchrewhousehotel.com
dir: W on A862. Hotel 2m after canal on right

Overlooking the Beauly Firth this impressive mansion house dates from the 17th century and retains much original character. Individually styled bedrooms are spacious and tastefully furnished. A wood-panelled restaurant is the setting for artfully constructed cooking and there is a choice of comfortable lounges complete with real fires.

Rooms 16 (4 fmly) (1 GF) ❦ **Facilities** FTV WiFi Fishing New Year **Conf** Class 30 Board 30 Thtr 80 **Parking** 40 **Notes** Closed 24-27 Dec Civ Wed 92

Glenmoriston Town House Hotel

★★★★ 75% ◉ TOWN HOUSE HOTEL

tel: 01463 223777 **20 Ness Bank IV2 4SF**
email: reception@glenmoristontownhouse.com **web:** www.glenmoristontownhouse.com
dir: On riverside opposite theatre

Bold contemporary designs blend seamlessly with the classical architecture of this stylish hotel, situated on the banks of the River Ness. Delightful day rooms include a piano bar and two eating options. Abstract Restaurant features accomplished modern Scottish cuisine based on the finest Scottish produce, and Contrast Brasserie is ideal for relaxed meals from breakfast through to dinner, and when possible for eating alfresco when the weather warms up. The sleek, modern, individually designed bedrooms have many facilities including free WiFi, DVD players and flat-screen TVs.

Rooms 30 (15 annexe) (1 fmly) (6 GF) ❦ **S** £65-£150; **D** £85-£210 (incl. bkfst)*
Facilities STV FTV WiFi ❧ ♫ Xmas New Year **Conf** Class 40 Board 60 Thtr 90 **Parking** 40 **Notes** LB ⊗ Civ Wed 70

The Columba Hotel

★★★★ 73% HOTEL

"bespoke"

tel: 0843 178 7112 **Ness Walk IV3 5NF**
email: reservations.columba@bespokehotels.com **web:** www.bespokehotels.com
dir: From A9, A96 follow signs to town centre, pass Eastgate shopping centre into Academy St, at bottom left into Bank St, right over bridge, hotel 1st left

Originally built in 1881 and with many original features retained, the Columba Hotel lies in the heart of Inverness overlooking the fast flowing River Ness. The bedrooms are very stylish, and public areas include a first-floor restaurant and lounge. A second dining option is the ever popular McNabs bar bistro, which is ideal for less formal meals.

Rooms 80 (3 fmly) ❦ **Facilities** FTV WiFi ❧ Xmas New Year **Services** Lift

Mercure Inverness Hotel

★★★ 79% HOTEL

Mercure
HOTELS

tel: 0844 815 9006 **Church St IV1 1DX**
email: info@mercureinverness.co.uk **web:** www.jupiterhotels.co.uk
dir: From A9 junct A82 (Kessock Bridge) join A82 Inverness. At rdbt 2nd exit, rdbt straight ahead next rdbt left onto B865. Right at lights continue past church Hotel on left

The Mercure Inverness Hotel is situated in an ideal location with the bustling Inverness city centre to one side, and the attractive River Ness running the length of the other. Spacious public areas, an inviting leisure centre and comfortable bedrooms can all be found here. The Brasserie serves a wide ranging selection of dishes. On-site parking and complimentary WiFi are added bonuses.

Rooms 106 **Facilities** WiFi ❧ ⊛ Gym Sauna Spa bath **Conf** Class 100 Board 80 Thtr 200 **Parking** 55 **Notes** Civ Wed 200

BEST WESTERN Inverness Palace Hotel & Spa

★★★ 78% HOTEL

Best Western

tel: 01463 223243 **8 Ness Walk IV3 5NG**
email: palace@miltonhotels.com **web:** www.invernesspalacehotel.co.uk
dir: A82 Glenurquhart Rd onto Ness Walk. Hotel 300yds on right opposite Inverness Castle

Set on the north side of the River Ness close to the Eden Court theatre and a short walk from the town, this hotel has a contemporary look. Bedrooms offer good levels of comfort and equipment, and a smart leisure centre attracts a mixed market.

Rooms 88 (48 annexe) (3 fmly) ❦ **Facilities** Spa FTV WiFi ⊛ supervised Gym Beautician Hairdresser Sauna Steam room Xmas New Year **Conf** Class 40 Board 30 Thtr 80 **Del** from £99.90 to £199.90* **Services** Lift **Parking** 18 **Notes** Civ Wed 100

Royal Highland Hotel

★★★ 73% HOTEL

tel: 01463 231926 & 251451 **Station Square, Academy St IV1 1LG**
email: info@royalhighlandhotel.co.uk **web:** www.royalhighlandhotel.co.uk
dir: From A9 into town centre. Hotel next to rail station & Eastgate Retail Centre

Built in 1858 adjacent to the railway station, this hotel has the typically grand foyer of the Victorian era with comfortable seating. The contemporary ASH Brasserie and bar is a refreshing venue for both eating and drinking throughout the day. The generally spacious bedrooms are comfortably equipped especially for the business traveller.

Rooms 86 (12 fmly) (2 GF) (10 smoking) ❦ **Facilities** FTV WiFi Xmas New Year **Conf** Class 80 Board 80 Thtr 200 **Services** Lift **Parking** 8 **Notes** Civ Wed 200

Premier Inn Inverness Centre (Milburn Rd)

BUDGET HOTEL

tel: 0871 527 8544 **Millburn Rd IV2 3QX**
web: www.premierinn.com
dir: From A9 & A96 junct (Raigmore Interchange, signed Airport/Aberdeen), take B865 towards town centre, hotel 100yds after next rdbt

High quality, budget accommodation ideal for both families and business travellers. Spacious, en suite bedrooms feature tea and coffee making facilities, and Freeview TV in most hotels. Internet access and WiFi are available for a small fee. The adjacent family restaurant features a wide and varied menu. See also the Hotel Groups pages.

Rooms 55

Premier Inn Inverness Centre (River Ness)

BUDGET HOTEL

tel: 0871 527 9302 **19-21 Huntly St IV3 5PR**
web: www.premierinn.com
dir: Exit A9 at Longman rdbt, 1st exit into Longman Rd (A82) follow Inverness/Fort William signs. Straight on at 3 rdbts. At Telford St rdbt 1st exit into Wells St. Right into Huntly St. Hotel on right

Rooms 98

Premier Inn Inverness East

BUDGET HOTEL

tel: 0871 527 8546 **Beechwood Business Park IV2 3BW**
web: www.premierinn.com
dir: From A9 follow Raigmore Hospital, Police HQ & Inshes Retail Park signs

Rooms 60

Premier Inn Inverness West

BUDGET HOTEL

tel: 0871 527 9338 **Glenurquhart Rd IV3 5TD**
web: www.premierinn.com
dir: From A9 exit at Kessock rdbt. At 4th rdbt 2nd exit into Kenneth St. Right at lights into Glenruquhart Rd, pass council offices, 1m, take A82 signed Fort William. Cross Caledonian Canal Bridge. Hotel on right

Rooms 76

INVERURIE
Aberdeenshire
Map 23 NJ72

Macdonald Pittodrie House

★★★★ 77% ◉◉ HOTEL

tel: 0870 1942111 & 01467 622 437 **Chapel of Garioch, Pitcaple AB51 5HS**
email: gm.pittodrie@macdonald-hotels.co.uk **web:** www.macdonald-hotels.com/pittodrie
dir: From A96 towards Inverness, pass Inverurie under bridge with lights. Turn left & follow signs

Set in extensive grounds this house dates from the 15th century and retains many historic features. Public rooms include a gracious drawing room, restaurant, and a cosy bar boasting an impressive selection of whiskies. The well-proportioned bedrooms are found in both the original house and in the extension that was designed to match the existing building.

Rooms 27 (6 fmly) **Facilities** STV FTV WiFi Clay pigeon shooting Quad biking Outdoor activities Xmas New Year **Conf** Class 75 Board 50 Thtr 150 **Parking** 200 **Notes** Civ Wed 120

IRVINE
North Ayrshire
Map 20 NS33

Menzies Hotels Irvine Ayrshire

★★★★ 77% HOTEL

tel: 01294 274272 **46 Annick Rd KA11 4LD**
email: irvine@menzieshotels.co.uk **web:** www.menzieshotels.co.uk
dir: From A78 at Warrix Interchange follow Irvine Central signs. At rdbt 2nd exit (town centre). At next rdbt right onto A71/Kilmarnock. Hotel 100mtrs on left

Situated on the edge of Irvine with good transportation links (including Prestwick Airport just seven miles away), this is a well-presented hotel that has an extremely friendly team with good customer care awareness. The decor is contemporary throughout, and there is a brasserie-style restaurant, cocktail bar and spacious lounge.

Rooms 128 (14 fmly) (64 GF) **S** £49-£139; **D** £49-£139 **Facilities** STV FTV WiFi ⑧ Fishing Xmas New Year **Conf** Class 140 Board 100 Thtr 280 Del from £95 to £180* **Parking** 180 **Notes** LB Civ Wed 200

KELSO
Scottish Borders
Map 21 NT73

The Roxburghe Hotel & Golf Course

★★★★ 81% ◉◉ COUNTRY HOUSE HOTEL

tel: 01573 450331 **Heiton TD5 8JZ**
email: hotel@roxburghe.net **web:** www.roxburghe-hotel.com
dir: From A68 Jedburgh take A698 to Heiton, 3m SW of Kelso

Outdoor sporting pursuits are popular at this impressive Jacobean mansion owned by the Duke of Roxburghe, and set in 500 acres of woods and parkland bordering the River Teviot. Gracious public areas are the perfect settings for afternoon teas and carefully prepared meals. The elegant bedrooms are individually designed, some by the Duchess herself, and include superior rooms, some with four posters and log fires.

Rooms 22 (6 annexe) (3 fmly) (8 GF) **D** £135-£330 (incl. bkfst)* **Facilities** Spa STV FTV WiFi ⑧ ♪ 18 Putt green Fishing ⑤ Clay shooting Health & beauty salon Mountain bike hire Falconry Archery Xmas New Year **Conf** Class 20 Board 20 Thtr 50 Del from £171 to £306* **Parking** 150 **Notes** LB Civ Wed 60

K

KILCHRENAN
Argyll & Bute

Map 20 NN02

The Ardanaiseig Hotel

★★★★ 86% ◉◉◉ COUNTRY HOUSE HOTEL

tel: 01866 833333 **by Loch Awe PA35 1HE**
email: info@ardanaiseig.com **web:** www.ardanaiseig.com
dir: A85 at Taynuilt onto B845 to Kilchrenan. Left in front of pub (road very narrow) signed 'Ardanaiseig Hotel' & 'No Through Road'. Continue for 3m

Set amid lovely gardens and breathtaking scenery beside the shore of Loch Awe, this peaceful country-house hotel was built in a Scottish baronial style in 1834. Many fine pieces of furniture are evident in the bedrooms and charming day rooms, which include a drawing room, a library bar and an elegant dining room. The bedrooms are individually designed including some with four posters, some with loch views and some with access to the garden; standing on its own by the water is the Boat Shed, a delightful one bedroom suite.

Rooms 18 (4 fmly) (5 GF) 🐾 **Facilities** FTV WiFi ⌇ Fishing 🦢 Boating Clay pigeon shooting Bikes for hire In house massage treatments Xmas New Year **Parking** 20 **Notes** Civ Wed 50

Taychreggan Hotel

★★★★ 74% ◉◉ COUNTRY HOUSE HOTEL

tel: 01866 833211 & 833366 **PA35 1HQ**
email: info@taychregganhotel.co.uk **web:** www.taychregganhotel.co.uk
dir: W from Crianlarich on A85 to Taynuilt, S for 7m on B845 (single track) to Kilchrenan

Surrounded by stunning Highland scenery this stylish and superbly presented hotel, once a drover's cottage, enjoys an idyllic setting in 40 acres of wooded grounds on the shores of Loch Awe. The hotel has a smart bar with adjacent courtyard Orangerie and a choice of quiet lounges with deep, luxurious sofas. A well earned reputation has been achieved by the kitchen for the skilfully prepared dinners that showcase the local and seasonal Scottish larder. Families, and also dogs and their owners, are welcome.

Rooms 18 (1 fmly) **Facilities** FTV WiFi Fishing 🦢 Air rifle range Archery Clay pigeon shooting Falconry Mock deer stalk Xmas New Year **Conf** Class 15 Board 20 **Parking** 40 **Notes** Closed 3 Jan-9 Feb Civ Wed 70

KILLIECRANKIE
Perth & Kinross — Map 23 NN96

INSPECTORS' CHOICE

Killiecrankie Hotel

★★★ SMALL HOTEL

tel: 01796 473220 **PH16 5LG**
email: enquiries@killiecrankiehotel.co.uk **web:** www.killiecrankiehotel.co.uk
dir: Exit A9 at Killiecrankie onto B8079. Hotel 3m on right

Originally built in the 1840s, Killiecrankie sits in fours acres of wooded grounds with beautifully landscaped gardens; it enjoys a tranquil location by the Pass of Killiecrankie and the River Garry. Public areas include a wood-panelled bar and a cosy sitting room with original artwork, and a blazing fire in colder months. All of the bedrooms are individually decorated, well equipped and have wonderful countryside views.

Rooms 10 (2 GF) ♦ **S** £85-£125; **D** £170-£290 (incl. bkfst & dinner)* **Facilities** FTV WiFi ⛄ Xmas New Year Child facilities **Parking** 20 **Notes** LB Closed 3 Jan-12 Mar

KILMARNOCK
East Ayrshire — Map 20 NS43

The Fenwick Hotel

★★★ 85% HOTEL

tel: 01560 600478 **Fenwick KA3 6AU**
email: info@thefenwickhotel.co.uk **web:** www.thefenwickhotel.co.uk
dir: M77 junct 8, B7061 towards Fenwick, follow hotel signs

The Fenwick Hotel benefits from a great location alongside the M77, with easy location to Ayr, Kilmarnock and Glasgow. The spacious bedrooms are thoughtfully equipped; complimentary WiFi is available throughout the hotel. The bright restaurant offers both formal and informal dining and there is an attractive lounge bar where you can relax and choose from the extensive cocktail list. The hotel also has extensive conference and function facilities.

Rooms 29 (2 fmly) (9 GF) ♦ **Facilities** STV FTV WiFi ⛄ Xmas New Year **Conf** Class 280 Board 150 Thtr 280 **Services** Lift **Parking** 64 **Notes** Civ Wed 110

Premier Inn Kilmarnock

BUDGET HOTEL

tel: 0871 527 8566 **Moorfield Roundabout, Annadale KA1 2RS**
web: www.premierinn.com
dir: M74 junct 8 signed Kilmarnock (A71). From M77 onto A71 to Irvine. At next rdbt right onto B7064 signed Crosshouse Hospital. Hotel on right

High quality, budget accommodation ideal for both families and business travellers. Spacious, en suite bedrooms feature tea and coffee making facilities, and Freeview TV in most hotels. Internet access and WiFi are available for a small fee. The adjacent family restaurant features a wide and varied menu. See also the Hotel Groups pages.

Rooms 40

KINCARDINE
Fife — Map 21 NS98

Premier Inn Falkirk North

BUDGET HOTEL

tel: 0871 527 8394 **Bowtrees Roundabout, Houghs of Airth FK2 8PJ**
web: www.premierinn.com
dir: From N: M9 junct 7 (or from S: M876) towards Kincardine Bridge. On rdbt at end of slip road

High quality, budget accommodation ideal for both families and business travellers. Spacious, en suite bedrooms feature tea and coffee making facilities, and Freeview TV in most hotels. Internet access and WiFi are available for a small fee. The adjacent family restaurant features a wide and varied menu. See also the Hotel Groups pages.

Rooms 40

KINCLAVEN
Perth & Kinross — Map 21 NO13

Ballathie House Hotel

★★★★ 78%  COUNTRY HOUSE HOTEL

tel: 01250 883268 **PH1 4QN**
email: email@ballathiehousehotel.com **web:** www.ballathiehousehotel.com
dir: From A9, 2m N of Perth, take B9099 through Stanley, follow signs. Or from A93 at Beech Hedge follow signs for hotel, 2.5m

Set in delightful grounds, this splendid Scottish mansion house combines classical grandeur with modern comfort. Bedrooms range from well-proportioned master rooms to modern standard rooms, and many boast antique furniture and art deco bathrooms. It might be worth requesting one of the Riverside Rooms, a purpose-built development right on the banks of the river, complete with balconies and terraces. The elegant restaurant has views over the River Tay.

Rooms 41 (16 annexe) (2 fmly) (10 GF) ♦ **Facilities** FTV WiFi Fishing ⛄ Xmas New Year **Conf** Class 20 Board 30 Thtr 50 **Services** Lift **Parking** 50 **Notes** Civ Wed 90

KINGUSSIE
Highland

Map 23 NH70

INSPECTORS' CHOICE

The Cross

 RESTAURANT WITH ROOMS

tel: 01540 661166 **Tweed Mill Brae, Ardbroilach Rd PH21 1LB**
email: relax@thecross.co.uk **web:** www.thecross.co.uk
dir: From lights in Kingussie centre take Ardbroilach Rd, 300yds left into Tweed Mill Brae

Built as a water-powered tweed mill in the late 19th century, The Cross is situated in the picturesque Cairngorm National Park and surrounded by four acres of riverside grounds that teems with an abundance of wildlife. Comfortable lounges and a selection of well-appointed bedrooms are offered, and dinners are served by an open fire in the stone-walled and wood-beamed restaurant.

Rooms 8 (1 fmly)

KINLOCH RANNOCH
Perth & Kinross

Map 23 NN65

Macdonald Loch Rannoch Hotel

★★★ 77% HOTEL

tel: 0844 879 9059 & 01882 632201 **PH16 5PS**
email: loch_rannoch@macdonald-hotels.co.uk **web:** www.macdonaldhotels.co.uk
dir: A9 onto B847 Calvine. Follow signs to Kinloch Rannoch, hotel 1m from village

Set deep in the countryside with elevated views across Loch Rannoch, this hotel is built around a 19th-century hunting lodge and provides a great base for exploring this beautiful area. The superior bedrooms have views over the loch. There is a choice of eating options - The Ptarmigan Restaurant and the Schiehallan Bar for informal eating. The hotel provides both indoor and outdoor activities.

Rooms 47 (25 fmly) **Facilities** FTV WiFi HL ⊕ Fishing Gym Xmas New Year **Conf** Class 80 Board 50 Thtr 160 Del from £95 to £145* **Services** Lift **Parking** 52 **Notes** Closed 24 Dec-2 Jan RS 1 Nov-1 Apr Civ Wed 130

KIRKCALDY
Fife

Map 21 NT29

Dean Park Hotel

★★★ 74% HOTEL

tel: 01592 261635 **Chapel Level KY2 6QW**
email: reception@deanparkhotel.co.uk **web:** www.deanparkhotel.co.uk
dir: Signed from A92 Kirkcaldy West junct

Popular with both business and leisure guests, this hotel has extensive conference and meeting facilities. The bedrooms are spacious, comfortable, well equipped and enjoy modern decor and up-to-date amenities. Public areas include the Dukes Bar & Bistro, and Grill Room which is well-known for its steaks

Rooms 33 (2 fmly) (5 GF) **Facilities** STV FTV WiFi Xmas New Year **Conf** Class 125 Board 54 Thtr 250 **Services** Lift **Parking** 250 **Notes** ⊗ Civ Wed 200

KIRKCUDBRIGHT
Dumfries & Galloway

Map 20 NX65

Arden House Hotel

★★ 76% HOTEL

tel: 01557 330544 **Tongland Rd DG6 4UU**
dir: Exit A75, 4m W of Castle Douglas onto A711. Follow Kirkcudbright signs, over Telford Bridge. Hotel 400mtrs on left

Set well back from the main road in extensive grounds on the northeast side of town, this spotlessly maintained hotel offers attractive bedrooms, a lounge bar and adjoining conservatory serving a range of popular dishes, which are also available in the dining room. There is an impressive function suite in the grounds.

Rooms 9 (7 fmly) ⌇ **S** £45-£55; **D** £65-£75 (incl. bkfst)* **Facilities** FTV WiFi **Conf** Class 175 Board 120 Thtr 175 **Parking** 70 **Notes** LB

LANARK
South Lanarkshire

Map 21 NS84

BEST WESTERN Cartland Bridge Hotel

★★★ 74% COUNTRY HOUSE HOTEL

tel: 01555 664426 **Glasgow Rd ML11 9UF**
email: sales@cartlandbridge.co.uk **web:** www.bw-cartlandbridgehotel.co.uk
dir: A73 through Lanark towards Carluke. Hotel in 1.25m

Situated in wooded grounds on the edge of the town, this Grade I listed mansion continues to be popular with both business and leisure guests. Public areas feature wood panelling, a gallery staircase and a magnificent dining room. The well-equipped bedrooms vary in size.

Rooms 18 (2 fmly) ⌇ **Facilities** FTV WiFi Xmas New Year **Conf** Class 180 Board 50 Thtr 250 **Parking** 120 **Notes** ⊗ Civ Wed 200

LARGS
North Ayrshire

Map 20 NS25

Willowbank Hotel

★★★ 74% HOTEL

tel: 01475 672311 & 675435 **96 Greenock Rd KA30 8PG**
email: iaincsmith@btconnect.com **web:** www.thewillowbankhotel.co.uk
dir: On A78

A relaxed, friendly atmosphere prevails at this well maintained hotel where hanging baskets are a feature in summer months. The nicely decorated bedrooms are, in general, spacious and offer comfortable modern appointments. The public areas include a large, well-stocked bar, a lounge and a dining room.

Rooms 30 (4 fmly) ⌇ **S** £75-£100; **D** £110-£150 (incl. bkfst) **Facilities** STV ♫ Xmas New Year **Conf** Class 100 Board 40 Thtr 200 Del from £100 to £150 **Parking** 40 **Notes** LB

K

LIVINGSTON
West Lothian

Map 21 NT06

Mercure Livingston Hotel

★★★ 75% HOTEL

tel: 0844 815 9102 **Almondview EH54 6QB**
email: info@mercurelivingston.co.uk **web:** www.jupiterhotels.co.uk
dir: From M8 junct 3 take A899 towards Livingston, exit at Centre Interchange, left at next rdbt, hotel on left

This large, modern hotel is conveniently located in the town centre with easy access to the M8. Bedrooms offer freedom of space and are comfortably appointed for both business and leisure guests. There is a large open-plan lobby and restaurant area; complementary WiFi is available throughout, and there is also a small but well-appointed leisure club.

Rooms 120 (15 fmly) (55 GF) **S** £60-£199; **D** £60-£199* **Facilities** FTV WiFi HL 🔄 Gym Xmas New Year **Conf** Class 55 Board 60 Thtr 100 Del from £99 to £250* **Parking** 130 **Notes** ⊗ Civ Wed 100

Premier Inn Livingston M8 Jct 3

BUDGET HOTEL

tel: 0871 527 8632 **Deer Park Av, Deer Park, Knightsbridge EH54 8AD**
web: www.premierinn.com
dir: At M8 junct 3. Hotel opposite rdbt

High quality, budget accommodation ideal for both families and business travellers. Spacious, en suite bedrooms feature tea and coffee making facilities, and Freeview TV in most hotels. Internet access and WiFi are available for a small fee. The adjacent family restaurant features a wide and varied menu. See also the Hotel Groups pages.

Rooms 83

LOCHGILPHEAD
Argyll & Bute

Map 20 NR88

Cairnbaan Hotel

★★★ 74% HOTEL

tel: 01546 603668 **Crinan Canal, Cairnbaan PA31 8SJ**
email: info@cairnbaan.com **web:** www.cairnbaan.com
dir: 2m N, A816 from Lochgilphead, hotel off B841

Located on the Crinan Canal, this small hotel offers relaxed hospitality in a delightful setting. Bedrooms are thoughtfully equipped, generally spacious and benefit from stylish decor. Fresh seafood is a real feature in both the formal restaurant and the comfortable bar area. Alfresco dining is popular in the warmer months.

Rooms 12 **Facilities** Xmas **Conf** Class 100 Board 80 Thtr 160 **Parking** 53 **Notes** Civ Wed 120

LOCKERBIE
Dumfries & Galloway

Map 21 NY18

Kings Arms Hotel

★★ 81% HOTEL

tel: 01576 202410 **High St DG11 2JL**
email: reception@kingsarmshotel.co.uk **web:** www.kingsarmshotel.co.uk
dir: A74(M), 0.5m into town centre, hotel opposite town hall

Dating from the 17th century this former inn lies in the town centre. Now a family-run hotel, it provides attractive well-equipped bedrooms with WiFi access. At lunch a menu ranging from snacks to full meals is served in both the cosy bars and the restaurant at dinner.

Rooms 13 (2 fmly) 🐾 **S** £60; **D** £90 (incl. bkfst) **Facilities** FTV WiFi Xmas New Year **Conf** Class 40 Board 30 Thtr 80 **Parking** 8

Ravenshill House Hotel

★★ 76% HOTEL

tel: 01576 202882 **12 Dumfries Rd DG11 2EF**
email: aaenquiries@ravenshillhotellockerbie.co.uk
web: www.ravenshillhotellockerbie.co.uk
dir: From A74(M) Lockerbie junct 14 North or 18 South. Follow signs for A709 Dumfries. Hotel 0.5m on right

Set in spacious gardens on the fringe of the town, this friendly, family-run hotel offers cheerful service and good value, home-cooked meals. Bedrooms are generally spacious and comfortably equipped, including a two-room unit ideal for families.

Rooms 7 (2 fmly) 🐾 **S** £45-£60; **D** £70-£80 (incl. bkfst)* **Facilities** FTV WiFi **Conf** Class 20 Board 12 Thtr 30 **Parking** 35 **Notes** LB Closed 1-7 Jan & 2 wks in Feb

LUSS
Argyll & Bute

Map 20 NS39

The Lodge on Loch Lomond

★★★★ 74% ◉◉ HOTEL

tel: 01436 860201 **G83 8PA**
email: res@loch-lomond.co.uk **web:** www.loch-lomond.co.uk
dir: Off A82, follow sign for hotel

This hotel is idyllically set on the shores of Loch Lomond. Public areas consist of an open-plan, split-level bar and fine dining restaurant overlooking the loch. The pine-finished bedrooms also enjoy the views and are comfortable, spacious and well equipped; some with saunas, DVDs and all with internet access. There is a stunning state-of-the-art leisure suite.

Rooms 47 (17 annexe) (20 fmly) (13 GF) 🐾 **Facilities** Spa STV FTV WiFi 🔄 Fishing Boating Xmas New Year **Conf** Class 80 Board 60 Thtr 150 **Parking** 120 **Notes** Civ Wed 100

L

MELROSE
Scottish Borders

Map 21 NT53

Burt's Hotel

★★★ 78% HOTEL

tel: 01896 822285 **Market Square TD6 9PL**
email: enquiries@burtshotel.co.uk **web:** www.burtshotel.co.uk
dir: A6091, 2m from A68 3m S of Earlston

Recognised by its distinctive black and white façade and colourful window boxes, in the heart of a small market town, this hotel has been under the same family ownership for almost 40 years. The genuine warmth of hospitality is notable. The smart bedrooms have been individually styled and include WiFi. Food is important at Burt's, and the elegant restaurant is well complemented by the range of tasty meals in the bar.

Rooms 20 ✿ **S** £70–£85; **D** £130–£145 (incl. bkfst)* **Facilities** STV FTV WiFi Salmon fishing Shooting New Year **Conf** Class 20 Board 20 Thtr 38 Del from £100 to £150* **Parking** 40 **Notes** Closed 24-26 Dec & 2-8 Jan

---

MILNGAVIE
East Dunbartonshire

Map 20 NS57

Premier Inn Glasgow (Milngavie)

BUDGET HOTEL

tel: 0871 527 8428 **103 Main St G62 6JQ**
web: www.premierinn.com
dir: M8 junct 16, follow Milngavie (A879) signs. Approx. 5m. Pass Murray Park Training Ground. Left at lights. Hotel on A81 adjacent to West Highland Gate Beefeater

High quality, budget accommodation ideal for both families and business travellers. Spacious, en suite bedrooms feature tea and coffee making facilities, and Freeview TV in most hotels. Internet access and WiFi are available for a small fee. The adjacent family restaurant features a wide and varied menu. See also the Hotel Groups pages.

Rooms 60

MONTROSE
Angus

Map 23 NO75

Links Hotel

★★★ 75% HOTEL

tel: 01674 671000 **Mid Links DD10 8RL**
email: ajames@parkmontrose.com **web:** www.linkshotel.com
dir: A935 to Montrose then right at Lochside junct, left at swimming pool and right by tennis courts for hotel 200yds

This Edwardian town house hotel lies in the centre of picturesque Montrose on the Angus coast and is popular with golfers, as it is convenient for many famous courses including the world's fifth oldest; Montrose Links. Hotel facilities include a coffee house, comfortable lounge bar and restaurant. Bedrooms and bathrooms are presented in a traditional style with WiFi and complimentary parking on-site.

Rooms 25 (1 GF) **S** £65–£88; **D** £74–£98 (incl. bkfst) **Facilities** 🎵 Xmas **Conf** Class 70 Board 70 Thtr 220 **Parking** 45 **Notes** Civ Wed 120

MOTHERWELL
North Lanarkshire

Map 21 NS75

Alona Hotel

★★★★ 74% HOTEL

tel: 01698 333888 **Strathclyde Country Park ML1 3RT**
email: gm@alonahotel.co.uk **web:** www.alonahotel.co.uk
dir: M74 junct 5, hotel approx 250yds on left

Alona is a Celtic word meaning 'exquisitely beautiful'. This hotel is situated within the idyllic beauty of Strathclyde Country Park, with tranquil views over the picturesque loch and surrounding forests. There is a very contemporary feel, from the open-plan public areas to the spacious and well-appointed bedrooms. WiFi is available throughout. M&D's, Scotland's Family Theme Park, is just next door.

Rooms 51 (24 fmly) (17 GF) ✿ **Facilities** FTV WiFi 🎵 Xmas New Year **Conf** Class 100 Board 76 Thtr 400 **Services** Lift Air con **Parking** 100 **Notes** ⊗ Civ Wed 250

Premier Inn Glasgow (Motherwell)

BUDGET HOTEL

tel: 0871 527 8430 **Edinburgh Rd, Newhouse ML1 5SY**
web: www.premierinn.com
dir: From S: M74 junct 5, A725 towards Coatbridge. Take A8 towards Edinburgh, exit at junct 6, follow Lanark signs. Hotel 400yds on right

High quality, budget accommodation ideal for both families and business travellers. Spacious, en suite bedrooms feature tea and coffee making facilities, and Freeview TV in most hotels. Internet access and WiFi are available for a small fee. The adjacent family restaurant features a wide and varied menu. See also the Hotel Groups pages.

Rooms 40

Ord House Hotel

  THE CIRCLE

★★ 74% SMALL HOTEL

tel: 01463 870492 **IV6 7UH**
email: admin@ord-house.co.uk **web:** www.ord-house.co.uk
dir: Exit A9 at Tore rdbt onto A832. 5m, through Muir of Ord. Left towards Ullapool (A832). Hotel 0.5m on left

Dating back to 1637, this country-house hotel is situated peacefully in wooded grounds and offers brightly furnished and well-proportioned accommodation. Comfortable day rooms reflect the character and charm of the house, with inviting lounges, a cosy snug bar and an elegant dining room where wide-ranging, creative menus are offered.

Rooms 12 (2 fmly) (3 GF) S £65-£75; **D** £110-£165 (incl. bkfst)* **Facilities** WiFi Putt green Clay pigeon shooting **Parking** 30 **Notes** LB Closed Nov-Apr

Barley Bree Restaurant with Rooms

  RESTAURANT WITH ROOMS

tel: 01764 681451 01764 910055 **6 Willoughby St PH5 2AB**
email: info@barleybree.com **web:** www.barleybree.com
dir: A9 onto A822 in centre of Muthill

Situated in the heart of the small village of Muthill, and just a short drive from Crieff, genuine hospitality and quality food are obvious attractions at this charming restaurant with rooms. The stylish bedrooms are appointed to a very high standard. The restaurant has a rustic feel with exposed stonework, wooden floors and a log-burning fire in the centre. Choices range from set, carte and tasting menus. Children are welcome too.

Rooms 6 (1 fmly)

Golf View Hotel & Spa

★★★★ 76%  HOTEL

tel: 01667 452301 **The Seafront IV12 4HD**
email: golfview@crerarhotels.com **web:** www.crerarhotels.com
dir: Exit A96 into Seabank Rd, hotel at end on right

This fine hotel has wonderful sea views and overlooks the Moray Firth and the Black Isle beyond. The championship golf course at Nairn is adjacent to the hotel and guests have direct access to the long sandy beaches. Bedrooms are of a very high standard and the public areas are charming. A well-equipped leisure complex and swimming pool are also available.

Rooms 42 (6 fmly) **Facilities** Spa FTV WiFi supervised Gym Sauna Steam room Xmas New Year **Conf** Class 40 Board 40 Thtr 100 **Services** Lift **Parking** 40 **Notes** Civ Wed 100

Boath House

★★★   HOTEL

tel: 01667 454896 **Auldearn IV12 5TE**
email: info@boath-house.com **web:** www.boath-house.com
dir: 2m past Nairn on A96, E towards Forres, signed on main road

Standing in its own 20-acre grounds, this splendid Georgian mansion was built in 1825 for the Dunbar family, but there has been occupation on this site since the 16th century. Guests are welcome to stroll around the gardens which have an ornamental lake, walled garden and secluded seating areas to relax in. The hospitality here is first class; the owners are passionate about what they do, and have an ability to establish a special relationship with their guests that will be particularly remembered. The food is also very memorable; head chef Charlie Lockley is devotee of slow and organic cooking which also includes using foraged produce. The five-course dinners are a culinary adventure, matched only by the excellence of breakfasts. The house itself is delightful, with inviting lounges and a dining room overlooking a trout loch. The bedrooms, with lake and woodland views, are striking and very comfortable; Orangerie Rooms have their own conservatory.

Rooms 8 (1 fmly) (1 GF) S £190-£260; **D** £260-£365 (incl. bkfst) **Facilities** FTV WiFi Fishing Beauty salon Treatment room Xmas New Year **Conf** Class 10 Board 10 Thtr 15 **Parking** 20 **Notes** LB Civ Wed 32

N

NETHY BRIDGE
Highland

Map 23 NJ02

Nethybridge Hotel

★★★ 67% HOTEL

tel: 01479 821203 **PH25 3DP**
email: salesnethybridge@strathmorehotels.com **web:** www.strathmorehotels.com
dir: A9 onto A95, onto B970 to Nethy Bridge

This popular tourist and coaching hotel enjoys a central location amidst the majestic Cairngorm Mountains. Bedrooms are stylishly furnished in bold tartans whilst traditionally styled day rooms include two bars and a popular snooker room. Staff are friendly and keen to please.

Rooms 69 (3 fmly) (7 GF) ↑ **S** £30–£80; **D** £50–£150 (incl. bkfst) **Facilities** FTV WiFi Putt green Bowling green ♫ Xmas New Year **Conf** Thtr 100 **Services** Lift **Parking** 80 **Notes** LB

See advert on page 499

NEWTON MEARNS
East Renfrewshire

Map 20 NS55

Premier Inn Glasgow Newton Mearns (M77 Jct 4)

BUDGET HOTEL

tel: 0871 527 9304 **Greenlaw Crookfur Rd G77 6NP**
web: www.premierinn.com
dir: From N exit M77 junct 4 towards Newton Mearns. At rdbt 1st left. Hotel on left

High quality, budget accommodation ideal for both families and business travellers. Spacious, en suite bedrooms feature tea and coffee making facilities, and Freeview TV in most hotels. Internet access and WiFi are available for a small fee. The adjacent family restaurant features a wide and varied menu. See also the Hotel Groups pages.

Rooms 60

NEWTON STEWART
Dumfries & Galloway

Map 20 NX46

Kirroughtree House

★★★ ◉◉ HOTEL

tel: 01671 402141 **DG8 6AN**
email: info@kirroughtreehouse.co.uk **web:** www.kirroughtreehouse.co.uk
dir: A75 onto A712, hotel entrance 300yds on left

This imposing mansion enjoys a peaceful location in eight acres of landscaped gardens near Galloway Forest Park. It is said that Robert Burns, a friend of the Heron family who owned the house at the time, sat on the staircase and recited his poetry. The inviting day rooms offer a choice of lounges with an elegant dining room. Bedrooms are traditional and generous in size, and many enjoy wonderful views of the grounds. Service is professional, warm and genuine.

Rooms 17 (1 GF) ↑ **S** £65–£80; **D** £130–£210 (incl. bkfst)* **Facilities** FTV WiFi Putt green 🎣 Xmas New Year **Conf** Class 15 Board 12 Thtr 28 Del from £130 to £160* **Services** Lift **Parking** 40 **Notes** LB No children 10yrs Closed 2 Jan–mid Feb

The Bruce Hotel

★★★ 73% HOTEL

tel: 01671 402294 **88 Queen St DG8 6JL**
email: mail@the-bruce-hotel.com **web:** www.the-bruce-hotel.com
dir: Exit A75 at Newton Stewart rdbt towards town. Hotel 800mtrs on right

Named after the Scottish patriot Robert the Bruce, this welcoming hotel is just a short distance from the A75. One of the well-appointed bedrooms features a four-poster bed, and popular family suites contain separate bedrooms for children. Public areas include a traditional lounge, a formal restaurant and a lounge bar, both offering a good choice of dishes.

Rooms 20 (2 fmly) **Facilities** FTV WiFi New Year **Conf** Class 50 Board 14 Thtr 100 **Parking** 14

NORTH BERWICK
East Lothian

Map 21 NT58

Macdonald Marine Hotel & Spa

★★★★ 81% ◉◉ HOTEL

tel: 0844 879 9130 & 01620 897300 **Cromwell Rd EH39 4LZ**
email: sales.marine@macdonald-hotels.co.uk **web:** www.macdonaldhotels.co.uk/marine
dir: From A198 turn into Hamilton Rd at lights then 2nd right

This imposing hotel commands stunning views across the local golf course to the Firth of Forth. Stylish public areas provide a relaxing atmosphere; creative dishes are served in the restaurant and lighter bites in the lounge/bar. Bedrooms come in a variety of sizes and styles, all are well equipped and some are impressively large. The hotel boasts extensive leisure and conference facilities.

Rooms 83 (7 fmly) (9 GF) 🐾 **Facilities** Spa STV FTV WiFi ⬇ ⬆ supervised ⬆ supervised Gym Indoor & outdoor salt water hydro pool Thermal areas Xmas New Year **Conf** Class 120 Board 60 Thtr 300 **Services** Lift **Parking** 50 **Notes** Civ Wed 150

OBAN
Argyll & Bute

Map 20 NM82

BEST WESTERN The Queens Hotel

★★★★ 72% ◉ HOTEL

tel: 01631 562505 & 570230 **Corran Esplanade PA34 5AG**
email: thequeenshoteloban@hotmail.co.uk **web:** www.thequeenshotel-oban.co.uk
dir: Into Oban on A85, down hill to mini rdbt. 2nd exit towards seafront. At next rdbt follow Ganavan Sands sign. Hotel 0.4m on right just after cathedral

The refurbished Queens Hotel enjoys a wonderful location with stunning views out over Oban Bay. The bedrooms are equipped with modern extras and some bathrooms feature chromatherapy spa baths. The Glen Campa restaurant serves award-winning food. A warm welcome is always forthcoming at this hotel.

Rooms 46 (2 fmly) 🐾 **S** £47.50-£80; **D** £70-£150* **Facilities** FTV WiFi New Year **Services** Lift **Parking** 15 **Notes** Closed 3-31 Jan Civ Wed 60

Manor House Hotel

★★★ 85% ◉ HOTEL

tel: 01631 562087 **Gallanach Rd PA34 4LS**
email: info@manorhouseoban.com **web:** www.manorhouseoban.com
dir: Follow MacBrayne Ferries signs, pass ferry entrance for hotel on right

Handy for the ferry terminal and with views of the bay and harbour, this elegant Georgian residence was built in 1780 as the dower house for the family of the Duke of Argyll. Comfortable and attractive public rooms invite relaxation, while most of the well-equipped bedrooms are furnished with period pieces.

Rooms 11 (1 GF) 🐾 **Facilities** FTV WiFi New Year **Parking** 20 **Notes** No children 12yrs Closed 25-26 Dec Civ Wed 30

Falls of Lora Hotel

★★★ 73% HOTEL

THE INDEPENDENTS
HOTEL ASSOCIATION

tel: 01631 710483 **PA37 1PB**
email: enquiries@fallsoflora.com **web:** www.fallsoflora.com

(For full entry see Connel)

OBAN *continued*

Royal Hotel

★★★ 72% HOTEL

tel: 01631 563021 **Argyll Sqaure PA34 4BE**
email: salesroyaloban@strathmorehotels.com **web:** www.strathmorehotels.com
dir: A82 from Glasgow towards Loch Lomond & Crianlarich then A85 (pass Loch Awe) to Oban

Well situated in the heart of Oban, just minutes from the ferry terminal and with all the shops on its doorstep, this hotel really is central. The comfortable and well-presented bedrooms differ in size, and all public areas are smart. There is a first-floor restaurant overlooking the town square.

Rooms 91 (5 fmly) ☏ **Facilities** FTV WiFi ♫ Xmas New Year **Conf** Class 60 Board 30 Thtr 140 **Services** Lift **Parking** 25 **Notes** ⊗ Civ Wed 70

See advert on page 499

See advert on page 499

OLDMELDRUM
Aberdeenshire
Map 23 NJ82

Meldrum House Country Hotel & Golf Course

★★★★ 83% ◉◉ COUNTRY HOUSE HOTEL

tel: 01651 872294 **AB51 0AE**
email: enquiries@meldrumhouse.com **web:** www.meldrumhouse.com
dir: 11m from Aberdeen on A947 - Aberdeen to Banff road

Set in 350 acres of wooded parkland this imposing baronial country mansion has a golf course as its centrepiece. Tastefully restored to highlight its original character

it provides a peaceful retreat. Bedrooms are massive, and like the public rooms, transport guests back to a bygone era, but at the same time provide stylish modern amenities including smart bathrooms.

Rooms 24 (13 annexe) (1 fmly) (6 GF) ☏ **D** £165-£325 (incl. bkfst)* **Facilities** FTV WiFi ♨ 18 Putt green ♨ Xmas New Year **Conf** Class 20 Board 30 Thtr 80 Del £295* **Parking** 70 **Notes** LB Civ Wed 150

ONICH
Highland
Map 22 NN06

Onich Hotel

★★★ 73% HOTEL

tel: 01855 821214 **PH33 6RY**
email: enquiries@onich-fortwilliam.co.uk **web:** www.onich-fortwilliam.co.uk
dir: Beside A82, 2m N of Ballachulish Bridge

Genuine hospitality is part of the appeal of this hotel, which lies right beside Loch Linnhe with gardens extending to its shores. Nicely presented public areas include a choice of inviting lounges and contrasting bars, and views of the loch can be enjoyed from the attractive restaurant. Bedrooms, with pleasing colour schemes, are comfortably modern.

Rooms 26 (6 fmly) ☏ **S** £45-£70; **D** £80-£160 (incl. bkfst) **Facilities** STV FTV WiFi Games room ♫ New Year **Conf** Board 40 Thtr 50 Del from £110 to £150 **Parking** 50 **Notes** LB Civ Wed 120

PEAT INN
Fife
Map 21 NO40

The Peat Inn

◉◉◉ RESTAURANT WITH ROOMS

tel: 01334 840206 **KY15 5LH**
email: stay@thepeatinn.co.uk **web:** www.thepeatinn.co.uk
dir: At junct of B940 & B941, 5m SW of St Andrews

This 300-year-old former coaching inn enjoys a rural location, and is close to St Andrews. The Peat Inn is spacious, very well appointed, and offers rooms that all have lounge areas. The inn is steeped in history and for years has proved a real haven for food lovers. The three dining areas create a romantic setting, and chef/owner Geoffrey Smeddle produces excellent, award-winning dishes. Expect welcoming open fires and a relaxed ambiance. An extensive continental breakfast selection is served to guests in their bedrooms each morning.

Rooms 8 (8 annexe) (3 fmly)

O

PEEBLES
Scottish Borders
Map 21 NT24

Cringletie House

★★★★ COUNTRY HOUSE HOTEL

tel: 01721 722510 **Edinburgh Rd EH45 8PL**
email: enquiries@cringletie.com **web:** www.cringletie.com
dir: 2m N on A703

This romantic baronial mansion, built in 1861, is set in 28 acres of beautiful gardens and woodland; there is a walled garden with a 400-year-old yew hedge (perhaps the oldest in Scotland), a waterfall, sculptures and croquet lawn. In 1971 Scottish Heritage granted the property a Grade B listing, and in the same year the house became a hotel. The delightful public rooms, with welcoming fires, include a cocktail lounge with adjoining conservatory, and there are service bells in each room which still work. The award-winning, first-floor restaurant has a magnificent hand-painted ceiling. The individually designed bedrooms have grace and charm, and for the ultimate luxury there's the Selkirk Suite.

Rooms 14 (1 annexe) (1 fmly) (2 GF) S £99-£169; **D** £125-£275 (incl. bkfst)*
Facilities FTV WiFi ❧ HL Putt green 🏊 Petanque Giant chess & draughts In room therapy treatments Xmas New Year **Conf** Class 20 Board 24 Thtr 45 Del from £192 to £242* **Services** Lift **Parking** 30 **Notes** Closed 2-27 Jan Civ Wed 100

Macdonald Cardrona Hotel, Golf & Spa

★★★★ 76% ◉ HOTEL

tel: 01896 833600 & 0844 879 9024 **Cardrona EH45 8NE**
email: general.cardrona@macdonald-hotels.co.uk
web: www.macdonald-hotels.co.uk/cardrona
dir: On A72 between Peebles & Innerleithen, 3m S of Peebles

The rolling hills of the Scottish Borders are a stunning backdrop for this modern, purpose-built hotel. Spacious bedrooms are traditional in style, equipped with a range of extras, and most enjoy fantastic views of countryside. The hotel features some impressive leisure facilities, including an 18-hole golf course, 18-metre indoor pool and state-of-the-art gym.

Rooms 99 (24 fmly) (16 GF) **Facilities** Spa FTV WiFi ❧ HL 🏊 ⚓ 18 Putt green Fishing Gym Sauna Steam room Xmas New Year **Conf** Class 120 Board 90 Thtr 250 Del from £99 to £175 **Services** Lift **Parking** 200 **Notes** Civ Wed 200

PERTH
Perth & Kinross
Map 21 NO12

Murrayshall House Hotel & Golf Course

★★★★ 76% ◉◉ HOTEL

tel: 01738 551171 **New Scone PH2 7PH**
email: info@murrayshall.co.uk **web:** www.murrayshall.co.uk
dir: From Perth take A94 (Coupar Angus), 1m from Perth, right to Murrayshall just before New Scone

This imposing country house is set in 350 acres of grounds, including two golf courses, one of which is of championship standard. Bedrooms come in two distinct styles: modern suites in a purpose-built building contrast with more classic rooms in the main building. The Clubhouse bar serves a range of meals all day, whilst more accomplished cooking can be enjoyed in the Old Masters Restaurant.

Rooms 41 (14 annexe) (17 fmly) (5 GF) S £85-£125; **D** £120-£210* **Facilities** STV FTV WiFi HL ⚓ 36 🏌 Putt green Driving range New Year **Conf** Class 60 Board 30 Thtr 150 Del from £125 to £165* **Parking** 120 **Notes** Civ Wed 130

Parklands Hotel

★★★★ 74% ◉◉ SMALL HOTEL

tel: 01738 622451 **2 St Leonards Bank PH2 8EB**
email: info@theparklandshotel.com **web:** www.theparklandshotel.com
dir: M90 junct 10, in 1m left at lights at end of park area, hotel on left

Parklands Hotel is ideally located close to the centre of town, with open views over the South Inch. The enthusiastic proprietors continue to invest heavily in the business and the bedrooms have a smart contemporary feel. Public areas include a choice of restaurants, with a fine dining experience offered in 63@Parklands and more informal dining at the No. 1 The Bank Bistro.

Rooms 15 (3 fmly) (4 GF) S £82.50-£149.50; **D** £105-£199.50 (incl. bkfst)
Facilities STV WiFi ❧ **Conf** Class 18 Board 20 Thtr 24 Del from £139.50* **Parking** 30 **Notes** LB Closed 26 Dec-6 Jan Civ Wed 40

The New County Hotel

★★★ 78% ◉◉ HOTEL

tel: 01738 623355 **22-30 County Place PH2 8EE**
email: enquiries@newcountyhotel.com **web:** www.newcountyhotel.com
dir: A9 junct 11 (Perth). Follow signs for town centre. Hotel on right after library

This is a smart hotel in the heart of the beautiful garden city of Perth. The bedrooms have a modern and stylish appearance and public areas include a popular bar and contemporary lounge area. No stay here is complete without a visit to the award-winning Opus One Restaurant, which has a well deserved reputation for fine dining.

Rooms 23 (4 fmly) **Facilities** STV FTV WiFi New Year **Conf** Class 80 Board 24 Thtr 120 **Parking** 10 **Notes** ⊗

P

PERTH *continued*

BEST WESTERN Lovat Hotel

★★★ 74% HOTEL

tel: 01738 636555 **90-92 Glasgow Rd PH2 0LT**
email: enquiry@lovat.co.uk **web:** www.lovathotel.co.uk
dir: M90 junct 10, 3rd exit, straight through next 3 rdbts, hotel on right 0.5m after 3rd rdbt

The Lovat Hotel offers a comfortable and relaxing atmosphere just a short walk from the centre of Perth. Accommodation consists of comfortable, modern bedrooms, and guests can enjoy a great dining experience in the 1747 Restaurant and Bar. Residents can also enjoy complimentary access to leisure facilities at the hotel's nearby sister property. Deluxe rooms are available for those looking to splash out on a little extra luxury.

Rooms 30 (1 fmly) (10 GF) ⚡ **S** £47-£89; **D** £65-£105 (incl. bkfst)* **Facilities** FTV WiFi ⌂ Xmas New Year **Conf** Class 60 Board 30 Thtr 150 Del from £115 to £135* **Parking** 30 **Notes** LB ⊗ Civ Wed 150

BEST WESTERN Queens Hotel

★★★ 74% HOTEL

tel: 01738 442222 **Leonard St PH2 8HB**
email: enquiry@queensperth.co.uk **web:** www.queensperth.co.uk
dir: From M90 follow to 2nd lights, turn left. Hotel on right, opposite railway station

This popular hotel benefits from a central location close to both the bus and rail stations. Bedrooms vary in size and style with top floor rooms offering extra space and excellent views of the town. Public rooms include a smart leisure centre and versatile conference space. A range of meals is served in both the bar and restaurant.

Rooms 50 (4 fmly) **Facilities** FTV WiFi 🏊 Gym Steam room Xmas New Year **Conf** Class 70 Board 50 Thtr 200 **Services** Lift **Parking** 50 **Notes** ⊗ Civ Wed 220

Mercure Perth Hotel

★★★ 74% HOTEL

tel: 0844 815 9105 **West Mill St PH1 5QP**
email: info@mercureperth.co.uk **web:** www.jupiterhotels.co.uk
dir: A93/A989 to city centre, left into Caledonian Rd, right at lights onto Old High St, hotel on left

This former 15th-century watermill has been converted into a modern hotel but still retains the mill stream running through reception under a glass floor. Central to Perth, the hotel is an ideal location for visiting the area or further afield. Contemporary rooms include satellite TV and free WiFi. The hotel has extensive conference facilities, and a popular brasserie where tempting meals are served.

Rooms 76 **Facilities** WiFi ⌂ **Conf** Class 50 Board 40 Thtr 120 **Parking** 40 **Notes** Civ Wed 300

Salutation Hotel

★★★ 71% HOTEL

tel: 01738 630066 **South St PH2 8PH**
email: salessalutation@strathmorehotels.com **web:** www.strathmorehotels.com
dir: At end of South St on right before River Tay

Situated at the heart of Perth, the Salutation is reputed to be one of the oldest hotels in Scotland and has been welcoming guests through its doors since 1699. It offers traditional hospitality with all the modern comforts. Bedrooms vary in size and are thoughtfully equipped. An extensive menu is available in the Adam Restaurant, with its impressive barrel-vaulted ceiling and original features.

Rooms 84 (5 fmly) ⚡ **Facilities** WiFi ♫ Xmas New Year **Conf** Class 180 Board 60 Thtr 300 Del from £80 to £120 **Services** Lift **Notes** Civ Wed 100

See advert on page 499

PETERHEAD
Aberdeenshire   Map 23 NK14

Buchan Braes Hotel

★★★★ 73% ⊛ HOTEL

tel: 01779 871471 **Boddam AB42 3AR**
email: info@buchanbraes.co.uk **web:** www.buchanbraes.co.uk
dir: From Aberdeen take A90, follow Peterhead signs. 1st right in Stirling signed Boddam. 50mtrs, 1st right

A contemporary hotel located in Boddam that is an excellent base for exploring the attractions of this wonderful part of Scotland. There is an open-plan lounge for drinks and snacks and the Grill Room with an open kitchen that offers a weekly changing, seasonal menu of locally sourced produce. All the bedrooms, including three suites, have 32" flat-screen TVs with satellite channels, king-sized beds and free WiFi.

Rooms 47 (1 fmly) (26 GF) ⚡ **S** £60-£100; **D** £95-£120 (incl. bkfst)* **Facilities** FTV WiFi Xmas New Year **Conf** Class 100 Board 130 Thtr 250 **Services** Lift **Parking** 80 **Notes** ⊗ Civ Wed 220

Palace Hotel

★★★ 75% HOTEL

tel: 01779 474821 **Prince St AB42 1PL**
email: info@palacehotel.co.uk **web:** www.palacehotel.co.uk
dir: A90 from Aberdeen, follow signs to Peterhead, on entering town turn into Prince St, then right into main car park

This town centre hotel is popular with business travellers and for social events. Bedrooms come in two styles, with the executive rooms being particularly smart and spacious. Public areas include a themed bar, an informal diner reached via a spiral staircase, and a newly refurbished restaurant called The Front Room.

Rooms 64 (1 fmly) (13 GF) ✿ **S** fr £65; **D** fr £75 (incl. bkfst)* **Facilities** STV FTV WiFi ⓑ Snooker & pool table 🎵 New Year **Conf** Class 100 Board 60 Thtr 250 **Services** Lift **Parking** 50 **Notes** Civ Wed 250

PITLOCHRY	Map 23 NN95
Perth & Kinross	

See also **Kinloch Rannoch**

Green Park Hotel

★★★★ 76% ⓜ COUNTRY HOUSE HOTEL

tel: 01796 473248 **Clunie Bridge Rd PH16 5JY**
email: bookings@thegreenpark.co.uk **web:** www.thegreenpark.co.uk
dir: Exit A9 at Pitlochry, follow signs 0.25m through town

Guests return year after year to this lovely hotel, situated in a stunning setting on the shores of Loch Faskally. Most of the thoughtfully designed bedrooms, including a splendid wing, the restaurant and the comfortable lounges, enjoy these views. Dinner utilises fresh produce, much of it grown in the kitchen garden.

Rooms 51 (3 fmly) (16 GF) ✿ **S** £78-£111; **D** £156-£222 (incl. bkfst & dinner)* **Facilities** FTV WiFi Putt green New Year **Services** Lift **Parking** 51 **Notes** LB

Knockendarroch House Hotel

★★★★ 75% ⓜⓜ SMALL HOTEL

tel: 01796 473473 **Higher Oakfield PH16 5HT**
email: bookings@knockendarroch.co.uk **web:** www.knockendarroch.co.uk
dir: Just off A9

This secluded hotel has outstanding views over the town and surrounding hills. The individually styled bedrooms are spacious and very well appointed - all have

plasma TVs. The traditional, country-style public rooms have large sofas, welcoming open fires and an excellent whisky cabinet. Dinner is served every evening in the award-winning restaurant with only the best of Scottish produce being used. The staff are friendly and attentive.

Rooms 12 (1 GF) ✿ **Facilities** FTV WiFi **Parking** 12 **Notes** No children 10yrs Closed Dec-Jan

Dundarach Hotel

★★★ 78% HOTEL

tel: 01796 472862 **Perth Rd PH16 5DJ**
email: inbox@dundarach.co.uk **web:** www.dundarach.co.uk
dir: S of town centre on main road

This welcoming, family-run hotel stands in mature grounds at the south end of town. Bedrooms come in a variety of styles, including a block of large purpose-built rooms that will appeal to business guests. Well-proportioned public areas feature inviting lounges and a conservatory restaurant giving fine views of the Tummel Valley.

Rooms 39 (19 annexe) (7 fmly) (12 GF) ✿ **Facilities** FTV WiFi **Conf** Class 40 Board 40 Thtr 60 **Parking** 39 **Notes** ⊗ Closed Jan RS Dec & early Feb

Fonab Castle Hotel

Ⓤ ⓜⓜ

tel: 01796 470140 **Foss Rd PH16 5ND**
email: reservations@fonabcastlehotel.com **web:** www.fonabcastlehotel.com
dir: Pitlochry A9 take Foss Rd junct. Hotel 1st on left

Nestled on the banks of Loch Faskally with stunning views, this hotel was originally built as a home for the Sandeman family, the sherry and port merchants. Stylish bedrooms are set across the main castle building and more modern annexe. The Brasserie, and lounge both offer panoramic views from the hotel's elevated position, and provide a wide choice of quality produce cooked to the highest standard. Due to open in late summer 2014 are a destination spa, pool and gym facilities. For further details please see the AA website: theAA.com

Rooms 26 (2 fmly) (6 GF) ✿ **S** £140-£600; **D** £160-£600 (incl. bkfst)* **Facilities** Spa STV FTV WiFi ⓑ Xmas New Year **Conf** Class 150 Board 40 Thtr 300 Del from £250 to £300* **Services** Lift **Parking** 50 **Notes** LB

POLMONT	Map 21 NS97
Falkirk	

Macdonald Inchyra Hotel and Spa

MACDONALD HOTELS & RESORTS

★★★★ 77% ⓜ HOTEL

tel: 01324 711911 **Grange Rd FK2 0YB**
email: inchyra@macdonald-hotels.co.uk **web:** www.macdonaldhotels.co.uk
dir: 2 mins from M9 junct 5

Ideally placed for the M9 and Grangemouth terminal, this former manor house has been tastefully extended. The hotel provides comprehensive conference facilities and guests will find that The Scottish Steak Club serves the highest quality produce in a contemporary style. The bedrooms are comfortable and most are spacious.

Rooms 97 (6 annexe) (35 fmly) (32 GF) **Facilities** Spa FTV WiFi ⓑ ⓢ Gym Steam room Sauna Aromatherapy shower Ice fountain New Year **Conf** Class 300 Board 80 Thtr 750 **Services** Lift **Parking** 500 **Notes** ⊗ Civ Wed 450

P

POLMONT *continued*

Premier Inn Falkirk East

BUDGET HOTEL

tel: 0871 527 8392 **Beancross Rd FK2 OYS**
web: www.premierinn.com
dir: M9 junct 5, Polmont A9 signs. Hotel on left

High quality, budget accommodation ideal for both families and business travellers. Spacious, en suite bedrooms feature tea and coffee making facilities, and Freeview TV in most hotels. Internet access and WiFi are available for a small fee. The adjacent family restaurant features a wide and varied menu. See also the Hotel Groups pages.

Rooms 40

PORT APPIN	Map 20 NM94
Argyll & Bute	

INSPECTORS' CHOICE

Airds Hotel and Restaurant

★★★★ ◉◉◉ SMALL HOTEL

tel: 01631 730236 **PA38 4DF**
email: airds@airds-hotel.com **web:** www.airds-hotel.com
dir: From A828 (Oban to Fort William road), turn at Appin signed Port Appin. Hotel 2.5m on left

The views are stunning from this small, luxury hotel on the shores of Loch Linnhe. The staff are delightful and nothing is too much trouble. The well-equipped bedrooms provide style and luxury whilst many bathrooms are furnished in marble and have power showers. Comfortable lounges with deep sofas and roaring fires provide the ideal retreat for relaxation. A real get-away-from-it-all experience.

Rooms 11 (3 fmly) (2 GF) ⚡ **S** £240-£325; **D** £290-£495 (incl. bkfst & dinner)* **Facilities** STV FTV WiFi ⌖ Putt green ⚐ In room massage available Xmas New Year **Conf** Class 16 Board 16 Thtr 16 **Parking** 20 **Notes** LB RS Nov-Jan Civ Wed 40

The Pierhouse Hotel

★★★ 80% ◉ SMALL HOTEL

tel: 01631 730302 & 730622 **PA38 4DE**
email: reservations@pierhousehotel.co.uk **web:** www.pierhousehotel.co.uk
dir: A828 from Ballachulish to Oban. In Appin right at Port Appin & Lismore ferry sign. After 2.5m left after post office, hotel at end of road

Originally the residence of the Pier Master, with parts of the building dating back to the 19th century, this hotel is located on the shores of Loch Linnhe with picture-postcard views to the islands of Lismore and Mull. The beautifully appointed, individually designed bedrooms have WiFi access and bathrooms which include Arran Aromatics toiletries. The hotel has a Finnish sauna, and also offers a range of treatments. Babysitting can be arranged.

Rooms 12 (2 fmly) (6 GF) ⚡ **S** fr £75; **D** £105-£225 (incl. bkfst)* **Facilities** FTV WiFi ⌖ Aromatherapy Massage Sauna Kayaking Walking Cycling New Year **Conf** Class 20 Board 20 Thtr 20 Del from £110* **Parking** 20 **Notes** LB Closed 25-26 Dec Civ Wed 80

PORTPATRICK	Map 20 NW95
Dumfries & Galloway	

INSPECTORS' CHOICE

Knockinaam Lodge

★★★ ◉◉◉ HOTEL

tel: 01776 810471 **DG9 9AD**
email: reservations@knockinaamlodge.com **web:** www.knockinaamlodge.com
dir: From A77 or A75 follow signs to Portpatrick. Through Lochans. After 2m left at signs for hotel

Any tour of Dumfries and Galloway wouldn't be complete without a stay at this haven of tranquillity and relaxation. Knockinaam Lodge is an extended Victorian house set in an idyllic cove with its own pebble beach (ideal for a private swim in the summer) and sheltered by majestic cliffs and woodlands. Surrounded by 30 acres of delightful grounds, the lodge was the location for a meeting between Churchill and General Eisenhower in World War II. Today, a warm welcome is assured from the proprietors and their committed team, and much emphasis is placed on providing a sophisticated but intimate home-from-home experience. There are just ten suites - each individually designed and all with flat-screen TVs with DVD players, luxury toiletries and complimentary bottled water. The cooking is a real treat and showcases prime Scottish produce on the daily-changing, four-course set menus; guests can always discuss the choices in advance if they wish.

Rooms 10 (1 fmly) ⚡ **S** £175-£310; **D** £285-£410 (incl. bkfst & dinner)* **Facilities** FTV WiFi Fishing ⚐ Shooting Walking Sea fishing Clay pigeon shooting Xmas New Year **Conf** Class 10 Board 16 Thtr 30 **Parking** 20 **Notes** Civ Wed 40

PRESTWICK
South Ayrshire   Map 20 NS32

Parkstone Hotel

★★★ 74% HOTEL

tel: 01292 477286 **Esplanade KA9 1QN**
email: info@parkstonehotel.co.uk **web:** www.parkstonehotel.co.uk
dir: From Main St - A79 W to seafront, hotel in 600yds

Situated on the seafront in a quiet residential area only one mile from Prestwick Airport, this family-run hotel caters for business visitors as well as golfers. Bedrooms come in a variety of sizes; all are furnished in a smart, contemporary style. The attractive, modern look of the bar and restaurant is matched by an equally up-to-date menu.

Rooms 30 (2 fmly) (7 GF) ⌇ **S** £59-£79; **D** £88-£98* **Facilities** FTV WiFi Xmas New Year **Conf** Thtr 100 **Parking** 34 **Notes** ⊗ Civ Wed 100

RENFREW

Hotels are listed under Glasgow Airport

RHU
Argyll & Bute   Map 20 NS28

Rosslea Hall Hotel

★★★ 78% ⊛ HOTEL

tel: 01436 439955 **Ferry Rd G84 8NF**
web: www.rossleahallhotel.co.uk
dir: On A814, opposite church

Overlooking the Firth of the Clyde and close to Helensburgh, this imposing mansion is set in its own well tended gardens. Bedrooms and bathrooms are of a good size, are well appointed and cater well for the modern traveller. The eating options include the Conservatory Restaurant which offers dishes cooked with imagination and flair, and overlooks the grounds and the Clyde. The hotel is a popular wedding venue.

Rooms 30 (3 fmly) (2 GF) ⌇ **S** £59-£109; **D** £59-£139 (incl. bkfst)* **Facilities** STV FTV WiFi Xmas New Year **Conf** Class 60 Board 80 Thtr 150 **Parking** 30 **Notes** ⊗ Civ Wed 120

ROY BRIDGE
Highland   Map 22 NN28

The Stronlossit Inn

★★★ 74% SMALL HOTEL

tel: 01397 712253 **PH31 4AG**
email: stay@stronlossit.co.uk **web:** www.stronlossit.co.uk
dir: Exit A82 at Spean Bridge onto A86, signed Roy Bridge. Hotel on left

Appointed to modern standards with the character and hospitality of a traditional hostelry, The Stronlossit Inn is quite a draw for the discerning Highland tourist. The spacious bar is the focal point, with a peat burning fire providing a warm welcome in cooler months; guests can eat in the attractive restaurant. Bedrooms come in a mix of sizes and styles, most being smartly modern and well equipped.

Rooms 10 (5 GF) ⌇ **S** £65-£85; **D** £77-£110 (incl. bkfst) **Facilities** WiFi ⌇ **Conf** Class 12 Board 10 Thtr 20 Del from £90 to £130 **Parking** 30 **Notes** LB ⊗ No children 17yrs Closed 1-15 Dec

ST ANDREWS
Fife   Map 21 NO51

INSPECTORS' CHOICE

The Old Course Hotel, Golf Resort & Spa

★★★★★ ⊛⊛⊛ HOTEL

tel: 01334 474371 **KY16 9SP**
email: reservations@oldcoursehotel.co.uk **web:** www.oldcoursehotel.co.uk
dir: M90 junct 8, A91 to St Andrews

A haven for golfers, this internationally renowned hotel sits adjacent to the 17th hole of the championship course. Bedrooms vary in size and style but all provide decadent levels of luxury. Day rooms include intimate lounges, a bright conservatory, a spa and a range of pro golf shops. The fine dining Road Hole Restaurant, the Sands Grill specialising in seafood and steaks, and the informal Jigger Inn are all popular eating venues. Staff throughout are friendly and services are impeccably delivered.

Rooms 144 (5 fmly) (3 GF) **S** £225-£400; **D** £305-£1410 (incl. bkfst)* **Facilities** Spa STV FTV WiFi ⌇⌇ ⌇ 18 Putt green Gym Thermal suite ⌇ Xmas New Year **Conf** Class 473 Board 259 Thtr 950 Del from £260 to £390* **Services** Lift **Parking** 125 **Notes** LB ⊗ Civ Wed 180

ST ANDREWS *continued*

Fairmont St Andrews, Scotland

★★★★★ 84%  HOTEL

tel: 01334 837000 **KY16 8PN**
email: standrews.scotland@fairmont.com **web:** www.fairmont.com/standrews
dir: Approx 2m from St Andrews on A917 towards Crail

Sitting just a few miles from St Andrews, overlooking the rugged Fife coastline and the championship golf courses, The Fairmont is situated on a 520-acre estate. There are spacious bedrooms and bathrooms. The eating options are The Squire for brasserie-style food, Esperante for Mediterranean dishes, and The Clubhouse and The Atrium with all-day menus. The hotel has an impressive spa and health club. Good standards of service are found throughout.

Rooms 209 (209 fmly) (68 GF) **Facilities** Spa STV FTV WiFi 36 Putt green Gym 106-seat cinema Nail salon Xmas New Year **Conf** Class 450 Board 168 Thtr 500 **Services** Lift Air con **Parking** 150 **Notes** Civ Wed 350

INSPECTORS' CHOICE

Rufflets Country House

★★★★  HOTEL

tel: 01334 472594 **Strathkinness Low Rd KY16 9TX**
email: reservations@rufflets.co.uk **web:** www.rufflets.co.uk
dir: 1.5m W on B939

Built in 1924 for a Dundee jute baron, this charming property is set in extensive gardens a few minutes' drive from the town centre. The stylish, spacious bedrooms are individually decorated, and include the Gilroy Suite, The Orchard Suite (separate from the main building), and Turret Rooms that have their own seating areas. Public rooms include a well-stocked bar, a choice of inviting lounges and the delightful Terrace Restaurant that serves imaginative, carefully prepared cuisine based on seasonal produce. Impressive conference and banqueting facilities are available in the adjacent Garden Suite. Families are very welcome, and the hotel is a popular wedding venue.

Rooms 24 (5 annexe) (3 fmly) (5 GF) **S** £120-£185; **D** £170-£295 (incl. bkfst)*
Facilities STV FTV WiFi Putt green Children's outdoor games New Year
Conf Class 60 Board 60 Thtr 200 Del from £185 to £235* **Parking** 50 **Notes** LB Civ Wed 130

Macdonald Rusacks Hotel

★★★★ 79%  HOTEL

tel: 0844 879 9136 & 01334 474321 **Pilmour Links KY16 9JQ**
email: general.rusacks@macdonald-hotels.co.uk **web:** www.macdonaldhotels.co.uk
dir: From A91 W, straight on at rdbt into St Andrews. Hotel 220yds on left

This long-established hotel enjoys an almost unrivalled location with superb views across the famous golf course. Bedrooms, though varying in size, are comfortably appointed and well equipped. Classically styled public rooms include an elegant reception lounge and a modern restaurant and brasserie bar.

Rooms 70 (1 annexe) **Facilities** STV FTV WiFi New Year **Conf** Class 35 Board 20 Thtr 80 **Services** Lift **Parking** 21 **Notes** Civ Wed 60

BEST WESTERN Scores Hotel

★★★ 80% HOTEL

tel: 01334 472451 **76 The Scores KY16 9BB**
email: reception@scoreshotel.co.uk **web:** www.bw-scoreshotel.co.uk
dir: M90 junct 2a, A92 E. Follow Glenrothes signs then St Andrews signs. Straight on at next 2 rdbts, left into Golf Place, right into The Scores

Enjoying views over St Andrews Bay, this well-presented hotel is situated only a short pitch from the first tee of the famous Old Course. Bedrooms are impressively furnished and come in various sizes; many are quite spacious. Smart public areas include Champions Grill, offering food all day from breakfast to dinner; Scottish High Teas are served here from 4.30-6.30pm. Alexander's Restaurant opens Thursday, Friday and Saturday evenings.

Rooms 36 (1 fmly) **S** £94-£219; **D** £140-£350 (incl. bkfst) **Facilities** FTV WiFi HL Xmas New Year **Conf** Class 60 Board 40 Thtr 180 Del from £144 to £203 **Services** Lift **Parking** 12 **Notes** LB Civ Wed 100

Russell Hotel

★★ 80% ⊕ HOTEL

tel: 01334 473447 **26 The Scores KY16 9AS**
email: enquiries@russellhotelstandrews.co.uk **web:** www.russellhotelstandrews.co.uk
dir: From A91 left at 2nd rdbt into Golf Place, right in 200yds into The Scores, hotel in 300yds on left

Lying on the east bay, this friendly, family-run Victorian terrace hotel provides well appointed bedrooms in varying sizes; some enjoy fine sea views. Cosy public areas include a popular bar and an intimate restaurant, both offering a good range of freshly prepared dishes. Situated in St Andrews, said to be 'The Home of Golf', this hotel offers a comprehensive range of golfing breaks, and is convenient for visits to the castle, cathedral and university.

Rooms 10 (3 fmly) **Facilities** WiFi ↳ New Year **Notes** ⊗

ST BOSWELLS
Scottish Borders   Map 21 NT53

Dryburgh Abbey Hotel

★★★★ 73% COUNTRY HOUSE HOTEL

tel: 01835 822261 **TD6 0RQ**
email: enquiries@dryburgh.co.uk **web:** www.dryburgh.co.uk
dir: Exit A68 at St Boswells. B6356 signed Scott's View & Earlston. Through Clintmains, 1.8m to hotel

This Victorian country house hotel is found in the heart of the Scottish Borders, sitting beside the ancient ruins of Dryburgh Abbey and the majestic River Tweed. It offers comfortable public areas and an array of bedrooms and suites, each still displaying original features. The award-winning Tweed Restaurant, overlooking the

river, showcases the chef's dedication to producing modern Scottish cuisine, and The Abbey Bistro offers food from noon until 9pm.

Rooms 38 (31 fmly) (8 GF) ⮐ **S** £50-£150; **D** £60-£200 (incl. bkfst)* **Facilities** FTV WiFi ↳ ⊗ Putt green Fishing ⟲ Sauna Xmas New Year **Conf** Class 80 Board 60 Thtr 150 **Services** Lift **Parking** 70 **Notes** Civ Wed 120

ST FILLANS
Perth & Kinross   Map 20 NN62

The Four Seasons Hotel

★★★ 85% ⊕⊕ HOTEL

tel: 01764 685333 **Loch Earn PH6 2NF**
email: info@thefourseasonshotel.co.uk **web:** www.thefourseasonshotel.co.uk
dir: On A85, towards W of village

Set on the edge of Loch Earn, this welcoming hotel and many of its bedrooms benefit from fine views. There is a choice of lounges, including a library, warmed by log fires during winter. Local produce is used to good effect in both the Meall Reamhar restaurant and the more informal Tarken Room.

Rooms 18 (6 annexe) (7 fmly) ⮐ **S** £66-£108; **D** £122-£166 (incl. bkfst)* **Facilities** FTV WiFi Xmas New Year **Conf** Class 45 Board 38 Thtr 95 Del from £102.50 to £148.50* **Parking** 40 **Notes** LB Closed 2 Jan-mid Feb RS Nov, Dec, Mar Civ Wed 80

SANQUHAR
Dumfries & Galloway   Map 21 NS70

Blackaddie House Hotel

★★★ 79% ⊕⊕ COUNTRY HOUSE HOTEL

tel: 01659 50270 **Blackaddie Rd DG4 6JJ**
email: ian@blackaddiehotel.co.uk **web:** www.blackaddiehotel.co.uk
dir: Exit A76 just N of Sanquhar at Burnside Service Station. Take private road to hotel 300mtrs on right

Overlooking the River Nith and in two acres of secluded gardens, this family run country house hotel offers friendly and attentive hands-on service. The bedrooms and suites, including family accommodation, are all well presented and comfortable with many useful extras provided as standard. The award-winning food, served in the restaurant, with its lovely garden views, is based on prime Scottish ingredients.

Rooms 7 (1 annexe) (1 GF) ⮐ **S** £80-£120; **D** £110-£220 (incl. bkfst)* **Facilities** FTV WiFi Xmas New Year **Conf** Class 12 Board 16 Thtr 20 **Parking** 20 **Notes** LB Civ Wed 24

S

SCOURIE
Highland   Map 22 NC14

Scourie Hotel

★★★ 72% SMALL HOTEL

tel: 01971 502396 **IV27 4SX**
email: patrick@scourie-hotel.co.uk **web:** www.scourie-hotel.co.uk
dir: N'bound on A894. Hotel in village on left

This well-established hotel is an angler's paradise with extensive fishing rights available on a 25,000-acre estate. Public areas include a choice of comfortable lounges, a cosy bar and a smart dining room offering wholesome fare. The bedrooms are comfortable and generally spacious. The resident proprietors and their staff create a relaxed and friendly atmosphere.

Rooms 20 (2 annexe) (2 fmly) (5 GF) 🕊 **S** £48-£59; **D** £92-£112 (incl. bkfst)*
Facilities WiFi Fishing **Parking** 30 **Notes** LB Closed mid Oct-end Mar

SELKIRK
Scottish Borders   Map 21 NT42

BEST WESTERN Philipburn Country House Hotel

★★★★ Ⓐ COUNTRY HOUSE HOTEL

tel: 01750 20747 **Linglie Rd TD7 5LS**
email: info@philipburnhousehotel.co.uk **web:** www.bw-philipburnhousehotel.co.uk
dir: From A7 follow signs for A72 & A707/Peebles & Moffat. Hotel 1m from town centre

Ideally located in a tranquil setting on the outskirts of Selkirk, this hotel dates back to 1751 and is surrounded by gardens and woodland. Bedrooms are individually designed and tastefully appointed to high standards; some feature jacuzzi baths, and some have a mezzanine floor and balcony dividing the lounge from the sleeping area.

Rooms 14 (2 annexe) (2 fmly) 🕊 **S** £95-£145; **D** £135-£185 (incl. bkfst)*
Facilities FTV WiFi ↺ �“ **Conf** Class 40 Board 40 Thtr 150 Del from £140 to £170*
Parking 55 **Notes** LB ⊗ Closed 3-20 Jan Civ Wed 200

SHIEL BRIDGE
Highland   Map 22 NG91

Grants at Craigellachie

Ⓐ RESTAURANT WITH ROOMS

tel: 01599 511331 **Craigellachie, Ratagan IV40 8HP**
email: info@housebytheloch.co.uk **web:** www.housebytheloch.co.uk
dir: From A87 exit for Glenelg, 1st right to Ratagan, opposite Youth Hostel sign

Sitting on the tranquil shores of Loch Duich and overlooked by the Five Sisters Mountains, Grants really does occupy a stunning location. The restaurant has a well deserved reputation for its cuisine, and the bedrooms are stylish and come with all the creature comforts. Guests are guaranteed a warm welcome at this charming house.

Rooms 4 (2 annexe)

SOUTH QUEENSFERRY
City of Edinburgh   Map 21 NT17

Premier Inn Edinburgh (Newcraighall)

BUDGET HOTEL

tel: 0871 527 8362 **91 Newcraighall Rd, Newcraighall EH21 8RX**
web: www.premierinn.com
dir: At junct of A1 & A6095 towards Musselburgh

High quality, budget accommodation ideal for both families and business travellers. Spacious, en suite bedrooms feature tea and coffee making facilities, and Freeview TV in most hotels. Internet access and WiFi are available for a small fee. The adjacent family restaurant features a wide and varied menu. See also the Hotel Groups pages.

Rooms 42

Premier Inn Edinburgh (South Queensferry)

BUDGET HOTEL

tel: 0871 527 8364 **Builyeon Rd EH30 9YJ**
web: www.premierinn.com
dir: M8 junct 2 follow M9 Stirling signs, exit at junct 1a take A8000 towards Forth Road Bridge, at 3rd rdbt 2nd exit into Builyeon Rd (NB do not go onto Forth Road Bridge)

Rooms 70

SPEAN BRIDGE
Highland   Map 22 NN28

Smiddy House

◉◉ RESTAURANT WITH ROOMS

tel: 01397 712335 🖹 01397 712043 **Roy Bridge Rd PH34 4EU**
email: enquiry@smiddyhouse.com **web:** www.smiddyhouse.com
dir: In village centre, A82 onto A86

Set in the Great Glen which stretches from Fort William to Inverness, this was once the village smithy, and is now a very friendly establishment. The attractive bedrooms, named after places in Scotland, are comfortably furnished and well equipped. A relaxing garden room is available for guest use. Delicious evening meals are served in Russell's restaurant.

Rooms 4 (1 fmly)

STEPPS
North Lanarkshire   Map 20 NS66

Premier Inn Glasgow North East (Stepps)

BUDGET HOTEL

tel: 0871 527 8452 **Crowwood Roundabout, Cumbernauld Rd G33 6HN**
web: www.premierinn.com
dir: M8 junct 12, A80 (becomes dual carriageway) to Crowwood rdbt, 4th exit back onto A80, hotel 1st left. Or exit M80 at Crowwood rdbt, 3rd exit signed A80 West. Hotel 1st left

High quality, budget accommodation ideal for both families and business travellers. Spacious, en suite bedrooms feature tea and coffee making facilities, and Freeview TV in most hotels. Internet access and WiFi are available for a small fee. The adjacent family restaurant features a wide and varied menu. See also the Hotel Groups pages.

Rooms 80

STIRLING	Map 21 NS79
Stirling	

The Stirling Highland Hotel

★★★★ 75% HOTEL

PUMA HOTELS
COLLECTION

tel: 01786 272727 **Spittal St FK8 1DU**
email: stirling@pumahotels.co.uk **web:** www.pumahotels.co.uk
dir: A84 into Stirling. Follow Stirling Castle signs to Albert Hall. Left, left again, follow Castle signs

Enjoying a location close to the castle and historic town, this atmospheric hotel was previously a high school. Public rooms have been converted from the original classrooms and retain many interesting features. Bedrooms are more modern in style and comfortably equipped. Scholars Restaurant serves traditional and international dishes, and the Headmaster's Study is the ideal venue for enjoying a drink.

Rooms 96 (4 fmly) (28 GF) **Facilities** Spa STV FTV WiFi ☆ HL ☒ supervised Gym Squash Steam room Dance studio Beauty therapist Xmas New Year **Conf** Class 60 Board 40 Thtr 120 Del from £120 to £169 **Services** Lift **Parking** 96 **Notes** Civ Wed 100

Premier Inn Stirling

BUDGET HOTEL

tel: 0871 527 9038 **Glasgow Rd, Whins of Milton FK7 8EX**
web: www.premierinn.com
dir: On A872, 0.25m from M9/M80 junct 9

High quality, budget accommodation ideal for both families and business travellers. Spacious, en suite bedrooms feature tea and coffee making facilities, and Freeview TV in most hotels. Internet access and WiFi are available for a small fee. The adjacent family restaurant features a wide and varied menu. See also the Hotel Groups pages.

Rooms 60

Premier Inn Stirling City Centre

BUDGET HOTEL

tel: 0871 527 9472 **Forthside Way FK8 1QZ**
web: www.premierinn.com
dir: Please see website for detailed directions

Rooms 60

STRACHUR	Map 20 NN00
Argyll & Bute	

The Creggans Inn

★★★ 78% HOTEL

tel: 01369 860279 **PA27 8BX**
email: info@creggans-inn.co.uk **web:** www.creggans-inn.co.uk
dir: A82 from Glasgow, at Tarbet take A83 towards Cairndow, left onto A815 to Strachur

Benefiting from a superb location on the shores of Loch Fyne, this well established family-run hotel caters well for both the leisure and corporate market. Many of the bedrooms are generous in size and enjoy wonderful views of the loch. During the cooler months open log fires are lit in the bar lounge and restaurant. WiFi is available throughout.

Rooms 14 (2 fmly) 🐾 **S** £75-£95; **D** £100-£140 (incl. bkfst) **Facilities** FTV WiFi New Year **Parking** 16 **Notes** Civ Wed 80

STRANRAER	Map 20 NX06
Dumfries & Galloway	

Corsewall Lighthouse Hotel

★★★ 80% HOTEL

tel: 01776 853220 **Corsewall Point, Kirkcolm DG9 0QG**
email: lighthousehotel@btinternet.com **web:** www.lighthousehotel.co.uk
dir: A718 from Stranraer to Kirkcolm (approx 8m). Follow hotel signs for 4m

Looking for something completely different? This is a unique hotel converted from buildings that adjoin a Grade A listed, 19th-century lighthouse set on a rocky coastline. Situated on the headland to the west of Loch Ryan, the lighthouse beam still functions to warn approaching ships. Bedrooms come in a variety of sizes, some reached by a spiral staircase, and like the public areas, are cosy and atmospheric. The cottage suites in the grounds offer greater space. The restaurant menus are based on Scottish produce such as venison and salmon.

Rooms 11 (5 annexe) (4 fmly) (2 GF) (3 smoking) 🐾 **S** £140-£210; **D** £160-£230 (incl. bkfst & dinner)* **Facilities** FTV WiFi Xmas New Year **Conf** Thtr 20 **Parking** 20 **Notes** LB ⊗ Civ Wed 28

STRATHAVEN	Map 20 NS74
South Lanarkshire	

Rissons at Springvale

 RESTAURANT WITH ROOMS

tel: 01357 521131 & 520234 📠 01357 521131 **18 Lethame Rd ML10 6AD**
email: info@rissons.co.uk **web:** www.rissonsrestaurant.co.uk
dir: A71 into Strathaven, W of town centre off Townhead St

Guests are assured of a warm welcome at this charming establishment close to the town centre. The bedrooms and bathrooms are stylish and well equipped. The main attraction here is the food - a range of interesting, well-prepared dishes served in Rissons Restaurant.

Rooms 9 (1 fmly)

S

STRATHYRE	Map 20 NN51
Stirling	

Creagan House

◉◉ RESTAURANT WITH ROOMS

tel: 01877 384638 📄 01877 384319 **FK18 8ND**
email: eatandstay@creaganhouse.co.uk **web:** www.creaganhouse.co.uk
dir: 0.25m N of Strathyre on A84

Originally a farmhouse dating from the 17th century, Creagan House has operated as a restaurant with rooms for many years. The baronial-style dining room provides a wonderful setting for the cuisine which is classic French with some Scottish influences. The warm hospitality and attentive service are noteworthy.

Rooms 5 (1 fmly)

STRONTIAN	Map 22 NM86
Highland	

Kilcamb Lodge Hotel

★★★ ◉◉ COUNTRY HOUSE HOTEL

tel: 01967 402257 **PH36 4HY**
email: enquiries@kilcamblodge.co.uk **web:** www.kilcamblodge.co.uk
dir: Off A861, via Corran Ferry

This historic house on the shores of Loch Sunart was one of the first stone buildings in the area, and was used as military barracks around the time of the Jacobite uprising. It is situated on the beautiful and peaceful Ardamurchan Peninsula where otters, red squirrels and eagles can be spotted. The suites and bedrooms, with either loch or garden views, are stylishly decorated using designer fabrics and have flat-screen TVs, DVD/CD players, plus bath robes, iced water and even guest umbrellas. Accomplished cooking, utilising much local produce, can be enjoyed in the stylish dining room. Warm hospitality is assured.

Rooms 10 (2 fmly) ⚒ **S** £80-£124; **D** £200-£404 (incl. bkfst & dinner)* **Facilities** FTV WiFi ⚓ Fishing Boating Hiking Bird/whale/otter watching Stalking Clay pigeon shooting Xmas New Year **Conf** Class 18 Board 18 Thtr 18 Del from £99 to £145* **Parking** 20 **Notes** LB No children 10yrs Closed 2 Jan-1 Feb Civ Wed 120

TAIN	Map 23 NH78
Highland	

The Glenmorangie Highland Home at Cadboll

★★★ ◉◉ COUNTRY HOUSE HOTEL

tel: 01862 871671 **Cadboll, Fearn IV20 1XP**
email: relax@glenmorangie.co.uk **web:** www.theglenmorangiehouse.com
dir: A9 onto B9175 towards Nigg. Follow tourist signs

This historic highland home superbly balances top class service with intimate customer care. Evenings are dominated by the highly successful 'house party' where guests are introduced in the drawing room, sample whiskies then take dinner (a set six-course meal) together around one long table. Conversation can extend well into the evening. Stylish bedrooms are divided between the traditional main house and some cosy cottages in the grounds. This is an ideal base from which to enjoy the world famous whisky tours.

Rooms 9 (3 annexe) (4 fmly) (3 GF) ⚒ **S** £250-£275; **D** £400-£430 (incl. dinner) **Facilities** FTV WiFi ⚓ Archery Beauty treatments Clay pigeon shooting Falconry Xmas New Year **Conf** Board 12 **Parking** 60 **Notes** ⊗ No children 15yrs Civ Wed 60

THORNHILL	Map 21 NX89
Dumfries & Galloway	

The Buccleuch and Queensberry Arms Hotel

★★★ 81% ◉ HOTEL

tel: 01848 323101 **112 Drumlanrig St DG3 5LU**
email: info@bqahotel.com **web:** www.bqahotel.com
dir: On A76 in centre of Thornhill

This small, family-run hotel is located in the heart of the small town of Thornhill. Inside the hotel has seen a massive refurbishment, bedrooms are extremely well appointed and of a high quality. Public areas are warm and welcoming with an open log fire adding to the charm. Food is a strong aspect to the operation with the award-winning chef using local produce where possible.

Rooms 12 (2 annexe) (2 GF) ⚒ **Facilities** STV FTV WiFi ♫ Xmas New Year **Conf** Class 60 Board 40 Thtr 120 **Parking** 12

THURSO
Highland
Map 23 ND16

Forss House Hotel

★★★★ 76% ◉◉ SMALL HOTEL

tel: 01847 861201 **Forss KW14 7XY**
email: anne@forsshousehotel.co.uk **web:** www.forsshousehotel.co.uk
dir: On A836 between Thurso & Reay

This delightful country house is set in its own 20 acres of woodland and was originally built in 1810. The hotel offers a choice of bedrooms from the traditional styled rooms in the main house to the more contemporary annexe rooms in the grounds. All rooms are very well equipped and well appointed. The beautiful River Forss runs through the grounds and is a firm favourite with fishermen.

Rooms 14 (6 annexe) (1 fmly) (7 GF) ⌇ **S** £99-£135; **D** £135-£185 (incl. bkfst)*
Facilities FTV WiFi ⌇ Fishing **Conf** Class 12 Board 14 Thtr 20 Del from £162.50*
Parking 14 **Notes** Closed 23 Dec-3 Jan Civ Wed 26

TIRORAN
Argyll & Bute
Map 20 NM42

Tiroran House Hotel

★★★★ 81% ◉◉ COUNTRY HOUSE HOTEL

tel: 01681 705232 **PA69 5ES**
email: info@tiroran.com **web:** www.tiroran.com
dir: Phone for directions

Tiroran House is delightfully located and sits in a splendid location, slightly elevated, with superb loch-side views, and walks and wild life all around. Rooms are very well appointed, with lots of thoughtful extra touches, and very comfortable beds. Dining is a must, with excellent local produce, skilled cookery and a friendly team, as well as charming hosts.

Rooms 10 (4 annexe) (1 fmly) (5 GF) ⌇ **S** £130-£220; **D** £185-£220 (incl. bkfst)*
Facilities STV FTV WiFi Fishing **Parking** 12 **Notes** LB Closed Dec-Feb

TORRIDON
Highland
Map 22 NG95

The Torridon

★★★★ ◉◉ COUNTRY HOUSE HOTEL

tel: 01445 791242 **By Achnasheen, Wester Ross IV22 2EY**
email: info@thetorridon.com **web:** www.thetorridon.com
dir: From A832 at Kinlochewe, A896 towards Torridon. (NB do not turn into village) 1m, hotel on right

Delightfully set amidst inspiring loch and mountain scenery, this elegant Victorian shooting lodge has been beautifully appointed to make the most of its many original features, and the 58 acres of surrounding parkland make it a perfect getaway destination. The attractive bedrooms are individually furnished and most enjoy stunning Highland views; expect to find Egyptian cotton sheets, duck down duvets, flat-screen satellite TVs, FM radios and iPod docks plus Victorian-style bathrooms; for complete privacy choose The Boathouse on the loch shore. Comfortable day rooms feature fine wood panelling and roaring fires in cooler months. The kitchen team creates award-winning menus based as much as possible on locally sourced ingredients; the hotel has its own herd of cattle. The whisky bar is aptly named, boasting over 300 malts and in-depth tasting notes. Outdoor activities include shooting, cycling and walking.

Rooms 18 (2 GF) ⌇ **Facilities** STV WiFi Fishing ⌇ Abseiling Archery Climbing Kayaking Mountain biking Clay pigeon shooting Xmas New Year **Conf** Board 16 Thtr 42 **Services** Lift **Parking** 20 **Notes** ⊗ Closed 2 Jan-9 Feb RS Nov-Mar Civ Wed 55

TROON
South Ayrshire   Map 20 NS33

Lochgreen House Hotel

★★★★ ◉◉◉ COUNTRY HOUSE HOTEL

tel: 01292 313343 **Monktonhill Rd, Southwood KA10 7EN**
email: lochgreen@costley-hotels.co.uk **web:** www.costley-hotels.co.uk
dir: From A77 follow Prestwick Airport signs. 0.5m before airport take B749 to Troon. Hotel 1m on left

Set in immaculately maintained grounds, Lochgreen House is graced by tasteful extensions which have created stunning public rooms and spacious, comfortable and elegantly furnished bedrooms. Extra facilities include a coffee shop, gift shop and beauty treatments in The Retreat. The magnificent Tapestry Restaurant provides the ideal setting for dinners that are immaculately presented.

Rooms 38 (7 annexe) (17 GF) **Facilities** STV WiFi Beauty treatments Xmas New Year **Conf** Class 180 Board 50 Thtr 200 **Services** Lift **Parking** 50 **Notes** ⊗ Civ Wed 140

The Marine Hotel

★★★★ 78% ◉◉ HOTEL

PUMA HOTELS COLLECTION

tel: 01292 314444 **Crosbie Rd KA10 6HE**
email: marine@pumahotels.co.uk **web:** www.pumahotels.co.uk
dir: A77, A78, A79 onto B749. Hotel on left after golf course

A favourite with conference and leisure guests, this hotel overlooks Royal Troon's 18th fairway. The cocktail lounge and split-level restaurant enjoy panoramic views of the Firth of Clyde across to the Isle of Arran. Bedrooms and public areas are attractively appointed.

Rooms 89 **Facilities** Spa FTV WiFi ⊠ supervised Gym Squash Steam room Beauty room Xmas New Year **Conf** Class 100 Board 40 Thtr 200 **Services** Lift **Parking** 200 **Notes** Civ Wed 100

TURNBERRY
South Ayrshire   Map 20 NS20

Turnberry Resort, Scotland

★★★★★ ◉◉◉ HOTEL

tel: 01655 331000 **KA26 9LT**
email: turnberry@luxurycollection.com **web:** www.turnberryresort.co.uk
dir: From Glasgow take A77, M77 S towards Stranraer, 2m past Kirkoswald follow signs for A719 & Turnberry. Hotel 500mtrs on right

Golf probably springs to mind when this hotel is mentioned, and with good reason. This famous establishment enjoys magnificent views over to Arran, Ailsa Craig, and the Mull of Kintyre. Facilities include a world-renowned golf course, the excellent Colin Montgomerie Golf Academy, a luxurious spa with pool, ESPA treatments and a techno fitness studio, as well as a host of outdoor pursuits for both adults and children. Some superbly modern rooms and more traditional, elegant bedrooms and suites are located in the main hotel, while adjacent lodges provide more space. The public areas are stunning and include the Grand Tea Lounge, Ailsa Bar and Lounge, the Duel in the Sun sports bar, 1906 restaurant, and the fine-dining James Miller room and chef's table.

Rooms 157 (40 annexe) (2 fmly) (14 GF) ☞ **S** £150-£405; **D** £170-£425 (incl. bkfst)*
Facilities Spa STV FTV WiFi ⊠ supervised ⅃ 45 Putt green Gym Leisure club Turnberry Adventures Turnberry Performance Academy Xmas New Year Child facilities **Conf** Class 145 Board 80 Thtr 300 Del from £179 to £385* **Services** Lift **Parking** 200 **Notes** LB Closed 1 wk Dec & 2 wks Jan Civ Wed 220

Malin Court

★★★ 80% HOTEL

tel: 01655 331457 **KA26 9PB**
email: info@malincourt.co.uk **web:** www.malincourt.co.uk
dir: On A74 to Ayr then A719 to Turnberry & Maidens

Forming part of the Malin Court Residential and Nursing Home Complex, this friendly and comfortable hotel enjoys delightful views over the Firth of Clyde and Turnberry golf courses. Standard and executive rooms are available; all are well equipped. Public areas are plentiful, with the restaurant serving high teas, dinners and light lunches.

Rooms 18 (9 fmly) **S** £70-£75; **D** £105-£130 (incl. bkfst)* **Facilities** STV WiFi Putt green **Conf** Class 60 Board 30 Thtr 200 Del from £115 to £125* **Services** Lift **Parking** 110 **Notes** ⊗ RS Oct-Mar Civ Wed 80

UPHALL
West Lothian Map 21 NT07

Macdonald Houstoun House
★★★★ 79% ◉◉ HOTEL

tel: 0844 879 9043 **EH52 6JS**
email: houstoun@macdonald-hotels.co.uk web: www.macdonaldhotels.co.uk
dir: M8 junct 3 follow Broxburn signs, straight over rdbt, at mini-rdbt turn right towards Uphall, hotel 1m on right

This historic 17th-century tower house lies in beautifully landscaped grounds and gardens, and features a modern leisure club and spa, a choice of dining options, a vaulted cocktail bar and extensive conference and meeting facilities. Stylish bedrooms, some located around a courtyard, are comfortably furnished and well equipped.

Rooms 73 (47 annexe) (12 fmly) (12 GF) ➤ S £65-£230; D £65-£230* Facilities Spa STV FTV WiFi ↕ 🎱 ♨ Gym Health & beauty salon Xmas New Year Conf Class 80 Board 80 Thtr 400 Del from £110 to £280* Parking 250 Notes Civ Wed 200

UPLAWMOOR
East Renfrewshire Map 20 NS45

Uplawmoor Hotel
★★★ 77% ◉ SMALL HOTEL

tel: 01505 850565 **Neilston Rd G78 4AF**
email: info@uplawmoor.co.uk web: www.uplawmoor.co.uk
dir: M77 junct 2, A736 signed Barrhead & Irvine. Hotel 4m beyond Barrhead

Originally a coaching inn, this friendly hotel is set in a village off the Glasgow to Irvine road. The relaxed restaurant (with cocktail lounge adjacent) features imaginative dishes, whilst the separate lounge bar is popular for freshly prepared bar meals. The modern bedrooms are both comfortable and well equipped.

Rooms 14 (1 fmly) ➤ S £70; D £95 (incl. bkfst) Facilities STV WiFi ↕ Parking 40 Notes ⊗ Closed 26 Dec & 1 Jan

WHITEBRIDGE
Highland Map 23 NH41

Whitebridge Hotel
★★ 69% HOTEL

tel: 01456 486226 **IV2 6UN**
email: info@whitebridgehotel.co.uk web: www.whitebridgehotel.co.uk
dir: A9 onto B851, follow signs to Fort Augustus. Or A82 onto B862 at Fort Augustus

Close to Loch Ness and set amid rugged mountain and moorland scenery, this hotel is popular with tourists, fishermen and deerstalkers. Guests have a choice of more formal dining in the restaurant or lighter meals in the popular cosy bar. Bedrooms are thoughtfully equipped and brightly furnished.

Rooms 12 (3 fmly) S £55-£60; D £86-£94 (incl. bkfst) Facilities WiFi Fishing Parking 32 Notes Closed 11 Dec-9 Jan

WICK
Highland Map 23 ND35

Mackay's Hotel
★★★ 74% HOTEL

tel: 01955 602323 **Union St KW1 5ED**
email: info@mackayshotel.co.uk web: www.mackayshotel.co.uk
dir: Opposite Caithness General Hospital

This well-established hotel is situated just outside the town centre overlooking the River Wick. MacKay's provides well-equipped, attractive accommodation, suited to both the business and leisure guest. There is a stylish bistro offering food throughout the day and the main bar offers a wide selection of whiskies.

Rooms 30 (2 fmly) ➤ Facilities FTV WiFi ↕ HL Free use of local gym & pool ♫ Conf Class 100 Board 60 Thtr 200 Services Lift Notes ⊗ Civ Wed 200

W

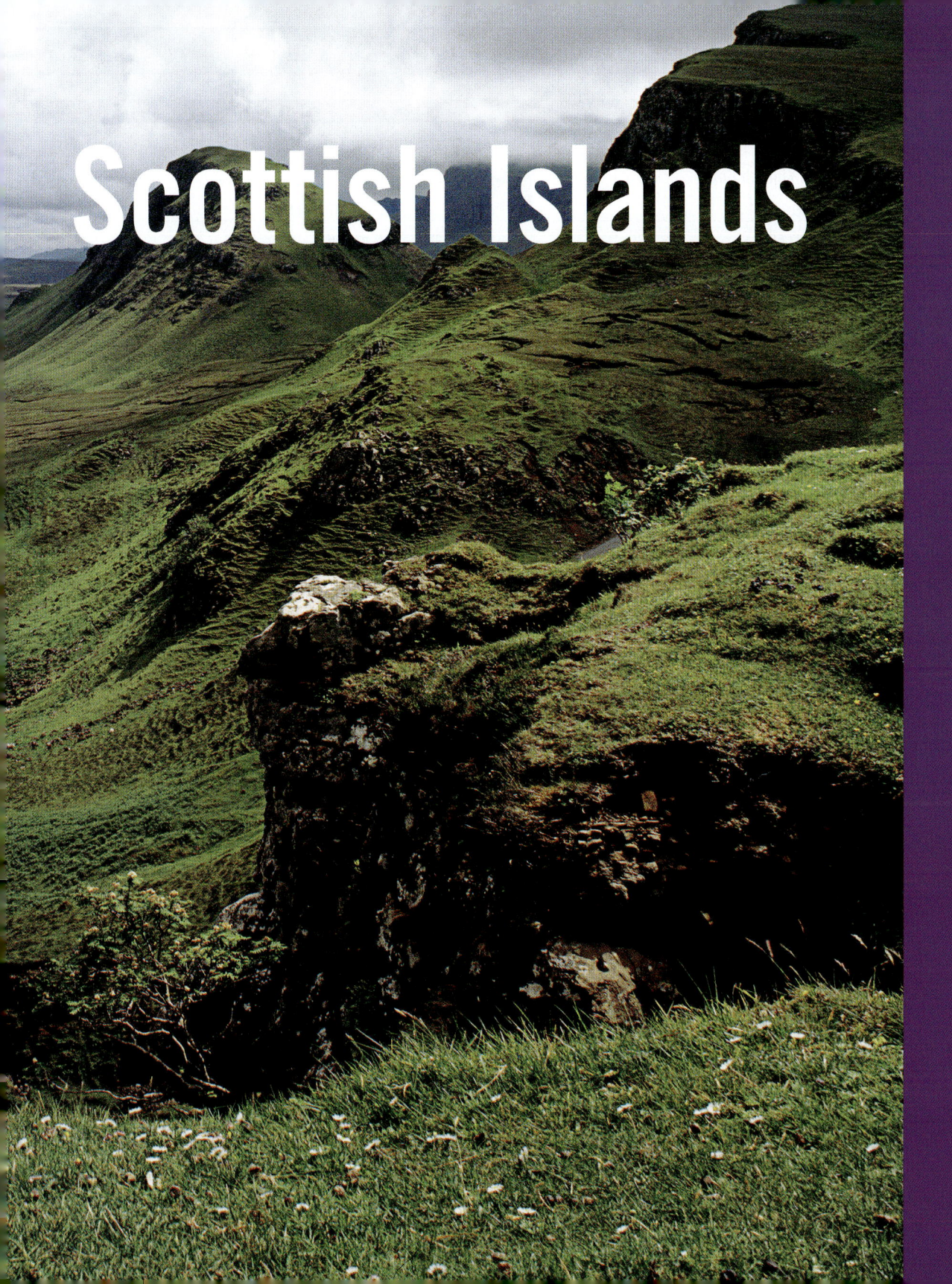

Scottish Islands

ISLE OF ARRAN

BLACKWATERFOOT — Map 20 NR92

BEST WESTERN Kinloch Hotel

★★★ 79% HOTEL

tel: 01770 860444 **KA27 8ET**
email: reservations@kinlochhotel.eclipse.co.uk **web:** www.bw-kinlochhotel.co.uk
dir: Ferry from Ardrossan to Brodick, follow signs for Blackwaterfoot, hotel in village centre

Well known for providing an authentic island experience, this long established stylish hotel is in an idyllic location. Smart public areas include a choice of lounges, popular bars and well-presented leisure facilities. Bedrooms vary in size and style but most enjoy panoramic sea views and several family suites offer excellent value. The spacious restaurant provides a wide ranging menu, and in winter when the restaurant is closed, the bar serves a choice of creative dishes.

Rooms 37 (7 fmly) (7 GF) ✆ **S** £40-£70; **D** £80-£140 (incl. bkfst)* **Facilities** STV WiFi ⬧ ⬧ Gym Squash New Year **Conf** Class 20 Board 40 Thtr 120 Del from £85 to £125* **Services** Lift **Parking** 24 **Notes** Civ Wed 150

BRODICK — Map 20 NS03

INSPECTORS' CHOICE

Kilmichael Country House Hotel

★★★ ◉◉ ◉ COUNTRY HOUSE HOTEL

tel: 01770 302219 **Glen Cloy KA27 8BY**
email: enquiries@kilmichael.com **web:** www.kilmichael.com
dir: From Brodick ferry terminal towards Lochranza for 1m. Left at golf course, follow signs

Reputed to be the oldest on the island, this lovely house lies in attractive gardens in a quiet glen less than five minutes' drive from the ferry terminal. It is a stylish, elegant country house, adorned with ornaments from around the world. The delightful bedrooms are furnished in classical style; some are contained in a pretty courtyard conversion. There are two inviting drawing rooms and a bright dining room where award-winning contemporary cuisine is served. The dishes include fresh eggs laid by the hotel's own ducks and hens, vegetables, fruit and herbs from the kitchen garden, and mushrooms and berries are foraged in season from the estate.

Rooms 8 (3 annexe) (7 GF) ✆ **S** £75-£98; **D** £120-£203 (incl. bkfst) **Facilities** WiFi **Parking** 14 **Notes** LB No children 12yrs Closed Nov-Feb (ex for prior bookings)

ISLE OF HARRIS

SCARISTA (SGARASTA BHEAG) — Map 22 NG09

Scarista House

◉◉ RESTAURANT WITH ROOMS

tel: 01859 550238 **HS3 3HX**
email: timandpatricia@scaristahouse.com **web:** www.scaristahouse.com
dir: On A859, 15m S of Tarbert

A former manse, Scarista House is a haven for food lovers and those who seek to explore this magnificent island. The house enjoys breathtaking views of the Atlantic and is just a short stroll from miles of golden sandy beaches. The house is run in a relaxed country-house manner by the friendly hosts. Expect wellies in the hall and masses of books and CDs in one of the lounges. Bedrooms are cosy, and delicious set dinners and memorable breakfasts are provided.

Rooms 6 (3 annexe) (1 fmly)

TARBERT — Map 22 NB10

Hotel Hebrides

★★★★ 75% ◉ HOTEL

tel: 01859 502364 **Pier Rd HS3 3DG**
email: stay@hotel-hebrides.com **web:** www.hotel-hebrides.com
dir: To Tarbert via ferry from Uig (Isle of Skye); or ferry from Ullapool to Stornaway, A859 to Tarbert; or by plane to Stornaway from Glasgow, Edinburgh or Inverness

Benefiting from an elevated position overlooking the town, this hotel is just a few minutes' walk from the centre. The small, hands-on team extend wonderful hospitality and customer care. The bedrooms are stylishly designed and include WiFi, high speed internet access and flat-screen TVs; the deluxe rooms have iPod docking stations and some rooms have loch and harbour views. Award-winning food is served in the Pierhouse Restaurant. A complimentary bus service is provided to the theatre in the summer months.

Rooms 21 (2 fmly) **S** £65-£85; **D** £130-£170 (incl. bkfst)* **Facilities** FTV WiFi ⬧ 🎵 **Conf** Class 35 Board 35 Del from £120 to £140* **Notes** LB ⊗

ISLE OF ISLAY

BOWMORE — Map 20 NR36

The Harbour Inn and Restaurant

◉◉ RESTAURANT WITH ROOMS

tel: 01496 810330 🖷 01496 810990 **The Square PA43 7JR**
email: info@harbour-inn.com **web:** www.harbour-inn.com
dir: Next to harbour

The humble whitewashed exterior of the Harbour Inn conceals a sophisticated environment that draws discerning travellers from all over the world. Spacious bedrooms are appointed to a high standard and the conservatory-lounge has stunning views over Loch Indaal to the peaks of Jura. The cosy bar is popular with locals, and the smart dining room showcases some excellent seafood. Welcoming peat fires burn in cooler months.

Rooms 7 (1 fmly)

PORT ASKAIG
Map 20 NR46

Port Askaig Hotel

★★ 64% SMALL HOTEL

tel: 01496 840245 **PA46 7RD**
email: hotel@portaskaig.co.uk **web:** www.portaskaig.co.uk
dir: At ferry terminal

The building of this endearing family-run hotel dates back to the 18th-century. The lounge provides fine views over the Sound of Islay to Jura, and there is a choice of bars that are popular with locals. Traditional dinners are served in the bright restaurant and a full range of bar snacks and meals is also available. The bedrooms are smart and comfortable.

Rooms 14 (2 annexe) (4 fmly) **Facilities** WiFi **Parking** 21 **Notes** ⊗

ISLE OF MULL

TOBERMORY
Map 22 NM55

INSPECTORS' CHOICE

Highland Cottage

★★★ ⑩⑩ SMALL HOTEL

tel: 01688 302030 **Breadalbane St PA75 6PD**
email: davidandjo@highlandcottage.co.uk **web:** www.highlandcottage.co.uk
dir: A848 Craignure/Fishnish ferry terminal, pass Tobermory signs, straight on at mini rdbt across narrow bridge, turn right. Hotel on right opposite fire station

Providing the highest level of natural and unassuming hospitality, this delightful little gem lies high above the island's capital. Don't be fooled by its side street location, a stunning view over the bay is just a few metres away. 'A country house hotel in town' it is an Aladdin's Cave of collectables and treasures, as well as masses of books and magazines. There are two inviting lounges, one with an honesty bar. The cosy dining room offers memorable dinners and splendid breakfasts. Bedrooms are individual; some have four-posters and all are comprehensively equipped to include TVs and music centres.

Rooms 6 (1 GF) **S** £95-£150; **D** £135-£165 (incl. bkfst)* **Facilities** FTV WiFi
Parking 6 **Notes** No children 10yrs Closed Nov-Mar

SHETLAND

LERWICK
Map 24 HU44

Shetland Hotel

★★★ 77% HOTEL

tel: 01595 695515 **Holmsgarth Rd ZE1 0PW**
email: reception@shetlandhotel.co.uk **web:** www.shetlandhotels.com
dir: Opposite ferry terminal, on main road N from town centre

This purpose-built hotel is centrally located opposite the main ferry terminal. Spacious and comfortable bedrooms are situated on three floors, and many look out over the harbour itself. The popular Waterfront Bar & Grill offers diverse, well executed and enjoyable dishes. There is also a new Sports Bar on the ground floor.

Rooms 64 (4 fmly) **S** £95; **D** £125 (incl. bkfst)* **Facilities** FTV WiFi **Conf** Class 75 Board 50 Thtr 300 **Services** Lift **Parking** 150 **Notes** ⊗ Closed 25-26 Dec, 1-2 Jan

SCALLOWAY
Map 24 HU33

Scalloway Hotel

★★★ 77% ⑩ SMALL HOTEL

tel: 01595 880444 **Main St ZE1 0TR**
email: info@scallowayhotel.com **web:** www.scallowayhotel.com
dir: 6m from main port of Lerwick on A970. Situated in Scalloway Main St

Scalloway is the ancient capital of Shetland; the Scalloway Hotel sits overlooking the waterfront and is currently undergoing a full refurbishment using high quality Shetland fabrics and materials. Also on offer is warm, friendly service and award-winning food using the best produce that the Shetland Larder can provide.

Rooms 24 **S** fr £80; **D** fr £115 (incl. bkfst)* **Facilities** FTV WiFi **Parking** 10

ISLE OF SKYE

ARDVASAR
Map 22 NG60

Ardvasar Hotel

★★★ 74% SMALL HOTEL

tel: 01471 844223 **Sleat IV45 8RS**
email: richard@ardvasar-hotel.demon.co.uk **web:** www.ardvasarhotel.com
dir: From ferry, 500mtrs, left signed Ardvasar

The Isle of Skye is dotted with cosy, welcoming hotels that make touring the island easy and convenient. This hotel ranks highly amongst its peers thanks to great hospitality and a preservation of community spirit. The hotel sits less than five minutes' drive from the Mallaig ferry and provides comfortable bedrooms and a cosy bar lounge for residents. Seafood is prominent on menus, and meals can be enjoyed in either the popular bar or the attractive dining room.

Rooms 10 (4 fmly) **Facilities** FTV WiFi Xmas New Year **Conf** Board 24 Thtr 50 **Parking** 30

SCOTTISH ISLANDS

SCOTTISH ISLANDS

COLBOST
Map 22 NG24

INSPECTORS' CHOICE

The Three Chimneys and House-Over-By

 RESTAURANT WITH ROOMS

tel: 01470 511258 **IV55 8ZT**
email: eatandstay@threechimneys.co.uk
web: www.threechimneys.co.uk
dir: 5m W of Dunvegan take B884 signed Glendale. On left beside loch

Crofters' cottages are as firmly rooted in the terroir as it is possible to be, synonymous with the island and its rugged and wild landscape. Two such crofts form the basis of Eddie and Shirley Spear's restaurant, which over the last 30 years has made its mark, too, on both the local economy and on the island's culinary reputation. This is destination dining. There are also classy bedrooms next door as staying over is a good option given the location. The decor reflects the natural environment, too, being proud of its origins, adding refined touches here and there but guaranteeing a sense of place. That sense of place is enhanced by the stunning views over land and loch. Michael Smith has been here for a decade in 2015, in which time he has cemented the reputation of the place and become a champion for Scottish produce. His is the kind of cooking that impresses with its technique and precision but somehow leaves the ingredients room to speak for themselves. There's a sensibly short carte - three or so options per course - alongside a tasting menu that packs quite punch. There's a table in the kitchen so diners' can get close to the action. The wine list is a fine piece of work, and even more reason to book one of those charming bedrooms.

Rooms 6 (1 fmly) (6GF)

ISLEORNSAY
Map 22 NG71

Duisdale House Hotel

★★★★ 81%  SMALL HOTEL

tel: 01471 833202 **Sleat IV43 8QW**
email: info@duisdale.com **web:** www.duisdale.com
dir: 7m S of Bradford on A851 towards Armadale. 7m N of Armadale ferry

This grand Victorian house stands in its own landscaped gardens overlooking the Sound of Sleat. The hotel has a contemporary and chic style which complements the original features of the house. Each bedroom is individually designed and the superior rooms have four-poster beds. The elegant lounge has sumptuous sofas, original artwork and blazing log fires in the colder months.

Rooms 18 (1 fmly) (1 GF) S £69-£200; D £70-£320* **Facilities** STV WiFi Private yacht Outdoor hydropool Xmas New Year **Conf** Board 28 Thtr 50 **Parking** 30 **Notes** Civ Wed 58

INSPECTORS' CHOICE

Kinloch Lodge

★★★ COUNTRY HOUSE HOTEL

tel: 01471 833214 & 833333 **Sleat IV43 8QY**
email: reservations@kinloch-lodge.co.uk **web:** www.kinloch-lodge.co.uk
dir: 6m S of Broadford on A851, 10m N of Armadale on A851

Owned and run in a hands-on fashion by Lord and Lady MacDonald and their family, this hotel enjoys a picture postcard location surrounded by hills and a sea loch. Bedrooms and bathrooms are well appointed and comfortable, and public areas boast numerous open fires and relaxing areas to sit. There is a cookery school run by Claire MacDonald and a shop that sells her famous cookery books and produce.

Rooms 15 (8 annexe) (1 GF) **Facilities** STV FTV WiFi Fishing Beauty treatment room Xmas New Year **Conf** Class 20 Board 20 Thtr 20 **Parking** 40

Toravaig House Hotel

★★★ 86% SMALL HOTEL

tel: 01471 820200 & 833231 **Knock Bay, Sleat IV44 8RE**
email: info@skyehotel.co.uk **web:** www.skyehotel.co.uk
dir: From Skye Bridge, left at Broadford onto A851, hotel 11m on left. Or from ferry at Armadale take A851, hotel 6m on right

Set in two acres and enjoying panoramic views to the Knoydart Hills, this hotel is a haven of peace, with stylish, well-equipped and beautifully decorated bedrooms. There is an inviting lounge complete with deep sofas and an elegant dining room where delicious meals are the order of the day. The hotel provides a sea-going yacht for guests' exclusive use from April to September.

Rooms 9 S £69-£190; D £70-£250 (incl. bkfst)* **Facilities** STV WiFi Daily excursions (Apr-Sep) on hotel yacht Xmas New Year **Conf** Board 10 Thtr 15 **Parking** 15 **Notes** LB Civ Wed 25

Hotel Eilean Iarmain

★★★ 79% SMALL HOTEL

THE CIRCLE

tel: 01471 833332 **Sleat IV43 8QR**
email: hotel@eileaniarmain.co.uk **web:** www.eileaniarmain.co.uk
dir: From Skye Bridge take A87 towards Broadford. Left onto A851 signed Armadale. 8m, left to hotel. Or From Armadale ferry take A851 signed Broadford. 7m to hotel

A hotel of charm and character, this 19th-century former inn sits by the pier and enjoys fine views across the sea loch. Bedrooms are individual and retain a traditional style, and a stable block has been converted into four delightful suites. Public rooms are cosy and inviting, and the restaurant offers award-winning menus showcasing the island's best produce, especially seafood and game.

Rooms 16 (10 annexe) (4 fmly) (3 GF) **S** £65-£110; **D** £100-£170 (incl. bkfst)
Facilities FTV WiFi Fishing Shooting Art exhibitions Whisky tasting Tweed Shop ♫ Xmas New Year **Conf** Class 10 Board 14 Thtr 25 Del from £130 to £180* **Parking** 20 **Notes** LB Civ Wed 30

▌ PORTREE   **Map 22 NG44**

Cuillin Hills Hotel

★★★★ 78% HOTEL

tel: 01478 612003 **IV51 9QU**
email: info@cuillinhills-hotel-skye.co.uk **web:** www.cuillinhills-hotel-skye.co.uk
dir: Right 0.25m N of Portree off A855. Follow hotel signs

This imposing building enjoys a superb location overlooking Portree Bay and the Cuillin Hills. Accommodation is provided in smart, well-equipped rooms that are generally spacious; some rooms are found in an adjacent building. Public areas include comfortable lounges, a Malt Whisky Bar and a newly refurbished restaurant that takes advantage of the views - 'The View'. Service is particularly attentive.

Rooms 29 (7 annexe) (4 fmly) (10 GF) ⋒ **Facilities** STV FTV WiFi HL Xmas New Year **Parking** 56 **Notes** Civ Wed 45

Rosedale Hotel

★★★ 74% HOTEL

tel: 01478 613131 **Beaumont Crescent IV51 9DF**
email: rosedalehotelsky@aol.com **web:** www.rosedalehotelskye.co.uk
dir: Follow directions to village centre & harbour

The atmosphere is wonderfully warm at this delightful family-run waterfront hotel. A labyrinth of stairs and corridors connects the comfortable lounges, bar and charming restaurant - all are set on different levels. The restaurant has fine views of the bay, and the modern bedrooms offer a good range of amenities.

Rooms 18 (1 fmly) (3 GF) ⋒ **S** £40-£65; **D** £70-£150 (incl. bkfst) **Facilities** FTV WiFi **Parking** 2 **Notes** ⊗ Closed Nov-mid Mar

---

▌ STAFFIN   **Map 22 NG46**

The Glenview

 RESTAURANT WITH ROOMS

tel: 01470 562248 **Culnacnoc IV51 9JH**
email: enquiries@glenviewskye.co.uk **web:** www.glenviewskye.co.uk
dir: 12m N of Portree on A855

The Glenview is located in one of the most beautiful parts of Skye with stunning sea views; it is close to the famous rock formation, The Old Man of Storr. The individually styled bedrooms are very comfortable and front-facing rooms enjoy the dramatic views. Evening meals should not to be missed as the restaurant has a well deserved reputation for its treatment of locally sourced produce.

Rooms 5

▌ STRUAN   **Map 22 NG33**

Ullinish Country Lodge

RESTAURANT WITH ROOMS

tel: 01470 572214 📠 01470 572341 **IV56 8FD**
email: ullinish@theisleofskye.co.uk **web:** www.theisleofskye.co.uk
dir: Take A863 N. Lodge signed on left

Set in some of Scotland's most dramatic landscape, with views of the Black Cuillin and MacLeod's Tables, this lodge has lochs on three sides. Samuel Johnson and James Boswell stayed here in 1773 and were impressed with the hospitality even then. Hosts Brian and Pam hope to extend the same welcome to their guests today. As you would expect, all bedrooms have amazing views, and come with half-tester beds. The AA Rosette award for the Ullinish Country Lodge is currently suspended due to a change in chef. AA Rosettes may be awarded once the inspectors have assessed the food created by the new kitchen regime.

Rooms 6

SCOTTISH ISLANDS

Wales

A

ABERAERON
Ceredigion   Map 8 SN46

INSPECTORS' CHOICE

Ty Mawr Mansion

RESTAURANT WITH ROOMS

tel: 01570 470033 **Cilcennin SA48 8DB**
email: info@tymawrmansion.co.uk **web:** www.tymawrmansion.co.uk
dir: On A482 (Lampeter to Aberaeron road), 4m from Aberaeron

Surrounded by rolling countryside in its own naturally beautiful gardens, this fine country mansion house is a haven of peace and tranquillity. Careful renovation has restored it to its former glory and, combined with lush fabrics, top quality beds and sumptuous furnishings, the accommodation is spacious, superbly equipped and very comfortable. Award-winning chefs create mouth-watering dishes from local and seasonal produce. There is also a 27-seat cinema with all the authenticity of the real thing. Martin and Cath McAlpine offer the sort of welcome which makes every visit to Ty Mawr a memorable one.

Rooms 9 (1 annexe) (1 fmly)

ABERDARE
Rhondda Cynon Taff   Map 9 SO00

Premier Inn Aberdare

BUDGET HOTEL

tel: 0871 527 8002 **Riverside Retail Park, Tirfounders Field CF44 OAH**
web: www.premierinn.com
dir: M4 junct 32, A470 signed Merthyr Tydfil. In approx 10m take A4059 signed Aberdare. Straight on at 1st rdbt, 3rd exit at next rdbt into Ffordd Tirwaun signed Riverside Retail Park, hotel in park

High quality, budget accommodation ideal for both families and business travellers. Spacious, en suite bedrooms feature tea and coffee making facilities, and Freeview TV in most hotels. Internet access and WiFi are available for a small fee. The adjacent family restaurant features a wide and varied menu. See also the Hotel Groups pages.

Rooms 28

ABERGAVENNY
Monmouthshire   Map 9 SO21

Llansantffraed Court Hotel

★★★★ 80% COUNTRY HOUSE HOTEL

tel: 01873 840678 **Llanvihangel Gobion, Clytha NP7 9BA**
email: reception@llch.co.uk **web:** www.llch.co.uk
dir: At A465 & A40 Abergavenny junct take B4598 signed Usk (NB do not join A40). Towards Raglan, hotel on left in 4.5m

In a commanding position and in its own extensive grounds, this very impressive property - a privately owned country-house hotel - has enviable views of the Brecon Beacons. Extensive public areas include a relaxing lounge and a spacious restaurant offering imaginative and enjoyable award-winning dishes. Bedrooms vary in size and reflect the individuality of the building; all are comfortably furnished and provide some thoughtful extras. Extensive parking is available.

Rooms 21 (1 fmly) S £80-£110; D £130-£190 (incl. bkfst)* **Facilities** STV FTV WiFi Putt green Fishing Clay pigeon shooting school Xmas New Year Child facilities **Conf** Class 120 Board 100 Thtr 220 Del from £160 to £220* **Services** Lift **Parking** 250 **Notes** LB Civ Wed 150

Angel Hotel

★★★ 80% HOTEL

tel: 01873 857121 **15 Cross St NP7 5EN**
email: mail@angelabergavenny.com **web:** www.angelabergavenny.com
dir: From A40 & A465 junct follow town centre signs, S of Abergavenny, past rail & bus stations

Once a coaching inn, this has long been a popular venue for both locals and visitors; the two traditional function rooms and the ballroom are in regular use. In addition there is a comfortable lounge, a relaxed bar and a smart restaurant. In warmer weather there is a central courtyard that is ideal for alfresco eating. The bedrooms include a four-poster room and some that are suitable for families.

Rooms 34 (4 annexe) (2 fmly) S £111-£178; D £111-£178 (incl. bkfst)* **Facilities** FTV WiFi New Year **Conf** Class 60 Board 60 Thtr 180 Del £140* **Services** Lift **Parking** 30 **Notes** LB Closed 25 Dec RS 24 & 26-30 Dec Civ Wed 180

ABERGELE
Conwy   Map 14 SH97

Kinmel Manor Hotel

THE INDEPENDENTS
HOTEL ASSOCIATION

★★★ 75% HOTEL

tel: 01745 832014 **St George's Rd LL22 9AS**
email: reception@kinmelmanorhotel.co.uk **web:** www.kinmelmanorhotel.co.uk
dir: A55 junct 24, hotel entrance on rdbt

In a rural location at the end of a long drive leading from the A55, parts of this notable, family-run hotel date from the 16th century. The smart bedrooms vary from standard to superior and executive rooms. The public areas include a popular lounge bar, the stylish Seasons Brasserie, and leisure facilities which include a gym, indoor pool, jacuzzi, steam room and sauna.

Rooms 42 (8 fmly) (18 GF) S £75-£100; D £90-£150 (incl. bkfst)* **Facilities** Spa FTV WiFi Gym Steam room Sauna Xmas New Year **Conf** Class 100 Board 100 Thtr 250 **Services** Lift **Parking** 120 **Notes** LB Civ Wed 250

The Kinmel Arms

RESTAURANT WITH ROOMS

tel: 01745 832207 01745 822044 **The Village, St George LL22 9BP**
email: info@thekinmelarms.co.uk **web:** www.thekinmelarms.co.uk
dir: From A55 junct 24a to St George. E on A55, junct 24. 1st left to Rhuddlan, 1st right into St George. 2nd right

This converted 17th-century coaching inn stands close to the church in the village of St George, in the beautiful Elwy Valley. The popular restaurant specialises in produce from Wales and north-west England, and friendly and helpful staff ensure you will have an enjoyable stay. The four attractive suites are luxuriously furnished and feature stunning bathrooms. Substantial continental breakfasts are served in the rooms.

Rooms 4

ABERSOCH
Gwynedd

Map 14 SH32

Porth Tocyn Hotel

★★★ 82% ◉◉ COUNTRY HOUSE HOTEL

tel: 01758 713303 & 07789 994942 **Bwlch Tocyn LL53 7BU**
email: bookings@porthtocyn.fsnet.co.uk **web:** www.porthtocynhotel.co.uk
dir: 2.5m S of Abersoch follow Porth Tocyn signs after Sarnbach

Located above Cardigan Bay with fine views over the area, Porth Tocyn is set in attractive gardens. Several elegantly furnished sitting rooms are provided and bedrooms are comfortably furnished. Children are especially welcome and a playroom is provided. Award-winning food is served in the restaurant.

Rooms 17 (1 fmly) (3 GF) **S** £77.50-£92.50; **D** £105-£185 (incl. bkfst)* **Facilities** FTV WiFi ⬩ ⬩ Table tennis **Conf** Class 15 **Parking** 50 **Notes** LB Closed mid Nov-week before Easter RS low season

ABERYSTWYTH
Ceredigion

Map 8 SN58

Nanteos Mansion

RESTAURANT WITH ROOMS

tel: 01970 600522 **Rhydyfelin SY23 4LU**
email: info@nanteos.com **web:** www.nanteos.com
dir: A487 onto A4120 signed Devil's Bridge then immediately right onto B4340 towards Trawscoed. Take 1st left fork, along narrow road, Nanteos Mansion signed

This historic mansion sits in delightfully peaceful countryside. Staff are keen to please, and proud of the cuisine served here. The restaurant offers good menu choices and a very pleasant wine list, and retains many of the grand features of the original house. The well-appointed bedrooms are splendid, and many are very spacious. Public areas are also roomy, and breakfast is taken in the Buttery, which was once the original kitchen.

Rooms 14 (4 annexe) (4 fmly)

BANGOR
Gwynedd

Map 14 SH57

Premier Inn Bangor

BUDGET HOTEL

tel: 0871 527 8046 **Parc Menai, Ffordd Y Parc LL57 4FA**
web: www.premierinn.com
dir: A55 junct 9 (Holyhead, Ysbyty Gwynedd Hospital). Take 3rd exit off rdbt. Hotel next left

High quality, budget accommodation ideal for both families and business travellers. Spacious, en suite bedrooms feature tea and coffee making facilities,

and Freeview TV in most hotels. Internet access and WiFi are available for a small fee. The adjacent family restaurant features a wide and varied menu. See also the Hotel Groups pages.

Rooms 40

BEAUMARIS
Isle of Anglesey

Map 14 SH67

The Bulkeley Hotel

★★★ 79% HOTEL

tel: 01248 810415 **Castle St LL58 8AW**
email: reception@bulkeleyhotel.co.uk **web:** www.bulkeleyhotel.co.uk
dir: A55 junct 8a to Beaumaris. Hotel in town centre

A Grade I listed hotel built in 1832, the Bulkeley is just 100 yards from the 13th-century Beaumaris Castle in the centre of town; the friendly staff create a relaxed atmosphere. Many rooms, including 18 of the bedrooms, have fine panoramic views across the Menai Straits to the Snowdonian Mountains. The well-equipped bedrooms and suites, some with four-posters, are generally spacious, and have pretty furnishings. There is a choice of bars, a coffee shop, a restaurant and bistro.

Rooms 43 (5 fmly) ⬩ **S** £40-£80; **D** £75-£160 (incl. bkfst)* **Facilities** FTV WiFi Xmas New Year **Conf** Class 40 Board 25 Thtr 180 **Services** Lift **Parking** 25 **Notes** Civ Wed 130

Bishopsgate House Hotel

★★ 85% ◉ SMALL HOTEL

tel: 01248 810302 **54 Castle St LL58 8BB**
email: hazel@bishopsgatehotel.co.uk **web:** www.bishopsgatehotel.co.uk
dir: From Menai Bridge onto A545 to Beaumaris. Hotel on left in main street

This immaculately maintained, privately-owned and personally-run small hotel dates back to 1760. It features fine examples of wood panelling and a Chinese Chippendale staircase. Thoughtfully furnished bedrooms are attractively decorated and two have four-poster beds. Quality cooking is served in the elegant restaurant and guests have a comfortable lounge and cosy bar to relax in.

Rooms 9 **Facilities** FTV WiFi ⬩ Xmas New Year **Parking** 8

B

BEDDGELERT	Map 14 SH54
Gwynedd	

The Royal Goat Hotel

THE CIRCLE

★★★ 78% HOTEL

tel: 01766 890224 **LL55 4YE**
email: info@royalgoathotel.co.uk **web:** www.royalgoathotel.co.uk
dir: On A498 at Beddgelert

An impressive building steeped in history, the Royal Goat provides well-equipped accommodation, and carries out an annual programme of refurbishment. Attractively appointed, comfortable public areas include a choice of bars and restaurants, a residents' lounge and function rooms.

Rooms 32 (4 fmly) **Facilities** FTV WiFi Fishing Xmas New Year **Conf** Class 40 Board 30 Thtr 70 **Services** Lift **Parking** 100 **Notes** Closed Jan-14 Feb

BETWS-Y-COED	Map 14 SH75
Conwy	

Craig-y-Dderwen Riverside Hotel

★★★★ 78% ⑥ COUNTRY HOUSE HOTEL

tel: 01690 710293 **LL24 0AS**
email: info@snowdoniahotel.com **web:** www.snowdoniahotel.com
dir: A5 to Betws-y-Coed, cross Waterloo Bridge, take 1st left

This Victorian country-house hotel is set in well-maintained grounds alongside the River Conwy, at the end of a tree-lined drive. Views down the river can be enjoyed from the restaurant and deck. Many of the bedrooms have balconies, and the feature rooms include a four-poster bed and a hot tub. There are comfortable lounges and the atmosphere throughout is tranquil and relaxing.

Rooms 18 (2 fmly) (1 GF) (1 smoking) ☏ **S** £105-£145; **D** £120-£230 (incl. bkfst)*
Facilities STV FTV WiFi ➘ Fishing ⚑ Badminton Volleyball New Year **Conf** Class 50 Board 50 Thtr 100 **Parking** 50 **Notes** LB Closed 23-26 Dec & 2 Jan-1 Feb Civ Wed 100

Royal Oak Hotel

★★★ 85% ⑥ HOTEL

tel: 01690 710219 **Holyhead Rd LL24 0AY**
email: royaloakmail@btopenworld.com **web:** www.royaloakhotel.net
dir: On A5 in town centre, adjacent to St Mary's Church

Centrally situated in the village, this elegant, privately owned hotel started life as a coaching inn and now provides very comfortable bedrooms with smart, modern en suite bathrooms. The extensive public areas retain much of their original charm

and character. The choice of eating options includes the Grill Bistro, the Stables Bar which is much frequented by locals, and the more formal Llugwy Restaurant.

Rooms 27 (1 fmly) ☏ **S** £77-£85; **D** £115-£195 (incl. bkfst) **Facilities** FTV WiFi ➘ ♫ New Year **Conf** Class 40 Board 20 Thtr 80 Del from £85 to £180 **Parking** 90 **Notes** LB ⊗ Closed 25-26 Dec Civ Wed 60

See advert on opposite page

BEST WESTERN Waterloo Hotel

Best Western

★★★ 80% HOTEL

tel: 01690 710411 **LL24 0AR**
email: reservations@waterloo-hotel.info **web:** www.waterloo-hotel.info
dir: On A5, S of village centre

This long-established hotel, named after the nearby Waterloo Bridge, is ideally located for visiting Snowdonia. Stylish accommodation is split between rooms in the main hotel and modern, cottage-style rooms located in buildings to the rear.

The restaurant serves traditional Welsh specialities, and the vibrant Bridge Inn provides a wide range of food and drink throughout the day and evening.

Rooms 42 (31 annexe) (13 fmly) (29 GF) 🌙 **S** £90–£100; **D** £93–£160 (incl. bkfst)* **Facilities** FTV WiFi ॐ Gym Steam room Sauna Beauty salon New Year **Conf** Class 18 Board 12 Thtr 40 Del from £90 to £150* **Parking** 100 **Notes** Closed 24 & 26 Dec RS 25 Dec

BRECON	Map 9 SO02
Powys	

Peterstone Court

 RESTAURANT WITH ROOMS

tel: 01874 665387 **Llanhamlach LD3 7YB**
email: info@peterstone-court.com **web:** www.peterstone-court.com
dir: 3m from Brecon on A40 towards Abergavenny

Situated on the edge of the Brecon Beacons, this establishment affords stunning views overlooking the River Usk. The atmosphere is friendly and informal; without any unnecessary fuss. No two bedrooms are alike, but all share comparable levels of comfort, quality and elegance. Public areas reflect similar standards, eclectically styled with a blend of the contemporary and the traditional. Quality produce is cooked with care in a range of enjoyable dishes.

Rooms 12 (4 annexe) (2 fmly)

BRIDGEND	Map 9 SS97
Bridgend	

BEST WESTERN Heronston Hotel

★★★ 77% HOTEL

tel: 01656 668811 **Ewenny Rd CF35 5AW**
email: reservations@bestwesternheronstonhotel.co.uk **web:** www.bw-heronstonhotel.co.uk
dir: M4 junct 35, follow signs for Porthcawl, at 5th rdbt left towards Ogmore-by-Sea (B4265), hotel 200yds on left

Situated within easy reach of the town centre and the M4, this large modern hotel offers spacious well-equipped accommodation, including ground-floor rooms. Public areas include an open-plan lounge/bar, attractive restaurant and a smart leisure and fitness club. The hotel also has a choice of function and conference rooms, and ample parking is available.

Rooms 75 (3 fmly) (36 GF) 🌙 **S** £70–£120; **D** £80–£130 (incl. bkfst) **Facilities** Spa STV FTV WiFi ॐ HL 🖹 Gym Steam room Sauna New Year **Conf** Class 80 Board 60 Thtr 250 Del from £105 to £125 **Services** Lift **Parking** 160 **Notes** LB Civ Wed 200

Court Colman Manor

★★★ 72% ⊛  COUNTRY HOUSE HOTEL

tel: 01656 720212 **Pen-y-Fai CF31 4NG**
email: experience@court-colman-manor.com **web:** www.court-colman-manor.com
dir: M4 junct 36, A4063 towards Maesteg, after lights 1st exit to Bridgend, under motorway, next right, follow hotel signs

Dating back to the Tudor times this fine mansion is set in its own peaceful grounds outside Bridgend, and is just a short distance from the M4. The spacious, comfortable bedrooms include ten themed rooms inspired by exotic locations - India, Japan, Morocco etc. The award-winning food served in Bokhara Brasserie is imaginative, and Indian and Mediterranean dishes are included in the choices. Diners can view their meals being prepared in the open-plan kitchen.

Rooms 30 (2 fmly) 🌙 **S** fr £52; **D** £85–£130 (incl. bkfst)* **Facilities** FTV WiFi ॐ HL Xmas New Year **Conf** Class 60 Thtr 100 Del from £95* **Parking** 180 **Notes** Civ Wed 150

Premier Inn Bridgend Central

BUDGET HOTEL

tel: 0871 527 8146 **The Derwen CF32 9ST**
web: www.premierinn.com
dir: M4 junct 36, A4061 (signed Bridgend & Pen-y-Bont). Hotel at next rdbt

High quality, budget accommodation ideal for both families and business travellers. Spacious, en suite bedrooms feature tea and coffee making facilities, and Freeview TV in most hotels. Internet access and WiFi are available for a small fee. The adjacent family restaurant features a wide and varied menu. See also the Hotel Groups pages.

Rooms 68

B

BRIDGEND *continued*

Premier Inn Bridgend M4 Jct 35

BUDGET HOTEL

tel: 0871 527 8144 **Pantruthyn Farm, Pencoed CF35 5HY**
web: www.premierinn.com
dir: At M4 junct 35, behind petrol station & McDonalds

Rooms 40

BUILTH WELLS	**Map 9 SO05**
Powys	

Caer Beris Manor Hotel

THE INDEPENDENTS
HOTEL ASSOCIATION

★★★ 78%  COUNTRY HOUSE HOTEL

tel: 01982 552601 **LD2 3NP**
email: info@caerberis.com **web:** www.caerberis.com
dir: From town centre follow A483/Llandovery signs. Hotel on the left (keep in left hand lane but bear right, straight over mini-rdbt)

Guests can expect a relaxing stay at this friendly and privately-owned boutique, country house hotel that has extensive and attractive landscaped grounds. Bedrooms are individually decorated and furnished to retain an atmosphere of a bygone era. The spacious and comfortable lounge, complete with log fire, and lounge bar continue this theme. Dining is available in the elegant 1896 Restaurant, complete with 16th-century panelling. Those aiming for total relaxation can also indulge in a well-being treatment including massages and facials.

Rooms 23 (2 fmly) (3 GF) ⚲ **Facilities** FTV WiFi ⤵ Fishing ⛳ Clay pigeon shooting Birdwatching Walking holidays Xmas New Year **Conf** Class 75 Board 50 Thtr 100 **Parking** 100 **Notes** Civ Wed 200

CAERNARFON	**Map 14 SH46**
Gwynedd	

INSPECTORS' CHOICE

Seiont Manor Hotel

HANDPICKED
HOTELS
BUILT FOR PLEASURE

★★★  COUNTRY HOUSE HOTEL

tel: 01286 673366 **Llanrug LL55 2AQ**
email: seiontmanor@handpicked.co.uk
web: www.handpickedhotels.co.uk/seiontmanor
dir: E on A4086, 2.5m from Caernarfon

A splendid hotel created from authentic farm buildings, set in the tranquil countryside near Snowdonia; the River Seiont flows through the 150-acre grounds. The bedrooms, including junior suites, are individually decorated and have luxurious extra touches; each has either a balcony or patio. The comfortable public rooms are cosy and furnished in country-house style. The kitchen team use the best local produce to provide exciting takes on traditional dishes, and guests can choose to eat in either the award-winning Llwyn y Brain Restaurant or the conservatory brasserie.

Rooms 28 (2 fmly) (14 GF) ⚲ **S** £95-£185; **D** £115-£205 (incl. bkfst)* **Facilities** STV FTV WiFi ⤵ HL ⚽ Fishing Gym Xmas New Year **Conf** Class 40 Board 40 Thtr 100 Del from £125 to £165* **Parking** 60 **Notes** LB ⊗ Civ Wed 100

Celtic Royal Hotel

★★★ 81% HOTEL

tel: 01286 674477 **Bangor St LL55 1AY**
email: reservations@celtic-royal.co.uk **web:** www.celtic-royal.co.uk
dir: Exit A55 at Bangor, take A487 towards Caernarfon

This large, impressive, privately owned hotel is situated in the town centre. It provides attractively appointed accommodation, which includes family rooms and bedrooms for less able guests. The spacious public areas include a bar, a choice of lounges and a pleasant split-level restaurant. Guests also have the use of the impressive health club.

Rooms 110 (12 fmly) ⚲ **Facilities** WiFi ⚽ Gym Steam room Sauna ♬ Xmas New Year **Conf** Class 120 Board 120 Thtr 300 **Services** Lift **Parking** 180 **Notes** ⊗ Civ Wed 200

Premier Inn Caernarfon

BUDGET HOTEL

tel: 0871 527 8180 **Victioria Dock, Balaclava Rd LL55 1SQ**
web: www.premierinn.com
dir: A55 junct 9, at rdbt 1st exit follow Caernarfon signs. In Caernarfon at rdbt (Morrisons on right) 1st exit, keep in right lane, at next rdbt 4th exit to mini rdbt, hotel opposite

High quality, budget accommodation ideal for both families and business travellers. Spacious, en suite bedrooms feature tea and coffee making facilities, and Freeview TV in most hotels. Internet access and WiFi are available for a small fee. The adjacent family restaurant features a wide and varied menu. See also the Hotel Groups pages.

Rooms 49

CAERPHILLY	**Map 9 ST18**
Caerphilly	

Premier Inn Caerphilly (Corbetts Lane)

BUDGET HOTEL

tel: 0871 527 8182 **Corbetts Ln CF83 3HX**
web: www.premierinn.com
dir: M4 junct 32, A470, 2nd left signed Caerphilly. At rdbt 4th exit, at next rdbt 2nd exit. Straight on at next rdbt & at Pwllypant Rdbt, hotel on left

High quality, budget accommodation ideal for both families and business travellers. Spacious, en suite bedrooms feature tea and coffee making facilities, and Freeview TV in most hotels. Internet access and WiFi are available for a small fee. The adjacent family restaurant features a wide and varied menu. See also the Hotel Groups pages.

Rooms 42

E

DEGANWY
Conwy   Map 14 SH77

Quay Hotel & Spa

★★★★ 86% ◎◎ HOTEL

tel: 01492 564100 **Deganwy Quay LL31 9DJ**
email: info@quayhotel.com **web:** www.quayhotel.co.uk
dir: M56, A494, A55 junct 18, straight across 2 rdbts. At lights bear left into The Quay. Hotel on right

This boutique hotel occupies a stunning position beside the estuary on Deganwy's Quay. What was once an area for railway storage is now a property of modern architectural design offering hotel-keeping of the highest standard. Spacious bedrooms, many with balconies and wonderful views, are decorated in neutral colours and boast a host of thoughtful extras, including up-to-the-minute communication systems. The friendly staff provide a fluent service in a charmingly informal manner.

Rooms 74 (15 fmly) (30 GF) **S** £95-£155; **D** £105-£225 (incl. bkfst)* **Facilities** Spa WiFi HL 🏊 supervised Gym Steam & sauna room Hydro therapy pool 🎵 Xmas New Year **Conf** Class 240 Board 90 Thtr 240 Del from £130 to £170* **Services** Lift **Parking** 96 **Notes** LB Civ Wed 150

DEVIL'S BRIDGE
Ceredigion   Map 9 SN77

The Hafod Hotel

★★★ 70% HOTEL

tel: 01970 890232 **SY23 3JL**
email: info@thehafodhotel.co.uk **web:** www.thehafodhotel.co.uk
dir: Exit A44 in Ponterwyd signed Devil's Bridge/Pontarfynach onto A4120, 3m, over bridge. Hotel opposite

This former hunting lodge dates back to the 17th century and is situated in six acres of grounds. Now a family-owned and run hotel, it provides accommodation suitable for both business and leisure guests. Family rooms and a four-poster room are available. In addition to the dining area and lounge, there are tea rooms.

Rooms 16 (2 fmly) **Facilities** WiFi 🎣 Xmas New Year **Conf** Class 70 Board 40 Thtr 100 **Parking** 200 **Notes** Civ Wed 40

DOLGELLAU
Gwynedd   Map 14 SH71

INSPECTORS' CHOICE

Penmaenuchaf Hall Hotel

★★★ ◎◎ COUNTRY HOUSE HOTEL

tel: 01341 422129 **Penmaenpool LL40 1YB**
email: relax@penhall.co.uk **web:** www.penhall.co.uk
dir: A470 onto A493 to Tywyn. Hotel approx 1m on left

Built in 1860, this impressive hall stands in 20 acres of formal gardens, grounds and woodland, and enjoys magnificent views across the River Mawddach. Sympathetic restoration has created a comfortable and welcoming hotel with spacious day rooms and thoughtfully furnished bedrooms, some with private balconies. Fresh produce cooked in modern British style is served in an elegant conservatory restaurant, overlooking the countryside.

Rooms 14 (2 fmly) 🐾 **S** £120-£185; **D** £180-£270 (incl. bkfst) **Facilities** STV FTV WiFi 🎣🏌 Complimentary salmon & trout fishing Coracling In-room massage treatments Xmas New Year **Conf** Class 30 Board 22 Thtr 50 Del from £133 to £200 **Parking** 30 **Notes** LB No children 6yrs Civ Wed 65

EBBW VALE
Blaenau Gwent   Map 9 SO10

Premier Inn Ebbw Vale

BUDGET HOTEL

tel: 0871 527 8356 **Victoria Business Park, Waunllwyd NP23 8AN**
web: www.premierinn.com
dir: M4 junct 28, A467 signed Risca, then Brynmawr. At rdbt at Brynithel 1st exit onto A4046, signed Ebbw Vale. At rdbt 3rd exit towards Waunllwyd. At rdbt 1st exit, next left. Hotel adjacent

High quality, budget accommodation ideal for both families and business travellers. Spacious, en suite bedrooms feature tea and coffee making facilities, and Freeview TV in most hotels. Internet access and WiFi are available for a small fee. The adjacent family restaurant features a wide and varied menu. See also the Hotel Groups pages.

Rooms 44

EGLWYS FACH
Ceredigion
Map 14 SN69

Plas Ynyshir Hall Hotel

★★★★ @@@ COUNTRY HOUSE HOTEL

tel: 01654 781209 & 781268 **SY20 8TA**
email: ynyshir@relaischateaux.com **web:** www.ynyshirhall.co.uk
dir: Exit A487, 5.5m S of Machynlleth, signed from main road

Set in beautifully landscaped grounds and surrounded by the RSPB Ynys-hir Nature Reserve, Plas Ynyshir Hall is a haven of calm. The house was once owned by Queen Victoria and is surrounded by mountain scenery. Lavishly styled bedrooms, each individually themed around a great painter, provide high standards of luxury and comfort. The lounge and bar, adorned with an abundance of fresh flowers, have different moods. The dining room offers highly accomplished cooking using the best, locally sourced ingredients including herbs, soft fruit and vegetables from the hotel's own kitchen garden, and wild foods gathered nearby. This hotel makes an idyllic location for weddings.

Rooms 10 (3 annexe) (4 GF) ♠ **S** £150-£655; **D** £205-£710* **Facilities** WiFi ⤷ 🦢 Xmas New Year **Conf** Class 20 Board 18 Thtr 25 **Parking** 20 **Notes** Closed 4-31 Jan Civ Wed 40

FISHGUARD
Pembrokeshire
Map 8 SM93

The Cartref Hotel

★★ 67% HOTEL

tel: 01348 872430 & 0781 330 5235 **15-19 High St SA65 9AW**
email: cartrefhotel@btconnect.com **web:** www.cartrefhotel.co.uk
dir: On A40 in town centre

Personally run by the proprietor, this friendly hotel offers convenient access to the town centre and ferry terminal. Bedrooms are well maintained and include some family rooms. There is also a cosy lounge bar and a welcoming restaurant that looks out onto the high street.

Rooms 10 (2 fmly) ♠ **S** £40-£50; **D** £70-£75 (incl. bkfst)* **Facilities** FTV WiFi **Parking** 4 **Notes** LB

HAY-ON-WYE
Powys
Map 9 SO24

The Swan-at-Hay Hotel

★★★ 74% @ HOTEL

tel: 01497 821188 **Church St HR3 5DQ**
email: stay@swanathay.co.uk **web:** www.swanathay.co.uk
dir: In town centre, on Brecon Road opposite cinema bookshop

This former coaching inn, now a privately owned hotel, has plenty of character and overlooks well-tended gardens. The bedrooms are comfortable, and a good range of guest extras are provided. The food, based on fresh local ingredients, is offered on a well-balanced menu. The Swan's location, between The Black Mountains and the Brecon Beacons, is ideal for walkers of course, but also convenient for leisure and business guests visiting the area. WiFi is available.

Rooms 17 (1 fmly) (2 GF) **Facilities** FTV WiFi Xmas New Year **Conf** Class 80 Board 60 Thtr 120 **Parking** 17 **Notes** RS Jan Civ Wed 80

HENSOL
Vale of Glamorgan
Map 9 ST07

Vale Resort

★★★★ 79% @ HOTEL

tel: 01443 667800 **Hensol Park CF72 8JY**
email: reservations@vale-hotel.com **web:** www.vale-hotel.com
dir: M4 junct 34 towards Pendoylan, hotel signed from junct

A wealth of leisure facilities is offered at this large and modern, purpose-built complex, including two golf courses and a driving range plus an extensive health spa with a gym, swimming pool, squash courts, orthopaedic clinic and a range of treatments. Public areas are spacious and attractive, while bedrooms, many with balconies, are well appointed. Meeting and conference facilities are available. Guests can dine in the traditional Vale Grill, a brasserie-style restaurant serving quality fresh ingredients.

Rooms 143 (114 annexe) (15 fmly) (36 GF) ♠ **Facilities** Spa STV WiFi ⤷ 🦢 ⤶ 36 🏊 Putt green Fishing Gym Squash Children's club (Sat am & school hols) Xmas New Year **Conf** Class 280 Board 60 Thtr 700 Del from £120 to £180* **Services** Lift Air con **Parking** 450 **Notes** ⊗ Civ Wed 700

| **KNIGHTON** | Map 9 SO27 |
| Powys | |

Milebrook House Hotel

★★★ 79% COUNTRY HOUSE HOTEL

tel: 01547 528632 **Milebrook LD7 1LT**
email: hotel@milebrookhouse.co.uk **web:** www.milebrookhouse.co.uk
dir: 2m E of Knighton, on A4113

Set in three acres of grounds and gardens in the Teme Valley, this charming house dates back to 1760. Over the years since its conversion into a hotel, it has acquired a well-deserved reputation for its warm hospitality, comfortable accommodation and the quality of its cuisine, which uses local produce and home-grown vegetables.

Rooms 10 (2 fmly) (2 GF) **Facilities** WiFi ↩ Table tennis Trout fly fishing Xmas New Year **Conf** Class 30 **Parking** 21 **Notes** ⊗ No children 8yrs RS Mon lunch

| **LAMPETER** | Map 8 SN54 |
| Ceredigion | |

The Falcondale Hotel & Restaurant

★★★★ 78% COUNTRY HOUSE HOTEL

tel: 01570 422910 **SA48 7RX**
email: info@thefalcondale.co.uk **web:** www.thefalcondale.co.uk
dir: 800yds W of High St (A475) or 1.5m NW of Lampeter - A482

Built in the Italianate style, this charming Victorian property is set in extensive grounds and beautiful parkland. The individually-styled bedrooms are generally spacious, well equipped and tastefully decorated. Bars and lounges are similarly well appointed with additional facilities including a conservatory and terrace. The award-winning restaurant, with a relaxed and friendly atmosphere, offers menus based on the best seasonal, locally sourced produce.

Rooms 18 (2 fmly) ⌕ **S** £100-£150; **D** £140-£190 (incl. bkfst)* **Facilities** FTV WiFi ↩ Xmas New Year **Conf** Class 26 Board 26 Thtr 60 Del from £142* **Services** Lift **Parking** 60 **Notes** LB Civ Wed 200

| **LLANBEDR** | Map 14 SH52 |
| Gwynedd | |

Ty Mawr Hotel

★★ 78% HOTEL

tel: 01341 241440 & 07717 080171 **LL45 2NH**
email: info@tymawrhotel.com **web:** www.tymawrhotel.com
dir: From Barmouth A496 (Harlech road). In Llanbedr turn right after bridge, hotel 50yds on left, follow brown tourist sigs

Ty Mawr means 'Big House' in Welsh. Located in a picturesque village within Snowdonia National Park, this family-run hotel has a relaxed, friendly atmosphere. The attractive grounds, opposite the River Artro, provide a popular beer garden during fine weather. The attractive, rustically furnished bar offers a blackboard selection of food and a good choice of real ales; a more formal menu is available in the restaurant. Bedrooms are smart and brightly decorated.

Rooms 10 (2 fmly) ⌕ **S** £55; **D** £85 (incl. bkfst)* **Facilities** STV FTV WiFi **Conf** Class 25 **Parking** 15 **Notes** Closed 24-26 Dec

| **LLANBERIS** | Map 14 SH56 |
| Gwynedd | |

The Royal Victoria Hotel Snowdonia

fOCUS hotels
management limited

★★★ 72% HOTEL

tel: 01286 870253 **LL55 4TY**
email: enquiries@theroyalvictoria.co.uk **web:** www.theroyalvictoria.co.uk
dir: On A4086 (Caernarfon to Llanberis road), directly opposite Snowdon Mountain Railway

This well-established hotel sits near the foot of Snowdon, between the Peris and Padarn lakes. Pretty gardens and grounds make an attractive setting for the many weddings held here. Bedrooms are well equipped. There are spacious lounges and bars, and a large dining room with a conservatory looking out over the lakes.

Rooms 106 (14 annexe) (7 fmly) ⌕ **Facilities** FTV WiFi ♫ Xmas New Year **Conf** Class 60 Board 50 Thtr 100 Del from £60 to £90* **Services** Lift **Parking** 107 **Notes** Civ Wed 100

| **LLANDEILO** | Map 8 SN62 |
| Carmarthenshire | |

The Plough Inn

★★★★ 77% HOTEL

tel: 01558 823431 **Rhosmaen SA19 6NP**
email: info@ploughrhosmaen.com **web:** www.ploughrhosmaen.com
dir: 0.5m N of Llandeilo on A40

This privately-owned hotel has memorable views over the Towy Valley and the Black Mountains. Bedrooms, situated in a separate wing, are tastefully furnished, spacious and comfortable. The public lounge bar is popular with locals, as is the spacious restaurant where freshly prepared food can be enjoyed. There are also conference facilities, a gym and a sauna.

Rooms 23 (11 fmly) (8 GF) ⌕ **S** £75-£100; **D** £95-£120 (incl. bkfst) **Facilities** FTV WiFi Gym Sauna Xmas New Year **Conf** Class 60 Board 30 Thtr 100 Del £100 **Services** Air con **Parking** 70 **Notes** Civ Wed 120

White Hart Inn

★★ 72% HOTEL

tel: 01558 823419 **36 Carmarthen Rd SA19 6RS**
email: info@whitehartinnwales.co.uk **web:** www.whitehartinnwales.co.uk
dir: A40 onto A483, hotel 200yds on left

This privately-owned, 19th-century roadside hostelry is on the outskirts of town. The modern bedrooms are well equipped and tastefully furnished, and family rooms are available. Public areas include a choice of bars where a wide range of grilled dishes is available. There are several function rooms, including a large self-contained suite.

Rooms 11 (6 fmly) ⌕ **Facilities** STV FTV WiFi New Year **Conf** Class 80 Board 40 Thtr 100 **Parking** 50 **Notes** ⊗ Civ Wed 70

L

Find out more about this country with the AA Guide to Wales see – theAA.com/shop

LLANDRINDOD WELLS
Powys

Map 9 SO06

The Metropole

★★★★ 77% HOTEL

tel: 01597 823700 **Temple St LD1 5DY**
email: info@metropole.co.uk **web:** www.metropole.co.uk
dir: On A483 in town centre

The centre of this famous spa town is dominated by this large Victorian hotel, which has been personally run by the same family for well over 100 years. The lobby leads to Spencers Bar and Brasserie and to the comfortable and elegantly styled lounge. Bedrooms vary in style, but all are spacious and well equipped. Facilities include an extensive range of modern conference and function rooms, as well as the impressive leisure centre. Extensive parking is provided to the rear of the hotel.

Rooms 114 (11 fmly) **S** £98; **D** £126-£175* **Facilities** Spa FTV WiFi ☃ ⊗ Gym Beauty & holistic treatments Sauna Steam room Xmas New Year **Conf** Class 200 Board 80 Thtr 300 **Services** Lift **Parking** 150 **Notes** Civ Wed 300

LLANDUDNO
Conwy

Map 14 SH78

INSPECTORS' CHOICE

Bodysgallen Hall and Spa

★★★★ ⊛⊛⊛ COUNTRY HOUSE HOTEL

tel: 01492 584466 **LL30 1RS**
email: info@bodysgallen.com **web:** www.bodysgallen.com
dir: A55 junct 19, A470 towards Llandudno. Hotel 2m on right

Situated in the idyllic surroundings of its own parkland and formal gardens, this 17th-century house is in an elevated position, with views towards Snowdonia and across to Conwy Castle. The lounges and dining room have fine antiques and great character. Accommodation is provided in the house, but also in delightfully converted cottages, together with a superb spa. Friendly and attentive service is discreetly offered, while the restaurant features fine local produce prepared with great skill.

Rooms 31 (16 annexe) (4 fmly) (4 GF) ☃ **S** £159-£349; **D** £179-£425 (incl. bkfst)*
Facilities Spa STV FTV WiFi ☃ ⊗ ⇨ Gym Beauty treatments Steam room Relaxation room Sauna Xmas New Year **Conf** Class 30 Board 22 Thtr 50 **Parking** 50 **Notes** LB ⊗ No children 6yrs Civ Wed 50

Imperial Hotel

★★★★ 80% HOTEL

tel: 01492 877466 **The Promenade LL30 1AP**
email: reception@theimperial.co.uk **web:** www.theimperial.co.uk
dir: A470 to Llandudno

The Imperial is a large and impressive hotel, situated on the promenade with lovely views out over the blue flag beaches to the bay, and within easy reach of the town centre and other amenities. Many of the bedrooms have sea views and there are also several suites available. The elegant Chantrey's Restaurant offers a fixed-price, monthly-changing menu that utilises local produce, and The Terrace is the place to relax and enjoy a leisurely lunch or a snack during the day.

Rooms 98 (10 fmly) ☃ **Facilities** FTV WiFi ☃ ⊗ Gym Beauty therapist Hairdressing ♫ Xmas New Year **Conf** Class 50 Board 50 Thtr 150 Del from £155 to £185* **Services** Lift **Parking** 25 **Notes** ⊗ Civ Wed 150

St George's Hotel

★★★★ 80% ◉ HOTEL

tel: 01492 877544 & 862184 **The Promenade LL30 2LG**
email: sales@stgeorgeswales.co.uk **web:** www.stgeorgeswales.co.uk
dir: A55, A470, follow to promenade, 0.25m, hotel on corner

This large and impressive seafront property was the first hotel to be built in the town. Restored to its former glory, the accommodation is of very high quality. The many Victorian features include the splendid, ornate Wedgwood Room restaurant. The terrace restaurant and main lounges overlook the bay; hot and cold snacks are available all day. Many of the thoughtfully equipped bedrooms enjoy sea views.

Rooms 76 (13 fmly) ⬧ **Facilities** STV FTV WiFi ⬧ In room beauty treatments Xmas New Year **Conf** Class 200 Board 45 Thtr 250 Del from £125 to £140* **Services** Lift Air con **Parking** 36 **Notes** ⊗ Civ Wed 200

See advert below

Empire Hotel & Spa

★★★★ 76% ◉ HOTEL

tel: 01492 860555 **Church Walks LL30 2HE**
email: reservations@empirehotel.co.uk **web:** www.empirehotel.co.uk
dir: From Chester, A55 junct 19 for Llandudno. Follow signs to Promenade, turn right at war memorial & left at rdbt. Hotel 100yds on right

Run by the same family for some 60 years, the Empire offers luxuriously appointed bedrooms with every modern facility. The 'Number 72' rooms in an adjacent house are particularly sumptuous. The indoor pool is overlooked by a lounge area where snacks are served all day, and in summer an outdoor pool and roof garden are available. The Watkins restaurant offers an interesting fixed-price menu.

Rooms 58 (8 annexe) (1 fmly) (2 GF) ⬧ **S** £72.50-£135; **D** £105-£155 (incl. bkfst)* **Facilities** Spa STV FTV WiFi ⬧ HL ⬧ ⬧ Gym Sauna Steam room Fitness suite New Year **Conf** Class 20 Board 20 Thtr 24 Del from £97.50 to £130* **Services** Lift Air con **Parking** 57 **Notes** LB Closed 20-30 Dec

L

LLANDUDNO *continued*

LLANDUDNO *continued*

INSPECTORS' CHOICE

Osborne House

★★★ ◉ TOWN HOUSE HOTEL

tel: 01492 860330 **17 North Pde LL30 2LP**
email: sales@osbornehouse.com **web:** www.osbornehouse.com
dir: Exit A55 junct 19. Follow signs for Llandudno then Promenade. Continue to junct, turn right. Hotel on left opposite pier entrance

Built in 1832, this Victorian house was restored and converted into a luxurious townhouse by the Maddocks family. Spacious suites offer unrivalled comfort and luxury, combining antique furnishings with state-of-the-art technology and facilities. Each suite provides super views over the pier and bay. Osborne's café grill is open throughout the day and offers high quality food, while the bar blends elegance with plasma screens, dazzling chandeliers and gilt framed mirrors.

Rooms 7 (1 fmly) ☎ **D** £115-£205 (incl. bkfst)* **Facilities** STV FTV WiFi ⬚ Use of swimming pool & sauna at Empire Hotel (100yds) New Year **Services** Air con **Parking** 6 **Notes** LB ⊗ No children 11yrs Closed 22-30 Dec

St Tudno Hotel and Restaurant

★★★ 83% ◉◉ HOTEL

WELSH RAREBITS *Hotels of Distinction*

tel: 01492 874411 **The Promenade LL30 2LP**
email: sttudnohotel@btinternet.com **web:** www.st-tudno.co.uk
dir: On Promenade towards pier, hotel opposite pier entrance

An excellent family-owned hotel with friendly and attentive staff, that enjoys fine sea views. The stylish bedrooms are well equipped with mini-bars, robes, satellite TVs and many other thoughtful extras. Public rooms include a lounge, a welcoming bar and a small indoor pool. The Terrace Restaurant, where seasonal and daily-changing menus are offered, has a delightful Mediterranean atmosphere. Afternoon tea is a real highlight.

Rooms 18 (4 fmly) ☎ **S** £80-£115; **D** £104-£230 (incl. bkfst) **Facilities** FTV WiFi HL Xmas New Year **Conf** Class 25 Board 20 Thtr 40 **Services** Lift **Parking** 12 **Notes** LB Civ Wed 70

Dunoon Hotel

★★★ 83% ◉ HOTEL

tel: 01492 860787 **Gloddaeth St LL30 2DW**
email: reservations@dunoonhotel.co.uk **web:** www.dunoonhotel.co.uk
dir: Exit Promenade at war memorial by pier into Gloddaeth St. Hotel 200yds on right

This impressive, privately owned hotel is centrally located and offers a variety of well-equipped bedrooms. Elegant public areas include a tastefully appointed restaurant where competently prepared dishes are served together with a good choice of notable, reasonably priced wines. The caring and attentive service is also noteworthy.

Rooms 49 (4 fmly) ☎ **S** £65-£107; **D** £110-£166 (incl. bkfst)* **Facilities** FTV WiFi Pool table **Services** Lift **Parking** 24 **Notes** LB Closed mid Dec-early Mar

Tynedale Hotel

★★★ 83% HOTEL

tel: 01492 877426 **Central Promenade LL30 2XS**
email: enquiries@tynedalehotel.co.uk **web:** www.tynedalehotel.co.uk
dir: On Promenade opposite bandstand

Tour groups are well catered for at this privately owned and personally run hotel, and regular live entertainment is a feature. Vibrant modern public areas create a unique and comfortable setting, and an attractive seafront patio garden is an additional asset. Bedrooms provide good comfort levels and the staff offer friendly and efficient service.

Rooms 54 (1 fmly) (10 GF) ☎ **S** £48-£59; **D** £92-£118 (incl. bkfst)* **Facilities** FTV WiFi ⬚ ♫ Xmas New Year **Services** Lift **Parking** 15 **Notes** LB ⊗

Cae Mor Hotel

★★★ 76% HOTEL

tel: 01492 878101 **5-6 Penrhyn Crescent LL30 1BA**
email: info@caemorhotel.co.uk **web:** www.caemorhotel.co.uk
dir: Exit A55 junct 19, follow A470/Llandudno/Town Centre signs. Straight on at 3 rdbts, right at 4th. Into right lane, right at next rdbt, follow Promenade signs. Straight on at next rdbt, left at next rdbt onto Promenade. 200yds, pass Venue Cymru

Located in a stunning seafront position adjacent to Venue Cymru, this tastefully renovated Victorian hotel provides a range of thoughtfully furnished bedrooms in minimalist style with smart modern bathrooms. Public areas include a choice of lounges and a stylish restaurant, the setting for imaginative dinners featuring the best of local seasonal produce.

Rooms 23 (2 fmly) (2 GF)  **S** £69-£102; **D** £95-£135 (incl. bkfst) **Facilities** FTV WiFi Xmas New Year **Conf** Board 28 Thtr 60 Del from £109 to £142 **Services** Lift **Parking** 26 **Notes** LB Civ Wed 50

Hydro Hotel

★★ 72% HOTEL

tel: 01492 870101 **Neville Crescent LL30 1AT**
email: hydro.llandudno@alfatravel.co.uk **web:** www.leisureplex.co.uk
dir: Follow signs for theatre to seafront, towards pier

This large hotel is situated on the promenade overlooking the sea, and offers good, value-for-money, modern accommodation. Public areas are quite extensive and include a choice of lounges, a games/snooker room and a ballroom where entertainment is provided every night. The hotel is a popular venue for coach tour parties.

Rooms 120 (4 fmly) (9 GF)  **Facilities** WiFi Table tennis Snooker ♫ Xmas New Year **Services** Lift **Parking** 10 **Notes** ⊗ Closed Jan-mid Feb RS Nov-Dec (ex Xmas) & mid Feb-Mar

Winchmore Hotel

★★ 69% SMALL HOTEL

tel: 01492 877458 & 878516 **7-8 Mostyn Crescent, Central Promenade LL30 1AR**
email: winchmore.hotel@gmail.com **web:** www.winchmore-hotel-llandudno.co.uk
dir: A55 (M6 & M56) take exit at Glan Conwy for Llandudno - A470, approx 5m. Upon arrival pass ASDA on left & Debenhams on right, keep to right. At level crossing go straight across towards seafront then take 1st right into Adelphi St along which is Hotel car park

This family-run establishment has a convenient foreshore location, and many of the public rooms as well as some bedrooms have sea views. The hotel has good parking, sufficient for all hotel guests, and is situated within easy walking distance of the town and attractions. Bedrooms are contemporarily styled and pleasantly appointed. Freshly cooked dinners are available and there is a cosy bar and two comfortable lounges.

Rooms 30 (5 fmly) (5 GF)  **S** £35-£45; **D** £60-£85 (incl. bkfst) **Facilities** FTV WiFi ♫ Xmas New Year **Conf** Class 80 Board 50 Thtr 50 Del from £60 to £75* **Services** Lift **Parking** 30

Premier Inn Llandudno North (Little Orme)

BUDGET HOTEL

tel: 0871 527 8636 **Colwyn Rd LL30 3AL**
web: www.premierinn.com
dir: A55 junct 20 follow Rhos-on-Sea/Llandrillo-Yn-Rhos/B5115 signs. Onto B5115 (Brompton Ave). Straight on at next 2 rdbts. Hotel on left

High quality, budget accommodation ideal for both families and business travellers. Spacious, en suite bedrooms feature tea and coffee making facilities, and Freeview TV in most hotels. Internet access and WiFi are available for a small fee. The adjacent family restaurant features a wide and varied menu. See also the Hotel Groups pages.

Rooms 19

The Lilly Restaurant with Rooms

 RESTAURANT WITH ROOMS

tel: 01492 876513 ▤ 01492 550100 **West Pde, West Shore LL30 2BD**
email: thelilly@live.co.uk **web:** www.thelilly.co.uk
dir: Phone for detailed directions

Located on the seafront on the West Shore with views over the Great Orme, this establishment has bedrooms that offer high standards of comfort, and good facilities. Children are very welcome here, and a relaxed atmosphere is found in Madhatter's Brasserie, which takes its name from Lewis Carroll's *Alice in Wonderland*, written while the author was staying on the West Shore. A fine dining restaurant is also available.

Rooms 5

LLANDUDNO JUNCTION Conwy	**Map 14 SH77**

Premier Inn Llandudno (Glan-Conwy)

BUDGET HOTEL

tel: 0871 527 8634 **Afon Conwy LL28 5LB**
web: www.premierinn.com
dir: A55 junct 19. Exit rdbt at A470 (Betws-y-Coed). Hotel immediately on left, opposite petrol station

High quality, budget accommodation ideal for both families and business travellers. Spacious, en suite bedrooms feature tea and coffee making facilities, and Freeview TV in most hotels. Internet access and WiFi are available for a small fee. The adjacent family restaurant features a wide and varied menu. See also the Hotel Groups pages.

Rooms 41

L

LLANELLI	Map 8 SN50
Carmarthenshire	

BEST WESTERN Diplomat Hotel and Spa

★★★ 79% HOTEL

tel: 01554 756156 **Felinfoel SA15 3PJ**
email: reservations@diplomat-hotel-wales.com **web:** www.diplomat-hotel-wales.com
dir: M4 junct 48, A4138 then B4303, hotel 0.75m on right

This Victorian mansion, set in mature grounds, has been extended over the years to provide a comfortable and relaxing hotel. The well-appointed bedrooms are located in the main house and there is also a wing of equally comfortable modern rooms. Public areas include Trubshaw's Restaurant, a large function suite and a modern leisure centre.

Rooms 50 (8 annexe) (2 fmly) (4 GF) ↑ **S** £70-£75; **D** £90-£110 (incl. bkfst)*
Facilities FTV WiFi ↻ 🏊 supervised Gym Sauna Steam room Beauty treatment room
♫ Xmas New Year **Conf** Class 150 Board 100 Thtr 450 **Services** Lift **Parking** 250
Notes LB Civ Wed 300

Ashburnham Hotel

★★★ 68% HOTEL

tel: 01554 834343 & 834455 **Ashburnham Rd, Pembrey SA16 OTH**
email: info@ashburnham-hotel.co.uk **web:** www.ashburnham-hotel.co.uk
dir: M4 junct 48, A4138 to Llanelli, A484 W to Pembrey. Follow brown information signs

American aviatrix, Amelia Earhart stayed at this friendly hotel after finishing her historic trans-Atlantic flight in 1928. Public areas include the brasserie restaurant and the conservatory lounge bar that serve an extensive range of bar meals. Bedrooms, varying from standard to superior, have modern furnishings and facilities. The hotel is licensed for civil ceremonies, and function and conference facilities are also available.

Rooms 13 (2 fmly) **S** £40-£65; **D** £50-£75 (incl. bkfst)* **Facilities** STV FTV WiFi ↻
Conf Class 150 Board 80 Thtr 150 **Parking** 100 **Notes** ⊗ RS 24-26 Dec Civ Wed 130

Premier Inn Llanelli Central East

BUDGET HOTEL

tel: 0871 527 8638 **Llandafen Rd SA14 9BD**
web: www.premierinn.com
dir: M4 junct 48, A4138, approx 3m. Hotel on left

High quality, budget accommodation ideal for both families and business travellers. Spacious, en suite bedrooms feature tea and coffee making facilities, and Freeview TV in most hotels. Internet access and WiFi are available for a small fee. The adjacent family restaurant features a wide and varied menu. See also the Hotel Groups pages.

Rooms 50

Premier Inn Llanelli Central West

BUDGET HOTEL

tel: 0871 527 9342 **Sandpiper Rd, Sandy Water Park SA15 4SG**
web: www.premierinn.com
dir: M4 junct 48, A4138 towards Llanelli town centre. Then follow Carmarthen signs to Sandy Park rdbt. Hotel on left

Rooms 28

LLANGAMMARCH WELLS	Map 9 SN94
Powys	

The Lake Country House & Spa

★★★ ◎◎ COUNTRY HOUSE HOTEL

tel: 01591 620202 **LD4 4BS**
email: info@lakecountryhouse.co.uk **web:** www.lakecountryhouse.co.uk
dir: W from Builth Wells on A483 to Garth (approx 6m). Left for Llangammarch Wells, follow hotel signs

Expect good old-fashioned values and hospitality at this Victorian country house hotel. In fact, the service is so traditionally English, guests may believe they have their own butler. The establishment offers a 9-hole, par 3 golf course, 50 acres of wooded grounds and a spa with a hot tub that overlooks the lake. Bedrooms, some located in an annexe, and some at ground-floor level, are individually styled and have many extra comforts. Traditional afternoon teas are served in the lounge, and award-winning cuisine is provided in the spacious and elegant restaurant.

Rooms 31 (12 annexe) (8 GF) ↑ **S** £145-£210; **D** £195-£260 (incl. bkfst)*
Facilities Spa FTV WiFi 🏊 ⅃ 9 ⚓ Putt green Fishing ⚓ Gym Archery Horse riding Mountain biking Quad biking Xmas New Year **Conf** Class 30 Board 25 Thtr 80 **Parking** 70 **Notes** LB No children 8yrs Civ Wed 100

LLANTRISANT	Map 9 ST39
Monmouthshire	

Premier Inn Llantrisant

BUDGET HOTEL

tel: 0871 527 8640 **Gwaun Elai, Magden Park CF72 8LL**
web: www.premierinn.com
dir: M4 junct 34, A4119 towards Llantrisant & Rhondda. At 1st rdbt take 2nd exit. At 2nd rdbt take 1st exit

High quality, budget accommodation ideal for both families and business travellers. Spacious, en suite bedrooms feature tea and coffee making facilities, and Freeview TV in most hotels. Internet access and WiFi are available for a small fee. The adjacent family restaurant features a wide and varied menu. See also the Hotel Groups pages.

Rooms 51

L

LLANWDDYN
Powys

Map 15 SJ01

Lake Vyrnwy Hotel & Spa

★★★★ 76% COUNTRY HOUSE HOTEL

tel: 01691 870692 **Lake Vyrnwy SY10 OLY**
email: info@lakevyrnwyhotel.co.uk **web:** www.lakevyrnwy.com
dir: On A4393, 200yds past dam turn sharp right into drive

This elegant Victorian country-house hotel lies in 26,000 acres of woodland above Lake Vyrnwy, and provides a wide range of bedrooms, most with superb views and many with four-poster beds and balconies. Extensive public rooms retain many period features, and informal dining is available in the popular Tower Tavern. Relaxing and rejuvenating treatments are a feature of the stylish health spa.

Rooms 52 (12 fmly) ♦ **S** £119-£235; **D** £145-£260 (incl. bkfst)* **Facilities** Spa STV FTV WiFi ♣ 🏊 Gym Archery Birdwatching Canoeing Kayaking Clay shooting Sailing Fly fishing Cycling Xmas New Year **Conf** Class 80 Board 60 Thtr 200 Del £155* **Services** Lift **Parking** 70 **Notes** LB Civ Wed 200

LLANWRTYD WELLS
Powys

Map 9 SN84

Carlton Riverside

◉◉ RESTAURANT WITH ROOMS

tel: 01591 610248 **Irfon Crescent LD5 4SP**
email: carltonriverside@hotmail.co.uk **web:** www.carltonriverside.com
dir: In town centre beside bridge

Guests are made to feel part of the family at this character property, set beside the river in the smallest town in Wales. Carlton Riverside offers award-winning cuisine which Mary Ann Gilchrist produces using the very best of local ingredients. The set menu is complemented by a well-chosen wine list and dinner is served in the stylish restaurant which offers a memorable blend of traditional comfort, modern design and river views. Four comfortable bedrooms have tasteful combinations of antique and contemporary furniture, along with welcome personal touches.

Rooms 4

Lasswade Country House

◉◉ RESTAURANT WITH ROOMS

tel: 01591 610515 📠 01591 610611 **Station Rd LD5 4RW**
email: info@lasswadehotel.co.uk **web:** www.lasswadehotel.co.uk
dir: Exit A483 into Irfon Terrace, right into Station Rd, 350yds on right

This friendly establishment on the edge of the town has impressive views over the countryside. Bedrooms are comfortably furnished and well equipped, while the public areas consist of a tastefully decorated lounge, an elegant restaurant with a bar, and an airy conservatory which looks towards the neighbouring hills. The kitchen utilises fresh, local produce to provide an enjoyable dining experience.

Rooms 8 (1 fmly)

LLYSWEN
Powys

Map 9 SO13

INSPECTORS' CHOICE

Llangoed Hall

★★★★ ◉◉◉ COUNTRY HOUSE HOTEL

tel: 01874 754525 **LD3 0YP**
email: enquiries@llangoedhall.com **web:** www.llangoedhall.com
dir: On A470 between Brecon & Builth Wells

Set against the stunning backdrop of the Black Mountains and the Wye Valley, this imposing country house is a haven of peace and quiet. The interior is no less impressive, with a noteworthy art collection complementing the many antiques in day rooms and bedrooms. Comfortable, spacious accommodation is matched by equally inviting lounges. In the kitchen, chef Nick Brodie and his team produce cooking that makes Llangoed Hall into something of a destination.

Rooms 23 ♦ **S** £150-£400; **D** £190-£500 (incl. bkfst) **Facilities** FTV WiFi ♣ HL 🏊 Fishing 🦅 Snooker table Outdoor chess Xmas New Year **Conf** Class 30 Board 30 Thtr 80 Del from £150 to £400 **Parking** 50 **Notes** LB ⊗ Civ Wed 80

MAESYCWMMER
Caerphilly

Map 9 ST19

Bryn Meadows Golf, Hotel & Spa

★★★★ 79% HOTEL

tel: 01495 225590 **CF82 7SN**
email: reception@brynmeadows.co.uk **web:** www.brynmeadows.com
dir: M4 junct 28, A467 signed Brynmawr, 10m to Newbridge. Take A472 signed Ystrad Mynach. Hotel off Crown rdbt signed golf course

Surrounded by its own mature parkland and 18-hole golf course, this impressive hotel, golf, leisure and function complex provides a range of high quality, well-equipped bedrooms; several have their own balconies or patio areas. The attractive public areas include a pleasant restaurant which, like many of the bedrooms, enjoys striking views of the golf course and beyond. There are impressive function facilities and the hotel is a popular venue for weddings.

Rooms 42 (4 fmly) (21 GF) ↟ **Facilities** Spa FTV WiFi ⓑ supervised ⌕ 18 Putt green Gym Sauna Steam room Aromatherapy suite Xmas New Year **Conf** Class 70 Board 60 Thtr 120 **Services** Air con **Parking** 120 **Notes** ⊗ Civ Wed 250

MANORBIER
Pembrokeshire

Map 8 SS09

Castlemead

RESTAURANT WITH ROOMS

tel: 01834 871358 ▤ 01834 871358 **SA70 7TA**
email: castlemeadhotel@aol.com **web:** www.castlemeadhotel.com
dir: A4139 towards Pembroke, B4585 into village, follow signs to beach & castle, establishment on left

Benefiting from a superb location with spectacular views of the bay, the Norman church and Manorbier Castle, this family-run business is friendly and welcoming. Bedrooms, which include some in a converted former coach house at ground floor level, are generally quite spacious and have modern facilities. Public areas include a sea-view residents' lounge and a restaurant accessed by stairs, which is open to non-residents, along with a cosy bar. There are extensive gardens to the rear of the property.

Rooms 8 (3 annexe) (2 fmly)

MERTHYR TYDFIL
Merthyr Tydfil

Map 9 SO00

Premier Inn Merthyr Tydfil

BUDGET HOTEL

tel: 0871 527 8768 **Pentrebach CF48 4BB**
web: www.premierinn.com
dir: M4 junct 32, A470 to Merthyr Tydfil. At rdbt right to Pentrebach (A4060). At next rdbt 3rd exit signed Abergavenny, (dual carriageway). Double back at next rdbt by Pentrebach Co-op onto A4060 towards Pentrebach. Left after layby, hotel adjacent to Pentrebach House

High quality, budget accommodation ideal for both families and business travellers. Spacious, en suite bedrooms feature tea and coffee making facilities, and Freeview TV in most hotels. Internet access and WiFi are available for a small fee. The adjacent family restaurant features a wide and varied menu. See also the Hotel Groups pages.

Rooms 40

MISKIN
Rhondda Cynon Taff

Map 9 ST08

Miskin Manor Country Hotel

★★★★ 75% ◉◉ COUNTRY HOUSE HOTEL

tel: 01443 224204 **Pendoylan Rd CF72 8ND**
email: reservations@miskin-manor.co.uk **web:** www.miskin-manor.co.uk
dir: M4 junct 34, A4119, signed Llantrisant, hotel 300yds on left

This historic manor house is peacefully located in 22-acre grounds, yet is only minutes away from the M4. Bedrooms are furnished to a high standard and include some located in converted stables and cottages. Public areas are spacious and comfortable and include a variety of function rooms. The relaxed atmosphere and surroundings ensure this hotel remains popular for wedding functions as well as with business guests. There is a separate modern health and fitness centre which includes a gym, sauna, steam room and swimming pool.

Rooms 43 (9 annexe) (2 fmly) (7 GF) **Facilities** FTV WiFi ⓑ ⩗ Gym Sauna Steam room Dance studio **Conf** Class 80 Board 65 Thtr 160 **Parking** 200 **Notes** Civ Wed 200

MOLD
Flintshire

Map 15 SJ26

Beaufort Park Hotel

★★★ 77% HOTEL

tel: 01352 758646 **Alltami Rd, New Brighton CH7 6RQ**
email: info@beaufortparkhotel.co.uk **web:** www.beaufortparkhotel.co.uk
dir: A55, A494, through Alltami lights, over mini rdbt by petrol station towards Mold, A5119. Hotel 100yds on right

This large, modern hotel is conveniently located a short drive from the North Wales Expressway and offers various styles of spacious accommodation. There are extensive public areas, and several meeting and function rooms are available. There is a wide choice of meals in the formal restaurant and in the popular Arches bar.

Rooms 106 (8 fmly) (32 GF) **Facilities** FTV WiFi Squash ♫ Xmas New Year **Conf** Class 120 Board 120 Thtr 250 **Parking** 200 **Notes** Civ Wed 250

MONMOUTH
Monmouthshire

Map 10 SO51

Bistro Prego

◉◉ RESTAURANT WITH ROOMS

tel: 01600 712600 ▤ 01600 716016 **7 Church St NP25 3BX**
email: enquiries@pregomonmouth.co.uk **web:** www.pregomonmouth.co.uk
dir: Travelling N A40 at lights left turn, T-junct left turn, 2nd right, hotel at rear of car park

Located in the middle of Monmouth, this Italian-style restaurant with rooms is open all day for a selection of teas, coffees, lunches and light snacks. At dinner, a delicious choice of dishes using local produce is available in the popular bistro-style dining area. Rooms are located above the dining room and come in a range of shapes and sizes.

Rooms 8 (2 fmly)

NARBERTH
Pembrokeshire — Map 8 SN11

The Grove

◉◉◉ RESTAURANT WITH ROOMS

tel: 01834 860915 **Molleston SA67 8BX**
email: info@thegrove-narberth.co.uk **web:** www.thegrove-narberth.co.uk
dir: A48 to Carmarthen, A40 to Haverfordwest. At A478 rdbt 1st exit to Narberth, through town towards Tenby. At bottom of hill right, 1m, The Grove on right

The Grove is an elegant 18th-century country house set on a hillside in 24 acres of rolling countryside. The owners have lovingly restored the building with care, combining period features with excellent modern decor. There are bedrooms in the main house, and additional rooms in separate buildings; all are appointed with quality and comfort. Some bedrooms are on the ground floor, and most have fantastic views out over the Preseli Hills. There are two sumptuous lounge areas, one with an open fire and a small bar, and two separate dining rooms that offer award-winning cuisine. Self-catering cottages are available.

Rooms 20 (6 annexe) (3 fmly)

NEATH
Neath Port Talbot — Map 9 SS79

Castle Hotel

★★★ 74% HOTEL

tel: 01639 641119 **The Parade SA11 1RB**
email: info@castlehotelneath.co.uk **web:** www.castlehotelneath.co.uk
dir: M4 junct 43, follow signs for Neath, 500yds past rail station, hotel on right. Car park on left in 50yds

Situated in the town centre, this Georgian property, once a coaching inn, has a wealth of history and plenty of character. Lord Nelson and Lady Hamilton are reputed to have stayed here, and it is where the Welsh Rugby Union was founded in 1881. The hotel provides well-equipped accommodation and pleasant public areas. Bedrooms include family bedded rooms and one with a four-poster. Green's restaurant provides a good range of dishes at both lunch and dinner. Function and meeting rooms are available.

Rooms 29 (3 fmly) (14 smoking) **Facilities** STV FTV WiFi ⬙ ♫ Xmas New Year **Conf** Class 75 Board 50 Thtr 160 Del from £80 to £190 **Parking** 26 **Notes** ⊗ Civ Wed 120

NEWCASTLE EMLYN
Carmarthenshire — Map 8 SN34

Gwesty'r Emlyn Hotel

★★★ 80% ◉ HOTEL

WELSH RAREBITS Hotels of Distinction

tel: 01239 710317 **Bridge St SA38 9DU**
email: reception@gwestyremlynhotel.co.uk **web:** www.gwestyremlynhotel.co.uk
dir: In town centre

This hotel, in the heart of a busy market town, dates back some 300 years. Appointed to a high standard, the stylish and comfortable bedrooms have luxury bathrooms. The public areas comprise a choice of bars, a cosy seating area and a modern restaurant offering dishes created from good, locally sourced ingredients. There is a gym, sauna and spa pool plus a large function suite for weddings and parties.

Rooms 24 (3 fmly) (1 GF) ⬙ **Facilities** FTV WiFi Gym Sauna Splash pool Xmas New Year **Conf** Class 100 Board 50 Thtr 150 **Parking** 25 **Notes** ⊗ Civ Wed 150

NEWPORT
Newport — Map 9 ST38

See also **Cwmbran**

The Celtic Manor Resort

★★★★★ 85% ◉◉◉ HOTEL

tel: 01633 413000 **Coldra Woods NP18 1HQ**
email: bookings@celtic-manor.com **web:** www.celtic-manor.com
dir: M4 junct 24, take B4237 towards Newport. Hotel 1st on right

This hotel is part of the outstanding Celtic Manor Resort. Here there are three challenging golf courses including the Twenty Ten Course specifically designed for the 2010 Ryder Cup; a huge convention centre; superb leisure clubs and two hotels. This hotel has excellent bedrooms, with suites and two Presidential suites, offering good space and comfort. Stylish extensive public areas are set around a spectacular atrium lobby that includes several eating options; Terry M is the award-winning, fine dining restaurant. There is a choice of shops and boutiques as well.

Rooms 334 (34 fmly) ⬙ **S** £123-£144; **D** £333-£370 (incl. bkfst) **Facilities** Spa STV FTV WiFi ⬙ ⊛ ♿ 54 ⛳ Putt green Gym Golf Academy Clay pigeon shooting Mountain bike trails Games room Archery ♫ Xmas New Year Child facilities **Conf** Class 600 Board 60 Thtr 1500 **Services** Lift Air con **Parking** 1300 **Notes** ⊗ Civ Wed 100

The Manor House

★★★★ 77% ◉ HOTEL

tel: 01633 413000 **The Celtic Manor Resort, Coldra Woods NP18 1HQ**
email: bookings@celtic-manor.com **web:** www.celtic-manor.com
dir: M4 junct 24, B4237 towards Newport. Hotel 1st on right

Part of the complex of the Celtic Manor Resort, this hotel, built in the 19th century, offers country house charm combined with modern comforts. Sitting in beautiful landscaped gardens it has traditionally styled bedrooms, three with four-posters. Several eating options are available both at Manor House and at the Celtic Manor Resort, where guests have access to all the hotel and leisure facilities; three challenging golf courses and superb leisure clubs among them.

Rooms 65 (3 fmly) ⬙ **S** £73-£85; **D** £241-£260 (incl. bkfst) **Facilities** Spa STV FTV WiFi ⊛ supervised ♿ 18 ⛳ Putt green Fishing Gym Golf academy Adventure golf Archery Clay pigeon shooting ♫ Xmas New Year **Conf** Class 80 Board 40 Thtr 200 **Services** Lift Air con **Parking** 1000 **Notes** ⊗ Civ Wed 180

N

NEWPORT *continued*

Premier Inn Newport South Wales

BUDGET HOTEL

tel: 0871 527 8814 **Coldra Junction, Chepstow Rd, Langstone NP18 2NX**
web: www.premierinn.com
dir: M4 junct 24, A48 to Langstone, at next rdbt return towards junct 24. Hotel 50mtrs on left

High quality, budget accommodation ideal for both families and business travellers. Spacious, en suite bedrooms feature tea and coffee making facilities, and Freeview TV in most hotels. Internet access and WiFi are available for a small fee. The adjacent family restaurant features a wide and varied menu. See also the Hotel Groups pages.

Rooms 63

NEWPORT
Pembrokeshire
Map 8 SN03

Llys Meddyg

 RESTAURANT WITH ROOMS

tel: 01239 820008 **East St SA42 0SY**
email: contact@llysmeddyg.com **web:** www.llysmeddyg.com
dir: On A487 in centre of town

Llys Meddyg is a Georgian town house offering a blend of old and new, with elegant furnishings, deep sofas and a welcoming fire. The owners of this property employed local craftsmen to create a lovely interior that has an eclectic style. The focus of the quality restaurant menu is the use of fresh, seasonal, locally sourced ingredients. The spacious bedrooms are comfortable and contemporary in design; bathrooms vary in style.

Rooms 8 (3 annexe) (3 fmly)

NORTHOP
Flintshire
Map 15 SJ26

Soughton Hall Hotel

★★★ 87% COUNTRY HOUSE HOTEL

tel: 01352 840811 **CH7 6AB**
email: info@soughtonhall.co.uk **web:** www.soughtonhall.co.uk
dir: A55/B5126, after 500mtrs turn left for Northop, left at lights (A5119-Mold). After 0.5m follow signs

Built as a bishop's palace in 1714, this elegant country house has magnificent grounds. Bedrooms are individually decorated and furnished with fine antiques and rich fabrics. There are several spacious day rooms designed in keeping with the style of the house. The trendy Stables bar and restaurant offer a good range of dishes at both lunch and dinner. Understandably, the hotel is a very popular venue for weddings.

Rooms 15 (2 fmly) (2 GF) ↻ **S** £79-£99; **D** £160-£190* **Facilities** FTV WiFi 🏊 🎣 Riding stables nearby Xmas New Year **Conf** Thtr 180 Del from £135* **Parking** 100 **Notes** LB ⊗ Civ Wed 100

NORTHOP HALL
Flintshire
Map 15 SJ26

Holiday Inn A55 Chester West

★★★ 75% HOTEL

tel: 01244 550011 **Westbound A55, Mold, nr Chester CH7 6HB**
email: bookings@holidayinnchesterwest.co.uk **web:** www.holidayinnchesterwest.co.uk
dir: M6 junct 20, M56 to Queensferry, follow signs for A55/Conwy. Hotel 500yds past A494 slip road

This modern hotel is ideally situated to explore Chester, Deeside and North Wales, and offers comfortable accommodation and warm hospitality. All rooms benefit from free WiFi, Freeview TV and Sky Sport channels. Meals are served in the conservatory restaurant with snacks and drinks available in the Lounge Bar.

Rooms 81 (24 fmly) (31 GF) (5 smoking) **S** £44-£85; **D** £44-£85 **Facilities** STV FTV WiFi ↻ HL Gym New Year **Conf** Class 130 Board 55 Thtr 220 Del from £99 to £119 **Services** Lift Air con **Parking** 200 **Notes** Closed 24-25 Dec Civ Wed 100

PEMBROKE
Pembrokeshire
Map 8 SM90

BEST WESTERN Lamphey Court Hotel & Spa

★★★★ 73% ⊛ HOTEL

tel: 01646 672273 **Lamphey SA71 5NT**
email: info@lampheycourt.co.uk **web:** www.lampheycourt.co.uk
dir: M4 then A477 to Pembroke. Left at Milton for Lamphey, hotel on right

This Georgian mansion, on an elevated site, is set in attractive countryside and is perfectly situated for exploring the stunning Pembrokeshire coast, the beaches and the Preseli Hills. Well-appointed bedrooms and family suites are situated in a converted coach house within the grounds. The elegant public areas include both formal and informal dining rooms that feature dishes inspired by local produce. Leisure facilities include a state-of-the-art spa with a swimming pool, gym, sauna, treatment rooms and much more.

Rooms 38 (12 annexe) (7 fmly) (6 GF) **Facilities** Spa FTV WiFi ↻ 🎣 🏊 Gym Sauna Steam room Beauty & therapy Xmas New Year **Conf** Class 40 Board 30 Thtr 60 **Parking** 50 **Notes** Civ Wed 80

Lamphey Hall Hotel

★★★ 77% HOTEL

tel: 01646 672394 & 07791 896191 **Lamphey SA71 5NR**
email: andrewjones1990@aol.com **web:** www.lampheyhallltd.co.uk
dir: From Carmarthen A40 to St Clears. Follow signs for A477, left at Milton

Set in a delightful village, this very friendly, privately owned and efficiently run hotel offers an ideal base from which to explore the surrounding countryside. Bedrooms are well equipped, comfortably furnished and include family rooms and ground floor rooms. Diners have a choice of three restaurant areas offering an extensive range of dishes. There is also a small lounge, a bar and attractive gardens.

Rooms 10 (1 fmly) (2 GF) **Facilities** FTV WiFi **Parking** 32

N

PONTYPOOL
Torfaen

Map 9 SO20

Premier Inn Pontypool

BUDGET HOTEL

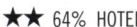

tel: 0871 527 8890 **Tyr'felin, Lower Mill Field NP4 0RH**
web: www.premierinn.com
dir: At junct of A4042 & A472

High quality, budget accommodation ideal for both families and business travellers. Spacious, en suite bedrooms feature tea and coffee making facilities, and Freeview TV in most hotels. Internet access and WiFi are available for a small fee. The adjacent family restaurant features a wide and varied menu. See also the Hotel Groups pages.

Rooms 49

PONTYPRIDD
Rhondda Cynon Taff

Map 9 ST08

Llechwen Hall Hotel

★★★ 74%  COUNTRY HOUSE HOTEL

tel: 01443 742050 & 743020 **Llanfabon CF37 4HP**
email: enquiries@llechwenhall.co.uk **web:** www.llechwen.co.uk
dir: A470 N towards Merthyr Tydfil. At large rdbt take 3rd exit. At mini rdbt take 3rd exit, hotel signed 0.5m on left

Set on top of a hill with a stunning approach, this country house hotel has served many functions in its 200-year-old history including time as a private school and a magistrates' court. The spacious, individually decorated bedrooms are well equipped; some are situated in the separate coach house nearby. There are ground-floor, twin, double and family bedrooms on offer. The Victorian-style public areas are attractively appointed and the hotel is a popular venue for weddings.

Rooms 20 (8 annexe) (6 fmly) (4 GF) **Facilities** FTV WiFi ♦ Xmas New Year **Conf** Class 80 Board 40 Thtr 200 **Parking** 150 **Notes** Civ Wed 80

PORTHCAWL
Bridgend

Map 9 SS87

Seabank Hotel

★★ 64% HOTEL

tel: 01656 782261 **Esplanade CF36 3LU**
email: seabank@alfatravel.co.uk **web:** www.leisureplex.co.uk
dir: M4 junct 37, A4229 to Porthcawl seafront

The Seabank Hotel stands in a prime location on the promenade of this seaside town, with panoramic sea views from the majority of bedrooms. Porthcawl has several beaches and coastal walks; the world famous Royal Porthcawl golf course is within easy distance and the cities of Swansea and Cardiff are only a short drive away. The spacious bedrooms are all en suite and there is a lift which serves most bedrooms. There is a spacious restaurant, a lounge bar and a choice of lounges with sea views. The hotel is a popular venue for coach tour parties, as well as weddings and conferences. There is ample parking around the hotel.

Rooms 89 (5 GF) ⬤ **S** £38-£57; **D** £60-£98 (incl. bkfst)* **Facilities** FTV WiFi 🎵 Xmas New Year **Services** Lift **Parking** 100 **Notes** LB ⊗ Closed 2 Jan-10 Feb

PORTHMADOG
Gwynedd

Map 14 SH53

Royal Sportsman Hotel

★★★ 82% HOTEL

tel: 01766 512015 **131 High St LL49 9HB**
email: enquiries@royalsportsman.co.uk **web:** www.royalsportsman.co.uk
dir: Located opposite rdbt where A487 meets A497

This hotel has a very convenient location handy for the coast or for those wishing to visit the national park or mountain railway. The hotel has a choice of dining options and food is a notable aspect here. Bedrooms are smartly appointed, and there is a spacious lounge. The staff are a friendly team and service is attentive. There is also covered parking available.

Rooms 28 (7 fmly) (4 GF) ⬤ **S** £65; **D** £94-£106 (incl. bkfst)* **Facilities** STV FTV WiFi ♦ Xmas New Year **Conf** Class 30 Board 30 Thtr 50 Del from £150 to £170 **Parking** 17 **Notes** LB

PORTMEIRION
Gwynedd

Map 14 SH53

The Hotel Portmeirion

★★★★ 79% ⬤⬤ HOTEL

tel: 01766 770000 & 772440 **LL48 6ET**
email: hotel@portmeirion-village.com **web:** www.portmeirion-village.com
dir: 2m W, Portmeirion village is S off A487

Saved from dereliction in the 1920s by Clough Williams-Ellis, the elegant Hotel Portmeirion enjoys one of the finest settings in Wales, located beneath the wooded slopes of the village, overlooking the sandy estuary towards Snowdonia. Many bedrooms have private sitting rooms and balconies with spectacular views. The staff, mostly Welsh-speaking, provide a good mix of warm hospitality and efficient service. Dinner and breakfast include the finest produce.

Rooms 44 (30 annexe) (6 fmly) ⬤ **S** £79-£279; **D** £119-£319 (incl. bkfst)* **Facilities** Spa FTV WiFi ♦ ⚡ Xmas New Year **Conf** Class 40 Board 30 Thtr 100 Del from £135* **Services** Lift **Parking** 44 **Notes** ⊗ Civ Wed 130

P

PORT TALBOT
Neath Port Talbot

Map 9 SS78

BEST WESTERN Aberavon Beach Hotel

★★★ 80% HOTEL

tel: 01639 884949 **Neath SA12 6QP**
email: sales@aberavonbeach.com **web:** www.aberavonbeach.com
dir: M4 junct 41, A48 & follow signs for Aberavon Beach & Hollywood Park

This friendly, purpose-built hotel enjoys a prominent position on the seafront overlooking Swansea Bay. Bedrooms, many with sea views, are comfortably appointed and thoughtfully equipped. Public areas include an all-weather leisure suite with swimming pool, open-plan bar and restaurant plus a choice of function rooms.

Rooms 68 (6 fmly) ⌨ **S** £50-£85; **D** £60-£120 (incl. bkfst) **Facilities** FTV WiFi ⌨ Sauna Xmas New Year **Conf** Class 200 Board 100 Thtr 300 Del from £110 to £120 **Services** Lift **Parking** 150 **Notes** LB Civ Wed 300

Premier Inn Port Talbot

BUDGET HOTEL

tel: 0871 527 8896 **Baglan Rd, Baglan SA12 8ES**
web: www.premierinn.com
dir: M4 junct 41 W'bound. Hotel just off 4th exit at rdbt. M4 junct 42 E'bound, left towards Port Talbot. Take 2nd exit off 2nd rdbt

High quality, budget accommodation ideal for both families and business travellers. Spacious, en suite bedrooms feature tea and coffee making facilities, and Freeview TV in most hotels. Internet access and WiFi are available for a small fee. The adjacent family restaurant features a wide and varied menu. See also the Hotel Groups pages.

Rooms 42

RAGLAN
Monmouthshire

Map 9 SO40

The Beaufort Raglan Coaching Inn & Brasserie

★★★ 77% ⬤ HOTEL

tel: 01291 690412 **High St NP15 2DY**
email: enquiries@beaufortraglan.co.uk **web:** www.beaufortraglan.co.uk
dir: M4 junct 24, A449/A40 junct Monmouth/Abergavenny, 0.5m into village opposite church

This friendly, family-run village inn dates back to the 15th century, and has historic links with nearby Raglan Castle. The bright, stylish and beautifully appointed bedrooms in the main house are suitably equipped for both tourists and business guests. Food is served in either The Brasserie restaurant or the traditional lounge, and both operations offer a relaxed service with an enjoyable selection of carefully prepared dishes.

Rooms 15 (5 annexe) (1 fmly) (5 GF) ⌨ **S** £60-£95; **D** £75-£115 (incl. bkfst)* **Facilities** FTV WiFi ⌨ Use of facilities at golf club in village Gliding Riding Fishing nearby ♫ **Conf** Class 60 Board 30 Thtr 120 **Parking** 30 **Notes** LB ⊗ RS 25-26 Dec

---

REYNOLDSTON
Swansea

Map 8 SS48

Fairyhill

⬤⬤ RESTAURANT WITH ROOMS

tel: 01792 390139 📠 01792 391358 **SA3 1BS**
email: postbox@fairyhill.net **web:** www.fairyhill.net
dir: M4 junct 47, A483, at next rdbt right onto A484. At Gowerton take B4295 for 10m

Peace and tranquillity are never far away at this charming Georgian mansion set in the heart of the beautiful Gower Peninsula. Bedrooms are furnished with care and are filled with many thoughtful extras. There is also a range of comfortable seating areas, with crackling log fires, to choose from. The smart restaurant offers menus based on local produce that are complemented by an excellent wine list.

Rooms 8

RHUDDLAN
Denbighshire

Map 15 SJ07

Premier Inn Rhuddlan

BUDGET HOTEL

tel: 0871 527 8932 **Castle View Retail Park, Marsh Rd LL18 5UA**
web: www.premierinn.com
dir: A55 junct 27, A525 signed Rhyl. At next rdbt 3rd exit into Station Rd. Next left into Marsh Rd. Hotel on left

High quality, budget accommodation ideal for both families and business travellers. Spacious, en suite bedrooms feature tea and coffee making facilities, and Freeview TV in most hotels. Internet access and WiFi are available for a small fee. The adjacent family restaurant features a wide and varied menu. See also the Hotel Groups pages.

Rooms 44

ROCKFIELD
Monmouthshire

Map 9 SO41

The Stonemill & Steppes Farm Cottages

⬤⬤ RESTAURANT WITH ROOMS

tel: 01600 775424 **NP25 5SW**
email: bookings@thestonemill.co.uk **web:** www.steppesfarmcottages.co.uk
dir: A48 to Monmouth, take B4233 to Rockfield. 2.6m

Located in a small hamlet just west of Monmouth, close to the Forest of Dean and the Wye Valley, this operation offers accommodation comprising six very well-appointed cottages. The comfortable rooms (for self-catering or on a B&B basis) have been lovingly restored to retain many original features. In a separate, converted 16th-century barn is Stonemill Restaurant with oak beams, vaulted ceilings and an old cider press. Breakfast is served in the cottages on request. This establishment's location proves handy for golfers with a choice of many courses in the area.

Rooms 6 (6 fmly)

ROSSETT
Wrexham   Map 15 SJ35

BEST WESTERN Llyndir Hall Hotel

★★★ 83% HOTEL

tel: 01244 571648 **Llyndir Ln LL12 0AY**
email: llyndirhallhotel@feathers.uk.com **web:** www.feathers.uk.com
dir: 5m S of Chester on B5445 follow Pulford signs

Located on the English/Welsh border within easy reach of Chester and Wrexham, this elegant manor house lies in several acres of mature grounds. The hotel is popular with both business and leisure guests, and facilities include conference rooms, an impressive leisure centre, a choice of comfortable lounges and a brasserie-style restaurant.

Rooms 48 (3 fmly) (17 GF) **Facilities** Spa FTV WiFi HL supervised Gym Beauty salon Sauna Xmas New Year **Conf** Class 60 Board 40 Thtr 120 **Parking** 80 **Notes** Civ Wed 120

SARN PARK MOTORWAY SERVICE AREA (M4)
Bridgend   Map 9 SS98

Days Inn Bridgend Cardiff - M4

BUDGET HOTEL

tel: 01656 659218 **Sarn Park Services, M4 Junct 36 CF32 9RW**
email: sarn.hotel@welcomebreak.co.uk **web:** www.welcomebreak.co.uk
dir: M4 junct 36

This modern building offers accommodation in smart, spacious and well-equipped bedrooms, suitable for families and business travellers, and all with en suite bathrooms. Continental breakfast is available and other refreshments may be taken at the nearby family restaurant. See also the Hotel Groups pages.

Rooms 40 (15 fmly) (20 GF) (8 smoking)

SAUNDERSFOOT
Pembrokeshire   Map 8 SN10

St Brides Spa Hotel

★★★★ 83% HOTEL

tel: 01834 812304 **St Brides Hill SA69 9NH**
email: reservations@stbridesspahotel.com **web:** www.stbridesspahotel.com
dir: A478 onto B4310 to Saundersfoot. Hotel above harbour

Set overlooking Carmarthen Bay this award-winning contemporary hotel and spa takes prime position. Many of the stylish, modern bedrooms enjoy sea views and

have balconies; there are also luxury apartments in the grounds. The hotel is open plan and has excellent views of the bay from the split-level lounge areas. Fresh local seafood is a speciality in the modern airy restaurant, which has a terrace for dining alfresco when the weather allows. The destination spa enjoys some of the very best views from the double treatment room and spa pool.

Rooms 46 (12 annexe) (6 fmly) (9 GF) **S** £130-£205; **D** £160-£310 (incl. bkfst)
Facilities Spa FTV WiFi Gym Thermal suite Hydrotherapy pool Steam & herbal rooms Ice fountain Xmas New Year **Conf** Class 40 Board 34 Thtr 100 Del from £130 to £200* **Services** Lift **Parking** 65 **Notes** LB Civ Wed 90

SKENFRITH
Monmouthshire   Map 9 SO42

INSPECTORS' CHOICE

The Bell at Skenfrith

 RESTAURANT WITH ROOMS

tel: 01600 750235 01600 750525 **NP7 8UH**
email: enquiries@skenfrith.co.uk **web:** www.skenfrith.co.uk
dir: On B4521 in Skenfrith, opposite castle

The Bell is a beautifully restored, 17th-century former coaching inn which still retains much original charm and character. It is peacefully situated on the banks of the Monnow, a tributary of the River Wye, and is ideally placed for exploring the numerous delights of the area. Natural materials have been used to create a relaxing atmosphere, while the bedrooms, which include full suites and rooms with four-poster beds, are stylish, luxurious and equipped with DVD players. Fresh produce from the garden is used by the kitchen brigade who produce award-winning food for relaxed dining in the welcoming restaurant.

Rooms 11 (2 fmly)

SOLVA
Pembrokeshire   Map 8 SM82

Crug-Glas Country House

RESTAURANT WITH ROOMS

tel: 01348 831302 **Abereiddy SA62 6XX**
email: janet@crugglas.plus.com **web:** www.crug-glas.co.uk
dir: From Solva to St Davids on A487. From St Davids take A487 towards Fishguard. 1st left after Carnhedryn, house signed

This house, on a dairy, beef and cereal farm of approximately 600 acres, is situated about a mile from the coast on the St Davids peninsula. Comfort, relaxation and flawless attention to detail are provided by the charming host, Janet Evans. Each spacious bedroom has the hallmark of assured design plus a luxury bathroom with both bath and shower; one suite on the top floor has great views. In addition there are two suites in separate buildings.

Rooms 7 (1 fmly)

S

SWANSEA
Swansea

Map 9 SS69

See also **Port Talbot**

Swansea Marriott Hotel

★★★★ 80% HOTEL

tel: 0870 400 7282 **The Maritime Quarter SA1 3SS**
web: www.swanseamarriott.co.uk
dir: M4 junct 42, A483 to city centre past Leisure Centre, then follow signs to Maritime Quarter

Just opposite City Hall in the bustling Maritime Quarter, this busy hotel enjoys fantastic views over the bay and marina. The air-conditioned bedrooms are spacious and equipped with a range of extras. Public rooms include a popular leisure club with a gym, whirlpool, sauna and swimming pool; and The Bayside Grill restaurant which overlooks the marina. It is worth noting, however, that lounge seating is limited.

Rooms 119 (49 fmly) (11 GF) **Facilities** STV WiFi 🖱 Gym New Year **Conf** Class 120 Board 30 Thtr 300 **Services** Lift Air con **Parking** 122 **Notes** ⊗ Civ Wed 220

The Dragon Hotel

★★★★ 77% 🌸 HOTEL

tel: 01792 657100 **The Kingsway Circle SA1 5LS**
email: info@dragon-hotel.co.uk **web:** www.dragon-hotel.co.uk
dir: A483 follow signs for city centre. After lights at Sainsbury's right onto The Strand then left. Hotel straight ahead

This privately-owned hotel is located in the city centre and offers spacious modern accommodation with well-equipped, comfortable bedrooms. There is a bar and lounge facility on the first floor along with the dining room for breakfast. On the ground floor, the Dragons Brasserie provides award-winning food from a vibrant continental menu for both residents and non-residents. The health and fitness club offers an excellent choice of facilities and there is a good range of conference rooms.

Rooms 106 (5 fmly) 🐾 **S** fr £75; **D** fr £75* **Facilities** STV WiFi 🏊 HL 🖱 supervised Gym Beauty therapist Xmas New Year **Conf** Class 120 Board 60 Thtr 230 Del from £125 to £175 **Services** Lift Air con **Parking** 52 **Notes** LB ⊗ Civ Wed 200

Mercure Swansea Hotel

★★★ 74% HOTEL

tel: 0844 815 9081 **Phoenix Way SA7 9EG**
email: info@mercureswansea.co.uk **web:** www.jupiterhotels.co.uk
dir: M4 junct 44, A48 (Llansamlet), left at 3rd lights, right at 1st mini rdbt, left into Phoenix Way at 2nd rdbt. Hotel 800mtrs on right

Located in the business park area just outside of Swansea, this is a popular hotel with both business and leisure guests. A wide range of dishes are available throughout the day and evening from the relaxing lounge, or the well furnished restaurant. Bedrooms and bathrooms are located over two floors and include standard and executive options. Leisure facilities and a large car park are also provided.

Rooms 119 (24 fmly) (55 GF) **D** £50-£150 (incl. bkfst)* **Facilities** FTV WiFi 🖱 Gym Xmas New Year **Conf** Class 80 Board 60 Thtr 200 Del from £99 to £189* **Parking** 180 **Notes** LB Civ Wed

Premier Inn Swansea City Centre

BUDGET HOTEL

tel: 0871 527 9060 **Salubrious Place, Wind St SA1 1EE**
web: www.premierinn.com
dir: M4 junct 42, A483 towards the city centre. Pass Sainsburys on left, right into Salubrious Place, 2nd right, then 3rd exit at mini rdbt

High quality, budget accommodation ideal for both families and business travellers. Spacious, en suite bedrooms feature tea and coffee making facilities, and Freeview TV in most hotels. Internet access and WiFi are available for a small fee. The adjacent family restaurant features a wide and varied menu. See also the Hotel Groups pages.

Rooms 116

Premier Inn Swansea North

BUDGET HOTEL

tel: 0871 527 9062 **Upper Forest Way, Morriston SA6 8WB**
web: www.premierinn.com
dir: M4 junct 45, A4067 towards Swansea. In 0.5m at 2nd exit left into Clase Rd. Hotel 400yds on left

Rooms 40

Premier Inn Swansea Waterfront

BUDGET HOTEL

tel: 0871 577 9212 **The Waterfront Development, Langdon Rd SA1 8PL**
web: www.premierinn.com
dir: M4 junct 42, A483 towards Swansea/Abertawe (signed Fabian Way). Approx 4.5m. At 2nd lights, left into SA1 Waterfront development. At rdbt take 2nd exit into Langdon Rd. Hotel on left

Rooms 132

TENBY
Pembrokeshire

Map 8 SN10

Atlantic Hotel

★★★ 80% HOTEL

tel: 01834 842881 **The Esplanade SA70 7DU**
email: enquiries@atlantic-hotel.uk.com **web:** www.atlantic-hotel.uk.com
dir: A478 into Tenby, follow town centre signs (keep town walls on left) right at Esplanade, hotel on right

This privately owned and personally run, friendly hotel has an enviable position looking out over South Beach towards Caldy Island. Bedrooms vary in size and style, but all are well equipped and tastefully appointed. The comfortable public areas include a choice of restaurants and, in fine weather, guests can also enjoy the cliff-top gardens.

Rooms 42 (11 fmly) (4 GF) **S** £79-£92; **D** £105-£194 (incl. bkfst) **Facilities** FTV WiFi 🖱 Steam room Spa bath **Conf** Board 8 **Services** Lift **Parking** 25 **Notes** LB ⊗ Closed early Dec-late Jan

S

Clarence House

★★ 67% HOTEL

tel: 01834 844371 **Esplanade SA70 7DU**
email: clarencehotel@freeuk.com **web:** www.clarencehotel-tenby.co.uk
dir: From South Parade (by town walls) into St Florence Parade & Esplanade

Owned by the same family for over 50 years, this hotel has superb views from its elevated position. Many of the bedrooms have sea views and all are comfortably furnished. The bar leads to a sheltered rose garden and a number of lounges. Entertainment is provided in high season, and this establishment is particularly popular with coach tour parties.

Rooms 76 (6 fmly) ♠ **S** £37-£45; **D** £72-£100 (incl. bkfst)* **Facilities** FTV ♫ New Year **Services** Lift **Notes** LB Closed 18-28 Dec

---

TINTERN PARVA	Map 4 SO50
Monmouthshire	

BEST WESTERN Royal George Hotel

★★★ 78% HOTEL

tel: 01291 689205 **Wye Valley Rd NP16 6SF**
email: royalgeorgetintern@hotmail.com **web:** www.bw-royalgeorgehotel.co.uk
dir: M48 junct 2, A466, 5m to Tintern, 2nd left

This privately owned and personally run hotel provides comfortable, spacious accommodation, including bedrooms with balconies overlooking the well-tended garden; there are also a number of ground-floor bedrooms. The public areas include a lounge bar and a large function room, and a varied and popular menu is available in either the bar or restaurant. This hotel is an ideal base for exploring the counties of Monmouthshire and Herefordshire.

Rooms 15 (14 annexe) (6 fmly) (10 GF) **S** £65-£110; **D** £75-£120 (incl. bkfst) **Facilities** FTV WiFi ♫ Xmas New Year **Conf** Class 40 Board 30 Thtr 80 Del from £95 to £135 **Parking** 50 **Notes** LB Civ Wed 70

TREARDDUR BAY	Map 14 SH27
Isle of Anglesey	

Trearddur Bay Hotel

★★★ 81% HOTEL

tel: 01407 860301 **LL65 2UN**
email: enquiries@trearddurbayhotel.co.uk **web:** www.trearddurbayhotel.co.uk
dir: A55 junct 2, left, over 1st rdbt, left at 2nd rdbt, right after approx 2m

This seaside hotel stands 100 yards from the Blue Flag beach, offering stunning views of the bay. The very comfortable bedrooms are well appointed and have flat-screen TVs. Guests have a choice of dining options: the more formal Bay Restaurant, or the Inn at The Bay, which also has an outdoor area for summer dining. Facilities include an indoor swimming pool and a children's play area.

Rooms 43 (6 annexe) (6 fmly) (3 GF) ♠ **S** £59-£150; **D** £69-£240 (incl. bkfst) **Facilities** FTV WiFi ♫ 🏊 **Conf** Class 80 Board 60 Thtr 200 Del from £80 to £140 **Parking** 200 **Notes** LB Civ Wed 140

TREFRIW	Map 14 SH76
Conwy	

Yr Hafod Country House and Grill

RESTAURANT WITH ROOMS

tel: 01492 642444 **LL27 ORQ**
email: enquiries@hafod-house.co.uk **web:** www.hafod-house.co.uk
dir: From N - A470 onto B5279, after 1m left onto B5106. 5.5m to Trefriw, over bridge 200mtrs on left. From S - A470 into Llanrwst, left over bridge onto B5106. 1.5m on right

Situated in tranquil countryside and ideally located for the Conwy valley and Snowdonia National Park, this cosy restaurant offers very well appointed bedrooms, which are tastefully designed and comfortably appointed, each with separate access and its own balcony. Dinner and breakfast are not to be missed, and dishes are freshly prepared using as much home-grown and local produce as possible. Proprietor-run, the small friendly team are particularly welcoming.

Rooms 3

USK	Map 9 SO30
Monmouthshire	

The Three Salmons Hotel

★★★ 79% ⚫⚫ HOTEL

tel: 01291 672133 **Bridge St NP15 1RY**
email: general@threesalmons.co.uk **web:** www.threesalmons.co.uk
dir: M4 junct 24, A449, 1st exit signed Usk. On entering town, hotel on main road

The Three Salmons is a 17th-century coaching inn located in the centre of a small market town with friendly, efficient staff that help create a welcoming atmosphere. The food in the contemporary restaurant is very popular. Bedrooms are comfortable and a good range of extras are provided. There is a large function suite ideal for weddings and parties. Parking is secure.

Rooms 24 (14 annexe) (3 fmly) (7 GF) **Facilities** FTV WiFi **Conf** Class 80 Board 40 Thtr 110 **Parking** 25 **Notes** Civ Wed 100

Glen-yr-Afon House Hotel

★★★ 78% HOTEL

tel: 01291 672302 & 673202 **Pontypool Rd NP15 1SY**
email: enquiries@glen-yr-afon.co.uk **web:** www.glen-yr-afon.co.uk
dir: A472 through High St, over river bridge, follow to right. Hotel 200yds on left

On the edge of this delightful old market town, Glen-yr-Afon is a unique Victorian villa, offering all the facilities expected of a modern hotel combined with the warm atmosphere of a family home. Bedrooms are furnished to a high standard and several overlook the well-tended gardens. There is a choice of comfortable sitting areas and a stylish and spacious banqueting suite.

Rooms 28 (1 annexe) (2 fmly) ♠ **Facilities** STV FTV WiFi 🏊 Complimentary access to Usk Tennis Club New Year **Conf** Class 200 Board 30 Thtr 100 **Services** Lift **Parking** 151 **Notes** Civ Wed 150

U

USK *continued*

Newbridge on Usk

 RESTAURANT WITH ROOMS

tel: 01633 451000 & 410262 **Tredunnock NP15 1LY**
email: newbridgeonusk@celtic-manor.com **web:** www.celtic-manor.com
dir: M4 junct 24, signed Newport, onto B4236. At Ship Inn turn right, over mini-rdbt onto Llangybi/Usk road. Turn right opposite Cwrt Bleddyn Hotel, signed Tredunnock, through village & down hill

This cosy, gastro-pub is tucked away in a beautiful village setting with the River Usk nearby. The well-equipped bedrooms, in a separate building, provide comfort and a good range of extras. Guests can eat at rustic tables around the bar or in the upstairs dining room where award-winning, seasonal food is served; there is also a small private dining room. Breakfast is one of the highlights of a stay with quality local ingredients offered in abundance.

Rooms 6 (2 fmly)

WELSHPOOL	Map 15 SJ20
Powys	

Royal Oak Hotel

★★★ 77% HOTEL

tel: 01938 552217 **The Cross SY21 7DG**
email: relax@royaloakhotel.info **web:** www.royaloakhotel.info
dir: By lights at junct of A483 & A458

This traditional market town hotel dates back over 350 years. The public areas are furnished in a minimalist style that highlights the many retained period features, including exposed beams and open fires. Three different bedroom styles provide good comfort levels and imaginative food is served in the elegant Red Room or in the adjacent all-day café/bar.

Rooms 25 (3 fmly) **S** £40-£65; **D** £55-£95 (incl. bkfst)* **Facilities** FTV WiFi Beauty treatment rooms ♫ Xmas New Year **Conf** Class 60 Board 60 Thtr 150 Del £150* **Parking** 19 **Notes** ⊗ Civ Wed

WHITEBROOK	Map 4 SO50
Monmouthshire	

The Crown at Whitebrook

RESTAURANT WITH ROOMS ⊚⊚⊚

tel: 01600 860254 **NP25 4TX**
email: info@crownatwhitebrook.co.uk **web:** www.crownatwhitebrook.co.uk
dir: 4m from Monmouth on B4293, left at sign to Whitebrook, 2m on unclassified road, on right

Peacefully located and surrounded by woods and rivers, this delightful restaurant with rooms offers a peaceful escape. All the bedrooms are located above the main restaurant and come in a range of shapes and sizes. All are very comfortably decorated and furnished. Dinner utilises the finest of local produce and the relaxing surroundings and friendly service provide a memorable dining experience.

Rooms 8

WOLF'S CASTLE	Map 8 SM92
Pembrokeshire	

Wolfscastle Country Hotel

★★★ 79%  COUNTRY HOUSE HOTEL

tel: 01437 741225 & 741688 **SA62 5LZ**
email: enquiries@wolfscastle.com **web:** www.wolfscastle.com
dir: On A40 in village at top of hill. 6m N of Haverfordwest

This large stone house, a former vicarage, dates back to the mid-19th century and is now a friendly, privately-owned and personally-run hotel. It provides stylish, modern, well-maintained and well-equipped bedrooms. There is a pleasant bar and an attractive restaurant, which has a well deserved reputation for its food.

Rooms 20 (2 fmly) ☞ **Facilities** STV WiFi New Year **Conf** Class 100 Board 30 Thtr 100 Del from £122.50* **Parking** 60 **Notes** Closed 24-26 Dec Civ Wed 70

WREXHAM	Map 15 SJ35
Wrexham	

Premier Inn Wrexham

BUDGET HOTEL

tel: 0871 527 9190 **Chester Rd, Gresford LL12 8PW**
web: www.premierinn.com
dir: On B5445, just off A483 (dual carriageway) near Gresford

High quality, budget accommodation ideal for both families and business travellers. Spacious, en suite bedrooms feature tea and coffee making facilities, and Freeview TV in most hotels. Internet access and WiFi are available for a small fee. The adjacent family restaurant features a wide and varied menu. See also the Hotel Groups pages.

Rooms 38

Premier Inn Wrexham Town Centre

BUDGET HOTEL

tel: 0871 527 9458 **Jacques Way LL11 2BY**
web: www.premierinn.com
dir: A55 junct 38. At Wrexham Road Interchange, A483. At rdbt 2nd exit signed Wrexham. Exit at junct 5, at next rdbt take A541. Pass football ground, right at lights

Rooms 83

Ireland

Additional Information for Northern Ireland & the Republic of Ireland

Licensing Regulations

Northern Ireland: Public houses open Mon-Sat 11.30-23.00. Sun 12.30-22.00. Hotels can serve residents without restriction. Non-residents can be served 12.30-22.00 on Christmas Day. Children under 18 are not allowed in the bar area and may neither buy nor consume liquor in hotels.

Republic of Ireland: General licensing hours are Mon-Thu 10.30-23.30, Fri & Sat 10.30-00.30. Sun 12.30-23.00 (or 00.30 if the following day is a Bank Holiday). There is no service (except for hotel residents) on Christmas Day or Good Friday.

The Fire Services (NI) Order 1984

This covers establishments accommodating more than six people, which must have a certificate from the Northern Ireland Fire Authority. Places accommodating fewer than six people need adequate exits. AA inspectors check emergency notices, fire fighting equipment and fire exits here.

The Republic of Ireland safety regulations are a matter for local authority regulations. For your own and others' safety, read the emergency notices and be sure you understand them.

Telephone numbers

Area codes for numbers in the Republic of Ireland apply only within the Republic. If dialling from outside check the telephone directory (from the UK the international dialling code is 00 353). Area codes for numbers in Britain and Northern Ireland cannot be used directly from the Republic.

For the latest information on the Republic of Ireland visit the AA Ireland's website: www.TheAA.ie

---

NORTHERN IRELAND

AGHADOWEY
Co Londonderry — Map 1 C6

Brown Trout Golf & Country Inn

★★★ 77% HOTEL

IRISH COUNTRY HOTELS

tel: 028 7086 8209 **209 Agivey Rd BT51 4AD**
email: jane@browntroutinn.com **web:** www.browntroutinn.com
dir: At junct of A54 & B66 junct on road to Coleraine

Set alongside the Agivey River and featuring its own 9-hole golf course, this welcoming inn offers a choice of spacious accommodation. Comfortably furnished bedrooms are situated around a courtyard area whilst the cottage suites also have lounge areas. Home-cooked meals are served in the restaurant and lighter fare is available in the charming lounge bar which has entertainment at weekends.

Rooms 15 (11 fmly) (15 GF) **S** £60-£100; **D** £90-£140* **Facilities** STV FTV WiFi 9 Putt green Gym Game fishing Xmas New Year **Conf** Class 24 Board 28 Thtr 40 **Parking** 80 **Notes** Civ Wed 40

ANTRIM
Co Antrim — Map 1 D5

Holiday Inn Express Antrim M2 Jct 1

BUDGET HOTEL

Holiday Inn Express

tel: 028 9442 5500 **Ballymena Rd BT4 1LL**
email: reception.antrim@holidayinnexpress.org.uk **web:** www.hiexpress.com/antrim
dir: At Junction One Shopping Outlet

A modern hotel ideal for families and business travellers. Fresh and uncomplicated, the spacious rooms include Sky TV, power shower and tea and coffee-making facilities. Continental buffet breakfast is included in the room rate; other meals may be taken at the nearby family pub or restaurant. See also the Hotel Groups pages.

Rooms 90 (52 fmly) (10 GF) **Conf** Class 20 Board 20 Thtr 40

BALLYMENA
Co Antrim — Map 1 D5

Galgorm Resort & Spa

★★★★ 85% ◉◉ HOTEL

tel: 028 2588 1001 **BT42 1EA**
email: mail@galgorm.com **web:** www.galgorm.com
dir: 1m from Ballymena on A42, between Galgorm & Cullybackey

Standing in 163 acres of private woodland and sweeping lawns beside the River Maine, this 19th-century mansion offers spacious, comfortable bedrooms. Public areas include a welcoming cocktail bar and elegant restaurant, as well as Gillies, a lively and atmospheric locals' bar. Also on the estate is an equestrian centre and a conference hall.

Rooms 75 (14 fmly) (8 GF) **D** £135-£205 (incl. bkfst)* **Facilities** Spa FTV WiFi Fishing Clay pigeon shooting Archery Horseriding Xmas New Year **Conf** Class 170 Board 30 Thtr 500 Del from £150 to £180* **Services** Lift **Parking** 300 **Notes** LB Civ Wed 300

BELFAST
Belfast — Map 1 D5

The Merchant Hotel

★★★★★ 85% ◉◉ HOTEL

tel: 028 9023 4888 **16 Skipper St BT1 2DZ**
email: info@themerchanthotel.com **web:** www.themerchanthotel.com
dir: In city centre, 2nd left at Albert Clock into Waring St. Hotel on left

The Merchant Hotel is a magnificent hotel situated in the historic Cathedral Quarter of the city centre. This Grade I listed building has been lovingly and sensitively restored to reveal its original architectural grandeur and interior opulence. All the bedrooms, including five suites, have air-conditioning, hi-speed internet access, flat-screen TVs and luxury bathrooms. There are several eating options including the grand and beautifully decorated Great Room Restaurant.

Rooms 62 (17 fmly) **S** £170-£230; **D** £180-£260 (incl. bkfst)* **Facilities** Spa FTV WiFi Gym Xmas New Year **Conf** Class 100 Board 60 Thtr 200 Del from £185 to £310 **Services** Lift Air con **Parking** 35 **Notes** Civ Wed 130

Malone Lodge Hotel

★★★★ 78% HOTEL

tel: 028 9038 8000 **60 Eglantine Av BT9 6DY**
email: info@malonelodgehotel.com **web:** www.malonelodgehotelbelfast.com
dir: At hospital rdbt exit towards Bouchar Rd, left at 1st rdbt, right at lights at top, then 1st left

Situated in the leafy suburbs of the university area of south Belfast, this stylish hotel forms the centrepiece of an attractive row of Victorian terraced properties. The hotel has undergone a massive transformation of the exterior, public areas, bar and restaurant, with a rolling bedroom refurbishment also undertaken. The new Knife and Fork restaurant offers relaxed and informal dining.

Rooms 54 (7 fmly) **Facilities** FTV WiFi **Conf** Class 100 Board 60 Thtr 190 **Services** Lift **Parking** 35 **Notes** ✖ Civ Wed 140

Radisson Blu Hotel Belfast

★★★★ 77% HOTEL

tel: 028 9043 4065 & 9082 0109 **3 Cromac Place BT7 2JB**
email: info.belfast@radissonblu.com **web:** www.radissonblu.co.uk/hotel-belfast
dir: On corner of Ormeau Rd & Cromac St

This modern hotel is in the centre of the regenerated urban area close to the city centre. The bedrooms are stylishly presented, well equipped and all have are air conditioning; there is a choice of business suites. Public areas include a spacious lounge bar and the Filini Restaurant, which serves good Italian and Sardinian cuisine. Ample secure parking, and free WiFi (throughout the hotel) are available.

Rooms 120 (11 fmly) **S** £75-£249; **D** £75-£249* **Facilities** FTV WiFi ⬇ Access to LA Fitness Xmas New Year **Conf** Class 70 Board 50 Thtr 150 **Services** Lift Air con **Parking** 120 **Notes** LB Civ Wed 90

Malmaison Belfast

Malmaison
hotels that dare to be different

★★★ 86% ⚫ HOTEL

tel: 0844 693 0650 **34-38 Victoria St BT1 3GH**
email: belfast@malmaison.com **web:** www.malmaison.com
dir: M1 along Westlink to Grosvenor Rd. Follow city centre signs. Pass City Hall on right, left onto Victoria St. Hotel on right

Situated in a former seed warehouse, this luxurious, contemporary hotel is ideally located for the city centre. Comfortable bedrooms boast a host of modern facilities, whilst the deeply comfortable, stylish public areas include a popular bar lounge. The 'Home Grown and Local' menu in the brasserie showcases local seasonal ingredients. The warm hospitality is notable.

Rooms 64 (8 fmly) **Facilities** STV WiFi Gym **Conf** Board 22 **Services** Lift **Notes** Civ Wed

Ramada Encore Belfast City Centre

★★★ 81% ⚫ HOTEL

tel: 028 9026 1800 & 9026 1809 **20 Talbot St BT1 2LD**
email: reception@encorebelfast.co.uk **web:** www.encorebelfast.co.uk
dir: On Dunbar Link behind St Annes Cathedral

This stylish modern hotel is ideally located in the city's Cathedral Quarter and is a short walk from the main shopping and business district. The open-plan public areas feature the SQ Bar & Grill, which is ideal for a relaxed lunch or an intimate dinner. The popular Hub Bar serves an extensive choice of cocktails and there's free WiFi in the bar area. The spacious bedrooms are very well appointed and have bathrooms with power showers.

Rooms 165 (20 fmly) ✎ **S** £50-£199; **D** £50-£199* **Facilities** FTV WiFi ⬇ HL ♫ Xmas New Year **Conf** Class 75 Board 30 Thtr 110 Del from £105 to £145* **Services** Lift **Notes** ✖

Premier Inn Belfast City Cathedral Quarter

BUDGET HOTEL

tel: 0871 527 8070 **2-6 Waring St BT1 1XY**
web: www.premierinn.com
dir: M1 or M2 to Westlink to Grosvenor Rd rdbt, signed city centre. Into Grosvenor Rd. At 2nd lights left, take right lane, right (pass City Hall on right). At end of Chichester St left into Victoria St. Through next 2 lights, left into Waring St. Hotel 300yds on right

High quality, budget accommodation ideal for both families and business travellers. Spacious, en suite bedrooms feature tea and coffee making facilities, and Freeview TV in most hotels. Internet access and WiFi are available for a small fee. The adjacent family restaurant features a wide and varied menu. See also the Hotel Groups pages.

Rooms 171

Premier Inn Belfast City Centre Alfred St

BUDGET HOTEL

tel: 0871 527 8068 **Alfred St BT2 8ED**
web: www.premierinn.com
dir: M1 or M2 to Westlink. Follow city centre signs. 1st right, 2nd left into Hope St. At 2nd lights left into Bedford St. At next lights right into Ormeau Ave. Left into Alfred St. Underground car park (chargeable) on left

Rooms 148

Premier Inn Belfast Titanic Quarter

BUDGET HOTEL

tel: 0871 527 9210 **2A Queens Rd BT3 9FB**
web: www.premierinn.com
dir: From all major routes follow Odyssey Arena signs. From M3 junct 1 exit onto Queens Island, to lights. Hotel on left

Rooms 102

BUSHMILLS
Co Antrim   Map 1 C6

AA HOTEL OF THE YEAR FOR NORTHERN IRELAND 2014–2015

Bushmills Inn Hotel

★★★★ 80% HOTEL

tel: 028 2073 3000 & 2073 2339 **9 Dunluce Rd BT57 8QG**
email: mail@bushmillsinn.com **web:** www.bushmillsinn.com
dir: On A2 in village centre

Enjoying a prominent position in the heart of the village, this hotel offers a range of bedroom styles including spacious, creatively designed rooms that have the latest technology and a small dressing room. The charming public areas feature inglenook turf-burning fires, cosy snugs along with a very popular traditional bar. The restaurant has a well deserved reputation for its food. The hotel is very popular with golfers; it is close to the Giants Causeway, Bushmills Distillery and the stunning scenery of the Antrim Coast.

Rooms 41 (2 fmly) (20 GF) ⚓ **S** £98–£278; **D** £128–£398 (incl. bkfst)* **Facilities** WiFi ♫ New Year **Conf** Class 30 Board 18 Thtr 40 Del from £148 to £218* **Services** Lift **Parking** 70 **Notes** ⊗ Closed 25 Dec

CARRICKFERGUS
Co Antrim   Map 1 D5

Premier Inn Carrickfergus

BUDGET HOTEL

tel: 0871 527 8214 **The Harbour, Alexandra Pier BT38 8BE**
web: www.premierinn.com
dir: Exit at M2 junct 2, take M5 N onto A2 towards Carrickfergus. Follow Castle/Maritime Area signs. Right at rdbt adjacent to castle. Hotel straight ahead, adjacent to harbour

High quality, budget accommodation ideal for both families and business travellers. Spacious, en suite bedrooms feature tea and coffee making facilities, and Freeview TV in most hotels. Internet access and WiFi are available for a small fee. The adjacent family restaurant features a wide and varied menu. See also the Hotel Groups pages.

Rooms 49

COLERAINE
Co Londonderry   Map 1 C6

Premier Inn Coleraine

BUDGET HOTEL

tel: 0871 527 8262 **3 Riverside Park North, Castleroe Rd BT51 3GE**
web: www.premierinn.com
dir: A26 towards Colraine. At rdbt left on A29 (ring road) signed Cookstown/Garragh. At rdbt A54 (Castleroe Rd). Hotel on right

High quality, budget accommodation ideal for both families and business travellers. Spacious, en suite bedrooms feature tea and coffee making facilities, and Freeview TV in most hotels. Internet access and WiFi are available for a small fee. The adjacent family restaurant features a wide and varied menu. See also the Hotel Groups pages.

Rooms 49

CRAWFORDSBURN
Co Down   Map 1 D5

The Old Inn

★★★★ 81% ❁❁ HOTEL

tel: 028 9185 3255 **15 Main St BT19 1JH**
email: info@theoldinn.com **web:** www.theoldinn.com
dir: A2 from Belfast (pass Belfast City Airport & Transport Museum). 2m, left at lights onto B20. 1.2m to hotel

This delightful hotel enjoys a peaceful rural setting just a short drive from Belfast. The property dates from 1614, and many of the day rooms exude charm and character. Individually styled, comfortable bedrooms, some with feature beds, offer modern facilities. The popular bar and intimate restaurant both offer creative menus, and staff throughout are keen to please.

Rooms 31 (1 annexe) (7 fmly) (6 GF) ⚓ **D** £79–£279* **Facilities** STV FTV WiFi ⇘ In room spa/massage treatments ♫ Xmas New Year **Conf** Class 120 Board 40 Thtr 150 **Services** Lift **Parking** 84 **Notes** ⊗ RS 25 Dec Civ Wed 100

DUNGANNON
Co Tyrone   Map 1 C5

The Cohannon Inn & Auto Lodge

★★ 74% HOTEL

tel: 028 8772 4488 **212 Ballynakilly Rd BT71 6HJ**
email: info@cohannon.com **web:** www.cohannon.com
dir: 400yds from M1 junct 14

Handy for the M1 and the nearby towns of Dungannon and Portadown, this hotel offers well-maintained bedrooms, located behind the inn complex in a smart purpose-built wing. Public areas are smartly furnished and wide-ranging menus are served throughout the day.

Rooms 42 (20 fmly) (21 GF) (5 smoking) **S** £42.95–£49.95; **D** £50–£59.95* **Facilities** FTV WiFi Hair & beauty salon New Year **Conf** Class 100 Board 40 Thtr 160 **Parking** 160 **Notes** RS 25 Dec

ENNISKILLEN
Co Fermanagh   Map 1 C5

Lough Erne Resort

★★★★★ 84% HOTEL

tel: 028 6632 3230 **Belleek Rd BT93 7ED**
email: info@lougherneresort.com **web:** www.lougherneresort.com
dir: A46 from Enniskillen towards Donegal, hotel in 3m

This delightful resort enjoys a peaceful and idyllic setting and boasts championship golf courses, a wonderful Thai spa and a host of outdoor and leisure pursuits. Bedrooms and en suites are spacious, particularly well appointed and include a number of luxury suites. Day rooms are spacious, luxurious and include lounges, bars and restaurants with splendid views. Service is friendly and extremely attentive.

Rooms 120 (61 annexe) **Facilities** Spa STV WiFi ⓒ ♨ 18 Fishing Gym ♫ Xmas New Year **Conf** Class 200 Board 80 Thtr 400 **Services** Lift **Parking** 240 **Notes** ⊗ Civ Wed 300

Manor House Country Hotel

★★★★ 80% ◎◎ COUNTRY HOUSE HOTEL

tel: 028 6862 2200 **Killadeas BT94 1NY**
email: info@manorhousecountryhotel.com **web:** www.manorhouseresorthotel.com
dir: On B82, 7m N of Enniskillen

This charming country house hotel enjoys a stunning location on the banks of Lower Lough Erne and is a short drive from the busy town of Enniskillen. Bedrooms are equipped to a very high standard with front-facing rooms having the fabulous lough views. There is a choice of restaurants, and afternoon tea is served in the comfortable lounge with its open fire. The hotel has first-class business, conference and leisure facilities including its own air-conditioned cruiser for tours and corporate events.

Rooms 79 (12 fmly) (12 GF) ⓒ **S** £70-£125; **D** £80-£325 (incl. bkfst) **Facilities** FTV WiFi ⓑ ⓒ Gym Sauna Steam room ♫ Xmas New Year **Conf** Class 120 Board 100 Thtr 400 Del £135 **Services** Lift **Parking** 300 **Notes** ⊗ Civ Wed 300

Killyhevlin Hotel & Health Club

★★★★ 79% HOTEL   IRISH COUNTRY HOTELS

tel: 028 6632 3481 **BT74 6RW**
email: info@killyhevlin.com **web:** www.killyhevlin.com
dir: 2m S of Enniskillen, off A4

This modern, stylish hotel is situated on the shores of Lough Erne, south of the town. The well-equipped bedrooms are particularly spacious and enjoy fine views of the gardens and lake. The restaurant, informal bar and comfortable lounges all share the views. Staff are friendly and helpful. There are extensive leisure facilities and a spa.

Rooms 70 (42 fmly) (22 GF) ⓒ **S** £60-£110; **D** £70-£160 (incl. bkfst)* **Facilities** Spa FTV WiFi ⓑ ⓒ Fishing Gym Aerobic studio Steam room Sauna Hydrotherapy area Relaxation room ♫ New Year **Conf** Class 160 Board 100 Thtr 500 **Services** Lift **Parking** 500 **Notes** LB ⊗ Closed 25 Dec RS 24 & 26 Dec Civ Wed 250

LIMAVADY
Co Londonderry   Map 1 C6

Roe Park Resort

★★★★ 75% HOTEL

tel: 028 7772 2222 **BT49 9LB**
email: reservations@roeparkresort.com **web:** www.roeparkresort.com
dir: On A2 (Londonderry-Limavady road), 1m from Limavady

This impressive, popular hotel is part of a modern golf resort. The spacious, contemporary bedrooms are well equipped and many have excellent views of the fairways and surrounding estate. The Greens Restaurant provides a refreshing dining experience and the Coach House brasserie offers a lighter menu. The leisure options are extensive.

Rooms 118 (15 fmly) (37 GF) (5 smoking) ⓒ **S** £63-£150; **D** £69-£260 (incl. bkfst)* **Facilities** Spa FTV WiFi HL ⓒ supervised ♨ 18 Putt green Fishing Gym Driving range Indoor golf academy ♫ Xmas New Year **Conf** Class 190 Board 140 Thtr 450 Del from £130* **Services** Lift **Parking** 350 **Notes** ⊗ Civ Wed 300

LISBURN
Co Antrim   Map 1 D5

Premier Inn Lisburn

BUDGET HOTEL   Premier Inn

tel: 0871 527 8606 **136-144 Hillsborough Rd BT27 5QY**
web: www.premierinn.com
dir: M1 onto A1 (Sprucefield Rd). Left into Hillsborough Rd. Approx 1.5m, hotel on left

High quality, budget accommodation ideal for both families and business travellers. Spacious, en suite bedrooms feature tea and coffee making facilities, and Freeview TV in most hotels. Internet access and WiFi are available for a small fee. The adjacent family restaurant features a wide and varied menu. See also the Hotel Groups pages.

Rooms 60

LONDONDERRY   Map 1 C5
Co Londonderry

City Hotel

★★★★ 76% HOTEL

tel: 028 7136 5800 **Queens Quay BT48 7AS**
email: reservations@cityhotelderry.com **web:** www.cityhotelderry.com
dir: Follow city centre signs. Hotel on waterfront

In a central position overlooking the River Foyle, this stylish, contemporary hotel will appeal to business and leisure guests alike. All bedrooms have excellent facilities including internet access; the executive rooms make particularly good working environments. Meeting and function facilities are extensive and there are good leisure options.

Rooms 158 (16 fmly) ☛ **Facilities** FTV WiFi ↳ ⊛ supervised Gym Steam room ♫ New Year **Conf** Class 150 Board 80 Thtr 350 **Services** Lift Air con **Parking** 48 **Notes** ⊛ Closed 25 Dec Civ Wed 350

Premier Inn Derry / Londonderry

BUDGET HOTEL

tel: 0871 527 9414 **Crescent Link BT47 6SA**
web: www.premierinn.com
dir: Telephone for detailed directions

High quality, budget accommodation ideal for both families and business travellers. Spacious, en suite bedrooms feature tea and coffee making facilities, and Freeview TV in most hotels. Internet access and WiFi are available for a small fee. The adjacent family restaurant features a wide and varied menu. See also the Hotel Groups pages.

Rooms 60

ARDMORE   Map 1 C2
County Waterford

Cliff House Hotel

★★★★ 83%  HOTEL

tel: 024 87800 & 87801
email: info@thecliffhousehotel.com **web:** www.thecliffhousehotel.com
dir: From Dungarvan: N25, signed Cork. Left onto R673. From Youghal: N25 signed Waterford. Right onto R673 signed Ardmore. In Ardmore take Middle Rd to hotel

This unique property, virtually sculpted into the cliff face overlooking Ardmore Bay, is just a few minutes' walk from the village. Most of the individually designed bedroom suites and the public rooms enjoy the spectacular views, as do the stunning spa and leisure facilities. Dinner in the award-winning House Restaurant is a particular highlight - the menus feature imaginatively cooked, seasonal and local produce.

Rooms 39 (8 fmly) (7 GF) ☛ **S** €160-€225; **D** €180-€495 (incl. bkfst)*
Facilities Spa STV FTV WiFi ↳ ⊛ Fishing Gym Sauna Steam room Relaxation room Outdoor pursuits New Year Child facilities **Conf** Class 30 Board 20 Thtr 50 **Del from** €225 to €395* **Services** Lift Air con **Parking** 52 **Notes** LB ⊛ Closed 24-26 Dec Civ Wed 60

BALLINA   Map 1 B4
County Mayo

Mount Falcon Estate

★★★★ 83%  HOTEL

tel: 096 74472
email: info@mountfalcon.com **web:** www.mountfalcon.com
dir: On N26, 6m from Foxford & 3m from Ballina. Hotel on left

Dating from 1876, this house has been lovingly restored to its former glory, and has a bedroom extension that is totally in keeping with the original design. Relaxing lounges look out on the 100-acre estate, which has excellent salmon fishing on The Moy plus well-stocked trout lakes. Dinner is served in the original kitchen with choices from a varied and interesting menu; for lunch there is also the Boathole Bar. An air-conditioned gym is available.

Rooms 32 (3 fmly) ☛ **Facilities** Spa STV WiFi ↳ ⊛ supervised Fishing Gym Sauna Steam room Driving range New Year **Conf** Class 120 Board 80 Thtr 200 **Services** Lift **Parking** 260 **Notes** ⊛ Closed 24-27 Dec Civ Wed 200

Belleek Castle

★★★ 73% HOTEL

tel: 096 22400 **Belleek**
email: info@belleekcastle.com **web:** www.belleekcastle.com
dir: In Belleek woods N of Ballina

This lovely manor house, formerly the ancestral home of the Earl of Arran, is set in wonderful parkland at the head of Belleek Wood on the River Moy estuary. The cosy public lounges are welcoming, and are complemented by a series of banqueting suites that are decorated in a nautical theme. Bedroom accommodation varies in style; all rooms are comfortably appointed. Dinner is the highlight of any visit, offered from a choice of Market or Gourmet set menus. The food is all locally sourced, and the chef has a keen eye for seasonality. The hotel is a popular wedding venue. There is also a museum specialising in armoury and memorabilia from the Spanish Armada.

Rooms 11 (2 fmly) **S** €50-€160; **D** €80-€220 (incl. bkfst)* **Facilities** STV FTV WiFi ☝ Xmas New Year **Conf** Class 60 Board 30 Thtr 100 Del from €80 to €300 **Parking** 200 **Notes** LB ⊗ Civ Wed 200

BALLINGEARY
County Cork   Map 1 B2

Gougane Barra Hotel

★★★ 78% HOTEL

tel: 026 47069 **Gougane Barra**
email: gouganebarrahotel@eircom.net **web:** www.gouganebarrahotel.com
dir: On L4643. Exit R584 between N22 at Macroom & N71 at Bantry

This charming hotel, run by the Lucey family for over five generations, is in an idyllic location on the shores of Gougane Barra Lake, overlooking the tiny Oratory of St. Finbarr, a popular venue for intimate weddings. The bedrooms vary in size, but they are all well decorated, very comfortable and ideal for leisure guests. Chef Katie Lucey prepares menus based on the best local and seasonal ingredients, some from artisan producers. The ground floor includes cosy lounge areas and a traditional bar, with a marquee theatre in the summer months for an innovative experience known as Theatre by the Lake.

Rooms 26 (12 GF) ☝ **Facilities** STV FTV WiFi Fishing Boating Cycling **Parking** 26 **Notes** ⊗ Closed 10 Oct-10 Apr Civ Wed

---

BALLYCOTTON
County Cork   Map 1 C2

Bayview Hotel

★★★ HOTEL

tel: 021 4646746
email: res@thebayviewhotel.com **web:** www.thebayviewhotel.com
dir: Exit N25 at Castlemartyr, through Ladysbridge & Garryvoe to Ballycotton

The gardens of this hotel seem to hang onto the cliffs overlooking the pier and Ballycotton Bay. The comfortable public rooms and bedrooms with balconies take in the breathtaking coastline views. Dinner in the Capricho Room is a special delight where guests will find locally-landed fish on the menu. More casual dining is available throughout the day in the bar. The warm and friendly team impress with their high standards of customer care.

Rooms 35 (5 GF) (10 smoking) **Facilities** STV WiFi Pitch and putt Sea angling Use of swimming pool at sister hotel **Conf** Class 30 Board 24 Thtr 60 **Services** Lift Air con **Parking** 40 **Notes** ⊗ Closed Nov-Apr Civ Wed 100

BALLYLICKEY	Map 1 B2
County Cork	

Seaview House Hotel

★★★  HOTEL

tel: 027 50073 & 50462
email: info@seaviewhousehotel.com **web:** www.seaviewhousehotel.com
dir: 5km from Bantry, 11km from Glengarriff on N71

Colourful gardens and glimpses of Bantry Bay through the mature trees frame this delightful country house. Owner Kathleen O'Sullivan's team of staff are exceptionally pleasant, and there is a relaxed atmosphere in the cosy lounges. Guest comfort and good cuisine are top priorities. Bedrooms are spacious and individually styled, and some on the ground floor are appointed to suit less able guests.

Rooms 25 (3 fmly) (5 GF) ✆ **Facilities** STV FTV WiFi **Conf** Class 30 Board 25 Thtr 25 **Parking** 32 **Notes** Closed mid Nov-mid Mar Civ Wed 75

BALLYLIFFIN	Map 1 C6
County Donegal	

Ballyliffin Lodge & Spa

★★★★ 77% HOTEL

tel: 074 9378200 **Shore Rd**
email: info@ballyliffinlodge.com **web:** www.ballyliffinlodge.com
dir: From Derry take A2 towards Moville, exit for Carndonagh at Quigleys Point. Ballyliffin 10km

Located in the heart of the village, this property offers a range of very comfortable bedrooms, many of which enjoy panoramic views of Malin Head and the famed Ballyliffin Golf Club. Dinner is served in the open-plan Jacks bar and restaurant, and less formal meals are served in the bar throughout the day. Guests are welcome to use the leisure facilities in the adjoining Crystal Rock Spa, where there is also a hairdressing salon.

Rooms 40 (28 fmly) ✆ **Facilities** Spa STV WiFi ⓑ supervised Gym Hair salon ♫ New Year **Conf** Class 200 Board 100 Thtr 300 **Services** Lift **Parking** 80 **Notes** ⊗ Civ Wed 150

BALLYVAUGHAN	Map 1 B3
County Clare	

Gregans Castle

★★★  COUNTRY HOUSE HOTEL

tel: 065 7077005
email: stay@gregans.ie **web:** www.gregans.ie
dir: 3.5m S of Ballyvaughan on N67

This hotel is a hidden gem in The Burren area, and the delightful restaurant and bedrooms enjoy splendid views towards Galway Bay. The Haden family, together with their welcoming staff, offer a high level of personal service. Bedrooms are individually decorated; superior rooms and suites are particularly comfortable; some are on the ground floor and have patio gardens. There are welcoming fires in the comfortable drawing room and the cosy cocktail bar where afternoon tea is served. Dinner is a highlight of any visit; the chef shows a real passion for food which is evident in his cooking of top quality local and organic produce. The area is rich in archaeological, geological and botanical interest, and cycling and walking tours can be organised. There is a beautiful garden to relax in.

Rooms 21 (3 fmly) (7 GF) ✆ **Facilities** WiFi ⓑ ♣ **Conf** Class 25 Board 14 Thtr 25 **Parking** 25 **Notes** Closed Jan-12 Feb & 30 Nov-Dec Civ Wed 65

BALTIMORE	Map 1 B1
County Cork	

Rolfs Country House

 RESTAURANT WITH ROOMS

tel: 028 20289 **Baltimore Hill**
email: info@rolfscountryhouse.com **web:** www.rolfscountryhouse.com
dir: Before village turn sharp left up hill. House signed

Situated on a hill above the fishing village of Baltimore, are the 400-year-old stone buildings that the Haffner family successfully converted into accommodation. Available are ten traditionally furnished en suite bedrooms in an annexe building, a cosy bar with an open fire, and a rustic restaurant on two levels. Dinner is served nightly during the high season and at weekends in the winter months; the menu features quality meats, artisan cheeses and fish landed at the busy pier. This is a lovely place to stay and the hosts are very friendly.

Rooms 10 (10 annexe)

BARNA (BEARNA)	Map 1 B3
County Galway	

The Twelve

★★★★ 80% ◉◉ HOTEL

tel: 091 597000 **Barna Village**
email: enquire@thetwelvehotel.ie **web:** www.thetwelvehotel.ie
dir: Coast road Barna village, 10 mins from Galway

Located just ten minutes west of Galway city, this hotel looks as if it has been on the site for decades. However, once inside the decor is striking and contemporary. The bedrooms come in a number of different sizes, but all are furnished with taste and with guest comfort in mind. The Pins is a vibrant and popular bar and bistro where food is served throughout the day. West Restaurant opens during the evening, and features fine dining from a well-compiled menu of local and seasonal produce. Le Petit Spa offers treatments based on seaweed products.

Rooms 47 (12 fmly) 🐾 **Facilities** STV FTV WiFi ⌇ Beauty treatment room Children's cookery programme Art classes Wine classes ♫ Xmas New Year **Conf** Class 70 Board 60 Thtr 80 **Services** Lift Air con **Parking** 140 **Notes** RS 22-27 Dec Civ Wed 100

BELMULLET	Map 1 A5
County Mayo	

The Talbot Hotel

★★★★ 79% ◉ HOTEL

tel: 097 20484 **Barrack St**
email: info@thetalbothotel.ie **web:** www.thetalbothotel.ie
dir: On left side as you enter the town

In the heart of Belmullet town, this family operated boutique property has evolved from humble beginnings of a grocery store with a bar, to what is now a warm and welcoming hotel. The simple exterior belies the contemporary opulence of the individually designed and decorated bedrooms and suites that make up this comfortable townhouse. It is very much a boutique hotel, with a really welcoming team that have great interest in their guests. The bar is a popular venue with the locals and visitors alike, where quality food is served throughout the day, with seafood a feature. The 1st floor Barony Restaurant opens from Easter to October, and at peak periods, offering an interesting menu of interesting combinations of local and seasonal produce.

Rooms 21 (4 fmly) (8 GF) 🐾 **S** €75-€180; **D** €160-€280 (incl. bkfst)* **Facilities** STV FTV WiFi ⌇ ♫ Xmas New Year **Conf** Class 100 Board 100 Thtr 180 Del from €120 to €215* **Services** Lift Air con **Notes** LB ⊗

BLARNEY	Map 1 B2
County Cork	

Blarney Golf Resort

★★★★ 78% HOTEL

tel: 021 4384477 **Tower**
email: reservations@blarneygolfresort.com **web:** www.blarneygolfresort.com
dir: Exit N20 for Blarney, 4km to Tower, right into Old Kerry Rd. Hotel 2km on right

This resort includes a John Daly designed golf course. The hotel is situated close to Tower village and the famous Blarney Castle. Bedrooms are well equipped and comfortable; some have balconies and spacious lounges. Early Bird and carte dinner menus are served nightly in the Inniscarra Restaurant, with more casual dining available in the golf club bar. There are excellent leisure facilities in the Sentosa Spa.

Rooms 117 (56 annexe) (56 fmly) (30 GF) **Facilities** Spa FTV WiFi ⊗ supervised ♨ 18 Putt green Gym Steam room Sauna ♫ Xmas New Year **Conf** Class 150 Board 40 Thtr 300 **Services** Lift Air con **Parking** 250 **Notes** ⊗

CARLOW	Map 1 C3
County Carlow	

Seven Oaks Hotel

★★★ 78% HOTEL

tel: 059 9131308 **Athy Rd**
email: info@sevenoakshotel.com **web:** www.sevenoakshotel.com

This hotel is conveniently situated within walking distance of the town centre. Public areas include comfortable lounges, library, bar and a restaurant where food is available all day. There is a traditional Irish music session on Monday nights in the Oak Bar. Bedrooms are spacious and very well appointed. There are extensive leisure and banqueting facilities and a secure car park.

Rooms 89 (5 fmly) (7 GF) 🐾 **S** €50-€85; **D** €90-€139 (incl. bkfst)* **Facilities** STV WiFi ⌇ ⊗ supervised Gym Aerobic studio Steam room ♫ **Conf** Class 150 Board 80 Thtr 400 Del from €110 to €130* **Services** Lift Air con **Parking** 200 **Notes** LB ⊗ Closed 25-26 Dec RS Good Fri Civ Wed 200

CARRICKMACROSS	Map 1 C4
County Monaghan	

Shirley Arms Hotel

★★★★ 76% ◉ HOTEL

tel: 042 9673100 **Main St**
email: reception@shirleyarmshotel.ie **web:** www.shirleyarmshotel.ie
dir: N2 to Derry, take Ardee Rd to Carrickmacross

Set at the top of the town, this long established hotel is an imposing stone building with a contemporary interior. Bedrooms, in a purpose-built block, are spacious and have clean, modern lines; there is also a comfortable suite in the original house overlooking the square. Food is an important element of the business here, with options available throughout the day.

Rooms 25 (2 fmly) 🐾 **S** €75-€95; **D** €110-€150 (incl. bkfst)* **Facilities** STV WiFi ⌇ ♫ New Year **Conf** Class 150 Board 200 Thtr 200 **Services** Lift **Parking** 80 **Notes** LB ⊗ Closed 24-26 Dec RS 6 Apr, Good Fri, 24-26 Dec Civ Wed 150

CASHEL
County Galway

Map 1 A4

INSPECTORS' CHOICE

Cashel House Hotel

★★★ ◉◉ COUNTRY HOUSE HOTEL

tel: 095 31001
email: res@cashel-house-hotel.com **web:** www.cashel-house-hotel.com
dir: S off N59, 1.5km W of Recess, well signed

Cashel House is a mid-19th century property, standing at the head of Cashel Bay in the heart of Connemara, set amidst secluded, award-winning gardens with woodland walks. Attentive service comes with the perfect balance of friendliness and professionalism from McEvilly family and their staff. The comfortable lounges have turf fires and antique furnishings. The restaurant offers local produce such as the famous Connemara lamb, and fish from the nearby coast.

Rooms 29 (4 fmly) (6 GF) ⚲ **S** €75-€105; **D** €120-€220 (incl. bkfst)* **Facilities** STV FTV WiFi Garden school Cookery classes Xmas New Year **Parking** 40 **Notes** LB Closed Jan-10 Feb Civ Wed 120

CAVAN
County Cavan

Map 1 C4

Radisson Blu Farnham Estate Hotel

Radisson BLU
HOTELS & RESORTS

★★★★ 79% ◉ HOTEL

tel: 049 4377700 **Farnham Estate**
email: info.farnham@radissonblu.com **web:** www.farnhamestate.com
dir: From Dublin take N3 to Cavan. From Cavan take Killeshandra road for 4km

Situated on a 1,300 acre estate, this 16th-century Great House combines old-world grandeur with modern glamour. Interiors are light, airy and contemporary with a relaxing atmosphere. The spacious bedrooms and suites are in the newer building. Interesting dining options are available in the Botanica Restaurant and Wine Goose Cellar Bar. There are extensive banqueting facilities and the health spa offers a range of treatments.

Rooms 158 (50 GF) ⚲ **S** €79-€200; **D** €99-€220 (incl. bkfst)* **Facilities** Spa STV WiFi ⟳ ⚲ ⚲ 18 Putt green Fishing ⚲ Gym In/Outdoor infinity pool Water mint thermal suite Relaxation rooms Walking ♫ Xmas New Year **Conf** Class 200 Board 44 Thtr 380 Del from €159 to €210* **Services** Lift **Parking** 600 **Notes** ⊗ Civ Wed 150

CLAREMORRIS
County Mayo

Map 1 B4

McWilliam Park Hotel

★★★★ 79% HOTEL

tel: 094 9378000
email: info@mcwilliamparkhotel.ie **web:** www.mcwilliampark.ie
dir: Take Castlebar/Claremorris exit from N17, straight over rdbt. Hotel on right

McWilliam Park Hotel is situated on the outskirts of Claremorris town just off the N17 between Galway and Sligo. It is approximately 20 minutes from the Knock Marian Shrine and Ireland West Airport Knock. There are comfortable lounges together with extensive conference, banqueting, and leisure and health facilities. The spacious bedrooms are well appointed, with good communication technology. Food is served all day in Kavanagh's bar, and dinner is available each night in J.G's Restaurant which also serves a popular Sunday lunch. Traditional music, social dancing and other entertainment events are held on a regular basis in the McWilliam Suite.

Rooms 103 (19 fmly) (15 GF) ⚲ **S** €95-€125; **D** €150-€190 (incl. bkfst)* **Facilities** Spa STV FTV WiFi ⟳ ⚲ Gym ♫ Xmas New Year Child facilities **Conf** Class 250 Board 80 Thtr 600 **Services** Lift **Parking** 320 **Notes** LB ⊗ Civ Wed 200

CLIFDEN
County Galway

Map 1 A4

Abbeyglen Castle Hotel

★★★★ 80% ◉ HOTEL

tel: 095 21201 **Sky Rd**
email: info@abbeyglen.ie **web:** www.abbeyglen.ie
dir: N59 from Galway towards Clifden. Hotel 1km from Clifden on Sky Road

The tranquil setting overlooking Clifden, matched with the dedication of the Hughes's father and son team and their attentive staff, combine to create a magical atmosphere. Now into its fifth decade, Abbeyglen Castle has a well earned reputation, with many guests returning year after year. Well-appointed rooms and very comfortable suites are available, together with a range of relaxing lounge areas. The restaurant features a daily-changing menu of traditional and more modern dishes; many guests enjoy impromptu sessions around the piano in the bar following dinner. Treatment rooms are available.

Rooms 45 (9 GF) ⚲ **S** €117-€141; **D** €180-€228 (incl. bkfst)* **Facilities** STV WiFi ⚲ Putt green Wellness & relaxation centre ♫ Xmas New Year **Conf** Class 50 Board 40 Thtr 100 Del from €190 to €220* **Services** Lift **Parking** 50 **Notes** LB ⊗ No children 10yrs Closed 4-29 Jan

CLONMEL
County Tipperary
Map 1 C2

Hotel Minella

★★★★ 80% ⊛ HOTEL

tel: 052 6122388
email: frontdesk@hotelminella.ie **web:** www.hotelminella.ie
dir: S of river in town

This family-run hotel is set in nine acres of well-tended gardens on the banks of the Suir River. The hotel originates from the 1860s, and the public areas include a cocktail bar and a range of lounges; some of the bedrooms are particularly spacious. The leisure centre in the grounds is noteworthy. Two-bedroom holiday homes are also available.

Rooms 90 (8 fmly) (14 GF) (10 smoking) ⚡ **Facilities** FTV WiFi ⇘ 🏊 ♨ Fishing ⛴ Gym Beauty treatment room Sauna Steam room **Conf** Class 300 Board 20 Thtr 500 **Services** Lift **Parking** 100 **Notes** ⊗ Closed 24-28 Dec

CONG
County Mayo
Map 1 B4

Ashford Castle

★★★★★ 86% ⊛⊛ HOTEL

tel: 094 9546003
email: ashford@ashford.ie **web:** www.ashford.ie
dir: In Cross left at church onto R345 signed Cong. Left at hotel sign, through castle gates

Set in over 300 acres of rolling parklands, this magnificent castle, dating from 1228, occupies a stunning position on the edge of Lough Corrib. Bedrooms and suites vary in style but all benefit from a pleasing combination of character, charm and modern comforts. Dinner in the elegant George V Dining Room is a treat, with creative cookery of seasonal ingredients. Less formal dining is available in other locations on the estate during peak periods. The hotel offers an extensive range of both indoor and outdoor leisure pursuits including falconry, golf, shooting, fishing and an equestrian centre.

Rooms 83 (6 fmly) (22 GF) ⚡ **D** €225-€535 (incl. bkfst) **Facilities** Spa STV WiFi ⇘ ⚘ 9 ♨ Putt green Fishing Gym Archery Clay pigeon Falconry Horse riding Bike hire Lake cruises Water sports ♫ Xmas New Year **Conf** Class 65 Thtr 110 **Services** Lift **Parking** 200 **Notes** Civ Wed 150

The Lodge at Ashford Castle

[U]

tel: 094 9545400 **Ashford Estate**
email: reception@thelodgeatashfordcastle.com **web:** www.thelodgeatashfordcastle.com
dir: N84 (either direction) take first turn for Cong, go through Ashford main gates, first left

Currently the rating for this establishment is not confirmed. This may be due to a change of ownership or because it has only recently joined the AA rating scheme. For further details please see the AA website: theAA.com

Rooms 50 (12 fmly) (15 GF) ⚡ **S** €155-€365; **D** €155-€365 (incl. bkfst) **Facilities** FTV WiFi ⇘ ⚘ 9 ♨ Fishing Gym Beauty treatment room Falconry Archery Equestrian Boating Canoeing Kayaking ♫ Child facilities **Conf** Class 80 Board 80 Thtr 210 Del from €200 to €400* **Services** Lift **Parking** 80 **Notes** LB Closed 1st week Jan to last week Feb RS Nov to 1st week of Jan Civ Wed 180

CORK
County Cork
Map 1 B2

Maryborough Hotel & Spa

★★★★ 80% ⊛ HOTEL

tel: 021 4365555 **Maryborough Hill, Douglas**
email: info@maryborough.com **web:** www.maryborough.com
dir: From Jack Lynch Tunnel 2nd exit signed Douglas. Right at 1st rdbt, follow Rochestown signs to fingerpost rdbt. Left, hotel on left in 0.5m

Dating from 1715, this house was renovated and extended to become a fine hotel with beautifully landscaped grounds featuring rare plant species. There are stylish suites in the main house and the bedrooms in the wing are comfortably furnished. The bar and lounge are very popular for the range of food served throughout the day; Zings restaurant offers a mix of classic and contemporary dishes. There are impressive spa, leisure and conference facilities, plus activities for children.

Rooms 93 (6 fmly) ⚡ **S** €145-€350; **D** €160-€500 (incl. bkfst) **Facilities** Spa STV WiFi ⇘ 🏊 supervised Gym Sauna Steam room New Year **Conf** Class 250 Board 60 Thtr 500 **Services** Lift **Parking** 300 **Notes** LB ⊗ Closed 24-26 Dec Civ Wed 100

Silver Springs Moran Hotel

★★★★ 78% HOTEL

tel: 021 4507533 **Tivoli**
email: silverspringsres@moranhotels.com **web:** www.moranhotels.com
dir: N8 S, take Silver Springs exit. Right, then right again, hotel on left

Located on the main approach to the city this hotel has spacious, contemporary public areas. The lobby lounge is very popular for all-day dining, with more formal meals served in the Watermarq Restaurant. Bedrooms and suites are comfortable, many offering good views over the River Lee. Excellent conference and leisure facilities are available in separate buildings in the grounds.

Rooms 109 (32 fmly) ⚡ **Facilities** WiFi ⇘ 🏊 supervised ♨ Gym Squash Aerobics classes Complementary use of leisure centre ♫ New Year **Conf** Class 520 Board 30 Thtr 800 **Services** Lift **Parking** 325 **Notes** ⊗ Closed 24-27 Dec Civ Wed 500

DELGANY
County Wicklow
Map 1 D3

Glenview Hotel

★★★★ 78% ⊛ HOTEL

tel: 01 2873399 **Glen O' the Downs**
email: sales@glenviewhotel.com **web:** www.glenviewhotel.com
dir: From Dublin city centre follow signs for N11, past Bray on N11 S'bound, exit 9

This hotel is set in lovely terraced gardens overlooking the Glen o' the Downs. The comfortable bedrooms are spacious, and many enjoy the great views over the valley. The impressive public areas include a conservatory bar, lounge and choice of dining options including the first-floor Woodlands Restaurant where dinner is served. The hotel has an excellent range of leisure and conference facilities. A championship golf course and horse riding can be found nearby.

Rooms 70 (11 fmly) (16 GF) ⚡ **Facilities** Spa STV WiFi 🏊 supervised ♨ Gym Aerobics studio Massage Beauty treatment rooms ♫ Xmas New Year Child facilities **Conf** Class 100 Board 80 Thtr 270 Del from €120 to €140 **Services** Lift **Parking** 200 **Notes** ⊗ Civ Wed 180

DINGLE (AN DAINGEAN)
County Kerry

Map 1 A2

Dingle Skellig Hotel & Peninsula Spa

★★★★ 80% ◎ HOTEL

tel: 066 9150200
email: reservations@dingleskellig.com **web:** www.dingleskellig.com
dir: N86 to Dingle, hotel on harbour

This modern hotel, close to the town, overlooks Dingle Bay and has spectacular views from many of the comfortably furnished bedrooms and suites. Public areas offer a spacious bar and lounge and a bright, airy restaurant. There are extensive health and leisure facilities, and many family activities are organised in the Fungi Kids Club.

Rooms 113 (10 fmly) (31 GF) 🐾 **Facilities** Spa STV FTV WiFi ↘ 🐕 supervised Gym 🎵 New Year Child facilities **Conf** Class 120 Board 100 Thtr 250 **Services** Lift **Parking** 110 **Notes** ⊗ Closed Jan RS Nov-Dec Civ Wed 250

Dingle Benners Hotel

★★★ 72% HOTEL

tel: 066 9151638 **Main St**
email: info@dinglebenners.com **web:** www.dinglebenners.com
dir: In town centre

Located in the centre of the town with parking to the rear, this long-established property has an old world charm. There are a selection of relaxing lounges, open turf fires and comfortable bedrooms that are furnished with antique pine; some have four-poster beds. Food is available in Mrs Benner's traditional bar.

Rooms 52 (2 fmly) (9 GF) **Facilities** STV FTV WiFi **Services** Lift **Parking** 32 **Notes** ⊗ Closed 19-27 Dec Civ Wed 90

DONABATE
County Dublin

Map 1 D4

The Waterside House Hotel

★★★ 75% ◎ HOTEL

tel: 01 8436153
email: info@watersidehousehotel.ie **web:** www.watersidehousehotel.ie
dir: Exit M1 junct 4 (Donabate/Portrane), 3rd exit at rdbt, pass Newbridge House Demesne on left, continue over rail bridge, right at sign for golf courses & hotel. Hotel on left

This family-run hotel is situated in an enviable position right on Donabate beach in north Co. Dublin. Overlooking Lambay Island, the public areas and bedrooms are appointed in a contemporary style, with the comfortable lounge bar and terrace taking advantage of the breathtaking views. The Signal Restaurant offers evening dining in a cosy environment at weekends and during peak seasons. Entertainment is provided on a regular basis, with tribute shows during the summer months. A popular wedding venue, it is close to Dublin Airport and a number of golf courses.

Rooms 35 (8 fmly) (8 GF) 🐾 **Facilities** STV FTV WiFi 🎵 Xmas New Year **Conf** Class 150 Board 100 Thtr 400 **Services** Lift Air con **Parking** 100 **Notes** ⊗ Civ Wed 250

DONEGAL
County Donegal

Map 1 B5

Harvey's Point Hotel

★★★★ 85% ◎◎ HOTEL

tel: 074 9722208 **Lough Eske**
email: stay@harveyspoint.com **web:** www.harveyspoint.com
dir: N56 from Donegal, then 1st right (Loch Eske/Harvey's Point)

Situated by the shores of Lough Eske, a short drive from Donegal, this welcoming hotel is an oasis of relaxation; comfort and attentive guest care are the norm here. A wide range of particularly spacious suites and bedrooms is on offer, together with smaller rooms in the courtyard annexe. The kitchen brigade maintains consistently high standards in The Restaurant at dinner, with less formal dining in the sun lounge throughout the day. A very popular Sunday buffet lunch is served weekly, with dinner and cabaret entertainment on selected dates during the summer. Breakfast is also a feature of a stay here. Pet friendly accommodation is available.

Rooms 64 (8 annexe) (17 fmly) (28 GF) 🐾 **Facilities** STV FTV WiFi ↘ Beauty treatment rooms Bicycle hire Walking tours 🎵 Xmas New Year **Conf** Class 200 Board 50 Thtr 200 **Services** Lift **Parking** 300 **Notes** Closed Mon & Tue Nov-Mar Civ Wed 250

Mill Park Hotel

★★★★ 76% HOTEL

tel: 074 9722880 **The Mullins, Donegal Town**
email: info@millparkhotel.com **web:** www.millparkhotel.com

The Mill Park is located within walking distance of Donegal town. It is a family owned and operated property, with a friendly and dedicated team that are sure to please with their natural and warm approach. All of the comfortable rooms and suites have been recently renovated in stylish contemporary décor schemes. All-Day dining is available in the Café Bar, a popular destination with the locals, with more formal evening dining in the 1st floor Granary Restaurant that overlooks the main lobby. There is a spacious leisure centre available on a complimentary basis to resident guests, together with treatments and pampering in the Wellness Centre. The hotel has an excellent reputation for its banqueting and conference facilities.

Rooms 115 (10 fmly) (40 GF) 🐾 **Facilities** Spa STV FTV WiFi ↘ 🐕 supervised Gym New Year **Conf** Class 100 Board 40 Thtr 300 **Services** Lift **Parking** 200 **Notes** ⊗ Closed 24-26 Dec Civ Wed 350

The Central Hotel Conference & Leisure Centre

★★★ 78% HOTEL

tel: 074 9721027 **The Diamond**
email: info@centralhoteldonegal.com **web:** www.centralhoteldonegal.com
dir: In town centre

Located right in the centre of the town, this long established hotel is a gem. The public rooms are decorated to a high standard; a popular carvery lunch is served in The Just William, and evening dining in the atmospheric Upper Deck Bar. Whites-on-The Diamond also serves dinner at peak periods. Afternoon tea is served on the first-floor mezzanine from which guests can look down on the bustling town below. Bedrooms vary in style and many have views over Donegal Bay. There is also a contemporary banqueting suite where occasional concerts and a programme of summer events are held.

Rooms 112 (26 fmly) 🐾 **S** €50-€70; **D** €90-€190 (incl. bkfst) **Facilities** STV FTV WiFi ↘ 🐕 supervised Gym 🎵 Xmas New Year **Conf** Class 160 Board 70 Thtr 380 Del from €160 to €500 **Services** Lift **Notes** ⊗ Civ Wed

REPUBLIC OF IRELAND

The Red Door Country House

◉ RESTAURANT WITH ROOMS

tel: 074 9360289 **Fahan, Inishowen**
email: info@thereddoor.ie **web:** www.thereddoor.ie
dir: In Fahan village, church on right, The Red Door signed on left

Nestled among mature trees and landscaped gardens, this warm and welcoming restaurant with rooms stands proudly on the shore of Lough Swilly in the historic village of Fahan, just south of Buncrana. Dating from 1789, the tradition of the house is cleverly combined with contemporary styling. The four guest bedrooms are cosy and comfortable, each individually decorated and all en suite. The house has a fine reputation in the region for the quality of its restaurant for evening dining, and al fresco lunches. Breakfast is also a highlight and is designed to be lingered over.

Rooms 4

DUBLIN
Dublin   Map 1 D4

INSPECTORS' CHOICE

The Merrion Hotel

★★★★★ ◉◉◉◉ HOTEL

tel: 01 6030600 **21 Upper Merrion St,**
email: info@merrionhotel.com **web:** www.merrionhotel.com
dir: At top of Upper Merrion St on left, beyond Government buildings on right

This terrace of gracious Georgian buildings, reputed to have been the birthplace of the Duke of Wellington, embraces the character of many changes of use over 200 years. Bedrooms and suites are spacious, some in the original house; others are in a modern wing overlooking the gardens. They all offer great comfort and a wide range of extra facilities. The lounges retain the charm and opulence of days gone by, while the Cellar bar area is a popular meeting point. Dining options include The Cellar Restaurant specialising in prime local ingredients and, for that very special occasion, the award-winning Restaurant Patrick Guilbaud is Dublin's finest. "Art Tea" is an afternoon tea experience with a difference, where delightful pastries are inspired by works from the hotel's vast art collection.

Rooms 142 (21 GF) (20 smoking) ⟋ **S** €495-€3400; **D** €515-€3400* **Facilities** Spa STV FTV WiFi ⇘ ⊠ Gym Steam room Relaxation area Xmas New Year **Conf** Class 25 Board 25 Thtr 60 **Services** Lift Air con **Parking** 60 **Notes** ⊗ Civ Wed 50

INSPECTORS' CHOICE

The Shelbourne Dublin, a Renaissance Hotel

RENAISSANCE. HOTELS & RESORTS

★★★★★ ◉◉ HOTEL

tel: 01 6634500 **27 St Stephen's Green,**
email: rhi.dubbr.reservations@renaissancehotels.com **web:** www.theshelbourne.ie
dir: M1 to city centre, along Parnell St to O'Connell St towards Trinity College, 3rd right into Kildare St, hotel on left

This Dublin landmark exudes elegance and a real sense of history, having been established in 1824. The public areas are spacious and offer a range of dining and bar options. There is a selection of bedroom styles and suites available, many with commanding views over St. Stephen's Green. No 27 is a popular bar and lounge for casual dining. The Saddle Room is the main restaurant featuring a steak and seafood menu with a contemporary twist, while afternoon tea is served in the elegant Lord Mayor's Lounge. An extensive leisure and fitness facility is also available.

Rooms 265 (7 smoking) ⟋ **S** €190-€2650; **D** €190-€2650 **Facilities** Spa STV FTV WiFi ⇘ ⊠ Gym Relaxtion room Thermal facilities Dance studio ♫ Xmas **Conf** Class 240 Board 60 Thtr 400 **Services** Lift Air con **Notes** ⊗ Civ Wed 350

The Westbury Hotel

★★★★★ 87% ◉◉ HOTEL

tel: 01 6791122 **Grafton St**
email: westbury@doylecollection.com **web:** www.doylecollection.com
dir: Adjacent to Grafton St, half way between Trinity College & Stephens Green

Located just off Grafton Street, Dublin's premier shopping district, this is an oasis of calm; guests are well cared for amid smart, contemporary surroundings. Spacious public areas include the relaxing Gallery Lounge where afternoon tea is popular with shoppers taking a break. Café Novo is the hotel's buzzing street-level brasserie bar, while Wilde-The Restaurant is an elegant grill with an emphasis on seasonal and artisan fare. A range of stylish suites and bedrooms is offered; many overlooking the roofs of the city. Valet parking is available.

Rooms 205 (9 fmly) ⟋ **Facilities** STV FTV WiFi ⇘ Gym **Conf** Class 100 Board 46 Thtr 200 **Services** Lift Air con **Parking** 100 **Notes** ⊗ Civ Wed 120

DUBLIN *continued*

Castleknock Hotel & Country Club

FBD Hotels & Resorts

★★★★ 83% ⊛ HOTEL

tel: 01 6406300 **Porterstown Rd, Castleknock**
email: info@chcc.ie **web:** www.castleknockhotel.com
dir: M50 from airport. Exit at junct 6 (signed Navan, Cavan & M3) onto N3, becomes M3. Exit at junct 3. At top of slip road 1st left signed Consilla (R121). At T-junct left. 1km to hotel

This modern hotel is set on a golf course only 15 minutes from Dublin. The bedrooms are very comfortable, with all expected modern guest facilities. The spacious public rooms have an airy feel, and some rooms open onto a terrace that overlooks the golf course. The range of food and beverage outlets includes The Park Room, a steak house, a busy all-day brasserie, and The Lime Tree which is open in the evening. Excellent conference and banqueting facilities are available, together with a popular leisure centre. Castleknock Hotel is the AA Hotel of the Year for the Republic of Ireland 2013-2014.

Rooms 138 (30 fmly) (5 smoking) ℮ **S** €69-€430; **D** €79-€440 (incl. bkfst)*
Facilities Spa FTV WiFi ⓠ ⓢ supervised ⓛ 18 Gym Sauna Steam room Children's pool ♫ Xmas New Year **Conf** Class 200 Board 80 Thtr 400 **Services** Lift **Parking** 200 **Notes** LB ⊛ Closed 24-26 Dec Civ Wed 200

Radisson Blu St Helens Hotel

★★★★ 82% ⊛ HOTEL

tel: 01 2186000 & 2186011 **Stillorgan Rd**
email: info.dublin@radissonblu.com **web:** www.radissonblu.ie/sthelenshotel-dublin
dir: On N11 Stillorgan dual carriageway

An early 18th-century period estate houses this hotel, carefully restored with much of the original décor and architectural features still intact. Just 5 Km south of the city, close to UCD, there are over a hundred and fifty suites and rooms from which to choose. They are in a modern block to the side and are all very well appointed, many with garden views. The spectacular Orangerie and the Ballroom are popular venues for all day dining, with the AA Rosette awarded Italian restaurant, Talavera, located in the original kitchens open each evening. Le Panto is a wonderfully decorated room available for private dining. Fitness suite and beauty facilities are provided, together with extensive meeting and event spaces for up to 300 delegates.

Rooms 151 (22 fmly) (38 GF) ℮ **S** €110-€349; **D** €110-€349* **Facilities** STV FTV WiFi ⓠ Gym Beauty salon ♫ Xmas New Year **Conf** Class 150 Board 70 Thtr 350 **Services** Lift Air con **Parking** 220 **Notes** ⊛ Civ Wed 240

Clontarf Castle Hotel

★★★★ 80% ⊛ HOTEL

tel: 01 8332321 & 8534336 **Castle Av, Clontarf**
email: mlong@clontarfcastle.ie **web:** www.clontarfcastle.ie
dir: M1 towards centre, left at Whitehall Church, left at T-junct, straight on at lights, right at next lights into Castle Ave, hotel on right at rdbt

Dating back to the 12th century, this castle retains many historic architectural features which have been combined with contemporary styling in the well-equipped bedrooms. Public areas offer relaxing lounges, and modern cuisine is served in Fahrenheit Grill, Indigo Lounge and Knights Bar. The Great Hall is a versatile venue for banqueting and conferences.

Rooms 111 (7 fmly) (11 GF) (23 smoking) ℮ **Facilities** STV WiFi ⓠ Gym Xmas New Year **Conf** Class 250 Board 90 Thtr 600 **Services** Lift Air con **Parking** 134 **Notes** ⊛ Civ Wed 400

Crowne Plaza Hotel Dublin - Blanchardstown

 CROWNE PLAZA HOTELS & RESORTS

★★★★ 79% ⊛ HOTEL

tel: 01 8977777 **The Blanchardstown Centre**
email: info@cpireland.crowneplaza.com **web:** www.cpireland.ie
dir: M50 junct 6 Blanchardstown

This landmark building is on the doorstep of a wide range of shops in Blanchardstown. Bedrooms are stylishly decorated with generously sized beds and well appointed en suites. The Sanctuary Bar serves an international range of informal dishes from lunchtime through to the evening, with Italian specialities (pasta dishes and pizzas) served in the evenings in Forchetta Restaurant. Secure underground parking is provided. There is a floor of dedicated boardrooms and meeting facilities, together with banqueting rooms. Secure underground parking is complimentary to resident guests.

Rooms 188 (60 fmly) (15 smoking) ℮ **S** €75-€380; **D** €85-€380* **Facilities** STV FTV WiFi ⓠ HL Gym Sauna New Year **Conf** Class 300 Board 300 Thtr 500 **Del** from €200 to €350* **Services** Lift Air con **Parking** 250 **Notes** ⊛ Civ Wed 300

Stillorgan Park Hotel

★★★★ 78% ⊛ HOTEL

tel: 01 2001800 **Stillorgan Rd, Stillorgan**
email: info@stillorganpark.com **web:** www.stillorganpark.com
dir: From N11 follow Wexford signs (pass RTE studios on left) through 5 sets of lights. Hotel on left

This modern hotel is situated on the southern outskirts of the city, close to UCD, Dundrum and Stillorgan shopping centres. Comfortable public areas include a spacious lobby, The Purple Sage Restaurant and a traditional style bar. There are extensive air-conditioned banqueting and conference facilities, a gym and a spa with treatment rooms.

Rooms 150 (8 fmly) (4 smoking) ℮ **S** €85-€220; **D** €85-€220* **Facilities** Spa STV WiFi ⓠ Gym ♫ New Year **Conf** Class 220 Board 130 Thtr 500 **Del** from €138 to €170* **Services** Lift Air con **Parking** 300 **Notes** LB ⊛ Closed 25 Dec RS 24 Dec Civ Wed 300

Ashling Hotel, Dublin

★★★★ 77% ⊛ HOTEL

tel: 01 6772324 **Parkgate St**
email: info@ashlinghotel.ie **web:** www.ashlinghotel.ie
dir: Close to River Liffey, opposite Heuston Station

Situated on the banks of the River Liffey close to the city centre, railway station and law courts, this hotel is on the tram route and just a five-minute walk from Phoenix Park. The property is appointed to a high standard in a contemporary style. The bedrooms are comfortably furnished; the newer ones are more spacious. Food is available in the Iveagh Bar throughout the day and a popular carvery is served at lunchtime; Chesterfield's Brasserie offers a carte in the evening. Staff are very friendly and service is attentive and professional. Secure multi-storey parking is available.

Rooms 225 (23 fmly) ℮ **Facilities** STV WiFi **Conf** Class 110 Board 50 Thtr 220 **Services** Lift **Parking** 100 **Notes** ⊛ Closed 24-26 Dec

Red Cow Moran Hotel

★★★★ 76% HOTEL

MORAN HOTELS

tel: 01 4593650 **Red Cow Complex, Naas Rd**
email: redcowres@moranhotels.com **web:** www.moranhotels.com
dir: At junct of M50 & N7 on city side of motorway

Located just off the M50, this hotel is 20 minutes from the airport and close to the city centre via the Luas light rail system. The dedicated team of staff show a genuine willingness to create a memorable stay. Bedrooms are well equipped and comfortable, and the public areas and conference rooms are spacious. Ample free parking is available.

Rooms 123 (21 fmly) (7 smoking) **Facilities** FTV WiFi ᕒ 𝄞 New Year **Conf** Class 350 Board 150 Thtr 750 **Services** Lift Air con **Parking** 700 **Notes** ⊗ Closed 24-26 Dec Civ Wed 400

Roganstown Hotel and Country Club

★★★★ 75% HOTEL

tel: 01 8433118 **Naul Rd, Sword**
web: www.roganstown.com

Developed from the original family home and farm some 10 years ago, Roganstown is now a quality hotel property surrounded by parkland encompassing a golf course and a well equipped leisure centre and spa. Some rooms are in the original farmhouse, with most in a separate modern block around a well landscaped courtyard. The public areas include a cosy bar that doubles as the golf member's area, a busy O'Callaghan's lounge where food is served throughout the day. Finer evening dining takes place in the award-winning McLaughlin's restaurant where the menu features carefully sourced seasonal ingredients cooked with flair. A multi-use conference and events centre is located on the first floor.

Rooms 52 (4 fmly) (20 GF) **Facilities** STV WiFi ᕒ ⊗ ⬇ 18 Putt green Gym Aerobics studio **Conf** Class 150 Board 128 Thtr 300 Del from €165* **Notes** ⊗ Civ Wed

Bewleys Hotel Ballsbridge

★★★ 78% HOTEL

tel: 01 6681111 **Merrion Rd, Ballsbridge**
email: ballsbridge@bewleyshotels.com **web:** www.bewleyshotels.com
dir: On corner of Merrion Rd & Simmonscourt Rd

This stylish hotel is a restored 19th-century Masonic school situated near the RDS, Aviva Stadium and the city centre. It offers comfortable, good-value, well-appointed accommodation. The Brasserie serves an interesting menu with a very popular carvery lunch and breakfast; snacks are available in Tom's Bar throughout the day. There is secure underground parking, and Thomas Prior Hall is a unique venue for banquets and conferences.

Rooms 304 (56 fmly) (50 GF) **Facilities** WiFi ᕒ Xmas New Year **Conf** Class 150 Board 80 Thtr 250 **Services** Lift **Parking** 220 **Notes** ⊗ Civ Wed 250

Bewleys Hotel Leopardstown

★★★ 77% HOTEL

tel: 01 2935000 & 2935001 **Central Park, Leopardstown**
email: leop@bewleyshotels.com **web:** www.bewleyshotels.com
dir: M50 junct 13/14, follow signs for Leopardstown. Hotel on right

This hotel is conveniently situated close to the Central Business Park and Leopardstown racecourse and is serviced by the Luas light rail system and

Aircoach. The bedrooms are spacious and well appointed. Contemporary in style, the open-plan public areas include a spacious lounge bar with snack food available throughout the day, while lunch and dinner are served in the Brasserie. There is a gym and a choice of conference rooms including the Power Suite. Underground parking is available.

Rooms 355 (84 fmly) (30 smoking) ᕒ **Facilities** STV FTV WiFi ᕒ Gym **Conf** Class 50 Board 50 Thtr 160 **Services** Lift **Parking** 228 **Notes** ⊗ Closed 23-25 Dec

Sandymount Hotel

★★★ 77% HOTEL

tel: 01 614 2000 **Herbert Rd, Sandymount**
email: info@sandymounthotel.ie **web:** www.sandymounthotel.ie
dir: Adjacent to Aviva Stadium, 200mtrs from Dart Rail Station

This hotel (previously known as the Mount Herbert Hotel) has been run by the Loughran family for three generations, and is located close to the Aviva Stadium, the RDS and Sandymount village. The comfortable bedrooms are well appointed, as are the lounge areas. The bistro restaurant and bar overlook the lovely garden. There are conference facilities and ample free parking is available.

Rooms 168 (3 fmly) (56 GF) **Facilities** STV WiFi ᕒ **Conf** Class 60 Board 40 Thtr 100 **Services** Lift **Parking** 90 **Notes** ⊗ Closed 21-27 Dec

Cassidys Hotel

★★★ 75% HOTEL

tel: 01 8780555 **6-8 Cavendish Row, Upper O'Connell St**
email: stay@cassidyshotel.com **web:** www.cassidyshotel.com
dir: In city centre at N end of O'Connell St

This family-run hotel is located at the top of O'Connell Street, in a terrace of red-brick Georgian townhouses, directly opposite the famed Gate Theatre. The warm and welcoming atmosphere created by the hospitable team in Groomes Bar and Bistro adds to the traditional atmosphere. Bedrooms are individually styled and well appointed; many have air conditioning. A residents' gym, conference facilities and limited parking are all available.

Rooms 113 (26 annexe) (3 fmly) (12 GF) (30 smoking) **Facilities** STV WiFi ᕒ Gym **Conf** Class 45 Board 45 Thtr 80 **Services** Lift **Parking** 8 **Notes** ⊗ Closed 24-26 Dec

Bewleys Hotel Newlands Cross

★★★ 74% HOTEL

tel: 01 4640140 & 4123301 **Newlands Cross, Naas Rd**
email: newlands@bewleyshotels.com **web:** www.bewleyshotels.com
dir: M50 junct 9, N7 (Naas road). Hotel near junct of N7 & Belgard Rd

This modern hotel is situated on the N7 and close to the M50 and Luas light rail to the city. Bedrooms are spacious and the pricing structure proves popular with families. The Brasserie restaurant is open through the day for casual dining and serves a carvery lunch; more formal meals are served in the evening. The hotel also has a comfortable bar where snacks are available, conference rooms, a gym and ample free parking.

Rooms 297 (182 fmly) (62 GF) ᕒ **Facilities** STV WiFi ᕒ Gym 𝄞 New Year **Conf** Class 18 Board 14 Thtr 50 **Services** Lift **Parking** 200 **Notes** ⊗ Closed 24-26 Dec

DUBLIN *continued*

Temple Bar Hotel

★★★ 74% HOTEL

tel: 01 6773333 **Fleet St, Temple Bar**
email: reservations@tbh.ie **web:** www.templebarhotel.com
dir: From Trinity College towards O'Connell Bridge. 1st left onto Fleet St. Hotel on right

This hotel is situated right in the heart of Dublin's Temple Bar area, and is close to the main shopping districts, restaurants and the nightlife of the city. Bedrooms are comfortable and well equipped, with more spacious executive rooms available at a small surcharge. Food is served throughout the day in Buskers themed bar, with the Rendezvous a more peaceful option. Alchemy is the smart night club which becomes a music venue at weekends and at other peak periods. Parking is available in a multi-storey opposite at a reduced rate for hotel guests.

Rooms 129 (6 fmly) (30 smoking) **S** €70-€250; **D** €70-€320 (incl. bkfst)* **Facilities** STV WiFi ↴ ♫ **Conf** Class 40 Board 40 Thtr 70 Del from €105.90 to €113.90* **Services** Lift **Notes** LB ⊗ Closed 23-25 Dec RS Good Fri

Ibis Hotel Dublin West

BUDGET HOTEL

tel: 01 464 1480 **Naas Rd, Monastery Rd, Clondalkin**
email: H0595@accor.com **web:** www.ibis.com
dir: On Red Cow rdbt M50 junct 9 off Naas Rd on Monastery Rd

Close to Dublin airport and the M50, this hotel is modern in style. Bedrooms have contemporary furnishings including large desks. Public rooms include a restaurant and a lounge. Breakfast is self-service and a 24-hour snack service is also available. See also the Hotel Groups pages.

Rooms 150 (39 fmly) (35 GF) **S** €31-€99; **D** €31-€99 **Conf** Class 25 Board 18 Thtr 35 Del from €90 to €110

DUBLIN AIRPORT	Map 1 D4
Dublin	

Crowne Plaza Dublin Northwood

★★★★ 80% 🏵 HOTEL

tel: 01 8628888 **Northwood Park, Santry Demesne, Santry**
email: info@crowneplazadublin.ie **web:** www.cpdublin.crowneplaza.com
dir: M50 junct 4, left into Northwood Park, 1km, hotel on left

Located within minutes of Dublin Airport, and served by a complimentary shuttle service, this modern hotel is located in Northwood Park, and benefits from an idyllic location overlooking 85 acres of mature woodlands of the former Santry Demesne. Bedrooms come in a variety of styles, and each is comfortable and well appointed. Guests in executive rooms have the use of a lounge facility where a light breakfast is served. The hotel offers a range of dining options, including full room service and a lobby café. There are extensive conference and event rooms at this property, together with a secure multi-storey car park. Guests also have use of a well equipped gymnasium.

Rooms 204 (17 fmly) (5 smoking) 🌂 **S** €89-€280; **D** €99-€300 **Facilities** STV FTV WiFi ↴ HL Gym Xmas New Year **Conf** Class 450 Board 100 Thtr 850 Del from €225 to €250 **Services** Lift Air con **Parking** 400 **Notes** LB ⊗ Civ Wed 300

Bewleys Hotel Dublin Airport

★★★ 77% HOTEL

tel: 01 8711000 & 8711200 **Baskin Ln**
email: dublinairport@bewleyshotels.com **web:** www.bewleyshotels.com
dir: At end of M50 N'bound, 2nd exit at rdbt (N32), left at next rdbt

Conveniently situated for Dublin Airport, this hotel has the added advantage of secure underground parking and a complimentary shuttle bus to the airport. Bedrooms are spacious and suitable for families; there is a comfortable lounge bar and brasserie with a wide selection of dishes on offer. Good quality meeting and banqueting rooms are available.

Rooms 466 (228 fmly) (36 smoking) 🌂 **Facilities** FTV WiFi ↴ Fitness room Xmas **Conf** Class 150 Board 12 Thtr 300 **Services** Lift **Parking** 1150 **Notes** Civ Wed 250

Premier Inn Dublin Airport

BUDGET HOTEL

tel: 0871 527 8312 **Airside Retail Park**
web: www.premierinn.com
dir: M1 junct 2 for Dublin Airport. At main airport rdbt 3rd exit, follow Drogheda & Belfast signs. 2nd exit at Cloghran rdbt. Right at lights signed Airside Industrial Estate/Retail Park. Hotel on right

High quality, budget accommodation ideal for both families and business travellers. Spacious, en suite bedrooms feature tea and coffee making facilities, and Freeview TV in most hotels. Internet access and WiFi are available for a small fee. The adjacent family restaurant features a wide and varied menu. See also the Hotel Groups pages.

Rooms 155

DUNBOYNE	Map 1 D4
County Meath	

Dunboyne Castle Hotel & Spa

★★★★ 79% 🏵🏵 HOTEL

tel: 01 8013500
email: info@dunboynecastlehotel.com **web:** www.dunboynecastlehotel.com
dir: In Dunboyne take R157 towards Maynooth. Hotel on left

Located within walking distance of Dunboyne village, this fine property is a successful combination of the traditional and contemporary. Set on over two acres of mature woodland and well tended grounds, the original house is home to a number of meeting rooms, with the spacious bedrooms in a modern block to the side. All day dining is offered in the Terrace Lounge, with evening meals and breakfast served in the newly refurbished Ivy Restaurant.

Rooms 145 (37 GF) 🅿 **Facilities** Spa STV WiFi ☾ Gym 🎵 Xmas New Year
Conf Class 200 Board 80 Thtr 450 Del from €119 to €229 **Services** Lift Air con
Parking 380 **Notes** ⊗ Civ Wed 250

See advert below

DUNDALK Map 1 D4
County Louth

Ballymascanlon House Hotel

★★★★ 80% HOTEL

tel: 042 9358200
email: info@ballymascanlon.com **web:** www.ballymascanlon.com
dir: M1 junct 18 onto N52 signed Dundalk North/R173 at Carlingford. Exit at Faughart rdbt. 1st left at next rdbt. Hotel in approx 1km on left

This Victorian mansion is set in 130 acres of woodland and landscaped gardens at the foot of the Cooley Mountains. The elegant house and the modern extension make this a very comfortable hotel that has really stylish bedrooms. Public areas include a spacious restaurant, lounge and bar, together with relaxing reading rooms that retain many original architectural features. There is a well-equipped leisure centre, and The Oak Room banqueting facility proves to be very popular for weddings and family occasions.

Rooms 90 (11 fmly) (5 GF) 🅿 **Facilities** STV FTV WiFi ☾ 🕸 supervised ⚓ 18 ⛳ Putt green Gym Steam room Sauna Plunge pool 🎵 Xmas New Year **Conf** Class 220 Board 100 Thtr 400 **Services** Lift **Parking** 250 **Notes** ⊗ Civ Wed 300

Dunboyne Castle Hotel & Spa

Hotel description
This breath-taking hotel is set on the original site of a 15th century castle. Comprising a total of 145 en suite rooms, the hotel offers impressive facilities, including a helicopter pad. Fully air-conditioned, the hotel features a lobby with 24-hour reception and check-out service, hotel safe, currency exchange facilities, cloakroom and lift access. Guests will find *Seoid Spa*, *The Sadlier Bar* & *The Terrace Lounge* plus *The Ivy Restaurant* on site which holds 2AA Rosettes. Conference facilities and WiFi Internet access are both available, along with a laundry service and 24-hour room service. Guests arriving by car can make use of the nearby parking facilities.

Room Description
Designed with space and comfort in mind, the over-sized guest rooms have either garden or forest views providing plenty of natural light. The rooms are en suite with bathtub/shower and include bathrobes and a hairdryer. All of the rooms come with an in-room safe, coffee tray, video on demand, flat-screen TV with satellite channels, fridge and ironing set. Further facilities include direct dial telephone, radio, complimentary Wi-Fi access, king-size bed, air conditioning and heating and some balcony/terrace.

Seoid Spa
The hotel grounds include a hot tub, sauna, steam room, solarium, gym and sun terrace, as well as 18 treatment rooms and a hydrotherapy pool. A wide range of spa and massage treatments are available. Guests looking to play a round of golf should look no further than the course in Luttrellstown, some 5 km from the hotel.

Meals
This hotel offers a large selection of packages including dinner, bed and breakfast.

Location
This country hotel is set in 21 acres of lush landscape in an ideal location, approximately 16 km from Dublin city centre. The centre of Dunboyne is just 100 metres from the hotel's doors and features restaurants, bars and pubs. Shops can be found 5 km away in Blanchardstown Shopping Centre, and Dublin Airport is 21 km from the accommodation.

How To Get There
On leaving Dublin Airport take the M50 heading south. Continue southbound until reaching the Blanchardstown exit (N3). Continue on this road until signs for Clonee and Dunboyne; take this exit. After driving through Clonee village, reach Dunboyne. Drive through the village, and on exiting the village take a left turn, signposted Maynooth. The hotel is on the left-hand side.

Maynooth Road, Dunboyne, Co. Meath • Tel: +353 1 801 3500 • Fax: +353 1 436 6801
Website: www.dunboynecastlehotel.com • **Email:** frontoffice@dunboynecastlehotel.com

DUNFANAGHY
County Donegal

Map 1 C6

Arnolds Hotel

★★★ 75% ⊚ HOTEL

IRISH
COUNTRY
HOTELS

tel: 074 9136208
email: enquiries@arnoldshotel.com web: www.arnoldshotel.com
dir: N56 from Letterkenny, hotel on left on entering village

This family-owned and run hotel, situated in a coastal village overlooking sandy beaches and beautiful scenery, is noted for its warm welcome and good food. The public areas and bedrooms are very comfortable; there is a traditional cosy bar with turf fires, a popular bistro that serves food throughout the day, and Seascapes Restaurant where local seafood features on the menu. There are stables attached to the hotel, with preferential terms for residents. Photographic and painting breaks are available, as is links-based golf.

Rooms 30 (10 fmly) ◈ S €85-€120; D €110-€180 (incl. bkfst)* Facilities FTV WiFi ♬ New Year Parking 60 Notes LB ⊗ RS Nov-Apr Civ Wed 90

DUNGARVAN
County Waterford

Map 1 C2

Lawlors Hotel

★★★ 70% HOTEL

tel: 058 41122
email: info@lawlorshotel.com web: www.lawlorshotel.com
dir: Off N25

This town centre hotel has very attractive and comfortable public areas with a busy bar where food is served throughout the day. A good value dinner menu is available in Davit's Restaurant. The bedrooms vary in size but all are well appointed. Conference and meeting rooms plus secure parking are available.

Rooms 89 (8 fmly) Facilities WiFi ♬ New Year Conf Class 215 Board 420 Thtr 420 Services Lift Notes Closed 25 Dec

DURRUS
County Cork

Map 1 B2

Blairscove House & Restaurant

⊚⊚ RESTAURANT WITH ROOMS

tel: 027 61127 ▤ 027 61487
email: mail@blairscove.ie web: www.blairscove.ie
dir: From Durrus on R591 towards Crookhaven, 2.4km, house (blue gate) on right

Blairscove comprises four elegant suites located in the courtyard of a Georgian country house outside the pretty village of Durrus near Bantry; each room is individually decorated in a contemporary style and has stunning views over Dunmanus Bay and the mountains. The restaurant is renowned for its wide range of hors d'oeuvres and its open wood-fire grill. The piano playing and candle light add to a unique dining experience.

Rooms 4 (4 annexe) (1 fmly)

ENNIS
County Clare

Map 1 B3

Temple Gate Hotel

★★★ 80% ⊚ HOTEL

tel: 065 6823300 The Square
email: info@templegatehotel.com web: www.templegatehotel.com
dir: Exit N18 onto Tulla Rd for 0.25m, hotel on left

This smart hotel is owned and run by the Madden family and is located in the centre of the town. It incorporates a 19th-century, Gothic-style Great Hall banqueting room. The public areas are well planned and include a comfortable library lounge, popular traditional pub and Legends Restaurant. Bedrooms are attractive and well equipped with some executive rooms and suites available.

Rooms 70 (3 fmly) (11 GF) (20 smoking) Facilities STV FTV WiFi ♘ ♬ New Year Conf Class 100 Board 80 Thtr 250 Services Lift Parking 52 Notes ⊗ Closed 25-26 Dec RS 24 Dec Civ Wed 200

ENNISKERRY
County Wicklow

Map 1 D3

Powerscourt Hotel

★★★★★ 89% ⊚⊚ HOTEL

tel: 01 2748888 Powerscourt Estate
email: info@powerscourthotel.com web: www.powerscourt.com/hotel
dir: From Dublin take M50, M11, then N11, follow Enniskerry signs. In Enniskerry left up hill, hotel on right

This very stylish hotel, built in the Palladian style, has a tranquil setting with stunning views over the gardens and woodlands to the Sugar Loaf. The bedrooms and suites are particularly spacious and well appointed with very impressive bathrooms that have TVs, deep tubs and walk-in showers. The luxuriously appointed public areas are airy and spacious with a variety of food options that includes the Gordon Ramsay at Powerscourt restaurant. The hotel also has a stunning spa, two golf courses, and includes fly fishing and equestrian pursuits among its many leisure facilities.

Rooms 200 (39 GF) Facilities Spa STV WiFi ♘ ⊛ ♿ 36 Putt green Fishing ⚲ Gym Cycling Mega chess Xmas New Year Conf Class 240 Board 72 Thtr 500 Services Lift Air con Parking 384 Notes Civ Wed 400

GALWAY
County Galway

Map 1 B3

The G Hotel

★★★★★ 87% ⊚⊚ HOTEL

tel: 091 865200 Wellpark, Dublin Rd
email: info@theg.ie web: www.theghotel.ie
dir: Telephone for detailed directions

Designed in association with the acclaimed milliner Philip Treacy who hails from the county, this hotel is the epitome of contemporary styling. The public areas include a series of eclectically furnished lounges, each with its own identity. The cutting-edge design is also apparent in the bedrooms and suites, which are very comfortable and appointed to a high standard. An interesting menu is on offer at dinner each evening in GiGi's, the atmospheric restaurant, and a very popular all-day menu is served in the lounges, including traditional afternoon tea. The hotel has a number of boardrooms, an events space and an Espa spa facility. Underground and valet parking is available.

Rooms 101 (2 fmly) ◈ Facilities Spa STV FTV WiFi HL Gym New Year Conf Class 42 Board 40 Thtr 120 Services Lift Air con Parking 349 Notes ⊗ Closed 23-26 Dec Civ Wed 90

Ardilaun Hotel & Leisure Club

★★★★ 81% ⚙ HOTEL

tel: 091 521433 **Taylor's Hill**
email: info@theardilaunhotel.ie **web:** www.theardilaunhotel.ie
dir: M6 to Galway City West, then follow signs for N59 Clifden, then N6 towards Salthill

This very smart country-house style hotel, appointed to a high standard, is located on the outskirts of the city near Salthill and has lovely landscaped gardens. The bedrooms have been thoughtfully appointed and the deluxe rooms and suites are particularly spacious. Public areas include a selection of comfortable lounges, the Camilaun Restaurant that overlooks the garden, Blazers bistro and bar, and extensive banqueting and leisure facilities.

Rooms 125 (17 fmly) (8 GF) (16 smoking) ☂ **Facilities** Spa STV WiFi ⓧ supervised Gym Beauty treatment & analysis rooms Beauty salon ♫ New Year **Conf** Class 280 Board 100 Thtr 650 **Services** Lift **Parking** 380 **Notes** Closed 23 Dec pm & 24-26 Dec Civ Wed 650

Park House Hotel & Restaurant

★★★★ 79% ⚙ HOTEL

tel: 091 564924 **Forster St, Eyre Square**
email: parkhousehotel@eircom.net **web:** www.parkhousehotel.ie
dir: In city centre/Eyre Sq

Situated just off Eyre Square, this well established hotel offers comfortable facilities to suit business or leisure guests. Public areas and bedrooms are well appointed and attractively decorated. The Park Restaurant has been a popular spot for the people of Galway for many years; less formal food is available throughout the day in Boss Doyle's bar. Parking for hotel guests is available at the rear.

Rooms 84 (4 smoking) ☂ **Facilities** STV FTV WiFi ↔ ♫ **Conf** Class 15 Board 15 Thtr 15 **Services** Lift Air con **Parking** 48 **Notes** ⓧ Closed 24-26 Dec

Garryvoe Hotel

★★★★ 79% ⚙ HOTEL

IRISH COUNTRY HOTELS

tel: 021 4646718 **Ballycotton Bay, Castlemartyr**
email: res@garryvoehotel.com **web:** www.garryvoehotel.com
dir: N25 onto L72 at Castlemartyr (between Midleton & Youghal). 6km to hotel

In a delightful location facing the beach and overlooking Ballycotton Island and Bay, this is a comfortable, family-run hotel with caring staff. The bedrooms are appointed to a very high standard; some have balconies. The popular bar serves light meals throughout the day, and a more formal dinner menu is available in the dining room. There are extensive banqueting and excellent health club facilities.

Rooms 82 (17 fmly) (5 smoking) **Facilities** STV WiFi ↔ ⓧ supervised Putt green Gym Sauna Steam room ♫ **Conf** Class 150 Board 12 Thtr 300 **Services** Lift **Parking** 100 **Notes** ⓧ Closed 24-25 Dec Civ Wed 150

The Lodge at Castle Leslie Estate

★★★★ 81% ⚙⚙ HOTEL

tel: 047 88100
email: info@castleleslie.com **web:** www.castleleslie.com
dir: M1 junct 14, N2 to Monaghan, N12 to N185 to Glaslough

Set in 1,000 acres of rolling countryside dotted with mature woodland, the lodge is the social hub of the Castle Leslie Estate which has been in the Leslie family since the 1660s. The comfortably furnished bedrooms are in the original hunting lodge and the converted stable block. Resident guests have two dining options - Snaffles Restaurant and Connors Bar. There is a Victorian spa, a successful equestrian centre and a private fishing lake. For those who enjoy country pursuits this hotel is ideal for the many walks and interesting flora and fauna that the area has to offer.

Rooms 29 (2 fmly) (10 GF) ☂ **S** €140-€210; **D** €160-€230 (incl. bkfst)*
Facilities Spa STV FTV WiFi 🏊 Fishing Horse riding Kayaking Clay Pigeon Falconry Boating Hot air balloon rides **Conf** Class 25 Board 24 Thtr 35 **Services** Lift **Parking** 100 **Notes** LB ⓧ Closed 24-27 Dec Civ Wed 40

The Glendalough Hotel

★★★ 73% HOTEL

tel: 0404 45135 & 45391
email: info@glendaloughhotel.ie **web:** www.glendaloughhotel.com
dir: N11 to Kilmacongue, right onto R755, straight on at Laragh, right onto R756

Mountains and forest provide the setting for this long-established hotel at the edge of the famed monastic site, and many of the comfortably appointed bedrooms have superb forest views. Food is served daily in the very popular bar and on the terrace when weather permits. The renovated Glendasan River Restaurant is a stylish bistro where dinner is served, while the atmospheric Glendalough Tavern is a popular meeting place for visitors and locals alike.

Rooms 44 (3 fmly) **Facilities** STV WiFi Fishing ♫ **Conf** Class 150 Board 50 Thtr 200 **Services** Lift **Parking** 100 **Notes** ⓧ RS Dec-Jan, Mon-Fri

Seafield Golf & Spa Hotel

★★★★ 80% ⚙⚙ HOTEL

tel: 053 942 4000 **Ballymoney**
email: reservations@seafieldhotel.com **web:** www.seafieldhotel.com
dir: M11 exit 22

This ultra-modern hotel is part of a village style resort that includes an 18-hole championship golf course, courtyard family suites and the award-winning Oceo Spa. Set in 225 acres of parkland with mature trees, river-side walks and access onto Ballymoney Beach, the hotel offers contemporary, spacious bedrooms and suites which have views of either the coastline or the golf course. There are two dining options - fine dining in the restaurant, and a more casual option in the bar or on the terrace.

Rooms 101 ☂ **Facilities** Spa STV WiFi ↔ ⓧ ♪ 18 Putt green Gym Playground ♫ New Year Child facilities **Conf** Class 220 Board 40 Thtr 300 **Services** Lift **Parking** 200 **Notes** ⓧ Civ Wed 280

GOREY *continued*

Amber Springs Hotel

★★★★ 80% HOTEL

tel: 053 9484000 **Wexford Rd**
email: info@ambersprings.ie **web:** www.ambersprings.ie
dir: 500mtrs from Gorey by-pass at junct 23

This hotel, on the Wexford road, is within walking distance of the town. Bedrooms are spacious and very comfortable, and guests have full use of the leisure facilities. Dining in Kelby's Bistro is a highlight of a visit, with a combination of interesting food and really friendly service.

Rooms 80 (34 fmly) (24 GF) **Facilities** Spa STV WiFi supervised Gym Mini golf Petting farm Kids train New Year **Conf** Class 450 Board 30 Thtr 700 **Services** Lift Air con **Parking** 178 **Notes** Closed 25-26 Dec Civ Wed 700

Ashdown Park Hotel

★★★★ 76% HOTEL

tel: 053 9480500 **The Coach Rd**
email: info@ashdownparkhotel.com **web:** www.ashdownparkhotel.com
dir: N11 junct 22, on approaching Gorey, 1st left (before railway bridge), hotel on left

Situated on an elevated position overlooking the town, this modern hotel has excellent health, leisure and banqueting facilities. There are comfortable lounge areas and two dining options - Ivy, a popular carvery bar, and The Rowan Tree, the first-floor fine dining restaurant open in the evenings. Bedrooms are available in a number of styles; all are spacious and well equipped. Close to a number of golf courses, this property is popular with golfers, and also with families as it is near the beaches.

Rooms 79 (17 fmly) (22 GF) **S** €80-€150; **D** €110-€300 (incl. bkfst)*
Facilities Spa FTV WiFi supervised Gym Leisure centre Massage rooms New Year Child facilities **Conf** Class 315 Board 100 Thtr 800 **Services** Lift **Parking** 150 **Notes** LB Closed 25 Dec Civ Wed 300

INSPECTORS' CHOICE

Marlfield House Hotel

★★★ COUNTRY HOUSE HOTEL

tel: 053 9421124
email: info@marlfieldhouse.ie **web:** www.marlfieldhouse.com
dir: N11 junct 23, follow signs for Courtown. At Courtown Rd rdbt left for Gorey. Hotel 1m on left

This Regency-style building has been gracefully extended and developed into an excellent hotel. An atmosphere of elegance and luxury permeates every corner of the house, underpinned by truly friendly and professional service led by the Bowe family who are always in evidence. The bedrooms are decorated in keeping with the style of the house, with some really spacious rooms and suites on the ground floor. Dinner in the restaurant is always a highlight of a stay at Marlfield.

Rooms 19 (3 fmly) (6 GF) **Facilities** FTV WiFi Beauty treatment room **Conf** Board 24 Thtr 60 **Parking** 100 **Notes** Closed 2 Jan-28 Feb RS Nov-Dec & Mar-Apr Civ Wed 120

INSPECTORS' CHOICE

Sheen Falls Lodge

★★★★★ COUNTRY HOUSE HOTEL

tel: 06466 41600
email: info@sheenfallslodge.ie **web:** www.sheenfallslodge.ie
dir: From Kenmare take N71 to Glengarriff over suspension bridge, take 1st left

This former fishing lodge has been developed into a beautiful hotel with a friendly team of professional staff. The cascading Sheen Falls are floodlit at night, forming a romantic backdrop to award-winning cuisine in La Cascade Restaurant. Less formal dining is available in Oscar's Bistro, and the Sun Lounge serves refreshments and light snacks throughout the day. The bedrooms are very comfortably appointed; many of the suites are particularly spacious. The leisure centre and beauty therapy facilities offer a number of exclusive treatments, and outdoor pursuits include walking, fishing, tennis, horse riding and clay pigeon shooting.

Rooms 66 (14 fmly) (14 GF) **S** €120-€240; **D** €160-€300 (incl. bkfst)*
Facilities Spa STV WiFi supervised Fishing Table tennis Steam room Clay pigeon shooting Cycling Vintage car rides Library Xmas New Year **Conf** Class 65 Board 50 Thtr 120 Del from €295 to €400* **Services** Lift **Parking** 76 **Notes** LB Closed 30 Nov-19 Dec & 2 Jan-1 Feb RS 24-27 Dec Civ Wed 100

KILKENNY
County Kilkenny — Map 1 C3

Kilkenny River Court Hotel

★★★★ 78% HOTEL

tel: 056 7723388 **The Bridge, John St**
email: reservations@rivercourthotel.com **web:** www.rivercourthotel.com
dir: In town centre, opposite castle

Hidden behind archways on John Street, this is a very comfortable and welcoming establishment. The restaurant, bar and many of the well-equipped bedrooms command great views of Kilkenny Castle and the River Nore. Attentive, friendly staff ensure good service throughout the hotel. Excellent corporate and leisure facilities are provided.

Rooms 90 (4 fmly) ⚡ **Facilities** Spa STV WiFi ⓢ 🞰 supervised Gym Steam room **Conf** Class 110 Board 45 Thtr 260 **Services** Lift **Parking** 84 **Notes** ⊗ Closed 23-26 Dec Civ Wed 210

Langton House Hotel

★★★★ 76% HOTEL

tel: 056 7765133 & 7721728 **69 John St**
email: reservations@langtons.ie **web:** www.langtons.ie
dir: N9 & N10 from Dublin, follow city centre signs on outskirts of Kilkenny, left to Langtons. Hotel 500mtrs on left after lights

This hotel, situated in the heart of the medieval city of Kilkenny, has long had a well-deserved reputation for its genuine hospitality as a vibrant entertainment venue with many strings to its bow. There is a nightclub with free access for resident guests and up to seven bars to choose from. The most recent addition is the much talked about Set Theatre, where leading performers take to the stage. There is a range of bedroom options, many in the garden annexe; all are very comfortable and smartly decorated, with the junior suites in the main house being particularly well appointed. Eating options include The Langton, a busy restaurant serving dinner, and the more casual, all-day '67', a lively bar popular with visitors and locals that features live music groups most evenings. The elegant Tea Room is open throughout the day.

Rooms 34 (16 annexe) (4 fmly) (8 GF) (22 smoking) **Facilities** STV FTV WiFi 🎵 New Year **Conf** Class 250 Board 30 Thtr 400 **Services** Air con **Parking** 60 **Notes** Closed 24-25 Dec Civ Wed 252

KILLARNEY
County Kerry — Map 1 B2

Muckross Park Hotel & Cloisters Spa

★★★★ 85% HOTEL

tel: 064 6623400 **Lakes of Killarney**
email: info@muckrosspark.com **web:** www.muckrosspark.com
dir: From Killarney take N71 towards Kenmare. Hotel is 4km from town centre

Dating originally from 1795, this fine property offers spacious accommodation and excellent public areas. Most of the bedrooms are in a recently developed block to the rear, with some in the original building, retaining many of the original features. All of the rooms and suites are beautifully appointed, with high quality fabrics and furnishings. Casual dining is available throughout the day in the old world atmosphere of Molly Darcy's pub, with more formal dining in the Blue Pool or GB Shaw's Restaurants. The Cloisters Spa is an oasis of calm and tranquillity, with a wide range of treatments available.

Rooms 68 (3 fmly) ⚡ **S** €90-€260; **D** €130-€300 (incl. bkfst) **Facilities** Spa STV WiFi ⓢ 🞰 Gym Cycling Yoga Pilates Free bike hire Guided walks Kayaking 🎵 New Year **Conf** Class 250 Board 60 Thtr 350 Del from €150 to €350 **Services** Lift Air con **Parking** 80 **Notes** LB ⊗ Closed Nov-Jan wkdays Civ Wed 270

Cahernane House Hotel

★★★★ 80% ◉◉ HOTEL

tel: 064 6631895 **Muckross Rd**
email: info@cahernane.com **web:** www.cahernane.com
dir: On N22 to Killarney, take 1st exit off rdbt then left at church, 1st exit at next rdbt to Muckross Rd

This fine country mansion, the former home of the Earls of Pembroke, has a magnificent mountain backdrop and panoramic views from its lakeside setting, yet is only a ten minute walk from the town centre. Elegant period furniture is complemented by more modern pieces to create a comfortable hotel offering a warm atmosphere with a particularly friendly team dedicated to guest care. A number of accommodation options are available, some in the original house, others in a more recent building accessed by a stunning conservatory. Dinner in the Herbert Room is a highlight of a stay at this property, with more casual fare on offer in the cosy Cellar Bar.

Rooms 38 (26 annexe) ⚡ **Facilities** WiFi 🎣 Fishing ⚓ **Conf** Class 10 Board 10 Thtr 15 **Services** Lift Air con **Parking** 50 **Notes** ⊗ Closed 21 Dec-Jan Civ Wed 60

The Lake Hotel

★★★★ 75% HOTEL

tel: 064 6631035 **Lake Shore, Muckross Rd**
email: info@lakehotel.com **web:** www.lakehotel.com
dir: N22 to Killarney. Hotel 2km from town on Muckross Rd

Enjoying a delightful location on the shores of Killarney's lake shore, this hotel is run by a second generation of the Huggard family together with a dedicated and friendly team. There is a relaxed atmosphere, with log fires and stunning views from the lounges and restaurant. Guests could be lucky enough to see a herd of red deer wander by. The smartly furnished bedrooms have either lake or woodland views; some have balconies and four-poster beds. The spa offers good facilities, and there are cycle paths and lovely walks to enjoy.

Rooms 130 (6 fmly) (23 GF) ⚡ **S** €75-€300; **D** €110-€350 (incl. bkfst)* **Facilities** Spa STV FTV WiFi 🎣 Fishing ⚓ Gym Sauna Steam room 🎵 **Conf** Class 60 Board 40 Thtr 80 Del from €230 to €250 **Services** Lift **Parking** 140 **Notes** LB ⊗ Closed 6 Dec-Jan Civ Wed 60

Castlerosse Hotel & Holiday Homes

★★★ 79% HOTEL

tel: 064 6631144 **Lakes of Killarney**
email: res@castlerosse.ie **web:** www.castlerosse.ie
dir: From Killarney take R562 signed Killorglin & The Ring of Kerry. Hotel 2.5km from town on left

This hotel is situated on 6,000 acres overlooking the Lakes of Killarney with the Magillycuddy Mountains as a backdrop. At times guests may be able to spot deer in Killarney National Park. Bedrooms and junior suites are well appointed and comfortable. There is live entertainment most nights in Mulligan's pub. Leisure facilities include a 9-hole parkland golf course, tennis courts, a leisure centre and treatment rooms.

Rooms 120 (27 fmly) ⚡ **S** €55-€110; **D** €80-€180 (incl. bkfst) **Facilities** STV FTV WiFi ⓢ 🞰 supervised ⚓ 9 ⚓ Putt green Gym Beauty treatment room Cycling Golf & horse riding arranged 🎵 **Conf** Class 100 Board 40 Thtr 200 Del from €85 to €110* **Services** Lift **Parking** 100 **Notes** LB ⊗ Closed Nov-Mar Civ Wed 80

REPUBLIC OF IRELAND

KILLINEY
County Dublin

Map 1 D4

Fitzpatrick Castle Hotel

★★★★ 81% HOTEL

tel: 01 2305400 & 2305556
email: reservations@fitzpatricks.com **web:** www.fitzpatrickcastle.com
dir: From Dun Laoghaire port turn left, on coast road right at lights, left at next lights. Follow to Dalkey, right at Ivory Pub, immediate left, up hill, hotel at top

This family-owned, 18th-century castle is situated in lovely gardens with mature trees and spectacular views over Dublin Bay. The original castle rooms are appointed to a high standard and have four-poster beds, while the rooms in the modern wing are spacious and some have balconies. Lounges are comfortably furnished, and PJ's restaurant serves dinner on certain days of the week; more casual fare is available each night in the trendy Dungeon bar and grill. There are extensive leisure and conference facilities.

Rooms 113 (36 fmly) (12 smoking) ⟨S €99-€270; **D** €109-€300 **Facilities** STV WiFi supervised Gym Beauty/hairdressing salon Sauna Steam room Fitness centre Xmas New Year **Conf** Class 250 Board 80 Thtr 500 Del from €170 to €250 **Services** Lift **Parking** 300 **Notes** LB RS 25-Dec Civ Wed 400

KILMESSAN
County Meath

Map 1 C/D4

The Station House Hotel

★★★ 75% HOTEL

tel: 046 9025239 & 9025586
email: info@stationhousehotel.ie **web:** www.stationhousehotel.ie
dir: M50, N3 towards Navan. At Dunshaughlin left at end of village, follow signs

While the Station House saw its last train in the early sixties, it still retains much of its railway history and atmosphere. Some of the accommodation is located in the old carriage house, and the signal box is the bridal suite; the station itself hosts diners in the station master's office. The bedrooms are comfortably appointed, and the lounge areas are very relaxing. Set in attractively landscaped gardens and woodlands, this is a popular wedding venue. Dinner is always a highlight, featuring well-sourced ingredients cooked with both flair and care.

Rooms 20 (14 annexe) (3 fmly) (5 GF) ⟨S €55-€95; **D** €130-€180 (incl. bkfst) **Facilities** WiFi In-room beauty/spa treatments Xmas New Year **Conf** Class 300 Board 100 Thtr 400 Del from €109 to €159 **Parking** 200 **Notes** LB Civ Wed 100

KINGSCOURT
County Cavan

Map 1 C4

Cabra Castle Hotel

★★★★ 80% HOTEL

tel: 042 9667030
email: sales@cabracastle.com **web:** www.cabracastle.com
dir: R165 between Kingscourt & Carrickmacross

Nestled in over 100 acres of parkland and manicured gardens, this family-run property offers a selection of accommodation styles. Some rooms are in the 19th-century castle building, with the balance in a number of courtyard buildings at the rear. Weddings are a particular feature of the business of the castle, due to really spectacular facilities and an outstanding reputation. The Courtroom is the principal dining area of the castle, a series of first floor elegantly appointed rooms where dinner is a highlight of a visit. All day dining is offered in The Derby Bar, or on the Terrace when weather permits. Leisure pursuits on the grounds include 9-hole golf and tennis, with horse riding and fishing available nearby.

Rooms 105 (88 annexe) (10 fmly) (48 GF) ⟨S €85-€142; **D** €110-€222 (incl. bkfst)* **Facilities** WiFi 9 **Conf** Class 160 Board 60 Thtr 200 Del from €155 to €195* **Parking** 200 **Notes** Closed 24-27 Dec Civ Wed 350

KINSALE
County Cork

Map 1 B2

Carlton Hotel Kinsale

★★★★ 79% HOTEL

tel: 021 4706000 **Rathmore Rd**
email: reservations.kinsale@carlton.ie **web:** www.carlton.ie
dir: R600 to Kinsale, turn left signed Charles Fort. 3kms, (pass rugby club), hotel on left

This recently-built hotel is set on an elevated position overlooking Oysterhaven Bay in 90 acres of mature parkland, approximately five kilometres from the town centre. All of the bedrooms are spacious and well appointed, many with spectacular views over the bay. Two-bedroom holiday apartment options are available in the grounds. The contemporary public rooms are on the first floor, with spacious terraces. They include the Rockpool Restaurant where guests can cook fine Angus steaks on lava stones at their table. The team at this property are all very guest focused, and make families particularly welcome.

Rooms 130 (60 annexe) (20 fmly) (24 GF) **Facilities** Spa STV FTV WiFi supervised Gym Sauna Steam room New Year **Conf** Class 150 Board 40 Thtr 250 **Services** Lift Air con **Parking** 140 **Notes** Closed 23-27 Dec Civ Wed 200

Blue Haven Hotel

★★★ 75% HOTEL

tel: 021 4772209 **3/4 Pearse St**
email: info@bluehavenkinsale.com **web:** www.bluehavenkinsale.com
dir: In town centre

At the heart of this historic town, this vibrant hotel offers a comfortable lounge and café, a very popular and stylish bar with an airy bistro plus an elegant restaurant. Live music is a feature seven days a week in high season, and five days in low season. Bedrooms vary in size and are furnished to a high standard.

Rooms 17 ⟨S €55-€95; **D** €70-€160 (incl. bkfst) **Facilities** FTV WiFi New Year **Conf** Class 35 Board 25 Thtr 100 **Notes** Closed 25 Dec Civ Wed 70

The White House

 RESTAURANT WITH ROOMS

tel: 021 4772125 📠 021 4772045 **Pearse St, The Glen**
email: whitehse@indigo.ie **web:** www.whitehouse-kinsale.ie
dir: In town centre

Centrally located among the narrow, twisting streets of the charming maritime town of Kinsale, this restaurant with rooms dates from 1850. It is a welcoming hostelry with smart, comfortably appointed contemporary bedrooms. The atmospheric bar and bistro are open for lunch and dinner, with Restaurant d'Antibes also open during the evenings. The varied menu features local fish and beef. The courtyard at the rear makes a perfect setting in summer and there is regular entertainment in the bar.

Rooms 10 (2 fmly)

LETTERKENNY Map 1 C5
County Donegal

Radisson Blu Hotel Letterkenny

★★★★ 79% 🅰 HOTEL

tel: 074 9194444 **Paddy Harte Rd**
email: info.letterkenny@radissonblu.com **web:** www.radissonblu.ie/hotel-letterkenny
dir: N14 into Letterkenny. At Polestar Rdbt take 1st exit, to hotel

Letterkenny is an ideal base for visiting the many peninsulas of County Donegal. Within walking distance of the town and the retail parks, this hotel offers a range of very comfortable rooms, with all the facilities that today's traveller expects. Guests can dine throughout the day in the popular Oakk Bar & Grill, or, in the evening, enjoy seafood delights and other good dishes in Brasserie TriBeCa. Well-equipped meeting rooms are available, together with a large conference and banqueting hall. The leisure facilities are complimentary to residents.

Rooms 114 (5 fmly) (6 smoking) **Facilities** STV WiFi Gym Sauna Steam room Sunbed Olympic weights room Xmas New Year **Conf** Class 270 Thtr 600 **Services** Lift **Parking** 150 **Notes** ⊗ Civ Wed 600

Downings Bay Hotel

★★★ 75% HOTEL

tel: 074 9155586 & 9155770 **Downings**
email: info@downingsbayhotel.com **web:** www.downingsbayhotel.com
dir: 23m N of Letterkenny on R245. Hotel in village centre

This friendly family-run hotel is situated on Sheephaven Bay in the picturesque village of Downings. There is a cosy lounge; JC's a traditional style bar where an extensive menu is available all day, and The Haven Restaurant which opens for dinner. The bedroom accommodation is spacious and all rooms are comfortable and well appointed. A popular location for families and within easy reach of a number of golf courses, this property hosts occasional musical events, and there is a nightclub open at weekends. Guests have complimentary use of the local leisure centre.

Rooms 40 (8 fmly) (4 smoking) S €40-€80; D €40-€75 (incl. bkfst) **Facilities** WiFi supervised Gym Sauna Steam room Indoor adventure play area New Year Child facilities **Conf** Class 175 Board 50 Thtr 350 Del from €80 to €120 **Services** Lift Air con **Parking** 40 **Notes** LB ⊗ Closed 24-26 Dec Civ Wed 80

LIMERICK Map 1 B3
County Limerick

Limerick Strand Hotel

★★★★ 79% 🅰 HOTEL

tel: 061 421800 **Ennis Rd**
email: info@strandlimerick.ie **web:** www.strandlimerick.ie
dir: From Shannon/Galway follow N18 to Limerick. At Coonagh rdbt follow Ennis road into city centre. Hotel on right on banks of river

This hotel enjoys stunning views over the River Shannon, and all bedrooms are spacious and fitted to a high standard. The public areas make the most of the views, with meeting rooms on the penthouse level. All-day dining is available in the bar, with innovative evening meals served in the River Restaurant. Secure parking is available at a reduced rate for residents.

Rooms 184 (13 fmly) **Facilities** Spa STV WiFi supervised Gym Xmas New Year **Conf** Class 400 Board 50 Thtr 600 **Services** Lift Air con **Parking** 203 **Notes** ⊗ Civ Wed 450

LISDOONVARNA Map 1 B3
County Clare

Sheedy's Country House Hotel

★★★ 78% 🅰🅰 HOTEL

tel: 065 7074026
email: info@sheedys.com **web:** www.sheedys.com
dir: 200mtrs from The Square in town centre

Dating in part from the 17th century and set in an unrivalled town centre location on the edge of The Burren, this house is full of character and has an intimate atmosphere. Fine cuisine can be enjoyed in the contemporary restaurant, and the bedrooms are spacious and well appointed. Sheedys makes an ideal base for touring as it is close to Doolin, Lahinch Golf Course, and the Cliffs of Moher.

Rooms 11 (1 fmly) (5 GF) S €80-€120; D €99-€170 (incl. bkfst)* **Facilities** STV FTV WiFi **Parking** 40 **Notes** LB ⊗ Closed mid Oct-Apr

Wild Honey Inn

 RESTAURANT WITH ROOMS

tel: 065 7074300 📠 065 7074490 **Kincora**
email: info@wildhoneyinn.com **web:** www.wildhoneyinn.com
dir: N18 from Ennis to Ennistymon. Continue through Ennistymon towards Lisdoonvarna, located on the right at edge of town

Set in a former hotel dating from the 1860s, when the town prospered as a Spa, The Wild Honey Inn has created a solid reputation for its cuisine. 'Modern bistro style' is Aidan McGrath's description of the food on offer, which is served in the comfortable atmospheric bar area at both lunch and dinner. Great attention is placed on the provenance of the ingredients, most of which is organic and sourced as close to County Clare as possible. Reservations are not taken. Bedrooms come in a number of styles, with the garden rooms benefiting from private patios. Resident guests have the use of a relaxing lounge, filled with reading material, not surprisingly featuring food and cookery. Breakfast is also a highlight of a visit, with a range of interesting options.

Rooms 14

LUCAN
County Dublin
Map 1 D4

Finnstown Country House Hotel

★★★ 79% HOTEL

tel: 01 6010700 & 6010708 **Newcastle Rd**
email: edwina@finnstown-hotel.ie **web:** www.finnstown.com
dir: From M1 onto M50 S'bound. 1st exit for N4. Take slip road signed Newcastle/
Adamstown. Straight on at rdbt, through lights, hotel on right

Set in 45 acres of wooded grounds and paddocks, Finnstown House is a calm and
peaceful country property in an urban setting. The elegant bar and drawing room is
where informal meals are served throughout the day, with more formal dining at
lunch and dinner in the Peacock Restaurant. There is a wide choice of bedroom
styles, situated both in the main house and in the annexes. The staff members are
very guest focussed, with a warm and friendly approach. This is a very popular
venue for small conferences and family celebrations. A fitness centre is available to
resident guests.

Rooms 82 (54 annexe) (6 fmly) (9 GF) (12 smoking) **Facilities** STV WiFi
Gym Steam room New Year **Conf** Class 150 Board 50 Thtr 300 **Services** Lift
Air con **Parking** 300 **Notes** Closed 24-26 Dec Civ Wed 200

Lucan Spa Hotel

★★★ 67% HOTEL

tel: 01 6280494
email: info@lucanspahotel.ie **web:** www.lucanspahotel.ie
dir: At N4 junct 4a, approx 11km from city centre

Set in its own grounds and 20 minutes from Dublin Airport, close to the M50, the
Lucan Spa is a lovely Georgian house with a modern extension. Bedrooms vary in
size and are well equipped. There are two dining options; dinner is served in Honora
D Restaurant, and The Earl Bistro is for more casual dining. A conference centre is
also available.

Rooms 71 (15 fmly) (9 GF) **S** €50-€80; **D** €65-€120 (incl. bkfst) **Facilities** STV
FTV WiFi Access to Lucan Golf Club opp hotel **Conf** Class 250 Board 80
Thtr 600 **Services** Lift Air con **Parking** 200 **Notes** Closed 24-26 Dec Civ Wed 250

MACREDDIN
County Wicklow
Map 1 D3

BrookLodge Hotel & Macreddin Village

★★★★ 87% HOTEL

tel: 0402 36444
email: info@brooklodge.com **web:** www.brooklodge.com
dir: N11 to Rathnew, R752 to Rathdrum, R753 to Aughrim, follow signs to Macreddin
Village

BrookLodge is a luxury country-house hotel in a village-style setting which includes
an 18-hole golf course, a pub, café and food shop. There is a choice of dining
options - the award-winning Strawberry Tree Restaurant specialising in organic and
wild foods and a more casual Italian restaurant. Bedrooms and lounges in the
original house are very comfortable; there are also bedrooms in Brookhall, tailored
for guests attending weddings and conferences. The Wells Spa offers extensive
treatments and leisure facilities, and there are many outdoor activities including
horse riding and off-road driving.

Rooms 86 (32 annexe) (27 fmly) (4 GF) **Facilities** Spa STV FTV WiFi 18
Putt green Gym Archery Clay pigeon shooting Off road driving New Year
Conf Class 170 Board 150 Thtr 300 **Services** Lift Air con **Parking** 200 **Notes** Closed
24-25 Dec Civ Wed 200

MALLOW
County Cork

Map 1 B2

Springfort Hall Country House Hotel

★★★ 77% HOTEL

tel: 022 21278
email: stay@springfort-hall.com web: www.springfort-hall.com
dir: N20 onto R581 at Two Pot House, hotel 500mtrs on right

This 18th-century country manor is tucked away amid tranquil woodlands located just six kilometres from Mallow. There is an attractive oval dining room, a cosy drawing room and lounge bar where bistro-style food is served. The spacious bedrooms are comfortably furnished. There are extensive banqueting and conference facilities. Local amenities include championship golf courses, fishing on the Blackwater and Ballyhass Lakes, and horseracing at Cork Race course.

Rooms 49 (5 fmly) (17 GF) Facilities STV FTV WiFi ♫ Conf Class 180 Board 50 Thtr 360 Parking 200 Notes ⊗ Closed 23-26 Dec Civ Wed 300

MAYNOOTH
County Kildare

Map 1 D4

Carton House Hotel Golf & Spa

★★★★ 79% HOTEL

tel: 01 5052000
web: olawlor@cartonhouse.com
dir: From Dublin Airport follow M50, N4 then M4 towards Sligo. At junct 6 take R449 to Leixlip. Continue to R148. Located 4m outside Maynooth

The Carton House dates from 1739 and many of the features of that period are reflected in the careful renovation of the fine public rooms and event spaces. While some suites of the hotel are also in the original house, most of the bedrooms are in a modern block to the side. They are all spacious and comfortable, fitted out to a high standard. There are a number of dining options on the estate, including The Coach House in the golf club and The Linden Tree. Set in over a thousand acres, there are plenty of walks and cycle paths to be enjoyed. The property has a strong reputation for its many sport training facilities and Spa treatment rooms.

Rooms 165 (12 fmly) (46 GF) ♠ S €85-€405; D €100-€420 (incl. bkfst)*
Facilities Spa STV WiFi ⊗ ⅃ 36 ⅃ Putt green Fishing ⅃ Gym ♫ Xmas New Year Conf Class 280 Board 90 Thtr 500 Del from €190 to €240* Services Lift Parking 500 Notes ⊗ Civ Wed

MOHILL
County Leitrim

Map 1 C4

Lough Rynn Castle

★★★★ 78% HOTEL

tel: 071 9632700 & 9632714
email: enquiries@loughrynn.ie web: www.loughrynn.ie
dir: N4 (Dublin to Sligo), hotel 8km off N4 & 2km from Mohill

Once the ancestral home of Lord Leitrim, set in 300 acres of parkland, the castle offers a range of luxurious rooms and suites. The award-winning Sandstone Restaurant is an elegant dining option, and the many lounges are individually decorated; some feature antique furniture.

Rooms 43 (16 annexe) (5 fmly) (6 GF) ♠ S €80-€165; D €99-€185 (incl. bkfst) Facilities STV FTV WiFi ♫ Xmas New Year Conf Class 200 Board 30 Thtr 450 Services Air con Notes LB ⊗ Civ Wed 320

MOVILLE
County Donegal

Map 1 C6

Redcastle Hotel, Golf & Spa Resort

★★★★ 79% HOTEL

tel: 074 9385555 Inishowen Peninsula
email: info@redcastlehotel.com web: www.redcastlehotel.com
dir: On R238 between Derry & Greencastle

Perched beside the sea in mature parkland just outside Redcastle, this hotel has an enviable position on the Inishowen Peninsula with great views over Lough Foyle. It offers spacious, well-equipped bedrooms; some on the ground floor and some with balconies. The public areas include a range of relaxing lounges with an atmospheric bar where food is served throughout the day, and a large terrace for relaxing when the weather permits. The Edge Restaurant is right on the water's edge, and offers a well thought out menu with interesting options. There is a conference centre and an extensive leisure club offering spa treatments. The hotel has its own private 9-hole golf course, with sea fishing available from the shore.

Rooms 93 (17 fmly) (16 GF) (8 smoking) ♠ Facilities Spa STV FTV WiFi ⊗ ⊗ ⅃ 9 Putt green Fishing ⅃ Gym Thalasso therapy pool ♫ New Year Conf Class 150 Board 50 Thtr 300 Services Lift Parking 200 Notes ⊗ Civ Wed 250

MULRANY
County Mayo

Map 1 B4

Mulranny Park Hotel

★★★★ 79% HOTEL

tel: 098 36000
email: info@mulrannyparkhotel.ie web: www.mulrannyparkhotel.ie
dir: R311 from Castlebar to Newport onto N59. Hotel on right

Set on an elevated site, this property has commanding views over Clew Bay. Originally a railway hotel dating from the late 1800s, it has a range of smart public rooms that retain many of the period features. Bedrooms vary in size but are comfortable and decorated in a contemporary style. Dinner in the Nephin Restaurant is a highlight of any stay, with casual dining available throughout the day in the Waterfront Bar. A programme of activities is offered weekly for resident guests, in addition to a well appointed leisure club.

Rooms 61 (25 fmly) ♠ S €75-€105; D €100-€170 (incl. bkfst) Facilities WiFi ⊗ ⊗ supervised Gym Steam room Health & beauty Hairdressing Cycling ♫ New Year Conf Class 140 Board 50 Thtr 400 Del from €110 to €150 Services Lift Parking 200 Notes LB ⊗ Closed 4-21 Jan Civ Wed 150

NAVAN
County Meath

Map 1 D4

Bellinter House

HOTEL

tel: 046 9030900
web: www.bellinterhouse.com
dir: N3 towards Navan, left at Tara Na Ri pub, travel 5 mins, hotel on right

Currently the rating for this establishment is not confirmed. This may be due to a change of hands or because it has only recently joined the AA rating scheme. For further details please see the AA website: theAA.com

Rooms 34 (5 fmly) (12 GF) Facilities Spa STV FTV WiFi Fishing Steam room Sauna Conf Class 30 Board 24 Thtr 50 Services Lift Parking 80 Notes ⊗ Civ Wed 200

NEWMARKET-ON-FERGUS
County Clare

Map 1 B3

INSPECTORS' CHOICE

Dromoland Castle Hotel

★★★★★ @@ HOTEL

tel: 061 368144
email: sales@dromoland.ie **web:** www.dromoland.ie
dir: N18 to Ennis/Galway from Shannon for 8km to 'Dromoland Interchange' signed Quin. Take slip road left, 4th exit at 1st rdbt, 2nd exit at 2nd rdbt. Hotel 500mtrs on left

Dromoland Castle, dating from the early 18th century, stands on a 375-acre estate and offers extensive indoor leisure activities and outdoor pursuits. The professional team are wholly committed to caring for guests, in a warm and informal manner. The thoughtfully equipped bedrooms and suites vary in style, but they all provide excellent levels of comfort. The magnificent public rooms, warmed by log fires, are no less impressive. The hotel has several dining options; the elegant fine-dining Earl of Thomond Restaurant, where award-winning cuisine is available together with the less formal Fig Tree in the golf clubhouse, and The Gallery, which offers a menu suitable for all day dining.

Rooms 99 (20 fmly) ↑ **S** €225-€588; **D** €225-€662 **Facilities** Spa STV WiFi ⌂ ⊗ supervised ↨ 18 ⤵ Putt green Fishing Gym Archery Clay shooting Mountain bikes Falconry Pony & trap Golf academy ♫ Xmas New Year **Conf** Class 220 Board 80 Thtr 450 Del from €295 to €482 **Services** Lift **Parking** 120 **Notes** ⊗ Civ Wed 70

Carrygerry Country House Hotel

U

tel: 061 360500
email: info@carrygerryhouse.com **web:** www.carrygerryhouse.com
dir: N18 towards Shannon Airport then N19 at town rdbt turn right to Newmarket-on-Fergus after 450mtrs at small rdbt turn left, opposite Shannon Aerospace

Currently the rating for this establishment is not confirmed. This may be due to a change of ownership or because it has only recently joined the AA rating scheme. For further details please see the AA website: theAA.com

Rooms 11 (5 annexe) (1 fmly) (3 GF) **S** €65-€85; **D** €130-€155 (incl. bkfst)* **Facilities** STV FTV WiFi ⌂ **Conf** Class 40 Board 20 Thtr 60 Del from €110 to €130* **Parking** 30 **Notes** ⊗ Closed 23-28 Dec Civ Wed 60

NEWTOWN MOUNT KENNEDY
County Wicklow

Map 1 D3

Druids Glen Resort

★★★★★ 84% @ HOTEL

tel: 01 2870800
email: reservations@druidsglenresort.com **web:** www.druidsglenresort.com
dir: N11 S'bound, off at Newtown Mount Kennedy. Follow signs for hotel

This hotel, situated between the Wicklow Mountains and the coast, has two fabulous golf courses and a range of smart indoor leisure facilities and treatment rooms. Bedrooms have been equipped to the highest standard and service is delivered in a most professional manner, and always with a smile. Guests may choose to dine in Druid's Brasserie or the more formal Flynn's Restaurant.

Rooms 145 ↑ **S** fr €139; **D** fr €139 (incl. bkfst)* **Facilities** Spa STV WiFi ⌂ ↨ 18 Gym Sauna Steam room Indoor playroom Outdoor playground Giant games **Notes** Civ Wed 220

RATHMULLAN
County Donegal

Map 1 C6

Rathmullan House

★★★★ 80% @@ COUNTRY HOUSE HOTEL

tel: 074 9158188
email: info@rathmullanhouse.com **web:** www.rathmullanhouse.com
dir: From Letterkenny, then Ramelton then Rathmullan, R243. Left at Mace shop, through village, hotel gates on right

Dating from the 18th century, this fine property has been operating as a country-house hotel for the last 50 years under the stewardship of the Wheeler family. It is in a magical setting leading right on the shores of Lough Swilly. Guests are welcome to wander around the well-planted grounds and the walled garden, where many of the ingredients for the Weeping Elm Restaurant's seasonal menus are grown. The numerous lounges are relaxing and comfortable, many have welcoming log and turf fires. The bedrooms vary in size, but they are furnished to a high standard; many feature balconies and patio areas.

Rooms 34 (4 fmly) (9 GF) ↑ **S** €70-€125; **D** €140-€250 (incl. bkfst)* **Facilities** WiFi ⊗ ⤵ ⤴ Treatment room New Year **Conf** Class 90 Board 40 Thtr 135 Del from €150 to €195* **Parking** 80 **Notes** LB Closed 11 Jan-5 Feb RS 15 Nov-12 Mar Civ Wed 135

RATHNEW
County Wicklow

Map 1 D3

Tinakilly Country House

★★★★ 78% @@ HOTEL

tel: 0404 69274
email: info@tinakilly.ie **web:** www.tinakilly.ie
dir: Follow N11/M11 to Rathnew, then R750 towards Wicklow. Entrance to hotel approx 500mtrs from village on left

An elegant oak-lined avenue leads to Tinakilly House, a Victorian mansion steeped in history. It was built in 1884 for Captain Robert Halpin, Master Mariner and Commander of *SS Great Eastern* who laid the telegraphic cable joining Europe to America. There are lovely garden views from the lounges that have open log fires. Some of the comfortable bedrooms and suites enjoy views over the Irish Sea and bird sanctuary at Broadlough Costal Lagoon. Furnishings throughout reflect the Victorian period yet provide all modern comforts. Fine dining is available in the dining room, and snacks and afternoon tea are served in the drawing room.

Rooms 51 (15 fmly) (14 GF) ↑ **Facilities** STV WiFi ⌂ ♫ New Year **Conf** Class 70 Board 35 Thtr 90 **Services** Lift **Parking** 60 **Notes** ⊗ Closed 24-26 Dec Civ Wed 100

Hunter's Hotel

 ★★★ 78%  HOTEL

tel: 0404 40106
email: reception@hunters.ie **web:** www.hunters.ie
dir: 1.5km from village of Rathnew. From Dublin, N11/M11 exit 15, turn left at bridge in Ashford, follow signs to hotel

One of Ireland's oldest coaching inns, this charming country house was built in 1720 and is full of character and atmosphere. The comfortable bedrooms have wonderful views over prize-winning gardens that border the River Vartry. The restaurant has a good reputation for carefully prepared dishes which make the best use of high quality local produce, including fruit and vegetables from the hotel's own garden.

Rooms 16 (2 fmly) (2 GF) **S** €65-€95; **D** €130-€190 (incl. bkfst)* **Facilities** WiFi **Conf** Class 40 Board 16 Thtr 40 Del from €110 to €130 **Parking** 50 **Notes** LB ⊗ Closed 24-26 Dec Civ Wed 40

RECESS (SRAITH SALACH)
County Galway

Map 1 A4

INSPECTORS' CHOICE

Lough Inagh Lodge Hotel

★★★ ◉◉ COUNTRY HOUSE HOTEL

tel: 095 34706 & 34694 **Inagh Valley,**
email: inagh@iol.ie **web:** www.loughinaghlodgehotel.ie
dir: From Recess take R344 towards Kylemore

Dating from 1880, this former fishing lodge is akin to a family home, where guests are encouraged to relax and enjoy the peace. Overlooking Lough Inagh, and situated amid the mountains of Connemara, it is in an ideal location for those who enjoy walking and fishing. Bedrooms are individually decorated, some with spacious seating areas, and each is dedicated to an Irish literary figure. There are two cosy lounges where welcoming turf fires are often lit. Informal dining from a bar menu is available during the day. Dinner is a highlight of a visit to the lodge; the menus feature locally sourced produce cooked with care - seafood is a speciality.

Rooms 13 (1 fmly) (4 GF) **Facilities** WiFi Fly fishing Cycling **Conf** Class 20 Board 20 Thtr 20 **Services** Air con **Parking** 16 **Notes** Closed mid Dec-mid Mar Civ Wed 50

ROSAPENNA
County Donegal

Map 1 C6

Rosapenna Hotel & Golf Resort

★★★★ 78% HOTEL

tel: 074 9155128
email: reservations@rosapenna.ie **web:** www.rosapenna.ie

Adjoining the 800-acre Dunes System and a number of links golf courses, The Rosapenna Hotel has been welcoming guests for over a century. Bedrooms come in a number of styles, with some having balconies making the most of the wonderful rugged views. The public rooms all offer great space, with lots of comfortable relaxing lounge options. The Vardon Restaurant offers a well compiled menu, featuring the best of Donegal produce, and of course, the freshest of seafood.

Rooms 63 (6 fmly) (31 GF) **Facilities** STV FTV WiFi ⌕ ⊛ supervised ⌘ 45 ⌁ Putt green Treatment room Snooker room Table tennis ♫ **Services** Lift **Notes** Civ Wed 100

ROSCOMMON
County Roscommon

Map 1 B4

Kilronan Castle Estate & Spa

★★★★ 78% HOTEL

tel: 071 9618000 **Ballyfarnon**
email: enquiries@kilronancastle.ie **web:** www.kilronancastle.ie
dir: M4 to N4, exit R299 towards R207 Droim ar Snámh/Drumsna/Droim. Exit R207 for R280, turn left Keadue Road R284

Located on the shores of Lough Meelagh, this recently restored Gothic revival castle dates from the early 19th century. It is set in almost 50 acres of rolling park and woodland. Great care has been taken in its restoration, with many of the fine bedrooms and suites in the adjoining sympathetically built modern block. The Drawing Room is now a cosy lounge serving food throughout the day. The highlight however is dinner in the Douglas Hyde Restaurant, where the friendly professional team go to great lengths to offer fine food in elegant surroundings. The impressive Spa has a wide range of treatments on offer. There is also a leisure centre together with a wonderful events centre accessed by a tunnel from the main building.

Rooms 84 (9 fmly) ⌕ **S** €99-€179; **D** €99-€199 (incl. bkfst) **Facilities** Spa FTV WiFi ⊛ Gym ♫ Xmas New Year **Conf** Class 360 Board 60 Thtr 500 Del from €199 to €249 **Services** Lift Air con **Parking** 300 **Notes** LB ⊗ Civ Wed 200

REPUBLIC OF IRELAND

ROSSLARE
County Wexford

Map 1 D2

INSPECTORS' CHOICE

Kelly's Resort Hotel & Spa

★★★★ ◉◉ ⦿ HOTEL

tel: 053 9132114
email: info@kellys.ie **web:** www.kellys.ie
dir: N25 onto Rosslare/Wexford road, signed Rosslare Strand

The Kelly family have been offering hospitality here since 1895, where together with a dedicated team, they provide very professional and friendly service. The resort overlooks the sandy beach and is within minutes of the ferry port at Rosslare. Bedrooms are thoughtfully equipped and comfortably furnished. The extensive leisure facilities include a smart spa, swimming pools, a crèche, young adults' programme and spacious well-tended gardens. Both the eating options, La Marine Bistro and Beaches restaurant, have been awarded AA Rosettes for the quality of their cuisine.

Rooms 118 (15 fmly) (20 GF) ⦿ **Facilities** Spa STV FTV WiFi ⦿ supervised ⦿ ⦿ Putt green ⦿ Gym Bowls Badminton Crazy golf Table tennis Snooker Sauna Steam room ⦿ **Conf** Class 30 Board 20 Thtr 30 **Services** Lift **Parking** 150 **Notes** ⊗ Closed early Dec-late Feb

SALTHILL

See Galway

SKIBBEREEN
County Cork

Map 1 B2

West Cork Hotel

★★★ 75% HOTEL

tel: 028 21277 **Ilen St**
email: info@westcorkhotel.com **web:** www.westcorkhotel.com
dir: In Skibbereen, N71 into Bridge St, with Baby Hannah's pub on left to right into Ilen St, hotel on right. From Cork Road, N71 to Schull, left at next rdbt towards town centre, hotel on left

This charming hotel was built in 1902 and is family owned and run. It is located in the centre of town beside the River Ilen, where guests can enjoy an outdoor drink while sitting on the historic old West Cork railway bridge. There is a cosy lounge with log fire and furnishings and decor that are a successful mix the best of old and new. Food is available throughout the day in the Railway Bar and in the evening in Kennedy's Restaurant. Bedrooms vary in size and are comfortably

furnished, some with riverside views. There are extensive banqueting facilities and ample car parking at the rear of the hotel.

Rooms 34 (4 fmly) ⦿ **Facilities** FTV WiFi Use of facilities at Skibbereen Sports Centre **Conf** Class 20 Board 24 Thtr 250 **Services** Lift **Parking** 100 **Notes** ⊗ Closed 24-28 Dec Civ Wed 300

SLANE
County Meath

Map 1 D4

Conyngham Arms Hotel

★★★ 74% HOTEL

tel: 041 984444 **Main St**
email: info@conynghamarms.ie **web:** www.conynghamarms.ie
dir: From N2 north in village at x-rds take N51 (left), hotel 100yds on left

This 17th-century coaching inn has been beautifully refurbished to a high standard of comfort and quality, and is situated in the centre of Slane village, close to Slane Castle and the World Heritage site of Newgrange and many other historical sites. The bedrooms vary in size due to the age of the house and are very smartly appointed with guest comfort in mind. Food is bistro style featuring the best of local produce, and breads and confectionary from their own bakery, served throughout the day in the cosy bar with an open log fire. There is private off-street parking available.

Rooms 15 ⦿ **Facilities** FTV WiFi **Conf** Class 100 Board 50 Thtr 200 **Parking** 20 **Notes** ⊗ Civ Wed 200

SLIGO
County Sligo

Map 1 B5

The Glasshouse

★★★★ 79% ◉ HOTEL

tel: 071 9194300 **Swan Point**
email: info@theglasshouse.ie **web:** www.theglasshouse.ie
dir: From N4 right at 2nd junct. Left at Post Office into Wine St. Hotel on right

This landmark building in the centre of town makes a bold statement with its cutting edge design and contemporary decor. Bright cheerful colours are used throughout the hotel; the bedrooms have excellent facilities including LCD TVs, workspace and internet access. There is a café bar serving food throughout the day, with a board walk for alfresco riverside dining. More formal evening dining takes place in the Kitchen restaurant. Secure underground parking is complimentary to residents, and preferential terms have been arranged at a nearby leisure and fitness facility.

Rooms 116 ⦿ S €70-€200; D €70-€200* **Facilities** STV FTV WiFi New Year **Conf** Class 100 Board 60 Thtr 120 **Services** Lift **Parking** 250 **Notes** LB ⊗ Closed 24-25 Dec Civ Wed 120

Radisson Blu Hotel & Spa Sligo

★★★★ 79% ◉ HOTEL

tel: 071 9140008 **Rosses Point Rd, Ballincar**
email: info.sligo@radissonblu.com **web:** www.radissonblu.ie/hotel-sligo
dir: From N4 into Sligo to main bridge. Take R291 on left. Hotel 1.5m on right

Located three kilometres north of the town overlooking Sligo Bay, this contemporary hotel offers standard and business class bedrooms which are all appointed with up-to-date facilities. The Benwiskin bar offers tasty casual dining throughout the day, and for formal dining in the evening there's Classiebawn Restaurant. Residents are welcome to use Healthstyles leisure club during their stay, and spa treatment facilities are also available. A range of eleven rooms are provided for meetings and events.

Rooms 132 (13 fmly) (32 GF) **Facilities** Spa STV WiFi Gym Steam room Thermal suite Sauna ♫ Xmas New Year **Conf** Class 420 Board 40 Thtr 750 **Services** Lift Air con **Parking** 320 **Notes** Civ Wed 750

Sligo Park Hotel & Leisure Club

★★★★ 76% HOTEL

tel: 071 9190400 **Pearse Rd**
email: sligo@leehotels.com **web:** www.sligopark.com
dir: N4 to Sligo take exit S2 (Sligo Sth) Carrowroe/R287. Follow signs for Sligo. Hotel 1m on right

Set in seven acres on the southern side of town, this hotel is well positioned for visiting the many attractions of the north west and Yeats' Country. Bedrooms are spacious and appointed to a high standard. There are two dining options, plus good leisure and banqueting facilities.

Rooms 136 (10 fmly) (52 GF) (23 smoking) **Facilities** WiFi supervised Gym Holistic treatment suite Plunge pool Steam room ♫ Xmas New Year **Conf** Class 290 Board 80 Thtr 520 **Services** Lift **Parking** 200 **Notes** RS 24-26 Dec Civ Wed 520

STRAFFAN
County Kildare

Map 1 D4

The K Club

★★★★★ COUNTRY HOUSE HOTEL

tel: 01 6017200
email: sales@kclub.ie **web:** www.kclub.ie
dir: From Dublin take N4, exit for R406, hotel on right in Straffan

The K Club is set in 550 acres of rolling woodland. There are two magnificent championship golf courses, and a spa facility that complements the truly luxurious hotel that is the centrepiece of the resort. Public areas, suites and bedrooms are opulently furnished, and many have views of the formal gardens that lead down to the banks of the River Liffey. Dining options include the elegant River Room, with more informal dining options offered in Legends in the Golf Pavilion. There is also a Thai restaurant in the resort.

Rooms 69 (10 fmly) **D** fr €220 (incl. bkfst)* **Facilities** Spa STV FTV WiFi supervised 36 Putt green Fishing Gym Beauty salon Fishing tuition Clay pigeon shooting Horse riding Falconry ♫ Xmas New Year **Conf** Class 300 Board 160 Thtr 300 **Services** Lift **Parking** 205 **Notes** LB

Barberstown Castle

★★★★ 80% HOTEL

tel: 01 6288157
email: info@barberstowncastle.ie **web:** www.barberstowncastle.ie
dir: R406, follow signs for Barberstown

With parts dating from the 13th century, this castle hotel provides the very best in standards of comfort. The inviting public areas range from the original keep, which houses one of the restaurant areas, to the warmth of the drawing room and its cocktail bar. Bedrooms, some in a purpose-built wing, are elegantly appointed with relaxing seating areas. The airy Tea Room serves light meals throughout the day. The Castle is a popular venue for weddings and other family occasions.

Rooms 55 (2 fmly) (21 GF) **Facilities** STV WiFi ♫ New Year **Conf** Class 100 Board 72 Thtr 200 **Services** Lift **Parking** 200 **Notes** Closed 24-26 Dec & Jan Civ Wed 300

THOMASTOWN
County Kilkenny

Map 1 C3

Mount Juliet Hotel

★★★★ COUNTRY HOUSE HOTEL

tel: 056 7773000
email: info@mountjuliet.ie **web:** www.mountjuliet.ie
dir: M7 from Dublin, M9 towards Waterford, exit at junct 9/Danesfort for hotel

Mount Juliet is set in 1,500 acres of parkland with a Jack Nicklaus-designed golf course and an equestrian centre. The elegant and spacious public areas retain many of the original architectural features including ornate plasterwork and Adam fireplaces. Bedrooms in the main house are elegant and comfortably appointed to a high standard, with more compact rooms available in the Clubhouse annexe. Fine dining is on offer in the ornate Lady Helen restaurant overlooking the river; with French Brasserie cuisine in Kendal's located in the golf clubhouse. The President's Bar is the location for all-day dining. The hotel has an excellent spa and health club, with equestrian and other activities also available.

Rooms 59 (28 annexe) (14 GF) **Facilities** Spa STV WiFi supervised 18 Putt green Fishing Gym Archery Cycling Clay pigeon shooting Equestrian Xmas New Year **Conf** Class 40 Board 20 Thtr 75 **Parking** 200 **Notes** Closed Sun-Wed eve Nov-1st wk Dec & Jan-Mar Civ Wed 60

THURLES County Tipperary	Map 1 C3

Horse & Jockey Hotel

★★★★ 79% HOTEL

tel: 0504 44192 **Horse & Jockey**
email: info@horseandjockeyhotel.com **web:** www.horseandjockeyhotel.com
dir: 800mtrs from M8 junct 6

Located just off the motorway, this hotel offers smart and well-appointed bedrooms which are very comfortable. Dining options are the Enclosure Bar with a varied menu, and for more formal dining in the evening there is Silks Restaurant. There is also a well-equipped leisure centre with spa treatments and an equestrian themed gift shop. The conference facilities include ten self-contained meeting rooms and a tiered auditorium seating 200 delegates.

Rooms 67 (4 fmly) (15 GF) (7 smoking) **Facilities** Spa STV FTV WiFi ⬆ supervised Gym Sauna Steam room Hydrotherapy area **Conf** Class 24 Board 25 Thtr 200 **Services** Lift **Parking** 450 **Notes** ⊗ Closed 25 Dec RS 24 & 26 Dec

TRALEE County Kerry	Map 1 A2

Ballygarry House Hotel and Spa

★★★★ 81% ⊛ HOTEL

tel: 066 7123322 **Leebrook**
email: info@ballygarryhouse.com **web:** www.ballygarryhouse.com
dir: 1.5km from Tralee, on N21

This charming hotel offers the complete country house experience, where courtesy and care is paramount. Located a short drive from the town centre, there are comfortably furnished lounges with open log fires. Food is served throughout the day in the Leebrook Lounge and fine dining is available in the evening in Brooks Restaurant which overlooks the lovely six-acre gardens. Bedrooms and suites are spacious and elegantly decorated. Spa treatments and relaxation areas are offered in the Nadur Spa. A recent addition is The Pavilion, a party venue where the outdoors is seamlessly brought indoors.

Rooms 64 (11 fmly) (12 GF) ⬏ **Facilities** Spa STV WiFi ⬇ Steam room Sauna ♫ New Year **Conf** Class 100 Board 50 Thtr 200 **Services** Lift **Parking** 200 **Notes** ⊗ Closed 20-26 Dec Civ Wed 350

Ballyseede Castle

★★★ ⊛⊛ HOTEL

tel: 066 7125799
email: info@ballyseedecastle.com **web:** www.ballyseedecastle.com
dir: On N21 just after junct of N21/N22

Located within minutes of Tralee town, Ballyseede Castle is steeped in history dating back to 1590 and has been fought over, lived in and lovingly restored to a high standard which still pays homage to its ancient grandeur. The spacious bedrooms are elegantly decorated; some have four-poster beds and antique furnishings. There are gracious receptions rooms with original ornamental cornices and marble fireplaces, a carved oak library, a cosy bar and a splendid banqueting hall. The castle stands in its own grounds at the end of a winding drive through formal gardens and natural woodland. All-day dining is available in the atmospheric Pappy's Bar, with more formal evening dining in the award winning O'Connell Room. The Castle is noted for the quality of its wedding celebrations and other family events.

Rooms 23 (4 fmly) (10 GF) ⬏ **Facilities** STV FTV WiFi **Parking** 180 **Notes** ⊗ Closed Jan-3 Mar Civ Wed 130

TRAMORE County Waterford	Map 1 C2

Majestic Hotel

★★★ 80% HOTEL

tel: 051 381761
email: info@majestic-hotel.ie **web:** www.majestic-hotel.ie
dir: Exit N25 through Waterford onto R675 to Tramore. Hotel on right, opposite lake

A warm welcome awaits visitors to this long established, family friendly hotel in the holiday resort of Tramore. Many of the comfortable and well-equipped bedrooms have sea views; some have balconies. Public areas offer relaxing comfortable lounges, a smartly decorated bar, a garden patio and a spacious restaurant where guests can enjoy the spectacular sea views. A discounted rate at Splashworld across from the hotel is available to residents.

Rooms 60 (8 fmly) ⬏ **Facilities** STV FTV WiFi ⬇ ♫ New Year **Conf** Class 100 Board 50 Thtr 100 **Services** Lift **Parking** 10 **Notes** ⊗ Civ Wed 250

TULLOW
County Carlow

Map 1 D3

Mount Wolseley Hotel, Spa & Country Club

★★★★ 80% ◉ HOTEL

tel: 059 9180 100 & 9151 674
email: info@mountwolseley.ie **web:** www.mountwolseley.ie
dir: N7 from Dublin. In Naas, take N9 towards Carlow. In Castledermot left for Tullow

Located on a vast, well landscaped estate long associated with the Wolseley family of motoring fame, this hotel has much to offer. Public areas are very spacious with a large range of suites and bedrooms. Leisure pursuits include a championship golf course together with a popular health centre and Sanctuary Spa. The hotel offers a number of dining options including Aaron's lounge, Fredrick's (1 AA Rosette), and The Wolseley Lounge in the Golf Pavillion.

Rooms 143 (10 fmly) (5 smoking) 🔌 **S** €70-€125; **D** €90-€220 (incl. bkfst)* **Facilities** Spa STV FTV WiFi 🏊 HL 🖱 supervised ⛳ 18 ⛳ Putt green Gym Childrens play areas Games room 🎵 Xmas New Year Child facilities **Conf** Class 288 Board 70 Thtr 750 Del €129* **Services** Lift Air con **Parking** 160 **Notes** LB 🚫 Closed 25-26 Dec Civ Wed 450

WATERFORD
County Waterford

Map 1 C2

Faithlegg House Hotel & Golf Resort

★★★★ 78% ◉ HOTEL

FBD Hotels & Resorts

tel: 051 382000 **Faithlegg**
email: reservations@fhh.ie **web:** www.faithlegg.com
dir: From Waterford follow Dunmore East Rd then Cheekpoint Rd

This hotel is surrounded by a parkland championship golf course and overlooks the estuary of the River Suir. The house has 14 original bedrooms, and the others in a more contemporary style are in an adjacent modern block. There is a range of comfortable lounges together with comprehensive meeting facilities. The leisure and treatment rooms are the perfect way to work off the food offered in the Roseville Restaurant. Lighter options are served throughout the day in the Piano Bar and in the golf Clubhouse.

Rooms 82 (6 fmly) (30 GF) **Facilities** FTV WiFi 🖱 supervised ⛳ 18 ⛳ Putt green Gym Sauna Steam room New Year **Conf** Class 90 Board 44 Thtr 180 Del from €125 to €225 **Services** Lift **Parking** 100 **Notes** 🚫 Closed 20-27 Dec Civ Wed 220

Granville Hotel

★★★★ 76% HOTEL

tel: 051 305555 **The Quay**
email: stay@granville-hotel.ie **web:** www.granville-hotel.ie
dir: N25 to waterfront, hotel opposite clock tower

Centrally located on the quayside, this long established hotel was originally a coaching house. It is appointed to a very high standard, and retains much of its original character. The bedrooms come in a choice of standard or executive grades; all are well equipped and very comfortable. The Meagher Bar offers food throughout the day, and is a popular lunch venue with shoppers and the business community of Waterford. The Bianconi is an elegant restaurant where evening dinner is served. Friendliness and hospitality are hallmarks of a stay here.

Rooms 100 (5 fmly) (10 smoking) 🔌 **S** €80-€120; **D** €90-€180 (incl. bkfst) **Facilities** STV 🎵 New Year **Conf** Class 150 Board 30 Thtr 200 Del from €135 to €160 **Services** Lift **Parking** 300 **Notes** LB 🚫 Closed 25-26 Dec Civ Wed 200

Tower Hotel

★★★ 79% ◉ HOTEL

FBD Hotels & Resorts

tel: 051 862300 **The Mall**
email: info@thw.ie **web:** www.towerhotelwaterford.com
dir: Opposite Reginald's Tower in town centre. Hotel at end of quay, in the heart of the Viking Triangle

With a commanding position on The Mall opposite Reginald's Tower, this well established hotel has much to offer. The spacious public areas include conference suites, a choice of dining options and a popular leisure club. Health and beauty treatments are available. A range of bedrooms is on offer; all are comfortably appointed and stylishly decorated. Secure parking is provided to the rear of the building.

Rooms 136 (27 fmly) 🔌 **S** €49-€110; **D** €49-€145 **Facilities** Spa STV FTV WiFi 🖱 supervised Gym Beauty treatment rooms 🎵 New Year **Conf** Class 250 Board 80 Thtr 500 **Services** Lift **Parking** 100 **Notes** 🚫 Closed 24-28 Dec Civ Wed 400

Dooley's Hotel

★★★ 78% HOTEL

tel: 051 873531 **30 The Quay**
email: hotel@dooleys-hotel.ie **web:** www.dooleys-hotel.ie
dir: Adjacent to N25, on the Quay on R680

This hotel has been family run for three generations. It is situated on the quay overlooking the River Suir at the harbour's mouth. Dinner is served in New Ship Restaurant and casual dining is available in the Dry Dock Bar. Bedrooms are attractively decorated and offer a good standard of comfort. There is a convenient public car park opposite the hotel.

Rooms 110 (3 fmly) (29 smoking) 🔌 **S** €70-€140; **D** €80-€198* **Facilities** STV WiFi 🏊 🎵 New Year **Conf** Class 150 Board 100 Thtr 240 Del from €110* **Services** Lift **Notes** 🚫 Closed 25-27 Dec RS 24 Dec

WESTPORT
County Mayo

Map 1 B4

Knockranny House Hotel

★★★★ 84% ◉◉ HOTEL

tel: 098 28600
email: info@khh.ie **web:** www.khh.ie
dir: On N5 Westport-Castlebar Rd

Perched on a height overlooking Westport, with Clew Bay and Croagh Patrick in the distance, this fine family-run property is set in well landscaped grounds. The reception rooms take full advantage of the stunning views, and include The Brehon, a lounge where food is served throughout the day, and La Fougére, the award-winning restaurant that is a real treat to visit. The comfortable furnishings create an inviting and relaxing atmosphere throughout the lounges, bar and restaurant. Bedrooms are very well appointed and come in a number of styles, with the newer ones being particularly spacious. Guests have complimentary use of extensive leisure facilities, with wellbeing treatments on offer in Spa Salveo. There are extensive banqueting and conference facilities.

Rooms 97 (4 fmly) (18 GF) 🔌 **Facilities** Spa STV FTV WiFi 🏊 HL 🖱 Gym 🎵 New Year **Conf** Class 350 Board 40 Thtr 600 **Services** Lift **Parking** 150 **Notes** 🚫 Closed 24-26 Dec Civ Wed 250

WESTPORT *continued*

Hotel Westport Leisure, Spa & Conference

★★★★ 80% ⊕ HOTEL

tel: 098 25122 & 0870 876 5432 **Newport Rd**
email: reservations@hotelwestport.ie **web:** www.hotelwestport.ie
dir: N5 to Westport. Right at end of Castlebar St, 1st right before bridge, right at lights, left before church. Follow to end of street

Located in seven acres of woodlands and just a short riverside walk from the town, this hotel offers spacious public areas, including The Islands restaurant and the all-day Maple Bar. Bedrooms come in a range of styles, and are all comfortable and well appointed. Both leisure and business guests are well catered for by the enthusiastic and friendly team who go to great lengths to ensure residents enjoy their stay. This hotel is a popular choice with special interest groups and also families, who enjoy the leisure facilities, and in summer time, the children's club.

Rooms 129 (67 fmly) (42 GF) (12 smoking) ↟ **S** €70-€159; **D** €120-€280 (incl. bkfst) **Facilities** Spa STV WiFi ⊳ HL ⊛ supervised Gym Children's pool Lounger pool Steam room Sauna Fitness suite ♫ Xmas New Year **Conf** Class 150 Board 60 Thtr 500 Del from €140 to €160 **Services** Lift **Parking** 220 **Notes** LB ⊗ Civ Wed 350

The Wyatt Hotel

★★★ 74% HOTEL

tel: 098 25027 **The Octagon**
email: info@wyatthotel.com **web:** www.wyatthotel.com
dir: Follow one-way system in town. Hotel by tall monument at Octagon

This stylish, welcoming hotel is situated in the famous town-centre Octagon. Bedrooms are attractively decorated and well equipped. Public areas are very comfortable with open fires and include a lively, contemporary bar and the traditional Cobblers Bar. JW Bistro serves food all day, and in high season The Wyatt Restaurant offers more formal dining.

Rooms 55 (10 fmly) (2 GF) (4 smoking) ↟ **Facilities** WiFi Complimentary use of nearby leisure park ♫ New Year **Conf** Class 200 Board 80 Thtr 300 **Services** Lift **Parking** 32 **Notes** Closed 25-26 Dec Civ Wed 200

Mill Times Hotel Westport

★★★ 73% HOTEL

tel: 098 29200 & 29130 **Mill St**
email: info@milltimeshotel.ie **web:** www.milltimeshotel.ie
dir: N59 signed town centre, in Bridge St keep in left lane, into Mill St, hotel on left

This family-run hotel is situated in the centre of Westport, close to the shops and many pubs of this bustling town. It is ideal for visiting north Mayo with its many beaches and golf courses, or as a base for climbing the pilgrimage mountain of Croagh Patrick. Bedrooms are traditional in style and public areas are comfortable. Uncle Sam's café bar is a lively venue with entertainment at weekends. Temptations Restaurant offers good value meals during the evening, and is the venue for a hearty breakfast. Underground parking is provided.

Rooms 34 (6 fmly) **Facilities** WiFi ♫ New Year **Conf** Class 100 Board 60 Thtr 180 **Services** Lift Air con **Parking** 25 **Notes** ⊗ Closed 24-25 Dec Civ Wed 200

WEXFORD
County Wexford   Map 1 D3

Whitford House Hotel Health & Leisure Club

★★★★ 77% ⊕ HOTEL

tel: 053 9143444 **New Line Rd**
email: info@whitford.ie **web:** www.whitford.ie
dir: Just off N25 (Duncannon rdbt) take exit for R733 (Wexford), hotel immediately left

This is a friendly family-run hotel just three kilometres from the town centre and within easy reach of the Rosslare Ferry. Comfortable bedrooms range from standard to the spacious deluxe rooms. Public areas include a choice of lounges and the popular Forthside Bar Bistro where a carvery is served at lunch. More formal meals are on offer during the evening in the award-winning Seasons Restaurant. Leisure and fitness facilities are complimentary to resident guests.

Rooms 36 (28 fmly) (18 GF) **S** €65-€120; **D** €80-€180 (incl. bkfst)* **Facilities** Spa FTV WiFi ⊳ ⊛ supervised Gym Children's playground Football area Hairdresser ♫ Xmas New Year **Conf** Class 12 Board 25 Thtr 50 **Parking** 200 **Notes** LB ⊗ Closed 25-26 Dec RS 24 & 27 Dec Civ Wed 100

Gibraltar

GIBRALTAR

O'Callaghan Eliott Hotel

★★★★ 79% HOTEL

tel: 00 350 200 70500 & 200 75905 **2 Governor's Pde**
email: eliott@ocallaghanhotels.com **web:** www.ocallaghanhotels.com

Located in the heart of the old town, this hotel provides a convenient central base for exploring the duty-free shopping district and other key attractions on foot. The bedrooms are stylish, spacious and well equipped. The roof-top restaurant provides stunning bay views, while guests can also take a swim in the roof-top pool.

Rooms 123 ☏ **Facilities** STV WiFi ⊰ **Gym** ♬ **Xmas New Year Conf** Class 80 Board 70 Thtr 180 **Services** Lift Air con **Parking** 17 **Notes** ⊗ Civ Wed 120

Caleta Hotel

★★★★ 78% ◉◉ HOTEL

tel: 00 350 200 76501 **Sir Herbert Miles Rd, PO Box 73**
email: reservations@caletahotel.gi **web:** www.caletahotel.com
dir: Enter Gibraltar via Spanish border & cross runway. At 1st rdbt turn left, hotel in 2kms

For travellers arriving in Gibraltar by plane, the Caleta is an eye-catching coastal landmark that can be spotted from the air if arriving from the east. This imposing and stylish hotel sits on a cliff top and all sea-facing rooms enjoy panoramic views across the straights to Morocco. Bedrooms vary in size and style; some have spacious balconies, flat-screen TVs and mini bars. Several dining venues are available, but Nunos provides an award-winning, fine dining Italian experience. The staff are friendly and service is professional.

Rooms 161 (89 annexe) (13 fmly) (80 smoking) **Facilities** Spa STV FTV WiFi ⊰ ⊰ supervised Gym Health & beauty club **Xmas New Year Conf** Class 172 Board 85 Thtr 216 **Services** Lift Air con **Parking** 32 **Notes** ⊗ Civ Wed 300

The Rock Hotel

★★★★ 78% ◉ HOTEL

tel: 00 350 200 73000 **Europa Rd**
email: reservations@rockhotel.gi **web:** www.rockhotelgibraltar.com
dir: From airport follow tourist board signs. Hotel on left half way up Europa Rd

Enjoying a prime elevated location directly below the Rock, this long-established art deco styled hotel has been the destination of celebrities and royalty since it was built in 1932. The bedrooms are spacious and well equipped, and many boast stunning coastal views that stretch across the Mediterranean to Morocco. The staff are friendly and service is delivered with flair and enthusiasm. Creative dinners and hearty breakfasts can be enjoyed in the stylish restaurant.

Rooms 104 ☏ S £130-£148; **Facilities** STV WiFi ⊰ supervised Gym **Xmas New Year Conf** Class 120 Board 30 Thtr 150 Del from £180 to £200* **Services** Lift Air con **Parking** 40 **Notes** ⊗ RS 5 Oct-1 Apr Civ Wed 200

Acknowledgments

The Automobile Association would like to thank the following photographers, companies and picture libraries for their assistance in the preparation of this book.

Abbreviations for the picture credits are as follows – (t) top; (b) bottom; (c) centre; (l) left; (r) right; (AA) AA World Travel Library

Front Cover: © Pavel Konovalov / Alamy

England Opener AA/Adam Burton;
London Opener AA/James Tims;
Scotland Opener AA/Jim Henderson;
Scottish Islands Opener AA/AJ Hopkins;
Wales Opener AA/Mari Sterling;
Ireland Opener AA/Stockbyte;
Gibraltar Opener © LOOK Die Bildagentur der Fotografen GmbH/Alamy

003 Courtesy of Bushmills Inn Hotel, County Antrim; 004 Courtesy of Dormy House Hotel & Spa, Worcestershire; 009 Courtesy of Stratford Manor, Warwickshire; 011 AA/Clive Sawyer; 011l Courtesy of Dormy House Hotel & Spa, Worcestershire; 011r Courtesy of Rosewood, London; 012-013 AA/Clive Sawyer; 012l Courtesy of Meldrium House, Aberdeen; 012r Courtesy of Plas Ynyshir Hall Hotel, Eglwys Fach; 013l Courtesy of Bushmills Inn Hotel, Co. Antrim; 013r Courtesy of Maryborough House Hotel, Cork; 015 AA/Clive Sawyer; 015tr Courtesy of Norton Park, Hampshire; 015br Courtesy of Stratford Manor, Warwickshire; 016 AA/Clive Sawyer; 016tr Courtesy of Brokencote Hall Worcestershire; 016cr Courtesy of The Greenway Hotel, Gloucestershire; 016b Courtesy of Mallory Court, Warwickshire; 018 Courtesy of The Midland, Greater Manchester; 020 Courtesy of The Hampshire Court Hotel, Hampshire; 021 Courtesy of The Cheltenham Chase Hotel, Gloucestershire; 022-023 © Loop Images Ltd / Alamy; 025 © funkyfood London - Paul Williams / Alamy; 026 © Richard Croft / Alamy; 241 © Alan Novelli / Alamy; 260 AA/James Tims; 484 AA/Peter Trenchard; 585 AA/Mark Bauer; 621 AA/Peter Wilson.

Every effort has been made to trace the copyright holders, and we apologise in advance for any unintentional omissions or errors. We would be pleased to apply any corrections in a following edition of this publication

COUNTY MAPS

England

1 Bedfordshire
2 Berkshire
3 Bristol
4 Buckinghamshire
5 Cambridgeshire
6 Greater Manchester
7 Herefordshire
8 Hertfordshire
9 Leicestershire
10 Northamptonshire
11 Nottinghamshire
12 Rutland
13 Staffordshire
14 Warwickshire
15 West Midlands
16 Worcestershire

Scotland

17 City of Glasgow
18 Clackmannanshire
19 East Ayrshire
20 East Dunbartonshire
21 East Renfrewshire
22 Perth & Kinross
23 Renfrewshire
24 South Lanarkshire
25 West Dunbartonshire

Wales

26 Blaenau Gwent
27 Bridgend
28 Caerphilly
29 Denbighshire
30 Flintshire
31 Merthyr Tydfil
32 Monmouthshire
33 Neath Port Talbot
34 Newport
35 Rhondda Cynon Taff
36 Torfaen
37 Vale of Glamorgan
38 Wrexham

Na h-Eileanan
an Iar

Orkney Islands

Shetland Islands

Highland

Moray

SCOTLAND

Aberdeenshire

City of
Aberdeen

Angus

Perth &
Kinross

City of
Dundee

Argyll &
Bute

Stirling

Fife

Argyll
& Bute

Stirling

18

22

Fife

North
Ayrshire

East
Lothian

25

20

Falkirk

19

24

Scottish
Borders

Inverclyde

23

17

North
Lanarkshire

West
Lothian

City of
Edinburgh

South
Ayrshire

Dumfries &
Galloway

North
Ayrshire

21

Midlothian

19

South Lanarkshire

Scottish
Borders

Northumberland

Tyne & Wear

Cumbria

Durham

Isle
of Man

North
Yorkshire

Lancashire

East Riding
of Yorkshire

Isle of
Anglesey

Merseyside

6

West
Yorkshire

Conwy

30

Cheshire

South
Yorkshire

Lincolnshire

29

38

Derbyshire

Gwynedd

ENGLAND

11

13

Norfolk

Shropshire

9

12

WALES

15

Cerédigion

Powys

16

14

10

5

Suffolk

Pembrokeshire

7

1

Carmarthenshire

Gloucestershire

4

8

Essex

Swansea

31

26

32

Oxfordshire

Greater
London

33

35

36

3

2

Kent

27

28

34

Wiltshire

Surrey

37

Cardiff

Wiltshire

West
Sussex

East
Sussex

Somerset

Hampshire

Devon

Dorset

Isle of
Wight

Cornwall

Isles of
Scilly

Guernsey

Jersey

0   20   40   60   80   100 miles

0   20 40 60 80 100 120 140 160 kilometres

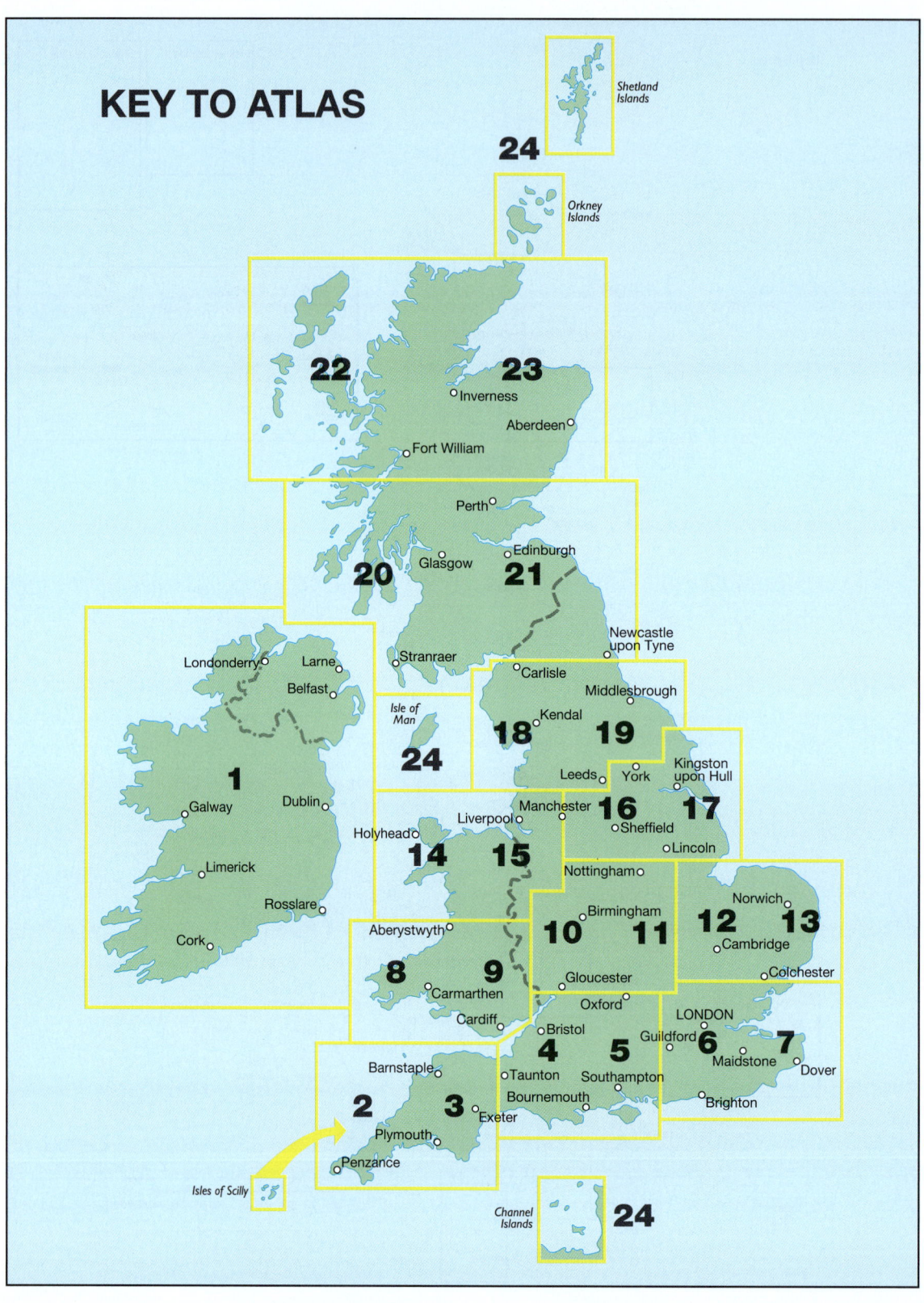

KEY TO ATLAS

Shetland Islands

24

Orkney Islands

22　　**23**

Inverness

Aberdeen

Fort William

Perth

Edinburgh

20　Glasgow　**21**

Newcastle upon Tyne

Stranraer

Londonderry　Larne

Belfast

Carlisle

Middlesbrough

Isle of Man

Kendal

18　　**19**

1

Leeds　York　Kingston upon Hull

Galway　Dublin

24

Manchester　**16**　**17**

Holyhead　Liverpool

Sheffield

Lincoln

Limerick

14　**15**

Rosslare

Nottingham

Cork

Aberystwyth

Birmingham　Norwich

10　**11**　**12**　**13**

Cambridge

8　**9**

Carmarthen　Gloucester　Colchester

Cardiff　Oxford

LONDON

Bristol　Guildford　**6**　**7**

Barnstaple　**4**　**5**　Maidstone

Taunton　Southampton　Dover

Bournemouth　Brighton

2　**3**　Exeter

Plymouth

Isles of Scilly　Penzance

Channel Islands　**24**

2

For continuation pages refer to numbered arrows

For continuation pages refer to numbered arrows

14

For continuation pages refer to numbered arrows

C EDIN	City of Edinburgh
C GLAS	City of Glasgow
CLACKS	Clackmannanshire
C DUND	City of Dundee
E DUNS	East Dunbartonshire
E RENS	East Renfrewshire
INVER	Inverclyde
MDLOTH	Midlothian
N LANS	North Lanarkshire
RENS	Renfrewshire
W DUNS	West Dunbartonshire
W LOTH	West Lothian

Hotel
AA Hotel of the Year
Town/Village name

0   10   20 miles

0 10 20 30 kilometres

Durness
Strathy Point
Scrabster Gills
Thurso
Duncansby Head
John o' Groats
Stromness V St Margaret's Hope
Dunnet Head
PENTLAND FIRTH
A836
A9
A99
Melvich
Bettyhill
A836
Tongue
A838
WICK
Wick

NC

ND

Altnaharra
A836
A838
Dunbeath
Lybster

Lairg
A839
A836
A839
Helmsdale
A837
Golspie Brora
A9
Bonar Bridge
Dornoch
A949
A836
Tain

HIGHLAND

NH

Alness
Invergordon
Dingwall
A835
A834
Fortrose
Muir of Ord
Beauly
A832
A862
INVERNESS
A9
MORAY FIRTH
Cromarty
V (Jun-Sept)
Nairn
Forres
A96

Lossiemouth
Buckie Cullen Portsoy
Banff
Fraserburgh
Elgin
A941
A98
A98
A98
A952
A90
Rothes
Keith
Aberchirder
Turriff
A950
A941
A95
A96
A920
Peterhead

MORAY

NJ

NK

Aberlour
Dufftown
A941
A920
Huntly
A97
A96
A920
Oldmeldrum
Ellon
Kirkwall V

Abriachan
A833
A9
A5
A939
Grantown-on-Spey
A938
Carrbridge
Nethy Bridge
A95
Tomintoul
Alford
Inverurie
Kintore
Aberdeen Airport
Dyce
Lerwick V

Drumnadrochit
Invermoriston
Whitebridge
Fort Augustus
A862
A82
Aviemore
A9
CAIRNGORMS
A944
A944
CITY OF ABERDEEN
ABERDEEN

Monadhliath Mountains
Kingussie
Newtonmore
CAIRNGORM MOUNTAINS
A939
A93
Ballater
Aboyne
A980
Petercalter
Banchory
A957

NN

NO

ABERDEENSHIRE

NATIONAL PARK
A86
Braemar
A93
Stonehaven

A889
G R A M P I A N   M O U N T A I N S
Laurencekirk
A90
Inverbervie
A9
A827
Blair Atholl
A924
Kinloch Rannoch
Killiecrankie
Pitlochry
A9
A93
A935
Brechin
Montrose
A934
A937

ANGUS

Fortingall
Kenmore
Aberfeldy
Kirriemuir
Forfar
Inverkeilor
A827
A821
A822
A923
A923
A932
A933
A934
Arbroath
Fortingall
Killin
A827
PERTH AND KINROSS
Blairgowrie
A93
A926
A94
A90
A92
A930
Carnoustie

21

Loch Earnhead
St Fillans
A85
Dunkeld
Kinclaven
Coupar Angus
SIDLAW HILLS
C DUND
DUNDEE
Newport-on-Tay
St Andrews Bay
Comrie Crieff
Perth
A9
A85
A90
A92
A822
A923
A94
A923
A9

24

HP

Herma Ness
Haroldswick
Unst
A968

Fetlar

Yell
A968

A970
A971
A968
A970

Papa Stour
Muckle Roe
Whalsay

SHETLAND
ISLANDS

Sandness

MAINLAND
A971

West Burra

LERWICK
Scalloway
Bressay

HU

A970

SUMBURGH
Aberdeen
Kirkwall
Sumburgh Head

Shetland Islands

0   10 miles
0   10   20 kilometres

Orkney Islands

0   10 miles
0   10   20 kilometres

● Hotel
○ AA Hotel of the Year
○ Town/Village name

Papa Westray
North Ronaldsay
Westray
Lerwick

Eday
Sanday

Brough Head
A966
Rousay

MAINLAND
A965
A961
A964
ORKNEY
KIRKWALL
ISLANDS

Stromness

Shapinsay
Stronsay

HY

Scapa Flow
HOY
Flotta
Burray
St Margaret's Hope
South Ronaldsay
A961
Aberdeen

ND

PENTLAND FIRTH

Dunnet Head
Duncansby Head
Scrabster
Gills
John o' Groats
A836
A9
Thurso
A9

Orkney Islands

Isle of Man

NX
Point of Ayre

0   5 miles
0   10 kilometres

Bride
A10
Jurby
A17
Andreas
Ramsey Bay
A14
Sulby
A3
Ballaugh
Ramsey
Maughold
A18
Kirk Michael
A3
A15
A1
B10
SC
Laxey
Peel
A3
A18
A2
St John's
Crosby
Onchan
Dalby
Foxdale
DOUGLAS
A36
A24
Heysham
St Marks
A26
A25
A5
Ballasalla
ISLE OF MAN (RONALDSWAY)
Birkenhead (Nov-Mar)
Liverpool (Mar-Oct)
Port Erin
Port St Mary
Castletown
Calf of Man

0   1   2   3 miles
0   1   2   3   4 kilometres

L'Ancresse
Grandes Rocques
Vale
Weymouth Poole
St Sampson
Cobo
Castel
St Peter Port
Herm
L'Erée
King's Mills
Jersey Portsmouth
Roquaine Bay
St Saviour
St Andrew
St Peter's
St Martin
Fermain Bay
Forest
Jersey
Jerbourg
Sark

Guernsey

ALDERNEY
FRANCE
Herm
Sark
GUERNSEY
JERSEY

La Grève de Lecq
St John
Bouley Bay
L'Etacq
B64
B63
A9
A8
St Mary
Trinity
Rozel
B31
A12
St Peter
A10
St Martin
B41
JERSEY
St Lawrence
A6
St Ouen's Bay
Beaumont
Millbrook
Five Oaks
St Brelade
A1
St Saviour
Gorey
A13
St Aubin
St Helier
A3
Grouville
Corbière
A4
St Clement
Poole
Weymouth via Guernsey
Guernsey, Portsmouth

Jersey

0   1   2   3 miles
0   1   2   3   4 kilometres

Readers' Report Form

Please send this form to:–
Editor, The Hotel Guide,
Lifestyle Guides,
AA Media,
Fanum House,
Basingstoke RG21 4EA

e-mail: lifestyleguides@theAA.com

Please use this form to recommend any hotel where you have stayed, whether it is included in the guide or not currently listed. You can also help us to improve the guide by completing the short questionnaire on the reverse.

Please note that the AA does not undertake to arbitrate between you and the hotel management, or to obtain compensation or engage in protracted correspondence.

Date

Your name (BLOCK CAPITALS)

Your address (BLOCK CAPITALS)

Post code

E-mail address

Name of hotel

Location

Comments

(please attach a separate sheet if necessary)

Please tick here ☐ if you DO NOT wish to receive details of AA offers or products   PTO

Readers' Report Form *continued*

Have you bought this guide before? ☐ YES ☐ NO

Do you regularly use any other, accommodation, restaurant, pub or food guides? ☐ YES ☐ NO
If YES, which ones?

Why did you buy this guide? (tick all that apply)

Holiday ☐   Short break ☐   Business travel ☐   Special occasion ☐

Overnight stop ☐   Find a venue for an event e.g. conference ☐

Other (please state)

How often do you stay in hotels? (tick one choice)

More than once a month ☐   Once a month ☐   Once in 2-3 months ☐

Once in six months ☐   Once a year ☐   Less than once a year ☐

Other (please state)

Please answer these questions to help us make improvements to the guide:

Which of these factors are the most important when choosing a hotel? (tick all that apply)

Price ☐   Location ☐   Awards/ratings ☐   Service ☐

Decor/surroundings ☐   Previous experience ☐ Recommendation ☐

Other (please state)

Do you read the editorial features in the guide? ☐ YES ☐ NO

Do you use the location atlas? ☐ YES ☐ NO

What elements of the guide do you find most useful when choosing somewhere to stay? (tick all that apply)

Description ☐   Photo ☐   Advertisement ☐   Star rating ☐

Is there any other information you would like to see added to this guide?

Readers' Report Form

Please send this form to:–
Editor, The Hotel Guide,
Lifestyle Guides,
AA Media,
Fanum House,
Basingstoke RG21 4EA

e-mail: lifestyleguides@theAA.com

Please use this form to recommend any hotel where you have stayed, whether it is included in the guide or not currently listed. You can also help us to improve the guide by completing the short questionnaire on the reverse.

Please note that the AA does not undertake to arbitrate between you and the hotel management, or to obtain compensation or engage in protracted correspondence.

Date

Your name (BLOCK CAPITALS)

Your address (BLOCK CAPITALS)

Post code

E-mail address

Name of hotel

Location

Comments

(please attach a separate sheet if necessary)

Please tick here ☐ if you DO NOT wish to receive details of AA offers or products

PTO

Readers' Report Form *continued*

Have you bought this guide before? ☐ YES ☐ NO

Do you regularly use any other, accommodation, restaurant, pub or food guides? ☐ YES ☐ NO
If YES, which ones?

_____

_____

Why did you buy this guide? (tick all that apply)

Holiday ☐   Short break ☐   Business travel ☐   Special occasion ☐

Overnight stop ☐   Find a venue for an event e.g. conference ☐

Other (please state)

How often do you stay in hotels? (tick one choice)

More than once a month ☐   Once a month ☐   Once in 2-3 months ☐

Once in six months ☐   Once a year ☐   Less than once a year ☐

Other (please state)

Please answer these questions to help us make improvements to the guide:

Which of these factors are the most important when choosing a hotel? (tick all that apply)

Price ☐   Location ☐   Awards/ratings ☐   Service ☐

Decor/surroundings ☐   Previous experience ☐   Recommendation ☐

Other (please state)

Do you read the editorial features in the guide? ☐ YES ☐ NO

Do you use the location atlas?   ☐ YES ☐ NO

What elements of the guide do you find most useful when choosing somewhere to stay? (tick all that apply)

Description ☐   Photo ☐   Advertisement ☐   Star rating ☐

Is there any other information you would like to see added to this guide?

_____

_____

_____

_____

_____

Readers' Report Form

Please send this form to:–
Editor, The Hotel Guide,
Lifestyle Guides,
AA Media,
Fanum House,
Basingstoke RG21 4EA

e-mail: lifestyleguides@theAA.com

Please use this form to recommend any hotel where you have stayed, whether it is included in the guide or not currently listed. You can also help us to improve the guide by completing the short questionnaire on the reverse.

Please note that the AA does not undertake to arbitrate between you and the hotel management, or to obtain compensation or engage in protracted correspondence.

Date

Your name (BLOCK CAPITALS)

Your address (BLOCK CAPITALS)

Post code

E-mail address

Name of hotel

Location

Comments

(please attach a separate sheet if necessary)

Please tick here ☐ if you DO NOT wish to receive details of AA offers or products   PTO

Readers' Report Form *continued*

Have you bought this guide before? ☐ YES ☐ NO

Do you regularly use any other, accommodation, restaurant, pub or food guides? ☐ YES ☐ NO
If YES, which ones?

Why did you buy this guide? (tick all that apply)

Holiday ☐   Short break ☐   Business travel ☐   Special occasion ☐
Overnight stop ☐   Find a venue for an event e.g. conference ☐
Other (please state)

How often do you stay in hotels? (tick one choice)

More than once a month ☐   Once a month ☐   Once in 2-3 months ☐
Once in six months ☐   Once a year ☐   Less than once a year ☐
Other (please state)

Please answer these questions to help us make improvements to the guide:
Which of these factors are the most important when choosing a hotel? (tick all that apply)

Price ☐   Location ☐   Awards/ratings ☐   Service ☐
Decor/surroundings ☐   Previous experience ☐   Recommendation ☐
Other (please state)

Do you read the editorial features in the guide? ☐ YES ☐ NO

Do you use the location atlas? ☐ YES ☐ NO

What elements of the guide do you find most useful when choosing somewhere to stay? (tick all that apply)

Description ☐   Photo ☐   Advertisement ☐   Star rating ☐

Is there any other information you would like to see added to this guide?

Readers' Report Form

Please send this form to:–
Editor, The Hotel Guide,
Lifestyle Guides,
AA Media,
Fanum House,
Basingstoke RG21 4EA

e-mail: lifestyleguides@theAA.com

Please use this form to recommend any hotel where you have stayed, whether it is included in the guide or not currently listed. You can also help us to improve the guide by completing the short questionnaire on the reverse.

Please note that the AA does not undertake to arbitrate between you and the hotel management, or to obtain compensation or engage in protracted correspondence.

Date

Your name (BLOCK CAPITALS)

Your address (BLOCK CAPITALS)

Post code

E-mail address

Name of hotel

Location

Comments

(please attach a separate sheet if necessary)

Please tick here ☐ if you DO NOT wish to receive details of AA offers or products

Readers' Report Form *continued*

Have you bought this guide before? ☐ YES ☐ NO

Do you regularly use any other, accommodation, restaurant, pub or food guides? ☐ YES ☐ NO
If YES, which ones?

_____

_____

Why did you buy this guide? (tick all that apply)

Holiday ☐   Short break ☐   Business travel ☐   Special occasion ☐
Overnight stop ☐   Find a venue for an event e.g. conference ☐
Other (please state)
_____

How often do you stay in hotels? (tick one choice)

More than once a month ☐   Once a month ☐   Once in 2-3 months ☐
Once in six months ☐   Once a year ☐   Less than once a year ☐
Other (please state)
_____

Please answer these questions to help us make improvements to the guide:

Which of these factors are the most important when choosing a hotel? (tick all that apply)

Price ☐   Location ☐   Awards/ratings ☐   Service ☐
Decor/surroundings ☐   Previous experience ☐   Recommendation ☐
Other (please state)
_____

Do you read the editorial features in the guide? ☐ YES ☐ NO

Do you use the location atlas? ☐ YES ☐ NO

What elements of the guide do you find most useful when choosing somewhere to stay? (tick all that apply)

Description ☐   Photo ☐   Advertisement ☐   Star rating ☐

Is there any other information you would like to see added to this guide?

_____

_____

_____

_____